Encyclopedia of Cryptozoology

Encyclopedia of Cryptozoology

A Global Guide to Hidden Animals and Their Pursuers

MICHAEL NEWTON

McFarland & Company, Inc., Publishers

Jefferson, North Carolina

The present work is a reprint of the illustrated casebound bound
edition of Encyclopedia of Cryptozoology: A Global Guide to
Hidden Animals and Their Pursuers, first published in 2005
by McFarland.

LIBRARY OF CONGRESS CATALOGUING-IN-PUBLICATION DATA

Newton, Michael, 1951–
Encyclopedia of cryptozoology : a global guide to hidden
animals and their pursuers / Michael Newton.
            p.   cm.
Includes bibliographical references and index.

ISBN 978-0-7864-9756-0 (softcover : acid free paper) ∞
ISBN 978-0-7864-9153-7 (ebook)

1. Cryptozoology — Encyclopedias.   I. Title.
QL88.3.N49   2014   001.944'03 — dc22   2004020826

BRITISH LIBRARY CATALOGUING DATA ARE AVAILABLE

On the cover (clockwise from upper left):
Gulf of Mexico sea serpent, Bigfoot, Beebe's manta ray,
giant Artrellia, Florida skunk ape
(artwork by William Rebsamen)

Printed in the United States of America

McFarland & Company, Inc., Publishers
Box 611, Jefferson, North Carolina 28640
www.mcfarlandpub.com

To the memory of
the pioneers of cryptozoology:

Antoon Oudemans
Bernard Heuvelmans
Tim Dinsdale
René Dahinden
Boris Porshnev

And to Dr. Karl Shuker,
preeminent cryptozoologist of a new millennium.

Table of Contents

Preface

The work in hand required 12 months to write, but research spanned the better part of half a century, beginning with a 1957 *Reader's Digest* article about Loch Ness. That brief report fired my imagination, and my fascination deepened when Bigfoot made his media debut in 1958. By the time my school library purchased Bernard Heuvelmans's *On the Track of Unknown Animals* in 1959, I was already hooked for life.

From humble childhood beginnings, my research continually broadened; ultimately, I amassed a substantial library on cryptozoology (including translations of various non–English sources) and undertook years of field work including seven visits to Loch Ness. This book, therefore, presents a synthesis of scholarship spanning 6,000 years and planet Earth at large.

The *Encyclopedia of Cryptozoology* is meant to be comprehensive on the subject. It includes 2,744 entries. The majority (1,583 entries) describe specific mystery creatures reported from every part of the world, throughout recorded history. Other entries include 742 places where unnamed cryptids are said to appear; profiles of 77 groups and 112 individuals who have made some contribution to the field of cryptozoology; descriptions of 12 specific objects or events important to the subject (e.g., the PANGBOCHE HAND); and two general essays on related subjects (CRYPTOTOURISM and HOAXES). Appendices include a timeline of zoological discoveries; annotated lists of movies and television series with cryptozoological themes; a list of cryptofiction titles; and a list of Internet websites devoted to cryptozoology. A comprehensive bibliography completes the work.

Every effort has been made to organize this volume for the reader's convenience. That said, certain explanations are required concerning style and methodology.

- *Scope of the text.* This work offers a "flesh-and-blood" view of cryptozoology. It does not include discussion of supernatural entities and phenomena. Thus excluded are fairies, ghosts, zombies, extraterrestrials and mythical beings (except where some flesh-and-blood creature accounts for the myth). Various sources are readily available on paranormal aspects of cryptozoology, but they do not concern us here.

- *Arrangement of entries.* All entries are arranged in a standard alphabetical format, with headers in **bold type**. Biographical entries are alphabetized by the individual's surname (e.g., **Sanderson, Ivan**). Organizations are listed by the first word of a group's proper name (e.g., **International Society of Cryptozoology**). Cryptids are alphabetized by the creature's most common or popular name (e.g., **Yeti**). Unnamed **Sea Serpents** are listed under the names of ships from which they were seen (e.g., ***Adamant***), or names of locations where they appeared (e.g., **Along Bay**). Treatment of adjectives depends on their normal use in an animal's common name: thus, readers will find an entry for the **Giant Squid**, while reports of giant anacondas will be found under the header **Anaconda (Giant)**.

- *Cross-references.* Cross-referencing in this work is accomplished by two means. First, subjects with their own discrete entries are presented in SMALL CAPITALS the first time they appear in another entry (e.g., "When the INTERNATIONAL SOCIETY OF CRYPTOZOOLOGY was formed in 1982"). Elsewhere, "see" references direct readers to other entries in the text; e.g., "**Father-of-All-Turtles** see **Turtles (Giant)**."

- *Sources.* While the work includes a comprehensive bibliography, each entry also has a short list of sources for the reader's immediate convenience. Sources found in the main bibliography are abbreviated when they appear with individual entries (e.g., "Sanderson, *Abominable Snowmen*"). Sources not included in the bibliography (chiefly short articles or sources of only peripheral interest to cryptozoologists) are presented at the end of specific entries with full information on place and date of publication.

Every effort has been made to ensure accuracy in this volume. Readers wishing to submit possible corrections or new material for future editions may contact the author in care of the publisher or by visiting his Internet website at http://www.michaelnewton.homestead.com/.

I owe thanks to the following individuals (listed alphabetically) for their valuable contributions to this volume: Danny Bamping; Matthew Bille; John Bindernagel; H.G. Cogger, deputy director of the Australian Museum in Sydney; Loren Coleman; David Frasier, reference librarian at Indiana University; Jeffrey Graf, at Indiana University; Bernard Heuvelmans; J. Richard Greenwell; Lenore Locken; Jeffrey Meldrum; Heather Newton; John W. Patterson; Michel Raynal; Bill Rebsamen; Bobbie Short; Karl Shuker; and Autumn Williams.

Introduction

Where be monsters?

On every continent, in every nation, animals unrecognized by modern science are reported on a daily basis. In the oceans, lakes and rivers; in the rain forests and desert wastes; on mountain pinnacles and in the everlasting night of caverns underground; in distant lands and in our own backyards, they wait. The men and women who pursue them are propelled by passion.

And their passion has a name: cryptozoology.

What does it mean?

Dr. BERNARD HEUVELMANS coined the term cryptozoology in the 1950s, though French author LUCIEN BLANCOU was first to use it in print, in his book *Géographie Cynégétique du Monde* (1959). Heuvelmans constructed the word from the Greek roots *kryptos* (hidden), *zoon* (animal) and *logos* (discourse) — thus, literally, the science of hidden animals. Decades later, he elaborated to define cryptozoology as "the scientific study of hidden animals, i.e., of still unknown animal forms about which only testimonial or circumstantial evidence is available, or material evidence considered insufficient by some." When the INTERNATIONAL SOCIETY OF CRYPTOZOOLOGY (ISC) was formed in 1982, with Heuvelmans as president, the founders declared that cryptozoology also concerns "the possible existence of *known* animals in areas where they are not supposed to occur (either now or in the past) as well as the unknown persistence of presumed extinct animals to the present time or to the recent past.... What makes an animal of interest to cryptozoology ... is that it is *unexpected*."

What is excluded?

As Heuvelmans explained, cryptozoology "is not an arcane or occult zoology." False claims by some dishonest critics notwithstanding, it has never been concerned with vampires, werewolves, zombies and the like. It has nothing to do with ghosts, UFOs or alleged close encounters with extraterrestrials. That said, some cryptozoologists do study mythical monsters, seeking to identify the flesh-and-blood creatures that spawned ancient legends. Prime examples of such work include Peter Costello's *The Magic Zoo* (1979) and KARL SHUKER'S *Dragons: A Natural History* (1995).

When did cryptozoology begin?

Before the 19th century, zoologists around the world focused as much on discovery of new species as on resolving mysteries of those already known to humankind. In effect, zoology itself *was* cryptozoology, and global exploration during the 15th to 17th centuries opened whole new worlds for study. Sadly, the rapid advance of knowledge bred a kind of scientific arrogance which survives to the present day. In 1812, Baron Georges Cuvier (1769-1832), a French biologist widely hailed as the "father of paleontology," boldly declared: "There is little hope of discovering new species of large quadrupeds." As for SEA SERPENTS and other unknown marine species, Cuvier wrote, "I hope nobody will ever seriously look for them in nature; one could as well search for the animals of Daniel or for the beast of the Apocalypse."

Those opinions, as Heuvelmans later observed, comprised a "rash dictum" indeed. Cuvier lived to see himself proved wrong with the discovery of the American TAPIR (1819) and the world's largest FISH, the whale SHARK (1828), but that was by no means the scope of his error. Thomas Jefferson, speaking for North America a mere 17 years before Cuvier's pronouncement, observed: "In the present interior of our continent there is surely space and range enough for elephants and LIONS, if in that climate they could subsist, and for MAMMOTHS and megalonyxes who may subsist there. Our entire ignorance of the immense country to the West and North-West, and of its contents, does not authorize us to say what it does not contain." The same could certainly be said of other continents as well, where post–Cuvier discoveries of the 19th century would include the CHIMPANZEE (1834), the lowland GORILLA (1847), the giant panda (1868), the pygmy hippopotamus (1870) and Grévy's zebra (1882). At sea, the GIANT SQUID'S existence was not scientifically confirmed until 1857.

Despite Cuvier's influence, early cryptozoologists persevered, inviting ridicule and ostracism from their peers. In Cuvier's own homeland, Pierre Denys de Montfort (1764-

1820) and Constantin Samuel Rafinesque (1783-1840) boldly maintained that large unknown creatures still thrived in the seas. In 1844, Hugh Falconer (1808-65) proposed that the survival of a giant prehistoric TURTLE (*Colossochelys atlas*) into historical times might explain the Hindu myth of a turtle supporting the Earth. Four years later, Charles Hamilton Smith (1776-1859) suggested that American aborigines may have hunted mammoths and the huge sloths known as *MEGATHERIUM*. Charles Carter Blake (1840-88) opined in 1863 that Brazilian legends of a giant APE called Cayaporé might be explained by survival of the primate *Protopithecus antiquus* into historical times. Heinrich Rathke (1793-1890) was another sea serpent believer, while fellow German Fritz Müller proposed the existence of parallel "freshwater sea serpents," more commonly known as LAKE MONSTERS. The Rev. John George Wood (1827-99) added a religious vote of confidence for sea serpents in his June 1894 article for *Atlantic Monthly*. Hard on the heels of that pronouncement, Dutch researcher ANTOON OUDEMANS devoted his career to studying aquatic cryptids. All these, and doubtless others since forgotten, were the intellectual forefathers of cryptozoology.

What are "cryptids"?

John E. Wall, writing to the ISC's quarterly newsletter in summer 1983, proposed that the term cryptid ("hidden animal") should replace the pejorative "monster" label in future discussions of animals studied by cryptozoology. Many such beasts, after all, are monstrous neither in appearance nor behavior. As cryptozoologist ROY MACKAL observes, "There are no monsters, just unidentified animals."

Discovery of the giant panda challenged Baron Cuvier's dictum on new species.

Accordingly, I have avoided application of the monster tag within this book unless it is part of a cryptid's popular name (e.g., the SYKESVILLE MONSTER) or where imputed behavior has made the term appropriate for many.

In further defining cryptids, Heuvelmans observed: "For an unknown animal to be reported, or for it to bring attention to itself, it is necessary that it should be *highly visible*, and hence must be of an *appreciable size*." He left that size unspecified, however, adding that his dictum "should perhaps be supplemented by that of *abnormal size* within a certain group." In 1985, J. RICHARD GREENWELL proposed a system of classification for cryptids that includes the following seven groups:

1. Individuals of a known, living species whose form, size, color or pattern is extraordinary for the species (e.g., giant ANACONDAS, spotted lions, etc.).

2. Extant and well-known species unrecognized as living in a particular area (e.g., KANGAROOS in North America).

3. Presumably extinct species, not fossil forms, known only from limited organic evidence (skin, bones, feathers, etc.), but without a complete type specimen.

4. Known species presumed extinct within historical times (e.g., the THYLACINE), which may have survived much longer and perhaps to the present day.

5. Representatives of fossil forms (e.g., DINOSAURS) presumed extinct during geologic times, which may have survived into historical times or to the present day.

6. New species known from anecdotal evidence, for which no known organic evidence exists.

7. New species not reported previously or known to aboriginal people, which may be accidentally discovered. A case in point is the megamouth shark (*Megachasma pelagios*), unknown and unsuspected before the first specimen was hooked near Oahu, Hawaii, in November 1976. Greenwell notes, however, that this final group "is not cryptozoological in the complete sense of the definition," since truly unknown creatures cannot be hunted.

Where do cryptids hide?

Skeptics commonly insist that every part of Earth, if not yet "settled" by humans, has nonetheless been thoroughly explored and mapped. Any good atlas seems to prove the point — but in this case, appearances are deceptive.

Some 71 percent of Earth's surface is covered by water, including lakes, rivers, oceans and seas. Parts of the vast Pacific Ocean are nearly seven miles deep, while the Atlantic's Puerto Rico Trench plummets to 5.4 miles, and even the relatively shallow Caribbean boasts depths of 4.8 miles off the Cayman Islands. Much of what happens below the surface is anyone's guess. As Jesse Ausubel, director of the ongoing Census of Marine Life (CML) project, told BBC News in October 2003, "Some 95 percent of the ocean is still unexplored biologically. We know more about the surface of the moon." During the first three years of its 10-year global survey, CML scientists cataloged 15,304 marine species worldwide, at least 500 of them formerly unknown to science. Ausubel hoped to identify another 2,000 to 3,000 species before the work ended in 2010. Meanwhile, in June 2003, marine biologists aboard the research vessel *Tangaroa* reported that they had found more than 400 new species of sea life—including 100-odd fishes and 300 invertebrates—during a four-week survey conducted in waters northwest of New Zealand.

What about dry land? Surprisingly, the global picture is not as clear as outspoken skeptics would have us believe. In December 2002, the Washington-based group Conservation International reported that 46 percent of Earth's land surface—more than 26.3 million square miles—still qualified as wilderness, a designation indicating blocks of 3,800 square miles or larger in size, with 70 percent or more of the original vegetation intact and fewer than 10 human dwellers per square mile. Nearly one-third of that wilderness area (some 8.9 million square miles) comprised Antarctica and the Arctic tundra, while other large tracts were found in the Sahara Desert and in the vast forests of Alaska, Canada, the Congo, Russia and Papua New Guinea. Already, the 21st century's surprises include the following:

January 2001— Some 500 years after European explorers "discovered" the Amazon River, scientists armed with satellite technology finally traced its source for the first time.

November 2001— Scientists in Ecuador announced discovery of a 123,500-acre "virgin forest never before seen by humans."

August 2002— Russian scientists in North Africa proclaimed the discovery of an underground river, deemed "a world miracle," flowing beneath the sands of the Sahara Desert. In the same month, Canadian workmen assigned to cap two old artesian wells found another large subterranean river flowing beneath Toronto.

November 2002— Archaeologists discovered evidence of a previously unknown civilization, dating from 750 BCE to A.D. 400, concealed by jungle on the Atlantic coast of Nicaragua.

February 2003— Satellite surveys revealed 1,000 previously unknown islands in the Indonesian archipelago. Of the country's 18,000 islands, only 6,000 are inhabited by humans, with more than half of Indonesia's population residing on Java.

September 2003— Yet another lost civilization was discovered in South America. This one, in the heart of the Amazon jungle, included "clusters of extensive settlements linked by wide roads and surrounded by agricultural developments" that flourished in pre–Columbian times.

At this point, skeptics may grant the possibility of cryptic habitats remaining in some "Third World" jungle, but they will insist that no such possibility exists in North America. And once again, they are mistaken.

Any schoolchild knows that Canada and the United States are mapped in thorough and meticulous detail. What they too often fail to grasp, however, is the way in which such maps are made. Before the invention of aircraft, wilderness regions were typically mapped by exploring rivers and coastlines, noting mountain peaks and other landmarks visible from shore, and filling in the rest by guesswork or by word of mouth from hardy individuals who traveled off the beaten track and lived to tell (or sometimes fabricate) the tale. It was a haphazard method at best, fraught with pitfalls. In 1961, author IVAN SANDERSON discovered that northern California had last been "surveyed" in 1859, while around the same time, a mountain range in South America was found to be misplaced by some 200 miles on standard maps. Modern maps are enhanced by aerial and satellite photography, but for all their marvelous applications in espionage, those high-tech methods reveal nothing of wildlife beneath the treetops, be it in Africa, Southeast Asia, or the Pacific Northwest.

What *is* the present state of exploration in "civilized" North America? Canada, sprawling over 3.9 million square miles, is the second largest country on Earth (after Russia). Its average population density of eight persons per square mile qualifies the whole nation as wilderness, but even that figure is deceptive, since 46 percent of Canada's people reside in nine large cities, all but one of them within 100 miles of the U.S. border. When we subtract the urban population from Canada's total, the country's population density drops to 4.7 persons per square mile. Ninety percent of British Columbia is virtually uninhabited, and the northern provinces are wilder still: the Yukon Territory boasts 16 persons per 100 square miles; the Northwest Territories has seven persons per 100 square miles; and Nunavut has only three per 100 square miles.

The United States, with an average of 80 persons per square mile, is more densely populated than Canada, but once again large urban populations skew the figures. Nationwide, huge tracts of wilderness—mountain ranges, deserts, forests, swamps and "bottomlands," state and national parks—remain largely uninhabited and unexplored. In July 2002, a *New York Times* report pinpointed "America's wildest valley" along the North Fork of Montana's Flathead River, abutting Glacier National Park and the Canadian border. (Statewide, rural Montana's population density is only 3.9 persons per square mile.) Other wilderness areas rival that site for remoteness, and a study of large-scale maps quickly reveals a correlation between U.S. cryptid sightings and the nation's underpopulated regions.

In short, there are countless places for cryptids to hide on Earth, particularly since most "mainstream" scientists refuse to look for them at all.

How many species remain undiscovered?

The short answer is, no one knows. Carolus Linnaeus counted 4,406 species when he prepared the first catalog of global fauna in 1758, and the numbers have grown dramatically over the past 247 years. Some of the tabulations:

> 1817 — Georges Cuvier: 5,738
> 1850 — Johannes Leunis: 108,897
> 1886 — Leunis and Hubert Ludwig: 273,220
> 1896 — Karl Möbius: 418,600
> 1911 — H.S. Pratt: 522,400
> 1928 — R. Hesse: 1,013,773
> 1946 — Ernst Mayr: 1,000,000
> 1950 — Bernard Heuvelmans: 1,040,000
> 2000 — Paul Massicot: 1,800,000

Despite Cuvier's prediction in 1812, new species were discovered at an average rate of 4,500 per year throughout the 19th century. That figure increased to 12,000 yearly in the first half of the 20th century and never fell below 9,000 per year in the century's latter half. Granted, most of those new species ranged in size from relatively small to microscopic, but large surprises still awaited discovery. A sampling includes the okapi (1901), the mountain gorilla (1902), the giant forest hog (1904), the Komodo DRAGON (1912), the kouprey (1937), the VU QUANG ox (1992), the giant muntjac (1994), and the leaf muntjac (1997). At sea, while Linnaeus listed only 23 species more than six feet long in 1758, Charles Paxton found 220 in

2001 and estimated that another 51 large species still awaited discovery.

Worldwide, scientific estimates of living species still unknown to humans range from 2 million to 20 million or more. Frederick Grassle, director of Rutgers University's Institute of Marine and Coastal Sciences, estimates that the deep sea alone may contain 10 million unknown species. The All Species Foundation, created in 2000, ambitiously aims to identify and catalog all life on earth by 2025 — the span of one human generation — but it offered no progress report at press time for this book.

How does cryptozoology work?

Heuvelmans called cryptozoology the "sister science" of paleontology, explaining that both "depend on reconstructions — through interpolation, extrapolation, or conjecture — on the basis of incomplete data." Three modes of proof are recognized, including *autopical* (that observed with one's own eyes), *testimonial* or anecdotal (events described by witnesses to non-observers), and *circumstantial* (analyzing bits of physical evidence). Science commonly demands autopical proof and rejects the anecdotal, while courts of law reverse the procedure completely. Heuvelmans outlined the following steps for an ideal cryptozoological investigation:

1. Collect all available evidence and information concerning a cryptid's alleged existence, including surveys of regional linguistics and mythology. Remember that legends and "native tales" sometimes describe real-life creatures, albeit in exaggerated terms.

2. Analyze the data, comparing any physical evidence with known organisms of similar appearance, while allowing for exaggeration in eyewitness reports and eliminating cases of mistaken identity or obvious HOAXES.

3. Create "a sort of identikit-picture" of the cryptid and attempt to place it within the known classes of animal

Left: **Mountain gorillas were unrecognized by science until 1902 (*William Rebsamen*). *Right:* The okapi was considered mythical until its official discovery in 1901.**

life. Once a creature and its habitat have been described, the final search begins.

What about the skeptics?

All true cryptozoologists are skeptics, normally defined as persons who question the validity or authenticity of purported factual data. However, as Professor Marcello Truzzi of Eastern Michigan University observes, the "skeptic" label has been hijacked and abused in many debates over cryptozoology and other unconventional subjects. Many self-styled skeptics are in fact professional debunkers, prejudging every subject they approach, devoted to ridicule and misrepresentation in lieu of detailed analysis. A skeptic's mind may change, but the debunker's mind is closed before debate begins. In essence, a skeptic says, "I'll believe it when I see it." The debunker's creed, by contrast, is entirely dogmatic: "I'll *see* it when I *believe* it."

Why does cryptozoology matter?

In August 2001, famed primatologist Richard Leakey warned a South African audience that Earth's plant, insect and animal species are dying off at a rate of some 50,000 to 100,000 species per year. "At that rate," he declared, "we are probably approaching a point similar to mass extinction." Some species vanish as a result of natural selection, but many more are threatened by the conscious acts of human beings — hunting, environmental pollution, and destruction of habitats in the name of "progress." Most scientists today accept the fact that mankind has unconsciously eradicated species without ever knowing they existed.

In order to protect new species, some of which are almost certainly endangered at the present time, those species first must be located and identified. The urgency of that effort increases with rare species, some of which may hold the keys to understanding human ancestry, while others

Discovery of the okapi and the saola, separated by almost a century, demonstrate the importance of cryptozoology today (**William Rebsamen**).

may provide undreamed-of benefits to all life on the planet. As Leakey observes, "It is easier to prevent [extinction] than to cure [it]." For some creatures, it may already be too late, but we will never known unless we try.

Despite the nay-sayers, we live, still, in a world of possibilities. The days of exploration and discovery are not behind us yet. But if we never seek, we cannot find. And if we never ask, how can we learn?

The most beautiful thing we can experience is the mysterious.
It is the source of all true art and all science.
He to whom this emotion is a stranger,
who can no longer pause to wonder and stand rapt in awe,
is as good as dead. His eyes are closed.
—*Albert Einstein*

The Encyclopedia

A

Aar River, Switzerland   Sightings of huge, eel-like creatures were reported from this river in central Switzerland during the 15th and 16th centuries, whenever the nearby lake of Luzern was flooded. A lack of sightings for this apparent LAKE MONSTER in modern times suggests that it is probably extinct.
Source: "Eel be back." *Fortean Times* 123 (June 1999): 44.

Abasambo *see* **Lions (Spotted)**

Åbborvatnet, Norway   Located in Oppland County, Åbborvatnet boasts a nearby lake where a gunsmith named Børse-Gunder reportedly shot an unidentified serpentine creature. Unfortunately, no details of the incident have been preserved, including the date, and it is thus impossible to evaluate.
Source: Erik Knatterud, "Sea Serpents in Norwegian Lakes." http://www.mjoesormen.no.

Abnauayu   An unknown HOMINID reported from the Caucasus Mountains, the Abnauayu takes its best-known local name from the Abkhaz language, meaning "forest man" or "shy boy" (reports vary). Alternate names in different parts of the Caucasus range are Bnahua and Ochokochi. The creature is described as man-sized and muscular, covered with reddish-black hair. The hair on its head is typically long and flowing in back. Facial features commonly described include a low jutting brow, reddish-tinted eyes, high cheekbones and prominent teeth. In female specimens, the breasts and buttocks are pronounced. Witnesses describe the Abnauayu as uttering garbled sounds, but it is seemingly incapable of speech. Some reports describe the creatures using sticks and stones as improvised tools or weapons.
Russian investigator BORIS PORSHNEV collected reports of the Abnauayu in the 1960s, including several accounts of a female specimen dubbed ZANA, who was reportedly captured in the late 19th century and who allegedly bore four mixed-breed children to human males in the village where she was confined. On the basis of reports collected from the region, Porshnev and BERNARD HEUVELMANS speculated that the Abnauayu might comprise a relict population of NEANDERTALS.
Sources: Bayanov, *In the Footsteps of the Russian Snowman*; Heuvelmans and Porshnev, *L'homme de Néanderthal est toujours vivant*.

Abominable Snowman   While the Himalayan YETI has been recognized by local residents for centuries, reported by Western visitors since the late 19th century, its best-known nickname was not coined until 1921, and only then by accident. Ironically, a simple error spawned global notoriety for a creature that otherwise might have remained virtually unknown outside Central Asia.
Lieutenant Colonel C.K. Howard-Bury was leading a British reconnaissance patrol on the north face of Mt. Everest (the Tibetan side) in September 1921, approaching the Lhapka-La pass at 17,000 feet, when he sighted several dark forms trudging across a snowfield high above. Howard-Bury watched them through binoculars, but observed no significant details. When his party reached the spot on 22 September, they found manlike tracks "three times those of normal humans" in size. Howard-Bury's Sherpa guides identified the creatures who had left the tracks as *metoh-kangmi,* a mixture of Nepalese (*meh-teh,* "man-sized wild creature") and Chinese (*kang-mi,* "snow creature") roughly translated as "man-sized snow creature."
Already strange enough, the tale took a bizarre turn when

Howard-Bury cabled his report to Calcutta. There, a telegrapher mistakenly transcribed the creature's name as *metch kangmi,* a term which no one in the office recognized. A local know-it-all, columnist Henry Newman of the *Calcutta Statesman,* volunteered to translate, declaring that *metch* was a Nepalese term meaning "horrible" or "abominable"—and so the "Abominable Snowman" was born in florid headlines flashed by teletype around the world.
"The result," as cryptozoologist IVAN SANDERSON wrote 40 years later, "was like the explosion of an atom bomb." It opened a floodgate of Yeti reports spanning decades and launched a series of investigations that continue to the present day. Despite exposure of its origins, the nickname was too colorful to die, reduced to a kind of shorthand in recent times, with many authors lumping Yeti and its fellow cryptic hominids together as "ABSMs." As late as 30 August 1992 one Yeti hunter claimed, on television's "Unsolved Mysteries," that the Abominable Snowman had been labeled for its loathsome body odor.
Sources: Coleman and Clark, *Cryptozoology A to Z*; Sanderson, *Abominable Snowmen*.

Abominable Snowmen Club of America   In 1966, BIGFOOT researcher Roger Patterson published a book titled *Do Abominable Snowmen of America Really Exist?* Around the same time, Patterson created the Abominable Snowmen Club of America, operating from his home in Yakima, Washington. The club offered membership certificates and sold phonograph recordings of eyewitness encounters with a creature Patterson called the "Giant Hairy APE." A few months later, in October 1967, Patterson captured on film the most compelling and controversial images of Bigfoot ever seen. Debate over the PATTERSON FILM'S authenticity continues to the present day, but Patterson's "club" dissolved some time before his death from cancer, in 1972.
Sources: Coleman, *Bigfoot!*; Keel, *The Complete Guide to Mysterious Creatures*.

Abonesi   A small HOMINID reported from the northern sector of Togo, in West Africa, the Abonesi is said to be a forest-dweller covered in dark hair. Suggested explanations for the sightings include an unidentified species of APE and a possible relict population of *Australopithecus.*
Source: Heuvelmans, *Les bêtes humaines d'Afrique*.

Abu Sotan *see* **Wobo**

Abyssal Rainbow Gar   Sighted only once to date, by submarine explorer WILLIAM BEEBE in the early 1930s, the abyssal rainbow gar was reported from the North Atlantic off Bermuda, seen at a depth of 2,500 feet. Beebe described the still-unclassified FISH as four inches long, with a crimson head, blue body and yellow tail. It was otherwise noteworthy for its long beak and its habit of swimming in a stiff, upright posture.
Source: Beebe, *Half Mile Down*.

Academy of Applied Science   Founded at Belmont, Massachusetts in March 1963, the Academy of Applied Science (AAS) is a nonprofit, tax-exempt educational group whose stated goal is "to ensure that innovation continues to flourish as the essence of human spirit and the foundation of the world's freedom and prosperity." From its present headquarters in Concord, New Hampshire, the AAS collaborates with various other foundations and public schools to promote scientific education at every grade level. Since 1970, founder and president ROBERT RINES has led a series of expeditions to Loch Ness, Scotland, where AAS members obtained some of the most dramatic photographs and sonar tracks of NESSIE yet recorded. In 1992, an AAS team also participated in the search for BIGFOOT, but without results. Cryptozoology is not the group's primary concern, and indeed receives no mention on the AAS Internet website, but its contribution to LAKE MONSTER research can scarcely be exaggerated.

Sources: Harrison, *Encyclopedia of the Loch Ness Monster*; Rines, "Summarizing a decade of underwater studies at Loch Ness"; Wyckoff, et al., "An unmanned motion-sensitive automatic infrared camera tested in a Pacific Northwest quest for possible large primates."

Acámbaro Figurines

Acámbaro, Mexico lies in an arid highland valley (formerly an Ice Age lake) in the state of Guanajuato, 175 miles northwest of Mexico City. In 1944 a huge cache of primitive figurines was discovered at Acámbaro by Waldemar Julsrud, a local merchant who had made another archaeological strike at nearby Chupícuaro, in 1923. The later find was far more spectacular, ultimately yielding 33,500 ceramic figurines, stone objects (including jade) and obsidian knives. The figurines were startling for their depiction of various races, Egyptian-Sumerian motifs, plus creatures resembling DINOSAURS and prehistoric mammals. One sculpture clearly depicts a long-tailed reptilian quadruped swallowing a man head-first. Another portrays a man standing beside an APE of nearly human size.

Heated controversy surrounds the Acámbaro figurines to this day. Archaeologist Charles DiPeso alleged that Julsrud was duped by a family of Mexican peasants (still unnamed) who prepared the objects as a HOAX. In 1952, after a four-hour visit with Julsrud, DiPeso claimed he had "minutely examined" Julsrud's full collection — then comprising some 32,000 pieces — and pronounced the objects fraudulent. Another archaeologist challenged that assertion, noting that DiPeso must have "minutely examined" 133 pieces per minute to complete his survey in the allotted time.

Charles Hapgood, a professor of history and anthropology at the University of New Hampshire, visited Julsrud for the first time in 1955 and pronounced the objects genuine. Cryptozoologist IVAN SANDERSON and mystery author Erle Stanley Gardner (creator of the Perry Mason series) collaborated with Hapgood and shared his opinion. Hapgood submitted three of Julsrud's artifacts to the Teledynes Isotopes laboratory in 1968, for radiocarbon dating. Those tests dated the objects between 1110 B.C. and 4530 B.C. Similar tests, performed at the University of Pennsylvania in 1972, dated other objects in Julsrud's collection at 2500 B.C. Two decades later, further tests (using thermoluminescence techniques) placed the age of tested figurines around 3,975 ± 55 years.

Some students of the Acámbaro figurines maintain that they are proof of dinosaur survival into relatively recent times — and by extrapolation, perhaps to the present day. Critics admit no such thing and insist that the whole cache is fake. John Tierney accused the Smithsonian Institution of mounting a "disinformation" campaign to discredit Julsrud's collection. Finally, after filing suit under the U.S. Freedom of Information Act, Tierney discovered that the Smithsonian's files on the Acámbaro collection had vanished.

Source: Hapgood, *Mystery in Acambaro*.

Acorn Worm (Giant)

Although recognized by a scientific name (*Planctosphaera pelagica*), the giant acorn worm has never been observed in adult form. It is known only from larvae (tornariae), much larger than those of other hemichordates in the class *Enteropneusta*, which appear as transparent spheres with the internal organs visible. Based on the normal ratio of development for other species, marine biologists calculate that the adult *Planctosphaera* might grow to a length of nine feet. It is believed to dwell in the North Pacific and the Eastern North Atlantic, thriving in mud at depths between 250 feet and 1,660 feet. Critics complain that the giant worm's classification was premature, suggesting that the *Planctosphaera* larvae might be abnormally enlarged tornariae of another species which failed to reach adulthood. A similar argument has been advanced against the theoretical existence of giant EELS.

Sources: M.G. Hadfield and R.E. Young, "Planctosphaera (Hemichordata: Enteropneusta) in the Pacific Ocean." *Marine Biology* 73 (1983): 151–153; C.J. van der Horst, "Planctosphaera and Tornaria." *Quarterly Journal of Microscopial Science* 78 (1936): 605–613.

Adamant sea serpent

In May 1818 several U.S. newspapers published reports of a sea monster sighting recorded by Capt. Joseph Woodward of the schooner *Adamant*, allegedly occurring on 10 May at a point ten leagues from the coast of Hingham, England. Woodward's letter described an animal "the size of a large boat," which he supposed to be ship wreckage until it was revealed as "a monstrous serpent." Woodward claimed to have fired a deck gun at the creature, whereupon the projectiles "rebounded as if they had struck against a rock." Woodward described the creature as twice the length of his schooner (i.e., 130 feet), with a head 12 to 14 feet long. Woodward's affidavit was also published in the *Quarterly Journal of Science, Literature and the Arts of the Royal Institute of London*, and reprinted 30 years later in the *Zoologist*. The latter publication evoked criticism of inconsistencies in Woodward's account, and BERNARD HEUVELMANS subsequently dismissed it as a HOAX.

Source: Huevelmans, *In the Wake of the Sea Serpents*.

Adam-Ayu

An unknown HOMINID reported from the Tian Shan Mountains in China's Xinjiang Uygur Autonomous Region, the Adam-Ayu draws its name from the Kazakh term "bear man." It appears to be similar, if not identical, to the Chinese YEREN or the Himalayan YETI. It is almost certainly identical to the ADAM-DZHAPAIS reported from the Kunlun Mountains of Xinjiang and from other parts of Central Asia.

Source: Tchernine, *The Yeti*.

Adam-Dzhapais

An unknown HOMINID reported from various regions of Central Asia, including the Pamir Mountains of Tajikistan and the Kunlun Mountains of China's Xinjiang Uygur Autonomous Region. Its common name means "wild man" in the Kyrgyz language; alternate regional names include Adamjapais, Adam-yapayisy, Adam-yavei, Japayi-kishi and Zhabayi-adam. The man-sized hairy creature may be identical to the ADAM-AYU reported from Xinjiang's Tian Shan Mountains.

Sources: Heuvelmans and Porshnev, *L'homme de Néanderthal est toujours vivant*; Tchernine, *The Yeti*.

Adelong sea serpent

In the last week of May 1903, crewmen on the fishing boat *Adelong* reported sightings of an unidentified "monster" on four successive nights, at Burra Haaf in the Shetland Islands. The creature destroyed ten of their nets and passed so close to the boat they had to push it away with a boat hook. They described its skin as covered with a foul-smelling slime. Around the same time, on 30 May 1903, witness

J.P. Jamieson sighted a similar creature off Scalloway, in the Shetlands. He described the beast as 30 feet long, shaped "like a sail," and claimed that "on its head it had what appeared to be a horn, and an enormous flipper-like appendage." Thirty years after the fact, a surviving *Adelong* crew member refused to discuss the event, apparently fearing that sea monster sightings produced bad luck for the witnesses. BERNARD HEUVELMANS accepted the sightings as genuine but believed the creature was a common basking shark; researcher TIM DINSDALE, in his report of the case, was less certain of the creature's identity.

Source: Dinsdale, *Monster Hunt*; Heuvelmans, *In the Wake of the Sea Serpents.*

Adirondack Research Organization

According to its Internet website, this group is dedicated to "investigating BIGFOOT in [the] upstate New York counties of Albany, Columbia, Essex, Fulton, Greene, Montgomery, Rennselaer [*sic*], Schenectady, Schoharie, Warren and Washington." Founder Paul Bartholemew is the coauthor (with brother Bob) of a book on New York's Bigfoot, *Monsters of the Northwoods* (1992). While the ARO's website lists only three sightings between 1989 and 2000, New York boasts a rich history of Bigfoot (or NORTH AMERICAN APE) encounters. In fact, one of North America's earliest Bigfoot sightings by a white settler was recorded near Ellisburgh, New York, in September 1818. Sightings continue sporadically, for a published total of 56 by autumn 1989.

Sources: Berry, *Bigfoot on the East Coast*; Bord and Bord, *The Bigfoot Casebook*; Rife, *Bigfoot Across America*; ARO website at http://squatchdetective.freeyellow.com/.

Adjulé

A large wolflike animal reported from the Sahara Desert, the Adjulé is described as distinct in appearance from known FOXES and JACKALS. Tuareg tribesmen call females of the species Tarhsit, while the name Adjulé is reserved for males. BERNARD HEUVELMANS opined in 1986 that the Adjulé is "obviously" identical with the *kelb-el-khela* (bush dog) found in neighboring Mauritania—which in turn has been identified as the African hunting dog (*Lycaon pictus*). If so, the desert habitat varies greatly from *Lycaon*'s usual range over savannas and the tropics farther south.

Source: Heuvelmans, "Annotated checklist of apparently unknown animals with which cryptozoology is concerned."

Adlekhe-Titin

An unknown HOMINID reported from the northwestern section of Russia's Caucasus Mountains, the Adlekhe-titin is described as man-sized and covered with hair. Its name is Ubykh for "mountain man"; alternate regional names include Lakhatet and Lakshir. It may be identical to the ALMAS, reported from other parts of the Caucasus range.

Sources: John Colarusso, "Ethnographic information on a wild man of the Caucasus," in Halpin and Ames, *Manlike Monsters on Trial.*

Aeronaut sea serpent

On 20 June 1879, Captain Wells of the ship *Aeronaut* reported sighting a large, unidentified creature swimming two miles off the coast of Cape Ann, Massachusetts. Details of the sighting are unfortunately vague, but the description apparently conformed to the "serpent" popularly dubbed *SCOLIOPHIS ATLANTICUS.*

Source: O'Neill, *The Great New England Sea Serpent.*

Afa

A large unidentified lizard, possibly a new species of MONITOR (family *Varanidae*), the Afa is said to inhabit marshes at the mouth of Iraq's Tigris River.

Source: Wilfred Thesiger, *The Marsh Arabs*. New York: Dutton, 1964.

Afanc

A LAKE MONSTER reported from Wales, the Afanc ("beaver") is variously described as a giant BEAVER or a CROCODILE. Reports date from Medieval times, when King Arthur allegedly killed an Afanc in Llyn Barfog (at Gwynedd, Wales). More recently, a witness named Oliver Vaughan, hiking on the slopes of Snowdon sometime in the 1930s, reported sighting the creature's pale head below him, in Lyn Glaslyn (near Powys). Afanc reports have also been filed from Llyn yr Afanc (Beaver Pond), at Conwy. The Afanc is said to attack humans and drag them underwater. More fanciful reports also blame the creature for occasional flooding.

Sources: Holiday, *The Great Orm of Loch Ness*; John Rhys, *Celtic Folklore, Welsh and Manx.* Oxford: Clarendon, 1901.

Åfjordvatnet, Norway

A lake near this town, in Finnmark County, is said to host a serpentine cryptid. Four witnesses reported a group sighting in 1977, describing the creature as 15 feet long, with several humps visible above the lake's surface.

Source: Erik Knatterud, "Sea Serpents in Norwegian Lakes." http://www.mjoesormen.no.

Afonya

A large HOMINID, described as seven or eight feet and covered with gray hair, the Afonya reportedly inhabits the Kola Peninsula of northern Russia (separating the White and Berents Seas). Witnesses describe the creature as having a round head and wrinkled face, with wide-set reddish eyes. It uses its long arms for knuckle-walking, apelike, and displays pale-colored buttocks when retreating. Reports suggest a nocturnal lifestyle and attribute loud mooing sounds to the Afonya. Some accounts describe the creature hurling rocks and sticks when frightened. It reportedly sleeps in abandoned cabins and sometimes steals dogs.

The most concentrated "flap" of Afonya sightings occurred in 1988, when several teenagers on a fishing trip to Lake Lovozero (near Murmansk) were allegedly harassed by the creature for several successive days in August and September. They coined the creature's nickname, variously described as a diminutive form of the Russian name Afanasii and as the title of a popular Russian film produced in 1975 (about an alcoholic plumber). Around the same time, a local game warden sighted the Afonya, and a team of researchers led by Maya Bykova also reported a sighting. Bykova's team returned in the summer of 1989, collecting feces, hair and local eyewitness reports. Bykova's team reportedly used different animal calls to lure the creature on two occasions, and while no photographs were taken, they recorded several whistling cries emitted by the Afonya in response. Footprints left by the creature during one such encounter measured 15 inches in length.

Source: Bayanov, *In the Footsteps of the Russian Snowman.*

Agatch-Kishi

A man-sized hairy HOMINID reported from Russia's Caucasus Mountains, the Agatch-kishi is probably identical to the more widely reported ALMAS. Its name is the Karachay-Balkar term for "wild man."

Source: Bayanov, *In the Footsteps of the Russian Snowman.*

Agnagna, Marcellin

A Congolese zoologist, educated in Cuba, Marcellin Agnagna served as director of the Brazzaville Zoo in the 1980s. From that post, he encouraged research on MOKELE-MBEMBE, described by witnesses as a DINOSAUR dwelling in the African jungle. Agnagna joined cryptozoologists ROY MACKAL and J. RICHARD GREENWELL on their 1981 expedition to search for the creature, and subsequently led the first Congolese expedition in 1983. With other members of the native team, Agnagna claimed a sighting of their quarry on 1 May 1983, but his camera apparently malfunctioned and the film was ruined.

Sources: Agnagna, "Results of the first Congolese Mokele-mbembe expedition"; Mackal, A Living Dinosaur?

Agogino, George Allen (1923–2000)

George Agogino graduated from high school in Philadelphia as a star athlete and was chosen for the U.S. Olympic track team for the 1940 summer Olympic Games (canceled by World War II in Europe). He volunteered for military service at age 20 and served in the Pacific, where he reported sighting an unknown freshwater shark in New Guinea's LAKE SENTANI. Upon discharge, Agogino earned a bachelor's degree in anthropology and a master's in sociology from the University of New Mexico, moving on from there to teach in Maine while completing his Ph.D. in anthropology at Syracuse University. In 1963 Agogino visited Portales, New Mexico to lead an archaeological dig and remained to create the anthropology department at Eastern New Mexico University (which he chaired for the next 11 years).

In addition to teaching and scholarly research, including publication of some 600 articles in various journals, Agogino nurtured a lifelong fascination for cryptozoology. He was an active colleague of researchers TOM SLICK, PETER BYRNE, CARLETON COON, IVAN SANDERSON and others. In 1959 he coordinated U.S. study of alleged YETI relics collected in Nepal and filed an insightful report on the PANGBOCHE HAND. Three decades later, Agogino regaled LOREN COLEMAN with tales of his covert service with the Central Intelligence Agency during the same period. Agogino retired from teaching as a Distinguished Research Professor in 1991. He died at his home in Portales on 11 September 2000.

Sources: Coleman, "Necrolog: Crypto-Crypt"; Coleman, Tom Slick and the Search for Yeti.

Agogwe

An unidentified HOMINID reported from Tanzania, in East Africa, the Agogwe is typically described as four feet tall and covered with reddish-brown hair. A report from witness William Hichens, published 10 years after the event, includes the following description:

In 1927 I was with my wife coasting Portuguese East Africa in a Japanese cargo boat. We were sufficiently near to land to see objects clearly with a glass of 12 magnifications. There was a sloping beach with light bush above upon which several dozen baboons were hunting for and picking up shell fish or crabs, to judge by their movements. Two pure white baboons were amongst them. These are very rare but I had heard of them previously. As we watched, two little brown men walked together out of the bush and down amongst the baboons. They were certainly not any known MONKEY and yet they must have been akin or they would have disturbed the baboons. They were too far away to see in detail, but these small human-like animals were probably between 4 and 5 feet tall, quite upright and graceful in figure. At the time I was thrilled as they were quite evidently no beast of which I had heard or read. Later a friend and big game hunter told me he was in Portuguese East Africa with his wife and three hunters, and saw a mother, father, and child, of apparently a similar animal species, walk across the further side of a bush clearing. The natives loudly forbade him to shoot.

BERNARD HEUVELMANS suggested that the Agogwe might comprise a relict population of Australopiths, inasmuch as world-famous discoveries of fossil footprints and remains have been made in Tanzania, at Laetoli (Australopithecus afarensis) and at Olduvai Gorge (Paranthropus boisei). Indeed, many anthropologists consider East Africa the birthplace of prehistoric hominids.

Sources: Hichens, "African mystery beasts"; Heuvelmans, Les bêtes humaines d'Afrique; Sanderson, Abominable Snowmen.

Ah-Een-Meelow

An unidentified SEA SERPENT reported from Ramat Bay, on the eastern shore of New Ireland, Papua New Guinea, the Ah-een-meelow ("fish eel") was named by local Barok tribesmen in an interview conducted by cryptozoologist J. RICHARD GREENWELL. Witnesses describe a serpentine creature some 50 feet long, capable of swimming at a speed of six knots (about 7 mph). The first sighting, recorded by an unnamed witness in August 1958, included four gray-green loops or humps seen above the ocean's surface, spaced roughly 10 feet apart. No head was seen, but the witness reported a frill on the creature's back and described a vertical, segmented tail about two feet long. A second sighting, by witness Bernie Gash and members of his family, occurred on 26 April 1981. Viewing the creature from an estimated distance of 600–900 feet, the Gashes described a raised neck and head "like a PYTHON'S," 10–15 feet long and two feet in diameter. After the head submerged, they saw several small humps moving briefly on the surface. Edward Gash, eight years old at the time of that incident, later described seven sightings of the Ah-een-meelow between 1981 and 1983.

Source: Cropper and Smith, "Some unpublicized 'sea serpent' reports."

Ahool

A nocturnal flying creature reported from the mountains of western Java, Indonesia, the Ahool is named for the sound of its haunting cry. It resembles a giant BAT, but its estimated wingspan of 11–12 feet and its torso the size of a one-year-old child's make it larger than any known species. Witnesses describe the Ahool as covered with dark gray fur and possessing a monkeylike face with large eyes. It is said to skim low over rivers, hunting for FISH, but attacks on human beings have also been reported. Dr. Ernest Bartels reported a sighting of the Ahool from the Salek Mountains, near Cijengkol, in 1925 or 1927 (reports vary).

Sources: Bartels and Sanderson, "The one true Batman"; Shuker, "A belfry of crypto-bats."

Ahuítzotl

A cryptid from Mesoamerican legend, the Ahuítzotl ("water dog") curiously shared its name with an Aztec ruler, the predecessor of famed Montezuma. It was described as a "small and smooth, shiny" canid with "small pointed ears, just like a small dog." In other respects, however, the Ahuítzotl was not distinctly canine. Its paws were said to resemble those of a raccoon or MONKEY, and some fanciful reports described its tail ending in an appendage "just like a human hand." The Ahuítzotl lived underwater, perhaps in caverns, and was said to drown human prey on occasion. Little more is known of the Ahuítzotl, which is presumed to be extinct. Christopher Columbus described a similar creature from Jamaica, in a letter written to the King and Queen of Spain on 7 July 1503:

A cross-bowman slew a beast that resembled a large CAT, but was much bigger and had a face like a man. He transfixed it with an arrow from the breast to the tail. Nevertheless it was so fierce that he had to cut off an arm and a leg. When a wild boar, which had been given to me as a present, caught sight of this beast its bristles stood on end and it fled with all speed....[The animal] immediately attacked the wild boar, encircled its mouth with its tail and squeezed it vigorously. With the one arm it had left, it throttled the wild boar's throat as one strangles a foe.

Similar (if less ferocious) "water dogs" also featured in the folklore of North America's Hopi and Shasta Indian tribes. Considering the Ahuítzotl's aquatic habits, author Andrew Gale suggests that it may have been an otter, possibly an unknown species.

Source: Gale, "Two possible cryptids from precolumbian Mesoamerica."

Aidakhar   The Aidakhar is an alleged LAKE MONSTER reported from Lake Kök-köl in the Dzambul region of Kazakhstan. Its local name, the Kazakh term for "huge SNAKE," befits descriptions of the Aidakhar as 45–50 feet long, with a head six feet long and three feet wide. The creature is described as having a long neck and displaying a single hump when it swims. Some reports include mention of a trumpeting call that announces the Aidakhar's appearance. Witnesses Anatolii and Volodya Pechersky reported a sighting of the Aidakhar in 1975, viewed from a distance of 25 feet, but skeptics insist that the "creature" is simply a transient whirlpool, caused by water flooding underground caverns. Between 31 January and 2 February 1977, ANTHONY SHIELS and Indian fakir Chandra Rao attempted to raise the Aidakhar by psychic means, but their effort was fruitless.

Sources: Bord and Bord, *Alien Animals*; "Muddying the waters." *ISC Newsletter* 5, no. 4 (Winter 1986): 10; Shuker, *From Flying Toads to Snakes with Wings*.

Aimak   An unidentified ungulate, the Aimak is said to inhabit portions of Mongolia's inhospitable Gobi Desert. Native inhabitants describe the Aimak as brown, the size of a goat, with short, spreading horns. The front part of its body is "bent forward and shaped like a saiga" (a species of Asian antelope), while the hindquarters resemble those of a musk deer. The Aimak reportedly runs faster than sheep or goats, but not as fast as an antelope.

Source: Karl Shuker, "Alien zoo." *Fortean Times* 147 (July 2001): 16.

***Albatros* sea serpent**   Initially published in 1905 by one Count Gauron, "a bearded dandy from Angers," this third-hand account of a sea monster sighting professed to relate the story of a Chinese seaman named Yan, serving aboard the *Albatros* [*sic*] in June 1897. No location for the sighting was provided, and BERNARD HEUVELMANS reveals that the story was copied verbatim (complete with illustrations) from the 1903 TRESCA SEA SERPENT report — itself exposed as a HOAX.

Source: Heuvelmans, *In the Wake of the Sea Serpents*.

Albatwitcher   This name was once applied to an unclassified species of primate or NORTH AMERICAN APE, said to inhabit wooded areas surrounding Pennsylvania creeks and rivers. Although primarily arboreal, Albatwitchers were described as bipedal when they descended from trees to feed on fruit or insects.

Eyewitness descriptions are similar to those of Tennessee's LITTLE RED MEN OF THE DELTA: tailless and covered with hair, the largest specimens roughly the size of a 10-year-old child. Like MONKEYS in other nations, the Albatwitchers were mischievous, sometimes stealing objects from travelers (and then displaying a preference for red things).

Source: Karl Shuker, "Alien zoo." *Fortean Times* 170 (June 2003): 20.

***Albeona* sea serpent**   The English brig *Albeona* was rounding the Cape of Good Hope on 4 September 1854, en route to China, when its crew sighted "an enormous sea-monster" at longitude 13° east and latitude 38° south. Capt. Charles Richardson described the creature rising 30 feet above the ocean's surface

This Aztec carving depicts the Mexican cryptid known as Ahuítzotl.

"at an angle of about 60. His head was long and narrow — eyes not discernible. From the top of his snout, about 12 ft. on each side of his head, was a white streak, about a foot in width, which I suppose to be his mouth which he kept shut. About 6 ft. from the termination of the white streak, (or jaw) there was a protuberance on his back, like a small water-cask. His body at the surface of the water was about the same size round as the long boat." Although Richardson compared his creature to the 1848 DAEDALUS SEA SERPENT sighting, it bares no real resemblance to the earlier "serpent." BERNARD HEUVELMANS interpreted the sighting as misidentification of a whale, specifically the common rorqual.

Source: Heuvelmans, *In the Wake of the Sea Serpents*.

Alcova Reservoir, Wyoming   Located in Natrona County, 20 miles southwest of Casper, Wyoming, Alcova Reservoir reportedly shelters a serpentine cryptid of indeterminate size. Witness Dawn Bruner reported a sighting in the summer of 1982, but no details are presently available.

Source: *Casper Star-Tribune* (15 April 1983).

***Alfred* sea serpent**   On 2 November 1839, Captain Sawyer of the schooner *Alfred* sighted a large unidentified SEA SERPENT off the coast of Boon Island, Newburyport, Massachusetts. Sawyer initially mistook the creature for a capsized boat, but recognized his error when the animal raised its neck and head 10 feet above the surface, then quickly sank out of sight. Aside from Sawyer's description of the creature's long neck, no details of the sighting are available today.

Source: O'Neill, *The Great New England Sea Serpent*.

Algerian Hairy Viper   Sighted only once, in January 1852, the Algerian hairy viper was described as a SNAKE about 22 inches long, covered with reddish-brown hair like a huge caterpillar. The unnamed witness saw the purported reptile coiled around a tree outside Draria, Algeria. It is uncertain why the witness assumed the creature must be a venomous serpent. Snakes have no hair, but the alternative suggestion of a giant caterpillar is equally perplexing.

Source: Shuker, "Hairy reptiles and furry fish."

Alice Hodges sea serpent

On 18 June 1888 a ship's mate from the *Alice Hodges*, George Thomas, told a reporter for the *Baltimore Sun* that he had recently seen a 100-foot SEA SERPENT off the coast of Nag's Head, North Carolina. "I am convinced it was a sea monster," Thomas proclaimed. "I have sailed for the past 16 years and I have seen some queer things, but the object was the most curious I ever saw." No further description of the creature is presently available.

Source: O'Neill, *The Great New England Sea Serpent.*

Alien Big Cats

In cryptozoological terms, an alien big CAT (ABC) is any large felid sighted, killed or captured far from its normal habitat — and typically on the wrong continent. Thus, a TIGER would be out of place in Africa, a COUGAR in Australia, or an African LION in North America — and all would truly "alien" in Europe. The term is loosely applied, without reference to the scientific definition of "big cats," which includes only those with a hyoid apparatus that permits roaring but prohibits continuous purring. (Thus, cougars are not "big cats," regardless of their size.) Popular reports use the ABC label indiscriminately, describing any "exotic" cat from LYNXES and ocelots to lions and leopards, as long as they are found in a radically alien environment.

While Africa, Asia and South America produce many reports of unidentified cats — including specimens of strange coloration, unusual size and behavior — the vast majority of ABC reports are filed from Europe, North America and Australia. In Europe, reports have been logged over time from at least eight nations. In the Czech Republic, ABCs have been reported from the neighborhood of Jinačovice. In Denmark, Meldungen is the center of ABC action. Finland's reports are more widespread, issuing from Imatra, Kekäleenmäki, Kristinestad, Ruokolahti and Vaasa. French reports are more numerous still, with ABC sightings reported from Cézallier, Corsica, Epinal, Estérel, Forêt de Chize, Île du Levant, Noth, Pindray, Pornic and Valescure. In Germany, reports issue from Bruchmühlbach-Miesau, Deggendorf, Erding, Ernsdorf, Fürth, Gelnhausen, Hannover, Heubach, Kalbach, Lindenfels, Odenwald, Rantrum, Saarland, Schwalbach, Soest, Steinach and Winterkasten. Italy records sightings from Bari and Foggia, while Russia boasts black cats in the Caucasus Mountains and Switzerland reports ABCs around Graubünden.

In Europe, Great Britain is the hands-down leader in ABC sightings, with reports dating back to Medieval times. Legend has it that Percival Cresacre fought to the death with a giant "wood cat" in 1475, at a site now known as Cat Hill (near Doncaster, South Yorkshire). In the 14th-century romance *Livre d'Artus*, legendary King Arthur stalks and slays a black cat of "monstrous proportions" that has terrorized the British countryside. In 1825, witnesses reported a wild cat prowling around Waverly, Surrey, which they compared to a Canadian puma. Sightings of the SURREY PUMA proliferated in the 1930s and continue to the present day, while sightings of other ABCs — including lynxes, leopards, cheetahs and black panthers (actually a melanistic leopard) — are filed in ever growing numbers throughout England, Scotland and Wales. The BRITISH BIG CAT SOCIETY, founded in March 2001, logged more than 1,000 reports in its first 18 months of existence, while the SCOTTISH BIG CAT SOCIETY reports nearly equal activity north of the border.

A majority of British ABC reports followed passage of the 1976 Dangerous Wild Animals Act, which restricted and financially penalized ownership of exotic pets. Several big-cat owners later admitted releasing their animals into the wild, in lieu of facing prosecution or high taxes. Authorities disagree on whether those cats may have survived to establish breeding colonies — but the sightings continue, despite assurances from the Ministry of Agriculture that only 16 big cats escaped to the wild in Britain between 1977 and 1998, with all but two of them recaptured.

In fact, as author Paul Sieveking reveals, there are plentiful "bodies of evidence" proving that ABCs roam at will throughout the United Kingdom. The roster of exotic cats captured or killed in the British Isles since 1975 includes five leopard cats (*Felis begalensis*), three jungle cats (*Felis chaus*), two leopards (*Panthera pardus*), two northern lynxes (*Felis lynx*), two pumas (*Puma concolor*), one clouded leopard (*Neofelis nebulosa*), one African lioness (*Panthera leo*), and one African caracal (*Felis caracal*).

All cats are technically alien to Australia, which had none prior to the arrival of European settlers. A cougar-sized marsupial "lion" (*Thylacoleo carnifex*) filled the gap, but it apparently became extinct around 10,000 years ago. Nonetheless, ABC reports are recorded with fair regularity from every Australian state except Tasmania — more than 1,000 sightings between 1885 and 1994, according to researchers Paul Cropper and Tony Healy. Two-thirds of those sightings involve "black panthers," while the remaining witnesses describe cats resembling pumas. Unlike the British Isles, there is no tradition of spotted ABCs at large — though one cat sighted between Badingarra and Nambung, in August 1982, had a "spotted or heavily striped tail." On 2 November 2003, state government spokesmen declared it "more likely than not" that a breeding colony of ABCs exists in New South Wales.

In North America, where cryptozoologist LOREN COLEMAN has documented ABC reports dating from the 18th century onward, mystery cats are more diverse than their counterparts Down Under. The Eastern Puma Research Network, while seeking evidence of a known species deemed extinct in the eastern U.S., logged 865 sightings of "black panthers" in the 1990s. Large striped cats have also been sighted in America, beginning with a "tyger" reported from Pepin County, Wisconsin in 1767. Maned cats — sometimes black and larger than the average African lion — have also been sighted across the U.S., and the ABCs sometimes appear in groups. A small pride of lions (including a male, female and three cubs) was reported from Clinton County, Pennsylvania in 1797. More than 150 years later, in 1953, two African lionesses were seen traveling with a "black panther" in New Brunswick, Canada. A black cat and a tawny specimen visited northern California together in 1972. Five years later, a maned lion and a black panther prowled the woods around Dierks, Arkansas. Residents of central Ohio saw a striped cat and a lioness together in 1994. In 2003, hunters were summoned to track the MAUI MYSTERY CAT of Hawaii.

Theories abound in regard to worldwide reports of elusive ABCs. Accidental or deliberate releases would account for most of the European sightings, if we acknowledge the feasibility of breeding populations living in the wild. The same is probably true in Australia, where several U.S. military units apparently kept pumas as mascots during World War II, and other exotics may have been secretly imported. Some theorists have suggested a relict population of *Thylacoleo* surviving Down Under, but researchers Cropper and Healy present compelling arguments against the notion. In North America, likewise, escapees or misidentified cougars may account for many reports (including melanistic specimens cast as "panthers"), but MARK HALL suggests an intriguing alternative—specifically, survival of a prehistoric lion (*Panthera leo atrox*) which resembled *P. leo* but grew 25 percent larger at maturity. Presumed extinct since the Pleistocene era, *P. l. atrox* tipped the scales at an average 520 pounds, compared to the modern male lion's 320, and it may explain American lion sightings from the 18th and early 19th centuries. Skeptics, meanwhile, attribute all ABC sightings to "zoo escapes" (even where none have occurred) or to feral dogs (even when zoologists identify pug marks as those of large cats).

Sources: Bord and Bord, *Alien Animals*; Brodu and Meurger. *Les félins-mystère*; Campion-Vincent, "Appearances of beasts and mystery-cats in France"; Coleman, *Mysterious America*; Eamonn Duff, "Big cats not a tall tale." *Sydney Sun-Herald* (2 November 2003); Healy and Cropper, *Out of the Shadows*; Pete Mella, "Legendary cats," *Fortean Times* 170 (June 2003): 76–77; "Residents on Maui spot large, catlike beast," Associated Press (14 June 2003); Rosen, "Out of Africa: Are there lions roaming Finland?"; Shuker, *Mystery Cats of the World*; Sieveking, "Big cats in Britain"; Smith, *Bunyips and Bigfoots*.

Alkali Lake, Nebraska *see* Walgren Lake

Allier River, France

A curious report from the Allier River, near Vichy in south-central France, describes a black three-headed monster seen swimming in the river, sometime during 1933 or 1934. Sadly, the witnesses were not identified and no further details are available.

Source: Albert van Hageland, *De Magische Zee*. Leuven, Belgium: Davidsfonds, 1961.

Alligator (Pink)

In the first week of March 1976, Florida tour guide Danny Decker reported two sightings of a pink alligator in the Everglades, near Andytown (in Broward County). No other witnesses were present, and no subsequent encounters with the creature(s) have been filed. Skeptics dismiss the reports as HOAXES, but another explanation may involve a rare case of albinism.

Source: *Fort Lauderdale* (FL) *News* (3–5 March 1976).

Alligators (Mislocated)

Alligators are reptiles belonging to the order *Crocodylia*. Other members of the order include CROCODILES and gharials. The family *Alligatorinae* includes seven species and four subspecies, all but two of which are CAIMANS native to Latin America. The Chinese alligator (*Alligator sinensis*) is normally found only in the lower Yangtze River and its tributaries, while the larger American alligator (*A. mississippiensis*) commonly ranges throughout the southeastern United States, from southern Virginia through the Carolinas and Florida, westward to the Rio Grande river in east Texas. Alligators may also be found along the Mississippi River, ranging into extreme southern Arkansas and the far southeast corner of Oklahoma (McCurtain County).

While alligators should not be found outside their normal range, and placement outside the southern U.S. puts them at risk of death from exposure to unhealthy climates, they habitually surface in areas far beyond their standard habitat. Discovery of misplaced alligators is typically explained with allusions to "lost pets" or "zoo escapees," but those theories are seldom (if ever) confirmed by authorities. A review of mislocated alligators (admittedly incomplete) would include the following U.S. states and foreign nations:

Arizona: Lost Lake—A 10-foot alligator was killed along the Colorado River (June 1943). Tucson—A 5-foot specimen was

Exotic cats of various species are reported from non-native habitats around the world (*William Rebsamen*).

caught at a motel (Spring 1950). Parker—Witnesses reported a "large" alligator at La Paz Slough (1950).

California: Corcoran—A 6-foot alligator was sighted at Tulare Lake Basin (Summer 1930). Sacramento County—Multiple sightings occurred around Folsom Lake (June 1957–September 1958). Lafayette—An 8-foot alligator was reported from Lafayette Lake (23 October 1975). Fresno—A 4-foot specimen was sighted in the Kings River (23 June 1981). San Francisco—An alligator was captured at Mountain Lake and shipped to a Louisiana game reserve (September 1996). Yuba City—Tracks were found after a 7-foot specimen was seen near the Feather River (8 May 1981).

Colorado: Aurora—A 3-foot alligator was found crawling on a city street (August 1984). Denver—Police scoured Washington Park after sightings of a "large reptile" (13 August 1998).

Connecticut: Darien—A 3-foot alligator was sighted at Collender's Point (2 October 1929). Turner—A 2-foot alligator was captured (13 September 2003).

Delaware: Dover—A 57-inch alligator was captured (1 April 1982).

Illinois: Decatur—An alligator was sighted in Lake Decatur (30 August 1937); 13 alligators averaging 12 inches long were captured in a hot-water ditch (24 October 1966); a 10-inch specimen was caught (26 June 1967). Lombard—An 18-inch gator was reported from a manmade pond (30 July 1970). Oakley—A sighting was reported from the Sangamon River (August 1971). Chenoa—A 3-foot specimen was found wandering on U.S. Highway 66 (22 September 1972). Antioch—An alligator was sighted and videotaped in the Chain o' Lakes (July 1999). Ottawa — A 39-inch specimen was found on a residential driveway (August 2003).

Indiana: Evansville — A 2-foot specimen was captured, witnesses claiming it fell from the sky (21 May 1911). Vincennes — A specimen of unrecorded size was sighted in Mariah Creek (December 1946). Indianapolis — Authorities dragged their fourth alligator of the summer, a 4-footer, from Fall Creek (26 August 1999).

Kansas: Newton — A 10-inch alligator was killed in a resident's basement drain (July 1970). Olathe — A sighting was reported from Interstate 70 (Summer 1978). Wichita — Multiple sightings of a 10-foot alligator were reported from the Little Arkansas River (30 June-7 July 1978). Stillwell — A 3-foot specimen was sighted (March 1979).

Maryland: Potomac River — A 3-foot alligator was sighted (1926); two alligators were seen along Herring Creek (18 November 1942). Riverdale — A 46-inch specimen was captured (4 December 1933).

Massachusetts: Ware — Multiple sightings in 1922 climaxed with the capture of a 2-foot specimen. Palmer — Two alligators, 15 and 18 inches long, were captured at a golf course (18 July 1937). Dedham — Multiple sightings were recorded around flooded gravel pits on Rustcraft Road (August-September 2002). Boston — Animal control officers sighted a 2-foot alligator in Jamaica Pond (21 August 2003).

Michigan: Detroit — A 22-inch specimen was reported from the Huron River (1938). Oakland County — A 24-inch specimen was caught at Elizabeth Lake (1953); another, five or six feet long, was caught at Island Lake (9 July 1955); sightings were reported and tracks found around Lower Long Lake (June-July 1955); a 17-inch specimen was caught at Harris Lake (June 1956); a 56-inch gator was reported from Lower Long Lake (10 July 1957); a 42-inch specimen was killed at Susan Lake (4 August 1957). Lansing — A 16-inch specimen was caught in a horticultural pond (31 May 1967); an 18-incher was captured at the state capitol building (6 June 1968).

Minnesota: Lakefield — An alligator, shot and wounded, still escaped (June 1941). Minneapolis — Canoers reported an alligator from Lake of the Isles (May 2000); multiple sightings were reported from Mooney Lake (July 2002).

New Jersey: Hackensack Meadows — Witnesses sighted a 31-inch specimen (September 1929). Red Bank — A 14-inch alligator was seen in the Shrewsbury River (7 July 1932). Passaic — Two 3-foot gators were sighted (11 September 1933). Morris and Sussex Counties — Multiple reports of a "giant" alligator were filed (Summer 1973). Linden — A 3-foot specimen was sighted (November 1978). Edison — A 5-foot gator was seen at Edison Board Basin (24 August 1980).

Alligators have been seen, killed and captured in many areas outside their normal range.

New Mexico: Hobbs — Two alligators were reported living in a nearby swamp (October 1976).

New York: Middleton — A "good-sized" alligator was captured (September 1927); witnesses saw six gators and killed two (November 1927). Jervis — A 2-foot 'gator was sighted (2 July 1929). Wolcott — A 2-foot specimen was captured (September 1929). Pleasantville — A 24-inch specimen was caught in shrubbery on an estate (22 March 1931). Westchester County — Multiple alligators were sighted in the Bronx River (28 June 1933); another sighting was reported from Crestwood Lake (1 July 1932); a 6-foot specimen was found dead at Grass Sprain (7 March 1935). New York City — A 90-inch alligator weighing 125 pounds was dragged from a sewer and killed (9 February 1935); a 3-foot specimen was caught in Yonkers (7 March 1935); 49-inch gator was pulled from the East River (1 June 1937); a 2-foot specimen was caught on a Bronx subway platform (6 June 1937); a 3-foot specimen was captured at Kissena Lake in Queens (1997); multiple sightings occurred at Harlem Meer, a lake in Central Park, climaxed with the capture of a 2-foot specimen (21 June 2001); police captured a 4-foot alligator in a Queens Park (28 August 2003). New Rochelle — Five alligators were caught at Huguenot Lake, the longest 19 inches (11 August 1938). Westfield — A 48-inch specimen was killed at Lake Mindowaskin (16 August 1942). Red Hook — A 48-inch alligator was killed in a pond (4 August 1970). Valhalla — A 2-foot specimen was sighted at Kensico Reservoir (9 August 1982). Berne — A 28-inch specimen was captured at a local lakeshore (18 June 1983). Staten Island — A 53-inch alligator was caught in a local stream (June 2000). Buffalo — A 4-foot alligator weighing 80 pounds was caught in Scajaquada Creek (26 June 2001).

Ohio: Akron — A 12-inch juvenile alligator was caught inside a store at Arlington Plaza (29 January 2003).

Oregon: Willamina — Witnesses reported an alligator eating ducks in Willamina Pond. Authorities confirmed that ducks had vanished, but they could not find the reptile (summer 2001).

Pennsylvania: Philadelphia — A specimen of unrecorded size was captured (1926). Harrisburg — Four months after witnesses first reported a 3-foot alligator living in a lake adjacent to Harrisburg High School, police failed in efforts to bait the reptile with pieces of chicken (18 July 2003).

Rhode Island: Little Compton — Hikers Philip and Laura Casey reported a 3-foot alligator sunning itself beside Simmons Pond (30 November 2003). Police failed to locate the reptile, but publication of the sighting prompted other witnesses to report encounters with the gator during the recent Thanksgiving holiday.

Washington: King County — Two alligators were reported chasing ducks at the southern end of Lake Washington (1967).

Wisconsin: Janesville — A 66-inch specimen was found frozen beside the Rock River (February 1892). Pewaukee — A 30-inch alligator was caught at Pewaukee Lake (9 July 1971). North Prairie — A 2-foot specimen was captured in a resident's front yard (26 September 2001).

Canada: Kootenay Lake, B.C. — A 12-foot alligator was sighted at Crawford Bay and left tracks on the shore (10 October 1900). Holy Cross Mountains, B.C. — Prospectors reported sightings at a location they named Alligator Lake (1915). Galt, Ontario — A 3-foot specimen was captured (17 June 1929). Windsor, Ontario — A 3-foot alligator was sighted (20 September 1970); a 24-inch specimen was caught in a resident's backyard (20 September 1980). Montréal, Québec — A 10.5-inch alligator was captured in a vacant lot (28 July 1973). Lethbridge, Alberta — An alligator attacked a dog along the Oldman River (July 1999). Victoria,

B.C.—Authorities searched in vain for a 3-foot specimen sighted at a Colwood park (28 March 2003). Other sightings in British Columbia have been logged from Chilliwack Lake, Cultus Lake, the Fraser River, Nitinat Lake and Pitt Lake (where locals dubbed their resident gator the Pitt Lake Lizard).

Sources: "A crop of crocodilians." *Fortean Times* 151 (November 2001): 17; "Alligator wrestler confident of catching New York's Nessie." Associated Press (22 June 2001); Arment and LaGrange, "Canadian 'black alligators'"; Bord, *Unexplained Mysteries of the 20th Century*; Pete Bowles, "This tale is no croc." *Newsday* (29 August 2003); Emily Bowers, "Elusive alligator subject of park search." *Victoria* (B.C.) *Times Colonist* (29 March 2003); Bruce Burdett, "Gator startles Little Compton hikers." *Barrington* (RI) *Times* (4 December 2003); Thomas Caywood, "A tiny monster surfaces in J.P." *Boston Herald* (22 August 2003); Dan Churney, "Alligator bag-ged." *Ottawa* (IL) *Daily Times* (22 August 2003); Coleman, *Mysterious America*; Jim Flaherty, "Gator makes unexpected house call in North Prairie." *Kettle Moraine* (WI) *Index* (27 September 2001); Andale Gross, "Wayward alligator's no crock." *Akron* (OH) *Beacon Journal* (20 January 2003); Chuck Haga, "Don't sweat the milfoil; we've got alligators, maybe." *Minneapolis Star Tribune* (20 July 2002); Wendy Kirkland, "Alligator pays visit to Quiet Corner yard." *Norwich* (CT) *Bulletin* (14 September 2003); Kavita Kumar, "Gator may lurk in Plymouth lake." *Minneapolis Star Tribune* (19 July 2002); Henry Miller, "The mystery of Willamina's gator." *Salem* (OR) *Statesman Journal* (15 May 2003); "Mystery gator spotted in central Pa. lake." *Harrisburg* (PA) *Patriot News* (18 July 2003); Ross, *Crocodiles and Alligators*; "See you later alligator...?" *Gloucester Echo* (19 June 2003); Liz Taurasi, "Elusive alligator evades authorities." *Dedham* (MA) *Daily News* (30 September 2002); Sheba Wheeler, "Gator may lurk in Wash Park." *Denver Post* (14 August 1998).

Almas/Almasti   An unidentified man-sized HOMINID, the Almas or Almasti is reported (with various regional names) over a wide Asian territory ranging from the Caucasus Mountains of Russia and Georgia, eastward through Kazakhstan, Siberia, Mongolia and China. While primarily a mountain dweller—in addition to the Caucasus, it is reported from Siberia's Sayanskiy Range, Mongolia's Altai Mountains, plus China's Qilian Shan and Tian Shan Mountains—the Almas is also sometimes reported from Mongolia's Gobi Desert. Witnesses describe a creature ranging from five to six and a half feet tall, covered with reddish-brown hair (except for hands and face, where dark skin is observed). The Almasti's face features a prominent brow ridge and cheekbones, flat nose, and a jutting lower jaw without visible chin. Long arms are standard. The creatures walk upright with knees bent, on feet whose big toes are shorter than the other four and markedly crooked inward.

Western reports of the Almas/Almasti date from the early 15th century, when Bavarian prisoner of war Johannes Schiltberger observed two specimens captured by Mongol soldiers in the Tian Shan Mountains. Russian scholar Badzar Baradin reported an encounter from the Gobi Desert in April 1906, though some researchers consider the report fictitious. (It was not recorded in Baradin's diary at the alleged time of occurrence.) Further sightings from the Gobi were logged in 1927 and 1930. Soviet physician Evan Ivlov claimed a sighting of three specimens—male, female and an apparent juvenile—while passing through the Altai range in 1963. Researcher MARIE-JEANNE KOFFMANN found a set of tracks in the northern Caucasus, in March 1978. Another Russian, biologist Gregory Panchenko, filed a curious report from the Kabardin-Balkar Republic in August 1991. Panchenko claimed he was hiding in a barn when an Almas entered through a window, proceeded to braid the mane of an unresisting horse, then left through an open door. Dr. Koffmann and French filmmaker

Sylvain Pallix failed to find the Kabardin-Balkar Republic's Almas in 1992, on an expedition sponsored by the RUSSIAN SOCIETY OF CRYPTOZOOLOGY, but they photographed tracks from a recent sighting and made plaster casts of the footprints.

Certain reports of the Almas/Almasti, beginning with Johannes Schiltberger's, are unusual for their claims of specimens captured or killed. A young female was reportedly killed in the Gobi Desert, sometime in the early 20th century, when it triggered a local hunter's crossbow snare. Many locals reportedly viewed the corpse, but reports of the incident were long suppressed because hunting with crossbow snares was illegal. A complete Almas skin was allegedly displayed at the Baruun Hural monastery, in Mongolia, during 1937, but no trace of it remains today. In October 1944, a group of policemen led by Erjib Koshokoyev "nearly" trapped a female Almas in a Caucasus hemp field, south of Nal'chik, but the animal eluded them. The tables were nearly turned on 8 June 2001, when a Mongol woman identified as Ts. Tuvshinjargal claimed she was attacked by a "strong and hairy" creature in the Eej Hairhan mountains of the Gobi-Altai Aimag. The animal was frightened off by Tuvshinjargal's traveling companions.

Cryptozoologists differ on proposed solutions for the riddle of the Almas/Almasti. BERNARD HEUVELMANS and BORIS PORSHNEV suggested that the creatures may comprise a relict population of NEANDERTAL MAN, while LOREN COLEMAN and MARK HALL suspect surviving specimens of *Homo erectus*. Fossil remains of both prehistoric hominids are found at various points throughout the Almasti's range. Skeptics dismiss all anecdotal evidence and tracks as worthless, pending collection of a type specimen.

Sources: Colarusso, "Ehtnographic information on a wild man of the Caucasus"; Heaney, "The Mongolian Almas"; Heuvelmans and Porshnev, *L'homme de Néanderthal est toujours vivant*; Korman, "Brief ecological description of the Caucasus relic hominoid (Almast) based on oral reports by local inhabitants and on field investigations"; Rinchen, "Almas still exist in Mongolia"; Sanderson, *Abominable Snowmen*; Shackley, *Still Living?*; Tchernine, *The Yeti*; "Yeti attacks woman." http://www.mongolnet.mn/gglmsg/last.htm.

Along Bay sea serpents   Along Bay, on northern Vietnam's Gulf of Tonkin, ranked among the world's most active venues for SEA SERPENT reports in the late 19th and early 20th centuries. The series of reports began in 1883, when remains of an unidentified pelagic creature washed ashore on the beach. A witness to the stranding, 18-year-old Tran Van Con, described the creature to Dr. A. Krempf, director of Indochina's Oceanographic and Fisheries Service, in 1921. According to that account:

It was a carcase in a very advanced state of putrefaction. The head had gone. The body alone was 60 feet long by 3 feet wide. The animal was formed of successive segments almost all alike one another. Each segment was 2 feet long and 3 feet wide and had a pair of appendages 2 feet 4 inches long. The teguments were of a remarkable consistency and rang like sheet-metal when hit with a stick. The color of this tegumentary envelope was dark brown on the dorsal surface and light yellow on the ventral surface. The stench that arose from this prodigious animal was such that even the Annamites would not go near it, and it was decided to tow the remains out to sea and sink them.

Natives called the creature CON RIT ("millipede"), and it roughly matched the description of an ancient sea DRAGON with many feet "like a centipede," described in a classic book of Vietnamese folklore, the *Chich-Quai*. According to legend, the beast attacked fishing boats on the Gulf of Tonkin, sinking them and devouring their crews. Lac-long-Quân, the second king of Viet, allegedly killed the dragon and cut it into pieces, which became the odd-shaped stones found on Along Bay's Ca-Ba Island. The monster's head, in turn, became Câu-Dâu Mountain, east of Quâng-Yên.

The *con-rit* stranding in Along Bay was followed by a series of at least eight "serpent" sightings spanning the 22 years between 1893 and 1915. Witnesses included officers and crewmen aboard the ships LA MUTINE (June 1893), *Héron* (1896), *Vauban* (July 1898), CHARLES-HARDOUIN (December 1903), the GUEYDON (two sightings, in December 1903 and March 1904), CHATEUX-RENAULT and LA DÉCIDÉE (both in February 1904), and the HANOI (June 1908). During the same period, officers and passengers aboard the AVALANCHE reported three separate sightings of two "serpents" swimming in tandem off the nearby Fâi-tsi-long archipelago (July 1897 and February 1898).

On 27 June 1904 Professor A. Giard read a report on the Along Bay cryptids to the Academy of Sciences in Paris. One day later, Giard told *Le Temps*, "The sea-serpent has emerged from legend and entered reality … We may suppose that the sea-serpent belongs to those groups thought to be extinct, for instance the Mosasaurs or Icthyosaurs." Noting the okapi's recent discovery in Africa, he added, "Why should we not also rediscover the Mosasaur and Icthyosaur, which, if they still exist, can only live at great depths in the sea and appear on the surface but rarely and by accident?"

Source: Heuvelmans, *In the Wake of the Sea Serpents*.

Alovot   This unidentified bird is reported from Pulau Simeulue (Simeulue Island), located 65 miles northwest of Sumatra, Indonesia. It is described as a forest-dwelling pheasant the size of a chicken, with short legs, dark-brown plumage showing lighter spots, and a comblike crest on its head. The Alovot is said to eat rice and nest on stumps or logs, laying brown eggs somewhat smaller than a hen's. Rocky, reef-bound Simeulue is 65 miles long and 20 miles wide, with a total area of 712 square miles. Its hills peak at 1,860 feet, their slopes covered with hardwood forests. Isolation has produced distinctive species and subspecies of birds and reptiles, thus encouraging cryptozoologists who hope the Alovot may yet be found and classified. At press time, a proposed Pulau Simeulue Wildlife Reserve, slated to encompass 27,000 hectares of the island's northwest interior, had not been approved by the Indonesian government.

Sources: Jacobson, "The Alovot"; Shuker, "Gallinaceous mystery birds."

***Alpha* sea serpent**   In May 1849, Captain Edwards of the ship *Alpha* recorded a SEA SERPENT sighting in his private log. It read:

Wednesday, May 30, P.M., strong breezes at N.N.W., and a sharp sea on; about 1:15 I felt a strange shaking of the ship. Mr. Thomson, my chief officer, Mr. George Park, civil engineer, cabin passenger on board, ran on deck as well as myself, when we beheld immediately under our lee quarter a monster of huge dimensions. It had no fins or broad tail, as whales have. It was of a light fawn color, with large brown spots behind the shoulders; the head pointed like that of a porpoise. It had large glossy eyes; the shoulder was much darker than the rest of the body, which was the thickest part of it, (say twenty feet in diameter), from thence diminishing to the tail, to about the size of our mainyard in the slings (say twenty-four inches diameter). He took a turn around, and we afterwards saw him astern, and he went away in a S.E. by S. direction, at about thirty miles an hour.

ANTOON OUDEMANS considered the *Alpha* creature identical to various "serpents" reported from the New England coast in the early 19th century, collectively dubbed SCOLIOPHIS ATLANTICUS, but BERNARD HEUVELMANS noted that the beast bore no resemblance to a giant SNAKE or EEL. Instead, Heuvelmans speculated that it may have been a large unknown species of manta ray.

Source: Heuvelmans, *In the Wake of the Sea Serpents*.

Altamaha-Ha   A variation on the classic LAKE MONSTER, this creature reportedly inhabits the Altamaha River near Darien, Georgia (seat of McIntosh County). Witnesses describe a small-headed creature ranging from 10 to 25 feet long, with gray or brown skin. Reports of a "long neck" are ambiguous, but most reports agree that the Altamaha-ha swims with undulating motions, typically displaying two or three humps above the water's surface. Reported sightings date from July 1969, with the most recent published description filed by witnesses Jim and Mary Marshall, on 6 July 1997.

Sources: Davis, *The Tale of the Altamaha "Monster"*; Karl Shuker, "Alien zoo," *Fortean Times* 106 (January 1998): 14.

Alula Whale   A mystery cetacean reported from the Gulf of Aden, the Alula whale takes its name from the Somali coastal town of Alula (or Caluula), located at the tip of Africa's "horn." Witnesses describe the creature as a brown variety of killer whale, some 20 feet long, with a 2-foot dorsal fin, a rounded forehead, and white star-shaped "scars" on its body. Naturalist Willem Mörzer Bruyns reported sightings of four specimens swimming together in the Gulf of Aden, but skeptics currently refuse to accept the Alula whale as a verified species.

Sources: W.F.J. Mörzer Bruyns, *Field Guide of Whales and Dolphins*. Amsterdam: Tor, 1971; Shuker, *From Flying Toads to Snakes with Wings*.

Alux   An unclassified species of APE or large MONKEY, reported from Mexico's Yucatán peninsula and neighboring Guatemala, the Alux is regarded by most cryptozoologists as similar (if not identical) to the DUENDE of South America. Aboriginal folklore treats the creatures as "little people," including references to clothing, weapons, and infliction of fever on unfortunate witnesses. The more fantastic elements of legend may be safely ignored in this case, although reports of occasional attacks on humans may suggest occasional aggressive specimens.

Sources: Scott Corrales, "Aluxoob: Little people of the Maya"; Virginia Rodriguez Rivera, "Los duendes en Mexico (el alux)."

Amali   A large semiaquatic creature, possibly reptilian, the Amali is said to inhabit remote jungle areas of Gabon, in West Africa. The legendary Alfred Aloysius ("Trader Horn") Smith was first to report the Amali in print outside Africa, in the 1920s. He considered it identical to the creature dubbed JAGO-NINI by aboriginal people of the same region, and cryptozoologist ROY MACKAL suggests that its name may be a variant of N'YAMALA, also reported from Gabon. The creatures are said to battle and kill elephants on occasion, prompting speculation that they may represent a relict form of DINOSAUR. Trader Horn reportedly chiseled out a cave painting of the Amali and sent it to ex-President Ulysses Grant sometime in the early 1880s.

Sources: Heuvelmans, *On the Track of Unknown Animals*; Mackal, *A Living Dinosaur?*

Åmännigen, Sweden   Located in Västmanland County, Sweden, Åmännigen was the site of multiple LAKE MONSTER sightings spanning a period between the 1830s and 1940. Reports ceased thereafter from this lake which measures only 35 feet at it deepest point.

Source: GLOBAL UNDERWATER SEARCH TEAM website (http://www. bahnhof.se/~wizard/cryptoworld/)

Amarok   Amarok is the Inuit word for "WOLF," also applied to a legendary canid of superior size and intelligence said to be a deadly man-eater. Because the name is used interchangeably, the "monster" Amaroks may have been simply rogue or rabid specimens of common wolf (*Canis lupus*).

Source: Blackman, *The Field Guide to North American Monsters.*

Ambon sea serpent   In October 1904, crewmen of the steamer *Ambon* sighted an unidentified SEA SERPENT in the Straits of Bab-el-Mandeb, between the Gulf of Aden and the Red Sea. Captain G.A. Zeilanga commanded the *Ambon*, but the best description of the creature is that offered by his third officer, J. Vollewens, to ANTOON OUDEMANS.

On 22 October 1904, at 11 o'clock in the morning, while we were passing through the Little Strait of Mandeb, or Eastern Passage, a strange animal was seen, which raised its head above the water for more than half a minute. This head had many points in common with a CAYMAN'S, but was, however, quite smooth above and below; the top was black in color, the bottom perfectly white; the eyes, not at all prominent, were dark. In the two jaws, upper and lower, were long pointed teeth about 4 inches long. The head was raised about 8 feet out of the water.

The body was dark on top, the belly white; on the back a fin was seen for a moment. The animal rose out of the water as shown in the drawing and sank in the same way. The diameter at the level of the neck was about 2 feet 6 inches. The beast was surrounded by a big shoal of little brown animals, about 20 inches long, which were very like young sharks. We saw the beast about six times.

BERNARD HEUVELMANS concluded from Vollewens's sketch of the creature that it must be a mammal, probably an unknown species of BEAKED WHALE. Strangely, then, in his final tally of "serpent" sightings, Heuvelmans described the *Ambon* cryptid as either a "merhorse" or a "marine saurian," two very different categories created by Heuvelmans for classification of unidentified pelagic cryptids.

Source: Heuvelmans, *In the Wake of the Sea Serpents.*

American Anthropological Research Foundation
BIGFOOT researchers WILLIAM ERNST, L.M. Hardy and ROBERT MORGAN founded the AARF in 1975 "to facilitate, conduct and augment progressive research into the emerging field of crypto-anthropology and those social and physical sciences which complement anthropology to the benefit of humankind." A 17-member science advisory board was subsequently created, including at various times GEORGE AGOGINO, CARLETON COON, GROVER KRANTZ and Russian hominologist Boris Sapunov. With the deaths of Ernst and Hardy, Morgan emerged as the AARF's sole shareholder and executive officer. According to the group's Internet website, Scott Robinson serves as director of communications and special projects, while scattered field offices are directed by Steve Jones (Ohio), Chris Kimball (Florida), Bill Lee (Idaho) and Richard Van Dyke (Texas). Morgan personally directs the AARF's subsidiary American YETI Expeditions, described as an exercise in "ongoing research to separate fact-from-fiction" with respect to the unknown HOMINIDS that Morgan calls Giant Forest People or "FGs."

Source: American Anthropological Research Foundation, http:// www.trueseekers.org/.

American Samoa carcass   In 1974, while visiting American Samoa (a U.S. protectorate in the South Pacific), Australian tourist Joseph Elkhorne snapped three photographs of a decomposing carcass he found washed up on the beach. The specimen—which measured roughly one meter (39 inches) in length—was not preserved, but marine biologists in Melbourne and Portugal later examined the photos. One expert opined that the creature was "some kind of sea bird," while the other found it "reminiscent of a Portuguese man-o-war." Publication of the photographs in *Fortean Times* magazine likewise failed to solve the mystery.

Source: "Sea creature." *Fortean Times* 142 (February 2001): 53.

American sea serpent   On 2 December 1893, First Officer Peters, aboard the steamer *American*, reportedly sighted a SEA SERPENT off the coast of Newfoundland at 43° 55' north, 56° west, southwest of Grand Bank. He estimated that the chocolate-brown creature was 100 feet long, with the diameter of a sugar barrel. Peters watched it swim with "arches" in its body for about five minutes, then ran to fetch his captain. By the time he returned, the animal had disappeared. His story, published in the *New York Herald* on 5 December, included the following comments:

I have been at sea man and boy these twenty-one years and I know that what I saw was a big fish or snake. He moved with a wavy motion. He bent his back into arches until he looked like a lot of crank shafts. You could see the humps plainly. They rose and fell with a steady beat.

Source: O'Neill, *The Great New England Sea Serpent.*

Amerika sea serpent   On 26 October 1934, as the Dutch ocean liner *Amerika* approached St. Thomas in the Virgin Islands, several passengers sighted a large, unidentified creature swimming some distance away. One of those witnesses, a British subject identified as G. Cooper, published his account in the *Listener* 19 years later.

The weather was bright and clear and at a distance of about a quarter of a mile, traveling on an opposite course, an elongated mass, sixty to eighty feet in length, broke surface in a flurry of foam and spray. It had a long serpentine neck thrust upwards, and a flattish head which, however, was flexed and gave it an equine appearance. Behind the neck a series of six or more large, protruding humps, chocolate brown in color, moved forward in sinuous motion, giving an illusion of speed which was probably not more than fifteen to twenty knots.

BERNARD HEUVELMANS opined that the *Amerika* creature "seems to be related to the pinnipeds," but he strangely omitted the incident from his final roster of SEA SERPENT sightings and thus failed to classify the creature from his own list of nine potential candidates.

Source: Heuvelmans, *In the Wake of the Sea Serpents.*

The *Ambon* sea serpent, after witness J. Vollewens.

Amhúluk   The Amhúluk is said to be a LAKE MONSTER of northwestern Oregon, inhabiting Forked Mountain Lake, west of Forest Grove in Washington County (near Portland). Aboriginal accounts of the creature, last reported in the 1890s, described it as a large, spotted animal with four legs and long horns sprouting from its head.

Source: Gatschet, "Water monsters of American aborigines."

Amikuk   Nineteenth-century Inuit natives of Alaska described the Amikuk as a giant OCTOPUS inhabiting the Bering Strait. If the beast was not in fact an octopus, it may have been a GIANT SQUID. An even larger cephalopod, the rare COLOSSAL SQUID, has been reported from Antarctic waters and might theoretically dwell in equally frigid seas of the far north.

Source: Edward Nelson, "The Eskimo about Bering Strait." *Annual Report of the Bureau of American Ethnology* 18, pt. 1 (1896–97): 442.

***Amsteldjik* sea serpent**   In August 1911 the Dutch steamer *Amsteldjik* encountered a SEA SERPENT in the North Atlantic, at latitude 47° 30' north, longitude 27° 11' west. The ship's second officer, J.A. Liebau, recorded the following information in the *Amsteldjik*'s log:

On Saturday, 19 August, at half past one in the afternoon an animal was observed which was very probably a sea-serpent. Our attention was suddenly drawn by something hitting the sea fairly violently; about 60 yards to port a great mass of foam was seen, in the middle of which was a dark colored sea-animal. Altogether it was very like a *Noordkaper* [Northern Right Whale] but without a dorsal fin.

A few seconds later, a body suddenly lifted above the water and rose about 8 feet above the surface; 30 feet further on the back of the sea-animal could be seen. After it had shown itself for ten seconds in this position, it fell back into the water, hitting it violently, and then disappeared into the depths and was seen no more.

This colossus was about 2 feet 6 inches in diameter (that is the part out of the water). A large proportion of the part that emerged seemed to belong to the head and sank progressively with the body. The diameter of the head seemed to our eyes to be a little greater than that of the rest of the visible part. The back was dark in color, while the ventral part was much lighter. Because it appeared so suddenly, and at a considerable distance, we could not observe it more closely.

Two months later, Liebau addressed a further description of the creature to ANTOON OUDEMANS: "Our general impression was that it was not a FISH, and the shape of the head was fairly like a seal's....On the head we could see a dark spot and line, which I think were the eye and mouth."

As BERNARD HEUVELMANS later noted, Liebau's account was inaccurate in one respect, at least: Right Whales (genus *Eubalaena*) have no dorsal fins. Heuvelmans finally classified the *Amsteldjik* creature as a specimen of his hypothetical "long-necked" sea serpent.

Source: Heuvelmans, *In the Wake of the Sea Serpents.*

Anaconda (Giant)   Anacondas are large South American SNAKES belonging to the family *Boidae*, genus *Eunectes*. Two universally recognized species are the green anaconda (*E. murinus*) and the much smaller yellow anaconda (*E. notaeus*). The status of two other proposes species, *E. barbouri* and *E. deschauenseei*, is disputed. Both have been reported only from Marajo Island, at the mouth of the Amazon River, and a majority of herpetologists refuse to acknowledge them as distinct species or subspecies. While typically describing *E. murinus* as the world's heaviest snake, most texts on herpetology name the reticulate python

(*Python reticulatus*) as attaining greater lengths. Officially, neither snake reaches a length of 30 feet or more, and a $50,000 reward offered by the American Museum of Natural History for any serpent attaining that size remains unclaimed today.

That said, Robert Lamon reported a green anaconda measuring 37 feet 6 inches, killed in Colombia in 1939 or 1940, and a Copley News Service article from February 1969 referred to a specimen "nearly 40 feet long" displayed at a museum in Belém, Brazil. Still, numerous reports from the Amazon basin describe much larger specimens, some allegedly more than 100 feet long. Accounts of those giants are often confused by local references to a monster snake called SUCURIJÚ GIGANTE or *cobra grande*, described in conflicting reports as a huge anaconda or an entirely different, unclassified species.

Spanish conquistadors reported sightings of giant snakes in the Amazon jungles from their earliest explorations. Friar Pedro Cimon sighted a 45-foot specimen near Coro, Venezuela, while Father Pedro Lozano examined a dead anaconda measuring between 60 and 70 feet. In February 1889, a 45-foot specimen was allegedly captured on the island of Martinique. Explorer PERCY FAWCETT reported the following encounter in 1907:

We were drifting easily along in the sluggish current not far below the confluence of the Rio Negro when almost under the bow of the *igarité* there appeared a triangular head and several feet of undulating body. It was a giant anaconda. I sprang for my rifle as the creature began to make its way up the bank, and hardly waiting to aim smashed a .44 soft-nosed bullet into its spine, ten feet below the wicked head. At once there was a flurry of foam, and several heavy thumps against the boat's keel, shaking us as though we had run on a snag.

With great difficulty I persuaded the Indian crew to turn in shorewards. They were so frightened that the whites showed all round their popping eyes, and in the moment of firing I had heard their terrified voices begging me not to shoot lest the monster destroy the boat and kill everyone on board, for not only do these creatures attack boats when injured, but also there is great danger from their mates.

We stepped ashore and approached the reptile with caution. It was out of action, but shivers ran up and down its body like puffs of wind on a mountain tarn. As far as it was possible to measure, a length of forty-five feet lay out of the water, and seventeen feet in it, making a total length of sixty-two feet. Its body was not thick for such a colossal length — not more than twelve inches in diameter — but it had probably been long without food....

Such large specimens as this may not be common, but the trails in the swamps reach a width of six feet and support the statements of Indians and rubber pickers that the anaconda sometimes reaches an incredible size, altogether dwarfing that shot by me. The Brazilian Boundary Commission told me of one killed in the Rio Paraguay exceeding eighty feet in length!

In 1923 explorer F.W. Up de Graff sighted an anaconda of similar size, lying in shallow water beneath his canoe. De Graff wrote: "It measured fifty feet for certainty, and probably nearer sixty. This I know from the position in which it lay. Our canoe was a twenty-four footer; the snake's head was ten or twelve feet beyond the bow; its tail was a good four feet beyond the stern; the center of its body was looped up into a huge S, whose length was the length of our dugout and whose breadth was a good five feet.

A giant anaconda was photographed in 1933, along the Rio Negro, by members of the Brazil-Colombia Boundary Commission. Witnesses report that the snake was 30 meters (97 feet 6 inches) long and 60 centimeters (23.4 inches) in diameter. They killed it with machine-gun fire and afterward reported that four men could not life the snake's head. The photo has long since been lost, but the technician who developed it in Manaus swore to his priest that the negative was not retouched.

In July 1945, a huge snake (called *Boiuda* by natives) was blamed for destroying the village of Capucema, near the Rio Abete. That predator escaped, but a massive anaconda was killed in April 1947, by members of an expedition tracking Indians between the Rio Manso and the Rio Cristalino. Witness Serge Bonacase later described the event to BERNARD HEUVELMANS:

> The guide pointed out an anaconda asleep on a rise in the ground and half hidden among the grass. We approached to within 20m of it and fired our rifles at it several times. It tried to make off, all in convulsions, but we caught up with it after 20 or 30m and finished it off. Only then did we realize how enormous it was; when we walked along the whole length of its body it seemed as if it would never end. What struck me most was its enormous head....
>
> As we had no measuring instruments, one of us took a piece of string and held it between the ends of the fingers of one hand and the other shoulder to mark off a length of one meter. Actually it could have been a little less. We measured the snake several times with this piece of string and always made it 24 or 25 times as long as the string. The reptile must therefore have been nearly 23 meters [75 feet] long.

Lethal encounters with huge anacondas continued through the late 1940s. In January 1948 a band of Indians lassoed a giant snake, which they found sleeping off a recent meal, and towed it behind their boat to Manaus. There, it was shot and photographed, with its picture published on 24 January in the newspaper *Diario de Pernambuco*. The photo's caption declared that "the snake weighed five tons, its diameter was 80 centimeters [31.2 inches], and it measured no less than 40 meters [130 feet]."

A second specimen was killed in 1948, after it crawled ashore from the Rio Oiapoc, in Brazil's Guyaporé territory, and invaded Fort Tabatinga. A one-sided battle ensued, with defenders firing 500 shots at the snake before it expired. The dead snake reportedly measured 114 feet from nose to tail, but no part of it was preserved before soldiers shoved it back into the river.

Guyaporé produced another monster—and substantial confusion—in April 1949. On the 28th of that month, the newspaper *A Provincia do Pará* published a photo of a dead snake, floating belly-up in a river, with houses in the distant background. The picture was credited to Joaquim Alencar, its caption describing a specimen 45 meters (146 feet 3 inches) long, photographed on the Rio Abuna, with the negative developed in Manaus on 27 April 1949. Some reports claim the photo depicts the snake killed at Fort Tabatinga in 1948, but discrepancies in size and location refute that theory.

Sightings continue to the present day. In the 1950s, CIA agents stationed in Bolivia reportedly killed a snake 34 feet 3 inches long, which "had eaten, at the very least, ten Indians." The skin was allegedly preserved, but its whereabouts are unknown and herpetologists note that snake skins commonly stretch by some 30 percent in the tanning process. In July 1962, witness Canciona Gomez reported a near-miss encounter with an even larger specimen in Argentina's Chaco Province (where it is called *lampalagua*). In February 1969, Italian naturalist Bruno Falcci announced his intent to capture an anaconda "more than 100 feet long and at least a yard wide," which he glimpsed at Surprise Lake, 180 miles southwest of Porto Velho, in western Brazil's Rondônia Territory. A member of the Falcci expedition, identified

Artist's conception of a clash between Brazilian soldiers and a giant anaconda (*William Rebsamen*).

only as "a Bolivian named Ramon," blamed the snake for devouring six of his relatives.

Falacci did not find his giant snake, but reports continued through the 1990s. On 19 August 1997, villagers from Nuevo Tacna, Peru (170 miles northeast of Lima) claimed a "boa constrictor" 130 feet long and 15 feet in diameter had passed through the forest near their village, en route to the nearby Rio Napo. The snake, described as "very black," allegedly toppled stout trees and left a deep ditch in its wake.

Efforts to bag a giant anaconda continue. Two Ohio-based expeditions were announced in July 1999, with plans to penetrate the Amazon jungle "next year." One, led by the Cincinnati Zoo's reptile curator, seemed content to photograph its quarry; the other, organized by an "adventure" travel agent, planned to catch the snake alive. Neither succeeded, but the quest goes on. In November 2002, Wisconsin leather dealer Paul Raddatz announced plans to capture a giant anaconda for profit. At the same time, Cincinnati lawyer Robert Manley organized another group to bag a specimen for his city's zoo. Thus far, the giants have eluded all pursuers.

Sources: "Boa! Boa! Boa!" *Fortean Times*; Dinsdale, *Monster Hunt*; Reid Epstein, "Businessman aims to charm world with giant anaconda." *Milwaukee Journal Sentinel* (29 November 2002); "Expedition formed to search for the world's largest snake," Associated Press (29 July 1999); Heuvelmans, *On the Track of Unknown Animals*; Theiss, "World's biggest snake"; Wade, "Snakes alive!"

Andaman Wood Owl   Described by witnesses as an unknown species of owl, this mystery BIRD is said to live in dense rain forests of the Andaman and Nicobar Islands, southwest of Myanmar (Burma) in the Andaman Sea. Several other owls are recognized from these islands, and the presence of a new species would come as no great surprise.

Source: Salim Ali and S. Dillon Ripley, *Handbook of the Birds of India and Pakistan, Together with Those of Nepal, Sikkim, Bhutan and Ceylon.* (3 volumes) New York: Oxford University Press, 1968–74.

Andean Wolf   Although named for the Andes Mountains of South America, this unrecognized wild dog is said to be a pampas dweller, known by natives from southern Brazil through Paraguay and into Argentina. The creature's distinctive long legs, which enable it to peer over tall pampas grass in search of prey, prompt locals to call it *aguara guaza* ("FOX on stilts"). In 1927, German animal collector Lorenz Hagenbeck purchased a peculiar pelt in Buenos Aires, described as resembling that of a maned wolf (*Chrysocyon brachyurus*), but with shorter, rounder ears. Hagenbeck observed three similar pelts at the same time, but did not acquire them. Back in Germany, mammalogist Ingo Krumbiegel studied the pelt and compared it to a strange canid skull—similar to a maned wolf's, but slightly larger than average—collected from the Andes in 1935. Upon pairing the specimens (perhaps incorrectly), Krumbiegel published a formal description of the animal in 1949, calling it a new species which he named *Oreocyon hagenbecki* (Hagenbeck's mountain wolf). The classification remains controversial, with no further specimens found to date. Skeptics note that canid cross-breeds are notoriously variable in appearance, and some suggest that Krumbiegel may have paired a maned wolf's skull with the pelt of an ordinary German shepherd (*Canis familiaris*). DNA tests performed on the Hagenbeck pelt in 2000 were inconclusive; the skin had been chemically treated, and it was also contaminated with a variety of human, dog, wolf and pig DNA.

Sources: Heuvelmans, *On the Track of Unknown Animals*; Shuker, *The Lost Ark*; Shuker, "Pity about the pelt."

Anfish Said to inhabit marshes at the mouth of Iraq's Tigris River, the Anfish is described as a FISH with hairy skin. No specimen has yet been captured, and while fish do not have hair, similar reports have been logged from various other parts of the world.

Source: Wilfred Thesiger, *The Marsh Arabs*. New York: Dutton, 1964.

Angeoa Dubawnt Lake, in Canada's Nunavut province, is one of the country's largest lakes (with a surface area of 1,600 square miles). Inuit natives report that the lake is—or once was—occupied by a LAKE MONSTER, dubbed Angeoa, which they describe as black, 50–60 feet long, and sporting a large dorsal fin. In the 1940s, one Inuit witness told author Farley Mowat that Angeoa had attacked his father's kayak in the late 19th century, overturning the boat and killing one passenger. No recent sightings have been filed, and Dubawnt Lake is icebound for much of the year.

Source: Farley Mowat, *People of the Deer*. Boston: Little, Brown, 1952.

Anghenfil *see* **Teggie**

Angola sea serpent In the fall of 1892, officers and crewmen of the *Angola* sighted a SEA SERPENT in the Gulf of Guinea, off the coast of Nigeria. Witnesses observed the creature for at least 10 minutes, claiming that it measured some 200 feet in length and traveled at a speed of six or seven knots (between 9 and 10 miles per hour). At one point, the animal reportedly raised its head above the surface and stared at the ship with "terrible green eyes." Inasmuch as the sighting occurred from a distance of one mile, the *Glasgow Weekly* (of 29 October 1892) reported that the witnesses "have been subjected to a great deal of ridicule." BERNARD HEUVELMANS stopped short of deeming the incident a HOAX, treating the creature as a possible specimen of his hypothetical "merhorse."

Source: Heuvelmans, *In the Wake of the Sea Serpents*.

Ankerdine Beast(s) On 5 April 2003, Sheila Harris saw a strange animal while passing by Ankerdine Hill, near Knightwick, Worcestershire, England. "It was a weird-looking thing," she told reporters. "My first reaction was that it was a hyena with a mane." In fact, the creature she described was com-

pletely bald, except for a thick red mane behind its long-snouted head. When the report was published, various locals opined that the beast was a deer or a "FOX with mange," but the riddle went unsolved as the animal remained at large. Four months later, on 1 August, Jo Morris was driving with her family on Hadley Heath, Worcestershire, when she glimpsed a small creature described as "half fox cub, half wild boar." On hearing the latest report, Sheila Harris insisted the creature she saw was larger than a fox, but she speculated that her beast might be the smaller one's parent. At press time for this volume, neither animal had been located or identified.

Source: "Sighting of second mystery beast." *Worcester Evening News* (5 August 2003).

Annie E. Hall sea turtle On 30 March 1883, while sailing off Newfoundland's Grand Bank, crewmen aboard the schooner *Annie E. Hall* saw an object which they thought to be a capsized boat. Drawing closer, they realized it was a giant TURTLE, some 40 feet long and 30 feet wide, with flippers close to 20 feet in length. Although BERNARD HEUVELMANS missed this case in his 1968 tabulation of SEA SERPENT sightings, the beast qualifies as an prime example of the hypothetical creature he called "Father-of-all-turtles." Heuvelmans speculated that occasional sightings of giant sea turtles may represent a relict population of *Archelon*, a pelagic turtle of the Late Cretaceous, known to reach 12 feet in length.

Source: Jerome Clark's Calendar of Unexplained Events, 2001.

Anny Harper sea serpent In June 1890, Captain David Tuits of the schooner *Anny Harper* reported a SEA SERPENT sighting off the coast of Connecticut, near Long Island, New York. Tuits described the unknown creature as 100 feet long, sporting a 40-foot tail that was brown with black spots. Strangely, Tuits claimed that the animal swam with its "tail" continuously raised above the water's surface—which logically should have rendered forward motion impossible. BERNARD HEUVELMANS hypothesized that Tuits mistook the creature's neck for its tail. With that in mind, Heuvelmans suggested that the animal might represent a specimen of his hypothetical "long-necked" sea serpent (or perhaps a "super EEL").

Source: Heuvelmans, *In the Wake of the Sea Serpents*.

Antarctic Killer Whale In 1980, Russian researchers A. Berzin and V.L. Vladimirov observed what they believed to be a new species of killer whale (orca) at Prydz Bay, on the coast of Antarctica adjoining the Indian Ocean. Three years later, still without a type specimen in hand, Berzin and Vladimirov named their discovery *Orcinus glacialis*. No specimen has yet been cap-

An unknown species of killer whale was reported from Antarctic waters in 1980.

tured, and most marine biologists consider the creature a sub-species of killer whale (*Orcinus orca*), if in fact it is distinct in any way.

Source: Michael Bigg et al., *Killer Whales: A Study of Their Identification, Genealogy, and Natural History in British Columbia and Washington State*. Nanaimo, B.C.: Phantom, 1987.

Antarctic Long-Finned Whale

Another unidentified cetacean reported from Antarctic waters, this presumed whale is described as 20 to 30 feet long and black overall, with occasional reports of white coloration around the mouth and chin. The animal's defining feature is a tall, slightly curved dorsal fin located near its tail. The first sighting was reported in 1841, by officers of the *Erebus*, in the Ross Sea. Six decades later, in January and February 1902, zoologist Edward Wilson sighted pods of long-finned whales during an Antarctic expedition aboard the *Discovery*. In November 1964, a group of cetologists led by Robert Clarke recorded eight separate sightings of a 20-foot specimen off the coast of Chile.

Source: Naish, "Multitudinous enigmatic cetaceans, or 'whales in limbo.'"

Ants (Giant)

Insects are rarely considered legitimate cryptids, due to their typically small size, but reports of FOX-sized ants from India and elsewhere in Asia clearly merit inclusion in this survey. Greek historian Herodotus (ca. 484–425 B.C.) filed the first report on such creatures, and while the ants described did not rival the Hollywood giants of *Them!* (1954), an encounter with them would still be quite startling. Herodotus wrote:

There is found in this desert a kind of ant of great size — bigger than a fox, though not so big as a dog. Some specimens which were caught are kept in the palace of the Persian king. As they burrow underground these animals throw up the sand in heaps, just as our own ants throw up the earth, and are very like ours in shape. The sand has a rich content of gold, and it is that the Indians are after when they make their expeditions into the desert.

Similar reports emerged from China's Yangtze Valley in the first century A.D., and while no such giant ants have yet been catalogued by science, cryptozoologists believe they have solved the riddle. In 1979, researcher Peter Costello nominated the red marmot (*Marmota caudata*) as a "giant ant" candidate. Two decades later, in 1997, French anthropologist Michael Peissel suggested an alternate marmot species (*Arctomys himalayanas*) as the culprit. Those 2-foot creatures burrow diligently on plains overlooking the Indus River, where gold-bearing strata of sand are found three feet below the surface. In the absence of true giant insects, the mystery seems to be solved.

Sources: Costello, *The Magic Zoo*; "Giant ants find gold," *Fortean Times*; Karl Shuker, "Menagerie of mystery," *Strange Magazine* 19 (Spring 1998): 23.

Ape Canyon, Washington

Located two miles east of Mount Saint Helens, in Skamania County, Ape Canyon is named for a series of remarkable events reported first in the Portland *Oregonian* of 13 July 1924. Under the headline "FIGHT WITH BIG APES REPORTED BY MINERS," the story read:

KELSO, Wash., July 12 — (Special) The strangest story to come from the Cascade mountains was brought to Kelso today by Marion Smith, his son Roy Smith, Fred Beck, Gabe Lefever and John Peterson, who encountered the fabled "mountain devils" or mountain gorillas of Mount St. Helens this week, shooting one of them and being attacked throughout the night by rock bombardments of the beasts.

The men had been prospecting a claim on the Muddy, a branch of the Lewis River about eight miles from Spirit Lake, 46 miles from Castle Rock. They declared that they saw four of the huge animals, which were about 400 pounds and walked erect. Smith and his companions declared that they had seen the tracks of the animals several times in the last six years and Indians have told of the "mountain devils" for 60 years, but none of the animals ever has been seen before.

Smith met with one of the animals and fired at it with a revolver, he said. Thursday Fred Beck, it is said, shot one, the body falling over a precipice. That night the animals bombarded the cabin with showers of rocks, many of them large ones, knocking chunks out of the log cabin, according to the prospectors. Many of the rocks fell through a hole in the roof and two of the rocks struck Beck, one of them rendering him unconscious for nearly two hours.

The animals were said to have the appearance of huge gorillas. They are covered with long, black hair. Their ears are about four inches long and stick straight up. They have four toes, short and stubby. The tracks are 13 to 14 inches long. These tracks have been seen by forest rangers and prospectors for years.

The prospectors built a new cabin this year and it is believed it is close to the cave thought to be occupied by the animals. Mr. Smith believes he knows the location of the cave.

The cave was never located, but a second *Oregonian* article (published on 14 July) confirmed ranger sightings of strange four-toed tracks around Spirit Lake and explained that the stones — some 200 in all — had been hurled into the cabin through a crude chimney hole in the roof.

Despite some obvious discrepancies — upright ears and four-toed footprints — the Ape Canyon report apparently describes the same creatures known in Canada as SASQUATCH, which would not be christened BIGFOOT until 1958. Fred Beck dictated his account of the battle to son Ronald in 1967, published that September as a booklet titled *I Fought the Apemen of Mount St. Helens, Wa.* Striving for "a spiritual and metaphysical understanding of the case," Beck described events preceding the attack as "filled with the psychic element." Beck called himself a visionary healer and declared that "the method [by which] we found our mine was psychic," involving "a spiritual being" who appeared in the guise of "a large Indian dressed in buckskin." The hostile apes themselves, Beck insisted, were "lower or grosser manifestations" of some psychic energy. In fact, Beck declared:

The Abominable Snowmen are from a lower plane. When the condition and vibration is at a certain frequency, they can easily, for a time, appear in a very solid body. They are not animal spirits, but also lack the intelligence of a human consciousness....The Snowmen are a missing link in consciousness, neither animal nor human. They are very close to our dimension, and yet are a part of one lower.

Despite such strange reasoning, most cryptozoologists still agree with LOREN COLEMAN, who wrote in 2001: "While I sense that Beck and his associates had actual experiences with real Bigfoot, this event has been screened through his and others' worldviews and retold with such heavy editing as to be confusing today." Primatologist JOHN NAPIER added to that confusion with the following passage from his book *Bigfoot: The Yeti and Sasquatch in Myth and Reality* (1972):

In 1918 a story appeared in the *Seattle Times* of July 16th concerning the "mountain devils" who attacked a prospector's shack at Mount St. Lawrence [*sic*], near Kelso, Washington State. These creatures were supposed to be members of the Seeahtik tribe. They were half-human, half-monster, were 7 ft.-8 ft. tall and possessed the gifts of hypnotism and the ability to make themselves invisible (a folktale characteristic).

At first glance, the report seems to be a garbled retelling of the standard Ape Canyon story, with Napier garbling the date (as he did the name of Mount St. Helens), but he goes on to relate Beck's account five pages later, with the correct date and details. Some researchers treat the passage as evidence of a second Bigfoot attack near Kelso, but documentation remains elusive.

Sources: Beck, *I Fought the Apemen of Mount St. Helens, Wa.* (Privately published, 1967); Coleman, *Bigfoot!*; Green, *Sasquatch: The Apes Among Us*; Napier, *Bigfoot*.

Ape-Faced Cat An unknown felid described by Christopher Columbus during his fourth voyage to the New World, this creature was reportedly captured in 1502, when Columbus sent a party of explorers to probe the interior of present-day Costa Rica.

Europe has but one indigenous simian, but reports of others continue.

Witnesses described the animal as a large CAT with an apelike face and a prehensile tail, which it used as a weapon to kill prey. Columbus reported that the cat killed a peccary before his men subdued it. An absence of further reports since the 16th century suggests that the creature may be extinct.

Source: Wendt, *Out of Noah's Ark.*

Apes (European) Apes and MONKEYS do not naturally occur in Europe or the British Isles (with the exception of the Barbary apes of Gibraltar, which are famous for being the only wild monkeys in Europe), yet simian sightings are nonetheless recorded on occasion. One notable case occurred in November 1938, when two apes were seen repeatedly in Neubrandenbury, Germany. Authorities failed to capture the creatures, but they reported that none were missing from local zoos. On 16 September 1996, a man walking his dog at Barlaston Downs, near Stoke on Trent, England saw a large apelike creature, light brown in color, with red eyes and visible fangs. The animal froze briefly in surprise, then bolted on all fours and disappeared into some nearby woods. The witness, described in press reports as "a keen naturalist," checked several books on apes without finding a match for the creature. Once again, police declared that no local wildlife sanctuary had reported any missing primates. Private ownership of exotic animals has been strictly regulated by law in Britain since 1976.

Sources: "Beast or baboon?" *Fortean Times* 94 (January 1997): 16.; Bord and Bord, *Unexplained Mysteries of the 20th Century.*

Apes (Giant) An unknown ape, depicted in primitive cave art and reported by modern eyewitnesses, this GORILLA-sized creature is said to inhabit portions of Namibia and South Africa, roughly 1,000 miles south of the nearest known gorilla colony. Cave art discovered near Goedgegeven, in South Africa's Free State Province, depicts a battle between spear-wielding Khoisan tribesmen and a pack of large apes bearing stones as weapons. More recently, multiple sightings of a similar creature were recorded around Outjo, Namibia in November 1959. Because the local environment is unsuitable for gorillas, it seems unlikely that one or more rogue individuals could have traveled from the Congo or survived long in the wild, although that theory was advanced in 1959. BERNARD HEUVELMANS and other cryptozoologists have speculated on the possible survival of relict Australopiths, who thrived in Africa during the Pliocene and early Pleistocene eras.

Sources: "Ape in SWA may be gorilla," *Salisbury* (Zimbabwe) *Evening Standard* (18 November 1959); Heuvelmans, *Les bêtes humaines d'Afrique.*

Apple Creature *see* Sykesville Monster

Arabian Ostrich The world's smallest known OSTRICH was the Arabian (or Syrian) ostrich (*Struthio camelus syriacus*), a flightless BIRD native to modern-day Syria, Jordan and Saudi Arabia. The birds were plentiful until the end of World War I, when proliferation of firearms made life more dangerous for native species in the Middle East. Various accounts of the ostrich's presumed extinction claim that the last known specimen was killed in Bahrain, in 1941, or by a German tank crew the following year. Most sources agree that the bird was extinct by the early 1950s, but an ostrich carcass was dragged from floodwaters in southwestern Jordan, in February 1966. Four years later, in June 1970, the species was declared officially "endangered," and while no specimens have yet been found alive, hope persists that a few may still exist.

In the 1990s, the National Wildlife Research Center began breeding wild ostriches in the 1,300-square-mile Mahazat as-Sayd

Protected Area in central Saudi Arabia. Because no Arabian ostriches were available, the Sudanese red-necked ostrich (*Struthio
camelus camelus*) was used as a substitute. Thirteen adult specimens were introduced between June 1994 and December 1996,
with free-range chicks successfully hatched in February and
March 1997.

Source: Bille, *Rumors of Existence.*

Arabian Sea serpent

In 1913, British journalist John
Scott Hughes sighted a SEA SERPENT in the Arabian Sea, one day's
travel eastward from the Gulf of Aden. Hughes was serving as
ship's lookout at the time, between 4:00 and 6:00 p.m. Forty
years later, in the *Observer*, he described the sighting as follows:

> Presently my idle-roving eyes were attracted to a slight and silent
> disturbance of the sea, distant between 200 and 400 yards, and in
> a position five to six points on the port bow. What made this slight
> disturbance was the emergence above the water of a series of some
> six to eight arches, which seemed to undulate as they (or It) pro-
> gressed on a course reciprocal to the ship's. What my eyes next saw
> … was the neck, higher and longer than the arches but of less
> thickness, supporting a disproportionately small head, wedge-
> shaped.

Source: Heuvelmans, *In the Wake of the Sea Serpents.*

Archie

A LAKE MONSTER resembling a giant otter with a
horselike head, Archie reportedly inhabits Loch Arkaig, in the
Scottish Highlands. Lord Malmesbury recorded the following report from October 1857 in his memoirs.

> This morning my stalker and his boy gave me an account of a
> mysterious creature, which they say exists in Loch Arkaig, and
> which they call the "Lake-Horse." It is the same animal of which
> one has occasionally read accounts in newspapers as having been
> seen in the Highland lochs, and on the existence of which Lord
> Assynt, the late Lord Ellesmere, wrote an interesting article, but
> hitherto the story has always been looked upon as fabulous. I am
> now, however, nearly persuaded of its truth. My stalker, John Stu-
> art, at Achnaharry, has seen it twice, and both times at sunrise on
> a bright sunny day, when there was not a ripple on the water. The
> creature was basking on the surface; he saw only the head and
> hindquarters, proving that its back was hollow, which is not the
> shape of any FISH or seal. Its head resembled that of a horse.

Source: Harrison, *Sea Serpents and Lake Monsters of the British Isles.*

Argus Pheasant (Unknown)

The single species of
argus pheasant recognized by modern science is the great argus
(*Argusianus argus*), which displays a single reddish-brown band
on its primary feathers. In 1871, T.W. Wood received a single
argus-type feather of unknown provenance that bore two bands
with white dots. On the strength of that evidence alone, he christened the unknown BIRD *A. bipunctatus*. It is unknown today
whether the bird survives or where on Earth it might be found,
although suggested habitats include Java and the Malaysian island
of Tioman. Most ornithologists believe the species is extinct.

Sources: G.W.H. Davison, "Notes on the extinct *Argusianus bipunctatus*." *Bulletin of the British Ornithologists Club* 103 (1983): 86–88;
Shuker, "A selection of mystery birds"; Shuker, "Gallinaceous mystery
birds"; T.W. Wood, "*Argus bipunctatus*, sp. n., described from a single
feather." *Annals and Magazine of Natural History* 8 (1871): 67–68.

Arizona Jaguar

A subspecies of JAGUAR, classified as *Pan-
thera onca arizonesis*, the Arizona jaguar was hunted to near-extinction in its native habitat by 1905. Sightings of jaguars continue to the present day, though some experts believe the
subspecies has been wiped out and witnesses have sighted stray

jaguars from Mexico. The Arizona jaguar was officially listed as
endangered by U.S. authorities in July 1997. Proof positive of
jaguars roaming Arizona was collected in December 2001, when
researcher Jack Childs photographed a specimen near the U.S.-
Mexico border. It remains uncertain whether a breeding population still survives in the Grand Canyon State. On 7 August 2003,
the same jaguar — identified by its distinctive markings — was
caught on film by another surveillance camera.

Sources: Lee Dye, "Where the jaguars roam." ABCNews.com (21 Feb-
ruary 2002); "Photo gives biologists new evidence of jaguars in Arizona."
Associated Press (2 February 2002); Mary Jo Pitzl, "Camera captures
elusive jaguar in southern Ariz." *Arizona Republic* (24 October 2003);
U.S. Fish and Wildlife Service, *Endangered and Threatened Wildlife and
Plants: Final Rule to Extend Endangered Status for the Jaguar in the United
States* (22 July 1997).

Arkansas Primate Encounter Studies

Based at Mena,
near the Oklahoma border in Polk County, Arkansas Primate Encounter Studies (APES) is described on the Internet as "an independent researcher [*sic*] dedicated to unraveling [*sic*] the mystery of
BIGFOOT sightings in Arkansas." According to its website, the unnamed founder of APES began active field research in April 2001
and founded the group in October 2002. APES "plans to maintain
frequent field outings in order to search for evidence of the creatures
and document their behaviors," but no activities to date are detailed. Membership is open to residents of Arkansas, northern
Louisiana, northern Mississippi, southern Missouri, western Tennessee and northeastern Texas, but the group's website has not been
updated since 25 January 2003 and its present status is unknown.

Source: Arkansas Primate Encounter Studies, http://www.geocities.
com/Arkansas_Bigfoot/index.html.

Armadillos (Giant)

Armadillos (Family *Dasypodidae*)
are xenarthran mammals, related to aardvarks and pangolins. Science recognizes 8 genera and 20 species, including the giant armadillo (*Priodontes maximus*) of South America, with a maximum length of 4 feet 10 inches and a record weight (in captivity)
of 132 pounds. The only known North American species is the
9-banded armadillo (*Dasypus novemcinctus*), reaching a record
length of 3 feet 6 inches and a maximum weight of some 20–25
pounds. Nonetheless, in October 2001 crypto-researcher Brad
LaGrange published the eyewitness account of a Florida resident
identified only as Jane, who reported a nocturnal encounter with
several "giant" armadillos, sometime in the late 1960s or early
1970s. Jane saw the creatures in an orange grove outside Tampa

**Recent photographs prove that Arizona jaguars (shown here in a
pen and ink sketch) are not extinct.**

and described them as 4–5 feet long, with "armored" backs and tails. The sighting was not unique; rather, the animals appeared so frequently that Jane's family considered their digging and rooting for food a perpetual nuisance. LaGrange suggests that specimens of *Priodontes* may have been introduced to Florida, as so many other exotic species have been through the years.

Source: Brad LaGrange, "Giant armadillos in Florida?" *North American BioFortean Review* 3 (October 2001): 26–27.

Armadillos (Illinois)   Prior to the early years of the 21st century, North America's species of 9-banded armadillos (*Dasypus novemcinctus*) naturally occurred only in the southeastern and south-central United States. In summer 2003, however, a faunal survey conducted by the Illinois Department of Natural Resources produced a surprising abundance of armadillo sightings throughout southern Illinois. Such sightings began in the 1970s and have multiplied exponentially over the past 30 years, with reports from 11 Illinois counties including one confirmed road-kill in Carbondale and 7 live captures during 2000. As state analyst Joyce Hoffman told the *Peoria Journal-Star*, "We used to have reports where somebody said they had seen an armadillo run across the road. Some of that was attributed to too much holiday cheer or not knowing the difference between an armadillo and an opossum. Initially, my reaction was that we possibly had some animals that stowed away in semis or train cars and made it up here. But after we found seven, it became apparent it wasn't random and accidental transport....I think we can officially count them as being part of the Illinois fauna." No similar survey has yet been conducted for states lying between the armadillo's normal range and Illinois.

Source: Jeff Lampe, "State can count on armadillos." *Peoria* (IL) *Journal-Star* (11 January 2004).

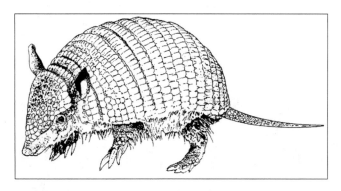

Reports of giant armadillos have been logged from Florida.

Arrow Lake, Canada   A LAKE MONSTER resembling OGOPOGO has been occasionally reported from both the upper and lower sections of this Canadian lake, ranging some 80 miles in length from Beaton and Shelter Bay in the north to Castlegar in the south.

Source: Kirk, *In the Domain of the Lake Monsters.*

Arroyo Salado, Argentina   The town of Arroyo Salado stands in a forested area four miles east of Rosario de la Frontera, the capital of Argentina's Salta province. In early 2003, local residents were terrorized by an unknown HOMINID described by witnesses as standing six feet six inches tall, with "a hairy body, large ears and eyes, [and] powerful claws in its upper extremities." The beast "issued deafening howls," but that was the least of its fright-

ening behavior. As reported by Salta's leading newspaper on 23 February 2003, the hairy prowler was "accused of having devoured medium and large-sized animals and of attacking an undetermined number of people." Police from Rosario de la Frontera interviewed various witnesses, and veterinarian Luis Calderon examined the remains of a colt allegedly killed by the creature, reporting that the colt "had been gnawed by an animal with sharp teeth, powerful jaws and sharp incisors which even perforated the horse's bones." Plaster casts made of the creature's footprints remain unidentified, and a search team organized by fire chief Jose Exequiel Alvarez failed to capture the beast. Investigators learned that the first report of Arroyo Salado's lurking predator was filed in 2001, when a pair of young lovers claimed the creature had attacked them in the forest.

A new report emerged from Arroyo Salado in mid-April 2003, when schoolteacher Hugo Rodas and businessman Raul Torres reported finding a strange carcass near El Duraznito. Fire chief Jose Alvarez interpreted the eyewitness accounts to reporters as follows:

A large unknown animal lay by the roadside, apparently run over by a vehicle. They got out of their car to take a look, turned it around using a stick, and were astonished. They had never seen anything like it. It had amazing claws, was like a human, measured 1.5 meters [4 feet 10 inches] in length. It had a bearlike snout with enormous fangs and genitals identical to those of a male human.

Alvarez — who claimed to have seen the Arroyo Salado predator himself and said it "resembled a GORILLA very closely" — planned to visit El Duraznito and view the remains, but no follow-up reports on the startling announcement are presently available.

Source: Juan Abarza, "Remains of colt devoured by large animal unknown species has population on edge." *El Tribuno Digital* (21 February 2003); "Unknown animal carcass found near Salta." *El Tribuno de Salta* (16 April 2003).

Artakourma *see* **Gnéna**

Artrellia   The Artrellia ("tree DRAGON") is described by witnesses as an arboreal lizard reaching lengths of 20 to 30 feet, which dwells in the trees of Papua New Guinea's dense rain forest. Reports by Western visitors date from the late 19th century, with multiple sightings recorded by soldiers during World War II. Another witness from the early 1940s, David Marsh, was the district commissioner when two government agricultural officers, Lindsay Green and Fred Kleckhan, allegedly recovered an Artrellia's skin and jawbone in 1960, from a village 70 miles northwest of Port Moresby, but the fate of the relics is unknown. A year later, explorers David George and Robert Grant reported their encounter with a 26-foot lizard in the Strachan Island District. The reptile was said to be gray, with a neck three feet long.

In 1978, researchers Jean Becker and Christian Meyer reportedly captured an Artrellia on film, but poor quality prevented identification. Two years later, John Blashford-Snell led an expedition, dubbed "Operation Drake," to trap the Artrellia. Aboriginal tribesmen initially refused to join the hunt, but they finally presented Blashford-Snell with a MONITOR LIZARD just over six feet long, which they identified as a young Artrellia. The captive lizard was identified as a specimen of Salvadori's monitor (*Varanus salvadorii*), and was said to be "very immature." The official record length for Salvadori's monitor is 15 feet 7 inches, but reports of Artrellia double that size continue to this day from the largely unexplored interior of Papua New Guinea.

Sources: Bayless, "The Artrellia"; Blashford-Snell, *Mysteries: Encounters with the Unexplained*; Shuker, *From Flying Toads to Snakes with Wings.*

ASA Monster On 17 January 1977, the *Potomac News* of Dumfries, Virginia reported that "[m]uch has been written about the monster at the ammunition storage area at Quantico Marine Corps Base," but no other sources were cited in the article. Instead, the piece paraphrased reports from two anonymous marines, one describing "a brown thing walking on two legs," while the other depicted a long-haired beast resembling "a cross between an APE and a bear." Loud screams had also been reported on the base. The article concluded:

> We called the ASA (Ammunition Storage Area) sergeant of the guard to determine whether there had been any more sightings or sounds in the area but were told that all information regarding the ASA monster is considered classified. When asked why that is so, the guard answered that he was not allowed to answer that question either. He later said that the information is not really "classified," but everyone at the compound has been ordered not to talk about the monster at all.

The ASA Monster is presumably the same BIGFOOT-type HOMINID seen by Luther Jackson and Dewey Thompson in summer 1977, while they were hunting raccoons near the Quantico base. Jackson and Thompson described the beast as 10 feet tall and covered with dark hair. In 1993, author Jason Berry asserted that "Marines in that area have reported seeing similar creatures for the past 40 years."

Sources: Berry, *Bigfoot on the East Coast*; Green, *Sasquatch: The Apes Among Us.*

Asamanukpa *see* Gnéna

Ashley Leopard One of many ALIEN BIG CATS reported from the English countryside, the Ashley leopard was reported from Kent in the 1990s. During January 1995, a female resident of Wingham reportedly rescued her house CAT from the creature in a dramatic and potentially perilous encounter.

Source: David Walker, "Big cats in the UK." ourworld.compuserve.com/homepages/DavidFWalker_3/ukpreyhb.htm.

Ashuaps A LAKE MONSTER reported from Lac St.-Jean, Québec, Ashuaps takes its name from an abbreviation of the Ashuapmouchouan River, which flows into the lake near St. Prime. Various witnesses describe the creature as ranging from 30 to 100 feet in length. Witness Marcel Tardif and his wife reported a sighting off Scott Point in 1978, estimating the animal's length between 50 and 60 feet. That same afternoon, some unseen object tipped a canoe occupied by Michel Verreault, his wife and daughter, near the same location. Skeptics note that a number of California sea lions (*Zalophus californianus*) were released into Lac St.-Jean in 1975. Sea lions reach a maximum length of eight feet, but it is suggested that several swimming in tandem might present the aspect of a larger serpentine creature. By the same token, sea lions clearly do not explain sightings of Ashuaps prior to 1975.

Source: Meurger and Gagnon, *Lake Monster Traditions.*

Assama sea serpent Sheer exaggeration marks this SEA SERPENT report from February 1897 as a probable HOAX. According to the Sumatra *Daily Courant* of 17 February, the steamer *Assama* was making its way through the Indian Ocean when the ship's captain and helmsman observed a huge creature as long as their vessel and 18 feet in diameter. The capper came when both witnesses claimed the animal raised its neck in an arc 150 above the ocean's surface.

Source: Heuvelmans, *In the Wake of the Sea Serpents.*

Natives of Papua New Guinea describe the Artrellia as a giant man-eating lizard (*William Rebsamen*).

Assyrian Monster Invasion In A.D. 774 the Assyrian empire (spanning portions of present-day Jordan, Syria and Iraq) suffered a frightening invasion of man-eating creatures as yet unidentified. The events were recorded by Denys of Tell-Mahre, a leader of the Syrian Jacobites, in his *Chronicles.*

> Before the reign of the Emperor Leo IV there raged a plague that was followed by the appearance of frightening and terrifying animals who feared nothing and no one. They fled from no man and, indeed, killed many people. A very little were they like wolves, but their face was small and long … and they had great ears. The skin on their spines resembled that of a pig.
>
> These mysterious animals committed great ravages on the people of the Abdin Rock region, near Hoh. In some villages they devoured more than one hundred people, and in many others from twenty, to forty or fifty. Nothing could be done to them because they were fearless of man. If a man did pursue them, in no ways did the monsters become scared or flee. Instead, they turned on the man. If men loosed their weapons on a monster, it leaped on the men and tore them to bits.
>
> These monsters entered houses and yards, and seized and kidnapped children and left, no one daring to offer resistance. They climbed in the night onto terraces, stole children from their beds and went off without opposition. When they appeared, dogs were afraid to bark.
>
> For these reasons, the country suffered a more terrible experience than it had ever known before. Two or three men were frightened to move around together. Cattle disappeared from the field because all of the livestock had been devoured by these dreadful monsters. Indeed, when one of these creatures attacked a heard of goats, or a flock of sheep, they took away several at one time….
>
> These monsters passed from the land and went into Arzanene [southern Armenia] and ravaged every village there. They also rav-

aged the country of Maipherk and along Mt. Cahai and caused great damage at Amida.

Source: Norman, *The Abominable Snowmen.*

Astor Monster   Astor, Florida is located in Lake County, on the eastern fringe of the Ocala National Forest. For more than a century, local residents and visitors have reported encounters with the Astor Monster, a "beast of the deep" that prowls the St. Johns River, sometimes surfacing in nearby lakes. The first reports date from 1896, when fishermen and passengers aboard a steamboat claimed sightings on Lake Dexter. Further reports were logged in the 1940s and 1950s. In 1953, boaters on Lake Dexter claimed a 35-foot creature swam along beside their craft, then veered toward shore, left the water, and vanished into the woods. In the late 1960s, fishing guide Buck Dillard and two of his clients encountered a beast the size of an elephant, which rose from the St. Johns River near Lake Dexter. Dillard says the creature *walked* along the river bottom, thereby ruling out confusion with a manatee. In 1987, two fishermen on Lake Dexter claimed that a large, unseen animal upset their boat from below, leaving a 4-foot dent in the hull.

Source: Mike Archer, "Old town by river holds rich, wise history." *Orlando (FL) Sentinel* (17 June 2002).

Astoria sea serpent   In 1939 the crew of a fishing boat, trolling for halibut near Astoria, Oregon, at the mouth of the Columbia River, reported sighting an unidentified SEA SERPENT. They described a 10-foot neck raised from the water, while the creature watched them with "astonished eyes." No further details were recorded, but BERNARD HEUVELMANS accepted the sighting as genuine, suggesting that British Columbia's CADBOROSAURUS may have been paying "a goodwill visit to the United States."

Source: Heuvelmans, *In the Wake of the Sea Serpents.*

Athenian sea serpent   In May 1863, crewmen of the mail-packet *Athenian* reported sighting a SEA SERPENT in the North Atlantic, while sailing between the Canary and Cape Verde Islands, off the west coast of Africa. One of the ship's officers described the creature in a letter to a friend, subsequently published in the *Zoologist* and the *Illustrated London News.*

> All doubts may now be set at rest about the great sea-serpent. On the 6th. of May The African Royal Mail Steam Ship *Athenian* on her passage from Teneriffe to Bathurst, fell in with one. At about 7 a.m. John Chapple, quartermaster, at the wheel, saw something floating towards the ship. He called the attention of the Rev. Mr. Smith and another passenger, who were on deck at the time, to it. On nearing the steamer it was discovered to be a large SNAKE about 100 feet long, of a dark brown color, head and tail out of water, the body slightly under. On its head was something like a mane or sea-weed. The body was about the size of our mainmast.

Source: Heuvelmans, *In the Wake of the Sea Serpents.*

Atlas Bear   A small subspecies of the Old World brown bear, *Ursus arctos faidherbianus*, once flourished throughout northern Africa, but unrestricted hunting decimated the population until only a small breeding colony remained in Morocco's Atlas Mountains by the early 19th century. During the 1820s, the Emperor of Morocco presented a specimen to the Marseilles Zoological Gardens, but its skin was lost sometime after 1830. An Englishman named Crowther supplied a description of the living animal to Edward Blyth, curator of the Royal Asiatic Society's museum at Calcutta, in 1841. Blyth's description, published in the Proceedings of London's Zoological Society for 1841, follows:

> Upon questioning Mr. Crowther respecting the Bear of Mt. Atlas, which has been suspected to be the *Syriacus* [*U. a. syriacus*], he knew it well, and it proves to be a very different animal. An adult female was inferior in size to the American Black Bear, but more robustly formed, the face much shorter and broader, though the muzzle was pointed, and both its toes and claws were remarkably short (for a Bear), the latter being also particularly stout. Hair black, or rather of a brownish black, and shaggy, about four or five inches long; but, on the under parts, of an orange rufous color; the muzzle black. This individual was killed at the foot of the Tetuan mountains, about twenty-five miles from that of the Atlas. It is considered a rare species in that part, and feeds on roots, acorns, and fruits. Does not climb with facility; and is stated to be very different-looking from any other Bear.

Three years later, in 1844, the Atlas bear was formally designated a separate subspecies (*Ursus arctos crowtheri*). Although the species has been deemed officially extinct since the late 19th century, sporadic eyewitness sightings continue to the present day. Skeptics suggest that confusion arises from the similarity of Arabic names for the bear (*dubb*) and hyena (*dubbah*), but the solution seems unlikely, since the *U. a. crowtheri* bears no resemblance to a hyena.

Source: Shuker, *From Flying Toads to Snakes with Wings.*

Attakourma *see* **Gnéna**

Atu Pandek *see* **Orang Pendek**

Atúnkai   An alleged LAKE MONSTER reported by aboriginal inhabitants of northwestern Oregon through the late 19th century, the Atúnkai was described by witnesses as resembling an oversized seal or sea otter. The dearth of modern reports suggests that it may be extinct.

Source: "Water-Monsters of American Aborigines," *Journal of American Folklore* 12 (1899): 255–60.

Au Angi-Angi   An unclassified species of giant MONITOR LIZARD, described reaching 20 feet or more in length, the Au Angi-angi is reported by aboriginal people of eastern Papua New Guinea. Typical descriptions include brown or green coloration; a long neck; a "cowlike" head with large eyes and sharp teeth; forelegs noticeably smaller than the hind legs; and a long, slender tail. The most recent sightings reported in the West were made by two separate groups of witnesses near Boboa, at Lake Murray, on 11–12 December 1999.

Sources: "Dinosaur-like reptile sighted at Lake Murray," *Boroko Independent* (30 December 1999); Heuvelmans, "An annotated checklist of apparently unknown animals with which cryptozoology is concerned."

Au Train Lake, Michigan   Located in Alger County, on Michigan's upper peninsula, Au Train Lake is the reported home of an unidentified LAKE MONSTER. A typical report, from the 1870s, describes a large animal circling a canoe in the middle of the lake, badly frightening the boat's lone occupant.

Source: Richard Dorson, *Bloodstoppers and Bearwalkers.* Cambridge, MA: Harvard University Press, 1952.

Audubon Bighorn Sheep   This subspecies of bighorn sheep (*Ovis canadensis auduboni*) was once commonplace throughout the river breaks and badlands of Nebraska, North and South Dakota, Wyoming and eastern Montana. Unrestricted hunting thinned the wild herds until the last known specimens were killed in the 1890s or early 1900s (reports vary), and the Audubon bighorn was officially declared extinct in 1916. That status is not

Some experts challenge the existence of the Audubon bighorn sheep.

disputed today, but in a curious twist on cryptozoology, two modern researchers now deny that the subspecies ever existed at all. Rob Ramey, curator of zoology at the Denver Museum of Natural History, collaborated with John Wehausen (University of California) to produce a 2000 report suggesting that taxonomists initially identified the Audubon bighorn by size variations linked to diet and environment of regional herds. That conclusion was reached after measuring 694 bighorn sheep skulls in various museum collections across North America, but Ramey and Wehausen admit that few samples of Audubon bighorns exist. In fact, they had only seven skulls to work with for the supposed subspecies, and thus definitive DNA testing was not performed. Based on measurements alone, the researchers concluded that Audubon bighorns did not deserve subspecies recognition. "It's really not a very surprising result to be honest," Wehausen told reporters. "We're just correcting some poor work from earlier days. People just eat this stuff up and keep repeating it. It was pretty well established that there were seven species of bighorn sheep. We'll narrow it down to three: Rocky Mountain, Sierra and Desert."

Source: Brett French, "Audubon sheep's existence disputed. *Billings* (MT) *Gazette* (2 October 2003).

Auli   A possible unclassified sirenian, the Auli has been reported at various times from Chad's Ounianga Lakes and Dagana Marshes, from Ethiopia's Lake T'ana, and from the tributaries of Eritrea's Mereb Wenz. Another sirenian, the West African manatee (*Trichechus senegalensis*) is presently recognized, but sightings of the Auli far exceed its normal range. Fossil remains of extinct sirenians found in Egypt suggest the possibility of a relict population in East Africa, as yet unrecognized by science.

Source: Heuvelmans, *Les derniers dragons d'Afrique.*

Australian Centre for Mystery Investigations *see* **Bull, Tim**

Australian Hominid Research   One of several cryptozoological groups active Down Under, the Australian HOMINID Research (AHR) organization devotes itself to pursuing the cryp-

tid known as YOWIE or Yahoo. Dean Harrison, of Brisbane, is frequently identified in media reports as the AHR's spokesman and "chief Yowie hunter," operating in collaboration with partner Steve Bott. Published accounts conflict on how and when Harrison developed his interest in Yowie: one story claims he has been stalking the creature since 1995; another says he joined the hunt after a Yowie chased him through the woods near his home, in 1997. In any case, Harrison believes the creatures reached Australia via a speculative land bridge from Asia, and he goes on to say, "The distinct difference between the BIGFOOT and the Yowie is that we've got two species here." He suggests that surviving specimens of *Australopithecus robustus* may be the smaller Yowie, while reports of a creature seven feet and taller refer to *Gigantopithecus*, an extinct APE known only from fossils found in Vietnam and China.

In April 2001, galvanized by a large reward offer from a group of self-proclaimed Australian Skeptics, the AHR launched an effort to catch Yowie on videotape. Dubbed Operation Rotation, the plan involved 24 Yowie hunters staking out a wilderness area near Esk, in southeastern Queensland, between 26 April and 4 May 2001. "That's the hot spot for Yowies," Harrison told reporters. "We've had so many sightings from reliable witnesses. Our information is that a least two clans or families of Yowies live in the area. All the witnesses are of the highest caliber and integrity." All the same, no cryptids were captured on film, but Harrison afterward claimed that a Yowie had rocked the camper van occupied by two of his hunters, leaving oversized footprints as it fled into the night.

Sources: Donnan, "On the trail of Yowie"; "Yowie hunters head for the hills near Glympie." *Farshores* website at http://www.100megs-free4.com/farshores/hairbear.htm.

Australian Rare Fauna Research Association   The ARFRA began life in June 1984, as Rare Fauna and Phenomena Research, and incorporated under its present name in 1993. Founder and president PETER CHAPPLE created the group with 12 charter members, pledged to "investigate and analyze reported sightings of unusual animals" throughout Australia. In THYLACINE research alone, the group has collected 3,800 eyewitness reports of "extinct" Tasmanian marsupials surviving on the Australian mainland. Aside from its cryptozoological work, the ARFRA also conducts fauna and flora survey work, data analysis, historical information searches, and studies of livestock and wildlife predation. According to the ARFRA's Internet website, membership "is available on three levels," and all members are required to sign legally binding confidentiality agreements. Chapple died in August 2002 and the group's last monthly bulletin (as of press time for this volume) was issued in December 2002.

Source: Australian Rare Fauna Research Association, http://www.arfra.org/.

Australian Yowie Research Centre *see* **Gilroy, Rex**

Avalanche sea serpents   Few sailors claim to have sighted SEA SERPENTS, and fewer still to have seen more than one. An unusual series of events involving the French gunboat *Avalanche*, assigned to coastal duty in Indochina (now Vietnam) during 1897–98 provides a rare exception to the rule. An officer of the *Avalanche*, Lieutenant Lagrésille described the first two encounters as follows:

In the month of July last [1897] the *Avalanche* saw for the first time, off ALONG BAY, two animals of weird shape and large dimensions;

their length was reckoned at about 65 feet and their diameter at 6 to 10 feet. The feature of these animals was that their body was not rigid like that of the known cetaceans, but made undulating movements similar to a SNAKE's, but in a vertical direction. A revolving gun was loaded and fired at 600 yards, at slightly too short range. They immediately dived, breathing loudly and leaving a wash on the surface like breakers. They did not reappear, but we thought we saw their heads, which we judged to be of small dimensions.

On 15 February of this year [1898], when crossing the Bay of Faî-tsi-long, I saw similar animals again. I at once gave chase and had the revolving gun loaded. Several shots were fired at one of them, at ranges between 300 and 400 yards, and at least two shots reached them without seeming to do them the least harm, the shells bursting on the surface. I also tried to reach them with the bow of the ship, but their speed was greater than that of the *Avalanche*. Each time, however, that this animal came into shallow water it turned back, which enabled me to gain upon it and confirm its great size. It frequently emerged, and always one noticed its undulatory movements. Each emergence was preceded by a jet of water, or rather of water vapour made by a loud breath, unlike the ordinary Blowers which inhale water and blow it out to a certain height.

The color of the animal was grey with several black fins. Its trail was easily followed by the release of its breath which formed circles of 4 to 5 yards in diameter of the surface of the sea, which was then perfectly calm. At one moment I thought I had reached it. The chase went on without success for an hour and a half and had to be abandoned as night was falling.

Lt. Lagrésille recounted his adventures to Paul Doumer, then governor of Indochina and later president of France, at a reception on 25 February 1898. One day later, while accompanied aboard the *Avalanche* by 10 officers from the *Bayard*, Lagrésille returned to the Faî-tsi-long archipelago and logged a third sighting of two unknown creatures swimming in tandem. As Lagrésille described the third encounter:

We gave chase to one of them for thirty-five minutes, and at one particular moment we saw it clearly about 200 yards on the beam, floating horizontally. It had three undulations without a break, which ended with the appearance of its head, which much resembled a seal's, but almost double the size. We could not see whether it had a neck, joining it to the body, of relatively much greater dimensions: this was the only time we saw the undulations appear without a break. Until then we might have thought that what we took for them were humps appearing in succession; but from the testimony of all the witnesses doubt is no longer permissible, for, before they appeared, we saw the animal emerging by the same amount all along its length. Two of the officers present possessed a camera; they ought to have been able to use it then, but they were so surprised by what they saw, that when they thought of aiming their cameras the animal dived, only to appear much further away in much less clear conditions unfavorable to taking a photograph.

To sum up, the animals seen by the *Avalanche* are not known. Their length is about 65 feet (minimum), their color grey and black, their head resembles that of a seal, and their body is subject to undulations that are sometimes marked: finally their back is covered with a sort of saw-teeth which removes any resemblance to known cetaceans; like the latter they reveal their presence by blowing noisily, but they do not spout a jet of inhaled water like the whales; it is, rather, their violent respiration which causes a sort of vaporization of water, which is ejected in drops and not in a jet. Undoubtedly these animals, known and feared by the Annamites, must have provided the idea of the DRAGON, which modified and amplified by legend, has been, if I may so term it, *heraldized* into the national emblem.

Source: Heuvelmans, *In the Wake of the Sea Serpents.*

Aye-Aye (Giant)   The aye-aye is a variety of lemur (*Daubentonia madagascariensis*) confined to the island of Madagascar, off the southeast coast of Africa. In 1930 a government official named Hourcq found and confiscated an unusually large aye-aye skin from the home of a villager at Andranomavo, in Madagascar's Soalala district. No living specimen has yet been taken, but some primatologists surmise that a lemur known only from fossil remains (*D. robusta*) might survive today in remote corners of the island. Presumably hunted to extinction some 2,000 years ago, *D. robusta* in life was three to five times larger than the modern aye-aye.

Source: W.C. Osman Hill, *Primates: Comparative Anatomy and Taxonomy.* Edinburgh: Edinburgh University Press, 1953.

Aypa   A variety of WATER TIGER, reported from Serra de Tumucumaque, in Brazil's Amapá State, the Aypa is described by witnesses as an aquatic creature with a head and neck resembling a TIGER's, boasting long fangs and a body covered in scales or shiny fur (reports vary). A Guyanese missionary described the creature in a letter written to his French superiors during the 18th century. Speculation persists that it may represent an aquatic form of SABER-TOOTHED CAT.

Sources: René Ricatte, *De l'Île du Diable aux Tumuc-Humac.* Paris: La Pensée Universelle, 1978; Shuker, *Mystery Cats of the World.*

Ayrshire Puma   This collective name is broadly applied to various ALIEN BIG CATS sighted in the Ayrshire district of Scotland from the late 1960s to the present day. Farmer John Stewart, of Ballageich, reported several of his geese slaughtered in 1973, by an unseen predator that ripped through a 6-foot wire fence and left his Alsatian guard dog cowering in fear. Richard O'Grady, then director of the Calder Park Zoo, examined tracks left at the scene and pronounced them those of a puma. Sightings multiplied rapidly through 1974, with witnesses reporting tan or black CATS roughly the size of an Alsatian or Labrador retriever, with tails the same length as their bodies. Police scoured the Ayrshire countryside, but failed to snare the elusive prowlers.

Many Ayrshire sightings preceded passage of Britain's Dangerous Wild Animals Act in 1976, which prompted some owners of exotic animals to release their pets in the wild. Big cat sightings proliferated thereafter, and have continued in the new millennium, suggesting the existence of a local breeding population. Some typical recent sightings include:

1 January 2000: A motorist driving from Irvine to Kilmarnock reported seeing a black cat "a little larger than a collie dog but longer in length," with a tail "nearly as long as its body."

28 February 2000: A woman walking her dog sighted a cat she described as "pure black, large as a fully grown Alsatian but longer, with a very long tail," which "seemed to be stalking something across the fields." She observed the animal for two minutes before it vanished into the woods.

Early March 2001: Dr. Fiona Fraser, driving from Sorn to Kilmarnock, observed a large black cat near Galston. Initially startled by the cat's orange eyes, Fraser recalled, "I slowed down to about five or ten miles an hour and it calmly moved off the road. It didn't appear to be frightened of the car at all."

A witness at Patna videotaped a large cat which she observed lounging near her home in October 1996. Researcher Di Francis examined the tape and reported its depiction of "a crouched heavily built animal silhouetted against the skyline and apparently filmed from a lower level and on maximum zoom. Definition is poor, the image is blurred, but the position against the light of the sky does reveal the outline of a massive lionlike animal with broad shoulders, unlike the lean shape of a domestic cat. Size scale is suggested by the posts of stock fencing in the background." Despite its overall poor quality, Francis concluded that "the footage is genuine and shows a large powerfully built feline,

though without further work, a large mastiff type dog is a possibility. If the ears can be defined as being erect, then I believe the footage is likely to be that of a large dark cat."

Source: Mark Fraser, "Big cats in Ayrshire." (December 2000) http://www.scottishbigcats.co.uk/articles.htm.

——— B ———

Babette   This name was borrowed from a cartoon CAT once popular in France and applied to the MYSTERY MAULER(S) that plagued farmers around Epinal, in Vosges Department, during 1977. Those raids were no laughing matter to the locals involved, with at least 289 sheep and 3 cows slaughtered between February and November. Witnesses described a sort of hybrid predator, said to have fur like a WOLF'S and eyes resembling those of a LYNX (*Felis lynx*). The killing stopped during the winter of 1977–78, and farmers hoped the beast — perhaps an ALIEN BIG CAT — had died from exposure to cold weather. Spring dashed those hopes, when multiple witnesses reported sightings of two jet-black animals, noteworthy for their short legs and large paws, but the raids on livestock did not resume and no sightings were reported after early 1979.

Sources: Brodu and Meurger, *Les Félins-Mystère: Sur Traces d'un Mythe Moderne.* Paris: Pogonip, 1984.

Baboons (Mislocated)   Baboons are the largest known MONKEYS on Earth. They belong to the subfamily *Cercopithecinae* and are divided into three genera, *Mandrillus*, *Papio* and *Theropithecus*. Scientifically, only members of the genus *Papio* are viewed as true baboons today, while their close relatives are termed mandrills and geladas, but all remain baboons in common speech. Regardless of their species, baboons are terrestrial omnivores, recognized by their long doglike muzzles, close-set eyes, powerful jaws, short tails and in some species by their brightly-colored buttocks. They are endemic to Africa and the Arabian peninsula, although their range once extended eastward to India. In the wild, they live in hierarchical troops of 5–250 baboons, with a 50–member troop considered average.

Baboon sightings in unexpected locations are rare, but not unknown. Some of the DEVIL MONKEYS described by U.S. witnesses are described as resembling baboons, and author LOREN COLEMAN suggests that rogue primates may explain some alleged KANGAROO sightings across North America. In 1972, 60 anubis baboons (*Papio anubis*) escaped en masse from a safari park in the Spanish province of Cadiz, and while 40 of the fugitives were subsequently shot by hunters, ecologists found a small population living wild there in 1998. On 8 August 1977, two witnesses reported a baboon walking on all fours along a road in Matthews, North Carolina. Several boys saw the primate leap from a tree the next day, but police searches proved fruitless. On 17 January 1999, a motorist approaching Prestwick Airport in Ayrshire, Scotland saw a baboon run across the highway. Again, police responded to the scene and this time saw the beast, closing within 30 yards before it vanished into thick brush. No Scottish zoos had baboons on exhibit at the time, nor had any owners of exotic pets reported an escape.

Sources: "Baboon loose in wilds of Ayrshire." *The Scotsman* (18 January 1999); Bord and Bord, *Unexplained Mysteries of the 20th Century*;

Witnesses report wild baboons in some surprising locations.

Coleman, *Mysterious America*; Callum Frew, "Police hunt for the Yeti of Ayr." *Scottish Daily Record* (18 January 1999); Karl Shuker, "Menagerie of mystery." *Strange Magazine* 20 (December 1998): 39.

Bachman's Warbler   The small BIRD known as Bachman's warbler (*Vermivora bachmanii*) is officially designated by the World Wildlife Fund as "the rarest native songbird in the U.S." In fact, modern ornithologists disagree as to whether the species still exists. The last known active nest was found in 1937, but another 30 years passed before the warblers were listed as endangered. By then, sporadic reports of lone specimens were chiefly concentrated in the Francis Marion National Forest, located in South Carolina's Berkeley County. The last reported sighting, of a female specimen, occurred in Cuba during 1981. Males of the species sported olive plumage on their backs, with a yellow face and underside offset by a black "cap" and "neckerchief" markings. Their vibrant call, now perhaps stilled forever, was described by one author as imbued with "a passion and intensity that impressed itself on all who heard."

Source: Bille, *Rumors of Existence*.

Back Bay sea serpent   In October 1921, a resident to Mumbai (formerly Bombay), India experienced a SEA SERPENT sighting while sailing on Back Bay. The witness later reported his encounter to RUPERT GOULD, on condition that his anonymity should be preserved. As he described the creature:

The upright neck stood some 10 feet, I should say, perpendicularly from the sea surface, tapering very slightly towards the head. The diameter of this column appeared to be about 18 inches near the water. It seemed to be covered with large scales and, in colour, was a light olive green at the back, shading off to a dirty yellow in front. The head was like that of a gigantic TORTOISE, or TURTLE, but any body to correspond with that head and neck would be, at least, fifty feet long, I should judge.

As BERNARD HEUVELMANS noted in 1968, that estimate would only be correct if the creature was serpentine in form. A turtle or PLESIOSAUR might be less than half the length proposed and yet support a 10–foot neck. Strangely, in light of that judgment, Heuvelmans later went on to suggest that the creature may have been a PYTHON.

Source: Heuvelmans, *In the Wake of the Sea Serpents.*

Badak Tanggiling   Natives of Sumatra, Indonesia describe the Badak tanggiling as a large ungulate, reaching lengths of 10 feet and sporting a single horn on its snout. They do not confuse it with the Sumatran RHINOCEROS (Dicerorhinus sumatrensis), reporting that the Badak tanggiling is larger. A specimen was allegedly shot sometime in the 1920s, by hunter J.C. Hazewinkel, but the specimen was not preserved. Some researchers believe the JAVAN RHINOCEROS (Rhinoceros sondaicus), believed extinct on its native island until 1999, may have survived on Sumatra until World War II or later.

Sources: Ley, *The Lungish and the Unicorn*; Shuker, *Extraordinary Animals Worldwide.*

Badigui   Another supposed living DINOSAUR of Africa, the Badigui or Ngakula-ngu ("water devil") is described by natives of the Central African Republic as a huge amphibious creature resembling the Congo's MOKELE-MBEMBE. Its most notable feature is a flexible neck, 10–12 feet long, terminating in a flat head resembling a SNAKE'S. Although herbivorous, it shares Mokele-mbembe's reputation for killing (but never eating) any hippopotamus that strays into its watery domain. Most reports emanate from Brouchouchou and Gounda Rivers, where drag marks 3–5 feet wide mark the creature's passing. Recorded sightings date from 1890 and continued at least until 1930, when one of LUCIEN BLANCOU'S future guides claimed discovery of tracks as wide as a truck, near Ndélé.

Sources: Heuvelmans, *Les Derniers Dragons d'Afrique*; Heuvelmans, *On the Track of Unknown Animals.*

Bahía Craker carcass   In mid-December 1957, Argentinean naval personnel found an unusual creature beached and dying at Bahía Craker, north of the Río Negro's mouth. Newspaper reports described the animal as having a head like an ARMADILLO'S, but with two great tusks, small lidless eyes, and a neck covered with hair three-quarters of an inch in length. Nearly seven weeks later, on 30 January 1958, the same papers announced that the creature was dead, claiming that it was "probably" some prehistoric mammal thawed out from Antarctic ice, whose long swim up the coast had finally exhausted it. No further information on the beast or its identity has yet been published.

Source: Picasso, "South American monsters and mystery animals."

Baitoushan Crater, China   Between August and October 1980, five sightings of an unknown LAKE MONSTER were reported from this 6,400-foot flooded volcano in northeastern Jilin Province, near China's border with North Korea. Witnesses had only seen the creature's head above water so far, glimpsed at ranges of 95–130 feet. They described it as having "the flat beak of a duck and a head shaped like that of a cow, but much larger."

Source: "Cousin of 'Ness' sighted in China." *Las Vegas Sun* (6 October 1980).

Bái-Xióng   Confusion surrounds the Chinese cryptid known as Bái-xíong ("white bear"), since its Mandarin name is also sometimes applied to the giant panda (*Ailuropoda melanoleuca*). Witnesses in China's Hubei Province describe the Bái-xíong as a white bear somewhat smaller than the polar bear (*Ursus maritimus*). Four specimens captured during the 1960s were reportedly displayed at zoos in Beijing and Wuhan, but no information is presently available concerning their status as a species. Skeptics note that the Shennongjia Forest, source of most reported sightings, has an unusually high incidence of albinism among known animals, thus concluding that the Bái-xíong is probably an albino brown bear (*Ursus arctos*).

Sources: Heuvelmans, "Annotated checklist of apparently unknown animals with which cryptozoology is concerned"; Shuker, *The Lost Ark.*

Bakanga *see* **Lions (Spotted)**

Bala Lake *see* **Teggie**

Balaena Whale   On 17 December 1892, while passing through the Bransfield Strait that separates Antarctica from the South Shetland Islands, crewmen aboard the vessel *Balaena* glimpsed a single-tusked cetacean resembling a narwhal (*Monodon monoceros*). However, those whales are found only in Arctic waters, at the opposite end of the Earth, prompting speculation that a corresponding, still-unclassified Antarctic species may also exist. Two possibly related sightings were reported from the South Atlantic in the early 17th century. Dutch explorer Willem Schouten reported that an unseen creature had rammed one of his ships in mid-Atlantic, on 5 October 1615, leaving a 12-inch horn broken off in the hull. On 3 February 1620, off the coast of South Africa, Augustin de Beaulieu reported a dark-blue animal, resembling a porpoise with a tall dorsal fin and a tusk 1–2 feet long. Since narwhals have no dorsal fins and are known only from frigid waters, some researchers believe the 17th-century sightings involved swordfish (*Xiphias gladius*).

Sources: Naish, "The walrus whales"; Shuker, *From Flying Toads to Snakes with Wings.*

Baldwinsville Mill Pond, New York   On 27 May 1871, the *New York Times* reported a LAKE MONSTER sighting from this pond, northwest of Syracuse in Onondaga County. Today, many researchers consider the incident a HOAX.

Source: Coleman, *Mysterious America.*

Bali Leopard   In 1978, two officers of the Indonesian Nature Protection and Wildlife Protection Service reported a "black panther" sighting from the Parpat Agung district on Bali. No such species of CAT exists in nature, though the label is applied equally to melanistic leopards (*Panthera pardus*) and JAGUARS (*P. onca*). The story was largely ignored at the time, but a year later, Bali residents complained of hearing distinctive nocturnal cries from a leopard. Zoologists were skeptical, since leopards are unknown on Bali, but investigation of the reports turned up leopard pawprints in a nearby dried-up river bed. Suddenly, it appeared that Bali had *two* big cat species in residence, also including survivors of the "extinct" BALI TIGER. Despite the initial excitement, however, no further evidence of leopards inhabiting Bali has yet been produced.

Source: Shuker, *Mystery Cats of the World.*

Bali sea serpent   On 31 October 1922, crewmen aboard the steamer *Bali* saw a SEA SERPENT in the Gulf of Mannar, between India and Sri Lanka, at 7° 23' north latitude and 77°52'

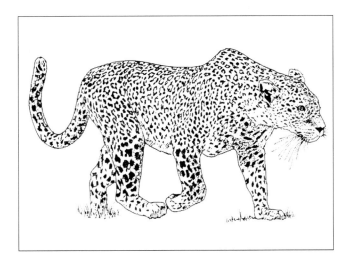

Physical evidence suggests that the Bali leopard may not be extinct.

east longitude. The ship's fourth officer, P. Kruyt, described the incident as follows in the *Bali*'s log:

At about 4:30, about half a mile to port, the water began to be very disturbed until a little later there appeared in the same place an animal with a head and neck recalling a giraffe's but larger. The monster remained visible for about two minutes, and then dived back into the water head first. After which nothing was to be seen except that there were many BIRDS above the place where the beast had disappeared. The serpent was about the same thickness everywhere, of circular section, the head ending in a blunt point. Its thickness was reckoned at about 18 inches, and the visible part about 15 feet long. It was gray-green in color.

Source: Heuvelmans, *In the Wake of the Sea Serpents.*

Bali Tiger   The Bali TIGER (*Panthera tigris balica*) was the smallest known subspecies of *P. tigris*, confined to the Indonesian island of Bali. Its ranks were decimated by unrestricted hunting between the World Wars, until the last known specimen was shot at Sumbar Kima on 27 September 1937. Swedish zoologist Kai Curry-Lindahl believed that several specimens survived on Bali in 1963, but he found no trace of them during an expedition two years later. In 1972, two tourists claimed that officers of the Balinese Forestry Department had admitted evidence of at least one tiger seen on the island "very recently." New hunts were launched

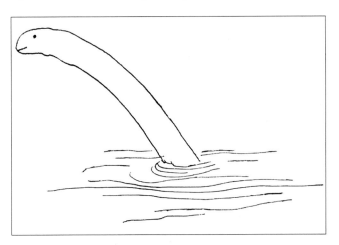

The *Bali* sea serpent, after witness P. Kruyt.

in 1975, but the searchers came back empty-handed, dismissing reports of apparent predation by tigers in northwestern Bali as unproven. Later still, in 1980, spokesmen for the World Wildlife Fund announced that feline claw marks had been found on trees in Bali, cut into the bark at heights that made tigers the most likely suspects. Experts dated the markings as 6–18 months old. Curiously, around the same time, WWF investigators reported evidence of a previously unknown BALI LEOPARD living on the island.

Sources: Bille, *Rumors of Existence*; Shuker, *Mystery Cats of the World.*

Ballynahinch Lake, Ireland   Sometime in the 1880s or 1890s (published accounts differ), a 30-foot serpentine creature "as thick as a horse" allegedly became stuck for two days beneath a bridge spanning the Ballynahinch River, near the castle of the same name in Ireland's County Galway. A blacksmith from Cashel forged a special harpoon to kill the beast, but before he arrived on the scene it was freed by an overnight flood and escaped. On another occasion, a LAKE MONSTER locally known as a horse-EEL appeared on the bank of Ballynahinch Lake, then fled back into the water when tenants of nearby homes approached.

Sources: Holiday, *The Dragon and the Disk*; McEwan, *Mystery Animals of Britain and Ireland.*

***Balmedic* Skull**   In June 1908, crewmen from the ship *Balmedic* found a curious skull beached on the northern coast of Scotland. No further information is available, and the fate of that specimen is unknown, but BERNARD HEUVELMANS dismissed it as a belonging to a whale of uncertain species.

Source: Heuvelmans, *In the Wake of the Sea Serpents.*

Balong Bidai   This predatory LAKE MONSTER of peninsular Malaysia closely resembles the CUERO reported from Chile. Both are said to be flat creatures, resembling an animal hide in the water, which rise to envelop and drown a variety of prey including human beings. Sightings are not restricted to any particular lake. Various explanations advanced for the reports include whirlpools, submarine eruptions of natural gas, and the possible existence of a large freshwater OCTOPUS.

Source: Ronald McKie, *The Company of Animals.* New York: Harcourt, Brace, World, 1966.

Baltic sea serpent   Sir Alexander Ball was a distinguished British sailor and one-time governor of Malta. During 1781, while serving as a junior naval officer in the Baltic Sea, he saw a SEA SERPENT but did not report it. Years later, as noted by friend and former secretary Samuel Coleridge, Ball regretted failing to report the incident. As Coleridge explained in January 1810, soon after Ball's death:

Having observed to me one day that the opposite errors of Credulity and Incredulity must necessarily meet in the same minds where Persons have no other grounds for their believing a thing true, but that they have been accustomed to believing it, he added, that many curious facts and it might be important Discoveries were kept secret by the Persons who had seen them [from] the fear of exciting doubts as to their veracity or judgement. I confess, says he, knowing the general opinion concerning the relations of [Scandinavian clergyman Hans] Egede I was ashamed when I was then indeed a much younger man on my return from the Baltic to avow publicly that I had myself, as was actually the case, seen a Creature resembling in all respects the Monster described by Egede [from Greenland, in 1741] under the name of the Sea Serpent. He then described to me the appearance expressing at the same time the probability that the size and height might have seemed greater with the perception and have remained uncorrected from the distance and the short time the Animal remained above the water. By comparing however my Notes with the Account lately transmitted from the North of Scotland of this same Animal [I think] that Sir Alexander Ball had distrusted the accuracy of his observation without reason.

Indeed, BERNARD HEUVELMANS, writing more than 150 years later, concluded that Egede and Ball had both seen the creature Heuvelmans described as the "super-otter" type of sea serpent.

Source: Heuvelmans, *In the Wake of the Sea Serpents.*

Bamping, Daniel M. (1975 —)
Wildlife researcher and photographer Danny Bamping, of Plymouth, England, founded the BRITISH BIG CAT SOCIETY in 2000 or 2001 (accounts vary). According to the group's Internet website, he is also the current president, though press reports sometimes refer to him as the society's secretary or media representative. In any case, since the society was formed Bamping has emerged as Britain's most frequently quoted authority on the subject of ALIEN BIG CATS at large. Bamping's goal is to prove the existence of exotic CATS living and breeding in the British countryside, as indicated by more than 1,000 eyewitness sightings the BBCS collected between March 2001 and August 2002.

Sources: Sieveking, "Big cats in Britain"; British Big Cat Society, http://www.britishbigcats.org/.

Bangenza
This unclassified African primate, reported from the Democratic Republic of Congo, is described by witnesses as brown in color and larger than a mature CHIMPANZEE (*Pan troglodytes*). Unlike chimps, it is also said to be a solitary creature, wandering alone through the jungle rather than in family groups. No specimens have yet been collected, but skeptics suggest that sightings may reflect encounters with "rogue" male chimpanzees.

Source: Heuvelmans, *Les Bêtes Humaines d'Afrique.*

Ban-Jhankri *see* Yeti

Ban-Manush
This unclassified primate or HOMINID of the Himalayas is reported under various names from Bangladesh, India and Nepal. Witnesses describe it as a forest-dwelling biped, 4–5 feet tall and covered in gray hair. The Ban-manush is aggressive toward humans and enjoys a reputation for kidnapping persons of both sexes. Natives of the creature's range do not confuse it with the YETI. Regional names for the Ban-manush include Bang, Bunmanus and Van-manas. Female specimens are sometimes called Lidini.

Sources: Lall, *Lore and Legend of the Yeti*; Tchernine, *The Yeti.*

Barceloneta Bird
Puerto Rico has emerged as an unexpected hotbed of cryptids in recent decades. The predatory CHUPACABRA terrorized residents during the 1990s, with its attacks on livestock and domestic pets, and a new millennium brought no respite. In spring 2001, reports from Barceloneta announced that a large and "very strange" BIRD had appeared in the Barrio Garrochales and Pozo Gratis neighborhoods. Witnesses described the avian intruder as 30 inches long and 12 inches tall, with a long thick neck and a 4-inch beak. Its mottled plumage was black, white and gray. Its feet resembled a chicken's, sans claws, but its legs were "similar to those of a CAT." Strangest of all, locals claimed, was the fact that it "feeds on blood." More specifically, observers told the press that the bird swallowed chickens alive, "feathers and all," then regurgitated its meal 10 minutes later "as a chewed-up, featherless and bloodless mass."

Remarkably, one of these unique specimens was allegedly captured by a Barceloneta resident in late April 2001. A reporter from *El Expresso* snapped photos (still unpublished) and told his readers that "the strange creature appears to have a tail that protrudes from its head and measures approximately eight inches." At last report, no scientists had taken time to examine the bird or speculate on its identity.

Source: "A 'bloodthirsty' bird swallows chickens." *El Expresso* (3–9 May 2001).

Bardin Booger
This local nickname is applied to the unknown HOMINID or NORTH AMERICAN APE allegedly seen in 1987 by residents of Bardin, Florida, a small logging village located north of Palatka, in Putnam County. It is a variation of the BOOGER label applied to various cryptids throughout the southern U.S., and serves here as a synonym for the more common name of SKUNK APE. Visitors report that Bardin residents have tapped a meager vein of CRYPTOTOURISM by developing "something of a cottage industry around it."

Source: "Bardin Booger." Posted to the Bigfoot-Sasquatch Internet newsgroup by "Bigfoot Searcher" (4 July 2003).

Barham sea serpent
At 2:30 p.m. on 28 August 1852, officers and crew aboard the vessel *Barham* met a SEA SERPENT south of the Mozambique Channel, at 37° 16' south latitude, 40° east longitude. One witness, a Captain Steele of the 9th Lancers, described the incident as follows:

We had all gone below to get ready for dinner, when the first mate called us on deck to see a most extraordinary sight. About five hundred yards from the ship there was the head and neck of an enormous SNAKE; we saw about sixteen or twenty feet out of the water, and he *spouted* a long way from his head; down his back he had a crest like a cock's comb, and was going very slowly through the water, but left a wake of about fifty or sixty feet, as if dragging a long body after him. The captain put the ship off her course to run down to him but as we approached him, he went down. His colour was green, with light spots. *He was seen by every one on board.*

Another witness penned an account of the sighting to *The Times* of London, which published the letter on 17 November 1852. He wrote:

You will be surprised to hear that we have actually seen the great sea-serpent, about which there has been so much discussion…. His head appeared to be about sixteen feet above the water, and he kept moving it up and down, sometimes showing his enormous neck, which was surmounted with a huge crest in the shape of a saw. It was surrounded by hundreds of BIRDS, and we at first thought it was a dead whale. He left a track in the water like the wake of a boat, and from what we could see of the head and part of his body, we were led to think he must be about sixty feet in length, but he might be more. The captain kept the vessel away to get nearer to him, and when we were within a hundred yards he slowly sank into the depths of the sea. While we were at dinner he was seen again, and a midshipman took a sketch of him, of which I will send you a copy.

The sketch was not published and has yet to surface in print.

Source: Heuvelmans, *In the Wake of the Sea Serpents.*

Bâri *see* Gnéna

Barking Snake
SNAKES have no vocal cords, and are thus incapable of making any oral sound except a hiss. That fact notwithstanding, serpents capable of anomalous vocalization are

reported both from Africa (the CROWING CRESTED COBRA) and from Paraguay, in South America. The latter nation, more specifically the rain forest surrounding the Upper Río Paraná, allegedly harbors a barking snake of curious description. Said to bark like a canid, the reptile is described as 10 feet long at maturity, with a doglike head, a visibly inflated abdomen, and four sharp hooks near the tip of its tail. A team of government surveyors allegedly captured one of the snakes in February 1972 and delivered it to the zoo at Asunción, but no trace or record of that specimen remains. Skeptics suggest it was a pregnant female of some known species, but that explanation fails to account for either the barking or tail-hooks unknown among extant snakes.

Sources: "The Paraguayan 'barking snake.'" *Pursuit* 21 (January 1973): 14; "The Paraguayan monster." *Pursuit* 20 (October 1972): 86–87.

Barloge sea serpent   In his 1968 tabulation of SEA SERPENT sightings, BERNARD HEUVELMANS includes a report filed from Barloge, Ireland in September 1861. He names the witness as one Robert Atkins and classifies the sighting as a HOAX, but despite listing page numbers (224–225) for the Barloge incident in his index, Heuvelmans strangely made no reference to it in the text. In fact, his tabulation of hoaxes from 1848–91 includes no cases at all from 1861.

Source: Heuvelmans, *In the Wake of the Sea Serpents.*

Barloy, Jean-Jacques (1939–)   French zoologist Jean-Jacques Barloy earned his Ph.D. in zoology, with specialization in ornithology. He is best known today as the author of numerous books and articles dealing with natural history. His first cryptozoological volume, dealing with SEA SERPENTS, was published in 1978 as *Serpent de Mer et Monstres Aquatiques.* Six years later, he followed that effort with *Les Survivants de l'Ombre,* reviewing evidence of relict HOMINIDS around the world. Between those efforts, he performed computer analysis of 18th-century data related to a French MYSTERY MAULER known as the BEAST OF GÉVAUDAN, which ranks among his most important contributions to the field. Barloy remains a popular guest on French radio and television programs, where his presentations often include cases drawn from cryptozoology.

Source: Coleman and Clark, *Cryptozoology A to Z.*

Bar-Manu   The Bar-manu is an unclassified primate or HOMINID of northwestern Pakistan. Although its name translates literally as "big hairy one," witnesses commonly describe the creatures as shorter than the average man, possessed of a muscular physique and covered head-to-toe with dark hair. The Bar-manu's head is said to be disproportionately large, with a prominent brow ridge, receding forehead and minimal chin. Its wide, humanoid footprints are often pigeon-toed. As in the case of many other hominids, witnesses are frequently impressed by the beast's foul body odor. Sightings are frequently reported from montane forests of the Hindu Kush at altitudes above 6,500 feet. Spanish cryptozoologist JORDI MAGRANER began a single-minded pursuit of the Bar-manu in the late 1980s, and was rewarded in 1994 when he personally found a set of the elusive creature's tracks. A year later American researcher LOREN COLEMAN was contacted by Pakistanis who claimed to know where one of the creatures was buried, but the informants then lapsed into silence, shunning efforts to pursue their lead. Magraner continued his quest for evidence until he was murdered in Pakistan, on 2 August 2002. Some authors claim that the MINNESOTA ICEMAN was in fact a Bar-manu specimen, although no evidence exists link-

A sketch of Pakistan's elusive Bar-manu, after researcher Jordi Magraner.

ing that supposed cryptid to Pakistan.

Source: Coleman and Clark, *Cryptozoology A to Z*; Michel Raynal, "Jordi Magraner's field research on the Bar-manu: Evidence for the authenticity of Heuvelmans's *Homo pongoides.*" *Crypto Hominology Special* 1 (7 April 2001): 98–103.

Barmi Birgoo *see* **Jogung**

Barwon River, Australia   Southern Victoria's Barwon River was known in the 19th century as a popular BUNYIP habitat, prompting speculation that those cryptids dined on the river's plentiful supply of EELS. Escaped convict William Buckley, whose memoirs were published in 1852, recalled attempting to spear bunyips along the river, but he finally desisted out of fear that local Aborigines might react adversely if one of the creatures was killed. No recent sightings from the Barwon are on file.

Source: Smith, *Bunyips & Bigfoots.*

Basajaun   This unknown HOMINID or WILDMAN of the Pyrenees Mountains was christened Basajaun ("forest man") by Basque herdsmen. Other names applied throughout its range in France and Spain include Basandre ("woods woman"), Mono careto ("ugly APE"), Peladits ("finger peeler") and Tártalo ("cyclops"). It appears to Western Europe's version of BIGFOOT or YETI, described by witnesses as 6–10 feet tall, thick-chested and covered with dark hair. In May 1979, several workmen in Spain's Huesca Province surprised a Basajaun at rest, whereupon it snarled and put them to flight by hurling a tree trunk at them. Fifteen years later, in spring 1994, mountaineer Juan Ramó Ferrer reported an encounter with a squealing hominid in Huesca Province, near Bielsa.

Source: Magin, "The European Yeti"; Sergio de la Rubia-Muñoz, "Wild men in Spain." *INFO Journal* 72 (Winter 1995): 22–25.

Basile Lake, Connecticut   Authors LOREN COLEMAN and JOHN KIRK include this supposed Connecticut lake on published lists of reported LAKE MONSTER habitats, but no details of sightings are included. An exhaustive search reveals no Basile Lake within the Nutmeg State.

Sources: Coleman, *Mysterious America*; Kirk, *In the Domain of the Lake Monsters*; Columbia Gazetteer of North America, http://www.bartleby.com/69/.

Basilisco   Residents of Argentina describe the Basilisco as a large toadlike creature that hatches from enigmatic black eggs. Recent sightings are recorded from Santiago del Estero, the Mapuche region, and parts of northwestern Argentina. The original basilisk of ancient mythology — from the Greek *basiliskos* ("little king") — was a composite creature combining elements of BIRD and SNAKE, capable of killing humans with a glance. No such evil power is attributed to the Argentinean version, but its sporadic appearances still serve to terrify witnesses.

Source: Adolfo Colombres, *Seres Sobrenaturales de la Culture Popular Argentina*. Buenos Aires: Del Sol, 1984.

This 17th-century sketch of a basilisk depicts a composite of bird and reptile.

Basilosaurus *see* **Zeuglodon**

Bass Lake, Indiana   Potawatomi Indian legends name Bass Lake, near Winona in Starke County, as the lair of a legendary LAKE MONSTER. No recent sightings of the creature(s) are on file.

Source: "The Logansport *Telegraph* and the monster of the Indiana lakes." *Indiana Magazine of History* 42 (1946): 249–267.

Basswood Lake   This international lake spans the U.S.-Canadian border, with roughly equal sections lying in Ontario and in northeastern Minnesota's Lake County. Vague aboriginal traditions of LAKE MONSTERS surround Basswood Lake, but the closest thing to a modern sighting is witness Bill Powell's report of a curious spouting by some unseen creature in the early 20th century.

Source: Richard Dorson, *Bloodstoppers and Bearwalkers*. Cambridge, MA: Harvard University Press, 1952.

Bathysphaera Intacta   Deep-sea explorer WILLIAM BEEBE named this abyssal FISH on the basis of a single sighting, recorded from his bathysphere off Bermuda, at a depth of 2,100

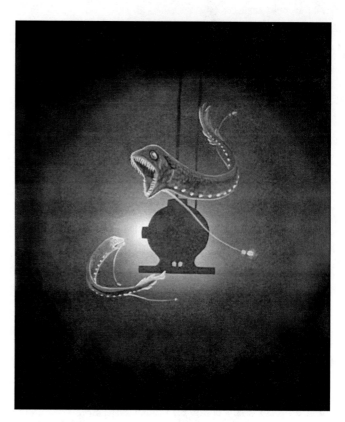

Explorer William Beebe remains the only witness to the deep-sea fish he named *Bathysphaera intacta* (William Rebsamen).

feet, on 22 November 1932. Beebe described the fish as six feet long, with a row of blue lights along each side of its serpentine body. The specimen observed also had two dangling ventral tentacles, each tipped with red and blue lights. Beebe classified it as a member of the scaleless dragonfishes (Subfamily Melanostomiidae), although the largest known member of that group is barely 15 inches long. No other specimens of Bathysphaera intacta have yet been observed or collected.

Source: Beebe, *Half-Mile Down*.

Bats (Giant)   Bats (Order *Chiroptera*) rank among the most plentiful and prolific mammals on Earth. Various published sources acknowledge 800–900 recognized species, divided into the suborders *Megachiroptera* and *Microchiroptera*. As implied by their name, members of the *Megachiroptera* include the largest known bats on earth, though experts disagree on which species deserves top honors. Leading candidates include the kalong (*Pteropus vampyrus*) of Indonesia and Malaysia, with a 5.5-foot wingspan and a record weight of 2 pounds; the New Guinea flying FOX (*P. neohibernicus*), with reported wingspans between 5 feet 3 inches and 5 feet 9 inches; and the Indian flying fox (*P. giganteus*), with a wingspan of 4 feet 9 inches and a record weight of 3.3 pounds. Africa's six species of *Megachiroptera* are relative PYGMIES by comparison, none boasting a wingspan beyond 3 feet 10 inches.

Despite their sometimes imposing appearance, all members of the *Megachiroptera* are gentle fruit-eaters, commonly kept as pets in tropical countries. Members of the *Microchiroptera* enjoy more diverse diets: most are insectivorous, but the sub-order also includes fruit-eaters (Family *Phyllostomidae*) and three species of true vampires (Family *Desmontidae*). The largest known mi-

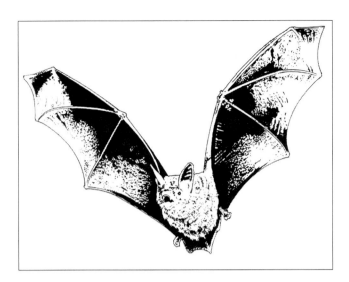

Giant unknown bats are reported from various countries around the world.

crochiropterid is Australia's giant false-vampire (*Macroderma gigas*), with a record wingspan of 2 feet 7 inches. True vampire bats are tiny creatures, with maximum 8-inch wingspans and bodies the size of a man's thumb.

No one denies the likelihood that more bat species wait to be discovered, but most scientists balk at the notion of truly giant bats cruising nocturnal skies, in search of tasty fruit or other prey less savory. Still, sightings of such giants continue around the world, without respite. Some of those covered elsewhere in this work include the AHOOL of Java, Mexico's CAMAZOTZ, Ethiopia's so-called DEATH BIRD, the GUIAFAIRO of Senegal and the OLITAU of Cameroon. Some cryptozoologists assert that modern reports of large flying reptiles, including Africa's KONGAMATO and Papua New Guinea's ROPEN, are more logically explained by reference to giant bats than relict PTEROSAURS. In the U.S., researcher MARK HALL writes with apparent confidence that "[t]he night skies of North America are visited by *Giant Bats*." (Emphasis in the original.) Unfortunately, his "best evidence of [their] survival here" involves a series of giant BIRD sightings reported from Texas in 1975–76. Hall disagrees with most of his colleagues in that respect, maintaining that the flying cryptids seen by multiple witnesses were "actually very large bats."

Ranchers in South America may well agree with Hall. For over 30 years, reports of giant vampire bats have circulated from the Río Ribeira valley in Brazil's São Paulo State to the Argentinean provinces of Jujuy and Mendoza. A priest in Argentina, Friar Salvador Giliz, reported vampires with a wingspan of 3 feet 3 inches from Jujuy, during a spate of alleged vampire attacks on livestock in 1972–73. Eight years later, in 1981, construction workers hired to demolish an abandoned house reputedly found the skeleton of a bat with an 11-inch-long body on the premises. No living bat fits the description of those predators, but fossil remains discovered in Brazil during 1988 document the existence of a relative "giant" from the Pleistocene period. Christened *Desmodus draculae*, this bat was 25 percent larger than modern vampires, boasting a wingspan of 17 inches. *D. draculae* is presumed extinct, with its fossil remains dated around 10,000 years ago, but survival of a relict population could explain the reports filed from Latin America.

Two recent giant-bat reports come from England and Chile, re-

spectively. In the first case, a witness known only as Simon claims he saw a bat with a wingspan of 3–4 feet flying over a cemetery in Exeter, a half-hour past midnight on 25 May 2000. His queries to local organizations of bat enthusiasts went unanswered, and Simon has withheld further details in an effort to avoid ridicule. The incident remains unexplained. On the night of 23 July 2003, three boys in the village of San Pedro de Atacama — near Calama, in northern Chile — were frightened by a shiny-black, 5-foot-tall creature with an 11-foot wingspan, which scratched at the windows of their grandfather's house. The case is complicated by a rash of CHUPACABRA sightings around Calama during the same period.

Sources: "Creature of the night." *Fortean Times* 138 (October 2000): 52; Mark Hall, "Giant bats." *Wonders* 6 (2001): 6–7; Picasso, "South American monsters and mystery animals"; Shuker, "A supplement to Dr. Bernard Heuvelmans' checklist of cryptozoological animals"; Shuker, "Lingering pterodactyls"; "Tales of terror." *Fortean Times* 176 (December 2003): 30–31; E. Trajano and M. de Vivo, "*Desmodus draculae* Morgan, Linares, and Ray, 1988, reported for southeastern Brazil, with paleoecological comments (Phyllostomidae Desmodontidae)." *Mammalia* 55 (1991): 456–459.

Batsquatch

On 19 April 1994, Brian Canfield was driving past Lake Kapowsin, near Eatonville in Washington's Pierce County, when his pickup truck suddenly died. Simultaneously, Canfield claims, a bizarre winged creature swooped from the sky to land on the road in front of him. He later described it as vaguely humanoid in form, nine feet tall, with batlike wings. If that was not strange enough, the beast sported a coat of blue fur, with pointed ears, yellow eyes, a mouthful of prominent teeth, and clawed feet resembling a BIRD'S. After staring at Canfield for several moments, the beast spread its wings and flew off slowly eastward, toward Mt. Rainier National Park. Canfield dubbed the thing Batsquatch, in honor of Washington's more familiar SASQUATCH or BIGFOOT. No other sightings of the creature are reported, and skeptics dismiss Canfield's report as a HOAX.

Source: Phyllis Benjamin, "Batsquatch, flap, flap." *INFO Journal* 73 (Summer 1995): 29–31.

Battle River, Canada

In June 1934, residents of Rosalind, Alberta reported a 30-foot serpentine creature navigating the Battle River. Newspapers at the time referred to the beast as OGOPOGO, a name more properly reserved for the supposed LAKE MONSTER of Okanagan Lake, British Columbia. No recent sightings of the river serpent are recorded.

Source: "Hundreds seek glimpse of Ogopogo at Rosalind." *Edmonton Journal* (10 June 1934).

Batûtût

An unclassified primate or HOMINID of Malaysia's Sabah State, in the northern portion of Borneo, the Batûtût or Ujit is described by witnesses as a 4-foot-tall biped of nocturnal habits. Despite their relatively small size, the creatures are said to be violently aggressive, killing humans on occasion and tearing out their livers. British zoologist John MacKinnon, later renowned for his discoveries in Vietnam's VU QUANG NATURE RESERVE, found a trail of Batûtût footprints in 1969. The prints were six inches long and four inches wide, manlike at toe and heel, but with soles too short and flat for a human foot. As MacKinnon later described his reaction to the find:

My skin crept and I felt a strong desire to head home....I found two dozen footprints in all [but] was quite happy to abandon my quest and shelter under a leaning tree-trunk waiting out a sudden rainstorm....I didn't want to follow them and find out what was at the end of the trail. I knew that no animal we known about could make those tracks. Without deliberately avoiding the area I realize I never went back to that place in the following months of my studies.

Cryptozoologist LOREN COLEMAN and others suggest that the Batûtût may be identical to the small form of YETI known as Teh-lma in the Himalayas, and perhaps synonymous with Vietnam's NGUOI RUNG. Regrettably, MacKinnon's lapse of courage spoiled the best chance yet on record to locate and finally identify the creatures.

Sources: Coleman and Clark, *Cryptozoology A to Z*; John MacKinnon, *In Search of the Red Ape*. New York: Ballantine, 1974.

Bauang sea serpent   In December 1966, a film crew operating at Bauang, in La Union Province on the Philippine Island of Luzon, detonated underwater charges as a part of their production. Moments later, they claimed that a large SEA SERPENT with a snakelike body and a flat head broke the surface, frightening actors and technicians out of the water. The creature allegedly bit the steel shaft of a spear while personnel scrambled into the nearest available boats, then submerged again before it could be caught on film.

Source: Bord and Bord, *Unexplained Mysteries of the 20th Century*.

***Bawean* sea serpent**   On 23 July 1925, soon after departing from Brisbane, Australia en route to Sydney, sailors aboard the Dutch ship *Bawean* saw a SEA SERPENT off the coast of New South Wales. According to Captain P. de Haan:

> We were suddenly aware of a violent disturbance in the water to starboard. A little later a long black body, estimated at 8 metres [26 feet] long, emerged at an angle of 45 degrees, then fell back into the water with a loud splash, making the sort of waves we had already seen. It reappeared again, closer to us, four times; the body, sticking out obliquely, which was about 1½ metres [4 feet 9 inches] thick and was more or less cylindrical, seemed to have a long head, with a beak and eye, and rounded at the end. When the animal fell back, a fin about 4 metres [13 feet] rose at an angle on the right side behind the head, and the body curved to this side when it fell. At the same time there rose out of the water, several metres away, a sort of tail, much thinner than the front part. On the top of the head the skin was black and pimpled, while underneath it was light and smooth. The erected "fin" was much lighter still: almost white with black patches. Its breath was very clearly seen and heard. To my great regret nobody had a camera handy, and it was very difficult to focus glasses on the animal, as we did not know exactly where it would appear next. The shortest distance at which it appeared was about 350 metres [380 yards].

Based on the captain's description, author Malcolm Smith concludes that the creature was an unknown species of beaked whale (Family *Ziphiidae*) or dolphin (Family *Delphinidae*), but the latter seems decidedly unlikely, since the largest known dolphin (*Grampus griseus*) do not exceed 13 feet in length.

Source: Smith, *Bunyips & Bigfoots*.

Bay of Quinte, Canada   An article published in 1978 refers to a LAKE MONSTER sighting allegedly reported from this backwater of LAKE ONTARIO, between Trenton and Belleville, sometime in the 19th century. No further details are presently available.

Sources: "Appearances in the lakes." *Res Bureaux Bulletin* 37 (17 August 1978).

Bay State Bigfoot Society   New England may seem an unlikely venue for BIGFOOT research, but Massachusetts witnesses

reported 11 sightings of large unknown HOMINIDS between December 1969 and summer 1980. Little information is presently available on the Bay State Bigfoot Society, based at Needham and led by John Horrigan. The group was active in December 1996, butnow appears to be defunct.

Source: Berry, *Bigfoot on the East Coast*; Bigfoot/Sasquatch FAQ, http://home.nycap.rr.com/wwilliams/BigfootFAQ.html.

Bayanov, Dmitri (1932–)   Russia's foremost cryptozoologist was born in Moscow and graduated from a teachers' college in 1955, with a major in humanities. After working as a teacher and a Russian-English translator, Bayanov studied under BORIS PORSHNEV, a founder of the SOVIET SNOWMAN COMMISSION, and P.O. Smolin, then chief curator of Moscow's Darwin Museum. He joined MARIE-JEANNE KOFFMANN'S initial search for the elusive ALMAS in the Caucasus Mountains, and later returned to the region for further research on his own. Bayanov joined the Darwin Museum's Relict Hominoid Research Seminar in 1964 and was elected chairman of the group 11 years later. During that time, he coined the term "hominology" to described the study of unknown HOMINIDS worldwide. In 1982, Bayanov was a founding member of the INTERNATIONAL SOCIETY OF CRYPTOZOOLOGY, and he served on that body's board of directors through 1992. His published works on hominology include *In the Footsteps of the Russian Snowman* (1996) and *America's BIGFOOT: Fact, Not Fiction—U.S. Evidence Verified in Russia* (1997). In 2001, Bayanov joined the heated debate over proper means of verifying Bigfoot's existence, with an impassioned plea to abstain from killing a type specimen. Two years later, he realized a lifelong dream by visiting U.S. for a SASQUATCH symposium convened at Willow Creek, California. On that occasion, he told a local reporter, "Today, here I am in front of you. If anybody doubts that Bigfoot is real, I trust that nobody doubts now that Bayanov is real—who does not doubt that Bigfoot is real."

Sources: Sara Arthurs. "Bigfoot fans flock to Willow Creek." *Eureka* (CA) *Times-Standard* (14 September 2003); Dmitri Bayanov, "Bigfoot: To kill or to film?" *The Anomalist* (1 August 2001); Coleman and Clark, *Cryptozoology A to Z*.

Beaked Whales (Unknown)   Beaked whales (Family *Ziphiidae*) are the most mysterious of cetaceans. The lack of current knowledge stems in equal parts from the apparent rarity of some species, and the general preference of beaked whales for deep water far from land. Nineteen species are presently recognized, ranging in length from 13 feet 6 inches to 42 feet 9 inches at maturity. Coloration is highly variable between individuals and is not considered a reliable means of identification. Unknown beaked whales are frequently proposed as SEA SERPENT candidates (e.g., the *BAWEAN* case), and they may also account for a fair number of vaguely identified GLOBSTERS. Two unclassified species are recognized by some cetologists, though debate continues on their legitimacy.

The first and more common unknown beaked whale is known from 30–65 sightings (tabulations differ) in the eastern Pacific, ranging along the coast of Latin America from Mexico to Peru. Generally described as 16–18 feet long, it shares characteristics of the recognized *Mesoplodon* species and has been granted the tentative scientific name *Mesoplodon* species A. This whale apparently displays sexual dimorphism, with presumed males wearing a broad white or cream-colored "saddle" pattern over a black-brown or chocolate color. Females and juveniles, by contrast, are uniformly bronze or gray-brown on top, with lighter undersides.

These whales have moderately long, wide beaks, and their relatively flat heads display a small but distinct melon.

The second supposed species of unknown beaked whale is more speculative, known only from a single sighting from the North Atlantic, in the 1840s. Witness Philip Gosse claimed that his ship was surrounded by the creatures for 17 hours one day, while en route to Jamaica. He described the whales as 30 feet long, on average, with pink tips on their beaks, black dorsal coloring, with white bellies and flippers. No other evidence to date supports Gosse's report.

Sources: Mark Carwardine, *Whales, Dolphins and Porpoises.* New York: DK Publishing, 1995; Philip Gosse, *A Naturalist's Sojourn in Jamaica.* London: Longman, Brown, Green, and Longmans, 1851.

Bear Lake   Bear Lake spans the border between northeastern Utah and southeastern Idaho. It is 20 miles long, 8 miles wide at its broadest point, and has a maximum recorded depth of 200 feet. When Mormon settlers reached Utah (then called Deseret) in the 1840s, Shoshone tribesmen told them that a fierce LAKE MONSTER had inhabited Bear Lake until 1830's great blizzard drove it away. As related by historian Austin Fife, "They represented it as being of the serpent kind, but having legs about eighteen inches long on which they sometimes crawl out of the water a short distance on the shore. They say it spouts water upward out of its mouth." Native assurances notwithstanding, Salt Lake City's *Deseret News* reported on 27 July 1868 that "reliable white testimony" described a beast still living in Bear Lake. Three weeks earlier, witness S.M. Johnson was driving along the lake's shore from South Eden to Round Valley:

> when about half-way he saw something in the lake which, at the time, he thought to be a drowned person. The road being some distance from the water's edge he rode to the beach and the waves were running pretty high. He thought it would soon wash into shore. In a few minutes two or three feet of some kind of animal that he had never seen before were raised out of the water. He did not see the body, only the head and what he supposed to be part of the neck. It had ears or bunches on the side of its head nearly as big as a pint cup. The waves at times would dash over its head, when it would throw water from its mouth or nose. It did not drift landward, but appeared stationary, with the exception of turning its head. Mr. Johnson thought a portion of the body must lie on the bottom of the lake or it would have drifted with the action of the water.

Four witnesses saw the creature one day later, reporting that it was "very large" and "swam much faster than a horse could run on land." On 26 July, a party of 10 persons was traveling between Fish Haven and St. Charles when:

> their attention was suddenly attracted to a peculiar motion or wave in the water, about three miles distant. The lake was not rough, only a little disturbed by light wind. Mr. [Thomas] Slight says he distinctly saw the side of a very large animal that he supposed to be not less than 90 feet in length. Mr. [Allen] Davis doesn't think he saw any part of the body, but is positive it must have been not less than 40 feet in length, judging by the wake it left in the rear. It was going south, and all agreed that it made a mile a minute easily. In a few minutes after the discovery of the first, a second one followed in its wake; but it appeared to be much smaller, appearing to Mr. Slight about the size of a house. A large one, in all, and 6 small ones hied southward out of sight. One of the large ones, before disappearing made a sudden turn to the west, a short distance; then back to its former track. At this turn Mr. Slight says he could distinctly see it was a brownish color. They could judge somewhat their speed by observing known distances on the other

side of the lake, and all agree that the velocity with which they propelled themselves through the water was astonishing.

At least three more sightings were reported in 1871, including the 19 July account of two Fish Haven witnesses who fired shots at a creature swimming with "a wavy serpentine motion." Hapless hunters Milando Pratt and Thomas Rich claimed that the beast had "a body in diameter like that of a man and a head which suggested a walrus without tusks." The same month brought reports that residents of Fish Haven had captured an unknown "creature some 20 feet long which propelled itself through the water by the action of its tail and legs," but the fate of that specimen is unknown and most researchers now regard the story as a HOAX.

On 15 May 1874, four witnesses reported a sighting of the creature three miles north of Laketown. After first mistaking the beast for "a very large duck," they soon concluded it was something very different. William Budge told Mormon leader Brigham Young that "its face and part of its head were distinctly seen, covered with fur, or short hair of a light snuff color." The face was flat, with "very full large eyes, and prominent ears....It did not look ferocious, and was in no hurry to go but kept moving slowly." After receiving that report, Young contracted with Phineas Cook of Swan Creek "to catch the serpent in the Lake at halves." Cook attached a barbed hook to a 20-foot cable and 300 feet of rope, anchored to a lakeside tree, but two years of trolling produced no results. Travel-writer Phil Robinson reported more sightings in October 1883, including one eyewitness claim that the beast was 200 feet long.

Though seen less frequently in modern times, Bear Lake's resident cryptids still make the occasional appearance. Witness Ronald Hansen reported a sighting in 1937, and a local contest held in 1996 resulted in the creature being christened Isabella. As recently as October 2003, an unnamed "veteran local navigator" warned the *Salt Lake Tribune* that it was vital to "let people know to be on the lookout for the Bear Lake monster, because it is still alive and lurking."

Sources: Will Bagley, "Bear Lake monster season is over for this year, but the legend lives on." *Sale Lake Tribune* (8 December 2002); Will Bagley, "Does monster lurk beneath Bear Lake?" *Salt Lake Tribune* (4 March 2001); Will Bagley, "Monster tale haunts shore of Bear Lake." *Salt Lake Tribune* (1 April 2002); Will Bagley, "Recent witness says Bear Lake monster 'is still alive and lurking.'" *Salt Lake Tribune* (5 October 2003); Costello, *In Search of Lake Monsters*; Alan Edwards, "Bear Lake monster gets no respect." *Deseret Morning News* (10 August 2003); Garner, *Monster! Monster!*; Kirk, *In the Domain of the Lake Monsters*.

Beast of Bala   Conflicting reports obscure the tracks of this MYSTERY MAULER from Wales. Its first lamb-killing raids occurred at Llanuwchllyn, near Bala in Snowdonia, and it had time to earn its famous nickname before it was killed by a local farmer in October 1995. Reports from the British Broadcasting Company claim the animal shot was "a pet lemur which had escaped from a nearby animal sanctuary," but those Madagascar primates are not known to slaughter livestock, and the shooting did not stop raiding in the district. In April 1997, 30 lambs were killed at Llanuwchllyn within a 2-week period, by a predator resembling an ALIEN BIG CAT.

Sources: "Catalogue of Wales' weird cats." BBC News (26 August 2000); "Cats in the hats." *Fortean Times* 111 (June 1998).

Beast of Ballybogey   In August 2003, reports of an ALIEN BIG CAT frightened residents of Ballybogey, a village near Portrush in County Antrim, Northern Ireland. Conflicting eyewitness testimony described the CAT as resembling either a COUGAR (*Puma concolor*) or a "black panther," and it was blamed for the mauling of several sheep. Police acknowledged the presence of one or more large cats in the area, threatening prosecution of some unidentified "rogue owner" whom they suspected of releasing it (or them) to roam free. Marksmen were summoned to scour the district, while agents of the Ulster Society for Prevention of Cruelty to Animals stood by with tranquilizer guns. By 24 September, authorities believed they had the cat trapped in a patch of woods near Ballybogey, but they were wrong. At press time for this volume, the animal and its alleged former owner were still at large.

Source: "Trackers close in on beast of Ballybogey." *Ananova* (24 September 2003).

Beast of Ballymeana   Six years before the BEAST OF BALLYBOGEY appeared to frighten residents and vex authorities in Northern Ireland, another ALIEN BIG CAT prowled the wilds of County Antrim. Dubbed the Beast of Ballymeana for the town where it was seen most frequently, the CAT appeared sporadically during 1996, eluding searchers at will, and finally vanished as mysteriously as it had come.

Source: Sieveking, "Watch out: Big cat about."

Beast of Balmoral   This ALIEN BIG CAT of northeastern Scotland earned its place in headlines by prowling near the British royal family's luxurious retreat at Balmoral Castle, seven miles west of Ballater. It was seen first in 1994, when Prince Charles blamed the CAT for snatching Pooh, his favorite Jack Russell terrier. Sheep were the predator's next target, while teams of gamekeepers patrolled the 55,000-acre royal estate in vain. On 7 September 1996, a large cat frightened Princess Olga Romanoff, a cousin of Queen Elizabeth II and great niece of Russian Tsar Nicholas II, at Banchory, 25 miles distant from Balmoral Castle. "It was sleek, black and had pointed ears," the princess reported. "I am convinced there is a panther on the loose. I've no doubt I saw the one that has been prowling Balmoral Estate. I know these animals can travel great distances in a day." By December 1997, some locals complained that royal employees had grown trigger-happy in their futile pursuit of the beast. As evidence, they cited the slaying of the Rev. Robert Sloan's pet cat, shot after it crossed the road in front of a gamekeeper's car. It may be significant that Balmoral Forest lies adjacent to territory where the BEAST OF BENNACHIE has roamed at large since 1995.

Sources: "Beast Of Balmoral Blunder." *Daily Mail* (15 December 1997); Chris Smith, "Cat Beast Purr-sues Princess." *News of the World* (8 September 1996).

Beast of Bangor   Sightings of this unknown cryptid in the Eithenog woods near Bangor, in Gwynedd, Northwest Wales, date from 1992. Some witnesses describe it as resembling a polecat (*Mustela putorius*), while others claim it is an ALIEN BIG CAT of indeterminate species. One of the earliest witnesses, Iori Williams, waited six years to report her sighting for fear of public ridicule. "I remember," she said in July 1998, "my husband and I were walking along a path next to trees in the Eithinog woods, when we spotted something in front of us. It was ginger coloured and was bigger than a CAT. We kept it to ourselves until now, but it looks like others have seen something there as well. I would hate to think this animal could be in danger if and when the building work starts, it wouldn't hurt to investigate I'm sure." Thus far, there has been no investigation and the mystery remains unsolved.

Some witnesses compare the Beast of Bangor to a polecat.

Source: "Beast of Eithenog Woods." *North Wales Chronicle* (3 July 1998).

Beast of Barnet   Witnesses described this ALIEN BIG CAT of Hertfordshire, England as sandy-colored, with a black ring around the tip of its tail. The first sightings occurred on 25 September 1998, at South Mimms, near the junction of the M25 and A1 highways. (Newspapers also dubbed the beast the Monster of the M25.) Police searched the area in vain, but two officers saw the CAT in nearby Potters Bar the following day. Once again, the beast escaped, but this time it left pawprints 3–4 inches long. Helicopters equipped with thermal imaging cameras then joined the search, but they were always in the wrong place while 10 more sightings were recorded through 29 September. A new sighting was reported from Childs Hill on 4 May 2002, whereupon police rushed to the scene and cornered a large cat beneath an apartment house staircase. A veterinarian armed with a tranquilizer gun subdued the animal, which proved to be a female northern LYNX (*Felis lynx*), presumed to be extinct in Britain. The cat, dubbed Lara, was transported to the London Zoo, where she was reportedly adjusting well four months later.

Sources: "'Beast' is recovering well." *This Is London* (8 July 2002); Sieveking, "Big cats in Britain"; Sieveking, "Nothing more than felines."

Beast of Barr Beacon   This ALIEN BIG CAT of the British Midlands made its first appearance on 10 June 2002, when a motorist saw it running along Beacon Road, toward Barbican Park in Walsall, with a RABBIT in its mouth. The CAT resembled a COUGAR (*Puma concolor*) in size and tawny hue. Sgt. Gary Iliff, speaking for Walsall's Community Safety Bureau, told reporters, "We've made some inquiries but we don't know of any such animals in that area so it's a bit of a mystery." Dr. David Breeston, of the Dudley Zoo, surmised that exotic predators "may live on disused railway lines and eat rabbits. They may come into gardens at night but they will stay away from human contact. They are usually spotted at night or on their way back in the morning." Thus far, the Beast of Barr Beacon has not been captured or identified.

Source: Andy Shipley, "It's the beast of Barr Beacon," *Birmingham Evening Mail* (11 June 2002).

Beast of Barton   Lancashire, England produced a rash of ALIEN BIG CAT sightings between March and July 2001, including reports from Barton, Broughton, Carnforth and Milnthorpe, where a motorist saw "a big brown CAT carrying a dead RABBIT" across the highway at 2:00 a.m. on 20 March. Early July brought a new report from Pilling, where the prowler was said to be "as big as a Labrador." Tabloids assumed there was only one creature at large, dubbing it the Beast of Barton.

Source: Alan Burrows, "Is this the Beast of Barton?" *Lancashire Evening Post* (14 July 2001).

Beast of Basingstoke   The first sighting of an ALIEN BIG CAT at Basingstoke, in Hampshire, England, was recorded in January 1994. More reports followed in March and May, when Basingstoke councilor Mem Fitzpatrick saw the CAT and found a mangled deer nearby. Another sighting was logged in August, and the story made headlines a month later. The cat was seen on 3 September at Old Basing, where two sheep were killed and one partially eaten. Eight witnesses reported sightings between 16 and 20 September. One of them, gamekeeper Gordon Lishcombes, watched the beast through binoculars for several minutes and told reporters it was "definitely a lioness" (*Panthera leo*). Armed police, supported by an airplane with thermal imaging equipment, mounted a hunt dubbed Operation Gordon on 22 September, but their prey eluded them. A confusing report of a male lion, complete with mane and a shaggy tuft at the tip of its tail, was reported on 20 November, south of Andover, before the cats vanished at last.

Source: Sieveking, "Beasts in our midst."

Beast of Bath   In May 2003, reports of an ALIEN BIG CAT emanated from Bath, in Somerset, England. Witnesses described the animal as a "black panther," prompting speculation that a melanistic leopard (*Panthera pardus*) might have settled in the neighborhood. Peter and Karen Hanley saw the CAT in mid-June, prowling the grounds of Bath's archery club. "I couldn't quite believe my eyes," Mrs. Hanley told reporters. "I didn't want to think it was a big cat but when we looked again there was no mistaking it. It was looking straight at me but as soon as it got sight of us, it turned and walked away. At first I thought it was just a moggy but when you looked at the cat in proportion to a barn it was next to, it was huge. It was black, had long legs, a long body and its tail was long and pointing straight out. I have seen enough wildlife programs to know a big cat when I see one." Local shepherd Richard Alvis blamed a similar predator for killing one of his lambs several years earlier. "The cats are around this area, there is no doubt about it," he declared. "The area is perfect for them—RABBITS, pheasants, deer—all perfect food sources for them, and I know many people who have spotted them." At last report, police remained skeptical and the Beast of Bath remained elusive.

Source: "Spate of sightings of mystery beast around Bath." *Bath Chronicle* (19 June 2003).

Beast of Bean   Between June 2000 and April 2001, at least 36 residents of Kent, England reported sightings of an ALIEN BIG CAT which they described as closely resembling a COUGAR (*Puma concolor*). Its unofficial nickname derives from frequent appearances at Bean, near Dartford. Two years later, while the jet-black BEAST OF BEXLEY agitated residents of that Kent neighborhood, a fawn-colored felid also appeared on the scene. Brad Clough, speaking for the BRITISH BIG CAT SOCIETY, speculated that Bean's beast may have traveled along railroad lines to find a new hunting ground, where searchers found pawprints 4.5 inches wide and 4 inches long. A videotape from Plumstead supported the case, but neither beast has yet been captured or positively identified.

Sources: Ed Hadfield, "Cats find a purr-fect county." Bexley News Shopper (20 April 2001); Toby Nation, "Beast number two." Scottish Big Cat Society, http://www.scottishbigcats.org.

Beast of Beckenham   In the 1990s, players at Langley Park Golf Course in Beckenham, South East London reported sightings of a 6-foot-tall bipedal creature with a head resembling a rodent's. It lurked in shrubbery and woodland around the greens, startling golfers and spoiling their shots with its surprise appearances. Some witnesses compared it to a KANGAROO, prompting speculation that the beast might be one of the WALLABIES known to be living wild in various parts of Great Britain.

Source: Beast of Beckenham, http://www.wetfloor.gothic.co.uk/the-beastofbeckenham.htm.

Beast of Belbroughton *see* **Pedmore Puma**

Beast of Bennachie/Beast of Braemar   Reports of a "black panther" at large in Aberdeenshire, Scotland date from 1995. While the ALIEN BIG CAT ranged over a fairly wide area, one of its popular nicknames derives from Bennachie hill at Donside, a tourist site where it had frequently appeared. Sheep are sometimes mauled by unseen predators within the beast's range, and a golfer was reportedly attacked by "a sleek black beastie" at Aberdeen's Westhill Golf Course on 9 January 2002, sustaining a bite on her thigh. Six weeks later, on 21 February, witnesses saw the CAT at Bennachie Centre, where it left pawprints 3 inches wide and 14 inches apart, with a distance of 42 inches between the front and rear paws. In June 2003, Richard Dougherty snapped photographs of a cat prowling the hills on Invercauld Estate, near Braemar, but the pictures proved inconclusive. A month later, on 23 July, Tracy Paterson videotaped a large black cat crossing a field near her home at Upper Carse. According to media reports, the footage shows "a creature about the size of a Labrador with a feline tail."

Source: Alistair Beaton, "Bus driver tells of close encounter with Beast of Bennachie." *Press & Journal* (23 February 2002); Alan Crawford, "Whatever it was I don't know. But this was no pussycat." *Sunday Herald* (20 January 2002); Clive Denner, "Family capture giant cat on video." Press & Journal (25 July 2003); Heather Greenaway, "Beast of Braemar." *Scottish Sunday Mail* (8 June 2003); Sieveking, "Watch out: Big cat about"; "ABC Survey 2001–2002." *Fortean Times*, http://www.fortean-times.com/articles/167_bigcats2002_2.shtml.

Beast of Bennington   At 7:10 p.m. on 24 September 2003, Ray Dufresne was driving north on Route 7 near Bennington, Vermont when a "big black thing" crossed the highway in front of his car. "It was hairy from the top of his head to the bottom of his feet," Dufresne said. "It was not walking like a normal person. The first thing I thought was this is a GORILLA costume. I thought it was a joke. Then, I put two and two together." His conclusion was that he had seen a SASQUATCH more than six feet tall, weighing some 270 pounds. Dane Hathaway, speaking for the Vermont Fish and Wildlife Department, suggested that Dufresne had merely seen a black bear (*Ursus americanus*), though that species is not known to walk bipedally for any significant distance. Still, speculation on the Beast of Bennington's identity sent local reporters off to their archives, where they discovered a history of BIGFOOT and WILDMAN sightings dating back to October 1879. The publicity also produced another sighting, this one occurring eight days before Dufresne's, when Doug Dorst saw a similar creature on Route 7, near Cavendish. Dorst initially thought the dark figure was a "homeless dude with a war wound in a snowsuit," then he "freaked out" on noting the creature's size. First impressions notwithstanding, he later told reporters, "My feeling is that it was a stunt, and I enjoy that. More power to the guy." Witnesses Ann Mrowicki and Sadelle Wiltshire next came forward, to report a sighting from Route 7 on the same night as Dufresne's. The figure they had seen was "definitely not a bear," Mrowicki said. Wiltshire believed it was "a guy in a gorilla suit, but it looked like it had a tail." Several locals named a Bennington prankster, 42-year-old Michael Greene, as the most likely perpetrator of a HOAX, but Greene denied it. "I pull some jokes on people," he admitted, "but not this one."

Sources: Noah Hoffenberg, "Reports of 'guy in gorilla suit' follow bigfoot sighting in Vt." *Berkshire* (MA) *Eagle* (3 October 2003); "Man spots 'Bigfoot,'" *Bennington* (VT) *Banner* (26 September 2003).

Beast of Bernera

Glen Bernera, in the northwestern Scottish Highlands, produced its first report of an ALIEN BIG CAT in February 1986. Forester Charles Greenlees was examining a load of fertilizer outside Ardintoul, when he saw a fawn-colored CAT the size of a deerhound watching him from a clump of heather 20 yards distant. Man and cat eyed each other for roughly two minutes, before the felid rose and ran into the nearby forest. Officials at the Kingussie Wildlife Park agreed with Greenlees that the cat resembled a COUGAR (*Puma concolor*), but at the time of his sighting no exotic cats had been reported north of Fort William, so his story was ignored. Over the next 12 months, residents of the sparsely populated district reported more sightings, and a deer was found partially eaten, with its skin rolled back to bare the flesh beneath as cougars sometimes do.

Source: Viv Alexander, "The Beast of Bernera." Scottish Big Cat Society, http://www.scottishbigcats.co.uk/benera.htm.

Beast of Bexley

British authorities received their first reports of ALIEN BIG CATS prowling near Bexley, Kent in October 2001. Frank Mortimer was walking his dog in the Princess Road section of Dartford, when a saw a large CAT watching him from 10–15 feet away. "It was black, about four-and-a-half feet long with a curly tail and it had yellowish eyes," he later told reporters. "My initial reaction was one of shock to come face to face with such a large animal....I have no doubt that it was a panther. I have seen them in the wild on various holidays in Africa. This was definitely not an ordinary cat, even an unusually large one." Fifteen months later, in January 2003, Steve Gardiner found a similar felid peering through the open patio doors of his home at Plumstead. "I was terrified," he said, "but it didn't seem the least bit concerned by me. What I remember about its size was that, as it walked away, its nose disappeared from the edge of one door while its back legs and tail were still visible in the other. Now, that's a big cat." As the beast retreated, Gardiner ran to fetch his video camera, but DANNY BAMPING of the BRITISH BIG CAT SOCIETY (BBCS) found the resultant tape inconclusive. Its central object proved to be a dark "blob," albeit "a very large blob indeed."

The reports were ominous, since Oxleas Wood in Bexley, only 10 miles from Westminster, is a popular weekend retreat for residents of Kent and southeast London. Between the Mortimer and Gardiner sightings, Kent emerged as England's third-busiest region for ABC reports in 2002, with a total of 92 sightings recorded. A month after Gardiner's encounter, a different cat was seen around Bexley. This one, as described by witnesses and videotaped in a Plumstead garden, was fawn-colored and resembled a COUGAR (*Puma concolor*). More significantly, it left pawprints behind at Crayford, measuring 4.5 inches wide and 4 inches long. Seven casts were made of the prints, delivered to Ellis Daw, founder-owner of the Dartmoor Wildlife Park. Daw pronounced himself "90 percent certain" that the prints belonged to a cougar, while Brad Clough, speaking for the BBCS, suggested a possible

suspect. The new Beast of Bexley, he opined, might be a far-ranging cougar last reported as the BEAST OF BEAN in 2000–01, which "travels long distances along railway lines."

Sources: Steve Boggan, "The Beast of Bexley." *London Evening Standard* (24 January 2003); Toby Nation, "Beast number two," Scottish Big Cat Society, http:// www.scottishbigcats.org.

Beast of Billericay

In December 1998, two "wild CAT-like creatures" were sighted roaming the streets of Ramsden Heath, near Billericay in Essex, England. Another witness soon reported a "grisly panther-like creature" lurking about the Barleylands and South Green area of Billericay itself. Described as black, bulky and strong, about the size of Doberman pincers, the animals were suspected of raiding a local homestead, where a pet RABBIT died of fright in its hutch. A different description was offered from Langdon Hills, where two witnesses watched another large cat through binoculars. One observer told the press, "I saw a big cat, like an American mountain lion [*Puma concolor*]. It had a long tail and was at least as big as a dog. I couldn't believe my eyes. I'm sure it could easily kill a little kid. Someone should be looking into the problem." As yet, no official investigation has been mounted and the cats remain at large.

Source: "'Beast of Billericay' sparks danger warning." *This is Essex* (January 1999).

Beast of Bin

In 1994, farmers blamed an ALIEN BIG CAT for a series of sheep-slaying incidents around Huntly, in the Grampian district of northeastern Scotland. Gamekeeper Norman Martin, assigned to the nearby Bin Forest, claimed two sightings of a large exotic CAT since 1992. Farmer Douglas Davidson lost his third sheep on 15 December 1994, a 90-pound ewe that was dragged more than 100 yards across a field before the predator settled down to pick its bones clean. Scientists at the Scottish Agricultural Society examined those remains and officially identified the culprit as "a large, non-native cat." That hardly solved the problem, nor were matters improved by the formation of a special police squad on 16 December, to track the sheep killer. More ewes were devoured at Auchindoun, 10 miles from the Davidson farm, on 20 December. Eight days later, when three sheep were killed and eaten at Aberlour, Moray, Grampian police wildlife liaison officer John Sellar blamed "a pack of domestic dogs gone wild. All the evidence points to canine rather than feline involvement." With that pronouncement, the investigation ceased — and so, apparently, did the predation.

Source: "The Purr-fect place to spot a big cat." *North Scotland Evening Express* (13 September 2003); Sieveking, "Beasts in our midst."

Beast of Bladenboro

This elusive MYSTERY MAULER appeared in North Carolina's Bladen County after Christmas 1953. It struck first at Clarkton, 10 miles southeast of Bladenboro, where it killed a dog on 29 December. Over the next week, it ranged at will through the surrounding countryside, mangling nine more dogs and a pet RABBIT. In each case, the beast crushed its victim's skull and drained the carcass of blood. Witnesses who glimpsed the creature claimed it was black, 3–4 feet long with a 14-inch tail, standing nearly 2 feet tall at the shoulder. Its tracks were "catlike," and while some researchers speculate that the beast was a rare EASTERN COUGAR (*Puma concolor*), melanistic COUGARS are unknown to science. A mob of some 1,000 hunters scoured southern Bladen County on 6–7 January 1954, and while their chaotic search proved fruitless, the predation ceased.

Sources: Michael Futch, "Beast of Bladenboro put town on map."

Fayetteville (NC) *Observer* (23 July 2000); Joseph Gallehugh Jr., "The vampire beast of Bladenboro." *North Carolina Folklore* 24 (1976): 53–58.

Beast of Blagdon   This ALIEN BIG CAT of Somerset, England announced its arrival in October 2000, with the first of several sheep slayings on Robert Harding's farm at Winford. Harding lost two more ewes by spring 2001, insisting to reporters that the predator "was not a dog, a FOX, or a badger. We are talking about throats, shoulders and ribs being ripped open. One of the ewes had her face skinned from her nose right across her head. It would have taken a very powerful animal to do that." On 17 August 2001, Susan Todd was parked with her daughter and granddaughter at a filling station south of Churchill, waiting for husband Ken to buy cigarettes, when she saw a large CAT climbing a hillside 300 yards distant. Ken Todd and sales clerk Karen Ritchings also saw the animal, as did two other passersby. Terry Hooper, coordinator of Britain's Exotic Animal Register, suggested that the beast was a COUGAR (*Puma concolor*), but Ken Todd disagreed. As a former employee of Longleat Safari Park, Todd concurred with other eyewitnesses that the cat was "definitely a lioness" (*Panthera leo*). In any case, it eluded searchers who found no trace of the animal, except for another mutilated sheep on Robert Harding's farm.

Source: Sieveking, "Big cats in Britain."

Beast of Blairadam   This ALIEN BIG CAT of Scotland is named for the Blairadam Forest near Kelty, in Fife. Its most recent sighting, as of press time for this book, occurred on 15 January 2004, when it frightened runner Iain Taylor into finishing a forest race 18 seconds ahead of his nearest competitor. "I'd never believed in the Beast of Blairadam," Taylor told reporters, "but there is a big CAT there. I would say it was about two foot high, three foot long and was black. It's probably the reason I won the race." No other runners saw the beast, but searchers found feline pawprints in the snow along Taylor's route the next day. George Redpath, speaking for the SCOTTISH BIG CAT TRUST, declared, "I wouldn't dispute the runner's sighting at all. It's probably a black panther."

Source: Scott Hussey, "Panther left me panting." Daily Record (16 January 2004).

Beast of Bodalog   This MYSTERY MAULER of Powys, Wales was named for the Bodalog farm near Rhayader, where it killed 35 sheep in October 1988. Evidence found at the scene of the killings suggested that some unknown predator crept from a nearby river, killed its victims by inflicting clean bites on their throats near the sternum, and then returned to the water after each attack. Some locals believed the beast to be a SNAKE, but no indigenous species is large enough to inflict similar wounds. Feral dogs were ruled out, on grounds that that they would neither kill so tidily nor leave prey undevoured. European otters (*Lutra lutra*) and naturalized minks (*Mustela vison*) are both carnivores, but neither normally attacks prey larger than itself. Whatever the hunter's identity, it soon tired of the game and vanished forever.

Source: Shuker, "A water vampire."

Beast of Bodmin Moor   This ALIEN BIG CAT of Cornwall, England first appeared on 26 October 1993, attacking Jane Fuller as she walked her dog on Bodmin Moor and stunning her with a blow to the head. A short time later, two sheep were found slaughtered in a nearby field, one beheaded and the other disemboweled. Two months later, Rosemary Rhodes videotaped an apparent black leopard (*Panthera pardus*) with two cubs at Jamaica

Inn. On 4 January 1994, Keith Farmer snapped a photo of the same CAT or its twin from a range of 400 yards, while it sipped water from a lake near Lanivet, Bodmin. Eight months later, on 27 August, a cat "the size of a small pony" was seen 10 miles west of Bodmin. That same month saw an official conference on the beast convened by Paul Tyler, a member of parliament for North Cornwall who had seen the cat himself, within 100 yards of his home at Rilla Mill. Among the speakers at the gathering was police dog-handler Peter Keen, who had seen big cats in the district on three occasions, one of them accompanied by two cubs. While many witnesses described the Beast of Bodmin Moor as a "black panther," Keen insisted that the animals he saw were COUGARS (*Puma concolor*).

On 12 January 1995, the British Ministry of Agriculture, Fisheries and Food launched an official hunt for the cat(s), funded to the tune of £8,500. Investigators Simon Baker and Charles Wilson dismissed the Rhodes videotape as depicting three domestic cats, while various sheep kills were blamed on a shifting cast of badgers, crows, dogs and FOXES. A skull found in the River Fowey near St. Cleer, Cornwall on 24 July 1995 was traced to an imported leopard-skin rug. The final government report, finding "no verifiable evidence" of big cats at large, was widely dismissed by Cornish farmers as a whitewash. Still, it had the desired effect of driving big-cat stories from the media until February 1998, when the Jamaica Inn videotape was finally aired on television. Commentator Mike Thomas, curator of the Newquay Zoo, opined that the tape depicted either a European wildcat (*Felis silvestris*), presumed extinct in England since the 1870s, or a hybrid of that animal and some exotic cat released by its owner after passage of the Dangerous Wild Animals Act in 1976.

Still, occasional reports of the beast continue to surface. In February 2001, a 3.5-inch feline pawprint was found in soft mud on the outskirts of Botusfleming, Cornwall. Around the same time, a resident of Saltash claimed a pre-dawn sighting near the China Fleet golf course, where a large cat clawed and bit a garden fence. The creature left behind a deep pawprint, splashes of blood and four black hairs. Witness Christopher Riddle told reporters, "We were amazed to see what I can only describe as a large jet-black cat approximately 5ft to 6ft in length with a long, cat-like tail. It stood 18 inches to 2ft high and was bounding through the grass of a small meadow. We all saw it." In October 2002, a black cat "the size of a small Labrador dog" was seen by a gardener in Trelissick. A Christmas Eve sighting in 2002 sent officers racing to catch a "cat" that proved to be a stack of telephone directories stored in a black plastic bag, but the laughter from that episode could not drown out later reports, including the May 2003 report of "a large white creature" seen in a field south of Bodmin. Rumors of a new film clip emerged from the Bodmin area in November 2003, but no frames from the film had surfaced at press time for this volume.

Sources: "'Beast of Bodmin' was black plastic bag." *Western Morning News* (24 December 2002); "Big-cat paw prints give life to the mystery of Bodmin Moor." *Nature* (10 May 2002); "Perplexing sightings of 'beast.'" West Briton (6 March 2003); "Puma-like cat seen at Trelissick." *West Briton* (31 October 2002); Sieveking, "Beasts in our midst"; Sieveking, "Cool cats"; Sieveking, "Nothing more than felines"; Sieveking, "Watch out: Big cat about"; Mark Fraser Internet posting (4 November 2003) to Scottish Big Cat Society, http://www.scottishbigcats.org.

Beast of Boncath   In January 1996, witnesses sighted an ALIEN BIG CAT at Llangoedmor, near Boncath in Ceredigion, Wales. Another sighting was reported on 22 August 1996. Descriptions of the large felid were vague, and no livestock predation was reported.

Source: "Catalogue of Wales' weird cats." BBC News (26 August 2000); Sieveking, "Cool cats."

Beast of Bont   October 1995 witnessed the first of many attacks on sheep in southern Wales by an ALIEN BIG CAT which farmers dubbed the Beast of Bont. The raids occurred primarily around Pontrhyfendigaid in Ceredigion, though sightings of a large fawn-colored CAT were also reported from the Llanddewi-Brefi area. Fifty sheep were dead by January 1996, when police marksmen combed Tywi Forest, near Aberystwyth, without spotting their quarry. London officials declined initial pleas for help, on grounds that no such predators exist in Britain. Veterinarians at the London Zoo disagreed, after performing necropsies on some of the butchered sheep in early 1997. According to that verdict, the wounds were unmistakably inflicted by a young COUGAR (*Puma concolor*), with frontal attacks employing large claws to rip open throats. Still, the government remained aloof until April 1998, when two young boys were frightened by a large cat in the woods near Pontarddulais, Swansea. South Wales police then scoured the forest and employed a helicopter to spot the beast, all in vain. Doug Richardson, assistant curator at London Zoo, deemed it "perfectly possible" that Welsh woodlands might harbor a small population of exotic felids, but the vote of confidence accomplished nothing. Welsh farmers still lose stock to the Beast of Bont. On 4 January 2004, farmer Diane Marshall lost a prize Torwen lamb to the prowler, which returned to confront her the following night. "It was dark," she told reporters, "but I saw two glowing eyes looking straight at me and knew it was not a dog. It did not seem afraid but it did run off quickly. I am just worried it will come back, as it was not concerned at all about my presence." Local police called the incident "a classic big cat attack."

Sources: "Annual cat-alogue of sightings." *Fortean Times* 128 (November 1999): 6; "Beast of Bont." *South Wales Argus* (14 April 1998); Gareth Morgan, "'Beast of Bont' bites leg off rare lamb." *Western Mail* (8 January 2004); Sieveking, "Watch out: Big cat about"; Dave White, "Beware Beast of Bont." *Yukon News* (11 April 1997).

Beast of Braemar *see* **Beast of Bennachie**

Beast of Brassknocker Hill   This enigmatic cryptid is sometimes confused with the ALIEN BIG CAT known in Britain as the BEAST OF BATH. The confusion dates from September 1979, when the Dutch newspaper *Het Binnenhof* ran a sensational story headlined "Beast of Bath Destroys British Wood." The wood in question surrounded Brassknocker Hill, in Somerset, and the beast was described as some kind of APE or MONKEY, compared by various witnesses to a BABOON, CHIMPANZEE, gibbon, lemur or spider monkey. Local resident Frank Green brandished a shotgun for reporters while declaring, "I am very fond of some animals, but I reckon this creature could be dangerous and I am taking no chances." No damages were specified, much less destruction of the forest, and officials closed the case in summer 1980, after a policeman reportedly glimpsed a stray chimp (*Pan troglodytes*) in the neighborhood. He failed to catch it, but Inspector Mike Price was satisfied, telling the press, "We were sure this mystery creature would turn out to be a monkey of some sort. After all, men from Mars aren't hairy, are they?"

Cryptid reports resumed from Brassknocker Hill in 1982, but this time witnesses described an exotic quadruped, resembling either a "stag polecat" (*Mustela putorius*) or a Japanese deer (*Cervus*

nippon). Sporadic sightings continued for the next two years, until summer 1984, when reporters from the *Bath Chronicle* answered a report of a strange-looking animal blocking traffic on a road near Brassknocker Hill. They arrived to find a stray alpaca (*Lamas pacos*) that had wandered from a nearby farmer's paddock. Thus the mystery was solved a second time, but the "solution" left nagging questions unanswered. Where had the mystery ape of 1979–80 come from, and where did it go? What kind of creatures were seen around Brassknocker Hill in 1982–83, before the fugitive alpaca made its great escape? Authorities, thus far, reveal no inclination to pursue those riddles further.

Source: Matthew Zuckerman, "'Beast of Bath destroys British wood'—or does it?" *Bath Chronicle* (9 September 2002).

Beast of Braunton   As in other parts of Britain, witnesses to the existence of an ALIEN BIG CAT at Braunton, in Devon, sometimes disagree about what kind of CAT it is. The first reports, in January 1999, described a tawny-colored predator resembling a COUGAR (*Puma concolor*). One month later, a "black panther" was seen prowling in the same area. The cougar was apparently forgotten by April 1999, when multiple witnesses saw "a large black cat" at Blackmoor Gate, Croyde and Georgeham. November shifted the action to Morthoe, near Woolacombe, where a 6-foot-long black cat spent 10 minutes circling a pub called the Smugglers Rest. Freelance photographer Barbara Fryer saw a smaller panther, "about the size of an Alsatian dog," at Heanton Court on 25 January 2000. She snapped a photo of the beast before it fled, and later told journalists that she suspected the cat was pregnant. Trevor Beer, a press-labeled nature expert from Barnstaple, assured reporters that both cougars and black leopards (*Panthera pardus*) were breeding in the neighborhood. "It's absolutely positive that they are around," he said, "because we've seen them and we've seen them with cubs. We know there's a history of them in Braunton through to Combe Martin, particularly at this time of the year."

Source: "New sighting of big cat reported in Braunton area." *North Devon Journal* (11 February 2000).

Beast of Brechfa   This ALIEN BIG CAT of Carmarthenshire, West Wales has been reported since 1996, when Professor Alan Perrott reported a COUGAR (*Puma concolor*) prowling around his farm. Two years later, August 1998, three horses were attacked on the same property. One foal vanished, while another died from shock with claw marks on its hindquarters and an adult mare suffered bites on its neck, described by a local veterinarian as "consistent with an attack by a large CAT." Prof. Perrott saw the predator again on 17 September 1998, describing it as "a large brown cat with a lighter underbelly." The missing foal's skeletal remains were found on 26 June 1999, and a search of the surrounding woods revealed the gnawed bones of several sheep. On 5 January 2003, a large cat killed a pensioner's dog at Llangadog. More sightings followed, including one reported by police equipped with night-vision goggles. On 14 January, spokesmen for the Dyfed Powys police told reporters that "a big cat expert has found prints bigger than her fist in Brechfa Forest which is not far from where the animal has been seen." At press time for this volume, the predator remained at large and unidentified.

Sources: "Beast of Brechfa exists." BBC Wales (21 October 2002); "Big cats on the prowl." *Fortean Times* 168 (April 2003): 7; F.A. Street-Perrot, "Attack on Bianca." Scottish Big Cat Trust: http://www.bigcats.org /index.html.

Beast of Broadoak This ALIEN BIG CAT of Gloucestershire, England is typically described as a "black panther." Its first appearance was reported from Framilode, along the River Severn, in May 1994. Chris Evans filmed a large black CAT in the Forest of Dean, on 29 March 1995. The following day he was lucky again, tracking two large cats on film for 10 minutes, at a distance of 400 yards. Skeptics dismissed his films as footage of domestic cats.

Sources: Sieveking, "Beasts in our midst"; Sieveking, "Cool cats"; Big Cats, http://www.darksites.com/souls/goth/heartshowl/Bigcats.html.

Beast of Brookmans Park Reports of an ALIEN BIG CAT prowling Brookmans Park, in Hertfordshire, England date from 23 January 1996, when Madelaine Dinsmore found her Range Rover damaged in a nocturnal attack. The car's front bumper was shredded by some large animal, prompting local police to consult experts at the London Zoo. After examining the evidence, zoo curators blamed the incident on "a large dog-like creature" of unknown species. Two locals contested that verdict in August 1997, reporting that they saw a large CAT near the site where a goat was found dismembered in a tree, several feet above ground. Police wildlife officer Dave Hodges was convinced by the evidence and "very lucid" testimony that a large exotic cat was prowling the vicinity. Professor Peter Ambrose offered further evidence on 7 January 1999. While driving between Brookmans Park and Essendon at 11:45 a.m., he "saw a creature about 40 yards ahead disappearing into the undergrowth on the right-hand side of the road. I saw only the back half and tail of the creature. It was black. The tail was quite full and was about half the length of the body. Our cat Jasper is very large but this thing could have had him for breakfast. As I got level with the point I looked to my right but saw nothing in the undergrowth."

Sources: "Cats in the hats." *Fortean Times* 111 (June 1998); Brookmans Park Newsletter, HTTP://BROOKMANS.COM/SAY/PUMA.SHTML.

Beast of Broomhill *see* **Penistone Panther**

Beast of Buchan The Beast of Buchan is a near-legendary ALIEN BIG CAT of northeastern Scotland, blamed since the 1990s for killing and devouring numerous sheep. Descriptions of the creature(s) vary, with some witnesses calling it a "black panther," while others compare it to a COUGAR (*Puma concolor*). Locals hoped the mystery might be solved on 30 April 2002, when farmer Bill Duffus found the partially decapitated carcass of a 3-foot-long CAT outside Boddam, but discovery of those remains only confused the issue further. Paul Paterson, at Glasgow Zoo, told reporters, "It seems it has been part of a private collection, perhaps from a local wildlife park. A European wildcat [*Felis silvestris*] would be about calf-height and would be about twice the size of a normal cat. It would be easier to tell had the head been intact because they have distinctive ears. The other thing it could be is a bobcat [*Felis rufus*], which is like a puma, very hairy, and almost indistinguishable from our wildcats." Ian Turner, of Longleat Safari Park near Bath, opined: "The tail and its coat instantly rule it out from being a LYNX although it is a similar size. Leopard cats [*Felis bengalensis*] can also be around this size. It seems very much like a Scottish wildcat [*F. s. grampia*], which are similar to domestic cats but bigger. But this is big even for them." Terry Wright of Boddam, meanwhile, spoke for many locals when he claimed the Beast of Buchan was still alive and well. "The cat which was found could possibly be one of its young," he suggested. "I have seen it with two younger ones before but I have never been very close to get a proper look at them." Wright de-

clined to reveal the location of his multiple sightings, fearing the cats would be killed, but he described the largest specimen as 5 feet long, estimating its weight at 90 pounds. He believed the cats were black, but had never seen them in daylight. A new sighting of the beast was reported from St. Fergus in December 2003.

Source: "Big cat sighting at St. Fergus." *Buchan Observer* (15 January 2004); "Theories abound over big cat found dead in Buchan countryside." *Press & Journal* (2 May 2002).

Beast of Bucks England's Buckinghamshire (or Bucks) district has not been immune to reports of ALIEN BIG CATS over the past two decades. Most witnesses describe the elusive Beast of Bucks as a tawny-colored CAT resembling a COUGAR (*Puma concolor*), but others claim that they have seen a LYNX (*Felis lynx*) or "black panther." Such confusion typified reports in the early years of the new millennium, thus complicating any efforts to identify the beast(s).

Wildlife photographer Keith Curtis found dead and mangled deer in Penn Wood on two successive days, in January 2002. He later told reporters, "It was horrible, especially as the FOXES had already found them, but there's no way a fox could have killed them. Alarm bells went off straight away. I've worked on gun and wildlife magazines and this is not natural causes. They were so close together and too far from the ring road to blame a car. There's something that's killing these little deer and we have to find out what." Public appeals to anyone who may have released big cats into the wild since 1976, when Britain's Dangerous Wild Animals Act became law, brought no response. The beast returned with a vengeance in early 2003, striking the same Saunderton farm three times and killing 40-plus chickens and other barnyard fowl between late January and early April. The farm's owner glimpsed a creature with "a brown sheen," allegedly resembling a lynx, but witnesses at nearby Princes Risborough believed the cat to be a cougar. By 9 October 2003, when Ernie and Barbara Carey saw the beast outside Cookham, it had morphed into a panther. He told the press:

> The animal was jet black and was at least 2ft high and about 4ft long. It had a very long black tail and little ears. It was huge and its paws were like a TIGER'S. It just strolled right in front and crossed the road....It was definitely not a cat. We weren't alarmed or anything like that, it wasn't doing anybody any harm. It wasn't threatening, it was like a cat walking across the road. It was so huge. We both saw it so it wasn't a case of mistaken identity. But we were still completely surprised to see such a big thing.

Sources: Michelle Fleming, "Photographer shocked by gruesome discovery." *Bucks Free Press* (31 January 2002); "Help to solve the Beast of Bucks mystery." *This is London* (4 July 2002); Clare Kelly, "Beast of Bucks spotted in Cookham." *Bucks Free Press* (10 October 2003); James Webb, "Beast of Bucks is back." *Bucks Free Press* (3 April 2003).

Beast of Buderim This elusive denizen of Queensland, Australia's Sunshine Coast was christened by the media after a series of sightings in spring 1995. Some witnesses compared the creature to a THYLACINE or Tasmanian TIGER, while others seemed convinced that they had seen an ALIEN BIG CAT. Buderim dentist Lance Mesh was driving with his 10-year-old daughter in June, when the creature ran in front of his car. "It was striped and like a combination of a goldy, brindly CAT and dog" he told reporters. "It was medium-sized and had a prominent bump above the eyes. My headlights froze him, he arched his back and crouched before running off the road into the rainforest. I couldn't believe it. For a moment I thought someone had painted a strange looking dog with stripes." Ron and Mandy West saw the animal sniffing at road-kill near Pomona. "We weren't imagining it," Ron insisted. "I can still see it in my mind's eye. It was maybe two feet tall and not at all like a dog. There wasn't much hair. It looked almost bald. The stripes were the arresting thing. We immediately thought 'Tasmanian Tiger.'" Karen Robinson disagreed emphatically, reporting on 2 July that she had struck the beast with her car two months earlier, on the road between Murgon and Nanango. As she described that incident:

> A thing with a big cat face and huge green eyes reared up on its hind legs in our headlights. We hit it at about 70kmph [42mph] at 6:30 at night. It was golden like a lioness [*Panthera leo*] and had a long, long tail and strong back legs. I'll never forget it as it reared and glared at us. It did $1,500 worth of damage to my car, pushing the guard into the wheel. I used my mobile to call for a tow. But when we looked there was no blood and just one little bit of fur. That was no dingo or KANGAROO we saw.

On 9 July 1995, the *Brisbane Sunday Mail* reported that witness Doris Crerar had snapped photos of the prowling creature on her property at Buderim West. Zoologist and thylacine tracker Eric Guiler studied the pictures and told the paper, "I've never seen anything like this. I need to see more. I really cannot tie it in with anything but there is definitely dog in it — and something else. Ask the local Aborigines. If it's lasted 20,000 years perhaps, they must have seen it, must know of it." Researcher Steve Rushton countered with a suggestion that the beast might be "a nocturnal descendant" of Australia's marsupial LION [*Thylacoleo carnifex*], presumed extinct for some 10,000 years. Motorist Ron Swaby described a rather different beast in late August, when it chased an adult kangaroo across the highway in front of his car, south of Bundaberg. He told reporters:

> This incredible sandy-coloured striped animal leapt out from the side of the road a full 15 feet and into the glare of my 100-watt halogen spots and four headlights. It stopped on the road, turned to look at me and fell back on to its huge hindquarters, its large green- yellow eyes glowing in the light, and then it opened its jaws and snarled at me. I have never seen anything like [it]. The white teeth were large and the jaws like a CROCODILE, like a mantrap. It took two steps and then suddenly crouched and sprang again, 15–20 feet, this time into the scrub. I was 20 metres [65 feet] away from it and my lights lit up the road and the creature like it was daylight. I could even see its whiskers.

Although he made no reference to the thylacine's trademark stripes in his statement, Swaby subsequently viewed a lithograph depicting that creature and assured journalists that "there is absolutely no doubt that is what I saw." Nonetheless, doubts remained, and they would only increase with autumn 1995, when the sightings ended as suddenly as they began.

Sources: Toni McRae, "Beast of Buderim." *Brisbane Sunday Mail* (18 June 1995); Toni McRae, "Beast of Buderim on the prowl." *Brisbane Sunday Mail* (2 July 1995); Toni McRae, "Beast on the prowl." *Brisbane Sunday Mail* (16 July 1995); Toni McRae, "'Buderim Beast' made man shake." *Brisbane Sunday Mail* (28 August 1995); Toni McRae, "Doris captures Buderim Beast." *Brisbane Sunday Mail* (9 July 1995); Toni McRae, "Odd beast seen again." *Brisbane Sunday Mail* (25 June 1995); "Sightings fuel search for tiger." *Sunshine Coast Sunday* (30 April 1995).

Beast of Bungoma   In early 1974, this MYSTERY MAULER was blamed for slaughtering hundreds of farm animals throughout Kenya's Bungoma district. Witnesses who glimpsed the nocturnal predator described it as having a TIGER's head, a leopard's spots and a LION's claws. Hunters tracked and killed a large leopard (*Panthera pardus*) in the same region, during mid-April, and while the raids ceased thereafter, no hard evidence linked that CAT to the killings.

Source: Shuker, *Mystery Cats of the World.*

Beast of 'Busco   Churubusco, in northeastern Indiana's Allen County, lends its abbreviated name to a supposed giant TURTLE reported from nearby Fulk's Lake since the late 19th century. Witness Oscar Fulk was first to claim a sighting at the lake on his family's farm, in 1898. (Some accounts call the reptile Oscar, in his honor.) The Beast of 'Busco reappeared in 1914 and in July 1948, when fishermen Ora Blue and Charles Wilson reported a sighting. The reptile made headlines in 1949, after farmer Gale Harris — Wilson's brother-in-law, then owner of the property — glimpsed it in March. He described it as larger than his boat, some six feet long and five feet wide, with a head "big enough to swallow a basketball." A sequence of events recalled as Churubusco's "Great Turtle Hunt" then ensued, with Harris importing divers, pumps, a dredging crane and a female sea turtle (as bait) to effect the capture. Churubusco enjoyed a rush of CRYPTOTOURISM as thousands of visitors came to watch the proceedings. On 13 October, an audience of 200 saw a large turtle leap from the water in pursuit of a duck employed as a lure, but it escaped and vanished once again. Some sources claim a 125-pound alligator snapping turtle (*Macroclemys temminckii*) was imported as a joke during the hunt, but if so, it likewise managed to elude searchers. The excitement waned in December, as cold weather set in, dredging efforts failed, and Gale Harris was stricken with appendicitis.

A footnote was added to the Beast of 'Busco's legend in July 1950, when workmen at Hammond, Indiana — a Gary suburb some 140 miles northwest of Churubusco, on the Illinois border — drained nearby Black Oak Swamp. Rumors claimed that a huge turtle with "a head as big as a man's" was seen entering a drain that led to the Little Calumet River, but it escaped and left no evidence behind. Residents of Churubusco still celebrate Turtle Days in June, and Terry Doran produced a documentary film about the 1949 search, titled *The Hunt for Oscar*, in 1994. Eight years later, the *Chicago Tribune* described the Beast of 'Busco as Indiana's "SASQUATCH in a shell." Some skeptics claim the turtle never existed, while others allow the possibility of alligator snappers far beyond its normal range. That said, the record specimen for that species measured 31.5 inches long and tipped the scale at 250 pounds, roughly half the size of Churubusco's alleged cryptid.

Sources: John Gutowski, Back Home in Indiana, http://english.sxu.edu/efl/news/gutowski.html; The Turtle in Missouri Folklore, http://websites.quincy.edu/~hoebiph/turtleman.html.

Indiana witnesses describe the Beast of 'Busco as a giant turtle.

Beast of Carsington ALIEN BIG CAT sightings are an old story in the Peak District of Derbyshire, England. The cryptids' latest incarnation is the Beast of Carsington, a supposed "black panther" sighted by a motorist at Two Dales at 1:30 p.m. on 19 April 2002. According to the witness, she saw a large black CAT cross the road in front of her car and leap across a stone wall separating the road from nearby woods. Police answered the report and found two dark hairs atop the wall, presumably left by the cat as it bounded across. The evidence was passed to a zoologist for study, but no verdict had been published at press time for this book. Police Constable Paul Hartshorn cautioned that the hairs might prove nothing, but he told reporters, "I think there is something out there. We have had sightings in the Peak District for at least 15 years and we take them seriously."

Sources: Rod Malcolm, "Panther puzzler." *Matlock Mercury* (2 May 2002); Sieveking, "Cool cats."

Beast of Castor Witnesses in Cambridgeshire, England first reported this ALIEN BIG CAT in late summer 1999. Researcher Ian Wilkinson of Thorney, near Peterborough in the CAT'S main stalking ground, began a concerted but ultimately fruitless search for evidence that December. He was still on the job after Christmas, when witness Derek Speechley reported a startling encounter from Lynch Island, near Castor at Ailsworth. As Speechley told the local press, "I got within 50 yards of the island when I saw a big, black cat jump out on to the bank. I was close enough to see its whiskers. My dogs started going mad and I had to tie them up. I didn't want them to try to attack the animal. It disappeared down the bank." Bill Dobbs, who glimpsed the beast at Peterborough three months earlier, described a rather different animal with "a long thin tail that curled up and a dark brown coat." The conflicting reports appeared to confirm Ian Wilkinson's theory that multiple exotic cats inhabit Cambridgeshire, including at least one black specimen and another resembling a COUGAR (*Puma concolor*).

Source: "Big Cat 'Lurking at Old Fishing Haunt.'" *Peterborough Evening Telegraph* (7 February 2000).

Beast of Cézallier The plain of Cézallier in Auvergne, France is a wild volcanic plateau flanked by the peaks of Cantal and Sancy. In the last quarter of the 20th century it produced reports of an ALIEN BIG CAT at large, but few details were published and the Beast of Cézallier has since passed into local legend.

Source: Brodu and Meurger, *Les Félins-Mystère*; Campion-Vincent, "Appearances of beasts and mystery-cats in France."

Beast of Chiswick Unlike so many British cryptids covered in this volume, the creature that stalked London's Chiswick suburb during June-August 1994 bore little or no resemblance to an ALIEN BIG CAT. Shaken witnesses described the Beast of Chiswick as a "scrawny-looking" animal, two feet long, with a dog's body, the pointed face of a KANGAROO, and a long slender tail. Its fur was gray, though a minority of witnesses recalled white spots. The beast was clearly carnivorous, leaving a trail of mutilated squirrels and pigeons around Chiswick. It also allegedly raided trash cans, ripping open plastic bags in search of sustenance. "It skulks around at night," witness Angela Vallis told reporters, "and just stands and stares at you." Whatever the beast may have been, it vanished with summer and has not returned.

Sources: "The Beast of Chiswick." *London Evening Standard* (9 August 1994); True News Animal Stories, http://www.top.net.nz/~tich/animal.html.

Beast of Dean ALIEN BIG CAT sightings have emerged from the Forest of Dean in Gloucester, England since the early 1990s. Most witnesses describe the creature as a "black panther," in keeping with other reports of the wide-ranging BEAST OF GLOUCESTER. Highway sightings are common, exemplified by the report of a motorist from Mitcheldean in May 2000. "It just sauntered across the road in front of us and was completely unafraid," she told reporters. Investigations by various British cryptozoologists have thus far failed to collect definitive evidence. The riddle was compounded on 5 December 2002, when motorist Richard Keevil struck and killed a large wild boar on the A40 motorway near Over. The pig measured six feet long, sported an impressive set of tusks, and was covered in shaggy black hair.

Source: "'Beast' experts combine." *Gloucestershire Echo* (17 February 2000); "Could death crash boar end theories?" *The Citizen* (7 December 2002); "New 'forest beast' sighting." Yowie Hunters, http://www.yowiehunters.com.

Beast of Durham County Durham, in northeastern England, reported its first ALIEN BIG CAT visitation in early 1994, when 6-inch pawprints with a stride greater than a man's were found in snow at Ferryhill, on 23 February. In August and September of that year, large cats resembling COUGARS (*Puma concolor*) were seen at Aycliffe, Crook and Sedgefield. Reports were sparse over the next decade, but the Beast of Durham returned in spring 2001, killing 12 of farmer Richard Wade's lambs within two weeks at New Brancepeth, near Durham City. In each case, the prey was killed with a crushing bite to the skull. Durham police sergeant Eddie Bell seemed confused when he addressed reporters on 10 April 2001, declaring that the predator was neither an exotic CAT nor an "indigenous UK animal." What was it, then? "That leaves a dog as the chief suspect," Bell said, "but taking all the circumstances into account I don't think it's a dog either. At this stage I couldn't say." Journalists mercifully refrained from asking Bell why he "dismissed the possibility of a big cat," if he had no idea what the creature might be. The mystery remains unsolved.

Source: "'Beast of Durham' on the loose — experts baffled." *Ananova* (11 April 2001).

Beast of Essex Reports of an ALIEN BIG CAT at large around Essex, England date from 1995, but descriptions of the animal(s) are by no means consistent. Farmer Don Gooding, from Raydon Hamlet near Harlow, described the beast that killed his CAT and left deep claw marks on his car in January 2001 as a "giant black puma." No such cat is known to science, since the puma or COUGAR (*Puma concolor*) appears to have no melanistic phase, but that is the least of the Essex riddles. In 2002, various local witnesses announced encounters with a JAGUAR (*Panthera onca*), a LYNX (*Felis lynx*), a ginger-colored cat of unknown species, and an unseen beast that uttered "deafening roars." Large feline pawprints were found on a farm near Maldon, in July 2002. Eight months later, two women in Black Notley brought the tally of sightings to 80, with their report of a "black panther-type creature" lurking outside Longmead Court Nursing Home. John Hancock's ESSEX BIG CAT RESEARCH PROJECT collects and analyzes reported sightings, but concrete evidence remains as elusive as the animals themselves.

Sources: "Giant Cat Has Eaten My Car." *London Mirror* (6 January 2001); "How beastly." Yellow Advertiser (5 July 2002); Sieveking, "Cool cats"; Sieveking, "Nothing more than felines"; Sieveking, "Watch out: Big cat about"; "Women see elusive Beast of Essex." Essex Evening Echo (6 March 2003).

Beast of Estérel   The Massif de l'Estérel is located at Cap Roux, along the Côte d'Azur of southern France. In the 1980s, residents of the mountains region reported an ALIEN BIG CAT at large, but organized hunts failed to locate the creature.

Sources: Brodu and Meurger, *Les Félins-Mystère*; Campion-Vincent, "Appearances of beasts and mystery-cats in France."

Beast of Exmoor   Sightings of an ALIEN BIG CAT around Exmoor, in the British counties of Devon and Somerset, date from summer 1971, when a couple driving along the Wistlandpound Reservoir Track glimpsed a creature they described as "very large, quite black, and shaped like a female LION" (*Panthera leo*). Four years later, a quartet of picnickers at Hacche Moor were startled by a similar animal. One witness told the press, "All four of us saw it clearly, no doubt about what it was, a very large, black CAT and I said at the time it had probably escaped from a zoo or circus." Before years end, the problem was compounded by multiple sightings of a large fawn-colored cat resembling a COUGAR (*Puma concolor*) around South Molton and West Buckland. A "black panther" was also seen around South Molton in 1978, while the tawny cougar resurfaced in February 1980. Both cats were seen in early 1981, the black one leaving large pawprints around Tedburn St. Mary. Alleged experts identified the tracks as a cougar's, though melanistic cougars are unknown to science.

Exmoor's predators hit the headlines in April 1983, with reports of 70–80 lambs slaughtered on four adjacent farms. In each case, the victims had their skulls crushed by powerful jaws. Locals mounted an organized hunt for the beast on 21 April, supported by a reward offer of £1,000 from one area newspaper, the *Daily Express*. Armchair naturalists blamed the predation on a variety of big cats, as well as WOLVES, badgers and feral dogs. When police and civilian efforts failed to bag the prowler, Royal Marines were deployed around South Molton, digging camouflaged trenches equipped with infrared tracking devices. On 4 May, marine sniper John Holden saw a large black creature but declined to shoot for fear his bullets might strike a nearby farmhouse. The troops withdrew in early July, having accomplished nothing, but police declared the Beast of Exmoor dead on 29 July. A large dog had been shot by one of their marksmen, they claimed, and while they had no carcass to prove it, they seemed confident the wounded animal had crawled away to die in hiding.

Be that as it may, cat sightings continued through 1983 and beyond. In summer 1984, witness Trevor Beer described an encounter in the Exmoor woods, where several deer had recently been killed.

> In the green, sun-dappled shadows of the wood it looked black and rather otter-like, a first impression I shall always remember, for the head was broad and sleek with small ears. The animal's eyes were a clear greeny-yellow as I stood still and stared at it. As it stared back at me I could clearly make out the thickish neck, the powerful-looking forelegs and deep chest and then without a sound it turned and moved swiftly away through the trees. That it was jet black I was sure, and long in the body and tail. I guessed at four-and-a-half feet in body length and about two feet at the shoulders.

On 6 March 1986, Beer told BBC reporters that he had seen the cat six more times since his original encounter. Cougar sightings continued throughout the same time span, as did sheep predation. Stranger still, hairs from a LYNX (*Felis lynx*) were found with one sheep carcass in 1986. In January 1987, zoologist Steven Harris examined a series of nine 3-inch pawprints discovered at Exmoor, declaring that they belonged either to a lynx or a wild-cat (*Felis sylvestris*), both presumably extinct in England. A short time later, cougar hairs were found and positively identified. Trevor Beer had three other witnesses with him in August 1987, when he photographed a black animal 4–4.5 feet long and 2 feet tall at the shoulder. A close-up photo of the "panther" was published on page one of the *Mid Devon Star*, on 1 January 1988, but the photographer remained anonymous, known only as "the Jungle Man." Sheep were still falling prey to the beast(s) in January 1990, when Lars Thomas led an expedition known as Operation Exmoor and recovered more cougar hairs from one of the kills. Eleven years later, at least one large cat was still at large in the region, sighted by motorist Maurice Jenkins near Barton Wood Quarry. He told the press:

> It was a big black pussycat. His eyes reflected in my headlights and I slowed down so I could get a better look and it sat watching me. It was dark but it was in the line of my headlights. It was the size of a collie dog with a jet black head and tail. He leapt away and made off into the fields. It was a beast of some kind and I have put my camera in the car just in case I see it again.

In mid-December 2003, after a big cat spooked a horse near Torridge, the BRITISH BIG CAT SOCIETY urged local farmers to report any sightings or unusual incidents. That plea produced evidence of an unidentified large animal sleeping in one farmer's barn, and pawprints found in fresh mud at a second location. Exmoor residents had new reasons for concern that month, after a British shooting magazine offered a prize of £1,000 pounds to the first hunter who could bag a big cat. Thus far, the bounty has not been collected.

Sources: Clark and Pear, *Strange & Unexplained Phenomena*; "Maurice spots the beast." E-mail posting to the Chupacabra Internet newsgroup (22 January 2001); McEwan, *Mystery Animals of Britain and Ireland*; "New hunt to find the Beast of Exmoor." *North Devon Journal* (23 December 2003); Shuker, *Mystery Cats of the World*.

Beast of Fife   Residents of eastern Scotland's Fife district, between the FIRTH OF FORTH and FIRTH OF TAY, filed their reports of ALIEN BIG CATS in 1995. A truck driver logged the first sighting, followed by 20 more reports from farmers, road workers and police officers over the next two years. A witness at Cupar videotaped one of the CATS, described as black and four feet long, in November 1997. Despite its color, local authorities seemed convinced that the beast was a COUGAR (*Puma concolor*) abandoned by some unknown private owner after passage of Britain's Dangerous Wild Animals Act in 1976. Police spokesman George Redpath told reporters he was "certain there is a puma living in the area," and Richard O'Grady, in charge of the Glasgow Zoo, seemed to agree. After viewing still photos taken from the Cupar video he said, "It could be a puma. I've seen pictures of other 'big cats' which turned out to be FOXES. But this one is very interesting." Melanistic cougars are unknown to science, but witnesses may be mistaken in regard to color of a creature briefly glimpsed, especially during nocturnal sightings. The same may not be said of Constable Redpath, who himself became a witness in spring 1999. That June, he admitted two recent sightings, one from a distance of 20 feet, of an animal he described as "a large black cat with a long tail."

Sources: Charles Morton, "Mystery 'cat' is caught on video." *The Sun* (17 November 1997); "Beast appears on the beat." Yowie Hunters, http://www.yowiehunters.com/crypto/reports/big_cats1999.htm.

Beast of Gala Hill   Gala Hill, in the Borders district of southern Scotland, has a longstanding tradition of ALIEN BIG CAT sightings that continue in the new millennium. Witnesses generally describe the CATS as large and black, some approaching the size of a mastiff or German shepherd. In July 2002, neighbors of Gala Hill reported that five domestic cats had recently vanished when left outdoors overnight, and others were confined to quarters as a preventive measure. Researcher Di Francis suggested that the area might host a breeding population of KELLAS CATS, but the case remains unproved at press time for this volume.

Source: Bob Burgess, "Scottish wildcat." *Southern Reporter* (25 July 2002).

Beast of Gévaudan

Gévaudan is the obsolete name of a mountainous region in southeastern France, roughly corresponding to the modern-day district of Lozère. In the mid-18th century, villagers throughout the area were terrorized by a ferocious MYSTERY MAULER that killed and mutilated an estimated 100 human victims within a 3-year period. The first victim, in June 1764, was a young girl tending cattle in the Fôret de Mercoire outside Langogne. Her dogs panicked and fled at the approach of a beast she described as resembling an oversized WOLF, and she survived a vicious mauling when her cattle charged the beast and frightened it away. Days later, on 30 June, the animal killed 14-year-old Jeanne Boulet as she watched her family's sheep. By year's end, the beast slaughtered 14 more women and children around Gévaudan, while eluding soldiers sent from Languedoc to kill it.

The new year started badly with another attack on children playing near Veleret d'Apcher, on 12 January 1765. The monster mauled an 8-year-old boy, but his playmates drove it off with knives and stones before it completed the kill. A mass hunt by soldiers and civilian volunteers killed 100 wolves over the next month, but the beast remained at large. King Louis XV sent professional hunters to Gévaudan in February and July 1765, but they also returned empty-handed. By mid-September 1765, 73 persons had been slain by a creature described in contemporary reports as "much higher than a wolf, low before, and his feet are armed with talons. His hair is reddish, his head large, and the muzzle of it is shaped like that of a greyhound; his ears are small and straight; his breast is wide and gray; his back streaked with black; his large mouth is provided with sharp teeth." Then, on 20 September, Parisian hunter Antoine, Sieur de Beauterne shot a large predator near the Abbey of Chazes in Auvergne. A

This 18th-century engraving depicts the Beast of Gévaudan in action.

necropsy was performed, to allay local fears of a werewolf at large, and the beast proved to be a wolf 5 feet 7 inches long, weighing 130 pounds. Its mounted remains were dispatched to the Museum of Natural History in Paris, but were subsequently lost.

King Louis, thus assured that the Beast of Gévaudan was dead, turned his attention to other problems of state. The royal confidence was misplaced, however, and two more children were slaughtered near Mont Moucher on 2 December 1765. More victims fell in February and March 1766, but appeals for royal aid were ignored. The monster claimed its 100th known victim, a young girl at Nozenolles, on 18 June 1767. A local nobleman, the Marquis d'Apcher, gathered a dozen hunters to pursue the creature. One of the party, Jean Chastel, confronted a large beast near Mont Chauvet on 19 June and killed it with a silver bullet, loaded just in case the werewolf rumors proved to be correct. The carcass was crudely preserved and displayed in Gévaudan for two weeks, then packed off to the Paris museum, where it gathered dust until it disappeared in 1810 or 1819 (reports differ). Descriptions of the monster vary, but the killings ceased after Chastel squeezed off his lucky shot.

What was the Beast of Gévaudan? A century after the events, French novelist Henri Pourrat and naturalist Gérard Ménatory proposed a hyena as the most likely candidate, noting contemporary claims that Antoine Chastel — son of beast-killer Jean — had at least one such specimen in his private menagerie. That theory seemed to be confirmed in summer 1997, when taxidermist Franz Jullien announced discovery of 18th-century museum records naming the vanished beast as a striped hyena (*Hyena hyena*). In the absence of the specimen itself, however, other researchers remain unpersuaded. Some still blame a large gray wolf (*Canis lupus*), while others point the finger of suspicion at a WOLVERINE, an ALIEN BIG CAT or a deranged serial killer clad in animal skins. JEAN-JACQUES BARLOY accepts the hyena hypothesis, while suggesting that Protestant zealots may have unleashed the man-eater on Catholic rivals during one of France's sectarian feuds. LOREN COLEMAN, meanwhile, questions the Chastel family's role in the affair, if they in fact maintained hyenas on their property.

Sources: Barloy, "Le Bête du Gévaudan soumise á l'ordinateur"; Coleman and Clark, *Cryptozoology A to Z*; Jullien, "La deuxième mort de la Bête de Gévaudan"; Ménatory, *La Bête du Gévaudan*; Karl Shuker, "Alien zoo." *Fortean Times* 104 (November 1997): 14–15.

Beast of Gloucester

This generic term has been applied since 1993 to a variety of ALIEN BIG CATS reported from the Cotswolds and Forest of Dean in Gloucestershire, England. One of the earliest sightings occurred near Longney, south of Gloucester, where a frightened witness described his encounter with a "huge black creature with blazing green eyes. It was going so fast that it crossed a five-acre field in about ten seconds. Then it ran across the road about six feet away from me. I could see it very clearly. It was about three feet long and two feet high and it was definitely a big CAT with very large teeth. I was terrified." In October 1994, Police Inspector David Morgan glimpsed a "black panther" near Staunton, which he vaguely described as "larger than a FOX but smaller than a small horse." Other witnesses have reported cats "three times the size of a fox" and "about the size of a large dog." Humans and livestock alike have suffered injury in clashes with the mystery felids. Local names for various Gloucestershire cryptids include the BEAST OF BROADOAK, the BEAST OF DEAN and the BLACK BEAST OF INKBERROW.

Source: Some Recent Sightings of the Beast(s) of Gloucester, http://www.deville.demon.co.uk/glosabc.htm.

Beast of Gravesham

One evening in July 2002, Mick Cole was working in his garage near Gravesend, in Kent, England, when he thought he saw a FOX run past him with a RABBIT clutched in its mouth. Cole ran after the creature, shouting in hopes it would release its prey, but he soon recognized his mistake. As he later told reporters: "I thought, 'Shit, it's a CAT the size of a Labrador with a live and kicking black and white rabbit in its mouth.' I recognised it as a LYNX [*Felis lynx*] from the black tips on the end of its ears. It swiped at me with its right paw and left three long deep scratches in my hand. It hurt like hell." The animal escaped with its meal, leaving Cole to bind his wounds and report the latest sighting of an ALIEN BIG CAT known locally as the Beast of Gravesham. Neil Arnold, spokesman for the KENT BIG CAT RESEARCH, reported a rash of sightings over the past month, including 45 sightings recorded in one 3-day period. Paul Paterson, curator of carnivores at Glasgow Zoo, told reporters, "People are dumping them. It's easy to import them illegally, especially if you are rich. They cross breed with domestic cats, and the hybrids seems to breed with each other, producing mongrels. The government is hushing it up, because it does not want a mass panic. No one wants to know."

Source: John Vidal, "Wild beast watchers pounce on new sightings." *The Guardian* (11 January 2003).

Beast of Hackney Marshes

Two variations on the story of this creature may be found on the Internet, and apparently nowhere else. The BEASTWATCH U.K. website offers a one-line reference to "well known reports of a bear-like animal, seen on the East London marshes during the 1970s." Another website, this one anonymous, claims that a group of boys were playing in the marshland on 25 December 1980, enjoying a surprise snowfall, when they were frightened by a large quadruped that rose to its hind legs while roaring at them. According to this source, adults discounted the story until a traveling circus announced that its GRIZZLY BEAR (*Ursus arctos horribilis*) was missing, whereupon police marksmen tracked it to the marsh and killed it. In either case, the episode was reduced to comedy in 1997, as an episode of BBC's television series *The Detectives*, aptly titled "The Beast of Hackney Marshes."

Source: Beast Watch U.K., http://homepage.ntlworld.com/chris.mullins/London.*htm*; Beast of Beckenham, http://www.wetfloor.gothic.co.uk/thebeastofbeckenh*am.htm*.

Beast of Hade Edge

Witnesses in Huddersfield, England describe the Beast of Hade Edge as a "black panther" believed responsible for mauling two lambs at Denby Dale in 1997. Sightings of the ALIEN BIG CAT continue, exemplified by the report filed from Hade Edge in November 2000, by witnesses Wilomena Roderick and Margaret Wainwright. They saw the CAT stalking sheep in a local farmer's field, initially mistaking it for a large dog. Roderick soon realized her mistake, afterward telling reporters, "It was a very big powerful-like cat. I saw the profile of its head and face. It belonged in a zoo. I was dumbfounded. The tail was a dead giveaway. It was really long and curled up at the end, and swishing like cats do swish their tail." Local police acknowledged other recent sightings and said they were "treating the case seriously," but so far they have failed to corral the predator(s).

Source: Andrew Baldwin, "Stalking beast in Hade Edge." *Huddersfield Daily Examiner* (8 November 2000).

Beast of Margam

This ALIEN BIG CAT of West Glamorgan, Wales raided sheep herds in 1995, prompting farmers to stand armed guard over their flocks while worried parents escorted their children to school. Motorists saw a large CAT crossing the M4 motorway at Margam, near Neath, on 25 May 1995, but hunters failed in their attempts to track the beast. In August 2002, newspaper reports claimed the beast had killed "hundreds" of RABBITS in Margam Country Park, near Port Talbot.

Sources: "Catalogue of Wales' weird cats." BBC News (26 August 2000); Sieveking, "Cool cats"; "ABC Survey 2001–2002." Fortean Times, http://www.forteantimes.com/articles/167_bigcats20*02_2*.shtml.

Beast of Milton Keynes

The Beast of Milton Keynes, in England's Buckinghamshire district, is an ALIEN BIG CAT variously described by witnesses as resembling a COUGAR (*Puma concolor*) or "black panther." It is not restricted to the neighborhood of Milton Keynes, but has been seen as far north as Olney and Newport Pagnell. The CAT made its first appearance in May 1995, and by late June had been reported in colors ranging from fawn to jet black. Seven more sightings were logged in May–June 1996, with a dwindling number reported in 1997–98. After a year-long hiatus, the animal(s) returned on 9 February 2001, for a sighting at Little Brickhill. Witnesses June Dungate and John Hurkett initially mistook the creature for a German shepherd, but Hurkett later told reporters, "It was definitely a panther."

Sources: "Return of the Beast of Milton Keynes." *Milton Keynes Citizen* (15 February 2001); Sieveking, "Cool cats"; Sieveking, "Watch out: Big cat about."

Beast of North Lincs

In December 2003, residents of Scunthorpe, North Lincolnshire, England were troubled by reports of an ALIEN BIG CAT at large. Witness Norman Robinson, of Barrow, encountered the creature on 29 December. "I was walking alongside some bushes," he told journalists, "and I could see something moving. I looked closer and there was a big black CAT peering through the bushes. It looked at me and I froze. It was just 35 to 40 metres [114–130 feet] away. It was a big, black cat with a round face and pinched ears, but with a big chin. It had big whiskers and it was very big—the size of an Alsatian [German shepherd] dog and in very good condition." Reporters dubbed Robinson's cat the Beast of North Lincs, but it may be identical with another ABC, the TERROR OF TRODS, reported from a nearby district around the same time.

Sources: "What is 'Beast of North Lincs'?" *Scunthorpe Telegraph* (1 January 2004).

Beast of Noth

During November and December 1982, farmers around Noth, in the Creuse Department of central France, reported attacks on their cattle and sheep by an ALIEN BIG CAT. Witnesses who glimpsed the beast described it as resembling a LION (*Panthera leo*) the size of a small calf. Hunters tracked the animal to no avail, but its depredations ceased at year's end.

Sources: Brodu and Meurger, *Les Félins-Mystère*; Campion-Vincent, "Appearances of beasts and mystery-cats in France."

Beast of Ongar

Variously described as a COUGAR (*Puma concolor*) or "black panther," this ALIEN BIG CAT of Essex, England is named for the town of Ongar, but it also roams as far afield as the Walthamstow marshes, where it was seen by a resident of St. James Village on 24 January 2001. The witness told reporters she saw the CAT nosing through trash bins beside a block of apartments. "It came to the front of the car," she said. "It looked like a dog but with the face of a cat and it had a long tail."

It was as big as a FOX. I thought this is a huge animal. It was looking for food and rooting around. I must admit I was not really scared even though I recognised it was a puma. I watched it go round the corner by the dustbins in Wickham Close. I am sure of what I saw." That testimony is somewhat curious, since foxes are rarely "huge," and adult cougars are much larger than the average fox. Still, John Hancock of ESSEX BIG CAT RESEARCH accepted the sighting as genuine, announcing: "We have noticed that these big cats seem to have lost their shyness and a lot of them have been seen going through people's rubbish. It is not unreasonable to think that it came from Walthamstow Marshes. It could have been passing through the area, and these animals do have quite large territories. It was probably on the look-out for an easy meal and they can pick out the smell of meat or fish in people's litter." Another sighting was reported from Stanford Rivers, near Ongar, on 25 October 2003. Witness Kay Hayden told the press, "All I can say is it was a great big leopard [*Panthera pardus*] size. It was a muscular, completely black, strong-looking animal, much, much larger than a dog."

Sources: "Beast of Ongar now prowls the marshes." *Waltham Forest Guardian* (25 January 2001); "Woman reports 'beast' sighting." BBC News (26 October 2003).

Beast of Ossett   The first reports of a "black panther" prowling around Ossett, in West Yorkshire, England, were filed in August 2000. Subsequent sightings expanded the ALIEN BIG CAT'S range to include Flockton and Middlestown. On 30 December 2000, bus driver David Crest saw the CAT on Heath Common. He returned with a video camera, hoping to catch the beast on tape, but had to settle for a trail of "strange paw prints" in the snow. Later, Crest told reporters, "There is no way that it could have been either a domestic cat or a FOX— it was just too big. Its body was around three feet long and it had a tail almost as long again. It appeared to be cowering from something as it crossed the road. It was like nothing I had seen before."

Source: "'Beast' is spotted by bus driver." *Wakefield Express* (5 January 2001).

Beast of Otmoor   This ALIEN BIG CAT of Oxfordshire, England made its first appearance in June 1994, at Fencott, eight miles from Oxford. Local residents accused it of snatching chickens from their yards, and witness Malcolm Warner had a camera ready when he saw the CAT reclining in a tree. He snapped its photo as the beast climbed head-first down the trunk and fled into the nearby undergrowth, but the resultant picture was too blurry to have much evidentiary value. Lewis Watson later met the "black panther" at close quarters, and another sighting was reported by farm workers at Stonesfield, 12 miles distant, on 21 July 1994.

Sources: Sieveking, "Beasts in our midst."

Beast of the Borders   This ALIEN BIG CAT of western Britain earned its tabloid name by prowling both sides of the boundary line between Shropshire, England and North Wales in September 1994. Numerous sightings were reported, including several claims that the creature menaced hikers in wooded areas, snarling from behind trees and bushes. Newspaper photographer Andy Compton snapped a picture of the CAT near Llandrinio on 29 September, but the long-distance shot through a 200mm lens provided no critical detail.

Source: "Catalogue of Wales' weird cats." BBC News (26 August 2000); Sieveking, "Beasts in our midst."

Beast of Tonmawr   Residents of Tonmawr, Wales reported their first sightings of an ALIEN BIG CAT in 1984, claiming that it growled and shrieked at walkers in the Neath and Afan Forests. Local officials made light of the reports until August 1994, when plaster casts were made of large pawprints found near Port Talbot. Experts at the London Zoo matched the prints to a jungle CAT (*Felis chaus*), whose normal range spans half the globe from North Africa to India. Jungle cats are brown, lynxlike felids three times the size of a domestic cat at maturity. Despite its identification, the Beast of Tonmawr has yet to be photographed or captured.

Sources: "Catalogue of Wales' weird cats." BBC News (26 August 2000); Sieveking, "Beasts in our midst."

Beast of Trellech   Brothers Josh and Jeremy Hopkins were playing in a field near their home at Trellech, South Wales on 26 August 2000, when they suddenly found themselves confronted by a 5-foot-long "black panther." As 11-year-old Josh later described the event, "The animal had blood on its jaws and its breath smelled as if it had just eaten something like a RABBIT. Then it got my head in its jaws and bit me. I was terrified and I thought it was going to kill me. I started screaming and ran. The animal ran away as well into some nearby fields." Police marksmen scoured the neighborhood, supported by a helicopter outfitted with heat-seeking gear, but they found no trace of the ALIEN BIG CAT, and an imported big-cat specialist had no better luck. The cat reappeared in late January 2001, sighted by Allan Austin while he was walking his dog in the snowy Gwent countryside, between Pant-y-Pwdyn and Cwm-Nant-y-Groes. "It was a black cat against a white background," Austin said. "It could not have happened in a better place. The area was clear, with no trees, snow was on the ground and the cat was easily visible. Its tail was the distinguishing feature. It was in the air and as long as your arm." More sightings were logged in June and July 2002, when a large black cat was seen prowling the grounds of a local school. After the second report, on 11 July, Inspector Mark Wheatsome told reporters, "Officers attended and with the assistance of staff made a search of the area that proved negative."

Sources: "'Beast of Trellech' spotted by teacher." *South Wales Argus* (12 July 2002); "Dog walker tells of panther sighting." *South Wales Argus* (7 February 2001); Sydney Young and Nick Servini, "The Beast of Trellech." Yowie Hunters, http://www.yowiehunters.com.

Beast of Truro   In September 1981, an unidentified MYSTERY MAULER began mauling livestock and pets around Truro, Massachusetts, on Cape Cod. A dozen domestic cats were killed and mutilated in the first wave of attacks, followed by multiple attacks on penned hogs in early January 1982. Police initially suspected feral dogs, until eyewitnesses reported sightings of "a large furry creature that they did not recognize." William and Marsha Medeiros provided the most dramatic report, after they met the prowler on a path near Truro's Head of the Meadow Beach, in October 1981. Mrs. Medeiros told reporters:

My husband put his arm out to stop me and said, "You see what I see?" Together we said, "It's not a FOX." It had a very definite long ropelike tail like the letter J. It hit the ground and went up. We figured it was about as tall as up to our knees and weighed 60 or 80 pounds. We were frightened and froze. He was in the path and didn't see us at first. As we made some noise, he turned and we saw his face and short ears.

The witnesses believed their creature was a COUGAR (*Puma concolor*), and a tourist from New York also reported sighting "something resembling a mountain lion" near Truro in December 1981. If true, the sightings offer further evidence of EASTERN COUGARS surviving in the wild, despite their supposed extinction in the late 19th and early 20th centuries.

Source: "Killer beast stalks town." *New York Times* (18 January 1982).

Beast of Tweseldown

Hampshire, England produced multiple sightings of ALIEN BIG CATS in 1994, with the most persistent prowler dubbed the Beast of Tweseldown in tabloid newspaper reports. The CAT made its first appearance at Fleet, in May, seen from a distance of 10 feet by one startled witness. A month later, five observers saw it mauling a collie and chasing ponies outside Brockenhurst. Tweseldown Racecourse was a particular favorite haunt, with multiple sightings reported by a list of witnesses that included two police officers. A visitor to the racetrack snapped photos of the cat from 30 yards in June 1994, but the resultant pictures were too murky to identify their subject.

Source: Seiveking, "Beasts in our midst."

Beast of Valescure

Valescure lies on the French Côte d'Azur, near St.-Raphael. In February 1983, local residents reported sightings of an ALIEN BIG CAT resembling a COUGAR (*Puma concolor*), but hunters had no more success in tracking it than they had with other French CATS, including BABETTE, the BEAST OF CÉZALLIER, the BEAST OF ESTÉREL and the BEAST OF NOTH. The animal departed in its own good time, for parts unknown.

Sources: Bord and Bord, *Unexplained Mysteries of the 20th Century*; Brodu and Meurger, *Les Félins-Mystère*; Campion-Vincent, "Appearances of beasts and mystery-cats in France."

Beast of Widnes

In 2000, an ALIEN BIG CAT announced its presence in the neighborhood of Widnes and Runcorn, North Cheshire, England. Witnesses described the animal as a "black panther" five times the size of an adult domestic CAT. James Mc-Dowall and Linda O'Mally were confronted by the growling beast in July 2003, in a field at Halton. McDowall later told reporters, "This huge black cat ran across our path. It came from a set of steps in the church field wall and stopped for a second to look at us and give out a loud, deep snarl. It ran into the bushes and for several minutes we could hear dogs barking in fear on the Castlefields estate." While some officials remained skeptical, big-cat expert Quentin Rose attempted to reassure frightened locals. "These cats are not yet common in Britain," he said. "They were released by their owners when the Dangerous Wild Animals Act of 1976 was brought in to make it harder to keep them as pets. It appears they are now breeding well and living off the land. At the moment they are not dangerous to humans because they are not attacking people. However, they could become extremely dangerous very quickly if people attempt to hunt them or hurt them."

Source: "Beast back on the prowl." *Runcorn Weekly News* (24 July 2003).

Beasts of Bardia

In the 1980s, reports of previously unknown elephants emerged from Nepal's Royal Bardia National Park. Not only were the pachyderms unexpected, but witnesses also claimed they were larger than normal Asian elephants (*Elephas maximus*), standing 13 feet tall at the shoulder, compared to an average specimen's height of 11 feet. Between 1991 and 1995, naturalist John Blashford-Snell led seven expeditions into the Bardia forest, discovering elephant footprints that measured 22.5 inches across. Finally, he found and photographed two male elephants, whom he dubbed Kancha and Rajah Gaj. Both were

adults, the larger of them estimated to be 11 feet 3 inches tall. DNA tests performed on dung samples confirmed their identity as specimens of *E. maximus*. Today, authorities believe as many as 100 seldom-seen elephants occupy the Bardia preserve.

Source: Blashford-Snell and Lenska, *Mammoth Hunt*.

Beastwatch U.K.

Organized in 2003, this British group is a clearinghouse for reports of cryptids throughout the United Kingdom. Its fascinating Internet website includes a contact list of affiliated researchers in England, Scotland and Wales, together with summaries of numerous cryptid sightings. Rather than duplicate the efforts of such pre-existing groups as the BRITISH BIG CAT SOCIETY and BRITISH HOMINID RESEARCH, Beastwatch lists encounters with a variety of often-overlooked BIRDS, mammals and reptiles. Unnamed members also mount expeditions pursue specific creatures on a strictly nonviolent, "no-kill" basis. As the website explains in a note to skeptics:

> We're not saying that all exotic species mentioned within these pages, are thriving in our environment, nor that they over-run our countryside. Some, after release or escape, either struggle to survive, or die soon after a very short period of freedom, so there may only be the odd one or two out there — but Out There they ARE.

Source: Beastwatch U.K., http://homepage.ntlworld.com/chris.mullins/.

Beaver (Giant)

Aboriginal folklore throughout North America includes tales involving giant beavers that were actively hostile to humans, and sometimes described as man-eaters. Tlingit natives around Sitka, on southeastern Alaska's Baranof Island, tell the story of a huge beaver that once ran amok and destroyed a whole village. Chilliwack natives of British Columbia likewise claimed that huge beaverlike creatures, called SLAL'I'KUM or Ts'ewálí, inhabited Cultus Lake. Across the continent, in Labrador, Newfoundland, Montagnais-Naskapi tribesmen named the Mishtamishku-shipu ("giant beaver river") after two rodents larger than seals, which the tribe once slaughtered to keep them from breeding. Farther south, in the CONNECTICUT RIVER Valley, legends of huge beavers are plentiful. Their great dams allegedly created several lakes in the region, around Deerfield and Northampton, Massachusetts. Pocumtuck tribesmen once believed that the mountain range which bears their name concealed the body of a giant beaver killed in battle with their gods.

In fact, there were giant beavers in Pleistocene North America. Members of the species (*Castoroides ohioensis*) rivaled bears in size, reaching 8 feet in length, weighing 600–700 pounds, and sporting wicked 4-inch incisors. Modern beavers (*Castor canadensis*), by contrast, attain peak weights under 70 pounds. Fossil remains of *C. ohioensis* dated at 70,000 years have been unearthed around Toronto, Canada and in the Yukon's Old Crow Basin. They presumably became extinct with MAMMOTHS and other Ice Age megafauna, around 10,000 years ago — but what are we to make of giant beaver sightings from the late 20th century? In August 2002, an Internet poster known only as Staci reported her family's encounter with a beaver "the size of a horse" at Lake Powell, spanning the Arizona-Utah border. In late March 1993, Tom Greene, horticulture superintendent for the town of Moline, Illinois reported that a 5-foot beaver weighing 80 pounds or more was gnawing down trees at the Marquis Harbor Yacht Club. The rodent, both clever and "quite strong," had sprung two traps and yet escaped. At last report, the beaver — dubbed "NESSIE" by the *Chicago Sun-Times* — was still at large. In 2000, witness J. Greenwald allegedly saw a horse-sized beaver near Bullfrog Marina, on

Aboriginal folklore and modern reports describe giant beavers in North America.

southern Utah's Lake Powell. Another two years passed before Greenwald reported her sighting to the National Institute of Discovery Science in Las Vegas, Nevada. She described the beast as brownish-black in color and weighing 700–900 pounds. "You wouldn't believe how big it was," Greenwald wrote. "It could kill you."

While America's giant beavers remain elusive, the search for a similar creature in Austria ended rather differently. In August 2003, police around Wiener Neustadt received several eyewitness reports of a huge beaver wandering about their city and a hunt was organized. The creature, finally cornered and caught in a parking garage, proved to be a KANGAROO of unknown origin.

Sources: Jane Beck, "The giant beaver: A prehistoric memory?" *Ethnohistory* 19 (Spring 1972): 109–122; "That's no giant beaver." *Sydney Morning Herald* (21 August 2003); Coleman and Huyghe, *The Field Guide to Lake Monsters, Sea Serpents, and Other Mystery Denizens of the Deep*; David Bolling, Whole Earth (Spring 2002), http://www.findarticles.com/cf_dls/m0GER/2002_Spring/84866371/p1/article.jhtml; Giant Beaver, HTTP://WWW.NATURE.CA/NOTEBOOKS/ENGLISH/GIANTBEV.HTM; Giant Prehistoric "Extinct" Beaver Alive in Lake Powell, Utah, http://www.nidsci.org/resources/forum/Read/627.html; Strange Magazine, http://www.strangemag.com/mixedbagarch2.html; Mishtamishku-shipu: Giant Beaver River, http://www.innu.ca/beaver1.html; Tammy Rittenour, Native American Legend of the Giant Beaver, http://www.bio.umass.edu/biology/conn.river/nalegend.html.

Beaver sea serpent   On 5 January 1878, the magazine *Land and Water* published an article on SEA SERPENTS written by Andrew Wilson, including the following entry from the log of the schooner *Beaver*, owned by Adam Scott and commanded by a Captain Boyle. The entry describes an event occurring at Sungyce, near Hamai on the west coast of China, on 2 August 1863. Captain Boyle wrote:

I came to anchor about twelve o'clock last night, about two miles out of this harbour. At half-past four o'clock this morning I went on shore with five young Chinese. The villages that are about three miles up the river were all in an uproar. I could not make out what was the matter with them — in fact, I thought it was another fight. A little while longer, I saw them dragging at something, but what it was I could not tell....When I got a little closer...I saw that it was some great FISH of some kind. He was not dead then.... There were about 3,000 men and boys on the spot, every one with a lance, spear, knife, or chopper. More than half of these men were cutting and haggling at this monster. By the time I had been looking on, and walking around it, they managed to cut about forty

feet off its tail or the small end of the monster, which is just the same as a SNAKE'S. I requested them to cut off its head, and said I would give them 500 cash to have a good look at the inside of its mouth. This was gladly accepted, while some were standing close to me as if they were out of wind from the hard work they had had with their choppers. I asked them how that fish came there. They told me that he came there at his own accord, and when on the sand made a fearful splashing and noise on the sand and water. At first every one of them were scared, until some of the fishermen ventured close to it, and called out that it was a large fish, and that it was theirs. This caused every one to run with whatever they could get to get a cut for himself. The fish ran on the bank at three o'clock....

By this time the monster's head was cut off, but very much disfigured. I had then to draw it up the bank out of the water, and had the lower jaw cut off so as I could examine the inside of the mouth. I found the inside of the mouth to be just the same as a snake's, but it had three rows of soft teeth all as even as anything could be, and exactly the same size. They were movable, that is, I could move them towards the lip and back. At the entrance of the throat I found a strange sort of gridiron-shaped, tough substance, up and down. It was covered with a sort of reddish flesh, which causes me to think this monster of the deep lives on suckson [*sic*]. The snout was flat, the cheek or eyebrow stuck out about two and a-half feet — at least two and a-half times the length of my boot. The skin was one and a-half inches thick only, but awful tough, of a dirty blue colour. I should think there must have been many tons of barnacles on this monster. Where the barnacles were taken off there was a dirty white spot to be seen. As near as possible, it was twenty seven yards long. The head is exactly like a snake's, but the eye was very like a hog's, till it was perfectly dead. My boots not being waterproof, and the sun being very hot, I was forced to leave, or I should have remained there until it was all cut up and weighed; but this I could not do. I have no idea of the weight. I left, and went ashore at a village close to the waterside, about two miles from the spot where the monster was being cut up. Here I found some tons of it upon the rocks being cut up into great junks [*sic*]. They were spoiling the bones by sawing them up as they were cutting the beef, as they call it.

When Capt. Boyle next went ashore, on 15 August, no trace remained of the creature. Discussing the case 105 years later, BERNARD HEUVELMANS proposed that the animal was either a large unknown SHARK or EEL, but he strangely omitted it entirely from his tabulation of sea serpent reports.

Source: Heuvelmans, *In the Wake of the Sea Serpents.*

Beaverton Bessie *see* **Igopogo**

Beckjord, Jon-Erik (n.d.-)   Jon-Erik Beckjord's Internet website describes him as "a real-life *Raiders of the Lost Ark* hero...a management consultant and also an investigator of anomalous phenomena world-wide, an adventurer, traveler, lecturer and author." At various times in the past two decades, Beckjord has billed himself as the leader-spokesman of National Cryptozoological Society, Project BIGFOOT, the SASQUATCH Research Project, and San Francisco's now-defunct "UFO, Bigfoot, NESSIE and Crop Circle Museum." His website cautions visitors: "REMEMBER! TRUST NO ONE IN THIS RESEARCH — EXCEPT US! We EXPOSE hoaxers, and act as YOUR guide." (Emphasis in the original.) Critics take a rather different view of Beckjord's efforts, and have not been reticent in saying so.

Beckjord burst onto the crypto-scene in August 1983, with a claim that he had videotaped three LAKE MONSTERS swimming together in Urquhart Bay, at Loch Ness. Skeptics deny that the tape shows any such thing, and other witnesses present at the scene saw only waterfowl. Eight years later, in July 1991, Beckjord re-captured headlines with a theory that "[s]pace travelers could have come to Earth and lost some of their pets. This pet could have been Nessie — which has grown through the ages." Thus began a long series of hit-and-run encounters on the fringes of cryptozoology, which often found Beckjord cited as a "leading expert" on various cryptids, ranging from Bigfoot and Nessie to MOTHMAN. Granted, the "expert" label was often self-applied (Beckjord facetiously describes himself as "Mr. Shy and Modest"), or else bestowed by professional debunkers seeking straw men to lampoon. After analyzing the controversial PATTERSON FILM, Beckjord claimed to see multiple unknown HOMINIDS lurking in the nearby woods, as well as a "white kid on [Bigfoot's] back, as [a] piggy-backer." In other statements, Beckjord claimed to have seen Bigfoot "on many occasions," and once declared that he had found the remains of a Sasquatch (never presented for study) near Lewiston, Idaho. In response to criticism of such statements, he tells the skeptics, "None of you are cryptozoologists."

Beckjord has sparked equivalent controversy in other fields, as well. During the murder trial of O.J. Simpson, he offered a "ghost photo" of victims Nicole Simpson and Ron Goldman for sale, but no takers met his $500,000 asking price. Two years later, speaking from his storefront museum, Beckjord told a CNN reporter, "We had a big party with belly dancers, and a UFO showed up. It stayed three hours and kept asking to plug into the wall. They were cheap aliens. They didn't want to pay for their own juice." Following the terrorist attacks of 11 September 2001, Beckjord advertised himself as a "security and management consultant" for the California firm of Beckjord, Hanson & MacGillivray. His prescription for foiling skyjackers was unique, to say the least. "Muslims abhor pig meat," he wrote. "Do not laugh, but if you bring on canned Spam, which is pig meat, you can open it and throw bits at them, to force them back. You must chant: 'Pig meat!' over and over. Some, not all, will recoil and back off."

Sources: "Don't believe in aliens? Visit San Francisco's UFO 'Museum.'" CNN (19 April 1997); Harrison, *The Encyclopaedia of the Loch Ness Monster*; "Mothman theories spark paranormal catfight." *Wireless Flash* (5 February 2002); Laurel Wellman, "Dog bites." *San Francisco Weekly* (2 June 1999); Aliens on Earth, http://www.aliensonearth.com/misc/1999/aug/d11–001.*shtml*; Beckjord.com, http://www.beckjord.com/; Cryptozoology, http://www.adam.com.au/bstett/PaCryptozoology77.htm; Erik Beckjord, http://www.ufowatchdog.com/beckjord.html; UFO Hall of Shame, http://www.ufowatchdog.com/hall2.html.

Bedfield Beast   In January 2003, a resident of Bedfield, near Framlingham in Suffolk, England, glanced through her bedroom window and was startled by an unexpected sight. She later told reporters, "My bedroom window overlooks nearby fields and recently I was convinced I saw a large black CAT. It was far too big to be a domestic cat and it moved differently from a dog." The witness did not report her sighting until 1 February, when she woke to find large pawprints in the snow shrouding her garden. Authorities granted that the 6-inch prints, spaced 40 inches apart, were made by "a sizeable creature," but they balked at blaming an ALIEN BIG CAT. Another Bedfield resident, Dominique Thomas, was less reticent. "I do not think there is any doubt about it," she said. "These pawprints are not those of a dog. We have not heard of any livestock being taken in the village, but farmers here keep a number of animals and BIRDS that could be attacked, including geese and black swans." The original witness, who preferred anonymity, reported, "It looks like it was after the food left on the bird table, but those scraps would not have been enough to

fill a large animal." At press time for this book, no further sightings were recorded from the Bedfield neighborhood.

Source: "Tracks of big cat in Suffolk village." *Evening Star* (3 February 2003).

Bedias Creek, Arkansas   Authors LOREN COLEMAN and JOHN KIRK include this supposed Arkansas waterway on published lists of sites generating aquatic cryptid reports. No details of the sightings are provided. A search conducted for this volume found no Bedias Creek in Arkansas, but there *is* one in Texas, where it feeds the Trinity River and serves as a southern boundary for Madison County. No cryptid sightings are reported from the Texas creek.

Sources: Coleman, *Mysterious America*; Kirk, *In the Domain of the Lake Monsters*; Columbia Gazetteer of North America, http://www.bartleby.com/69/.

Beebe, Charles William (1877–1962)   Brooklyn native William Beebe inherited a lifelong interest in nature from his parents and pursued it to the end of his remarkable life. Frequent family visits to the American Museum of Natural History sparked an enduring friendship with museum president Henry Osborn, who designed the Bronx Zoo and doubled as a professor at Columbia University. Beebe spent three years at Columbia (1896–99) but left without graduating, though some biographers erroneously credit him with a B.S. degree. (In 1928, Beebe received an honorary Ph.D. in science from Tufts College and Colgate University.) From Columbia, Beebe went to work as a curator of BIRDS at the Bronx Zoo, where he remained until 1903. Extensive travels with wife Mary followed over the next eight years, including research expeditions to Britain and 14 nations in Asia, Africa and South America. In 1916, Beebe established the Bronx Zoo's research station in British Guiana (now Guyana), then joined the fledgling French air force in 1917. A new round of scientific expeditions followed World War I, including visits to the Galápagos Islands, where Beebe observed an unknown species of MANTA RAY in 1923. By the late 1920s, he had become a deep-sea diving enthusiast, and thus achieved his most lasting fame.

In 1928, Beebe was approached by Otis Barton, inventor of a deep-water exploration vehicle that Beebe dubbed a bathysphere. Between 1930 and 1934, Beebe and Barton repeatedly plumbed the Atlantic depths off Bermuda's Nonsuch Island, setting a record for the time with their descent to 3,028 feet. In the process, Beebe reported sightings of several deep-sea denizens which no other human has seen to this day. They included the ABYSSAL RAINBOW GAR, a serpentine fish he called *BATHYSPHAERA INTACTA*, the FIVE-LINED CONSTELLATION FISH, the PALLID SAILFIN and the three-starred anglerfish. While engaged in that research, Beebe was named director of the Bronx Zoo's department of tropical research, a post he maintained until July 1952. Beebe's classic works include *Jungle Peace* (1919), *Edge of the Jungle* (1921), *Jungle Days* (1925), *The Arcturus Adventure* (1926), *Beneath Tropic Seas* (1927), *Galápagos: Worlds End* (1928), *A Round Trip to Davy Jones's Locker* (1931), *Half Mile Down* (1935) and *High Jungle* (1949). He died on 4 June 1962 and was buried in Trinidad.

Sources: Beebe, *Half Mile Down*; Jonathan Maslow, *Footsteps in the Jungle*. Chicago: Ivan R. Dee, 1996; The Official William Beebe Website, http://hometown.aol.com/chines6930/mwl/beebe1.htm.

Beithir   Ancient Celtic folklore describes the Beithir ("serpent" or "beast") as a large cave-dwelling SNAKE most often seen near Loch a' Mhuillidh, in the Scottish Highlands. It seems not to have been a LAKE MONSTER, but rather a terrestrial serpent 9–10 feet long, principally active in summer months. The common grass snake (*Natrix natrix*) of Europe and the British Isles sometimes exceeds six feet in length, but it has not officially inhabited the Highlands during modern times. No recent sightings of the Beithir are on file.

Source: Karl Shuker, "Sideshow." *Strange Magazine* 15 (Spring 1995): 32.

Bekk-Bok *see* **Kra-Dhan**

Benbecula carcass   In 1990, an unidentified GLOBSTER washed ashore on the island of Benbecula, in Scotland's Outer HEBRIDES. Louise Witts, a 16-year-old babysitter, found the carcass and was photographed beside it, sitting on a rock. As she later described the creature:

It had what appeared to be a head at one end, and a curved back with eaten-away flesh or even a furry skin and was about 12 feet long. It smelled absolutely disgusting, but the weird thing was that it had all these shapes like fins along its back, like a DINOSAUR or something.

The snapshots were forgotten until 1996, when Witts rediscovered them while moving and showed them to Alan Coles, curator of natural sciences at the Hancock Museum in Newcastle upon Tyne, England. Coles placed the photos on display that August, reporting in December 1996 that none of the botanists, zoologists or marine biologists who had viewed the pictures could identify their subject.

Source: "The beast of Benbecula." *Fortean Times* 93 (December 1996): 9.

***Bengkalis* sea serpent**   At 1:00 p.m. on 15 August 1928, crewmen aboard the steamer *Bengkalis* spied a SEA SERPENT in the Indian Ocean west of Sumatra, at 2° 25' north latitude and 95° 47' east longitude. The creature initially resembled a floating tree trunk, some 400 yards off the starboard bow, with the surrounding water disturbed as if by a shoal of fish. Pilot J.R.A. Swaan wrote the following description in the ship's log, countersigned by Capt. J.F. Straakenbroek:

We saw through binoculars that it was not a tree-trunk but a living creature which moved, and of which some four portions of the body (probably the back) were above water. These portions did not look like fins; they shone in the sun, they were smooth and not very arched, and their color was very like that of a seal. Suddenly there rose out of the water a part which looked like a big round branch, about 2 feet in diameter and 6 feet long and making an angle of 30° with the sea; the end was rounded. Slowly this part dived under the water again, while the sea became very disturbed. Nothing in particular could be seen on this portion out of the water — nothing the shape of eyes or anything similar — and the color was the same as that of the other parts. The distance by then was 250 yards. The quartermaster, who was from the British East Indies and was at the helm, also saw what had appeared in the sea, without my drawing his attention to it, and cried: "*Barry machli* (big FISH)."

Source: Heuvelmans, *In the Wake of the Sea Serpents*.

***Benjamin* sea serpent**   At 2:00 p.m. of 8 March 1854, while anchored at Singapore aboard the clipper *Benjamin*, French poet Joannis Morgon saw a SEA SERPENT passing nearby. As he later recalled the incident:

I was the first to be able to draw the attention of the crew…to the presence of this phenomenal ophidian. It seemed to us to be about 55 feet in length: it had a great resemblance to the boa; its head

which it kept raised, sometimes causing its pointed and arched tongue to tremble, was flattened: its body, of a surprising diameter, formed two series of circles or knots on the surface, diapered with patches of black and pale yellow; one of these series, below its raised withers, was separated from the other series of these coils or rings, of which I was able to count eleven, by a prolongation of its majestic body.

BERNARD HEUVELMANS, writing 114 years later, questioned Morgon's veracity, yet he stopped short of declaring the report a HOAX.

Source: Heuvelmans, *In the Wake of the Sea Serpents*.

Bennett Lake, Canada   Fortean authors Colin and Janet Bord include this lake, spanning the border between British Columbia and the Yukon, as a source of LAKE MONSTER reports. No dates or details of sightings are provided.

Source: Bord and Bord, *Unexplained Mysteries of the 20th Century*.

Bennington Monster   A dearth of details hampers any effort to identify this cryptid, once reported from the neighborhood of Bennington, in southern Vermont. Local historian Joseph Citro reports that sometime in the 19th century, during a nocturnal rainstorm, a stagecoach was stopped outside Bennington when its horses refused to proceed. The driver stepped down and found "huge circular imprints" on the unpaved roadway, forming "a line of tracks, as if something gigantic had passed by." The driver called his passengers to see the prints, and as they stood out in the rain, some unseen monster toppled the coach with "a savage, thunderous blow." The five witnesses later claimed they had seen "a huge beast, partly obscured by tree branches" as it retreated, roaring, into the forest. No more was ever heard of it, and the story has passed into legend — where, perhaps, it belongs.

Source: Citro, *Green Mountain Ghosts, Ghouls & Unsolved Mysteries*.

Bensbach's Bird of Paradise   Bensbach's BIRD of paradise (*Janthothorax bensbachi*) is one of six species collected from Papua New Guinea in the 19th century and never seen again by Western eyes. In 1930, Erwin Stresemann dismissed all six as hybrid specimens of known species, but some modern ornithologists believe his verdict may have been faulty. The question remains unanswered, pending discovery of another specimen.

Source: Fuller, *The Lost Birds of Paradise*.

Benson, Robert (n.d.-)   Physicist Robert Benson received his B.S. from Southwest Texas University in 1976, followed by his Ph.D. from Texas A&M University in 1985. He remained to teach at Texas A&M- Corpus Christi, where he also directs the university's Center for Bioacoustics and serves as curator of the center's Natural Sounds Collection, documenting the vocalizations of various mammals and BIRDS. In that capacity, Benson was retained in 2002 to analyze alleged recordings of BIGFOOT for the Discovery Channel's production *SASQUATCH: Legend Meets Science*. As a longtime skeptic, Benson had rejected several previous offers to review supposed tapes of unknown HOMINIDS crying in the wilderness, and he admitted that his final agreement in 2002 "wasn't a hasty decision." Benson was among a dozen experts recruited to analyze several supposed Bigfoot recordings, comparing the calls with those of known animals, including elk, coyotes, WOLVES and various primates. "It's a visual picture of the sound," he explained to reporters, "so we can make measurements of the temporal frequencies. This is a mammal, at least we suspect. There is a whole range of things that it might possibly be. There is the possibility that this could be human. We have recordings but what the source might be, we don't know. It is evidence but it might be negative evidence." In the final broadcast, Benson declared that the creature making the sounds was "probably primate." "We've been able to compare this sound with the obvious animals that it might be," he said. "In our analysis so far, it does not seem that this source fits into those groups." As Benson later told *USA Today*, "I've gone from being a raving skeptic to being curiously receptive."

Source: Marco della Cava, "Bigfoot's indelible imprint." *USA Today* (31 October 2002); Tricia Schwennesen, "A&M-CC prof searches for the sounds of Sasquatch." *Corpus Christi* (TX) *Caller-Times* (28 May 2002); Robert Benson, Ph.D., http://www.sci.tamucc.edu/pals/faculty/benson.html.

Berens Lake, Canada   A LAKE MONSTER resembling an oversized ALLIGATOR was reported from this lake, near Kenora, Ontario, in the early 20th century. No modern sightings are on file.

Source: Richard Lambert, *Exploring the Supernatural*. Toronto: McClelland and Stewart, 1955.

Bergman's Bear   Officially, the largest bears living on Earth today are the mighty brown bears of Alaska's Kodiak Island (*Ursus arctos middendorffi*). Males of that subspecies reach eight feet in length, but some researchers are convinced that even larger specimens may be found in Russian territory, on the Kamchatka Peninsula. In autumn 1920, while visiting the region, Swedish zoologist Sten Bergman examined a huge, black bear's pelt, estimating that the live animal must have weighed between 1,100 and 2,500 pounds. Another Swedish scientist, Rene Malaise, spent nine years in Kamchatka and reported personal observations of a giant bear's skull, along with a pawprint measuring 14.5 inches long and 10 inches wide. Siberian brown bears (*U. a. berringianus*) are not black and do not approach the size of Bergman's bear. Sadly, no further information on the unknown bears of Kamchatka has been reported since Bergman published his initial treatise in 1936.

Source: Shuker, *From Flying Toads to Snakes with Wings*.

Bergsjø, Norway   Tourists and residents of Norway's Buskerud County report occasional LAKE MONSTER sightings from this lake. The creature is typically described as serpentine, gray in color, with a slender 3-foot neck and 7–8 humps showing above the surface as it swims with undulating movements.

Source: Skjelsvik, "Norwegian lake and sea monsters."

Berkeley Lake, Georgia   In July 2003, residents of Berkeley Lake, Georgia — located northeast of Atlanta in Gwinnett County — reported sightings of a huge TURTLE in the 88-acre lake that shares their town's name. Witnesses compared the reptile to "a big boulder with a head attached," insisting that it must weigh 150 pounds or more. One local who glimpsed the turtle, Joe Voyles, told reporters, "His head was as big as mine." State wildlife biologist Jim Ozier rejected all such claims without a visit to the site, declaring that region's largest turtle, the common snapper (*Chelydra serpentina*) weighs no more than 75–80 pounds. In fact, captive specimens have reached 86 pounds, but a much larger turtle is native to parts of Georgia. The alligator snapping turtle (*Macroclemys temminickii*) often weighs 150 pounds, and its record weight is 251 pounds. Officially, that species is not found in northern Georgia, though they range much farther north along the MISSISSIPPI RIVER valley, and a stray specimen in the Atlanta suburbs is hardly inconceivable.

Source: Roger Conant and Joseph Collins, *Reptiles and Amphibians: Eastern/Central North America*. New York: Houghton Mifflin, 1998; "Lake residents swear there's an enormous turtle nearby." Atlanta Journal Constitution (19 July 2003).

Berreador   The Río Uruguay rises in southern Brazil and flows 1,000 miles southwestward to the Río de la Plata estuary. Along the way, it forms part of the boundary between Brazil and Argentina, and most of the border separating Argentina from Uruguay. The Berreador is said to be a giant creature of the forest pressing close along the Río Uruguay, where boatmen sometimes glimpse its great fanged mouth, pushed through the undergrowth and roaring at them as they pass. No further description of the beast is available, since none who have confronted it on land survived to tell the tale.

Sources: Picasso, "South American monsters and mystery animals."

Berry Head sea serpent   On 31 July 1906, witness A.J. Butler sighted a "strange creature" swimming on the surface of the ocean 30 feet from his sailboat, off the coast of Berry Head, near Brixham, in Devon, England. As he described the animal:

It was, as nearly as I could judge, about 6 feet long, four or five inches broad, tapering to about two inches at the tail, and quite flat — like a long broad sword blade. It was not more than an inch in thickness, and of a buff colour. The edges were all serrated and gave the impression of being set along with tiny fins.

Though positively minuscule by normal SEA SERPENT standards, the Berry Head creature still found its way into BERNARD HEUVELMANS'S 1968 tabulation of unknown pelagic creatures. He classified it as a "ribbon-like FISH," but stopped short of suggesting its species.

Source: Heuvelmans, *In the Wake of the Sea Serpents*.

***Bertie* sea serpent**   In spring of 1882, a report issued from the Shetland Islands that a fishing boat, the *Bertie*, had narrowly survived a SEA SERPENT'S attack offshore from Fetlar. As described in a letter to the press, from the boat's supposed captain, the beast was 150 feet long, its massive head decorated with barnacles "the size of herring barrels" and "whiskers hanging down around its mouth and seemingly about seven or eight feet long, of a pretty green colour." Though the boat was nearly swallowed — "of course, with the mast laid" — it somehow managed to escape. Skeptic Arthur Stradling, discussing the report in *Land and Water* (1 July 1882), asked rhetorically:

Does the marine ornithology of the Shetlands abound with such *rare aves* as fishing-boat skippers who talk about scenes that "baffle description" (twice), who call their boat a "frail craft," and a sea monster an "unwelcome visitor," and nice things of that sort, and who indulge in such expressions as "an order not long in being executed," "I candidly confess," and other high-class conversation? Why, it beats the sea-serpent hollow!

BERNARD HEUVELMANS, reporting the case 83 years later, joined Stradling in dismissing it as a HOAX.

Source: Heuvelmans, *In the Wake of the Sea Serpents*.

Beruang Rambai   Semantics complicate efforts to identify the Beruang rambai ("long-haired bear") of Borneo, since its name is also sometimes used for the familiar sun bear (*Helarctos malayanus*). Nonetheless, natives describe it as a large primate or HOMINID, six feet tall when standing erect and four feet tall at the shoulder when walking on all fours. Its black hair is reportedly 3–4 inches long (while the sun bear's is short), and the Beruang rambai has a bullet-shaped head on a short neck, reminiscent of a GORILLA or BIGFOOT. When standing erect, the creature sometimes beats its chest, after the manner of an APE. Explorer Leonard Clark met a Beruang rambai in the Borneo mountains, sometime in the early 1930s, and eyewitness sightings continued into the 1960s, at least. Some researchers feel that witnesses have misidentified orangutans (*Pongo pygmaeus*), but those apes are smaller than the Beruang rambai and their hair is normally red.

Sources: Leonard Clark, *A Wanderer till I Die*. New York: Funk and Wagnalls, 1937; Tchernine, *The Yeti*.

Bésonroubé *see* Gnéna

Bessie   Lake Erie is the southernmost of North America's Great Lakes. Sightings of a large LAKE MONSTER, affectionately nicknamed Bessie, have been filed periodically since 1793. In 1881, a "big SEA SERPENT" 25 feet long and 12 inches in diameter, was allegedly captured in Sandusky Bay, Ohio. Two fishermen clubbed the beast unconscious and forced it into a packing crate, which was "inspected" by police from a safe distance. After an initial spate of stories in the press, no more was heard of the creature, strongly suggesting that the story was a HOAX. Six years after that fiasco, two other fishermen allegedly found a "glowing" creature 30–40 feet long, writhing in agony on the shore near Toledo. They ran home for ropes to secure it, but the beast was gone when they returned.

In July 1892, Captain Jenkins of the steam barge *Fenton* sighted an apparent wreck in the middle of the lake, then discovered the hulk was a serpent 30 feet or more in length. Jenkins described the animal for the *Chicago Sunday Tribune*:

> The tail of the monster was laterally compressed thus adapting it to the same purpose in locomotion through the water as the caudal fin in fishes. The head was nearly a foot in length, the nostrils being placed not as in ordinary serpents at the end of the snout, but above and the eyes, blazing like two balls of fire, were about two and a half inches in diameter. The neck was very short and thick set and the mouth, turned upward instead of downward, was of huge cavernous dimensions when the animal opened its jaws so as to display its forked tongue. The color was black with yellowish white bands on the body and white patches upon the head.
>
> On passing the huge reptile it was observed to rear its head and neck out of the water and fall into the wake of the boat as if in pursuit of prey. For twenty or more miles the chase continued, the serpent equaling the speed of the steamer and swimming gracefully most of the time with its head and neck only out of the water, but occasionally rearing upon its abdomen so that it seemed to stand up straight above the water for about fifteen feet, as if to take a survey of the deck and see if there was any prey there worth seizing. At intervals, the animal approached the ship closely and rearing itself, as it were, on its haunches seemed disposed to dart on board and seize some of the persons on deck. At such times, the experience was thrilling in the extreme.

In the summer of 1990, a 40- to 50-foot blackish creature with bulging eyes was sighted repeatedly along the Ohio shore. College teacher Mary Landoll, at Huron, said its head "was probably twice the size of a football." Others reported the animal swimming in serpentine patterns, while one described "two small horns sticking up from what I took to be its head." Tom Solberg Sr., owner of the Huron Lagoons Marina, offered $150,000 for Bessie's capture "alive and unharmed." His stipulations: The beast must measure 30 feet or longer, weigh at least 1,000 pounds, and represent a new species. A giant holding pen was built for Bessie, and it waits today, still empty.

In October 1994, another mystery beast surfaced on the Cana-

dian side of the lake, at Port Dover, Ontario. Nine years later, in August 2003, three swimmers at Port Dover suffered bites on their legs from some large, unseen predator swimming beneath the lake's surface. Dr. Harold Hynscht treated the victims at a local hospital, suggesting that the 6-inch bite marks were inflicted by a "big, honking FISH." Examination of the wounds ruled out snapping turtles and various fish known to live in Lake Erie, though Hynscht suggested the culprit might be a primitive bowfin (*Amia calva*). Hynscht told reporters, "One of the consistent elements of the stories I've heard is that it happened so fast they hardly had time to react. Whatever is doing this is doing so because of territory. It's not doing this because it's hungry." Photos of the bite marks were sent for study at Toronto University, but no verdict on their identity has been announced.

Sources: Garner, *Monster! Monster!*; "Mystery 'big, honking' fish bites Canadian swimmer' legs." *London* (Ontario) *Free Press* (13 August 2001); Paula Schleis, "If Scotland has Nessie, does Ohio have Bessie?" *Akron* (OH) *Beacon Journal* (31 October 2002); Gerald Tebben, "Ohio mileposts: Sailors sight 'monster' in Lake Erie." *Columbus* (OH) *Dispatch* (7 July 2003).

Big Alkali Lake, Nebraska   Big Alkali Lake lies 15 miles south of Valentine, in northern Nebraska's Cherry County. Author Betty Garner reports that a 4-man party sighted a horned, reptilian LAKE MONSTER here in July 1923, but her description of the incident clearly refers to a sighting at Wagner (formerly Alkali) Lake, located 100 miles further west in Sheridan County.

Sources: Garner, *Monster! Monster!*; Mark Swatek, "Nebraska's famous lake monster." *INFO Journal* 10 (Spring 1973): 8–11.

Big Chapman Lake, Indiana   Big Chapman Lake lies five miles northeast of Warsaw, in Indiana's Kosciusko County. Some maps show it simply as Chapman Lake. On 16 August 1934, W.H. Scott was fishing from a boat when a LAKE MONSTER surfaced nearby, revealing a 2-foot-wide head with eyes resembling cow's.

Sources: Clark and Coleman, "America's lake monsters"; Garner, *Monster! Monster!*

Big Grey Man   Modern reports of BIGFOOT-type HOMINIDS in the British Isles are infrequent, but they still occur. A case in point is Scotland's Big Grey Man, said to inhabit Ben MacDhui, at 4,296 feet the tallest peak in the Grampian district's Cairngorm Mountains. Sporadic encounters with this cryptid, usually atop the mountain's misty crest, have been recorded since 1891, when hiker Norman Collie heard the crunch of heavy footsteps on a path behind him and fled home in terror. In the early 1920s, Tom Crowley glimpsed a huge gray figure with pointed ears and clawed feet on the slopes of nearby Braeraich. Two decades later, in 1942, Sydney Scroggie recorded a sighting while camped on Ben MacDhui. An unnamed friend of mountaineer Richard Frere allegedly met a 20-foot hairy biped on Ben MacDhui in January 1950 or 1951. On 2 December 1952, James Rennie photographed a series of humanoid footprints on Ben MacDhui. The prints measured 19 inches long by 14 inches wide, with a 7-foot stride. The trail was straight and at one point "jumped" 30 feet across a road.

Sources: Coleman and Huyghe, *The Field Guide to Bigfoot, Yeti, and Other Mystery Primates Worldwide*; Gray, *The Big Grey Man of Ben MacDhui*.

Big Lake, Alaska   Aptly-named Big Lake, north of Anchorage in Denali National Park, produced an unexpected LAKE MONSTER sighting on 13 September 1970. That afternoon, witness Manne Landstrom saw a 30-foot creature resembling a floating log, with a long, flat head resembling that of a CROCODILE.

Source: Coleman, *Mysterious America.*

Big Mo   In January 1974, several residents of Aurora, Illinois reported encounters with a SASQUATCH-type HOMINID covered in dirty white hair. Newspapers dubbed the beast Big Mo, but it soon dropped from sight. Eight months later, a 7-foot-tall hominid with brown hair was reported from Carol Stream, eight miles northeast of Aurora, where it left a trail of 4-toed footprints 13 inches long and 6 inches wide. At least a dozen witnesses reported sightings of the beast around Carol Stream.

Sources: Bord and Bord, *The Bigfoot Casebook*; Green, *Sasquatch: The Apes Among Us.*

Big Muddy Monster   This BIGFOOT or NORTH AMERICAN APE of Murphysboro, Illinois made its first appearance in June 1973. Teenagers Randy Needham and Judy Johnson were parked near the Big Muddy River on 25 June, when they heard snarling in the night and saw a 7-foot-tall HOMINID run past their car. Reporting the incident to police, they described the creature as covered in dirty-white hair smeared with mud, emitting a stench "like dead FISH and river slime." On 26 June, three more witnesses reported a "big white ghost" in their yard, and police found a trail of slime at the scene. Five days later, several carnival workers saw the Mud Monster lurking near a pen filled with Shetland ponies. Subsequent sightings were recorded in July 1974 and July 1975. Two days before Halloween 2003, Illinois journalist Jeff Smyth suggested promoting the Mud Monster as a draw for CRYPTOTOURISM, but the tongue-in-cheek suggestion was ignored.

Source: Bord and Bord, *The Bigfoot Casebook*; Hauck, *Haunted Places*; Jeff Smyth, "A monster of an idea to boost tourism." *Southern Illinoisan* (29 October 2003).

Big Pine Lake *see* **Oscar**

Big Rideau Lake, Canada   Three witnesses who encountered a LAKE MONSTER at Big Rideau Lake, north of Kingston, Ontario in 1957 waited 43 years to report the event, and even then they refused to identify themselves. The trio's spokesman described the incident as follows, in a 2000 Internet posting:

> It suddenly appeared in front of us as we were going to our island. I had to do a U-turn so as not to run into it. It was about 20 feet out of the water. It seemed to have a serpent like body, but it's head and jaw were in at an angle to the neck like a mammal. We were three in the boat and we all saw it very clearly but we didn't speak about it together or mention it to anyone else at the time. I didn't think anyone would believe us and was afraid of ridicule.

Source: The Shadowlands Sea Serpent Page, http://theshadowlands.net/sightings.htm.

Big Sandy Lake, Minnesota   This lake, in central Minnesota's Aitkin County, was the scene of a curious LAKE MONSTER sighting in August 1886. Witness Chris Engstein claimed that he saw a horned creature emerge from the lake and that he fired several shots to drive it back underwater. His effort must have been successful, since no further sightings are on file.

Source: Fort, *The Complete Books of Charles Fort.*

Big Swan Pond, Indiana   Big Swam Pond lies 10 miles south of Vincennes, in southwestern Indiana's Knox County. On 17 June 1892, the *Vincennes Commercial* reported that Robert Hedges and other "men of good repute for veracity" had seen a LAKE MONSTER 25–30 feet long in the pond. The creature was serpentine in form, with a white head and throat reminiscent of a dog's, while its skin was "spotted or mottled, red and yellow, like the side of a large water SNAKE."

Source: "Sea-serpent, werewolf, etc." *The Valley Advance* (6 October 1981).

Big Wally   Big Wally is the supposed LAKE MONSTER of Wallowa Lake, located on the eastern edge of the Eagle Gap Wilderness Area in Oregon's Wallowa County. Early aboriginal accounts describe a creature vaguely resembling a manatee (Family *Trichechidae*), while a prospector's tale from November 1885 refers to a 100-foot beast with a 10-foot neck and a head like that of a hippopotamus. In the 1950s, several witnesses reported giant FISH in the lake, including a July 1952 description of three fish "longer than any boat in the lake." In 1978, witnesses glimpsed a 25-foot creature with three humps or coils visible above water. The last sightings to date, from 1982, described a 50-foot serpentine animal resembling British Columbia's OGOPOGO. Skeptics explain all the sightings with reference to a large white sturgeon (*Acipenser transmontanus*), and while those fish reach lengths approaching 20 feet, none have been confirmed as inhabiting Lake Wallowa.

Sources: Dash, "The reporting of a lake monster." *Fortean Times* 44 (Summer 1985): 42–43; Kirk, *In the Domain of the Lake Monsters.*

Bigfoot   With Scotland's NESSIE and the Himalayan YETI, the North American HOMINID commonly known as Bigfoot or SASQUATCH ranks as one of cryptozoology's reigning "superstars." And like those other famous cryptids, Bigfoot has apparently been playing hide-and-seek with humankind throughout recorded history. Long before the first European explorers "discovered" the Americas, aboriginal tribes knew the hairy, bipedal giants under a bewildering array of names including Atahsaia (Zuni), Boqs (Bella Coola), Choanito (Wenatchee), Dzozavits (Shoshoni), Esti capcaki (Seminole), Gougou (Micmac), Hecaitomixw (Quinault), Iariyin (Hare), Kushtaka (Tlingit), Loo-poo-oi'yes (Miwuk), Manabai'wok (Menomini), Nalusa falaya (Choctaw), Omah (Yurok), Pa-snu-ta (Omaha), Rugaru (Ojibway), Seeahtkch (Clallam), Toké-mussi (Algonquin), Urayuli (Inuit), Windago (Athabascan), Xi'lgo-nehalem (Tillamook), and Ye'iitsoh (Navajo).

European colonists in North America not only heard the native names and legends of those beasts, but also saw the animals themselves. From the first years of the 19th century, sightings of unknown hominids or APES continue to the present day. Sometimes they come in trickles, fits and starts, while other periods produce a veritable flood of sightings. California highway workers coined the Bigfoot name in 1958, and persistent lurkers in other regions are often tagged with local nicknames. From Tennessee's WILDMAN of the Woods in 1878 to Vermont's BEAST OF BENNINGTON in 2003, the shambling parade is endless. No definitive tabulation of Bigfoot/Sasquatch sightings presently exists. Researcher JOHN GREEN enumerated 1,692 sightings for the continental U.S. and Canada in 1978. Two years later, authors Colin and Janet Bord listed 1,000 for the same area. Rick Berry, writing in 1993, counted 1,050 sightings from 15 East Coast states, where Green found only 233 in 1978. (Berry claims 350 sightings from Pennsylvania and 232 in Maryland, where Green found only 24 and 12, respectively.) The problem is compounded further by a careful reading of the detailed lists, which reveals several inadvertent duplications of sightings.

Rendering of Bigfoot based on eyewitnesses (*William Rebsamen*).

Whatever the final tally of sightings, and the more common discovery of large humanoid footprints with no beast at hand, Bigfoot reports have been filed from every Canadian province and from every continental U.S. state except Rhode Island. The Pacific Northwest produces a majority of sightings — Green logged 58 percent of his sightings between northern California and British Columbia — but there seems to be no shortage of cryptic hominids nationwide. Based on eyewitness descriptions, a "typical" Bigfoot ranges from 6–12 feet tall, with estimates of weight falling between 300 and 1,000 pounds. Reports of a bullet head and "no neck" are routine, mounted atop a massive torso. The creature's arms are longer in proportion to its body than a human's, and adult females are readily identified by their prominent breasts. The creatures are covered with hair, its hue ranging from reddish-brown to gray or black, although occasional white specimens have also been reported. Witnesses often remark on the animal's foul body odor. Most describe solitary sightings, but reports of paired couples and "families" with juveniles in tow are common enough to imply social life of some kind.

The famous footprints from which Bigfoot derives its name vary in size like the creatures themselves. The average print, based on thousands of samples, is 14–18 inches long, 7.2 inches wide at the ball and 4.8 inches wide at the heel. The largest on record to date reportedly measured 27 inches long and was 13.5 inches wide at the ball. (By comparison, the foot of a basketball player 7 feet

3 inches tall is 16.5 inches long and 5.5 inches wide.) The depth of footprints naturally varies with the surface walked upon, but many leave impressions suggesting body weights beyond the normal human range. The admission of various HOAXES by RANT MULLENS, RAYMOND WALLACE and various lesser-known fakers prompt skeptics to suggest that *all* Bigfoot tracks should be disqualified as evidence without examination. Less biased researchers insist that only study can reveal a fraud, and that most fake footprints are easily detected by their uniformity, rigidity, and so forth. Cryptozoologists also note that a standing reward of $100,000 is offered by the proprietors of California's Willow Creek-China Flat Museum for anyone who can dupe a panel of experts with manufactured footprints. "Nobody can do it," John Green says. "If somebody proves us wrong, then that's very worthwhile to know. But I don't expect it." Thus far, the offer has drawn no takers.

Since skeptics automatically discount eyewitness evidence — ironically, the very kind preferred above all else in courts of law — what proof of Bigfoot's physical existence then remains? Physical evidence may be divided into several categories. They include:

Bodies: The ultimate proof of a creature's existence is collection of a type specimen for scientific study. While there have been multiple reports of unclassified hominids killed or captured in the U.S. and other nations throughout history, no trace of those alleged bodies remains. So far, the nearest thing to a type specimen of Bigfoot is the enigmatic MINNESOTA ICEMAN, variously described as the find of the century, a showman's hoax or a combination of both. Whatever the facts of that case, the original specimen examined by BERNARD HEUVELMANS and IVAN SANDERSON in 1969 has likewise gone missing. Skeptics often suggest that road kills should provide Bigfoot specimens, but while several vehicular collisions with large hominids are on file since the 1960s, none proved fatal. A report issued in 2000 by the U.S. Forest Service emphasizes the rarity of road kills involving large predators such as grizzly bears and wolverines "due to their general avoidance of highways and their low population numbers and densities."

Bones: If no complete carcass is available, some researchers still believe we may have fragments of a Sasquatch stashed in museums or in the hands of private collectors. Bones are susceptible to DNA testing that would reveal their origin, or eliminate known animal species as possible donors. Between the 19th century and the 1960s, skeletal remains of GIANTS 7–9 feet tall were unearthed in 12 U.S. states and in British Columbia, but few were preserved and none have yet undergone DNA analysis. In August 1965, Dr. Robert Denson found part of a "massive" skull in a marshy region of northern California's Minarets Wilderness. Pathologist Gerald Ridge deemed it "a rather interesting specimen," whose "unusual length" and "unusual development of the nuchal ridge in the occipital zone" suggested "some anthropoid species other than human." Analysts at UCLA nonetheless concluded that the partial skull belonged to "a young, ancient Indian male" — and then promptly lost the specimen. Another missing bone, described by John Green as a humanoid jawbone "so large that it fits over a normal human head," was likewise misplaced at the British Columbia Museum, presumed to be "crated and in storage" at some unknown location. In February 2002, RAYMOND CROWE related the story of an elk poacher in Washington State who allegedly shot a Sasquatch near the Klickitat River in 1996 but kept silent for fear of prosecution. Two months later, he returned to the site and retrieved the only bone remaining, a giant femur which he buried in his yard. Attempts to retrieve it, if it exists, have thus far been futile.

Hair samples: Like bones and other organic remains, hair may be subjected to DNA analysis and thus determine the donor's identity, or at least eliminate known species. In Asia, hair allegedly collected from the Yeti and ORANG PENDEK has been tested and classified as belonging to unknown primates. Sasquatch researcher ROBERT MORGAN has twice collected suspect hairs in the Pacific Northwest. His first sample was analyzed at the Smithsonian Institution in 1970, where experts said the hairs were "possibly from bears." Four years later, Oregon microbiologist Mary Florey diagnosed a second Morgan hair sample as "humanoid, but not human." Around the same time, hunting guide Wayne Twitchell found six hairs at the scene of a Bigfoot sighting near French Creek, Idaho. A crime laboratory technician declared that the hairs came from "no known animal." An environmental atlas of Washington State, published by the U.S. Army Corps of Engineers in 1975, claims that an FBI analysis of alleged Sasquatch hairs "resulted in the conclusion that no such hair exists on any human or presently-known animal for which such data are available." That report may refer to an alleged auto collision with a Bigfoot in Harford County, Maryland during 1975. Author Philip Rife quotes a *York* (Pennsylvania) *Daily Record* article of 23 February 1978 as saying that hair retrieved from the car "was not bovine. It was from a primate. It did not compare with hair samples from over a hundred common primates." Rife also sites an anonymous, undated Internet posting as his source for a claim that alleged Bigfoot hairs recovered from Carter County, Oklahoma in 1983 did not match those of "humans or any known animal." Hairs extracted from the plaster cast of a Sasquatch footprint, found in Vermont during 1985, produced "inconclusive" DNA results. One year later, the Fortean journal *Pursuit* claimed that hairs found at the site of a Hampshire County, West Virginia sighting was analyzed in Washington, with the following result: "We can only conclude that they came from some primate species. The hair did not come from a GORILLA or from one of the more common species of MONKEY. It did not come from a human or non-primate." In 1995, Bigfoot hunter Paul Freeman and two companions glimpsed a Sasquatch in the Blue Mountains of southeastern Washington, then found clumps of black and brown hair at the site. Tests performed at Ohio State University determined that the hair came "from two individuals of the same species" and "was indistinguishable from human hair by any criterion," but that "DNA extracted from both hair shaft or roots (hair demonstrably fresh) was too fragmented to permit gene sequencing." In May 2002, Ohio geneticist John Lewis analyzed alleged Bigfoot hairs collected in Kentucky and pronounced them "hominid," more closely related to bonobo APES (*Pan paniscus*) than to *Homo sapiens*. In 2003, cryptozoologist AUTUMN WILLIAMS collected suspect hairs from Alabama's BOOGER which were analyzed as belonging to an "unknown primate."

Scatology: In addition to suspect hair samples, Robert Morgan also collected samples of alleged Bigfoot feces during 1974. DNA tests were unknown at the time, and study of the droppings could only determine the donor's diet. An anthropologist attached to Morgan's team suggested that the creature's diet was consistent with an that of an elk (*Cervus elaphus*), but he doubted that elk could produce such large droppings. The sample was not preserved, but any future specimens should clearly be subjected to DNA analysis.

Castings: While some doubters dismiss all Sasquatch footprints

as the products of hoaxes, they may yet serve to document Bigfoot's existence. Experts JOHN NAPIER and GROVER KRANTZ were persuaded by analysis of the BOSSBURG TRACKS, collected in Washington State during 1969, which apparently were made by a biped with a crippled foot. On 10 June 1982, U.S. Forest Service patrolman Paul Freeman saw an 8-foot-tall Sasquatch in Washington's Umatilla National Forest and made casts of its footprints. Six days later, two more sets of tracks were cast at nearby Elk Wallow, by Forest Service biologist Rodney Johnson and Joel Hardin, a tracker for the U.S. Border Patrol. All three sets of tracks revealed dermal ridges and sweat pores consistent with the friction skin from soles of higher primates. Hardin and Johnson still dismissed the tracks as a practical joke, but Grover Krantz pronounced them genuine. Eleven years later, Texas forensic scientist James Chilicutt examined an 18-inch footprint cast made in Washington, in 1987. Chilicutt told reporters that the cast "has dermal ridges, and the flow and texture matches the ridge flow texture of [a cast] from California. The ridges are about twice as thick as in a human being. The ridges run down the side of the foot, [while] in humans, the ridges run across the width of the foot. The only other animal I've seen this in is a howler monkey [*Alouatta palliata*] in Costa Rica. As a crime scene investigator, I don't deal in what I believe or what I think....I know there's an animal out there, because I've seen the physical evidence." Similar opinions were advanced in 2000 for the SKOOKUM CAST, which may show the outline of a reclining Bigfoot imprinted in mud.

Audio recordings: Acoustics experts can analyze recorded sounds to determine their source, the size and species of animate noisemakers, and the individual identity of human speakers. Many Bigfoot witnesses remark on the creature's distinctive cries, and several audio recordings of alleged Bigfoot calls now exist. Alan Berry made the first such recording on 21 October 1972, at an altitude of 8,500 feet in California's Sierra Nevada Mountains. Pitch-frequency analysis of the tape, performed in 1977, concluded that the sounds were made by more than one creature, each having a 10-inch larynx, while that of a 6-foot-tall man is typically 6.5 inches long. Extrapolating from the larynx size, the "speaker" should be 8 feet tall or larger. Researcher Rich LaMonica claims that he recorded a Bigfoot's call in 1994, in Guernsey County, Ohio. Analysts at Kent State University's Speech Pathology and Audiology Department analyzed the tape, reporting that the sound fell within a tenor range, produced by a speaker roughly 6 feet tall, with a large head and body. Attempts to duplicate the tone with human subjects failed. Subsequently, an interpreter of ancient Indian dialects claimed that the taped sounds could translate as "We are watching" or "We are being watched." More persuasive, perhaps, are the analyses performed on other tapes by Texas acoustic expert ROBERT BENSON in 2002, their results converting Benson from "a raving skeptic to...curiously receptive."

Photographic evidence: As with eyewitness sightings, no comprehensive list of alleged Bigfoot photos, films and/or videotapes presently exists. Because such evidence is readily faked, skeptics often dismiss it sight-unseen. It must be granted that some Bigfoot photographs and films, including most or all of those produced by IVAN MARX, are clearly fakes. The 1967 PATTERSON FILM remains a subject of heated controversy four decades later, with arguments continuing as this book went to press. The first alleged still photo of Bigfoot was published by the *San Francisco Chronicle* on 14 December 1965, five years after woodsman Zack Hamilton left the undeveloped film at a local camera shop and never returned. Nine years later, Ohio tourist Rosemary Tobash snapped a supposed shot of Bigfoot in British Columbia's Kootenay National Park. Others have followed through the years, including the anonymous MYAKKA PHOTOGRAPHS of Florida's SKUNK APE, but most are indistinct at best. Several alleged videotapes of Bigfoot are known to exist. One is a 5-second clip taken on 28 August 1995, in northern California's Jedediah Smith Redwoods State Park, which appears to show a large black creature brandishing a prominent erection. Another, taken in northeastern Washington by Laurie Pate on Memorial Day 1996, shows a hairy biped running and walking across a hillside. Analysis by a team of surveyors and measurement experts in 2002 revealed that the figure was 5 feet 4 inches tall, with legs 2 feet 6 inches long and a stride slightly over 4 feet. Although perceived by Pate to run at "inhuman speed," it actually traveled at half the speed of an athlete hired to recreate the sequence. No further light was shed on the subject's identity.

If Bigfoot exists, do the creatures pose a threat to man? In 1970, author JOHN KEEL published a global tally of 36 "hostile acts" committed against humans by unknown hominids, but his tabulation is faulty: the chart lists 8 persons attacked and injured, while four pages earlier Keel cites 18 attacks with injury in three South American countries alone. The total number of attacks reported—including damage to vehicles or property and harm inflicted on domestic animals—is clearly much higher, but the injuries claimed by humans are relatively minor. John Green's survey of 1,692 Sasquatch sightings included only three cases with alleged human fatalities—one in Idaho during the mid-19th century, and two more from Alaska, in 1920 and 1943. On balance, humans have more to fear from lightning or their own pet dogs. Skamania County, Washington bans Bigfoot hunting under pain of a $10,000 fine, but the ordinance exists primarily to guard human residents against trigger-happy monster hunters.

Sources: Berry, *Bigfoot on the East Coast*; "Bigfoot bangs may prove presence in Bluegrass State." Wireless Flash News (20 May 2002); Bord and Bord, *The Bigfoot Casebook*; Byrne, *Big Foot*; Alex Breitler, "Big reward offered for Bigfoot phonies." *Redding* (CA) *Record Searchlight* (9 March 2003); Coleman, *Bigfoot!*; David Giffel, "Bigfoot enthusiast is true believer." *Akron* (OH) *Beacon Journal* (18 January 2001); Green, *Sasquatch:: The Apes Among Us*; Guenette and Guenette, *The Mysterious Monsters*; Keel, *The Complete Guide to Mysterious Beings*; "Police expert claims Bigfoot 'proof.'" BBC News (2 October 2003); "Promising hair found by Bigfoot searcher." *Lakes Region Free Press* (6 June 2003); Rife, *Bigfoot Across America*; Slate and Berry, *Bigfoot*; The Relationship Between Rare Carnivores and Highways: An Update for Year 2000, http://www.fs.fed.us/r1/wildlife/igbc/Linkage/Relationships.htm.

Bigfoot Busters   According to its Internet website, active at press time for this volume, the group known as BIGFOOT Busters was founded by Bill Riley, self-described survivor of a SASQUATCH attack in eastern Missouri's Pike County, during July 1972. The unknown HOMINID dubbed MOMO was reported throughout the district that summer, but Pike's case does not appear in any standard literature on the subject. No further details on that incident are presently available, beyond the fact that it inspired Riley to undertake study of martial arts four years later. Likewise, no information is offered concerning Bigfoot Busters, beyond the fact that it is "dedicated to the search for the flesh and blood bigfoot orginating [*sic*] from the mid-west and then migrating to the Pacific Northwest." Techniques employed include "field expeditions, evidence collection, investigations of reported sightings, [and] exposing fraud"—but once again, no details of the group's activities are furnished. Riley and his anonymous

members (if any) "believe that Gigantipithecus Blaki [*sic*] migrated down from Asia during the last Ice Age and followed the Mississippi down into the midwest basin ending up in Missouri." Interested parties are invited to join the group and "hunt for a Legend with us!"

Source: Bigfoot Busters, http://www.bigfootbusters.com/.

Bigfoot Central Foundation   Based at Bothell, Washington, the BCF is dedicated to "peaceful" pursuit of BIGFOOT. The group's leader, since 1 February 2000, is Cary Crook, son of longtime SASQUATCH researcher CLIFF CROOK. The BCF's Internet website defines Bigfoot as a "phenomenon" and "someting [*sic*] that defies pat explanation," suggesting that "if the Sasuatch [*sic*] are creatures actually merging [*sic*] from an invisible spirit realm, they shall continue to remain elusive," thus reducing any searches to "a time wasted effort in futility." Curiously, the website then proclaims:

> The Bigfoot Central Foundation it's [*sic*] researchers and investigators, are not interested in any "Bigfoot-type creature" apparitions claims from anywhere, let alone, from any of the unlikely or tongue-in-cheek Sasquatch stomping grounds of North America. We do not accept Bigfoot reports form [*sic*] the following areas of North America: Central or Eastern Canada, New England, Mid Atlantic States, Great Lakes States, or the Heartland of the USA.

Having thus restricted its field of interest to the Pacific Northwest, the BCF next dismisses the PATTERSON FILM as the "Bigfoot HOAX of the century" and discounts the SKOOKUM CAST as an imprint left by a reclining elk. All other alleged Sasquatch photos are likewise rejected, leaving certain footprint casts and eyewitness testimony as the BCF's only accepted evidence of Bigfoot's existence.

Source: Bigfoot Central Foundation, http://www.angelfire.com/biz/bigfootcentral/.

Bigfoot Field Researchers Organization   The BFRO, led by southern California attorney Matt Moneymaker, bills itself as "the only scientific organization probing the BIGFOOT/SASQUATCH mystery." Moneymaker, whose interest in cryptozoology stems from a personal Bigfoot sighting in eastern Ohio, claims 3,000 members or associates of the BFRO nationwide. The group's Internet database of Bigfoot sightings was launched in 1995 as the first website soliciting eyewitness reports of unknown HOMINIDS. Competing websites are dismissed as being "filled with fabricated sighting reports, sometimes written by the webmasters themselves, in order to generate updated site content." According to Moneymaker, the BFRO's mission:

> is multifaceted, but the organization essentially seeks to resolve the mystery surrounding the Bigfoot phenomenon, that is, to derive conclusive documentation of the species' existence. This goal is pursued through the proactive collection of empirical data and physical evidence from the field and by means of activities designed to promote an awareness and understanding of the nature and origin of the evidence.

Sighting reports submitted to the BFRO are "analyzed, evaluated and investigated with techniques and approaches derived from the legal profession, law enforcement, and investigative journalism." Other "compelling evidence" is presented to unnamed "scientific and forensic specialists" for evaluation and eventual publication of findings. Unlike those scientists who dismiss all anecdotal evidence, BFRO leaders believe that "the collecting of credible sighting reports is an essential part of the scientific process."

Source: Bigfoot Field Researchers Organization, http://www.bfro.net/.

Bigfoot Investigations No detailed information is presently available on this BIGFOOT research group, once directed by Tom Morris from headquarters in Pleasant Hill, California. The organization was active in December 1996, but is now defunct.

Source: "Bigfoot investigation is alive and well." *Fortean Times* 93 (December 1996), http://www.forteantimes.com/articles/093_bigfoot.shtml.

Bigfoot Research Group of the Northeast No detailed information is presently available on this organization, led by Chris Julian with headquarters in Sanford, Maine. Ten sightings of unknown HOMINIDS or NORTH AMERICAN APES were reported in Maine between the early 1800s and October 1987, while across New England another 125 reports are on file from Connecticut, Massachusetts, New Hampshire and Vermont. Julian's group was reported active in December 1996, but it is now apparently defunct.

Source: Berry, *Bigfoot on the East Coast*; Bigfoot/Sasquatch FAQ, http://home.nycap.rr.com/wwilliams/BigfootFAQ.html.

Bigfoot Research Project Founded in 1992 by veteran HOMINID researcher PETER BYRNE, with headquarters at Mount Hood, Oregon, the BRP was funded by private donations and a grant from the ACADEMY OF APPLIED SCIENCES to conduct field research on BIGFOOT. At one point, the project reportedly had four 4-wheel-drive vehicles, a snowmobile and two helicopters equipped with infrared tracking equipment on 24-hour standby. Refunding was declined in 1997, with Byrne explaining to reporters, "They were disappointed with the extent of our findings, and they felt that we had spent enough money." Most of the BRP's staff (minus Byrne) transferred to the NORTH AMERICAN SCIENCE INSTITUTE.

Source: "Bigfoot research project ends." *Skeptic* 5 (1997): 28; "Bigfoot investigation is alive and well." *Fortean Times* 93 (December 1996), http://www.forteantimes.com/articles/093_bigfoot.shtml.

Bighoot *see* **Owls (Giant)**

Bili Apes/Bondo Ape In 1900 or 1908 (accounts differ), two APES of uncertain species were shot near a place called Bondo, in the Bili Forest of the northern Congo. Their crested skulls, and two others subsequently found in native villages, were unusual enough for zoologists of the era to consider them a new subspecies (*Gorilla gorilla uellensis*, after the Uele River), but no further information on those primates emerged from Africa during the next 90 years. In 1996, Swiss wildlife photographer Karl Ammann launched a 4-year search for the Bili or Bondo apes, collecting native reports of two separate CHIMPANZEE species inhabiting the region.

Normal chimps (*Pan troglodytes*) are known to Bili Forest hunters as "tree beaters," easily slain, while a larger breed of "lion killers" avoid human trackers with superior speed and evasive maneuvers. In March 2001, collaborating with an expedition mounted by National Geographic Radio, Ammann found another crested skull and several ape nests, complete with feces and hair samples. DNA analysis of that evidence suggests that the donors were not GORILLAS after all, but rather CHIMPANZEES, "perhaps of an unknown subspecies."

Sources: Karl Ammann, "The Bondo mystery apes." *The Economist* (17 October 2002); John Roach, "Elusive African apes: Giant chimps or new

species?" *National Geographic News* (14 April 2003); "Scientists hunt for 'mystery ape.'" *CNN Sunday Morning* (3 February 2002).

Bille, Matthew A. (1959–) Matthew Bille holds degrees in public administration and space systems management from the University of Southern California, Webster University and the University of North Dakota. He served 12 years as a U.S.

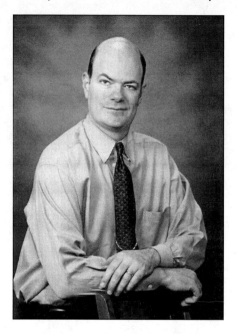

Cryptozoologist Matthew Bille.

Air Force officer before returning to civilian life in 1994 and settling at Colorado Springs, Colorado. There, he spent seven years with the nonprofit research firm ANSER before joining the consulting firm Booz Allen Hamilton in 2001. Bille is also a freelance science writer, specializing in topics that range from aerospace technology and the history of space exploration to cryptozoology. In the latter field, he edited the quarterly newsletter *Exotic Zoology* from 1994 to 1999.

His first book-length work on cryptozoology, *Rumors of Existence*, was published in 1995. His forthcoming books include a sequel, *Shadows of Existence*, and two volumes on the history of space exploration co-authored with satellite engineer Erika Lishock. Bille has also published many articles on space history, policy and technology. He is an active member of the American Institute of Aeronautics and Astronautics, the Colorado-Wyoming Academy of Science, the National Association of Science Writers, and the Science Writers Association of the Rocky Mountains.

Source: Matt Bille, http://hometown.aol.com/mattwriter/.

Billiwack Monster BIGFOOT-type HOMINIDS are less common in southern California than throughout the Pacific Northwest, but the region is not without its share of reports. One persistent source of sightings, in the mid-20th century, was Aliso Canyon, located west of Santa Paula in Ventura County, on the southern edge of the Los Padres National Forest. For over 20 years, local residents reported encounters with a tall, hairy biped whose fingers were tipped with sharp claws.

The Billiwack Monster was named for an early sighting at the abandoned Billiwack Dairy, closed in 1943 after its owner mysteriously vanished. In 1964, a group of hikers told police that the creature had stalked and terrorized them over a period of several hours.

Sources: Mike Marinacci, *Mysterious California*. Los Angeles: Pan-pipes Press, 1988; Richard Senate, *Ghosts of the Haunted Coast*. Ventura, CA: Pathfinder Publishing, 1986.

Billy Holler Booger This BIGFOOT-type HOMINID or NORTH AMERICAN APE was reported by residents of northern Georgia's Lumpkin County in summer 1974. The last reported sighting occurred on 2 September, when three campers at Blackburn State Park, near Dahlongea, saw an 8-foot-tall biped feeding from garbage bins in the predawn hours.

Source: Bord and Bord, *The Bigfoot Casebook*.

Bilungi This large unclassified primate or HOMINID reportedly inhabits the jungle surrounding Lac Tumba, in the Democratic Republic of Congo. Witnesses describe the creature as six feet tall, broad-chested, tailless and covered in brown hair.

Source: Heuvelmans. *Les Bêtes Humaines d'Afrique.*

Bindernagel, John A. (1941–) Wildlife biologist John Bindernagel dates his interest in BIGFOOT from 1963, when he was a third-year student in wildlife management at the University of Guelph in Ontario, Canada. Exposure to stories of the elusive creatures sparked a fascination with unknown HOMINIDS, followed by active field work after Bindernagel moved his family to British Columbia in 1975.

Thirteen years later, Bindernagel and his wife found several SASQUATCH footprints near their home on Vancouver Island and preserved them as plaster casts. The same year saw publication of Bindernagel's book *North America's Great Ape: The Sasquatch*. He continues field work in the Pacific Northwest and is an honorary member of the TEXAS BIGFOOT RESEARCH CENTER. In January 2004, Bindernagel announced a foray into CRYPTOTOURISM, inviting customers to join him on an environment-friendly BigFoot Safari.

Source: BigFoot Safari, http://www.bigfootsafari.com/bigfoot/; North America's Great Ape: The Sasquatch, http://www.bigfootbiologist.org/.

Birds (Giant) Folklore and mythology are replete tales of giant birds, including the Roc of Madagascar and the Indian Ocean, Scandinavia's KUNGSTORN, the PIASA of Illinois, and the THUNDERBIRDS memorialized by various Native American tribes. The largest living bird known to science is the Andean condor (*Vultur gryphus*), with a body length exceeding 4 feet and a record wingspan of 10 feet 6 inches. North America's reigning giant is the California condor (*Gymnogyps californianus*), with an official maximum wingspan of 9 feet 4 inches. The harpy eagle (*Harpia harpyja*) of Latin America boasts a wingspan approaching 10 feet, while Africa's largest bird, the white-backed vulture (*Gyps africanus*), boasts a record span of 7 feet 10 inches. The golden eagle of North America and Europe does not officially exceed a 7-foot wingspan.

Author Roger Caras notes, in *Dangerous to Man* (1975), that "the stories about eagles carrying off human babies, and even small children, are absolutely endless." Still, modern ornithologists deny the reality of such reports, as well as eyewitness accounts of truly giant birds reported from around the world. A partial list of those sightings includes the following:

12 July 1763— A German couple left their 3-year-old daughter unattended while cutting grass in a mountain meadow and returned to find her missing. Searchers followed the child's cries to a peak 1,400 feet away, where they found her suffering from gashes on one arm. She claimed that an eagle had snatched her, and members of the search party reported a "huge" bird circling over the spot.

1868— A less fortunate child, Marie Delex, was reportedly snatched and killed by an eagle in the French Alps.

1868— A similar incident occurred in Tippah County, Mississippi, where 8-year-old Jemmie Kenney was snatched from a schoolyard by a "large eagle," dying when the bird dropped him from a great height. Previously, local farmers had complained of eagles taking pigs, lambs and other barnyard animals.

1870— A black "monster bird, something like [a] condor" landed on James Pepples's barn at Stanford, Kentucky. Pepples shot the bird and captured it alive, reporting that its wingspan measured 7 feet. The fate of that specimen is unknown.

1895— Ten-year-old Landy Junkins vanished in the woods near Bergoo, West Virginia. The child was never found, but locals soon reported a "huge eagle" nesting atop nearby Snaggle Tooth Knob. A link between those sightings and the disappearance was assumed, but never proved.

1898— A native guide for explorer Stephen Bagge reported seeing several black birds "as large as sheep" in Uganda's Ruwenzori Range, south of Mount Speke, at an elevation of about 9,000 feet.

July 1910— French witnesses saw a large, black "bird-like object" plunge into the sea off the Normandy coast. They watched and waited, but it did not surface.

July 1925— Two climbers in Alberta's Canadian Rockies observed what they took for an eagle, circling a peak at 7,500 feet. As it approached, they realized the brown bird was much larger than a normal eagle, and that it carried an animal clutched in its claws. Their shouts caused it to drop the carcass of a 15-pound fawn.

5 June 1932— Svanhild Hansen, a 5-year-old child weighing 42 pounds, was snatched by a large bird on the Norwegian island of Neka, then dropped alive on a high mountain ledge.

1940— Pennsylvania writer Robert Lyman Sr. saw a huge bird sitting in the road near Coudersport. As he approached, it flew into some nearby woods, revealing a 20-foot wingspan. Three decades later, writing of the Keystone State's Thunderbird population, Lyman claimed "their present home is in the southern edge of the Black Forest....All reports for the past 20 years have come from that area. Thunderbirds are not a thing of the past. They are with us today, but few will believe it except those who see them."

27 February 1954— Gladie Bills and her daughter observed what they took for six jet fighter planes performing low-altitude maneuvers near Hillsboro, Oregon. Closer observation via telescope revealed the objects to be giant birds with glossy white wings.

27 March 1957— Witness Hiram Cranmer saw a grayish-colored bird with a wingspan of about 25–30 feet flying over Renovo, Pennsylvania. Local sightings then continued for the next three weeks.

6 December 1966— A mail carrier at Marysville, Kentucky reported seeing a giant bird in flight along his route. On the same day, MOTHMAN was sighted in Point Pleasant, West Virginia.

11 January 1967— Point Pleasant's famous cryptid faced competition with reports of a bird "the size of a small airplane" flapping around town.

July 1968— David St. Albans saw a giant bird fly over a cornfield

A golden eagle attacks in California, circa 1870.

at Keeneyville, Illinois. He described it as black, with a bare head and neck, and white tufts at the point where its neck joined the body.

1969— The wife of Clinton County, Pennsylvania sheriff John Boyle watched a gray bird land near the family's cabin on Little Pine Creek. She later said, "Its wingspread appeared to be as wide as the streambed, which I would say was about 75 feet." In summer of this year, three men claimed they saw a huge bird snatch a 15-pound fawn at nearby Kettle Creek.

28 October 1970— Several motorists reported a "gigantic winged creature" flying over the highway west of Jersey Shore, Pennsylvania. Witness Judith Dingler told reporters, "It was dark colored, and its wingspread was almost like [that of] an airplane."

Summer 1971— While driving through Mansfield, Massachusetts at a point ironically called Bird Hill, police sergeant Thomas Downey sighted a bird more than 6 feet tall, with a wingspan of 8–12 feet. Fellow officers thereafter ridiculed Downey by calling him "Bird Man."

31 March 1973— Joseph and Wanda Kaye were driving near the Oregon Hill ski area in Pennsylvania's Lycoming County, when they saw a huge black bird take wing from the roadside.

1975— Puerto Rican witnesses reported a "whitish-colored gigantic condor or vulture" circling and shrieking around the sites where farm animals were found slaughtered.

1975— Witnesses at Mount Adams, Washington reported sightings of a brown bird seven feet tall.

October 1975— A bird with a 15-foot wingspan and a "head like a vulture" was seen flying over Walnut Creek, California and perched on a rooftop at nearby East Bay.

1 January 1976— A black bird more than 5 feet tall, with red eyes and a 6-inch beak, was reported by two children from a plowed field near Harlingen, Texas. Sightings along the Rio Grande valley continued for the next two months, including a report from three teachers who saw a bird with a wingspan of 15–20 feet flying near San Antonio. Descriptions of the flying creatures varied. Some witnesses compared the beasts to PTEROSAURS, while researcher MARK HALL insists that they were giant BATS.

Spring 1977— Schoolteachers Sue Howell and Debbie Wright saw a bird described as "very dark, with a huge beak," near Drocker's Woods while driving toward Du Bois, Pennsylvania.

25 July 1977— Two huge birds attacked three children playing in a yard at Lawndale, Illinois. One of the birds lifted 10-year-old Marlon Lowe 2 feet off the ground and carried him 40 feet before the cries of approaching spectators caused it to drop him.

December 1977— A woman driving to work in Beason, Illinois was frightened by a man-sized bird standing in the road. LOREN COLEMAN reports that a group of men rushed to the site, killed the bird and burned its body, leaving no remains for study.

September 1982— Sightings of a "monster bird" or "flying DINOSAUR" were reported from the Yorkshire, England communities of Eldwick, Pudsey, Shipley Glen and Thackley.

1985— Italian farmer Gianpiero Balzi reported finding giant bird's footprints on his property at Brescia, near Milan. He described the tracks as being "in the exact shape of a chicken footprint, but enormous, as if some gigantic bird had swooped down, landed and then taken off again." Each print, he said, was 8 feet long and 5 feet wide, separated by a 16-foot stride. Balzi told reporters, "We are protecting the prints until experts arrive," but they never came.

September 1986— Three children reported a huge bird flying low over Crete's Asteroussia Mountains. Their description of its batlike wings leads some researchers to suggest it may have been a living pterosaur.

July 1993- Three members of the Fisher family reported a bird resembling an oversized eagle flying near Larry's Creek, Pennsylvania.

1994— Author Joseph Citro reported the undated sighting of a giant bird at Shelburne, Wisconsin. The unnamed witness glanced through her kitchen window to see the creature standing in her yard. It was 3–4 feet tall, with a long neck resembling a vulture's, and revealed a wingspan of 8–10 feet when it flew into some nearby woods.

23 April 1995— Reynaldo Ortega saw a bird 3–4 feet tall perched atop his roof in Naranjito, Puerto Rico. It had a thick neck, "piercing" eyes, and a muzzle resembling a WOLF'S in place of a beak.

September 1995— A resident of Weston, Massachusetts sighted a flying object which he initially mistook for a man in a hangglider. Moments later, he realized the creature was "a giant eagle-like bird with black eagle-like wings and some white colors, with a head resembling that of an eagle." Its wingspan was "at least 20 feet," while its body was "the size of an adult human." Based on size, he estimated the bird's weight at 175–200 pounds.

6 July 2000— Robin Swope saw a dark-gray bird with a wingspan of 15–17 feet flying over the Erie County Memorial Gardens, outside Erie, Pennsylvania.

13 June 2001— A resident of Greenville, Pennsylvania saw a bird "the size of a small airplane" land in a tree 300 yards from his home. It had dark brown or black plumage and a 15-foot wingspan. It remained in place for 15–20 minutes before departing.

Artist's depiction of attack on Marlon Lowe, 1977 (*William Rebsamen*).

25 September 2001— Witness Mark Felice saw a bird with a wingspan of 10–15 feet, flying at an altitude of 50–60 feet above Route 119, near South Greensburg, Pennsylvania. During a 90-second observation, it also landed briefly in a nearby tree.

26 September 2001— Several witnesses in Wyoming County, Pennsylvania reported sightings of two black birds, each 6 feet tall at rest, with reported 12-foot wingspans.

October 2001— While searching for their lost dog, two residents of New Wilmington, Pennsylvania saw a "huge grayish-white like bird" with a wingspan of 13–16 feet swoop low above their car and land in a nearby tree. In flight, it seemed to have unusually long legs that "dangled like a man's legs."

15 October 2002— The *Anchorage Daily News* announced sightings of a bird twice the size of a normal eagle, winging about the remote villages of Manoikotak and Togiak in southwestern Alaska. Witness Moses Coupchiak mistook the creature for a small airplane at first, while pilot John Bouker estimated its wingspan at 14 feet. Phil Shemf, a spokesman for the U.S. Fish and Wildlife Service in Juneau, told reporters, "As far as we know, nothing with a 14-foot wingspan has been alive for the last 100,000 years or so."

As far as we know. But huge birds of prey known as teratorns (Family *Teratornithinae*) did exist from Late Miocene to the Pleistocene times. The largest species yet discovered, known from fos-

sil remains in Argentina, was *Argentavis magnificens*. It stood 5–6 feet tall at rest, with a wingspan of 23–25 feet. Although presumed extinct for some 5 million years, that giant had more recent kin in North America. *Teratornis incredibilis*, a native of California and Nevada, boasted a 19-foot wingspan, while the smaller *T. merriami* had a 12-foot 6-inch wingspan and tipped the scales around 36 pounds. Cryptozoologists speculate that a relict population of such giants may survive in certain wilderness areas of the Americas, and perhaps on other continents as well.

Sources: "Alaska's big bird." *Fortean Times* 166 (February 2003): 6; Angela Barnes, "The hills are alive…with weird stories of ghosts, UFOs, fairies and flying dinosaurs." *Leeds Today* (23 June 2003); Bord and Bord, *Unexplained Mysteries of the 20th Century*; Citro, *Green Mountain Ghosts, Ghouls & Unsolved Mysteries*; Coleman, *Mysterious America*; Garner, *Monster! Monster!*; Hall, *Thunderbirds*; Keel, *The Complete Guide to Mysterious Beings*; Robert Lyman Sr., *Amazing Indeed!* Coudersport, PA: Potter Enterprise, 1973; Gerald Musinsky, "Return of the Thunderbird: Avian mystery of the Black Forest." *Fate* 48 (November 1995): 48–51; John Preston, *Tracking the Moon*. London: Mandarin, 1990; Karl Shuker, "Alien zoo." *Fortean Times* 103 (October 1997): 15; Bob F., Amazing Thunderbird Sighting, http://paranormal.about.com/library/blstory_july03_15.htm.

Bir-Sindic   Reports of this unclassified primate issue from the Indian state of Assam. Witnesses describe an APE closely resembling an orangutan (*Pongo pygmaeus*), though none of that Indonesian species are presently believed to inhabit the Asian mainland. However, orangutan fossils from the Pliocene period have been found in Laos, Vietnam and southern China, prompting cryptozoologists to argue that some of the creatures may yet survive in remote mainland hideaways. Alternate names for the Bir-sindic include Olo-banda and Iu-wun (in neighboring Myanmar).

Source: Heuvelmans, "Annotated checklist of apparently unknown animals with which cryptozoology is concerned."

Bis-Cobra   Despite its common name, suggestive of a SNAKE, reports from northern India describe this cryptic reptile as a lizard armed with venom equivalent in strength to that of 20 cobras. Worse yet, the Bis-cobra can allegedly spit venom with deadly accuracy, thus blinding its victims from a distance. The only venomous lizards presently known on Earth are the Gila monster (*Heloderma suspectum*) and the beaded lizard (*H. horridum*), found in the southwestern U.S. and northern Mexico. Neither is a spitter, and their painful bites are rarely fatal to human adults.

Source: Shuker, *From Flying Toads to Snakes with Wings*.

Bitarr *see* **Junjadee**

Black Annis   This legendary MYSTERY MAULER of Britain, commemorated in an 18th-century poem, was an ill-defined black creature armed with long talons, said to spring upon its victims from overhanging trees and drink their blood. Skeptics dismiss it as entirely mythical, but some researchers believe Black Annis was an early specimen of ALIEN BIG CAT. Their view is partially supported by the fact that later tales dubbed the creature Cat Annis.

Source: Shuker, *Mystery Cats of the World*.

Black Beast of Inkerberrow   This ALIEN BIG CAT of Gloucestershire, England is one of a relative few that have attacked human beings. It was initially reported during 1993, when residents of Inkerberrow, near Reddich, reported sightings of a large "black panther." Researchers Nick and Sally Dyke went searching for the creature in December, leaving bait in St. Peter's churchyard and prowling the woods with flashlights after sundown. Their second night on the hunt brought more adventure than they bargained for, when Nick stepped on the CAT and it bowled him over, leaping toward Sally and slashing her side with its claws before it escaped. Despite several layers of cold-weather clothing, she suffered three 5-inch scratches across her right side that required months to heal. Police reported other sightings, and the same beast may have killed a goat at Strenham, north of Tewksbury, although the evidence was not preserved for scientific study.

Source: Sieveking, "Beasts in our midst"; Some Recent Sightings of the Beast(s) of Gloucester, http://www.deville.demon.co.uk/glosabc.htm.

Black Beast of South Derbyshire   Witnesses describe this ALIEN BIG CAT as a "black panther." It was reported during 1997 from various sites in South Derbyshire, England, including Hartshorne, Measham and Moira. The heaviest concentration of sightings occurred near Overseal, at an old pipeworks on the A444 motorway. The third time it was seen at that location, a witness followed the CAT'S pawprints into dense shrubbery, where he lost his quarry but found several RABBITS partially buried, their heads bitten off.

Source: "Cats in the hats." Fortean Times 111 (June 1998).

Black Lake, Canada   Author Betty Garner reports that a serpentine LAKE MONSTER 20–30 feet long was sighted at Black Lake, Québec in 1894 and again in 1896. Curiously, research for this volume revealed that while Black Lakes exist in five Canadian provinces (British Columbia, Newfoundland, Ontario, Prince Edward Island and Saskatchewan), there is no lake by that name in Québec. There is, however, a *town* named Black Lake in Québec, and a nearby river feeds LAC WILLIAMS, where large cryptids have also been seen.

Sources: Garner, *Monster! Monster!*; Meurger and Gagnon, *Lake Monster Traditions*.

Black Panthers *see* **Cougars (Melanistic)**

Black River, New York   In 1951, witnesses reported a large cryptid swimming in this river of northwestern New York. They described the creature as 15 feet long, dark brown in color, with a serpentine body, visible fins, and "eyes like silver dollars." No subsequent sightings are recorded.

Source: Garner, *Monster! Monster!*

Blancou, Lucien (n.d.-)   From 1930 onward, Lucien Blancou served his nation's civil service in French Equatorial Africa (including the present-day nations of Chad, Gabon, the Central African Republic and the Republic of Congo). In 1949–53 he served as the colony's chief game inspector, while penning various articles on natural history. He was among the first Western authors to record native reports and observations of such cryptids as the BADIGUI, EMELA-NTOUKA and PYGMY ELEPHANT. Blancou also carried on a long-term correspondence with BERNARD HEUVELMANS, contributing significant material to Heuvelmans's first book, *On the Track of Unknown Animals* (1958). A year later, Blancou became the first author to use the term "cryptozoology" in print, when he dedicated his *Cynergetic Geography of the World* to "Bernard Heuvelmans, master of cryptozoology."

Sources: Lucien Blancou, *Géographie Cynégétique du Monde*. Paris: Presses Universitaires de France, 1959; Lucien Blancou, "Notes sur les mammifères de l'Equateur Africain Français: Un rhinocéros de fôret?" *Mammalia* 18 (December 1954): 358–363; Heuvelmans, *On the Track of Unknown Animals*; Mackal, *A Living Dinosaur?*

B'lian   Natives of southern peninsular Malaysia describe the B'lian as an unclassified jungle-dwelling HOMINID or WILDMAN. It differs scarcely, if at all, from other hominids of the same region, including the HANTU SAKAI and MAWAS, and on balance there is no clear reason to consider them a separate species.

Source: Heuvelmans, "Annotated checklist of apparently unknown animals with which cryptozoology is concerned."

Block Ness Monster   In June 1996, fishermen Gary Hall and J.T. Pinney netted a strange specimen near Block Island, 14 miles off the Rhode Island coast. The 13-foot serpentine carcass was badly decomposed, revealing a skeletal spine with no ribs, attached to a narrow head with empty eye sockets and "weird whiskers." Hall and Pinney hauled their catch to Block Island, where it was displayed for two days on the waterfront, then transferred for safekeeping to the summer home of part-time island resident Lee Scott, a New York State park biologist. Unable to identify the creature, Scott placed it in his freezer, pending delivery to the National Marine Fisheries Service in Narragansett, Rhode Island. When Gary Hall arrived to pick up the carcass and place it aboard the mainland ferry, however, Scott found that it had been stolen by persons unknown. It remains missing today, while researchers speculate on the creature's identity. Some suggest that it was a decomposed basking shark (*Cetorhinus maximus*), but Scott countered by noting that the animal's snout was 12 inches long, compared to a 6-inch norm in basking sharks. He proposed a new species of shark, as yet unknown to science, but without the evidence no final solution is possible. Locals, meanwhile, enjoyed a brisk trade in T-shirts advertising their here-and-gone cryptid as the Block Ness Monster.

Sources: "Good month for monster hunters." Fortean Times 95 (February 1997): 18; Janet Kerlin, "Block Island shrouded by mystery of the deep." USA Today (27 June 1996).

Blossom sea serpent   Details are lamentably sparse for this SEA SERPENT sighting in the South Atlantic. Recalling it long after the fact, Capt. Frederick Beechey, a surveyor for the Royal Navy, could only say that it took place sometime between 1825 and 1828, while he was in transit from Britain to the South Pacific aboard the *Blossom*. No description of the animal or the precise location where Beechey saw it are available today. Nonetheless, BERNARD HEUVELMANS opined in 1968 that the creature was one of his hypothetical sea serpents, either the "long-necked" species or the "super EEL."

Source: Heuvelmans, *In the Wake of the Sea Serpents*.

Blue Lakes, California   The small Blue Lakes are located in northern California's Lake County. Upper Blue Lake covers 73 acres, while Lower Blue Lake spans 52. In 1870–71, a 20-foot LAKE MONSTER resembling a DRAGON was reported from the lakes, but no moderns sightings are on file.

Source: Hector Lee, *Heroes, Villains and Ghosts: Folklore of Old California*. Santa Barbara: Capra Press, 1984.

Blue Mountain Lion *see* **Warrigal**

Blue Mountains Cryptid Research   The BMRC was a self-described "small group of people dedicated to the search for and study of a cryptic APE/ relict HOMINID species" known as YOWIE in the Blue Mountains of New South Wales, Australia.

The same region has also produced many sightings of ALIEN BIG CATS and THYLACINES. Identified members of the group included Michael Hallett, David McBean and Mick Meskers, supported by an unnamed cast of "silent locals." The BMRC's Internet website suggests that the group was organized in early 2001, while the absence of updates since April 2002 indicates that it may now be defunct.

Source: Blue Mountains Cryptid Research, http://members.ozemail.com.au/~mhallett/.

Blue-Nosed Frog

In July 1997, while visiting an animal fair at Newton Abbot, in Devon, England, Jonathan Downes of the CENTRE FOR FORTEAN ZOOLOGY found several curious frogs on sale. Each had a blue spot on its nose that glowed in the dark. The vendor claimed that the luminous amphibians came from the West African nation of Cameroon. Downes declined to pay the asking price of £25 each, and only later learned that no such species is known to modern science. Subsequent attempts to trace the owner and the animals have thus far been fruitless.

Source: Karl Shuker, "Menagerie of mystery." *Strange Magazine* 19 (Spring 1998): 23.

Blue sea serpent

On 12 May 1964, crewmen aboard the *Blue Sea* sighted what they first believed to be a whale, 30 miles south of Round Shoal buoy, off the coast of Nantucket, Massachusetts. Drawing closer, the sailors recognized their mistake. The SEA SERPENT they later described was at least 50 feet long, with several large humps on its back and "a blowhole in the top of the ALLIGATOR-like head." It seemed to "skim along the top of the water" at nine miles per hour before it submerged and disappeared. BERNARD HEUVELMANS considered the creature a probable specimen of his hypothetical "merhorse," while author J.P. O'Neill omits the case entirely from her survey of New England sea serpents.

Sources: Heuvelmans, *In the Wake of the Sea Serpents*; O'Neill, *The Great New England Sea Serpent*.

Blueberry Hill Monster

In 1964, while building Pretty Boy Dam outside Parkton, in northern Maryland's Baltimore County, workmen saw an unknown hairy HOMINID or NORTH AMERICAN APE emerge from the surrounding woods. Locals nicknamed the BIGFOOT-type creature after a nearby landmark.

Source: Bord and Bord, *The Bigfoot Casebook*.

Bnahua *see* Abnauayu

Bobo

On 7 November 1946, a curious creature appeared off the coast of Cape San Martin, California. The witnesses, a group of Portuguese fishermen, reported that the creature had a face resembling a GORILLA'S. They called it Bobo, which in Portuguese means "silly." Some authors treat Bobo as synonymous with another SEA SERPENT, the OLD MAN OF MONTEREY BAY, 50 miles farther north. Both locations lie within California's Monterey Bay National Marine Sanctuary.

Sources: Heuvelmans, *In the Wake of the Sea Serpents*; Reinstedt, *Mysterious Sea Monsters of California's Central Coast*.

Bohpoli *see* Nalusa Falaya

Boiling Water Lake, Canada

Aboriginal folklore cites this small lake, located south of Fort Fraser, British Columbia as a habitat of giant FISH. Research conducted for this volume in various gazetteers found no such lake listed in Canada.

Source: Diamond Jenness, "Myths of the Carrier Indians of British Columbia." *Journal of American Folklore* 47 (1934): 97, 256.

Bokyboky/Votsosoke

Natives of southwestern Madagascar describe the Bokyboky as a broad-faced civet the size of a mature domestic CAT. It preys on SNAKES, which it allegedly kills by backing up to their burrows and suffocating the reptiles with a kind of lethal flatulence. Skeptics suggest that the creature is actually a narrow-striped mongoose (*Mungotictus decemlineata*), which kills snakes by the more conventional means of biting through their necks.

Source: Burney and Ramilisonina, "The *Kilopilopitsofy, Kidoky*, and *Bokyboky*."

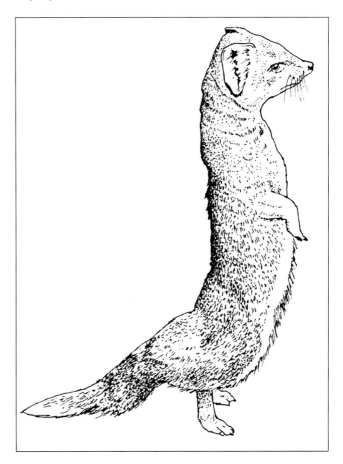

Witnesses describe the Bokyboky as an unknown mongoose with lethal flatulence.

Bolam Lake Yeti

In November 2002, hikers reported encounters with an unknown HOMINID at Bolam Lake Country Park in Northumberland, England. Witnesses described the YETI-type creature as a hairy biped, 7–8 feet tall and heavyset, with prominent teeth and fluorescent eyes. British cryptozoologist Jonathan Downes led members of the CENTRE FOR FORTEAN ZOOLOGY to Bolam Lake in January 2003 and reported a near-miss personal encounter with some hulking thing that crashed through trees and undergrowth, fleeing before their headlights. The team collected three sets of hair samples, but two were lost in the mail, while the third apparently belonged to a small carnivore. (Experts could not agree if they were CAT or dog hairs.) At the same time, however, CFZ investigators uncovered eyewitness reports predating the November flap by a full two years. That story had barely broken when skeptics weighed in with bad news. Two teenagers from Newcastle confessed to renting an ape suit and running amok in the Kielder Forest during summer 2002, but they denied any pranks at Bolam Lake. Ten days after that confession was published, local officials claimed the Bolam Lake Yeti was in fact an unidentified poacher, but they offered no evidence to prove their case.

Sources: "Bolam Lake Bigfoot, please lurch forward." *Hexham Courant* (14 February 2003); Jonathan Downes, "The big hairy monster of Bolam Lake." *Fortean Times* 169 (May 2003): 24–25; Ian Valentine, "Eight-foot Yeti sighting?" *Country Life* (24 January 2003); Zavian Friday, "In the footsteps of the Geordie Bigfoot." *Fortean Times* (5 February 2003), http://www.forteantimes.co.uk/exclusive/geordiefoot.*shtml.*

Bonita sea serpents

On 25 August 1910, the *Gloucester* [Massachusetts] *Times* reported New England's latest SEA SERPENT sighting as follows:

The captain of the fishing steamer *Bonita*, which arrived at Portland [Maine] on Monday with 100 barrels of sardine herring, reports that when off the Brown Cow, just this side of Small Point, on Saturday last [20 August], he passed within 50 yards of an immense sea serpent, apparently 80 to 90 feet in length, the color of the FISH being black with large white spots. The serpent was plainly visible for several minutes, and evidently has a penchant for the *Bonita*, as her captain was the first to see it in the summer of 1909.

The location described is in Maine's Casco Bay, off Portland. No location was offered for the sighting in 1909.

Source: O'Neill, *The Great New England Sea Serpent.*

Booaa

The Booaa of Senegal is said to be a large, unclassified species of hyena, named for the sound of its eerie nocturnal cry. The beast's aggressive temperament suggests that it may be a western version of East Africa's predatory NANDI BEAR.

Source: Shuker, "Death birds and dragonets."

The Booaa of Senegal is said to be a large unclassified hyena.

Boobrie

This large BIRD reported sporadically from the Scottish Highlands is generally described as a loon (Family *Gaviidae*) of exaggerated proportions. Witnesses claim its neck is 3 feet long and its beak measures 18 inches or more. It stands on short black legs and its feet possess both claws and webbing. However, some accounts describe the Boobrie's beak as resembling an eagle's, which bears no resemblance to the straight, pointed beak of a loon. Likewise, the largest known loons reach a total length of 36 inches at maturity.

Source: John Campbell, *Popular Tales of the West Highlands.* Edinburgh: Edmonston and Douglas, 1862.

Booger

This term was once used as a synonym for "ghost,"

primarily in the southern U.S., but it is also generically applied to various cryptids, ranging as far north as Indiana. The Booger Dogs of Arkansas are one example, combining supernatural elements with modern accounts of MYSTERY MAULERS. Since 1960, the "booger" label has been used more selectively for BIGFOOT-type HOMINIDS in various locations. Some examples include:

Alabama: Residents of Chilton County organized hunting parties to stalk a local Booger, described as resembling "a giant APE" that prowled the swamps along Walnut Creek, near Clanton, in 1960–61. The beast raided local orchards for peaches and uttered nocturnal cries "like a woman screaming." The Rev. E.C. Hand complained that his hunting dogs would not pursue the creature, whose footprint cast in concrete was "about the size of a person's foot but looking more like a hand."

Florida: Reports of a lurking SKUNK APE are old news in the Sunshine State, but newspaper reports from March 1972 reveal that commercial fishermen in Dade County also know the creatures as "buggers."

Georgia: Neighbors of the Okefenokee Swamp, in southeastern Georgia's Charlton and Clinch Counties, report that large apes known as Boogers inhabit the region, competing for space with another hairy hominid known as the PIG MAN. Farther north, in Lumpkin County, hunters pursued the elusive BILLY HOLLER BOOGER in September 1974.

Indiana: A shaggy, 10-foot-tall Booger Man terrorized residents of Pike County in August 1970, seen repeatedly around Petersburg and Winslow. Witnesses reported that the massive creature could run at speed approaching 60 miles per hour.

Kentucky: In the state's eastern counties, large bipedal creatures are sometimes called Bear Boogers, though witnesses describe beasts resembling SASQUATCH.

Sources: Frederic Cassidy, ed., *Dictionary of American Regional English.* Cambridge, MA: Harvard University Press, 1985; Christopher Coleman, *Strange Tales of the Dark and Bloody Ground.* Nashville, TN: Rutledge Hill, 1988; Graham, "Monsters of the Ozarks"; Green, *Sasquatch: The Apes Among Us*; Keel, *The Complete Guide to Mysterious Beings*; Having a Gas in Okefenokee Swamp, http://www.wired.com/news/roadtrip/0,2640,61284,00.*html.*

Borneo sea serpent

Sometime in 1890, a Singapore ship's pilot identified only as Mr. Mustard allegedly sighted a 45-foot SEA SERPENT off the coast of Borneo, Indonesia. No further details of the sighting are available. The case was not reported until 14 September 1903, and then only in the sketchiest of terms.

Source: Heuvelmans, *In the Wake of the Sea Serpents.*

Borrego Sink, California

For 60-odd years, campers and prospectors in this region of southern California's San Diego County have reported close encounters with unidentified shaggy bipeds resembling red-eyed, albino APES. Sometimes dubbed Sandmen, in homage to the ABOMINABLE SNOWMAN of the Himalayas, these unknown HOMINIDS or NORTH AMERICAN APES were first reported in 1938. Other reports were filed in 1964 and 1967, with the 1964 account including reference to humanoid footprints 14 inches long and 9 inches wide at the instep.

Sources: Mike Marinacci, *Mysterious California.* Los Angeles: Panpipes Press, 1988; Smith, *Strange Abominable Snowmen.*

Bossburg Tracks

Bossburg is a small town in northeastern Washington's Stevens County, midway between Colville and the Canadian border. On 24 November 1969, Colville butcher Joseph Rhodes found a peculiar set of SASQUATCH footprints in the soft soil surrounding Bossburg's community garbage dump. The left foot measured 17.5 inches long and was 6.5 inches wide at the ball; the right foot was crooked or "clubbed," a full inch shorter than the left and 7 inches wide across the ball. Both feet measured 5.5 inches wide at the heel. Local resident and BIG-FOOT hunter IVAN MARX began tracking the creature, while word of the find reached JOHN GREEN in neighboring British Columbia. Green, in turn, alerted colleague RENÉ DAHINDEN, who rushed south to join in the hunt. Dahinden found all but two footprints obliterated by human traffic. Those two, one representing each foot, were preserved under cardboard boxes. Dahinden photographed both and prepared plaster casts to preserve them for study. ROBERT TITMUS soon arrived and laid out bait in hopes of luring the creature within rifle range, but the trap got no takers.

On 13 December, Marx and Dahinden found an astounding new trail of 1,089 footprints in snow along Roosevelt Lake, near Grand Coolie Dam. Measurements and the right foot's deformity perfectly matched the original Bossburg tracks. At one point, the Sasquatch stepped over a 43-inch barbed-wire fence, then apparently paused to relieve itself and marked the trail with urine-yellowed snow. (In those days before DNA testing existed, the critical evidence was not collected.) Dahinden believed the footprints were no more than 15 hours old, but their maker eluded the hunters. Five days later, a U.S. Border Patrol officer found more "crippled" Sasquatch footprints on the far side of the Columbia River, again with no creature in evidence. Bigfoot hunters flocked to the vicinity, including Roger Patterson, producer of the still-controversial 1967 PATTERSON FILM. Ohio millionaire Tom Page bankrolled a hunt extending into January 1970, complete with snowmobiles, 4-wheel-drive vehicles and aerial searches, all in vain. In the midst of that furor, on 27 January, local prospector Joe Metlow claimed to have a severed Sasquatch foot in his freezer (viewable for a mere $5,000) and a "cream-colored" Bigfoot trapped in a cave at some undisclosed location, which he offered for sale to the highest bidder. Tom Page offered $55,000 before the HOAX was finally exposed. Ivan Marx rebounded from that charade in October 1970, announcing that he had captured the "Bossburg cripple" on film, but most viewers of his cinematic effort now regard it as another fraud.

As for the "crippled" prints, some experts still regard them as the best of Bigfoot's existence to date. GROVER KRANTZ studied Dahinden's casts in January 1970 and later wrote, "Before I examined these prints, I would have given you ten to one odds that the whole thing was a hoax. But there is no way that everything could have been tied together so perfectly in a fake." Primatologist JOHN NAPIER agreed, declaring: "It is very difficult to conceive of a hoaxer so subtle, so knowledgeable — and so sick — who would deliberately fake a footprint of this nature. I suppose it is possible, but it is so unlikely that I am prepared to discount it." John Green was more reserved, writing in 1978:

> Whether there ever was a [S]asquatch around Bossburg I'm sure that I don't know. It depends on whether Ivan [Marx] took over as producer before the curtain opened or half way through the third act. Whichever it was, he starred in the show from the first.

More than three decades after the fact, in May 2002, researcher DANIEL PEREZ added a new twist to the Bossburg story, claiming that several hairs of unknown origin — described as "thick and heavy and black" — were found where Bigfoot apparently straddled the barbed-wire fence in December 1969. The hairs have long since disappeared, if they ever existed, and we must note that

Unique footprints were found where a Sasquatch, dubbed the "Bossburg cripple," stepped across a fence (*William Rebsamen*).

Dahinden's account of the episode, published in 1973, mentions no such crucial evidence.

Sources: Coleman, *Bigfoot!*; Green, *Sasquatch: The Apes Among Us*; Hunter and Dahinden, *Sasquatch*; Krantz, *Big Footprints*; Napier, *Bigfoot*; Daniel Perez e-mail communication to Bigfoot newsgroup (10 May 2002).

***Boston* sea serpent**   On 13 March 1804, Captain George Little of the frigate *Boston* replied by letter to an inquiry from the Rev. Abraham Cummings, concerning reports of SEA SERPENT sightings along the coast of Maine. His letter, describing an event that occurred midway between Portland and Penobscot, read:

> In answer to yours of the 30th of January last, I observe that in May 1780 I was lying in Round Pond in Broad Bay, in a public armed ship. At sunrise, I discovered a large Serpent, or monster, coming down the Bay, on the surface of the water. The Cutter was manned and armed. I went myself in the boat and proceeded after the Serpent. When within a hundred feet, the marines were ordered to fire on him, but before they could make ready, the Serpent dove. He was not less than from 45 to 50 feet in length; the largest diameter of his body, I should judge, 15 inches; his head nearly the size of that of a man, which he carried four or five feet above the water. He wore every appearance of a common black SNAKE. When he dove he came up near Muscongus Island — we pursued him, but never came up within a quarter mile of him again. A monster of the above description was seen in the same place by Joseph Kent, of Marshfield, 1751. Kent said he was longer

and larger than the main boom of his sloop, which was 85 tons. He had a fair opportunity of viewing him, as he was within ten or twelve yards of his sloop.

Source: O'Neill, *The Great New England Sea Serpent.*

Botnvatnet, Norway   Ancient LAKE MONSTER traditions surround this lake, in Norway's Nordland County, but no modern cryptid sightings are on file.

Source: Erik Knatterud, Sea Serpents in Norwegian Lakes, http://www.mjoesormen.no.

Boulmer carcass   On 21 March 1961, a rotting GLOBSTER washed ashore at Boulmer, Northumberland, England. Locals speculated that it might prove to be an unidentified sea monster, but analysis of the remains identified the creature as a basking shark (*Cetorhinus maximus*).

Source: Heuvelmans, *In the Wake of the Sea Serpents.*

Bowen Harbour sea serpent   On 21 August 1934, the *North Queensland Register* reported a SEA SERPENT sighting at Bowen Harbour, on the coast of Queensland, Australia. The report read:

> A sea monster appeared in the Bowen Harbour this week. Mr. H. Hurst, a very well-known local fisherman, was making his way towards Bowen when he saw a dark object floating on the surface of the water, about two hundred yards away. The sea was dead calm at the time. He pointed it out to his two mates, C. Hunt and J. Ayles. At first they thought it was a whale as these have been fairly plentiful in these waters lately, but whilst they were approaching it suddenly lifted its head about eight feet out of the water, and the launch party called a halt.
>
> Mr. Hurst did not like the look of it at all. It appeared to be about thirty feet long and had a head like a large TURTLE just as has been described further north, and a body like a huge armoured horse. So they decided not to stop any longer, as they had no rifle on board, but went on to town. Mr. Hurst did not mention the incident at first, for fear of being disbelieved. When first seen the monster was between Sinclair Bay and Gloucester Passage, and was heading in the direction of Sinclair Bay.

Source: Smith, *Bunyips & Bigfoots.*

Bowness Lagoon, Canada   Calgary, Alberta's Bowness Lagoon is fed by the Bow River, a watercourse that rises from the Rocky Mountains and flows southeastward for 315 miles. In winter, the lagoon freezes over and is used as an outdoor ice-skating rink. In late July 1942, a creature resembling a huge CATFISH or EEL was sighted in Bowness Lagoon, but reports of its "capture" were decidedly premature. It remains unidentified today.

Sources: Grant MacEwan, "Marine monsters great boon to tourism." *Calgary Herald* (15 December 1984); "'Ogopogo' captured in Bowness Lagoon." *Calgary Herald* (30 July 1942).

Boyden Lake, Maine *see* **Wiwilámecq'**

Bozho   Bozho is a shortened version of the name Manabozho, applied by early Potawatomi tribesmen to a supernatural "trickster" or demon who played pranks on human beings. Today, the abbreviated name belongs to a supposed LAKE MONSTER residing in Madison, Wisconsin's Lake Mendota. Sightings of the creature date from 27 June 1883, when a huge green SNAKE allegedly menaced Billy Dunn and his wife on a boating excursion. The Dunns defended themselves by striking the beast with an oar and a hatchet when it tried to enter their boat. Thirty-four years later, in autumn 1917, a local fisherman reported a large serpentine creature swimming with its head and neck above water, off Picnic Point.

Source: Charles Brown, *Sea Serpents: Wisconsin Occurrences of These Weird Monsters.*

Bras d'Or Lake, Canada   Author Betty Garner reports that serpentine LAKE MONSTERS have been reported from these lakes on Nova Scotia's Cape Breton Island, but no dates or details of sightings are provided. She concluded that various unnamed witnesses probably glimpsed masses of EELS similar to those sometimes reported from LAKE AINSLIE.

Source: Garner, *Monster! Monster!*

Braxton Monster   This unclassified HOMINID or NORTH AMERICAN APE of Braxton County, West Virginia is known from a single sighting in December 1960. Witness Charles Stover was returning home from work, along a backwoods road near Hickory Flats, when he saw a 6-foot tall "monster, standing erect, with hair all over his face and body." The beast bore no resemblance to a red-face, 10-foot-tall creature reported from Flatwoods in 1952, though newspapers still lumped them both together as the Braxton Monster. No further sightings of the creature(s) are on file.

Sources: Bord and Bord, *The Bigfoot Casebook*; Green, *Sasquatch: The Apes Among Us.*

Bray Road Beast   Throughout the 1990s, residents of rural Walworth County, Wisconsin reported encounters with a menacing cryptid that lurked along Bray Road, east of Elkhorn. Lorianne Endrizzi was among the first witnesses, in autumn 1989. She described an animal resembling a large WOLF, crouched beside the highway as if feeding. Farmer Scott Bray saw a "strange-looking dog" on his property that October, while later witnesses reported a beast walking on its hind legs, snarling with a canine muzzle. Some claimed the creature had pursued them with malicious intent. On 31 October 1991, Doristine Gipson had a near-miss with the beast while parked along Bray Road, reporting that it slammed into her car's trunk as she sped away. HOAXES were suspected in some of the cases — Gipson's case, for instance had occurred on Halloween — while superstitious locals claimed the beast was a bona fide werewolf. Various "logical" explanations fell short of the mark, since coyotes (*Canis latrans*) are too small to match the beast's dimensions and gray wolves (*Canis lupus*) are presumably extinct throughout Wisconsin. Likewise, neither canid walks upright. A black bear (*Ursus americanus*) may do so on occasion, but they rarely trespass in Waltham County and none are full-time residents. Other suggestions include a BIGFOOT-type HOMINID or NORTH AMERICAN APE. In September 2003, researcher Linda Godfrey told the press, "I think that in the end, what we have come to call 'The Beast' may actually be a conglomeration of creatures and people's interpretations of them. On the other hand, many of the sightings were so compelling that it's hard to explain them rationally. It's arrogant to say we know all there is to know about this world. I guess I prefer just to live with the mystery."

Sources: Jackie Loohauis, "Beastly good story." Milwaukee Journal Sentinel (15 September 2003); Scarlet Sankey, "The Bray Road Beast: Wisconsin werewolf investigation." *Strange Magazine* 10 (Fall-Winter 1992): 19–21, 44–46.

Brazos River, Texas   On 23 May 1853, the *Burlington* (Vermont) *Free Press* ran the following story, which it attributed to a Texas newspaper, the *Columbia Democrat*:

> On Friday last, several of our citizens had a full view of a monster in our river, answering to the description of the SEA SERPENT. They

say it was from sixteen to eighteen feet long, with a large head resembling the ALLIGATOR. The circumference of its body near its head was about twenty-five or twenty-six inches, and its motions in the water were similar to those of a SNAKE. It moved with incredible swiftness, sometimes raising its body out of the water three or four feet at a time. When a mile below our town, his snakeship took a resting spell, and was seen plainly by a gentleman living immediately on the river. There can be no doubt that this individual is either a lineal descendant of the sea serpent, or in some way related to that monstrosity.

The former town of Columbia (now West Columbia) lies west of the Brazos in Brazoria County. Considering its place in Texas history—first meeting place of the Texas Republic's legislature, first seat of Brazoria County—it seems strange that reports of the dramatic cryptid sighting are known only from reports in far-off Vermont. Still, the alleged sighting location is only 30 miles inland from Freeport, where the Brazos meets the Gulf of Mexico.

Source: "From the past: Brazos River serpent." *North American Bio-Fortean Review* 3 (May 2001): 23.

Brentford Griffin   In ancient mythology, the griffin was a composite beast boasting an eagle's wings and head — often with horns — and the body of a LION. It was known as a fierce predator and man-eater, ranging from the Mediterranean through Central Asia to China and Mongolia. No less likely habitat for griffins is imaginable than the streets of modern London, yet such a creature was reported from that teeming city's Brentford neighborhood in 1984–85.

Kevin Chippendale saw it first, in June or July 1984, flying over the aptly-named Green DRAGON housing project on Braemar Road. Friends were skeptical, and all the more so when Chippendale reported a second sighting at the same place, in February 1985. Only then did he remark upon the beast's resemblance to the logo of a nearby pub, The Griffin. There the story might have ended, in a boozy haze, but witness Angela Keyhoe saw a similar cryptid that month, outside the Watermans Art Centre. Days later, psychologist John Olssen reported a sighting, while jogging beside the Thames River. Other witnesses spoke up in March, but the press soon lost interest. A decade later, novelist Robert Rankin admitting fabricating some of the newspaper reports as a HOAX without apparent motive.

Sources: Collins, *The Brentwood Griffin*; McEwan, *Mystery Animals of Britain and Ireland*.

Griffin sightings were reported in London in 1984–85.

Briagolong Tiger   This ALIEN BIG CAT of Victoria, Australia harassed ranchers around Briagolong for two decades, from the mid-1930s until the 1950s. Rod Estoppey, a veteran trapper for the Fisheries and Game Department, pursued the beast for years without result. Reports from the predator's heyday claim that it often devoured adult ewes in one sitting and killed 110 sheep on a single farmer's property. The CAT was never caught or positively identified.

Source: Healy and Cropper, *Out of the Shadows*.

Briaou *see* **Nguoi rung**

Bribie Island sea serpent   Bribie Island lies off the coast of southeastern Queensland, Australia. In the early 1960s, its surrounding waters produced a series of SEA SERPENT reports that remain unexplained to this day. The first was filed in September 1960, when Dave Tanner and his mother spied a 25-foot creature swimming parallel to the shore at Woody Bay, on the island's southern tip. They tracked the creature for 1.5 miles before giving up and returning home for breakfast. As Tanner described the animal to reporters:

The head is round, something like a man's, at least 2 ft. 6 in. across and 2 ft. long, with a flat nose and sort of semi-detached to the body….It was a dirty brown colour and appeared to have a body about 2 ft. across and a queer-looking fin 18 ft. from the head. It kept surfacing about every 50 yards.

Author Malcolm Smith surmises that Tanner meant to say the fin was 18 *inches* behind the head, but the point remains unproved. Two years later, in late September 1962, Robert Duncan was beach-combing on Bribie Island when he spied a "horrible" monster 1.8 miles offshore from Woorim. Duncan watched it for a full four minutes through binoculars, describing it as "something out of a nightmare." More specifically:

It was whitish-grey in colour, about 12 feet long, and seemed to have a swan's neck, a whale's body, and a FISH's tail and fins. It repeatedly raised its neck out of the water, and then flipped its strange tail. Two weeks later, on 6 October, Duncan saw the same beast or its twin swimming off the island's northern point. This time, he reported, "Its snout, instead of being pointed, is flat like a pig's. It has two little holes near the centre. They'd be nostrils, I suppose." Additionally, Duncan noted a dorsal fin appended to the creature's swanlike neck. BERNARD HEUVELMANS interpreted the fin as "a hairy crest" and judged the Bribie Island beast to be one of his hypothetical "long-necked" sea serpents.

Sources: Heuvelmans, *In the Wake of the Sea Serpents*; Smith, *Bunyips & Bigfoots*.

***Brilliant* sea serpent**   On 12 May 1843, Captain Cotton and his crew aboard the schooner *Brilliant* saw a SEA SERPENT swimming in the North Atlantic, 15 miles offshore from Cape Ann, Massachusetts. They watched the beast for an hour, later describing it as 70–80 feet long. It swam with its head held eight feet out of the water.

Source: O'Neill, *The Great New England Sea Serpent*.

Brisbane River, Australia   On 1 February 1999, Queensland residents Doug Harvey and Chris Johnson were fishing on the Brisbane River when some large, unseen creature snagged the anchor of their 16-foot boat. Suddenly, in full view of other fishermen and an officer from the Department of Fisheries, Harvey and Johnson found themselves racing through the water, their boat zigzagging and spinning in circles "like a cork." After several terrifying moments, the invisible beast dived deeper, swamping the boat's prow before it snapped the anchor cleat.

Shaken, Harvey and Johnson made their way to shore and safety. The creature that had taken them on the wild ride never revealed itself.

Source: "Fishermen taken on 'Jaws' river ride." *Brisbane Courier Mail* (1 February 1999).

Bristol Channel sea serpents

On 11 October 1883, the Rev. E. Highton glimpsed a large SEA SERPENT swimming down the Bristol Channel near Bude, Cornwall. He estimated that the creature was traveling at 25 miles per hour, leaving a "greasy trail" on the water as it traveled toward the North Atlantic. Nearly a quarter-century later, in April 1907, a more dramatic incident was reported from the same waters. According to the *Liverpool Echo* of 30 April, one M. M'Naughton had been fishing peacefully when his small boat was attacked by a creature "like a huge mummy with sunken eyes enveloped in a sort of hairy flap." M'-Naughton told the press:

> What happened after I can only dimly recollect. The flabby monster seemed to leap out of the water and straight as an arrow for me. I hardly know what I did. I think I must have ducked and crashed the oar into the creature. At any rate I was flung violently into the water. When I regained the surface I managed to clamber into my boat. My terrible enemy was nowhere in sight. In a dazed condition, scarcely knowing what I was doing, I succeeded in reaching Portishead.

BERNARD HEUVELMANS, writing 50 years after the fact, suggested that M'Naughton simply fell overboard when a large creature surfaced beside him, later inflating the tale to make it an epic battle. Still, Heuvelmans considered the sighting legitimate and ranked both Bristol Channel cryptids as specimens of his hypothetical "long-necked" sea serpent.

Source: Heuvelmans, *In the Wake of the Sea Serpents.*

British Banner sea serpent

On 25 April 1859, the vessel *British Banner* was allegedly attacked by a ferocious SEA SERPENT. According to the ship's commander, Capt. William Taylor, the huge beast began its assault by "shaking the bowsprit with his mouth," then "swallowed the foretopmast staysail and flying jib with the greatest apparent ease; he also snapped the thickest of the rigging asunder like a thread." Nearly sated, it smashed in the starboard quarter galley before submerging. Later the same day, Capt. Taylor claimed a juvenile specimen was captured, subsequently delivered to a museum at Melbourne, Australia. The museum confirmed delivery, but reported that the creature was a common sea SNAKE (*Pelamis bicolor*). As for the rest, Taylor further compromised his credibility by claiming the attack occurred at the impossible coordinates of 12° 7' *east* latitude and 93°52' *south* longitude. If we correct "east" to south and "south" to east, the site becomes a point in the Indian Ocean, between the Cocos Islands and Western Australia. On balance, it is safer to agree with BERNARD HEUVELMANS that the story was a HOAX.

Source: Heuvelmans, *In the Wake of the Sea Serpents.*

British Big Cat Society

The British Big Cat Society was founded in 2000 or 2001 (accounts differ) by current leader DANNY BAMPING, of Plymouth, England. Chris Moiser serves as the group's scientific and historical officer. The society's first meeting was held at the Dartmoor Wildlife Park, named as the society's official base of operations in 2003. The BBCS maintains working relationships with various police departments and government agencies, processing reports of ALIEN BIG CATS, which the society's Internet website term "Britain's zoological Holy Grail." Some 600 members scattered throughout the United Kingdom collaborate in an effort to "scientifically identify, quantify, catalogue and protect the Big Cats that freely roam the British countryside." To that end, the BBCS collects, analyzes and publishes reported CAT sightings in various forums, while attempting to pursue its own investigations in the field. The society collected more than 1,000 ABC sightings from various British venues between March 2001 and August 2002. In 2003, the BBCS was in the process of attaining tax-exempt charity status in England.

Sources: "Big cat sightings continue to grow." *Ananova* (24 January 2002); Sieveking, "Big cats in Britain": British Big Cat Society, http://www.britishbigcats.org/.

British Centre for Bigfoot Research

Name notwithstanding, this organization does not collect reports of unknown HOMINIDS in Great Britain. Rather, as explained by its Internet website:

> The British Centre for Bigfoot Research is a project founded in order to bring together people in the UK and other countries alike who have an interest in the phenomena of large hairy bipedal APES stalking the remote forests of the world. This project concentrates mostly on the creatures nicknamed BIGFOOT or SASQUATCH which are reported to live in the forests of North America.

To that end, the BCBR's unnamed members announced plans to mount an expedition in the Pacific Northwest, with assistance from the SOUTHERN OREGON BIGFOOT SOCIETY. "The main purpose of this expedition is to make a documentary film on the Bigfoot creatures and also to live out our childhood fantasies of acting like Indiana Jones and finding a 'monster'!" Since that message is undated, no information is presently available on that project's status.

Source: British Centre for Bigfoot Research, http://british-bigfoot.tripod.com/.

British Columbia Scientific Cryptozoology Club

The BCSCC was founded in 1989 by author JAMES CLARK, marine biologist PAUL LEBLOND and journalist JOHN KIRK. While maintaining that British Columbia hosts more cryptids per capita than any other region on Earth — including SASQUATCH, multiple LAKE MONSTERS, ALIEN BIG CATS and offshore SEA SERPENTS — the club does not restrict its membership to Canadian residents. Citizens of all nations are invited to join the BCSCC and to investigate reports of cryptids in their respective homelands, as long as they accept the club's guidelines for research. More specifically, the club's Internet website defines the BCSCC as:

> a scientific body which follows the accepted principles of orthodox zoology in regard to establishing the existence of new species of animals. Our mandate is to ascertain where they fit into the greater picture in the realm of natural history. We do not subscribe in any way, shape or form to any ludicrous paranormal, occultic or supernatural viewpoints when discussing the nature and origins of such animals.

Furthermore, the BCSCC declares itself "a conservation and preservation-oriented organisation and reject the need to kill for the sake of science." Prospective members "must be of attestable good character," and they are "expected to play a part in the life, development and growth of the club. This is not a club for sedentary individuals. We strongly encourage members to be involved in cryptozoological research wherever they may live." Founder LeBlond is renowned for his research and writings on the sea serpent known as CADBOROSAURUS, while BCSCC members have participated in four expeditions seeking proof of OGOPOGO's existence in Okanagan Lake. The club's director of BIGFOOT research, Anthony Vanzuilekom, has collected footprints and alleged hair samples from that elusive HOMINID in the Pacific Northwest.

Source: British Columbia Scientific Cryptozoology Club, http://www.cryptosafari.com/bcscc/index.htm.

British Hominid Research   Unlike the BRITISH CENTRE FOR BIGFOOT RESEARCH, this group investigates sightings of BIGFOOT-type HOMINIDS within the British Isles. The BHR's Internet website, designed and maintained by apparent group leader Geoff Lincoln, includes brief summaries of hominid sightings from England, Scotland and Wales, dating from 1879. Investigators from the BHR follow a strict "no-kill" policy in pursuing evidence of British cryptids. The website acknowledges ongoing debate between "flesh-and-blood" Bigfoot advocates and those who opt for supernatural theories, without taking sides in the argument. "Whatever the answer," Lincoln writes, "these elusive 'WILDMEN' and their habitats deserve serious research and most of all, our total respect for their possible existence."

Source: British Hominid Research, http://www.lincolns.org.uk/.

***British Princess* sea serpent**   At dawn on 4 May 1889, two officers aboard the American liner *British Princess* saw a SEA SERPENT in mid-Atlantic, at 44° north latitude and 42°40' west longitude. Captain Smith described the creature as a "large black obstacle, sticking out of the water in a perpendicular position — like a long spar or river buoy."

Source: O'Neil, *The Great New England Sea Serpent.*

Brookton Tiger   In the mid-1960s, ranchers around Brookton, Western Australia suffered a sudden increase in predation against their sheep herds, which they blamed on a skulking beast nicknamed the Brookton TIGER. As suggested by its name, the creature was alleged to be an ALIEN BIG CAT. Wildlife expert Harry Butler stalked the predator for two full years and finally killed it, still uncertain what it was even as he pulled the trigger. Post-mortem examination revealed that the "tiger" was a mutilated dingo (*Canis familiaris* var. *dingo*) that had once been trapped, clubbed, scalped and left for dead with its tail cut off. Somehow, it had survived that ordeal and returned to seek a measure of revenge before Butler cut short its sheep-killing career.

Source: Healy and Cropper, *Out of the Shadows.*

Brosnie   Brosnie is the supposed LAKE MONSTER of Russia's Lake Brosno, located 250 miles northwest of Moscow, in the wild and sparsely-populated Tver' district. The lake is 10 miles long, with a maximum recorded depth of 130 feet. Local sightings date from 1854 and typically describe a serpentine creature 16 feet long, with an "enormous tail" and a flat head resembling that of a FISH or a SNAKE. Residents of Benyok, a village situated on the lake's shore, were disturbed in 1996 after a Muscovite visitor photographed a "DRAGON monster" in the lake. His photo was inconclusive at best, and while locals speculated that Brosnie might be a living DINOSAUR, spokesmen for the Moscow Institute of Paleontology dismissed the notion as "a fairy tale, the kind of story told over the years in the countryside." Russian cryptozoologists noted that no representatives from the institute had visited Lake Brosno prior to passing judgment, and the "expert" verdict failed to explain why such sightings are common in various parts of Russia.

Sources: Kirk, *In the Domain of the Lake Monsters*; Nikolai Pavlov, "Russia's 'Nessie' frightens villagers." Reuters (14 December 1996); Ben Roesch, "A Russian lake monster." *Cryptozoology Review* 2 (Summer 1997): 4.

Brown Jack *see* **Junjadee**

Brown's Lake, Wisconsin   On 4 August 1876, three witnesses reported a LAKE MONSTER sighting from Brown's Lake, at Burlington, in southeastern Wisconsin's Racine County. They described the creature as 27 feet long, blue and green in color, with prominent fangs and two stiff dorsal fins. Thus far, no other sightings are on file.

Source: "An aquatic or amphibious demon rises on Brown's Lake." *Burlington Standard-Press* (10 August 1876).

Brush Monkey   Brush MONKEY is a regional nickname applied to unknown primates or HOMINIDS reported from Michigan's upper peninsula, sandwiched between LAKE MICHIGAN and LAKE SUPERIOR. According to local tradition, the creatures have thick coats of fur that enable them to survive Michigan's harsh winters. Accounts differ as to whether they Brush Monkeys are typically large, BIGFOOT-type creatures or smaller beasts in the mold of so-called DEVIL MONKEYS.

Source: Ted Barnhart, "Heard & seen." *Cambridge* (OH) *Daily Jeffersonian* (14 April 2003).

Bryngarw Beast   In 1983, three sightings of an ALIEN BIG CAT were reported from Bryngarw, near Croesyceiliog, Cwmbran, Wales. All the reports were filed within a 2-week period, after which the CAT apparently moved on to other hunting grounds.

Source: "Catalogue of Wales' weird cats." BBC News (26 August 2000).

Bubble Gum Dolphin   This enigmatic cetacean, reported most often from the waters surrounding Hong Kong, earns its nickname from the fact that while its coloration is gray or black at birth, adults of the species mature with a pink hue resembling bubble gum. Pink dolphins (*Inia geoffrensis*) are known from the Amazon River system, where natives call them boto, but no marine species recognized by science achieves the same color. Some researchers believe the Bubble Gum Dolphin represents an unrecognized color morph of the Indo-Pacific hump-backed dolphin (*Sousa chinensis*), found in coastal waters from East Africa through Asia to Papua New Guinea and eastern Australia. Others believe it may represent a new species.

Source: Shuker, *From Flying Toads to Snakes with Wings.*

Buckinghamshire Serpent   Sometime in the mid-18th century, a British gentleman of leisure wrote to a London magazine, describing an apparent LAKE MONSTER report from the county of Buckinghamshire (or Bucks) some 200 years earlier. The letter described a painting found on the wall of an old village meeting hall. It read:

In the year 1578, which appears above the painting, in a pond surrounded with briars near the house, a water-serpent of an uncommon size was frequently seen by a woman, who belonged to the house, when she went to get water. The creature, whenever she came, made advances to her....The woman, terrified at his appearance, told the story to neighbours, who advised her one day to sit near the pond side, while some of them stood behind the briars, with an intention to shoot it, if possible, when it advanced towards her. The thing was accordingly effected, and the skin of the creature, according to the tradition of the place, was hung up withoutside the house, stuffed with straw, for many years; but in process of time, by being so exposed, decayed. Ever since the year when this thing happened, the story has been painted on the wall of the refectory or hall....As it cannot be supposed that the first painting could continue to this time on the bare wall, as often as it has been in a state of decay, so often has it been renewed. The present painting was done about forty years since, by the famous Rowell, the glass-stainer.... The imagination of the painter has given the serpent wings and legs, which made some people suppose the whole fabulous, but that the story, exclusive of these emendations by the painter, is in every respect true, is plain from the traditional accounts of sensible judicious people hereabouts, and from the pencilled record of it on the wall of the house.

Source: G.L. Gomme, ed., *The Gentleman's Magazine Library: English Traditional Lore.* London: Elliott Stock, 1885.

Buffalo Lions Kenyan natives describe Buffalo LIONS as large male lions (*Panthera leo*) without manes, so large and fierce that they commonly stalk buffalo and other prey much larger than themselves. Legend has it that they also prefer solitude and shun socialization in prides. Two maneless lions harassed railroad construction crews around Tsavo in 1898, killing 140 laborers before they were tracked down and shot, with their mounted remains exhibited to this day at Chicago's Field Museum. (A 1996 film based on that episode, *The Ghost and the Darkness*, portrayed both CATS with full manes.) A century later, in 1998, two maneless lions were photographed with a bull calf they killed in Tsavo National Park. Most mammalogists blame genetic or hormonal defects for the occasional lack of a mane in male lions, but some cryptozoologists speculate that relict cave lions (*P. l. spelaea*) may explain sightings of lions much larger than normal.

Sources: Philip Caputo, *Ghosts of Tsavo.* Washington, DC: National Geographic, 2002; Peter von Buol, "'Buffalo lions': A feline missing link?" *Swara: The Magazine of the East African Wildlife Society* 23 (July-December 2000): 20–25.

Buin Monster CHUPACABRA researcher SCOTT CORRALES was first to report the presence of an unknown creature dubbed the Buin Monster, prowling the vicinity of Santa Filomena, Chile. On 5 January 2004, bus driver Juan Berrios was passing through Santa Filomena when a mysterious creature leaped across the road in front of his vehicle, grazing the windshield as it passed. Shaken, Berrios drove on to the bus terminal in Viluco, and only there discovered that several hairs — described as "hard, ringleted, black on the ends and white toward the center" — were stuck to one of his windshield-wiper blades. Berrios later described the beast as follows:

It was an animal I'd never seen before. It's tall, well over a meter and a half, standing at least 1.80 [5 feet 11 inches], I would say. And its eyes weren't red — they were black. When I saw that something crossed my path I hit the brakes. The animal was on the right side of my vehicle. Its muzzle was longer than a WOLF'S, it had a small hump on the back of its neck and had a creature in its maw. It looked at me, crouched into a fetal position and jumped, vanishing instantly.

Another driver for the La Cuarta bus line, Juan Espinoza, claimed that a pair of "gringo" foreigners visited Santa Filomena a short time later and photographed the scene of Berrio's encounter. The creature's hairs were reportedly submitted for scientific analysis, but no verdict was available at press time for this volume.

Source: Scott Corrales, "Hairs from mystery Chile creature recovered." Institute of Spanish Ufology press release (6 February 2004).

Bull, Tim (n.d.) Paranormal researcher Tim Bull is better known in his native Australia as "Tim the YOWIE Man," after his publicized pursuit of unknown HOMINIDS Down Under. In 2001, he became the official Australian representative of Britain's CENTRE FOR FORTEAN ZOOLOGY. Nickname notwithstanding, Bull's interests are not limited to Yowies or even to cryptozoology per se. In November 2001 he turned his attention to extraterrestrial puzzles, asserting that publicity agents for Disney Studios had faked numerous crop circles to advertise the Mel Gibson movie *Signs.*

Sources: "Disney accused of planting fake crop circles." *Wireless Flash* (11 November 2001); Richard Freeman, "Twilight Worlds 2001." Centre for Fortean Zoology, http://www.cfz.org.uk/projects/geordie.htm.

Bull Lake, Wyoming On 11 September 1906, a Wyoming newspaper called the *Land Clipper* reported a LAKE MONSTER sighting from Bull Lake, located 10 miles west of Morton in Fremont County. The story read:

While fishing in Bull Lake last week, O.L. Middlekauf claims to have seen the SEA SERPENT discovered some time ago by City Marshal Peter Peralta and John Mason. All of the parties describe the monster as bearing some resemblance to the gigantic saurians the books tell of. They say it was 40 to 50 feet long and swims with its head out of the water. Middlekauf says its head is as large as a candy bucket but does not claim to have been closer than a quarter of a mile.

The Shoshone Indians it is said, have always been afraid of the lake because they claim it is inhabited by devils. They claim that they hear bellowing like that of a bull especially in the winter time, but local scientists say this probably comes from gas escaping through the ice, the lake being near the big oil and gas bearing anticlinal that runs through the country from the Beaver divide beyond Bull Lake. The fishermen who claim to have seen the PLESIOSAUR or whatever it is, all deny that they had been imbibing any sea serpent whiskey or other strong waters calculated to make men see things.

Sadly, no further details are presently available on what appears to be a long-running lake monster tradition at Bull Lake. No recent sightings of the creature(s) are recorded.

Source: Kirk, *In the Domain of the Lake Monsters.*

Bullaresjön, Sweden This lake in Sweden's Västra Götaland County, also known to some as Norra, has a maximum recorded depth of 50 feet. In 1810, local witnesses reported sightings of a calf-sized LAKE MONSTER with an incongruous 12-foot head and neck. No modern sightings of the creature or its offspring are on file.

Sources: Costello, *In Search of Lake Monsters;* Global Underwater Search Team, http://www.cryptozoology.st/.

Bung Bung *see* **Lions (Spotted)**

Bunyip Bunyip is a generic name applied to various aquatic cryptids reported from various Australian rivers, lakes and swamps since the late 18th century. In 1812, the *Sydney Gazette* published a pamphlet by James Ives, in which the local "bahnuip" was described as "a large black animal like a seal, with a terrible voice which creates terror among the blacks." The term's origin is uncertain, but its wide application extended even into 19th-century Australian politics, as a synonym for "impostor." In 1852, the phrase "bunyip aristocracy" was used in Sydney to describe a class of conservative snobs.

Aborigines of the 19th century believed that two species of bunyip inhabited their native land. One kind was said to be "in shape similar to a low-set sheep dog, the colour of a PLATYPUS, [with] head and whiskers resembling an otter." The other was a quadruped, calf-size or larger and covered with long hair or feathers. It had a long neck with a flowing mane, and a small head resembling an EMU'S. Some witnesses also described tusks and a

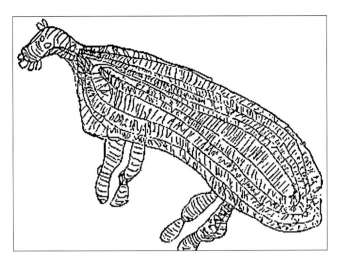

Aboriginal rock art depicts a typical Bunyip.

horselike tail. Both species were amphibious and spent most of their time in water. White settlers initially dismissed those native claims as superstition run amok, but they soon recorded their own bunyip sightings. Researchers Paul Cropper and Tony Healy report that 60 percent of non-Aboriginal witnesses described "seal-dog" bunyips, while 20 percent sketched long-necked cryptids resembling the traditional LAKE MONSTERS of Europe and North America. (The other 20 percent of sightings defied easy classification.) Regional names for bunyips include Kajanprati, Kianpraty, Toor-roo-don and Tumbata (in Victoria); Mirree-ulla and Wouwai (New South Wales); Moolgewanke (Queensland); Tunatpan and Wangul (Western Australia).

On 19 February 1847, the *Sydney Morning Herald* published a letter from William Hovell, announcing that his friend Atholl Fletcher had found a bunyip skull on the bank of the lower Murrumbidgee River, where local tribesmen called the beast Katenpai. Fletcher took the 9-inch partial skull, sans lower jaw and with the crown missing, to Melbourne, where it was examined by a battery of scientists. "Those skilled anatomists, Dr. Hobson and Mr. Greeves," declared that it belonged to an unknown species, but their judgment was not taken as the final word. Naturalist W.S. Macleay first said it was the skull of a giant BIRD, then changed his mind, declaring that it came from a young CAMEL or "a misshapen foal." Professor Richard Owen of London's Hunterian Museum never saw the skull, but after viewing sketches of it he proclaimed the beast to be a common calf. Thus denigrated, the relic was consigned to the Colonial (now Australian) Museum — where it disappeared after a brief term on display.

Whatever the source and/or final destination of the Murrumbidgee skull, theories abound in regard to the bunyip's identity. Proposed candidates from the roster of known animals include wandering Elephant seals (*Mirounga leonina*), Australian fur seals (*Arctocephalus pusillus doriferus*), Australian sea lions (*Neophoca cinerea*), Indo-Pacific crocodiles (*Crocodylus porosus*), 5-foot Murray cod (*Maccullochella peelii peelii*), and even the modest musk duck (*Biziura lobata*). KARL SHUKER and other researchers suggest that some bunyip legends may reflect Aboriginal memories of large, extinct marsupials, including *Diprotodon* and *Palorchestes*, though neither was amphibious. Other hypotheses include a still-unknown species of freshwater pinniped native to Australia and a variation on the long-necked lake monsters reported from other parts of the Earth.

Sources: Healy and Cropper, *Out of the Shadows*; Heuvelmans, *On the Track of Unknown Animals*; Shuker, *In Search of Prehistoric Survivors*; Smith, *Bunyips & Bigfoots*.

Burgingin *see* **Junjadee**

Bu-Rin In 2001, zoologist Alan Rabinowitz published a memoir of his explorations in Myanmar (formerly Burma), which included the following report from that country's northern quadrant.

In Putao, there were stories about a giant water SNAKE, the bu-rin, 40 to 50 feet long, that attacked swimmers or even small boats. Sounding somewhat like a larger, aquatic version of the Burmese PYTHON [*Python molurus bivittatus*], this snake was considered incredibly hostile and dangerous. No one had firsthand knowledge of the creature, yet because of it, children were often discouraged from spending long periods of time in the water.

Source: Alan Rabinowitz, *Beyond the Last Village: A Journey of Discovery in Asia's Forbidden Wilderness*. Washington, DC: Island Press, 2001.

Burmese witnesses describe the Bu-rin as a large aquatic snake.

Burrum Heads sea serpent On 14 September 1995, the Australian periodical *Isis Town & Country* published an anonymous letter and sketch purporting to describe a SEA SERPENT recently seen at Burrum Heads, on the Queensland coast between Bundaberg and Maryborough. The letter read:

During the first week of September a friend and myself were fishing from a tinnie. It was about three in the afternoon and we were near the junction of the Isis and the Burrum Rivers, when I spotted something unusual. I called my companion's attention to it and for what seemed about a minute we watched what appeared to be an enormous SNAKE with a bulbous head. I really do mean enormous: the neck/body was upright out of the water and was topped by a head the size of a labrador dog, while the neck seemed about half the girth of a timber power pole. It was very dark grey, almost black, and neither of us noticed any teeth, tongue, ears, fur or scales. There did seem to be a small wash as it moved slowly upstream but neither of us became aware of any swimming motion. After a while it just slipped under the water and that was it, we didn't see it again. It definitely did not dive, it slid away. Has anyone else seen anything similar or can offer an explanation? I can say it wasn't a snake or an EEL (too big), dead stock, vegetation or BIRDS (familiar with Darters, Cormorants, etc.). It wasn't a dog, roo or mirage. We weren't drunk or smoking dope and aren't seeking money of fame. In fact, this account is anonymous because of the ridicule that usually goes with anything out of the ordinary. My friend says we should forget it and just put it down as an unexplained incident, and that if we came forward we would end up as the Forrest Gumps of the Isis. Me, I'm full of curiosity and just want to know.

Source: Smith, *Bunyips & Bigfoots.*

Burrunjor
Aborigines in Arnhem Land, in the far north of Australia's Northern Territory, describe the Burrunjor as a large predatory lizard that walks primar-

The Burrum Heads sea serpent, from sketches by an unnamed witness.

ily on its hind legs, after the fashion of *Tyrannosaurus rex* and similar DINOSAURS. Some researchers equate the Burrunjor with Australia's MUNGOON-GALLI, noting the MONITOR LIZARDS of various sizes frequently rise to their hind legs while running.

Source: Gibbons, *Missionaries and Monsters.*

Artist's depiction of the Burrunjor (*William Rebsamen*).

Buru
Natives of the Apatani Valley, in northern India's Arunachan Pradash Union Territory, describe the Buru as a large aquatic lizard, dwelling in the lakes and swamps around Ziro. In 1945–46, zoologists James Mills and Charles Stonor visited the region and collected eyewitness accounts of the reptile, summarizing its description as follows:

The length of a *buru* was about three and a half to four metres [11–13 feet], and it was "long shaped." The *head* was about fifty centimetres [19.5 inches] long, and was elongated into a great

snout, flattened at the tip. The eyes were behind the snout. The teeth were "flat like those of a man," except for a pair in the upper and lower jaws, which were large and pointed "like those of a TIGER or a boar." The *neck* was rather under a metre [39 inches] in length, and could be stretched out or drawn in....The *body* was roundish and "the breadth of a man's arm and body across the back," with a girth "such as a man could just put his arms round." The *tail* was rounded and tapering, and about one and a half metres [4 feet 10 inches] in length. The general opinion is that it was not very pointed. It was fringed "from where the animal excreted" (i.e., the base) with broad and deeply fringed lobes which ran the whole length on either side, and sprang from the dorsal surface of the tail....The *legs* were fifty centimetres long, with claws on the feet, and they and the feet looked like "the forefeet of a burrowing mole." The *skin* was like that of a scale-less FISH. There were no hairs, but three lines of short, blunt spines ran down the back and along each side. The colour was dark blue blotched with white, and a broad band of white ran down the belly.

In 1948, the London *Daily Mail* sponsored a Buru-hunting expedition led by Stonor and RALPH IZZARD. The team found no concrete evidence of the creatures' existence, but returned with enough anecdotal accounts to convince BERNARD HEUVELMANS that the species was recently extinct. Izzard believed the Buru was a form of relict DINOSAUR, but other researchers have proposed their own candidates through the years. TIM DINSDALE thought the beasts might represent an unknown species of CROCODILE, while ROY MACKAL proposed a new species of giant MONITOR LIZARD (*Varanus* sp.) and KARL SHUKER suggests a large swamp-dwelling lungfish (Order *Lepidosireniformes*). If the Buru is truly extinct, the riddle seems unlikely to be solved.

Sources: Dinsdale, *Monster Hunt*; Izzard, *The Hunt for the Buru*; Mackal, *Searching for Hidden Animals*; Shuker, *Extraordinary Animals Worldwide.*

Bushbaby (Giant)
Bushbabies or galagos (Genus *Galago*) are primates of northern Africa, related to the lemurs. The largest of five known species is the silver galago (*Otolemur argentatus*), with a maximum recorded body length (minus tail) of 15 inches. The more common Senegal galago (*Galago senegalensis*) does not exceed a body length of 6.5 inches, though it can leap more than 7 feet from a standing start. Sightings of an unknown "giant" bushbaby have been reported from Senegal's Casamance Forest, where witness Owen Burnham saw a CAT-sized specimen with smaller offspring in June 1985, and from Cameroon, where a specimen of similar size was photographed by one of zoologist Simon Bearder's aides in 1994. Senegal galagos occur in both countries, while the larger silver galagos are officially unknown. Some researchers believe an unknown giant species of bushbaby may exist in West Africa, but KARL SHUKER suggests that witnesses may actually have encountered MARTIN'S FALSE POTTO.

Sources: Shuker, "A supplement to Dr. Bernard Heuvelmans' checklist of cryptozoological animals"; Shuker, "The secret animals of Senegambia."

Buster sea serpent
In early 1944, a SEA SERPENT sighting was reported from the Atlantic off Sierra Leone, by crewmen aboard H.M.S. *Buster*, a vessel of the Freetown Escort Force. Near dusk, while searching for German submarines, the *Buster*'s men were startled to see a large ray, 5–6 feet wide, leap high out of the water. Seconds later, the lookout shouted, "Huge object on port beam!" As second officer John Drummond later recalled:

That was gentle understatement. I have seen something of the like since — in horror movies, but this thing, in slow motion, heaved

Sightings of giant bushbabies are reported from West Africa.

itself out of the depths, remained suspended for four to five seconds and then fell forward with a thunderous splash. I think Able-
Seaman Fitzgerald of Pimlico was the look-out concerned. I think
that, because when I interviewed him afterwards, he described the
manifestation as:—"Like the side of a big building rumbling down
in the London blitz." The asdic [sonar] operator on duty…held a
sharp underwater contact on his set, then lost it on the recorder
as the thing dived.

Convinced that the beast was not a whale, Drummond asked
rhetorically, "Then what was it? Distances at sea are often very
deceptive. Out main mast was well over sixty feet high. The thing
seemed about that height, at a guess. In the dusk I could see no
eyes. The suggestion of a tail, yes. But the most vivid impression
was the thinness of the creature." In 1968, BERNARD HEUVELMANS
concluded that the animal was a specimen of his hypothetical
"super-EEL."

Source: Heuvelmans, *In the Wake of the Sea Serpents.*

Bynoe Harbor sea serpent   On 2 February 1980, the
Northern Territory News published an article about PLESIOSAURS
allegedly inhabiting Bynoe Harbor, southwest of Port Darwin, on
the coast of Australia's Northern Territory. The story examined
claims made by Burge Brown, a "beach sands prospector" who
glimpsed SEA SERPENTS twice during 1977–78. On the first occasion, while searching for a shipwreck with his son, Brown was
startled by a roaring noise that frightened his dogs. Some 15 minutes later, he watched through binoculars as three reptilian creatures passed by, swimming 1,000 yards off shore. He estimated
that the largest of the three was 30 feet long.

A year later, while fishing in deep water off Rankin point,
Brown was again surprised when FISH and sea SNAKES began leaping from the water around his boat, as if terrified. Soon, he saw
a large animal "with a tail and a front like an elephant's head, and
pairs of fins running down the length of its back." The creature
stayed within 65 feet of Brown's boat for the next 20 minutes,
thus permitting Brown and his companions to examine it in some
detail. One of Brown's friends, police sergeant Kevin Maley, ini-

tially described the beast as "black, about 30m [98 feet] long with
a head the size of a football." When author Malcolm Smith interviewed Maley, years later, Maley scaled the animal's length
back to 25 feet, with a S-shaped neck 8–10 feet long. He also recalled three rows of floppy triangular serrations along the animal's
back, each spike or fin about six inches high.

Source: Smith, *Bunyips & Bigfoots.*

Byrne, Peter Cyril (1925–)   An Irish native, born in
Dublin, Peter Byrne served in the Royal Air Force during World
War II, then moved on to work as a planter for the British Tea Company in India. In 1948, while enjoying a holiday in northern
Sikkim, he discovered a large humanoid footprint identified by natives as belonging to a YETI. The event captured Byrne's imagination, and he sought backing for a full-scale Yeti expedition in the
early 1950s, after he quit the tea trade to become a big-game hunter.
Terminally short of sponsors, Byrne moved to Sydney, Australia in
1954 and found work as a journalist. Local businessmen offered
backing for a Yeti hunt in August 1955, but that adventure was still
on the drawing board when Byrne met Texas millionaire TOM SLICK
in spring 1956. Their correspondence blossomed into friendship,
and Byrne joined the Slick Yeti Reconnaissance in March-April
1957. On 2 April, at an altitude of 10,000 feet, he found a line of
presumed Yeti tracks stamped in snow.

Byrne's association with Slick continued until the oilman's
death in 1962. Accompanied by brother Bryan, Byrne was a leading member of the Slick-Johnson Snowman Expeditions in 1958
and 1959. On the second trip, Byrne stole a portion of the PANG-
BOCHE HAND and smuggled it out of Nepal to the U.S. with help
from movie star James Stewart. Late 1959 found the Byrne brothers dwelling in a cave, in Nepal's Chhoyang Valley, but they were
rescued when Slick shifted his focus to North America and the
search for BIGFOOT. As members of Slick's Pacific Northwest Expedition, the brothers reported a dozen set of SASQUATCH in 1960
alone. The hunt continued until Slick's death in 1962, whereupon Burn retired from cryptozoology for nearly a decade. He returned to the hunt in 1971 and kept at it until 1979, during which
time he founded the International Wildlife Conservation Society
and published a book, *The Search for Big Foot* (1975).

As in 1962, the 1979 reports of Byrne's "permanent" retirement
from tracking unknown HOMINIDS proved premature. He returned to the quest in 1992, as leader of the BIGFOOT RESEARCH
PROJECT, described in press releases as a privately funded 5-year
program of field research based near Mount Hood, Oregon.
Funding sources included the ACADEMY OF APPLIED SCIENCE and
an unidentified "consortium of businessmen." Sponsors declined
refunding in 1997, and Byrne retired again, this time to the Los
Angeles area, after telling reporters, "We've confirmed to our satisfaction that these things do exist. Bigfoot is out there. Of this
I am certain."

Sources: "Bigfoot research project ends." *Skeptic* 5 (1997): 28; Phil
Busse, "Looking for Mr. Bigfoot." *Portland* (OR) *Mercury* (14 September 2000); Byrne, *The Search for Big Foot*; Coleman, *Tom Slick and the
Search for the Yeti*; Martha Goodavage, "Hunt for Bigfoot attracts true
believers." *USA Today* (24 May 1996).

—C—

Caá-Porá   The Caá-porá ("mountain lord") is a BIGFOOT-type HOMINID reported by natives in Brazil's Goiás and Paraná States, as well as the Misiones Department of neighboring Paraguay. Witnesses agree that the creatures are large hairy bipeds with oversized heads, who leave *pisadas grandotas* ("big footprints") wherever they travel.

Source: Picasso, "South American monsters and mystery animals."

Cabbage Head Man   According to researcher RAYMOND CROWE'S *Track Record* newsletter, this nickname is applied to BIG-FOOT in parts of Maryland.

Source: "Around the weird: Bizarre news briefs." *Wireless Flash Weird News* (4 June 2002).

Cabelludos *see* **Morcegos**

Cadborosaurus   Aboriginal artwork from Vancouver Island and neighboring portions of British Columbia demonstrate that early tribesmen were familiar with SEA SERPENTS in the coastal waters, variously known as Hiyitl'iik (to the Manhousat people), Numske lee Kwala (to the Comox), or T'chain-ko (among mainland Sechelts). The first recorded sighting by white visitors may have been logged by crewmen aboard the fur-trading vessel *CO-LUMBIA* in 1791, and reports have continued to the present day. Researchers PAUL LEBLOND and Edward Bousfield have compiled a list of 178 sightings between summer 1881 and June 1994, involving creatures that were "unambiguously alive and clearly not a known animal, because of its appearance or dimensions." More than half of those incidents involved multiple witnesses, including a report of 26 October 1895 wherein 17 persons saw the beast in Bellingham Bay.

Descriptions from the sightings collected by LeBlond and Bousfield vary widely, involving estimates of length ranging from 8 to 300 feet. Many reports include references to a long neck, a mane, a humped back or coils in the water, and a large head resembling that of a CAMEL or horse. Large eyes are frequently described, while some accounts include whiskers, fins, and a serrated ridge along the creature's back. Two of the serpents have been seen together on at least four occasions, in March 1934, December 1938, March 1939 and July 1993. On the latter occasion, pilots Don Berends and James Wells landed their sea plane close to the pair of gray-blue creatures they sighted at Saanich Inlet, but the animals escaped by swimming rapidly with vertical undulations.

Cadborosaurus (or Caddy) was christened by *Victoria* (B.C.) *Daily Times* editor Archie Wills in 1933, after a spate of sightings at Cadboro Bay. Throughout their long tenure in nearby coastal

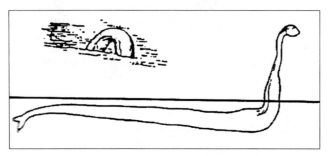

A sketch of Cadborosaurus prepared by witnesses in 1897.

waters, the creatures have also been dubbed Edizgiganteus (after Washington's Ediz Hook Light), Klahmahsosaurus (by residents of Texada Island), Penda (for Pender Island), the Sea Hag and the Serpent of Second Narrows. Although its most common popular name suggests a reptilian identity, virtually all researchers who have studied Cadborosaurus agree that if it exists, it must be a mammal. Diagnostic features in that regard include eyewitness descriptions of hair and vertical movements impossible for reptiles, as well as Caddy's seeming preference for cold water.

Aside from its numerous public appearances, Caddy is also remarkable for the dozen instances where alleged specimens were stranded or captured between 1930 and 1991. Most of the GLOB-STERS washed ashore on various beaches, from Alaska's GLACIER ISLAND in 1930 to Washington's WHIDBEY ISLAND in 1963, were tentatively identified as decomposed cetaceans, pinnipeds or SHARKS, yet tantalizing mysteries remain. A serpentine creature beached at CAMP FIRCOM, British Columbia on 4 October 1936 was photographed, its picture reproduced on postcards, but it remains unidentified today. Nine months later, an equally curious 10-foot carcass was taken from the stomach of a sperm whale at NADEN HARBOUR, British Columbia. Once again, the remains were photographed, and again they defied classification.

In addition to strandings, two witnesses claim that they captured "baby" specimens of Cadborosaurus, but both took pity on the animals and set them free without taking photos or submitting them for scientific study. William Hagelund reportedly made his catch in August 1968, at DE COURCY ISLAND and kept the 18-inch anomaly in a bucket of water while sketching it freehand, before he returned it to the sea. Nearly a quarter-century later, in July 1991, Johns Island resident Phyllis Harsh allegedly found a 2-foot "baby dinosaur" beached near her home, and placed it back in the surf. On other occasions, Harsh claimed to have seen an adult Cadborosaurus swimming offshore (summer 1990) and to have found a "small dinosaur" skeleton near a bald eagle's nest. Researchers Aaron Bauer and Anthony Russell suggest that Hagelund may have mistaken a crayfish or lobster for Caddy, while the Harsh reports resist simple solutions.

No photos of Cadborosaurus at sea have yet been produced, but a ship's captain reported sonar hits accompanied by a sighting of a 3-humped serpent at Becher Bay, in Juan de Fuca Strait, on 1 March 1987. In May 2001, the BRITISH COLUMBIA SCIENTIFIC CRYPTOZOOLOGY CLUB established Project Caddyscan, employing motion-sensitive digital cameras planted at various "hot" locations along the B.C. coastline. The effort had produced no results at press time for this volume, but BCSCC spokesman JOHN KIRK encouraged the hunt by telling reporters, "For anyone who captures a Cadborosaurus, we offer a $500 reward." In regard to Caddy's identity, Paul LeBlond once suggested (based on 30 reports filed between 1862 and 1969) that three separate cryptids were involved. In 1995, he retreated from that position, asserting that all British Columbia reports involve a single species, though LeBlond acknowledged that "it is not impossible that more than one animal might be hiding under the label 'Caddy.'"

Sources: Marke Andrews, "Tracking Caddy the sea serpent and a few of his monstrous pals." *Vancouver Sun* (25 June 2002); Todd Babiak, "Have you seen this serpent?" *Edmonton Journal* (21 May 2001); Bauer and Russell, "A living plesiosaur?"; "Caddy continues." *Strange Magazine*

20 (December 1998): 50; Garner, *Monster! Monster!*; LeBlond and Bousfield, *Cadborosaurus*; Shuker, *The Unexplained*.

Caddo Critter
Caddo, Texas lies in Stephens County, some 60 miles west of Fort Worth. In the mid-1970s, residents were agitated by sightings of a BIGFOOT-type HOMINID or NORTH AMERICAN APE, described by witnesses as seven feet tall and four feet wide, covered completely in dark hair. Rancher Charlie Gantt reportedly fired 10 shots at the creature one night, without slowing it down. An alleged film of the beast was broadcast on WBAP-TV in Fort Worth, but the murky footage revealed nothing of substance. Some Texans maintain that the Caddo Critter is identical to the HASKELL RASCAL and the beast called HAWLEY HIM, reported from nearby Haskell and Jones Counties.

Source: Green, *Sasquatch: The Apes Among Us.*

Caddy *see* Cadborosaurus

Cadmore Cat
Sightings of this ALIEN BIG CAT were reported from Gloucestershire, England in the early weeks of 2000, supplanting for the moment such notorious feline predators as the BEAST OF DEAN and BEAST OF BROADOAK. As with its predecessors and the unidentified CATS reported later, it eluded trackers and remains unidentified today.

Source: Big Cats in the UK?, http://www.cryptozoo.fsnet.co.uk/ABCs.htm.

Caesar sea serpent
Late in life, Vice-Admiral Robert Anstruther recalled that he had once seen a SEA SERPENT in the Irish Sea, between the coast of Ireland and the Isle of Man. Anstruther could not recall the date, but the event occurred while he was serving as commander of HMS *Caesar*, between October 1908 and April 1910. He described the incident as follows:

> In the first dog-watch I was standing on the bridge, when suddenly something shot out of the water right in front of me, about half a ship's length off, straight up into the air to about the height of the foremast head, about fifty feet. I, of course, had my galilee-glasses handy, and quickly fixed them on the quadruped—for a four-footer or, at any rate, a four-legged, beast it proved to be. In appearance it gave me the impression of a skinned chow-dog, such as one sees hanging up in the butchers' shops of Canton. In shape it reminded me of a chameleon, though a shortened one; the head and short tail also had a chameleon-like appearance. With outstretched neck and legs it fell, or rather dived, into the sea again.
>
> I had never seen such a creature before in all my long experience at sea, so I hastily called the navigating officer, who was at the standard compass, to come to my end of the bridge, in case the reptile, or whatever one may call it, should show itself again. No sooner had he got to my side than it shot up again, and I had another good look at it, and this time the navigating officer, Lieutenant-Commander (now Captain) H.J.L.W.K. Wilcox saw it as well. It did not appear to have scales, but rather the shiny skin of a reptile. Its feet seemed like the claws one sees represented in figures of Chinese DRAGONS. We waited and waited, but it never rose again.

Since all reptiles have scales, BERNARD HEUVELMANS concluded that the creature seen by Anstruther and Wilcox must have been some unknown mammal. He finally classified it as a specimen of his hypothetical "merhorse" or "long-necked" sea serpent.

Source: Heuvelmans, *In the Wake of the Sea Serpents.*

Cahore Point sea serpent
On 23 January 1976, witnesses at Cahore Point, on the coast of Ireland's County Wexford, reported sightings of a long-necked SEA SERPENT that moved through the water like "a big worm."

Source: Bord and Bord, *Unexplained Mysteries of the 20th Century.*

Cai-Cai-Filu
Araucanian folklore described the Cai-cai-filu as a SEA SERPENT native to Chile's coastal waters, typically described half SNAKE and half horse. In fact, the horselike head is a common element of many sea serpent and LAKE MONSTER sightings throughout the world.

Source: Julio Vicuna Cifuentes, *Mitos y Supersticiones Recogidos de la Tradicion Oral Chilena.* Santiago de Chile: Imprenta de la Universidad, 1915.

Caimans (Mislocated)
Caimans are crocodilians (Subfamily *Alligatorinae*) closely related to ALLIGATORS and CROCODILES. Three living genera are recognized, with five species and four subspecies, all normally confined to Latin America between southern Mexico and northern Argentina. Discovery of caimans outside that tropical range constitutes an anomaly, typically explained with reference to exotic pets released by their owners. Locations of recent sightings and captures include:

Arizona: Spokesmen for the state's Game and Fish Department report that 10–12 alligators and caimans are caught in the Grand Canyon State each year. They also suggested that the crocodile reported from Glendale (but never captured) in March 2002 was "probably" a caiman.

California: Castro Valley—A caiman was captured at Lake Chabot in 1996. Six years later, fishermen reported another reptile at large in the lake, but it eluded searchers (July 2002).

Florida: State wildlife officials acknowledge that populations of spectacled caimans are established in at least four counties. Dade was the first county infested (in 1960), followed by Broward (1966), Palm Beach (1966) and Seminole (1970s).

New York: New York City—A 2-foot spectacled caiman (*Caiman crocodilus*) was captured at Harlem Meer, a lake at the northeast corner of Central Park (16 June 2001).

Mexico: Piedras Negras—Local residents of this border town, facing Eagle Pass, Texas across the Rio Grande, found four caimans living in a local canal. One of the reptiles was caught on videotape, while neighbors tossed chickens into the water (August 2002). The cite lies roughly 1,000 miles north of the nearest known caiman habitat.

England: Finchley, North London—A resident walking his dog found the skull and flesh of a large reptile, identified by experts at the London Zoo as remains of a spectacled caiman (May 1996). Gloucestershire—Witnesses reported a caiman inhabiting a local canal, near Sellars Bridge. Police and members of BEASTWATCH UK investigated without apprehending the creature (June 2003).

Sources: "Croc creek." *Fortean Times* 90 (September 1996): 8; "A crop of crocodilians." *Fortean Times* 151 (November 2001): 17; David Madrid, "Glendale gator?" *Arizona Republic* (1 March 2002); "The 'monster' of Loch Chabot." *Contra Costa* (CA) *Times* (11 July 2002); Wendy Phillips, "Fisherman claims he's seen caiman prowl Lake Chabot." *Oakland* (CA) *Tribune* (5 July 2002); Dick Reavis, "Are reptile sightings a croc?" *San Antonio* (TX) *Express-News* (24 August 2002); "See you later alligator…?" *Gloucestershire Echo* (19 June 2003); "Gloucestershire croc." Beastwatch UK, http://www.beastwatch.co.uk; Florida's Exotic Wildlife, http://wld.fwc.state.fl.us/critters/exotics/resultsclass.asp?taxclass=r

Cait Sìth
The Cait sìth ("fairy cat") of the Scottish Highlands was described in Gaelic folklore as a dog-sized CAT, jet black except for a dramatic white patch on its chest. It marks the first

appearance of an ALIEN BIG CAT on Scottish soil, and while some skeptics consign it entirely to legend, most researchers now believe that Cait sìth sightings represented early contact between humans and the Scottish KELLAS CAT.

Source: James MacKillop, *Oxford Dictionary of Celtic Mythology*. New York: Oxford University Press, 1998.

Caitetu-Mundé   Tupí natives in Brazil's Mato Grosso State described the Caitetu-mundé as an piglike ungulate midway in size between the well-known white-lipped peccary (*Tayassu pecari*) and the smaller collared peccary (*T. tajucu*). Witnesses describe it as roughly 3 feet long and 20 inches tall at the shoulder. Semantic confusion derives from the fact that Tupís call the collared peccary *caitetu*, while the suffix *mundé* ("trap") is commonly added to the name of any game animal. Seen most often in forests along the Rio Aripuanã, the Caitetu-mundé reportedly lives in pairs or groups of four, rather than the larger herds preferred by other peccaries.

Source: Shuker, "New beasts from Brazil?"

Calcasieu River, Louisiana   Authors LOREN COLEMAN and JOHN KIRK include this river, in southwestern Louisiana, on published lists of supposed aquatic cryptid habitats. No dates or details of sightings are provided.

Sources: Coleman, *Mysterious America*; Kirk, *In the Domain of the Lake Monsters*.

California Giant Labels   In October 2000, while browsing items offered for sale on eBay, cryptozoologist LOREN COLEMAN discovered a packing crate label for lettuce once sold under the brand-name California Giant. The GIANT in question was artfully depicted as a burly HOMINID, completely hair-covered except for its face, posed with a wooden crate of vegetables tucked underneath one arm. Assisted by researcher Thomas Jacobsen, Coleman discovered that the labels were printed for a Salinas, California produce firm between 1925 and 1950. Based on calculations from the mirror-image label on the crate beneath the giant's arm, Coleman determined that the creature (if alive) would have been 10 feet tall, with feet 20–24 inches long. He thus concluded that the labels might depict an early image of SASQUATCH, printed 30-odd years before that elusive creature was nicknamed BIGFOOT in 1958.

Source: Coleman, *Bigfoot!*

***Calvin Austin* sea serpent**   On 9 September 1921, the *Boston Herald* reported a SEA SERPENT sighting off the coast of Scituate, Massachusetts. According to that story:

The annual sea serpent yarn has been spun a little late, but Capt. W.T. Holmes of the steamship *Calvin Austin*, whose veracity in 43 years of seafaring has never been questioned, uncorks a gem about what he saw off Scituate the other morning. He was bound here from New York when through the fog a ship's length ahead he observed a creature with a head as big as a cask and glassy eyes. The barnacled body, that tapered to a tail with a knob, was propelled by two flippers. The body was about 29 feet long and may have weighed a ton. If it's [*sic*] wrinkled warty mass could be appraised in years it may have antedated Methuselah. Capt. Holmes speaks about the creature reluctantly and refers to the pilot, lookout and quartermaster, who were equally amazed that Boston bay should be invaded [by] so repulsive a monster.

Source: O'Neill, *The Great New England Sea Serpent*.

Camahueto   The Camahueto ("sea elephant") is a sup-

posed SEA SERPENT of Chile, described by Mapudungun natives as a dangerous man-eating predator. The creatures allegedly spawn in various lakes, then migrate to the sea via rivers. The Camahueto's horselike head resembles descriptions of sea serpents and LAKE MONSTERS from other parts of the world, but its vicious temperament is distinctive. Most sightings are reported from the waters around Isla Grande de Chiloé, 400 miles south of Concepción.

Source: Julio Vicuña-Cifuentes, *Mitos y Supersticiones Recogidos de la Tradicion Oral Chilena*. Santiago de Chile: Universitaria, 1915.

Camazotz   Around 100 BCE, Zapotec natives of Oaxaca, Mexico developed a strange religious cult that revered a giant BAT known as Camazotz ("death bat" or "snatch bat"). By the time Spanish invaders arrived in the late 15th and early 16th centuries, the night-flying "neck-cutter" was widely known, christened with various names across its tropical range. Tribesmen in Chiapas, Mexico called it H'ik'al ("black man"); the Mayans dubbed it Zotzilaha chamalcan; in Ecuador it was Tin tin; on Trinidad, Soucouyant; in Peru and Chile, Chonchon. Since folktales clearly described the bat's nocturnal call—"Eek-eek" or "Tui-tui"—it was seemingly more flesh and blood than superstition. From descriptions of the Camazotz, some modern researchers belief it may have been a spear-nosed bat (Subfamily *Phyllostominae*) or a false vampire bat (*Vampyrum spectrum*), the latter a harmless but impressive species with a 3-foot wingspan. Others suggest that a relict population of giant vampire bats (*Desmodus draculae*) may have survived beyond the Pleistocene epoch to prey on humans and domestic animals.

Sources: Gable, "Two possible cryptids from Precolumbian Mesoamerica"; Eduard Seler, "The bat god of the Maya race." *Bulletin of the Bureau of American Ethnology* 28 (1904): 231–241.

Camel (Australian)   Camels (*Camelus* sp.) are not endemic to Australia, but a few were imported in 1840, and larger numbers—estimated at 10,000 to 12,000—were delivered between 1860 and 1907. Automobiles replaced them as a common means of Outback transportation by 1930, while some were released to create naturalized herds in the wild. By 2001, Australian authorities estimated that 150,000–300,000 camels roamed free across the country, with half their number found in Western Australia and the rest scattered throughout the Northern Territory, Queensland and South Australia. An enduring mystery surrounds Aboriginal sightings of camels in northern Australia prior to 1830, when none supposedly existed on the island continent. Researchers differ in opinion as to whether Australia once hosted an indigenous camel species, or unrecorded specimens were introduced prior to the first known importation.

Source: Australian Camel Information, http://www.austcamel.com.au/inform'n.htm.

Camp Fircom carcass   On 4 October 1936, the skeletal remains of an unknown sea creature washed ashore at Camp Fircom on Gambier Island, in British Columbia's Howe Sound. Two photos of the carcass, twisted in a pretzel shape, were made into postcards at the time, then vanished until KARL SHUKER published one of them anew in 1996. Shuker suggests that it may represent remains of the Pacific Northwest SEA SERPENT known as CADBOROSAURUS. Researcher Darren Naish disputes that view, maintaining that the photos are a HOAX, depicting a mussel shell posed as a skull, with the curving spine constructed from "the stem of a large plant, most probably a kelp." Naish grants, how-

Aborigines reported sightings of camels in Australia prior to their importation in the 19th century.

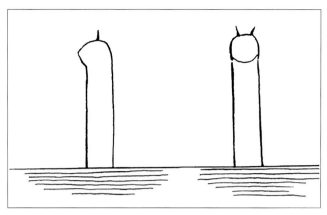

The *Campania* sea serpent, after witness Arthur Rostron.

ever, that other viewers of the photos dispute his diagnosis, and he admits that little can be said with certainty concerning reproductions of an old black-and-white photographs.

Sources: Darren Naish, "Another Caddy carcass?" *Cryptozoology Review* 2 (Summer 1997): 26–29; Shuker, *The Unexplained.*

Campania **sea serpent**   In 1931, the Sir Arthur Rostron published his memoirs of a life at sea, including the night in April 1912 when he rescued 700 survivors from the doomed *Titanic.* An incident more fascinating to cryptozoologists occurred on 26 April 1907, when Rostron was chief officer of the *Campania,* plying the coast of Ireland. As he told the story:

[W]e were coming one Friday evening into Queenstown when, off Galley Head, I noticed something sticking out of the water. "Keep clear of that snag right ahead," I called out to the junior officer who was with me on the bridge. We swung away a point but gradually grew nearer so that we were able to make out what the unusual thing was. It was a sea monster! It was no more than fifty feet from the ship's side when we passed it and so both I and the junior officer had a good sight of it. So strange an animal was it that I remember crying out: "It's alive!" One has heard such yarns about these monsters and cocked a speculative eye at the teller, that I wished as never before that I had a camera in my hands. Failing that, I did the next best thing and on the white "dodger board" in front of me made sketches of the animal, full face and profile, for the thing was turning its head from side to side for all the world as a BIRD will on a lawn between its pecks. I was unable to get a clear view of the monster's "features" but we were close enough to realize its head rose eight or nine feet out of the water while the trunk of the neck was fully twelve inches thick.

When interviewed by reporters, he further recalled that "[t]here were two protuberances where eyes might have been, but I could see no eyes....It had very small ears in comparison with its enormous bulk." When Rostron's book was published, the other witness — Captain H.C. Birnie — confirmed the commander's story.

Source: Heuvelmans, *In the Wake of the Sea Serpents.*

Campbell River, Canada   Researchers LOREN COLEMAN and JOHN KIRK include this river, on British Columbia's

Vancouver Island, on published lists of aquatic cryptid habitats, but no dates or details of sightings are offered.

Sources: Coleman, *Mysterious America;* Kirk, *In the Domain of the Lake Monsters.*

Campbeltown Loch sea serpent   Campbeltown Loch is a sea loch or inlet located on the southeastern coast of western Scotland's Kintyre Peninsula. One afternoon in 1934, local naturalist John MacCorkindale was conversing with postman Charles Keith beside Kilkerran Bay, when they heard a loud splash from the water nearby. Looking out to sea, they saw a huge SEA SERPENT thrashing the surface some 300 yards offshore, raising the forepart of its body 12 feet from the water and splashing down repeatedly before it finally submerged. MacCorkindale later told a reporter from the *Scotsman* that the visible part of the creature resembled a giraffe, complete with long neck, small head and little ears. Its skin was silvery in color, with dark lateral streaks or bands. A dorsal fin was barely visible, but no more of the body or tail was observed. The witnesses estimated its total length at 30 feet.

Source: Heuvelmans, *In the Wake of the Sea Serpents.*

Canandaigua Lake, New York   Aboriginal folklore identifies this lake, 25 miles southeast of Rochester, as the former abode of a large, serpentine LAKE MONSTER. No modern sightings of the creature are on file.

Source: Charles Skinner, *Myths and Legends of Our Own Land.* Philadelphia: Lippincott, 1896.

Canavar   In November 1995, a team of government researchers visited Turkey's Van Province to investigate sightings of a LAKE MONSTER in Van Gölü (Lake Van). Multiple witnesses — including provincial deputy governor Bestami Alkan and Zeki Ergezen, member of parliament from Bitlis Province — had reported personal encounters with the beast over the past six months. Most described a black creature 24–30 feet long, with a hairy, horned head and a row of triangular spines running the length of its back, but some witnesses sketched a white beast with a black-striped back and few claimed sightings of both animals together. Locals dubbed the creature Canavar ("monster"), with a handful preferring the more affectionate name Vanna. Matters were further complicated by reports of another cryptid at ERÇEK GÖLÜ, 12 miles east of Van Gölü. The state investigation solved nothing, but interest in the Canavar was rekindled on 10 June 1997, when Unal Kozak produced an alleged videotape of the creature. Kozak's footage shows a dark-colored object of indeterminate size moving through the water near shore, then submerging. When enlarged, the image seems to show a brown hump, and some viewers profess to see an eye.

Sources: "Sea monster or hoax?" *CNN News* (12 June 1997); Shuker, *From Flying Toads to Snakes with Wings.*

Canip Monster In July 1975, residents of Trimble County, Kentucky reported multiple sightings of a giant lizard along Canip Creek, near Milton. Witnesses Clarence and Garrett Cable allegedly saw the reptile three times, lurking around a local junkyard. Those who saw the animal described it as 15 feet long, with black-and-white stripes and a long forked tongue. Some of the sightings were accompanied by clawed footprints, 5 inches long and 4.5 inches wide. While the creature generally resembled a MONITOR LIZARD in form, its size exceeded that of the largest known species on Earth (*Varanus komodoensis*).

Source: Arment, "Dinos in the U.S.A."

Cannich Puma On 27 October 1979, Edward Noble saw an ALIEN BIG CAT stalking ponies on his farm near Cannich, in the Scottish Highlands. He reported the sighting to police and described the beast as resembling a lioness (*Panthera leo*), noting that livestock had inexplicably vanished from his property since mid-1978. Officers mounted a search but found nothing, yet Noble's livestock losses and big-cat sightings continued for another 12 months. At last, he built a steel cage which he baited each night with fresh meat, and on 29 October 1980 the effort succeeded. That morning, Noble found a 5-foot female COUGAR (*Puma concolor*) in his trap, and thus his claims were verified at last.

Or, were they?

Wildlife experts who examined Noble's catch found the CAT to be elderly, arthritic, and so tame that it purred while total strangers scratched its head. Authorities suspected that an unlicensed exotic pet owner had placed the cat in Noble's trap, either as a prank or as a cheap means of disposal. One opinion in Noble's favor came from Hans Kruuk, at Banchory's Institute of Terrestrial Ecology, who examined fecal samples from the cat and found them to contain remains of deer and sheep, presumably devoured in the wild. The cat, christened Felicity, was lodged at the Highland Wildlife Park, where she died in February 1985. Perhaps significantly, cougar sightings persisted in the Cannich region long after Felicity's capture. Ed Noble died on 11 December 1998, still regarded by many researchers as the victim of a HOAX.

Source: Karl Shuker, "Alien zoo." *Fortean Times* 121 (April 1999): 19; Shuker, *Mystery Cats of the World.*

Canyon Monster Between 1960 and 1975, numerous reports of a BIGFOOT-type HOMINID were filed from north-central West Virginia's Tucker County. Local journalists dubbed the creature the Canyon Monster. Witnesses included campers, hikers and horseback riders who met the beast in woodlands around Davis.

Source: Berry, *Bigfoot on the East Coast.*

Cape Breton sea serpent On 23 June 2003, lobster fisherman Wallace Cartwright reported a SEA SERPENT sighting from the waters off Cape Breton Island, Nova Scotia. At first, he mistook the 26-foot creature for a floating log, until it raised its head to scrutinize his boat. "It had a head on it like a sea TURTLE," Cartwright said, "and it had a body like a SNAKE, about as big around as a five-gallon bucket. I was kind of leery of ap-

proaching it. God knows, the thing might have been able to jump out of the water, you know? And I'm sure it could have swallowed you whole." Cartwright followed the brown beast for 45 minutes, while it dived and resurfaced a half-dozen times, finally vanishing into deep water. "I've been a lobster fisherman for 30 years, and I know what a bunch of seals or EELS on the surface look like," Cartwright told reporters. "This was one distinct animal. One I've never seen before." A spokesman for the Nova Scotia Museum, Andrew Hebda, suggested that Cartwright had seen an oarfish (*Regalecus glesne*), which may exceed 36 feet in length. "There aren't too many eight-meter-long FISH in the world," Hebda said. "It could only be one of a few known things, if it's a known species at all." On the other hand, Hebda admitted, "We have some specimens here at the museum taken from waters off Labrador and the Scotian Shelf, and we have no idea what they are."

Sources: "Arr, thar be sea serpents yonder." *CBC News* (24 June 2003); Matt Gardner, "C.B. lobster fisherman follows 'sea monster.'" *Halifax Herald* (25 June 2003).

Cape Charles sea serpent In February 1846, a sea captain named Lawson, ship unknown, reported a SEA SERPENT sighting between Cape Charles and Cape Henry, Virginia. He described the beast as having a small head and a row of "sharp projections" on its back. Proximity suggests that the beast may be identical to CHESSIE, of Chesapeake Bay, but Lawson's description bears no resemblance to other reports of that cryptid.

Source: Heuvelmans, *In the Wake of the Sea Serpents.*

Cape May carcasses Cape May lies at the extreme southwestern tip of New Jersey's Cape May County, on Delaware Bay. It holds the distinction of hosting two decomposed GLOBSTERS, the first washed ashore in October or November 1887, the other 34 years later, in November 1921. The first case is shrouded in mystery, mentioned briefly by BERNARD HEUVELMANS in his 1968 survey of SEA SERPENT sightings and strandings. Regrettably, Heuvelmans supplied no details beyond a passing reference to his source, an undated November article from the *Boston Courier* which remains as elusive as the stranded beast's identity.

Author F.A. Mitchell-Hedges reported the second incident in 1923, as follows:

[I]n November 1921, off Cape May, a great beast was washed ashore. This mammal, whose weight was estimated at over 15 tons…was visited by many scientists, who were unable to place it, and positively stated that nothing yet known to Science could in any way compare with it. The photographs which were published in many newspapers showed that this modern leviathan somewhat resembled the elephant — in fact, it could be best described as a sea-elephant, but of huge proportions.

Eight years later, author CHARLES FORT described his own research into the case.

I investigated the story of the Cape May monster, wherever I got the idea that I could find out anything in particular. Somebody in Cape May wrote to me that the thing was a highly undesirable carcass of a whale, which had been towed out to sea. He said that, if I'd like to have it, he'd send me a photograph of the monster. After writing of having seen something with a tusk twelve feet long, he sent me a photograph of something with two tusks, each six feet long. But only one of the seeming tusks is clear in the picture, and it could be, not a tusk, but part of the jaw bone of a whale, propped up tuskwise.

Heuvelmans concluded that Fort was correct and more specifically identified the second Cape May carcass as belonging to a baleen whale (Family *Balaenopteridae*) of unknown species.

Sources: Fort, *The Complete Books of Charles Fort*; Heuvelmans, *In the Wake of the Sea Serpents*; F.A. Mitchell-Hedges, *Battles with Giant Fish*. London: Duckworth, 1923.

Cape Province sea serpent

An unidentified SEA SERPENT was reportedly seen off the shore of South Africa's Cape Province, near Hawston, sometime in 1903. Unfortunately, the sighting was not reported until 1960, by which time all significant details had been lost.

Source: Heuvelmans, *In the Wake of the Sea Serpents*.

Cape Rosier sea serpent

In 1817, when a rash of SEA SERPENT sightings filled New England newspapers, the Rev. Abraham Cummings reported a sighting of his own, made off the coast of Maine 15 years earlier. As he described the incident:

It was sometime in July 1802 that we saw this extraordinary sea monster, on our passage to Belfast, between Cape Rosoi [now Cape Rosier] and Long Island. His first appearance was near Long Island. I then supposed it to be a large shoal of FISH with a seal at one end of it, but wondered that the seal should rise out of the water so much higher than usual; but, as he drew nearer to our boat, we soon discovered that this whole appearance was but one animal in the form of a serpent. I immediately perceived that his mode of swimming was exactly such as had been described to me by some of the people on Fox Islands [now North Haven and Vinalhaven Islands], who had seen an animal of this kind before, which must confirm the veracity of their report. For this creature had not the horizontal, but an ascending and descending serpentine motion. This renders it highly probable that he never moves on land to any considerable distance and that the water is his proper element. His head was rather larger than that of a horse, but formed like that of a serpent. His body we judged was more than sixty feet in length. His head and as much of his body as we could discover was all of a blue colour except a black circle around his eye. His motion was at first but moderate, but when he left us and proceeded toward the ocean, he moved with the greatest rapidity. This monster is the sixth of the kind, if our information be correct, which has been seen in this bay within the term of eighteen years. Mrs. Cummings, my daughter and Miss Martha Springs were with me in the boat at that time and can attest to the above description.

A colleague, the Rev. Alden Bradford, wrote to Cummings, asking if he could have mistaken several porpoises swimming in single file. Cummings replied:

Who ever saw fifty or sixty porpoises moving after each other in a right line and in such a manner that those who formed the rear were no larger than a haddock and mackerel, and none but the foremost showed his head? Who ever saw a serpent's head upon a porpoise or a whale? We saw him swim as far as from Long Island to the Cape before he disappeared. His head and neck all the time out of the water. Now whoever saw a porpoise swim so great a distance without ever immerging at all?

Two young men on Fox Island, intelligent and credible, saw an animal of this kind about five years since, as they then informed me. They told me that the serpent which they saw was about sixty feet long, and appeared to have an ascending and descending motion. A few years before, perhaps ten years since, two of those animals were seen by two other persons on that island, as their neighbors informed me. About twenty years since, two of those serpents, they say, were seen by one Mr. Crocket, who then lived upon Ash Point.

Sources: Heuvelmans, *In the Wake of the Sea Serpents*; O'Neill, *The Great New England Sea Serpent*.

Artist's conception of the Cape Rosier sea serpent (*William Rebsamen*).

Cape Town sea serpents

Cape Town, South Africa lies at the extreme southwestern tip of the continent, on the Cape of Good Hope. Local residents recorded two SEA SERPENT sightings in the 19th century, the first occurring in the summer of 1845 or 1846. C.D. Brunette and C. Fairbridge were fishing at Camp's Bay when they saw a large unknown creature in the water nearby. No detailed description has survived, but Fairbridge, considered "a considerable authority on marine life," opined that the beast belonged to no known species. The second incident occurred on 12 November 1881, when harbor official C.M. Hansen was working in his garden near Mouille Point. Glancing up from his labor, he saw a large beast swimming near the point where a ship, the *Athens*, was earlier wrecked. Hansen called his wife and children to see the beast, and they all watched it "viewing the coast at its ease for half an hour" before it swam out to sea. According to a local newspaper report: "Mr. Hansen describes this sea-monster as being about 75 feet long, of a dark colour and with a head the size of a 54 gallon hogshead, resembling that of a bull-dog, and provided with a long and brown mane, hanging down."

Source: Heuvelmans, *In the Wake of the Sea Serpents*.

Carabuncle

This serpentine aquatic cryptid derived its name from the Latin *carbunculus* ("gem"), based on alleged eyewitness reports of a glowing jewel or pearl sprouting from its skull. Luminous appendages are sometimes found on deep-sea denizens, who use them as lures while hunting in the abyss, but the Carabuncle supposedly surfaced before witnesses in both lake and salt water. During the 16th century, reports of Carabuncles were recorded from widely-scattered sites, including Loch Geal in County Kerry, Ireland; from landlocked Paraguay; and from Argentina's Strait of Magellan. No modern sightings of the beasts are known.

Sources: Martín del Barco Centenera, *The Argentine and Conquest of the River Plate*. Buenos Aires: Instituto Cultural Walter Owen, 1965; Nathaniel Cogan, "Field notes on the folklore of Irish plants and animals." *Irish Naturalist* 23 (March 1914): 53–64.

Carcharodon Megalodon

The largest living SHARKS known to science are the whale shark (Rhincodon typus), assumed to reach a length of 50 feet, and the basking shark (Cetorhinus maximus), which may reach 40 feet. Both are inoffensive plankton feeders, harmless to man despite their great size. The largest predatory shark—and presumed third-largest FISH on Earth—is the great white (Carcharodon carcharias). Undersea explorer Jacques Cousteau claimed to have seen a great white 25 feet long, and while other published claims range from 26 to 43 feet, none are supported by physical evidence or official documentation. The undated photograph of an alleged 30-footer caught near the Maldive Islands is almost certainly a HOAX, and the official record holder at press time for this volume is a 23 foot specimen caught in the Mediterranean, off Malta, in 1987.

Some 50 million years ago, during the Tertiary Period, a much larger ancestor of the great white roamed prehistoric seas. *Carcharodon megalodon* ("big tooth") was a king-sized version of *C. carcharias*, with teeth up to seven inches long and jaws so large that a man could pass upright between them. Estimates of *C. megalodon*'s size were initially inflated by an error in reconstruction at New York's Museum of Natural History. There, in 1940, technicians prepared a replica of *C. megalodon*'s jaws, using only the largest teeth available. The resultant extrapolation produced descriptions of a shark 120 feet long, but a revision by John Randall in 1973 corrected the monster's size to 45 feet. David Davies, director of the Oceanographic Research Institute in Durban, South Africa regards that estimate as too conservative, and credits *C. megalodon* with a length of 60–80 feet. In any case, it was a formidable predator, and while most ichthyologists maintain that *C. megalodon* became extinct some 1.5 million years ago, sporadic sightings of huge unidentified sharks challenge that conventional wisdom. In 1875, the British oceanographic vessel *CHALLENGER* dredged up two *C. megalodon* teeth from the sea bed at a depth of 14,000 feet. They were not "fresh," as once claimed by BERNARD HEUVELMANS, but when Russian scientist D. Tschernezky analyzed their manganese dioxide coating in 1959, he declared that one tooth was 24,000 years old, the other no more than 11,000 years. That verdict made *C. megalodon* a contemporary of *Homo sapiens*, and some cryptozoologists suspect that the giant fish may still survive today. The encouraging reports include:

1918—A group of Australian fishermen from Port Stephens, New South Wales reported an encounter with a giant shark near Broughton Island. The beast swallowed several crayfish traps, each

Carcharodon megalodon **was comparable in size to a sperm whale (*William Rebsamen*).**

3 feet 6 inches wide, "pots, mooring lines, and all." Estimates of the shark's length ranged from 115 to 300 feet, with all witnesses agreeing on its ghostly white color. Ichthyologist David Stead interviewed the fishermen, reporting that: "They were all familiar with whales, which they had often seen passing at sea, but this was a vast shark." Stead emerged from the interviews with "little doubt that in this occurrence we had one of those rare occasions when humans have been vouchsafed a glimpse of one of those enormous sharks of the White Death type, which we know to exist or to have existed in the recent past, in the vast depths of the sea."

1927–28—Western novelist and ardent fisherman Zane Grey was sailing off Rangiroa, in Polynesia's Tuamotu Archipelago, when he saw a shark longer than his 40-foot boat. His description of a squarish head and greenish-yellow body marked with white spots suggests a whale shark, though Grey thought otherwise and KARL SHUKER suggests that the "spots" may have been barnacles.

1933—Grey's son Loren saw a near-identical shark while sailing 100 miles northwest of Rangiroa. He described the fish as 40–50 feet long, with a head 10–12 feet wide, and insisted that it was not a whale shark. Skeptics disagree, while South Pacific islanders speak confidently of a mythic giant shark they call Lord of the Deep.

1950s—Sailor-author Thomas Helm was shipping with a crew of fishermen along Florida's west coast, in the Gulf of Mexico, when one crewman described his encounter with a shark whose mouth was "as big as two barrel hoops." The fish allegedly swallowed a hard-hat deep sea diver whole, then spit him out again. Ironically, next morning Helm watched "the biggest shark I have ever seen" swim under the crew's 60-foot boat, off Tarpon Springs. He watched the shark for an hour, unable to determine its species. Helm reported that it "may have been black, dark brown or dark blue, and in general conformation he most closely resembled the white shark. The pectoral fins or flukes could be seen on either side of the trawler when the shark was directly under us, and once when his huge tail was even with the stern his head was just below the midship booms! By actual measurement the shark was not an inch less than thirty feet!"

March 1954—While riding out a storm near Timor, Indonesia, sailors aboard the *Rachel Cohen* felt a violent jolt and imagined they had struck a floating log. Later, in dry dock at Adelaide, Australia, the boat's captain found 17 shark's teeth embedded in the hull. They reportedly averaged 4 inches long and 3 inches wide, dispersed in a pattern suggesting a mouth 3 feet wide. Based on calculations by ichthyologist John Randall, at Hawaii's Bishop Museum, the owner of those jaws would be 36–46 feet long.

In 1976, hot on the heels of Steven Spielberg's record-breaking movie *Jaws*, a supposed nonfiction book appeared describing encounters with a living *C. megalodon*. In *Killer Sharks: The Real Story*, author "Brad Matthews" described himself (like Captain Quint in *Jaws*) as a survivor of the U.S.S. *Indianapolis*, torpedoed on 29 June 1945 with a loss of some 900 men, many killed by sharks after the ship went down. In 1946, Matthews claimed, natives of Papua New Guinea described 100-foot man-eating sharks known as Aru, banishing skepticism with the revelation of a "new" 6-inch shark tooth. Matthews stole the tooth and subsequently showed it to "about 22,000" experts, all of whom agreed that it was not a fossil. Sidetracked by various adventures for the next quarter-century, Matthews resumed the hunt for *C. megalodon* following a sensational incident. As described in the book:

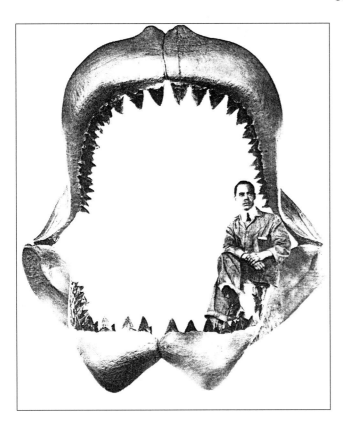

Reconstructed jaws of *Carcharodon megalodon*.

[I]n April of 1968, I read an account of the sinking of an Australian sloop named the *Mary Crowley*. It was a 90-foot sporting yacht and it was lost one night in the Torres Straits, south of New Guinea, with 18 people on board. The only survivor, a passenger named Baldridge, claimed that the ship was attacked by a white shark that was at least as long as the *Mary Crowley*, and that the shark smashed the wood hull and ate everyone on board. Baldridge was in shock and spoke incoherently. The Australian authorities surmised that the boat had been hit by a whale, which sometimes happens. As for the eating part, they assumed that Baldridge was slightly mad as a result of his experience. He died a few days afterward.

September 1968 found Matthews and his son collaborating with "a Dr. Barfoot" from the Australian Museum in Sydney, preparing to launch the research vessel *Rosinante*. The team sailed on 11 January 1969, on a mission "to find evidence of, or to kill *Carcharodon* [*sic*]." Late on the night of 21 March, near Timor, the crew encountered a shark "at least 100 feet long," which devoured one of the crew, then fled at speeds approaching 60 miles per hour. Matthews spent the next three months on a futile vengeance quest, then gave up the hunt. Shortly before his memoir's publication, in August 1975, he was reportedly killed by a normal-sized shark off Montauk, Long Island.

Such dramatic claims demand verification, and to that end in August 1976 I contacted the Australian Museum directly. Deputy Director H.G. Cogger responded on 31 May 1977, reporting that the museum had no record of Matthews, Dr. Barfoot or the *Rosinante*, nor of any expedition launched to capture *C. megalodon*, in 1969 or any other year. Likewise, no record existed of the ill-fated yacht *Mary Crowley*, but the surname of its short-term survivor "coincidentally" matched that of Prof. H. David Baldridge,

founder of the International Shark Attack File. Likewise, no record exists of shark-hunter Brad Matthews in the U.S. or anywhere else, and no shark attacks were reported off Long Island during August 1975. *Killer Sharks*, in short, was a transparent hoax.

By contrast, a front-page report from the tabloid *Weekly World News* of 23 August 1988 was pure comic relief. According to the paper's headline, a Soviet nuclear submarine had been attacked by a 120-foot shark in the South China Sea. The tabloid, which frankly admits concocting its stories from thin air and moonshine, included an apt quotation from a nonexistent Russian marine biologist, Alexei Pedko: "There is much about the ocean we don't know."

That much, at least, is indisputably true.

Sources: H.G. Cogger, personal correspondence with the author (31 May 1977); Coleman and Clark, *Cryptozoology A to Z*; Coleman and Huyghe, *The Field Guide to Lake Monsters, Sea Serpents, and Other Mystery Denizens of the Deep*; Richard Ellis and John McCosker. *Great White Shark*. Stanford, CA: Stanford University Press, 1991; Thomas Helm, *Shark!* New York: Collier Books, 1961; Heuvelmans, *In the Wake of the Sea Serpents*; Brad Matthews, *Killer Sharks: The Real Story*. New York: Manor Books, 1976; Peter Matthiessen, *Blue Meridian*. New York: Random House, 1971; Shuker, *In Search of Prehistoric Survivors*; Smith, *Bunyips & Bigfoots*.

***Carlisle Castle* sea serpent**   In 1880, while approaching Melbourne, Australia, crewmen aboard the vessel *Carlisle Castle* saw a large aquatic "varmint" swimming nearby. They reported the SEA SERPENT sighting to the Melbourne *Argus*, which published the story with a sketch of the creature. Facetious comments published in London's *Daily Telegraph* so angered Captain Austin Cooper that he told a friend, "I don't see any more sea-serpents. It is too much to be told that one of Green's commanders can't tell the difference between a piece of seaweed and a live body in the water. If twenty serpents come on the starboard, all hands shall be ordered to look to port. No London penny-a-liner shall say again that Austin Cooper is a liar and a fool."

Source: Heuvelmans, *In the Wake of the Sea Serpents*.

Carmarthen Cats   In the 1990s, wildlife biologists blamed several livestock attacks around Carmarthen, Wales on a prowling "family" of COUGARS (*Puma concolor*). The first victims were lambs, slaughtered on a farm at Whitemill. The most recent attacks, in 1999, claimed sheep, a calf and a horse at the Penbryn Park Farm. Thus far, none of the CATS have been captured or photographed.

Source: "Catalogue of Wales' weird cats." BBC News (26 August 2000).

Anecdotal evidence described a family of lions prowling Carmarthen, Wales in the 1990s.

Carmel River sea serpent   In April 1948, three witnesses strolling on a beach near the mouth of this river, in California's Monterey County, sighted a 40-foot SEA SERPENT swimming a short distance offshore. They described the animal as covered with grayish-green hair, although its 8-foot head and neck were pink. A row of "glassy" green spines was visible along its back.

Source: Bord and Bord, *Unexplained Mysteries of the 20th Century*.

***Carnatic* sea serpent**   On 26 January 1858, Captain Suckling of the ship *Carnatic* reported a SEA SERPENT sighting from the South Atlantic, midway between SAINT HELENA and CAPE TOWN, South Africa. He described the creature as resembling "a large spar sticking out of the water and one some thirty feet above the level of the sea." Writing 110 years later, BERNARD HEUVELMANS was torn between considering the beast a specimen of his hypothetical "long-necked" serpent or a giant "super-EEL."

Source: Heuvelmans, *In the Wake of the Sea Serpents*.

***Carol Ann* sea serpent**   On 25 July 1962, Massachusetts fishermen aboard the *Carol Ann* reported a SEA SERPENT sighting off the coast of Marshfield. Witnesses described the creature as having a head like an ALLIGATOR'S, a body resembling a nail keg, and two large fins protruding from the vicinity of its tail. Archie Lewis told reporters that the beast "was gulping up the FISH in the area and did not concern itself with fishermen in any way." He added that he had seen all kinds of whales "but never one that resembled this creature."

Source: O'Neil, *The Great New England Sea Serpent*.

Carolina Parakeet   At its discovery in 1891, the Carolina parakeet (*Conuropsis carolinensis*) was North America's only indigenous member of the parrot family (*Psittacidae*). A small BIRD, it was nonetheless dramatic with its green plumage, yellow head and orange face. Because they were fruit-eaters, Carolina parakeets were killed on sight by orchard growers throughout its range in South Carolina, Florida and Georgia. Those who managed to survive that slaughter were trapped for pets or killed for use as ornaments on women's hats. The last confirmed wild specimens were shot at Lake Okeechobee, Florida in April 1904, while the last captive parakeet — a male named Incas — died at the Cincinnati Zoo on 21 February 1918.

Although officially extinct, Carolina parakeets were still reported from the wild over the next two decades. In 1920, witness Henry Redding reported a flock of 30 birds along Fort Drum Creek, in Florida's Okeechobee County. Six years later, at Grapevine Hammock in Okeechobee County, Charles Doe glimpsed three pairs of Carolina parakeets. The birds fled at his approach, whereupon Doe took their eggs for the collection he maintained as curator of birds for the state university. That thoughtless act may have doomed the species in Florida, but bird wardens at South Carolina's Santee Swamp, in Sumter County, reported further sightings in the 1930s. During 1933–34, George Melamphy saw as many as nine birds together at once. In 1936, ornithologists Robert Allen and Alexander Sprunt Jr. reported a flock of green, yellow-faced birds in the swamp, and a woodsman named Shokes sighted three together near Wadmacaun Creek, two years later. Those reports did not deter construction workers from draining the swamp in 1938, to construct the Santee-Cooper Hydroelectric Project. Meanwhile, in Georgia's Okefenokee Swamp, Oren Stemville took a color film of a bird

resembling the Carolina parakeet in 1937. A strange footnote to the parakeet's story was recorded in 1949, when witness Robert Allen expressed a newfound belief that the birds he saw with Alexander Sprunt in 1936 were actually mourning doves (*Zenaida macroura*), buff-colored birds bearing no resemblance whatever to parakeets.

Sources: Bille, *Rumors of Existence*; Fuller, *Extinct Birds*.

Witnesses suggest that the Carolina parokeet did not become extinct in 1918.

Carrowmore Lake, Ireland   Irish folklore names Carrowmore Lake, in County Mayo, as the ancient abode of a fearsome LAKE MONSTER. No modern sightings of the creature(s) are recorded.

Source: Holiday, *The Dragon and the Disc*.

Carska Bara, Yugoslavia The Carska Bara nature reserve is a large swamp located in the Ramsar region of Serbia, Yugoslavia. It sprawls over 3,954 acres, providing sanctuary for an estimated 150 BIRD species, including 8 different species of herons. The marshland also produces sporadic reports of LAKE MONSTERS, most recently in June 2001. On that occasion, a Bosnian sailor named Slaven heard bubbling and croaking sounds in the swamp, accompanied by noises like numerous tails or whips striking the water. A park warden named Sima also heard the sounds and fired several shots into the night, with no apparent target. He later told Serbian researcher Marko Sciban that a large squidlike creature inhabits Carska bara, sometimes surfacing at night.

Source: Karl Shuker, "Alien zoo." *Fortean Times* 150 (October 2001): 21.

Carter Lake, Michigan Details are regrettably sparse concerning claims that a 20-foot SNAKE of unknown species was once seen in this lake, near Hastings in Michigan's Barry County. No reptile native to North America is known to reach such lengths.

Source: Coleman, "On the trail of giant snakes."

Carvana This insidious predator of swamplands and lagoons in eastern Texas was described by a Mexican migrant named Aluna, who allegedly lost livestock to the creature in the mid-19th century. According to Aluna's story, no Carvana was ever seen alive, though its remains were sometimes found during droughts, when its marshy habitat evaporated. On those occasions, local settlers and aboriginal tribesmen allegedly discovered skeletons resembling those of huge TURTLES, with shells 10–12 feet long and 6 feet wide, while the beast's head and tail resembled an ALLIGATOR'S. In life, the Canavar lay submerged in mud, waiting to pounce on prey that included livestock and human beings. Skeptics suggest that tales of monsters "never seen alive" refer to early discovery of fossil DINOSAURS or Ice Age megafauna.

Source: "'California as I saw it': First-person narratives of California's early years, 1849–1900." Library of Congress, http://memory.loc.gov/ammem/cbhtml/cbhome.html.

Cascade Hominology Research Project Steven and Heller James became fascinated with BIGFOOT in early 1996, after a "run-in" with an unknown HOMINID at their campsite in Oregon's Cascade Range. They subsequently founded the Cascade Hominology Research Project and established an Internet website for reported Bigfoot sightings, with an emphasis on analyzing hair samples. The CHRP is now apparently inactive. The last website update, from 2002, notes that the Jameses were attending an unnamed Texas university, where Steven was pursuing a biology degree, while Heller majored in ecology. No other members of the group (if such it was) are publicly identified.

Source: Cascade Hominology Research Project, http://www.geocities.com/cascadehominid/cascade1.html.

Cash sea serpent On 13 August 1821, the *Eastport* (Mass.) *Sentinel* published an account of the Bay State's latest SEA SERPENT sighting. According to that story, the creature:

[w]as seen yesterday about ½ past 12 o'clock by the officers, crew and passengers of the schooner *Cash* (Capt. Beal) from Bowdoinham. He was first seen by Mr. Asa B. Hagins, a passenger, about 1½ miles northeast of the Graves [a series of rock ledges in Massachusetts Bay] moving toward Nahant; his motion was slow and apparently playful, with his head raised from the water about three feet. The circumference of the animal was about the size of a common barrel; his head shaped like that of a horse and the protuberances on his back were about six feet apart. The sail on the schooner was taken in, and the Serpent kept in distinct view more than 30 minutes; his length appeared about 60 feet, but having no glass on board it could not be ascertained with certainty.

Source: O'Neill, *The Great New England Sea Serpent*.

Caspian Tiger The Caspian TIGER (*Panthera tigris virgata*) is one of three subspecies, with the BALI TIGER and the JAVAN TIGER, presently believed to be extinct. Once ranging widely through Afghanistan, Kazakhstan, Turkmenistan, Uzbekistan, Iran and Turkey, these CATS were hunted ruthlessly until the last known specimen was shot in 1970. Nonetheless, C.J. Peers subsequently informed KARL SHUKER that he and three companions collected eyewitness tiger sightings from eastern Turkey in 1979. Seven years later, Bulgarian zoologist Nikolai Spassov reported claims from several hunters that the tigers still existed in Afghanistan, as well. Later still, Turkish zoologist Guven Eken claimed personal sightings in the Cudi Mountains, prompting Turkey's Society for the Protection of Nature to mount a formal expedition in 2001. Thus far, no results of that search have been published.

Source: Shuker, "Tracking a Turkish tiger."

Cassie Cryptozoologist LOREN COLEMAN coined the popular nickname for this SEA SERPENT of Maine's Casco Bay in 1986, but the first recorded sighting from those waters predated that christening by 168 years. On 21 June 1818, a group of fishermen reported a large serpentine animal swimming in Casco Bay. It reappeared in the summer of 1909, sighted by crewmen aboard the fishing steamer *BONITA* who reckoned its length at 80 feet. And fishermen were again the witnesses on 5 June 1958, reporting a prolonged encounter off Cape Elizabeth, during which they spent 45 minutes observing a long-necked beast in excess of 100 feet long.

Sources: Bord and Bord, *Unexplained Mysteries of the 20th Century*; Loren Coleman, "Casco Bay's sea serpent." *Portland Monthly* (May 1986); O'Neill, *The Great New England Sea Serpent*.

Catala Chief sea serpent On 6 December 1938, three crewmen aboard the coastal tug *Catala Chief* saw two SEA SERPENTS swimming in Chemainus Bay, on the southeastern coast of British Columbia's Vancouver Island. Witnesses William Higgs, George Macfarlane and John Shaw reported that the larger of the creatures was 40 feet long and the second slightly smaller, with round bodies and snakelike heads. Both swam with vertical undulations, indicative of mammals. Researcher PAUL LEBLOND considers the incident a sighting of the marine cryptid known as CADBOROSAURUS.

Source: LeBlond and Bousfield, *Cadborosaurus*.

Catfish (Giant) Catfish (Order *Siluriformes*) are freshwater FISH characterized by an absence of scales and whiskerlike barbels surrounding the mouth, for which they are named. Modern science recognizes 37 families of catfish worldwide, subdivided into 436 genera and 2,734 confirmed species, while speculative literature suggests another 873 species. Bona fide giant species, described in various conflicting publications as the largest freshwater fish on Earth, include the wels catfish (*Siluris glanis*) of Europe and Russia, with a record length of 15 feet 6 inches; Thailand's Chao Phrya giant catfish (*Pangasius sanitwongsei*), at 11 feet 4 inches; the 10-foot Mekong River giant catfish (*Pangasianodon gigas*); India's devil catfish (*Bagarius bagarius*), at 6

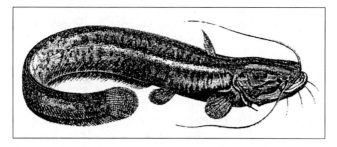

Encounters with giant catfish are reported from numerous world-wide locations.

feet 6 inches; and the Amazon's red-tailed catfish (*Phractocephalus hemioliopterus*), topping 5 feet in length. North America's record-holder, the blue catfish (*Ictalurus flurcatus*), is puny by comparison, with an average length of 2–3 feet and a record size of 4 feet 3 inches. Nonetheless, reports of much larger catfish persist from various parts of the U.S. and from other nations where no large species are recognized.

Cryptozoologist LOREN COLEMAN has collected U.S. tales of giant catfish dating from the 19th century to the present day. Specific sites with persistent stories of such whoppers include LAKE DECATUR, Illinois; LAKE MEAD, Nevada; LAKE OF THE OZARKS, Missouri; LAKE OF THE PINES, Texas; LOST LAKE, California; SAGUARO LAKE, Arizona; and TABLE ROCK LAKE, Missouri. Mark Twain claimed a personal sighting of a catfish "more than six feet long and weighing 250 pounds" in the MISSISSIPPI RIVER, where rumors claim that children have been snatched while swimming and welders allegedly refuse to work underwater on certain bridges after close encounters of the finny kind. Similar stories are told along the OHIO RIVER, where researcher Marc DeWerth reports that his grandfather once saw a dead catfish longer than his 20-foot fishing boat. In South America, predatory fish larger than *P. hemioliopterus* were described by explorer PERCY FAWCETT, and TIM DINSDALE recounted stories of swimmers devoured by giant catfish in various rivers. BERNARD HEUVELMANS and JOHN KIRK report sightings of the 18-foot MANGURUYÚ, said to ply the waters of Brazil's RIO PARAGUAI. In Africa's Congo basin, WILLIAM GIBBONS claims that a U.S. missionary, the Rev. Eugene Thomas, once caught a catfish weighing more than 200 pounds, which fed Thomas and 10 PYGMY families for more than a week.

Sources: Coleman, *Mysterious America*; "Dog-eating catfish dies." Reuters (25 July 2003); "Killer catfish croaks." *Fortean Times* 176 (December 2003): 16; "Terrors of the deep." *Fortean Times* 85 (February-March 1996): 12; Wright Thompson, "In pursuit of the giant catfish." Kansas City Star (6 July 2003); "Trying to save a catfish as big as a bear." CNN News (1 December 2003); All Catfish Species Inventory, http://clade.acnatsci.org/allcatfish/.

Cat-Headed Snake

A measure of confusion surrounds this supposed reptilian cryptid of 18th-century Europe. In April 1711, at Hauwelen in the Swiss Alps, brothers Jean and Thomas Tinner allegedly killed a 7-foot gray-and-black SNAKE with a head resembling a CAT'S and a sharp ridge running the length of its spine. Further west, the Cat-headed snake of France's Vienne Department was no snake at all, but rather an aggressive lizard with four obvious legs, a feline head, short tail, and a furry mane. Frenchmen also called the reptile a Dar, meaning "forked tongue." Some researchers suggest that both creatures are synonymous with the elusive TATZELWURM.

Sources: Henri Ellenburger, "Le monde fantastique dand le folklore de la Vienne." *Nouvelle Revue des Traditions Populaires* 1 (1949): 407–435; Johan Scheuchzer, *Helvetica*. Leiden: Petri Vander Aa, 1723.

Catherine sea serpent

On 3 October 1892, five Scottish fishermen aboard the *Catherine* saw a SEA SERPENT in the FIRTH OF TAY near Angus. Witness Thomas Gall described a large slate-blue SNAKE'S tail with a white tip thrashing the surface some 30 yards from the vessel. Soon after it submerged, a round blackish-brown head appeared above water 30 feet distant, prompting the observers to peg the beast's length around 40 feet.

Source: Heuvelmans, *In the Wake of the Sea Serpents*.

Catherine Burke sea serpent

On 18 May 1931, a SEA SERPENT was sighted in Massachusetts Bay. A newspaper report described the incident as follows:

Report of the first "sea serpent" of 1931 was the news of the day at the Boston Fish Pier — and vouched for by twenty-three fishermen, the captain and crew of the Gloucester schooner *Catherine Burke*. They all had a look at the "serpent," or what you will, last Monday, twenty miles east of Boston Lightship while bound for Georges Bank. The creature described as forty or fifty feet long, with a head about five feet long resembling that of a horse, appeared on the surface 100 yards astern the schooner. It remained in sight several minutes traveling at [an] estimated speed of seven to eight knots per hour [8–9 mph]. In this interval, the "serpent" sounded twice, giving the fishermen a view of its "broad black back and SHARK-like tail." It was a clear morning and observation was perfect, according to Captain Ray Marsden's report of the incident to the secretary of the Boston Fish Bureau.

Source: O'Neill, *The Great New England Sea Serpent*.

Cats (Winged)

BATS are the only flying mammals recognized by science, but reports of winged felids have emerged from three continents over the past 140 years. The first came from India, where hunter Alexander Gibson shot a winged cat in the late 1860s and displayed its skin at a gathering of the Bombay Asiatic Society. Three decades later, in November 1899, London's *Strand Magazine* published a photo of a cat owned by a resident of Wiveliscombe, Somerset. The animal had two furry growths on its back that flapped like wings whenever it moved. Another London publication, the *Daily Mirror*, published the following story from a special correspondent on 9 June 1933:

A few days ago neighbours of Mrs. Hughe Griffiths of Summerstown, Oxford, saw a strange black and white cat prowling round their gardens. Last evening Mrs. Hughes Griffiths saw the animal in a room of her stables. "I saw it move from the ground to a beam — a considerable distance which I do not think it could have leaped — using its wings in a manner similar to that of a BIRD," she said to me. Mrs. Hughes Griffiths at once telephoned the Oxford Zoo, and Mr. Frank Owen, the managing director, and Mr. W.E. Sawyer, the curator, went to her home and captured the animal in a net. I carefully examined the cat tonight, and there is no doubt about the wings. They grow just in front of its hindquarters.

The Oxford Zoo no longer exists, and the only relic of its curious feline is a photograph published in 1933. Six years later, another black-and-white cat with a 2-foot wingspan was photographed in Attercliffe, Sheffield. This one was a domestic pet, named Sally by its owner, and it resembled the Oxford specimen so closely that some researchers suspect a blood relationship between them. In June 1949, another cat with a 23-inch wingspan was reportedly shot and killed in northern Sweden, when it attacked a child. Once again, the remains were discarded. A third British specimen, a tortoiseshell cat named Sandy, was exhibited at Sutton-in-Ashfield, Nottinghamshire in the 1950s. Sandy reportedly developed wings as an adult, and while she flapped them energetically, she could not fly.

Teenager Douglas Shelton was hunting near his Pinesville, West Virginia home in May 1959, when his dog treed a peculiar animal. About to shoot it, Shelton realized the creature was a cat with wings and spared its life. He caught the animal and took it home, naming it Thomas, though it proved to be a female. Reporter Fern Miniacs of the Beckley *Post-Herald* examined Thomas, and told her readers: "It's thirty inches long, has a tail like a squirrel, and two perfectly shaped wings, one on each side. The wings are boneless but evidently have gristles [*sic*] in them. Each wing is about nine inches long." Shelton told the press, "It wasn't wild. It acted like it was used to people. And its manners were pretty good until you pulled those wings. Then it would get mad and start clawing." An unnamed Baltimore veterinarian examined Thomas and declared, "I thought at first that the wings were the result of a freak of nature, an attempt to grow an extra pair of legs. But now I don't know what they are." Shelton and Thomas appeared on NBC's *Today* show on 8 June 1959, then returned to Pinesville, where Shelton charged the curious 10 cents a head to see his cat. One of the visitors was Mrs. Charles Hicks, a widow who claimed she had purchased the cat — named Mitzi — at a California pet shop some years earlier. Shelton refused to surrender the animal, and Mrs. Hicks filed a lawsuit for possession. On 5 October 1959, Shelton appeared in court with Thomas/Mitzi and a small box containing its wings, which were shed sometime in July. Mrs. Hicks accused Shelton of trickery, but the judge dismissed her claim, allowing the plaintiff one dollar "for her trouble."

A strikingly similar case was reported from England in the early 1960s, where a newspaper advertisement offered the mounted remains of "Thomas Bessy, the Famous Winged Cat" for sale in a glass-and-mahogany showcase. According to the ad, the cat had been displayed in a 19th-century British circus, whereupon its original owner filed a lawsuit for recovery. The plaintiff won that case, but the cat was dead on arrival at home, allegedly poisoned in transit. Author Peter Dance wrote to the address given in the ad, but he received no answer and the specimen's fate (if it ever existed) remains a mystery.

On 24 June 1966, Jean Revers glanced outside his home at Alfred, Ontario and saw a creature "looking like a big black cat, but with hairy wings on its back" pursuing a neighbor's cat. Revers grabbed a rifle and ran outside, whereupon the beast "screamed like hell, and it tried to get away by making gliding jumps of 50 or 60 feet — wings extended — after a good running start. It could stay a foot or so above the ground." Revers shot it five times, then called the police. Constable Terence Argall told reporters, "I couldn't believe my eyes when I saw the thing. Its head resembled a cat's, but a pair of needle-sharp fangs five-eights of an inch long protruded from the mouth. It had a cat's whiskers, tail, and ears, and its eyes were dark, greenish and glassy." The cat weighed 10 pounds, its pelt was glossy black, and its wingspan measured 14 inches. Revers buried the carcass in his backyard, then unearthed it for study at Kemptville Agricultural School, where lab technicians reported: "The bat-like wings protruding from its back were found to be growths of thick, matted fur. It was just an ordinary black cat." Strangely, Canadian papers carried two more reports of winged cats killed that year — one near Ottawa, Ontario and another at Lachute, Québec — but details are hopelessly vague in both cases.

One last report of a winged cat was filed from Japan in May 1998. Witness Rebecca Hough was visiting Kumamoto, on the island of Kyūshū, when she saw a cat with a strange "bumpy" back. "I realized," she said, "that it had weird growths — not fat or bones, but jutting-out fur-covered wing-like growths. In all other respects it seemed quite normal. The growths were triangular and covered in soft fluffy fur. They felt like the wings of a chicken."

Cryptozoologist KARL SHUKER suggests that cats with "wings" are actually afflicted with a condition known to veterinarians as feline cutaneous asthenia (FCA), characterized by abnormally delicate, flexible skin that may result in furry winglike flaps. While plausible enough in cases where the wings remain immobile, FCA would not explain reports of cats using dorsal appendages to leap or glide long distances above the ground.

Sources: "Can a cat fly?" *Strand Magazine* 18 (November 1899): 599; Peter Dance, *Animal Fakes and Frauds*. Maidenhead, England: Sampson Low, 1976; Keel, *The Complete Guide to Mysterious Beings*; Rickard and Michell, *Unexplained Phenomena*; Shuker, "Cat flaps"; Karl Shuker, "Menagerie of mystery." *Strange Magazine* 17 (Summer 1996): 24; R.B.W., "Flying cat." *Naturalist's Note Book* 5 (1868): 318.

Cauldshields Loch, Scotland

While writing to a friend in 1815, novelist and poet Sir Walter Scott had this to say about a small lake in his native Borders region of southern Scotland:

> A monster long reported to inhabit Cauldshields Loch, a small sheet of water in this neighborhood, has of late been visible to sundry persons. If it were not that an otter swimming seems a very large creature, I would hardly know what to think of it, for a very cool-headed, sensible man told me he had seen it in broad daylight. He scouted my idea of an otter and said the animal was more like a cow or a horse.

Scott never saw the beast himself, but "by a sort of instinct" he took a rifle with him on his next stroll past the loch.

Source: Costello, *In Search of Lake Monsters*.

Cax-Vinic

Ancient Mayans described the Cax-vinic ("bush man") as a WILDMAN of the forest, covered in brown or black hair. Historically, sightings were concentrated in the southern state of Chiapas, but scattered reports have also emerged from other parts of Mexico. In the 1930s, explorer W.C. Slater found humanoid footprints "the size of a small woman's hand" in a snowfield on Volcán Popocatépetl, near Mexico City, at an altitude of 6,500 feet. Local residents identified the tracks with elusive "men of the snows." Alternate names for the Cax-vinic throughout its range include Fantasma humano ("human phantom") and Hombre oso ("bear man").

Source: Sanderson, *Abominable Snowmen*.

Cecil

Walker Lake, in western Nevada's Mineral County, is said to be inhabited by a LAKE MONSTER known as Cecil, presumably in homage to the *Beany and Cecil* TV cartoon series (1950–67) featuring "Cecil the sea-sick SEA SERPENT." Aboriginal tribesmen regarded Walker Lake's serpentine cryptids as predatory man-eaters, but legend has it that their shamans struck a bargain with the beasts, whereby the animals restricted their predation to white settlers. As recently as April 1956, two witnesses described a creature 45–50 feet long in Walker Lake, swimming on the surface at a speed of 35 miles per hour.

Sources: Baumann, *Monsters of North America*; J.K. Parrish, "Our country's mysterious monsters." *Old West* (Fall 1969): 25, 37–38.

Cedar Lake, Canada

Manitoba's Cedar Lake, located four miles north of Lake Winnipegosis and linked to Lake Winnipeg by the Saskatchewan River, has long been a source of LAKE MONSTER reports. In 1909, fur trader Valentine McKay was canoeing across Cedar Lake, near Graves Point, when he saw "on the glossy surface of the water 400 yards from shore...a huge creature traveling at about 2 mph. It had a dark upper surface which glistened, and part of its body projected about four feet in the air, vertically. The water was considerably disturbed." Canadian cryptozoologist JOHN KIRK reports that a duck hunter, Oscar Frederickson, saw the beast in April 1918, but other sources (including TIM DINSDALE) place that sighting at Lake Winnipegosis. The confusion may be forgiven, perhaps, since some researchers consider the Cedar Lake creature(s) identical with WINNIPOGO, reported from neighboring lakes.

Sources: Dinsdale, *Monster Hunt*; Kirk, *In the Domain of the Lake Monsters.*

Cenaprugwirion/Genaprugwirion

This unidentified foot-long lizard is reported from the neighborhood of Aber Sôch, on the Lleyn Peninsula of Gwynedd, Wales. Witnesses describe the reptile as dark brown in color, with a head the size of a ripe orange, a long tongue, and a prominent dewlap. Modern sightings are rare, but locals claim the Cenaprugwirion ("daft flycatcher") was common during the early 20th century. Cryptozoologist KARL SHUKER notes that specimens of the New Zealand tuatara (*Sphenodon punctatus* or *S. guntheri*) were commonly imported as exotic pets in the 19th century. suggesting that escapees may have established a naturalized population. Tuataras live 100 years or more in the wild and may survive on a meager diet of two earthworms per week. Unless a specimen is captured, however, the Cenaprugwirion's identity cannot be confirmed.

Source: Shuker, "Land of the lizard king."

Centipede (Giant)

Centipedes (Family *Chilopoda*) are arthropods distantly related to crabs and lobsters. Although their common name means "hundred-legged worm," they are not worms and none has 100 legs. In fact, until October 1999, all of the 3,000 recognized centipede species on Earth had odd-numbered pairs of legs, ranging from 15 (or 30 legs total) to 191. That rule was broken when Chris Kettle found a new species with 48 pairs of legs at Whitburn, near Sunderland, England. All centipedes are predators, injecting venom into prey through their first pair of legs, but few species have fangs large enough to pierce human skin. Among those that do, we include North America's largest species, the giant desert centipede (*Scolopendra heros*) of the U.S. Southwest and Mexico, with a record length exceeding 8 inches. A related species, Florida's *S. altermans*, may exceed 7 inches. Yet another relative, the Galápagos centipede (*S. galapagensis*), doubles those records with a documented length of 17 inches. The largest centipede (and largest arthropod) yet known to science was found in April 1999, in Early Permian fossil beds at Thueringen, in central Germany. That flesh-eating monster (Genus *Anthropleura*) measured 7 feet 6 inches and possessed a pair of fangs resembling ice tongs.

Thankfully, such giants need not trouble us today, but relatively "giant" centipedes have been reported in the U.S. Ozarks region, where they have no place, and some of those allegedly rival the size of *S. galapagensis*. Ozark folklorist Silas Turnbo records several incidents from the 19th century, in which large centipedes were killed or captured in Arkansas and Missouri, well outside the range of *Scolopendra*. According to Turnbo, an 8-inch specimen was caught near Gainesville, Missouri and preserved in alcohol by a local physician who displayed it at his office. Another cen-

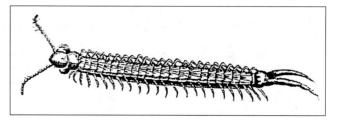

Giant centipedes are said to inhabit Arkansas and Missouri.

tipede, 7–8 inches long, was captured between Gainesville and Dugginsville by "an old settler who managed to sell it to someone for a half pint of whisky." In Stone County, Missouri a 7.5-inch centipede allegedly bit a child who "lay a year before he recovered" and "remained a cripple" after the wound had healed. During autumn 1861, a woodcutter in Taney County, Missouri found an 8-inch centipede curled around a clutch of young in an attitude commonly displayed by *Scolopendra* females.

Thus far, the specimens described were all within normal size limits for North American centipede species, albeit far from home. The same cannot be said about the even larger centipedes described by Turnbo, however. A ferocious 12-incher allegedly pursued a young boy near Bradley's Ferry, Missouri, then menaced a man who came to his aid before it was shot and killed. Another 12-inch specimen was burned alive by frightened witnesses who saw it run into a tree stump on Mountain Creek, in Marion County, Arkansas. In 1855, Marion County spawned another giant, killed outside the town of Powell. Its slayer reported, "I had no way of measuring it accurately, but a close examination proved it was not less than fourteen inches long and over an inch wide." And even worse lay in store for local arachnophobes, as Turnbo reported:

> The biggest centipede found in the Ozarks I have a record of was captured alive by Bent Music on Jimmie's Creek in Marion County in 1860. Henry Onstott, an uncle of mine, kept a drug store in Yellville and collected rare specimens of lizards, serpents, spiders, horned frogs and centipedes, and kept them in a large glass jar which sat on their counter. The jar was full of alcohol and the collection [*sic*] was put in the jar for preservation as they were brought in. Among the collection was a monster centipede. It was of such unusual size, it made one almost shudder to look at it. Brice Milbum, who was a merchant at Yellville when Mr. Music brought the centipede to town, said he assisted in the measuring of it, before it was put in the alcohol, and its length was found to be eighteen inches. It attracted a great deal of attention and was the largest centipede I ever saw. The jar with its contents was either destroyed or carried off during the heat of the [Civil] war.

Source: Arment, "Giant centipedes in the Ozarks."

Centre for Fortean Zoology

Britain's Centre for Fortean Zoology, based at Devon, was founded in 1992 by author and cryptozoologist Jonathan Downes. He continues as director to the present day, although renowned explorer John Blashford-Snell is listed as the group's honorary president for life. The CFZ's Internet website describes it as "the only full time scientific organization dedicated to the study of mystery animals in the world." Since its formation, members of the CFZ have conducted nationwide field investigations into sightings of mislocated CROCODILES, the BOLAM LAKE YETI and the MONSTER OF MARTIN MERE, while launching an ALIEN BIG CAT Study Group in 2003. Various CFZ members have also led cryptozoological expeditions to Mexico, Central America, Thailand and Sumatra during recent years.

In addition to editing the CFZ journal, *Animals & Men*, director Downes has published several books in the field, including *The Owlman and Others* (1998), *The Rising of the Moon* (1999), *Weird Devon* (2000) and *The Monster of the Mere* (2003). As research for this volume neared completion, the CFZ announced a triumph of sorts over mainstream zoology. Specifically, society spokesmen had long disputed claims by herpetologists that only three species of lizard are found on the British mainland. The CFZ was vindicated in August 2003, when a thriving population of European green lizards (*Lacerta viridis*) was found in Bournesmouth, within 100 yards of headquarters for the skeptical Herpetological Conservation Trust.

Source: Centre for Fortean Zoology, http://www.cfz.org.uk/.

Ceram Civet While the mammalian carnivores known as civets (Family *Viverridae*) are found in various countries, including 34 species in 20 genera, none are presently recognized from the Indonesian island of Ceram. In 1986, however, Tyson Hughes collected an 18-inch mammal's tail, covered in fur with dark rings, which Ceram's Moluccan natives identified as belonging to a beast half CAT and half dog. Zoologists employed by the World Wildlife Fund identified the tail as a civet's, but its species and point of origin remain unknown.

Source: Shuker, "A surfeit of civets?"

Ceram's elusive civet is known only from a severed tail.

***Ceramic* sea serpent** In 1932, crewmen aboard the vessel *Ceramic* saw "a monster with a thick neck with flippers on either side, and a head like a TURTLE" in the Indian Ocean, midway between Sydney, Australia and Durban, South Africa. BERNARD HEUVELMANS considered the creature a specimen of a hypothetical SEA SERPENT he dubbed "father-of-all-turtles."

Source: Heuvelmans, *In the Wake of the Sea Serpents.*

***Ceres* sea serpent** On 25 July 1881, crewmen aboard the ship *Ceres* allegedly attacked and wounded a large, spotted SEA SERPENT in Mariveles Bay, on the Philippine island of Manila. BERNARD HEUVELMANS speculated that their victim was probably a whale shark (*Rhincodon typus*).

Source: Heuvelmans, *In the Wake of the Sea Serpents.*

Chadburn Lake, Canada Fortean authors Colin and Janet Bord include this Canadian lake, located near Whitehorse in the Yukon Territory, on a published list of supposed LAKE MONSTER habitats. Unfortunately, no dates or details of sightings are provided, and they also misplace the lake in British Columbia.

Source: Bord and Bord, *Unexplained Mysteries of the 20th Century.*

Chagljevi The Chagljevi is a small, unidentified canid of timid nocturnal habits, reported from the Republic of Montenegro (formerly a part of Yugoslavia). Researchers suggest that the reports may involve the golden JACKAL (*Canis aureus*), which ranges widely over southeastern Europe.

Source: Marcus Scibanicus, "Strange creatures from Slavic folklore." *North American BioFortean Review* 3 (October 2001): 56–63.

Chain Lakes, Maine Ancient legends of the Passamaquoddy tribe describe these lakes, along the border with Québec, as the domain of a 50-foot amphibious SNAKE. No modern sightings of the creature are recorded.

Source: Charles Skinner, *American Myths and Legends*. Philadelphia: Lippincott, 1903.

***Chalcedony* sea serpent** On 5 June 1880, Captain M.D. Ingalls and the crew of the *Chalcedony* sighted a creature they described as "the original SEA SERPENT" near Monhegan Island, off the coast of Maine. According to Ingalls:

It was dead, and floated on the water, with its belly, of a dirty brown color, up. Its head was at least 20 feet long, and about 10 feet through at the thickest point. About midway of the body, which was, I should guess, about 40 feet long, were two fins, of a clear white, each about 12 feet in length. The body seemed to taper from the back of the head down to the size of a small log, distinct from the whale tribe, as the end had nothing that looked like a fluke. The shape of the creature's head was more like a tierce [a 42-gallon wine keg] than anything I can liken it to. I have seen almost all kinds of shapes that can be found in these waters, but never saw the like of this before.

Capt. Ingalls further reported that some of his sailors "got on this dead creature, and one of the boys cut a double-shuffle on its belly." Writing nine decades later, BERNARD HEUVELMANS concluded that Ingalls was "no doubt" mistaken in misidentifying a decomposed whale carcass.

Source: Heuvelmans, *In the Wake of the Sea Serpents.*

Chalk Point Creature A SASQUATCH-type HOMINID visited Maryland's Anne Arundel County for the first time in 1968, when motorist Carl Drury reported a 10-foot-tall creature covered with "dark mangy hair," wandering along Patuxent Road. By year's end, at least 25 sightings were recorded from the area, and local newspapers dubbed their visitor the Chalk Point Creature. Sightings continued for nearly a decade, often sparse in detail, with the last on record reported by witness Ronald Jones. On 30 August 1977, Jones claimed an 8-foot, 500-pound monster attacked his pickup truck near Tracy's Landing, forcing Jones to defend himself with a tire iron and flee at top speed.

Source: Berry, *Bigfoot on the East Coast.*

Challenger Deep Flatfish The MARIANA TRENCH, located east of the Mariana Islands in Micronesia, is some 1,500 miles long and has an average width of 42 miles. It is the deepest submarine chasm on Earth, and its greatest depth is found near Guam, in the Challenger Deep (named for oceanographic vessel HMS CHALLENGER II). On 23 January 1960, undersea explorers Jacque Piccard and Donald Walsh plumbed the abyss of the Challenger Deep in a bathysphere, touching bottom at 35,800 feet below sea level. As they touched down, a large flat FISH resembling a sole (Family *Cynoglossidae*) swam away from the bathysphere and soon vanished beyond the range of their lights. Both witnesses reported that the unknown fish had two visible eyes, though skeptics say they would be useless at such depths. Researcher Torben

Wolff proposed that the creature might have been an oval-shaped sea cucumber (*Galatheathauria aspera*), though that species has no eyes.

Source: Eberhart, *Mysterious Creatures*; Jacques Piccard and R.S. Dietz, *Seven Miles Down*. New York: G.P. Putnam's Sons, 1961.

Challenger sea serpent

In 1963, while conducting research off the coast of New Jersey, scientists aboard the U.S. Fish and Wildlife vessel *Challenger* observed a strange, nearly transparent creature 40 feet long and 5 inches wide. Some of those present believed it was a Venus girdle (*Cestum veneris*), but that ribbon-shaped marine invertebrate (Phylum *Ctenophora*) has an official 5-foot record length. No other giants of the same description have been found during the intervening decades.

Source: Bille, *Rumors of Existence*.

Chambers, John (1922–2001)

Chicago native John Chambers spent 30 years in Hollywood as a special-effects makeup artist, renowned for his work on such diverse films as *Showdown on Boot Hill* (1958), *The List of Adrian Messenger* (1963), *Slaughterhouse Five* (1972), *The Island of Dr. Moreau* (1977) and *National Lampoon's Class Reunion* (1982). His television credits included work on *Lost in Space*, *Mission Impossible*, *The Outer Limits* and *Star Trek*, where he reportedly created Mr. Spock's distinctive ears. Chambers is best known, though, for the APE makeup that won him an Academy Award for *Planet of the Apes* (1968). In preparation for that film and its sequels, Chambers studied primates at the Los Angeles Zoo and developed a new type of foam rubber to create more expressive facial prosthetics. The timing of those events is auspicious, since the controversial PATTERSON FILM depicting an alleged BIGFOOT appeared in October 1967. Over the next three decades, rumors circulated that Chambers was involved in production of that film, and also in sculpting a model of the MINNESOTA ICEMAN. In summer 1996, magician-author Mark Chorvinsky took the rumors public in *Strange Magazine*, claiming that it was "general knowledge" among Hollywood insiders that Chambers built "the Patterson ape suit" and that he may have aided further in production of the film.

"Common knowledge" it may be—but is it true? Chorvinsky, by his own account, first heard the Chambers-Patterson rumor from a young summer intern at the Smithsonian Institution in 1992. Three years later, he picked up its echo from makeup artist Dave Kindlon, who in turn heard the tale from colleague Howard Berger in 1983–84. Berger's source was makeup artist Rick Baker, who relayed the rumor when they worked together on a Bigfoot movie, *Harry and the Hendersons* (see Appendix B). Kindlon later heard the story from Baker himself in 1987, while collaborating on *Gorillas in the Mist*. Baker's source was unknown, but Berger speculated that Baker "probably heard if from John Chambers." An outspoken critic of the Patterson film, Baker told talk-show host Gerald Rivera in 1992 that Patterson's SASQUATCH "looked like cheap fake fur." Still, he refused Chorvinsky's interview request, a circumstance which prompted Chorvinsky to write: "It is highly significant that Baker believed the film to be a fake. He, if anyone, would know."

That logic is fatally flawed, unless Baker himself collaborated on the film, which he did not. Still, others stood ready to buttress the rumor with second- and third-hand assertions. "Ape impersonator" Bob Burns deemed the Patterson film a HOAX and told Chorvinsky, "I heard a rumor once that John Chambers might have built that suit." Sadly, despite "racking [his] brains," Burns could not remember his source. John Vulich, owner of a Cali-

fornia makeup studio, repeated the Chambers-Patterson tale in a series of 1995 Internet postings. Vulich heard the rumors "from at least two or three people," including FX artist Bart Mixon and makeup man Jim McPherson. While acknowledging that Patterson could not have afforded a decent Hollywood ape suit in 1967, McPherson theorized, "He probably called Chambers to rent a suit." Makeup sculptor took the hearsay game a step further, telling Chorvinsky that the rumors came from "reputable sources" who vowed that friends and relatives of Chambers "knew that he worked on the Patterson suit." Chorvinsky mentioned "a source very close to John Chambers"—but again, the informants remained anonymous. In October 1997, director John Landis told reporter Scott Essman that Chambers had built the Patterson ape suit and later confessed it to Landis, when they worked together on *Beneath the Planet of the Apes* (1970).

But what of Chambers himself? Essman traced him to a Los Angeles nursing home on 25 October 1997, and reported his comments to Chorvinsky. As recalled by Essman, "Chambers said that he didn't do it. He said that it was not his project, and that if he had done it, he would have done a better job." Nurse and Bigfoot researcher BOBBIE SHORT spoke to Chambers the following day, receiving a somewhat different response. Again, Chambers denied involvement with the Patterson film, explaining to Short that he was "good, but he was not *that* good." Chorvinsky, perhaps predictably, ignored the denials. "I did not expect Chambers to tell Scott that he made the Patterson suit," Chorvinsky wrote, "any more than I would expect Patterson's associate Bob Gimlin to suddenly reveal that the film was hoaxed." Again, the logic was faulty, since Chambers had nothing to gain by keeping the secret, and he was rapidly nearing the end of his life.

Chorvinsky next pursued John Landis, who had known Chambers for almost 30 years and once directed him in a low-budget Bigfoot comedy called *Schlock* (Appendix B). Chorvinsky claims that Landis said he "thought that I deserved to know the truth about the case," but it was not to be. "Unfortunately," Chorvinsky wrote in 1998, "something occurred that made it impossible for him to publicly discuss the case any further." Landis allegedly consented to discuss the matter privately and off the record, but no further information is available concerning those disclosures, if in fact the conversation(s) ever happened. John Chambers died from complications of chronic diabetes on 25 August 2001, at the Motion Picture and Television Fund retirement home in Woodland Hills, California. In respect to his supposed involvement with the Patterson film, we have his personal denials ranged against speculative guesswork and third- or fourth-hand rumors, frequently derived from unnamed sources.

Sources: Chorvinsky, "The makeup man and the monster"; Chorvinsky, "Update: Makeup master John Chambers and the Patterson Bigfoot suit"; Chambers Affair, http://www.n2.net/prey/bigfoot/; Loren Coleman, "Forever linked to Bigfoot: John Chambers passes away." http://www.lorencoleman.com/john_chambers_obituary.*html*; Loren Coleman, John Chambers Denies Involvement in Patterson Bigfoot Film, http://www.n2.net/prey/bigfoot/.

Champ

Lake Champlain lies on the New York-Vermont border, extending into Québec as Missisquoi Bay. The lake is 109 miles long and 11 miles across at its widest point, with a surface area of 440 square miles and a maximum recorded depth of 400 feet. It is named for French explorer Samuel de Champlain, who "discovered" the lake in July 1609 and may have been the first white man to glimpse the LAKE MONSTER now known as Champ. Abnaki, Algonquin and Iroquois tribesmen recognized a great horned serpent in the lake, whom they dubbed Tatoskok, long before Champlain arrived. As to what, if anything, Champlain himself observed, the record is confused and controversial. Historian Marjorie Porter, writing for *Vermont Life* in summer 1970, cited no source for her claim that Champlain "recorded his impression of a serpent-like creature about twenty feet long, as thick as a barrel and with the head of a horse." Another suspect quotation from Champlain's journal refers to "a great monster, lying in the lake, allowing BIRDS to land on its beak, then snapping them in whole." Likewise, no documentation supports published claims that local natives presented Champlain with a souvenir monster's head. Champlain *did* record a sighting of a 5-foot creature known to the Iroquois as *chousarou*, still unidentified but generally believed to be a lake sturgeon (*Acipenser fulvescens*) or long-nosed gar (*Lepisosteus osseus*).

Whether Champlain saw the great serpent or not, other European settlers were soon aware of its presence. Abel Horsmer, a soldier stationed at lakeside Crown Point in September 1760 carved a DRAGON on his powder horn, while residents of Westport, New York named the nearby harbor Big Snake Bay. The first official sighting was logged on 24 July 1819, at Bulwagga Bay, New York. A boat captain named Crum reported a creature 187 feet long, bearing its flat head 15 feet above water, thus revealing a white star on its forehead and a bright-red ring around its neck. Another 315 sightings were recorded by November 1992, describing beasts that ranged from 10 to 75 feet long, dark in color, frequently displaying humps or coils and swimming with an upraised head. At least 219 sightings involved multiple witnesses, including groups of 50 (1870), 19 (July 1973), 30 (6 October 1982), 35 (7 July 1983), 14 (16 August 1983), 62 persons (28 July 1984), 10 (19 July 1992) and 25 persons (19 May 2003). As with Scotland's NESSIE, several sightings between 1886 and 1992 describe large cryptids seen on land, beside the lake.

Showman P.T. Barnum offered a $50,000 reward for Champ's capture in 1873 and repeated the bid (albeit reduced to $20,000) in 1887. Those offers got no takers, but two alleged captures of juvenile specimens were reported in the 20th century. Writing in 1970, Marjorie Porter quoted a 1945 newspaper headline — "Baby SEA SERPENT Taken in Vermont Waters — May Be Offspring of Lake Monster"— but she provided no further dates, details or sources for the sensational story. Three decades later, Dennis Hall reportedly caught a strange 12-inch reptile at an unspecified location beside Lake Champlain. As author JOHN KIRK states the case:

> The creature looked like no other living reptile and possessed a strange forked tongue. Upon inspecting the creature, Dennis's father thought the beastie strange enough to be worthy of examination by the scientists at the University of Vermont who indicated that it was unlike any living reptile in the catalog. Like many a cryptozoological creature, this one was somehow lostthereby ensuring that the monster would remain an enigma.

Not only was the specimen misplaced, but there appears to be no record of its visit to the university. Likewise, while Dennis Hall claims several sightings of Champ, he is entirely omitted from JOSEPH ZARZYNSKI'S 1984 tabulation of 224 sightings at Lake Champlain. John Kirk reports that Hall subsequently found "the spitting image" of his missing reptile in a book on prehistoric fauna. Hall identified his catch as *Tanystropheus*, a long-necked reptile of the Middle Triassic period, known from fossils found in Israel, Germany and Switzerland. Some paleontologists believe the 10-foot creature may have been amphibious, though its re-

mains display no specific adaptations to an aquatic lifestyle. In any case, it is presumed extinct for some 220 million years.

While specimens remain elusive, there is other evidence of Champ's existence. On 5 July 1977, Sandra Mansi was picnicking with her fiancé and children in a lakeside field north of St. Albans, Vermont when a long-necked creature surfaced 100–160 feet offshore. Before fleeing the scene, Mansi snapped a photo of the beast with her Kodak Instamatic camera, producing a picture that remained secret until its publication by the *New York Times* on 30 June 1981. Prior to publication, the photo was studied by multiple experts. Dr. George Zug, with the Smithsonian Institution's Department of Vertebrate Zoology, reported in July 1980 that while he could offer "no unequivocal

Showman P.T. Barnum offered rewards for Champ's capture.

identification" of the creature depicted, "[c]ertainly all our examinations cast no doubts on the authenticity of their photograph and report." In April 1981, J. RICHARD GREENWELL arranged for study of the Mansi photo at the University of Arizona's Optical Sciences Center, where Dr. B. Roy Frieden opined: "The picture appears to be a valid print, not a superposition, of a real object somewhere out on a fairly large body of water." Cryptozoologist PAUL LEBLOND performed a dynamics analysis of the photo in 1982, calculating that the creature caught on film was somewhere between 16 and 60 feet long. Another photo of Champ was allegedly taken by Bev Piche's daughter, from the Fort Ticonderoga ferry on 5 August 2001, but it has not been published.

Multiple alleged videotapes of Champ existed at press time for this book. The first was taken at Arnold's Bay by witness Mark Palmer, in late September 1992. According to analyst Dennis Hall, the tape depicts an animal "popping up and down very quickly, then moving through the water, and diving forward." Hall concluded that Palmer had seen an aquatic bird, but he has no such doubts concerning his own supposed videotapes of Champ. One 45-minute tape, taken by Hall near the mouth of Otter Creek, Vermont on 6 July 2000, reportedly shows two long-necked cryptids swimming in tandem. Hall claims to have at least five other tapes of Champ in action, taken between October 2000 and June 2003, but no scientific analyses of the videotapes is presently available.

As at Loch Ness, sonar technology also suggests the presence of one or more sizeable cryptids inhabiting Lake Champlain. Joseph Zarzynski's Lake Champlain phenomena investigation has employed sonar in search of Champ since the late 1970s, while encouraging private parties to do likewise. Zarzynski and colleague Jim Kennard scored their first sonar "hit" on a large submerged object in Whallon Bay, New York, on 3 June 1979. It traveled at a depth of 175 feet, and while the reading was consistent with a single organism, the hunters could not rule out a school of fish. On 1 May 1982, Raymond Sargent saw Champ on the surface, followed by a sonar reading after the creature submerged. In June 2003, multiple sonar recordings taken by a Discovery Channel television crew at Button Bay, Vermont were analyzed by Fauna Communications Research in Hillsborough, North Carolina. According to team spokesperson Elizabeth von Muggenthaler, "What we got was a biological creature creating biosonar at a level that only a few underwater species can do." The recordings were 10 times louder than sounds made by any known species of fish in Lake Champlain, while irregular sequence ruled out mechanical devices such as fish finders.

Skeptics insist that Champ sightings arise from HOAXES or mistaken observations of various objects ranging from logs to large sturgeons. Stray harbor seals (*Phoca vitulina*) have also been proposed, with specimens documented from Lake Champlain in 1810, 1846 and 1876. KARL SHUKER suggests that the creatures may be relict PLESIOSAURS, while ROY MACKAL and GARY MANGIACOPRA cast their votes in favor of surviving ZEUGLODONS. Whatever it may be, Champ is protected by law in both New York and Vermont. Port Henry's board of trustees set the tone on 6 October 1980, with a resolution declaring local waters "off limits to anyone who would in any way harm, harass or destroy the Lake Champlain Sea Monster [*sic*]." After a false start in 1981, Vermont's state legislature passed a similar resolution (drafted by Joseph Zarzynski) on 20 April 1982. Two weeks later, a Champ-protection resolution passed New York's state senate, followed by an identical measure's passage in the New York state assembly on 18 April 1983.

Sources: Daniel Bader, "Fisherman reports encounter with lake creature." *Plattsburgh* (NY) *Press-Republican* (10 August 2003); Citro, *Green Mountain Ghosts, Ghouls and Unsolved Mysteries*; Coleman and Huyghe, *The Field Guide to Lake Monsters, Sea Serpents, and Other Mystery Denizens of the Deep*; Diane Foulds, "New evidence on Champ is luring sea-monster fans to Vermont." *Boston Globe* (24 August 2003); Garner, *Monster! Monster!*; Sam Hemingway, "Lake's first 'Champ-hearing' recorded." *Burlington* (VT) *Free Press* (20 July 2003); Kirk, *In the Domain of the Lake Monsters*; "Magazine disputes legend of Champlain monster." *Newsday* (30 June 2003); Lohr McKinstry, "Champ found!" *Plattsburgh* (NY) *Press-Republican* (16 August 2003); Lohr McKinstry, "Champ surfaces for best fan." *Plattsburgh* (NY) *Press-Republican* (23 September 2002); Lohr McKinstry, "Camera-shy Champ the focus." *Plattsburgh* (NY) *Press-Republican* (16 May 2003); Lohr McKinstry, "'Discovery' Champ hunt true to name?" *Plattsburgh* (NY) *Press-Republican* (6 June 2003); Lohr McKinstry, "Mystery resurfaces." *Plattsburgh* (NY) *Press-Republican* (20 December 2000); Lohr McKinstry, "Owner of Champ suit skinned." *Plattsburgh* (NY) *Press Republican* (6 August 2003); Lohr McKinstry, "Shy Champ getting national TV exposure." *Plattsburgh* (NY) *Press-Republican* (31 August 2002); Wilson Ring, "Biologists find baby denizens of Lake Champlain." *Newsday* (23 May 2003); Zarzynski, *Champ*; Zarzynski, "LCPI work at Lake Champlain"; Champ: A Brief History, http://mistwebdesign.com/history.html.

Champ Quest   According to founder Dennis Hall, the Vermont-based CHAMP Quest organization was created in 1991 or 1992 (accounts differ) "to collect data, search for, record sightings and protect the animals living in Lake Champlain known as Champ." Hall claims the group has been remarkably successful, though questions surround its operations and discoveries. Par-

ticularly controversial are Hall's claims of personal sightings, videotapings and capture of a "baby" LAKE MONSTER at Lake Champlain.

The latter event allegedly occurred sometime in the 1970s, when Hall caught an unidentified 12-inch reptile at an undisclosed point along the lake's shore. As explained to author JOHN KIRK, Hall's father sent the specimen to the University of Vermont, where unnamed scientists pronounced it "unlike any living reptile in the catalog"—and then promptly lost it. No trace of the creature or its supposed laboratory analysis remains today, but Hall claims that he subsequently identified his catch from pictures in an unnamed text on prehistoric animals. Specifically, he chose *Tanystropheus*, a long-necked lizard of the Middle Triassic period, known from fossil deposits in Europe and the Middle East. Aside from its presumed extinction some 220 million years ago, *Tanystropheus* displayed no features of aquatic life and seemingly did not exceed 10 feet in length. Champ, by contrast, is a lake-dweller described by witnesses as ranging from 10 to 187 feet long.

Hall's early brush with baby Champ did not see light until Kirk published it in 1998, six or seven years after Hall and colleague Richard Deuel began research at Lake Champlain. By that time, Hall had glimpsed a grownup specimen at Button Bay, Vermont, in 1985. Champ Quest supplanted the Lake Champlain phenomena investigation, created in the 1970s by pioneer researcher JOSEPH ZARZYNSKI, and while the LCPI boasted modest results, Champ Quest's were quite the reverse. Of 30 eyewitness sightings reported in 1992, Hall claimed 5 for himself, including an alleged sighting of 4 creatures seen together near Kent's Island, on 8 November. Thus, within five months, Hall doubled the record of multiple sightings by any known witness in Champ's 400-year history—nor was he finished, yet. According to Hall, he has also videotaped Lake Champlain's cryptids on at least seven occasions, between 6 July 2000 and 23 June 2003. In the first instance, Hall produced a 45-minute videotape purportedly showing two long-necked creatures swimming near the mouth of Otter Creek, Vermont. On 8 September 2002, Hall and his wife spent 10 minutes taping three large cryptids in the lake between Ferrisburgh and Westport, Vermont.

Some skeptics consider Hall's record of multiple sightings—and sightings of multiple creatures—too good to be true. Indeed, Hall himself sounded incredulous as he described yet another videotaping of Champ, at Button Bay, on 30 May 2003. He told the press, "I have so much work to do that is not Champ-related, but job-related, so I should not have gone to the lake Saturday for just a few minutes. But I did, and guess who showed up as soon as I pulled in, long enough to capture five minutes of video? The video is convincing, as it is closest yet, and the head pops in and out of the water several times." Fuzzy still photos lifted from various videotapes are displayed on Champ Quest's Internet website, but no independent analysis of the tapes has yet been published.

Sources: Deuel and Hall, "Champ Quest at Lake Champlain, 1991–1992"; Kirk, *In the Domain of the Lake Monsters*; Lohr McKinstry, "Champ surfaces for best fan." *Plattsburgh* (NY) *Press-Republican* (23 September 2002); Lohr McKinstry, "'Discovery' Champ hunt true to name?" *Plattsburgh* (NY) *Press-Republican* (6 June 2003); Champ Quest: The Ultimate Search, http://www.champquest.com/.

Chan   The Mexican LAKE MONSTER known as Chan reportedly divides its time among seven lakes of the Valle de Santiago, in Guanajuato State, northwest of Mexico City. Witnesses describe the creature as resembling a long-necked sauropod DI-NOSAUR, similar in form to Africa's MOKELE-MBEMBE. Most sightings are reported from Lago La Alberca, but natives of the region maintain (without supporting evidence) that all seven lakes are linked by flooded subterranean caverns. Chan was known to ancient Aztecs, who revered it as a deity and offered gifts to win the beast's favor. That ritual persists in modern times, and researcher Leopoldo Bolaños allegedly captured Chan on film during one such offering, in September 1997. Sadly, the photo reveals no conclusive detail, a problem familiar to crypto-photographers worldwide. Forty years earlier, 6 September 1958, a more dramatic picture of Chan had been snapped in the wake of a local earthquake. Analysts with the BRITISH COLUMBIA SCIENTIFIC CRYPTOZOOLOGY CLUB have classified that photo as a probable HOAX.

Source: Kirk, *In the Domain of the Lake Monsters.*

Changhai Lake, China

The mysterious East is never more inscrutable than when discussion turns to cryptozoology. A case in point is Changhai ["colorful"] Lake, located in central China's Sichuan Province at 32° 4' north latitude and 104° 1' east longitude. Changhai is 4.8 miles long, with a mean depth of 143 feet and a maximum recorded depth of 289 feet. On 12 October 1984, a Chinese scientist working at Changhai Lake sighted a "miracle animal," which he described as having a horse's head and a body resembling that of a DINOSAUR or a RHINOCEROS. When reporting that incident, in 1989, Fortean authors Colin and Janet Bord unaccountably moved Changhai Lake to Tibet (or Zizang Province), roughly 1,000 miles west of its actual location. That confusion may derive in part from Changbai Lake, more commonly called Tianchi ("DRAGON Lake"), allegedly inhabited by the LAKE MONSTER known as GUÀI WÙ. However, that site lies in Jilin Province, near China's border with North Korea, some 1,200 miles east of Changhai Lake. Author JOHN KIRK compounds the mystery by treating Changbai and Tianchi as two entirely separate lakes.

Source: Bord and Bord, *Unexplained Mysteries of the 20th Century*; Kirk, *In the Domain of the Lake Monsters.*

Channel Islands sea serpent

In August 1923, while hunting for lobsters along the coast of Herm, one of the smaller Channel Islands between England and France, 14 witnesses encountered a remarkable creature. Witness Hilda Bromley later described the event to TIM DINSDALE as follows:

After walking and running for some time, we came to a large pool — but what held us spellbound were marks on the seaweed as if something huge had come out of the pool and had dragged itself over the seaweed covered sand and away to our right — we one and all turned, and followed these drag marks…for some considerable distance, and then we came to an enormous pool — far larger than the first one, into which the drag marks 5–6 ft. in width, disappeared! We all stood amazed, 14 of us, what could it be? Then slowly, away in the middle of the pool, a large head appeared and a huge neck — but we did not see the body; there it stayed with its great black eyes gazing at us without fear — then slowly it sank back into the water. It was evident it had never seen a human being before. We joined hands and all stepped into the pool, to see if we could disturb the creature, but it was too large and deep for us to make any real impression.

The tide came in at that point, causing the intrepid monster-stalkers to retreat. Mrs. Bromley further described the beast as black, with a thick neck 3–4 feet long, and a wide mouth like that of a sea elephant (*Mirounga leonina*). Writing of the incident 65 years later, BERNARD HEUVELMANS speculated that the creature was

either a specimen of his hypothetical "long-necked" sea serpent, or perhaps the similar "merhorse."

Source: Heuvelmans, *In the Wake of the Sea Serpents.*

Chapel St. Leonards sea serpent

On 16 October 1966, while strolling on the beach at Chapel St. Leonards in Lincolnshire, England, George and May Ashton saw a large SEA SERPENT swimming 100 yards offshore. As it moved parallel to the coast, the creature revealed six or seven "pointed" humps above the surface.

Source: B.M. Bayliss, "Those sea monsters." *Skegness Standard* (26 October 1966).

Chapple, Peter (1954–2002)

Cryptozoologist and singer Peter Chapple founded the AUSTRALIAN RARE FAUNA RESEARCH ASSOCIATION in 1984, after his personal encounter with an ALIEN BIG CAT in the Dandenong Range. With Chapple as president, the group proceeded to investigate sightings of ABCs, relict THYLACINES and other cryptids reported from the island continent Down Under. Chapple pursued that quest for 18 years, including trips to England where he lectured on Australian cryptids in 2000 and 2001. In his spare time, Chapple frequently participated in Welsh eisteddfod festivals, winning 38 events and placing in 57 more between 1985 and 1993. He also joined the Victoria State Opera in 1985 and cut four albums during 1993–96. In 1997, Chapple placed first while representing Australia at the Fifteenth International April Spring Music Festival in North Korea. He was pursuing a master of science degree at Monash University when a heart attack claimed his life on 26 August 2002. Colleague Mike Cleeland told the press, "Peter's rare qualities of inspiration, ability, and persistence resulted in the assembly of a loyal band of colleagues at ARFRA who will be determined to ensure that his work will be continued."

Source: Loren Coleman Internet obituary of Peter Chapple, 28 August 2002.

Charles-Hardouin sea serpent

In December 1903, while en route from France to Hong Kong, the French ship *Charles-Hardouin* was caught in a typhoon and forced to seek shelter in Vietnam's Tourane [now Da Nang] Bay. As the vessel sought shelter, the helmsman pointed out a large, dark object in the water. According to a report from the ship's mate:

15 to 20 yards from the ship a double mass appeared. The length of each part must have been about 25 feet and the distance between them about 18. The bulk of each of these coils could be compared to that of a big half-hogshead barrel. A spiky crest gave the coils a quite singular appearance. It all undulated like a SNAKE in motion, and its speed was markedly greater than that of the ship, which was doing 9 knots [10 mph] so far as I recall. The color was "dirty black." A few seconds later the animal dived horizontally, churning the water violently.

Reviewing the case 65 years later, BERNARD HEUVELMANS concluded that the creature was a specimen of his rare hypothetical "many-finned" SEA SERPENT, seen most often in coastal waters of tropical Asia.

Source: Heuvelmans, *In the Wake of the Sea Serpents.*

Charles Mill Lake, Ohio

In 1959, witnesses reported a "strange animal" swimming in this lake, east of Mansfield in northern Ohio's Richland County. No other sightings of the supposed LAKE MONSTER are on file.

Source: Bord and Bord, *Unexplained Mysteries of the 20th Century.*

***Charles of Provincetown* sea serpent**　At 10:00 a.m. on 5 July 1833, officers and crew aboard the schooner *Charles of Provincetown* sighted a large SEA SERPENT in Massachusetts Bay, 1.5 miles east of Nahant. The sighting corresponded with a report of three large, serpentine creatures seen from the steamboat *CONNECTICUT*, approximately three miles distant.

Source: O'Neill, *The Great New England Sea Serpent.*

Charlie　Charleston Lake lies 30 miles northeast of Kingston, Ontario, between Lyndhurst and Mallorytown. In 1897, settler Noah Shook claimed that a LAKE MONSTER pursued him on the surface of the lake, hissing loudly as it thrashed the water. A half-century later, three fishermen reported their encounter with a beast resembling a DINOSAUR, near Tallow Bay Rock. In 1994, a visitor who came to scatter his father's ashes at Charleston Lake sighted a cryptid resembling "a large rain slick." Three years later, a couple passing the lake at night saw unexplained waves 3–4 feet high breaking on the shore, although there was no wind and no boats were visible.

Source: Shadowlands Sea Serpent Page, http://theshadowlands.net/serpent2.htm#ontario.

***Châteaux-Renault* sea serpent**　On 12 February 1904, officers and crew aboard the French steam-launch *Châteaux-Renault* saw a SEA SERPENT in ALONG BAY, on the northern coast of Vietnam. While approaching a waterway known as Crapaud (Toad) Roads, Lieutenant Péron, commanding the vessel, was alerted by a warning cry of "a rock dead ahead," whereupon:

> I stood up and stopped the engines. Then I saw, not very far ahead, a gray mass shaped like a TURTLE'S back, which we reckoned to be more than 12 feet across. Almost at once it disappeared. I supposed it was a sperm-whale. The launch still having way on her, we came near where it had surfaced, and I saw that there was a big patch of oil on the water. I still remained stopped, and am glad I did. Soon afterwards we heard the water churning to the west, and we saw, almost touching the nearby shore a little south of Chandelier Rock, two huge coils which I supposed must belong to a monstrous EEL at least 3 feet in diameter. I saw to my great surprise that the skin of this beast and the rocks on the shore were the same color; dark gray with patches of dirty yellow. From the distance that I was the skin seemed smooth and even. It appeared briefly, [then] the two coils disappeared with a repetition of the noise we had already heard. Once again we looked all around us. There was not a breath of wind, the surface of the water was smooth. In the end we saw ripples rather far away in the direction of the Crapaud. We could not see clearly, for we were too low down. All the same I got the impression that the animal was just awash and moving by vertical undulations.

Péron pursued the creature but was unable to catch it, later estimating its speed in excess of 10 miles per hour. During the futile chase, he said, "from time to time a jet of water came out of the head," and he "saw that there were patches of oil in the animal's wake." Despite the eyewitness comparison to a giant turtle, BERNARD HEUVELMANS later concluded that the creature was one of his hypothetical "many-finned" sea serpents.

Source: Heuvelmans, *In the Wake of the Sea Serpents.*

Chats Lake, Canada　Located on the Ottawa River at Arnprior, Ontario, Chats Lake is also known in Québec as Lac des Chats ("lake of CATS"). On 13 November 1874, witness R. Young reported a LAKE MONSTER sighting from Chats Lake, but no other reports are on file. The creature, if it existed, was presumably in transit.

Source: "A monster in the Ottawa." *New York Times* (18 November 1874).

Chattahoochee Bigfoot Organization　No background information is presently available on this Georgia-based organization of BIGFOOT researchers. The CBO's Internet website describes the group as "a layman's organization that primarily prides itself with amateur researchers and field investigators." The organization's stated goal is "to gather information… to document the existence of an endangered species, known as Bigfoot in the southeast [*sic*] and Sasquatch in the northwest United States." At press time for this volume, the CBO's 27 identified members — all committed to a "no-kill" research philosophy — included 14 in Tennessee; 4 in Georgia; 2 each in Alabama and Kentucky; and 1 each in the states of Connecticut, Hawaii, New Hampshire, Texas and Virginia. The CBO's website declares: "We are not out for fame, fortune and glory. We are out for the real glory and that being 'KNOWING.'"

Source: Chattahoochee Bigfoot Organization, http://www.chattahoocheebigfoot.org/.

Chattahoochee River, Georgia　Cryptozoologists LOREN COLEMAN and JOHN KIRK included northern Georgia's Chattahoochee River on published lists of supposed aquatic cryptid habitats, but they provide no dates or details of sightings.

Sources: Coleman, *Mysterious America*; Kirk, *In the Domain of the Lake Monsters.*

Chelovek Mishka *see* **Yeti**

Chemosit *see* **Nandi Bear**

Chepitchkaam/Chepitkam *see* **Ktchi Pitchkayam**

Chessie　SEA SERPENT sightings from Chesapeake Bay and adjacent rivers date from the 19th century and have continued into modern times. One of the first reports, filed on 26 July 1840 by crewmen aboard two schooners, described a 12-foot creature resembling a giant TURTLE, seen swimming on the surface near North Point, Maryland. At least 77 other reports were filed by 1884, most of them describing dark-colored serpentine creatures 12–35 feet long. In 1963, a helicopter pilot from Aberdeen Proving Grounds saw one such beast in the Bush River. Two years later, witness Pam Peters reported a sighting from the Hillsmere section of South River, near Annapolis. Chessie's nickname was coined by a reporter for the *Richmond* (VA) *Times Dispatch* in July 1977, after Gregg Hupka snapped a fuzzy photo of the beast near the Potomac River's mouth. Sightings multiplied thereafter, and Robert Frew produced the first Chessie videotape at Love Point, on Kent Island, on 31 May 1982. A panel of scientists from the Smithsonian Institution and Maryland's Department of Natural Resources studied the tape on 20 August 1982, and while their final verdict was inconclusive, spokesman George Zug declared: "All viewers of the tape came away with a strong impression of an animate object….These sightings are not isolated phenomena, for they have been reported regularly for the past several years [*sic*]." Three years later, in September 1985, two fishermen were trolling for flounder near the Hampton Roads Bridge when:

> Suddenly, something rose and broke the surface, rolling over. It appeared to be large with no dorsal fins; only a large curved back was visible. Puzzled, we didn't know what it was. A short time later, we observed a long neck protruding from the water of the stern of our boat, toward the northwest, with a short, horse-like head, looking away from us at an angle….I looked at my friend and

asked what it was. He said that maybe it was a turtle. I said I had never seen a turtle with an 8-ft. neck! The creature submerged when I wasn't looking. About 15 to 20 minutes later, while I was putting bait on my hook, my friend shouted that he had something big on his line. I looked over and his rod was bent over double, his line moving in the water from our right to our left, steady, as though something big was on. Suddenly, a head, long neck, and large body erupted from the water behind us. I could see a greenish yellow-colored body, rounded back with a number of barnacles on it, and large diamond-shaped fins on the front, stroking frantically. My friend's fishing line, which was draped over the chest of the animal, snapped. The animal took several frantic thrusts in the water and dove down. A large wash of several waves rose our boat up and slammed us down.

The year 1985 witnessed a legislative effort to encourage scientific study of Chessie, with a resolution placed before the Maryland state senate's Committee on Economic and Environmental Affairs. That resolution was defeated by senators unable to accept Chessie's "possible existence," but their negative votes failed to discourage the creature(s), and sightings continued into the 1990s.

Sources: "Chessie videotape analysis inconclusive." *ISC Newsletter* 2 (Spring 1983): 9; Clark and Pear, *Strange & Unexplained Phenomena*; Michael Frizzell, "The Chesapeake Bay serpent." *Crypto Dracontology Special* 1 (November 2001): 129–137; Garner, *Monster! Monster!*; Russ Robinson, "Chessie may have made video debut." *Baltimore Sun* (11 July 1982); Close Encounter with Chessie, http://paranormal.about.com/library/blstory_july03_som.htm.

Chester carcass   On 8 May 1782, a curious GLOBSTER washed ashore near Chester, England from the River Dee. A local newspaper, the *Chester Courant*, described the carcass as follows:

The length of it is 25 feet; the girth proportionally large, though very unequal; it has two dorsal and six pectoral fins—two of the latter of a vast singular form, partaking of the nature of feet. The tail is perpendicular, of prodigious size and strength; there are five gills on each side. The mouth, when open to its extremity, is three feet wide; there are not any teeth, but a vast quantity of small, irregular sharp protuberances, which are evidently given it for the purpose of comminuting its food, the orifice of the throat being astonishingly narrow for a creature of such magnitude. The upper and under jaws are each furnished with ten strong protuberant bones, horizontally placed, which meet when the mouth closed, in such a manner as to appear capable of breaking almost any substance. The eye is situated very near the mouth, and scarcely larger than that of an ox; the nose is hard and prominent; the whole body is covered with a very thin skin, and the weight of the FISH is between four and five tons.

The report ended with an observation that "We have been thus particular, as it is probable that some Naturalist may favour the public with the certain information of its real species." Sadly, that appeal went unanswered and the beast remains unidentified today.

Source: Richard Holland, "Beached leviathans." *Fortean Times* 119 (February 1999): 52.

Cheval Marin   The Cheval marin ("sea horse") was a SEA SERPENT reported from Canadian waters in the 16th century. French explorer Jacques Cartier was first to report the fishlike beasts with heads resembling those of horses, in 1534. He saw them swimming in the St. Lawrence River, near the mouth of an unnamed tributary generally believed to be the modern-day Rivière-St.-Jean. Cartier's description roughly corresponds with aboriginal accounts of various Canadian LAKE MONSTERS. On the far side of the Earth, French pioneers in Africa applied the same

name to large aquatic creatures they met along that continent's west coast. Today, most researchers believe those animals were either West African manatees (*Trichecus senegalensis*) or hippopotamuses (*Hippopotamus amphibius*).

Sources: Awnsham Churchill, ed., *A Collection of Voyages and Travels*. London: A. and J. Churchill, 1704; Meurger and Gagnon, *Lake Monster Traditions*.

Chicken Man   Beginning in December 1970, residents of El Reno, Oklahoma suffered nocturnal raids upon their chicken coops by a MYSTERY MAULER that initially left only bloodstains and feathers behind. As the attacks continued into 1971, however, some victims reported finding oversized humanoid footprints and handprints at the scenes of various attacks, prompting local wags to dub the prowler Chicken Man. Author W. Haden Blackman claims that investigators found tracks "in huge numbers" at various scenes, yet the case is entirely omitted from standard works of BIGFOOT-SASQUATCH lore published over the next two decades. Blackman published a photo of one handprint, credited to LOREN COLEMAN, and claims it was examined by Oklahoma City Zoo director Lawrence Curtis. The print measured 7⅝ inches long by 4⅛ inches wide, with a badly deformed thumb.

Source: Blackman, *The Field Guide to North American Monsters*.

Chiemsee, Germany   Fisherman Max Pertl reportedly hooked and then lost a giant FISH at this lake, in Germany's Bayern State, on 22 June 1991. While no one else saw the reputed whopper, most zoologists agree that he may have caught a wels CATFISH (*Siluris glanis*), which attains a record length of 15 feet 6 inches in some European lakes and rivers.

Source: Magin, *Trolle, Yetis, Tatzelwürmer*.

***Chillagoe* sea serpent**   On 13 July 1902, Captain W. Firth and his crew aboard the steamer *Chillagoe* met a SEA SERPENT off the coast of Victoria, Australia. Witnesses later agreed that the beast was 30–35 feet long, with four visible fins each 4–5 feet tall and spaced 6 feet apart. Its head resembled a seal's but was larger, roughly 2 feet wide. When the *Chillagoe* approached within 100 yards, the creature raised its head, stared briefly at the vessel, then submerged. Captain Firth told reporters, "All agree that it resembled the serpent seen by those on board the *PRINCESS*, illustrated in the *Strand Magazine*, the only visible difference being the fins, which seemed more angular than those in the magazine." Nearly seven decades later, BERNARD HEUVELMANS sited the creature as a specimen of his theoretical "many-finned" sea serpent.

Source: Heuvelmans, *In the Wake of the Sea Serpents*.

Chilludo   Natives of Argentina's Nuequén Province describe the Chilludo as a SASQUATCH-type HOMINID who inhabits mountain peaks and lobs boulders at human trespassers. While legends of the creatures predate the arrival of Spanish conquistadors, a Chilludo sighting was reported from Colo Michi Co as recently as 1950.

Source: Gregorio Alvarez, *El Tronco de Oro*. Nuequén, Argentina: Pehuen, 1968.

Chimpanzee (Giant) *see* **Bili Apes**

Chimpanzee (Pygmy)   Natives of Gabon report that certain forests of their nation are inhabited by troops of chimpanzees (*Pan troglodytes*) much smaller than normal members of that species. The average mature pygmy chimp allegedly weighs only six pounds, and some are said to lack thumbs or big toes.

Pygmy chimpanzees allegedly inhabit the forests of Gabon.

Any personal deficiencies are overcome by the APES' habit of traveling in groups that include 100 or more individuals. Explorer Phillip Carroll collected a specimen in August 1957, after it fell from a tree and was fatally injured. Carroll shipped its remains to the University of Zürich's Anthropological Institute, where it was dissected and identified as a juvenile chimpanzee with severe skeletal deformities. No other specimens have been collected to date, although the pygmy chimps have been graced with a zoological catalog number (AIZ 6624). Some published accounts refer to these apes as Gabon orangutans, despite their complete dissimilarity from actual orangutans (*Pongo pygmaeus*).

Source: Michael Diamond, "Setting the record straight on the 'Gabun orangutan.'" *Pursuit* 48 (Fall 1979): 142–145.

Chipekwe
This supposed living DINOSAUR of southern Africa has been known to aboriginal inhabitants from time immemorial, and to Western readers since the first decade of the 20th century. Famed animal collector Carl Hagenbeck was first to mention the creature in print, in 1909. He wrote:

> Some years ago I received reports from two quite distinct sources of the existence of an immense and wholly unknown animal said to inhabit the interior of Rhodesia [now Zambia and Zimbabwe]. …The natives, it seemed, had told both my informants that in the depths of the great swamps there dwelt a huge monster, half elephant, half DRAGON. This, however, is not the only evidence for the existence of the animal. It is now several decades ago since [Hagenbeck associate Joseph] Menges, who is, of course, perfectly reliable, heard a precisely similar story from the [N]egroes; and still

more remarkable, on the walls of certain caverns in Central Africa there are to be found actual drawings of this strange creature.

It remained for another of Hagenbeck's agents, Hans Schomburgk, to furnish the Chipekwe's native name in 1910. Schomburgk described visits to Zambia's Lake Bangweulu and the Dilolo marshes, located where Zambia and Angola border the Democratic Republic of Congo. In both places, natives described the Chipekwe as a huge amphibious creature that killed and ate hippopotamuses. "Unfortunately," Schomburgk wrote, "I thought this story was a fable and did not pursue my inquiries further. Later I talked to Carl Hagenbeck, and now I am convinced that it is some kind of saurian. Hagenbeck has received from other sources reports which entirely agree with my own observations and with what I was told by the natives I questioned."

Natives were not the only witnesses to the Chipekwe, however. One night in 1906, Rhodesian magistrate H. Croad was camped beside an unnamed lake when he heard loud splashing sounds, and sunrise revealed huge, unidentified footprints on shore. Later that year, Croad met a settler from Lulimala, R.M. Green, who described a hippo killed by the Chipekwe, with its throat torn out, on the nearby River Lukulu. Neither story was published until 1933, but London's *Daily Mail* printed a letter from correspondent C.G. James on 26 December 1919 which described the Chipekwe, albeit with various typographical errors. James wrote:

> Sir, I should like to record a common native belief in the existence of a creature supposed to inhabit huge swamps on the borders of the Katanga district of the Belgian Congo [now the DRC]—the Bangmeolo [Lake Bangweulu], Minero [Lake Mweru], [and] the Kafue swamps. The detailed descriptions of this creature vary, possibly through exaggerations, but they all agree on the following points: It is named the Chipekure [*sic*]; it is of enormous size; it kills hippopotami (there is no evidence to show that it eats them, rather the contrary); it inhabits the deep swamps; its spoor (trail) is similar to a hippo's in shape; it is armed with one huge tusk of ivory.

Maps reveal that Lakes Bangweulu and Mweru are linked by the Luapala River system, and that both are linked to Tanzania's Lake Tanganyika by the Lualaba River. Five years after James's letter was published, author John Millais provided further corroboration for the Chipekwe and its range. He wrote:

> I have met only one practical hunter and man of observation actually believing in the existence of a great beast that is unknown to science. This is Mr. Denis Lyell, who has written many books on the game of Central Africa. He is convinced that there is, or was till recently, some large pachyderm, somewhat similar in habits to the hippopotamus, but possessing a horn on the head, which frequents the great marshes and lakes of Banguelu [*sic*], Mweru, and Tanganyika. He calls it a water RHINOCEROS, and can adduce good evidence for his theory.

On 15 July 1932, the *Rhodesian Herald* published a letter from South African big-game hunter Franz Grobler, describing the great cryptid of the Dilolo swamps. Grobler wrote:

> It is known by the native name "Chepekwe." [*sic*] The natives in Central Africa used to call it the water lion. It can best be described as a huge leguan [IGUANA], the weight of which is estimated at about four tons or more. It was discovered about six months ago by a German scientist in the Dilolo swamps in Angola, and while I was in that country I saw photographs of it. I went to Lake Dilolo myself to look for it, but I did not see it. The natives say it is extremely rare and seldom seen, but they are convinced as I am of its existence. It lives only in the swamps, and from what I was told it attacks rhino, hippo, and elephant. I have seen a photograph of the "Chepekwe" on top of a hippo it had killed.

The *Herald* subsequently printed another letter, this one from J.C. Johansen, an overseer on a Belgian rubber plantation in the Congo. The letter described a hunting trip to the Kasai valley, where Johansen allegedly met a Chipekwe on 16 February 1932. As he described the incident:

> No game was in sight. As we were going down to the water, the boy suddenly call out "elephants." It appeared that two giant bulls were almost hidden by the jungle. About 50 yards away from them I saw something incredible — a monster, about 16 yards in length, with a lizard's head and tail. I close my eyes and reopened them. There could be no doubt about it, the animal was still there. My boy cowered in the grass whimpering.
>
> I was shaken by hunting-fever. My teeth rattled with fear. Three times I snapped [a camera]; only one attempt came out well. Suddenly the monster vanished, with a remarkably rapid movement. It took me some time to recover. Alongside me the boy prayed and cried. I lifted him up, pushed him along and made him follow me home. On the way we had to traverse a big swamp. Progress was slow, for my limbs were still half-paralysed with fear. There in the swamp, the huge lizard appeared once more, tearing lumps from a dead rhino. It was covered in ooze. I was only about 25 yards away. It was simply terrifying. The boy had taken French leave, carrying the rifle with him. At first I was careful not to stir, then I thought of my camera. I could plainly hear the crunching of rhino bones in the lizard's mouth. Just as I clicked, it jumped into deep water.

The latter photo was published in various magazines and newspapers, and again by BERNARD HEUVELMANS in the 1950s. Heuvelmans dismissed it as a "crude fake," wherein a Komodo dragon [*Varanus komodoensis*] was "transplanted somewhat clumsily into an African swamp scene, where it is perched ballerina-like on the tips of its toes on the carcass of a hippopotamus or rhinoceros, thus making it look enormous." In any case, the beast depicted has no horn, and thus clearly was not the classic Chipekwe.

The year after that HOAX, British settler Joseph Hughes published a book describing his 18 years on Lake Bangweulu, including a report of a Chipekwe killed by Wa-Ushi tribesmen on the Luapula River. Hughes wrote:

> A good description of the hunt has been handed down by tradition. It took many of the best hunters the whole day spearing it with their large "Viwingo" harpoons — the same as they use today for the hippo. It is described as having a smooth dark body, without bristles, and armed with a single smooth white horn fixed like the horn of a rhinoceros, but composed of smooth white ivory, very highly polished. It is a pity that they did not keep it, as I would have given them anything they liked for it.

Witness Alan Brignall reported a LAKE MONSTER sighting at Lake Bangweulu in May 1954, but the long-necked creature he described had no horns and more closely resembled accounts of the beast known as MOKELE-MBEMBE. A year later, author Frank Lane published what may be the last contemporary Western account of the Chipekwe, quoting a letter from big-game hunter H.C. Maydon. "I met a man," Maydon wrote, "an old hunter-prospector in Livingstone, Rhodesia, who swore that he had seen a water monster in Lake Mweru and had studied its tracks." KARL SHUKER notes that the Chipekwe bears a strong resemblance to the Congo's elephant-killing EMELA-NTOUKA.

Sources: Heuvelmans, *On the Track of Unknown Animals*; Shuker, *In Search of Prehistoric Survivors*.

Chippewa Lake, Wisconsin   Authors LOREN COLEMAN and JOHN KIRK include this lake, located 22 miles southeast of Hayward in Wisconsin's Bayfield County, on published lists of supposed LAKE MONSTER habitats. No dates or details of sightings are provided.

Sources: Coleman, *Mysterious America*; Kirk, *In the Domain of the Lake Monsters*.

Chitapo   Native folklore in Zambia described the Chitapo as a LAKE MONSTER inhabiting Lake Kashiba. Mythology invests it with the supernatural power to devour human shadows. No modern sightings of the creature are reported.

Source: Brian Siegel, Water Spirits and Mermaids, http://www.ecu.edu/african/seras/Siegel400.htm.

***Chitral* sea serpent**   In April 1933, while traveling from Japan to England, passengers aboard the British liner *Chitral* glimpsed a SEA SERPENT in the Indian Ocean. A quarter-century later, witness Lilian Rawlings described the event to her grandson as follows:

> The bell had gone for lunch. Nearly all the passengers (2nd class) had left the deck. Only a few of us remained, leaning on the rail. Then I saw something moving, parallel with the ship, in the same direction (apparently only a few yards from the ship but that I was not competent to judge) a small head on a long neck sticking out of the water and behind the neck a gap and then a hump — the whole seeming to be about the length of our ship. (It would be absurd I think not to assume that the humps belonged with the neck and head, especially as they moved with it.) We watched it for (I should guess) from anything from a minute to a minute and a half and then the whole thing quietly sank out of sight. I expected a fuss to be made of what had been seen....But I heard nothing of it....When I *saw* the beast, and realized I was looking at a creature which was generally supposed not to exist, I had the sensation that it was not so very wonderful after all, and that, having once seen it, I might see it again and that others would. Once assured of its existence, my mind accepted the fact and got rid of its astonishment entirely.

Thus fearing ridicule, Rawlings did not recount her experience until 1953, when a report of other sightings in the press moved her to go public. The description penned for her grandson was not offered until 1957. In such fashion, other potentially important sightings have doubtless been lost or delayed so long that crucial details are lost.

Source: Heuvelmans, *In the Wake of the Sea Serpents*.

Choccolocco Monster   During summer 1969, residents of Choccolocco, in northeastern Alabama's Calhoun County, reported multiple encounters with an unknown creature they described as resembling a gray or black hump-backed cow. The beast was glimpsed on highways, by approaching motorists, but sightings ceased after one local fired several shots at the prowler. Thirty-two years later, on Halloween 2001, prankster Neal Williams confessed to the *Anniston Star* that the Choccolocco Monster was a HOAX, concocted as a practical joke. According to Williams, he donned a sheet and cow's skull on four occasions, traipsing into the street as cars approached, but the near-miss with death discouraged him from further outings. The newspaper confession earned Williams a 3-minute guest spot on Comedy Central's *Daily Show* and a round of applause at his high school reunion in December 2001.

Sources: Matthew Creamer, "Choccolocco monster?" *Anniston* (AL) *Star* (31 October 2001); Matthew Creamer, "'Choccolocco monster' goes national on Daily Show." *Anniston Star* (30 November 2001).

Choga *see* **Koolookamba**

Chollier's Ape   In 1938, while on a safari in southeastern

Mali, hunter Louis Chollier glimpsed a man-sized APE unknown to modern science. The beast escaped into rocky terrain before Chollier could shoot it, leaving only his first impression of a shaggy black creature the size of a bear or GORILLA. No primates of that size or description are known to inhabit the region.

Source: Heuvelmans, *Les Bêtes Humaines d'Afrique*.

Christina   This Canadian LAKE MONSTER is named for Christina Lake, located near Conklin, Alberta. The fisherman who reported its first appearance in June 1984 described the beast as 30–40 feet long, with a horselike head mounted atop a 3-foot neck. In that respect, at least, it conforms to descriptions of other lake monsters reported across the continent and in parts of Europe.

Source: Stephen Lequire, "Sunday showcase." *Calgary Sunday Sun* (28 July 1985).

Chuchunaa   This unclassified primate or HOMINID of eastern Siberia is a described by witnesses as a BIGFOOT-type creature, 6–7 feet tall, with a heavy build, prominent brow ridge, and a full-body coat of dark hair. Reported sightings include both solitary specimens and small groups traveling together. Occasional stories of creatures dressed in animal skins may refer to some primitive mountain tribe, rather than actual cryptids. The Chuchunaa is said to be omnivorous, dining on foods that range from wild berries to FISH and reindeer. Siberian folktales allude to "many" Chuchunaa being killed by Russian troops in czarist times, during the country's civil war (1918–21) and during World War II, but some of those stories probably result from linguistic confusion, since an alternate name for the beasts—Mulen—translates as "bandit." In its classic form, the Chuchunaa may be identical to other Siberian hominids including the ALMAS, KÉÉDIEKI, KHEYAK, KILTANYA, KUL, MECHENY, MIRYGDY, PIKELIAN, TUNGU and ZEMLEMER. BERNARD HEUVELMANS and BORIS PORSHNEV considered the Chuchunaa a relict NEANDERTAL MAN, while researcher MARK HALL suggests that they may represent surviving specimens of *Homo gardarensis*.

Sources: Bayanov, *In the Footsteps of the Russian Snowman*; Heuvelmans and Porshnev, *L'Homme de Néanderthal est Toujours Vivant*.

Chum-Chum   Chum-Chum is the nickname applied, for reasons unknown, to a BIGFOOT-type HOMINID reported from Maine. Sightings date from the early 1800s, but the creature's nickname is a 20th-century media creation. Eyewitnesses in the 1980s described Chum-Chum as 7 feet tall and weighing roughly 400 pounds. Witness Dick Perkins photographed a series of the beast's footprints in October 1985. The prints measured 12¾ inches long by 6¼ inches wide.

Source: Berry, *Bigfoot on the East Coast*.

Chu-Mung *see* Yeti

Chunucklas/Shunuklas   Salishan tribesmen describe the Chunuklas as a LAKE MONSTER inhabiting British Columbia's Harrison Lake and the adjacent Harrison River. Reports of the creature are not limited to aboriginal folklore, however. Crewmen aboard a tugboat saw the beast swimming across Harrison Lake in 1908, with its long neck raised above water. Nearly three decades later, on 24 August 1936, multiple witnesses watched Chunuklas cavorting in the Harrison River, at the mouth of Old Jim's Slough. Two days later, the *Chilliwack Progress* carried the following report of that sighting:

An OGOPOGO, thought on account of its enormous length to be

the granddaddy of all its mysterious species in the British Columbia waters, made its appearance on the Harrison River above the rapids about 8 o'clock Monday morning and caused much excitement among the river folk. Unlike the reputed, but elusive, monster of the same name reported to have been seen from time to time in Okanagan Lake and elsewhere along the coast of British Columbia, the Harrison River Ogopogo came down the river in three sections, about a hundred feet in length and about the same distance apart from each other.

According to that report, the beast was a "radiant silver" color, 300 feet long from head to tail, but its titanic size did not prevent it from nearly being trapped by floating logs near Hatchery Island. Upon becoming snagged, the creature reportedly leapt from the water and then plunged back into the river "like a flaming meteorite" to vanish beneath the surface.

Source: Kirk, *In the Domain of the Lake Monsters*.

Chupacabra(s)   Peasants in rural Puerto Rico are no strangers to cryptozoology. For over a century, one of their popular songs has included the verse *Líbranos, señor, de este terrible animal* ("Deliver us, Lord, from this terrible beast!"). Folklorists long assumed that the lyrics referred to Satan, but that view was challenged in March 1975, when a ferocious MYSTERY MAULER slaughtered cows, geese, goats and pigs around Moca. In each case, the barnyard victims were marked with deep puncture wounds and virtually drained of blood by a creature soon christened the Moca Vampire. Spokesmen for Puerto Rico's Agricultural Commission blamed BIRDS and SNAKES, even as they called for a police investigation. Juan Muñiz became the first human victim on 25 Mary 1975, when he was mauled by a "horrible creature covered in feathers." Other towns reported livestock losses during April, then the raids ceased and the hysteria faded—for a while.

Nocturnal attacks resumed in March 1991, with another spate of livestock and poultry deaths around Lares. Locals there blamed the attacks on an unknown apelike creature, while police accused dogs. Three months later, predation began around Aguada, then ceased again until March 1995, when eight sheep were found exsanguinated at Orcovis. By that time, Puerto Ricans had renamed their elusive predator El Chupacabra ("the goat-sucker"). Another 150 animals were dead at Canóvanas, Puerto Rico by August 1995, when witness Madelyne Tolentino described her encounter with a 4-foot-tall biped, dark gray in color, with spindly limbs, a row of spikes or feathers down its back, and abdominal marks resembling burn scars. On 15 November 1995, a witness in Caguas claimed the Chupacabra had invaded her home to maul a teddy bear, leaving a pool of foul-smelling liquid behind. Puerto Rican sightings continued into March 1996, although descriptions varied widely. Osvaldo Rosado, manhandled by a cryptic predator at Guánica on 23 December 1995, claimed his assailant resembled a GORILLA. A farmer at Fajardo, meanwhile, described the slayer of his livestock as "a giant falcon with a human face." Attacks in Puerto Rico have continued to the present day, including a raid that slaughtered 27 guinea hens at Barceloneta on Christmas Day 2001; another that killed 19 chickens, ducks and RABBITS at Ponce on 22 September 2002; a third that claimed more rabbits in Aguas Buenas on 6 October 2002; and yet another massacre of 20 rabbits near Ponce, on 22 February 2003.

Meanwhile, the Chupacabra menace had gone international. The various regions thus far affected include:

Guatemala: Attacks on livestock and poultry date from 11 November 1995, when Alicia Fajardo lost 150 chickens in a single night. Two months later, cattleman Vicente Sosa reported his encounter with a black doglike predator, while other witnesses described a large bird or BAT. On 18 May 1996, numerous chickens, dogs, sheep and horses were killed and wounded on a farm owned by Oscar Padilla, 20 miles outside Guatemala City. Investigators found that coops and cages had been opened to attack smaller prey, with the wire mesh torn and twisted on some enclosures. Surviving victims appeared weak and listless, while Padilla and his employees displayed signs of illness after handling the carcasses. A veterinarian's report dismissed coyotes and WOLVES as suspects in the slaughter, suggesting that a heavy "winged creature" equipped with large claws. The unseen killer returned subsequently to kill Padilla's rabbits.

Mexico: The nation's first alleged Chupacabra attacks were reported from Puebla on 16 February 1996. On 6 March, sheep were found drained of their blood at Nayarit. Eight days later, reports announced the slaughter of four goats and several dozen chickens at Altamira, near Tampico. By early April, the Chupacabra was blamed for cattle deaths and mutilations across the northern states of Chihuahua, Coahuila and Sinaloa. May 1996 witnessed the death of 45 fighting cocks at Pánuco, Veracruz, while farmers at Laguno de Hermosillo, Sinaloa paraded a drowned cat as the late Chupacabra. Sinaloa witness Benigno Cano described a creature 35 inches tall, "with large, sharp fangs, red eyes, scales, and a DRAGON-like appearance." Others, in their turn, spoke of black hair, pointed ears and wings. As elsewhere throughout the elusive predator's range, attacks persist to the present. Recent incidents include the slaying of 23 chickens and turkeys at Chan Cenote, in the Yucatán peninsula, on 12 April 2001; the persecution of a farming family which lost 63 sheep and 1 pig killed, with another 14 sheep wounded at Bocoyna, Chihuahua between 10 and 31 October 2001; harassment of sheep by a "strange humanoid" with large ears near Payogasta on 11 February 2002; and the alleged mauling of Guadalupe policeman Leonardo Samaniego on 16 January 2004.

Florida: Sweetwater resident Teide Carballo reported an "inhuman shape" traversing her property on 10 March 1996, two weeks before neighbor Olimpia Govea found 2 goats and 27 chickens drained of blood in her backyard. Barbara Martinez lost more than 40 birds the same night. On 11 March, a Miami witness glimpsed a creature "neither human nor simian" near the site where several chickens were killed in their pen. Perhaps typically, Miami responded by producing Chupacabra video games, T-shirts, and a fast-food restaurant named for the beast. Still the slaughter continued, with a dozen goats and sheep killed on Rafael Moreno's farm at Hialeah Gardens, on 2 May 1996.

Spain: In April 1996, 600 sheep were killed and drained of blood in the Spanish Pyrenees. Insurance adjustors visited the stricken farms and unanimously blamed the attacks on "an unknown species of predator — definitely not a wolf." A month later, on 25 May, 163 sheep simply vanished from a heard of 700 near Celadas. Police dubbed that case "the strangest theft we've ever investigated," reporting a total absence of vehicle tracks at the scene. A local prosecutor told journalist Bruno Cardeñosa, "It's strange, very strange. Yes, they might well have been carried off upward."

Arizona: Tucson police responded to a call from José Espinoza on 1 May 1996, claiming the Chupacabra had invaded his home, attacked his 7-year-old son, then fled through the boy's bedroom window. Numerous hand- and footprints were found in the house, but detectives said all were traceable to Espinoza's 3-year-old.

Texas: In mid-May 1996, Sylvia Ybarra claimed that Chupacabra had drained her goat of blood at Donna, upriver from Brownsville on the Rio Grande. Veterinarians blamed the attack on a dog, but rumors persisted and blossomed again in July 2002, with reports of a dog killed in Brownsville. Owner Luis Duran told reporters, "It couldn't be a coyote because they usually fight around the house and there should be blood. If it was a wildcat, there should be wounds, but there was only marks like fingernails." Brownsville police and public health director Jose Ramirez insist the dog was struck and killed by an automobile.

California: Conservative Orange County was the scene of an alleged Chupacabra attack in May 1996. Construction worker Roberto García fell asleep beside an open window and woke to the pain of fangs piercing his hand, glimpsing "a sizable, shadowy figure" as it fled. Farther north, at Mendota, a rooster was killed and drained of blood around the same time.

Costa Rica: Details are sparse concerning the alleged near-abduction of Erlinda Vega from Bijagual de Turrubares in 1996. Vega described her nocturnal assailant was a winged creature with "a small face and eyes," which tried to snatch her from her yard. Vega's husband responded to her screams and found her hysteri-

The skeleton of an alleged Chupacabra, found in Chile (*La Estrella del Loa*).

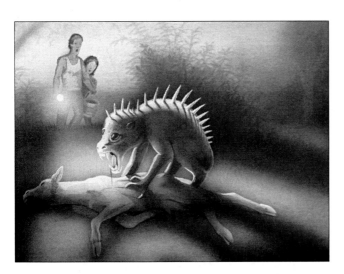

Artist's conception of the Chupacabra (*William Rebsamen*).

Chilean scientists examine an alleged Chupacabra (*La Estrella del Loa*).

cal, but he missed glimpsing the creature. Around the same time, a cow was drained of blood in the same village. Investigators from the Ministry of Agriculture blamed that slaying on a vampire bat (*Desmodus rotundus*), a small creature that rarely, if ever, inflicts fatal wounds on large prey.

Portugal: On 7 September 1996, the newspaper *Jornal de Noticias* published a story linking the Chupacabra to recent deaths of sheep around Idanha-a-Nova, all found drained of blood through punctures in their necks. Biologist Pedro Sarmento countered with a declaration that the predator was "an extremely intelligent and experienced wolf." The newspaper *Povo da Beira* took Sarmento's theory one step closer to absurdity, proclaiming that the killings were all committed by "one old wolf with a single canine tooth."

Brazil: In the early hours of 24 May 1999, 11 pigs and a dog were attacked on a farm at Araçoiaba da Serra. Nine of the pigs died from their wounds, while a tenth, sent to the butcher, reportedly "didn't have a single spoonful of blood" remaining in its veins. Farm manager Valdelei dos Santos told reporters, "The most intriguing thing is that there are 11 dogs and none of them barked." Dos Santos also claimed that another farm dog was killed under similar circumstances, with three puncture marks on its neck, in 1988.

Argentina: Alleged Chupacabra activity in this nation began at San Antonio, on Tierra del Fuego, in July 1999. Forty sheep were killed and drained of blood in that spate of slaughter, but Agricultural and Livestock Service spokesman blamed the trouble on wild dog packs. The raids resumed around Porvenir, Tierra del Fuego on 9 June 2000, leaving more than 100 animals dead and dozens wounded. According to published reports on that case, the unknown predator(s) left "no traces which pointed to the presence of dogs, FOXES or game." On 23 June 200, five cats were slain at Maria Elena, 300 miles northwest of Buenos Aires. Each was drained of blood, via puncture wounds around the heart, and one victim's lungs were extracted. Fresh reports of Chupacabra activity circulated through northern Argentina during April 2002.

Chile: Worse hit than anyplace outside Puerto Rico, Chile dates its first alleged Chupacabra attacks from mid-April 2000, when more than 200 chickens, goats, pigs, sheep and rabbits were drained of blood around Calama. Farmers rejected all official claims that dogs were responsible for the assaults. On 15 May 2000, the newspaper *Crónica* reported that a troop of soldiers had surprised a family of Chupacabras in a mine shaft, in Chile's

Second Region, losing one man before the three creatures were captured and confined to an army barracks. Before Chilean scientists could study them, however, the beasts were allegedly whisked away by a flying squad from the U.S. National Aeronautics and Space Administration. Still, other specimens survived, killing chickens at Calama (19 January 2001); chasing a car at 70 mph down the Cuesta de Montecristo (24 June 2001); slaughtering poultry at Tocopilla (13 August 2001); harassing miners outside Antofagasta (9 April 2002); killing 15 inmates of a mini-zoo at Pillanlelbun (3 July 2003); brawling with residents of Vina del Mar (9 July 2003); killing 59 birds and a pig at Los Lagos (18 August 2003); sucking dogs dry "from within" at Lota (23 August 2003); and draining 15 canaries at Pan de Azucar (15 October 2003). Two more Chupacabras have allegedly been caught in Chile. One, trapped in a cave near Huasco by soldiers and customs officers, in November 2001, was described as "a strange giant bat." Private researcher Darwin Godoy told reporters, "According to descriptions, the creature was about 80 centimeters [31 inches] in height and it had a wingspan of approximately 1.7 meters [5 feet 5 inches]." Another unknown beast was caught in the act of drinking a chicken's blood at Pinchulao, 414 miles south of Santiago de Chile, and delivered to the manager of a TV station in nearby Togue. That creature, killed and embalmed to preserve it pending study by veterinarians, was said to be 12 inches long. Researchers in Chile were hampered by agents of "unidentified agencies" who bribed or threatened witnesses into silence. Even inquisitive senator Carlos Cantero failed to launch an official inquiry, when state police ignored his protests and arbitrarily closed their investigation.

Nicaragua: After losing more than 70 goats and sheep on his

The remains of an alleged Chupacabra killed in Nicaragua (*La Prensa de Nicaragua*).

farm near Malpaisillo, Jorge Talavera laid an ambush and allegedly shot a Chupacabra on 28 August 2000. The wounded beast escaped, but Talavera recovered its body several days later, packing it off to the National Autonomous University in Leon. On 30 August, the newspaper *La Prensa de Nicaragua* described the animal as having "yellow hair on its short tail, large eye-sockets, soft skin like that of a bat, large claws and fangs, and a crest on its main vertebrae." Nonetheless, after a curious delay of nearly 16 months, zoologist Edmundo Torres declared on 18 January 2002, "It's a dog, without any room for doubt." Colleague Carlos Gomez agreed, "This is a common dog. There are no fangs or anything that could suck blood." As in other nations, though, the official pronouncement solved nothing. Chupacabra attacks were reported from Rio Blanco on 19 August 2002 (9 sheep killed, 7 wounded), and several small communities of northern Nicaragua during August 2003 (55 goats and sheep drained of blood).

Theories abound concerning the Chupacabra's possible identity. Many accounts in the popular media treat the creature(s) as supernatural entities or link them to UFO sightings as possible extraterrestrial drop-ins. Local authorities, as we have seen, prefer to blame a range of normal predators, sometimes including human practitioners of occult blood rituals. Researcher SCOTT CORRALES notes that the Spanish name *chotocabras* is commonly applied to a well-known harmless bird, the band-winged nightjar (*Caprimulgus longirostris*), whose range extends from Venezuela to Argentina. "Fugitive" rhesus MONKEYS (*Macaca mulatta*) are sometimes proposed as Chupacabra candidates in Puerto Rico, although they have never been known to attack livestock or humans. Authors LOREN COLEMAN and PATRICK HUYGHE challenge tradition by dubbing Chupacabra a MERBEING, but their brief description of the creature strangely mentions no sightings in or near water. Debunkers blame the entire phenomenon on mass hysteria, as with the Indian reports of MONKEY MAN, MUHNOCHWA and the CRAWLING GHOST.

Sources: Juan Abarzúa, "Strange humanoid allegedly seen." *El Tribuno* (30 March 2002); "Agency offers money in exchange for silence on Chupacabras." *La Estrella de Calama* (6 January 2001); Dudley Althaus, "'Goatsucker' spreading fear across Mexico." *Houston Chronicle* (12 May 1996); "Another mysterious attack: Chupacabra returns." *Primera Hora* (7 October 2002); "Another mysterious Chupacabra attack in Puerto Rico." *Primera Hora* (11 October 2002); María Besnier, "'The Chupacabras Must Be Taken Very Seriously.'" *Diario Las Ultimas Noticias* (24 June 2001); "Carabineros closed Chupacabras case." *La Estrella del Loa* (3 August 2001); "Children with face-to-face encounter with a Chupacabra." *La Estrella del Loa* (1 February 2001); "Chilean senator backs down." *La Estrella del Loa* (30 July 2001); "Chupacabra attack reported." *El Lider de San Antonio* (19 August 2003); "Chupacabra bares its fangs yet again." *Crónica* (18 August 2003); "Chupacabra cavorts on a rooftop in Calama, Chile." *Mercurio de Calama* (23 June 2003); "Chupacabra exsanguinates chickens." *Primera Hora* (23 March 2001); "Chupacabra gets a beating." *La Estrella de Valparaiso* (12 July 2003); "Chupacabra kills farm animals in the Yucatan." *Por Esto!* (13 April 2001); "Chupacabra raids a family home in central Chile." *Diario Lider de San Antonio* (14 February 2002); "Chupacabra researcher in the crosshairs of the Men In Black." *La Estrella del Loa* (26 April 2001); "Chupacabras Attacks Coastal Chilean Town." *Diario Lider de San Antonio* (15 February 2002); "Chupacabras Attacks Continue in Chile." *La Estrella de Calama* (21 April 2001); "Chupacabras Claims Five Victims in Tocopilla." *La Estrella del Loa* (27 August 2001); "Chupacabras fever." *Fortean Times* 140 (December 2000): 22–23; "Chupacabras Reappears In Puerto Rico." *Primera Hora* (23 September 2002); "Chupacabras rides again." *Fortean Times* 156 (April 2002): 7; "Chupacabras strikes again." *Fortean Times* 129 (December 1999): 24; Coleman and Huyghe, *The Field Guide to Bigfoot, Yeti, and Other Mystery Primates Worldwide*; Corrales, *Chupacabras and Other Mys-*

teries; Corrales, *The Chupacabras Diaries*; Corrales, *Chupacabras Rising*; Corrales, "How many goats can a goatsucker suck?"; "Eyewitness account of a Chupacabras encounter." *La Estrella del Loa* (30 January 2001); "Intriguing death of 20 rabbits." *El Nuevo Dia* (23 February 2003); Maricely Linarte and Clarissa Altamirano, "Chupacabras remains found." *La Prensa de Nicaragua* (30 August 2000); "Mysterious beast slays 50 hens, 9 geese, 1 pig." *Diario Austral de Valdivia* (19 August 2003); Gonzalo Pizarro, "Dogs sucked dry from within in Lota." *Crónica* (4 September 2003); "A revealing study of the Chupacabras case." *La Estrella de Loa* (25 April 2001); Jessica Rocha, "Chupacabra blamed for dog's mysterious death." *Brownsville* (TX) *Herald* (9 July 2002); Jessica Rocha, "Chupacabra report prompts fear, doubt from local residents." *Brownsville* (TX) *Herald* (11 July 2002); Sánchez-Ocejo, *Miami Chupacabras*; "Senator Asks for Information on Chupacabras Case." *La Estrella del Loa* (11 June 2001); "'Something Fishy' Going On With Chupacabras." *La Estrella del Loa* (15 June 2001); Jim Steinberg, "Mendota rooster's demise stirs talk of Chupacabras." *Fresno* (CA) *Bee* (18 May 1996); "Strange animal caught: The Chupacabra?" *La Nueva Provincia* (20 April 2003); "Strange animal mystery continues." *Diario Austral de Araucania* (21 April 2003); "Terrified of the Chupacabras." *La Prensa* (17 August 2003); "Terror spreads among farmers of La Palmilla." *La Cuarta de Temuco* (17 July 2003); "US Chupacabra researcher reveals new information on Chile attacks." *La Estrella del Loa* (24 March 2001); "Vampires or Chupacabras?" *El Nuevo Diario de Nicaragua* (19 August 2002); "Winged Chupacabra paces frightened family in car at 120 kmh." *La Estrella del Loa* (29 June 2001); "Yellow monster Chupakabra." *Pravda* (23 October 2002).

Churchill sea serpent

On 31 August 1884, while the steam-tug *Churchill* rode anchor at Port Natal (now Durban), South Africa, members of its crew observed a frightening SEA SERPENT. As Captain Wellington described the incident:

[A] huge beast suddenly appeared level with the bulwarks presenting the most terrific appearance. It seemed covered with large sea shells and to have a big, hairy head; twice it appeared, and as suddenly plunged down again. The second time the whole of its body passed under the ship, and in doing so all on board assert positively that its head could be seen some distance at one side while the tail was still visible many yards away at the other. Its length was estimated at 60 feet.

Source: Heuvelmans, *In the Wake of the Sea Serpents*.

The ***Churchill*** sea serpent, based on crew members' descriptions.

Chuti This unidentified Nepalese predator is described as having a tigerlike body, complete with dramatic stripes, and a head like that of a large dog. Its feet are said to be peculiar, bearing four claws on each forefoot, and only one each on the hind feet. In the 1970s, various lamas told mountaineer Hamish MacInnes that the creatures commonly inhabit the Choyong and Iswa Valleys of Nepal's Makalu-Barun National Park. Russian zoologist Vladimir Tschernesky suggests that the Chuti may be striped hyenas (*Hyaena hyaena*), whose broad range includes parts of Nepal. The weakness of that argument is the hyena's normal preference for open country and avoidance of montane forests.

Source: Hamish MacInnes, *Look Behind the Ranges.* London: Hodder and Stoughton, 1979.

Chūzenji-Ko, Japan On 21 December 1933, the *Times* of London published a letter from Asian traveler Kathleen Conyngham, describing the mysterious "night tides" that raise water levels at this lake in Honshū's Tochigi Prefecture. Lakes normally have no tides, and local residents blamed the anomaly on submerged movements of a huge LAKE MONSTER. No actual sightings of the beast itself are recorded.

Source: *The Times* (21 December 1933).

Cigau Sumatran natives describe the Cigau as an aggressive man-killer, half APE and half TIGER, found most often in the neighborhood of Bangko and Mount Kerinci. The beast has tan or yellow fur, a short tail, and a bushy ruff around its neck. During her long search for Sumatra's ORANG PENDEK, British explorer Debbie Martyr has also collected tales of the Cigau, which describe its unprovoked attacks on humans. The beast is reportedly smaller than a Sumatran tiger, but more heavily muscled and displays unfailing aggression.

Sources: Bernard Heuvelmans, "Le bestiaire insolite de la cryptozoologie ou le catalouge de nos ignorances." *Criptozoologia* 2 (1996): 3–18; Shuker, "Blue tigers, black tigers, and other Asian mystery cats."

Cincinnati Bigfoot Research Group Unfortunate confusion surrounds this organization, also sometimes called the Cincinnati SKUNK APE Research Group. Founded by Ohio geneticist John Lewis in April 1989, to investigate sightings of unknown HOMINIDS, the group(s) established an Internet website in 1998. Two years later, Lewis reportedly embarked on an expedition to South America, seeking evidence for the modern-day existence of the prehistoric ground sloth *MEGATHERIUM*. The results of that trek are unknown. While claiming 137 members across North America, Lewis also described his group as "an appendage" of the larger SOCIETY FOR THE SEARCH FOR CRYPTOZOOLOGICAL ORGANISMS AND PHYSICAL EVIDENCE. All three organizations seemingly passed from existence at the same time, concurrent with an Internet posting from Lewis on 6 July 2003 that read: "The skunk ape site is no more. I'm still interested in cryptozoology, but there are more pressing matters which need to be addressed at this time."

Sources: "Tristater searches for giant sloth." *Cincinnati Enquirer* (31 May 2001); Cincinnati Bigfoot Research Group, http://skunkape.veryweird.com.

***City of Baltimore* sea serpent** On 28 January 1879, while traveling aboard the *City of Baltimore* in the Gulf of Aden, Major H.W.J. Senior of the Bengal Staff Corps glimpsed a SEA SERPENT from the ship's afterdeck. As he described the animal:

So rapid were its movements that when it approached the ship's wake, I seized a telescope, but could not catch a view as it darted rapidly out of the field of the glass before I could see it. I was thus prevented from ascertaining whether it had scales or not but the best view of the monster obtainable when it was about three cables' length, that is about 500 yards' distant [actually 1,824 feet], seemed to show that it was without scales. I cannot, however, speak with certainty. The head and neck, about two feet in diameter, rose out of the water to a height of about twenty or thirty feet, and the monster opened its jaws wide as it rose, and closed them again as it lowered its head and darted forward for a dive, reappearing almost immediately some hundred yards ahead. The body was not visible at all, and must have been some depth under water, as the disturbance on the surface was too slight to attract notice, although occasionally a splash was seen at some distance behind the head. The shape of the head was not unlike pictures of the DRAGON I have often seen, with a bull-dog appearance of the forehead and eyebrow.

Two other witnesses, including the ship's surgeon and another passenger, co-signed Major Senior's description of the unknown creature.

Source: Heuvelmans, *In the Wake of the Sea Serpents.*

***City of Manila* sea serpent** Seaman Alec Gracie waited nearly 30 years to report a SEA SERPENT sighting he experienced in 1926 or 1927, while passing through the Great Australian Bight aboard the *City of Manila*, en route from Melbourne to Freemantle. By that time, Gracie had lost the ship's log with details of the incident, but he reconstructed it as follows in a letter to author/witness John Hughes:

It was about six bells on a Sunday morning [3:00 a.m.] when I noticed about a mile away just as you recall [i.e., "six to eight arches, which seemed to undulate"] but also no discernible head....I took a quick look with my glasses and then moved quickly to the white quartermaster, handed him the binoculars and asked him what he saw. He said something to the effect that it was "damn funny," but agreed that it could be a sea-serpent "if there *was* such a thing." I said, "But hang it all man, what else *was* it?" For by this time, nearly half a minute, the thing had gone....When I told the mate at eight bells [5:00 a.m.] he displayed the usual incredulity and then suggested porpoises. Well, you know *your* serpent wasn't porpoises and I know *mine* wasn't!

Source: Heuvelmans, *In the Wake of the Sea Serpents.*

Clark, Eugenie (1922–) New York native Eugenie Clark earned her B.A. in zoology from Hunter College in 1942, followed by an M.A. from New York University in 1946 and a Ph.D. (also from NYU) in 1950. Clark's distinguished career includes a 9-year stint as founding director of the Cape Haze Marine Laboratory at Sarasota, Florida (1955–67), followed by 24 years on the University of Maryland faculty (1968–92). In addition to those achievements, Clark is a world-renowned diver whose ground-breaking research on SHARKS earned her the nickname "Shark Lady." She has conducted 71 deep submersible dives, and four species of FISH were named in her honor between 1978 and 1987. Clark's longstanding interest in cryptozoology prompted her to organize a course titled Sea Monsters and Deep-Sea Sharks, which she taught for the last time in 1997. Clark is the author of more than 160 scholarly articles and several books, including *Lady with a Spear* (1953), *The Lady and the Sharks* (1969), *Shark Lady: True Adventures of Eugenie Clark* (1978), and *Adventures of the Shark Lady: Eugenie Clark Around the World* (1979). The last three volumes were co-authored with Clark's frequent diving partner, Ann McGovern. Today, while the University of Maryland ranks Clark as a professor emerita and senior research scientist, she continues her research at Florida's Mote Marine Laboratory.

Source: Dr. Eugenie Clark, http://www.sharklady.com/.

Clark, James Alexander (1960–89)
Canadian author James Clark was a prodigious researcher who compiled a massive archive of cryptid sightings for his home province of British Columbia. In May 1989, he teamed with colleagues JOHN KIRK and PAUL LEBLOND to found the BRITISH COLUMBIA SCIENTIFIC CRYPTOZOOLOGY CLUB. Two months later, Clark's efforts were rewarded when he and others from the BCSCC recorded a sighting of OGOPOGO at Okanagan Lake. That experience prompted Clark and wife Barbara to relocate in August 1989 from Coquitlam to Kelowna, on the Okanagan shore, in hopes of seeing the creature again. Sadly, within two weeks of the move, Clark suffered a fatal heart attack. Before year's end, the BCSCC created a Jim Clark Memorial Prize for elementary school students who complete research projects on subjects related to cryptozoology.

Source: Coleman and Clark, *Cryptozoology A to Z.*

Clark, Jerome (1946–)
Minnesota native Jerome Clark is a prolific author and tireless researcher in the field of Forteana, nationally recognized for his published work in the fields of cryptozoology, unidentified flying objects and anomalous phenomena. His articles have appeared in numerous magazines, and since 1985 he has edited the *International UFO Reporter,* a quarterly journal produced by the J. Allen Hynek Center for UFO Studies. Clark's books in the field of cryptozoology include *The Unidentified* (1975, with LOREN COLEMAN), *Creatures of the Outer Edge* (1978, also with Coleman), *Earth's Secret Inhabitants* (1979), *Creatures of the Goblin World* (1984, with Coleman), the *Encyclopedia of Strange and Unexplained Phenomena* (1993), *Strange & Unexplained Phenomena* (1997, with Nancy Pear), *Unexplained!* (1998), and *Cryptozoology A to Z* (1999, again with Coleman). Today, Clark lives and works in his hometown of Canby, Minnesota.

Source: Clark, *Unexplained!*; Coleman and Clark, *Cryptozoology A to Z.*

Clark, Ramona (1932–97)
Brooksville, Florida resident Ramona Clark was one of the Sunshine State's earliest SKUNK APE investigators, briefly allied with the YETI RESEARCH SOCIETY before she severed that affiliation to pursue the quest on her own. She subsequently married fellow Skunk Ape hunter Duane Hibner, but continued to use her maiden name when writing for BIGFOOT newsletters. In correspondence with JOHN GREEN, Clark claimed several personal sightings, in addition to discovery of humanoid footprints 19 inches long. In regard to the Skunk Ape's notorious odor, she told Green, "It will actually gag you, it is so disgusting." Clark-Hibner's fascination with unknown HOMINIDS continued until her death at age 65, in December 1997.

Sources: Coleman and Clark, *Cryptozoology A to Z*; Green, *Sasquatch: The Apes Among Us.*

Claveria carcass
On 25 December 1996, a large unidentified carcass washed ashore at Claveria, on the Philippine island of Masbate, located south of Luzon. According to media reports, the creature was 26 feet long, with an EEL-like body and a skull resembling a TURTLE'S, albeit with a blowhole suggesting the beast was a cetacean. Despite that evidence, however, the animal's skeleton was strangely incomplete. In February 1997, Philippines University zoologist Perry Ong told reporters, "Judging from what I see now, it's an eel-like FISH. It must be an ancestral or primitive fish. It had fins. But if it's a fish, where are the

ribs? It is not a mammal." Several unnamed scientists called for carbon-dating of the beached remains, a clearly futile exercise since desiccated flesh still clung to some of the bones. At press time for this volume, the animal's identity remained unknown.

Source: Karl Shuker, "Alien zoo." *Fortean Times* 105 (December 1997): 16–17.

Clear Lake, California
In October 1993, fisherman Lyle Dyslin pulled a peculiar FISH from this lake, in northern California's Lake County. Its lobed fins resembled legs, and its head reminded Dyslin of a dog's, though dangling barbels were more reminiscent of a CATFISH. Its prominent scales were also odd-looking, while the creature's tail was flattened horizontally like a cetacean's. The fish reminded Dyslin of his dachshund, so he released it after snapping several photographs. It remains unidentified today, though some researchers believe it was a deformed specimen of Clear Lake's famous channel catfish (*Ictalurus punctatus*), an exotic species introduced in the late 19th century.

Source: Shuker, "Sounds fishy to me!"

Clearwater River, Canada
Canada's Clearwater River spans the provincial border between Alberta and Saskatchewan. On 18 October 1946, Alberta resident Robert Forbes reported an encounter with a 20-foot aquatic cryptid, gray in color and sporting horns on its head, which surfaced to pluck a calf from the river's bank. A front-page report of the event in the *Calgary Herald* referred to the predator as OGOPOGO, more properly identified with British Columbia's Okanagan Lake. No other sightings of the river beast are presently on file.

Source: "Ogopogo raises ugly head, snatches calf." *Calgary Herald* (18 October 1946).

Cleopatra sea serpent
On 15 September 1849, while en route to Singapore, crewmen aboard the British ship HMS *Cleopatra* saw a 30-foot SEA SERPENT in the Indian Ocean. No further details of the creature's appearance were published until 1892, when witness George Lucas recalled: "The head of the monster was much like a dog's, the body being about eight feet in circumference, as far as we could judge. Its colour was of a greenish brown."

Source: Heuvelmans, *In the Wake of the Sea Serpents.*

Clyde River serpent
On 3 February 1962, the *Scottish Daily Mail* reported that Jack Hay had seen a huge SEA SERPENT on the Clyde River's bank, during a late-night stroll near Helensburgh, Ayrshire. Hay described the creature as 30–40 feet long, with a 3-foot head, a slender neck and stout body. It slithered back into the river as Hay approached within 40 yards, but a large single footprint remained on the sand.

Sources: Heuvelmans, *In the Wake of the Sea Serpents*; McEwan, *Mystery Animals of Britain and Ireland.*

Coelacanth
The coelacanth (*Latimeria chalumnae*) is the "poster child" of cryptozoology, at once a triumph and an ongoing enigma. This lobe-finned FISH, whose former genus name means "hollow spine" in Greek, apparently evolved during the Devonian period, some 350 million years ago. Its first fossil remains were found in 1836, at which time scientists assumed it had been extinct for at least 65 million years. That assumption was torpedoed on 23 December 1938, when Captain Hendrick Goosen of the fishing trawler *Nerine* delivered his latest catch to market at East London, South Africa. Present on the docks that

day was Marjorie Courtenay-Latimer, curator and taxidermist at a local museum. As she later described the event:

> I went onto the deck of the trawler *Nerine* and there I found a pile of small SHARKS, spiny dogfish, rays, starfish, and rat tail fish. I said to the old gentleman, "They all look much the same, perhaps I won't bother with these today"; then, as I moved them, I saw a blue fin and pushing off the fish, the most beautiful fish I had ever seen was revealed. It was 5 feet long and a pale mauvy blue with iridescent silver markings. "What is this?" I asked the old gentleman. "Well, lass," said he, "this fish snapped at the Captain's fingers as he looked at it in the trawler net. It was trawled with a ton and a half of fish plus all these dogfish and others." "Oh," I said, "this I will definitely take to the museum and I shall not worry with the rest." I called Enoch, my native boy, and with a bag we had brought down he and I placed it in the bag and carried it to the taxi. Here to my amazement, the taxi man said, "No stinking fish in my taxi!" I said, "Well you can go, the fish is not stinking. I will call another taxi." With that, he allowed us to put it in the boot [trunk] of the taxi."

The specimen weighed 12 pounds, and ichthyologist J.L.B. Smith identified it as a coelacanth, which he named in honor of Courtenay-Latimer. The bombshell discovery of a genuine "living fossil" rocked the scientific world and launched an epic hunt for further specimens, fueled by a reward offer of £100 for the next coelacanth. Another 14 years elapsed before fisherman Ahmed Hussein caught the next specimen off Comoros — a chain of volcanic islands between Mozambique and Madagascar — on 20 December 1952. The new catch was briefly dubbed *Malania anjouanae*, in honor of South Africa's prime minister, but that name was discarded upon recognition that both fish represented a single species.

Between 1952 and 1975, another 203 coelacanths were hauled from the depths, all from Comoros or East African waters, with the latter presumed to be strays from a localized population. Most coelacanths were caught at depths between 600 and 1,200 feet, with some netted as deep as 2,000 feet, and none survived in captivity. Marine biologists concluded that females hatched their grapefruit-sized eggs internally, then gave birth to live young, but as of press time for this book, no juvenile specimens have yet been caught or seen. In 1987, German naturalist Hans Fricke scored another breakthrough, when he observed and photographed six living coelacanths during dives off Grand Comoro Island. Fricke's observations disproved the belief that coelacanths

The coelacanth is a classic example of a "living fossil" (*William Rebsamen*).

walked on the ocean floor with their leglike fins, while revealing that the fish generate electric fields around their bodies, in the manner of electric EELS.

There the matter rested until September 1997, when American marine biologist Mark Erdmann embarked on a honeymoon trip to Celebes (or Sulawesi), Indonesia. There, he observed a coelacanth en route to a local fish market and snapped its picture. Assuming that the fish were known to inhabit those waters, Erdmann posted the photo on his Internet website and thought no more of it, until he received an urgent message from coelacanth specialist E.K. Balon of Ontario's Guelph University. Unrecognized by Erdmann, the discovery of Indonesian coelacanths was yet another scientific breakthrough. Funded by the Smithsonian Institution and the National Geographic Society, Erdmann led a team back to Celebes, in search of further evidence. He soon discovered that Indonesian fishermen knew the fish as Rajalut ("king of the sea"), but further specimens remained elusive until 30 June 1998, when another was caught near Manado Tua. A report of the discovery, published in *Nature* on 24 September 1998, noted that while Indonesian coelacanths were brown with gold flecks (versus blue and silver in Comoros waters), they inhabited similar deep-water caves on the slopes of submerged volcanoes.

The first coelacanth scandal broke in July 2000, when a team of French researchers from the National Museum of Natural History in Paris claimed prior discovery of the Indonesian fish. According to their story, they had captured one off Java in 1995, but it was seized by government officials and delivered to a wealthy private collector as a personal trophy. As evidence, the French team submitted a photo suspiciously similar to one of those published in *Nature* two years earlier. Erdmann's coauthor denounced the picture as a fake, lifted from the journal, and *Nature* refused to accept the French report for publication. The team's leader, variously identified as Bernard Séret and George Serre in conflicting media accounts, confessed that the matter was "very embarrassing." Although the Frenchmen went on to name "their" find *L. menadoensis*, many ichthyologists do not recognize the Indonesian fish as a separate species.

Three months after that scandal broke, in October 2000, divers Peter Timm and Pieter Venter glimpsed a coelacanth in Sodwana Bay, on the coast of South Africa's KwaZulu Natal Province. Over the next month, they claimed sightings of 6–7 specimens, distinguished by their markings, and 3 coelacanths were videotaped while swimming together on 27 November. The expedition ended tragically, when team member Dennis Harding ascended too swiftly and died from a cerebral embolism, but his loss did not deter the hunters. A specimen 5 feet 6 inches long was netted off Kenya in 2001, pronounced a stray from the Comoros colony, but attention now focused on Sodwana Bay. Passengers aboard the submersible craft *Jago*, funded by the South African government, saw a coelacanth on their first day of exploration, 30 December 2001. A new expedition was launched in April 2002, reporting that the Sodwana Bay coelacanths deviated from normal routines for their species. Although cave dwellers, they apparently prefer depths around 300 feet, thus making study a less cumbersome affair.

The coelacanth's saga is sufficient to rate it star billing in cryptozoology, but further mysteries surround the ancient fish — including controversial claims of specimens inhabiting the Western Hemisphere. In 1949, ichthyologist Isaac Ginsburg received a letter from a Tampa, Florida souvenir vendor, including a distinctive fish scale purchased from an unnamed local fisherman. The vendor typically purchased scales by the barrel load, for use in crafting trinkets, but this one from the Gulf of Mexico was unique in her experience. Ginsburg recognized the large, thick scale as similar to a coelacanth's, but the Florida vendor never replied to his request for further samples, and Ginsburg subsequently lost the scale.

Fifteen years later, Argentinean chemist Ladislao Reti bought a silver figurine resembling a carved coelacanth at a village near Bilbao, Spain. A second, nearly identical figurine was found in 1965, by a college student shopping for antiques in Toledo, Spain. Hans Fricke, still 22 years from his first-ever photos of live coelacanths, was intrigued by the figurines and consulted an art expert in Madrid, one Professor Valdavinus, who diagnosed the silver fish as artifacts crafted in Mexico, under Spanish colonial rule (1519–1810). Long afterward, in August 2001, Fricke and coauthor Raphaël Plante published a paper contending that the Spanish figurines were in fact modern sculptures, modeled from coelacanths captured since 1938.

If accurate, that finding still does not resolve the claims of New World coelacanths. In the early 1970s, naturalist Sterling Lanier saw a necklace composed of apparent coelacanth scales, displayed at an art show on Florida's gulf coast. The owner claimed he had found the scales aboard a Mexican shrimp boat, mixed with other marine detritus, and while he refused to sell it, Lanier was permitted to sketch the necklace. (He later lost the sketch.) In 1992, French naturalist Ronald Heu bought three large scales resembling a coelacanth's from a souvenir shop in Biloxi, Mississippi. In fact, Heu believed the scales were those of *Latimeria*, but critics insist that they came from a large South American species known as arapaima or pirarucu (*Arapaima gigas*).

Equally strange, and far from the New World, is the report of an 18th-century Indian miniature painting that depicts a Moslem holy man standing beside a large, peculiar fish. In a 1972 article for *Naturwissenschaftliche Rundschau*, German professor B. Brentjes proposed that the fish was a coelacanth stranded far from its normal waters. KARL SHUKER disagreed and showed the painting to French ichthyologist François de Sarre, who opined that the fish depicted was an Indian climbing perch (*Anabas testudineus*). That judgment may be accurate, but on balance there seems to be no prima facie reason why coelacanths should be exclusively restricted to the Eastern Hemisphere.

Sources: Paul Chambers, "Indonesian coelacanths." *Fortean Times* 144 (April 2001): 66; Coleman and Clark, *Cryptozoology A to Z*; Rena Singer, "South Africa on mission to find 'dinofish' at sea." *USA Today* (8 May 2002); Karl Shuker, "Alien zoo." *Fortean Times* 138 (October 2000): 19; Shuker, *In Search of Prehistoric Survivors*; "Silver surprise." *Fortean Times* 153 (January 2002): 21; "Sodwana fossil fish find." *Fortean Times* 144 (April 2001): 23; Stoddard, "Expedition to study South Africa's living fossils." Reuters (3 April 2002); Ward, *On Methuseleh's Trail*.

Coffin Bay carcass   The strange tale of an alleged SEA SERPENT carcass washed ashore at Coffin Bay, South Australia begins with an apparent case of editorial ineptitude. On 6 November 1891, the *Times* of London ran a story reporting the death of the Rev. G.W. Kennion, bishop of Adelaide, which sprang from a telegram sent by an Australian correspondent of Dalziel's Press Agency. That cable read: "INFLUENZA EXTENSIVELY PREVALENT WALES VICTORIA NUMEROUS DEATHS BISHOP ADELAIDE FOUND DEAD SEA SERPENT SIXTY FEET COFFIN BAY." A *Times* competitor, the *Saturday Review*, soon discovered that Re. Kennion was alive and well, but the follow-up was even more peculiar. On 16 December 1891, the *Times* printed another story, this one reading:

Yesterday's Australian mail brought news of the finding by the Bishop of Adelaide of the carcase of a sea serpent at Avoid Point, near Coffin Bay, South Australia. The Bishop, in writing to an Adelaide friend, states that while riding along the beach he came across a dead sea serpent about 60 ft. in length. It had a head 5 ft. long, like that of an immense SNAKE, with two blow holes on top. There were no teeth in the jaws. The body was round, and the tail resembled that of a whale. The Bishop described his "find" as the most peculiar animal he has ever seen.

Thus the incident was seemingly validated, perhaps with discovery of a decomposed whale carcase, until the Rev. Kennion himself denied that any such creature was found, by himself or anyone else. Most modern researchers dismiss the second *Times* report as a HOAX prompted by the original telegram.

Sources: "The Bishop of Adelaide and the sea monster." *The Times* (16 December 1891); Roesch, "A review of alleged sea serpent carcasses worldwide (Part Two—1881–1891)."

Coff's Harbour sea serpent   The year 1934 produced multiple SEA SERPENT reports from Australia. The last sighting, from New South Wales, was announced in the *Sydney Morning Herald* of 14 September. That story read:

Charles Blanche and Alfred Jackson, of Coff's harbour, two well-known deep-sea fishermen, report that about four miles from the entrance to Coff's harbour they saw from their launch yesterday what they first took to be a log. Then they saw two legs which were about a foot in diameter, and were about 20 feet apart. They turned their craft to make a closer inspection, but when nearing the object, they saw it roll over and a head, which both men declare resembled that of a horse, appeared. With a snort the creature plunged down to the depths, disappearing in a cloud of spray. Blanche and Jackson declare that the monster was up to 40 feet in length, and that in all their years of the sea they had never seen before such a weird-looking sea dweller.

Source: Smith, *Bunyips & Bigfoots*.

Coje Ya Menia   *see*   **Water Leopard**

Cold Lake, Canada   *see*   **Kinosoo**

Coleman, Loren (1947–)   Virginia native Loren Coleman was raised in Decatur, Illinois from three months of age, nurturing a lifelong fascination with animals and nature that included maintenance of a home zoo in childhood. His interest in cryptozoology dates from a 1960 viewing of the Japanese YETI film *Half Human* (see Appendix B). Henceforth, Coleman collected all available reports of cryptids seen in Illinois and elsewhere, soon graduating to active field investigations. In 1962, he discovered 10-inch footprints of an unknown apelike creature near Decatur and soon coined the term NORTH AMERICAN APE to describe unclassified primates whose tracks and other features differ significantly from those of BIGFOOT/SASQUATCH. In the course of subsequent investigations, Coleman visited every state in the U.S., as well as Canada, Mexico, Scotland and the Virgin Islands.

Academically, Coleman earned his B.A. in anthropology and zoology from Southern Illinois University-Carbondale, with an M.A. in psychiatric social work from Boston's Simmons College. He later enrolled in doctoral programs at Brandies University (social anthropology) and the University of New Hampshire (sociology) without completing Ph.D. requirements. Coleman published the first of 300-plus magazine articles in 1969 and went on to write numerous books. His cryptozoological titles include *The Unidentified* (1975, with JEROME CLARK), *Creatures of the Outer*

Edge (1978, also with Clark), *Mysterious America* (1983, revised edition 2001), *Creatures of the Goblin World* (1984, with Clark), *Tom Slick and the Search for the Yeti* (1989), *Cryptozoology A to Z* (1999, with Clark), *The Field Guide to Bigfoot, Yeti, and Other Mystery Primates Worldwide* (1999, with PATRICK HUYGHE), *Bigfoot!* (2003) and *The Field Guide to Lake Monsters, Sea Serpents and Other Mystery Denizens of the Deep* (2003, with Huyghe).

Coleman is a life member of the INTERNATIONAL SOCIETY OF CRYPTOZOOLOGY and an honorary member of the

Crytpzoologist and author Loren Coleman (*Emily Weir, 2003*).

BRITISH COLUMBIA SCIENTIFIC CRYPTOZOOLOGY CLUB. He lectures frequently at various cryptozoology symposiums and conventions, in addition to various TV appearances and serves as a consultant on programs including *In Search Of* and *Unsolved Mysteries*. On 20 October 1997, marking the 30th anniversary of the controversial PATTERSON FILM, Coleman was among the first 10 inductees into the still-incomplete Roger Patterson Memorial Bigfoot Museum at Portland, Oregon. Six years later, he opened his own cryptozoology museum at his home in Portland, Maine. "I've put half my retirement savings in this," Coleman told reporter Buck Wolf, as he posed beside an 8.5-foot replica of Bigfoot. "This museum represents a lifetime of work."

Sources: Coleman and Clark, *Cryptozoology A to Z*; Buck Wolf, "Gross museums." ABCNews.com (9 September 2003); The Cryptozoologist, http://www.lorencoleman.com/.

Colossal Claude   Colossal Claude is the supposed SEA SERPENT reported since 1934 from the mouth of Oregon's Columbia River and adjacent coastal waters. The first known witnesses included crewmen aboard the Columbia River lightship and its tender, *Rose*, who described a 40-foot creature with a snakelike head, an 8-foot neck, a bulky body and long tail. The observers watched through binoculars but were dissuaded from lowering a boat to chase the beast by orders from their captain. Three years later, fishermen aboard the *Viv* encountered a hairy, tan-colored creature 40 feet long and 4 feet wide, with the head of "an over-grown horse." Another fishing captain, Chris Anderson of the *Argo* accused Colossal Claude of raiding his lines and snatching a 20-pound halibut. In 1963, while conducting a search of the Oregon Coast, divers for the Shell Oil Company filmed a 15-foot creature with barnacle-encrusted skin swimming at a depth of 180 feet.

Sources: Peter Cairns, "Colossal Claude and the sea monsters." Portland *Oregonian* (24 September 1967); Garner, *Monster! Monster!*

Colossal Squid   On 1 April 2003, media reports announced that a huge "killer squid" had attacked a New Zealand

fishing boat in the Ross Sea, off the coast of Antarctica. As described in those accounts, the 19-foot, 330-pound beast appeared while crewmen were hauling in their catch and tried to snatch FISH from the net, whereupon it was gaffed and hauled aboard to die. Journalists described the creature as "larger, quicker and more formidable than a GIANT SQUID [*Architeuthis*]," equipped with "eyes as big as dinner plates, swiveling, razor-sharp hooks and a taste for anything that swims by." Although the specimen was immature, reports suggested that might reach 40 feet and 2,000 pounds as an adult.

Steve O'Shea, a senior research fellow at Auckland University of Technology, fueled the fire with a series of statements replete with superlatives. "I've seen 105 giant squid," he told reporters, "but I've never seen anything like this before. It's a true monster of the deep. This thing leaves the giant squid for dead. It would kill you if you fell in [the water]. I'm not exaggerating. This is a killer squid. From a science point of view, this is absolutely priceless. Now we can say that it attains a size larger than the giant squid. Giant squid is no longer the largest squid that's out there. We've got something that's even larger, and not just larger but an order of magnitude meaner. When this animal was alive, it really has to be one of the most frightening predators out there. It's without parallel in the oceans. This discovery raises questions about what else lives down deep in the ocean. If animals like this are turning up in waters that are 6,000 feet deep, what is going on at 10,000 feet?"

In fact, the predator which O'Shea dubbed the colossal squid was not new to science. It was initially described in 1925, from fragments of two specimens found in the stomachs of sperm whales harpooned off the South Shetland Islands. A new genus was created for it, as the only large squid known to have hooks on its eight arms, as well as on its two longer tentacles. Its scientific name, *Mesonychoteuthis hamiltoni*, translates as Hamilton's middle-hooked squid, a reference to the swivel-based hooks that can turn in all directions while clutching at prey. Some confusion surrounds the history of specimen discoveries for *Mesonychoteuthis*. Media reports from spring 2003 claim that only six specimens were known to science, five of them retrieved from inside sperm whales, but Steve O'Shea mentioned a 4-foot "baby" dredged from Antarctic waters in the 1970s. No trace of that capture survives in current squid literature, but the Russian trawler *Evrica* did net a juvenile specimen nearly 17 feet long in 1981, at a depth of 2,500 feet off Droning Maud Land, Antarctica.

How large does *Mesonychoteuthis* grow? While no adult has yet

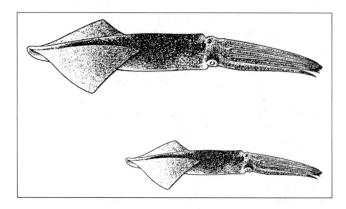

Some experts claim the colossal squid is substantially larger than *Architeuthis*, while others disagree.

been seen intact, it appears that O'Shea's 40-foot estimate was somewhat overstated. In 1959, author Gilbert Ross credited the species with a maximum length of 24 feet, scaled back to 20 feet by RICHARD ELLIS in 1998. The confusion seemingly arises from its mantle (body) length, which may indeed surpass the comparable measurement of *Architeuthis* species recognized by science, but the colossal squid's tentacles (according to Ellis) are proportionately "much shorter." A necropsy performed on the Ross Sea specimen suggested that may be transparent in sea water, and that "its waste system leaves a little to be desired." Nothing is known to date about its reproduction, and speculative efforts to minimize its adult size may prove to be as vain as in the case of *Architeuthis*.

Sources: Ellis, *The Search for the Giant Squid*; Kim Griggs, "Super squid surfaces in Antarctic." BBC News (2 April 2003); Bernie Napp, "Giant sea monsters are real." *Dominion Post* (3 April 2003); Bernie Napp, "Sighting raises fear of giant killer squid." *Dominion Post* (1 April 2003); Paula Oliver, "Colossal squid a formidable customer." *New Zealand Herald* (3 April 2003); Kathleen O'Toole, "Squid gives scientists chance to check out fish tales." *Lincoln* (NE) *Journal-Star* (2 April 2003); Richard Shears, "Colossus of the deep." *Daily Mail* (4 April 2003); "Squid secrets revealed." New Zealand TV One News (23 May 2003); Karl Shuker, "The enormous hype over the colossal squid." *Fortean Times* 172 (August 2003): 56.

Colovia   The Colovia is a large, unclassified SNAKE reported from the island of Sicily. It reportedly exceeds 10 feet in length, a size far greater than the largest recognized serpents of Europe. On 27 December 1933, the *Times* of London reported that one such specimen was allegedly killed in a swamp outside Siragusa. By the time reporters followed up on the story two days later, villagers frightened by folklore that named the Colovia as a harbinger of catastrophe had burned the carcass.

Source: *The Times* (27 and 29 December 1933).

***Columbia* sea serpent (1791)**   Details are sparse concerning this report of a SEA SERPENT from the coastal waters of British Columbia, regarded by some cryptozoologists as the earliest known sighting of CADBOROSAURUS. The witness was a crewman aboard the *Columbia*, a fur-trading ship commanded by U.S. captain Robert Gray, and while the vague description of a large serpentine animal generally conforms to other accounts of Caddy, researchers PAUL LEBLOND and Edward Bousfield exclude it from their list of sightings published in 1995.

Sources: Frederic Howay, ed., *Voyages of the "Columbia" to the Northwest Coast, 1787–1790 and 1790–1793*. Portland, OR: Oregon Historical Society, 1990; LeBlond and Bousfield, *Cadborosaurus*.

***Columbia* sea serpent (1839)**   On 3 September 1839, seaman Concord Patten reported a SEA SERPENT sighting from the schooner *Columbia*, while traveling along the southern coast of Maine, en route from Newburyport, Massachusetts to the mouth of the Kennebec River. Aside from his description of a large, serpentine animal, no details of the creature's appearance have survived.

Source: O'Neill, *The Great New England Sea Serpent*.

***Columbia* sea serpent (1879)**   On 25 September 1879, the *Manchester Guardian* published a report from a certain Captain Larson, claiming that his vessel, the *Columbia*, had collided with a huge SEA SERPENT in the North Atlantic on 4 September, while en route from London to Québec. Not only was the creature gravely wounded, bleeding profusely, but Larson claimed the ship was so badly damaged that it sank. Subsequent research un-

covered no trace of any such nautical calamity in official records, and most researchers now dismiss the report as a HOAX.

Source: Heuvelmans, *In the Wake of the Sea Serpents*.

***Columbian* sea serpent**   On 1 December 1904, crewmen aboard the steamer *Columbian* sighted a SEA SERPENT 40 miles off Sable Island, in the Gulf of Maine. A sworn statement from the ship's second officer, H.A. Dawes, was summarized in the *Boston Transcript*. That story read:

> The sky was overcast, but the air was clear, and he had a perfect view of the creature. He says that it was about 80 feet long, 5 feet across the back, while twenty feet from the head was a fin about three feet across and twelve feet high, pointed at the top. The head was high and pointed, and tapered down to a flat nose, with a wide mouth and thick lips. The eyes were about the size of a saucer, and were bright and glaring....When the creature was abreast of the ship, it raised itself from the water, shook itself and then sank its body under the water, leaving the fin still sticking out. Mr. Dawes is a perfectly matter-of-fact, unimaginative steamship officer, and there seems not the slightest reason to doubt the statement.

Source: O'Neill, *The Great New England Sea Serpent*.

Committee for the Search of Strange and Rare Creatures   On 27 October 1994, China's official Xinhua news agency announced the formation of a scientific body to investigate reports of unclassified primates or WILDMEN commonly known as YEREN. The new Committee for the Search of Strange and Rare Creatures was staffed by researchers from the Institute of Vertebrate Paleontology and Paleoanthropology of the Chinese Academy of Sciences. Already in hand for review were casts of 16-inch humanoid footprints allegedly made by 7-foot HOMINIDS weighing more than 650 pounds, plus suspect hair samples from various regions of China. Some of the hairs were black (from Yunnan Province), while others were white (from Tibet) or reddish-brown (Hubei Province). The latter were described in Xinhua press releases as belonging to "a kind of unknown primate, possibly the offspring of a branch of anthropoid APE, who is said to have extinguished on the planet [*sic*], or even a group of ape men who have lagged behind evolution." In April 1995, a 30-member team led by Wang Fangchen launched a two-month search for Yeren in the Shennongjia National Forest of western Hubei Province. No cryptids were seen, but more hairs were gathered for study. A new search of Shennongjia was planned for later in the year, complete with helicopters, but no further word of the committee's progress has been published.

Sources: "China searches for human-like creatures." Reuters (27 October 1994); "Chinese wildman returns." *Fortean Times* 139 (January 2000): 8–9; Louise Evans, "Chinese are hot on snowman's trail." *Sunday Telegraph* (6 November 1994); "Man-beast hunts in the Far East." *Fortean Times* 83 (October-November 1995): 18–19; Karl Shuker, "Menagerie of mystery." *Strange Magazine* 15 (Spring 1995): 32; Karl Shuker, "Menagerie of mystery." *Strange Magazine* 16 (Fall 1995): 29.

Con Rit   The Con rit ("millipede") was described by natives of 19th-century Vietnam as a peculiar SEA SERPENT resembling a giant CENTIPEDE, whose 60-foot body, dark brown above and yellow underneath, was composed of armored segment 2 feet long and 3 feet wide, each sprouting lateral appendages 2 feet 4 inches long. A dead Con rit reportedly washed ashore at ALONG BAY, on Vietnam's northern coast, in 1883. According to witness Tran Van Con, the carcass had no head, and it rang with a metallic sound when struck with a stick. It stank so badly in decay that local villagers towed the body out to sea and let it sink. In Sep-

tember 1921, Dr. A. Krempf, director of Indochina's Oceanographic and Fisheries Service, sketched a diagram of the creature based on Tran's description and others. BERNARD HEUVELMANS considered the Con rit an example of his hypothetical "many-finned" sea serpent, writing in 1968 that it "is probably therefore the prototype of the oriental DRAGON. It could well also be that of the Western dragon, since it is no doubt what the Jews described as the leviathan." KARL SHUKER counters with the suggestion that it may be an unknown species of giant crustacean.

Sources: Heuvelmans, *In the Wake of the Sea Serpents*; Shuker, *In Search of Prehistoric Survivors*.

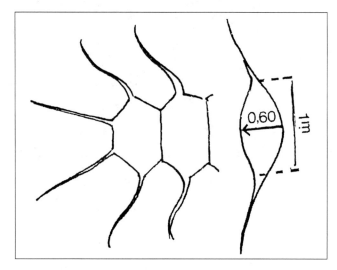

Dr. A. Krempf sketched the Con rit's body segments in 1921.

Concord sea serpent

At 5:00 a.m. on 6 June 1819, officers and crew aboard the sloop *Concord*, en route from New York City to Salem, saw "something that resembled a SNAKE" 15 miles northwest of Race Point, within sight of Cape Ann, Massachusetts. As Commander Hawkins Wheeler later told reporters, "I had a fair and distinct view of the creature, and from his appearance am satisfied that it was of the serpent kind." Another witness, Gersham Bennett, provided a more detailed description of the beast:

> I saw a serpent of enormous size and uncommon appearance upon the water. His head was about the length of the anchor stock above the surface of the water, viz. about seven feet. I looked at the anchor stock at the time, and formed my opinion by comparing the two objects....I had I think as good a view of the animal as if I had been within two rods [33 feet] of him. The color of the animal throughout, as far as could be seen, was black, and the surface appeared to be smooth, without scales—there was a degree of flatness, with a slight hollow on the top of his head—his eyes were prominent, and stood out considerably from the surface, resembling in that respect the eyes of a toad, and were nearer to the mouth of the animal than to the back of the head. I had a full view of him for seven or eight minutes. He was moving in the same direction as the sloop, and about as fast. The back was composed of bunches about the size of a flour barrel, which were apparently three feet apart— they appeared to be fixed but might be occasioned by the motion of the animal, and looked like a string of casks or barrels tied together— the tail was not visible, but the part which could be seen was, I should judge, fifty feet in length— the motion which of the bunches was undulatory, but the wake of his tail, which he evidently moved under the water, showed a horizontal or sweeping motion, producing a wake as large as the ves-

sel made. He turned his head two or three times slowly round, toward and from the vessel, as if taking a view of some object on board. I went up on the rigging, for the purpose of taking a view of him from above; but before I had reached my station, he sunk below the surface of the water, and did not appear again.

Source: O'Neill, *The Great New England Sea Serpent*.

Congella sea serpents

On 1 December 1959, Captain Bill Nichols of the South African fishing boat *Congella* reported that his vessel had encountered a troop of 20 SEA SERPENTS offshore from Durban. The gray, dome-headed creatures "escorted" the boat for some distance and nearly capsized it in the process, terrifying Nichols's two crewmen. Nichols initially thought they were whales, then changed his mind. Writing of the incident nine years later, BERNARD HEUVELMANS suggested that the captain's first impression was correct, and that the beasts were beaked whales of the family *Ziphiidae*, species unknown.

Source: Heuvelmans, *In the Wake of the Sea Serpents*.

Connecticut River

New England's longest river rises from the Connecticut Lakes of northern New Hampshire, near the Canadian border, and follows a 407-mile course to the south, along the Vermont–New Hampshire boundary, across Massachusetts and Connecticut, to enter LONG ISLAND SOUND at Saybrook. In 1968, New Hampshire residents Douglas and Dorothy Grove were canoeing from Rygate to Brattleboro, Vermont when they saw an unidentified "small animal" keeping pace with their boat. They described it as bright green and scaly, 18–24 inches long and weighing about 2 pounds. After tracking the creature for some distance, the Groves watched it wriggle under a tree stump on the Vermont shoreline, leaving tracks and drag marks from its tail. No further description is available of the apparent reptile. Authors LOREN COLEMAN and JOHN KIRK include the river's Connecticut segment on published lists of supposed aquatic cryptid habitats, but they provide no dates or details of any sightings from the Nutmeg State.

Sources: Citro, *Green Mountain Ghosts, Ghouls & Unsolved Mysteries*; Coleman, *Mysterious America*; Kirk, *In the Domain of the Lake Monsters*.

Connecticut sea serpents

At 10:00 a.m. on 5 July 1833, passengers and crew aboard the steamboat *Connecticut* saw three large SEA SERPENTS in Massachusetts Bay, four miles northeast of Nahant. Captain Porter, commanding the vessel, reported that the largest of the beasts was about 100 feet long, while the other two measured 60–70 feet. An anonymous passenger wrote to the *Boston Evening Transcript* on 6 July, describing the creatures as ranging "from 80 or 90 to 120 or 130 feet." He went on to say:

> They were lying full length on the water occasionally lifting their heads four or five feet above the surface and showing twenty or thirty bunches of SNAKE-like undulations at a time. Their heads bore a resemblance to the pickerel's, and the crease of their mouths, marking the division of the jaws, was like that of a common snake. The engine of the boat was stopped, and for three quarters of an hour we had a cool and deliberate view of the monsters. Officers aboard the schooner CHARLES OF PROVIDENCETOWN confirmed a sighting of one large serpent off Nahant, around the same time, while other passengers aboard the *Connecticut* described "three or four...Serpents, one of which was certainly 100 feet in length."

Another vessel named *Connecticut* reported a sea serpent sighting 64 years later, in July 1895, from the Connecticut side of LONG ISLAND SOUND. Unfortunately, no further details are presently available concerning that incident, the ship or its crew.

Source: O'Neill, *The Great New England Sea Serpent*.

Connemara sea serpent   In 1910, Howard St. George and his son saw an unidentified SEA SERPENT off the coast of Connemara, Ireland, in Kilkerrin Bay. Their story was not published until 1932, at which time they described the beast floating on an ebb tide, exposing a brown, hairy body "as big as a 2-horse lorry." The creature's small head sat atop a 6-foot neck, raised swanlike above the surface and swaying as if the animal was searching for something.

Source: Heuvelmans, *In the Wake of the Sea Serpents*.

Conway's Marsh, Canada   An anonymous magazine article published in spring 1981 identified this Ontario site as a source of LAKE MONSTER reports. Sadly, no dates or details were provided, and a diligent search of various Canadian atlases and gazetteers reveals no such place in the country. There *are* three "unincorporated areas" named Conway scattered across the eastern half of Canada, including one located east of Belleville, Ontario at 44° 12' north latitude, 76°92' west longitude. Without more information, the claim for this supposed site cannot be validated.

Source: "A brief survey of Canadian lake monsters." *INFO Journal* 39 (March-June 1981): 2–5.

Cook Islands sea serpent   In September 1993, a Polynesian clergyman named Solomona and his son were fishing off the twin atolls of Manihiki and Rakahanga, in the Cook Islands chain, when they saw a flock over BIRDS circling over the water nearby. Hoping to find a school of FISH, they sailed toward the spot and soon beheld a SEA SERPENT which they described as resembling "a lizard bigger than a whale." The Solomonas panicked when the creature raised its head above water, sending them back to dry land at top speed. A Cook Islands newspaper, the *News Daily*, reported their sighting on 29 September, with a notation that no one else had thus far seen the animal.

Source: "Remote sea monster." *Strange Magazine*, http://www.strangemag.com/mixedbagarch2.html.

Cookie Monster   Residents of Somerset County, Pennsylvania borrowed the name of a popular *Sesame Street* character in October 1972, and applied it to an aggressive SASQUATCH-type HOMINID seen by members of one family at Champion. The witnesses endured repeated visits by the creature, which on one occasion grabbed their car and rocked it violently from side to side. Later, they found the family dog torn nearly in half by some unseen predator. It lived long enough to reach the veterinarian's office, then died. A 5-year hiatus then ensued, broken on 23 December 1977, when two young hikers saw a large hairy biped near Trent.

Source: Berry, *Bigfoot on the East Coast*.

Coole Lough, Ireland   Irish legends identify this lough, in County Galway, as the ancient hunting ground of a predatory LAKE MONSTER. No recent sightings of the creature are recorded.

Source: Isabella Gregory, *Visions and Beliefs in the West of Ireland*. New York: G.P. Putnam's Sons, 1920.

Coon, Carleton Stevens (1904–61)   Anthropologist Carleton Coon was a Massachusetts native who earned his B.A., M.A. and Ph.D. from Harvard University, the latter degree completed in 1948 after a stint with the cloak-and-dagger Office of Strategic Services in World War II. Upon receiving his doctorate, he taught briefly at Harvard, then accepted a professorship at the University of Pennsylvania (1949–63), where he also served as curator of ethnology at the University Museum. That post re-

quired extensive field work, and the year 1956 found Coon in India, engaged in projects for the museum and New York's Wenner-Gren Foundation of Anthropological Research. There, he became fascinated with reports of the YETI and was hired as a consultant by Texas oilman TOM SLICK in 1956. Coon met with PETER BYRNE and others at Darjeeling, in January 1957, to plan Slick's first Yeti-hunting expedition, and he analyzed evidence collected on subsequent hunts. In May 1959, after examining casts of HOMINID footprints obtained in Nepal, Coon opined, "If it is a primate, it is an exceedingly unusual one." He went on to suggest that the Yeti might be "a completely unknown animal, close to primate or halfway between bear and primate." Conversely, Coon was first to analyze the supposed Yeti forearm preserved at Makalu lamasery as the mummified leg of a carnivorous quadruped.

Coon never lost his interest in unknown hominids, and his book *The Story of Man* (1962) included a chapter on "Giant APES and Snowmen." In 1978, he was a keynote speaker at the University of British Columbia's Symposium on SASQUATCH and Similar Phenomena." Coon died at Gloucester, Massachusetts on 6 June 1981, but his work lived on. A chapter by Coon titled "Why there has to be a Sasquatch" appeared three years later, in Vladimir Markotic's *The Sasquatch and Other Unknown Hominids* (1984).

Sources: Coleman, *Tom Slick and the Search for the Yeti*; Carleton S. Coon, Science Daily, http://www.sciencedaily.com/encyclopedia/Carleton_Coon.

Copanello sea serpent   In August 1958, a party of foreign tourists was spear-fishing in the Mediterranean near Copanello, in the Italian province of Calabria, when they met a serpentine creature resembling a giant EEL 80 yards offshore. Badly frightened, the witnesses fled to their boat and swiftly returned to dry land.

Source: Heuvelmans, *In the Wake of the Sea Serpents*.

***Coral* sea serpent**   Details are sadly lacking for this report of a SEA SERPENT glimpsed by Captain Sherman, of the schooner *Coral*, at the mouth of the CONNECTICUT RIVER on 23 March 1888. We know nothing of the beast today, except that it was large and serpentine in form.

Source: O'Neill, *The Great New England Sea Serpent*.

Cordering Cougars   Ranchers in the neighborhood of Cordering, Western Australia have long been accustomed to predation by dingoes and other local carnivores. In 1977, however, they confronted a new menace in the form of ALIEN BIG CATS, dubbed the Cordering COUGAR. Shrieks in the night were followed by slaughter of sheep on various ranches. Brothers Dennis and Ross Earnshaw lost $3,000 worth of lambs in one season alone, but the deaths were not merely expensive. As described by authors Paul Cropper and Tony Healy:

> The new predators appeared to kill for the sheer pleasure of it: most of their victims were not eaten. When they did pause to nibble, however, their eating habits were quite distinctive and radically different from those of dogs, FOXES or pigs. The bellies of the victims were neatly slit open and their entrails consumed. When, more rarely, additional flesh was eaten, this was done in an extremely thorough and very unusual manner: the skin was neatly peeled back and the ribs were stripped of every last shred of meat.

KANGAROOS also fell victim to the hunters, found with their necks broken and internal organs "almost surgically removed." Eyewitness sightings began in June 1978, when Jim Putland met a tawny, 200-pound CAT in his backyard. Soon afterward, motorist

Mike Drew saw one of the creatures at Darkan, 12 miles north of Cordering. It was "a big, thickset, sandy-colored thing with a small head and a long tail. It moved like a cat with its body close to the ground and showed no fear at all." Its luminous eyes, Drew said, were "as big as saucers." The Earnshaw brothers saw two large ginger-colored cats together in broad daylight, during one of their patrols. A short time later, Dennis and his wife saw "something like a lioness" cross the road in front of their car. Large pawprints marked the ground around some kills, and ranchers found large gum trees scarred with scratch marks where the predators had climbed aloft. By that time, local ranchers were convinced they had at least one cougar (*Puma concolor*) on their hands.

A spokesman for Australia's Agricultural Protection Board admitted to journalist David O'Reilly that if cougars were present "it would be our job, I guess, to do something about it and I'm not sure what we could do." That said, the APB denied that any such problem existed. To prove its point, the board hired Bob Neumann, a transplanted American cat-hunter, to debunk the cougar "myth," but his final verdict was not reassuring. "Man," Neumann told his employers, "you sure got cougars." O'Reilly spent $7,000 on a Starlite night-vision scope and soon reported his own sighting of "a robust cat-like figure moving at startling speed, in huge bounds, into the scope's view." A hunt was finally organized, and while shooter Bert Pinker claimed to have wounded a cougar from 217 yards, no cats were killed or captured. Sightings continue in Western Australia, including both cougars and occasional "black panthers."

Sources: Healy and Cropper, *Out of the Shadows*; O'Reilly, *Savage Shadow*; Smith, *Bunyips & Bigfoots*.

Corinthian sea serpent

At 4:30 a.m. on 30 August 1913, a SEA SERPENT was sighted off the Grand Banks of Newfoundland by G. Batchelor, second officer of the transatlantic liner *Corinthian*, en route from London to Montréal. Watching from a distance of one mile, Batchelor first believed the object was a capsized fishing boat, but when the gap had closed to 200 feet, he realized it was alive. He described the animal as follows:

> First appeared a great head, long fin-like ears and great blue eyes. The eyes were mild and liquid, with no indication of ferocity. Following sad eyes came a neck, it was a regular neck all right, all of twenty feet in length which greatly resembled a giraffe. The monster took its time in emerging, but it kept emerging so long that I wondered what the end would be. The neck…seemed to be set on a ball-bearing, so supple was it and so easily and rhythmically did it sway while the large liquid blue eyes took in the ship with a surprised, injured and fearful stare. The creature was well fixed for side arms. Three horned fins surmounted its bony head, probably for defence and attack or for ripping things up. The body was about the same length as the neck, very much like that of a monster seal or sea-lion with short water-smoothed fur. The tail was split into two large fins. Its colour scheme was good, although some might think it giddy; light brownish-yellow tastefully spattered with spots of a darker hue.

Despite his enumeration of various mammal characteristics, Batchelor went on to speculate that the creature was a PLESIOSAUR, further suggesting that is was "either a native of the Arctic regions which has come down with the stream…or else of the mile-down bottom of the sea." Having determined that much, at least to his own satisfaction, Batchelor then advanced the curious notion that the animal's appearance was somehow occasioned by the wreck of the liner *Titanic* nearby, on 14 April 1912.

Source: Heuvelmans, *In the Wake of the Sea Serpents*.

Cork sea serpents

Between 28 August and 25 September 1850, a series of extraordinary SEA SERPENT sightings were reported from the coast of Ireland's County Cork. Witness R.W. Travers set the ball rolling with two successive reports, from Old Head of Kinsale on 28 August and from Dunwoody Head, three days later. On 2 September, seamen aboard the vessel *Antelope* claimed to have found the beast's discarded skin, shed like that of a SNAKE, floating off Old Head of Kinsale. Witness John Good reported a sighting from the offshore Sovereign Islands on 9 September, followed by alarms from fishermen at Ballycottin Bay a week later. The story ended on 24 September, when anonymous heroes at Youghal claimed they had killed the creature after a fierce battle, during which it vomited dozens of FISH and "being handled, gave the crew the most terrific electric shocks." Nothing remained of its carcass when journalists came snooping, and BERNARD HEUVELMANS later dismissed the whole series of sightings as HOAXES.

Source: Heuvelmans, *In the Wake of the Sea Serpents*.

Corpach Lock carcass

Details are sadly lacking in the case of an "odd animal" reportedly found dead in Corpach Lock, on Scotland's Caledonian Canal, near the turn of the last century. Corpach is situated near Fort William and LOCH EIL, 20-odd miles below Loch Ness. No description of the carcass is available today, nor is the date of its discovery confirmed. Peter Costello reports that the animal was found "before 1899," while Mike Dash later placed the event "around 1900."

Sources: Costello, *In Search of Lake Monsters*; Dash, "Status report: Lake monsters."

Corrales, Scott (1963–)

Pennsylvania resident Scott Corrales is an author and translator who attended Rutgers and George Washington Universities. His fascination with unexplained phenomena, including cryptozoology and UFOs, dates from childhood. Today, he is recognized worldwide as the leading researcher of CHUPACABRA sightings and a tireless translator of anomalous reports from Latin America. Corrales edits *Inexplicata*, a Spanish-language journal of mysterious events. His books, based on extensive field research, thus far include *Chupacabras and Other Mysteries* (1997) and *Flashpoint: High Strangeness in Puerto Rico* (1998).

Sources: Coleman and Clark, *Cryptozoology A to Z*; Corrales, *Chupacabras and Other Mysteries*.

Corsican sea serpents

The French island of Corsica produced two still-unexplained SEA SERPENT sightings in the first quarter of the 20th century. A group of fishermen from Calvi logged the first report in October 1907, when they saw a 200-foot creature resembling a string of floating barrels in the Gulf of Porto, west of the Île de Beauté. They raced to land in a panic, and watched from the dock with local villagers, while the beast cavorted on the surface. So frightened were the fishermen that they remained ashore for several days, until a gunboat arrived from Ajaccio to kill the creature, but the hunters found no trace.

Seventeen years later, at 9:00 a.m. on 6 May 1924, a serpentine creature 100 feet long was seen in the Gulf of Ajaccio, reported by G. Juranville, Corsica's Inspector of Public Assistance at Agosta. A week after the sighting, Dr. J. Pellegrin read Juranville's description of the animal at a meeting of the Zoological Society of France. Juranville wrote: "It showed a raised head, and the rest of the body seemed to roll in vertical undulations."

Source: Heuvelmans, *In the Wake of the Sea Serpents*.

Corsican Wildcat In December 1929, French scientist L. Lavauden published a report concerning the supposed existence of an unidentified wildcat (*Felis silvestris*) species on Mediterranean island of Corsica. Lavauden named the elusive species *Felis reyi*, later downgraded to subspecies *F. s. reyi*, based on a skull and three pelts collected since February 1929 by a Corsican schoolteacher named Rey-Jouvin. The skull and one skin were delivered to Lavauden, while two other skins were lodged at Isère's Musée de Grenoble. Lavauden noted that the Corsican specimens differed from most European wildcats in its dark pelage, and further from Sardinian wildcats (*F. s. sarda*) by its short tail and lack of russet coloring behind its ears. Strangely, although Rey-Jouvin and other witnesses described the Corsican CATS as fairly common, no other specimen has yet been collected, and KARL SHUKER suggests that the subspecies may be extinct.

Source: Shuker, *Mystery Cats of the World.*

Cougars (Melanistic) The term "black panther" has no scientific meaning. It is typically applied to melanistic specimens of JAGUAR (*Panthera onca*) or leopard (*P. pardus*) whose background pelage is dark enough to obscure the CAT'S characteristic spots or rosettes. Feline melanism is most common in moist tropical regions of Africa, Asia and Latin America, but black panthers are also reported from other regions where no jaguars or leopards naturally occur. Panther sightings are fairly common in the U.S. and Canada, where cougars (*Puma concolor*) are the largest known cats, but no melanistic cougar has ever been confirmed, either in captivity or in the wild. Reports of alleged black cougars from eastern North America are further complicated by official insistence that the EASTERN COUGAR is now extinct throughout that range.

How common are black panther sightings across North America? No two published sources agree on the number of panthers reported, but a survey of estimates suggests the scope of the phenomenon. Researcher JOHN LUTZ recorded 615 Eastern cougar reports between 1983 and 1989, of which 37 percent referred to black cats; for 1990–99, Lutz counted 865 panther reports out of 3,948 total (22 percent); and by 2001 he listed 1,101 panther reports among 4,882 total (23 percent). Author Gerry Parker, writing in 1998, declared that 15–25 percent of all Eastern cougar reports described black cats. EASTERN COUGAR NETWORK spokesman Todd Lester logged 673 sightings during 1995–99, of which 177 (26 percent) described black panthers. In California, where an estimated 2,500 cougars survive in the wild, a newspaper tabulation of sightings between 1957 and 1975 found 15 percent describing black cats. The U.S. states reporting black panthers include:

Alabama: John Lutz lists 16 panther sightings as of 2001, but only one — from Nauvoo in May 1987 — is specified in the standard literature. A new rash of sightings was reported around Talladega in July 2003, prompting false rumors that a circus train had derailed in the area.

Arizona: Multiple sightings were logged around Tucson between 16 September and 26 October 1976. In April 2003, a "black lion" with a cub was seen near Mayer, in Yavapai County. Ten months later and 20 miles to the northwest, Brenda Patton of Prescott glimpsed a "sleek, black" cat equal in size to her 100-pound dog. Local newspapers refer to "rare black mountain lions," while state wildlife authorities dub melanistic cougars "the YETI of the Southwest."

Arkansas: Panther reports have emerged from Green County (September 1968), Fayetteville (December 1972), and Little Rock

Though frequently reported, melanistic cougars remain undocumented by science.

(November 1976). On some unspecified date in the 1970s, a group of raccoon hunters allegedly killed a black cat "with a long round body and an even longer tail" in the Black River Bottoms of northeastern Arkansas. One witness claimed the animal was "smaller than a cougar, but bigger than a bobcat," with a tail 5–6 feet long. The carcass was not preserved. In 1977, residents of Dierks and Dover reported a black panther traveling with a maned LION (*Panthera leo*). Another sighting was filed from Russellville in January 1980, and cryptozoologist WILLIAM REBSAMEN recorded sightings at Fort Smith in 1999.

California: Marin County residents reported multiple sightings in June 1963 and September 1964. Ventura County produced a series of sightings between 1964 and 1968, including one report (in 1964) of two black panthers seen together. A panther was seen with a tawny-colored cougar in Contra Costa County, during 1972. Other black cat sightings have been logged from Thousand Oaks (January 1968), Mount Diablo (fall 1972), Concord and Danville (March 1973), San Jose (December 1973), San Dimas (May 1984), and Fairfield (April 1988).

Colorado: A Utah hunter named Bruce Hartman allegedly killed a black cougar on 8 December 1912, south of Gunnison, and while its pelt was reportedly examined by various unnamed experts, no trace of the cat or any contemporary reports of the incident survive today.

Connecticut: John Lutz lists no panther sightings from the Nutmeg State, but author GARY MANGIACOPRA records encounters spanning nearly a century, from 1869 to 1963. Specific incidents listed in Mangiacopra's report include a sighting from Tolland County (1869) and another from Hartford (1939), where black and tawny cats were seen together.

Delaware: Lutz notes 9 black panther reports among 69 Eastern cougar sightings reported from Delaware during 1993–2001, but he provides no details of the incidents.

Florida: Lutz lists 9 sightings from the Sunshine State, while Todd Lester acknowledges one. The only case detailed in current literature emerged from Fort Myers in 1959 or 1960, where a motorist and his wife saw a "large, long, black cat" cross the road in front of their car. They described the beast as "quite black and very large, much more so than a dog but not necessarily big for a panther."

Georgia: Lutz reports 23 sightings from this venue, while Lester counts 2. Three cases described in some detail include a Cedartown sighting (April 1958) and multiple reports from Stockbridge (September 1975). Local hunter James Rutledge claimed to have killed a panther at Stockbridge in spring 1975, but he refused to disclose where the carcass was buried. Witness Gerald Cameron Jr. claimed two sightings of a panther at Savannah, in 1988. He described the cat as 4–4.5 feet long, roughly 2 feet 6 inches tall at the shoulder, weighing 100–140 pounds.

Illinois: With 47 panther reports on file through 2001 (according to Lutz), Illinois has recorded some of the country's most dramatic — and peculiar — panther sightings. The earliest dates from October 1946, when two black cats eluded 150 hunters and three airplanes at Oquawka. Decatur and surrounding Macon County have been visited repeatedly, in 1955, 1960, 1963, 1965, 1970, 1976 and 1995. St. Clair County is similarly blessed, with sightings in 1976, 1986 and 1987. Alexander County produced a rash of sightings during 1966–70, including one of the strangest on record. Motorist Mike Busby had stopped to stretch his legs along the highway south of Olive Branch, on 10 April 1970, when he was attacked by a 6-foot-tall panther walking on its hind legs. Before another vehicle frightened it off, the beast shredded Busby's shirt, leaving cuts on his arm, chest and stomach that required hospital treatment. The most recent sighting to date, in 2001, featured claims from Carl and Debbie Johnson that a "black cougar" was living on their property at Sheldon, in Iroquois County.

Indiana: Lutz acknowledges 21 panther reports from the Hoosier State, dating from the end of World War II. Hunter Roy Graham allegedly shot one of the cats near Lebanon, on 4 September 1946, but it fell into a swift-flowing creek and was not recovered. Two years later, residents of eastern Indiana and neighboring Ohio reported a panther traveling with a maned lion and a tawny lioness or cougar. "Panther trouble" hit Perry County in 1978, where a local farmer allegedly wounded a jet-black predator 5–6 feet long. He assumed the cat was dead, based on circling vultures seen two days later, but the shooter did not confirm his kill or report it to authorities. Crypto-researcher Brad LaGrange logged his own panther sighting in February 2001, when a large black cat crossed the highway in front of his car near tiny Leavenworth, in Crawford County.

Iowa: Multiple residents of Council Bluffs sighted a panther during June 1978.

Kansas: Todd Lester reports one sighting, but no details are presently available.

Kentucky: Lutz records 16 panther sightings from the Bluegrass State, while Lester admits only 6. No specific cases are described in either report.

Louisiana: Motorist Wanda Dillard reported the state's only black panther sighting to date in November 1945, while driving through swampy St. Mary Parish on Highway 90. A "huge black cat" crossed the highway in front of her car, whereupon Dillard stopped to watch it. Lit by her headlights, the creature "simply sat down like any common old house cat and began to groom himself." Dillard described it as "a bit smaller" than an average cougar and "jet black, very sleek looking and well muscled, with a long black tail that he wrapped around himself as he sat there." She watched the cat for 10 minutes, until traffic forced her to proceed.

Maine: Todd Lester reports a single sighting from Maine, compared to 21 in Lutz's file. One witness, in 1955, was the father of cryptozoologist MATTHEW BILLE. A quarter-century later, in May 1981, a game warden's wife reported a sighting from Harrington Lake, in Baxter State Park. She told reporters, "There is absolutely no doubt in my mind that what I saw was a black panther."

Maryland: John Lutz reports 86 Maryland panther sightings, versus a single report from Todd Lester's files. Loren Coleman enumerates two alleged cases without details, one from Flintstone in 1970 and the other from Fairfax County (actually located in Virginia) during February 1971.

Massachusetts: LOREN COLEMAN reports a 1948 sighting at Pittsfield, but Lutz found no black panthers in his survey of 43 Bay State cougar sightings logged during 1993–2001.

Michigan: Lutz records 46 panther sightings from Michigan, with particular concentration in Chippewa and Oakland Counties since the early 1950s. A flurry of reports emerged from Livingston, Oakland and Washtenaw Counties during 1984–87. In December 2003, a White Lake witness reported sighting a "gorgeous" black cat weighing about 150 pounds.

Minnesota: According to researcher MARK HALL, a black panther was killed near Bemidji in the early 1970s. A photo of the carcass was allegedly published in local newspapers, but state conservation officers urged witnesses "not to talk about it." Three decades later, a "large and ever elusive black cat" disturbed residents of Forest Lake, 125 miles southeast of Bemidji. Police glimpsed the beast but were unable to trap it.

Mississippi: John Lutz records 16 panther sightings statewide out of 77 Eastern cougar reports, between 1993 and 2001, but details are sadly omitted.

Missouri: The Show-Me State recorded its first known panther sighting in July 1957, when Walter Bigelow and his wife saw a 3-foot-long creature, tailless and "rather stubby," cross the highway outside Chillicothe. Two decades later, in June 1976, a hunter watched a 4-foot-long specimen, estimated weight 100–110 pounds, drinking from a pond two miles north of Wellsville. It was, he said, "without question a panther." Another sighting was filed from Lone Jack, in February 1980.

Nebraska: On 18 February 1897, the *Omaha Daily News* reported a panther sighting from Fairmont, in southern Nebraska's Fillmore County.

New Hampshire: A panther was reportedly sighted at Wilton, in 1948. John Lutz found no black cats listed among the state's 59 cougar sightings for 1993–2001.

New Jersey: Lutz records 61 panther sightings for the Garden State, compared with 17 from Todd Lester's files. Neither author provides details, Loren Coleman reports a sighting from Mountainside in January 1957, with another spate from Cumberland and Salem Counties during 1987.

New York: Black-cat encounters in New York date from 1962, when a panther was sighted at Delhi. Another visited Eaton Corners in March 1971, and a swamp-dwelling cat terrorized Van Etten residents, feeding on their pets and dodging hunters between July and December 1977. John Lutz records a further 146 panther sightings from the Empire State between 1993 and 2001.

North Carolina: Panther reports from North Carolina began in May 1899, with a sighting in Wilkes County. Other regions with reported sightings prior to creation of the Eastern Puma Research Network include Iredell County (1934), Bladensboro (1953–54), Mecklenburg County (1959) and Cleveland County (1978). John Lutz reports another 22 panther encounters between 1993 and 2001. On 27 January 2004, witness Denise Williams videotaped a large black cat behind her home in Asheboro, but police and zoo employees could not find the animal.

Ohio: Sightings in the Buckeye State began early, with a report from Lamartine in 1890. Neighboring Clark and Montgomery Counties produced multiple reports between May and July 1962, while Allen County logged a visit in 1977 and Cincinnati hosted an urban panther in late 1984. By 2001, John Lutz listed another 26 panther sightings statewide.

Oklahoma: The year 1977 brought a spate of panther sightings to Oklahoma, including reports from Talihina (19 January) and Oklahoma City (25–26 October).

Pennsylvania: Panther sighting tabulations from the Keystone State vary widely. Researcher Helen McGinnis claims encounters dating from the mid-19th century, with, 35 sightings collected between 1957 and 1981. Todd Lester, writing in 1998, found only 5 reports, but John Lutz placed Pennsylvania at the top of his panther list three years later, with 282 sightings between 1993 and 2001. On October 2003, Ronald and Brenda Graham saw a large black cat beside Elk Creek, in Franklin's Girard Borough Park.

South Carolina: Panther sightings in South Carolina date from autumn 1948, when witnesses reported a curious bipedal specimen from White Oak Swamp. John Lutz records 10 more sightings statewide, between 1993 and 2001. "Black cat fever" hit Mauldin in October 2003, with police mobilized to set traps for a cryptid seen by multiple witnesses. Their bait vanished, but the cat remained at large as this volume went to press.

Tennessee: Todd Lester reported one panther sighting from the Volunteer State in 1998, but John Lutz collected 29 more by 2001. Hunters around Indian Mound complained that panthers were snatching their deer in the 1990s, and Nashville authorities failed to bag the black cat seen by witness Connie Scheitlin in December 2003.

Texas: The Lone Star State has a relative paucity of black panther sightings, but reports have been filed from Fort Worth (1960), Big Thicket (1975), Nobility (May 1975) and Houston (April 2001). In the latter case, police were alerted by witnesses who saw a large black cat lurking around the garbage bins at an apartment complex.

Vermont: Witness Marian Peduzzi reported a black panther four feet long near Berlin, in 1946. John Lutz records one more sighting, sometime between 1993 and 2001, but no further details are available.

Virginia: Todd Lester counted 16 panther sightings from Virginia in 1998, while John Lutz ran the tally up to 35 in 2001. Chincoteague Island residents were panicked on 15 January 2003, after 76-year-old Helen White was attacked in her home by "a huge, sleek, black cat wearing a thick, red collar," with eyes "shaped like almonds and green as poison." The cat bit and clawed White's leg, while she fought back with a broom, but White eventually held no grudge, despite an admonition to reporters that the beast "had murder in his heart." At least 10 other witnesses reported less traumatic sightings over the next two weeks, while police scoured the island in vain. Estimates of the animal's size ranged from "twice that of a domestic cat" to "bigger than most dogs." Sightings continued through March, then ended as mysteriously as they began. Helen White suffered further injuries, this time from an ordinary domestic cat, on 10 April 2003.

West Virginia: In a curious reversal of the norm, John Lutz notes 76 black panther reports from West Virginia between 1993 and 2001, while Todd Lester claimed 122 by 1998. The only case detailed involves a flurry of sightings in mid-September 1978 around Point Pleasant, formerly notorious for sightings of the creature known as MOTHMAN.

Wisconsin: Mark Hall, writing in 1994, referred to a series of black panther sightings occurring in 1991–93. John Lutz takes up the cause thereafter, citing another 98 cases between 1993 and 2001. Unfortunately, neither researcher provides a detailed list of incidents.

Canada, like the U.S., once boasted indigenous cougars from sea to sea — and like its neighbor to the south, Canadian officialdom now claims the cats are extinct in the eastern half of the country. Still, black panther sightings in New Brunswick date from 1948 (at least), and local researcher Bruce Wright catalogued 20 seemingly reliable sightings between 1951 and 1970. Another "eastern black panther" surfaced in December 2002, on Barry Campbell's property at Miramichi, New Brunswick. A sighting was also recorded at Sudbury, Ontario in August 1959.

Latin America has melanistic jaguars to explain black panther sightings, but reports of jet-black cougars still persist. In 1843 or 1845 (accounts vary), Canadian hunter William Thomson allegedly killed a black cougar in Brazil, at some ambiguous point 250 miles from Rio de Janeiro. According to Thomson's description of that animal, "Everything was total black, head, back, rump, shoulders and tail. Its undersides and throat were an ashen-grey." No remains were preserved to corroborate the story. More than a century later, in 1957, explorer Leon Mott reportedly examined the pelts of several black cougars in Nicaragua, but again, none were collected for study. Native hunter Miguel Ruiz Herrero claimed to have slain a black cougar in Costa Rica's Guanacaste Province, during 1959, and while a photo of the cat's pelt was published 28 years later, the skin remains elusive and the story unsupported by hard evidence. The 1990s brought reports of a YANA PUMA ("black mountain lion") twice the size of a jaguar, said to inhabit Peru's montane forests, but remains are distressingly ephemeral.

Australia has no indigenous cats, but reports of feline predators continue, and many of the ALIEN BIG CATS described by witnesses are black. In fact, as noted by researchers Paul Cropper and Tony Healy, the continent Down Under reverses normal trends, with more than 65 percent of its ABC sightings involving black cats. Australia's close proximity to Asia's thriving leopard population leads some investigators to identify the island nation's panthers as melanistic leopards, but Cropper and Healy raise three telling objections to that conventional wisdom. First, they observe that while many Australian panthers are seen at close range and in broad daylight, no witnesses to date have reported the underlying spots found on all melanistic leopards. Second, leopards are not historically difficult to trap or shoot, as witnessed by their near-extinction in parts of their range. Third, leopards are not known to kill for sport, without feeding, as do Australian predators like the EMMAVILLE PANTHER and others. Finally, the authors note that Australian panthers frequently run at high speed for long distances, another trait unknown amongst leopards. A long-standing rumor in Western Australia traces panther sightings to 1942, when two cougars — a black male and tan female — allegedly leaped or were thrown from a U.S. warship near Denmark, where they swam ashore and vanished, but that tale still does not prove that black cougars exist.

If they do not, then how may we explain the ever-growing number of "panther" sightings, especially in North America? One common explanation is mistaken identity, involving large black dogs, oversized domestic cats, or some other known animal. HOAXES are also possible, either in the form of false reports or cougar pelts dyed black, though none have thus far been discovered. Black jaguars might explain occasional sightings in the U.S.

Southwest, though melanism is unlikely in a desert environment. John Lutz suggests that early slave traders may have imported and released African leopards in America sometime before the Civil War. Loren Coleman takes another tack, proposing that a relict population of Pleistocene cave lions (*P. atrox*) has survived to modern times in North America. That theory also explains the occasional sighting of black panthers with maned lions since, Coleman writes, "The *atrox* males may have manes, and the females sometimes, perhaps often, are black." In fact, however, since *P. atrox* is known only from fossil remains, no data exists concerning melanistic specimens, and there is no clear reason why females of the species should display uncharacteristic melanism in a temperate climate.

Sources: Chad Arment, "Black panthers in North America." *North American BioFortean Review* 3 (2000): 38–56; Chad Arment, "Eyewitness account: A mystery cat in Missouri." *North American BioFortean Review* 1 (April 1999): 16; John Boyanoski, "Mysterious cat 'like a UFO' around Mauldin." *Greenville* (SC) *News* (20 October 2003); Citro, *Green Mountain Ghosts, Ghouls & Unsolved Mysteries*; Clark and Pear, *Strange & Unexplained Phenomena*; Loren Coleman, "Black 'mountain lions' in California?" *Pursuit* 46 (Spring 1979): 61–62; Coleman, *Mysterious America*; Coleman and Clark, *Cryptozoology A to Z*; CHRISTOPHER COOTE, "MANGALO CAT MYSTERY." *EYRE PENINSULA TRIBUNE* (20 NOVEMBER 2002); Jennifer Cording, "Woman recounts mauling by panther." *Chincoteague* (VA) *Beacon* (29 January 2003); Jennifer Cording, "Chincoteague—Cat nips continue for 'panther' victim." *Chincoteague* (VA) *Beacon* (23 April 2003); Joanna Dodder, "Local woman is among few to see rare black mountain lion." *Prescott* (AZ) *Daily Courier* (10 February 2004); "Dogs routed by 'panther.'" *Kansas City Star* (23 July 1957); "Elusive black cat shows itself again in FL." *Forest Lake* (MN) *Times* (5 March 2003); Bill Geroux, "Oversize black cat roaming island?" *Richmond* (VA) *Times-Dispatch* (11 March 2003); Bob Gross, "Woman says she saw black cat." *Daily Oakland* (MI) *Press* (10 January 2004); Healy and Cropper, *Out of the Shadows*; Hocking, "Large Peruvian mammals unknown to zoology"; Mitchell Kline, "Too big to be a dog, too small to be Bigfoot." *Nashville Tennesseean* (18 December 2003); Brad LaGrange, "An old black panther report." *North American BioFortean Review* 2 (2000): 40; Brad LaGrange, "Black panther sighting." *North American BioFortean Review* 3 (May 2001): 27–28; Brad LaGrange, "Black panthers in Perry County, Indiana." *North American BioFortean Review* 2 (December 2000): 4; John Lutz, "The black panther mystery." *North American BioFortean Review* 4 (March 2002): 25–40; John Lutz and Linda Lutz, "Century-old mystery rises from the shadows." *North American BioFortean Review* 3 (October 2001): 30–50; Mangiacopra and Smith, "Connecticut's mystery felines"; George Miller, "House cat or cougar?" *Erie* (PA) *Times-News* (30 October 2003); "Mysterious panther found in Miramichi?" *New Brunswick Telegraph Journal* (24 December 2002); Parker, *The Eastern Panther*; Bo

Researcher Loren Coleman suggests that U.S. "panther" sightings may indicate survival of *Panthera leo atrox*.

Petersen, "Are cat tales really just fish stories?" *Charleston* (SC) *Post and Courier* (16 November 2003); Sue Anne Pressley, "Animal attack has residents of Virginia island on alert." *Washington Post* (26 February 2003); Sue Anne Pressley, "Hunting for the truth." *Washington Post* (23 February 2003); Robert Prevo, "Arkansas' 'black panthers.'" *North American BioFortean Review* 3 (October 2001): 51–52; Darryl Ray, "Talladega panthers remain phantoms." *Birmingham* (AL) *News* (12 July 2003); Shuker, *Mystery Cats of the World*; April Silvaggio, "Big cat moving south along Golden Strip." *Greenville* (SC) *News* (22 October 2003); April Silvaggio, "Something is taking bait set for big cat." *Greenville* (SC) *News* (24 October 2003); Christine Sima, "Houston panther sighting prompts alert." *Medina* (OH) *Gazette* (6 April 2001); Smith, *Bunyips & Bigfoots*; Bob Themer, "'Big cat' believed to be prowling rural Watseka garden." *Watseka* (IL) *Daily Journal* (27 June 2002); "Tigers and lions and bears, oh my." Greenville (SC) News (22 October 2003); Chip Womick, "Mysterious creature baffles officials." *Asheboro* (NC) *Courier-Tribune* (28 January 2004); Jason Zacher, "Big cat reported seen in Mauldin." *Greenville* (SC) *News* (17 November 2003).

Counfea Lough, Ireland Celtic legends name this lake, in Ireland's County Waterford, as the one-time habitation of a large LAKE MONSTER. No modern sightings of the cryptid(s) are reported.

Source: Holiday, *The Dragon and the Disc*.

County Clare sea serpent On 9 December 1871, *Harper's Weekly* published a report of an Irish SEA SERPENT sighting drawn from an undated issue of the *Limerick Chronicle*. According to that second-hand account, the beast had been seen by several witnesses—including a "well-known clergyman in the north of Ireland"—on the coast of County Clare, near Kilkee. The beast had a head resembling a horse's and "a huge mane of seaweed-looking hair, which rose and fell with the motion of the water." Its glassy eyes were so intimidating that one female witness "nearly fainted at the sight." Unable to resist a jibe, *Harper's* suggested that there was "far more reason to expect that the serpent himself will be overcome by faintness at some of the sights to be witnessed at many of the watering-places on the English and Irish coasts."

Source: Heuvelmans, *In the Wake of the Sea Serpents*.

Cow Lake, Canada Aboriginal traditions maintain that Cow Lake, nestled in the Canadian Rockies less than a mile from Rocky Mountain House, Alberta, was one the home of a ferocious LAKE MONSTER. No modern sightings of the creature are recorded.

Source: Benedict, "The unknown lake monsters of Alberta."

Cowal Lake, Australia Cowal Lake is a marshy wetland area of central New South Wales, fed by Manna and Yeo Yeo Creeks. In 1873, a party of surveyors crossing the lake in a boat glimpsed a peculiar BUNYIP at a distance of 163 yards. They described the beast as looking "like an old man blackfellow, with long dark-coloured hair." It swam in a straight line across the lake, rising to reveal its shoulders every 20–30 feet. When they approached it, the animal evaded them and finally submerged, albeit without showing any sign of fear.

Source: Smith, *Bunyips & Bigfoots*.

Cradley Cat *see* **Pedmore Puma**

Craigsmere sea serpent In July 1920, while navigating along the Florida coast between Miami and Fort Lauderdale, sailors aboard the merchant vessel *Craigsmere* spied a SEA SERPENT swimming in tandem with their vessel. As witness Charles Blackford III later described the incident to IVAN SANDERSON, "The captain, mate on watch, helmsman and some others of the crew saw it. As I remember it they say it was long, with dorsal fins somewhat like a porpoise only several in number with its head some distance ahead of the body and partly submerged." Analyzing the report half a century later, BERNARD HEUVELMANS assumed that the fins were lateral, rather than dorsal as described, thus making the creature a specimen of his hypothetical "many-finned" sea serpent.

Source: Heuvelmans, *In the Wake of the Sea Serpents.*

Cranberry Lake, Canada

Canadian researcher JOHN KIRK reports that LAKE MONSTER sightings from Cranberry Lake span more than a century, beginning in the 1890s. The heaviest concentration of reports date from the 1920s and 1950s, when witnesses described encounters with a 12-foot SNAKE. Earlier accounts referred to larger creatures with horselike heads, resembling aquatic cryptids found in other North American and European lakes. Strangely, Kirk places Cranberry Lake in Nova Scotia, where no such body of water seems to exist. Canadian atlases and gazetteers list two Cranberry Lakes, one in Ontario and the other in New Brunswick (at 46°12' north latitude and 65°63' west longitude).

Source: Kirk, *In the Domain of the Lake Monsters*; The Atlas of Canada, http://atlas.gc.ca/site/english/find_a_place/index_html.

Crater Lake, Oregon

Crater Lake is located in southwestern Oregon's Cascade Range, at the heart of Crater Lake National Park. It dates from the Ice Age, some 7,000 years ago, when the peak of volcanic Mount Mazama collapsed, leaving a crater 1,938 feet deep. Although the lake has no known outlets and no feeder streams, year-round precipitation keeps the water level virtually constant. Early Klamath tribesmen regarded the lake as a divine creation, populated with "water demons" that dragged unwary humans to a grisly death beneath the surface. White settlers also reported occasional LAKE MONSTER sightings, but no modern reports are on file. In 1977 a low-budget horror film, *The Crater Lake Monster*, depicted a living DINOSAUR emerging from the lake to seek human prey. Georgia tourist Mattie Hatcher reported a sighting of the elusive beast in the 1980s. "That thing must have been a block long," she said. "I have never been so scared in my life. What we saw that day was a monster. To me, it looked like a DRAGON." In October 2003, an Internet poster known only as Zathan reported an undated sighting of the creature, which he dubbed CASSIE (no relation to the SEA SERPENT of Casco Bay, Maine). As described in that account, "Her body resembled a vary large lizard. She had a long tail about as long as her body. She was a dark brown color. Cassie swam back and forth like a SNAKE. I could have sworn that I heard a faint peeping sound."

Sources: Garner, *Monster! Monster!*; Charles Herndon, "Georgia woman discovers the mystery of Crater Lake." Fort Meyers (FL) News-Press (2 May 2002); "I saw the Crater Lake monster." *Farshores* (15 October 2003); Charles Skinner, *Myths and Legends of Our Own Land.* Philadelphia: Lippincott, 1896.

Crawling Ghost

Close on the heels of panic sparked by India's predatory MONKEY MAN and MUHNOCHWA, in summer 2002, came reports of yet another MYSTERY MAULER at Biswan, in the Sitapur district of Uttar Pradesh. Locals called their latest nemesis the Crawling Ghost, noting its predilection for attacking women from behind and clawing their buttocks. Twenty complaints were on file by early August, and some women armored themselves with "padded posteriors" to ward off injury. Magis-

trate Akhilesh Singh dismissed any suggestion that the reports were spawned by mere hysteria, telling journalists, "The incidents are for real." Dr. S.P. Verma, at Lucknow's government hospital, observed that "the entire town has turned insomniac," with Biswan families standing watch outside their homes by night, armed with torches to repel the unseen prowler. According to Verma, all victims of the Crawling Ghost bore "identical scratches." Police inspector R.D. Yadav acknowledged the flood of complaints and answered with one of his own: "We can arrest a man but not a ghost." The attacks ceased with autumn's arrival and had not resumed at press time for this book.

Sources: "Monster madness." *Fortean Times* 163 (November 2002): 7; Alka Rastogi, "The ghost who crawls." Hindustan Times (1 August 2002).

Creature (St. Paul)

When residents of St. Paul, Minnesota mention The Creature, they are referring to a cryptid of uncertain size or form which prowls by night around the greens and fairways of local golf courses. Over the past decade or longer, according to St. Paul newspaper columnist Joe Soucheray, the unknown beast "has been described as everything from an Urban Jackelope, whatever that is, to a FOX, to a prehistoric PIASA bird and even an UNICORN." Soucheray, it should be noted, claims several sightings of The Creature since March 1992. The most recent identified witness, 52-year-old computer technician Walt Mills, was walking his dog on Como Golf Course in early December 2001, when he met The Creature. As he explained to Soucheray, "I thought it was a dog, but no one was with it. Also, it looked kind of tall and skinny for a dog. Then I decided that it was a short deer." Questioned further, Mills confirmed that the beast had matted fur "about the color of dirty snow," with "long feet" and "ears pinned back." Soucheray suggests that The Creature may be a coyote (*Canis latrans*), but admits that his proposed solution "doesn't diminish its mysterious presence in the middle of the city."

Source: Joe Soucheray, "Creature returns, and a club member is initiated," *St. Paul* (MN) *Pioneer Press* (10 December 2001).

Crescent City sea serpent

On 21 August 1896, London's *Shipping Gazette* published this startling item from Carrabelle, Florida, located on the Gulf of Mexico in Franklin County:

A SEA-SERPENT is reported to have been captured at Carabelle [*sic*], Florida, by a fishing steamer named the *Crescent City*, which it towed wildly for some time before it was killed. The thing measures 49 feet long and 6 feet in circumference. It is EEL shaped, with a SHARK-like head and a tail armed with formidable fins. It was caught with a shark-hook, but after being tired out it had to be shot.

Incredibly, the item languished forgotten in dusty archives until BERNARD HEUVELMANS rediscovered it in the case in the 1960s. No follow-up report was ever published, and today no one knows what became of the specimen, assuming it ever existed.

Source: Heuvelmans, *In the Wake of the Sea Serpents.*

Crescent Lake, Oregon

Crescent Lake lies in Oregon's Klamath County, at the southeastern corner of the Diamond Park Wilderness Area. As with CRATER LAKE, 30 miles farther south, aboriginal tribesmen believed Crescent Lake was inhabited by malign "water demons," and sightings of LAKE MONSTERS were reported by white settlers in the 19th century. A dearth of modern sightings suggests that the creature(s) may now be extinct.

Sources: "Colossal Claude and the sea monsters." *Portland Oregonian* (24 September 1967); Garner, *Monster! Monster!*

Cressie Newfoundland's Crescent Lake is located near Robert's Arm, 150 miles northwest of St. John's on Notre Dame Bay. Aboriginal folklore describes it as the lair of a LAKE MONSTER variously known as Haoot tuwedyee ("swimming demon") or Woodum haoot ("pond devil"). Early European settlers logged their own sightings of the creature(s) now called Cressie, and modern reports have been fairly consistent since the mid-1950s. In June 1960, four loggers saw a "floating log" on Crescent Lake, which came alive and forced its way through a sandbar, revealing 10 feet of its serpentine body in the process. Spring 1990 brought a daylight sighting of a "huge creature" that reared 5 feet above the surface while thrashing the water into foam. Shortly after noon on 9 July 1991, teacher and journalist Fred Parsons saw a dark-colored serpentine beast more than 20 feet long swimming across the lake by means of vertical undulations. Two months later, on 5 September, witness Pierce Rideout glimpsed a black, 15-foot animal passing 150 yards offshore. Locals worried that Cressie might be dead, when 2002 passed without a reported sighting, but the creature(s) came back strong in 2003. Witness Vivian Short saw a beast large enough to "eat four or five people if they were swimming, like," while Robert's Arm town clerk Ada Rowsell recorded several other sightings "of a huge monster or SEA SERPENT or some kind of a FISH."

Sources: John Braddock, "Monsters of the Maritimes." *Atlantic Advocate* 58 (January 1968): 12–17; "'Cressie' sightings in Newfoundland." CBC News (1 August 2003); Kirk, *In the Domain of the Lake Monsters*.

Creve Coeur Lake, Missouri Spring-fed Creve Coeur Lake, located west of St. Louis, Missouri, is described in Native American legends as the habitat of ferocious LAKE MONSTERS. As recently as 1987, witnesses sighted a curious FISH in the lake, described as 2–4 feet long, with large scales, a long tail, and "a fierce-looking reptilian head." It remains unidentified today.

Sources: Graham, "Monsters of the Ozarks"; Charles Skinner, *Myths and Legends of Our Own Land*. Philadelphia: Lippincott: 1896.

Crisfield Monster This BIGFOOT-type HOMINID of southern Maryland's swampy Somerset County is named for its frequent appearances around the town of Crisfield. Sightings date from the 1940s, resulting in fruitless searches of the Jenkins Creek marshes. After a 30-year hiatus, sightings briefly resumed in October 1976, but police and civilian hunters proved no more adept at tracking the beast than the prior generation of searchers. At press time for this volume, no hominid reports had been filed from Somerset County in nearly three decades.

Source: Berry, *Bigfoot on the East Coast*.

Crocodile (Celebes) In 1935, zoologist Karl Schmidt reported an unclassified species of CROCODILE inhabiting certain lakes on the Indonesian island of Celebes (or Sulawesi). No specimens were collected, and science presently acknowledges no crocodilians on Celebes, although Siamese crocodiles (*Crocodylus siamensis*) once inhabited the neighboring islands of Java, Kalimantan and Sumatra. Another crocodilian, the false gharial (*Tomistoma schlegelii*) presently exists on Kalimantan and Sumatra, suggesting that specimens may have found their way to Celebes as well. Some cryptozoologists believe that a Pleistocene species, known from fossils uncovered on Celebes and presumed extinct, may yet survive in certain isolated lakes.

Sources: Heuvelmans, "Annotated checklist of apparently unknown animals with which cryptozoology is concerned"; D.A. Hooijer, "Crocodilian remains from the Pleistocene on Celebes." *Copeia* (1954): 263–266; Karl Schmidt, "A new crocodile from the Philippine Islands." *Zoological Series of the Field Museum of Natural History* 20 (1935): 67–70.

Crocodiles (Mislocated) Crocodiles are amphibious reptiles (Family *Crocodylidae*, Subfamily *Crocodylinae*), closely related to ALLIGATORS and CAIMANS. Modern science recognizes 3 genera and 14 species, naturally occurring in tropical regions of both hemispheres. Four species inhabit narrow ranges in the western hemisphere, while Africa boasts three species and Australasia has seven. The American crocodile (*Crocodylus acutus*) occasionally surfaces in the marshlands of southern Florida, but is otherwise confined to Mexico, Central America and the Caribbean islands. No crocodilians are indigenous to Europe, and specimens found outside their normal range qualify as cryptids. As in the case of other mislocated animals, authorities commonly dismiss errant crocodiles as fugitives from zoos, sideshows or private menageries. Their presumed owners are rarely identified, and the beasts themselves often outwit pursuers. A sampling of anomalous cases includes the following:

Arizona: Glendale—Authorities responded to multiple sightings of a crocodile roaming the streets, but no reptile was found, leaving searchers to squabble over the elusive reptile's species (1 March 2002).

California: Long Beach—A 5-foot crocodile inexplicably appeared in a resident's backyard, prompting speculation that it "fell from the sky" (late 1960).

Indiana: Vincennes—A crocodile was killed in Mariah Creek (December 1946). Indianapolis—Another specimen was found in Fall Creek (September 1959).

Massachusetts: Dedham—Dozens of would-be croc hunters responded to sightings at a local pond, but officers from the Animal Rescue League failed to snare their quarry (20 August 2002).

Ohio: Xenia—A 3-foot specimen was caught at Huffman Pond (6 July 1936).

Texas: Brownsville—An 18-inch juvenile croc was found inside a cotton bin (21 September 1970). Eagle Pass—Reports of 13-foot crocodiles swimming in the Rio Grande alarmed residents of this border city and nearby Piedras Negras, Mexico. Searches proved fruitless, prompting police chief Tony Castañeda to announce, "There are no crocodiles here, though I imagine that story would help us with our immigration and dope problems." (July-August 2002).

Australia: While *Crocodile Dundee* and TV "Croc Hunter" Steve Irwin present an image of a land swarming with ravenous reptiles, Australia's two indigenous crocodile species (*C. johnsoni* and *C. porosus*) are normally confined to the far north of the continent Down Under. Areas outside that range reporting crocodiles include: Blackwater, Queensland—Located 150 miles from the nearest natural croc habitat, this mining town has produced reports of crocodiles inhabiting the Burdekin and Herbert Rivers (December 2002). Lismore, New South Wales—Local rumors claim that six "pet crocodiles" were released into the Richmond River in the 1960s, with one (nicknamed Hector) sighted and photographed through 1974. Rumors of local crocodile infestation resurfaced in August 2003. Tewantin, Queensland—Fishermen and swimmers reported sightings of an 8-foot croc in the Noosa River, near Munna Point (21 September 2003). Wyndham, Western Australia—A specimen of *C. porosus*, 6 feet 6 inches long, was caught outside town (6 January 2004). It subsequently escaped and was reported wandering the town's streets.

Austria: Vienna—Firefighters hauled a 2-foot specimen from a downtown Danube canal and delivered it to Schonbrunn Zoo (19 July 2001).

Belgium: Ombret-Rawsa — Local witnesses reported a 3-foot crocodile, nicknamed MAASIE, swimming in the River Maas (6 August 1979).

Britain: More than 100 cases of errant crocodilians have been reported from the United Kingdom since the mid-19th century. A few of the sites include: Chipping Norton, Oxfordshire — A 12-inch croc allegedly pursued several hikers, until one crushed its skull with a stone (1836). Over Norton, Oxfordshire — *The Field* reported a juvenile specimen sighted nearby (23 August 1862); an August 1896 report in *Gentleman's Magazine* describes other specimens killed near the same town, circa 1866 and 1886. River Ouse, Yorkshire — A crocodile was sighted but eluded searchers (1970). River Stour, Kent — Another specimen outwitted hunters (1975). Caerphilly, Wales — A dead 5-footer was found by local residents (21 March 1978). Preston, Lancashire — Police received three reports of a 6-foot crocodile crossing the M55 motorway at Lightfoot Lane, including one call from a driver who thought he had run over the animal's tail. Searches proved fruitless (May 1980). Congleton, Cheshire — Searchers failed to locate a crocodile sighted in a flooded quarry (June 1995). Cannock, Staffordshire — Witnesses reported a 7-foot reptile hunting swans in the scenic pool at Roman View, Churchbridge. Police and members of the CENTRE FOR FORTEAN ZOOLOGY investigated without locating the predator (June 2003).

Germany: Cologne — passengers aboard the Munich-Cologne Express found a crocodile in one of the train's public washrooms (February 1973). Ketch — A cyclist pausing to relieve himself beside the Rhine saw a 5-foot specimen that hissed and fled when he threw dirt at it. Another sighting two days later prompted police searches employing boats and helicopters, but only a joker's carved model was found. A third sighting, by boaters on the Rhine, was reported one day after the search ended (22–27 June 2001).

Hong Kong: Chinese conservation workers armed with bait, cages and tranquilizer guns hunted a 5-foot crocodile reported by multiple witnesses. Police saw the reptile, but failed to capture it. Croc-hunter John Lever, imported from Australia, had no better luck and finally returned home empty-handed. Ten days after his departure, local journalists caught the beast on film (4–30 November 2003).

Russia — A report from 1582 claims that crocodiles attacked residents of Pskov, located on the Vilikaya Rover, 400 miles northwest of Moscow and 150 miles southwest of St. Petersburg. According to the chronicle, "many people were bitten" before several of the reptiles were killed and the rest fled the area. No crocodiles are normally found above 32° north latitude, where the Nile River enters the Mediterranean — some 2,200 miles south of Pskov.

Singapore: Wildlife experts were baffled by sightings of four separate crocodiles, including one seen near a busy downtown bank. Authorities speculated that the reptiles may have come from neighboring Malaysia (August-September 2003).

Spain: Madrid — Hunters searched in vain for two crocodiles seen at a reservoir in suburban Valdemorillo, near the popular Valmayor dam. Wildlife expert Luis Dominguez confirmed that crocodile nests were discovered, but baited traps failed to snare the reptiles (June 2003).

Sweden: Dalsland — Children playing at Lilla Le, a nearby lake, found a 2-foot crocodile dead on the shore (25 June 2001).

A witness sketched this crocodile, found at Oxfordshire, England in 1836.

United Arab Emirates: Dubai — A dead crocodile of indeterminate species was found on the beach near this city, washed ashore from the Persian Gulf (February 2003). No crocodiles are native to the area.

Sources: Bord and Bord, *Unexplained Mysteries of the 20th Century*; Faye Casey, "Mystery as 'croc' spotted at pool." *Wolverhampton Express & Star* (16 June 2003); "The Congleton 'croc.'" *Fortean Times* 82 (August-September 1995): 15; Martin Corben, "Crocodiles on the NSW North Coast?" ABC News (21 August 2003); "Croc Beats Hunter." *Sydney Morning Herald* (21 November 2003); "Croc hot spots." *Fortean Times* 174 (October 2003): 9; "Croc makes surprise appearance." Australian Associated Press (5 November 2003); "Croc on the loose sparks calls for professional catcher." *Sydney Morning Herald* (10 November 2003); "Croc 1, Dundee 0 as Aussie reptile hunter goes home." *Sydney Morning Herald* (28 November 2003); "Croc shock in Cannock." BBC News (19 June 2003); "Crocodile sightings baffle Singapore experts." Reuters (18 September 2003); "A crop of crocodilians." *Fortean Times* 151 (November 2001): 19; Dash, *Borderlands*; Andrew Dawson, "Saltwater crocs roam 250km inland…or do they?" *Brisbane Courier Mail* (19 December 2002); Jimmy Din, "Hunt is on for the Cannock crocodile." *Birmingham Evening Mail* (19 June 2003); Jon Downes, "The Cannock croc." *Fortean Times* 176 (December 2003): 38–39; "Expert Calls Off Hong Kong Crocodile Hunt." Reuters (15 November 2003); Peter Hartzel, "Croc hunters flock to Dedham pond." *Metro West Daily News* (21 August 2002); Chris Hogg, "Croc hunter heads for Hong Kong." BBC News (11 November 2003); "Hong Kong Steps Up Hunt for Elusive Crocodile." Reuters (4 November 2003); "Huge crocodile spotted in British country lake." BBC News (16 June 2003); "Journos spot stray Hong Kong croc." *Sydney Morning Herald* (1 December 2003); David Madrid, "Glendale gator? Or was it a croc?" *Arizona Republic* (1 March 2002); Leah Moore, "Fishing mates support Noosa croc sighting." *Brisbane Courier Mail* (26 September 2003); Nasouh Nazzal, "Crocodile found dead on beach." *Gulf News* (16 February 2003); Dick Reavis, "Are reptile sightings a croc?" *San Antonio Express-News* (24 August 2002); "Sixteenth century Russian crocodile account." *ISC Newsletter* 12 (1993–1996): 9–10; Giles Tremlett, "Croc alert at Spanish reservoir." *Guardian* (9 June 2003).

Crook, Cliff (1940–)

Washington resident Cliff Crook dates his pursuit of unknown HOMINIDS from age 16, when he and three companions were allegedly frightened out of their backwoods camp near Duvall by a snarling SASQUATCH that emitted cries like "Ee-gor-lar-gor." The boys ran home barefoot, abandoning their gear, but Crook has been coming back for more ever since, renowned in the Pacific Northwest as either a tireless researcher (to his fans) or "a sometimes thorn in the side of the BIGFOOT community" (according to author LOREN COLEMAN). In the 1960s, Crook emerged as an outspoken "no-kill" rival of RENÉ DAHINDEN and others, who advocated shooting a Sasquatch to identify the species and thus secure its legal protection. In 1976, Crook developed a 7-point test to detect HOAX footprints, and he subsequently organized the BIGFOOT CENTRAL FOUNDATION (now led by his son). His various commercial products and publications include Sasquatch postcards, buttons, bumper sticker, the *Bigfoot Map* (1973, 1995), *Bigfoot Trailblazer* (1980), *Bigfoot Trails Newsletter* (launched in 1992), and *Bigfoot and the Moon* (1995). In June 2000, Crook cast two sets of supposed Sasquatch footprints found by Gene Sampson near Port Angeles, Washington. One set measured 17.5 inches long and 8 inches wide, while the others were 14 by 7 inches, prompting GROVER KRANTZ to interpret them as the prints of a male-female couple walking together.

By accident or design, Crook has spent much of his cryptozoological career mired in controversy. He has denounced the PATTERSON FILM as "the Bigfoot hoax of the century" and claims to have a book in progress that will prove his case. In January 1999, Crook declared that one "enhanced" frame of the film revealed a nondescript metal fastener dangling from the creature there portrayed. "When the guy in the suit turned to look at the camera," Crook said, "it probably snapped loose and dangled from the fur." Undismayed by the fact that most viewers saw no such object, enhanced or otherwise, Crook went on in 2000 to attack the SKOOKUM CAST, discovered by members of the BIGFOOT FIELD RESEARCHERS ORGANIZATION, as another hoax. Crook dubbed it the "Spoofem" or "Wapiti" cast, insisting that the print was made by a reclining elk.

Crook's quarrel with the BFRO dates from November 1995, when spokesmen for that group denounced publication of a "new fake bigfoot photo by hoaxer Cliff Crook." The photo in question was said to be one of 14 snapped on 11 July 1995, by an unidentified forest ranger hunting poachers in the Wild Creek wilderness near Mount Rainier. Crook told reporters that he purchased seven of the best photos, but only one was released for public scrutiny. (A second surfaced five years later, to revive the controversy.) BFRO spokesmen were not alone in calling the photo a fraud, but when Crook suggested that the unnamed ranger may have fooled him, the BFRO's Internet website replied:

> This is also not true. The photo itself and story of how Crook obtained it are both hoaxes by Mr. Crook himself....Although it is not certain how this latest fake photo was produced, many conclude that is was produced the same way as many of his previous fake photos—a sculpture model placed in an outdoor setting.

Crook's defense of the photo claimed that "over a dozen photo specialists from Seattle to Spokane" studied the ranger's pictures on 27 August 1996 and "unanimously determined that the photographs and negatives were free from any sign of super-imposement, altering, or photo fakery." None of those experts were identified, but another Bigfoot Central report from February 1997 quoted Noriyuki Kurokawa, a supposed expert from Tokyo, as saying, "I did not find any kind of tampering or doctoring of the photos." In response to those statements, the BFRO responds: "These reports only prove that the photos were not faked, and that the subject is real—a real 7'10" dummy."

Sources: Coleman, *Bigfoot!*; Coleman and Clark, *Cryptozoology A to Z*; Bigfoot Central, http://www.geocities.com/tomkinson99/hoaxes/wildcreekreports.txt; Bigfoot Field Researchers Organization, http://www. bfro.net/REF/hoax.asp; Cliff Crook Is No Hoax!!, http://www.angelfire. com/wa3/cliffcrook/; Cliff Crook: The Wild Creek Photographs, http://www.geocities.com/tomkinson99/hoaxes/hoaxes.html.

Crooked Island Snakes   Christopher Columbus reported more than his share of encounters with still-unknown cryptids while he was exploring the so-called New World. On 21 October 1492, some of his crewmen killed a 5-foot amphibious SNAKE in a freshwater lagoon on the northwestern coast of Crooked Island, in the Bahamas. A sailor from the *Pinta*, Martin Pinzón, killed a second specimen the following day and planned to preserve its skin for study in Spain, but no trace of that relic has survived. The snakes described by Columbus match no species presently known in the Bahamas. Modern researchers have suggested that the animals were not snakes at all, but rather IGUANAS (Family *Iguanidae*). When the site of a 15th-century village on Crooked Island was excavated in 1987, archaeologists recovered the femur of a 4-foot American CROCODILE (*Crocodylus acutus*), but recent theories fail to explain why Columbus would mistake any 4-legged reptile for a serpent.

Source: Shuker, "Close encounters of the cryptozoological kind."

Crosswick Monster   In the late 19th century, two boys fishing at a stream near Crosswick, in southwestern Ohio's Warren County, were reportedly menaced by a huge lizard. Several men ran to their aid, whereupon the reptile retreated into a nearby hollow tree. When townsfolk returned to cut the tree down, the lizard allegedly fled into the nearby woods, running erect on its hind legs, and disappeared. While MONITOR LIZARDS sometimes run on their hind legs, Crosswick witnessed estimated this creature's length at 12–16 feet, exceeding that of the largest known living lizard on Earth (*Varanus komodoensis*). Coincidentally or otherwise, Crosswick is located near the site where 20th-century witnesses reported encounters with the LOVELAND FROG.

Source: Arment, "Dinos in the USA."

Crosswind Lake, Alaska   Alaska's Crosswind Lake, near Glennallen, is reportedly inhabited by giant FISH resembling ILLIE of Iliamna Lake, but no dates or details of sightings are presently available.

Source: Garner, *Monster! Monster!*

Crowe, Raymond (1941–)   Portland, Oregon native Raymond Crowe held many jobs prior to launching a mid-life career as a full-time researcher of unknown HOMINIDS. Variously employed as an electrician, dye lab assistant and computer technician, he was running a bookstore in 1991, when a friend invited him to join a weekend BIGFOOT-hunting expedition. While the giant biped remained elusive, Crowe returned from the field trip with eight half-inch reddish-brown hairs of unknown origin, thereby astounding his companions with beginner's luck. Before year's end, Crowe founded the Western Bigfoot Society, subsequently relocated to Hillsboro, Oregon and renamed the International Bigfoot Society. The IBS remains active today as a taxexempt nonprofit organization, with Crowe as president and Patti Reinhold as vice-president. Crowe's journal, *The Track Record*, is published 10 times per year. Crowe and the IBS maintain an active Internet website where Bigfoot sightings may be reported, in addition to hosting periodic SASQUATCH symposiums.

Sources: Coleman, *Bigfoot!*; International Bigfoot Society, http://www.internationalbigfootsociety.com/.

Crowing Crested Cobra   SNAKES have no vocal cords and are incapable of making any oral sound except a hiss, but witnesses from sub-Saharan Africa claim that one large species of venomous serpent crows like a rooster as a warning to its enemies. Only male specimens possess that talent, but both sexes allegedly emit grunting sounds like "chu-chu-chu" when cornered or alarmed. As if their vocalizations were not strange enough, males of the species also allegedly sport red facial wattles like a turkey's. These snakes are said to be extremely venomous, producing near-instant death in humans from their bite. At lengths approaching 20 feet, they would also be the longest venomous snakes on Earth. Arboreal by preference, they supposedly strike at the head and shoulders of passersby, with unfailing lethal results. Despite their great size, some reports claim the snakes feed chiefly on maggots, killing larger prey only to produce rotting flesh that will breed their food of preference. Sightings are reported over a wide range, from the Central African Republic southward through Tanzania, Zambia, Malawi, Mozambique, Zimbabwe and South Africa. Alternate names throughout that range include Bobo, Hongo, Inkhomi, Kovoko, Mbobo, N'gokwiki, Ngoshe and Songo. Explorer J.O. Shircore allegedly obtained skeletal remains of at least two specimens from a Malawi witch doctor in the early 1940s, but the bones were not preserved for study. Likewise, John Knott reportedly killed a specimen with his car in May 1959, near Zimbabwe's Lake Kariba, and while he described the 7-foot reptile's bony crest in some detail, Knott regrettably kept neither remains nor photographs.

Sources: John Knott, "Crowing snake." *African Wildlife* 16 (September 1962): 170; J.O. Shircore, "Two notes on the crowing crested cobra." *African Affairs* 43 (1944): 183–186; Shuker, *Extraordinary Animals Worldwide.*

Cryptofiction *see* **Appendix D**

Cryptotourism Monsters, in modern media parlance, are "sexy." They are sensational by definition, stimulating the imagination and attracting curious observers wherever sightings are reported in accessible locations. A sudden influx of gawkers typically benefits local service industries, as fresh money flows to hotels, restaurants, gas stations, gift shops and the like. When cryptid sightings persist over time at a given location, a full-fledged tourist industry sometimes evolves, complete with guided tours, museums or other exhibitions, and a wide range of memorabilia offered for sale. In some cases, skeptics maintain that sightings are fabricated specifically to create a fertile environment for tourism, and a handful of documented HOAXES demonstrate that the charge is sometimes accurate.

The first well-documented incident of cryptotourism in the U.S. occurred in July 1855 at SILVER LAKE, NEW YORK, where proprietors of the Walker House Hotel manufactured a LAKE MONSTER to enhance their failing business. Nearly a quarter-century later, in October 1878, a "WILDMAN of the woods" was allegedly captured in Tennessee and shipped off to public exhibition in Louisville, Kentucky. Scotland's Loch Ness was the first major cryptotourism draw of the 20th century, beginning with global announcements of NESSIE sightings in 1933. Today, the loch boasts multiple boat tours, thriving gift shops, and two competing Nessie exhibitions — one "original," the other "official" — at Drumnadrochit. In 1958, after road workers at Willow Creek, California coined the BIGFOOT nickname for a mystery HOMINID formerly known as SASQUATCH, the local chamber of commerce commissioned sculptor Jim McClarin to carve a redwood likeness of the Golden State's most famous cryptid. Other elusive creatures honored with statues include British Columbia's OGOPOGO (Okanagan Lake), ISSIE of Japan's Lake Ikeda, and the MOTHMAN of Point Pleasant, West Virginia. CHAMP makes do with a stylish billboard at Bulwagga Bay, on Lake Champlain, while competition for bragging rights over MEMPHRÉ, at Québec's Lake Memphrémagog, has inspired litigation. Interest may have waned for guided tours of Louisiana's HONEY ISLAND SWAMP, but gift shops still celebrate the FOUKE MONSTER in Miller County, Arkansas.

In 1995, critics accused South African restaurateur Bob Teeney of fabricating INKANYAMBA sightings to increase his clientele at Howick Falls. More recently, in June 2002, Guyana's Pan-Tribal Confederacy of Amerindian Tribal Nations launched an Internet website soliciting cryptotourism. Beneath a photo of a native with an unfurled ANACONDA skin, the caption read:

The man holding this skin is six feet tall. The Indians that killed it to save 2 children's lives call it a "small" one. The interior of Guyana is 95% untouched and all the tribes in these remote areas boast of encounters with SNAKES well over 30 feet in length. For those willing to spend the 14 days required to get into these far out locales the opportunity exists to photograph or video one of these giant serpents. You will not be allowed to kill one of these full grown monsters for they are religious icons in the native cultures. There is only one place that caters to cryptozoologist travelers in South America. It is also the only native Indian run entity that can by-pass the red-tape and no-go hoopla, and take you safely in and out of this unknown and officially restricted areas [*sic*].

While no 30-foot serpents have thus far been officially documented in Guyana — or anywhere else, for that matter — wealthy risk-takers with a taste for the mysterious may well find such excursions the adventure of a lifetime.

Sources: Sara Arthurs, "Record number of tourist inquiries this month." *Eureka (CA) Times-Standard* (1 May 2003); Sian Hall, "Legend of the falls"; Herbert Hawley, "The sea serpent of Silver Lake." *New York Folklore Quarterly* 2 (1945): 191–196; Jeff Smyth, "A monster of an idea to boost tourism." *Southern Illinoisan* (29 October 2003); Chris Stirewalt, "Mothman lives." *Charleston (WV) Daily Mail* (23 September 2003); Andrew Stuttaford, "Loch Roswell?" *National Review* 49 (15 September 1997): 24–25; "W.Va. town revels in Mothman legend, erects statue in winged apparition's honor." Associated Press (23 September 2003); Giant Snakes Await Cryptozoologist Traveler In South America, http://www.guidedculturaltours.com/cryptozoology.htm.

***Cuba* sea serpent** In July 1934, three officers aboard the French liner *Cuba* saw a SEA SERPENT in the North Atlantic, 250 miles southwest of the Azores. The principal witness, second captain P. Maguerez, recalled the incident as follows:

It was broad daylight by 5:20 [a.m.], and I had my eyes down on my notebook, in front of the window, when the lookout-helsman called to me: "Captain, *a steamer ahead!*" Now a few seconds before there had been nothing, for I had been looking up from time to time. You'll see how big the animal was when I say that at that moment it was a good 2 miles from us. I looked up and saw the beast in question *completely* out of the water, before it dived without making the least splash. This is what attracted my attention, for a great whale makes as much splash as a 305 shell when it leaps like that. I took my glasses and followed its wake. The sea was smooth as oil. It had dived in the same direction as the ship and, a few minutes later, it reappeared on the port bow about a mile off, swimming fast in the opposite direction. I reckoned its speed as being at least ours, that's to say 15 knots [17 miles per hour]. At that moment its neck and two humps appeared com-

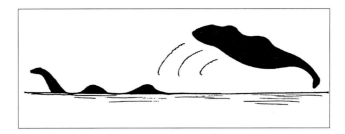

Sketches of the *Cuba* sea serpent after witness P. Maguerez.

pletely. At the helmsman's shout the other free seaman ran for his glasses too. It dived again four times at very short intervals, and during one of its appearances, about 800 yards abeam, we could watch it at leisure, for it remained on the surface several seconds and bent its neck forward before diving....The head turned and looked at the ship, but the body was *absolutely rigid* and black in colour, not the least undulation. If I had had a camera or a little ciné-Kodak I could have had a 30- second film, for 800 yards is not far when one is 56 feet up....It was certainly not a serpent, for it was too thick for its length. I reckon its diameter at 12 to 16 feet, and I assure you it was no mirage.

Source: Heuvelmans, *In the Wake of the Sea Serpents*.

Cuero   The South American aquatic cryptid known as Cuero ("cowhide") is reported from various lakes in Argentina and Chile. Witnesses describe it as flat and circular, resembling a large animal's hide, with claws and/or eyes ringing the perimeter of its body. The Cuero lies immobile until prey approaches, then rises to envelop and devour its meal of choice — allegedly including human beings on occasion. Variant names throughout the creature's range include Manta ("blanket") and Trelquehuecuve ("devil's hide"). In Argentina, most Cuero reports issue from LAGO LACAR and LAGO NAHUEL HUAPI, where the creatures reportedly share space with other LAKE MONSTERS. Lago Lacar boasts a resident MERBEING, while Lago Nahuel Huapi is the home of a serpentine creature called NAHUELITO. Argentina's CUERO UNUDO seems to be a different, though admittedly similar cryptid. Author Jorge Borges suggests that the Cuero is a freshwater OCTOPUS, while KARL SHUKER favors an unknown giant JELLYFISH and MARK HALL proposes a surviving prehistoric SEA SCORPION.

Sources: Borges, *The Book of Imaginary Beings*; Mark Hall, *Natural Mysteries*; Picasso, "South American monsters and mystery animals"; Shuker, *From Flying Toads to Snakes with Wings*.

Cuero Unudo   This predatory LAKE MONSTER of Argentina has no specific habitat, but rather is described by Araucanian natives as lurking in various lakes. Unlike the CUERO or Hide, which rises from lake beds to envelop prey with its elastic body, the Cuero Unudo resembles a log and lies buried in silt near the water's edge. When a potential meal steps on the beast, the Cuero Unudo uses its many claws to drag the victim underwater. Humans are reportedly include on its menu.

Source: Gregorio Alvarez, *El Tronco de Oro*. Nuequén, Argentina: Pehuen, 1968.

Cuino   This unclassified ungulate, reported from Oaxaca State in southern Mexico during the 19th and early 20th centuries, was described as sporting a thick coat of curly black-and-white or brown-and-white hair. Early theorists suggested that Cuinos were produced by cross-breeding between rams (*Ovis aries*) and domestic sows (*Sus scrofa scrofa*), but their exclusive presence in the wild was unexplained. Zoologist W.B. Tegetmeier examined a supposed Cuino skull in 1902 and identified it as belonging to a normal pig. Today, the same name is applied to a miniature breed of pig found in Yucatán State. No modern sightings of the original Oaxaca Cuinos are reported.

Source: Shuker, *Mysteries of Planet Earth*.

Cuitlamitzli   In 1520, during the invasion of Mexico by Spanish conquistador Hernán Cortés, Bernal Diaz del Castillo reported seeing a long-legged "wolf-cat" in the personal menagerie of Aztec emperor Moctezuma, at Teotihuacan. Natives called the strange creature Cuitlamitzli ("glutton cat"). Some modern re-

searchers believe the creature seen by Diaz was a specimen of the enigmatic ONZA.

Source: Shuker, *Mystery Cats of the World*.

Cullercoats sea serpent   On 26 March 1849, British fishermen at Cullercoats, Northumberland caught a strange creature 12 feet 3 inches long, 11¼ inches deep (measured vertically) and 2¾ inches thick. Eight weeks later, on 19 May, the *Illustrated London News* touted the beast as a SEA SERPENT, but naturalists Dennis Embleton and Albany Hancock disagreed. After examining the animal, they declared it a new species of oarfish (*Regalecus glesne*). In fact, only one species of oarfish is recognized today.

Sources: Heuvelmans, *In the Wake of the Sea Serpents*; Roesch, "A review of alleged sea serpent carcasses worldwide (Part One —1648–1880."

Cunarid Din   Amuesha tribesmen in Peru's Pasco Department describe the Cunarid din as a "speckled TIGER" that inhabits montane forests along the lower Río Palcazú valley, around Cuchurras. They describe the CAT as equal in size to a jaguar (*Panthera onca*), but with a larger head. Its coat is gray, covered with solid black speckles, in contrast to the jaguar's golden coat with dark rosettes. The Cunarid din is found most often at altitudes around 1,600 feet, and researcher interviewed two native hunters who allegedly killed and skinned specimens between the 1970s and late 1980s. One source promised Hocking a skull and pelt, but the objects were never delivered.

Sources: Hocking, "Further investigation into unknown Peruvian mammals"; Hocking, "Large Peruvian mammals unknown to science."

Curinquéan   This large, unclassified primate or HOMINID of South America allegedly reaches heights in excess of 11 feet at maturity, leaving humanoid footprints 21.5 inches long. It enjoys a ferocious reputation for attacking cattle, which it kills by ripping out their tongues while leaving no other wound on the bodies. In the early 1950s, more than 100 cattle were reportedly killed by such means on ranches in the neighborhood of Ybitimi, Paraguay. Similar depredations were reported from Brazil's Mato Grosso State, along the Rio Araguaya.

Source: Heuvelmans, *On the Track of Unknown Animals*.

Curupira   Tupí tribesmen in Brazil describe this unclassified primate or small HOMINID as being 3–4 feet tall and covered with reddish hair. The creatures are primarily arboreal, emitting birdlike whistles as they forage in the jungle. Aggression against humans is reported, including abduction of children and sexual assault against females. Alternate names throughout the creatures' range include Kurupi and Yurupari. Some researchers speculate that the Curupira may comprise a relict population of *Protopithecus*, a prehistoric form of spider MONKEY known from Pleistocene fossil deposits in eastern Brazil.

Source: Karl Shuker, "Alien zoo." *Fortean Times* 102 (September 1997): 17.

Cushpij *see* **Yoshi**

Cusworth Hall Jaguar   On 9 August 2003, while riding home from a visit to Cusworth Hall Museum at Doncaster in Yorkshire, England, 9-year-old Charlotte Clarke saw an ALIEN BIG CAT resembling a JAGUAR (*Panthera onca*) in a grassy field beside the road. She alerted the car's other occupants, a cousin and her grandmother, but neither saw the CAT and they dismissed her story as a joke. Charlotte convinced her mother, who notified Yorkshire police, and while several newspapers reported the sighting, no trace of the beast could be found. A local member of the

CENTRE FOR FORTEAN ZOOLOGY, Dave Baker, visited Cusworth Hall and interviewed the Clarkes, but his search for physical evidence proved fruitless. A Yorkshire press photographer claimed that a jaguar had attacked a farmer near Cusworth Hall the previous year, but no record of that incident was found. Likewise, rumors that "someone down the lane" once kept a menagerie of big cats proved untraceable.

Source: Dave Baker, "The Cusworth cat." Scottish Big Cats Society, http://www.scottishbigcats.co.uk/cusworthcat.htm.

—D—

***Daedalus* sea serpent**   On 6 August 1848, officers and crew aboard the British frigate H.M.S. *Daedalus* experienced one of the 19th centuries most famous SEA SERPENT encounters. The incident was not reported for another two months, when the ship arrived at Plymouth from the East Indies. As rumors of the sighting spread, Admiral Sir W.H. Gage demanded an accounting from Captain Peter M'Quhae. In response to that order, M'Quhae penned the following letter on 11 October:

Sir,— In reply to your letter of this day's date, requiring information as to the truth of a statement published in *The Times* newspaper, of a sea-serpent of extraordinary dimensions having been seen from Her Majesty's ship *Daedalus*, under my command, on her passage from the East Indies, I have the honour to acquaint you, for the information of my Lords Commissioners of the Admiralty, that at 5 o'clock p.m. on the 6th of August last, in latitude 24° 44' S., and longitude 9° 22' E., the weather dark and cloudy, wind fresh from the N.W., with a long ocean swell from the S.W., the ship on the port tack heading N.E. by N., something very unusual was seen by Mr. Sartoris, midshipman, rapidly approaching the ship from before the beam. The circumstance was immediately reported by him to the officer on the watch, Lieut. Edgar Drummond, with whom and Mr. William Barrett, the Master, I was at the time walking the quarter-deck. The ship's company were at supper.

On our attention being called to the object it was discovered to be an enormous serpent, with head and shoulders kept about four feet constantly above the surface of the sea, and as nearly as we could approximate by comparing it with the length of what our main- topsail yard would show in the water, there was at the very least 60 feet of the animal *à fleur d'eau*, no portion of which was,

to our perception, used in propelling it through the water, either by vertical or horizontal undulation. It passed rapidly, but so close under our lee quarter, that had it been a man of my acquaintance, I should easily have recognized his features with the naked eye; and it did not, either in approaching the ship or after it had passed our wake, deviate from its course to the S.W., which it held on at the pace of from 12 to 15 miles per hour, apparently on some determined purpose.

The diameter of the serpent was about 15 or 16 inches behind the head, which was, without any doubt, that of a SNAKE, and it was never, during the 20 minutes that it continued in sight of our glasses, once below the surface of the water; its colour a dark brown, with yellowish white about the throat. It had no fins, but something like a mane of a horse, or rather a bunch of seaweed, washed about its back. It was seen by the quartermaster, the boatswain's mate, and the man at the wheel, in addition to myself and the officers above mentioned.

Source: Heuvelmans, *In the Wake of the Sea Serpents.*

Dahinden, René (1930–2001)

Swiss native René Dahinden moved to Canada in 1953, and within two months of his arrival was enthralled by tales of SASQUATCH. By 1956, two years before the elusive HOMINID was christened BIGFOOT in the U.S., Dahinden was devoting much of his spare time to research on the creature's history and modern sightings (often in collaboration with journalist JOHN GREEN). In 1959–62, Dahinden, Green, PETER BYRNE and IVAN MARX were members of millionaire TOM SLICK'S Pacific Northwest expedition seeking Bigfoot. From 1967 onward, Dahinden ranked among the most outspoken champions of the PATTERSON FILM, and he was the first to screen it in Russia after the collapse of Soviet Communism. Legal sparring over rights to the film and recurring bouts of cancer limited Dahinden's field work in the 1990s, and the disease finally claimed his life on 18 April 2001.

Sources: Coleman, *Bigfoot!*; Coleman and Clark, *Cryptozoology A to Z.*

Dakuwaqa/Dakuwaqua

Fijian natives report this large SHARK from the Koro Sea, of Vanua Levu, claiming that it sometimes attacks canoes and devours the inhabitants. Descriptions in-

Artist's depiction of the *Daedalus* sea serpent, 1848.

The Fijian Dakuwaqa resembles a whale shark.

clude a turtlelike head, spotted hide, and a huge dorsal fin. In 1912, the Rev. A.J. Small reportedly glimpsed such a shark from the deck of a passing ship. The spotted whale shark (*Rhincodon typus*) is an obvious Dakuwaqa candidate, exceeding 40 feet in length, but it is an inoffensive plankton feeder with a relatively small dorsal fin.

Sources: Colman Wall, "Dakuwaqa. *Transactions of the Fijian Society* (1917): 6–12, 39–46; Sieveking, "The Dakuwaqua."

Dakwa Cherokee legends describe the Dakwa as a large aquatic serpent, prone to capsizing canoes and devouring humans. Its favorite habitats were said to be the LITTLE TENNESSEE RIVER, in eastern Tennessee's Monroe County, and the French Broad River in western North Carolina (Buncombe County). A garbled reading of those folktales may account for unsupported modern references to "river monsters" infesting North Carolina's branch of the Little Tennessee River.

Source: Gatschet, "Water monsters of American aborigines."

Dà-Mao-Rén *see* **Mao-Rén**

Damasia According to Kikuyu tribesmen, the Aberdare Highlands of Kenya are home to a large unclassified CAT called Damasia, resembling a leopard with dark pelage. The Kikuyus are familiar with leopards (*Panthera pardus*) in both normal and melanistic morphs, and they insist that the Damasia is a separate species. G. Hamilton-Snowball reported shooting such a cat in the 1920s, but its pelt was not preserved. KARL SHUKER notes that African natives frequently different names to members of a known species based on differences in color, size or behavior, thus granting that the Damasia may be a normal leopard of aberrant size or color.

Source: Shuker, *Mystery Cats of the World.*

Witnesses in Kenya compare the Damasia to a dark-colored leopard.

Danau Poso, Indonesia A 30-foot LAKE MONSTER with a head resembling that of a cow was reported in February 1977, from this lake on the island of Celebes (Sulawesi). It apparently bore no resemblance to the large CROCODILES sighted in other lakes on the same island.

Source: Munich *Süddeutsche Zeitung* (22 February 1977).

Dao Van Tien (1920–1995) Vietnam's premier cryp-

tozoologist, Dao Van Tien, was a native of Nam Dinh Province. He graduated from the Université de l'Indochine in 1942 and earned his Master's degree in zoology two years later, subsequently serving as a professor of zoology at Viet Minh and Hanoi Universities from 1946 to 1986. In 1963, while visiting the village of Thuan Chau on a research expedition, Dao heard stories of a 5-foot hairy WILDMAN known locally as Pí Cang Co'i. He initially dismissed the creature as "a burglar disguised as a wildman," but subsequent events changed his mind. In 1979, at Sa Thây, Dao was told of another HOMINID, this one "taller than an ordinary person, ferocious looking, hairy, and walking upright on his legs," which the natives called NGUOI RUNG. Two years later, a university colleague loaned Dao a copy of *L'Homme de Néanderthal est Toujours Vivant*, by BERNARD HEUVELMANS and BORIS PORSHNEV. In making its case for survival of NEANDERTAL MAN, that book discussed the MINNESOTA ICEMAN and Frank Hansen's claims that the creature had been killed in Vietnam. As Dao described the impact of that work:

> When I finished Heuvelmans' and Porchnev's book, my doubt about the wildman's presence in Vietnam had begun to lessen. The body which Hansen exhibited could well have been that of a genuine wildman. However, the unclear origin of the body and the fact that Hansen would not sell it to the Smithsonian Institution, could be because he was worried about breaking some kind of law and would be caught. Eventually, Hansen closed down the exhibition and announced that the body had been destroyed. It is a great shame!

Dao spent the rest of his life trying to solve the riddle of Southeast Asia's unknown hominids. He led two expeditions in search of the creatures, and his series of articles on the subject, entitled "The Facts About Forest Man," were published in Hanoi's forestry journal *Tap Chi' Lâm Nghiêp* during 1990. Dao died of a heart attack in May 1995, leaving a new generation of Vietnamese zoologists to carry on his work.

Sources: Coleman and Clark, *Cryptozoology A to Z*; Dao Van Tien, "Wildman in Vietnam." http://coombs.anu.edu.au/~vern/wildman/tien.txt.

***Daphne* sea serpent** On 26 October 1848, soon after reports of the *DAEDALUS* SEA SERPENT were published in *The Times* of London, the *Globe* printed a letter allegedly penned by one James Henderson, self-described captain of the ship *Mary Ann*. According to the letter, on 30 September, Henderson's vessel met a Boston brig, the *Daphne*, off the coast of Portugal. In passing, Captain Mark Trelawney of the *Daphne* reported his meeting, 10 days earlier, with "a huge serpent, or SNAKE, with a DRAGON'S head" in the Atlantic, off the Congo coast at 4° 11' south latitude and 10° 15' east longitude. Sailors aboard the *Daphne* reportedly loaded a deck gun with nails and scrap iron, wounding the 100-foot creature before it escaped at a speed of 24 miles per hour. The story was sensational — and false. Subsequent research proved there was no *Mary Ann* or Captain Henderson. The episode had simply been a HOAX.

Source: Heuvelmans, *In the Wake of the Sea Serpents.*

Dard *see* **Cat-Headed Snake**

Darky Lake, Canada Ojibwa rock paintings of a horned LAKE MONSTER are found near this small lake in Ontario's Quetico Provincial Park, suggesting that aboriginal inhabitants once viewed it as a habitat the serpent MISHIPIZHIW.

Source: Selwyn Dewdney and Kenneth Kidd, *Indian Rock Paintings of the Great Lakes.* Toronto: University of Toronto Press, 1967.

Dart sea serpent

Early in 1898, Captain John Dawson and five crewmen aboard the sloop *Dart*, allegedly met a huge SEA SERPENT in the North Sea, off the Scottish coast. Dawson described the incident as follows:

> The animal was over fifty feet long — what we saw of it — and there must have been a great length of body beneath the sea. In appearance it resembled nothing we can describe, nearer than the ancient animals of prehistoric existence that we sometimes find described and illustrated by scientific men.
>
> Altogether it must have been 180 feet long. The head was of a long tapering shape. The mouth being open, we saw the full size of it. It must have been large enough to swallow at least a cow or a horse. The teeth shone in the faint light and gave the animal a fearful and terrifying appearance. A long flipperlike appendage seemed to dangle from its body about 15 or 20 feet from the head. The eyes shone with a green light, shifting from green to blue and often crimson and drove terror into our hearts. Its body had a mane-like fin running down the full length of the back and breast. It was of a dark colour and unlike any monster we in a natural way could ever have dreamt of.

BERNARD HEUVELMANS concluded, from the melodramatic style and the creature's improbable method of raising its body so far above the ocean's surface, that the sighting was a HOAX.

Source: Heuvelmans, *In the Wake of the Sea Serpents.*

The *Dart* sea serpent, as sketched by alleged witnesses.

Darwin Harbor sea serpents

For half a century, reports of strange SEA SERPENTS or other pelagic cryptids have emerged from Darwin, on the coast of Australia's Northern Territory. The first sighting was logged in 1955, by two women (one of them a nun) who allegedly saw a 100-foot creature with a string of undulating humps along its back, racing across Darwin Harbor in 10 minutes flat. Four years later, in October 1959, another report was filed by Allan Carter, proprietor of the local Mandorah resort hotel. The *Northern Territory News* declared that:

> Mr. Carter saw the object late one evening. He reported by radio that it was "a long black shallow object travelling just above or close to the surface" of the sea between Mandorah and Doctor's Gully. He thought it was moving at 80 or 90 miles an hour. When it was moving toward Delissaville a green light shot into the sky. The next morning Mr. Carter saw the strange object again and it headed towards one of the creeks on his side of the harbour.

Ten days later, the creature was seemingly airborne, when wit-

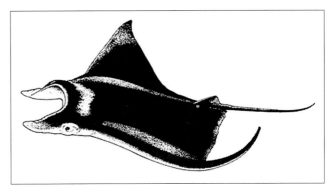

Some witnesses compared the Darwin Harbor sea serpent to a giant manta ray.

ness J.G. Slaggert reported "some kind of low flying object or monster" near Mandorah. It produced "a queer swooshing noise like giant wings or a new type of jet." No further details were elicited, beyond the fact that Carter and Slaggert agreed the creature was 80–100 feet long. A naval search for the "Mandorah Monster" was underway when Darwin fisherman Ted Maloney told the *News*: It's my old mate the giant devil ray, and it is 40 feet long, 25 feet across, and weighs several tons....It's the biggest ray I have ever seen, and would look even bigger in clear water. Seen from a distance with its shadow behind, it could easily seem 70 to 80 feet long. It has a top speed of 40 m.p.h.— but this also looks a lot faster when you see it ploughing through the water.

Maloney greatly exaggerated the length of the largest known MANTA RAY (*Manta birostris*), though his estimated width is not far off the acknowledged record of 22 feet. Another fisherman, Ian Harper, chimed in to report that a large manta had ripped his nets a few days earlier. Stung by the implied criticism of his peers, Allan Carter lashed back with a claim that the object he saw was not an animal at all, but seemed to be a mechanical contraption of some kind.

No such confusion surrounds the sighting at Darwin Harbor on 19 February 1980. Terry Annesley was working on the third floor of the Hooker Building, with a clear view of the harbor, when he saw a large creature swimming toward shore "at about the same speed as a whale." Annesley summoned a friend, John Hamilton, and they watched the animal while telephoning the nearby office of the *Northern Territory News*. A reporter and photographer arrived, but the distance proved too great for snapshots with the gear available. Still, the four witnesses watched through binoculars for 30 minutes as the black, 65-foot creature swam around the harbor, displaying five or six loops the size of auto tires, each surmounted by a dorsal fin. By the time it disappeared, the watchers were convinced that it was neither a whale nor a school of dolphins swimming in tandem.

Sources: Heuvelmans, *In the Wake of the Sea Serpents*; Smith, *Bunyips & Bigfoots.*

Das-Adder

The curious reptile known as the Das-Adder makes its home in South Africa's Drakensberg ("DRAGON Mountain") Range, where witnesses describe it as a SNAKE with red and yellow stripes on its tail, and a head resembling that of a HYRAX. In fact, the local name for the rock hyrax (*Procavia*) is "dassie," suggesting a degree of confusion from vague sightings. A curious feature is the frequent reference to external ears (snakes have none), whose flaps extend into a frill or crest around the creature's head. Many natives believe the Das-Adder is highly venomous, and superstitious tales grant it the power to hypnotize its prey — including the occasionally unlucky human. Sporadic efforts to collect a specimen since the 19th century have all proved fruitless. Today, some herpetologists believe that Das-Adder sightings result from misidentification of the Cape rock MONITOR (*Varanus albigularis*), a lizard common in the area. However, as KARL SHUKER notes, the monitor's head bears no resemblance to a hyrax's, and its body does not bear the Das-Adder's colorful stripes.

Sources: Shuker, *From Flying Toads to Snakes with Wings*; W.L. Speight, "Mystery monsters of Africa."

Dato/Datobu *see* **Gnéna**

Daufuskie Island Apes   Daufuskie Island lies off the coast of South Carolina, at the mouth of the Savannah River. Inhabitants of the largely undeveloped island have reported multiple sightings of large, BIGFOOT-type HOMINIDS or NORTH AMERICAN APES over a period of years. The creatures have been seen and tracked (without result) near the Daufuskie Lighthouse and around the Moss Creek Plantation on Highway 278.

Source: Hauck, *Haunted Places.*

Dauphin Lake, Canada   Manitoba is well known for its LAKE MONSTERS, including MANIPOGO and WINNIPOGO, but the cryptid of Dauphin Lake (east of Dauphin) has yet to be named. In 1948, witness C.P. Alarie followed the sound of wailing cries to a marsh at the south end of the lake, near St. Rose du Lac, and saw a strange creature from a distance of 400 yards. Alarie described it as large and brownish-black, rearing six feet out of the water.

Source: Chris Rutkowski, *Unnatural History: True Manitoba Mysteries.* Winnipeg: Chameleon, 1993.

Dav/Dev   These names, with local variations, are applied to an unclassified primate or HOMINID reported from the Caucasus Mountains of Georgia through Armenia and northern Iran, as far east as the Pamir Mountains in Tajikistan. The various forms of its name translate as "demon," but the hairy biped is not typically invested with supernatural powers. Eyewitness descriptions are similar (if not identical) to those of the ALMAS and KAPTAR from neighboring regions. A spate of reports from Tajikistan in the 1930s suggests that Soviet authorities were familiar with the creatures. An adult specimen was reportedly captured near Tutkaul in 1933 and caged for two months before it finally escaped. A year later, geologist B.M. Zdorik and his guide stumbled on a sleeping Dev near the Dondushkan River, in the Pamirs. Frightened, the men turned and fled before the beast woke.

Sources: Bayanov, *In the Footsteps of the Russian Snowman*; Sanderson, *Abominable Snowmen.*

De Courcy Island sea serpent   In 1987, William Hagelund published a memoir of his youth as a whaler, including various adventures experienced after he retired from slaughtering cetaceans. One such incident, from August 1968, allegedly included the live capture of a "baby" SEA SERPENT at Pirate's Cove on De Courcy Island (off the coast of British Columbia, 20 miles west of Vancouver). Hagelund described the incident as follows:

> We spotted a small disturbance in the calm anchorage where we had dropped the hook for the night. Lowering the dinghy, my youngest son Gerry and I rowed out to investigate. We found a small EEL-like sea creature swimming along with its head completely out of the water, the undulation of its long, slender body causing portions of its spine to break the surface. My first thought

that it was a sea-SNAKE was quickly discarded when, on drawing closer, I noticed the dark limpid eyes, large in proportion to the slender head, which had given it a seal-like appearance when viewed from the front. When it turned away, a long, slightly hooked snout could be discerned. Scooping the animal up in a net, Hagelund took it aboard his yacht and placed it in a bucket of water, planning to drop it off next morning at Nanaimo's Pacific Biological Station. Up close, Hagelund wrote, "We found that he was approximately sixteen inches long, and just over an inch in diameter. His lower jaw had a set of sharp tiny teeth, and his back was protected by platelike scales, while his undersides were covered in a soft yellow fuzz. A pair of small, flipper-like feet protruded from his shoulder area, and a spade-shaped tail proved to be two tiny flipper-like fins that overlapped each other." That night, feeling guilty while the captive creature splashed in its bucket, Hagelund allegedly returned it to the sea.

Fact or fiction? Another chapter of Hagelund's memoir — this one supported by photos and independent testimony — describes the discovery of a similar specimen 21 years earlier, cut from the stomach of a sperm whale at Naden Harbor. Today it is impossible to know if Hagelund fabricated the De Courcy Island incident, but some researchers (including PAUL LEBLOND) consider it a hopeful sign that CADBOROSAURUS may yet be identified along the coast of the Pacific Northwest.

Sources: William Hagelund, *Whalers No More.* Madeira Park, B.C.: Harbour Publishing, 1987; LeBlond and Bousfield, *Cadborosaurus.*

De Loys's Ape   In 1920, while traveling along the Río Tarra (on the border between Colombia and Venezuela), members of an expedition led by Swiss geologist François De Loys met two large, tailless APES. The animals reportedly displayed aggression, and the female was shot, while its mate fled into the jungle. Several photographs were taken of the creature, propped upright on a wooden crate, before it was skinned, with the pelt and skull preserved for future study. Sadly, only one photo survived the expedition, found among De Loys's papers by a friend, anthropologist George Montandon, in 1929. Montandon named the ape *Ameranthropoides loysi*, proposing that it was the "missing link" ancestor of the western hemisphere's "red" peoples. (Montandon also believed that blacks evolved from GORILLAS, while Asians sprang from orangutans.) A critic of Montandon, Arthur Keith, believed the animal depicted in the photo was a new species of spider MONKEY, which he named *Ateles loysi* (also in 1929).

Controversy endures surrounding the photo and identity of the animal depicted therein. IVAN SANDERSON believed it was a white-bellied spider monkey (*A. belzebuth*), bloated by decomposition and photographed on a crate smaller than 16 inches, rather than the 18–20 inches estimated by Montandon. LOREN COLEMAN and MICHEL RAYNAL go even further, proclaiming the photo a HOAX on Montadon's part, intended to promote his racist views on human origins. Other cryptozoologists note that stories of a large ape, called MONO GRANDE, have been recorded into modern times throughout the region traversed by De Loys. KARL SHUKER compounded the mystery in the 1990s, uncovering three sources who recalled seeing a *second* photo of the phantom ape, published in some unknown book decades earlier. In November 1997, one of those witnesses, U.S. anthropology professor Susan Ford, described the picture to Shuker as:

> a black and white photo of the animal (looking a lot like a big spider monkey), dead, propped between two native males who were standing. They appeared to be adult but of possibly short stature; I recall no scale in the picture or reference in the text to the height

Heated controversy still surrounds this 1920 photograph of an unknown primate dubbed De Loys's ape.

of the humans. It was a chapter specifically dealing with this animal, in a book about unusual animal discoveries. I seem to recall it being hardbound with a dark cover, and not a large or thick book. It was small, the size perhaps of an average journal today. I recall neither title nor author of the book. I really am usually much more organized about references than this, and feel embarrassed that I did not keep better track of this reference and a copy. I can visualize the picture quite clearly, however, and there were two males on either side of the dead monkey.

In 1999, the first expedition to explore the southern hemisphere's longest cave — Brazil's 60-mile-long Toca da Boa Vista, in Bahía State — discovered large numbers of fossilized animal bones, including the skull of a 55-pound spider monkey (twice the size of known, living species). Researcher JEFF MELDRUM, meanwhile, suggests that De Loys's ape (and perhaps Mono Grande) may represent a relict population of *Propithecus brasiliensis*, a South American species twice the size of any living New World monkey, known only from a fossil leg bone found in 1836. Debate continues, and the issue is far from resolved.

Sources: Coleman, "Debunking a racist hoax"; Karl Shuker, "Alien zoo." *Fortean Times* 134 (June 2000): 21; Shuker, "Another missing photo?"; Shuker, "Monkeying around with memories?"

Dead Creek, Vermont   The cryptid said to reside in this creek near Swanton, in northeastern Vermont's Franklin County, surfaced for the first time in 1909. The witnesses, three local fishermen, claimed the beast chased them out of their row-

boat and up a tall tree. The frightened men claimed their adversary was as "big around as a sugar barrel," with "shiny gray scales about the size of a baseball on the throat, with big ones toward the belly. When it opened its terrible mouth we could see several rows of glittering white teeth ten inches long." Soon giving up the chase, the animal yet lingered long enough to give the men a good look. "The top of its head was black and hairy," one said, "and shaded down to the ears to a dirty moss green. It stuck its head out of the water...and sniffed a good deal like a bird dog."

Source: Citro, *Green Mountain Ghosts, Ghouls & Unsolved Mysteries.*

Deception Bay sea serpent   Deception Bay lies on the east coast of Queensland, Australia, below Bundaberg. In 1959, local fisherman Ron Spencer claimed five sightings of an inquisitive SEA SERPENT that reared its brown head three feet out of the water to gape at his boat with "strange, staring eyes." Spencer was accompanied by his wife on one such occasion, and on another by fisherman John Belcher. After Spencer's story was published, in January 1960, 10 other witnesses came forward with similar reports of their own. Nigel Tutt, his daughter and a friend had seen the animal on New Year's Day, estimating its length at 22 feet. The creature's head was square, Tutt said, and roughly two feet wide. Two foot-long fins or flippers were located 6–8 feet behind the head. Tutt's rough sketch of the creature resembled an EEL.

Source: Smith, *Bunyips & Bigfoots.*

Dediéka/Dodiéka   An unclassified primate reported from the jungles of Gabon and the neighboring Republic of Congo, the Dediéka is also known as Tschimpênso in some portions of its range. Witnesses describe it as resembling an oversized CHIMPANZEE (*Pan troglodytes*), but with the prominent sagittal crest of a GORILLA (*Gorilla gorilla*). Several skins and skulls were collected in the 19th century, prompting European scientists to speculate that the Dediéka might be a gorilla-chimpanzee hybrid. That theory has since been discarded, some primatologists claiming the relics come from female gorillas, while others insist they belong to large male chimpanzees.

Source: Heuvelmans, *Les Bêtes Humaines d'Afrique.*

Deepdale Holm carcass   On 20 January 1942, a large GLOBSTER washed ashore at Deepdale Holm, on Mainland, in Scotland's Orkney Islands chain. Local naturalist J.G. Marwick examined the carcass and published the following description of it in the *Orcadian*, on 29 January:

The outstanding features to me, were its small head, long thin neck; massive hump; long sinuous back and tail parts. We made a fairly thorough examination of the carcase, commencing at the head.

The lower jaw was missing; no teeth or the appearance of any in the upper jaw: skull being bare of skin was of gristle, very much resembling the gristly bones of a skate, but certainly not like the skull bones of any land animal; head rounded on top with very large eye sockets on either side; apparently its eyes had been large. Down the centre of the skull was a hole which I took to be for breathing purposes, and above this was a slight cavity in which appeared two tiny holes in its upper part. Head 18 inches from snout to back and 10–12 inches across....

The neck from base of skull to where it joined the body was 3½ feet roughly and 6 inches broad. A small hump was visible along the back, less than a foot high; then came the large hump or dorsal fin, which was quite intact and one of the most prominent features. This hump was 2½ feet high — and on its upper edge were several thick hairs much worn and broken by rubbing on the beach. Proceeding towards the tail were a whole series of small projections plainly visible for several feet along the back, but not at all in the nature of the large hump already mentioned. Then, 7½ feet from the centre of the large hump was a third hump, not quite so prominent as the smaller one in front, but a distinct hump nevertheless. From this to the tail were more of the small projections, but at the extreme end of the tail the flesh was all gone, leaving the backbone in sight, several sections of which were broken off and what had been the utmost end of the tail was a piece of gristle—as I saw it the total length of the creature was 25 feet. I should have stated the detached tail-piece fitted lengthwise to the backbone, not across it as in the case with the tail-flukes of a whale.

Proceeding from the tail towards the head …on the side of the body was a projection, obviously the stump of what had been a tail flipper.…[P]assing the entrails, we came to the front flipper which was 3 feet 9 inches long and fully a foot broad, curving to a point. …This flipper was strongly attached to the shoulder of the creature, all of which was composed of the same gristly substance already mentioned. The shoulder appeared to be massive and strong and the front then curved up to the neck.…The body being devoid of skin through action of BIRDS and weather was of yellowish-white colour, the white being mostly fat, or so it appeared. The only skin I saw was on the tail portion and was in the nature of a hard horny substance, yellowish-grey in colour.… The tail portion was not round, but more flat like as it lay on the stones, and the widest part of the body I estimated to have been 3 to 4 feet deep, apart from the large hump.… In giving an estimate of weight I ventured to suggest half a ton…but my brother doubled it easily.

In a second article for the *Orcadian*, published on 5 February 1942, Marwick suggested that the carcass belonged to "one of a species considered extinct many ages ago—a marine saurian in fact, or marine reptile." He proposed that the creature be named *Scapasaurus*, after nearby Scapa Flow, but experts from Edinburgh's Royal Scottish Museum torpedoed that prospect the same afternoon, reporting that their study of photos taken at Deepdale Holm identified the beast as a decomposed basking shark (*Cetorhinus maximus*).

Source: Dinsdale, *Monster Hunt*.

Déguédégué *see* Gnéna

Delake, Oregon carcass

On 5 March 1950, the rotting carcass of a 22-foot "hairy monster" washed ashore at Delake, Oregon (now Lincoln City). Townspeople secured the remains to a piling with chains and examined its soft, white flesh. One local, as reported in the press, "stuffed his arm into the creature's 'mouth' up to the elbow without learning anything particularly interesting." Seagulls refused to eat the animal—which some wit christened "Jughead"—and the stench prompted beachfront residents to burn the carcass a week or so later. Before it was incinerated, a biologist from Oregon State University took samples of the flesh and pronounced it whale blubber. Delakers rejected that verdict, and 53 years later the *Medford Mail Tribune* declared, "To this day there is no definitive explanation of what the sea monster really was."

Source: "Since you asked." *Medford* (OR) *Mail Tribune* (2 July 2003).

Delavan Lake, Wisconsin

Rumors of lurking LAKE MONSTERS issued from this lake, in southern Wisconsin's Walworth County, in the late 19th century, but no modern reports suggest that the creatures still survive.

Sources: Brown, *Sea Serpents: Wisconsin Occurrences of These Weird Water Monsters*; Mackal, *Searching for Hidden Animals*.

Delia sea serpent

On 21 June 1818, officers and crew aboard the packet *Delia* (or *Delta*, in some reports) allegedly saw a SEA SERPENT battling with a large humpback whale (*Megaptera novaeangeliae*), six miles offshore from Cape Ann, Massachusetts. As they watched, the unknown creature whipped the cetacean with its tail, rising some 30 feet out of the water before each blow. Captain Shubael West, commanding the ship, swore to the story under oath on 27 June, before a justice of the peace in Kennebec County, Maine, but many researchers still dismiss the tale as a HOAX. "Serpent" sightings were so common along the Massachusetts coast in 1817–18 that the creature(s) earned a scientific name, *SCOLIOPHIS ATLANTICUS*.

Sources: Heuvelmans, *In the Wake of the Sea Serpents*; O'Neil, *The Great New England Sea Serpent*.

Delta sea serpent

In 1861, sailors aboard the British vessel *Delta* sighted an unknown SEA SERPENT off the coast of France, near Ushant, Brittany. No report was filed at the time, for fear of inviting ridicule, but a crewman (later captain) named Anderson told the story in 1880, claiming the creature was seen by all on board from a distance of five miles. Perhaps he misspoke, or his listener misunderstood; in any case, it seems improbable that anyone could see the animal from such a distance, much less in the detail claimed by Anderson's report:

It resembled a SNAKE with a large fringe round the neck. It appeared to be traveling, and moved its head to and fro like a snake. It never spouted, and was observed for a quarter of an hour.

Despite calling attention to the account's implausibility, BERNARD HEUVELMANS nonetheless accepted it as genuine, classifying the creature as one of his hypothetical "long-necked" or "merhorse" sea serpents.

Source: Heuvelmans, *In the Wake of the Sea Serpents*.

Densmore Hill Monster

Densmore Hill stands near Hartland, in eastern Vermont's Windsor County. Reports of a predatory cryptid date from 1763, when the vaguely-described monster carried off a woman named Rood, prompting her husband to take his own life. Whatever the facts of that case, sporadic sightings continued into the early 20th century, but the creature is seldom mentioned today.

Source: Citro, *Green Mountain Ghosts, Ghouls & Unsolved Mysteries*.

Detector sea serpent

In the summer of 1831, a SEA SERPENT was sighted in Boothbay Harbor, Maine, by Captain Walden and the crew of the revenue cutter *Detector*. Witnesses agreed that the creature was roughly 100 feet long.

Sources: Heuvelmans, *In the Wake of the Sea Serpents*; O'Neil, *The Great New England Sea Serpent*.

Devil Bird

Since the late 17th century, travelers and ornithologists have squabbled over the identity of a nocturnal hunter known to natives of Ceylon (now Sri Lanka) as the Devil BIRD. The first English-language account of Ceylon, published by Robert Knox in 1681, includes a claim that "oftentimes the Devil doth cry with an audible Voice in the Night; 'tis very shrill, almost like the barking of a dog." In 1849, Charles Pridham identified the Devil Bird as an inoffensive brown wood owl (*Strix gaulama*), while William Legge proposed the gray nightjar (*Caprimulgus indicus*) in 1880, and George Henry suggested the forest eagle owl (*Bubo nipalensis blighi*) in 1955. James Tennent, writing in 1861, concurred with Pridham's identification of the devil bird as a brown wood owl, but strangely reported that native islanders "regard it literally with horror, and its scream by night in the vicinity of a village is bewailed as the harbinger of impending disaster." He also recorded the opinion of a Mr. Mitford, a British official stationed on Ceylon whose avocation was birdwatching. Mitford declared:

The Devil-Bird is not an owl. I never heard it until I came to Kornegalle, where it haunts the rocky hill at the back of Government house. Its ordinary note is a magnificent clear shout like that of a human being, and which can be heard at a great distance, and has a fine effect in the silence of the closing night. It has another cry like that of a hen just caught, but the sounds which have earned for it its bad name, and which I have heard but once to perfection, are indescribable, the most appalling that can be imagined, and scarcely to be heard without shuddering; I can only compare it to a boy in torture, whose screams are being stopped by being strangled. I have offered rewards for a specimen, but without success. The only European who had seen and fired at one agreed with the natives that it is of the size of a pigeon, with a long tail. I believe it is a Podgarus or Night Hawk.

KARL SHUKER notes that the "podgarus" name is applied in Sri Lanka both to nightjars and to the related frogmouth (*Batrachostormus moiniliger*), none of which grow longer than nine inches. However, Tennent himself reportedly sighted a much larger specimen, supposed to be a Death Bird. As he described that incident, "I have since seen two birds by moonlight, one of the size and shape of a cuckoo, the other a large black bird, which I imagine to be the one which gives these calls." Richard Spittel, writing a century after Tennent, reported that remains of supposed Death Birds collected by hunters actually represented four different species: the forest eagle owl, the Sri Lankan hawk-eagle (*Nisaetus cirrhatus ceylonensis*) Hodgson's hawk-eagle (*Nisaetus nipalensis kelaarti*), and the crested honey buzzard (*Pernis ptilorhynchus ruficollis*).

Sources: Shuker, *From Flying Toads to Snakes with Wings*; Richard Spittel, "The Devil Birds of Ceylon." *Loris* 11 (December 1968): 1–14; James Tennent, *Sketches of the Natural History of Ceylon*. London: Longman, Green, Longman and Roberts, 1861.

Devil Monkeys

Cryptozoologists LOREN COLEMAN and MARK HALL apply this name to certain large, unidentified primates reported from various points across North America. These cryptids differ are typically brown or gray in color, and while they may stand 5–6 feet tall on their hind legs, they also travel on all fours. Devil MONKEYS are distinguished from various unknown HOMINIDS and NORTH AMERICAN APES by protruding snouts and long tails (sometimes described as being hairless). Coleman suggests that they may be identical to the Choctaw NALUSA FALAYA, and furthermore that Devil Monkeys may account for some reports of wild KANGAROOS at large in Canada and the U.S. Some of the better-known Devil Monkey sightings include:

1959— Members of the Boyd family logged their first sighting of a giant monkey while driving through the mountains near their home at Saltville, Virginia. The piebald creature attacked their car, leaving three clear scratches in the paint. Various Boyds recorded monkey sightings over the next four decades.

1969— Canadian cryptozoologists JOHN GREEN and RENÉ DAHINDEN investigated reports of a large, long-tailed monkey around Mamquam, British Columbia. The creature left distinctive three-toed tracks.

1973— A trio of giant, bushy-tailed monkeys killed livestock at Albany, Kentucky. Loren Coleman investigated, reporting three-toed tracks similar to those found in British Columbia four years earlier.

Artist's conception of a devil monkey reported by a U.S. witness (*William Rebsamen*).

1973— A friend of the Boyd family (see above) was attacked by a large monkey while driving between Marion and Tazewell, Virginia. The animal rushed at his car and tried to grab the driver's arm through an open window.

1997— Debbie Cross was roused at 1:00 a.m. on 26 June, by dogs barking outside her home in Dunkinsville, Ohio. Peering outside, she saw a large monkey knuckle-walking and "skipping" across her yard. Cross told investigators, "It was about three to four feet tall and gray in color. It had large, dark eyes and rounded ears extended above the head. It had real long arms and a short tail. It made a gurgling sound. From the available light, the animal appeared to have hair or fur all over its body about 1½ inches long."

Sources: Coleman, *Mysterious America*; Coleman and Huyghe, *The Field Guide to Bigfoot, Yeti, and Other Mystery Primates Worldwide*.

Devil's Lake, North Dakota

Confusion surrounds the issue of LAKE MONSTER reports from Devil's Lake, located near a town of the same name in North Dakota's Ramsey County. In 1903, author Charles Skinner recorded aboriginal legends of a green, 90-foot SNAKE said to inhabit the lake, but Dennis Hauck links those reports to LAKE SAKAKAWEA, 80 miles farther west. According to Hauck, indigenous tribes used "Devil's Lake" as an alternate name for Lake Sakakawea.

Sources: Hauck, *Haunted Places*; Charles Skinner, *American Myths and Legends*. Philadelphia: Lippincott, 1903.

Devil's Lake, Wisconsin

In August 1889, witnesses reported two huge, serpentine LAKE MONSTERS with fins or paddles battling on the surface of this lake near Baraboo (Sauk County). The outcome of the epic struggle is unknown, but no modern reports are on file to suggest that a winner survived.

Source: "Western lake resorts have each a water monster." *Chicago Tribune* (24 July 1892).

Devon sea serpent

In 1911, while traveling with three women to Westward Ho! on the south coast of Devon, England, William Cook of Instow alleged met a SEA SERPENT. Their boat was veering to avoid some offshore rocks, when all aboard discovered that the "boulders" were alive. Cook recalled:

The boatman was so terrified that he immediately hauled down the sails, and, with the oars, pulled the boat towards the shore.... The thing then stretched itself out in an undulating coil, lashing the water. We calculated its length at from 60 to 90 feet, as its head did not appear. The body was round, and about the size of a 30-gallon cask. Almost black fins, with short intervals, ran the whole length of its back. Its body was of a brownish gray, with scales, very similar to a gigantic SNAKE.

The creature then swam off toward Clovelly, trailing a foamy wake and showing three or four coils of its body above water at a time. Six decades later, BERNARD HEUVELMANS seemed skeptical of the tale, yet he finally accepted it as genuine and classified the beast as one of his hypothetical "super EELS."

Source: Heuvelmans, *In the Wake of the Sea Serpents.*

Dhulough, Ireland

This small Irish lake is located near Gort, in County Galway. Lady Augusta Gregory describes the resident LAKE MONSTER, which she glimpsed in the late 19th century.

> I was coming home with my two brothers from Tirneevin School, and there as we passed Dhulough we heard a great splashing, and we saw some creature put its head up, with the head and mane like a horse. And we didn't stop but ran.

Source: McEwan, *Mystery Animals of Britain and Ireland.*

Diablito

Between September 2000 and February 2001, residents of Pitrufquen, Argentina (250 miles west of Buenos Aires) were terrorized by reports of small humanoid creature they called Diablito (Spanish for "imp"). The 20-inch nocturnal predator was seen first by children, who claimed that it lived in a cave outside town. Adults dismissed the tales until they heard the creature's "crying baby" wail and noted injuries inflicted on domestic animals, including dogs and poultry. By early 2001, the Diablito had been glimpsed by firefighters and agents of the state police, though it eluded all pursuers. False rumors spread that the creature was caught and packed off to Temuco for medical examination. Local farmer Hernan San Martin lost several chickens to the lurking hunter, and his wife saw it in the yard, describing it as "a little man with wizened features, hairy pig-like ears and shining eyes." Investigator SCOTT CORRALES noted similarities between the Diablito and the CHUPACABRA reported from various points throughout Latin America since 1995.

Source: "Local residents terrified of 'Imp.'" *Diario Austral de Temuco* (18 February 2001).

Didi

These unclassified primates or HOMINIDS of northern South America are reported under various names from Guyana, Suriname and French Guiana. Spanish conquistadors were the first Europeans to collect native reports of the Didi, and Edward Bancroft wrote of them in 1769, describing the creatures as five feet tall, bipedal and covered with black hair. British surveyor Charles Brown collected more native reports in 1868, from the region of present-day Guyana. A British resident magistrate, named Haines, allegedly sighted two of the creatures in 1910, near Rupununi, Guyana. In 1931, members of an Italian scientific expedition to Guyana heard more such tales in the same area. Without exception, witnesses agree that the Didi is tailless, matching the general description of DE LOYS'S APE and the creature known farther west as MONO GRANDE.

Sources: Heuvelmans, *On the Track of Unknown Animals*; Sanderson, *Abominable Snowmen.*

Dientudo

An unclassified HOMINID or large primate of Argentina, the Dientudo ("big teeth") is described as a ferocious half-man, half-bear, boasting a mouthful of prominent fangs. Numerous sightings have been reported from Buenos Aires Prov-

ince, within a 30-mile radius of the nation's capital. The beast appears most frequently around Toloso and along El Gato Creek in Ringuelet.

Source: Picasso, "South American monsters & mystery animals."

Dildo Pond, Canada

Various published accounts list this strangely-named Newfoundland lake as a source of LAKE MONSTER reports, but none provide any dates or details of sightings. Against all odds, the province has *two* Dildo Ponds, separated by 100 miles, thus rendering the mystery virtually insoluble.

Sources: "A brief survey of Canadian lake monsters." *INFO Journal* 39 (March-June 1981): 2–5; Kirk, *In the Domain of the Lake Monsters.*

Dinderi *see* Junjadee

Dinosaurs (Living)

The term dinosaur ("terrible reptile") was coined by Richard Owen in 1842, to describe a class of prehistoric reptiles living between the Late Triassic Period to the end of the Cretaceous (225–65 million years ago). Common perceptions notwithstanding, the superorder *Dinosauria* does not properly include any reptiles living prior to the Triassic Period, nor does it include all reptiles living at the same time as the dinosaurs. It does not include marine reptiles (the PLESIOSAURS, Ichthyosaurs and Mosasaurs), flying reptiles (PTEROSAURS), SNAKES, lizards, TURTLES or crocodilians that were contemporaries of the dinosaurs. Dinosaurs are properly defined by skeletal characteristics, primarily their ball-and-socket hip joints later shared by mammals. The superorder *Dinosauria* is divided into two orders, the *Saurischia* (including bipedal, carnivorous therapods such as *Tyrannosaurus* and herbivorous sauropods such as *Diplodocus*) and the *Ornithischia* (including various horned and armored dinosaurs such as *Triceratops* and *Stegosaurus*). If mainstream science is correct, no dinosaurs have walked the Earth for 65 million years, though various other life forms (ranging from cockroaches to CROCODILES) have survived virtually unchanged to the present day.

Many cryptozoologists dispute that view and actively pursue reports of creatures resembling prehistoric reptiles, collected from Africa, Asia, South America and various Pacific islands. Some of those cryptids, such as KONGAMATO and the ROPEN of Papua New Guinea, are commonly lumped together with dinosaurs despite their close resemblance to pterosaurs. Likewise, some accounts of SEA SERPENTS and LAKE MONSTERS describe them as resembling ancient reptiles. The best-known alleged living dinosaur, pursued by various expeditions from 1920 through the 1990s, is Africa's MOKELE-MBEMBE, described as resembling *Apatosaurus* (formerly *Brontosaurus*). Others include the CHIPEKWE, EMELA-NTOUKA,

Are dinosaurs truly extinct, or did some species survive into modern times?

JAGO-NINI, LI'KELA-BEMBE, LINGUIN, MBIELU-MBIELU-MBIELU, N'YAMALA, and SILWANE MAZZI. Aboriginal tribesmen in Africa and Papua New Guinea have selected drawings of various prehistoric reptiles to depict large creatures reportedly sharing their forests today, but all outside attempts to prove those cryptids exist have so far been fruitless. The latest effort, on 11 March 2004, sent armed police in Papua New Guinea searching for a dog-eating "dinosaur" near Rabaul, New Ireland. Hunters failed to bag the beast, described as gray, 10 feet tall, "with a head like a dog and a tail like a crocodile."

It should not be supposed, however, that dinosaur sightings are limited to the Old World. In January 1911, the *New York Herald* ran a story written by Franz Schmidt, describing an adventure he had experienced in eastern Peru four years earlier, with companion Rudolph Pfleng and several Indian guides. While hiking along the Río Amazonas (or Río Solimões), the party came upon huge tracks and toppled trees, following the trail until they found a "frightful monster" hunting MONKEYS on the bank of a jungle lake. Schmidt estimated that the creature was "35 feet long, with at least 12 of this devoted to head and neck." The animal's head was "about the same size as a beer keg and was shaped like that of a TAPIR, as if the snout was used for pulling things or taking hold of them." Aside from the serpentine neck, it had "great heavy clawed flippers," a "heavy blunt tail," and its skin was covered with "rough horny lumps" that left it "knotted like an ALLIGATOR's hide." Schmidt and Pfleng opened fire with their rifles, but the creature fled without apparent injury. Pfleng died of fever a few months later, leaving Schmidt's tale uncorroborated.

Closer to home, in 1934, a farmer in Brookings County, South Dakota claimed a giant four-legged reptile had forced his tractor off the road before plunging into nearby Campbell Lake. A year later, in May 1935, Myrtle Snow allegedly sighted five "baby dinosaurs" near Pagosa Springs, Colorado (Archuleta County, near the New Mexico border). A farmer shot one of the reptiles a few months later, when it attacked his sheep. "My grandfather took us to see it the next morning," Snow recalled in 1982. "It was about seven feet tall, was gray, had a head like a snake, short front legs with claws that resembled chicken feet, large stout back legs and a long tail." Incredibly, Snow glimpsed another of the creatures in 1937, and again in October 1978.

If dinosaur sightings from the U.S. Southwest sound bizarre, what should we make of similar reports from Italy? In December 1970, a resident of Forli told police that he had been attacked by a "15-foot reptile, like a dinosaur." Fifty miles to the northwest, in June 1975, farmer Maurizio Tombini was frightened by a "gigantic lizard" that left "remarkable tracks" in his tomato patch. Local authorities said several other witnesses had sighted the reptile, which uttered "wolflike" howling sounds. Farmer Tombini, described in press reports as a respected citizen with "a reputation for seriousness," staunchly denied that the creature he saw was a crocodile.

Sources: Clark and Pear, *Strange & Unexplained Phenomena*; Heuvelmans, *Les Derniers Dragons d'Afrique*; Heuvelmans, *On the Track of Unknown Animals*; Mackal, *A Living Dinosaur?*; "Police hunt 'dinosaur' in PNG." *The Age* (12 March 2004); Shuker, *In Search of Prehistoric Survivors*.

Dinsdale, Tim (1924–87)

Born to British parents living in China, Tim Dinsdale graduated from King's School in Worcester and served as a Royal Air Force pilot in Africa during World War II. Subsequently employed as an aeronautical engineer, Dinsdale read a magazine article about NESSIE in 1955 and was instantly captivated by the mystery. He spent the next five years devising a "master plan for a campaign of observation" at Loch Ness, and visited Scotland for the first time in April 1960. There, at 9:00 a.m. on 23 April, he sighted an unknown object in the loch near Foyers Bay and grabbed his small Bolex camera, producing the first-ever movie film of Nessie at a range of 1,300 yards. The Royal Air Force Joint Air Reconnaissance Intelligence Center (JARIC) analyzed Dinsdale's film in 1966, concluding that it showed:

> ...a solid, black, approximately triangular shape with no impression of perspective. If the shape is assumed to be a plane triangle...it is a triangle with a base 5.5 ft. approx. and height 3.7 ft. approx....A reasonable assumption would be that during the complete film sequence the object was travelling at or approaching 10 mph.

As to the subject of the film, JARIC's experts concluded that it was neither a boat nor submarine, "which leaves the conclusion that it is probably an animate object ...with some body....Even if the object is relatively flat bellied, the normal body 'rounding' in nature would suggest that there is at least 2 feet under the water from which it may be deduced that a cross section through the object would be not less than 6 feet wide and 5 ft. high."

Encouraged by his initial success, Dinsdale conducted 55 more expeditions to Loch Ness over the next quarter-century. In 1970, he supervised the LOCH NESS INVESTIGATION BUREAU's survey and resided for a time at the loch. His career as a self-styled monster-hunter also produced four books: *Loch Ness Monster* (1961), *The Leviathans* (1966), *Monster Hunt* (1972), and *Project Water Horse* (1975). Six years after his death, in 1993, Dinsdale's film was subjected to computer enhancement, revealing a previously unseen shadow beneath the object on the loch's surface, clearly attached to the body Dinsdale filmed and suggesting a large submerged form.

Sources: Coleman and Clark, *Cryptozoology A to Z*; Costello, *In Search of Lake Monsters*; Harrison, *The Encyclopaedia of the Loch Ness Monster*.

Dirty Water Lake, Canada

Omitted from most maps, Dirty Water Lake lies in western Manitoba at 52° 41' north latitude and 101° 23' west longitude. Fishermen F. Ross and Tom Spence allegedly sighted a LAKE MONSTER here in 1935. As author JOHN KIRK describes the incident:

> At the back of the periscope-like head and neck, they observed a single horn-like protuberance raised up from the animal's small flat head. The men described the animal as looking like a DINOSAUR and possessing a slate-colored hide similar to that of an elephant.

Source: Kirk, *In the Domain of the Lake Monsters*.

Discovery mystery fish

Britain's Royal Oceanographic Vessel *Discovery* gathered much new information on marine life during its travels, and it left some unanswered questions as well. A member of the ship's crew, biologist P.G. Corbin, described for BERNARD HEUVELMANS the unknown creature he sighted one afternoon, in 1952 or 1954, near the Azores in mid-Atlantic. After watching the beast through binoculars for 5–8 minutes, Corbin said:

> I can't identify it as any kind of animal and it there remains entirely as the private sea-monster. All I would go as far as to say is that I'm convinced it was animal, because it was moving, it didn't break surface, it was large, very roughly quadrangular, I would say about 10 feet long by six, seven or eight feet broad, of the usual monster greyish colour below the surface of the water. It could

only, of the known large animals, have been a very large sunfish, but, I think of the known records, it appeared to be far too large to be identified as a sunfish.

Heuvelmans concluded that the creature *was* in fact a sunfish, since lengths of 11 feet have been recorded for both species (*Mola mola* and *Masturus lanceolatus*).

Source: Heuvelmans, *In the Wake of the Sea Serpents.*

Divi-Te Zeni *see* **Sumske Dekle**

Divji Moz *see* **Sumske Dekle**

Divozenky *see* **Sumske Dekle**

Dja River, Cameroon Shortly after World War II, a long-necked cryptid with a head resembling a TURTLE'S and a body the size of a car was reported from this tropical river, near southern Cameroon's border with the Republic of Congo. The description is generally consistent with those offered for MOKELE-MBEMBE, further to the south and east.

Source: Gaston Grandclément, "Le monstre du Dja." *Bulletin des Chasseurs du Cameroun* (October 1947): 19.

Dobhar-Chú Irish folklore describes the Dobhar-chú as a rare, very large otter, typically attended by smaller common specimens dubbed *madra usice* ("water hounds"). Its size and entourage earned the Dobhar-chú such alternate names as "king otter" and "master otter," though it was rarely seen by humans. The Dobhar-chú was sometimes vicious, as alleged in an 18th-century case from Glenade Lough, County Leitrim. There, on 24 September 1722, a fierce specimen allegedly killed Grace Connolly while she was washing clothes in the lake. Her husband slew the creature, whereupon its own mate burst from the water and attacked, waging a terrible struggle before it was killed in turn. Connolly's gravestone may be seen today in Congbháil (Conwall) Cemetery, in the township of Drumáin (Drummans). It bears the carved likeness of a Dobhar-chú, combining features of an otter and a dog. As recently as May 1968, sightings of an animal resembling the Dobhar-chú were reported from GLENDARRY LOUGH on Achill Island, off the western coast of County Mayo.

Eyewitness accounts describe the Dobhar-chú as a giant otter.

Sources: Cunningham, "The legend of the Dobhar-chú"; Shuker, *From Flying Toads to Snakes with Wings*; Patrick Tohall, "The Dobhar-chú tombstones of Glenade, Co. Leitrim." *Journal of the Royal Society of Antiquaries of Ireland* 78 (1948): 127–129.

Dobsegna This doglike predator of New Guinea closely resembles the THYLACINE, from its light-brown fur and striped flanks, to its yawning jaws and long, slender tail. Paleontologists recognize that Thylacines once inhabited the island of New Guinea — now politically divided between Irian Jaya, Indonesia (on the west) and Papua New Guinea (to the east) — but they presumably became extinct by the end of the Late Pleistocene, some 10,000 years ago. Natives of New Guinea tell a different story, reporting that packs of these nocturnal hunters still raid farms for livestock and poultry. Sightings were reported in the 1990s from Mount Giluwe, in Papua New Guinea, and from Irian Jaya's Gunsung Lorentz National Park. In 1993, Dani tribesmen in Irian Jaya's Baliem Valley identified photos of a Thylacine as depicting the Dobsegna.

Source: "More Tasmanian tigers." *Cryptozoology Review* 2 (Winter-Spring 1998): 5–6; Shuker, "Thylacines in New Guinea?"

Dodo The dodo (*Ralphus cucullatus*) was a large (3 foot 3 inch) flightless BIRD related to pigeons, which once inhabited Mauritius (one of the Indian Ocean's Mascarene Islands). Man's arrival in 1598 was disastrous for the inoffensive birds, as captive specimens were shipped off to Europe and the remainder were hunted to extinction by 1690.

Or were they?

In the 1930s, natives of Mauritius told Lawrence Green that dodos might still be found living in some of the island's remote mountain caves. Fifty years later, WILLIAM GIBBONS heard similar stories from his wife (a Mauritius native) and others living on the island. According to those tales, dodos are sometimes glimpsed in the coastal rain forests of the Plain Champagne. Gibbons mounted two expeditions in the 1990s, seeking dodos, but returned empty-handed both times. The possibility of dodo survival in another venue has been suggested by ROY MACKAL, based on study of 17th-century reports of birds sighted by Portuguese explorers on Nazareth Island (now Île Tromelin), located 375 miles northwest of Mauritius at 15° 51' south latitude and 54° 25' east longitude. Explorer François Cauche described birds resembling dodos from that island in 1638, but thus far no expedition has searched Île Tromelin for remains or living specimens. Other

Despite its presumed extinction, dodo sightings persist into modern times (*William Rebsamen*).

islands of the Indian Ocean, including the heavily forested Carajos Shoals (235 miles north of Mauritius) are still essentially unexplored today. Plans to clone dodos from DNA samples, announced on Mauritius in September 2002, have thus far produced no results.

Sources: Jonathan Fryer, "Bringing the dodo back to life." BBC News (14 September 2002); Gibbons and Hovind, *Claws, Jaws and Dinosaurs*; Mackal, *In Search of Hidden Animals*; Anna Salleh, "Dead as a dodo? Not necessarily." ABC Science Online (20 November 2003); Karl Shuker, "Alien zoo." *Fortean Times* 99 (July 1997): 17; Shuker, *From Flying Toads to Snakes with Wings*; Shuker, "Menagerie of mystery." *Strange Magazine* 19 (Spring 1998): 22.

Dodu   In April 2000, while searching for MOKELE-MBEMBE in Carmeroon, WILLIAM GIBBONS collected native stories of an altogether different cryptid, known to the Bantu people and Baka pygmies alike as Dodu. Witnesses describe the creature as a large primate, six feet tall and dark gray in color, which is normally bipedal but sometimes travels on all fours. Bad tempered and aggressive, the Dodu sometimes attacks adult GORILLAS. The natives interviewed by Gibbons noted two other peculiarities about the Dodu. First, they claim the creatures have only three fingers on each hand and three toes on each foot—a striking parallel with certain three-toed tracks left by unknown HOMINIDS or primates on other continents. Second, the beasts display odd dietary habits. After killing an animal, the Dodu allegedly leaves it uneaten to rot, then returns later to feed on maggots infesting the carcass. On another trip to Cameroon, in 2001, Gibbons heard that a

The Dodu of Cameroon is said to be a large, aggressive primate (**William Rebsamen**).

group of unidentified white men had captured a Dodu near Moloundou, but he could not verify the story, and the creature's fate (if it ever existed) remains unknown.

Source: Karl Shuker, "Alien zoo." *Fortean Times* 169 (May 2003): 16.

Doglas   Cross-breeding between leopards (*Panthera pardus*) and TIGERS (*Panthera tigris*) has not been documented in the wild, but Indian folklore maintains that large male leopards sometimes mate with a tigress, producing a hybrid CAT called the Doglas. In 1910, Frederick Hicks encountered such a specimen and later described the incident as follows:

[T]he spotted head of a panther [*sic*] of extraordinary size pushed its way through the grass, followed by the unmistakable striped shoulders and body of a tiger, though looking a bit dirty as if it had been rolling in ashes. I succeeded in dropping this extraordinary creature dead with a shot in the neck, and, on examining it, I found it to be a very old male hybrid, with both its teeth and claws much worn and broken; its head and tail were purely that of a panther, but with a body, shoulders and neck-ruff unmistakably that of a tiger, the black stripes being broad and long though somewhat blurred and breaking off here and there into a few blurred rosettes, the stripes of the tiger being most predominant on the body. One of the peculiarities of this creature which I particularly noticed was that, though it was male, it had the feet of a female and measured a little over 8 feet in length.

Cryptozoologist KARL SHUKER suggests that the cat may have been both a hybrid and a hermaphrodite. The creature's pelt was later lost or stolen, and is thus unavailable for scientific study.

Sources: Frederick Hicks, *Forty Years Among the Wild Animals of India from Mysore to the Himalayas*. Allahabad, India: Pioneer Press, 1910; Shuker, *Mystery Cats of the World*.

Doko   This unclassified primate or HOMINID of Kenya is reported from the region east of Lake Turkana. Witnesses describe the Doko as four feet tall, with the general appearance of a human PYGMY. Reports date from the 19th century, when some European travelers claimed the Doko were enslaved by local tribes. The creatures were sometimes said to practice a form of religion, yet native tribesmen of the region viewed them as subhuman. No Pygmies are known from this part of East Africa today.

Source: Roumeguère-Eberhardt, *Dossier X.*

***Don* sea serpent**   On 10 August 1881, passengers aboard the Royal Mail packet *Don* alleged saw a SEA SERPENT in the North Atlantic, at 30° north latitude, 42° 40' west longitude. A letter to *Le Monde Illustré*, published on 8 October, described the beast:

From the bottom of the throat where there was a sort of swelling, emerged a rigid pointed tongue, garnished with what seemed to be suckers and shining with reflections which were at once blue as steel and phosphorescent as the sea at certain times; the eye was round, very luminous, very mobile and seemed to be endowed with the faculty of seeing backwards, so rapid and well-coordinated were the animals evolutions.

It gave off an odour as fetid as that of a sick creature; this odour, which persisted more than half an hour seemed to be the result of a great combined operation of the house of Lesage, of the heat of the main sewer at Asnières, and half a dozen bone-black factories like those at Billancourt. It would need the shops of several of our best perfumers put together to counteract it. The monster seemed to be old, as much because of its size as the colour and roughness of its integument.

Le Monde's editors offered the letter "with every reserve," and 80 years later, BERNARD HEUVELMANS agreed that it was almost certainly a HOAX.

Source: Heuvelmans, *In the Wake of the Sea Serpents.*

Dongus *see* **Bunyip**

Dorothy Alexander sea serpent

On 26 May 1934, officers aboard the steamer *Dorothy Alexander* sighted a SEA SERPENT off Cape Flattery, Washington, at the mouth of the Juan de Fuca Strait. Captain Landstrom and First Officer Connolly described it as having a head the size of a 40-gallon barrel. Most modern researchers treat the sighting as an encounter with the cryptid known as CADBOROSAURUS.

Source: LeBlond and Bousfield, *Cadborosaurus.*

Doubs River, Switzerland

Switzerland's Canton Jura was the alleged haunt of flying DRAGONS in Medieval times, and this local river maintained the monstrous tradition as recently as June 1934, when a long-necked cryptid with a blue back and yellow underside was seen navigating its waters. Witnesses claimed that the beast swam by means of undulation, but their descriptions failed to specify whether its spine curved vertically (in mammalian style) or in a lateral plane (as with reptiles).

Source: *New York Herald Tribune* (20 June 1934).

Doudo *see* **Gnéna**

Dove sea serpent

On 17 November 1835, while sailing from Boston to Kennebunk, Maine, the fishing schooner *Dove* "fell in with his marine majesty, the SEA SERPENT, cruising near the half-way rock." Captain Peabody watched the creature from a distance of 65 feet, reported that "several protuberances appeared along his head, which was elevated three or four feet above the water; but as the schooner neared him he settled under the water, his wake indicating him to be sixty or seventy feet in length."

Source: O'Neill, *The Great New England Sea Serpent.*

Dover Castle sea serpent

On 17 October 1912, passengers aboard the British ship *Dover Castle* met a SEA SERPENT in the equatorial Atlantic off the coast of Gabon, at 1° 31' north latitude, 9° 31' west longitude. A spokesman for the several witnesses, one A. Wilmot, reported that the beast was serpentine in appearance, raising its head and long neck 14 feet above the ocean's surface.

Source: Heuvelmans, *In the Wake of the Sea Serpents.*

Dowa Predators

On 8 August 2002, an unrecognized animal appeared in the Dowa district of Malawi (sixty miles from the capital, Lilongwe), launching a reign of terror that left one person dead and 18 others injured. Chaos ensued as the beast roamed over a 12-mile radius, striking at random, leaving its victims with severed hands or fingers and deep gashes on their bodies. Police and big-game hunters failed to stop the MYSTERY MAULER, but native tribesmen emboldened by traditional magic finally cornered and killed a strange specimen on 20 August. Even with the carcass in hand, however, questions remained. District Commissioner Charles Kalemba told reporters the animal was "hyenalike," then added: "A hyena has shorter hind legs, but this animal has legs which are the same length. It has hyena fur in some parts of its body but it has fur like that of a wild pig in other parts. In fact it has also got a bigger and wider tail with lots of fur compared to that of a hyena." A district wildlife officer sent to identify the creature confused matters further when he announced, "Some people say it is a human creation, others say it is a resurrected human being. But preliminary assessments based on footprints indicated that it might be a LION."

On 21 August 2002, Malawi's deputy director for parks and wildlife, Humphrey Nzima, declared that the Dowa beast was simply a hyena, after all. A necropsy revealed that "the hyena died from a combination of beatings it received as it went about biting people and starvation as it appeared not to have eaten anything from the 11th of this month." As for discrepancies in its appearance, Nzima said, "It's true a hyena has shorter hind legs and it is easier to tell while it is standing but people saw it while it was lying down. As for the hairs it is natural in every animal that hairs on the tail are longer." Nzima did not address the discrepancy in pawprints.

Calm returned to Dowa for a while, but it was shattered once again in March 2003, when another "terror beast" ran amok in the district. By 5 March, three persons were dead and 16 gravely injured, while 4,000 others fled four local villages and sought refuge at the district headquarters in Blantyre. Dowa's district health officer, Dr. Matius Joshua, identified the dead as two elderly women and a 3-year-old child, all killed when "the beast crushed their skulls and ate their intestines and private parts." A survivor "lost her mouth and nose" to the creature, while others were likewise "completely maimed and disfigured." At last report, on 10 March, all efforts to trap or shoot the beast had failed. Refugees returned to their homes under armed guard, but the identity and fate of their four-legged nemesis remains a mystery.

Sources: "Malawi police guard against 'terror beast.'" BBC News (10 March 2003); Denis Mzembe, "Strange beast was a hyena." *Malawi Nation* (22 August 2002); Denis Mzembe, "Strange Dowa creature killed." *Malawi Nation* (21 August 2002); Raphael Tenthani, "Malawians flee 'terror beast.'" BBC News (5 March 2003); "Traditional hunters track down killer beast." Sapa-AFP (21 August 2002).

Dragons

All known cultures have traditions referring to large reptilian creatures, commonly called dragons, which interacted in various ways with human beings at some distant time in history. Around 8000 B.C., a Chinese artist painted the earliest known portrait of a dragon on a cliff in Shanxi Province. The name we use today for such monsters derives from the Greek *dracones*, a reference to large SNAKES found near tombs and said to embody the spirits of dead heroes. Unknown to Europeans and Asians, meanwhile, ancient Aztecs worshipped a huge flying serpent named Quetzalcoatl, and their kinsfolk to the north spoke of aquatic monsters called NAITAKA. In A.D. 1109, Chinese emperor Huizong formally classified dragons into five color-coded families—black, white, yellow, red and blue. While Asian dragons were sacred beasts, their British cousins were reviled as symbols of Satan. Continental Europe hosted dragons in black, white, red and yellow, uniformly lethal from their fangs and crushing coils to the toxic slime left in their wake. Many dragons could fly, including some without wings, but others crawled like snakes or swam in lakes and rivers. Some dined on livestock and humans (frequently preferring virginal young women), while others drank milk or ate nothing at all. Fire-breathers were apparently unknown in Asia, but relatively common in the West. For all their mythic qualities, some dragons entered history as flesh-and-blood predators. Some examples include:

8th century— King Charlemagne reportedly killed a lake-dwelling dragon at LAGO BANYOLES, SPAIN.

714— Basque hero Don Teodosio killed a winged dragon on the slopes of Mount Aralar, Spain.

774— "Horrid serpents" were seen in the sky over Sussex, England, filling residents with "great amazement."

793— Another flight of "fiery dragons" over Sussex were followed in short order by "a great famine."

Some dragons are depicted in folklore as huge serpents or lizards.

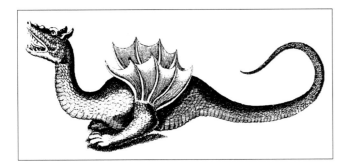

Other dragons are winged and capable of flight.

Middle Ages—A bull-sized, hairy dragon with fiery breath emerged from the Huisne River to terrorize villagers at La Ferté-Bernard, in France's Sarthe Department. A local hero killed the beast by slicing off its tail.

1171—According to the *Genealogies of the Kings of England*, "A great dragon…flew through the air not far from the ground, and in his flight raised a great fire in the air which burnt a house to ashes, with all that was about it."

1304—A dragon crawled from the French lake Belchensee during a flood, wreaking havoc around Issenheim.

April 1388—A "flying dragon was seen…in many places" over the British Isles.

14th century—Lord Lambton of Durham (England) caught a hideous "worm" while fishing in the River Wear and threw it down a well without recognizing its true nature. Over time, the beast grew large and terrorized the countryside, devouring cattle and humans alike. Peasants placated the creature with offerings of milk until Lord Lambton finally killed it, donning a spiked suit of armor that fatally lacerated the monster's gullet. A piece of the Lambton Worm's scaly hide was displayed at the family castle until the 19th century.

15th century—Sir Maurice de Berkeley allegedly killed a scaly fire-breather near Bisterne, Hampshire (England). The site of their epic battle is called Dragon Field.

1405—Townspeople of Wormingford (or Bures), on the Essex/Suffolk border, killed a large unidentified reptile near town.

16th century—Sir Thomas Venables reportedly shot a dragon that was attacking a child in Bache Pool, near Moston, Cheshire. A carving displayed in the local church vestry, circa 1632, reveals the Venable family crest as a picture of a dragon swallowing a child.

17th century—A loathsome dragon was blamed for an outbreak of plague around Lac Pavin, France in Puy-de-Dôme Department.

August 1614—A modest 9-foot dragon capable of spitting venom hunted for prey in St. Leonard's Forest, near Horsham, Sussex. It reportedly killed two persons, two dogs and several cattle in serial attacks, but made no effort to devour its victims.

May 1669—A winged dragon 8–9 feet long was sighted by peasants near Henham, Essex. On the second day of its appearance, townsfolk armed with guns and pitchforks rallied to destroy the creature, but it escaped into nearby Birch Wood.

July 1713—A farmer named Zander reportedly killed a snake 17 feet 4 inches long near Wroclaw, Poland. No reptiles approaching that size are native to Europe.

1783—A German silversmith and his daughter were chased by a "fiery dragon with gaping jaws" on Rattlesnake Hill, near Silver Run, Maryland.

1857—Passengers aboard a MISSOURI RIVER steamboat, slowing for a landing on the Nebraska shore, sighted "a great undulating serpent, in and out of the lowering clouds, breathing fire, it seemed, with lighted streaks along the sides." The incident was remarkable enough to inspire a folk song.

June 1873—Residents of Fort Scott, Kansas claimed that "when the disc of the sun was about halfway above the horizon [at sunrise], the form of a huge serpent, apparently perfect in form, was plainly seen encircling it and was visible for some moments."

June 1873—Within days of the Kansas sighting, farmers outside Bonham, Texas were "seriously frightened" by an "enormous serpent" flying overhead. According to the *Bonham Enterprise*, "It seemed to be as large and as long as a telegraph pole, was of a yellow striped color, and seemed to float along without effort. They could see it coil itself up, turn over, and thrust forward its huge head as if striking at something, displaying the maneuvers of a genuine snake." A *New York Times* editorial dismissed the incident as "the very worst case of delirium tremens on record."

November 1883—A resident of Frederick, Maryland, while passing through the nearby Catoctin Mountains, reported a near-miss with "a monstrous dragon with glaring eye-balls, and mouth wide open displaying a tongue, which hung like a flame of fire from its jaws" while the creature "feared and plunged."

May 1888—Residents of Darlington County, South Carolina reported a winged reptile, 15 feet long, flying over their homes and uttering loud hissing sounds. Witnesses claimed the creature was "sailing through the air with a speed equal to that of a hawk or buzzard but without any visible means of propulsion." Reports from neighboring counties were logged on the same day.

September 1891—A reptilian monster, 20 feet long and 8 feet wide, appeared in the sky over Crawfordsville, Indiana on two successive nights. Witnesses said it "flapped its fins violently" and swooped from 100 feet to ground level, where frightened burghers felt its "hot breath."

1890s—German scientists schemed to embarrass British rivals by sculpting an intricate 12-inch "baby dragon" and sending photos of the model to Oxford University. A necropsy was scheduled, but officials at England's Natural History Museum suspected a HOAX and ordered the specimen destroyed without removing it from its jar of formaldehyde. Unknown to his employers, a museum clerk kept the model and it surfaced in January 2004, to create a new media stir.

1902—During the Russo-Japanese War, a group of Chinese soldiers told Elder Barsanuphius that they had several times glimpsed a winged, cave-dwelling dragon 40 miles from Muling, in Heilongjiang Province.

1913— A large, fire-breathing cryptid eluded hunting parties around MCCLINTOCK LAKE, in Canada's rugged Yukon territory.

1917— A combat pilot in World War I reported a frightening encounter with "a curiously coloured dragon-like animal apparently floating in the air," which rushed at his plane in mid-air.

1933— Maryland resident Helen Kay reported a dragon swimming in the Patuxent River, near a children's waterfront camp.

By the mid-19th century, many scholars had decided that dragon legends sprang from early discovery of fossilized DINOSAUR remains. Indeed, some Chinese apothecaries still sell petrified "dragon's bones" and "dragon's eggs" laid by an extinct OSTRICH, excavated from the Gobi Desert. Some cases of man-eating dragons in Europe — including the Wormingford reptile of 1405 and a voracious predator in France's Rhône Valley — are now widely explained as mislocated CROCODILES, perhaps escaped from some wealthy eccentric's private menagerie. Charles Gould, writing in 1886, was among the first to disagree, suggesting that some "mythical" dragons were creatures of substance. Gould wrote:

> We may infer that it was a long terrestrial lizard, hibernating and carnivorous with the power of constricting with its snake-like body and tail; possibly furnished with wing-like expansions of its integuement, after the fashion of *draco volans* and capable of occasional progress on its hind legs alone when excited in attack....Probably it preferred sandy open country to forest land.... Although terrestrial, it probably, in common with most reptiles, enjoyed frequent bathing, and when not so engaged, or basking in the sun, secluded itself under some overhanging bank or cavern.

Vestigial wings aside, Gould's description is a fair match for certain giant MONITOR LIZARDS reported to this day from parts of Australia, Papua New Guinea, and elsewhere. Seven years later, an expert on Asian folklore, Nichols Dennys, had "little doubt" that Chinese dragons were based on real-life creatures representing the "most fearful embodiment of animal ferocity to be found." In respect to European dragons, cryptozoologist MARK HALL suggests that some may have been an evolved form of *Kuehneosaurus*, a winged reptile that inhabited the British Isles during the Late Triassic period (200 million years ago). Granted, *Kuehneosaurus* was only two feet long and apparently glided rather than flapping its wings, but Hall suspects it may have grown larger and learned true flight over time. Reports of aquatic dragons worldwide may represent sightings of the same creatures known in modern times as SEA SERPENTS and LAKE MONSTERS.

Sources: Benedict, "The dragons that stalked America"; Chorvinsky, "Here be dragons!"; Costello, *The Magic Zoo*; Gould, *Mythical Monsters*; Holiday, *The Dragon and the Disk*; Humfrey Hunter, "Enter the dragon." *London Evening Standard* (23 January 2004); Kirk, *In the Domain of the Lake Monsters*; Shuker, *Dragons: A Natural History*.

Drekavac   The Drekavac is a creature of Slavic folklore which has survived to wreak havoc in modern Serbia, Yugoslavia. During 1956–58, a night-prowling Drekavac emerged repeatedly from the Djikina bara swamp to disturb residents of nearby Srbobran with its unearthly wailing, compared by some observers to the cry of a peacock. That visitor eluded hunters, but another surfaced at Bashaid in the early 1990s, prompting some locals to vacate their homes. On 9 December 1992, the newspaper *Vecernje Novosti* reported that a Drekavac's carcass had been found beside the Kravicka River. It resembled "something between a dog and a FOX with legs similar to a KANGAROO," rousing suspicions that

it was "a product from a NATO laboratory." The beast was not identified, but one of its kin reportedly roused sleepers in Kula and three neighboring villages during early April 2001. Semantic confusion surrounds the Drekavac in some regions where residents recognize "land" and "swamp" species. The former is deemed mammalian, while the latter may include any BIRD, amphibian or other animal possessed of a loud voice. The sound-alike name *bukavac* is also applied in some districts to a species of marsh-dwelling heron.

Source: Marcus Sibanicus, "Strange creatures from Slavic folklore." *North American BioFortean Review* 3 (October 2001): 62–63.

Dre-Mo   The Himalayas suffer from an embarrassment of riches where cryptozoology is concerned. The famous YETI offers mystery enough, and comes in several sizes which various cryptozoologists regard as distinct and separate species of HOMINIDS, and the elusive BURU entices herpetologists. If this were not enough, the region also hides the Dre-mo, an unclassified primate or bear sometimes confused with the Yeti, a nocturnal hunter said to walk on all fours and bipedally. Alternate names throughout its range include Chemo ("big") and Dredmo ("brown bear"). Mountaineer-author Reinhold Messner sighted a Dre-mo near Alamdo, Tibet in July 1986, and emerged from the experience convinced that he had solved the larger riddle of the Yeti. Linguistic confusion leaves the matter decidedly unsettled, but two brown bears are known to inhabit the Himalayas. The common brown bear (*Ursus arctos*) may be found in red varieties throughout the range, and is known in the neighboring Karakorams as Dreng mo. A "blue" subspecies of brown bear, also called the "horse bear" (*U. a. pruinosis*), inhabits eastern Tibet.

Sources: Messner, *My Quest for the Yeti*; Tchernine, *The Yeti*.

***Drift* sea serpent**   In 1886, spokesmen for the U.S. Coast and Geodesic Survey published a report of a SEA SERPENT sighting filed eight years earlier, in August 1878, by Captain Robert Platt of the survey schooner *Drift*. Platt's report read:

> August 29, while becalmed off Race Point, Cape Cod [Massachusetts], almost four hundred yards from the vessel, we saw a sea monster, or what I suppose has been called a sea-serpent. Its first appearance was that of a very large round spar two or three feet in diameter, from twelve to fifteen feet high, standing upright in the sea, but in a few minutes it made a curve and went down. It was visible about three minutes; the second appearance, about half an hour after the first, the monster came out of the water about twenty-five feet, then extended to about thirty-five or forty feet and about three feet in diameter; when out about forty feet, it curved and went down, and as it did so a sharp dorsal fin of about fifteen feet in length came up. This fin was connected to the monster, for the whole animal moved off with the same velocity. I looked at it with a good pair of glasses. I could not tell whether it has a mouth or eyes; it was brownish color. I enclose to you a sketch made by me and submitted to all on board who saw the animal, and they all agree that it is a fair representation of the animal as it appeared.

Source: O'Neil, *The Great New England Sea Serpent*.

Drop Bear   Australia's Drop Bear is typically described as resembling an oversized koala (*Phascolarctor cinereus*), 3–5 feet tall, armed with sharp claws and teeth. The creatures allegedly lurk in trees, then drop onto passing humans in a fierce, sometimes fatal attack. Its supposed fondness for tackling foreign tourists mark the Drop Bear as a HOAX dreamed up by some joker Down Under. One of the more extreme Internet websites devoted to Drop Bears describes the creatures as follows (with grammatical errors intact):

> The drop bear, or Pangkala as its known as by the aborigenies, is smilar to the koala. It has the same basic shap of the koala except it is about 8 foot tall, it has a lethery back-side, long razor sharpe claws and has 40cm [15-inch!] long incisor teeth. The drop bear hunts by sitting in a tree until a victim walks under it. The drop bear would then fall out of the tree onto its victim, breaking its neck. If the drop bear misses it would them use its long claws to kill the victim. The drop Bear hunts in packs, with upto 4 bears in one tree at a time! Once the victim has been killed the rest of the bears would then fall and fight over the kill. These fights can be made up of upto 30 bears.

Source: Drop Bears: Terror of the Australian Bush, http://library.trinity.wa.edu.au/subjects/english/*fant/drop.htm*.

Australia's Drop Bear is a mythical variation on the innocuous koala.

Dry Harbor carcass   In June 1956, a large carcass washed ashore at Dry Harbor, south of Yakutat, Alaska. Initial reports described it as 100 feet long and 15 feet wide, covered with 2-inch reddish-brown hair. The beast was swiftly decomposing, but observers still noted its bright-red flesh, prominent teeth, and syrupy blood. One of the first examiners, Trevor Kincaid, declared that its "description fits no known animal." Six months later, W.A. Clemens, director of the University of British Columbia's Institute of Oceanography, announce that the creature was in fact a specimen of Baird's beaked whale (*Berardius bairdii*). While common to Alaskan waters, however, *B. bairdii* attains a maximum official length of 42 feet, less than half the reported size of the Dry Harbor carcass. The discrepancy remains unexplained.

Sources: Heuvelmans, *In the Wake of the Sea Serpents*; LeBlond and Bousfield, *Cadborosaurus*.

Du   New Caledonia, 700 miles east of Australia in the South Pacific, was once inhabited by large flightless BIRDS (*Sylviornis neocaledoniae*) resembling the OSTRICH and EMU. They stood 5–6 feet tall, and presumably behaved in manners similar to those of their cousins in Africa and Australia. Subfossil remains discovered on the Isle of Pines in 1974 date from approximately 1500 B.C., after Melanesian tribesmen arrived to settle the islands. Officially, the great birds were hunted to extinction no later than A.D. 300, but reports of living specimens still circulated in the 1990s. French biologist François Poplin speculates that large earthen mounds discovered on New Caledonia and the Isle of Pines, measuring 5 feet tall and 30–50 feet in diameter, may be Du nesting sites.

Sources: Cécile Mourer-Chauviré and François Poplin, "Le mystère des tumulus de Nouvelle-Calédonie." *La Reverches* 16 (September 1985): 1094; Lars Thomas, *Mysteriet om Havuhyrerne*. Copenhagen: Gyldendal Boghandel, 1992.

Duah *see* **Ropen**

Dublin Lake, New Hampshire   Author Philip Rife reports that LAKE MONSTER sightings have been logged at Dublin Lake, near Keene in southwestern New Hampshire's Cheshire County. According to Rife, "[A] skindiver who'd set out to explore the lake's underwater caverns in the early 1980s emerged badly shaken and mumbling something about 'monsters.'" Rife provides no further details, and his source for the story is an anonymous Internet posting, traced by researcher Craig Heinselman to the website of a defunct New Hampshire organization, the Granite State BIGFOOT Society. Heinselman concluded that many alleged reports posted to that site were "mere rumors" and "completely unsubstantiated."

Sources: Craig Heinselman, "A lake monster in New Hampshire?" *North American BioFortean Review* 4 (March 2002): 14–15; Rife, *America's Loch Ness Monsters*.

Duende/Dwendi   These unclassified primates or small HOMINIDS of Central and South America are known by a variety of names throughout their range. The most common name, Duende, apparently derives from a Spanish word for "dwarf" or "goblin." Other names include Dueno del monte ("lords of the mountain"), Silborcito ("little whistler") and Sombrero'n ("big hat"). The latter names refer, respectively, to the Duende's whistling cry and its alleged habit of holding large palm fronds over its head to make shade. IVAN SANDERSON observed identical behavior in adult CHIMPANZEES (*Pan troglodytes*) during a visit to Africa. Witnesses typically describe the Duende as 3–4 feet tall, covered by hair ranging from blonde to red or gray, with long arms and thick calves. Their feet are relatively small, with pointed heels, and (in common with reports of other unknown hominids) are frequently described as pointing backward. The Duende inhabit forests, caves, mine shafts and abandoned houses, sometimes attacking dogs and livestock during their nocturnal hunts. A few reports describe them wearing primitive articles of clothing. Based on those descriptions, Sanderson suggested that they might be relics of a pygmy Mayan race.

Sources: Sanborne, "An investigation of the Duende and Sisimite of Belize: Hominoids or myth?"; Sanborne, "On the trail of the Duende and Sisimite of Belize"; Sanderson, *Abominable Snowmen*.

Duivenbode's Riflebird   The tropical BIRD of paradise known as Duivenbode's riflebird (*Parypheporus duivenbodei*) was identified from a single specimen shot in Papua New Guinea during the late 19th century, with no information recorded on the precise date or place of collection. In 1930, Erwin Stresemann dismissed *P. duivenbodei* and five other species as simple hybrids, but some ornithologists now reject that verdict. Speculation persists that the species may still survive.

Source: Fuller, *The Lost Birds of Paradise*.

Dulugal *see* **Yowie**

Dunbar Castle **sea serpent**   In 1955, South African big-game hunter Tromp van Diggelen published his memoirs, including a brief account of a SEA SERPENT he glimpsed a quarter-century earlier. The passage reads:

> While returning from England in 1930 on the ill-fated *Dunbar Castle*, I actually saw a sea-serpent. It was 11 o'clock on a sunny November morning.
>
> The neck of the "thing" was very plainly visible through my Zeiss marine glasses (it was only a few hundred yards away), and it was sticking out of the water some 12 or 15 feet and was travelling fast, as if in terror.
>
> The movement was much more like that of a cormorant as it swims away from a boat when frightened. I saw no pronounced head, neither were there any coils or flippers visible....
>
> The passengers were all crowded on the port side of the ship to watch nearby Robben Island, and my only companion was an American lady.
>
> I handed her my glasses and said, "Look at that."
>
> "Good heavens, it must be a sea serpent," she exclaimed. I had not put the suggestion to her.

Source: Tromp van Diggelen, *A Worthwhile Journey.* London: William Heinemann, 1955.

Dundrum Bay sea serpent   According to Celtic folklore, legendary hero Fergus mac Léti killed a SEA SERPENT at Dundrum Bay, Northern Ireland (formerly Lough Rudraige) around 39 B.C. Different versions of the tale say the creature was locally known as Muirdis or Sínach.

Source: James MacKillop, *Dictionary of Celtic Mythology.* New York: Oxford University Press, 1998.

Dungarvon Whooper   The Dungarvon River is a tributary of the Miramichi, in eastern New Brunswick, Canada. It reportedly harbors an unknown creature dubbed the Dungarvon Whooper, after its eerie howls that "have sent chills up the spines of lumberjacks for more than a century." Some naturalists suggest the sounds are made by EASTERN COUGARS, themselves officially extinct in eastern Canada, but local guides and woodsmen tend to disagree.

Source: Garner, *Monster! Monster!*

Dungeness Bay sea serpent   In mid-March 1961, multiple witnesses sighted a SEA SERPENT in Dungeness Bay, 15 miles west of Port Townsend, Washington. Various published descriptions say the creature was dark brown and/or orange in color, long-necked, with a mane and three humps visible above the

water. PAUL LEBLOND includes the report on a list of CADBOROSAURUS sightings, while others claim the animal resembled pictures of "swamp-dwelling DINOSAURS."

Sources: Guiley, *Atlas of the Mysterious in North America;* LeBlond and Bousfield, *Cadborosaurus.*

Durham Puma   Between 1986 and 1994, at least 170 sightings of this ALIEN BIG CAT were reported from County Durham, England. Most witnesses agree that the animal resembles a COUGAR (*Puma concolor*). On 16 August 1992, Philip Nixon photographed a large CAT carrying a rabbit in its jaws, near St. John's Chapel in County Durham. Animal droppings were found beside a mutilated sheep at Whorlton, in September 1993, and a sample was sent to the Institute of Terrestrial Ecology in Aberdeen. There, carnivore specialist Hans Kruuk studied the feces and reported in August 1994: "My examinations all point to a puma or leopard, but since no sightings exist in Durham of a spotted creature my conclusion would favour a puma. I really have little doubt." Occasional sightings continue from the region, with the most recent—of a jet-black, dog-sized cat—reported on 29 October 2003.

Sources: "Possible sighting of legendary Durham puma." *Northern Echo* (30 October 2003); Sieveking, "Beasts in our midst"; Sieveking, "Big cats in Britain."

Durham **sea serpent**   On 26 February 1878, everyone aboard the steamer *Durham* saw an unidentified 30-foot SEA SERPENT in the South Pacific, near "Nerowa Island." No such island is presently known, but Nauru (the world's smallest republic, with a total area of 21 square miles) lies 1,000 miles east of Papua New Guinea.

Source: Heuvelmans, *In the Wake of the Sea Serpents.*

Dwayo/Dwayyo   Dwayo is the name sometimes applied to a BIGFOOT-type HOMINID or NORTH AMERICAN APE reported at various times from northern Maryland's Frederick County. Initial sightings were made in the 1920s, by visitors to Gambrill State Park (northwest of Frederick). In November 1965, local resident John Becker claimed to have grappled with a man-sized hairy biped in his yard, 10 miles from Frederick. Various sources disagree on when the Dwayo name was coined, and none suggest a meaning. In some accounts, the creature is also called Wago.

Sources: Bord and Bord, *The Bigfoot Casebook;* Chorvinsky and Opsasnick, "Notes on the Dwayyo."

Dziwo-Zony *see* **Sumske Dekle**

Dzu-Teh *see* **Yeti**

— E —

Eagle Creek, Indiana   Cryptozoologists LOREN COLEMAN and JOHN KIRK include Eagle Creek (near Gary, in Lake County) on lists of North American waterways hosting LAKE MONSTERS, but neither source provides any details of sightings or descriptions. Their listings may have confused Eagle Creek with EAGLE LAKE, in Noble County (60 miles to the east), but no final determination is possible without further information.

Sources: Coleman, *Mysterious America;* Kirk, *In the Domain of the Lake Monsters.*

Eagle Lake, California   This lake in Lassen County, 90 miles northeast of Sacramento, is reportedly the home of a large, unidentified LAKE MONSTER. Modern descriptions are hopelessly vague, but the creature survives (at least in local legend) to titillate fishermen and summer residents of the nearby Lassen County Youth Camp. This location should not be confused with EAGLE CREEK or EAGLE LAKE, INDIANA.

Source: Wildlife, http://www.lcoe.org/YouthCamp/YouthCamp-Wildlife.htm.

Eagle Lake, Indiana   One of the Internet's best websites on aquatic cryptids lists this lake, in Indiana's Noble County (northwest of Fort Wayne), as the reputed home of a LAKE MONSTER. Unfortunately, no further details are offered and the stories are untraceable. A possibility exists that Eagle Lake has been confused with EAGLE CREEK, listed in two published books (also without supporting evidence) as a source of Indiana "monster" reports.

Source: Katie Sullivan, The Online Lake Cryptid Directory, http://dive.to/lakemonsters.

***Eagle* sea serpent**   At 11:00 a.m. on 23 March 1830, officers and crew aboard the schooner *Eagle* met a SEA SERPENT resembling a huge reptile a mile offshore from Charleston, South Carolina. According to witnesses, the creature was sighted 300 yards from the ship, but Captain Deland sailed within 20-25 yards of the animal and shot it with a musket, whereupon it dived and struck several hard blows against the *Eagle*'s hull before fleeing the scene. A Charleston newspaper summarized the crew's observations:

> They all had opportunity to see their enemy and agree that its length was about 70 feet. The body was as thick as or thicker than a sixty-gallon keg, of a gray color, EEL-shaped, without visible fins and apparently covered with scales, the back full of joints or bunches, the head and beak resembled an ALLIGATOR'S, the former 10 feet long, and as big as a hogshead.

Witnesses aboard the *Eagle* also saw a smaller specimen, which submerged when fired upon, and the two creatures were later seen swimming together.

Source: Heuvelmans, *In the Wake of the Sea Serpents.*

Earth Hound   A Scottish cryptid, the Earth Hound (also known as a Yard Dog or Yird Swine) is described by witnesses as a curious composite creature. It is ferret-sized, perhaps a rodent, though its head resembles a dog's (except for a snout like a pig's). It sports prominent incisors, has feet like a mole's, and possesses a short busy tail. Worse than its unlovely conglomerate appearance is the Earth Hound's reputed habit of frequenting graveyards,

where it allegedly burrows into graves and eats human flesh. Specimens were reportedly killed in 1867 and 1915 (the latter in a parish churchyard at Mastrick, Abderdeenshire), and Alexander Fenton collected reports of Earth Dogs from Keith (Banffshire) as recently as April 1990.

Sources: Fenton and Heppell, "The Earth Hound"; Shuker, *Mysteries of Planet Earth.*

Earwig (Giant)   Earwigs are beetlelike insects of distinctive appearance, featuring a curved set of pincers at the rear of the abdomen. Their appearance and occasional foul odor alarms some homeowners who find them in the house, but common earwigs do not grow beyond 1¼ inches long.

In 1798, a Danish zoologist named Fabricus discovered a species of "giant" earwig, ranging from 2½ to 3 inches long, on the South Atlantic island of Saint Helena. He named the species *Labidura herculeana*, but entomologists then lost track of it for nearly 200 years. In 1962, members of an expedition seeking BIRD remains on Saint Helena found body parts belonging to a giant earwig. Three years later, another party found several living specimens, but none have been sighted in the past four decades. The insects are presumably still living, but their whereabouts remains unknown.

Source: Jonathan Downes, Mystery Insects of the World, http://www.eclipse.co.uk/cfz/features/insects.htm.

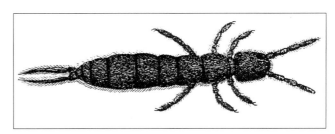

Giant earwigs have been reported from Saint Helena since the 18th century.

Scotland's Earth Hounds reportedly eat human corpses (*William Rebsamen*).

East Caroga Lake, New York   This lake in the southern part of New York's Adirondack Park (Fulton County) produced a LAKE MONSTER report on 30 August 1983, when Lewis Decker and 15 other witnesses observed an unidentified creature thrashing about on the surface. Suggestions that they may in fact have seen a large muskellunge (*Esox masquinongy*) remain unconfirmed.

Source: Dan Lowenski, "Was it a fish, or...?" *Pursuit* 64 (1985): 184-185.

East River, New York   On 29 June 1856, two New York City policemen reported a serpentine creature swimming in the East River off Greenpoint, Queens. The officers claimed it was yellow, with a forked tail and a head resembling that of an ALLIGATOR. No other sightings were recorded, and the beast remains unidentified.

Source: *Brooklyn Daily Eagle* (1 July 1856).

Easter Bunny   Oregon BIGFOOT researcher RAYMOND CROWE reports that this nickname is occasionally used for unknown HOMINIDS in certain parts of Michigan. No more specific information is presently available.

Source: "Around the weird: Bizarre news briefs." *Wireless Flash Weird News* (4 June 2002).

Eastern Cougar   While still surviving in the western half of North America today, the COUGAR (*Puma concolor*, formerly *Felis concolor*) is officially extinct throughout the eastern half of the continent, except for small numbers acknowledged in southern Florida. In most of the eastern U.S., cougars vanished—at least from the official records—in the latter years of the 19th century. The last acknowledged wild cougar in eastern Canada was shot in 1938, along the border between Maine and Québec or New Brunswick (reports differ). Nonetheless, thousands of sightings have been logged over the past century, throughout the CAT'S original range. Today, wildlife officials in a few locations grudgingly admit that cougars are returning to their former habitats, but others stubbornly refuse to change their minds, even in the face of pawprints, photographs and carcasses. Volumes could be filled with modern sightings of the Eastern cougar, but the following roster of sightings may suffice to prove the point.

Arkansas: Hot Springs—Multiple sightings were recorded, while authorities denied the existence of any cougars in the state (March 2003). Little Rock—an automatic camera set up near the Winona Wildlife Management Area captured a cougar on film (August 2003).

Connecticut: Salisbury—a hiker met a cougar on the Appalachian Trail (1979); Somers—three sightings in a single week were dismissed by the Department of Environmental Protection as encounters with "escaped pets" (September 2002); Pomfret—a cougar appeared in the Connecticut Audubon Society's bird sanctuary (spring 1999); Torrington—witnesses reported a "mammoth mountain LION" (November 2002); New Fairfield—a cougar was seen near a public school (February 2003); Winsted—a motorist sighted a cougar on the highway outside town. DEP spokesmen acknowledged receiving cougar reports "once a month or more frequently," but denied any proof of cats living wild in the state (April 2003).

Delaware: Scattered reports were logged throughout the northern sector of the state in the 1990s; Bear—an elementary school employee saw a cougar prowling near campus (May 2002). Hockessin—residents sighted a cougar 5-6 feet long and 3 feet tall at the shoulder (9 October 2003); Wilmington—motorists reported a cougar near Christiana Mall (26 November 2003).

Evidence suggests the Eastern cougar survives in North America.

Georgia: Clayton—multiple witnesses reported a "huge" cougar passing through a residential neighborhood (October 2002); Jonesboro—sightings outside town prompted a fruitless search by the Department of Natural Resources (November 2002).

Illinois: Fort Kaskaskia State Historical Site—a 110-pound male cougar was killed by a train nearby, with necropsy results finding all claws intact and venison in the cat's stomach (July 2000); Darrow—a large cat left 4-inch pawprints around a rural neighborhood (June 2002); Central Illinois—multiple sightings were reported from Congerville, East Peoria, Lacon, Lilly, Manito, Pekin and Sheffield (December 2002).

Indiana: South Bend—sightings were recorded in an area where cougars were allegedly wiped out in 1900 (July 2002); Fairland—an unknown "large cat" killed a local resident's domestic cat, then returned two days later and inflicted $1,700 damage on a car parked in her driveway. Several domestic animals were killed at a nearby home, while authorities set traps without result (July 2002); Wabash County—a cougar sighting was reported (August 2003); South Bend—residents reported a cougar on the prowl in suburban neighborhoods (October 2003).

Iowa: Shelby County—a 7.5-foot adult male cougar was struck and killed by a car on a rural highway (August 2001); Mondamin—an adult cougar with a cub was sighted and videotaped (May 2003); Carroll, Freemont, Monoa, Ringgold and Shelby Counties—confirmed sightings were acknowledged by the Department of Natural Resources, even as state spokesmen denied the existence of wild cougars in Iowa (June 2003); Allamakee, Carroll, Cherokee, Fremont, Lyon, Monoa, Ringgold, Shelby and Webster Counties—confirmed cougar tracks supported eyewitness sightings (June 2003); Bagley (Greene County)—farmers blamed cougars for the recent disappearance of a dog and lamb, and for injuries suffered by a horse (August 2003); Ireton—farmers shot and killed a cougar five miles outside town (24 October 2003); Solon—multiple sightings in November 2003 were followed by discovery of a pawprint 5-6 inches wide, found six miles west of town (6 December 2003).

Kentucky: Floyd County—an 8-pound female cub was struck and killed by a truck. DNA testing suggested South American lineage, leading authorities to dismiss the cat as an escaped pet (June 1997); Kenton County—a prowling cougar frightened dogs and residents (April-August 2003).

Maine: Bangor—a forest ranger on fire-watch duty saw a cougar at Blue Hill Mountain, south of town (April 1989); Hartland—a cougar was photographed outside town (December 1993).

Maryland: Street—an adult cougar was seen and photographed in a residential district, followed by more sightings across Hartford County (August 1992).

Massachusetts: Truro—hikers met a cougar on a trail in Cape Cod National Seashore (September 1981); Rochester—another cat was seen beside the Mattapoisett River (August 2002); Chincoteague—multiple sightings were reported to police, who failed to catch the cat (January 2003); Chelmsford—multiple witnesses logged sightings, prompting another futile search (June 2003); Westford—a cougar was seen roaming the streets of this Boston suburb (June 2003); Beverly—reports of a "baby mountain lion" at large climaxed with discovery of a partially-devoured deer (September 2003); Rutland—residents reported multiple sightings of a cat the size of a large dog (September 2003).

Michigan: Leonard and Oakland Counties—sightings were recorded throughout the 1940s and 1950s; Manchester—another sighting was logged (1985); Waterford — witnesses reported a cougar on the prowl (1986); Emmet County — 20 sightings were reported to authorities within a decade (1990-2001); Delta and Menominee Counties — further sightings prompted the Michigan Wildlife Habitat to declare that 10-20 adult cougars live wild in the state's upper peninsula, with "a few" in the lower peninsula. Evidence includes a recent photo of a female with two cubs (March 2001); Chippewa County — a cougar skull of unknown origin was found beside 15 Mile Road (summer 2001); Niles — a cougar surfaced in a residential neighborhood; Holland Township — Ottawa County authorities claim a cougar sighted in the area is an "escaped pet," insisting no wild cougars have existed in the region "for more than 100 years" (February 2002); Lakeshore — the National Park Service recorded a "very reliable" sighting (June 2002); Ludginton — a cougar was reported on a nearby farm (August 2002); Kalkaska County — cougars mauled horses on two different farms (September 2002); French Township — state authorities ignored cougar pawprints found by an animal control officers (June 2003); Westford — numerous sightings were reported by local residents (July 2003); Macomb County — authorities searched in vain for a cougar seen in Ray Township, finally dismissing the reports as "unlikely" (15-16 September 2003); Traverse City — another cougar sighting was reported (16 September 2003); Van Buren Township — state authorities declared that a cougar seen in the vicinity "is not a threat to people and will not attack unless provoked," though it subsequently mauled a cocker spaniel (October-December 2003). In response to state claims that any and all cougars seen in Michigan, Mike Zuidema, a retired forester for the state Department of Natural Resources, says: "It's a real dumb thing on the part of the [government] to say that they're pets. Where did they come from? My god, does everybody with cougar pets come to the Upper Peninsula to release them? Almost every cougar pet is declawed. So how would they be killing deer?"

Minnesota: Minneapolis — a security camera photographed a cougar in one of the city's western suburbs (July 1996); Jacobson — a homeowner shot a female with two cubs after the cat attacked his dog (August 2001); Savage — a cougar tripped an infrared camera while eating a deer outside town, 10 miles from Minneapolis (April 2002); Bloomington — a security guard shot a cougar on a popular walking path (May 2002); Big Detroit Lake — the Department of Natural Resources admitted a cougar was responsible for injuring a horse (June 2002); Courtland — a large cat killed a goat and eight RABBITS on a farm outside town. State spokesmen agreed that it was "probably" a cougar (July 2002); La Salle — further sightings were recorded (July 2002); Kent — multiple sightings were reported to authorities (March 2003).

Missouri: Houston — a cougar pelt with head and feet attached was found beside a highway outside town. DNA tests were ordered to trace the cat's origin, but no results were published (November 1998); Lewis County — a cougar was videotaped in the wild (January 2002); Kansas City — a motorist on the north side of town struck and killed a male cougar (October 2002); Fulton — a 105-pound male cougar with "no signs of having been in captivity" was killed by a hit-and-run motorist (11 August 2003); Overland Park — residents reported another cougar prowling residential neighborhoods (22 August 2003); King City — yet another cougar sighting was recorded (24 August 2003); Independence — police answered reports of a "dead lion" beside Interstate 70 but found no cat (25 October 2003).

Nebraska: Grand Island — a cougar was killed near a public school (2000); Howard County — at least seven more sightings followed the school incident (2000-02); Saline County — 24 farmers reported cougar sightings (2000-02); Friend — a cougar was seen, and a 3.5-inch pawprint was found, near the site where a calf was partially devoured (November 2002); state authorities acknowledged 11 "confirmed" cougar sightings between 1991 and July 2002; Omaha — zoo employees armed with tranquilizer guns captured an 80-pound male cougar in a city park (1 October 2003); Lincoln — two residents sighted a cougar near their home (6 November 2003)

New Hampshire: Stewardstown — repeated sightings of a 3-foot cougar were recorded (winter 1992-93); Moultonboro — a biologist found suspected cougar scat in the woods outside town (December 2001). A year later, he was still waiting for DNA test results from the Michigan Wildlife Foundation.

New Jersey: Although cougars have been officially extinct in the Garden State for over 100 years, an average of 12-15 sightings are reported each year from the Pinelands in southern New Jersey; Salem County — David Owens, a member of the EASTERN COUGAR NETWORK, sighted a cat at Carneys Point (January 2002); Burlington County — two witnesses sighted a cougar near Mount Misery (April 2002).

New York: Rouses Point — large pawprints were found at a local cemetery (June 2002); Morrisonville — three witnesses reported a cougar at large (18 August 2003); Oneida — multiple witnesses reported a large cat on the northwest side of town (October 2003); despite ongoing reports from six Catskills counties, the state Department of Environmental Conservation dismisses all reports, comparing wild cougars to BIGFOOT and NESSIE as mythical creatures.

North Carolina: After reviewing "hundreds of reports" spanning a quarter-century, the Division of Wildlife Management publicly admitted that cougars were returning to the Tarheel State (December 2001). Private researcher Charles Humphreys Jr., a member of the Eastern Cougar Network, reported that half of the 500 sightings contained in his personal files describe sightings of "black panthers."

Ohio: St. Clairesville — multiple witnesses reported a cougar prowling farms on the outskirts of town (September 2003).

Oklahoma: Roger Mills County — a deer hunter killed a cougar (1982); Cimarron County — two more cougars were shot (1990s); Newkirk — a cougar twice appeared at Karina Jackson's home on the Arkansas River, attacking her the second time, when she tried to defend some puppies (September 2002).

Pennsylvania: Tarentum — a long series of cougar sightings by local residents began (July 1979); Tarentum — a Pittsburgh TV film crew captured a cougar on videotape (June 1982); Philadelphia — multiple sightings were reported from the city's western suburbs (1990s); Thornberry — two residents reported a cougar in their backyard (May 1998); Woodland Township — a cougar trespassed on the grounds of Chatsworth Elementary School (May 2001); Wayne County — in the midst of multiple cougar sightings, a large tan-colored cat was photographed by local residents (August 2003); Northampton Township — Bucks County police searched in vain for another reported cougar roaming in Tyler State Park (October-November 2003); Lancaster County — residents reported cougar sightings around Welsh Mountain (October 2003); Philadelphia — a veteran hunter reported a cougar near his home in Kennett Square (10 November 2003).

Rhode Island: South County — three residents reported cougar sightings, while authorities insisted they had actually seen coyotes (September 2003); Saunderstown — witness Steven Kelly reported a cougar mauling a deer outside his home, but police once again blamed coyotes (10 September 2003).

South Carolina: Mauldin — a resident reported a cougar with cubs prowling around her property (October 2003).

Tennessee: Great Smoky Mountains National Park — multiple sightings were recorded, spanning a decade (1990s); Sugarlands — a cougar was seen nearby (May 2002); Great Smoky Mountains — a park wildlife biologist told the press, "We've had some observations, reports, of big cats every year, every single year. Nothing's confirmed" (August 2002).

Vermont: Berlin — a 4-foot cougar was reported (1946); Craftsbury — game wardens found scat, pawprints and other confirmed evidence of cougar activity (1994-95).

Virginia: Dickenson County — the state legislature authorized payment of $2,500 to a farmer whose 25 goats were killed by a cougar (1998); Blue Ridge Parkway — motorists sighted an adult cougar (summer 2002); Wytheville — Professor Don Linzey, a member of the Eastern Cougar Network, reported that he has collected 384 cougar sightings since the early 1970s. Linzey rated 167 as reliable, including 69 with multiple witnesses (2002).

West Virginia: Pocahontas County — a large male cougar was killed after mauling a farmer's sheep. A pregnant female was captured alive two days later, but the state Department of Natural Resources has "lost" its records of the case (April 1976).

Wisconsin: Manitowoc County — more than a dozen sightings were recorded, while state DNR spokesmen insisted, "There are no wild cougars in Wisconsin" (summer 2001); Vernon County — two hikers met a cougar on the Bad Axe River (June 2002); Romance — another sighting was recorded (June 2002); Marinette County — two fishermen watched a large fawn-colored cat run across an open field (August 2003); Two Rivers — police recorded two cougar sightings along the West Twin River (September 2003); Sturgeon Bay — multiple reports were filed of a cougar prowling the city's northwest side (September 2003); Berlin — another cougar was reported at large (September 2003); Green Lake — cougar reports spread to this community while police searched in vain (October 2003)

Canada: Albert and St. John Counties, New Brunswick — clear tracks of an adult cougar and two cubs were found (March 1947); Fredericton, New Brunswick — motorists reported a daylight sighting on the highway west of town (September 1966); Waasis, New Brunswick — a cougar was videotaped in the nearby forest (spring 1990); Gaspé Peninsula, Québec — officials from the Ministry of Natural Resources found cougar fur and feces (Mary 1999); Vinton, Ontario — multiple cougar sightings were reported (April-October 2002); Braeside, Ontario — local residents sighted a cougar in the neighborhood (October 2002); Arnprior, Ontario — more sightings were recorded (October 2002); St. Andrews West, Ontario — an "immense cat" was seen in the area where a horse was fatally mauled. MNR spokesmen admitted it was "probably" a cougar (October 2002); St. Martins, New Brunswick — a cougar sighting rallied police, who searched in vain for the cat (September 2003).

Sources: Mike Ackerman, "Neighbors warily watch for cougar." *Oneida* (NY) *Dispatch* (9 October 2003); Stephanie Arnold, "Cougars again making tracks, residents say." *Philadelphia Inquirer* (3 December 2003); Daniel Bader, "Residential sighting of mountain lion spurs concern." *Plattsburgh* (NY) *Press-Republican* (19 August 2003); Peter Becker, "'Big cat' sightings continue." *Wayne* (PA) *Independent* (29 August 2003);

Peter Becker, "Mountain lion on the loose?" *Wayne* (PA) *Independent* (21 October 2003); Marilyn Bellemore, "Deer-killing mystery: A 'big cat' or coyotes?" *Kent County* (RI) *Daily Times* (18 September 2003); Marilyn Bellemore, "More 'cougar' sightings reported to newspaper." *Wakefield* (RI) *Standard Times* (25 September 2003); Paul Bird, "Ferocious wildcat chews up Buick." *Indianapolis Star* (8 May 2003); Elizabeth Boch, "Mystery cat has Westford wondering about mountain lions." *Boston Globe* (20 June 2003); Karen Bouffard, "Mystery feline tangles with dogs." *Detroit News* (2 January 2004); Scott Brand, "Local discovery offers few clues." *Sault Ste. Marie* (MI) *Evening News* (7 May 2002); Greg Breining, "Are cougars moving east?" *Minneapolis Star-Tribune* (29 June 2003); Paul Brinkmann, "Latest 'cougar' sighting steps up hunt in Sturgeon Bay area." *Green Bay* (WI) *Press-Gazette* (26 September 2003); Ed Brock, "Cat catch fever is on." *Clayton County* (GA) *News Daily* (15 November 2002); Ed Brock, "Huge feline spotted in Clayton subdivision." *Henry County* (GA) *Daily Herald* (9 November 2002); Ed Brock, "State wildlife officials to take over search for cat." *Clayton County* (GA) *News Daily* (22 November 2002); "Car hits, kills mountain lion in Missouri." *Lawrence* (KS) *Journal-World* (13 August 2003); Eric Carlson, "Cougar verified in Lakeshore; one may live near Empire." *Leelanau* (MI) *Enterprise* (25 January 2003); Tom Carney, "State has cat fight on its hands." *Michigan Outdoor News* (7 March 2003); Jesse Claeys, "Ireton farmers kill mountain lion." *Sioux City* (Iowa) *Journal* (25 October 2003); Jennifer Cording, "Search for panther continues on island." *Chincoteague* (MA) *Beacon* (29 January 2003); Tom Dalton, "Mysterious cat kills deer." *Salem* (MA) *News* (23 September 2003); Barbara Dempsey, "Mystery cat seen near Niles home." *South Bend* (IN) *Tribune* (11 February 2002); "Door County stays wary of possible loose cougar." *Appleton* (WI) *Post-Crescent* (18 September 2003); James Dornbrook, "Dead lion spotted." *Independence* (MO) *Examiner* (27 October 2003); Pat Durkin, "Cougar study not viable option." *Oshkosh* (WI) *Northwestern* (2 November 2003); Dan Egan, "Cougar sightings: Ghosts of a predator past." *Milwaukee* (WI) *Journal-Sentinel* (29 November 2003); Dan Egan, "Residents report big cat sightings." *Milwaukee Journal-Sentinel* (4 October 2003); Kelly Egan, "Farmer says cougar did it." *Ottawa Citizen* (7 December 2002); Kelly Egan, "'Immense feline' spotted near Arnprior." *Ottawa Citizen* (18 October 2002); Kelly Egan, "Ontario's great cougar mystery." *Ottawa Citizen* (22 October 2002); Henry Farber, "Sightings of Clayton County's exotic big cat mount." *Atlanta Journal Constitution* (16 November 2002); Erin Fitzgerald, "Overland Park investigates cougar sighting." *Kansas City Star* (26 August 2003); Thomas Fraser, "Study may answer questions about cougars in park." *Maryville* (TN) *Daily Times* (30 May 2002); Austin Gelder, "Hunter's remote camera captures picture of mountain lion." *Arkansas Democrat-Gazette* (23 August 2003); "The 'ghost' cat of Michigan." WXMI-TV, Grand Rapids (7 November 2002); Eric Hahn, "Cougar on the prowl?" *Detroit Lakes* (MN) *Tribune* (19 June 2002); Robin Harned, "More sightings of cat-like animal in Rutland." *Holden* (MA) *Landmark* (9 October 2003); Janel Hartman, "Residents encounter mountain lion." *Martins Ferry* (OH) *Times Leader* (24 September 2003); Syd Herman, "Cougar stories sound familiar." *Manitowoc* (WI) *Herald Times Reporter* (13 October 2002); Mitch Hotts, "Cougar unlikely in north Macomb." *Macomb* (MI) *Daily* (26 September 2003); Mitch Hotts, "Police investigate cougar sighting in north Macomb." *Macomb* (MI) *Daily* (16 September 2003); Isak Howell, "Mountain lions are the Sasquatch of the Appalachians." *Roanoke* (VA) *Times* (21 October 2002); Erica Jacobson, "Sightings keep Vermont's catamount debate alive." *Burlington* (VT) *Free Press* (18 August 2002); Cathy Johnston, "Additional mountain lion sightings are reported." *Lowell* (MA) *Sun* (9 July 2003); Ray Kisonas, "Cougar sightings lack proof, DNR officials say." *Monroe* (MI) *Evening News* (17 June 2003); Bob Lamb, "Cougar sighting near Romance second in area." *La Crosse* (WI) *Tribune* (28 June 2002); Jeff Lampe, "Mountain lion sightings no joke anymore." *Peoria* (IL) *Journal Star* (20 December 2002); Jim Lee, "Mountain lions in Michigan?" *Wisconsin Rapids Daily Tribune* (5 January 2003); Mary Loden, "Are large predator cats returning to Iowa?" *Mitchell County* (IA) *Press-News* (12 June 2003); Suzanne Moore, "Wild-cat signs found." *Plattsburgh* (NY) *Press Republican* (9 June 2002); "Mountain lion killed in western Iowa." KETV-7, Omaha (28 August 2001); Robb Murray, "Dealing with a hidden predator." *Mankato* (MN) *Free Press* (21 July 2002); "Mysterious visitor roaming western Iowa." KETV-7, Omaha (1 August 2003); "Mystery feline blamed for damage, animal deaths." WRTV Indianapolis (13 May 2003); "Officials clawing for answers in cat attack." *Fort Wayne* (IN) *News-Sentinel* (8 May 2003); Bill O'Brien, "Man reports seeing cougar on side of road." *Traverse City* (MI) *Record-Eagle* (17 September 2003); Elaine O'Connor, "Unsolved mysteries: Can you help?" *Ottawa Citizen* (2 January 2003); Jamie Olmstead, "Lion seen in city." *Torrington* (CT) *Register Citizen* (9 November 2002); Mike Penprase, "Cougars are here, but difficult to find, track." *Springfield* (MO) *News-Leader* (7 September 2003); Don Porter, "Developer says he, too, has spotted a cougar." *South Bend* (IN) *Tribune* (6 July 2002); Phil Potter, "'Extinct' animals may not be gone." *Evansville* (IN) *Courier Press* (5 October 2003); Krista Primrose, "Wabash man reports seeing cougar." *Kosciusko County* (IN) *Times-Union* (23 August 2003); Neil Rhines, "Have cougars 'invaded' Two Rivers?" *Manitowoc* (WI) *Herald Times Reporter* (16 September 2003); Terri Sanginiti, "Cougar-like cat seen near Hockessin." *Wilmington* (DE) *News Journal* (10 October 2003); Terri Sanginiti, "Cougar sightings reported near mall." *Wilmington* (DE) *News Journal* (27 November 2003); Steve Sansone, "Biologist: Cougar sightings no shock." *St. Joseph* (MO) *News-Press* (21 September 2003); Steve Sansone, "Now, I'm a believer." *St. Joseph* (MO) *News-Press* (31 August 2003); Brian Saxon, "Mountain lion sighting reported." *Danbury* (CT) *News-Times* (21 February 2003); Mark Schieldrop, "Does a 'big cat' prowl South County?" *Narragansett* (RI) *Times* (17 September 2003); Chris Sebastian, "Cougar sighting adds to state's big-cat debate." *Muskegon Chronicle* (2 August 2002); Sonia Sharigian, "More people claim to see mountain lion." *Westford* (MA) *Eagle* (19 June 2003); Eric Sharp, "Odd cat fight breaks out after animal attacks." *Detroit Free Press* (28 September 2002); Eric Sharp, "Officials deny cougars in Michigan." *Detroit Free Press* (6 October 2002); Eric Sharp, "Tracking down the ghost cats of the north woods." *Detroit Free Press* (15 November 2001); Ruth Sheehan, "Cougar reports mount." *Jefferson City* (MO) *News Tribune* (4 February 2001); Ruth Sheehan, "Sightings of panthers spur talk of big cat's return to N.C." *Raleigh* (NC) *News & Observer* (7 December 2001); Karl Shuker, "Alien zoo." *Fortean Times* 121 (April 1999): 18-19; April Silvaggio, "Greenville County natives say big cats have been here for years." *Greenville* (SC) *News* (25 October 2003); Tom Spoth, "Wildlife expert doubts area's cougar craze." *Lowell* (MA) *Sun* (21 June 2003); Tom Spoth and Jack Minch, "Meandering mountain lion apparently crosses the border." *Lowell* (MA) *Sun* (19 June 2003); Don Stacom, "Big cat sighting reported by driver." *Hartford* (CT) *Courant* (10 April 2003); Rebecca Svec, "Big cat sighting outside Friend is unconfirmed." *Lincoln* (NE) *Journal Star* (7 December 2002); Deborah Swift, "The wildest of all." *Hartford* (CT) *Courant* (8 June 2003); Marie Szaniszlo, "Mountain lion sightings raise roar in Rochester." *Boston Herald* (18 August 2002); Roselyn Tantraphol, "Cat sightings 'phantoms.'" *Hartford* (CT) *Courant* (12 September 2002); Roselyn Tantraphol, "A dogged pursuit of the big cat." *Hartford* (CT) *Courant* (17 September 2002); Roselyn Tantraphol, "3rd mountain lion sighting reported by Somers resident." *Hartford* (CT) *Courant* (11 September 2002); Bob Themer, "'Big cat' believed to be prowling rural Watseka garden." *East St. Louis* (IL) *Daily Journal* (27 June 2002); Kate Thompson, "Cougars return to a changed Iowa." *Boston Globe* (31 March 2002); Dave Toplikar, "Big game on campus." *Lawrence* (KS) *Journal-World* (8 October 2003); Mac Trueman, "Hunter sure of cougar sighting." *St. John* (N.B.) *Telegraph-Journal* (6 September 2003); Rebecca Tsaros. "Could a cougar lurk among us?" *Concord* (NH) *Monitor* (1 December 2002); Anthony Twyman, "Big cat-and-mouse game." *Newark* (NJ) *Star-Ledger* (6 May 2002); Todd Von Kampen, "Big-cat tales get warden's support." *Omaha* (NE) *World-Herald* (22 June 2003); Jolene Walters and Mike Ackerman, "Woman says she's seen 2nd cougar." *Oneida* (NY) *Dispatch* (17 October 2003); Wayne White, "Was it a cougar?" *Newkirk* (OK) *Herald Journal* (27 September 2002); Shelly Whitehead, "Cougar sightings reported in Kenton County." *Cincinnati Post* (19 September 2003); "Wild animal caught." *Topeka* (KS) *Capital-Journal* (2 October 2003); Greg Wilkerson, "Biologist suspects cougars

live in Smokies." *Maryville* (TN) *Daily Times* (11 August 2002); Garvey Winegar, "Cougar sighting worth believing." *Richmond* (VA) *Times-Dispatch* (29 October 2003); Heather Yakin, "No lions? Oh my! Catskills have no big cats, DEC says." *Middleton* (NY) *Times Herald-Record* (18 December 2002); Kevin Zimmerman, "Lion sighting calls continue this week." *Chelmsford* (MA) *Independent* (25 June 2003).

Eastern Cougar Network The EASTERN COUGAR Network (ECN) was created in 2002 by founders Jim Close, Mark Dowling, Ken Miller and Bob Wilson. Its goal is documentation of surviving cougars (*Puma concolor*) in the eastern half of North America, where the CATS are officially deemed extinct. Reports of cougar sightings, pawprints and the like are collected and published on the ECN's Internet website. The group credits its ongoing success in data collection to the support of government and private wildlife professionals in the U.S. and Canada. Witnesses may report sightings to the ECN via e-mail at info@eastern-cougarnet.org.

Source: Eastern Cougar Network, http://www.easterncougarnet.org/.

Eastern Ohio Bigfoot Investigation Center The EOBIC was founded by DONALD KEATING of Newcomerstown, Ohio (Tuscarawas County) after a personal BIGFOOT sighting in September 1985. In addition to maintaining an Internet website for reports of Bigfoot sightings, Keating has hosted the Annual Bigfoot Conference in Newcomerstown since 1989. Keating stresses that the EOBIC is "not just looking for reports from Ohio, but anywhere in the United States or Canada!" An online reporting form is provided at the Center's website. At some point in the 1990s, Keating changed the group's name to the Tri-State Bigfoot Study Group. By 2002, he appeared to use the names interchangeably.

Source: Eastern Ohio Bigfoot Information Center, http://www.angelfire.com/oh/ohiobigfoot/home.html; Tri-State Bigfoot Study Group, http://www.angelfire.com/oh/ohiosasquatch/tsbsg.html.

Eastern Puma Research Network *see* **Lutz, John**

Eccles Cheetah A resident of Eccles, in Norfolk, England reported an ALIEN BIG CAT sighting in July 1987. According to the witness, the creature most closely resembled an African cheetah (*Acinonyx jubatus*).

Source: Wallis, "British big cats."

A cheetah sighting was reported from Norfolk, England in 1987.

Eccles sea serpent On 5 August 1936, five witnesses observed an unknown SEA SERPENT swimming off the coast of Eccles, Norfolk, England. Those present included H.E. Witard (chairman of the Norwich Watch Committee and former Lord Mayor of Norwich), Charles Ammon (a member of Parliament), and a former M.P. named A. Gosling. According to Witard's report in the *Daily Mirror*:

We were standing on the beach at 7:25 in the evening when I noticed an unusual form travelling swiftly about one mile from the shore in a northerly direction. I am an old sailor and could not be deceived by a shoal of porpoises. It was a serpent beyond question.

Looking at it from a distance, it appeared to be about thirty or forty feet in length and was skimming the surface of the water in a wormlike movement. Its speed was terrific. It would not be an exaggeration to say it was anything from ninety to 100 miles an hour. It was a perfectly clear evening and we watched it take a straight line parallel with the coast.

Upon reading Witard's account, Colin King wrote to report a sighting at Eccles between 2:00 and 3:00 p.m., when he saw "a black SNAKE or wormlike object travelling at a terrific speed on the surface of the water, about half a mile or so out, going in the direction of Happisburgh." While reluctant to dismiss the sightings entirely, BERNARD HEUVELMANS concluded that Witard's estimate of the creature's speed was greatly exaggerated, suggesting that he may have seen a flight of sea BIRDS skimming the surface.

Source: Heuvelmans, *In the Wake of the Sea Serpents*.

Edgerton, Harold Eugene (1903–1990)

Harold ("Doc") Edgerton enrolled as a student at the Massachusetts Institute of Technology in 1926 and was affiliated with the school in various capacities for the remainder of his life. In the late 1920s, he invented stop-motion photography by means of flashing stroboscopic light that enabled cameras to "freeze" bullets and hummingbirds in flight. During World War II, Edgerton devised a process of aerial night-flash photography that proved invaluable for surveillance of Normandy's beaches before the D-Day invasions of 6 June 1944. A generation later, in the 1970s, his techniques were applied to the search for NESSIE by ROBERT RINES and the ACADEMY OF APPLIED SCIENCE. Edgerton encouraged Rines (a lifelong family friend) in his research at Loch Ness, and his last article — concerning underwater photography at the loch — was published in Volume 8 of the journal *Cryptozoology* (1989). Edgerton died of a heart attack at age 86, on 4 January 1990.

Source: Robert Rines, "Harold E. 'Doc' Edgerton, 1903-1990." *ISC Newsletter* 9 (Spring 1990): 8-9.

Edward Waite sea serpent

On 18 February 1884, sailors aboard the schooner *Edward Waite* spent 30 minutes watching an unidentified SEA SERPENT in the Atlantic near Cape Henry, North Carolina (north of Cape Hatteras). Witnesses estimated the creature's length at 90 feet, saying it swam with its horselike head above water, leaving a long, broad wake. Ship's mate William Page told reporters the animal's saffron-colored eyes were "half as big as a man's hand."

Source: O'Neill, *The Great New England Sea Serpent*.

Eelpoot

This foul-smelling resident of Maryland's Zekiah Swamp (in Charles County) is also sometimes called the Hane-turtle, the Hoopinflinder, or the Lun. The swamp is 20 miles long and a half-mile wide at its broadest point. Descriptions of the Eelpoot are vague, supporting suggestions that it may belong more to rural folklore than to science.

Source: Amy Compton, "Tales of the Zekiah Swamp." *Maryland Magazine* 7 (Spring 1975): 14-17.

Eels (Giant)

Throughout history, various witnesses have compared unknown SEA SERPENTS to gigantic eels. The serpentine shape is correct, and for many theorists it is easier to imagine a common creature grown to freakish size than to speculate on species as yet unknown. Authors Maurice Burton and ROY MACKAL have also proposed that huge eels may account for sightings of NESSIE and other LAKE MONSTERS. The largest known eels are the conger and the moray. Congers (*Conger conger* or *Conger oceanicus*) typically reside in the Atlantic and the Mediterranean, attaining an official maximum length of nine feet, though author Charles Gould has cited anecdotal reports of 20-foot specimens caught off Singapore. Most morays (*Muraenidae* sp.) do not exceed six feet in length, but a Pacific species (*Thyrsoidea macrurus*) may reach 11.5 feet. Even those whoppers fall far short of "monster" dimensions, but a potential candidate emerged from the Atlantic depths in 1930.

On 31 January of that year, oceanographers aboard the *Dana* made a surprising catch between Saint Helena and the Cape of Good Hope, at 35° 42' south latitude and 18° 37' east longitude. Rising from a depth of 900 feet, their net revealed a leptocephalus (eel larva) six feet long. Marine biologist Anton Bruun calculated that if the leptocephalus grew at a rate common to known pelagic eels, its adult form would measure 18-30 times the larva's length, for a mature length of 108 to 180 feet! A critic of Bruun's, French ichthyologist Léon Bertin, dismissed those calculations as "absolutely absurd," noting that different eel species mature at various rates. The controversy endured for 40 years, until 1970, when Miami ichthyologist David Smith finally identified the *Dana* specimen as the larva of a spiny eel (Order *Notacanthiformes*), which barely exceeds the length of its larva at maturity.

Still, speculation on the possible existence of giant eels at sea continues. BERNARD HEUVELMANS, writing two years before the Miami University discovery, listed a "Super-Eel" among his nine categories of hypothetical sea serpents. Heuvelmans suspected giant eels in 23 of 401 apparently reliable "serpent" sightings logged between 1666 and 1966, but he acknowledged that eyewitness estimates of size were probably exaggerated by as much as 100 percent, leaving the true Super-Eel with a maximum length around 50 feet. Heuvelmans believed they were responsible for most reports of sea serpents coiled on the surface, a habit common to some conger eels.

And indeed, reports of giant eels are not confined to the oceans of the world. In August 1997, reporters in Birmingham, England headlined accounts of a of a 20-foot eel, "black, with little beady eyes," reported lurking in the city's Gas Street canal. Several local fishermen reported sightings of the creature, but it managed to avoid their baited hooks.

Sources: "Dutch whopper." *Fortean Times* 91 (October 1996): 10; Ellis, *Monsters of the Sea*; Heuvelmans, *In the Wake of the Sea Serpents*; Karl Shuker, "Alien zoo." *Fortean Times* 107 (February 1998): 15; Shuker, "Bring me the head of the sea serpent!"

Effingham Inlet carcass

On 2 December 1947, Canadian fisherman Henry Schwarz found the skeletal remains of a huge sea creature on the rocky shore of Effingham Inlet, a part of Barkley Sound, on the west coast of Vancouver Island, British Columbia. As described by BERNARD HEUVELMANS in 1968:

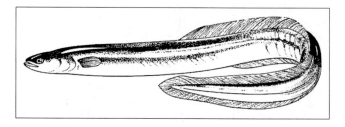

Giant eels are often suggested as sea serpent candidates.

It had a head the size of a sheep's attached to a spinal column at least 40 feet long…. There was a skull 1 foot 2 inches long by 8½ inches wide, and oddly lacking in teeth, and some 145 cylindrical vertebrae, the largest being 6 inches in diameter, and the smallest, at the end, only 1½ inches.

PAUL LEBLOND'S brief account of the case confirms the number of vertebrae but adds 5 feet to the skeleton's length. On 8 December, the *Vancouver Daily Press* reported that two staffers from the Dominion fisheries biological station at Nanaimo had examined the skeleton *in situ* and removed two vertebrae for further study. Those experts, R.E. Foerster and A.L. Tester, initially opined that the creature was a large oarfish (*Regalecus glesnae*), then stated that "[t]he skeleton is definitely not of the whale family. Some parts are of a type similar to a SHARK skeleton, but the head is too small and the vertebrae too numerous for it to be a shark." Nonetheless, Heuvelmans reports that Foerster and Tester finally identified the specimen as a basking shark (*Cetorhinus maximus*)—despite the troublesome fact that such sharks normally possess only 103 vertebrae. If it was not in fact a SEA SERPENT, a basking shark with 42 extra vertebrae clearly qualifies as a cryptid in its own right.

Sources: Heuvelmans, *In the Wake of the Sea Serpents*; LeBlond and Bousfield, *Cadborosaurus.*

Egilsstadirvatn, Iceland

Ancient reports of a local LAKE MONSTER are memorialized with a serpentine form on Egilsstadirvatn's official coat of arms, but no modern sightings suggest that the creature survives today.

Source: A Trip to Iceland, http://www.chez.com/barkokhba/fire.htm.

Elbst

A Swiss LAKE MONSTER, reported over a span of four centuries from the Selisbergsee (in Canton Uri), the Elbst made its first appearance in 1585 and was sighted sporadically thereafter until 1926. The last witnesses to report a sighting were construction workers building a new road beside the lake. In its heyday, locals described the Elbst as a reddish-colored reptile, covered with scales, whose head was the size of a pig's. Some reports include short legs and clawed feet. According to folklore, the creature sometimes came ashore at night, to prey on cattle. The Elbst's overall resemblance to other long-necked cryptids is emphasized by the origin of its name, apparently derived from the old German *albiz* ("swan").

Source: Josef Müller, *Sagen aus Uri aus dem Volksmunde Gesammelt.* Basel, Switzerland: Gesellschaft für Folkskunde, 1926.

Electra sea serpent

In 1935, crewmen aboard the U.S. Coast Guard vessel *Electra* sighted a SEA SERPENT off the coast of Norfolk, Virginia. Lieutenant W.C. Hogan described the creature as 40-50 feet long, with six dorsal fins, each 2 feet tall and 2 feet 6 inches wide at the base. Despite several shots being fired, the animal seemed unconcerned.

Source: Heuvelmans, *In the Wake of the Sea Serpents.*

Elephant sea serpent

On 15 November 1819, sailors aboard the British brig *Elephant* allegedly met a school of SEA SERPENTS in the North Sea. Reports of the incident later reached France, where this account was published in the *Censeur Européen* of 3 February 1820.

Yesterday, about 5 o'clock in the morning, under shortened sail, our ship received a great shock: the men on watch thought that we had struck a rock or shoal. We were, however, more than 300 miles from land. At once everyone rushed on deck, and, as we sought the cause of our alarm, we saw in the light of the moon,

several sea-monsters of dreadful size which were thrashing about around us. One of them was so near the ship, that it threw up such a strong wake that it broke on deck and knocked two men off their feet. At break of day we saw more than 20 of these monsters around us. We noticed one in particular which was more than 50 feet long. It advanced with fury towards the ship on the starboard side. A gunlayer, seizing the instant when it opened its mouth, aimed so well that the ball went straight in. The monster swam and expired, the noise of the cannon putting the others to flight. We then lowered the longboat and succeeded in towing the animal, which we recognized as a Sea-Serpent like those that have been talked about; it was 100 feet long: we cut it up, and I have preserved the tusks to make you a present when I return to England.

BERNARD HEUVELMANS noted that no part of the creature was ever delivered, to England or anywhere else, and he rightly dismissed the report as a HOAX.

Source: Heuvelmans, *In the Wake of the Sea Serpent.*

Elephant-Dung Bat

This curious cryptid, reported from Mount Kulal and the Marsabit Forest of Kenya, is known only from two brief sightings by explorer Terence Adamson in the 1950s. Adamson described the animal as a small BAT with silver or gray fur on its back, lighter on the underside. The specimens observed had a wingspan of five inches or less. Adamson named the bat for its alleged practice of roosting on the ground, in piles of dried elephant dung, but two sightings hardly qualify the behavior as habitual. KARL SHUKER suggests that Adamson may have seen the horn-skinned bat (*Eptesicus floweri*), which typically nests on the ground amongst acacia roots. Horned-skin bats inhabit Mali and Sudan, the latter country being one of Kenya's northern neighbors.

Sources: John Williams, "An unsolved mystery." *Animals* 10 (June 1967): 73-75; Shuker, "A belfry of crypto-bats."

Elisabeth sea serpent

On 26 July 1883, officers aboard the German corvette *Elisabeth* sighted a SEA SERPENT in the South Atlantic off Libreville, Gabon (West Africa). Captain Hollmann noted the incident in his log as follows:

Five p.m. Saw a school of cetaceans of various sizes and among them an animal the shape and movements of which recalled a big serpent. Its colour was whitish, and it often raised its head and neck 10 to 18 feet above the waves, while the rest of its body appeared in the form of numerous coils.

One of the ship's officers, Kapitän-Leutnant Wislicenus, watched the creature through binoculars for 20 minutes, afterward reporting that it was 50-65 feet long, with a spear-shaped head and a black-and-white "double tail" some 20 feet long.

Source: Heuvelmans, *In the Wake of the Sea Serpents.*

Elizabeth Lake, California

Elizabeth Lake, in Los Angeles County, produced reports of a predatory LAKE MONSTER throughout the 19th century. Don Chico Lopez allegedly sighted the creature in the early 1880s, describing it as possessing both flippers and wings like a BAT'S. In 1886, Don Felipe Rivera reported that a veritable DRAGON, 45 foot long, with wings and six pairs of legs, had killed and partially devoured one of his steers. Other tales describe a more "conventional" giant SNAKE, renowned for eating calves and sheep. On balance, those stories gave the lake a dark reputation that endures to this day, although no modern sightings are on file.

Source: Jason Song, "At a remote forest lake, monstrous legends spawn." *Los Angeles Times* (6 January 2001).

Elkhart Lake, Wisconsin   Located 15 miles west of Sheboygan, in the northwest corner of Sheboygan County, Elkhart Lake was the reputed home of a LAKE MONSTER in the 19th century. The best-known eyewitness account, from the 1890s, stressed the creature's large jaws without providing further significant details. The absence of modern reports suggests extinction, if the animal(s) ever existed.

Source: Brown, *Sea Serpents: Wisconsin Occurrences of These Weird Water Monsters.*

Elli   Elli was the media nickname of an ALIEN BIG CAT reported in the summer of 1992, from the forests around Ruokolahti, Finland. The first sighting, logged on 22 June by forestry official Martti Arvinen, described a felid resembling a female LION. Numerous reports were filed over the next week, including reports of large pawprints and the discovery of a half-eaten juvenile moose. The CAT was never photographed, and sightings tapered off in mid-July.

Source: Rosén, "Out of Africa: Are there lions roaming Finland?"

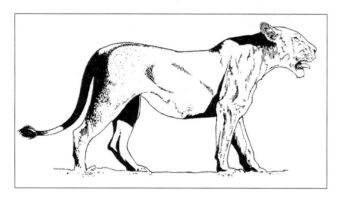

Finnish witnesses sighted a lioness, nicknamed Elli, in 1992.

Ellinggårdskilen, Norway   Legend has it that this lake, in Norway's Østfold County, once hosted a night-prowling LAKE MONSTER prone to crawling from the water after sundown, leaving tracks "as deep as a ditch" in the surrounding fields. If true, the creature and its progeny are now presumably extinct, since no reports are known from modern times.

Source: Skjelsvik, "Norwegian lake and sea monsters."

Elliott's Sicklebill   Elliott's sicklebill (*Epimachus ellioti*) is one of six BIRDS discovered on Papua New Guinea in the 19th century and never seen again. In 1930, Erwin Stresemann dismissed all six as hybrids of other species, but modern ornithologists believe his judgment may have been hasty. The sicklebill's present status is unknown.

Sources: Fuller, *The Lost Birds of Paradise*; Shuker, *The Beasts That Hide From Man.*

Ellis, Richard (1938–)   New York native Richard Ellis graduated from the University of Pennsylvania in 1959 and soon established himself as a renowned artist, specializing in illustrations of marine animals. His paintings have appeared in the *Encyclopaedia Britannica* and numerous magazines. In 1975 Ellis published his own lavishly-illustrated *Book of Sharks*, hailed in critical reviews as the most popular book ever written on sharks. His interest in cryptozoology dates from the following year, when the first specimen of the new and wholly unexpected megamouth shark (*Megachasma pelagios*) was snared in the Pacific. Commu-

nication with fellow shark researcher EUGENIE CLARK alerted Ellis to the fledgling INTERNATIONAL SOCIETY OF CRYPTOZOOLOGY in 1982, and he soon became a member. Ellis's subsequent publications of interest to cryptozoologists include the books *Great White Shark* (1991, with a chapter on CARCHARODON MEGALODON), *Monsters of the Sea* (1994), and *The Search for the GIANT SQUID* (1998).

Sources: Coleman and Clark, *Cryptozoology A to Z*; Ellis, *Monsters of the Sea.*

Eman River, Sweden   Giant EELS and CATFISH reportedly inhabit this river in southern Sweden. Witness Rolf Rosenkvist met one of the eels at age eight, and described his encounter 70 years later to Swedish cryptozoologist JAN-OVE SUNDBERG. In the early 1930s, Rosenkvist's father took him on a fishing trip "to capture the largest eel you're likely to ever see, my son." By torchlight they found — but failed to catch — a creature "15 feet long, 4 feet wide, with an unusual fin along its body. It had a menacing head, thick and repulsive with large black eyes and wide nostrils." The eel escaped both spear and noose, though Rosenkvist claimed it was later caught by others and proved to be inedible, whereupon its remains were dumped in a swamp to rot. Sundberg's GLOBAL UNDERWATER SEARCH TEAM planned an expedition on the Eman River in July 2003, dubbed Operation Catfish, but the worst flooding since 1928 forced GUST to reschedule the effort for spring 2004.

Source: Global Underwater Search Team, http://www.cryptozoology.st/.

***Emblem* sea serpent**   On 5 August 1885, sailors aboard the Canadian ship *Emblem* met an unidentified SEA SERPENT in the North Atlantic, south of the Azores. Captain Roberts reported that the incident began when a ship's mate saw an object standing upright from the water. A newspaper account continues:

> As the vessel approached the object was discovered to be a large monster with a serpent's head, with from 10 to 12 feet of its body, was raised above the surface of the water as if the animal was leisurely surveying his surroundings. When the *Emblem* approached within a few yards of the monster, he dived his head under the water, allowing, however, his body to float on the surface. Judging from the length of his vessel, Captain Roberts estimates the length of the serpent at about 60 feet, while his girth is equal to that of a large pork barrel. His back was barred, pink and white, but his belly was all white.

Source: Heuvelmans, *In the Wake of the Sea Serpents.*

Emela-Ntouka   An element of confusion surrounds this large cryptid of Central Africa. Witnesses describe the animal as elephant-sized or larger, with thick legs, a stout tail like a CROCODILE'S, and a long horn on its snout. Opinions differ on whether the hairless, reddish-brown creature is a reptile or mammal, but all accounts confirm its herbivorous diet and fondness for lurking in water. Like the RHINOCEROS and hippopotamus, the Emela-Ntouka is frequently foul-tempered and attacks on slight provocation, wielding its horn with sufficient force to disembowel an adult elephant. Its most common name, in fact, is a Bantu phrase meaning "killer of elephants." Other names applied to the creature throughout its broad range translate as "water-elephant" and "forest rhinoceros." Some tribes apparently confuse it with another, MOKELE-MBEMBE, or use that name generically for all large unknowns in the jungle.

The first known report of Emela-Ntouka emerged from Liberia in 1913, when Hans Schomburgk related stories of a from the

Klao tribe, but most accounts come originate farther east and south, from Cameroon, Gabon, the Central African Republic, Congo and Zambia. Cryptozoologists ROY MACKAL and J. RICHARD GREENWELL collected reports of the creature during expeditions in 1980-81. No modern animal matches the Emela-Ntouka's description, but several prehistoric candidates have been proposed. Mackal proposed a relict population of *Centrosaurus* (formerly *Monoclonius*), a 20-foot ceratopsid DINOSAUR from the late Cretaceous period (presumed extinct for 65 million years). A mammalian candidate is *Elasmotherium*, a 16-foot Pleistocene rhinoceros that boasted a 7-foot horn (but no appreciable tail, as described in most reports of the Emela-Ntouka).

Source: Mackal, *A Living Dinosaur?*

Africa's Emela-ntouka resembles a horned dinosaur (***William Rebsamen***).

***Emily Holden* sea serpent**   On 22 August 1875, Captain Frederick York sighted a SEA SERPENT from the schooner *Emily Holden*, in the North Atlantic off Matinicus, Maine. York claimed the animal resembled a cross between a whale and a giant EEL. While trying for a closer look, York struck the creature with his ship, whereupon it lashed at the *Emily Holden* with its tail, then sank out of sight.

Source: O'Neill, *The Great New England Sea Serpent.*

Emmaville Panther   For over half a century, reports of ALIEN BIG CATS have emerged from the region between Emmaville and Uralla (sometimes called New England), in the northeastern corner of New South Wales, Australia. The CATS are typ-

ically (but not always) described as jet black, hence their popular designation as "panthers." Feline pawprints are reported from the district, ranging from the size of a large dog's to those of an adult TIGER. While investigator Paul Cropper notes a sighting from 1911, most reports come in more recent waves: the first lasted from 1956 through 1962; another ran from 1969 to 1973; and yet another occurred during 1988-90. Livestock predation is also reported on occasion, with one rancher claiming 340 sheep killed in 1956–57. A typical witness, Merv Thompson of Kootingal, wrote to Cropper:

> On the 28th of July 1988, I was walking along the New England Highway. At 6:30 a.m. in the morning, I noticed [the panther] walking in the paddock next to the road. It was about 50 m away from me. I sneaked up behind a pine tree on the edge of the road to get a better look at it. The animal was walking very casually, then it kneeled down on all four paws. It was eating something. I watched it for about two minutes. It got up and started to walk towards the fence that was running up the hill to a corner post. It leapt on to the post and over the other side. The animal I saw that morning was too big to be a domestic cat. It was black all over. It was about 2 ft. high, his tail about a metre [39 inches] long. Its body was about one metre long. I had a very clear look at this animal.

Sources: Healy and Cropper, *Out of the Shadows*; Smith, *Bunyips & Bigfoots.*

Emus (Mislocated)   Emus (*Dromaius novaehollandiae*) are the world's second-largest flightless BIRDS, after OSTRICHES. Mature adults may stand 6 foot 6 inches tall and weigh up to 100 pounds, yet run at speeds approaching 40–50 miles per hour. Though native only to Australia, emus are dispersed worldwide to zoos and commercial ranches that raise them for slaughter. It may logically be assumed, therefore, that reports of emus roaming at large across North America refer to escapees from private menageries. And indeed, while several such cases were reported in the 1990s, other documented cases of emus in the wild remain unexplained, with no legal owners identified. A sampling of those incidents includes the following:

23 July 1999—An emu of unknown origin was captured in Waukesha, Wisconsin after dodging cars in the drive-through lane of a local Burger King restaurant. Police corralled the bird after a wild chase on Highway 59.

15 February 2002—A 5½-foot emu appeared at Terry Beedie's home outside Bedford, Indiana, showing no inclination to flee when offered food. Public appeals to the bird's hypothetical owner were fruitless, prompting Beedie to declare, "If someone owns him, I want him to go back to them, but if nobody does, then we want him."

April 2002—Residents of Gillsville, Georgia reported an emu at large, but animal control officers were unable to locate the bird.

29 June 2002—Stearns County sheriff's deputies in Rockville, Minnesota shot and killed an emu after tranquilizer darts failed to bring it down alive. An official statement to the press declared: "Residents of the area have reported emu sightings recently, but authorities have received no reports of missing emus."

28 November 2002—Two more emus were killed by police after fruitless efforts to capture them alive, this time in a farmer's field east of Petersburg, Ontario. Authorities expressed fear that the emus would dart into traffic on a nearby road and cause drivers to crash their cars. Press reports announced that "[t]he owner of the long-legged birds has not been found."

13 April 2003—An emu ran wild through backyards in

Jefferson and Mount Arlington, New Jersey. Police were summoned, but the bird eluded them, finally dashing into traffic on busy Route 80, in Roxbury, where it was struck by a vehicle and killed. Once again, media reports acknowledged, "No one knows where it came from."

4 August 2003— Rick Barnes reported an emu of unknown origin prowling his yard in Hall County, Georgia. Animal control officers deemed the bird too large to transport and made no attempt to capture it. Sightings continued over the next week, while public appeals to the bird's presumed owner went unanswered.

17 October 2003— A 6-foot emu was sighted running at large through the Little Creek subdivision of Pensacola, Florida. Another bird that escaped from its owner on 15 October had already been recaptured. The 17 October sighting remains unexplained, and police failed to locate the emu.

27 October 2003— Police in Atlantic County, New Jersey searched in vain for an emu seen prowling the outskirts of Buena Vista Township. Another bird had been captured in Hamilton Township the previous week, its origin unknown. John Hill, chief of Tri-County Animal Control Services, told reporters, "They've been seen all along, but they just got some publicity. Now everybody's calling. There is nothing in the world we can do but chase them into the woods."

3 March 2004— Two free-roaming emus created a traffic jam in Boyertown, Pennsylvania. One was struck by a car and fatally injured, while the other escaped and was last sighted at nearby New Hanover on 4 March. Media reports described the feathered fugitive as an "escaped emu," while admitting that "exactly where the two birds hail from remains a mystery."

Sources: Pearce Adams, "Homeless emu is on the loose in eastern Hall." *Gianesville (GA) Times* (11 August 2003); John Brand, "Here, emu, emu—yet another loose." Press of Atlantic City (28 October 2003); Brady Gillihan, "Emu 'lands' at area farm." *Bedford (IN) Times-Mail* (16 February 2002); "It gets weird in Wisconsin." *Milwaukee Journal Sentinel* (24 July 1999); Jason McKee, "Authorities can't find evasive emu." *Pottstown (PA) Mercury* (5 March 2004); "Ontario emus evade officers before being shot." *Kitchener-Waterloo Record* (28 November 2002); "Runaway emu shot by Stearns County deputies." *Minneapolis Star Tribune* (1 July 2002); Michael Stewart, "Jogger claims to have seen emu." Pensacola (FL) News Journal (18 October 2003); Bill Swayze, "Big bird meets its maker on Rt. 80." *Newark (NJ) Star-Ledger* (15 April 2003).

Endres Pond, Connecticut On 8 July 1999, a resident of Guilford, Connecticut (10 miles east of New Haven), reported witnessing a "large, scaly creature" snatch a Canada goose below the surface of Endres Pond. He Huang, a genetic biologist at Yale University, announced three sightings of an ALLIGATOR in the pond since summer 1998, but spokesmen for the state's Department of Environmental Protection remained skeptical. "Alligators are not native to Connecticut," said David May, director of the DEP's Wildlife Division. "Often times, what is originally thought to be an alligator turns out to be a snapping TURTLE." Guilford Public Works Director John Volpe was more open-minded, noting that local fishermen had seen the reptile several times. "They said they saw a duck fly onto the pond," Volpe reported, "and the alligator grabbed the duck and did whatever it is that alligators do to ducks." The controversy endures, and the reptile of Endres Pond remains elusive.

Source: "Pond creature remains a mystery." WVIT-TV 30, New Britain, Connecticut (9 July 1999).

Engbé This unclassified primate or HOMINID is said to inhabit the forests of West Africa, specifically parts of Côte d'Ivoire and Sierra Leone (where it is also called Egbéré). The long-haired animal has been mythologized to the point where some accounts describe it building villages and kidnapping humans as prisoners. Confusion is exacerbated by use of the Engbé name to describe a known primate, the mustached MONKEY (*Cercopithecus cephus*) further east, in the Central African Republic.

Source: Gaston Joseph, "Notes sur les Avikams de la lagune de Lahou et les Didas de la région du Bas-Bandama." *Bulletins et Mémoires de a Société Anthropologique de Paris* 1 (1910): 234-247.

Engledow, Bob *see* **Operation Big Cat**

English Rose III sea serpent In the summer of 1966, Captain John Ridgway and Sergeant Chay Blyth rowed across the Atlantic in the *English Rose III.* Shortly before midnight on 25 July, they experienced a remarkable encounter, later described by Ridgway in his book *A Fighting Chance.*

I was lulled by the unending monotony. It was an idyllic night.

I was shocked to full wakefulness by a swishing noise to starboard. I looked out into the water and suddenly saw the writhing, twisting shape of a great creature. It was outlined by the phosphorescence in the sea as if a string of neon lights were hanging from it.

It was an enormous size, some thirty-five or more feet long, and it came towards me quite fast. I must have watched it for some ten seconds. It headed straight for me and disappeared right beneath me.

I stopped rowing. I was frozen with terror at this apparition. I forced myself to turn my head to look over the port side. I saw nothing, but after a brief pause I heard a most tremendous splash.

I thought that this might be the head of the monster crashing into the sea after coming up for a brief look at us. I did not see the surfacing—just heard it.

I am not an imaginative man, and I searched for a rational explanation for this incredible occurrence in the night as I picked up the oars and started rowing again. Chay and I had seen whales and SHARKS, dolphins and porpoises, flying FISH—all sorts of sea creatures but this monster in the night was none of these. I reluctantly had to believe that there was only one thing it could have been—a SEA SERPENT.

Source: John Ridgway and Chay Blyth, *A Fighting Chance.* London: Hamlyn, 1966.

Engôt A large, aggressive primate or HOMINID reported from Gabon, the Engôt is reputed to kill and devour humans on occasion. As with other unknown hominids around the world, some accounts claim that the creature's feet point backwards. Its most common name is the Bantu word for "ogre"; alternate names throughout the animal's reported range include Éngunguré, Enzinzi, Ézôzôme and Ntyii. Some anthropologists believe that legends of the Engôt represent distorted tribal memories of ancient interaction with GORILLAS.

Source: Heuvelmans, *Les bêtes humaines d'Afrique.*

Enkidu This prototypical Middle Eastern WILDMAN appears in the Sumerian *Epic of Gilgamesh*, recounting the adventures of a king who ruled Uruk (modern Erech, Iraq) around 2800 B.C. The shaggy man-beast's name translates roughly from Sumerian as "wild one." Cryptozoologists note the similarity between Enkidu and modern descriptions of mystery HOMINIDS throughout West Asia, including the ABNAUAYU and KAPTAR.

Source: Shackley, *Still Living?*

Ensut-Ensut A large primate or HOMINID of Malaysia, the Ensut-ensut is reported primarily from the Endau-Rompin

Park on the peninsula's east coast. Eyewitnesses describe the creature as bipedal, 9-10 feet tall, and covered in dark brown hair. Its bare footprints average 17.5 inches in length, and once again — as we find so often in Asia and Africa — some witnesses claim the creature's feet are inverted or "backwards." A spate of sightings was reported to forestry officials in spring 2001, after several campers discovered large tracks or claimed personal encounters with the creature(s). A thorough search of the parks 384 square miles proved impractical. A Malaysian press report of May 2001 claimed the most recent sighting was "of the creature running out of a burning jungle with its young one in search of shelter."

Source: Sager Ahmad. "Big-foot sightings." *New Straits Times* (25 April 2001).

Er Hai Lake, China Cryptozoologist JOHN KIRK lists high-altitude Er Hai Lake, in the Cang Shan Mountains of Yunnan Province, as one of several Chinese lakes with modern LAKE MONSTER reports to their credit, but he provides no details and it seems no sightings are available in English-language sources. The lake's secret, like so much else about the Far East cryptid scene, remains shrouded in mystery.

Source: Kirk, *In the Domain of the Lake Monsters.*

Erçek Gölü, Turkey In 1995, witnesses reported a LAKE MONSTER resembling a white amphibious horse from this lake in Turkey's Van Province. No further sightings have been publicly recorded, though another lake 12 miles to the east, Van Gölü, has produced sightings and an alleged videotape of a creature known as the CANAVAR.

Source: Shuker, *From Flying Toads to Snakes with Wings.*

Ernst, William (1945–1998) Florida attorney William ("Ted") Ernst joined colleague ROBERT MORGAN to incorporate the nonprofit AMERICAN ANTHROPOLOGICAL RESEARCH FOUNDATION (AARF) on 11 July 1974. Over the next quarter-century, Ernst and Morgan sponsored numerous searches for Florida's elusive SKUNK APE, as well as expeditions seeking unknown HOMINIDS in Central Asia. The partners retired from public life during the 1980s, while Morgan pursued metaphysical studies "under the auspices of Native American holy men," but they resurfaced in 1991 for an expedition to Moscow, the Russian Caucasus and the Crimea. Accompanied by an exiled Tibetan lama, Ernst and Morgan pursued spiritually-based solutions for the riddle of the ALMAS and YETI. A Mongolian expedition was planned for 1999, but Ernst drowned in the swimming pool at his Key West home on 21 May 1998. Morgan noted Ernst's skill as a swimmer and called the accident "bizarre." A police report on the event called it "unexplainable."

Source: Coleman and Clark, *Cryptozoology A to Z.*

Erongo skeleton In early 2002, while prospecting for crystals in Namibia's Erongo Mountains, a resident of Usakos found the skeleton of an unknown animal embedded in sandstone. The specimen measured 9¾ inches long, with long hind legs and short forelegs, and still had portions of its skin intact. The finder, identified only as "Theophillus," delivered the skeleton to Namibia's Ministry of Environment and Tourism, where it was later examined by an unnamed geologist. That individual declared that the specimen "was definitely not older than 10,000 years," and thus dismissed local speculation that it might be the remains of a DINOSAUR. Beyond that pronouncement, and speculation from a Swakopmund merchant that the creature "might be an unborn animal," the Erongo skeleton remains unidentified today.

Source: Maggi Barnard, "Mystery animal skeleton found." *The Namibian* (3 February 2003).

Esakar-Paki This mystery ungulate of Ecuador resembles a smaller-than-average peccary or javelina (*Tayassu tajacu*), with reddish-brown hair. Witnesses report the animals traveling in groups of 50 to 60, which attack human beings on occasion. Although no specimens have been collected, sightings range from Ecuador's Sangay National Park eastward to the Peruvian border.

Source: Angel Forés, "An investigation into some unidentified Ecuadorian mammals." http://perso.wanadoo.fr/cryptozoo.expeditions/ecuador _eng.htm.

Witnesses describe the Esakar-paki of Ecuador as resembling a miniature peccary.

Essex Big Cat Research Project Reports of an ALIEN BIG CAT, known as the BEAST OF ESSEX, prompted Braintree resident John Hancock to establish the Essex Big Cat Research Project. At one point, early in his research, Hancock was reportedly collecting witness statements at a rate of 12 per month. With 80 sightings on file by March 2003, Hancock felt confident in stating that Essex was home to at least two "black panthers," one lurking near Braintree and another at Stansted. The EBCRP maintained no Internet website at press time for this book, but Hancock invited reports and inquiries to his home. Strangely, despite the project's focus on cryptozoology, it somehow rated listing on multiple Internet directories of UFO groups.

Sources: "Black Notley: New Beast of Essex sighting claim." This is Essex (6 March 2003); International UFO Groups, http://www.aliengif-centre.com/UFOGroups.htm.

Étables sea serpent In the summer of 1939, British subject A.F. Waymark vacationed with his wife and daughter at Étables, on the French Côte-du-Nord (Brittany). One morning, from his balcony, Waymark observed an unknown creature swimming in the English Channel and called to his family. Mrs. Waymark later told BBC correspondent Maurice Brown:

We dashed out and saw what one or two of your contributors to "The Great SEA SERPENT" programme accurately described and what looked like the picture on page 15 of *The Radio Times* (though after this length of time I don't remember the white underneath). A huge creature like a serpent was swimming rapidly along on the surface of the water, weaving in and out and leaving quite a wake after it. We estimated it would be at least 20 feet long—had a splendid view of it and watched it till it was out of sight, swimming towards the Atlantic.

The picture to which Mrs. Waymark referred was a drawing of the creature sighted from the *DAEDALUS* in 1848.

Source: Heuvelmans, *In the Wake of the Sea Serpents.*

Etchemin River, Canada

The Etchemin River, in southeastern Québec, connects Lac Etchemin to the St. Lawrence Seaway. In the early days of European exploration, native Abenaki tribesmen reported a fierce monster dwelling in the river, but severe industrial pollution and a dearth of modern sightings relegate the creature to history (or mythology).

Source: Henry Masta, *Abenaki Indian Legends.* Victoriaville, Québec: La Voix des Boisfrancs, 1932.

Ethiopian Death Bird

In the 1930s, adventurer Byron de Prorok traveled through Ethiopia, collecting native legends and exploring their roots. In the Welega district, locals spoke of an evil site called Devil's Cave, near Nek'emte, said to be infested with hyena-men and blood-drinking "death BIRDS." Prorok found the cave and satisfied himself that flesh-and-blood hyenas occupied the area. He also witnessed swarms of BATS, with wingspans of 12–18 inches, locally described as vampires that preyed on humans and livestock alike. Unfortunately, Prorok took no specimens, and no subsequent investigation of the bats has yet been undertaken. Officially, vampire bats are confined to the Western Hemisphere.

Sources: Byron de Prorok, *Dead Men Do Tell Tales.* New York: Creative Age Press, 1942; Shuker, "A belfry of crypto-bats."

Ethiopia's "death bird" may in fact be an unknown species of vampire bat.

Ethiopian Deer

In 1986 BERNARD HEUVELMANS noted recent sightings of a small ungulate, resembling a deer, from southern Ethiopia. Ancient Egyptian art suggests the creature (or one remarkably similar) once ranged farther north, along the Nile. Heuvelmans suggested that the animals sighted might comprise a relict population of *Climacoceras*, a creature with branched antlers known from Miocene fossils (presumed extinct for 6 million years).

Paleobiologist Christine Janis subsequently has noted that *Climacoceras* was not in fact a deer, but rather a prehistoric ancestor of the giraffe. Janis also suggested an alternate candidate, proposing that the animals sighted may be specimens of fallow deer (*Dama dama*), known in Ethiopia and Egypt during the late Pleistocene (10,000 years ago). Thus far, no specimen of Ethiopian deer has been collected, and the animal remains officially unrecognized.

Sources: Heuvelmans, "Annotated checklist of apparently unknown animals with which cryptozoology is concerned"; Christine Janis, "A reevaluation of some cryptozoological animals." *Cryptozoology* 6 (1987): 115-118.

Etta Mac sea serpent

On 30 April 1937, crewmen aboard the barge *Etta Mac* reported a SEA SERPENT sighting east of Gabriola Island, in British Columbia's Strait of Georgia. They described the beast as long and serpentine in form, approximately 18 inches thick, with brown and yellow stripes, a mouth bristling with teeth, and a "friendly eye." Some researchers consider the event a sighting of CADBOROSAURUS.

Source: LeBlond and Bousfield, *Cadborosaurus.*

Eufaula Lake, Oklahoma

Eufaula Lake is 40 miles long, sprawling over parts of four counties in eastern Oklahoma. Fortean authors Colin and Janet Bord report that LAKE MONSTER sightings emanated from the lake in 1973, but they provide no further dates or details. Another lake of the same name, also known as Walter F. George Reservoir, lies on the border between Alabama and Georgia.

Sources: Bord and Bord, *Unexplained Mysteries of the 20th Century*; Columbia Gazetteer of North America, http://www.bartleby.com/69/13/E03713.html.

Eumeralla River, Australia

On 18 July 1848, an Australian newspaper—the *Argus*—reported two consecutive cryptid sightings from the Eumeralla River, near Port Fairy, Victoria. The first account described an unknown hairy HOMINID swimming in the river, while witnesses on the following day described a long-necked BUNYIP with a head resembling a KANGAROO's, a huge mouth, and a flowing mane. Neither beast was seen again, and both remain unidentified today.

Sources: Healy and Cropper, *Out of the Shadows*; Smith, *Bunyips & Bigfoots*; Whitley, "Mystery animals of Australia."

Evansville Tiger-dog

On 29 November 1903, the *Evansville Courier & Press* published the following account of a strange beast captured in southwestern Indiana:

Edward Smith of Long Branch is the possessor of a strange animal that was captured near his home yesterday. Dozens have seen it, but no one has been able to tell what it is. Smith said: "It is as big and ferocious as a TIGER. Its head resembles a coon, but the rest of the body looks more like a dog. It is about 2 feet long, has a long, bushy tail and bright-red eyes." The strange animal will be brought to Evansville and placed on exhibition in a few days.

A 2-foot-long tiger might be ferocious, but it could not qualify as "big." In fact, Smith's description more closely resembles a coatimundi (*Nasua nasua*), like the one killed near Falls City, Nebraska in 1968. Sadly, the specimen was not preserved, no further information on the case is now available.

Source: "Strange animal 'ferocious as a tiger' baffles community." *Evansville* (IN) *Courier & Press* (29 November 1903).

Was the Evansville tiger-dog a misplaced coatimundi?

Everett sea serpent   On 30 August 1875, sailors aboard the steamer *Everett* sighted an unknown SEA SERPENT near the Isles of Shoals, off the coast of New Hampshire. The same day brought a report from Salisbury Beach, Massachusetts (north of Newburyport), where a small crowd watched the creature (or its twin) circling offshore for 20 minutes.
Source: O'Neill, *The Great New England Sea Serpent*.

Ezitapile Exotic   In September 2000, KARL SHUKER alerted the world to recent sightings of "a decidedly weird wotzit" reported from the neighborhood of Ezitapile, in South Africa's Eastern Cape Province. Eyewitness accounts of the creature, which Shuker dubbed the Ezitapile Exotic, described it as yellow and serpentine in form, "but with a horse-like head, a mane running down its back, and a body the shape of a 20-quart barrel." Captain Mpofana Skwatsh, of the Aliwal North police, observed that the beast was an apparent forest-dweller, most often seen with its long tail wrapped around a tree. Livestock were visibly agitated by the animal, which remains at large and unidentified today.
Source: Karl Shuker, "Alien zoo." *Fortean Times* 137 (September 2000): 18.

F

Faeroe Islands sea serpents   The Faeroe Islands are a Danish dependency in the North Atlantic, located some 250 miles north of Scotland and the same distance southeast of Iceland. In the 19th century, waters surrounding the Faeroes produced two intriguing SEA SERPENT reports.

The first sighting was logged by the commander of an unnamed ship, one Captain Brown, while passing between the Faeroes and the Shetland Islands in July 1818, while en route from the U.S. to St. Petersburg, Russia. A description of the creature follows:

> In swimming the head, neck and forepart of the body stood upright like a mast: it was surrounded by porpoises and fishes. It was smooth, without scales, and had eight gills under the neck; which decidedly evinces that it is not a SNAKE, but a new genus of FISH....Dark brown above, muddy white beneath: head obtuse. Capt. Brown adds, that the head was two feet long, the mouth fifteen inches, and the eyes over the jaws, similar to a horse's; the whole length might be 58 feet.

Three decades later, in 1845, British M.P. Philip Gosse related the following report of a cryptid seen by Captain Christmas of the Danish Navy, while sailing between the Faeroes and Iceland:

> He [Christmas] was lying to in a gale of wind, in a frigate of which he had the command, when an immense shoal of porpoises rushed by the ship, as if pursued, and lo and behold a creature with a neck moving like that of a swan, about the thickness of a man's waist, with a head like a horse, raised itself slowly and gracefully from the deep, and seeing the ship it immediately disappeared again, head foremost, like a duck diving. He saw it only for a few seconds; the part above the water seemed about eighteen feet in length. He is a singularly intelligent man, and by no means one to allow his imagination to run away with him.

Based upon these two reports from seamen well familiar with the denizens of waters frequently traversed, it would appear that some large, unknown creature in the North Atlantic makes a habit of hunting fish and porpoises close to the surface. The animals remain unknown, though BERNARD HEUVELMANS classified both creatures as specimens of his hypothetical "long-necked" sea monster.
Source: Heuvelmans, *In the Wake of the Sea Serpents*.

Fangalabolo   This unknown giant BAT of Madagascar is named Fangalabolo ("one that seizes the hair") for its alleged habit of swooping at humans and tearing hair from their scalps. Witnesses describe it as significantly larger than the native flying FOX (*Pteropus rufus*), which has a 5-foot wingspan.
Source: Heuvelmans, *On the Track of Unknown Animals*.

Fantasma de los Riscos   A mystery HOMINID reported from the Andean region of Argentina's San Juan and Mendoza Provinces, the Fantasma de los Riscos ("ghost of the badlands") is described as a naked, howling man covered with hair from head to foot. Author Fabio Picasso calls it the "ABOMINABLE SNOWMAN" of the Pie de Palo region, and thus far the Fantasma has proved as elusive as the Himalayan YETI.
Sources: Octavio Gill, *Tradiciones Sanjuaninas*. Buenos Aires: Peuser, 1948; Picasso, "South American monsters & mystery animals."

Farishta   An unknown HOMINID or WILDMAN of the Pamir Mountains in Tajikistan, the Farishta (Arabic for "angel") resembles Central Asia's ALMAS in all particulars. There is no clear-cut reason to believe it represents a different cryptid.
Source: Heuvelmans and Porshnev, *L'homme de Néanderthal est toujours vivant*.

Farrisvatnet, Norway Local traditions maintain that this lake, in Norway's Vestfold County, was once inhabited by a LAKE MONSTER. Unfortunately, no specific information is available and it seems no sightings have been recorded since the late 19th or early 20th century.

Source: A. Fonahan, "Sjøormen i Farrisvatnet." *Tidens Tegn* (20 December 1933).

Father-of-All-Turtles *see* **Turtles (Giant)**

Fating'ho This unclassified primate or HOMINID of West Africa reportedly inhabits jungle areas of Senegal and northern Guinea. Witnesses describe it as man-sized, covered in black hair which grows longest on the animal's large head. One story of the Fating'ho from Diaroumé, Senegal bears striking similarity to tales of ZANA in the country of Georgia, some 4,000 miles to the northeast. That story describes a hunter who captured a female Fating'ho and tamed it to the point that the creature bore him several children. One of their offspring, a daughter named Na Fancani, was supposedly a great beauty whose children lived at Diaroumé through the end of World War II. Entomologist Malang Mane glimpsed a similar creature in November 1992, while collecting insects in a mountainous region of northern Guinea.

Sources: Coly Dembo, "Étrange métissage (Casamance)." *Notes Africaines* 27 (July 1945): 18-19; Shuker, "The secret animals of Senegambia." *Fate* 51 (November 1998): 46-50.

Fawcett, Percy Harrison (1867–?) A British subject, born at Devon in 1867, Percy Fawcett was commissioned as an officer of the Royal Artillery at 1886 and served for several years in Ceylon (now Sri Lanka), where he met and married his wife. Fawcett later performed secret service work in North Africa and trained as a surveyor.

In 1906, the president of the Royal Geographical Society offered Fawcett a job mapping the frontier boundary between

Before his 1925 disappearance, explorer Percy Fawcett described several encounters with South American cryptids.

Bolivia and Brazil, a region then (as now) unsettled by whites and largely unexplored. Fawcett's numerous adventures on that expedition included an incident of enduring interest to cryptozoologists, wherein Fawcett reportedly met and killed a 62-foot ANACONDA.

Fawcett emerged from the arduous 3-year adventure with many fascinating stories, including the tale of his futile attempt to scale the Ricardo Franco Hills — a string of plateaus in the tropic wilderness whose description by Fawcett inspired Sir Arthur Conan Doyle to write his classic novel of surviving DINOSAURS, *The Lost World* (1912). Along the way, he also logged more reports of strange cryptids.

> In the Paraguay River there is a freshwater SHARK, huge but toothless, said to attack men and swallow them if it gets the chance. They talk here of another river monster —FISH or BEAVER— which can in a single night tear out a huge section of the river bank. The Indians report the tracks of some gigantic animal in the swamps bordering the river, but allege that it has never been seen. The shark exists beyond doubt; as for the other monsters — well, there are queer things yet to be disclosed in this continent of mystery, and if strange, unclassified insects, reptiles and small mammals can still exist here, mightn't there be a few giant monsters, remnants of an extinct species, still living out their lives in the security of the vast unexplored swamp areas? In the Madidi, in Bolivia, enormous tracks have been found, and Indians there talk of a huge creature described at times as half submerged in the swamps.

On another exploration, during 1914, Fawcett encountered a tribe of the elusive MARICOXI. He returned to England and to military service during World War I, but afterward renewed his exploration of the South American jungles. When the British press announced a hunt for living dinosaurs in Africa, he penned a letter to the London *Daily Mail* (17 December 1919) that read, in part:

> The Congo swamps are not the only region suspected of harbouring relics of the Miocene age. As I hinted in lectures in London some years ago, a similar beast is believed to exist in South American swamps. A friend of mine, a trader in the rivers and for whose honesty I can vouch, saw in somewhere about Lat. 12 S and Long. 65 W [the Brazil-Bolivia frontier] the head and neck of a huge reptile of the character of the brontosaurus. It was a question of who was scared most, for it precipitously withdrew, with a plunging which suggested an enormous bulk. The savages appear to be familiar with the existence and tracks of the beast, although I have never come across any of the latter myself.

In 1925, after seven expeditions Fawcett enlisted his oldest son, Jack, for a journey to discover an ancient lost city in the wilds of Brazil, which Fawcett called simply "Z." Before departing, Fawcett left word that should he fail to return, no search should be mounted, since the terrain was too perilous. Father and son embarked on 29 May 1925, after Fawcett penned a last message to his wife: "You need have no fear of failure." None of the party returned, and their fate remains a mystery.

Several searches were conducted in spite of Fawcett's final warning, and theories on his fate abound. As late as 1996, an expedition led by René Delmotte and James Lynch went looking for traces of Fawcett, but it ran out of steam after hostile Indians intercepted the party, held its members captive for several days, then released them after confiscating $30,000 worth of equipment.

Sources: Fawcett, *Exploration Fawcett*; Heuvelmans, *On the Track of Unknown Animals*; Sanderson, *"Things"*; Shuker, *In Search of Prehistoric Survivors*; Virtual Exploration Society, http://www.unmuseum.org/fawcett.htm.

Fei-Fei As if the search for unknown HOMINIDS in Asia were not already confusing enough, with the ALMAS, KAPTAR, YEREN and YETI vying for attention, we must also contend with the Fei-fei ("BABOON") reported from China's Sichuan and Zhejiang Provinces. Based on descriptions dating from the 16th century, this 10-foot shaggy creature may be nothing more than a Yeren renamed, but some accounts draw particular attention to its "long lips" and "backwards feet" (the latter a curious description applied to mystery hominids by aboriginal people throughout the world). As some Chinese appear to differentiate between the Fei-fei and the Yeren (or WILDMAN), it may in fact represent a different unknown primate.

Sources: Bernard Read, *Chinese Materia Medica: From the Pen ts'ao kang my Li Shih-chen, A.D. 1597.* Beijing: Peking Natural History Bulletin, 1931; Napier, *Bigfoot.*

***Felix* sea serpent** In June 1910, officers and crewmen aboard the three-master *Felix* saw an unidentified SEA SERPENT near Rathlin Island, six miles offshore from Ballycastle (on the northeast coast of Ireland). Captain Jorgenson reported that the animal was only briefly seen. He estimated its length at a minimum of 14 feet.

Source: Heuvelmans, *In the Wake of the Sea Serpents.*

Feltham, Steven (n.d.–) Cryptozoologist Steve Feltham made his first visit to Loch Ness at age seven, on a family vacation. There, he purchased a book on NESSIE and henceforth devoted every spare moment to study of Scotland's most famous cryptid. As an adult, he returned to the loch many times, and finally moved there in 1991, selling his home and business to purchase an old mobile library which he parked at Dores, on the northeastern shore of Loch Ness. There, as the founder and sole member of Nessie-Sery Independent Research, Feltham divides his time between scanning the loch for Nessie (he claims one sighting so far, from the shore near Fort Augustus) and making models of the creature which he sells to local gift shops for the tourist trade.

Source: http://www.lochnessresearch.co.uk/steve.htm.

Fen Tiger This ALIEN BIG CAT of Cambridgeshire, England has been sighted repeatedly since the early 1980s. Witness William Rooker videotaped a lurking felid at Cottenham, in June 1994, but the creature remained elusive despite several organized hunts. William Rooker captured the CAT on film a year later. Multiple sightings were logged at Fulbourn, where one witness claimed the cat had invaded her house, and three more reports came from Ely. Linton Zoo director Kim Simmons, without visiting the scene, dismissed the reports as "far-fetched." In June 2003, Oakington farmer Dianne Morris saw a large black cat chasing a normal-sized domestic cat across one of her fields, 400 yards from the site where the "tiger" was filmed in 1995. The next morning, Morris found a prize lamb dead, with one leg severed and missing from the scene.

Sources: Terry Dye, "The Cambridgeshire 'Fen Tiger.'" http://www.scottishbigcats.co.uk/fentiger.htm; Sieveking, "Beasts in our midst"; "Tails of the unexpected." *Cambridge News* (5 July 2003).

Fence Rail Dog A quasi-legendary canid reported from the neighborhood of Frederica, Maryland, the fence rail dog is named for its prodigious size, said to equal the height of a standard fence rail at the shoulder. Seen sporadically since the turn of the 20th century, the creature normally appears along Highway 12, between Frederica and Felton. Local tales of a "ghost dog"

make the sightings difficult to evaluate, but reports of the animal's glowing eyes may easily be explained by the reflection of oncoming headlights. If it truly exists, the creature might be akin to the SHUNKA WARAK'IN reported from the U.S. Midwest.

Source: Hauck, *Haunted Places.*

Fernando de Noronha sea serpent Sometime in 1905, British traveler C.H. Prodgers reported a SEA SERPENT sighting near the island of Fernando de Noronha, 250 miles northeast of Cape São Roque, Brazil. It was allegedly his second sighting in the same vicinity, the previous incident dating from 1901. Of the latter beast, observed from 50 yards, Prodgers wrote: "It had a head as big as a cow's head, and the body looked as large round as a flour barrel. I saw only one coil of the latter, and that was a matter of eight to ten yards away from the head, and raised above the water a foot or so." The unnamed ship's captain was skeptical, but he acknowledged to Prodgers "that he had often heard of the monster, and that my description of it tallied with what he had been told."

Source: Heuvelmans, *In the Wake of the Sea Serpents.*

Fiji Islands sea serpents Located in the South Pacific, roughly 1,000 miles north of New Zealand, the Fiji Islands produced two SEA SERPENT sightings in the late 19th and early 20th centuries. The first was recorded in 1881, by Major James Harding, while his gunboat was in service of King Cakobau, against rebel tribesmen on Vanua Levu. Harding's vessel was entering Suva Bay on Viti Levu one afternoon, when an unknown creature reared its maned neck and horselike head above the waves for several moments, then submerged and disappeared. Another Fiji sighting was reported in August 1903, mentioned briefly in the London *Daily Express* (14 September), but no details of that encounter have survived to the present day.

Source: Heuvelmans, *In the Wake of the Sea Serpent.*

Filey Brig sea serpent On 28 February 1934, British fishermen along the coast of Filey, in Yorkshire, reported sighting a SEA SERPENT three miles offshore. Later that night, another incident occurred, reported in the London *Daily Telegraph* of 1 March.

Mr. Wilkinson Herbert, a Filey coastguard, says he saw the thing on shore last night; a dark moonless night. He was walking along Filey Brig, a long low spur of rocks running out into the sea, when:

"Suddenly I heard a growling like a dozen dogs ahead, walking nearer I switched on my torch, and was confronted by a huge neck, six yards ahead of me, rearing up 8 feet high!

"The head was a startling sight—huge, TORTOISE eyes, like saucers, glaring at me, the creature's mouth was a foot wide and its neck would be a yard around. "The Monster appeared as startled as I was. Shining my torch along the ground, I saw a body about 30 feet long. I thought 'this is no place for me' and from a distance I threw stones at the creature.

"It moved away growling fiercely, and I saw the huge black body had two humps on it and four short legs with huge flappers on them. I could not see any tail. It moved quickly, rolling from side to side, and went into the sea. From the cliff top I looked down and saw two eyes like torchlights shining out to sea 300 yards away. It was a most gruesome and thrilling experience. I have seen big animals abroad, but nothing like this."

Source: Heuvelmans, *In the Wake of the Sea Serpents.*

Finnsnesvatnet, Norway Located in Nord-Trøndelag County, this Norwegian lake reportedly hosts a curious pink cryptid. Witnesses include a youth returning from a local discotheque, who claimed he saw the animal burst through the lake's lair of winter ice. Skeptics suggest that pink LAKE MONSTERS, like elephants of the same hue, owe more to alcohol than to cryptozoology.

Source: Erik Knatterud, "Sea serpents in Norwegian lakes." http://www.mjoesormen.no.

Fireti *see* Ufiti

Firth of Clyde sea serpents
Two SEA SERPENT reports were recorded from the Firth of Clyde, on Scotland's west coast, during the first half of the 20th century. The first incident, vaguely described in a newspaper report of 30 August 1911, says merely that an unnamed tourist on Wee Cumbrae, an island in the Firth, had glimpsed a "monster of the deep" 100 yards offshore. Because no details were provided, and the report was followed by a poem heralding the advent of the "silly season," BERNARD HEUVELMANS logically dismissed the sighting as a HOAX.

The next report, also anonymous, declared that a group of Ayrshire fishermen had seen an unknown creature in the Firth during August 1953. They described the cryptid as 30 feet long, including a 12-foot tail. Its overall description, including a CAMEL's head, giraffe's neck and tail sporting long hair, generally conforms to reports of a creature Heuvelmans dubbed the "merhorse."

Source: Heuvelmans, *In the Wake of the Sea Serpents.*

Firth of Forth sea serpents
The Firth of Forth, on Scotland's east coast, has produced three intriguing SEA SERPENT reports. The first, from the mid-19th century, was related as follows by BERNARD HEUVELMANS:

Around 1848 the fishing smack *Sovereign* of Hull, fishing in the Firth of Forth for Lord Norbury, caught a huge serpentine FISH, "which when spread out at length on the deck, extended beyond the limits of the vessel at stem and stern." The fishermen were not surprised at its length, for they had come across an even larger one, dark brown in color. The present fish was was only from 4 to 9 inches thick with a dorsal fin 7 to 8 inches high.

Heuvelmans is almost certainly correct in regarding this specimen as an oarfish (*Regalecus glesnae*), though the larger dark-brown creature described to Lord Norbury does not match the oarfish's description. A second cryptic encounter, occurring on 18 November 1873, was recorded as follows in the *Scotsman*:

Near the middle of Belhaven Bay, about a quarter of a mile from the place where we were standing, there certainly appeared "a long and large black animal" in the water, having all the appearance of the Saurian described by Dr. [James] Joass [from Sutherland in September 1873]. When first observed it was proceeding shorewards, with what seemed to be its head and various undulated portions of the body above the surface. After getting near the shore it turned to the westwards, and kept moving about in that position for a considerable time. Sometimes it appeared to stretch itself out to its full length, at which times both its head and tail were seen above water, only a small portion of the middle of the creature being submerged. Most frequently, however, it was the undulations or apparent coils of the body that were observed, two or three of them being occasionally visible at the same time. These coils had all the appearance to the observers at the distance mentioned above of the coils or folds of a serpent, the sea and the black masses being distinctly separated. Occasionally the creature seemed to take a header, and disappeared altogether, but it seldom remained longer than two of three minutes beneath the surface without exposing some part or other of its body. When fully stretched out, as it appeared several times during the period of ob-

servation, it seemed to be upward to a hundred feet in length, with an apparent breadth of from two to three feet. No doubt the dimensions must have been very much larger. As it was in sight for upwards of a quarter of an hour, ample opportunity was afforded to watch its movements.

Eight years later, in early July 1939, another large crowd watched some unknown creature swimming in the Firth, off West Wemyss. This time, witnesses described the animal as large and brown, with a horselike head and prominent eyes.

Source: Heuvelmans, *In the Wake of the Sea Serpents.*

Firth of Tay sea serpent
At 11:30 p.m. on 30 September 1965, while driving to Perth (in northeastern Scotland), Maureen Ford and a party of friends observed a strange creature on the roadside. It was crawling along the bank of the River Tay, near the point where that river empties into the Firth of Tay (an inlet of the North Sea). Ford described the animal as "a long gray shape. It had no legs but I'm sure I saw long pointed ears." Ninety minutes later, at 1:00 a.m. on 1 October, motorist Robert Swankie passed by in the opposite direction and saw the same creature on the other side of the road. The Scottish *Daily Express* quoted his description on 5 October 1965:

The head was more than two feet long. It seemed to have pointed ears. The body, which was about 20 feet long, was humped like a giant caterpillar. It was moving very slowly and made a noise like someone dragging a heavy weight through the grass.

Skeptics maintain that the various witnesses in this case were deceived by an optical illusion, produced by car headlights and shadows. Researchers F.W. Holiday and KARL SHUKER disagree, noting that a trick of lighting produces no sound. They argue instead that the witnesses observed an unknown "SEA SERPENT" making a rare (but not unique) visit to dry land.

Source: Shuker, *In Search of Prehistoric Survivors.*

Fish (Giant)
The first report of a giant fish unknown to science comes from the Old Testament (Jonah 1:17–2:10). Sinbad and other mythical sailors encountered fish so large they were mistaken for islands, until hapless shore parties awoke the monsters by treading too roughly or kindling a fire. The largest known fish is the whale shark (*Rhincodon typus*), with a maximum acknowledged length of 18 meters (58 feet 6 inches) and weighing 10 tons. Another pelagic giant, the basking shark (*Cetorhinus maximus*), may reach 12 meters (39 feet), though its average length is 10 feet less. The largest saltwater bony fish is the oddly-shaped ocean sunfish (*Mola mola*), with a record specimen from 1908 measuring 10 feet long and 14 feet vertically. Freshwater giants include the rare Beluga sturgeon (*Huso huso*), with a record specimen exceeding 29 feet and 3,000 pounds; the white sturgeon (*Acipenser transmontanus*), ranking as North America's largest fish with a record length of 20 feet; the wels CATFISH (*Siluris glanis*), which may attain a length of 15 feet 6 inches; and the Amazonian pirarucu (*Arapaima gigas*), with a record length of 15 feet.

None of those monster fish explains the huge specimen beached near Licata, Sicily in September 1741. It measured 45 feet 6 inches long, and 23 feet 7 inches in circumference, with its tail measurement cited as 10 feet 2 inches (presumably referring to the fins). It had two dorsal fins, large teeth — and a blowhole on top of its head. That feature confounds ichthyologists, since no fish has a blowhole and no known whale sports two dorsal fins. Some cryptozoologists speculate that the creature may have been a magenta whale, but that still-unidentified cryptid has never been reported from the Mediterranean. Author Samuel Rafinesque gave

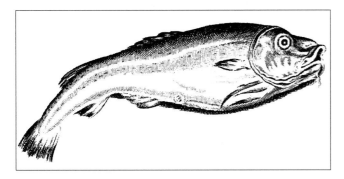

Huge unidentified fish are frequently reported from lakes and rivers around the world.

the huge unknown a Latin name (*Oxypterus mongitori*) in 1814, but it remains unrecognized by science. On 15 August 2003, residents of Little Armier, Malta reportedly sighted a fish of unknown species "about 20 feet long."

Numerous lakes around the world spawn reports of huge, unidentified fish to this day. In Europe, they include: Austria's GOGGAU SEE; England's Bomere pool (in Shropshire); Finland's LOUKUSAJÄRVI; Germany's WEIßE ELSTER and ZWISCHENAHNER MEER; Italy's LAGO DI COMO; with the Swedish lakes MYLLESJÖN and STORE LE. China boasts giant mystery fish in LAKE HANAS, while Argentina floats a similar claim for LAGO GUTIÉRREZ. At least eight Canadian lakes produce giant fish reports. They include: BOILING WATER LAKE (British Columbia); TURTLE LAKE (Saskatchewan); and six different lakes in Quebec—LAC-À-LA-TORTUE, LAC MÉKINAC, LAC RÉMI, LAC ST.-FRANÇOIS, LAC SIMON, and LES TROIS LACS. Alleged giant fish in the U.S. include "ILLIE" (of Lake Illiama, Alaska) and "OSCAR" (Big Pine Lake, Minnesota), along with unnamed whoppers in the following bodies of water: SAGUARO LAKE, Arizona; LAKE CONWAY, Arkansas; LOST LAKE, California; LAKE DECATUR, Illinois; Rangeley Lake, Maine; LAKE OF THE OZARKS, Missouri; FLATHEAD LAKE, Montana; LAKE SAKAKAWEA, North Dakota; FOWLER LAKE, Wisconsin; Koshkonong Lake, Wisconsin; LAC LA BELLE, Wisconsin; and OKAUCHEE LAKE, Wisconsin.

Sources: Costello, *In Search of Lake Monsters*; Ellis, *Monsters of the Sea*; Massimo Farrugia, "Large fish at Little Armier measured around 20 feet." *Malta Independent* (17 August 2003); Garner, *Monster! Monster!*; Kirk, *In the Domain of the Lake Monsters*; Antonio Mongitore, *Della Sicilia ricercata nelle cose piu memorabili*. Palermo: Francesco Valenza, 1742-43; Constantin Samuel Rafinesque, *Précis des découvertes et travaux somiologiques de C.S. Rafinesque-Schmaltz entre 1800 et 1814*. Palermo: Royale Typographie Militaire, 1814.

Fish (Hairy)   Only mammals grow hair, but knowledge of that scientific fact has not prevented witnesses around the world from reporting encounters with hairy fish over centuries past. In fact, no fewer than six different species of hairy fish have been described since the early 19th century, and while one of them—a mounted specimen of "Canadian fur-bearing trout" prepared by Ontario taxidermist Ross Jobe—has been exposed as a tongue-in-cheek HOAX, the other five remain open to speculation.

The first, reported from Japan in the early 19th century, was described as an amphibious species with a 4- to 5-foot scaly body and a bristling head of hair resembling a human's. The creatures were fond of playing on shore, but allegedly turned vicious if people approached, savagely attacking and disemboweling hapless victims. KARL SHUKER and researcher David Heppell suggest

that this hairy-fish story may have some basis in fact, resulting from exaggerated tales of Japan's native fur seal (*Callorhinus ursinus*).

An equally peculiar species is reported from Iceland, where a hairy trout called the *lodsilungur* was allegedly used as a tool of wrathful demons to torment mankind. Periodically, the legends say, Icelandic lakes and rivers would be overrun with inedible *lodsilungur*, driving out game fish and leaving the local populace to starve. Shuker suggests that the legends once again may be rooted in fact, this time referring to sporadic outbreaks of fungal infections in fish, which produce external overgrowth of mycelia resembling hair.

Explorer Marco Polo (1254–1324) logged a sighting of a very different hairy fish, during his 13th-century travels in China. This specimen was "fully 100 paces long," and its hairy corpse had dammed a local river, causing shortages of water to surrounding villages. When peasants tried to make the best of their misfortune by devouring the monster, Polo reported that its flesh proved toxic and killed many of the diners.

A smaller specimen of more recent vintage is said to dwell in an unnamed lake near Viitna, in Estonia's Lääne-Viru County. More startling yet, the fish's hair is reportedly yellow.

Finally, the only "hairy" fish recognized by modern science was not classified until 1956. A tiny creature found in the North Atlantic, around the Azores, *Mirapinna esau* ("hairy wonderfinned") measures 2.5 inches in length and appears at first sight to be covered with genuine hair. A closer look, however, reveals that the pelage actually consists of tiny filaments containing secretory cells, which make *Mirapinna* distasteful to predators.

Source: Oskar Loorits, *Grundzüge des estnischen Volksglaubens*. Lund, Sweden: Carl Bloms Boktryckeri, 1951; Shuker, "Hairy reptiles and furry fish."

Fish (Invisible)   It is difficult to imagine anything more preposterous than an invisible animal, yet even this may be found in the annals of cryptozoology. In July 1990, the late Gerald Wood (author of *The Guinness Book of Animal Feats and Facts*) addressed a query to KARL SHUKER, seeking information on an invisible fish, reportedly discovered near the Seychelles, in the Indian Ocean. Wood reported that the fish were capable of changing colors and more, typically shifting from black to gray before they "disappeared." A mated pair reportedly sold for £15,000 ($24,300), but Wood died before he could pursue his inquiry and Shuker has thus far obtained no more information on the elusive fish.

Source: Karl Shuker, "Menagerie of mystery." *Strange Magazine* 18 (Summer 1997): 52.

Fish, LeRoy (1943–2002)   Zoologist LeRoy Fish was an Oregon native, born at Portland on 10 February 1943. He obtained his bachelor's and master's degrees from Walla Walla College (in Washington), and earned his Ph.D. from Washington State University. As an active member of the BIGFOOT FIELD RESEARCHERS ORGANIZATION, Fish participated in discovery and analysis of the SKOOKUM CAST, in September 2000. With colleague GROVER KRANTZ, Fish believed the cast depicted the figure of a BIGFOOT reclining on soft earth. Debate concerning the cast's significance continues. Fish died at home, of congestive heart failure, on 20 March 2002.

Sources: Coleman, *Bigfoot!*; LeRoy Fish obituary. *Eugene* (OR) *Register-Guard* (23 March 2002).

Fiskerton Phantom   This jet-black ALIEN BIG CAT of Lincolnshire, England was nicknamed for the village where it first appeared in 1996. Witnesses included a group of four teenage girls who met the CAT while it was feeding. "We saw something moving in some bushes, so we went to take a look," one girl told the press. "When we saw what it was, we just froze. It was very frightening, with very big teeth. It looked like it was eating a pheasant." The cat soon fled,, but hours later it was seen by a motorist near the same spot. It surfaced at Dunholme in March 1997, and at Short Derry, near Lincoln, the following month.

Sources: "Cats in the hats." *Fortean Times* 111 (June 1998), http://www.forteantimes.com/articles/111_abc.shtml; Fiskerton, Lincolnshire, http://www.lincolns.org.uk/fiskerton.html.

Five-Lined Constellation Fish

This abyssal FISH has been seen only once, by WILLIAM BEEBE, while exploring the waters off Bermuda in the 1930s. Beebe was in a bathysphere at 1,900 feet below the Atlantic's surface when he glimpsed the creature, afterward describing it as a round-bodied fish with prominent eyes and small pectoral fins. Beebe named it *Bathysidus pentagrammus*, after the five lines of purple and yellow photophores on each side. Ichthyologist Carl Hubbs discounted the sighting, suggesting that Beebe's view of some passing jellyfish had been distorted by condensation of his own breath on the thick glass of the bathysphere's porthole.

Source: William Beebe, *Half Mile Down*. New York: Harcourt, Brace, 1934.

Five-Toed Llama

No living witnesses have thus far reported this mystery ungulate from the Andes. It is known only from pottery fragments, found near Pisco, Peru in the 1920s. Archaeologists believe the pottery, which includes painted depictions of llamalike creatures with five distinct toes on each foot, represents the work of a pre-Inca culture dating from 600 B.C. to A.D. 200. All known llamas and related camelids have cloven hooves, with only two toes. The curious detail of five-toed feet on creatures otherwise resembling modern llamas in all particulars remains unexplained.

Source: Shuker, "Hoofed mystery animals and other crypto-ungulates, Part 3." *Strange Magazine* 11 (Spring-Summer 1993): 25-27, 48-50.

Peru's five-toed llama is known only from depictions in ancient art.

Flat Pond, Illinois *see* Stump Pond

Flathead Lake, Montana

Flathead Lake, located in northwestern Montana between Kalispell and Polson, is the largest U.S. freshwater lake west of the Mississippi River. The island-dotted lake is 28 miles long and 15 miles across at its widest point, with a maximum depth of 386 feet. It is also one of North America's most active "monster" lakes, with traditions involving what seem to be two different cryptids.

Reports of the creature some locals call "Flattie" or "Montana NESSIE" are traceable to Kalispell Indian folklore. The first white witness, in 1885 (or 1889, reports vary) was Captain James Kern, who encountered a whale-sized creature while piloting his steamboat across Flathead Lake. The animal submerged when one of Kern's passengers opened fire with a pistol. Another steamboat sighting, this one with 50 witnesses, was logged in 1919. Statements described the creature as resembling a log, until it came alive and started swimming rings around the boat. Montana's Department of Fish and Wildlife had 78 sightings on file by 1998; a year later, *Flathead Courier* publisher Paul Fugleberg claimed to have 90 reports spanning the past century. About two-thirds of those reports describe a serpentine animal 20–40 feet long, sometimes displaying humps above the water's surface or raising a doglike head to ogle witnesses; the rest apparently describe a FISH, ranging from 8 to 12 feet long.

The latter reports may be explained by a population of large sturgeon in the lake. Montana's largest known white sturgeon (*Acipenser transmontanus*) measured 7 feet 6 inches and weighed 181 pounds. It was caught on 28 May 1955 and is displayed at the Polson-Flathead Historical Museum, but some skeptics dispute its source to this day, insisting that sturgeons are not found in Flathead Lake. If they are wrong, white sturgeons may explain some of the local "monster" sightings, since the largest specimen on record measured 20 feet. Still, they would hardly account for Ronald Nixon's sighting in 1963, of a creature he described as:

> something at least 25 feet long and with enough substance to it that as it moved near the surface it threw up a two-foot head wave. It was perfectly black, and it didn't have any sign of a fin on the back. It couldn't have been a fish, and I'm sure it wasn't manmade.

Dean Powell and his wife saw a similar animal swimming between Birs Island and the lake's eastern shore. Powell recalled, "It was huge and black, but it couldn't have been a boat, as it went up and down in the water, splashed around and circled." Witness Dan Knight reported a "giant fish" sighting in August 1983, but the creature he met bore no resemblance to a sturgeon. "Its fin was two feet out of the water and cutting the water like a SHARK," Knight said. In passing, it "sent a wave off that would put my 15-foot boat to shame."

The year 1964 witnessed a spate of attempts at solving the riddle. Montana skin diver Fuller Laugher spent four consecutive days in the lake without sighting anything monstrous, while an unnamed fisherman trolled Flathead's waters, baiting his oversized hook with whole chickens. A company called Big Fish Unlimited offered $1,400 for Flattie or any fish measuring longer than 14 feet, but that reward—like Paul Fugleberg's offer for a photo of the creature(s)—remains unclaimed today.

Sources: Church, "Flathead Lake monster"; Church, "Flathead Lake monster update"; Costello, *In Search of Lake Monsters*; Fugleberg, *Flathead Lake Nessie Log*; Fugleberg, *Montana Nessie of Flathead Lake*; Garner, *Monster! Monster!*; Kirk, *In the Domain of the Lake Monsters*; Mangiacopra, "The two monsters of Flathead Lake, Montana."

Flåvatnet, Norway   Though once reputedly the home of a LAKE MONSTER, this lake in Norway's Telemark County apparently lost its claim to fame in 1880, when the steamboat *St. Olaf* collided with the creature. Legend has it that the boat's paddle wheel tore the creature apart. No modern sightings are reported.

Source: Erik Knatterud, "Sea serpents in Norwegian lakes." http://www.mjoesormen.no.

Flora M. sea serpent   On 9 June 1914, crewmen aboard the schooner *Flora M.* sighted a SEA SERPENT off the coast of Massachusetts. An account in the *Gloucester Times* described the incident three days later.

> The crew of the British sch. *Flora M.* told an amazing story when their vessel reached Boston late Wednesday from Port Wade, N.S. [Nova Scotia]. Off Cape Ann Tuesday afternoon, while the two-master was sailing with a fair wind, there suddenly appeared above the surface of the water the head and part of the body of a huge marine monster.
>
> Every man on board from Capt. George Brooks to the cook saw the animal, and they are willing to take oath to the fact. They declare that it was no hallucination, and any suggestion that the monster may have been a whale or porpoise is resented. Capt. Brooks declared it was the worst looking "animal" he had ever seen and the six other men bear him out.
>
> Capt. Brooks was averse to telling the story to reporters, fearing ridicule, but finally gave the facts. The skipper has never been a believer in sea serpents and has never before seen anything in his long years at sea that could in any way be mistaken for one....
>
> "At first I thought it was a big gas buoy adrift. It was slanted at a sharp angle and the water appeared to be boiling under it. Then it lifted its great head which resembled more than anything the head of a horse. It gradually rose out of the water until we could plainly see fully 25 feet of its enormous back. The mate sprang for his glass and ran up the rigging to get a better view, while most of the crew followed him.
>
> "I stood on the deck too astonished to move. Suddenly the monster plunged beneath the surface and its entire body disappeared. In an incredibly short time it came up directly ahead of the schooner and closer than before....
>
> "I gave the wheel a twist to swing the schooner away from the monster, and just as we changed course he disappeared, stirring up the water for some distance. If I had a camera I could easily have taken a snap shot of the creature."
>
> Capt. Brooks was so impressed by what he saw that he told the boarding officer about it. He said in his opinion the animal must have been 75 feet long.

Source: O'Neill, *The Great New England Sea Serpent.*

Fluorescent Freddie   This facetious nickname was applied to a green 10-foot HOMINID with glowing red eyes, which frightened a group of children at French Lick, Indiana in March 1965. Most accounts list the incident among Indiana's various BIGFOOT sightings, although the creature's color remains unexplained. Researcher JOHN GREEN suggests that the report may be a HOAX.

Sources: Bord and Bord, *The Bigfoot Casebook*; Coleman, "The colour of mystery"; Green, *Sasquatch: The Apes Among Us.*

Fly sea serpent   Specific dates are lacking for this SEA SERPENT sighting, recorded from Mexican waters, but research indicates that the primary witness serves as a lieutenant aboard the *Fly* between 1836 and 1840. The following account was published long afterward, in the *Zoologist* of February 1849.

> Captain the Hon. George Hope states that, when in H.M.S. Fly, in the gulf of California, the sea being perfectly calm and trans-

The *Fly* sea serpent, sketched from eyewitness descriptions.

parent, he saw at the bottom a large marine animal, with the head and general figure of an ALLIGATOR, except that the neck was much longer, and that instead of legs the creature had four large flappers, somewhat like those of TURTLES, the anterior part being larger than the posterior: the creature was distinctly visible, and all its movements could be observed with ease: it appeared to be pursuing its prey at the bottom of the sea: its movements were somewhat serpentine, and an appearance of annulations or ring-like divisions of the body was distinctly perceptible.

Source: Heuvelmans, *In the Wake of the Sea Serpents.*

Foam sea serpent   On 24 May 1925, crewmen aboard the fishing trawler *Foam* observed a large SEA SERPENT off the coast of Massachusetts. The *Boston Herald* described that incident four days later.

> Returning to this port yesterday after a weeks [*sic*] fishing in South Channel, Captain Richard Tobin and the crew of the steam trawler *Foam* told of seeing a 125-foot sea serpent last Sunday afternoon, when the *Foam* was about 85 miles southeast of Boston Light. They insisted it was no "pipe dream" and expressed belief that the sea monster had been forced out of its lair by an upheaval of the bed of the ocean during one of the recent earthquakes in this part of the world.
>
> Capt. James Doyle, acting mate of the trawler, was the first to see the serpent. It came to the surface about 100 yards off the starboard bow of the *Foam*, and at first view he thought it was a naval submarine out hunting rum smuggling craft. But when about 20 feet of the submarine's bow bent upward at a right angle to its body, he gave a shout that brought every man on deck.
>
> They shook like aspen leaves or juniper berries in the November winds, while the monster, propelled by eight fins on each side of his EEL-like body, approached near.
>
> As it rapidly swam a circle around the trawler, the men observed that it had an almost perfectly smooth skin, battleship gray, excepting for a stretch of 15 feet at the back of the head and 10 feet of the tip of the tail. On these parts were green scales about the size of tea trays.
>
> The trawler steamed for a while in the wake of the serpent but soon lost sight of it. Capt. Doyle estimated that the serpent was 125 feet long, but Capt. Tobin believes it was nearer 150. It was the first sea serpent to be reported off the New England coast this season.

Source: O'Neill, *The Great New England Sea Serpent.*

Folsom Lake, California   Large reptilian quadrupeds were several times reported from this 18,000-acre man-made lake, northeast of Sacramento, between September 1957 and January 1958. Cryptozoologists disagree on possible explanations for the sightings: LOREN COLEMAN contends that the creatures were mislocated CROCODILES, while JOHN KIRK suggests the presence of giant SALAMANDERS, similar to those reported from California's Trinity Alps.

Sources: Coleman, *Mysterious America*; Kirk, *In the Domain of the Lake Monsters*.

Fontoynont's Tenrec   Tenrecs are small insectivorous mammals (family *Tenrecidae*) which inhabit Madagascar. Subfamilies include the spiny tenrecs (*Tenrecinae*) and the furred tenrecs (*Oryzoryctinae*). The largest species, *Tenrec ecaudatus*, grows to a maximum length of 14 inches. In 1929, French zoologist Guillaume Grandidier claimed the discovery of a new tenrec species in eastern Madagascar, distinguished by its ocher-colored coat, with black-and-white banded spines on its back and flanks. The creature, which Gradidier named *Dasogale fontoynonti*, is known only from two specimens, both poorly preserved in the 1920s. Some modern zoologists believe Grandidier misidentified juvenile specimens of the greater hedgehog tenrec (*Setifer setosus*), while others concede that *Dasogale* represents a new species of tenrec. Better specimens, which might resolve the controversy, have thus far proved elusive.

Sources: Guillaume Grandidier, "Un nouveau type de mammifère insectivore de Madagascar, le *Dasogale fontoynonti* G. Grand." *Bulletin de l'Academie Malgache* 11 (1929): 85–90; Ross MacPhee, "Systematic status of *Dasogale fontoynonti* (Tenrecidae, Insectivora)." *Journal of Mammalogy* 68 (1987): 133–135.

Forés, Angel Morant (n.d.)   A widely traveled Spanish cryptozoologist, Angel Forés collected information from Burundi on the cryptid known as MAMBU MUTU in 1995. Four years later, on a visit to Ecuador's Morona-Santiago Province, Forés saw and photographed the stuffed remains of a curious specimen found in a local shop. The animal vaguely resembled a mole but measured 15 inches long, with webbed feet, white fur with brown dorsal markings, and a short but distinct nasal trunk. The shop owner refused to sell the specimen, but Shuar Indians from the Macas region claimed such creatures were commonly seen in local rivers. Four mammalogists who examined Forés's photos failed to identify the animal, while a fifth suggested it might be a yapok or water opossum (*Chironectes minimums*). Forés solved the mystery by recruiting Ecuadorian biologist Didier Sanchez to examine the creature, determining that it was a HOAX concocted by a clever taxidermist.

Sources: Karl Shuker, "Alien zoo." *Fortean Times* 128 (November 1999): 18; Shuker, "Menagerie of mystery." *Strange Magazine* 15 (Spring 1995): 32.

Forked Deer River, Tennessee   On 27 October 1871, a Canadian newspaper, the *Perth* (Ontario) *Courier*, published the following account of an aquatic cryptid sighting:

A.A. Freeman, member elect from Hyewood County to the next Legislature, told the editor of this paper, in the presence of several well-known gentlemen, the following remarkable story: J.B. Maxey, an intelligent citizen of Bell's Depot, in this county, and keeper of a hotel at that place, and for whom A.A. Freeman vouches as a reliable truthful man, was fishing in a canoe on July 17, in Forked Deep River, and in that part of the river between the railroad bridge and dirt road bridge, when his attention was called to an object in the river, some fifty yards distant, which presented the appearance of a man drowning. Maxey rowed his boat within ten feet of the object, and saw a remarkable creature, as the following description will testify: It had a face perfectly white, with features like those of a human being. It had something like moss on its head instead of hair, and its neck was longer than the neck

of a man. Its body down to the waist, or so much of it as was exposed, was covered with black and white spots. It was as large as an ordinary man, and had large black eyes. Maxey was within ten feet of it for ten minutes. He did not see any arms. It looked at him and slowly turned around and disappeared into the water. Thomas Neal, Esq., told Mr. Freeman that he saw the same thing at the same place about three years ago, but did not tell of it because he thought that he would be laughed at. James Neal and Isaac Ward say they saw the same creature.

While the publication of that story in Ontario has prompted some researchers to list it as a Canadian sighting, there is no Bell's Depot, Forked Deep River or Hyewood County anywhere in Canada. There *is*, however, a Forked *Deer* River in western Tennessee, whose south fork flows past Bells in Haywood County. We may assume that the incident occurred there, if indeed it occurred at all, but thus far no corroboration from Tennessee newspapers has been discovered.

Source: "From the past: Ontario aquatic cryptid." *North American BioFortean Review* 3 (May 2001): 32.

Forsanvatnet, Norway   Located in Hamarøy County, this Norwegian lake has a tradition of LAKE MONSTER sightings involving a creature that sometimes basks on the surface, resembling the pontoon of a seaplane.

Source: Erik Knatterud, "Sea serpents in Norwegian lakes." http://www.mjoesormen.no.

Fort, Charles Hoy (1874–1932)   Born at Albany, New York on 9 August 1874, journalist Charles Fort spent much of his life researching scientific literature at the New York Public Library and the British Museum Library, in search of "damned" date — defined by Fort as "data that science has excluded." While not a cryptozoologist per se, he chronicled many reports of SEA SERPENTS, MYSTERY MAULERS and other anomalous creatures in four astounding volumes: *The Book of the Damned* (1919), *New Lands* (1923), *Lo!* (1931) and *Wild Talents* (1932). A true skeptic (as opposed to the modern crop of professional debunkers), Fort challenged conventional wisdom in every field of study. "I conceive of nothing," he wrote, "in religion, science or philosophy, that is more than the proper thing to wear for a while." He also hailed the "courageous persistence of science: Everything seemingly found out is doomed to be subverted — by more powerful microscopes and telescopes; by more refined, precise, searching means and methods — the new pronouncements irrepressibly bobbing up, their reception always as Truth at last, always the illusion of the final." Fort died on 3 May 1932. His work continues in an excellent monthly magazine, *Fortean Times*, and through Britain's CENTRE FOR FORTEAN ZOOLOGY.

Sources: Clark, *Unexplained!*; Fort, *The Books of Charles Fort*.

Fort Salisbury sea serpent   In October 1902, sailors aboard the *Fort Salisbury* logged their encounter with a SEA SERPENT in the tropical Atlantic, off Africa's Congo coast. A.H. Raymer, the ship's second officer, described the incident.

October 28, 3.5 a.m. — Dark object, with long, luminous trailing wake, thrown in relief by a phosphorescent sea, seen ahead, a little on starboard bow. Look-out reported two masthead lights ahead. These two lights, almost as bright as a steamer's lights, appeared to shine from two points in line on the upper surface of the dark mass.
     Concluded dark mass was a whale and lights phosphorescent. On drawing nearer dark mass and lights sank below the surface. Prepared to examine the wake in passing with binoculars.

Passed about forty to fifty yards on port side of wake, and discovered it was the scaled back of some huge monster slowly disappearing below the surface. Darkness of the night prevented determining its exact nature, but scales of apparently 1 ft. diameter and dotted in places with barnacle growth were plainly discernible. The breadth of the body showing above water tapered from about 30 ft. close abaft where the dark mass had appeared to about 5 ft. at the extreme end visible. Length roughly about 500 ft. to 600 ft.

Concluded that the dark mass first seen must have been the creature's head. The swirl caused by the monster's progress could be distinctly heard, and a strong odour like that of a low-tide beach on a summer day pervaded the air. Twice along its length the disturbance of water and a broadening of the surrounding belt of phosphorous indicated the presence of huge fins in motion below the surface.

The wet, shiny back of the monster was dotted with twinkling phosphorescent lights, and was encircled by a band of white phosphorescent sea.

Such are the bare facts of the passing of the sea serpent in latitude 5 deg. 31 min. S., longitude 4 deg. 42 min. W., as seen by myself, being officer of the watch, and by the helmsman and lookout man.

Upon considering the mixture of fine detail and vague generality contained in the report, together with estimates of size deemed greatly exaggerated, BERNARD HEUVELMANS dismissed the *Fort Salisbury* sighting as a HOAX.

Source: Heuvelmans, *In the Wake of the Sea Serpents.*

Fortune Bay sea serpent On Sunday afternoon, 4 May 1997, fishermen Charles Bungay and C. Clarke sighted a string of floating objects in Fortune Bay, on the southern coast of Newfoundland, Canada. They first mistook the things for plastic garbage bags and decided to haul them aboard, to sift through the contents. As they approached within 50 or 60 feet, however, the "garbage bags" surprised them by raising a head above water. As Bungay later told reporters, "It turned its head and looked right at us. All we could see was a neck six feet long, a head like a horse, but his dark eyes were on the front of its face…like a human….He just looked at us and slid under the water and disappeared." Bungay estimated that the animal was 30–40 feet long, with scaly hide and ears or horns projecting 6–8 inches from its head.

Source: O'Neill, *The Great New England Sea Serpent.*

Fossa (Giant) Although it resembles a CAT, the Madagascan fossa (*Cryptoprocta ferox*) is actually related to the civets. A much larger species, the cave fossa (*C. spelia*), once measured nine feet long (tail included) and tipped the scales at 200 pounds, but that ferocious predator is now officially extinct. In keeping with Madagascar's cryptic tradition, however, natives still report occasionally encounters with giant fossa in the island's hinterlands. Biologist Luke Dollar visited Madagascar's Zahamena National Park — also known as the Impenetrable Forest — in November 1999, but he failed to sight the rumored cryptid or obtain proof of its modern existence. Investigation continues in the country that has spawned so many zoological mysteries.

Source: Karl Shuker, "Alien zoo." *Fortean Times* 135 (July 2000): 22-23.

Fotsiaondré The Fotsiaondré ("white sheep") is yet another cryptid said to inhabit the dense forests of Madagascar's Isalo Massif. Also known to natives as Hadéby, this creature is an unknown primate, deriving its popular name from reports of its size and woolly white coat (spotted with black or brown). If the prospect of an undiscovered sheep-sized APE were not puzzling enough, witnesses credit the Fotsiaondré with bulging eyes, a long muzzle, floppy ears and cloven hooves. The latter trait is clearly mythical, but otherwise the creature may be hypothetically explained as a large new species of lemur, already well known from Madagascar with the families *Cheirogaleidae, Indriidae* and *Lemuridae.*

Source: Raymond Decary, *La Faune Malgache, son Rôle dans les Croyances et les Usages Indigènes.* Paris: Payot, 1950.

Fouke Monster Reports of an Arkansas creature resembling BIGFOOT date from 1834, but the state's most famous mystery HOMINID did not appear at Fouke (in Miller County, 10 miles south of Texarkana) until 1953. Sporadic sightings span the next four decades, with the enigmatic Fouke Monster returning despite a tendency of local human residents to meet it with gunfire. Fourteen-year-old James Crabtree was apparently the first to try bagging the creature, in 1965, after an 8-foot beast covered in 4-inch reddish-brown hair interrupted his squirrel hunt. Six years later, the beast returned to Fouke with a persistence that would land it on the silver screen.

The Fouke Monster siege began on the night of 1 May 1971, when the beast attacked Bobby Ford's rural home. Ford's wife was dozing on the living room couch when she "saw the curtain moving on the front window and saw a hand sticking through the window. At first, I thought it was a bear's paw, but it didn't look like that. I could see its eyes. They looked like coals of fire — real red." Her screams summoned her husband and his brother, Douglas Ford. Running outside, the men opened fire on a 6-foot hairy creature as it fled into the nearby woods. A constable was sum-

The Fouke Monster is an Ozarks version of Bigfoot (*William Rebsamen*).

moned and reported finding strange footprints, but he did not see the animal. It returned an hour later, kicking at Ford's front door until more gunshots drove it away. In the predawn hours of 2 May, Bobby Ford went out to check his yard and was attacked in the darkness, escaping with such desperate speed that he literally ran through his closed front door. Sheriff's deputies returned with daylight and found more tracks, but this time the creature did not return. Three weeks later, on 23 May, multiple witnesses reported sightings along Highway 71, outside town.

Those events inspired the first in a series of low-budget films about the Fouke Monster, titled *The Legend of Boggy Creek* (see Appendix for further details). Soon after the movie's release, in late November 1973, Orville Scoggins, his son and grandson met a 4-foot-tall version of the creature slowly walking through the woods near Fouke. The last recorded sighting (as of press time for this volume) was filed when a Louisiana couple traveling through Fouke saw the beast jump from a highway bridge, in 1991.

Sources: "Arkansas has a problem." *Pursuit* 4 (October 1971): 89–90; Bord and Bord, *The Bigfoot Casebook*; Green, *Sasquatch: The Apes Among Us*; Melissa Nelson, "Ghosts, monsters, unexplained phenomena, haunt state." Associated Press (28 October 2002); Rife, *Bigfoot Across America*.

Four Lakes Village Quarry, Illinois

Manmade reservoirs and quarries are unlikely habitats for LAKE MONSTERS, but this body of water near Lisle, Illinois (in Cook County) produced a sighting in October 1970. Witness Robert Seeger snapped a photograph of a dark shape displaying two humps on the surface, but the picture failed to convince investigators, and no further sightings have been recorded so far.

Source: Kirk, *In the Domain of the Lake Monsters*.

Fowler Lake, Wisconsin

This lake in Wisconsin's Waukesha County produced a series of LAKE MONSTER reports in the 19th century. Unfortunately, witnesses could not agree on whether they had seen an oversized BEAVER, FISH or otter. The mystery remains unsolved, and sightings are no longer reported.

Sources: Kirk, *In the Domain of the Lake Monsters*; "Western lake resorts each have a water monster." *Chicago Tribune* (24 July 1892).

Fox (Black Norwegian)

In early 2003, residents of central Norway's mountainous Sogn og Fjordane County reported a new breed of fox at large in their forests. The foxes were black, larger than the familiar red fox (*Vulpes vulpes*), and viciously dis-

Norway's black fox is said to be a bold, aggressive predator.

posed toward slaughtering domestic animals for pleasure. Farmers feared the prowling foxes would menace their sheep herds in summer, but county wildlife consultant Jon Jordanger noted that foxes could be shot during the normal hunting season, from 15 July to 15 April.

Jordanger surmised that the "new species" comprised hybrids of wild and tame foxes, noting that "a half-tame animal will always be more aggressive because it's not shy around people." One local resident claimed to have trapped a black fox, reporting that it collapsed and died in its cage from sheer anger. Sadly, the specimen was not preserved and no other black foxes had yet been caught or photographed by January 2004.

Source: "Mysterious black fox spreads fear." *Afternposteen Nettugaven* (10 March 2003).

Fox sea serpent

In early August 1836, Captain Black and two crewmen aboard the schooner *Fox* spied a SEA SERPENT swimming off the coast of Maine, between the mainland an Mount Desert Rock (near Bar Harbor). As described in the *Bangor Commercial Advertiser*, the witnesses were within 50 yards of the creature and watched it for roughly an hour. They described the animal as 60 feet long, swimming with its snakelike head held two or three feet above water. When at last the *Fox* drew closer, the animal sank out of sight, then resurfaced at a greater distance from the ship.

Source: O'Neill, *The Great New England Sea Serpent*.

François Lake, British Columbia

If local stories may be trusted, unidentified "water grizzlies" once inhabited this large lake, 60 miles northwest of Prince George. Whatever the true nature of the cryptids, no LAKE MONSTER sightings have been reported since the early 20th century.

Source: Diamond Jenness, "Myths of the Carrier Indians of British Columbia." *Journal of American Folklore* 47 (1934): 97, 256–257.

Fraser, Mark (n.d.)

A resident of Ayrshire, Scotland, Mark Fraser ranks among Britain's most active researchers in recording accounts of ALIEN BIG CATS. While tracking the elusive felids since 1994, Fraser founded the SCOTTISH BIG CATS SOCIETY as an affiliate of the BRITISH BIG CATS SOCIETY, and has served at various times as a spokesman for both organizations. He maintains an active Internet website and contributes frequent articles to various newspapers and periodicals. Fraser described his quest to the *Ayrshire Post* in September 2002:

> I've been doing this as a hobby for eight years now and its a bit frustrating to say the least. Even my wife Hannah has spotted a couple over the years which is a bit ironic really. This is a real passion for me and I spend as much time on it as possible. After reports of sightings come in I will investigate and perhaps even stake out the area with infrared cameras overnight. I recently spent a full week out in the country near Galston after a sighting, but CATS aren't stupid and it never appeared again. But over the years I've collected tree scratchings, hairs, paw prints and feces, so I believe there is a big cat of some kind out there.

Sources: Alan Campbell, "Big cat stalker." *Ayrshire* (Scotland) *Post* (24 September 2002); Scottish Big Cats Society. http://www.scottishbig-cats.org.

Freeman, Paul (d. 2003)

Washington resident Paul Freeman was working as a watershed patroller for the U.S. Forest Service on 10 June 1982, when he encountered BIGFOOT near Walla Walla. Freeman later told reporter David Foster that the creature "was 60 yards away. I watched him walk the length of two football fields. He'd take a few steps, look back at me, and take a few more steps. Then he went up over a hill and disappeared." Freeman made plaster casts of the animal's footprints, on which researcher JEFF MELDRUM later discovered dermal ridges of the kind found on human footprints and fingerprints. Foster described the aftermath of Freeman's sighting in a 1997 article:

> When word got out, Freeman became an instant celebrity, but the fame was spiked with ridicule. Reporters hounded him. His supervisors doubted him. Anonymous callers said he was crazy and threatened to take his three children away. Freeman quit his Forest Service job and moved away, drifting through a series of jobs. A gnawing need for vindication, he says, drew him back to Walla Walla in 1984.

Over the next two decades, Freeman found more Bigfoot tracks, and in August 1995 he found two clumps of alleged Bigfoot hair in Washington's Blue Mountains. Scientists at Ohio State University accepted the hairs for DNA analysis in November 1995 and promised a full report by the end of the month, but they later reneged, claiming that hairs without roots cannot be tested. (In fact, they routinely yield DNA results in police laboratories around the world.)

Skeptical journalists unfairly seized on the announcement as "proof" that Bigfoot does not exist, but Freeman remained tireless in his pursuit of the creature. He claimed to have photographed Bigfoot on several occasions, and his best-known video footage was analyzed in 2003, on the Discovery Channel's program *Sasquatch: Legend Meets Science.*

Fellow Bigfoot researchers remain divided on the value of Freeman's evidence. Investigators RENÉ DAHINDEN and JOHN GREEN were frankly skeptical, while LOREN COLEMAN opined that Freeman "personifies the individual who has an extraordinary encounter." Freeman died on 2 April 2003, from complications related to diabetes.

Sources: Thomas Clouse, "Bigfoot believer kept on searching." Spokane (WA) *Spokesman-Review* (3 April 2003); Coleman, *Bigfoot!*; Loren Coleman, "Paul Freeman, Bigfoot dermals discoverer, has died." Bigfoot Internet newsgroup (2 April 2003).

Freeman, Richard (n.d.)

A British cryptozoologist affiliated with the CENTRE FOR FORTEAN ZOOLOGY, Richard Freeman visited Thailand in autumn 2001 to investigate legends of the NĀGA, a legendary giant SNAKE. He collected eyewitness accounts of the creature and explored caves said to be the lair of an 18-meter (59-foot) specimen. While Freeman failed to meet the Nāga, he discovered Thailand's first known colony of luminous midge larva, similar to the famous "glow worms" of New Zealand's Waitomo cave system (*Arachnocampa luminosa*). Upon his return to Britain, Freeman speculated that the Nāga (if it exists) might be a larger relict form of prehistoric boa (*Wonambi naracoortensis*). Based on fossil remains from Australia, *Wonambi* reached a length of 20 feet, with a disproportionate girth of 29 inches.

Sources: Karl Shuker, "Alien zoo." *Fortean Times* 141 (January 2001): 23; Shuker, "Alien zoo." *Fortean Times* 144 (April 2001): 23.

Frickenhausen, Germany

During the 18th and early 19th century, LAKE MONSTER reports were filed from an unnamed body of water near this town in Germany's Bayern State. Whatever the source of those sightings, incidents have not continued to the modern day.

Source: Johann Sepp, *Altbayerischer Sagenschatz zur Bereicherung der indogermanischen Mythologie.* Munich: E. Stahl, 1876.

Friendship sea serpent

On 21 May 1964, the fishing boat *Friendship* was trawling off Nantucket, Massachusetts, 40 miles east-southeast of the Great Round Shoal buoy, when its crew observed a mysterious SEA SERPENT. A New Bedford newspaper described the animal on 22 May.

> The body was deep blue or blackish and "where the neck joined the body was irregularly scalloped." … [I]t had a light gray dorsal projection, triangular in shape and rounded on top. This was about four feet long and meaty looking. On the back were two blow-holes, pear shaped or oval….[W]here the mouth area might be was a very light color.

Source: Heuvelmans, *In the Wake of the Sea Serpent.*

Frog Lake, Alberta

Cryptozoologist JOHN KIRK included this Canadian lake, 20 miles southeast of Bonnyville, in a list of North American sites with reported LAKE MONSTERS, but no details are forthcoming from his work or any other available source. The listing may refer to aboriginal traditions, but any evidence of modern sightings has yet to be published.

Source: Kirk, *In the Domain of the Lake Monsters.*

Frogs (Giant)

In the summer of 1987, a team of nine biologists from Beijing University visited Wuhnan, in Hubei Province, to film and study wildlife at some deep freshwater pools nearby. While setting up their video equipment, the scientists saw three huge froglike creatures surface in the nearest pool, advancing toward their position on shore. The animals were grayish-white, with gaping mouths six feet across and eyes larger than rice bowls. One of the monsters lashed out with its tongue seizing a tripod-mounted camera, which disappeared into its gaping mouth. The other two animals, meanwhile, emitted shrieking cries before all three retreated to the pond and sank from view. As noted by KARL SHUKER, the incident sounds like a preposterous HOAX, until we recall that all nine witnesses were trained scientists from China's top university, serving a regime that does not appreciate practical jokes.

Source: Shuker, *From Flying Toads to Snakes with Wings.*

Chinese scientists reported giant frogs from Hubei Province in 1987.

Funkwe   In 1900, while traveling in Northern Rhodesia (now Zambia), William Kennelly collected native stories of a monster called Funkwe, inhabiting Lake Chilengwa. Kennelly's informants described Funkwe as a giant SNAKE with a ravenous appetite for human beings. Kennelly visited the lake, 10 miles southeast of Ndola (at Zambia's border with the Democratic Republic of Congo), but he failed to glimpse the creature.

   Source: C.P. Chesnaye, "A journey from Fort Jameson to the Kafue River." *Geographical Journal* 17 (1901): 42-48.

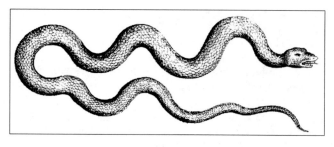

The African Funkwe is a huge man-eating snake.

—G—

Gaal, Arlene (1937–)   A native of British Columbia, Arlene Gaal is recognized as the principal chronicler of OGOPOGO, the LAKE MONSTER reported for decades from Lake Okanagan. Gaal's interest in the creature dates from 1968, when she settled at Kelowna with her husband and three children, working as a teacher and columnist for the *Kelowna Daily Courier*. Intrigued by ongoing reports of Ogopogo, Gaal began intensive personal research, resulting in the publication of three books: *Up from the Depths* (1976); *Ogopogo: The True Story of the Okanagan Lake Million Dollar Monster* (1994); and *In Search of Ogopogo: Sacred Creature of the Okanagan Waters* (2001). She has also served as a consultant to television programs aired in the U.S. and Japan. Gaal is an honorary lifetime member of the BRITISH COLUMBIA SCIENTIFIC CRYPTOZOOLOGY CLUB.

   Sources: Coleman and Clark, *Cryptozoology A to Z*; Arlene Gaal interview, "Welcome to Ogopogo Country," http://collections.ic.gc.ca/ogopogo/interviews/arlene.html.

Gair Loch, Scotland   This sea loch on Scotland's west coast was reportedly the scene of a fatal attack by an unknown beast in the early 16th century. According to sketchy reports, a cryptid the size of a greyhound emerged from the loch and killed three men before it was driven back into the water.

   Source: Hector Boece, *Scotorum historiae a prima gentis origine*. Paris: Josse Bade, 1527.

Gambo   On 12 June 1983, while strolling near the Bungalow Beach Hotel at Kotu, Gambia, Owen Burnham found a mysterious creature washed up on the beach. Local residents were cutting off its head, for sale as a curiosity, when Burnham arrived to interrupt them. Cryptozoologist KARL SHUKER subsequently dubbed the beast "Gambo," and published the following description: It measured 15 feet long and five feet wide. Its smooth skin, devoid of scales or fur, was brown on top and white along the belly. Its head resembled a dolphin's, but without a blowhole. The beast had small brown eyes, 18-inch jaws with nostrils at the tip, and 80 conical teeth. The animal had four paddle-shaped flippers, each 18 inches long. Its 5-foot pointed tail possessed no flukes, and the body had no dorsal fin.

   As Shuker observed, the combination of features displayed by Gambo ruled out identification as any known mammal, reptile or FISH. Prehistoric whales such as the ZEUGLODON, meanwhile, had only 40 teeth. Speculation continues that Gambo may represent a surviving prehistoric reptile of the pliosaur family (pre-sumed extinct for 65 million years, as was the COELACANTH), but its remains sadly were not preserved for further study.

   Source: Shuker, "Gambo: The beaked beast of Bungalow Beach"; Shuker *In Search of Prehistoric Survivors*.

Gander Lake, Canada   In the 1930s, Newfoundland's Gander Lake produced reports of a foot-long creature with six legs, 3-inch pincers, and eyes resembling those of a FISH. Skeptics claimed that hysterical locals had simply failed to identify an American lobster (*Homarus americanus*), native to Newfoundland waters, but witnesses insisted that the creature lacked the lobster's typical segmented tail.

   Source: "A mari usque ad mare." *Fortean Times* 46 (Spring 1986): 44-51.

Gasparilla Lake, Florida   In July 2003, several residents of Boca Grande, in southwestern Florida's Lee County, reported sightings of a dolphin (Family *Delphinidae*) in Gasparilla Lake. Kristine Barr saw the creature every day for two weeks, while lounging on the porch of her lakeside home, and other witnesses confirmed her impression of a marine mammal chasing FISH across the lake. Tom Farrish, an employee of a local landscaping company, also recorded multiple sightings. Both Barr and

Artist's conception of Gambo, beached on the Gambian coast in June 1983 (*William Rebsamen*).

Farrish described a small, gray, smooth-skinned creature, 2-4 feet long, aggressively pursuing fish toward shore. However, Gasparilla Lake is landlocked, with no inlet from the nearby Gulf of Mexico, thus prompting questions as to how a dolphin could arrive there. Marine mammal expert Randall Wells discounts the reports, suggesting that misguided witnesses have simply seen an otter or a large fish swimming in the lake. Unconvinced, Barr replies, "I know how dolphins swim and absolutely it is a dolphin." Farrish, meanwhile, told reporters, "It's like the Loch Ness monster here." At press time for this book, the creature was at large and unidentified.

Sources: "Residents say there is something 'fishy' in their lake." *Boca Beacon* (29 August 2003); Karl Shuker, "Alien zoo." *Fortean Times* 178 (January 2004): 26.

Gassingram This mystery CAT of the Central African Republic (also known as Vassoko) is described by natives as larger than a mature LION, reddish-brown in color, with small doglike ears and long fangs protruding from its upper jaw. It is a mountain-dwelling nocturnal hunter, reported primarily from the Massif des Bongos, near Ouanda Djallé. The Gassingram's presence is signaled by roars resembling the sounds made by elephants. Its overall description inspires speculation on the possible survival of SABER-TOOTHED CATS in remote parts of Africa.

Sources: Heuvelmans, *Les derniers dragons d'Afrique*; Heuvelmans, *On the Track of Unknown Animals*.

Gatineau River, Canada The Gatineau River rises in the Laurentian Mountains of southwest Québec and flows southward for 240 miles to meet the Ottawa River at Hull. Local witnesses report occasional sightings of an aquatic cryptid in the river, described as ranging from six to 30 feet in length, with a head resembling that of a horse. That description generally agrees with the appearance of several LAKE MONSTERS reported from Québec.

Source: Meurger and Gagnon, *Lake Monster Traditions*.

Gauarge This curious Australian cryptid allegedly combines traits of a BIRD and LAKE MONSTER. Aboriginal traditions describe the Gauarge as resembling a large EMU without feathers, dwelling in various Outback water holes where it springs upon its prey and drowns hapless animals or humans. With no recent sightings on record, cryptozoologists suggest the legendary creature may have sprung from ancient discovery of fossilized DINOSAUR remains.

Sources: Heuvelmans, *On the Track of Unknown Animals*; Whitley, "Mystery animals of Australia."

Gausbuvatnet, Norway Local tradition describes this lake as the home of a LAKE MONSTER that once attacked and killed a horse. The date and details of that incident are unclear, however, and no recent sightings are recorded.

Source: Skjelsvik, "Norwegian lake and sea monsters."

Gazeka Witnesses in Papua New Guinea describe the Gazeka as a large mammal or marsupial, resembling a TAPIR or oversized pig. Sightings occur primarily among the mountains of the Owen Stanley Range, but crewmen from HMS *Basilisk* reported finding huge piles of unidentified (and perhaps unrelated) excrement along New Guinea's northern coast in the 1870s. More recently, in 1962, ancient carvings of unknown animals with long snouts were discovered in the Ambun Valley. BERNARD HEUVELMANS suggested that "[f]rom its outer appearance, it could well be related to the Australian *Diprotodon*"—a 10-foot Pleistocene marsupial presumed extinct for 6,000 years.

Sources: "A remarkable stone figure found in the New Guinea highlands." *Journal of the Polynesian Society* 74 (1965): 78-79; Laurent Forges, "Un marsupial géant survit-il en Nouvelle Guinée?" *Amazone* 2 (January 1983): 9-11; Heuvelmans, "Annotated checklist of apparently unknown animals with which cryptozoology is concerned."

Gean *see* **Giant Water Hen**

Gecko (Giant) Sometime between 1833 and 1869, at a time when record-keeping was apparently ignored, the Marseilles (France) Natural History Museum received a unique reptilian specimen. It was a mounted lizard of unknown species and origin, brown with reddish stripes, measuring a fraction more than two feet long. The creature was displayed, but otherwise ignored, until herpetology curator Alain Delcourt "discovered" it in 1979. Delcourt sent photos of the lizard to colleagues around the world, drawing swift responses from Canadian biologist Anthony Russell and Pennsylvania herpetologist Aaron Bauer. Both agreed that the lizard was a gecko, albeit more than twice the size of the largest known species. In Delcourt's honor, the reptile was formally named *Hoplodactylus delcourti*, but investigators still had no idea where it came from or if any more of the breed were still living. Bauer's research suggested New Zealand as a point of origin, where a legendary lizard called the KAWEKAWEAU (or simply Kaweau) had been rumored since the 19th century. A 2-foot specimen closely resembling *H. delcourti* was allegedly killed in 1870, in the North Island's Waimana Valley, but it was not preserved. Bauer supposed the species was extinct until an article in the Wellington *Dominion* reported a North Island sighting in the 1960s. Searches continue in New Zealand, but no other specimens of the giant gecko have thus far been found.

Sources: Bauer and Russell, "Recent advances in the search for the living giant gecko of New Zealand"; Shuker, *The New Zoo*.

New Zealand's giant gecko is known only from a French museum specimen.

Genaprugwirion *see* **Cenaprugwirion**

***General Charles Humphreys* sea serpent** In 1935, while traveling aboard the *General Charles Humphreys*, a soldier named Silas King sighted a SEA SERPENT swimming in New York's Upper Bay, near Governor's Island. The creature was killed and hauled aboard, whereupon it proved to be a large PYTHON of unrecorded species. This case provides a rare example of a "sea serpent" that actually *was* a serpent—and it raises the question of how the snake found its way to the wrong side of the Atlantic Ocean.

Source: Heuvelmans, *In the Wake of the Sea Serpents*.

***General Coole* sea serpent**   On 1 August 1786, while traveling northeast of the Azores at 42° 44' north latitude and 23° 10' west longitude, British officers aboard the *General Coole* encountered a curious SEA SERPENT. The ship's log reported: "A very large SNAKE passed the ship; it appeared to be 16 or 18 feet in length, and 3 or 4 feet in circumference, the back of a light ash-colour and the belly thereof yellow."

Source: Heuvelmans, *In the Wake of the Sea Serpents.*

Geographe Bay sea serpent   On 30 March 1879, the Rev. H.W. Brown and a friend named M'Guire observed a SEA SERPENT swimming in Geographe Bay, near the southwestern tip of Western Australia. As Brown described the incident to *Nature*:

Just as I met (M'Guire) the FISH...came to the surface, showing gradually more and more of his length, till, when he was almost at rest, and all was apparently in view, I estimated the length to be 60 feet, straight and taper, like a long spar, with the butt end, his head and shoulders, showing well above the surface.

I can only describe the head as like the end of a log, bluff, about two feet in diameter; on the back we noticed, showing very distinctly above the water, several square-topped fins.... I saw no lateral fins and no fish-tail.

His description notwithstanding, Brown's crude sketch of the creature bears no resemblance to any known fish, and the animal remains unidentified. BERNARD HEUVELMANS considered it a specimen of his hypothetical "many-finned" sea serpent.

Source: Heuvelmans, *In the Wake of the Sea Serpents.*

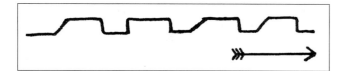

The Rev. H.W. Brown sketched the Geographe Bay sea serpent in 1879.

Georges River, Australia   Australian cryptozoologist REX GILROY claims sightings of a large freshwater cryptid from the Georges River in New South Wales, but no published details are presently available.

Source: Gilroy, "Search for the Hawkesbury River monster." *Australasian Ufologist* 4 (2003): 25-28.

***Georgina* sea serpent**   On 21 May 1877, crewmen aboard the *Georgina* sighted an unidentified creature in the Indian Ocean west of Sumatra, Indonesia. Their report described the animal as "a large serpent about forty or fifty feet long, grey and yellow in colour, and ten or eleven inches thick." Nine years later, officers aboard a Malaysian ship saw another SEA SERPENT in the same area, but no further details are available for that encounter.

Source: Heuvelmans, *In the Wake of the Sea Serpents*

Gerit   An unknown APE or HOMINID reported from western Kenya, the Gerit is described as bipedal, covered in reddish-yellow hair, and somewhat taller than a man. Natives describe the Gerit as a cave-dweller fond of stealing honey from rural beehives. Alternate local names for the creature throughout its range include Gereet, Kereet, N'gugu and Tiondo.

Source: Heuvelmans, *Les bêtes humaines d'Afrique.*

Geteit *see* **Nandi bear**

***G.F.B.* sea serpent**   In 1961, Maurice Brown produced a program on SEA SERPENTS for the British Broadcasting Corporation. Soon after it aired, Brown received a letter from H. Hodgson that read: "I listened with a certain amount of interest to your programme, 'The Great Sea Serpent.' I have seen a PLESIOSAURUS." When asked for further details, Hodgson explained that he had seen the beast in 1925, while working as a crewman on the vessel *G.F.B.*, owned by G.F. Birch of Spalding, Lincolnshire. In his third and last letter to Brown, Hodgson wrote:

First of all let's clear the deck. This thing was no sea serpent. It was of great bulk, as big as a 500-ton ship and with a very long neck and small head. The head must have been turned away from me because I thought "it looks like a football!" It had a terrific turn of speed.

Hodgson provided names and addresses of other crewmen from the *G.F.B.*, but no further details of the sighting were forthcoming.

Source: Heuvelmans, *In the Wake of the Sea Serpents.*

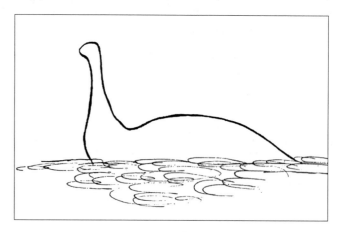

The *G.F.B.* sea serpent, after witness H. Hodgson.

Ghost Ape of Marwood   An elusive primate reported from Devon, in England, the so-called Ghost APE of Marwood has acquired a mythic quality over time. Local legends claim the creature was initially a rich landowner's pet, which escaped at some uncertain date and kidnapped its late owner's son in the process. Occasional sightings have continued into recent times, as with the report of a large apelike creature seen by three boys near Kings Nympton, Devon in 1978.

Source: Downes, "Born to be wild."

Ghost Deer   Northern California's elusive Ghost Deer allegedly dwells in the wilderness canyons of Mount Eddy, located west of Mount Shasta in Siskiyou County. Legend and a handful of eyewitnesses describe it as a huge buck, weighing at least 240 pounds and sporting antlers with 12 points on one side, 10 points on the other. Journalist Tom Stienstra reports finding hoofprints twice the size of a normal buck's in meadows surrounding Mount Eddy, and hunters who have tracked the Ghost Deer tell even stranger stories, claiming that it seems impervious to bullets. On 22 February 2004, Stienstra reported that the Ghost Deer was in fact a stray specimen of Roosevelt's elk (*Cervus elaphus roosevelti*), the largest subspecies of elk and a creature well known to California hunters.

The Ghost Deer of Mount Eddy, California is reportedly impervious to bullets.

Source: Tom Stienstra, "Sightings may ignite debate over 'natives.'" *San Francisco Chronicle* (22 February 2004); Tom Stienstra, "Tracking the legendary ghost deer of northern California." *San Francisco Chronicle* (9 November 2003).

Giant Sloth *see* **Megatherium**

Giant Squid Long before it was recognized by science, the giant squid maintained a fierce grip on the human imagination. It was 12-armed Scylla in the *Odyssey* and the fearsome Kraken of Norse legend, large enough to be mistaken for a chain of islands. Pliny the Elder (A.D. 23–79) described a huge "polyp" that raided FISH ponds at Casteia (now Rocadillo, Spain): it boasted 30-foot arms sprouting from a head the size of a 90-gallon cask. At least 11 giant squids were stranded on beaches from Scandinavia and Newfoundland to the Bahamas and Tasmania between 1545 and 1855. The huge cephalopod's existence was finally acknowledged in 1857, named *Architeuthis dux* by Danish Japetus Steenstrup. Working from fragmentary remains and ancient descriptions of sea monsters, Steenstrup went on name a second species *A. monachus*, and other researchers added 17 more provisional species by 1935, but most zoologists today treat *Architeuthis* as one of a kind.

Much of the confusion surrounding giant squids stems from the fact that none has ever been captured and studied alive. Earth's largest invertebrate and fifth-largest known animal (surpassed in length only by four great whales) is still known only from carcasses stranded on beaches or dredged from the sea in fishing nets. By 2003, at least 195 specimens had been collected from around the world. Dead squids are found most frequently in New Zealand (39), Newfoundland (36), Norway (16), and South Africa (16). Nearly all are incomplete, most badly mutilated or decomposed, but enough remain substantially intact to permit a rough estimate of the creature's adult size. Two 55-foot specimens hold the official record, found respectively at Thimble Tickle, Newfoundland (1878) and Island Bay, New Zealand (1880). A close runner-up, at 52 feet, was found at Coombs Cove, Newfoundland in 1872. Other truly giant squids include a 47-footer snared

in the Bahamas (1958); two 46-foot specimens found at Bonavista Bay, Newfoundland (1872) and Ranheim, Norway (1928); a 45-foot specimen from Lamaline, Newfoundland (1871); two 44-footers from Newfoundland's Conception Bay (1873) and Lance Cove (1877); a 41-foot squid from Kaikoura, New Zealand (1930); and a 40-footer from Lamaline, Newfoundland (1870).

Most *Architeuthis* specimens are substantially smaller than those giants, and they are not alone among the sea's great squids. Controversy still surrounds the maximum size attained by the so-called COLOSSAL SQUID (*Mesonychoteuthis hamiltoni*), said by some to outgrow *Architeuthis*, but most experts concede a length of 20 feet. A still-unidentified "MYSTERY SQUID" measuring 21 feet was reported from the Pacific Ocean in 2001. The "Pacific giant squid" (*Moroteuthis robusta*) certainly reaches 19 feet, and a subspecies (*M. japanica*) may exceed 14 feet. The Humboldt or "jumbo" squid (*Dosidicus gigas*) may not exceed six feet, but it hunts in voracious packs, making up in ferocity whatever it lacks in size.

So far, all efforts to study *Architeuthis* in its native habitat have proved fruitless. Deep-sea vessels have been used in vain attempts to lure the giant squid from hiding, and a fanciful effort involving attachment of a camera to the head of a sperm whale (known

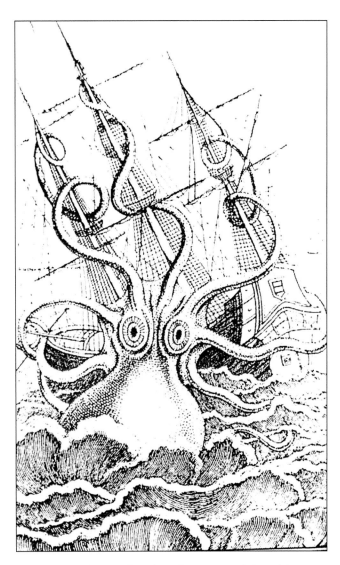

Pierre Denys de Montfort drew this giant cephalopod in 1801.

to feed on giant squids in the abyssal depths) likewise failed. A team of New Zealand researchers did capture several juvenile specimens on film, in February 2002, and while the experience was fascinating, the 4- and 5-inch "giants" revealed nothing of substance concerning their elders. *Architeuthis* is presumed to be a solitary hunter, but a very different picture was offered by Captain C.A. McDowall in the January 1998 issue of London's *Marine Observer*. McDowall recalled that "some years ago...in the Arabian Sea at night":

> ...we were visited by a large school of giant squid — I think. They just rose out of the deep to look at us, about 200 of them. There were babies the size of a bucket, and adults, the biggest having bodies 3-4m [10-13 feet] long with two long tentacles about 6m [19.5 feet] long. We lowered the loading ramp to get a good look, and the Captain's granddaughter took photographs — which probably didn't come out because of the very bright lights and the creatures being in shadow. The eyes were very large, bigger than a dinner plate, but the most remarkable thing was the colour. The top of the head was red, like a Ferrari, and the tentacles were white covered with red spots which made them look pink. Where the red back joined the white area around the eyes, there was a pattern of interlocking spots. The crew tried to catch the babies but once hooked they broke free, and that individual could not be hooked again, which was interesting. They stayed for about an hour and a half, and then slowly sank from view.

Any giant predator rates cautious treatment, but does *Architeuthis* truly pose a threat to humans at sea? Divers attacked by giant squid would likely not survive to tell the tale, and while it is fruitless to speculate on the fate of vanished swimmers or boaters, there are cases on file involving aggressive (even deadly) behavior by giant squids. They include:

1801— Pierre Denys de Montfort published the account of a retired Danish sea captain, Jean-Magnus Dens, who claimed he had once lost three crewmen in a battle with a huge squid off the coast of Angola. One of the monster's severed arms measured 25 feet and had "suckers as large as a ladle."

October 1873— Fishermen Daniel and Theophilus Piccot, with Piccot's 12-year-old son, were attacked by a giant squid at Portugal Cove, Newfoundland. The animal retreated after a fierce struggle, leaving behind a severed tentacle 19 feet long.

10 May 1874— The schooner Pearl was allegedly attacked and

sunk at in the Indian Ocean at 8° 50' north latitude and 84° 5' east longitude, by a huge squid with "monstrous arms like trees." *The Times* of London published alleged survivor James Floyd's account of the incident on 4 July, but no trace of the *Pearl* is found in any British shipping registry, and the report was almost certainly a HOAX.

1930-33— Commander Arne Grönningsaeter of the Royal Norwegian Navy reported (in December 1946) that his 15,000-ton tanker, the *Brunswick*, was attacked three times by giant squids in the South Pacific, each time while traveling between Hawaii and Samoa. In each case, the squid attacked from the stern and was killed by the *Brunswick*'s propellers. Grönningsaeter speculated that the animals mistook his ship for a whale.

25 March 1943— The troop ship *Britannia* was sunk by a German warship in the tropical Atlantic, 1,400 miles west of Freetown, Sierra Leone. Twelve surviving crewmen clung to a tiny raft, taking turns in the water. One night, a large squid dragged one of the sailors below, and moments later a tentacle briefly gripped the leg of Lieutenant R.E.G. Cox, leaving him scarred with marks of toothed suckers one inch in diameter.

12 January 2003— A large squid reportedly attacked the trimaran *Geronimo* in the Atlantic west of Gibraltar, clutching the boat for an hour. Captain Olivier de Kersauson claimed the squid's tentacles were 23-26 feet long and "as thick as my arm." The animal released *Geronimo* and retreated when crewmen stopped the boat, prepared to do battle with knives.

What is the maximum size attained by giant squids? Most authors grant a length of 60 feet but refuse to budge from that benchmark without a larger specimen in hand. Meanwhile, reports of much larger specimens are plentiful in maritime literature. A suggestion of size may be gained from fragmentary remains and sucker scars found on sperm whales, but even there controversy is rife. A 46-foot *Architeuthis* beached in 1872 had suckers 2.5 inches wide, and BERNARD HEUVELMANS calculated that in squids recovered prior to 1968, the diameter of the largest sucker was equal to $\frac{1}{100}$ of the total head-and-body length. A giant squid's eight arms normally equal the head-body length (if they do not exceed it), and the two much longer tentacles may stretch double that distance. We may calculate, therefore, that a squid with 1-inch suckers could easily measure 25 feet overall.

But how big do the *suckers* get?

In 1801, naturalist Pierre Denys de Montfort recorded interviews with two Dunkirk whaling captains who described huge tentacles regurgitated by dying sperm whales. One witness, a Captain Benjohnson, referred to an arm 35 feet long and over 6 inches thick at its severed narrow end; he estimated that a 10-foot section was missing from the arm's tip and 10-20 feet from the base. A Captain Reynolds, meanwhile, described an arm 45 feet long, 2 feet 6 inches in diameter and 7 feet 6 inches in circumference, with suckers as large as a plate. In 1892, a report from agents of the Hudson Bay Company described a huge squid found dead at Port Simpson, British Columbia. Before it was towed out to sea, one arm was measured at a length of 98 feet, with suckers "as big as a basin plate, to saucer-size at the ends." In his 1938 monograph on sperm whales, L. Harrison Matthews wrote, "Nearly all male Sperm whales carry scars caused by the suckers and claws of large squids, scars caused by suckers up to 10 cm. [3.9 inches] being common." In *Follow the Whale* (1956), IVAN SANDERSON reported: "The largest rings from the largest squids have a diameter of about four inches, yet scars left by such suckers on the skin of captured sperm whales have measured over eighteen inches in diameter."

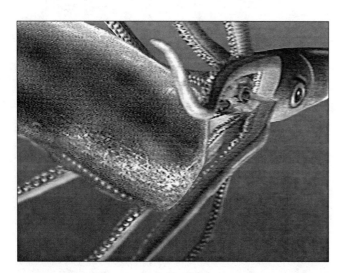

***Architeuthis* battles to the death with a sperm whale (*William Rebsamen*).**

In theory, 18-inch suckers would suggest a monster measuring 450 feet long with tentacles extended, but most experts dismiss reports of such huge scars as fantasy. As Heuvelmans acknowledged:

> [T]here are other squids which relatively speaking have much larger suckers. *Stenoteuthis caroli*, for instance, is only 2 feet 8 inches long, but its suckers are ¾ inch across. But these other squids are all small, and it seems likelier that there should be an *Architeuthis* less than twice as large as the biggest known specimen than a *Stenoteuthis* five times as big.

Even diligent skeptic RICHARD ELLIS granted the possible existence of truly huge squids, after reading the eyewitness account of Dennis Braun. Braun was a U.S. Marine in early 1969, training for amphibious assaults on Vieques Island, Puerto Rico, when he and two shipmates saw a huge squid drifting on the surface. Based on distance and the size of the vessel, Braun estimated that the squid was at least 100 feet long. Ellis asserts that squids beyond that length would likely starve for lack of prey, but Heuvelmans suggests that monster specimens might turn the tables on predatory whales. In fact, huge squids may account for reports such as those logged by crewmen aboard the *PAULINE* (1875) and *KIUSHIU MARU* (1879), wherein SEA SERPENTS were allegedly observed killing whales.

Whatever size is finally attained by giant squid, they are successful predators. So successful, in fact, that a July 2002 report in *Australasian Science* claimed large cephalopods were "taking over the world." A decline in natural predators was credited with the increasing size and frequency of specimens hauled from the deep. In fact, the authors claimed, cephalopods have overtaken man in terms of bio-mass, meaning that squid take up more space on Earth than human beings.

Sources: Ellis, *Monsters of the Sea*; Ellis, *The Search for the Giant* Squid; "Giant squid attack." *Fortean Times* 169 (May 2003): 7; Heuvelmans, *In the Wake of the Sea Serpents*; Heuvelmans, *The Kraken and the Colossal Octopus*; Frank Lane, *Kingdom of the Octopus*. New York: Pyramid Publications, 1960.

Giant Water Hen   In 1691, François Legaut led a French expedition to colonize Rodrigues Island, in the Mascarene group (east of Madagascar). After two years on the island, Legaut returned to France and subsequently published an account of his travels in 1708. One entry described a large marsh-dwelling BIRD, resembling a 6-foot goose with long legs and oversized feet, which Legaut called a Gean. The birds, all white except for red patches under their wings, lived primarily on nearby Mauritius, where they were hunted by settlers' dogs.

Legaut met one specimen on Rodriguez, but he shot and ate it, instead of preserving the remains for study. No other witnesses reported sightings of the birds, but Legaut was considered reliable enough that his discovery was named the giant water hen (*Legautia gigantea*). It is presumed extinct today, but some researchers hope a few survivors may remain on one of the Indian Ocean's remote islands.

Source: Bille, *Rumors of Existence*.

Giants   Cryptozoologists normally do not consider human beings as subjects of study, but *Homo sapiens* is after all a species of mammal, and the investigation of anomalous remains or races seems to have found no other niche in modern science. Human remains discovered in at least 10 countries (and in 12 U.S. states) over the past 2,600 years strongly suggest that giant humans belong as much to reality as to legend. An admittedly incomplete list of those discoveries, presented chronologically, includes:

560 B.C. — A blacksmith at Aléa, Arcadia (Greece) unearthed a 10-foot coffin containing the remains of a very large human. Locals presumed they were the bones of legendary Spartan hero Orestes, while some classical scholars today suggest the bones were those of some prehistoric animal, found earlier and ritually interred.

Middle Ages (500-1500) — An otherwise undated report by Hugh Hodson of Thorneway, Cumberland, England described the unearthing of a "gyant" 13 feet 6 inches tall, with teeth 6 inches long and 2 inches wide, whose "chin bone could contain three pecks of oatmeal." The skeleton was buried in armor, with various oversized weapons.

1509 — Ditch diggers outside Rouen, France revealed a tomb containing a large but incomplete human skeleton. From the 4-foot shinbone, examiners estimated the man's height at 17 feet. The hollow skull was large enough to hold a bushel of corn. A copper plate affixed to the tomb identified its occupant as Chevalier Ricon de Vallemont.

1578 — Sir Francis Drake lost two sailors in a battle with "men of large stature" at Port San Julian, on the coast of Argentina's Santa Cruz Province. Drake claimed the native warriors were 7 feet 6 inches tall.

1592 — While navigating the Strait of Magellan, explorer Anthony Knyvet saw huge Patagonians and reportedly measured some of their corpses at Port Desire. The bodies ranged from 10 feet 6 inches to 12 feet tall.

1598 — Another explorer, Sebald de Weert, reported seeing 10-foot natives in the same part of southern Argentina.

1764 — While anchored in the Strait of Magellan, Commodore Byron of the *Dolphin* met with a tribe of supposed giants, whose chief was close to 7 feet tall. Four years later, writing for the *Annual Register*, one of Byron's officers claimed the natives were even larger. "Some of them are certainly nine feet," he wrote, "if they do not exceed it....[T]here was hardly a man there less than eight feet, most of them considerably more; the women, I believe, run from seven and a half to eight."

1800 — According to the *Historical Encyclopedia of Illinois and History of Lake County* (1902), excavations performed in this year around Conneaut revealed "human bones...belonging to men of gigantic structure. Some of the skulls were of sufficient capacity to admit the head of an ordinary man, and jaw bones that might have been fitted on over the face with equal facility; the other bones were proportionally large."

1826-36 — During his travels on the *Beagle*, Charles Darwin visited a tribe of "so-called giant Patagonians" at Cape Gregory, Argentina. He reported that "on average their height is six feet, with some men taller and only a few shorter; and the women are also tall; altogether they are certainly not the tallest race that we anywhere saw."

1829 — During construction of a hotel at Chesterville, Ohio (Morrow County), a "large" human skeleton was unearthed. It was not measured, but witnesses reported that the mandible "fit easily over that of a citizen of the village, who was remarkable for his large jaw." A physician examined the skull, reporting that it had "more teeth than the white race of today." The skeleton was sent to Mansfield, but its fate and whereabouts are unknown today.

1833 — Soldiers at Rancho Lompoc, in southern California's Santa Barbara County, reportedly unearthed a 12-foot-tall human skeleton, buried with giant weapons and carved sea shells. The massive skull possessed a double row of teeth.

1868— Minnesota settlers began a series of excavations, opening Indian burial mounds at multiple locations over the next two decades. Several skeletons measuring 7-8 feet tall were unearthed. The largest, a "petrified" skeleton found at Sauk Rapids, reportedly measured 10 feet 9½ inches; its skull was flat on top, with a 31.5-inch circumference; the femur measured 26¼ inches, while the fibula was 25½ inches long.

1872— Excavation of Indian mounds at Seneca Township, Ohio (Noble County) revealed three partial skeletons whose height was estimated at eight feet. Examiners reported that the skulls had double rows of teeth in both jaws.

July 1877— Local newspapers announced the discovery of a giant skeletal foot and foreleg, found by prospectors near Eureka, Nevada. The leg reportedly measured 39 inches from knee to ankle.

1878— Diggers in Ashtabula County, Ohio penetrated more Indian burial mounds, uncovering multiple human skulls so large they fit over the head of a normal-sized man in the manner of a football helmet, with the skeletal lower jaw enveloping his face. Contemporary accounts state that "the bones of the upper and lower extremities were of corresponding size."

1882— Skeletal remains of 10 "gigantic" men and women were excavated from a prehistoric burial mound outside Warren, Minnesota.

1883— *The History of Marion County, Ohio* was published, referring to prior discoveries of "gigantic skeletons, with the high cheek bones, powerful jaws and massive frames peculiar of the red man."

1883— *The History of Brown County, Ohio* described excavation of three 8-foot human skeletons which turned black and crumbled after several days' exposure to the elements.

1890-91— The *12th Annual Report of the Bureau of Ethnology to the Secretary of the Smithsonian Institution* (1894) reported excavation of an Etowah burial mound in Bartow County, Georgia, that contained "a seven-foot skeleton having a heavy frame."

1890-91— The same Smithsonian report related the discovery of another giant "Indian" skeleton in Roane County, Tennessee. As described in the text: "The length from the base of the skull to the bones of the toes was found to be 7 feet 3 inches. It is probable, therefore, that this individual when living was fully 7½ feet high."

1890-91— Yet another giant find recorded in the same report — this one from Dunleith, Illinois — was described as follows: "Near the original surface, 10 or 12 feet from the center, on the lower side, lying at full length on its back, was one of the largest skeletons discovered by the Bureau agents, the length as proved by actual measurement being between 7 and 8 feet."

1890-91— The Smithsonian's report includes still more giant skeletons, these extracted from the Great Smith Mound in Kanawha County, West Virginia. The smaller of the two measured "fully seven feet long," while the larger "represented a man conceivably approaching eight feet in height when living."

1890-91— From burial mounds in Union County, Mississippi, the Smithsonian reported discovery of an 18-inch femur that "would indicate a man of above average height, perhaps approaching seven feet." The same report acknowledged that "femurs exceeding twenty inches have been found" in the same area.

1891— Workmen uncovered a granite burial vault outside Crit-

tenden, Arizona (now a ghost town, north of Patagonia, in Santa Cruz County). The sarcophagus, though empty, was 12 feet long and bore a carving on its lid depicting a 6-toed giant.

12 August 1896— A Minnesota newspaper, the St. Paul *Globe*, reported that a "huge man" had been unearthed on the Beckley farm at Lake Koronis, near Paynesville in Stearns County.

1930— Four human skeletons 7-9 feet tall were allegedly unearthed from two burial mounds outside Salem, West Virginia, but most of the bones disintegrated or were "lost" by the time anthropologist D.T. Stewart arrived to examine the find. Stewart reported that the remaining bones were average size.

1942— U.S. Army engineers on Shemya Island, in the Aleutians, uncovered a number of giant human skulls, with brow ridges measuring 22-24 inches from base to crown. The average human has a 6-inch brow ridge, prompting IVAN SANDERSON to calculate that the owners of the Shemya skulls must have been 20 feet tall.

1965— A "perfectly preserved" human skeleton measuring 8 feet 9 inches was found beneath a rock ledge near Holly Creek, Kentucky. The skull had a 30-inch circumference, with narrow slits in place of normal eye and nostril sockets, while the mandible was fused to the skull. Kentucky folklorist Michael Henson examined the skeleton briefly, but it was later reburied at an unknown location by the man who discovered it.

16 May 1966— London's *Daily Mirror* reported that "a ferocious band of savages more than seven feet tall are terrorising neighbouring tribes in the Amazon jungle" of Brazil's Mato Grosso State. Members of the victimized Calapalos tribe referred to their attackers as Krem-Akarore. Their existence was allegedly confirmed by Brazilian soldiers on a training exercise in the rain forest. An expedition to contact the strange tribe was announced, including three Britons, but no results of that effort were published.

May 1969— Archaeologists at Stretton-on-Fosse, Warwickshire, England discovered a 4th- or 5th-century Saxon cemetery. Over subsequent months, 31 graves were opened, including those of several "very big chaps" ranging from 6 feet 10 inches to 8 feet tall. The giant warriors were buried with shields, swords and spears.

1970s— Archaeologists at Repton, Derbyshire excavated a mound on the grounds of the Repton vicarage, disclosing skeletal remains of 200 men and 50 women. A "significant number" of the male remains were so large that standard British Museum long-bone boxes would not hold their femurs. Carbon-testing on four of the oversized bones dated them from A.D. 660 to 770, while another set dated from A.D. 770 to 870. Those tests scuttled a theory that the giants were unusually large Vikings, since Norsemen did not reach Repton until A.D. 873.

May 1976— Reports of violent "red-haired, hunchback giants" emerged from Peru's San Martin Province, where native guide Encarnacion Napuri claimed a gang of 15 warriors clad in animal skins, armed with clubs and stone-headed axes, had raided a hunter's camp on 26 April. The newspaper *La Prensa* claimed five men were injured in the raid and three women kidnapped; *Ultima Hora*, meanwhile, referred to 10 injuries but omitted any mention of abductions. Carlos Torrealza, who had discovered a lost ancient city in San Martin Province, also reported meeting the giants while he was lost in the jungle, but claimed they fled at his approach. Relatively modest by "giant" standards, the club-wielding hunters were described as 6 feet 6 inches tall and unanimously hunchbacked. No further information on the supposed lost tribe was forthcoming.

Sources: "A nine-foot skeleton," *Scientific American* 124 (1921): 203; "Ancient American giants," *Scientific American* 43 (1880): 106; "Archaeological no-man's land," *Science News-Letter* 18 (1930): 6; Jack Clayton, "The giants of Minnesota." *Doubt* 35 (1952(: 120-122; "Giant skeleton," *New York Times* (25 December 1868); "Giant skeletons," *Pursuit* 23 (July 1973): 69-70; Mark Hall, "Giant bones." *Wonders* 2 (March 1993): 3-13; "Peruvian tale of giant hunchbacks." *St. Louis Post-Dispatch* (23 May 1976); Phyla Phillips, "Giants in ancient America." *Fate* 1 (Spring 1948): 126-127; Sanderson, *More "Things"*; Henry Splitter, "The impossible fossils." *Fate* 7 (January 1954): 65-66; Serpent Mound Mysteries, http://greatserpentmound.org/articles/giants3.html.

Gibbons, William J. (1958–)

A childhood viewing of *The Lost World*, based on Sir Arthur Conan Doyle's novel of living DINOSAURS, inspired William Gibbons to pursue the study of cryptozoology. At age 27, in 1985, Gibbons organized his first expedition to Africa, in search of MOKELE-MBEMBE. While he failed to sight his quarry, Gibbons met a missionary on the trip and converted to fundamentalist Christianity. Gibbons subsequently earned his bachelor's and master's degrees in religious education from Immanuel Baptist College and received a Ph.D. in "creation science apologetics" from Emmanuel College of Christian Studies (Springdale, Arkansas).

Since his conversion, Gibbons has pursued cryptozoology as a form of evangelism, preaching the "young Earth" doctrine that condemns evolutionary theory as a "lie" while maintaining that the Earth is approximately 6,000 years old. In pursuit of that philosophy, Gibbons founded and led Creation Generation, a self-described "new ministry for the new millennium," whose "sole purpose is to educate and equip all true Christians worldwide with the tools to fight the rising tide of a destructive, one-

Cryptozoologist and author William Gibbons (*William Rebsamen*).

world religious system known as evolution." Gibbons's website lists crypto-artist WILLIAM REBSAMEN as the vice president of Creation Generation, and researcher SCOTT NORMAN is also associated with the effort.

Unlike most creationists, Gibbons continued field work after his conversion to the faith of creationism. His further expeditions include a second hunt for Mokele-mbembe (1992) and two expeditions to Mauritius in search of relict DODOS (1990 and 1997). Plans for Operation Congo III and Project Dodo III were announced in 1999, but no further information on their progress is available.

Gibbons is the author of two books on cryptozoology: *Claws, Jaws & Dinosaurs* (with KENT HOVIND), and *Missionaries and Monsters* ("devoting a book on cryptozoology to eye-witness accounts by missionaries from around the world").

Sources: Coleman and Clark, *Cryptozoology A to Z*; Creation Generation website, http://www.creationgeneration.org.

Gibraltar sea serpents

On 29 November 1892, the London journal *Answers* included the following account from an unnamed "captain," concerning a sighting of two SEA SERPENTS in the Mediterranean.

About three years ago when going up the Mediterranean, and when half-way between Gibraltar and Algiers, and 20 miles from land, I saw, as I thought at first, two masts or wreckage of some ship standing out of the water, but presently seeing that they were moving, and evidently something alive, I was naturally very intent in watching them. They gradually drew nearer, until they got within half a mile or so of me.

I saw then that they were large SNAKES or sea-serpents. They kept up on a parallel line with us for fully half an hour (ship going 8½ knots). They then struck off in another direction.

I had a good view of them with the naked eye, but with the telescope I could see them as distinctly as if they had been on the ship's deck. One was a little longer than the other. I judged the longer to be not less than 30 feet, the other four or five feet shorter. The longer carried its head from four to five feet out of the water, the shorter one not so high by a foot. Their heads in shape were not unlike a greyhound's head without ears. Their bodies were about nine inches in thickness, of a dark brown colour on the back, but of a gray underneath.

Source: "People who have seen the sea serpent." *Answers* (29 November 1892).

Gigantopithecus

The largest APE known to science, *Gigantopithecus blacki*, appeared in the fossil record during the Miocene epoch, about 6.3 million years ago. It thrived in Southeast Asia until the Middle Pleistocene (about 800,000 years ago), when *Homo erectus* invaded the great primate's territory. A deadly conflict then presumably ensued, with early humans hunting the apes, while "Giganto" was forced to compete with men and giant pandas for bamboo, its primary food source. Most researchers believe Giganto was driven to extinction sometime within the past 500,000 to 1 million years — but is it true?

Giganto was unknown to science until 1935, when German paleontologist Ralph von Koenigswald found a "DRAGON tooth" offered for sale in a Hong Kong pharmacy. He recognized it as the molar of an unknown primate, and a search of local shops revealed three more similar teeth. The proprietors told von Koenigswald that the teeth came Guanxi Province, in China. Their mixture with Middle Pleistocene panda and elephant fossils prompted von Koenigswald to date the teeth between 125,000 and 700,000 years old.

World War II interrupted von Koenigswald's research, but he survived a Japanese prison camp to resume his studies in 1946. In the 1950s, several Giganto mandibles were uncovered, and while no more complete remains have yet been found, the samples in hand permit scientists to reconstruct Giganto's skull, and thus to calculate the creature's overall size based on formulae from known primates. According to those calculations, Giganto stood 10 feet tall at maturity, resembling a giant GORILLA. Estimates of its mature weight range from 650 to 1,250 pounds.

The major controversy surrounding Giganto today concerns the date of its extinction — or whether it may still survive in the modern world. Cryptozoologists including BERNARD HEUVELMANS and GROVER KRANTZ speculate that Giganto was not wiped out by *Homo erectus* in Asia, but instead withdrew to more remote areas, perhaps including the Himalayas of Nepal, where it survives today as the YETI. An extension of that theory sees Giganto crossing the frozen Bering Strait from Asia to North America, establishing viable populations in wilderness regions where it would later be known as BIGFOOT.

Sources: Heuvelmans, *On the Track of Unknown Animals*; Krantz, *Big Footprints*; Krantz, *Bigfoot Sasquatch Evidence*; Sanderson, *Abominable Snowmen*; Shackley, *Still Living?*; University of Iowa Museum of Natural History, http://www.uiowa.edu/~nathist/Site/giganto.html.

Gilroy, Rex (1943–)

Rex Gilroy is Australia's best-known cryptozoologist, and one of the most controversial now living. Based in New South Wales, he has long maintained a private museum and archive of data related to cryptids throughout Oceania, and he founded the Australian YOWIE Research Centre. Another renowned investigator Down Under, Malcolm Smith, described Gilroy as follows in 1996:

Mr. Gilroy must be regarded as one of Australia's true eccentrics, and he is certainly the most enthusiastic and relentless cryptozoologist in the country. He manages to turn up wherever mystery animals are reported, with the result that a great deal of useful information falls into his hands. At flushing out *yowie* stories he has no equal….

Nevertheless, my impression has been that his enthusiasm overreaches his critical abilities. On the occasions I've followed up his accounts, I've found them to be incorrect. When he has commented on classical SEA SERPENT reports, for instance, the facts have been twisted to support preconceived theories. Furthermore, if we take him at his word, he has had some remarkable experiences: he claims to have seen a mainland THYLACINE, the KANGA-ROO VALLEY PANTHER, and the LAKE TAUPO monster of New Zealand; sometimes he will claim to have had only one *yowie* experience, at other times several — as well as having seen a *yowie* skeleton at a farm. In short, I am not prepared to accept any of Mr. Gilroy's stories unless they can be independently confirmed.

Gilroy's lifelong Yowie hunt began in 1958, but by his own account he did not glimpse the elusive cryptid until 7 August 1970, at the Ruined Castle, a rock formation in the Blue Mountains between Narrowneck and Mount Sydney. As Gilroy later described that encounter:

All was quiet, but I had a strange feeling that I was being watched. Then, almost immediately, this APE-like creature about as high as a small man broke from cover and ran across the open ground and disappeared into the bush on the far side.

Gilroy soon began advertising for Yowie reports in various magazines and newspapers, compiling a private archive that allegedly contained more than 3,000 sighting reports by 1978. It is chiefly through Gilroy's efforts that the Yowie name has replaced the ear-lier label of Yahoo for Australia's mystery HOMINIDS. His museum once displayed a supposed fossilized footprint of *GIGANTO-PITHECUS*, which Gilroy claimed to have found near Kempsey, New South Wales, but critics complained that "Giganto" is known only from fossil teeth and mandibles, thereby casting doubt on Gilroy's ability to recognize the creature's footprints.

Sources: Healy and Cropper, *Out of the Shadows*; Smith, *Bunyips & Bigfoots*.

Girt Dog

In the spring and summer of 1810, an elusive MYSTERY MAULER ravaged flocks of sheep around Ennerdale Water in Cumbria, England. Aside from simply killing sheep, the creature bit into their throats and apparently sucked blood from their jugular veins in a manner anticipating that of Puerto Rico's CHU-PACABRA. Farmers glimpsed the fleeing predator on numerous occasions, naming it the Girt Dog despite its deviation from normal canine behavior and the fact that it never barked. Repeated hunts were organized in vain, until the final party killed a supposed dog on 12 September 1810. The carcass was displayed at a museum in Keswick, but subsequently vanished. Despite the popular belief that a dog committed the raids, eyewitness Will Rotherby — who was knocked off his feet by the beast in its last hour of life — insisted that the carcass was feline, resembling a LION.

Sources: Fort, *The Books of Charles Fort*; Shuker, *Mystery Cats of the World*.

Girvan carcass

In August 1953, fishermen at Girvan, Scotland (in Ayrshire) found the beached carcass of a 30-foot creature, described as possessing a CAMEL'S head, a giraffe's neck, a 12-foot tail, and a body covered entirely in bristles. Tabloid journalists drew an immediate link to NESSIE, while London scientists proclaimed the carcass that of a "large whale." In fact, it was almost certainly a basking shark (*Cetorhinus maximus*), which in advanced decomposition resembles a long-necked cryptid.

Source: Heuvelmans, *In the Wake of the Sea Serpents*.

Gjevstroll

The Gjevstroll is an alleged LAKE MONSTER, said to inhabit Fyresvatn, in Norway's Telemark County. The last reported sighting was in 1918, when two men spied a large animal in the lake and one of them fired at it with a high-powered rifle. No clear description of the cryptid was recorded.

Source: Erik Knatterud, "Sea serpents in Norwegian lakes." http://www.mjoesormen.no.

Glacier Island carcass

One of history's most intriguing "GLOBSTERS" was discovered on Alaska's desolate Glacier Island, in Prince William Sound. A *New York Times* report hailed the find on 26 November 1930, reporting that the unknown animal was 42 feet long. That measurement included a 6-foot head, a 20-foot body, and a 16-foot tail. Two days later, a report in the *New York Sun* declared that the animal also had a "long snout."

W.J. McDonald, supervisor of the Chugash National Forest, led a seven-man party to investigate the reports. He found the carcass with little flesh remaining, but estimated its live weight at 1,000 pounds. McDonald measured the carcass precisely, reporting that its head ("much like that of an elephant") as 59 inches long. The snout measured 39 inches from its tip to the center of the beast's forehead; it was 11 inches long, with a 29-inch circumference. The body measured 24 feet long, with a 14-foot tail. The near-skeletal remains were 38 inches wide at the broadest point. The creature remains unidentified to this day.

Sources: Mark Chorvinsky, "Creature on ice." *Strange Magazine* 15

(Spring 1995): 17; "Confirm finding of pre-historic monster in ice." *New York Evening World* (28 November 1930); "Ice bares strange animal; Alaskans suggest prehistoric origin." *New York Times* (26 November 1930); "Monster in ice has long snout." *New York Sun* (28 November 1930).

Glastonbury Glawackus　　In January 1939, a large black CAT was sighted several times around Glastonbury, Connecticut. Locals reported its shrieking cries in the night, and large feline pawprints were also discovered. A massive hunt was organized on 14 January, but the beast eluded its pursuers. The last evidence of its appearance was reported on 24 February 1939, when resident Harold Roberts followed "panther" tracks over a four-mile trail, east of Glastonbury. Explanations for the spate of sightings include possible survival of the EASTERN COUGAR in Connecticut; the escape or deliberate release of a pet cougar around Glastonbury; or the survival of a Pleistocene American LION (*Panthera atrox*), suggested by cryptozoologist LOREN COLEMAN.

Sources: Coleman, *Mysterious America*; Mangiacopra and Smith, "Connecticut's mystery felines: The Glastonbury Glawackus, 1939-1967."

Glaucus Macaw　　A South American BIRD of the parrot family (*Psittacidae*), the glaucus macaw (*Anodorhynchus glaucus*) was scientifically described by Louis Vieillot in 1818. It lived in wet river valleys and fed primarily on the Yatay palm (*Butia yatay*). Widespread destruction of that food source evidently doomed the species to extinction. The last confirmed specimen died at the London Zoo in 1912. Another allegedly survived at the Buenos Aires Zoo until 1936, but some ornithologists insist that specimen was actually a Lear's macaw (*A. leari*). Lear's macaw grows slightly larger than the 29-inch *A. glaucus*, and its plumage is marginally brighter.

Although the glaucus macaw has been officially extinct since 1936, sporadic sightings continue over a wide range of territory in South America. Unconfirmed sightings of the bird were logged in 1951, 1970 and 1988. In 1992, a living specimen was reportedly found in captivity, but once again nay-sayers maintained that it was actually *A. leari*. Sporadic ongoing reports have issued from Corrientes and Misiones Provinces in Argentina; the Brazilian states of Rio Grande do Sul and Santa Caterina; and Uruguay's Artigas department. The bird has gray and turquoise plumage, with a brownish-gray throat and a black beak in a sooty face.

Sources: Pittman, "The glaucus macaw: Does it still survive?" Pittman, "Some new information on the glaucus macaw."

Glenade Lough, Ireland　　Glenade Lough, in Ireland's County Leitrim, was reportedly inhabited by a vicious DOBHAR-CHÚ in the early 18th century. Legend has it that a local woman named Grace (or Grainne) Connolly was attacked and killed by the creature on 24 September 1722, while she was washing clothes in the lake. A dearth of modern sightings suggests that the creature (if it existed) either died or moved on following the Connolly attack.

Source: Patrick Tohall, "The Dobhar-chú tombstones of Glenade, Co. Leitrim." *Journal of the Royal Society of Antiquaries of Ireland* 78 (1948): 127-129.

Glendarry Lough, Ireland　　Glendarry (or Sraheens) Lough is located on Achill Island, a popular tourist resort off the west coast of Ireland. Reports of a resident LAKE MONSTER have been logged sporadically since 1933, but the creature only gained true fame in 1968. On 1 May of that year, two men driving by the loch were startled when the animal crossed in front of their van. According to witness John Cooney:

It was between 8 and 12 feet long, I thought, with a long neck like a swan only much bigger. The tail was very thick. It was moving at an angle to us and we couldn't see exactly how long it really was. And it was weaving and curving. We could see it clearly. It was dark brown in colour and was slimey and scaley. The eyes were glittering. I don't know whether it actually looked at us, but it disappeared in an instant into the thick undergrowth — and we didn't stop to make further enquiries.

A month later, on 2 June 1968, three more witnesses saw the creature and one of them, a Dundalk businessman, allegedly snapped its picture with a Polaroid camera. Estimates of the animal's size ranged from 20 to 40 feet, with witness Mary O'Neill claiming "it was just like a DINOSAUR." Dublin's *Evening Herald* published the photo three days later, revealing a fearsome creature peering from behind a bush. When researcher Peter Costello requested a copy of the photo in November 1970, however, the *Evening Herald*'s editor had neither picture nor any record of the photographer's name. Costello dismissed the photo as a HOAX, while concluding that the creature itself may exist.

Sources: Costello, *In Search of Lake Monsters*; Katie Sullivan, "The Online Lake Cryptid Directory," http://dive/to/lakemonsters.

Glenfarg Lynx　　On the evening of 9 August 1976, a resident of Glenfarg, Scotland (in Perthshire) left her home to investigate her dog's frantic barking. Outside, she found a large CAT with tufted ears and "burning orange" eyes crouched atop the garden wall, snarling at her terrier. Frightened, the woman grabbed her dog and retreated to her house, whereupon the cat jumped down and fled into a nearby field. The witness estimated that the cat stood three feet tall at the shoulder, but fear may have

A lynx was seen at Glenfarg, Scotland, in 1976.

produced exaggeration. LYNX sightings comprise a significant minority of ALIEN BIG CAT reports from the United Kingdom.

Source: Shuker, *Mystery Cats of the World.*

Glengrant sea serpent

On 9 September 1903, fishermen aboard the Scottish trawler *Glengrant* met a SEA SERPENT in the North Sea, 80 miles off the Moray Coast. As their captain described the incident:

> A huge dark body rose and made for the steamer… with a swaying motion….When 20 ft. off the vessel it reared to a great height above, and with a loud hissing noise plunged down again…. The vessel took a great dip by the bow and shipped a huge sea, washing the deck clear and flooding the engine-room, cabin and forecastle ….Wiseman…the only one who had not lost his head… dashed below and got a gun. When the animal was 15 yards away he fired at the head. Whether he hit it is not known, but it dived, and a long sinuous body followed, wriggling like a serpent.

Crewmen described the creature as 200 feet long, with a head like a seahorse and "a long mane or fin down the back, great green glistening eyes, an enormous mouth and teeth." Five days later, an article in the London *Daily Express* heaped ridicule on the witnesses, claiming that the creature sighted had "a head like a Chinese DRAGON" and "rested his chin reflectively on the truck of the mainmast" before slithering below decks, where it "scorched the steward's whiskers and the paintwork with his fiery breath."

Source: Heuvelmans, *In the Wake of the Sea Serpents.*

Glenmore Reservoir, Canada

Alberta's Glenmore Reservoir, located at Calgary, is a popular tourist attraction, enjoyed by boaters and fishermen alike. In the early 1980s, reports of a resident LAKE MONSTER also sparked interest. Cryptozoologists note that it is difficult (if not impossible) for cryptids to inhabit manmade bodies of water, and they suggest that local cryptid sightings (if not outright HOAXES) may be explained by the presence of large pike in the reservoir.

Source: Grant MacEwan, "Marine monsters great boost for tourism." *Calgary Herald* (15 December 1984).

Global Underwater Search Team

The Global Underwater Search Team (GUST), created and led by Swedish cryptozoologist JAN-OVE SUNDBERG, is devoted to investigation of alleged European LAKE MONSTERS. Since 1975, Sundberg and various associates have staged 18 expeditions to various "monster" lakes, including:

July 1975—GLENDARRY LOUGH, on Ireland's Achill Island. Sponsored by a Swedish weekly newspaper, Sundberg and an aide spent 14 days observing the lake and interviewing local witnesses.

July 1977— Seljordsvatnet, Norway. With two associates and Sonar tracking gear, Sundberg spent 21 days tracking the elusive SELMA.

July 1979— Seljordsvatnet, Norway. A two-man, seven-day excursion included surface observations and eyewitness interviews.

July 1981— Seljordsvatnet, Norway. Sundberg and Fredrik Samuelson conducted another week-long session of interviews and surface observation.

July 1997— Lake Storsjön, Sweden. With two associates, Sundberg conducted three days of witness interviews and visual searches for STORSJÖODJURET.

August 1998— Seljordsvatnet, Norway. Sundberg's most ambitious expedition to date included 11 collaborators from six nations, searching nonstop for Selma over an 18-day period. "GUST 98" employed FISH finders, side-scan sonar and underwater cameras in an ultimately futile search. Dissension within the team

prompted Sundberg to say that "most of the members had been too young, uneducated, uncertain and uninterested."

August 1999— Seljordsvatnet, Norway. The team's fifth hunt for Selma included Sundberg and nine assistants armed with a Swedish Navy hydrophone. Sundberg claims the gear "registered a number of remarkable sounds in the lake that scientists from five countries could not explain."

September 1999— Lake Råsvalen, Sweden. With two aides and a DolphinEar mobile hydrophone, Sundberg conducted a one-day search for the cryptid locally known as RASSIC or Malen. The effort was foiled by equipment malfunctions.

December 1999— Seljordsvatnet, Norway. Storms scuttled this two-man effort to track Selma with GUST's repaired DolphinEar hydrophones.

March 2000— Loch Ness, Scotland. GUST's second expedition outside Scandinavia took Sundberg and four associates on a seven-day search for NESSIE with Swedish Navy hydrophones. The team recorded several "strange and interesting sounds" reminiscent of others taped in Norway the previous year.

August 2000— Seljordsvatnet, Norway. "GUST 2000" included 11 hunters, four navy hydrophones, sonar equipment, and a custom-made "SEA-SERPENT trap." While Selma failed to appear, the team recorded "new and amazing sounds from the depth[s]." Sundberg claims that "a scientific institution in the USA has recently confirmed that these sounds suggests that an unknown species live in the lake."

September 2000— Lake Råsvalen, Sweden. Three GUST members and their DolphinEar hydrophone achieved admittedly meager results. One tape recording of a rumbling sound like "an approaching nuclear sub" proved to be the echo of a distant freight train passing through Lindesberg.

September 2000— Seljordsvatnet, Norway. Collaborating with Fox Television on a project coordinated by LOREN COLEMAN, Sundberg and Goran Rajala spent two days interviewing witnesses, tracking Selma by hydrophone, and filming unidentified objects on the lake's surface.

October 2000— Loch Ness. Sundberg and four associates spent seven days in Scotland with their hydrophones, in an expedition dubbed "Nessie 2000, Part 2." Once again, stormy weather frustrated the team's best efforts.

April 2001— Loch Ness. "Operation CleanSweep" brought Sundberg an and four aides back to Scotland with SIMRAD multibeam sonar, underwater cameras, and their untested monster trap. The trap sparked complaints from PETA (People for the Ethical Treatment of Animals), and the effort was foiled, in Sundberg's words, by "storms, malfunctioning technology and broken promises."

June 2001—LOUGH REE, Ireland. GUST broke new ground with "Operation Horse EEL," a five-day expedition involving Sundberg, two assistants, and DolphinEar hydrophones. Sundberg concluded that the local cryptid is "most likely a primitive species of lamprey."

July 2001— Lake Storsjön, Sweden. Sundberg and four aides staged another week-long expedition, this one sponsored by a local trade association called What's On in Ostersund.

August 2001— Seljordsvatnet, Norway. GUST's ninth search for Selma, dubbed "Operation Gizmo," found Sundberg and Inge Falk packing sonar, DolphinEar hydrophones, and SIMRAD Aberdeen underwater cameras. Sundberg afterward claimed he had captured the creature on videotape, as well as in a "spectacular" still photo which he calls "the best ever taken of an unknown animal." Concerning his failure to publish the photo, Sundberg writes: "I have not released the picture yet and will keep it hidden for some time yet, but I can reveal that it got the thumbs up from Kodak in Sweden and a laboratory in America has found that it shows an unknown animal 20 feet long."

June 2002— Lake Rommen, Norway. A seven-day search, christened "Operation Sea Serpent," sent Sundberg and two associates, armed with hydrophones and echo-sounders, to seek a cryptid reported since the 18th century. Team members claimed no positive results.

Source: GUST Website, http://www.cryptozoology.st/.

Globsters

IVAN SANDERSON coined the term "globster" in the early 1960s, to describe the many nondescript, putrescent carcasses that wash up on beaches around the world each year. Such remains are often mystifying to the casual observer, and sometimes likewise to reputed experts. Throughout history, large stranded carcasses have been identified as the remains of SEA SERPENTS or living DINOSAURS, but most are finally identified as known creatures of the deep. The most frequent misidentified "sea serpent" is probably the basking SHARK (*Cetorhinus maximus*), which rots to resemble a long-necked animal covered with bristly hair. Other common culprits include the GIANT SQUID (known to science only from its beached or netted corpses), the oarfish (*Regalecus glesne*), large rays, and various cetaceans. Since

A typical "globster," resembling a long-necked cryptid.

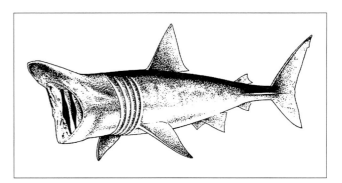

Many such carcasses are identified as decomposed basking sharks.

the 1990s, DNA analysis has proved itself a priceless tool for pinning names on otherwise unidentifiable remains.

It should not be supposed, however, that all globsters are so easily unmasked. Some of the cadaverous cryptids remain mysterious, including the strange creature beached at ALONG BAY, Vietnam in 1883; a headless whopper stranded at NEW RIVER INLET, Florida in 1885; St. Augustine, Florida's globster of 1896 (probably an unknown giant OCTOPUS); a floating carcass sighted from the *TROPPER* in 1906; the giant creature swept ashore at MARGATE, Natal in 1922; a reptilian cryptid found in the GULF OF FONSECA (1928); the alleged remains of a young CADBOROSAURUS pulled from the stomach of a whale in 1937; and the unique African carcass dubbed GAMBO by KARL SHUKER (1983).

Oceans are not the only source of globsters, as it happens. Lakes also offer up their rotting dead from time to time, including some bodies of water renowned as the homes of LAKE MONSTERS. Some of the "monster" lakes with reported strandings include Norway's GRESSKARDFOSSEN, REINSVATNET, and Lake Mjøsa (home of MJOSSIE); LOUGH MASK in Ireland; Scotland's LOCH LINNHE; Iceland's Lögurinn Lake (home of the SKRIMSL); BEAR LAKE, in Utah; at Lewis, in the HEBRIDES, and Canada's Lake Okanagan (home of OGOPOGO).

Sources: Costello, *In Search of Lake Monsters*; Dinsdale, *Monster Hunt*; Heuvelmans, *In the Wake of the Sea Serpents*; Moore, "What are the globsters?"; Sanderson, "Monster on the beach." *Fate* 15 (August 1962); Sanderson, *More "Things"*; Alexandra Witze, "DNA tests solving sea mysteries." *Dallas Morning News* (20 March 2002).

Glowing Lizard

In his book *Caribbean Adventure* (1938), naturalist IVAN SANDERSON reported that a rare lizard found only in Trinidad's Aripo Caves emitted light from a series of vents on its flanks. The reptile in question (*Proctoporus shrevi*) was known to science, but no other researcher had observed its luminescent quality. All efforts to confirm Sanderson's report over the next six decades proved fruitless, but the initial report was finally confirmed in 2000, when British herpetologist Mark O'Shea videotaped the glowing lizards and broadcast their image on television. O'Shea's investigation demonstrated that only male specimens are luminescent, whereas several previous researchers had conducted their experiments with females.

Sources: Karl Shuker, "Alien zoo." *Fortean Times* 133 (April 2000): 20-21; "Where de lizard?" *Trinidad Express* (15 May 2001); Mark O'Shea, "Exotic Island," http://www.markoshea.tv/series1/series01-10.html.

Gnéna

An unclassified APE or small HOMINID of West Africa, the Gnéna is reportedly bipedal, covered in long black or gray hair. Witnesses describe it as standing 2-4 feet tall; they often remark on the creature's long arms, and its oversized head with striking yellow eyes. The Gnéna reportedly walks with a knock-kneed gait, placing most of its weight on the outside of its feet (which, like those of other mystery hominids worldwide, are sometimes said to point backwards). Many accounts describe the Gnéna sleeping in trees, and some credit it with a malicious dislike for humans. Reports of the creatures firing arrows at animals and men are probably garbled ancient accounts of conflicts with forest-dwelling pygmies. The Gnéna are reported over a wide range in West Africa, from Senegal through Mali, Guinea, Burkina Faso, Côte d'Ivoire, Ghana, Niger, Cameroon and the Central African Republic. Across that range, the creatures are known by numerous local names, including Asamanukpa, Attakourma, Bâri, Datobu, Gotteré, Kélékongbo, Mokala, Nyama, Ouokolo, Pori, Sonkala, Tikirga, Wokolo, Yamana and many others.

Sources: Heuvelmans, *Les bêtes humaines d'Afrique*; Mamby Sidibé, "Légendes autour des génies nains en Afrique noir." *Notes Africaines* 47 (1950): 100.

Goat-Antelope   A cryptid reported from Mongolia's Dundgov? Province, this animal is described by witnesses as a brown, goat-sized ungulate with small, spreading antlers. It prefers hillsides and rocky canyons, where it typically grazes in small groups of four or five. When frightened, observers say, it runs faster than a sheep but slower than most antelopes.

Source: "Unknown animals." *Mongolia Online,* http://www.mongoliaonline.mn/.

Goatman   Cryptozoology collides with urban legends in pursuit of this mysterious hominid, reported since the late 1950s from Prince George's County, Maryland. At first glance, reports of Goatman seem to describe a BIGFOOT-type creature or NORTH AMERICAN APE, 6-8 feet tall and covered with dark hair, but some witnesses insist that the biped's legs resemble a goat's, thus casting it in the mold of a classical satyr. Sightings began in early August 1957, with a rash of reports around Upper Marlboro, Forestville and Ritchie. Goatman then enjoyed a 10-year hiatus, before returning to the county in 1967. Hunts were organize, resulting in claims that searchers were chased by the creature, but no hard evidence was collected. In January 1969 a motorist reported a 7½-foot monster crossing Route 197 near Beltsville. Summer 1971 brought several Goatman reports to police in Bowie, and local resident April Edwards blamed the creature for beheading her dog on 3 November 1971. In January 1973 an all-white hairy creature reportedly menaced teenagers at Oxon Hill. That summer produced another highway sighting near Beltsville, followed by another three-year lapse. Subsequent sightings were logged from Beltsville, Calverton and Laurel, between 1976 and 1985. Overall, Prince George's County produced 25 of Maryland's 198 hominid reports between 1957 and 1985. A curious twist was added to the Goatman legend in 1998, when the name was applied to a "hairy, horned monster" sighted in northern McLennan County, Texas.

Sources: Brian Anderson, "Texas Goatman terror." *Waco Tribune-Herald* (19 June 1998); Berry, *Bigfoot on the East Coast*; Mark Opasnick, "On the trail of the Goatman."

Goazi/Guayazi   An unknown APE or small HOMINID reported from the jungles of Brazil and Colombia by 17th-century explorers, the Goazi has not been sighted in modern times. Speculation persists that Portuguese and Spanish pioneers may have seen Indians of small stature — tribes of New World PYGMIES, in effect — but no evidence exists to prove the case.

Source: Simão de Vasconcellos, *Noticias curiosas, y necessarias das cousas do Brasil.* Lisbon: I. da Costa, 1668.

Goggau See, Austria   Prior to World War II, this lake in Austria's Kärnten State produced occasional reports of large unknown FISH, distinctive for their serrated dorsal crests. A cessation of reports since the 1930s suggests that the species may be extinct.

Source: Georg Graber, *Sagen aus Kärnten.* Graz, Austria: Lekym-Verlag, 1944.

***Gold Hunter* sea serpent**   On 25 December 1826, while traveling from Wales to New York City, passengers and crew aboard the *Gold Hunter* spied a SEA SERPENT in the North Atlantic, at 40° 30' north latitude, 63° west longitude. Captain Knowles later told the *New York Gazette* that when the creature was first seen, "its head was elevated about six feet out of the water, and directed towards the bow of the vessel. Night coming on, it was lost sight of. Its color was black." He further described the animal as "80 or 90 feet long, its head about the size of a bullock's without the horns; the circumference of the body was about equal to that of a barrel, tapering to the tail to about the thickness of a topmast, and smooth; it was suddenly rounded at the end and was destitute of fins."

Source: O'Neill, *The Great New England Sea Serpent.*

***Golden Flame* sea serpent**   In August 1958, 17 crewmen aboard the coaster *Golden Flame* reported meeting a brown SEA SERPENT a few miles offshore from East London, South Africa. As witness Ernie Stoltz described the event, "It reared up, stretched its neck, then looked at the coaster. After that it slowly sank down into the sea and swam off." Pressed for further details, Stoltz said that when it surfaced, the animal resembled a "giant LION sitting up on its haunches."

Source: Heuvelmans, *In the Wake of the Sea Serpents.*

Goldsborough Growler   Queensland, Australia's Goldsborough Valley, located south of Cairns, is said to be inhabited by an elusive predator that hunts by night, raiding livestock herds and rousing farmers from their sleep with eerie cries in the darkness. Reported sightings date from the 1930s and continue sporadically to the present day. Valley resident Mark Camplon described his close encounter with the beast in 1995. "I was sitting here on the back verandah, watching television," Camplon told the *Brisbane Sunday Mail.* "Rusty, my dog, was sitting on the bed next to me. Rusty's afraid of nothing, but all of a sudden he started shaking like mad. His hair was standing up along his back and he was staring out into the night, through the shade cloth. I looked out but I couldn't see a thing. Then it growled. It was unlike anything I'd ever heard, really deep and big sounding." Pat Shepherd, leader of a local group pledged to track the Goldsborough Growler, notes that hunters of past generations faced technical disadvantages. "They didn't have the knowledge or equipment we have, so on that basis we're off to a head start," he explains. "We have some sophisticated traps and tracking methods so we can do what people in the past didn't dream of — track this creature back to its lair. It's there we'll get the scientific evidence to support or debunk any theory." Thus far, however, efforts to locate the Growler have been fruitless. Skeptics dismiss the creature as a myth, while some researchers speculate that it may represent a relict form of the marsupial predator *Thylacaleo carnifex,* a CAT-like animal presumed extinct for some 10,000 years.

Source: Stephen Yates, "Chasing a myth." *Brisbane Sunday Mail* (12 November 1995).

Golub-Yavan   An unknown HOMINID of central Asia, the Golub-yavan is reported from a wide range including the Pamir Mountains of Tajikistan (where it is also known as Gul); the Karakoram Range of northern Pakistan; the Hindu Kush of eastern Afghanistan; the Tien Shan Mountains of eastern Kyrgyzstan and northwestern China; the Kunlun Shan, dividing China from Tibet; China's Nan Shan Highlands; and the Tsinling Mountains on China's border with Russia. Alternate local names applied throughout that range include Khaivan-akvan, Voita, and multiple variant spellings of Golub-yavan. The creature's broad geographical range overlaps those of the ALMAS and YETI, suggesting that witnesses may be describing the same animal.

Most Golub-yavan reports describe a bipedal creature ranging in height from five feet to six feet six inches, covered in black or gray hair. The bare face features a prominent brow and cheek bones, a flattened nose, and large teeth. Some accounts mention prominent ears. Like its Yeti neighbor, the Golub-yavan emits a whistling cry and a strong, unpleasant odor. Its footprints are humanoid, but shorter and wider than normal, with thick toes.

The most dramatic Golub-yavan reports have been logged from Tajikistan, where Russian Major General Mikhail Topilski claimed to have killed one in 1925, while hunting guerrillas in the Vanch District. An army physician examined the creature, but it could not be transported or preserved for further study. Fourteen years later, a Golub-yavan allegedly attacked a hunter near Imeni Kalinina, knocking the man unconscious but leaving him otherwise unharmed. As recently as August 1957, Russian researcher Alexander Pronin claimed a sighting in the Balyandikiik Valley, where he allegedly watched a Golub-yavan walk in and out of a cave. Sightings continued into the early 1980s, at least, and witness Vadim Makarov found four-toed footprints measuring 19_ long beside Tajikistan's Varzob River on 29 September 1981.

Sources: Bayanov, "A field investigation into the relict hominoid situation in Tajikistan, USSR"; Bayanov, *In the Footsteps of the Russian Snowman*; Heuvelmans and Porshnev, *L'homme de Néanderthal est toujours vivant*; Sanderson, *Abominable Snowmen*; Shackley, *Still Living?*

Goodenough Island bird   Goodenough Island is a possession of Papua New Guinea, located at 9° 22' south latitude and 150° 16' east longitude. (It should not be confused with the former *Goodenough's* Island, now Raratonga, capital of the independent Cook Islands.) For half a century, sporadic reports of an unknown BIRD have emerged from Goodenough. A member of the fourth Archbold Expedition was first to report it, in 1953, describing a jet-black BIRD the size of a crow, with long tail feathers. On 28 December 1975, zoologist James Menzies sighted several specimens on Mount Oiamadawa, but none were captured and the bird remains officially unrecognized. KARL SHUKER suggests the bird may be a paradise crow (*Lycocorax pyrrhopterus*), which is officially confined to Indonesia. Other researchers speculate that it may comprise a new species of honeyeater (*Meliphaga*) or bird of paradise (*Astrapia*).

Sources: Bruce Beehler, *A Naturalist in New Guinea*. Austin, TX: University of Texas Press, 1991; Shuker, *Mysteries of Planet Earth*.

Goonyak   This vaguely-described 8-foot HOMINID allegedly terrorized farmers in north-central Vermont during 1978. Sightings were reported from Craftsbury, Morrisville and Wolcott, including the claim that the Goonyak invaded an unnamed farmer's barn and killed a 1,000-pound bull. According to some reports, the creature was then shot and killed, either by the same anonymous farmer or by game warden John Kapusta, of Crafts-

bury (who denies any knowledge of the incident). While Vermont has produced nearly a score of BIGFOOT reports through the years, with the earliest dating from 1879, investigator Joseph Citro concluded that the Goonyak story was a HOAX.

Sources: Berry, *Bigfoot on the East Coast*; Citro, *Green Mountain Ghosts, Ghouls & Unsolved Mysteries*.

Goose Creek Lagoon, South Carolina   In 1928, while boating on Goose Creek Lagoon (12 miles north of Charleston), Herbert Sass observed a pink, thick-bodied creature five or six feet long, moving underneath the surface. He used an oar to fish it out, noting the animal's smooth tail and short legs before it wriggled off the oar and dived to safety. Sass described the creature as resembling a hellbender (*Cryptobranchus alleganiensis*), but those brown-and-gray amphibians are unknown in eastern South Carolina, and they attain a maximum official length of 29 inches.

Sources: Shuker, *In Search of Prehistoric Survivors*; "The pink what-is-it?" *Saturday Evening Post* (4 December 1948).

Gorillas (Mislocated)   Gorillas are the largest living primates known to modern science. Three subspecies are recognized, including the mountain gorilla (*Gorilla gorilla beringei*), the western lowland gorilla (*G. g. gorilla*), and the larger eastern lowland gorilla (*G. g. graueri*). All are native to Africa and naturally occur nowhere else, yet reports of errant gorillas were once fairly common across North America, emerging in the latter 19th century to supplant tales of hairy WILDMEN. A sampling of reported sightings includes the following:

23 January 1869—A presumed gorilla assaulted the driver of a carriage outside Gallipolis, Ohio.

Summer 1869—Residents of Arcadia Valley, Kansas (Crawford County) claimed sightings of a "wild man or gorilla" in the area.

October 1870—A newspaper in Antioch, California published an article listing multiple gorilla sightings from 1849 to 1870. The most recent sighting, in September 1870, involved a hunter's report of multiple gorillas seen near Orestimba Creek.

1900—An aggressive simian pursued a sleigh in North Dakota's Kildeer Mountains.

Gorilla sightings in North America date from 1869.

1913— Canada logged its first gorilla reports, when a white-maned APE was sighted near Labrador's Traverspine River. Witnesses described the creature alternately walking on two legs and on all fours.

December 1920-February 21— A rash of gorilla sightings was reported from Adams, Blair, Snyder and York Counties, Pennsylvania. Authorities blamed a simian escapee from an unnamed circus.

25 July 1929— A "huge gorilla" was seen in the woods near Elizabeth, Illinois.

June 1931— Another "escaped ape" terrorized residents of Mineola, Long Island. Subsequent investigation showed that no gorillas were missing from local zoos, and no circus was in the vicinity.

1949— A brown gorilla was sighted by fishermen along Sugar Creek, in Boone County, Indiana.

Autumn 1951— Multiple ape sightings prompted residents of Charlotte, Michigan to name a nearby marshy region "Gorilla Swamp."

American gorilla sightings waned after 1958, when a California reporter coined the name BIGFOOT for large unknown HOMINIDS, but occasional witnesses still revert to the traditional nomenclature. A farmer in Trimble County, Kentucky reported his encounter with a 6-foot gorilla in 1962. Six years later, stories of a gorilla at large were published in the *Arkansas Gazette*. As recently as 1996, witness Andrew Montoya reported an encounter with a "white ape" in the desert 10 miles north of Santa Fe, New Mexico. The creature's eyes "seemed to glow as if there was a fire behind them," and Montoya estimated that it ran at speeds approaching 50 miles per hour.

Sources: Coleman, *Bigfoot!*; Coleman, "Gorillas in the midst"; Keel, *The Complete Guide to Mysterious Beings*; Andrew Montoya, "White gorilla." *Strange Magazine* 17 (Summer 1996): 29.

Gotteré *see* **Gnéna**

Gougou   Arguably North America's most confusing cryptid, the Gougou of New Brunswick, Canada is described in varying accounts as either a SEA SERPENT (found in Chaleur Bay) or as a large, aggressive version of BIGFOOT. Samuel de Champlain recorded Aboriginal accounts of the creature, invariably described as a female man-eater cast "in the form of a woman," boasting a pouch where remains of its victims were kept. If not entirely mythical, the Gougou is presumably extinct, with no sightings on file since the early 17th century.

Sources: Guiley, *Atlas of the Mysterious in North America*; Wright, "The Gougou: The Bigfoot of the east."

Goulburn River, Australia   During the mid-19th century, the Goulburn River of New South Wales produced multiple sightings of unknown creatures collectively labeled BUNYIPS. Witness W.H. Barrett was a youth in 1849-50, when a cryptid from the Goulburn frightened residents of Mooriling Station. Years later, he recalled that several Aborigines were paid to kill the creature and waded into the river, firing shots at the animal, but its body was not recovered. In April 1857, the *Moreton Bay Free Press* published this account of the river's mysterious inhabitants.

Mr. Stocqueler informs us that the bunyip is a large freshwater seal, having two small paddles or fins attached to the shoulders, a long swan-like neck, a head like a dog, and a curious bag hanging under the jaw, resembling the pouch of a pelican. The animal is covered with hair like the platypus, and the colour is a glossy black. Mr. Stocqueler saw no less than six of the curious animals at different

times; his boat was within thirty feet of one, near M'Guire's Point, on the Goulburn, and fired at the bunyip, but did not succeed in capturing him. The smallest appeared to be about five feet in length, and the largest exceeded fifteen feet. The head of the largest was the size of a bullock's head and three feet out of the water.

Sources: "The bunyip." *Moreton Bay Free Press* (15 April 1957); W.H. Dudley LeSouef, *Wild Life in Australia*. Melbourne: Whitcombe & Tombs, 1907; Smith, *Bunyips and Bigfoots*.

Gould, Rupert Thomas (1890-1948)   A British subject who spent many years in the Royal Navy and retired with the rank of commander, Rupert Gould also shared CHARLES FORT'S fascination with anomalies of nature, though it is fair to say Gould approached his subjects more selectively and scientifically than Fort. His first two books on natural mysteries, both best-sellers, were *Oddities* (1928) and *Enigmas* (1929). In 1930 Gould published *The Case for the SEA SERPENT*, later described by BERNARD HEUVELMANS as "a model of scientific rigour." In 1933, Gould purchased a motorcycle to explore Loch Ness and collect first-hand sightings of NESSIE. That investigation led to publication of the first book on the subject, *The Loch Ness Monster and Others* (1934). Gould initially believed that Nessie was a pelagic creature adapted to fresh water, but he later changed his mind, declaring:

On the whole, despite the advocates of a "surviving plesiosaur," this and other "sea-serpent" cases suggest to me nothing so much as a vastly enlarged, long-necked marine form of the common newt. However that is a matter for a qualified zoologist with an open mind.

Sources: Clark and Pear, *Strange & Unexplained Phenomena*; Heuvelmans, *In the Wake of the Sea Serpents*.

Gower Peninsula sea serpent   In 1950, British author A.G. Thompson published his book *Gower Journey*, relating details of his visit to the Gower peninsula of Wales in 1946-47. Among the events he described, Thompson included an undated sighting of a 30-foot SEA SERPENT that he reportedly saw from the cliffs at Fall Bay. Thompson initially mistook the creature for a floating log, until:

Suddenly one end moved and it became plain that a head like that of a Horse [*sic*] with a mane was standing out of the water and watching something on the rocks at the foot of the cliff. What a thrill!! After staring for what seemed minutes the monster appeared to be satisfied and dived with what looked like two distinct undulations of the hind portion. What an uncanny feeling! The writer waited some half-hour or more but there was no reappearance. A local expert was of the opinion that it was a real Sea Horse, so Lockness [*sic*] cannot boast that they have a monopoly of Monsters.

Source: Heuvelmans, *In the Wake of the Sea Serpents*.

Gowrow   The Gowrow of rural Arkansas is described as a 20-foot cave-dwelling lizard with long tusks or fangs, reported by witnesses in the Razorback State for over a century. A traveling salesman named William Miller allegedly killed one near Marshall, in 1879. Miller claimed that he sent the reptile's carcass to the Smithsonian Institution in Washington, D.C., but it never arrived. Fifty-odd years later, in the early 1930s, another Gowrow was reported (but not actually seen) from Devil's Hole, a deep cavern on the Boone County estate of E.J. Rhodes. Upon hearing strange noises below ground, Rhodes lowered himself on a rope to a depth of 200 feet, where the passage proved too narrow for his body. Subsequently, workmen dropped a rope weighted with a flatiron to the same depth, whereupon they heard loud hissing sounds. The experiment was repeated, this time with a large stone, and the unseen creature bit through the rope.

Sources: LaGrange, "The Gowrow vs. Occam's razor"; Shuker, *From Flying Toads to Snakes with Wings.*

Grahamstown Cat   A unique and mysterious CAT was killed at Grahamstown, South Africa sometime in the 1880s, and its pelt was later sent to Dr. A. Günther, who described it for the *Proceedings of the Zoological Society of London* in March 1885. According to Günther, the skin measured 6 feet 7 inches in length, including a 30-inch tail. Its tawny color lightened to a rich orange gloss on the shoulders, and was marked by numerous spots, while a jet-black dorsal stripe ran from the head to the base of the tail. The cat's underside was white with large black spots, typically found in leopards (*Panthera pardus*). In 1886 Günther received a second, darker pelt from another Grahamstown hunter, apparently representing the same breed of cat. Günther concluded that the skins represented pseudo-melanistic leopards, but no further specimens have been collected to date.

Source: Shuker, *Mystery Cats of the World.*

***Granada* sea serpents**   On 21 December 1879, witnesses aboard the *Granada* reported a SEA SERPENT sighting from the Pacific Ocean off Cabo San Lucas, at the southernmost tip of Baja California. They described the creature's neck as three feet long and roughly the thickness of a man's forearm. In reporting that incident, the *Granada's* second officer also recalled sighting an unknown creature "several yards long" off the coast of Australia, in 1871, but no further details of that sighting are available. BERNARD HEUVELMANS speculated that the 1879 creature "could have been a large EEL— or a baby long-necked sea serpent."

Source: Heuvelmans, *In the Wake of the Sea Serpents.*

Granby Panther   In the 1950s, a series of livestock attacks by one or more large CATS was reported from Granby, Connecticut. Some witnesses described a predator resembling a COUGAR (*Puma concolor*), while others claimed the prowling cat was black. Killings of livestock apparently ended in 1959, but sightings of the elusive "panther" continued through 1967.

Source: Mangiacopra and Smith, "Connecticut's mystery felines."

Grand Lake, Canada   New Brunswick's largest lake, located 20 miles east of Fredericton, produced a brief spate of LAKE MONSTER sightings in the late 1960s. Witnesses claimed the creature resembled Scotland's NESSIE.

Source: Bord and Bord, *Unexplained Mysteries of the 20th Century.*

***Grangense* sea serpent**   In May 1901, while traveling from New York City to Belém, passengers aboard the steamer *Grangense* saw a SEA SERPENT. Nearly half a century later, witness Charles Seibert described the incident after reading an article by IVAN SANDERSON in the *Saturday Evening Post.* As Seibert recalled the event, he was walking on deck when a ship's officer shouted, "My God, look there!"

Looking as directed we saw some sort of an amphibian, grayish brown in color. The forward part, which was all we could see, was similar to the monster illustrated in the *Post;* however its neck was not so thick or long. Its head was a trifle longer, more like a CROCODILE'S. When it opened its mouth, we could see rows of regular teeth, maybe four to six inches long. It appeared to be playing on the surface, and would swirl in circles, bending its neck until it looked toward its tail, if it had one. It would gambol for maybe half a minute, then dive. This it did three times. We asked the captain if he was going to log the encounter. His reply was, "No fear. They will say we were all drunk, and I'll thank you mister, not to mention it to our agents at Para or Manaus."

Source: Heuvelmans, *In the Wake of the Sea Serpents.*

Grant County Monster   In July 1964, northern Kentucky's Grant County was visited by a 7-foot HOMINID with fluorescent eyes, seen prowling around a garbage dump off U.S. Highway 36. Soon, carloads of young monster-hunters from Grant and neighboring counties thronged the region, "shouting and shooting" to the annoyance of local farmers. Police moved in after two teenage boys were wounded by gunfire, and the local hysteria soon faded. When the smoke cleared, authorities suggested that the initial sightings involved "an eccentric man, well known to police," who was never publicly named.

Source: Jim Reis, "Carloads hunted monster in Grant County." *Kentucky Post* (27 August 2001).

Grassman   "Grassman" is a name applied by some researchers to a BIGFOOT-type creature (or NORTH AMERICAN APE) reported from Ohio. The term was coined by members of the OHIO BIGFOOT RESEARCH AND STUDY GROUP in early 1995, after they discovered nine alleged "Bigfoot nests" in Summit County, outside Akron. The "nests" were crude structures built from tree branches, then covered with grass and leaves to form an igloolike structure. Joedy Cook, a Cincinnati member of the OBRSG, claims he has received telephone calls from an unnamed U.S. Army officer, asserting that the Army and the FBI maintain secret files on Grassman/Bigfoot which were supposed to be declassified "in two years" (i.e., 1998). Thus far, no such documents have surfaced, but Bigfoot sightings in the Buckeye State continue.

Source: Murphy, "Grassman— the Ohio conspiracy."

Great Auk   (*See illustration next page.*) A large flightless BIRD classified by Carl von Linné in 1758, the great auk (*Alca impennis*) once occupied a wide range from Canada and Greenland to Iceland, Scotland and Norway. Ruthless hunting and predation by settlers' dogs decimated the species, and the last known breeding pair was killed by fishermen on Eldey Island, Iceland, on 3 June 1844. Although officially extinct, unconfirmed sightings have continued into modern times. A great auk was reportedly captured and eaten by residents of Qeqertarsuaq Tunua, Greenland, in 1867. More sightings were logged from the Lofoten Islands, off Norway's coast, in the 1920s and 1930s, but investigators found the birds were penguins imported by whalers. Most zoologists believe the great auk is now truly extinct.

Sources: Errol Fuller, *The Great Auk.* New York: Harry N. Abrams, 1999; "The end of the auk." *Fortean Times* 145 (May 2001): 48; "Raiders of the lost auk." *ISC Newsletter* 6 (Spring 1987): 5-7.

Great Gull Lake, Canada   This lake in southern Newfoundland is said to harbor a LAKE MONSTER, but no clear description of the creature is available.

Source: "A brief survey of Canadian lake monsters." *INFO Journal* 39 (March-June 1981): 2-5.

Great Lake, Tasmania   While most BUNYIP sightings emanate from mainland Australia, Tasmania's Great Lake also produced its share of reports in the mid-19th century. The first was recorded at 11:00 a.m. on 25 January 1863, while Charles Headlam was boating on the lake with his son Andrew. As Headlam described the event in his journal:

The lake was very rough, and we were pulling our boat against a strong head sea, when my oar nearly came in contact with a large-looking beast, about the size of a fully-developed sheep dog. The animal immediately started off at great speed towards an island in the Great Lake known as Helen Island. It appeared to have two small flappers, or wings, which it made good use of, as I should think it went at the rate of 30 miles per hour. We watched it as far as the eye could reach, and it appeared to keep on the face of the water, never appearing to dive.

Headlam waited six years to make his experience public, by which time witness Francis McPartland had reported several sightings of the beast(s) during 1868. McPartland saw them most often at Swan Bay, once watching three of the creatures splashing near shore. He described them as 3-4 feet long, dark in color, with round heads resembling a bulldog's. Chief Constable James Wilson interviewed several other witnesses around Great Lake who described black creatures 4-5 feet long, resembling sheepdogs in the water. Despite vehement contradictions from every witness, Wilson concluded that the Great Lake creatures were simply oversized PLATYPUSES.

Source: Smith, *Bunyips & Bigfoots.*

Sightings of the "extinct" great auk continued through the 1930s.

Great Lakes *see* **individual lakes by name**

Great Salt Lake, Utah   Utah's Great Salt Lake is the largest natural lake west of the Mississippi River, measuring 75 miles long and 50 miles across at its widest point. It is also the saltiest body of water on Earth, with a salinity five times that of any ocean. LAKE MONSTER sightings at Great Salt Lake date from 8 June 1877, when employees at the Monument Point salt works, near Kelton, observed a large creature thrashing offshore. Frightened away from their camp, the workers returned next morning to find their tents flattened, with large tracks leading to and from the water. The *Salt Lake Semi-Weekly Herald* carried this description of the creature on 14 July:

> It was a great animal like a CROCODILE or ALLIGATOR …said J.H. McNiel, one of the witnesses. It must have been seventy-five feet long; but the head was not like an alligator's[,] it was more like a horse's.

Reporters investigating that story found another witness, Judge Dennis Toohy of Corinne, who had been frightened by the beast while swimming, several years earlier. Another spate of sightings occurred in 1882, prompting one journalist to write: "It has frightened men — and far better evidence than that, it has been seen by children while playing on the shore. I say 'better,' because children are not likely to invent a plausible horror in order to explain their sudden rushing away from a given spot with terrified countenances and a consistent narrative."

Locals speculated that the creature might have migrated from BEAR LAKE (site of cryptid reports dating from 1863), but four dams erected on the river in the 1920s apparently solved that problem, and no further sightings have been logged at Great Salt Lake.

Source: Garner, *Monster! Monster!*

Greater Sandplover (Mislocated)   The greater sandplover (*Caradrius leschenaulti*) is well known to science as a species found in Asia, through Australia, to East Africa. While its existence is not questioned, the 7-inch wading BIRD still managed to cause a stir in early 2001, when it was sighted on the beach at Bolinas Lagoon, in northern California's Marin County. The first sighting came on 29 January 2001, reported by two employees of the Point Reyes Bird Observatory. Publication of the announcement brought a rush of avid birdwatchers from around the U.S. and Canada, armed with cameras and binoculars. By mid-February, photos of the bird were posted on the Internet, but experts retained an air of cautious skepticism. Initial witness Sue Abbot told the press, "There's a lot of evidence suggesting it's a greater [sandplover], but no absolute proof." In fact, while the specimen sighted bore all the general characteristics of a greater sandplover, experts noted that it was two inches smaller than average. Ornithologist Joe Morlan suggested that the bird may have strayed 6,000 miles across the Pacific from its normal range because of an irregularity in plumage or "a genetic defect that causes mirror-image orientation."

Source: "Bird never seen in Western Hemisphere makes sudden appearance." Associated Press (25 February 2001).

Greatstone carcass   On 14 April 1998, two beachcombing British youths found the decomposed remains of a strange sea creature beached at Greatstone, Kent. The body measured eight feet long, with vertebrae plainly visible through rotting flesh. The creature's head possessed a long triangular snout, with two thin antennae sprouting from its base. Cryptozoologist KARL SHUKER examined photos of the carcass and quickly determined that the remains were those of a small basking shark (*Cetorhinus maximus*). The animal's "antennae" were actually strips of rostral cartilage that raise the shark's snout.

Source: Karl Shuker, "Alien zoo." *Fortean Times* 114 (September 1998): 18-19.

Greek Chameleon Discovered by biologist-photographer Andrea Bonetti in 1996, this controversial population of chameleons lives around the Pylos Lagoon, on the southwestern coast of Peloponnesus. Bonetti considers the lizards a new species, larger than the European chameleon (*Chamaeleo chamaeleon*), yet slightly different in appearance from the African chameleon (*C. africanus*). Pending further study, the Greek chameleons are not recognized as a separate species.

Sources: Andrea Bonetti, "New life from Roman relics." *BBC Wildlife* 16 (July 1998): 10-16; Shuker, "A supplement to Dr. Bernard Heuvelmans' checklist of cryptozoological animals."

Andrea Bonetti reported discovery of an unknown Greek chameleon in 1996.

Greek Dolphin While studying pelagic life forms of the Mediterranean in the 1960s, Willem Mörzer Bruyns observed an unclassified cetacean similar in appearance to the striped dolphin (*Stenella coeruleoalba*), but lacking that animal's characteristic "halter" pattern of dark stripes and its pale-gray markings beneath the dorsal fin. No type specimen has yet been collected, and some marine biologists believe Mörzer Bruyns simply observed a striped dolphin with aberrant coloration.

Sources: Heuvelmans, "Annotated checklist of apparently unknown animals with which cryptozoology is concerned"; Willem Mörzer Bruyns, *Field Guide of Whales and Dolphins*. Amsterdam: Tor, 1971.

Green, John (1927–) A native of Vancouver, British Columbia, John Green is widely recognized as one of the pivotal figures in BIGFOOT research. His quest for North America's elusive HOMINID began in 1957, the year before Green earned his master's degree in journalism from Columbia University. Over the next five years, Green worked in collaboration with researchers TOM SLICK, PETER BYRNE, RENÉ DAHINDEN, ROBERT TITMUS and others on expeditions in California and British Columbia. Employed for over three decades as journalist, Green used his talents and spare time to produce a series of books about Bigfoot, including *On the Track of Sasquatch* (1968), *Year of the Sasquatch* (1970), *The Sasquatch File* (1973), and the classic *Sasquatch: The Apes Among Us* (1978). With more than 2,000 Bigfoot sightings and hundreds of discoveries of giant footprints, Green remains among the field's more active researchers, continuing on-site investigations and eyewitness interviews throughout the Pacific Northwest. In May 2002 he told Canada's Global National radio, "I'm not a believer, I'm an in-

vestigator. My investigation has convinced me that the existance of [Bigfoot] is the simpler explanation than trying to conjure up the worldwide everlasting conspiracy that would be necessary if all this is of human manufacture."

Sources: Coleman, *Bigfoot!*; Coleman and Clark, *Cryptozoology A to Z*; John Green radio interview (24 May 2002).

Green Hill Monster In 1970, multiple sightings of a BIGFOOT-type HOMINID were reported from the neighborhood of Talihina, in southeastern Oklahoma's Latimer County. Witnesses describe a hairy biped, nicknamed after one of its appearances on Green Hill Road. Local legends claim that police dispatched to investigate the sightings found several deer dead, their necks broken as if by a large predator. Roger Roberts, a private investigator and amateur Bigfooter, has tracked the Green Hill Monster since 2001. In November 2003 he told reporters, "The evidence I have in Oklahoma is very, very compelling, otherwise I wouldn't waste my time and money." That evidence allegedly includes 16-inch footprints and hair samples from an unknown primate. "It is definitely not bear hair," Roberts insists. He also claims a personal encounter with the beast. "It was a foggy, cold rainy night in January," he explained to Oklahoma City's KFOR-TV. "I shined my light and said, 'Damn, what is this?' At least 9- to 10-feet off the ground, the best you could tell in the fog. I illuminated the eyes with a light. I never seen any eyes like that. They just pulsated for about four seconds, and then they blinked and they were outta there. I say to the skeptics, just give us a little more time. I think the truth will come out. There's something out here leaving evidence."

Sources: Bord and Bord, *The Bigfoot Casebook*; Lance West, "Beast or bunk: Researchers chase mysterious creature." KFOR-TV, Oklahoma City (9 November 2003).

Green Island sea serpent (*See illustration next page.*) In 1924 an unidentified SEA SERPENT was sighted near Green Island, between Cairns, Queensland and the Great Barrier Reef. The incident was not publicized until June 1930, when an anonymous witness wrote to the Sydney *Daily Pictorial* (now the *Daily Telegraph*). As the writer described that encounter:

It was only a few oars' length from the launch, and about 9 feet of an arched neck was exposed. With a diameter about 15 inches, its colour was a mottled brown and yellow. The whole body must have been of great length. It was assuredly a member of the serpent order, and not a porpoise, seal, dugong, or TORTOISE, with all of which I am familiar. Others saw the animal. It was no optical illusion, and there was no liquor on board.

Source: "Sea serpents do exist! 'Saw one…no liquor aboard.'" Sydney *Daily Pictorial* (16 June 1930).

Greenland sea serpent (*See illustration next page.*) On 6 July 1734, a large SEA SERPENT was sighted in Baffin Bay, off the west coast of Greenland. One witness, Povel Egede, related the story to his father, the Rev. Hans Egede, who published an account of the incident seven years later. As described in that report:

This Monster was of so huge a Size, that coming out of the Water, its Head reached as high as the Mast-Head; its Body was bulky as the Ship, and three or four times as long. It had a long pointed Snout, and spouted like a Whale-Fish; great broad Paws, and the Body seemed covered with shell-work, its skin very rugged and uneven. The under Part of its Body was shaped like an enormous huge Serpent, and when it dived again under Water, it plunged backwards into the Sea, and so raised its Tail aloft, which seemed a whole Ship's Length distant from the bulkiest part of its Body.

Source: Heuvelmans, *In the Wake of the Sea Serpents*.

Hans Egede's depiction of the Greenland sea serpent.

Greenwell, J. Richard (1942–)

Originally from Surrey, England, J. Richard Greenwell spent two years in Spain and six years in Peru, during which time he explored the Andes and the Amazon. In 1975, he was appointed research coordinator of the Office of Arid Lands Studies at the University of Arizona, in Tucson. In 1982, with BERNARD HEUVELMANS and ROY MACKAL, he was instrumental in founding the INTERNATIONAL SOCIETY OF CRYPTOZOOLOGY (ISC), and has served as its secretary since that time. He is also editor of the *ISC Newsletter* and the Society's scholarly journal *Cryptozoology*. In 1984, he formulated a new classification system for cryptozoology, which is now considered the standard in the field.

A member of numerous scientific organizations, including the American Society of Mammalogists and the American Society of Primatologists, Greenwell is also a Fellow of both the Explorers Club in New York--serving on its Expeditions Committee and as its Southwest Chapter Chairman — and the Royal Geographical Society in London. He has traveled to over 30 countries in the course of his exploration and zoological work, and in 1991 he was awarded an honorary doctorate by the University of Guadalajara, Mexico. The author of over 100 technical and popular publications on cryptozoology, he has also been the cryptozoology columnist for *BBC Wildlife Magazine*, Britain's leading animal conservation publication.

Greenwell's cryptozoological expeditions around the world have included: searching for new evidence of MOKELE-MBEMBE in the swamps of the Congo Basin (with Mackal); investigating evidence for the RI in Papua New Guinea (with anthropologist Roy Wagner); seeking physical evidence of the legendary ONZA in Mexico (with mammalogist Troy L. Best); and searching for new YEREN evidence in the mountains of Central China (with anthropologist Frank E. Poirier). Since 1997, he has directed four field projects in Northern California's Six Rivers National Forest to test the "unverified primate hypothesis" for BIGFOOT. These projects represent the only long-term, deep-wilderness attempts by professional zoologists to acquire such evidence. A total of 38 incidents/finds have so far been documented, and a major new

J. Richard Greenwell.

project is in the planning stage. Greenwell is now a research associate in mammalogy in the Department of Zoological Collections of the International Wildlife Museum, in Tucson, where the Secretariat of the ISC is also based.

Sources: J. Richard Greenwell, "Preliminary report of the 1999 Six Rivers National Forest expedition" (30 August 1999); personal communication with the author (31 January 2004).

Greers Ferry Lake, Arkansas

One of the largest lakes in the Razorback State, Greers Ferry Lake sprawls across the border between Cleburne and Van Buren Counties. Local residents claim that a "water panther" inhabits the lake, and that its "huge yellow eyes" are sometimes visible from shore on summer nights. Wind may be responsible for groaning sounds attributed to the creature, but no breeze can account for the report of a scuba diver menaced by a creature — "big, hairy, and horrid" — during exploration of an underwater grotto in the 1970s. A similar snarling animal harassed construction workers at the lake, while they were converting a lakeside cave into a boathouse.

Source: Graham, "Monsters of the Ozarks."

Greiss Bay sea serpent

On 6 January 1893, *The Times* of London published a letter from W.M. Russell, a Scottish physician, describing a SEA SERPENT encounter from Greiss Bay, Scotland, some time before 1851. Russell wrote:

In 1851 I happened to be on a visit to the house of Mrs. M'Iver (mother of Mr. Evandu M'Iver, of Sourie, who is still living, the respected factor of the Duke of Sutherland at Loch Inver), and I not only herd from her a detailed account of the recent appearance of a great sea-serpent in the little bay of Greiss, opposite her residence, but I actually became the possessor of a number of scales about the size and shape of a scallop shell, which were found on the reef of rock in the bays whereon the monster had comforted itself by scratching its head. Mrs. M'Iver had not merely heard of the strange creature; she had seen it taking a leisurely swim along the beach, to the great alarm of the FISH, shoals of which leaped out of the water in front of it; and the venerable lady, whose words would be received with perfect faith by any one who knew her, said that she had watched the sea-serpent making for the reef, when the fishermen belonging to the cottages close at hand, having recovered their presence of mind, fired upon and apparently wounded it, and that she had seen it thrust its head and some eight or ten feet of its body up on the rocks, where it rested for some time till the shore boats approached, whereupon it slid into the water and disappeared seawards, leaving a long wake or furrow behind it. The fishermen found the scales of which I speak on the rocks, and gave some of them to Mrs. M'Iver. Many years afterward, in conversation with Sir Richard Owen at East Sheen, I happened to mention the circumstance. He asked if I could let him see the scales. On looking for them next day in the place in my collection of "curios" where they ought to have been, I was crestfallen at the discovery that my *pièces justificatives* had gone, for Sir Richard, then Professor Owen, was evidently incredulous, and I was, and am, a believer. In arguing the matter with him, I remarked that "I had seen sea SNAKES 5 ft. or 6 ft. long, and that there was no reason to suppose there might not be snakes 50 ft. or 60 ft. long." Sir Richard replied—"Well, well, if you told me you had seen men 7 ft. or 8 ft. high I would believe you, but I fear I could not accept a statement from you that you had seen men 70 ft. or 80 ft. in height." Even the scales would not have convinced him.

Source: Heuvelmans, *In the Wake of the Sea Serpents*.

Gresskardfossen Lake carcass   Author Peter Costello reports that the remains of a presumed LAKE MONSTER were beached on the shore of this lake, in Norway's Rogaland County, sometime in the mid-16th century. Unfortunately, no further details are available, and the tale is thus impossible to judge.

Source: Costello, *In Search of Lake Monsters*.

Grimm, Jack (1925–1998)   A native of Abilene, Texas, "Cadillac Jack" Grimm earned millions from his Grimm Oil Company, but his passion for unsolved mysteries rivaled his pursuit of black gold. Following the example of fellow Texan TOM SLICK, Grimm supported various investigations through the 1970s, including expeditions seeking BIGFOOT, NESSIE, and the putative remains of Noah's Ark. In the 1980s, Grimm shifted his focus to the *Titanic*, spending $2 million to locate and salvage the world's most famous shipwreck, collecting 1,700 objects from the ship by 1987. Sadly, Grimm's cryptozoological expeditions failed to deliver the same concrete results. Grimm died on 8 January 1998, at age 72.

Source: Coleman and Clark, *Cryptozoology A to Z*.

Grimsby Growler   On 1 August 2001, a resident of Grimsby, Lincolnshire, England reported sighting a large black animal in the town's Cartergate district. He described it as resembling a hyena (*Hyena hyena*), but media statements from local police referred to a "CAT-type creature." As noted in the press, North East Lincolnshire had become a "hot-spot" for cryptid sightings during recent years, with other witnesses reporting JACK-ALS, KANGAROOS and ALIEN BIG CATS. None of the beasts have yet been captured or identified, and Grimsby's curious black prowler is no exception to that rule. When two more sightings were reported in October 2003, police declared the beast "a large Newfoundland dog which had recently had its fur clipped." That attitude began to change on 16 January 2004, after a local security guard observed the creature through binoculars from 160 feet, describing it as "something large and feline," black and 5 feet long. A truckdriver saw the cat on 21 January, crossing the A180 motorway near near Great Coates, but renewed attention brought authorities no closer to capturing the Grimsby Growler.

Source: Rob Burman, "Grimsby 'big cat' is sighted again." *Grimsby Telegraph* (21 January 2004); Rob Burman, "'Growler' spotted on A180." *Grimsby Telegraph* (24 January 20024); "Hyena-like creature roams Grimsby." *Ananova* (2 August 2001).

Grizzly Bear (Giant)   In October 2001, 22-year-old hunter Ted Winnen shot a grizzly bear (*Ursus arctos horribilus*) on Alaska's Hinchinbrook Island (in Prince William Sound). The bear measured 10 feet 6 inches from nose to tail, and Winnen's guide estimated its weight at 1,200 pounds—more than twice the weight of the average Hinchinbrook grizzly. Photos snapped of Winnen with his trophy confirm the bear's awesome size—but Internet pranksters soon inflated the creature into a mind-boggling monster. Spurious e-mails claimed that Winnen's prize kill stood 12 feet 6 inches at the shoulder and weighed more than 1,600 pounds. As the cyberspace rumor evolved, the bear became

a certified killer with multiple human victims to its credit. By late 2002, some of the Internet messages bore a photo attachment purportedly depicting one of the bear's mangled victims. The HOAX persists, despite accurate media reports and formal denials from the U.S. Forest Service. In Juneau, on 29 May 2003, Forest Service spokesman Ray Massey told reporters, "I've gotten calls from media all over the world. I got a call from London today. It's like the Energizer bunny. I have no doubt the Internet is keeping it moving. Otherwise it would have died a long time ago."

Source: Peter Porco, "Actual killing of bear morphs into Internet urban myth." *Anchorage Daily News* (30 May 2003).

Grizzly Bears (Remnant)   Grizzly bears (*Ursus arctos horribilis*) once roamed at will over most of the western United States, from the Great Plains to the Pacific coast. The westward movement of white settlers was disastrous for grizzlies, as for so

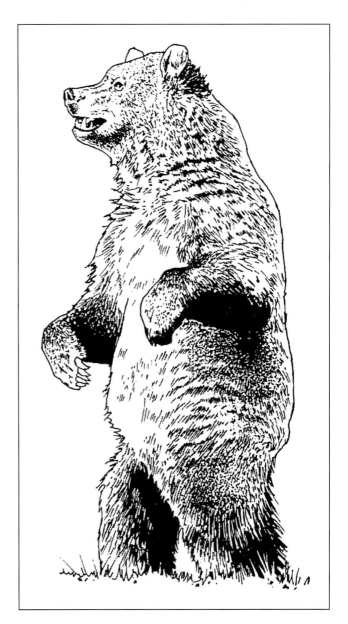

Reports of grizzly bears persist from regions where they are presumed extinct.

many other species, witnessing a ruthless slaughter wherever the great bears were found. Between 1850 and 1920, grizzlies were eradicated from 95 percent of their original range; between 1920 and 1970, the bear's range was slashed by another 52 percent, leaving grizzlies officially extinct across 98 percent of their original U.S. range. While healthier populations survived in Canada and Alaska, the 1,200 grizzlies known to exist in the "Lower 48" by 2001 represented 1 percent of the original population. According to U.S. government spokesmen:

> Grizzly bears persist as identifiable populations in five areas: the Northern Continental Divide, Greater Yellowstone, Cabinet-Yaak, Selkirk, and North Cascade ecosystems. All these populations except Yellowstone's have some connection with grizzlies in southern Canada, although the current status and future prospects of Canadian bears are subject to debate. The U.S. portions of these five populations exist in designated recovery areas, where they receive full protection of the Endangered Species Act....
>
> We have only rough estimates of size for U.S. grizzly bear populations. Many grizzlies exist only in the Northern Continental Divide and Yellowstone ecosystems. We can be confident that there are at least 175 bears in the Northern Continental Divide ecosystem and 142 in the Yellowstone ecosystem, and a minimum of about 360 in the entire contiguous United States (Table). On the other hand, it is unlikely that more than 75 animals inhabit each of the Cabinet-Yaak, Selkirk, and North Cascade populations.

Two areas where grizzly bears "potentially occur"—the realm of interest to cryptozoologists—are the San Juan Mountains of southern Colorado and the Bitterroot Range of eastern Idaho and western Montana. Officially, no grizzlies presently exist in either area. And yet ....

Colorado witnessed a series of brutal "grizzly wars" between 1821 (when the first white settler was killed by a bear) and 1953 (when the state banned private hunting of grizzlies). Congress escalated the carnage in 1931, with passage of the Animal Damage Control Act, creating a federal agency "to conduct campaigns for the destruction or control" of wild predators. Between 1916 and 1970, hunters killed at least 5,148 bears in Colorado, with 304 slaughtered in 1946-47 alone. The state's last "official" grizzly was killed by trapper Lloyd Anderson in September 1952, and a federal search in 1956 produced no grizzlies, but sightings persist to the present day. Anderson himself reported seeing San Juan grizzlies or their distinctive tracks in 1962, 1964, 1965 and 1967. A deer hunter met a grizzly near Raspberry Gulch, in 1965. Two government searches in 1970-71 failed to find any bears, but bow hunter Ed Wiseman killed a 400-pound female grizzly near Chimney Rock in September 1979. (Faced with poaching charges, Wiseman claimed the bear attacked him first and he passed a polygraph test to that effect.) Four grizzlies were seen by a Chromo County rancher in October 1990; game wardens found "an interesting track" at the site but deemed it inconclusive. Sportsman Arthur Trujillo reported four grizzly sightings between 1990 and 1993, but his photograph of the 1993 specimen was also dismissed as "inconclusive."

Similar reports from the Bitterroot Range have also met stubborn resistance from state officials and ranchers opposed to local imposition of the Endangered Species Act. Federal plans for returning grizzlies to the Bitterroots were scuttled in June 2001, after wealthy ranchers told President George W. Bush that it "makes about as much sense as reintroducing the polio virus." Ironically, a live grizzly surfaced at Ninemile Valley (northwest of Missoula) a few weeks later, killing 35 barnyard fowl at a local farm. Agents

of Montana's Department of Fish, Wildlife and Parks killed the bear on 6 July 2001, but confirmation of its presence launched a massive search by civilian researchers. Biologist Chuck Jonkel, in charge of the hunt, told reporters in July 2001, "The federal government's official position is, 'We have searched for grizzlies, and we found nothing.' But they searched maybe 5 percent of an area that's 200 miles by 200 miles."

Chris Servheen, in charge of the U.S. government's grizzly recovery program, countered Jonkel's claims with a prediction that the likelihood of finding more Bitterroot grizzlies is "extremely low." "We've looked really hard for bears in there," Servheen insists. "We've searched the records and followed up on all possible sighting reports, and we've never been able to validate anything. What they end up being is someone saying, 'I thought I saw a grizzly bear.' And when you come down to, 'Where's the evidence? Do you have a photograph or do you have some tissue?' None of that exists."

Sources: "The great grizzly search." *Los Angeles Times* (28 July 2001); Peterson, *Ghost Grizzlies.* David Mattson, "Grizzly bears." http://biology.usgs.gov/s+t/noframe.c032.htm.

Groot Slang This aquatic cryptid of South Africa is named "great serpent" in Afrikaans. Alternate (African) names within its range include Kayman, Ki-man, !Koo-be-eng, and !Koouteign !koo-rou ("master of the water"). It is typically described as a large, dark-colored reptile, though witnesses disagree on whether or not it has legs. Cryptozoologists note the apparent similarity between descriptions of the living Groot Slang and ancient rock paintings of huge serpents found in Brakfontein Cave (near Koesberg), in the cave of the Great Black Serpent (at Rockwood Glen, on the Upper Orange River), and in a cave near Klein Aasvogelkop. That impression is strengthened by the fact that multiple Groot Slang sightings have been reported from the Orange River itself.

Reports of the creature date from 1867, when witness Hans Sauer met a large, dark-colored SNAKE in the Orange River, near Aliwal North. Three decades later, near Upington (in Northern Cape Province), G.A. Kinnear saw an unknown creature lift its head from the Orange River atop a 10-foot neck. In 1910, three campers were frightened by a massive aquatic serpent near Augrabiesvalle, in Northern Cape Province. Ten years later, several witnesses reported a huge snake swimming at the confluence of the Orange and Great Fish Rivers. Witness John Clift reported a 20-foot lizard at the Big Hole, an abandoned mine shaft outside Kimberley, in November 1947. Another spate of sightings was recorded from the Vaal Dam (Free State Province) between November 1963 and February 1964. Skeptics maintain that the witnesses merely saw PYTHONS, CROCODILES or large MONITOR LIZARDS.

Sources: Frank Day, "Police fire on mysterious Vaal 'monster.' *Rand Daily Mail* (11 November 1963); Heuvelmans, *Les derniers dragons d'Afrique*; "Monster lurking in 'Big Hole' at Kimberley." *Johannesburg Sunday Times* (30 November 1947); "River monster with a 10 ft. neck." London *Daily Mail* (8 February 1921).

Ground Shark Initially reported in 1941, this unclassified man-eating SHARK of the Timor Sea (off Australia's northern coast) allegedly grows larger than the great white shark (*Carcharodon carcharias*) but lacks that certified killer's prominent dorsal fin. In further contrast to most predatory sharks, this creature refrains from cruising near the surface and prefers lying in wait at the bottom of the sea, from which its common name derives. KARL SHUKER suggests that ground shark sightings may in fact describe an unknown giant species of carpet shark or wobbegong (Family *Orectolobidae*). These bottom feeders reach a maximum official length of 10.5 feet, and while they normally subsist on a diet of crustaceans and small FISH, a few attacks on humans have been documented. A giant species might be more aggressive, but its existence remains unproven.

Sources: Ley, *The Lungfish and the Unicorn*; Shuker, *From Flying Toads to Snakes with Wings*.

Gryttie
Gryttie is the name applied to an unidentified LAKE MONSTER said to dwell in Sweden's Gryttjen Lake (Gävlesborg County, between Ljusdal and Hudiksvall). Systematic investigation of the sightings began in the mid-1980s, but no conclusive evidence has yet been found. Some researchers speculate that the creature may be a relict sea cow, but that theory fails to explain reports of an animal 100 feet long.

Sources: Karl Shuker, "Alien zoo." *Fortean Times* 106 (January 1998): 14; Gryttie Homepage, http://hem.passagen.se/gryttie/index.html.

Guài Wù
The Guài Wù ("strange beast" in Mandarin Chinese) is a LAKE MONSTER reported from Tianchi Lake (also variously called Changhai, Chon-Ji or Dragon Lake), in the Changbai Mountains of northeast China's Jilin Province. Tianchi is China's deepest volcanic lake, with a charted depth of 1,243 feet. Cryptid reports date from the 19th century and continue to the present day, with 100 sightings recorded between 1962 and 1994. Witnesses typically describe the Guài Wù as the size of an ox or larger, sporting a head like a seal's on a long, swanlike neck. Skeptics note that a nearby volcano erupted in 1702 and presumably destroyed all life in Tianchi Lake, suggesting that any cryptids dwelling in the lake cannot have prehistoric origins.

Cryptozoologists and members of the local Tianchi Monster Society respond to doubters by confirming that aquatic life is plentiful in the lake, and that the Guài Wù frequently appears before multiple witnesses. A party of meteorologists saw the creature in August 1980, and a group of 50 tourists watched it splashing near the eastern shore in January 1987. The first photos and videotape of the Guài Wù were taken on 2 September 1994, as the animal spent 10 full minutes gliding across the lake's surface. More photos were reportedly taken in 1996, while a crowd of some 200 witnesses watched four of the creatures swimming in broad daylight. Another group of 200-plus tourists observed the animal for 10 minutes in July 2002, reporting that it "jumped out of the water from time to time like a seal." A year later, on 11 July 2003, local government cadres watched for 50 minutes as a school of Guài Wù played on the lake's surface, splashing and diving. Zhang Lufeng, vice-director of the provincial forestry bureau, told the *Beijing Youth Daily* that near the end of the startling display, "as many as 20" of the creatures were simultaneously visible. Three weeks later, on 30 July, a lone specimen was sighted by 12 Chinese soldiers passing by the lake.

Sources: "Another Chinese lake monster," *Fortean Times* 48 (Spring 1987): 27-28; "China lays claim to its own Nessie." ABC News Australia (31 July 2002); "China's 'Loch Ness Monster' resurfaces." Reuters (15 July 2003); "Chinese lake monster." *INFO Journal* 77 (Spring 1997): 43; "Lake 'monster' jumps back to sight." *China Daily News* (31 July 2002); "Lake monsters ahoy!" *Fortean Times* 77 (October-November 1994): 16; Moore, "Water dragons"; Shuker, "Freshwater monsters: the next generation"; Shuker, *In Search of Prehistoric Survivors*; "Soldiers spot 'Chinese Nessie.'" BBC News (31 July 2003).

Guaraçai Air-Breather
An unclassified FISH reported from Brazil, this cryptid is described as five inches long, with barbels like a CATFISH, one visible gill, and two small legs with webbed toes on the feet. If its appearance were not strange enough, the fish allegedly surfaces periodically to breathe above the surface and is reportedly capable of surviving indefinitely on dry land. According to reports from Brazil, a single specimen was captured in September 1995, at a lake near Guaraçai (in São Paulo State), but its fate and whereabouts are presently unknown.

Source: Eberhart, *Mysterious Creatures*; "Fish caught walking underwater." *Fortean Times* 86 (May 1996): 40.

Guaurabo River, Cuba
In June 1998, the *Cuba Free Press* reported that Mayra Chaviano and her two small children had been attacked by an unknown "long-shaped marine animal" while swimming in the Guaurabo River near the town of Trinidad. All three were allegedly hospitalized in critical condition, including partial paralysis. Bystanders "gave differing descriptions" of the creature, some claiming the beast was new to the region while others said they had seen it before over several years. No further information is available on this mysterious case, but researcher Brad LaGrange suggests that the Chavianos may have been stung by a Portuguese man-of-war (*Physalia physalis*).

Source: Brad LaGrange, "Two Gulf cryptids?" *North American Bio-Fortean Review* 2 (December 2000): 33-34.

Was the Guaurabo River's lethal cryptid a Portuguese man-of-war?

Gueydon sea serpents
Officers and crew aboard the French cruiser *Gueydon* were among the many witnesses who reported SEA SERPENT sightings from ALONG BAY, Vietnam in the early 20th century. Details are lacking, but witnesses claimed to have seen the cryptids twice, in December 1903 and again in March 1904. Roughly 100 persons on the ship witnessed the second encounter.

Source: Heuvelmans, *In the Wake of the Sea Serpents*.

Guiafairo
Residents of Senegal describe this night-flying cryptid as a large gray BAT with clawed feet and a "human" face. Its intimidating size and appearance are augmented by a repul-

sive odor and a reputation (perhaps undeserved) for invading homes. The Guiafairo's name translates roughly as "the fear that flies by night." Despite its reputation, no attacks on human beings have been documented.

Source: Shuker, "The secret animals of Senegambia."

Güije/Jigüe

The Güije are unclassified APES or small HOMINIDS reported from the eastern quarter of Cuba. Witnesses describe the creatures as three feet tall and "half-MONKEY, half-man." Black skin is visible beneath dark hair, and on bare portions of the face. The Güije's head seems oversized, topping a body notable for its protruding belly and prominent navel. These nocturnal creatures are said to be quite strong, and defend themselves if cornered with a set of wicked claws.

Sources: Corrales, "Aluxoob: Little people of the Maya"; Antonio Bachiller y Morales, "Jigues: Tradición Cubana." *Archivos del Folklore Cubano* 2 (1926): 169-173.

Guirivilu

This supposed LAKE MONSTER of South America is not confined to a single body of water, but reportedly inhabits various lakes in southern Chile and neighboring Argentina's Neuquén Province. Its name means "FOX serpent" in the Araucanian dialect; alternate names throughout its range include Glyryvilu and Neguruvilu. All refer to creature's description, including a foxlike head on a large SNAKE's body. The Guirivilu's tail allegedly sports a double row of spikes, with a barb at the tip. The animal was predatory, known for attacking humans and livestock, but a dearth of reports since the early 20th century suggests that the Guirivilu may now be extinct (if it ever existed).

Sources: Hartley Alexander, *Latin American Mythology*. New York: Cooper Square, 1964; Robert Lehmann-Nitsche, "La pretendia existencia actual del Grypotherium." *Revista del Museo de La Plata* 10 (1902): 277-279.

Gul see Golub-Yavan

Gulebaney

An unclassified primate or HOMINID reported from the Talysh Mountains of Azerbaijan, the Gulebaney may be identical to the KAPTAR, whose range it shares. Eyewitnesses describe a hairy biped, roughly the size of an adult human, with a dietary preference for FISH, FROGS, and vegetables taken from rural gardens. Recorded sightings date from the 1890s, when zoologist Konstantin Satunin observed a female specimen at close range. A soldier named Ramazan claimed he was kidnapped by a pair of Gulebaney, one summer night in 1947. The creatures allegedly held him captive overnight, examining his body and clothing, then released him unharmed at sunrise. Alternate names for the Gulebaney include Biabanguli, Kulieybani, and Vol'moshin' (referring to females).

Sources: Heuvelmans and Porshnev, *L'homme de Néanderthal est toujours vivant*; Konstantin Satunin, "Bianbanguli." *Priroda i Okhota* 7 (1899): 28-35; Tchernine, *The Yeti*.

Gulf Coast Bigfoot Research Organization

The Gulf Coast BIGFOOT Research Organization (GCBRO) was founded in February 1997, by Bobby Hamilton of Warren, Texas. Its mission is to investigate Bigfoot reports from the southern U.S., thereby redressing a perceived imbalance in reports from the Pacific Northwest. In May 2003, Hamilton told the *Florida Sun* that his group had 18 members, but membership soon "exploded." A month later, the GCBRO's Internet website named 24 members, with a reference to "many others who...prefer to keep a lower profile." In addition to eyewitness interviews, GCBRO members pursue their own searches for Bigfoot, employing night-vision equipment, infrared heat sensors, thermal imaging devices, passive wireless microphones, and directional microphones with parabolic boosters.

Sources: "Stalking the southern Sasquatch." *Florida Sun* (24 May 2003); Gulf Coast Bigfoot Research Organization, http://www.gcbro.com.

Gulf of Aden sea serpent

In 1934 a dozen witnesses reported sightings of an unidentified SEA SERPENT at Largs Bay, Somalia, on the Gulf of Aden. No detailed descriptions are available from the sighting, which occurred six years after two cryptids were seen swimming in tandem off nearby Cape Guardafui, by crewmen aboard the Royal Mail Ship ORONSAY.

Source: Heuvelmans, *In the Wake of the Sea Serpents*.

Gulf of Alaska carcass

The London *Daily Mail Yearbook* for 1957 included the following account of a strange animal carcass washed ashore from the Gulf of Alaska the previous summer. It read:

Mystery Monster: A giant hairy Monster, with 6 foot tusks was washed ashore on the coast of Alaska in July 1956. The carcase which was more than 100 feet long and 15 feet wide, had crimson flash. Its origin and species were a complete mystery. Experts said that it fitted no known description of prehistoric beasts and that the 2-inch reddish-brown hair which covered the thick decaying hide excluded any relationship to whales.

The Monster was discovered by a veteran Alaskan hunting guide, and was apparently washed ashore during a gale in the Gulf of Alaska. Explorers who flew northward to view the carcase said the Monster had a huge head measuring 5½ feet across, with eye sockets 9 inches wide and about 42 inches apart. Its teeth were 6 inches long and 5 inches wide at the base. Clusters of ribs extended 6 feet from the spinal column, and the moveable upper jaw, a solid tusk-like bone protruded several feet beyond the end of the fixed lower jaw.

BERNARD HEUVELMANS failed to discuss this carcass in his classic study of SEA SERPENTS, but a chronology of strandings in that volume does mention a carcass found at Yakutak, Alaska (on the gulf) in "spring" 1956. Heuvelmans dismissed those remains as belonging to a specimen of Baird's BEAKED WHALE (*Berardius bairdii*), but that identification raises more questions than it answers. The maximum acknowledged length of *B. bairdii* is 42 feet; the whale's skin is gray, without visible hair; it has no tusks; and its four teeth (all on the lower jaw) are much smaller than those of the Alaska cryptid.

Sources: Dinsdale, *Monster Hunt*; Heuvelmans, *In the Wake of the Sea Serpents*.

Gulf of Fonseca carcass

In June 1928, a large, mysterious carcass washed ashore on the coast of El Salvador, from the Gulf of Fonseca. Observers at the time described it as the body of a "prehistoric reptile," 89 feet long and "very corpulent." The body was marked by dramatic black-and-white stripes. The creature's head sported a horn on top, and its mouth bristled with teeth 1.5 inches long. No relics of the creature were preserved, and it remains unidentified today.

Sources: Heuvelmans, *In the Wake of the Sea Serpents*; "Dubious Globsters," http://www.geocities.com/capedrevenger/dubiousglobsters.html

Gulf of Mexico sea serpents

Sightings of alleged SEA SERPENTS in the Gulf of Mexico are relatively rare. One very peculiar case was reported on 6 November 1973, when two Mississippi fishermen encountered a small but startling creature near the mouth of the Pascagoula River. As later described by Fortean au-

Divers in the Gulf of Mexico report encounters with huge, unknown creatures (*William Rebsamen*).

thors Colin and Janet Bord, the thing was "3 feet long, 3 or 4 inches wide and shiny like stainless steel," with an amber light winking sporadically on top. The witnesses summoned Coast Guard officers, who allegedly joined the fishermen in beating the unknown object with oars and boat hooks. At that point, the creature — or "craft," as the Bords suggest, apparently presuming it to be a tiny UFO — doused its light and escaped at high speed.

A later, equally mysterious encounter from the Gulf was reported to an Internet newsgroup in 2000. It read:

I used to have a friend who was at one time an undersea welder for Gulf Oil in the 70's and did work on the oil rigs way out in the Gulf of Mexico. He gave it up because he was seeing things that were beyond his ability to comprehend and even describe. And he wasn't the only one. At one oil rig, the welding crew were getting used to seeing this "giant headless glowing living firehose" that would zoom in from out of nowhere at incredible Nascar speeds and would keep on zooming past the welders for up to fifteen minutes! My friend then said he finally saw what ate the giant headless glowing living firehoses one scary day and caught the first helicopter back to shore.

Researcher Chad Arment traced the post's author and learned that the witness in question, one George Hale, had died in 1994. As further explained in their correspondence, Hale had been unable to describe the final beast he saw because:

It was too big and too close to him. It was as big to him as you are to an ANT. As a matter of fact, he had to ascend PDQ because he was in fear of being crushed like a bug. But the predator had a pallor and skin texture like a sea anemone and it might have been built along the lines of a starfish or a freshwater pond hydra [i.e., with multiple arms or tentacles]. And it was eating the firehose entity by swallowing it. Its method of propulsion was a mystery.

Sources: Chad Arment, "Lovecraftian beasts in the Gulf of Mexico." *North American BioFortean Review* 2 (2000): 28-29; Bord and Bord, *Unexplained Mysteries of the 20th Century*; Brad LaGrange, "Two Gulf cryptids?" *North American BioFortean Review* 2 (December 2000): 33-34.

Gulnare sea serpent   On 15 July 1877, artist George Wasson was piloting his yacht *Gulnare* off Gloucester, Massachusetts when he sighted a still-unidentified SEA SERPENT. A friend

aboard the yacht, B.L. Fernald, confirmed the sighting. Wasson describes the incident:

The day was hazy, with light breeze from the southeast. When we were, as I should judge, about two miles off the mouth of Gloucester harbor, the monster came to the surface about the eighth of a mile to leeward of us. I was looking that way, and saw him appear, but Mr. Fernald did not, the first time. He immediately noticed the surging noise made, and turning, exclaimed, "What ledge was that which broke?" This is exactly what the sound most resembled — a heavy ground-swell breaking over a submerged ledge; and the creature itself looked, both in shape and color, more like a ledge covered with kelp than anything else we could think of, though from the extreme roughness of the surface I remember that we both spoke of its being somewhat like a gigantic ALLIGATOR. The skin was not only rough, but the surface was very uneven, and covered with enormous humps of varying sizes, some being as large as a two-bushel basket. Near one end was a marked depression, which we took to be the neck. In front of this, the head (?) rose out of the water perhaps half as high as the body, but we saw no eyes, mouth, fins, or the slightest indication of a tail. It impressed us above all as being a shapeless creature of enormous bulk. I suppose its extreme height out of the water might have been ten feet, certainly not less; and as it disappeared the water closed over it with a tremendous roar and surge and spray, many feet into the air. The water for a large space where it had been remained white and seething with foam for some little time. From the way the water closed in over it, and the great commotion caused by its disappearing, we judged of its immense bulk, and we also concluded that it went down perpendicularly. It apparently rose in the same way. The largest whale I ever saw did not make a quarter part of the noise and disturbance in the water that this creature did. In concluding I will add that Mr. Fernald has followed the sea for fifteen years as a fisherman, and is perfectly familiar with all the cetaceans that appear on our coast.

Woods subsequently told the Boston Society of Nautical History that the visible part of the creature was brown and measured 40 to 60 feet long. He estimated its speed between five and six knots (six to seven miles per hour).

Source: Heuvelmans, *In the Wake of the Sea Serpents*.

Gunni   The Gunni (pronounces "goon-eye") is a legendary Australian cryptid, said to resemble a wombat (*Vombatus* sp.) with a long tail and growths on its head resembling horns. Initial sightings by gold prospectors in the 1860s were dismissed as a product of alcohol and "fertile imagination," but sporadic reports of the unlikely creatures have continued into modern times. In 1999, witness Frank Murphy claimed to have seen a Gunni near Marysville, Victoria, 60 miles northeast of Melbourne. "I got the fright of my life," Murphy told reporters. "I thought it might have been somebody's dog lost, and then it turned around and had antlers on top of its head. It stayed still for 30 to 40 seconds and then it went into the bush." Although he had not been drinking before the encounter, Murphy said, "After I saw it, I went home and had quite a few." In September 2003, local ranger Miles Stewart-Howie employed his talents as a taxidermist to create a fake Gunni, which he labeled *Turpis maialis cimex* and placed on display at the Marysville visitors' center. A minor rush of CRYPTOTOURISM ensued, notwithstanding the obvious HOAX, but most Australians today rank the Gunni with the DROP BEAR as a purely mythical creature.

Source: Paul Heinrichs, "Gunni legend proves hit and myth." *The Age* (5 October 2003).

Gurnet sea serpent   On 18 July 1915, the *Boston Sunday*

Herald published a melodramatic account of a SEA SERPENT sighted near Black Rock, off Cohasset, Massachusetts, by crewmen of the steamer *Gurnet.* Quartermaster Roy Litchfield was first to see the animal, described as a wild-eyed "leviathan." Captain Edward Edson confirmed the encounter, claiming that the creature "pretty near come aboard of us. I could have reached out and tickled her under the chin, we were so close." Edson was struck by the animal's speed, adding, "The long black mane stuck straight out from the back of her neck like a pennant on a yacht and she rolled her eyes horrible [*sic*] and the drool was running off her cruel mouth like foam."

Source: O'Neill, *The Great New England Sea Serpent.*

Gu-Ru-Ngaty *see* Bunyip

Gyedarra This elusive Australian cryptid was reported from Queensland, around Gowrie Station, in the latter 19th century. Witnesses described it as an herbivorous, semiaquatic mar-

supial the size of a horse, which lived in burrows it dug beside rivers and creeks. No modern sightings are recorded, and the creature is presumed to be extinct. Some investigators believe the 19th century sightings indicate a relict population of *Diprotodon optatum*, a Pleistocene marsupial resembling an oversized TAPIR; others maintain that descriptions of the long-dead creatures were handed down among Aborigines by word of mouth, related by tribal storytellers as if the animals were still alive.

Source: George Bennett, "A trip to Queensland in search of fossils." *Annals and Magazine of Natural History* 9 (1872): 315.

Gyona Pel A large unknown HOMINID reported from the Komi Republic of northern Russia, the Gyona Pel takes its name from a phrase in the Komi dialect meaning "hairy-eared." In fact, the creature (if it exists) is probably identical to the KAPTAR reported from other parts of Russia and Western Asia.

Source: Bayanov, *In the Footsteps of the Russian Snowman.*

——H——

Haas, George F. (1906-78) California cryptozoologist George Haas published the first issue of his *Bigfoot Bulletin* on 2 January 1969, and he continued to distributed the newsletter free of charge for the remainder of his life. His home in Oakland became a veritable BIGFOOT archive, housing more than 3,000 newspaper articles related to North America's elusive HOMINID. With founder Archie Buckley, Haas served as a spokesman for the Bay Area Group, a nonprofit Bigfooter's organization. Haas staunchly opposed suggestions that Bigfoot should be shot on sight to prove the species exists, but he supported a plan for live trapping "with strong reservations." He died of cancer on 16 February 1978.

Sources: Coleman, Bigfoot!; Bayanov, *Bigfoot: To Kill or to Film?,* http://www.n2.net/prey/bigfoot/biology/db5.htm.

Hadjel The Hadjel is an unclassified CAT, said to inhabit the mountains around Temki, in Chad. Witnesses describe it as larger than a LION, with a mane, unusually long fangs, and a short tail resembling a hyena's. Researchers speculate that it may be a relict form of SABER-TOOTHED CAT surviving from prehistoric times.

Source: Jeanne-Françoise Vincent, *Le Pouvoir et le Sacré Chez les Hadjerau du Tchad.* Paris: Éditions Anthropos, 1975.

Haietluk This SEA SERPENT reported from the coast of British Columbia takes its name from a Nootka Indian word meaning "wriggler." Its likeness is found in tribal petroglyphs, and while it apparently once shared coastal waters with the pelagic cryptid known as CADBOROSAURUS, the Haietluk was much smaller. Traditional descriptions make it 7-8 feet long, with four legs, a head and mane resembling a horse's, and a mouthful of large teeth. "Caddy," by contrast, is typically described as ranging from 16 to 100 feet long — raising the possibility that the Haietluk may be a juvenile specimen.

Source: Beth and Ray Hill, *Indian Petroglyphs of the Pacific Northwest.* Saanichton, B.C.: Hancock House, 1974.

Hairy Man Repeated sightings of an unknown HOMINID or NORTH AMERICAN APE in Round Rock, Texas (a northeastern

suburb of Austin) prompted local residents to dub a local highway Hairy Man Road. Dozens of witnesses claimed fleeting encounters with the Hairy Man during the 1960s, including one motorist who allegedly watched the beast chasing a goat down the middle of the road. In the 1980s, the highway's name was formally changed to Hairy *Mann* Road.

Source: Hauck, *Haunted Places.*

Hai-Ryo Mythology and cryptozoology clash in the case of this legendary Japanese "DRAGON bird." According to tradition, a dragon or LAKE MONSTER dwelling in a lake near Kyoto undergoes a magic transformation every 50 years, becoming a golden-plumed BIRD called the Hai-ryo. The quasi-reptilian bird utters blood-chilling cries, and its appearance normally precedes catastrophes. Could the Hai-ryo represent a real-life bird? We may never know, since most sources agree that the creature has not been seen since April 1834.

Sources: Gould, *Mythical Monsters*; Shuker, *Dragons: A Natural History.*

Hall, Mark A. (1946–) A childhood fascination with unsolved mysteries propelled Minnesota native Mark Hall into lifelong study of cryptozoology and other natural anomalies, which he simply calls "wonders." In that pursuit, Hall has traveled widely, interviewed scores of witnesses, and logged countless hours perusing historical archives. His work has paid off in discoveries of Native American folklore and early settlers' tales describing BIGFOOT, the THUNDERBIRD, LAKE MONSTERS, SEA SERPENTS, and various other cryptids. Hall worked closely with IVAN SANDERSON on various projects, notably including Sanderson's investigation of the MINNESOTA ICEMAN, and in the 1970s Hall served as director of Sanderson's SOCIETY FOR THE INVESTIGATION OF THE UNEXPLAINED. Hall's theories on the nature and variety of unknown living HOMINIDS remain controversial among cryptozoologists. Hall is the author of several self-published books, and of the journal *Wonders,* issued periodically.

Source: Coleman and Clark, *Cryptozoology A to Z.*

Hallandsvatnet, Norway In 1969, two fishermen reported a LAKE MONSTER sighting from this lake in Norway's Vest-Agder County. The creature, briefly glimpsed, apparently resembled those reported from other Norwegian lakes.

Source: Eric Knatterud, Sea Serpents in Norwegian Lakes, http://www.mjoesormen.no.

Hamilton sea serpent   On the afternoon 10 July 1839, Captain Sturgis of the revenue cutter *Hamilton* sighted an unidentified SEA SERPENT while cruising in fine weather between Cape Ann and Boston, Massachusetts. The *Boston Centinel* [*sic*] reported the incident, but no detailed description of the creature was provided.

Source: O'Neill, *The Great New England Sea Serpent*.

Hamlet   Hamlet is the name facetiously applied (from Shakespeare's play) to the alleged LAKE MONSTER of Lake Elsinore, California (Riverside County). Less literary-minded locals sometimes call the creature Elsie. First sighted in 1884, Hamlet appeared to witnesses sporadically over the next six decades, but Mother Nature seemed to pull the plug when droughts dried up Lake Elsinore in 1951 and 1955. That should have been the end for any aquatic cryptids, but witness Bonnie Pray claims to have seen Hamlet twice in 1970, describing a "SNAKE-like" creature 12 feet long and three feet in diameter. Three park rangers subsequently reported sighting an unknown creature in Lake Elsinore, swimming 50 feet from their boat, but contradictory descriptions left the mystery unsolved.

Sources: "The endless search." *Fate* 23 (November 1970): 32-36; Kirk, *In the Domain of the Lake Monsters*.

Hampshire Panther   Between March 1972 and January 1973, multiple witnesses reported sightings of a "black panther" from the New Forest region of Hampshire, England. A typical witness, John McPherson, was driving on the A35 near Lyndhurst when the CAT crossed in front of his car. McPherson said:

If it was a cat it was the largest cat I have ever seen in my life. It was large, black and low slung, rather longer than a Labrador but about the same height. It had a short head. It was cat-like, but much too big to be one and was definitely not a FOX or a badger.

Reports of ALIEN BIG CATS continue from Hampshire, including attacks on livestock. A supposed LION was seen at Basingstoke in September 1994, at the same time authorities were pursuing the elusive BEAST OF TWESELDOWN.

Sources: McEwan, *Mystery Animals of Britain and Ireland*; Sieveking, "Beasts in our midst."

Hanoi sea serpent   In 1922, a French sailor identified through *Lloyd's Register* as P. Merlees, a deep-sea captain from Granville, wrote to the newspaper *Ouest-Éclair* concerning a SEA SERPENT sighting from June 1908. The incident occurred in ALONG BAY, on the northern coast of Vietnam. Merlees described the event as follows:

I saw, some way ahead, a black mass which at first I took for a capsized boat. On approaching and examining it with binoculars, I found it had a strange shape. This resembled a framework over which a sail had been tightly stretched. The ribs were very marked. Seen from the side and from some way off it would certainly look indented, for the ridges were very sharp. I had a three-quarter view which enabled me to make a rough estimate of its size.

As I wondered what it could be I kept coming closer and clearly distinguished all its features. When I reached some thirty yards away a huge head emerged some 4 or 5 yards from what I could see, and therefore nearer to me.

Although surprised by this sudden apparition, I could observe

The *Hanoi* sea serpent, after witness P. Merlees.

it very well, and it was very like the head of a TURTLE, but longer and certainly 2 feet wide by 3 feet long; it had two big very bright black and white eyes and large nostrils. It was blackish like the rest. I could not see the jaw, the mouth being shut, but the mouth was clearly marked on the sides and of large dimensions.

The head turned to look at the ship, blew noisily without spouting water and at once dived, the rest following and making a big wash.

Source: Heuvelmans, *In the Wake of the Sea Serpents*.

Hantu Jarang Gigi *see* **Orang Dalam**

Hantu Sakai   The Semang people of Malaysia use this term to describe an alleged race of hairy, jungle-dwelling HO-MINIDS that spend most of their time in trees, but who walk bipedally when they descend. The name is clearly pejorative, as *hantu* means "devil" and *sakai* translates as "degenerate." Some confusion stems from the fact that nomadic Senoi hunters are sometimes also dubbed Sakai, in a show of contempt for their primitive lifestyle. IVAN SANDERSON classed the Hantu Sakai as "proto-PYGMIES," though witnesses describe some specimens as standing 5 feet 10 inches tall. Thick body hair is capped by long hair on the creatures' heads and prominent mustaches on male specimens. A few reports allude to Hantu Sakai wearing loincloths made of tree bark. Traditional accounts differ as to whether the creatures are timid or stalk humans for food. Some stories claim the Hantu Sakai use sharp bones on their forearms to cut thick foliage. Traveler Aug Frederickson saw and sketched a captive specimen while visiting the maharajah of Johor, in the 1870s. The creature was slated for shipment to India, but its fate is unknown. In late December 1953, a trio of Hantu Sakai, including two males and a female, were sighted by multiple witnesses at a rubber plantation near Terolak, in Perak State. Observers reported a strong odor emanating from the creatures, similar to that reported in some sightings of BIGFOOT and other unknown hominids.

Sources: "Abominable jungle-men." *Pursuit* 10 (April 1970): 36-37; Aug Frederickson, *Ad Orientem*. London: W.H. Allen, 1889; Heuvelmans, *On the Track of Unknown Animals*; Sanderson, *Abominable Snowmen*.

Hanush *see* **Yoshi**

Hapyxelor   The curious name of this Ontario LAKE MON-STER was coined in 1968, by witness Donald Humphreys, after he glimpsed a 24-foot creature paddling along near the southern end of Muskrat Lake (40 miles northwest of Ottawa). Humphreys claimed the name just "popped into his head," but many locals still call the animal Mussie (in tribute to Scotland's NESSIE). By the time Humphreys reported his encounter with the Hapyxelor, Muskrat Lake's resident cryptid had 65 years of sightings on record. A logger claimed to have fire at the beast with a rifle in 1903, from cliffs on the lake's northern shore, and resident Stewart Childerhose logged the first of several sightings in 1916. Ottawa resident A.W. Peever saw a horse-sized animal crossing the lake in 1941. Don Humphreys later revised his estimate of the creature's size, placing it between 14 and 16 feet, but larger specimens may also inhabit the lake. In 1974, the Hapyxelor allegedly overturned one boat and towed another for some distance after a Pennsylvania fisherman hooked it with his line. A 1976 witness described the animal as a giant FISH "walking on its tail." Twelve years later, in July 1988, four women claimed a sighting of a "baby" creature near the mouth of the Snake River, where it enters Muskrat Lake. Longtime researcher Michael Bradley dismisses claims that the Hapyxelor is a large sturgeon, since none have ever been hooked or reported from Muskrat Lake. Cryptozoologist JOHN KIRK speculates that the animals comprise a relict population of seals. Bradley himself sighted an 8-foot reddish-brown animal swimming in the lake on 3 October 1988. Two days later, his fishfinder tracked two objects of similar size, swimming at a depth of 54 feet, and while he followed them for half an hour, neither surfaced.

Sources: Bradley, *More Than a Myth*; Kirk, *In the Domain of the Lake Monsters.*

Harimau Jalor

The Harimau Jalor ("striped TIGER") is described by natives of Malaysia's Trengganu State as a larger-than-average tiger, distinguished from normal specimens of *Panthera tigris* by stripes that run longitudinally (from head to tail) rather than downward (from back to belly). Several sightings of the Harimau Jalor were reported to Lieutenant-Colonel Arthur Locke, during his service with the British army in Malaysia, after World War II, but in the absence of a specimen Locke presumed the witnesses had suffered from optical illusions.

Sources: Arthur Locke, *The Tigers of Trengganu.* London: Museum Press, 1954; Shuker, *Mystery Cats of the World.*

Harrum-Mo

This unidentified WILDMAN or HOMINID of Nepal's Lunak Valley, reported in the late 19th century, differs from the more familiar YETI by its alleged use of bows and arrows to hunt small animals. Some witnesses also report the Harrum-mo apparently conversing in an unknown language. It is conceivable that a small tribe of primitive humans may live undiscovered amid the Himalayas of Nepal.

Source: Joseph Hooker, *Himalayan Journals.* London: Ward, Lock, Bowden, 1891.

Haskell Rascal

Hominologist JOHN GREEN reports that sightings of a BIGFOOT-type creature around Haskell, Texas date from the 1890s, including reports of livestock predation during harsh winter seasons. Green cites no specific cases, but he notes that some residents of western Texas consider the so-called Haskell Rascal identical to the CADDO CRITTER, known in Stephens County.

Source: Green, *Sasquatch: The Apes Among Us.*

Haslar Lake, England

In September 1987, a 12-foot EEL was allegedly sighted in this lake at Gosport, Hampshire. The animal was never caught, but its reported size exceeds the maximum recorded length of Britain's largest eel (*Conger conger*) by two feet—and congers are, in any case, pelagic eels.

Source: *The Sun* (15 September 1987).

Hattak Chito *see* Nalusa Falaya

Hattie F. Walker sea serpent

In 1887, several U.S. newspapers reported that sailors aboard the schooner *Hattie F. Walker* had captured and killed a SEA SERPENT off the New-

foundland Banks, on 11 October 1886. Reporters claimed the unknown animal was stuffed and publicly displayed on Peake's Island, Maine (offshore from Portland). The animal was allegedly 47 feet 3 inches long and tipped the scales at 700 pounds. However, queries on the subject went unanswered, and none among the crew tried to claim showman P.T. Barnum's offer of $20,000 for a genuine sea monster. Today, most researchers dismiss the reports as a HOAX.

Source: Heuvelmans, *In the Wake of the Sea Serpents.*

Havhest

Havhest ("sea horse") is the generic name for a Norwegian SEA SERPENT or LAKE MONSTER described as a hybrid of horse and FISH. Descriptions typically include a flowing mane and a large mouth filled with double rows of large teeth. An eyewitness account published in 1934 described the Havhest as follows:

Its thick forefeet were like the limbs of a seal, and it swam with them. Its hind quarters were under the water and could not be seen clearly, but it had a long slippery tail with which it whipped the sea to foam.

Some researchers suggest that Havhest sightings may represent grossly exaggerated descriptions of a common walrus (*Odebenus rosmarus*).

Source: Meurger and Gagnon, *Lake Monster Traditions.*

Hawk Moth (Giant)

In 1862, after examining the deep rostrellum of Madagascar's comet orchid (*Angraecum sesquipedale*), Charles Darwin predicted that a moth with a 10-inch proboscis must exist to pollinate the flower. Darwin did not live to see it, but his prediction was validated in 1903, with the discovery of the hawk moth (*Xanthopan morgani praedicta*). Nine decades later, U.S. entomologist Gene Kritsky made a similar prediction, based on studies of a Madagascan orchid with an even deeper rostrellum (*A. longicalcar*). The new moth, still undiscovered, would require a 15-inch proboscis to fulfill its mission. Kritsky insists that the insect must exist, in order for the epiphytic orchid to thrive.

Sources: Natalie Angier, "It may be elusive, but moth with 15-inch tongue should be out there." *New York Times* (14 January 1992); Jonathan Downes, Mystery Insects of the World, http://www.eclipse.co.uk/cfz/features/insects.htm.

Hawkesbury River, Australia

Australian cryptozoologist REX GILROY reports that SEA SERPENTS have been sighted repeatedly near the mouth of this river in New South Wales. A married couple, fishing offshore in May 1976, saw a long-necked creature pass close to their boat, raising its head three feet above the water as it swam out to sea. Several weeks later, an Ettalong resident watched for 15 minutes through binoculars as a similar creature paddled upstream. Witness Rosemary Turner reported an animal with a 9-foot neck and a 20-foot humped back from the Hawkesbury headwaters, in May 1979. Aborigines interviewed by Gilroy claim the animals bury their eggs in beach sand along the river. Fortean authors Colin and Janet Bord refer to "numerous other sightings in the 1970s," but furnish no details.

Sources: Bord and Bord, *Unexplained Mysteries of the 20th Century*; Gilroy, "Search for the Hawkesbury River monster"; Smith, *Bunyips & Bigfoots.*

Hawley Him

Hawley Him is the local name for a BIGFOOT or NORTH AMERICAN APE sighted by three witnesses at the Abilene Boys' Ranch, near Hawley, Texas (north of Abilene, in Jones County). An adult employee of the ranch and two teenage boys claimed that the hairy HOMINID lobbed rocks at them on 6 July 1977. Some accounts relate that incident to reported Bigfoot sightings around Peerless, Texas (Delta County) in September 1973, but no compelling link is apparent between the two sites, separated by some 175 miles.

Sources: Blackman, *The Field Guide to North American Monsters*; Bord and Bord, *The Bigfoot Casebook*; Green, *Sasquatch: The Apes Among Us*.

Hayman Island sea serpent   Hayman Island lies between the coast of Queensland, Australia and the Great Barrier Reef, two miles from HOOK ISLAND. In 1933, SHARK fisherman Boyd Lee was trolling for prey 16 miles northeast of Hayman Island, when the largest TURTLE he had ever seen emerged from the depths below his boat. Lee later estimated that the turtle was four feet long and weighed about 500 pounds. That sight was surprising enough, but as Lee watched the turtle rising, a giant snake-like head flashed up from the shadows, engulfed the turtle, and retreated out of sight. Friends of Lee later vouched for his veracity, though author Paul Smith dismisses the tale as a HOAX.

Source: Smith, *Bunyips & Bigfoots*.

Hayman Lake, Canada   Cryptozoologist JOHN KIRK reports that he once found an Internet website (no longer active) describing reports of a LAKE MONSTER inhabiting this lake in northern Saskatchewan. The website's unnamed author supposedly snapped several photographs of the creature, swimming away from the camera. Kirk, in turn, digitally enhanced one "clear photograph," and while he found no sign of tampering, Kirk concluded that the photo revealed a "rather large" SNAKE of indeterminate species. He further reports that that while tales of the Hayman Lake cryptid are not widely known, "visitors to the lake usually find out about the beast fairly quickly and are known to exercise considerable caution when venturing out on the lake."

Source: Kirk, *In the Domain of the Lake Monsters*.

Hazard sea serpent   The SEA SERPENT dubbed *SCOLIOPHIS ATLANTICUS* made daily appearances off the Massachusetts coast in mid-August 1817. On 15 August it was seen by crewmen of the schooner *Hazard*, anchored off Kettle Island in Gloucester's Magnolia Harbor. Witness Joseph Lee described the event as follows [with errors uncorrected]:

I judge that I was abought one hundred and fifty yards from him. But to have a better view of him I went into the boat and went as near him as I thought it safe. I was within twenty yards of him. I thought it not safe to go any further. I then turned back on bord of the schooner again. I saw him in the above fashen. He was about one hundred feet in length as nie as I could judge. His bigness around I could not essertain. I saw him twenty minutes.

Lee also drew a sketch of the creature's head, complete with

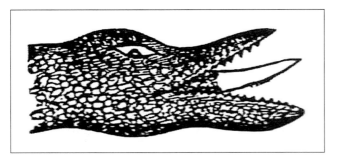

The *Hazard* sea serpent, after witness Joseph Lee.

gaping jaws and a sharp protruding tongue. The inclusion of scales in the drawing presumably derives from observation, rather than assumption that the "serpent" must be a reptile.

Source: O'Neill, *The Great New England Sea Serpent*l

Hazenwind sea serpent   At 2:30 p.m. on 24 November 1917, crewmen aboard the Dutch government schooner *Hazenwind* sighted an alleged SEA SERPENT in the Macassar Strait, between Borneo and Celebes. Four days later, in a letter to the Dutch Chief Inspector of Navigation, Commander H. Kievit described the animal as dirty white in color, with a longitudinal red line on its head. Witnesses on board estimated the creature's dimensions at 50-80 feet long and 2-3 feet thick. A half-century later, BERNARD HEUVELMANS concluded that the sailors had seen an oarfish (*Regalecus glesne*).

Source: Heuvelmans, *In the Wake of the Sea Serpents*.

Heart Lake, Canada   LAKE MONSTER legends are known from this Alberta lake, located between Imperial Mills and the eastern boundary of the Primrose Lake Air Weapons Range, but no modern reports are on file.

Source: "A list of bodies of water in Canada reportedly inhabited by monsters." *INFO Journal* 45 (November 1984): 30-31.

Hebrides sea serpents and lake monsters   The Hebrides (also called the Western Isles) are a group of some two dozen islands off the west coast of Scotland. Since the mid-18th century, several SEA SERPENT and LAKE MONSTER sightings have been reported from the area. Peter Costello reports that an unknown creature was captured on the Isle of Lewis "70 or 80 years" before 1821 and carried into Stornoway (on the island's east coast), but he provides no further details of the case. The next encounter, offshore from Coll in June 1808, was described as follows by the Rev. Donald Maclean:

Rowing along that coast, I observed, at about the distance of half a mile, an object to windward, which gradually excited astonishment.

At first view, it appeared like a small rock. Knowing there was no rock in that situation, I fixed my eyes on it close. Then I saw it elevated considerably above the level of the sea, and after a slow movement, distinctly perceived one of its eyes....

Its head was rather broad, of a form somewhat oval. Its neck was somewhat smaller. Its shoulders, if I can so term them, considerably broader, and thence it tapered towards the tail, which last it kept pretty low in the water, so that a view of it could not be taken so distinctly as I wished. It had no fin that I could perceive, and seemed to me to move progressively by undulation up and down. Its length I believed to be from 70 to 80 feet.

Around the same time, Maclean later heard, crewmen aboard 13 different fishing boats had seem a similar creature near the island of Canna. Ten years later, in July 1818, one Captain Brown, aboard an unnamed ship, reportedly sighted another cryptid between the Hebrides and the Faroe Islands, farther north. Samuel Rafinesque later paraphrased Brown's description.

In swimming the head, neck and forepart of the body stood upright like a mast: it was surrounded by porpoises and fishes. It was smooth, without scales, and had eight gills under the neck; which decidedly evinces that it was not a SNAKE, but a new genus of FISH! ... Dark brown above, muddy white beneath: head obtuse. Capt. Brown adds, that the head was two feet long, the mouth fifteen inches, and the eyes over the jaws, similar to a horse's; the whole length might be 58 feet.

In September 1821, a party of five hunters on Lewis reported sighting a strange beast in an unnamed loch, but they provided no further description. It may have been the same beast described in the following report from *The Times* of London, published on 6 March 1856.

> The village of Leurbost, Parish of Lochs, Lewis, is at present the scene of an unusual occurrence. This is no less than the appearance in one of the inland fresh-water lakes of an animal which from its great size and dimensions has not a little puzzled our island naturalists. Some suppose him to be a description of the hitherto mythological water-kelpie; while others refer it to the minute descriptions of the "sea-serpent," which are revived from time to time in the newspaper columns. It has been repeatedly seen within the last fortnight by crowds of people, many of whom have come from the remotest parts of the parish to witness the uncommon spectacle. The animal is described by some as being in appearance like "a large peat sack," while others affirm that a "six-oared boat" could pass between the huge fins, which are occasionally visible. All, however, agree in describing its form as that of an EEL; and we have heard one, whose evidence we can rely upon, state that in length he supposed it to be about 40 feet. It is probable that it is no more than a conger eel after all, animals of this description having been caught in Highland lakes which have attained huge size. He is currently reported to have swallowed a blanket inadvertently left on the bank by a girl herding cattle. A sportsman ensconced himself with a rifle in the vicinity of the loch during a whole day, hoping to get a shot, but did no execution.

A saltwater cryptid appeared once more, in late January 1895, off Bernera on the Isle of Lewis. Witness Angus Macdonald described it as resembling "a huge hornless bull," about 60 feet long, showing two "coils" 10 feet apart on the surface. A few days later, on 7 February, the Rev. Berners saw the creature from the Butt of Lewis, at the island's southern tip. As Berners described the sighting:

> 200 yards out, [I] saw a neck rise 15 feet out of the water, like a giraffe's, with a sort of ruffle 2 feet behind the ears....It had two great staring eyes, like a bull's, fixed upon me, and I then saw three joints of its body 120 feet long fitting into each other like the joints of a lobster's tail.

On 13 September 1959, while vacationing on the small island of Soay, SHARK fisherman Tex Geddes and engineer James Gavin observed a strange creature offshore, swimming with some killer whales toward the Isle of Skye. Geddes did not think it was another whale because:

> It was too high out of the water in the first place and it remained on the surface for several minutes at a time. When the object appeared to be steaming towards us we both stood up for a better view. I can't remember exactly how close it was when I heard the breathing, but I certainly could hear it before I could definitely have said that the object was alive. It was not making much speed, maybe 3 or 4 knots [4–5 mph]. We were soon able to make out two distinct objects, one larger than the other, and began making guesses at what it might be....

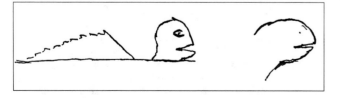

Sketches of a sea serpent seen at Soay, in the Hebrides, after witnesses Tex Geddes (left) and James Gavin.

The head was definitely reptilian, about two feet six [inches] high with large protruding eyes. There were no visible nasal organs, but a large red gash of a mouth which seemed to cut the head in half and which appeared to have distinct lips. There was at least two feet of clear water behind the neck, less than a foot of which we could see, and the creature's back which rose sharply to its highest point some three to four feet out of the water and fell away gradually towards the after end. I would say we saw 8 to 10 ft. of back to the water line.

Gavin elaborated on his friend's description, while both prepared sketches of the animal. According to Gavin:

> At the waterline the body was 6 to 8 ft. long. It was hump-shaped rising to a centrally-placed apex about two feet high. The line of the back was formed by a series of triangular-shaped spines, the largest at the apex and reducing in size to the waterline. The spines appeared to be solid and immobile — they did not resemble fins....
> The neck appeared to be cylindrical in shape, about 8 ins. in diameter. It arose from the water about 12 ins. forward of the body. I could not see where they joined; about 15 to 18 ins. of neck was visible. The head was rather like that of a TORTOISE with a snake-like flattened cranium running forward to a rounded face. Relatively it was as big as the head of a donkey. I saw one laterally placed eye, large and round like the eye of a cow. When the mouth was opened I got the impression of large blubbery lips and could see a number of tendril-like growths hanging from the palate. Head and neck arose to a height of about two feet. At intervals the head and neck went forward and submerged. They would then re-emerge, the large gaping mouth would open (giving the impression of a large melon with a quarter removed) and there would be a series of very loud whistling noises as it breathed.

Two years after that encounter, in July 1961, a desiccated carcass washed ashore on the small island of Barra. Photos of the animal appeared to show a long neck and reptilian skull, but zoologist Peter Usherwood identified the remains as belonging to a male BEAKED WHALE of uncertain species. By contrast, the BENBECULA CARCASS, discovered in 1990, remains unidentified today.

Sources: Costello, *In Search of Lake Monsters*; Dinsdale, *Monster Hunt*; Heuvelmans, *In the Wake of the Sea Serpents*.

Hell's Gate sea serpent On 10 August 1902, a startling encounter with a SEA SERPENT allegedly occurred within sight of the New York coastline. Captain Alexander Banta was guiding his tug boat through the passage known as Hell's Gate, between City Island and Hart Island, when a black creature "bigger than a whale" twice rammed the vessel with terrific force. Withdrawing for a third assault, the beast was distracted by a passing steamer and swam off in pursuit of that new target, while Banta made swiftly for shore. If the report was not a HOAX, it marks one of the rare occasions where pelagic cryptids have displayed aggression toward ships or the humans aboard.

Sources: Bord and Bord, *Unexplained Mysteries of the 20th Century*; "Sea serpent hits Hell Gate pilot." *New York Herald* (11 August 1902).

Hendaye carcass In February 1951, a 16-foot GLOBSTER washed ashore with the tide at Hendaye, in the Basses-Pyrénées district of France. Photographs were taken, but the case was otherwise largely ignored until 1962, when witness Léon Ducourau saw BERNARD HEUVELMANS on television and sent him a report of the incident. According to Ducourau, the beast looked "just like a prehistoric animal," with a head like that of a TORTOISE, two cartilaginous antennae, a long neck resembling a PLESIOSAUR'S, brown skin with scales visible in places, and four short, webbed fins like those of a seal or sea TURTLE. After examining the pho-

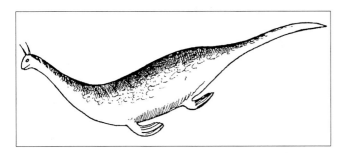

The Hendaye carcass, after witness Léon Ducourau.

tos, Heuvelmans concluded that the carcass belonged to a basking shark (*Cetorhinus maximus*).

Source: Heuvelmans, *In the Wake of the Sea Serpents*.

Henderson Island sea serpent

One of the strangest SEA SERPENT encounters on record was reported in the *Tacoma Daily Ledger* on 3 July 1893. According to that story, a fishing party and a team of surveyors were camped on Henderson Island, offshore from Tacoma in Henderson Bay, on 1 July, when "a most horrible noise rang out…and instantly the whole air was filled with a strong current of electricity that caused every nerve in the body to sting with pain." At first, the startled campers thought a surprise thunder storm was beginning, but they soon beheld "a most horrible-looking monster" in the bay, a few yards distant. As the witnesses stood gaping, "The monster slowly drew in toward the shore, and as it approached, from its head poured out a stream of water that looked like blue fire. All the while the air seemed to be filled with electricity, and the sensation experienced was as if each man had on a suit of clothes formed of the fine points of needles."

One of the surveyors advanced toward the creature, but another spout of water struck him and "he instantly fell to the ground and lay as though dead." The others hastily retreated, while the "demon of the deep sent out flashes of light that illuminated the surrounding country for miles, and his roar — which sounded like the roar of thunder — became terrific." The beast soon withdrew and submerged, but the frightened witnesses "were able to trace its course by the bright luminous light that was on the surface of the water." Returning to camp, they found their fallen comrade unconscious but breathing, and he recovered fully by daybreak. The men described their adversary as a "monster FISH" 150 feet long and 30 feet in diameter. Its head resembled that of a walrus, but with six eyes the size of dinner plates, while "two hornlike substances" atop the head spouted "the electrically charged water." As for the rest, "At intervals of about every eight feet from its head to its tail a substance that had the appearance of a copper band encircled its body, and it was from these many bands that the powerful electric current appeared to come." As a finishing touch, the creature's tail "was shaped like a propeller and seemed to revolve." No animal yet found in nature matches the description of this creature, which was doubtless either much exaggerated or the product of a HOAX.

Source: Clark and Pear, *Strange & Unexplained Phenomena*.

Hendrik Ido Ambacht sea serpent

On 11 July 1858, the Dutch ship *Hendrik Ido Ambacht* was allegedly menaced by a huge SEA SERPENT that showered the decks with vile-smelling fluid and hammered the vessel with blows from its powerful tail. The story is revealed as a HOAX, however, when one plots the ship's supposed position — 27° 27' north latitude and 14° 51' east

longitude — on a map. Based on those coordinate, the *Hendrik Ido Ambacht* must have been sailing across the Libyan desert when the supposed attack began.

Source: Heuvelmans, *In the Wake of the Sea Serpents*.

Henry Buck sea serpent

On 25 September 1888, officers and crewmen aboard the tug *Henry Buck* sighted a 50-foot SEA SERPENT in Winyah Bay, near Georgetown, South Carolina. Captain Springs, in charge of the boat, reported that the creature swam with its bright-red head held three feet out of water, with a long mane flowing in its wake.

Source: "The sea serpent." *St. Louis Globe-Democrat* (27 September 1888).

Henry Island carcass

In December 1934, a rotting carcass was beached on Henry Island, British Columbia. Reports described it as 30 feet long, with reddish-colored flesh, skin sprouting hair mixed with quills, a horselike head and four fins or flippers attached to its spine. The GLOBSTER was examined by various experts at Prince Rupert, with conflicting results. Neal Carter, director of the nearby Dominion Experimental Fisheries Station, declared it a mammal which "in life…must have been slender and sinewy."

One Dr. Clemens, at Nanaimo's government biological station, examined the skull and spine before pronouncing it a basking SHARK (*Cetorhinus maximus*). Curators at the Provincial Museum of Victoria disagreed, branding the creature a relict specimen of STELLER'S SEA COW (*Hydrodamalis stelleri*), long since presumed extinct. On 15 December, the *Illustrated London News* published photos of the Henry Island specimen beside photos of a sea cow's bones, revealing that they had little or nothing in common.

Three decades after the fact, BERNARD HEUVELMANS reviewed those photos and concurred in calling the beast a large decomposed shark, most likely *C. maximus*.

Source: Heuvelmans, *In the Wake of the Sea Serpents*.

Hermanus sea serpent

In 1903, while fishing 4-5 miles off Hermanus (on the coast of South Africa's Cape Province), crewmen aboard four boats allegedly observed a SEA SERPENT at close range. Thirty-five years after the fact, one of the unnamed witnesses described how he had seen the men on nearby boats rowing hastily toward shore.

> Our crew was dumbfounded and at a loss to understand what had suddenly gone wrong — particularly as the fishing was so good. We soon found out. I looked across the sea, and to my horror, I saw the most awful-looking monster with its head about four feet above the water, rapidly approaching our small boat. We were petrified and there was nothing we could do.
>
> Suddenly, about ten yards away, the snake-like creature raised its head still further to a height of more than 20 feet and looked down on us with eyes like saucers — not once but three times — for periods of about 15 seconds, and it was at least 120 feet long. It had a head the size of a paraffin tin and was covered with long hair that looked like seaweed. It appeared to be the thickness of an 8-10 inch water pipe. The body was black-brown, and the throat a whitish brown color; it swam very fast and then very slowly. It suddenly made one terrific dive and that was the last we saw of it.

Source: Heuvelmans, *In the Wake of the Sea Serpents*.

Herring Hogg

In 1636, a frightening sea beast washed ashore at Wirral, Cheshire, England, on the Irish Sea. According to the only brief description presently available:

It was 15 yards high, and 20 yards and one foot in length. Its voice was evidently powerful, for its cry could be heard six or seven miles away, and was "so hideous that none dared come near it for some time."

Locals dubbed their stranded monster the Herring Hogg, but nothing is recorded of its fate or final disposition.

Source: Christina Hole, *Traditions and Customs of Cheshire*. London: Williams and Norgate, 1937.

Herrington Lake, Kentucky

In 1972, college professor Lawrence Thompson claimed several sightings of a 15-foot LAKE MONSTER at this lake, located 20 miles southwest of Lexington, Kentucky. Sporadic reports continued into 1973. Descriptions of the "prehistoric" animal provided no significant details beyond its apparent length.

Sources: Garner, *Monster! Monster!*; Alan Markfield, "Professor says he's seen a prehistoric creature swimming in a Kentucky lake." *Cincinnati Enquirer* (12 November 1972); Joe Ward, "Monster reported swimming in Herrington Lake." *Louisville Courier-Journal* (7 August 1972).

Hertfordshire Lioness

This ALIEN BIG CAT caused a stir around Cuffley, Hertfordshire, England in May 1983. The first sighting was reported at 6:00 a.m. on 16 May, when a large sandy-colored CAT appeared in David Messling's garden, on the outskirts of town. Messling later told police that the cat resembled a lioness (*Panthera leo*), standing 2 feet 6 inches tall at the shoulder, and measuring about 4 feet between the front and hind legs. An officer called to Messling's home saw the cat leap over a nearby hedge, 5 feet 6 inches tall.

A massive hunt was organized, including curators from the Bronxbourne Zoo, but only vague pawprints were found. Police canvassed zoos and animal collectors, without confirming any recent escapes. Authorities then dismissed the incident as a mistaken sighting of a large Rottweiler, though no such dog was found at large in the neighborhood.

Source: McEwan, *Mystery Animals of Britain and Ireland*.

Hessie

This supposed SEA SERPENT of Hessafjorden, Norway (offshore from Ålesund, Møre og Romsdal County) is named in the tradition of NESSIE, ISSIE and other aquatic cryptids. Witnesses describe it as 80-100 feet long and 5 feet in diameter, brown, with a head resembling that of a huge SNAKE and a square dorsal fin 15 inches tall. Unlike many Scandinavian cryptids, Hessie boasts a list of recent sightings. On 2 June 1999, Arnt Molvær of Ålesund allegedly watched the creature with binoculars, while it fed on the floating carcass of a dead whale. Hessie was still feeding an hour later, when Molvær returned from home with a video camera and taped the strange scene. Two years later, on 18 March 2001, fishermen aboard the *Klaring* saw a large beast with two humps on its back swimming rapidly past nearby Sula Island.

Source: Eric Knatterud, Database of Norwegian Sea Serpents, http://www.mjoesormen.no/english.htm.

Heuvelmans, Bernard Joseph (1916–2001)

The "father of cryptozoology" was born at Le Havre, France on 10 October 1916, to a Belgian father and a Dutch mother. His lifelong interest in unclassified animals was sparked by childhood readings of such novels as Sir Arthur Conan Doyle's *The Lost World* and Jules Verne's *Journey to the Center of the Earth*. Heuvelmans earned his Ph.D. in zoology shortly before the outbreak of World War II, then joined the French army and was captured by Nazi troops in Belgium.

A fanciful drawing of Bernard Heuvelmans, the "father of cryptozoology."

Liberated in 1945, Heuvelmans supported himself as a science writer and jazz singer while searching for some greater goal. He found it in January 1948, after reading an article by IVAN SANDERSON in the *Saturday Evening Post*, titled "There could be DINOSAURS."

Henceforth, Heuvelmans resolved to pursue the vague, unfocused study of "monsters" in a scientific manner, combining archival research with field work international correspondence. By 1955, he had collected enough material to fill a two-volume work, published in France as *Sur la Piste des Bêtes Ignorées*. Three years later, condensed and translated to English, it appeared as *On the Track of Unknown Animals*.

One critic of that work declared, "Because his research is based on rigorous dedication to scientific method and scholarship and his solid background in zoology, Heuvelmans's findings are respected throughout the scientific community." And while that was not strictly true — some mainstream scientists would ridicule Heuvelmans for his perceived gullibility — the book has had a tremendous impact on readers. In subsequent correspondence, Heuvelmans coined the term *cryptozoology*, which he defined and revised in various writings over the following three decades.

Heuvelmans's next two books, *Dans le Sillage des Monstres Marins — Le Kraken et le Poulpe Colossal* (1958) and *Le Grand-Serpent-de-Mer* (1965), dealt with pelagic cryptids, including the GIANT SQUID, giant OCTOPUS, and SEA SERPENTS. They were combined and translated in 1968 as *In the Wake of the Sea Serpents*, wherein Heuvelmans proposed nine separate species of large marine animals awaiting discovery. At the same time Heuvelmans joined Sanderson and anthropologist GEORGE AGOGINO as behind-the-scenes advisors to millionaire TOM SLICK in his searches for YETI, BIGFOOT and other unidentified creatures. In 1968, with Sanderson, Heuvelmans examined the MINNESOTA ICEMAN and emerged from the experience convinced that NEANDERTAL MAN has survived into modern times. His book on that subject, co-authored with BORIS PORSHNEV, was published in 1974 as *L'homme de Néanderthal est Toujours Vivant*.

In 1975, Heuvelmans established a Center for Cryptozoology at Le Bugue, in the south of France (moved closer to Paris, at Le Vésinet, in the 1990s). His archive consisted of numerous books and some 18,000 articles clipped from magazines and newspapers. From that foundation, he wrote two more books, *Les Derniers Dragons d'Afrique* (1978) and *Les Bêtes Humaines d'Afrique* (1980), as well as numerous articles. When the INTERNATIONAL SOCIETY OF CRYPTOZOOLOGY was founded in 1982, Heuvelmans became president and served in that post for the remainder of his life. He also collaborated freely with the BRITISH COLUMBIA SCIENTIFIC CRYPTOZOOLOGY CLUB and other international efforts to resolve the mysteries of nature.

In 1984, Heuvelmans announced plans to write a 20-volume encyclopedia of cryptozoology, but failing health and other distractions prevented him from completing the epic work. In February 1997, when he received the Gabriele Peters Prize for Fantastic Science from the Zoological Museum of the University of Hamburg, Heuvelmans sent colleague Werner Reichenbach in his place to collect the $6,000 award. Two years later, Heuvelmans donated his vast archive to the Museum of Zoology in Lausanne, Switzerland. The last year of his life found Heuvelmans bed-ridden at home, where he died on 22 August 2001. Regrettably, the bulk of his groundbreaking work has not been translated to English.

Sources: Loren Coleman, "Bernard Heuvelmans: An appreciation of a friend" (24 August 2001); Coleman and Clark, *Cryptozoology A to Z*; Heuvelmans, various works.

Hibagon

The crowded islands of Japan seem an unlikely hunting ground for cryptids, but several unknown creatures are reportedly at large throughout the islands. The most startling is Hibagon, an unknown primate or HOMINID said to inhabit the forests around Mount Hiba, in Hiroshima Prefecture's Hiba-Dogo-Taishaku-Quasi National Park (on Honshu). Hibagon resembles a GORILLA, with dark hair and a chocolate-brown face, but it also emits a foul odor familiar from some BIGFOOT and SKUNK APE reports in the U.S. The first published sighting was logged in autumn 1972, by Reiko Harada and her son. The following year, a Saijo merchant named Sazawa saw a creature "about 5 feet tall, with a face shaped like an inverted triangle, covered with bristles, having a snub nose and large, deep, glaring eyes." Tabloid newspaper articles suggested that Hibagon might be a mutant created by radiation from the Hiroshima bombing of August 1945, while skeptics insisted it must be a stray Japanese macaque (*Macaca fuscata*).

Source: Bord and Bord, *Alien Animals*.

Hide

A strange, elastic sea monster reported from Chilean coastal waters, the Hide is named for its resemblance to a cow's hide stretched out flat. Countless eyes surround the animal's perimeter, with four larger ones at dead-center. The Hide is a bottom-dweller that rises to engulf its prey (including humans), then sinks once more to digest its struggling meal. Various authors have suggested that the beast may be an unknown species of OC-TOPUS or JELLYFISH, the many "eyes" perhaps colored spots or (in the jelly's case) sensory organs called rhopalia. Matters grow more confused, however, with reports of a similar freshwater creature, called Cuero or Trelque Huecufe ("Devil's Hide"), said to inhabit some Chilean lakes and rivers. In place of many eyes, the Cuero reportedly has sharp claws all around the edges of its body, used to grip and subdue its victims.

Sources: Gregorio Alvarez, *El Tronco do Oro*. Nuequén, Chile: Pehuen, 1968; Picasso, "South American monsters & mystery animals"; Karl Shuker, "Giant jellyfish," in *Monsters and Mysteries of the Sea*. Frank Spaeth (ed.), pp. 124-130.

High Desert Bigfoot Research Project

According to an e-mail from Raymond Ambrosin, posted to the White Mountain Online news group on 17 February 2003, the High Desert BIGFOOT Research Project is "a nonprofit, civilian Bigfoot investigative and research organization, offers its assistance to investigate observations by the public of unusual animal sightings." Ambrosin goes on to say that "[o]ur members are trained to single out cases of misidentification and thereby relieve your staff of such matters so as to allow concentration on more pertinent duties." To that end, the HDBRP "employs a centralized response system, the investigator closest to the scene being assigned to contact the witness(es) who report a claimed encounter." Ambrosin, the self-described "project coordinator," listed a telephone number and a post office box in Fountain Hills, Arizona as contact points for the group. Unfortunately, two website addresses offered for the HDBRP were both inactive when checked in July 2003.

Source: Raymond Ambrosin to White Mountain Online, HTTP://WWW.WMONLINE.COM/DISCUSSION/DISPLAY_MESSAGE.ASP?MID=1031.

High-Finned Whales

Whales are the largest known animals on Earth, and the giant species are critically endangered by human predation, but the world of cetaceans may still hold some secrets in store. In 1692, two unknown whales were stranded on the Shetland Islands, 150 miles north of Scotland. One specimen measured 60 feet, the other 45 feet. They resembled sperm whales (*Physeter macrocephalus*), down to their toothless upper jaws, except for their tall dorsal fins. Pioneer cetologist Sir Robert Sibbald viewed the specimens and named them *Physeter tursio*, but no more were ever beached or captured.

Fully 150 years later, in 1841, Captain James Ross spied a black whale with a tall dorsal fin near Antarctica's Ross Island, described in the memoirs he published six years after the fact. On 7 April 1868, while becalmed in the Gulf of Mannar (between India and Sri Lanka), Edmund Holdsworth saw a grayish-black whale, some 25 feet long, with a 5-foot dorsal fin. Indian sailors on his boat knew it as a Palmyra FISH, so called for the resemblance of its tall fin to the Palmyra palms (*Borassus flabelliformis*) of India's Mallabar Coast. One of the Antarctic specimens was seen again, by members of the *Discovery* expedition, on 28 January and 8 February 1902. In August or September 1946 (accounts vary), a high-finned black whale was seen for two days in Nova Scotia's Annapolis Basin. Eyewitness estimates of the animal's length varied radically, from 10 to 100 feet. Most recently, in November 1964, cetologist Robert Clarke and a group of colleagues claimed eight separate sightings of similar whales off the coast of Chile.

Sources: Edmund Holdsworth, "Note on a cetacean observed on the west coast of Ceylon." *Proceedings of the Zoological Society of London* (15 April 1872): 583-586; "No such animal." *Doubt* 16 (1946): 237; Shuker, *From Flying Toads to Snakes with Wings*.

Highland Puma   This name is applied generically to various ALIEN BIG CATS sighted in the Scottish Highlands since the 1960s, often without regard for a specific animal's size, color, or overall resemblance to an actual COUGAR (*Puma concolor*).

Source: "Scottish puma: Saga or farce?" *Fortean Times* 34 (Winter 1981): 24–25.

***Hilary* sea serpent**   At 9:00 a.m. on 22 May 1917, while patrolling the Atlantic 70 miles southeast of Iceland, officers aboard the British cruiser H.M.S. *Hilary* saw an object rising from the water which they mistook for the periscope of an enemy submarine. Further examination revealed to Captain F.W. Dean:

> an object which at first glance suggested to my mind a tree trunk with only the knobby ends (from which branches and roots had been cut) visible. A careful look through my glasses, however, made it clear that the thing was alive, and that the "knobby ends" were in fact its head and dorsal fin.
>
> We never missed a chance in those days to do a bit of anti-submarine practice, and it at once struck me that here was a good target; so I turned to the 1st lieutenant…and told him to get our three 6-pounder guns' crews up, so that each one in turn should have a run….
>
> Before taking the liberty of using the stranger as a target, however, I thought it would be a good thing to have a closer look at it. In due course we approached our object end on, and when we were about a cable [608 feet] from it, it quietly moved out of our way, and we passed it about thirty yards off on our starboard side, getting a very good view of it while doing so.
>
> The head was about the shape of, but somewhat larger than, that of a cow, though with no observable protrusions such as horns or ears, and was black, except for the front of the face, which could be clearly seen to have a strip of whitish flesh, very like a cow has, between its nostrils. As we passed, the head raised itself two or three times, apparently to get a good look at the ship. From the back of the head to the dorsal fin no part of the creature showed above the water, but the top edge of the neck was just level with the surface, and its SNAKE-like movements could be clearly seen.
>
> The dorsal fin appeared like a black triangle, and when the creature was end-on, this fin was seen to be very thin and apparently flabby, as the upper part turned over sometimes like the top of a terrier's ear when cocked. The fin was estimated to be about four feet high when in the position highest out of the water.

Captain Dean guessed that the animal was 60 feet long, while four other witnesses placed its length between 15 and 28 feet. Within moments, the *Hilary*'s guns opened fire on the inoffensive creature and left it thrashing briefly on the surface before it sank out of sight. Days later, a German U-boat sank the *Hilary*, but Dean and company survived to tell their story upon reaching shore. Some researchers have concluded from Dean's description that the animal killed was an ordinary basking SHARK (*Cetorhinus maximus*).

Source: Heuvelmans, *In the Wake of the Sea Serpents*.

Hilston sea serpent   In early August 1945, B.M. Baylis and other witnesses observed a SEA SERPENT swimming offshore from Hilston, in Yorkshire, England. As Baylis described the event:

> [W]e were sitting on the edge of the low mud cliffs…between Hornsea and Withernsea. There we saw a creature with a head and four or five humps each of which was leaving a wake. It was moving rapidly but quite silently along shore northwards in face of a northerly wind.

Source: Heuvelmans, *In the Wake of the Sea Serpents*.

Himalayas Riddle Investigation Society   Little information is presently available on this Chinese group dedicated to investigation of YETI reports from Tibet. An April 2001 press release identified Yan Zhenzhong as the organization's vice president, implying that the group may be working in concert with China's Academy of Sciences and the Beijing Nature Museum to collect information from the Himalayas.

Source: "Tibetan Abominable Snowman remains unsolved riddle." Sinhua News Agency (30 April 2001).

Hippogriff   This alleged LAKE MONSTER of Lake George, New York (Warren County) was the product of a classic HOAX. In 1904, local artist Harry Watrous devised a mechanism for manipulating a 10-foot log from the lake's wooded shoreline. Soon, reports of the lurking "Hippogriff" inspired a short-term rush of CRYPTOTOURISM around Lake George. Upon exposure of the fraud, good-natured townsfolk lodged Watrous's toy at the Lake George Historical Association, where tourists may view it today.

Sources: Harry Henck, "The Lake George monster." *Adirondack Life* (March-April 1980): 37–41; Joseph Zarzynski, "The Lake George monster hoax of 1904." *Pursuit* 51 (Summer 1980): 99–100.

Hippoturtleox   This curious LAKE MONSTER, reported from Tibet's Lake Duobuzhe, was named for its alleged combination of physical features resembling three widely varied creatures. Specifically, witnesses claimed that the beast had a horned head and body resembling an ox, but with the shiny-smooth skin of a hippopotamus and the stubby legs of a TURTLE. Chinese soldiers stationed in Tibet claimed to have killed such a creature at Lake Duobuzhe in 1972, but no evidence was forthcoming.

Source: Greenwell, "Hippoturtleox."

Hoaxes   Hoaxes are a perpetual risk in the field of cryptozoology. They are distinguished from honest mistakes, which may still have embarrassing consequences — as in the 1920s, when archaeologists mistook a seashell for the 2.5-inch fang of a giant prehistoric viper, erroneously christened *Bothrodon pridii*. Hoaxers, by contrast, intend to deceive, either for sport or for personal gain. If the latter, their motives may range from simple exhibitionism to financial profit (via sales of relics, photographs, or promotion of CRYPTOTOURISM). Hoaxes may even have an ideological motive, as when some creationists promote the long-discredited PALUXY TRACKS as evidence of human cohabitation with DINOSAURS in a "young Earth" scenario. Frankly commercial hoaxes include the promotion of INKANYAMBA sightings by a South African hotelier and the "Coleman FROG," a supposed giant amphibian fabricated to promote the sale of sore-throat remedies in New Brunswick, Canada.

No aspect of cryptozoology has been immune to fraud or practical jokes. BERNARD HEUVELMANS, in his classic 1968 study of SEA SERPENTS, dismissed 42 of 587 reports as deliberate hoaxes, while deeming 187 others mistaken sightings of known animals. LAKE MONSTER sightings are likewise suspect, with some reports clearly exaggerated, if not fabricated outright. In New York State alone, pranksters fabricated cryptids in Lake George (the HIPPOGRIFF) and SILVER LAKE, in the early 20th century, while a hoaxer armed with a stuffed hippopotamus foot faked NESSIE tracks around Scotland's Loch Ness. Researcher GEORGE HAAS suggested that 90 percent of all reported BIGFOOT sightings were either hoaxes or simple mistakes. The sham "evidence" produced by individuals such as IVAN MARX, RANT MULLENS and RAY WALLACE cast doubts on legitimate cryptozoologists, and pranks continue to the present day. A few examples include:

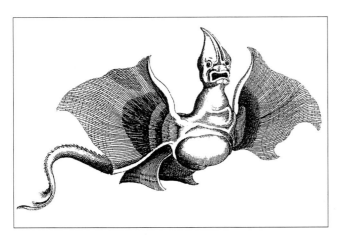

Hoaxers often created "dragons" by mutilating dead rays, skates or guitarfish.

October 1985— Craig Brashear was charged with disorderly conduct in Harrisburg, Pennsylvania, after donning an APE suit to frighten residents of rural East Pennsboro Township.

July 1997— Police cautioned and released a teenage boy who dressed as BIGFOOT, using fishnet and shrubbery, to shock motorists on a country road in Fauquier County, Virginia.

February 2002— Brothers Dennis and Steven Gates reported hundreds of "very clear" HOMINID tracks around a reservoir in Waynesboro, Pennsylvania. LOREN COLEMAN and MARK HALL examined photos of the footprints, deciding they had been produced by someone wearing fabricated "monster" feet.

April 2002— A spate of GORILLA sightings around Scotland's Loch of Skene came to nothing, after two local men admitted creating an ape suit to frighten their neighbors.

Hoaxes and urban legends of all kinds, many including fabricated photographs, have proliferated on the Internet. Two cryptozoological examples are the story of the OZARK HOWLER and the supposed slaying of a giant GRIZZLY bear. Others will doubtless be discovered over time, as various websites solicit eyewitness accounts of Bigfoot and lake monster sightings.

Claims of fakery and heated controversy still surround some of the most intriguing cryptozoological reports. Prime examples, covered elsewhere in this volume, include the MINNESOTA ICE-MAN, the PATTERSON FILM of Bigfoot, the SURGEON'S PHOTO of Nessie, and the Florida cryptid dubbed THREE-TOES. A curious phenomenon, in that respect, is the "skeptical" media's rush to accept any tale of a hoax, no matter how far-fetched. Thus, in 1994, reporters worldwide trumpeted a hoaxer's claim that he had faked a famous Nessie photograph with a model built from "plastic wood"— years before that product was invented. Likewise, in 2002, journalists were happy to proclaim that well-known hoaxer Ray Wallace "invented" Bigfoot in 1958 (a mere 150 years after the first reported sighting of an unknown hominid in North America). In such cases, the "exposé" itself becomes a hoax, assuming a life of its own and passing into the dubious realm of "common knowledge," immune to refutation. Thus, ironically, admitted liars have the final word and so pass into history as champions of "truth."

Sources: "Bigfoot? No, big joke." *Strange Magazine* 19 (Spring 1998): 38; Coleman, *Bigfoot!*; David Heppell, "Gigantic serpent really a gastropod!" *Conchologists' Newsletter* 16 (March 1966): 108-109; Heuvelmans, *In the Wake of the Sea Serpents*; Joe Nickell, *Real-Life X-Files*. Lexington, KY: University Press of Kentucky, 2001; "Reservoir hominids." *Fortean*

Times 158 (June 2002): 9; Shuker, "For crying out loud: It's the Ozark Howler!"; Shuker, "Alien zoo." *Fortean Times* 160 (August 2002): 20; Zarzynski, "The Lake George monster hoax of 1904." *Pursuit* 51 (Summer 1980): 99-100.

Hodag   This supposed Wisconsin swamp-dweller is described in folklore as a fierce quadruped, three feet tall at the shoulder, with a ride or series of spines along its back. Once facetious account compares it to "a cross between a mastiff and a DINOSAUR." Tales of the Hodag circulated among loggers in the 1890s, but reports of specimens captured and domesticated smack of the fantastic. A carved wooden model of a Hodag — complete with claws, tusks, curving horns and mouselike ears — resides in a logging museum at Rhinelander, Wisconsin.

Sources: Cohen, *The Encyclopedia of Monsters*; "States fight for 'beast.'" *Las Vegas Review-Journal* (24 August 1984).

Holadeira   Brazil's elusive Holadeira borrows its name from a large saw used to fell trees in the Amazon jungle, a reference to the serrated "teeth" displayed on the animal's back when it breaks the surface of murky jungle waters. British author Jeffrey Wade snapped photos of the creature in August 1993, at an unnamed Brazilian lake, but found no trace of it when he returned to the site in 1997. Some who viewed Wade's photographs suggested that the creature was a river dolphin (*Inia geoffrensis*) wounded by a predator or boat propeller, while others insist no dolphin could survive such wounds in waters teeming with CAIMANS and piranhas. Wade suspects the Holadeira (or "sawtooth dolphin") is an unknown species of freshwater dolphin, but proof awaits collection of a type specimen.

Sources: Wade, "Hell's teeth."

Holandsvatnet, Norway   Norwegian folklore identifies this lake, in Nordland County, as the one-time lair of a LAKE MONSTER, but a dearth of modern sightings frustrates up-to-date research.

Source: Skjelsvik, "Norwegian lake and sea monsters."

Hollow Block Lake, Indiana   In August 1960, this lake near Portland, Indiana (Jay County) briefly produced reports of a 7-foot LAKE MONSTER that uttered shrill screams. Eyewitness descriptions of the creature as roughly square in shape failed to clarify its possible identity.

Sources: *Cincinnati Enquirer* (7 August 1960); Coleman, *Mysterious America*.

Hollow Block Lake, Oregon   Multiple books and Internet websites list this supposed Oregon lake as a source of LAKE MONSTER reports, but extensive research fails to reveal any such lake in the state. The simplest explanation is a garbled reference to the screaming cryptid reported from HOLLOW BLOCK LAKE, INDIANA.

Sources: Coleman, *Mysterious America*; Kirk, *In the Domain of the Lake Monsters*.

Homer Lake, California   Native American legends identify this mountain lake, in California's Tahoe National Forest, as an ancient habitat of LAKE MONSTERS. Fishermen still ply these waters, but no modern reports of aquatic cryptids have emerged from Lake Homer or its two sister lakes on Keddie Ridge.

Sources: Coleman, *Mysterious America*; Charles Skinner, *American Myths and Legends*. Philadelphia: Lippincott, 1903.

Hominids/Hominology   Uneducated laymen often refer to cryptids as if only one of each species exists, immortal and immutable—i.e., *the* YETI, *the* SEA SERPENT, and so forth. Cryptozoologists discount such sophistry, recognizing from the outset that (a) no creature lives forever; (b) no single specimen, however durable, could possibly account for widely separated sightings or radically different descriptions; and (c) reports of multiple creatures together, including both genders and various sizes, indicates a viable breeding population. As with aquatic cryptids, so it is with unknown hominids or primates, those hairy denizens reported from six continents under a bewildering variety of names.

IVAN SANDERSON was first to propose a system for classifying unknown hominids, in 1961. After compiling and collating reports from every corner of the Earth, he proposed the following four categories:

1. *Sub-humans.* Sanderson included in this group various hominids reported from Asia, including the ALMAS, HANTU SAKAI, KSY-GIIK and YEREN. All are typically of average human size and are sometimes described as using primitive tools, while attempting verbal communication (albeit without true speech). The most likely candidate for such creatures, in Sanderson's view, was NEANDERTAL MAN (*Homo neanderthalensis*).

2. *Proto-Pygmies.* This category encompasses the smaller hominids reported worldwide, including the AGOGWE, DUENDE, ORANG PENDEK, SÉHITÉ, SHIRU, and the small Yeti sometimes called Teh-lma. All are known for below-average stature, bodies covered with red or black hair, and small feet with narrow (sometimes pointed) heels.

3. *Neo-giants.* In this group, Sanderson included BIGFOOT, the KUNG-LU, MAPINGUARI, SISEMITÉ, TOK, and the large Yeti known throughout much of its range as Dzu-Teh. All tower a foot or more above the average human, and some are dangerously aggressive. Sanderson identified these creatures with the prehistoric APE *Gigantopithecus*.

4. *Sub-hominids.* Describing these as "in every way the least human," Sanderson restricted this group to certain primates of south-central Eurasia, including the GOLUB-YAVAN and the Yeti most commonly known as Meh-teh. He considered these creatures representatives of an ape unknown from the present fossil record.

Four decades after Sanderson offered his list of hominids to the

Unknown hairy hominids are reported from every inhabited continent (*William Rebsamen*).

world, cryptozoologist MARK HALL published a new taxonomy. Hall's creatures, in order of ascending size, include:

1. *Shorter hominids.* Averaging five feet in height, this group includes the Golub-yavan and Nakani, identified by Hall as relict populations of *Homo neanderthalensis*.

2. *Least hominids.* Despite Hall's choice of terms, members of this group may stand 12 inches taller than specimens from the first category. Least hominids include the Almas and BAR-MANU of Central Asia, identified by Hall as surviving representatives of *Homo erectus* (presumed extinct for 125,000 years).

3. *Taller hominids.* Averaging seven feet in height, this group includes such cryptids as the CHUCHUNAA, KUL, MARICOXI and tornit. Hall suggests surviving prehistoric candidates *Homo gardarensis* and *Homo sapiens rhodesiensis*, though most anthropologists today regard the former (found in Greenland) as a Viking afflicted with acromegaly, and the later as an archaic specimen of *H. sapiens*. Hall replies that the Greenland skull's teeth show no evidence of acromegaly, suggesting instead that it may be a descendant of *Homo ergaster* (an East African fossil specimen presumed extinct for 1.5 million years).

4. *True giants.* This group, analogous to Sanderson's Neo-giants, includes Bigfoot, the Kung-lu, QUINKIN and other towering hominids, identified by Hall as an evolved form of *Gigantopithecus*.

Authors LOREN COLEMAN and PATRICK HUYGHE combined the Hall-Sanderson lists in 1999, adding refinements of their own to create the most elaborate list of unknown hominids to date. That list includes:

1. *Neo-giants.* Found in the Americas and parts of Asia, this group of 6- to 9-foot hominids includes Bigfoot, the UCUMAR, and the Gin-sung version of Yeti. Candidates suggested are *Gigantopithecus* and *Paranthropus robustus*.

2. *True giants.* Measuring 10 feet or taller, often leaving broad 4-toed footprints, this category includes such creatures as the BIG GREY MAN of Ben Macdhui, the NYALMO, ORANG DALAM and the TANO GIANT. Once again, *Gigantopithecus* stands as the only known candidate from the fossil record.

3. *Marked hominids.* These creatures average seven feet in height, but they are distinguished from Bigfoot-type Neo-giants by piebald coloration. This group includes the Chuchunaa, with MOMO and OLD YELLOW TOP from the U.S.

4. *Neandertaloids.* Borrowing from Hall's shorter hominids, this group includes the MINNESOTA ICEMAN, Nakani and Europe's WUDÉWÁSÁ as examples of surviving *Homo neanderthalensis*.

5. *Erectus hominids.* Analogous to Hall's least hominids, these presumed representatives of relict *Homo erectus* include the Almas, KAPTAR, Hantu Sakai and NGUOI RUNG, dwelling in Asia and parts of Oceania.

6. *Proto-Pygmies.* Borrowed from Sanderson, this category features cryptids reported from both hemispheres, including the Agogwe, DIDI, NITTAEWO and Orang Pendek.

7. *Unknown pongids.* Truly simian, rather than human, this group of unclassified apes spans the globe. Coleman and Huyghe believe it to include such cryptids as the GOATMAN, HIBAGON, the LAKE WORTH MONSTER, Mapinguari, MUHALU, NORTH AMERICAN APES, SKUNK APE, Yeren, Yeti and YOWIE.

8. *Giant monkeys.* Sometimes distinguished by their three-toed footprints, these denizens of Asia, Africa and the Americas include the ISNACHI, NALUSA FALAYA and the voracious NANDI BEAR (whose descriptions vary widely enough to suggest multiple cryptids).

9. *MERBEINGS.* This surprise inclusion covers all manner of

aquatic hominids reported throughout history, as well as some not commonly associated with the water. Along with traditional mermaids, the authors include STELLER'S SEA APE, the CHUPACABRA and various LIZARD MEN in this amphibious group.

While some scientists balk at the notion of *any* large primates still undiscovered on Earth — much less nine! — eyewitness sightings continue throughout the world. More persuasive still are the DNA tests performed on hairs allegedly collected from Orang Pendek and Yeti, in each case revealing that the hairs come from no animal presently known to science. This much, at least, is certain: in the Himalayan forests and Sumatra's jungles, *something* waits to be identified.

Sources: Coleman and Huyghe, *The Field Guide to Bigfoot, Yeti, and Other Mystery Primates Worldwide*; Hall, *Living Fossils: The Survival of* Homo gardarensis, *Neandertal Man, and* Homo erectus; Hall, *The Yeti, Bigfoot and True Giants*; Sanderson, *Abominable Snowmen*.

Honey Island Swamp

Honey Island Swamp spans the state border between Pearl River County, Mississippi and Washington Parish, Louisiana. It sprawls over 250 square miles, some 70,000 acres of that expanse comprising a government wildlife preserve. Portions of the swamp are virtually impenetrable and doubtless hold surprises in store for hardy zoologists. Sightings of the IVORY-BILLED WOODPECKER have been reported from the swamp, but its greatest notoriety derives from reports of an unidentified HOMINID or NORTH AMERICAN APE said to dwell in the murky bayou country.

Local hunters Harlan Ford and Billy Mills were the first to report sightings of a BIGFOOT-type creature in Honey Island Swamp. Their story, publicized in 1974, described alleged events from 1963. Harlan recalled that when he first glimpsed the animal, from behind, it was walking on all fours and reminded him of a LION (*Panthera leo*). That view swiftly changed as the beast rose to stand on two legs, revealing itself as a 7-foot monster covered in dingy gray hair, with massive shoulders and piercing amber eyes. The creature fled a moment later, leaving behind three-toed footprints. Eleven years later, Ford and Mills found similar tracks near the bodies of three mangled boars, and they made plaster casts to support their strange story. The prints were relatively small, only 9.75 inches long, and appeared to reveal three webbed toes.

Since the news of those sightings broke, 30 years ago, Honey Island Swamp has enjoyed sporadic waves of CRYPTOTOURISM exceeding the appeal of simple nature tours. The swamp was featured on TV's *In Search of...* series and in several published surveys of U.S. "monsters." Elderly Ted Williams came forward in 1976, claiming eight or nine sightings of the animal(s) over the past five years. His version of the creature weighed about 800 pounds and gave off "an awful scent, worse than a skunk to my thinking. You can smell that stink for a quarter of a mile." Skeptics, meanwhile, insist that any sighting of peculiar fauna in the Honey Island Swamp constitutes a deliberate HOAX or a case of mistaken identity.

Sources: Blackman, *The Field Guide to North American Monsters*; Coleman, "Three toes are better than five"; Landsburg, *In Search of Myths and Monsters*; Joe Nickell, "Tracking the swamp monsters." *Skeptical Inquirer* 4 (1 July 2001): 15; Honey Island Swamp Monster, http://jmichaelms.tripod.com/HIS/.

Hong Kong mystery cats

In July 1965, students from the Diocesan Girls' School in Hong Kong's New Territories were startled to see a large CAT resembling a TIGER (*Panthera tigris*) while picnicking on Taimoshan mountain. Their alarm was compounded by the fact that tigers do not exist (at least, officially) in Hong Kong. Search parties returned empty-handed from hunting the cat, while sightings from the nearby Shing Mun valley multiplied over the next three months. In the last week of October 1965, a carpenter named Chan Pui reported seeing the beast at Shatin, on the Chinese border, where a verified tiger sighting was recorded in the 1920s. Chan made matters worse, however, by insisting that the creature was a WOLF. When naturalists rejected that identification, Chan set out to vindicate himself by catching the "wolf," but instead bagged a friendly Alsatian-chow hybrid. The "solution" solved nothing, but the lurking cat disappeared — for a while.

Eleven years later, a new feline mystery vexed Hong Kong authorities. During the last two weeks of October 1976, more than 20 dogs (including some large ones) were fatally mauled by an unknown predator in Pik Uk and Junk Bay, in the Hang Hau district of Hong Kong's New Territories. By month's end, several villagers reported sightings of a large catlike creature, blackish-gray in color, with a long tail. Police scoured the region. The last known witness was a man who claimed two sightings of the creature in late November and early December 1976. Although he called the animal a tiger, he described an animal "about 3 ft. high, 4 ft. long, and of a dark colour." Whatever it was, it remains unidentified today.

Source: Shuker, *Mystery Cats of the World*.

Hong Kong sea serpent

In March 1969, a group of Hong Kong students enjoying a beach barbecue saw an unidentified SEA SERPENT passing offshore. They estimated the creature's length at 20–30 feet, reporting that it was black, with green eyes, and that it made a loud wailing noise.

Source: Bord and Bord, *Unexplained Mysteries of the 20th Century*.

Hook Head sea serpent

In 1975, fishermen trawling offshore from Hook Head, Ireland (County Wexford) reported sightings of a 20-foot SEA SERPENT resembling a long-necked lizard with a humped spine. The creature remains unidentified.

Source: Bord and Bord, *Unexplained Mysteries of the 20th Century*.

Hook Island sea serpent

In 1965, reports of a SEA SERPENT seen and photographed at Hook Island, near Australia's Great Barrier Reef, caused a worldwide sensation. The story broke on 31 March, in *Everybody's Magazine*, published in Sydney. According to that article and those which followed, French photographer Robert le Serrec, his wife and three children were on a 5-year cruise around the world in December 1964, when their 70-foot vessel sank and left them briefly stranded on Hook Island. The castaways were accompanied by Sydney skin-diver Hank de Jong, and they still had an 18-foot boat at their disposal. On 12 December, while crossing Stonehaven Bay to wash their clothes at a nearby waterfall, the party allegedly spied a huge serpentine creature lying still in the water offshore. After snapping photographs and filming the stationary beast with a movie camera, observing what appeared to be a large wound behind its head, le Serrec and de Jong mustered their courage to approach the creature underwater. Le Serrec describes the adventure:

It was only when we got to within 20 feet of the serpent that we could see its head clearly. The head was large — about 4 feet from top to bottom — with jaws about 4 feet wide. The lower jaw was flat like that of a sandfish. The skin was smooth but rather dull, brownish-black in color, the eyes seemed pale green, almost white. The skin looked more like that of a SHARK than an EEL. There

Photograph of the alleged Hook Island sea serpent (*Robert le Serrec*/True *Magazine*).

A close-range photograph of the Hook Island sea serpent's head (*Robert le Serrec*/True *Magazine*).

were no apparent scales. Nor did we see any parasites around. We supposed the flexible tail would have shaken any off. There were no fins or spines, nor were there any apparent breathing openings — although there must have been some. Perhaps we didn't see them because our attention was focused mainly on the creature's menacing mouth — the inside of which was whitish. The teeth appeared to be small. A fragment of some dark substance hung from the upper row of teeth — possibly a FISH. As the Monster was lying on the sandy bottom, we could not see the colour of its belly. The creature was about 70 feet long. Behind the head the body was about 2 feet 4 inches thick and remained that way for about 25 feet, then it gradually tapered to a whip-like tail. The general colour of the body was black with 1 foot-wide brownish rings every 5 feet — the first starting just behind the head. The skin was smooth but dull.

As le Serrec prepared to film the beast again, it raised its head and frightened the divers away. The animal turned and fled toward deeper water as the men reached their boat and started the motor. Le Serrec waited three months before selling his story and photos to the media, whereupon predictable dissection of the incident began. NESSIE-hunter TIM DINSDALE praised le Serrec's "moral courage" and suggested that "few...can really doubt the authenticity of his discovery." BERNARD HEUVELMANS took a different tack, researching le Serrec's background, and had this to say about the case in 1968:

I did my own checking on Le Serrec in France and found that he had left unpaid creditors in France and did not seem very trustworthy. IVAN [SANDERSON] had the photographs...examined by the experts at Fawcett publications, and they could find no sign that the pictures had been tampered with....

When the film did not arrive in Europe my suspicions increased. Then I heard from correspondents in New Caledonia, who had seen it, that the underwater shots were so fuzzy and vague that one could see nothing at all.

Finally I learnt that Robert Le Serrec, who in 1959 had tried to tempt some young men to come with him, and pay a handsome "share of his expenses," had promised that the expedition would be financially fruitful. "Besides," he said one day, "I have another thing in reserve which will bring in a lot of money ... [I]t's to do with the sea-serpent."

As for the alleged witnesses themselves, the rest is silence. Le Serrec had planned to write a book describing his adventures, but the volume never found its way to print, and he soon dropped from sight. In June 2003, Swedish cryptozoologist JAN-OVE SUNDBERG announced that LeSerrec, now 75 years old, had been found living in Asia. Sundberg hoped to schedule an interview, but nothing further was revealed by press time for this volume.

Sources: Dinsdale, *Monster Hunt*; Heuvelmans, *In the Wake of the Sea Serpents*; Karl Shuker, "Alien zoo." *Fortean Times* 174 (October 2003): 28.

***Hope On* sea serpent**   In autumn 1883, crewmen aboard the U.S. whaling ship *Hope On* met a SEA SERPENT near the Las Perlas archipelago, off the Pacific coast of Panama. At first, the sailors mistook it for a whale, and boats were lowered to pursue the animal, but the harpooners retreated when they recognized their mistake. A newspaper account of the incident read:

> A head like that of a horse rose from the water and then dived. The creature was seen by all the boat's crew. Captain Seymour describes the animal as almost 20 feet in length, with a handsome horse-like head, with two unicorn-shaped horns protruding from it. The creature had four legs or double-jointed fins, a brownish hide, profusely speckled with large black spots, and a tail that appeared to be divided into two parts.

Source: Richard Proctor, "A marine monster." *Newcastle Weekly Chronicle* (6 October 1883).

Horizon City Monster   Since the early 1970s, residents of Horizon City, Texas (southeast of El Paso) have reported sightings of a large unknown HOMINID or NORTH AMERICA APE. Witnesses typically describe the creature(s) as 7-8 feet tall, with broad shoulders, an "elongated" head, and strong body odor. Cecelia Montañez claims two sightings of "a big GORILLA-like thing" since 2001, reporting that the bulldog-faced creatures "have very short hair and are a faded brownish-maroon color." Montañez believes the creatures live in caverns beneath Horizon City, but geology professors at the University of Texas in El Paso deny that any such caverns exist. Deputy sheriff Bill Rutherford investigated alleged monster tracks at a local golf course in 1975, but said the footprints "appeared to have been dug" by human hands. Tony Aguilar, Horizon City's police chief, dismissed any monster reports in July 2003 with the claim that an unidentified hermit may have lived in the nearby mountains 30 years ago. "He had long hair and he was unshaven," Aguilar recalled of the unnamed suspect. "A lot of hunters at one point found a little cave, and found old cans, and like he had been living off the land."

Source: Adriana M. Chávez, "Some residents believe in Horizon City's monster." *El Paso Times* (31 July 2003).

Horse (Blue)   In 1860, a South African hunter named Lashmar saw a blue horse grazing with a herd of QUAGGAS and captured it alive, transporting the creature to Cape Town. From there, it was sold to a dealer in London, and by 1863 it resided in Lord Stamford's stable. London veterinarian Charles Spooner examined the horse, but could find no explanation for its aberrant hue. By February 1868, when Lord Stamford sold the horse for exhibition at the Crystal Palace, its striking blue color had faded to gray. No other specimens of blue horse have been found, so far. KARL SHUKER suggests that the animal's unique color may have derived from the pigment eumelanin, released in excessive quantities by a mutant gene. Mysteries surrounding the blue horse's origin and its presence in the quagga herd remain unsolved.

Source: Shuker, "A horse of a different color."

Horse-Headed Snake   The sole report of this curious cryptid emerged from the Lukolweni region of South Africa's Eastern Cape Province, in April 2000. Garbled eyewitness accounts described a large yellow SNAKE with a head and mane resembling those of a horse, its body as thick as a 5-gallon drum. South Africa's largest known snake is the rock PYTHON (*Python sebae*), which may reach 20 feet in length on rare occasions, though it bears no obvious resemblance to a horse.

Source: "South African 'horse-headed snake.'" *Cryptozoology Review* 4 (Summer 2000): 4.

Horseshoe Pond, Indiana   In April 1892, Isaac Daines reported a 60-foot LAKE MONSTER resembling a SNAKE with a dog's head from this lake located south of Vincennes, in Knox County. Identified in press reports as "a highly respected farmer, whose veracity cannot be questioned," Daines described the beast as follows:

> Its color is black on the back and sides. It inhabits the water and does not seem to venture any distance on shore. It glides through the waters of the pond with that easy and graceful movement peculiar to a snake swimming....When approached it becomes alarmed and swims away; if pursued it flees with wonderful rapidity. The creature's haste was doubtless inspired by Daines attempting to shoot it on several occasions. He claimed that bullets made no impact on the serpent, and his plan to return with a squad of riflemen apparently was never carried to fruition. More than a century without fresh sightings suggests that the creature is no longer present.

Source: Richard Day, "Sea-serpent, werewolf, etc." *Valley Advance* (6 October 1981); "A sea serpent." *Vincennes* (IN) *Commercial Weekly* (22 April 1892).

Hovind, Kent (1954–)   A resident of Pensacola, Florida and self-described cryptozoologist, Kent Hovind might be more appropriately termed a crypto-evangelist. As an outspoken "young earth Creationist"— one who takes the Bible literally and believes that God created Earth around the year 4004 B.C.— he lectures frequently ("over 700 times each year"!) on "the tremendous need for exposing evolution as a dangerous, religious world-view, and for arming Christians with scientific evidence that there are no contradictions between true science and the Bible." Billing himself as "Dr. Dino," Hovind also maintains an Internet website which offers fossil replicas for sale (including facsimiles of the PALUXY TRACKS, alleged to prove human-dinosaur interaction, that were conclusively discredited in 1984). Hovind is the co-author, with WILLIAM GIBBONS, of *Jaws, Claws and Dinosaurs*, a 72-page "cryptozoology book written for young adults from a creationist perspective!"

While mainstream cryptozoologists generally ignore Hovind, critics of his ministry and message have established several websites which attack his credentials (a mail-order Ph.D. from Patriot University, "a ministry of Hilltop Baptist Church" with no faculty or fixed address), his dissertation (untitled, sans footnotes, with "rampant misspellings"), and his standing $250,000 reward offer for anyone who can "prove evolution" (to Hovind's personal satisfaction). Some of that criticism verges on abuse, but Hovind's case is not enhanced by intemperate and unfounded assertions, such as his published claim that: "The Smithsonian Institute has 33,000 sets of human remains in their basement. Many of them were taken while the people were still alive. They were so desperate to find missing links, so desperate to prove their theory that they murdered people to prove it. It was the philosophy of evolution that drove them."

Sources: Dr. Dino website, http://www.drdino.com/; "Analysis of Kent Hovind," http://www.geocities.com/kenthovind/; The Kent Hovind Page, http://home.austarnet.com.au/stear/kent_hovind_page.htm

Huáng Yáo   An unclassified mustelid reported from various points in China, the Huáng Yáo is described by witnesses as a weasel with a catlike head. Its dorsal pelage is yellow, while the underside is black.

Source: Muirhead, "Some Chinese cryptids (Part Two)."

Hudson River, New York   Author Betty Sanders Gardner reports that in March 1969, a slimy, black-and-gray animal

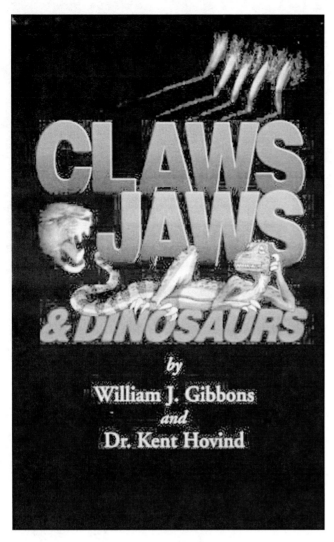

Kent Hovind co-authored this children's book with cryptozoologist William Gibbons (*William Rebsamen*).

"bigger than a whale" was sighted in the Hudson River, from "City Island Bridge, Bronx, New York." Unfortunately, there is no such bridge across the Hudson. City Island lies east of the Bronx, between Long Island Sound and Eastchester Bay, near the point where the HELL'S GATE SEA SERPENT reportedly attacked a tug boat in August 1902. Garner cites no source for the report, and it has proved impossible to trace.

Source: Garner, *Monster! Monster!*

Hughenden Puma   Sightings of this ALIEN BIG CAT around Hughenden, Buckinghamshire, began in 1994, when two women walking their dogs on a local soccer field met an animal described as five feet long, with a "CAT-like face" and a long tail. More sightings followed, spanning a range from Upper Dean to the northern outskirts of High Wycombe. Locals dubbed their elusive felid the Hughenden Puma, though some accounts described a jet-black animal bearing no real resemblance to a COUGAR (*Puma concolor*). Members of the Wycombe Heights Golf Club reported a large cat on their grounds in May 2001, and trackers confirmed that its pawprints matched those of a "young puma." Two weeks later, a half-eaten deer was found on Gomm Road, in High Wycombe. Sightings resumed in February 2003,

when workers at a furniture factory in Princes Risborough saw a large black cat prowling the area. Witness Brian Wratten told reporters, "It was jet black, much bigger than a cat. I would put money on it being some kind of puma." Another witness, Steve Lomas, found tracks in soft dirt where the cat was last seen. "I measured the distance between the front and back legs," Lomas said, "and it was the length of my golf club."

Source: James Webb, "Big cat on the prowl again." *Buckinghamshire Free Press* (26 March 2003).

Huia   The huia (*Heteralocha acutirostris*) is yet another victim of mankind's rapacious appetite for slaughter. When European settlers arrived on New Zealand's North Island, these 19-inch BIRDS were fairly common in the region between East Cape and modern-day Wellington. They received their scientific name in 1836, noted as remarkable for their black plumage with a metallic green tint, and for the differing bills of male and female specimens: the female's bill was long and curved, the male's short and straight. Nonstop hunting and competition with imported bird species decimated the huia population, and the last confirmed specimens (two males and a female) were seen on 28 December 1907. Still, 23 unsubstantiated sightings were reported in the 1920s, and an official search in 1924 found signs of huias (though no living birds were discovered). Witness Margaret Hutchinson reported a huia sighting from Lake Waikareti, in the Urewera State Forest, on 12 October 1961. Thirty years later, Dutch zoologist Lars Thomas claimed a sighting in the South Island's Pureora Forest. In July 1999, a conference of biologists, bioethicists and Maori tribal representatives agreed to clone huia's from DNA samples found in taxiderm specimens. Critics of the plan claimed that the huia's extinction was a natural process, proving it an unviable species. At press time for this book, no progress in the cloning effort was apparent.

Sources: Margaret Hutchinson, "I thought I saw a huia bird." *Birds* 3 (September-October 1970): 110-113; William Phillipps, *The Book of the Huia*. Christchurch, New Zealand: Whitcombe and Tombs, 1963; Shuker, *The New Zoo*.

Huillia   The Huillia of eastern Trinidad is said to be a large aquatic SNAKE, inhabiting the River Ortoire and surrounding forests. Witnesses from the early 19th century described the animal as 25-50 feet long, covered with scales and capable of swimming at a steamboat's speed. Frequent descriptions of the Huillia swimming with vertical undulations, however, eliminate all known reptiles from the list of candidates. An expedition was mounted to capture the Huillia in January 1934, complete with an Indian snake-charmer, but the hunters returned empty-handed.

Sources: Edward Joseph, *History of Trinidad*. London: A.K. Newman, 1838; Shuker, *In Search of Prehistoric Survivors*.

Humboldt River, Nevada   In July 1911, G.P. Griffith and Alex Hay reportedly met a bizarre creature while fishing along the Humboldt River, northeast of Elko, Nevada (Elko County). The *Elko Free Press* described the incident as follows on 11 July:

Griffith said he saw something coming down the stream, which he thought at first was a flock of wild ducks following one another in a long line. Being a sportsman, he was interested in the sight, and stepped back into a clump of bushes to watch them pass, and called to his companion at the sight.

But to his wonder and amazement, when the object got opposite them, it was a huge serpent, swimming on the surface of the water, with its head, or heads, held high and its long, huge, black, glistening, undulating body gracefully cleaving the pure, limpid mountain water, the reptile searching the banks on either side for prey.

About 20 feet was visible and the monster had four heads shaped something like a dog's head, the body of a black color and as large as a man's leg. Fascinated, they watched the huge SNAKE, but as soon as one of them spoke it disappeared on the instant.

Source: "Humboldt 'monster' described." *Las Vegas Sun* (18 October 1981).

Hün Garees/Hün Göröös *see* Khün Görüessü

Hunda carcass
In January 1942, around the same time that a large GLOBSTER washed ashore at DEEPDALE HOLM, in the Orkney Islands, a second carcass was discovered on nearby Hunda Island. Because Hunda was uninhabited, "several weeks" elapsed prior to arrival of a 3-man research team on 5 February. W. Campbell Brodie wrote the team's report, published in the *Orcadian* on 12 February 1942. It read:

> We were rather skeptical of the reported dimensions of the second Orkney "Monster" and we intended to verify these for ourselves; but on arrival at the very stony beach on the island a strange sight met our eyes. A huge elongated yellowish-colored creature lay embedded in the sea-wrack, wedged firmly between the boulders. Closer inspection revealed that this was indeed no ordinary denizen of the deep, but truly a creature of "Monster" proportions. All that remained was the skull and vertebral column, together with several appendages or fins consisting of cartilaginous material.
>
> There were suggestions of a hump of a fatty nature, on the top of which was another cartilaginous fin, similar in structure to the larger fins lying beneath the vertebral column. The back of the latter was covered with greyish-black tough skin with a hairy appearance. From some parts we obtained hair of a coconut fibre nature, about four to six inches in length. The skull of the creature was composed of a gristly substance, definitely not bony and there was no evidence of teeth. On the anterior part were two antennae, four inches long, and laterally two large sockets which may have contained the eyes. On a raised part of the skull was a large cavity, possibly a blower hole, about midway along its dorsal surface. Immediately behind this were two smaller holes, all communicating with the mouth region. Of a mouth or lower jaw there was no sign although we found a cartilaginous part, somewhat like a horse saddle in shape. We could not discover the articulations for this part or any part of the skeleton.
>
> We proceeded to measure the carcase — the length was 28 feet approximately, there being 65 vertebrae making up the spinal column. The head alone measured 2 feet long and 1 foot broad at its widest part. The appearance of the vertebrae was unusual, there being no spinous processes present. Each individual vertebra was bamboo-like in appearance and was joined to the preceding one with an elastic-like membrane. One of the large flipper parts measured 3 feet in length. We were so convinced that the creature was of a similar species to that found at Deepdale Holm, that we hired a boat from Mr. John McBeath and removed the skeleton in sections to St. Margarets Hope, and now are exhibiting it locally in aid of the Red Cross.

Spokesmen for Edinburgh's Royal Scottish Museum agreed that both carcasses belonged to the same species, but they found nothing mysterious about the creatures. In fact, both were proclaimed to be basking sharks (*Cetorhinus maximus*), and not particularly large ones at that. TIM DINSDALE observed that basking sharks normally have 103 vertebrae, begging the question as to whether 38 were lost during decomposition or the museum experts were mistaken in their diagnosis. As Dinsdale remarked, if the Hunda carcass *was* a basking shark, 28 feet long with more

than one-third of its skeleton missing, in life it must have rivaled the largest specimens on record.

Source: Dinsdale, *Monster Hunt.*

Hungary Bay carcass
On 22 January 1860, a serpentine creature was stranded at Hungary Bay, on Hamilton Island, Bermuda. Captain Hawtaigne of the British Royal Navy sent this report of its discovery to the *Zoologist*:

> *A sea-serpent in the Bermudas.*— I beg to send you the following account of a strange sea-monster captured on these shores, the animal being, in fact, no less than the great SEA-SERPENT which was described as having been seen by Captain M'Quhae, of H.M.S. "DAEDALUS," a few years since. Two gentlemen named Trimingham were walking along the shore of Hungary Bay, in Hamilton Island, on Sunday last, about eleven o'clock, when they were attracted by a loud rushing noise in the water, and, on reaching the spot, they found a huge sea-monster, which had thrown itself on the rocks, and was dying from exhaustion in its efforts to regain the water. They attacked it with large forks which were lying near at hand for gathering sea-weed, and unfortunately mauled it much, but secured it. The reptile was sixteen feet seven inches in length, tapering from head to tail like a SNAKE, the body being a flattish oval shape, the greatest depth at about a third of its length from the head, being eleven inches. The colour was bright and silvery; the skin destitute of scales but rough and warty; the head in shape not unlike that of a bull-dog, but it is destitute of teeth; the eyes were large, flat, and extremely brilliant, it had small pectoral fins, and minute ventral fins, and large gills. There were a series of fins running along the back, composed of short, slender rays, united by a transparent membrane, at the interval of something less than an inch from each other. The creature had no bone, but cartilage running through the body. Across the body at certain intervals were bands, where the skin was of a more flexible nature, evidently intended for the creature's locomotion, screw like, through the water. But its most remarkable feature was a series of eight long thin spines of a bright red colour springing from the top of the head and following each other at an interval of about an inch; the longest was in the centre: it is now in the possession of Colonel Munro, the acting Governor of the Colony; and I had the opportunity of examining it very closely. It is two feet seven inches long, about three eighth of an inch in circumference at the base, and gradually tapering, but flattened at the extreme end, like the blade of an oar.

As BERNARD HEUVELMANS noted, more than a century later, Captain Hawtaigne's description and accompanying sketch of the beast bear no resemblance whatever to the 1848 *Daedalus* sea serpent, but they present a near-perfect likeness of a large oarfish (*Regalecus glasne*). That finding is corroborated by British naturalist J. Mathew Jones, who examined the carcass and identified it on the spot. Colleague Edward Newman considered the Hungary

The Hungary Bay "sea serpent" was almost certainly an oarfish.

Bay specimen a new species of oarfish, but his judgment on that point was overruled, as in the case of the cullercoats carcass.

Sources: Heuvelmans, *In the Wake of the Sea Serpents*; Roesch, "A review of alleged sea serpent carcasses worldwide (Part 1—1648-1880)."

Huntington Lake, Indiana   Three books and several Internet websites list this Hoosier lake (unanimously misspelled "Huntington's") as a source of LAKE MONSTER reports, but none provides any dates or details of sightings. Also known as J. Edward Roush Lake, it lies two miles south of Huntington, in Huntington County.

Sources: Bord and Bord, *Unexplained Mysteries of the 20th Century*; Coleman, *Mysterious America*; Kirk, *In the Domain of the Lake Monsters*.

Hutton Lake, Wyoming   Native American folklore names this lake, in southeastern Wyoming (Laramie County), as the home of a fearsome "serpent queen." No modern sightings of the supposed LAKE MONSTER are on file.

Source: Charles Skinner, *Myths and Legends of Our Land*. Philadelphia: Lippincott, 1896.

Huyghe, Patrick (1952–)   Virginia native Patrick Huyghe holds a bachelor's degree in social psychology from the University of Virginia and a master's in journalism from Syracuse University, in New York. After working at *Newsweek* and *Us* magazines, he turned freelance in 1980, subsequently placing articles with magazines including *Audubon*, *Discovery*, *Omni*, *Psychology Today* and *Reader's Digest*. Huyghe's pieces on cryptozoology have thus reached a wide popular audience, further expanded by his own semi-annual journal, *The Anomalist*. His published books include *Glowing Birds: Stories from the Edge of Science* (1985); *The Big Splash* (with Louis Frank, 1990); *Columbus Was Last* (1992); *The Field Guide to Extraterrestrials* (1996); *The Field Guide to Bigfoot, Yeti, and Other Mystery Primates Worldwide* (with LOREN COLEMAN, 1999); *The Field Guide to UFOs* (with Dennis Stacy, 2000); *The Field Guide to Ghosts and Other Apparitions* (with Hilary Evans, 2000); *Swamp Gas Times* (2001); and *The Field Guide to Lake Monsters, Sea Serpents, and Other Mystery Denizens of the Deep* (with Coleman, 2003). In addition to writing, Huyghe also performs occasional field research. In 1993, inspired by a conversation with J. RICHARD GREENWELL, he traced "lost" remains that represent the only known physical evidence of the PYGMY ELEPHANT. Huyghe is presently the editor-in-chief of Paraview Press.

Source: Patrick Huyghe, http://homepage.mac.com/patrickhuyghe/bio.html.

Hvaler, Norway   According to legend, this lake in Norway's Østfold County once harbored a 60-foot LAKE MONSTER, dark gray in color, that possessed a mouthful of prominent yellowish teeth. No modern sightings are recorded.

Source: Skjelsvik, "Norwegian lake and sea monsters."

Hvítá, Iceland   In late November 2002, Radio One journalist Thorvaldur Fridriksson announced a dramatic increase in "sea monster" sightings around Hvítá, on the western coast of Iceland. Most of the creatures were harmless, according to Fridriksson, who described them as animals with long necks and tails. A few, however, were said to be dangerous. Fridriksson warned, "They are mermen and eat humans."

Source: "Around the weird: Bizarre news briefs." *Wireless News* (20 November 2002).

Hylophagos   In classical times, Greek authors described the Hylophagos ("wood eater") as an African WILDMAN known for its diet of wood and seeds. BERNARD HEUVELMANS suspected that the ancient Greeks were recording bastardized accounts of APES or unknown HOMINIDS from second-or third-hand reports. Vernon Reynolds assumed that the tales referred to CHIMPANZEES (*Pan troglodytes*), which include the bark of some trees in their diet.

Sources: Heuvelmans, *Les Bêtes humaines d'Afrique*; Vernon Reynolds, *The Apes*. New York: E.P. Dutton, 1967.

Hym-Che *see* **Yemische**

Hyraxes (Giant)   Hyraxes (Order *Hyracoidea*) are small, herbivorous mammals resembling guinea pigs. Although they resemble rodents, and grow no larger than RABBITS, their nearest living relatives are elephants. Three living species are presently recognized by science, all confined to Africa. They include the bush hyrax (*Heterohyrax*), rock hyrax (*Procavia*), and tree hyrax (*Dendrohyrax*). As humble as they are today, hyracoids were the dominant herbivores of Africa in the early Cenozoic era, when some species (*Kvabebihyrax* and *Titanohyrax*) grew as large as a modern RHINOCEROS. But did the giants all die out some 40 million years ago?

Bronze carvings from Shaanxi Province, China, depicting stocky quadrupeds of hyracoid appearance have been dated from 403-221 B.C., well after the last prehistoric specimen presumably expired. KARL SHUKER suggests that *Pliohyrax*, a pig-sized species from the Late Pliocene, may have survived into historic times instead of dying off 2 million years ago (though it is likely now extinct). A more recent survivor, according to modern reports, is a large herbivore of the Ethiopian desert. Witnesses describe it as four feet long and two feet high at the shoulder, prompting BERNARD HEUVELMANS to suggest an unknown giant species of bush or rock hyrax.

Sources: Heuvelmans, "Annotated checklist of apparently unknown animals with which cryptozoology is concerned"; Shuker, "A giant owl and a giant hyrax...?" *Strange Magazine* 21 (Fall 2000), http://www.strangemag.com.

—— I ——

Iemisch   The Iemisch is one of South America's several "WATER TIGERS," also known within its range as *tigre de agua*. More than a dozen local names are also applied to the creature, including Chimchimen, Erefilú, Guarifilu, Hymché, Jemechim, Jemisch, Ñerrefilu, Nervelu, Ngúrüvilu, Ñiribilu, Nürüfilu, Yem'chen, Yemische, and Zorro-víbora. Further confusion derives from the fact that marine otters (*Lontra felina*) are also frequently called "water tigers" in various parts of Latin America. Finally, researchers are unable to agree on whether or not the Iemisch and another aquatic cryptid, the YAQUARU, are identical.

By any name, witnesses describe the Iemisch as a puma-sized creature with brown hair, webbed toes, a long tail, and a round head with oversized canine teeth. It puts those fangs to use slaughtering humans and animals seized while crossing streams or rivers, dragging them below the surface and inflicting gruesome injuries. Florentino Ameghino believed the Iemisch was a relict form of prehistoric sloth (*Mylodon*), and so named it *Neomylodon listai* in 1898, but that designation remains unofficial. BERNARD HEUVELMANS and ROY MACKAL considered the Iemisch a kind of giant otter, and while one rare South American otter (*Pteronura brasiliensis*) may reach eight feet in length, its behavior does not match the Iemisch's fearsome reputation. Other researchers suggest the possibility of a relict SABER-TOOTHED CAT (*Smilodon*), which may have adapted to hunt in the water.

Sources: Ameghino, "An existing ground-sloth in Patagonia"; Heuvelmans, *On the Track of Unknown Animals*; Mackal, *Searching for Hidden Animals*; Shuker, *Mystery Cats of the World*.

Igopogo   Ontario's Lake Simcoe, located 40 miles north of Toronto, is home to a LAKE MONSTER dubbed Igopogo — presumably in imitation of Canadian cryptids MANIPOGO (Lake Manitoba) and OGOPOGO (Lake Okanagan). Reports of a "SEA SERPENT" in Lake Simcoe begin with aboriginal traditions and continue with reports from European settlers that continue to the present day. A group of witnesses including the Rev. L.B. Williams observed Igopogo on 22 July 1963, describing it as a charcoal-covered animal, 30 to 70 feet long, with multiple dorsal fins. Twenty years later, on 13 June 1983, sonar readings taken by William Skrypetz from Lefroy's Government Dock and Marina revealed the outline of "a long-necked, heavy-bodied creature not unsimilar to Scotland's Loch Ness monster." In 1991, the captain of a powerboat stalled on Lake Simcoe shot videotape of a large seallike animal as it twice emerged from the water.

Igopogo is famous enough to be known by various names around Lake Simcoe. In the lake's western extension, Kempenfelt Bay, the creature is sometimes dubbed Kempenfelt Kelly. On the eastern shore, residents of Beaverton prefer the name Beaverton Bessie, while Simcoe Kelly is an alternate nickname used throughout the area. Skeptics dismiss the sonar evidence from 1983, insisting that all Igopogo sightings involve "occasional seals" slipping into Lake Simcoe via lakes and rivers linking it to Georgian Bay and Lake Huron.

Sources: Costello, *In Search of Lake Monsters*; Garner, *Monster! Monster!*; "Igopogo, a mystery solved," at http://www.ultranet.ca/bcscc/igopogo,htm.

Iguanas (Mislocated)   Iguanas (Family *Iguanidae*) are diverse and widely distributed lizards, divided into 55 genera and 650 recognized species. Most are native to the Western Hemisphere, but three genera dwell in Madagascar and Fiji. In the New World, various species are found from southern Canada to Tierra del Fuego, with island-dwelling species throughout the Caribbean and the Galápagos chain. Species indigenous to the U.S. are uniformly small, but larger tropical species are often sold as pets. Escapees from private collections account for most reports of big iguanas at large, from the U.S. to Britain and continental Europe, but breeding populations of three exotic species are established in the state of Florida. The largest, with a record length of 6 feet is the green iguana (*Iguana iguana*) of Central and South America, described as thriving by the "hundreds, maybe thousands" throughout the subtropical Florida Keys. Chris Bergh, a spokesman for the Florida Fish and Wildlife Conservation Commission, told reporters in March 2003, "There is plenty of evidence that they are causing problems in people's residential and

Large iguanas have established breeding populations in several Florida counties.

commercial landscapes, just from the destruction of vegetation. The friends group for the U.S. Fish and Wildlife Service here in the Keys planted a butterfly garden at the Blue Hole park on Big Pine [Key]. Immediately afterward, the green iguanas moved in and ate pretty much everything."

Two species presently established and breeding on Florida's mainland include 4-foot Mexican spinytail iguana (*Ctenosaura pectinata*) and the 36-inch black spinytail iguana (*C. similis*), native to Mexico and Central America. Stable breeding populations of *C. pectinata* have been recognized in Dade County since 1972, while *C. similis* has maintained thriving colonies in four counties (Charlotte, Collier, Dade and Lee) since 1978, with recent expansion into Broward County during 2002. Unlike the strictly herbivorous green iguana, both *Ctenosaura* species include eggs and small vertebrates in their diet, thus posing a potential threat to various native species, including sea TURTLE hatchlings and various nesting BIRDS.

Sources: Jennifer Babson, "Scaling New Frights: Iguanas Invade Keys." *HerpDigest* (9 March 2003); Eric Staats, "Whatever Happened To: The spiny-tailed iguanas on Keewaydin Island." *Naples* (FL) *News* (25 December 2003); Florida's Exotic Wildlife, http://wld.fwc.state.fl.us/critters/exotics/resultsClass.asp?taxclass=R.

Ikal   An unidentified primate, reported from Chiapas State in southern Mexico, the Ikal (Mayan for "black spirit") is described as three feet tall, gracile in form, with a coat of curly dark hair over predominantly black skin. Erect ears are sometimes mentioned, and eyewitness accounts stress the creature's nocturnal habits. Based on appearance and proximity, the Ikal may be identical to the ALUX and/or the DUENDE reported from southern Mexico and Central America.

Sources: Stross, "The Ihk'als"; Stross, "Demons and monsters of Tzeltal tales."

Ikimizi *see* **Lions (spotted)**

Île du Levant wildcat   An unidentified CAT reported from Île du Levant — one of the Îles d'Hyères, off the southern coast of France — this felid remains officially unrecognized by science, though BERNARD HEUVELMANS graced it with a Latin name (*Felis silvestris levantina*) in 1986. Witnesses describe the cat as weighing between 20 and 30 pounds. One specimen, observed repeatedly in 1932, was so large that locals named it *le lynx de la Paille* ("haystack LYNX"). Several wildcats were reportedly caught in RABBIT traps during World War II, one of them tipping the scales at 22 pounds, but none were preserved for scientific study. Heuvelmans himself observed one of the predators in 1958, savagely attacking smaller feral cats. He considered it a subspecies of the African wildcat (*F. s. libyca*) and named it accordingly, but the classification remains unofficial.

Sources: Heuvelmans, "Annotated checklist of apparently unknown animals with which cryptozoology is concerned"; Shuker, *Mystery Cats of the World.*

Île Kergulélen sea serpent

On 17 July 1814, Samuel Mitchill sent the following letter to John Waterhouse, editor of the *Medical Repository* in Philadelphia:

A commander of a ship with whom I am particularly acquainted, performed a voyage from New York to Canton in 1809. Being outward bound during the month of September, he steered from the Cape of Good Hope towards Kerguelen's Land [now Île Kergulélen, a French possession]. In the latitude of about 41° south, the man in the fore-top cried out that there was a rock ahead, distant about a league [3 miles]. A lump of mass was distinguished in the direction the vessel was then going, directly forward, and having exactly the appearance of a rock.

On approaching it, the captain was soon convinced it was not a rock, but a body possessing motion of its own, and unquestionably a large animal. It was ascertained that the creature made progress toward the ship. They kept her somewhat away to avoid running foul; but at the same time sailed near enough to allow observations to be made. The animal continued its course without intimidation, and crossed the vessel's wake just behind the rudder. The part that was above the water, seemed to the captain as large as the floor of a parlour in which we were then sitting; which was a chamber of about twenty feet by fifteen.

The guns had been loaded to shoot it; but on drawing near, the view was so terrible that not a single piece was discharged. It was judged most prudent to sail by without offering any disturbance, or even hoisting out a boat. Its motion was steady, but slow and heavy. Another gentleman, Mr. Robert Cornwell, who was on board, possessed of good eyes and quick perceptions, told me it would have been easy to have run the ship on board of it. This was avoided by keeping her away. The appearance, as far as I could gather from these two respectable witnesses, was such as to refer this monster to the same class with the others [discussed in a previous letter]. It was longer than the ship, and her length on deck was one hundred and ten feet....The skin was totally destitute of hair; but was black and distinguished by spots, or rather seemed to be covered with barnacles. Mr. C. thought the part above water was forty feet in length. This was roundish or gibbous. The elevation might be four feet from the level of the sea. The captain thought he saw a knob or head. On the part above water, he distinguished a wrinkles or folded appearance, which he compared to an umbrella. And the wrinkles or folds seemed to possess living motion.

Source: Samuel Mitchill, "Additional proof in favour of the existence of huge animals in the ocean, different from whales, and larger than they." *Medical Repository* 17 (July 1814): 398.

Illankanpanka *see* Jogung

Illie

Illie is the common nickname for LAKE MONSTERS said to inhabit Lake Illiamna, located 150 miles southwest of Anchorage, Alaska. Inuit natives know the creatures as Jig-ik-nak

and report that they sometimes attack boats (preferring those with red hulls). The first modern report dates from September 1942, when aviators Babe Alsworth and Bill Hammersley sighted a school of gray, blunt-headed animals swimming on the surface of Lake Illiamna. Average length exceeded 20 feet, and the creatures swam like FISH, by sweeping their tails from side to side. In 1947, surveyor Lawrence Rost reported a fish more than 20-feet long and "the color of dull aluminum." Millionaire cryptozoologist TOM SLICK went looking for Illie in the 1950s, but retrieved only anecdotal evidence. In the 1960s, NASA astronauts on training flights over the lake reported Illie sightings, and a biologist from the Alaska Department of Fish and Game observed a lone specimen in 1963: it was 25-30 feet long and swam submerged for 10 minutes without surfacing to breathe. In 1977, pilot Tim LaPorte and two of his passengers saw a 12- to 14-foot specimen in Pedro Bay, in 1977. It dived as they passed overhead, flashing vertical tail fins. An aberrant sighting in 1985, by witness George Wilson, described a 3-foot dorsal fin swimming in the Kvichak River, at the south end of Lake Illiamna. The mystery was compounded in 1987-88, by sightings of tall dorsal fins *and* an unknown animal resembling a giant seal. So far, Illiamna — which measures 80 miles long and 25 miles across at its widest point, has managed to preserve its secret.

Sources: Bille, "What lies beneath Lake Illiamna?"; Coleman, *Tom Slick and the Search for the Yeti*; Kirk, *In the Domain of the Lake Monsters.* Paust, "Alaska's monster mystery fish."

Illigan Dolphin

An unclassified cetacean, the Illigan dolphin was named by Willem Mörzer Bruyns, who reported sighting schools of 30 individuals swimming in Illigan Bay, on the Philippine island of Mindanao. Mörzer Bruyns described his find as similar in shape and size to the melon-headed whale (*Peponocephala electra*), but more brightly colored, with a brown back, yellow flanks, and a pink underside. (The melon-headed whale is black.) No type specimen has yet been collected.

Sources: Heuvelmans, "Annotated checklist of apparently unknown animals with which cryptozoology is concerned"; Willem Mörzer Bruyns, *Field Guide of Whales and Dolphins.* Amsterdam: Tor, 1971.

Illinois River, Arkansas

The Illinois River, in northwestern Arkansas, is cited in various cryptozoology texts as a source of occasional "monster" reports, but none of the accounts name any witnesses or provide even a brief description of the creature. On balance, it seems likely that one author mistook PIASA reports from the Illinois River in *Illinois* for an Arkansas cryptid, and subsequent accounts repeated the mistake by including the Arkansas waterway in their "definitive" lists of LAKE MONSTERS.

Sources: Bord and Bord, *Unexplained Mysteries of the 20th Century*; Coleman, *Mysterious America*; Kirk, *In the Domain of the Lake Monsters.*

Imap Umassouroa

A huge sea creature said to inhabit the icy waters of the North Atlantic and Labrador Sea, the Imap Umassouroa is described in Inuit folklore as being the size of a small island. Since Inuit tribesmen were well acquainted with whales from the earliest times, this creature presumably represents some other species. Unfortunately, mythical exaggeration and a dearth of modern sightings makes identification impossible.

Source: "Water monsters: Greenland." *Fortean Times.*

Imogen sea serpent

In March 1856, crewmen aboard the British ship *Imogen* sighted a SEA SERPENT in the North Atlantic. Captain James Guy later sent the following extract from his log to the *Illustrated London News*, with three sketches of the creature.

> *Imogen*, from Algoa Bay, towards London. Sunday 30th March, 1856. Lat. 29 deg. 11 min. N; Long., 34 deg. 36 min. W; bar. 30.50; calm and clear. Four vessels visible to southward and westward.
>
> About five minutes past eleven, a.m., the helmsman drew our attention to something moving through the water, and causing a strong ripple about 400 yards distant from our starboard quarter.
>
> In a few minutes it became more distinct, presenting the appearance represented in Fig. 1, and showing an apparent length of about forty feet (above the surface of the sea), the undulations of the water extending on each side to a considerable distance in its wake. Mr. Statham immediately ascended to the main-topsail-yard, Captain Guy and Mr. Harries watching the animal from the deck with the telescope.
>
> After passing the ship about half-a-mile, the serpent "rounded to" and raised its head, seemingly to look at us (Fig. 2), and then steered away to the northward (N.E.), possibly to the neighbourhood of the Western Islands [the Azores], frequently lifting its head (Fig. 3). We traced its course until nearly on the horizon, from the topsail-yard, and lost sight of it from the deck about 11h. 45m. a.m.
>
> No doubts remained in our minds as to its being an immense snake, as the undulations of its body were clearly perceptible, although we were unable to distinguish its eyes. The weather being fine and the glassy surface of the sea only occasionally disturbed by slight flaws (catspaws) of wind we had a perfect opportunity of noticing its movements.

Contrary to Captain Guy's assumption, SNAKES and other reptiles are incapable of undulating horizontally, a fact which led BERNARD HEUVELMANS and other cryptozoologists to conclude that the *Imogen* "serpent" must have been an unknown mammal.

Source: Heuvelmans, *In the Wake of the Sea Serpents*.

Imperator sea serpent   In early September 1935, while trawling for halibut, fishermen aboard the schooner *Imperator* sighted an unknown SEA SERPENT off the Western Bank of Nova Scotia. Captain Albert Williams did not see the creature, but he accepted the word of seven crewmen, as reported in the *Boston Transcript* (12 September) and the *Boston Globe* (13 September). According to those reports, "The serpent had a round body about eight inches in diameter, dark brownish-blue in color, large round eyes, and a long snout.... [W]hile alongside the vessel, it raised its head and about fifteen feet of its body above the sea, gazed nonchalantly around, apparently ignoring the *Imperator* entirely, then glided away."

Source: O'Neill, *The Great New England Sea Serpent*.

India sea serpent   On 30 October 1923, sailors aboard the tanker *India* sighted an unknown SEA SERPENT off the Pacific coast of Costa Rica, at latitude 9° 23' north, longitude 86° 26' west. Captain F. Van de Biesen described the incident in his log.

> Suddenly to port, and almost abeam, there rose obliquely out of the water, at least 300 yards away, a gigantic pillar, 25 to 35 feet long and of a good thickness which we reckoned must be at least 3 feet and perhaps as much as 6.
>
> The thing fell back into the water with a violent splash, greater even than the commotion made by a whale. After which it must have appeared again momentarily for we (5 people) were aware for several minutes of the effects of the spout of water that it raised.
>
> My first impression was that it was a gigantic garfish, but with a blunter head. The rear end was not visible, but the diameter of the animal was greater than that of one of our masts. Its colour was much lighter than a whale's.

While four of the witnesses saw no sign of "blowing," the first pilot maintains that it "blew." But I watched carefully and could see no "blowing."

It was not a whale's tail, nor anything of that kind, but the front part of an animal more or less circular in section, on which there were no large excrescences in the shape of fins.

Source: Heuvelmans, *In the Wake of the Sea Serpents*.

Indian Devil   Maine produced some of North America's earliest SASQUATCH sightings by white settlers, and its residents have called their unknown HOMINIDS by various names over time. In eastern Maine, around Topsfield, BIGFOOT is commonly known as the Indian Devil. A report filed with the SOCIETY FOR THE INVESTIGATION OF THE UNEXPLAINED described it as a 7-foot-tall "almost-human-looking creature," covered in reddish-brown fur. The correspondent also claimed that locals "almost take the existence of this animal for granted, just as a New Yorker may believe in the fact that taxi-cabs exist."

Source: Green, *Sasquatch: The Apes Among Us*.

Ingruenfisi River, South Africa   A witness named Atherstone reported a large aquatic cryptid was from this river, in South Africa's Eastern Cape Province, during 1950. No further details of the sighting are presently available.

Source: Costello, *In Search of Lake Monsters*.

Ink Monkey   An enigmatic primate, the Chinese ink MONKEY (or pen monkey) derived its name from the fact that various ancient scholars allegedly trained the mouse-sized animal to prepare ink for writing. Author Evangeline Edwards provided the West's first glimpse of the ink monkey in 1938:

> This creature is common in the northern regions and is about four or five inches long. It is endowed with an unusual instinct; its eyes are like cornelian stones, and its hair is jet black, sleek and flexi-

Ancient Chinese scholars allegedly trained small monkeys to prepare ink for writing.

ble, as soft as a pillow. It is very fond of eating thick Chinese ink, and whenever people write it sits with folded hands and crossed legs, waiting till the writing is finished, when it drinks up the remainder of the ink; which done, it squats as before, and does not frisk about unnecessarily.

The Chinese reportedly trained ink monkeys from 2000 B.C. onward, and the scholar Zhu Xi (1130-1200 A.D.) allegedly owned one. Despite Edwards's claim that they were "common" in the 1930s, however, ink monkeys seem to have vanished from daily Chinese life sometime before the 19th century. The reason for their passing, when they proved so useful to the country's higher classes, is unknown.

On 5 April 1996, the *Times* of London reported the discovery in China of a fossil jawbone from *Eosimias centennicus*, a tiny primate weighing less than four ounces, which lived in the Eocene period (40 million years ago). Strangely, less than three weeks later, a story in the Chinese *People's Daily* (22 April) announced that living ink monkeys had been rediscovered in the Wuyi Shan Mountains of Fujian Province. The animals were said to weigh seven ounces, measuring four to five inches long. Thus far, no specimens have been produced for study, and KARL SHUKER suggests that the *People's Daily* report was in fact a garbled account of the earlier fossil discovery. As for the ink monkey, it remains unidentified, with an unknown species of tarsier (*Tarsius* sp.) suggested as the most likely candidate.

Sources: Shuker, "Menagerie of mystery." *Strange Magazine* 18 (Summer 1997): 52-53.

Inkanyamba   A LAKE MONSTER reported from South Africa's KwaZulu-Natal Province, the Inkanyamba is said to inhabit several bodies of water, including the Umgeni and Mkomazi Rivers, various dams in the vicinity of Dargle, and a pool below Howick Falls (where it is sometimes nicknamed "Howie"). In 1962, a game warden named Buthelezi sighted a serpentine creature with a horselike head basking on a sandbank in the Umgeni River. A year later, the Inkanyamba was blamed for drowning a Zulu child at Howick Falls. Johannes Hlongwane, caretaker of a trailer park at the falls, saw the resident cryptid in 1974 and again in 1981; he described a serpentine body thicker than his own, with a neck that towered over 30 feet above the water's surface. Bob Tweeney, owner of a restaurant at Howick Falls and a member of the Howick Publicity Association, reported a sighting in September 1995 and offered R1,000 ($140) for a photo of the creature, and two were produced by unidentified photographers, but most researchers dismiss the pictures as a HOAX designed to stimulate CRYPTOTOURISM. Publicity stunts aside, researchers have suggested that the Inkanyamba may be a CROCODILE (which bears no resemblance to a serpent) or a large freshwater eel. The largest known African EEL (*Anguilla marmorata*) attains a maximum length of six feet.

Sources: Hall, "Legend of the falls"; "Of ducks and plesiosaurs: Howick Falls' monster." *Cryptozoology Revies*.

International Bigfoot Society *see* **Crowe, Raymond**

International Dracontology Society of Lake Memphrémagog   Founded at Magog, Québec (10 miles southwest of Sherbrooke) on 19 June 1986, the International Dracontology Society was created by cryptozoologist Jacques Boisvert to collect and publicize reports of MEMPHRÉ, the LAKE MONSTER said to inhabit Lake Memphrémagog. Boisvert previously established the Historical Society of Lake Memphrémagog (in 1980) and completed more than 1,000 scuba dives in the lake by 1983.

That year launched his collection of historical reports on Memphré, dating from the 19th century. In 1995 he designed a pictogram of Memphré, mounted at various points around the lake to encourage tourist vigilance. By 2000, Boisvert and the IDS had recorded 50 new sightings involving 124 witnesses, for a total of 229 sightings on file.

Source: Vermont Northeast Kingdom Guide, http://www.vermonter.com/nek/memphre.asp.

International Society of Cryptozoology   The International Society of Cryptozoology (ISC) was founded on 8-9 January 1982, during a conference held at the Smithsonian Institution, in Washington, D.C. BERNARD HEUVELMANS was elected president, a post he held for the remainder of his life; ROY MACKAL was named vice president, while J. RICHARD GREENWELL was elected secretary and editor of publications. Other founding board members included DMITRI BAYANOV (of Moscow's Darwin Museum), Eric Buffetaut (University of Paris), Joseph Gennaro (New York University), Philippe Janvier (University of Paris), GROVER KRANTZ (Washington State University), PAUL LEBLOND (University of British Columbia), Nikolai Spassov (Bulgarian Academy of Science), Phillip Tobias (University of the Witwatersrand, South Africa), Leigh Van Valen (University of Chicago), FORREST WOOD (U.S. Naval Ocean Systems Center), ZHOU GUOXING (Beijing Natural History Museum), and George Zug (Smithsonian Institution's National Museum of Natural History).

The ISC's stated purpose was to serve "as a focal point for the investigation, analysis, publication, and discussion of all matters related to animals of unexpected form or size, or unexpected occurrence in time or space." In addition to annual meetings, the group published a quarterly *ISC Newsletter* and an annual scholarly journal, *Cryptozoology*. While a 1984 policy statement declares that the ISC takes no official position on the existence of specific cryptids, various members have participated in wide-ranging field investigations of creatures including BIGFOOT, the ONZA, the RI and MOKELE-MBEMBE. Persistent financial difficulties delayed ISC publications between 1993 and 2004, but the society hopes to conquer those problems in the next decade. At press time for this volume, four founding members — Buffetaut, Greenwell, Spassov and Zhou — remained on the ISC's board of directors. Other board members included president Christine Janis (of Rhode Island's Brown University), vice president Angelo Capparella (Illinois State University, at Normal), Aaron Bauer

ISC headquarters is housed at Tucson's International Wildlife Museum (*International Society of Cryptozoology*).

(Pennsylvania's Villanova University), Troy Best (Auburn University, Alabama), C.K. Brain (Transvaal Museum, South Africa), Susan Cachel, (Rutgers University, New Jersey), EUGENIE CLARK (University of Maryland), Gabriel Francescoli (National University of Uruguay), Colin Groves (Australian National University, Canberra), and Anthony Russell (University of Calgary, Alberta).

Sources: *Cryptozoology*, Vol. 1-13 (1982-98); "Formation of the society." *ISC Newsletter* 1 (Spring 1982): 1-3; personal communication with J. Richard Greenwell (14 February 2004).

***Intrepid* sea serpent** In May 1751, while traveling aboard the sloop *Intrepid*, Joseph Kent sighted a SEA SERPENT near Muscongus Island, off Round Pond, Maine. Observing the creature from a distance of 30 to 40 feet, Kent described it as "longer and larger than the main boom of [the] sloop, which was 85 tons." A similar cryptid was seen at the same place in May 1780, by officers of the frigate *BOSTON*.

Source: O'Neill, *The Great New England Sea Serpent*.

***Iris* sea serpent** On 17 June 1826, Captain Charles Godspeed and seven crewmen aboard the sloop *Isis* encountered a SEA SERPENT in the North Atlantic, three leagues (nine nautical miles) south of Cape Cod, Massachusetts. Captain Peter Daggett, aboard a nearby (unnamed) ship confirmed the sighting. Captain Godspeed described the creature as 40 to 50 feet long, and provided this account of his experience to the *Hartford Times*:

> As he neared us we perceived his head about 4 feet above the level of the water, making his course athwart our bow....We stood for him with about a three knot [5 mph] breeze, but found we could not overtake him. The above can be testified to by myself and seven others on board.

Source: O'Neill, *The Great New England Sea Serpent*.

Irish Elk One of the largest deer that ever lived, the Irish elk (*Megaloceros giganteus*) stood five feet tall at the shoulder and sported antlers with a 12-foot span, weighing 100 pounds in some specimens. The animal's common name is misleading, since it was only a distant relation of true elk (or moose), and it was not restricted to Ireland, roaming a broad sector of the Palaearctic Region from Great Britain to Siberia and China. Officially, the Irish elk became extinct sometime before the onset of the Holocene period, around 11,000 years ago, but some anthropologists disagree. Fossil remains found on the ISLE OF MAN have been carbon-dated from 9430 B.C., and much more recent skulls — believed by some to represent female *Megaloceros*— were excavated at Ireland's Loch Gûr (near Limerick) in 1846. Those skulls bore the marks of heavy blunt instruments, similar to the pole-axes used by butchers to slaughter animals through the late 1800s. From that evidence and Irish folktales of giant black deer, naturalist Philip Gosse surmised that early Celtic tribesmen hunted (and perhaps domesticated) the Irish elk as recently as 1,000 years ago. Critics dispute that theory, maintaining that the Loch Gûr skull actually belong to female moose (*Alces alces*).

Sources: Gonzalez, et al., "Survival of the Irish elk into the Holocene"; Karl Shuker, "Alien zoo." *Fortean Times* 138 (October 2000): 19; Shuker, *In Search of Prehistoric Survivors*.

Irish Wildcat While Ireland produces few reports of ALIEN BIG CATS, inhabitants have long described a smaller wildcat still unrecognized by modern science. It is typically described as twice the size of a domestic CAT and usually gray. Irish naturalist William Thompson investigated wildcat reports in the early 19th century, and personally examined the carcass of a specimen

Did the "extinct" Irish elk survive into the 19th century?

shot at Shane's Castle Park, near Randalstown in County Antrim, Northern Ireland. The dead cat weighed 10 pounds 9 ounces and resembled a typical European wildcat in all respects except for its tail (which lacked a bushy tip) and its fur (of finer texture than normal in wildcats). Decades later, on 28 January 1885, W.B. Tegetmeir displayed the skin of a wildcat from County Donegal before the Zoological Society of London, but a report in the Society's *Proceedings* (3 March 1885) dismissed it as the pelt of a feral domestic cat. There the matter might have rested, but for the 1904 discovery of subfossil felid remains in the Edendale and Newhall Caves near Ennis, County Clare. Dr. R.F. Scharff examined the remains and reported in the *Irish Naturalist* (April 1905) that wildcats were not long extinct in Ireland; in fact, he suggested, a few might still be living. Curiously, Scharff also reported that the cave remains belonged to an African wildcat (*Felis silvestris lybica*), rather than the Scottish species earlier suspected. Author A.W. Stelfox reexamined Scharff's work in July 1965 and dismissed the specimens as feral domestic cats, but sightings of larger-than-average felids continue from Ireland to the present day.

Sources: Shuker, *Mystery Cats of the World*; Stelfox, "Notes on the Irish 'wild cat'"; Thompson, "On the former occurrence of the African wild cat (*Felis ocreata*, Gmel.) in Ireland."

Irizima One of several African cryptids said to resemble a living DINOSAUR, the Irizima is described as a swamp-dweller found in the neighborhood of Lake Edward, straddling the border of Uganda and the Democratic Republic of Congo (formerly

Zaire). Lake Edward is 39 miles long and 23 miles across at its widest point, with a mean depth of 55 feet (364 feet at its deepest point). The eastern half of the lake lies within Uganda's Queen Elizabeth National Park, while the west end is surrounded by the

African witnesses describe the Irizima as resembling a long-necked dinosaur (*William Rebsamen*).

DRC's Virunga National Park. Five rivers feed the lake — including the Ishasha, the Nyamugasani, the Rutshuru, the Rwenzoris and the Rwindi — while the Kazinga Channel connects Lake Edward to Lake George. Ample marshland is thus available for the Irizima, described by witnesses as a black, long-necked animal whose body is larger than that of a hippopotamus. Some accounts also refer to a horn on the Irizima's snout. Author Eric Temple-Perkins suggested, *Kingdom of the Elephant* (1955) that the Irizima might be nothing more than an occasional water spout on Lake Edward, but local natives insist that the creature exists.

Sources: Hichens, "On the trail of the brontosaurus: Encounters with Africa's mystery animals"; Shuker, "How dead are the dinosaurs?"

Irkuiem/Irquiem   An unidentified bear reported from Russia's Kamchatka peninsula, the Irkuiem is described standing 4 feet 6 inches tall at the withers and weighing up to a ton. Despite that hulking weight, it is said to have a slender body mounted on long legs, all covered in white fur. A bulge or flap of fat hanging between the Irkuiem's hind legs explains its name (Kamchatkan for "trousers pulled down"). Russian hunter Rodion Sivolobov began pursuing stories of the Irkuiem in the 1970s, and in 1987 he obtained the pelt of an alleged Irkuiem, resembling that of a huge polar bear (*Ursus maritimus*). After reviewing Sivolobov's evidence, Soviet zoologist Nikolaj Vereshchagin suggested that the Irkuiem might comprise a relict population of the short-faced bear (*Arctodus simus*), believed extinct since the Pleistocene (10,000 years ago). *Pravda* broadcast Vereshchagin's opinion in September 1987, but no further evidence of the Irkuiem's existence has yet been collected.

Sources: "Giant bear sought by Soviets." *ISC Newsletter* 6 (Winter 1987): 6-7; Shuker, *From Flying Toads to Snakes with Wings*.

***Isabel* sea serpent**   In the spring of 1854, crewmen aboard the *Isabel* sighted an unidentified SEA SERPENT off Savannah, Georgia, at the mouth of the Savannah River. The *Isabel's* commander, Captain Rollins, reported that the creature raised its head above the water on a long neck that reached as high as the ship's funnel. A similar creature was seen one day earlier, by crewmen of the *WILLIAM SEABROOK*, as it navigated the Savannah River.

Source: Heuvelmans, *In the Wake of the Sea Serpents*.

Isabella *see* **Bear Lake**

Isiququmadevu   Another of Africa's mysterious neo-DINOSAURS, the Isiququmadevu inhabits swamps and tributaries along the Zambezi River, ranging from Zambia's Victoria Falls to

the Barote floodplain. During World War I, King Lewanika of Barotseland (the northwestern sector of modern Zambia) received word from his subjects that an Isiququmadevu had been sighted in a local marsh. Witnesses described "a gigantic lizard, with a neck like a giraffe, legs like an elephant's, a small snakelike head and a tail thirty feet long." Lewanika traveled to the spot, and while he failed to see the Isiququmadevu, he reported to the British Resident, on Colonel Hardinge, that the beast's passage left drag marks "as large as a full-sized wagon from which the wheels had been removed."

In the summer of 1925, a river-transport manager named V. Pare saw a slate-gray serpentine creature, 30 to 40 feet long, sunning itself beside the flooded Zambezi, near Victoria Falls, but it fled into a cave as he approached. More than three decades later, in January 1960, witness E.C. Saunders reported two long-necked creatures, each 20-25 feet long, from the Zambezi River near Katombora, Zambia. While critics insist that he witnessed two PYTHONS, perhaps caught in the act of mating, Saunders insisted that the animals he saw resembled no known SNAKES.

Cryptozoologist ROY MACKAL notes that descriptions of Isiququmadevu are virtually identical to those of Africa's elusive MOKELE-MBEMBE, suggesting that the creatures may be one and the same. BERNARD HEUVELMANS once suggested an oversized African otter (*Aonyx capensis*) to explain Pare's sighting in 1925, but the otter would be overgrown indeed which surpassed its maximum 5-foot length by a factor of 600 to 800 percent.

Sources: Brelsford, "Some northern Rhodesian monsters"; Heuvelmans, *Les derniers dragons d'Afrique*; "Le monstre des chutes Victoria." *Atlas*; Mackal, *A Living Dinosaur?*; Shuker, "How dead are the dinosaurs?"

Isle of Man sea serpents   In the early 20th century, two SEA SERPENT reports were logged from waters near the Isle of Man, located in the Irish Sea between England and Ireland. The first was recorded sometime between 1880 and 1910, by Commander Robert Anstruther, aboard H.M.S. *CAESAR*. Eighteen years later, in 1928, Major W. Peer Groves was on vacation with his wife and children when he saw a "sea monster" swimming off the Isle of Man. Groves wrote: "The beast was obviously large — many feet in length — though only the head was visible. The head was about as big as that of a large bull, but rather broader between the ears, ending in a long, dog-like snout."

Source: Heuvelmans, *In the Wake of the Sea Serpents*.

Isle of Serpents   In his seminal study of SEA SERPENT sightings, BERNARD HEUVELMANS recounts the experience of wit-

The Isle of Man sea serpent, after eyewitness descriptions in 1928.

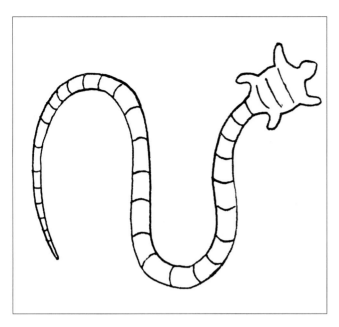

The Isle of Serpents beast, after witness A.G.L. Jourdan.

ness A.G.L. Jourdan, recorded in the early 1920s. The location is difficult to plot, since Heuvelmans places it simultaneously in "the China Sea" and 25 miles northwest of Port Arthur, Tasmania—i.e., the Indian Ocean. In any case, Jourdan's account of the sighting, published in *La Nature*, read as follows:

> When we had reached the meridian of a little island called "Isle of Serpents" which will be found on any large-scale map, but was too far off for us to see from where we were, I was surprised to see on the surface of the water, hardly immersed, at the very close distance of about 30 yards, an animal looking like a 10-foot SNAKE, with a maximum diameter of 7 to 8 inches, decreasing towards the tail, the body regularly annulated from one end to the other, alternatively light yellow and black, the length of each ring being about 4½ to 6 inches. The rather small head was immediately followed by a swelling about 12 to 14 inches in diameter, as thick as the body which followed it, and with four feet, two each side, recalling the shape of a TURTLE, but without a shell, striped in yellow and black and with an annulated tail about 10 feet long. I could not see whether this body was round like a snake's, or, as I supposed, slightly flattened.
>
> The animal seemed able to move only slowly, for despite the approach of the ship it was tossed by her wash and disappeared in her wake; a few moments later I saw two other snakes of similar appearance but with the yellow rings darker in colour; on none of them did I see appendages like those mentioned [by a previous writer] in *La Nature*: as they were further away from the ship than the first one I could not see any other details.

Jourdan went on to suggest that the Isle of Serpents might be named for the frequency of such creatures found in nearby waters. Based on his description and a sketch Jourdan prepared of the animal, Heuvelmans concluded that Jourdan had seen a pelagic sea snake (*Pelamis platurus*) in the act of swallowing a small turtle. Unfortunately, while that reptile indeed has black and yellow stripes, they run longitudinally (lengthwise) and do not present the appearance of rings. A more likely suspect is the yellow sea snake (*Hydrophis spiralis*), known for its gold and black rings, with an average length of six feet and a record length of nine feet. Little is known of the reptile's habits, but it frequents deep water and is often seen basking on the surface.

Sources: Heuvelmans, *In the Wake of the Sea Serpents*; U.S. Department of the Navy, *Poisonous Snakes of the World*. New York: Dover Publications, 1991.

Isnachi   An unknown primate reported from Peru, the Isnachi is described as a large MONKEY, roughly twice the size of the common spider monkey (*Ateles paniscus*). Its 4-foot height rivals the African CHIMPANZEE, witnesses describing a barrel-chested creature with arms thicker than those of most men and thighs of nearly human size. Covered with short black hair, the Isnachi has a thick, short tail about six inches long. Its exposed skin is black, the face extended in a snout with large teeth resembling a mandrill's. For all its fearsome appearance, Peruvian natives describe the Isnachi as a vegetarian that prefers tender shoots from the chonta palm (*Euterpe precatoria*). When seen, the Isnachi is usually alone, but pairs have been sighted on infrequent occasions, and whole troops of the creatures are described in a handful of reports.

The Isnachi's is a mountain dweller, living at altitudes between 500 and 1,500 meters (1,625 to 4,900 feet). It has been reported from mountain ranges all over Peru, including the Cerros de Canchahuaya (Loreto Province), Cerros de Orellana (Loreto and San Martin Provinces), Cordillera de Bagua (Amazonas Province), Cordillera de Yanachaga (Cerro de Pasco Province), Cordillera Sira (Ucayali Province), Cordillera Urubamba (Cuzco Province)Cordillera Vilcamba (Cuzco Province), and from mountains lining Peru's borders with Brazil and Ecuador. Researcher Peter Hocking failed to sight the Isnachi during a July 1992 expedition, but native witnesses confirmed the creature's existence in the Yanachaga Mountains of Pasco Province. While most researchers acknowledge the possibility of new monkey species living in South America—several have been discovered since the early 1990s—some critics maintain that Isnachi witnesses have misidentified the native spectacled bear (*Tremarctos ornatus*). While it is true that the bear sometimes climbs trees in search of fruit, the prominent white rings around its eyes have never been described on the Isnachi.

Sources: Hocking, "Large Peruvian animals unknown to zoology"; Hocking, "Further investigations into unknown Peruvian mammals"; Karl Shuker, "Menagerie of mystery." *Strange Magazine* 17 (Summer 1996): 22; Shuker, "Puzzling monkeys."

Issie   This Japanese LAKE MONSTER, reported from Lake Ikeda in Kyushu's Kagoshima Prefecture, is named in imitation of Scotland's famous "NESSIE." Lake Ikeda is a drowned volcano, home to a thriving population of EELS which many Japanese consider a prized delicacy. They may also feed the creature witnesses describe as ranging from 16 to 90 feet long, dark in color, typically displaying two 12-inch humps above the water's surface. A spate of sightings in 1978 climaxed on 16 December, when investigator Tokiashi Matsubara spied the creature through a 50-power telescope and snapped a series of photographs. Analysts reported that the photos depicted an unknown object roughly 30 meters (98 feet) long. Tourist authorities from nearby Isubuki awarded Tokiashi a prize of ¥100,000 ($1,000) for being the first to catch Issie on film, and Tokiashi went on to sight the creature four more times. Witness Hideaki Tomiyasu videotaped the creature for nine minutes, on 4 January 1991, then watched it submerge as a motorboat approached.

Sources: Chōno, "Issie of Japan's Lake Ikeda"; Kirk, *In the Domain of the Lake Monsters*; "Long, dark and humpsome." *Fortean Times*.

Itoshi   Residents of eastern Zambia describe this inhabitant of the Kafue River as a 50-foot CROCODILE with a man's head and fins like a FISH. Although apparently reptilian, the Itoshi does not match descriptions of the equally mysterious CHIPEKWE, said to inhabit the Kafue Flats.

Source: Edwin Smith and Andrew Dale, *The Ila-Speaking Peoples of Northern Rhodesia.* London: Macmillan, 1920.

Itsena *see* Koolookamba

Itzcuintlipotsotli

The Itzcuintlipotsotli ("hunchbacked dog") is an unclassified canid reported from south-central Mexico's Michoacán State through the mid-19th century. Witnesses described it as the size of a small dog, with a wolflike head, and small limp ears. The animal's forelegs were shorter than its hind legs, the color a mixture of black and brown with prominent white spots. The Itzcuintlipotsotli got its name from a fatty hump extending the full length of its back, from the short neck to the base of its tail. The last published report, in 1843, involved a dead specimen seen in a Guajimalco Valley town.

Source: Frances Calderón de la Barca, *Life in Mexico, during a Residence of Two Years in That Country.* London: Chapman and Hall, 1843.

Iu-Wun

The Iu-wun is an unclassified APE reported from Myanmar (Burma). BERNARD HEUVELMANS suggested that the creature may a relict mainland orangutan surviving from the Pleistocene era. Thus far, no specimen has been obtained.

Source: Heuvelmans, "Annotated checklist of apparently unknown animals with which cryptozoology is concerned."

Ives, Gordon Langley (n.d.)

In August 2002 a small press called Floating Island Publications announced the release of a 16-page chapbook titled *Conversations with Bigfoot.* The ad is so unusual that it deserves to be quoted in full.

> A lovely chapbook with a recorded conversation between Dr. Gordon Langley Ives, a Professor of Zoology at Portland University and "Priorian" as the creatures we call "BIGFOOT" call themselves. For anyone who has ever wondered whether the myth of Bigfoot is authentic, whether there are other mammals out there who are sentient beings like ourselves, this chapbook is an extraordinary interview. Bigfoot proves himself to be as wise as a Shaman and as knowing as the Dalai Llama. We are convinced of the authenticity of the tape and Dr. Ives' credibility. We submitted a copy of the tape to Dr. Spenser Grissom of the University of California Linguistic Studies Institute. Dr. Grissom is a widely recognized authority on voice prints and voice printing techniques. We quote his response: "Although the patterns and configurations are indisputably mammalian, it is impossible that they were produced by human vocal cords. It is my considered opion [*sic*], therefore, that you are dealing with a very clever HOAX or an astoundingly articulate bear." Dr. Grissom's wit neglects the obvious — that it is possible that the tape is authentic, that it is entirely conceivable that another variety of life could master our language. We leave it to our reader and posterity to decide.

That sound advice inspired an Internet search for further details, conducted on 11 May 2003, which revealed the following facts. There is no "Portland University" in the U.S., but the University of Portland may be found in Willamette, Oregon. Its website includes a search function, which revealed no faculty member named Ives in any department. The University of California has eight campuses, while 12 more bear the title of California State University. Floating Island's editors fail to identify the campus housing a Linguistic Studies Institute, and no such institution was revealed by Internet searches — except within the chapbook advertisement. An identical finding climaxed the search for

any reference to "Dr. Spenser Grissom." Floating Island's website offers no mailing address but links to the website of Valentine Publishing Group, a distributor for small press and self-published works based in Northridge, California. Based on those findings, it appears that *Conversations with Bigfoot* is indeed a hoax — and not a "very clever" one, at that.

Source: Internet advertisement for *Conversations with Bigfoot*, http://www.vpg.net/bigfoot.htm.

Ivory-Billed Woodpecker

The mystery surrounding this large (20-inch) woodpecker is not its physical existence, but rather its survival to the present day. Initially classified as *Campephilus principalis principalis* by Carl von Linné in 1758, the ivory-billed woodpecker received an alternate scientific name (*C. p. bairdii*) from John Cassin in 1863, based on specimens taken

The "extinct" ivory-billed woodpecker may still survive in Louisiana's bayou country.

from Cuba. A victim of man's depredations, the distinctive black-and-white, red-crested bird was declared extinct throughout the United States in the 1960s, while its Cuban subspecies officially passed from existence in 1990. Still, sightings continue in both countries, with most of the U.S. reports emerging from Louisiana. On 1 April 1999, zoology student David Kulivan sighted a pair of ivory-bills at close range in the Bayou State's 35,000-acre Pearl River Wildlife Management Area. A search was organized in January 2002, and while the hunters failed to glimpse their quarry, they heard and recorded what they believed were the woodpecker's distinctive rapping sounds. Six months later, ornithologists at Cornell University declared that the recorded sounds were in fact distant gunshots. In Cuba, at least five unsuccessful hunts for the ivory-bill were conducted between 1991 and 1999. Despite the failure of those expeditions, Cuban experts now believe a relict population may survive in the rugged Sierra Maestra mountains. Skeptics in the U.S. maintain that Kulivan and other witnesses have mistaken a pileated woodpecker (*Dryocopus pileatus*) for the extinct ivory-bill.

Sources: "A woodpecker's revenge." *New York Times* (11 June 2002); Karl Shuker, "Alien zoo." *Fortean Times* 157 (May 2002): 21; Eric Pianin, "Searching the bayous for an avian treasure." *Washington Post* (21 January 2002); "Sounds were gunshots, not rare woodpecker." Associated Press (10 June 2002); Rex Springston, "No proof yet that ivory-bill still lives." *Richmond* (VA) *Times-Dispatch* (21 February 2002).

Izzard, Ralph William Burdick (1910–92)   British adventurer and journalist Ralph Izzard attended Cambridge University from 1928 to 1931, there becoming friends with classmates W.M. (GERALD) RUSSELL and IVAN SANDERSON. Upon graduation, he joined the staff of London's *Daily Mail* as a foreign correspondent serving in Germany and Czechoslovakia. At the onset of World War II, Izzard joined the Royald Navy and qualified as a gunner, but old friend Ian Fleming (author of the James Bond novels) recruited him for intelligence work and Izzard was subsequently honored with an OBE for his service, including in a commando raid at Walcheren, Holland. At war's end he returned to the *Daily Mail*, as foreign correspondent in New Delhi. There, in 1946-47, he collected reports of the BURU, a 20-foot reptile said to inhabit certain remote valleys along India's northeastern frontier. In 1948, the *Daily Mail* financed a Buru-hunting expedition led by Izzard and zoologist Charles Stonor, which collected many eyewitness reports of the creatures but failed to retrieve a specimen. Izzard's report of that effort, *The Hunt for the Buru*, was published in 1951.

By the time that book went to press, Izzard was busy ducking bullets as a war correspondent in Korea. With the ceasefire, in 1953, he returned to India and covered the first British attempt to scale Mount Everest. That exercise, in turn, exposed him to reports of the YETI or ABOMINABLE SNOWMAN and prompted another *Daily Mail* expedition in 1954. That effort, led by Izzard and Gerald Russell, was described by Ivan Sanderson as "a curious outfit." Although it was the first Yeti hunt to include experienced zoologists (Stonor among them), the team was still directed by mountaineers who largely ignored Russell's tracking suggestions and focused their search on high-altitude snowfields unlikely to support large mammals. Izzard later complained that a climbing party in such terrain "is as conspicuous as a line of black beetles on a white tablecloth," but the group still found Yeti tracks in four widely separated locations, along with suspect hair and fecal samples. Izzard emerged from the campaign to write *The Abominable Snowman Adventure* (1955), and for the rest of his life remained convinced that there was "vastly more evidence to prove that [Yeti] does exist, than there is to prove that he does not."

Izzard met Texas millionaire and avid cryptozoologist TOM SLICK in the mid-1950s, and while he regarded Slick as "a bit of a showman, anxious to promote a big American prestige success," he still agreed to serve as a consultant on Slick's Yeti-hunting expeditions during 1957-59. In that capacity, despite his lack of formal scientific training, Izzard examined feces (judging its depositor to be "a hungry wolf") and supposed Yeti footprints (disputing analyst Adolph Schultz's suggestion that the Yeti was a new species of giant panda). Izzard never lost his enthusiasm for Eastern mysteries and cryptids, frequently reminding his acquaintances that "you will find information in the strangest places." He died on 2 December 1992, at age 82.

Sources: Coleman, *Tom Slick and the Search for the Yeti*; Izzard, *The Abominable Snowman Adventure*; Izzard, *The Hunt for the Buru*; Ralph Izzard, "The Snowman may be in for a shock." *Daily Mail* (29 September 1958); Sanderson, *Abominable Snowmen*; Tom Stacey, "One of Fleet Street's finest." *Daily Mail* (8 December 1992).

——— J ———

Jackal (Horned)   A legendary canid reported from Sri Lanka, the horned jackal (or *narric comboo*) is described in folklore as the leader of a pack, distinguished by a small horn on top of its skull. No dogs known to science have horns, including the golden jackals (*Canis aureus*) native to Sri Lanka, yet a sketch prepared by J. Emerson Tennent in 1861 depicts a jackal's skull with a small bony horn at the rear. Tennent's model was preserved for years as Specimen No. 4362A at London's Museum of the College of Surgeons, but it was ultimately lost. Singhalese tribesmen believed that the horn brought good luck, illustrated by the following example from Tennent:

> A gentleman connected with the Supreme Court of Colombo has repeated to me a circumstance, within his own knowledge, of a plaintiff who, after numerous defeats, eventually succeeded against

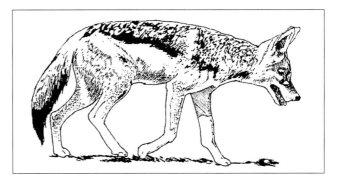

Karl Shuker suggests that horned jackals are simply aberrant members of a known species.

his opponent by the timely acquisition of this invaluable charm. Before the final hearing of the cause, the mysterious horn was duly exhibited to his friends; and the consequence was, that the adverse witnesses, appalled by the belief that no one could possibly give judgment against a person so endowed, suddenly modified their previous evidence, and secured an unforeseen victory for the happy owner of the narric-comboo!

Superstition aside, KARL SHUKER suggests that the occasional presence of a bony growth on individual jackal skulls may result from a simple deformity or from a kind of genetic mutation.

Sources: Shuker, *From Flying Toads to Snakes with Wings*; J. Emerson Tennent, *Sketches of the Natural History of Ceylon*. London: Longman, Green, Longman and Roberts, 1861.

Jacko   This nickname was applied to a creature resembling a GORILLA, supposedly captured in British Columbia in 1884. The initial press report has been widely published in BIGFOOT literature, but many authors sadly ignored the follow-up stories, which prove the incident to be a HOAX. The original item appeared in the Victoria (B.C.) *Daily Colonist* on 4 July 1884. It read:

WHAT IS IT?
A Strange Creature Captured Above Yale
A British Columbia Gorilla

YALE, B.C., July 3rd, 1882 [*sic*] — In the immediate vicinity of No. 4 tunnel, situated some twenty miles above this village, are bluffs of rock which have hitherto been unsurmountable, but on Monday morning last were successfully scaled by Mr. Onderdonk's employees on the regular train from Lytton. Assisted by Mr. Costerton, the British Columbia Express Company's messenger, and a number of gentlemen from Lytton and points east of that place who, after considerable trouble and perilous climbing, succeeded in capturing a creature which may truly be called half man and half beast. "Jacko" as the creature has been called by his capturers, is something of the gorilla type standing four feet seven inches in height and weighing 127 pounds. He has long, black, strong hair and resembles a human being with one exception, his entire body, excepting his hands (or paws) and feet are covered with glossy hair about an inch long. His fore arm is much longer than a man's fore arm, and he possesses extraordinary strength, as he will take hold of a stick and break it by wrenching or twisting it, which no man living could break in the same way.

Since his capture he is very reticent, only occasionally uttering a noise which is half bark and half growl. He is, however, becoming daily more attached to his keeper, Mr. George Tilbury, of this place, who proposes shortly starting for London, England, to exhibit him. His favorite food so far is berries, and he drinks fresh milk with evident relish. By advice of Dr. Hannington raw meats have been withheld from Jacko, as the doctor thinks it would have a tendency to make him savage. The mode of his capture was as follows:

Ned Austin, the engineer, on coming in sight of the bluff at the eastern end of the No. 4 tunnel saw what he supposed to be a man lying asleep in close proximity to the track, and as quick as thought he blew the signal to apply the brakes. The brakes were instantly applied, and in a few seconds the train was brought to a standstill. At this moment the supposed man sprang up, and uttering a sharp quick bark began to climb the steep bluff. Conductor R.J. Craig and Express Messenger Costerton, followed by the baggageman and brakemen, jumped from the train and knowing they were some twenty minutes ahead of time immediately gave chase. After five minutes of perilous climbing the then supposed demented Indian was corralled on a projecting shelf of rock where he could neither ascend nor descend. The query now was how to capture him

alive, which was quickly decided by Mr. Craig, who crawled on his hands and knees until he was about forty feet above the creature. Taking a small piece of loose rock he let it fall and it had the desired effect of rendering poor Jacko incapable of resistance for a time at least. The bell rope was then brought up and Jacko was now lowered to terra firma. After firmly binding him and placing him in the baggage car "off brakes" was sounded and the train started for Yale. At the station a large crowd who had heard of the capture by telephone from Spuzzum Flat were assembled, each one anxious to have the first look at the monstrosity, but they were disappointed, as Jacko had been taken off at the machine shops and placed in charge of his present keeper.

The question naturally arises, how came the creature where it was first seen by Mr. Austin? From bruises about its head and body, and apparent soreness since its capture, it is supposed that Jacko ventured too near the edge of the bluff, slipped, fell and lay where found until the sound of the rushing train aroused him. Mr. Thos. White and Mr. Gouin, C.E., as well as Mr. Major, who kept a small store about half a mile west of the tunnel during the past two years, have mentioned having seen a curious creature at different points between Camps 13 and 17, but no attention was paid to their remarks as people came to the conclusion that they had either seen a bear or stray Indian dog. Who can unravel the mystery that now surrounds Jacko! Does he belong to a species hitherto unknown in this part of the continent, or is he really what the train men first thought he was, a crazy Indian!

Another paper, the *Columbian*, reprinted the story on 5 July. Four days later, a rival newspaper, the *Mainland Guardian*, carried this item:

THE "WHAT IS IT"

Is the subject of conversation in town this evening. How the story originated, and by whom, it is hard for one to conjecture. Absurdity is written on the face of it. The fact of the matter is, that no such creature was caught, and how the "Colonist" was duped in such a manner and by such a story, is strange: and stranger still, when the Columbian reproduced it in that paper. The "train" of circumstances connected with the discovery of "Jacko" and the disposal of same was and still is, a mystery.

Embarrassed, the *Columbian*'s editors had what should have been the last word on Jacko, with this article of 12 July 1884.

THE WILD MAN — Last Tuesday it was reported that the wild man, said to have been captured at Yale, had been sent to this city and might be seen at the gaol. A rush of citizens instantly took place, and it is reported that not fewer than 200 impatiently begged admission into the skookum house. The only wild man visible was Mr. Moresby, governor of the gaol, who completely exhausted his patience answering enquiries from the sold visitors.

Ironically, even as the hoax was exposed, use of the term "SKOOKUM" (a Chinook Indian term originally meaning "evil god of the woods") prefigured another sensational piece of Bigfoot lore nearly 120 years later.

Sources: Coleman, *Bigfoot!*; Green, *Sasquatch: The Apes Among Us*.

Jago-Nini   The Jago-nini ("giant diver") is another of Africa's mysterious neo-DINOSAURS, described by witnesses as a huge reptilian creature inhabiting the swamps of Gabon, where it dines on manatees and occasional unlucky humans. Alfred ("Trader Horn") Smith provided the West's first glimpse of the Jago-nini in 1927, with publication of memoirs that described his African travels during the 1870s.

Aye, and behind the Cameroons there's things living we know nothing about. I could 'a' made books about many things. The

Jago-Nini they say is still in the swamps and rivers. Giant diver it means. Comes out of the water and devours people. Old men'll tell you what their grandfathers saw, but they still believe it's there. Same as the AMALI I've always taken it to be. I've seen the amali's footprints. About the size of a good frying pan in circumference and three claws instead o' five. There are some very big lakes behind the Cameroons. Used to be full of nice seal at one time. Manga they call it. But the Jago-Nini's wiped 'em almost out, the old natives say.

As ROY MACKAL notes, Smith erred in his application of the "manga" label, which in fact applied to manatees (*Trichechus senegalensis*) rather than seals. As for the Jago-nini, its identify and present status are unknown.

Sources: Heuvelmans, *On the Track of Unknown Animals*; Mackal, *A Living Dinosaur?*

Jaguar (Speckled)

This mystery CAT of Peru is also called the speckled TIGER and the *cunard din* (in the Wapishána dialect). Native hunters describe it as a mountain dweller, preferring altitudes around 500 meters (1,625 feet). Witnesses say the creature is equal in size to a normal jaguar (*Panthera onca*), but with a somewhat larger head. Where jaguars sport yellow pelage with prominent dark rosettes, this unknown cat is gray with solid black speckles. Researcher Peter Hocking made two Peruvian expeditions in 1992-93, seeking proof of the creature's existence, and while one hunter promised to send him the skin of a specimen killed in 1991, the pelt was somehow lost.

Sources: Hocking, "Large Peruvian mammals unknown to zoology"; Hocking, "Further investigation into unknown Peruvian mammals."

Jaguar (Striped)

Another unrecognized CAT reported from Peru by researcher Peter Hocking, the striped jaguar (or striped TIGER) apparently prowls both hilly terrain and lowland rain forest in search of its prey. Witnesses describe the animal as equal in size to a jaguar (*Panthera onca*), but tan in color with tigerlike stripes. Hocking collected only two reported sightings and judged the creature very rare, but in 1992 a Peruvian hunter furnished the skull of a cat killed near Puerto Bermudez (in Pasco Province). Hocking noted some unspecified "interesting differences" between that specimen and a known jaguar skull, whereupon he shipped the skull to paleontologist Steven Conkling, at the Natural History Museum of Los Angeles County. Conkling, in turn, reported to Hocking "that a number of anatomical features seem to distinguish the skull from jaguar skulls, and that the evidence warrants further careful study to determine if a new species is involved." Thus far, more than a decade later, no such designation has been registered.

Sources: Hocking, "Large Peruvian mammals unknown to zoology"; Hocking, "Further investigation into unknown Peruvian mammals."

Jaguar (White)

Throughout South America, aboriginal people report sightings of "ghost jaguars" described as white or grayish-white, so pale that the animal's trademark rosettes may only be discerned in certain lights. The skin of one such specimen, displayed to German naturalist J.R. Rengger in the 1820s, bore only faint markings on the flanks and underside against a pallid background. The hunters who killed the beast told Rengger that its claws were also white, apparently confirming KARL SHUKER'S suggestion that the "ghost jaguars" are albinos. A concentration of sightings in Paraguay further indicates the possibility of a small breeding population as yet undiscovered.

Source: Shuker, *Mystery Cats of the World.*

Jaguareté

Some confusion surrounds this unrecognized CAT, reported from Brazil and Guyana. Its name derives from *yaguarete* ("great beast"), and while that term is frequently used in Brazil to describe ordinary JAGUARS (*Panthera onca*), the Jaguareté is distinguished by its color and its fondness for prowling seashores, where it dines on FISH and TURTLE eggs. Naturalist Thomas Pennant published this description of the Jaguareté (also known as *cougar noire*) in 1781:

Head, back, sides, fore part of the legs, and the tail, covered with short and very glossy hairs of a dusky-color; sometimes spotted with black, but generally plain; upper lips white: at the corner of the mouth a black spot: long hairs above each eye, and long whiskers on the upper lip: lower lip, throat, belly, and the inside of the legs, whitish, or very pale ash-color: paws white: ears pointed. Grows to the size of a heifer of a year old: has vast strength in its limbs. Inhabits Brazil and Guiana: is a cruel and fierce beast; much dreaded by the Indians; but happily is a scarce species."

Scarce it remains, despite attempts to establish the Jaguareté's identity. Some researchers believe that eyewitness accounts refer to a melanistic jaguar. KARL SHUKER suggests a black-and-tan mutation, but no such specimens have been documented.

Sources: Thomas Pennant, *History of Quadrupeds.* London: B. White, 1781; Shuker, *Mystery Cats of the World.*

Jamberoo Tiger

An ALIEN BIG CAT reported from New South Wales, Australia, the so-called Jamberoo TIGER was actually described by witnesses as a jet-black felid the size of a mastiff. An article in the *Robertson Advocate*, dated 23 April 1909, reported that the beast was prowling the hills near Kiama, 12 miles north of Kangaroo Valley. The creature eluded hunters, and so passed into local history.

Source: Healy and Cropper, *Out of the Shadows.*

Jane Eliza sea serpent

On 2 January 1979, Captain Dalton and two officers aboard the *Jane Eliza* sighted a SEA SERPENT near Captain's Island, off the coast of Greenwich Point, Connecticut. Unfortunately, no detailed description of the creature has survived, but all three witnesses agreed that it was nothing known to them from long years of experience at sea.

Source: O'Neill, *The Great New England Sea Serpent.*

Japayi-Kishi *see* Adam-Dzhapais

Java sea serpent

In October 1906, passengers and crew aboard the steamer *Java* observed a SEA SERPENT in the Indian Ocean, 600 miles off the coast of Somalia. Ship's officer J. Vollewens (who had observed another unknown creature from the AMBON two years earlier) wrote this description in the *Java*'s log:

In 10° 7.5' N. latitude, 59° 23' E. longitude on 15 October 1906 seaman J.A. Spruijt, saw the head of a sea-monster raised some 6 feet out of the water, by his reckoning at 200 yards; it was shaped like a cayman, brown in color, with a smooth skin, and was followed directly by the beginning of a body of the same colour.

The animal remains unidentified, since CAIMANS are a kind of crocodilian restricted to the western hemisphere. BERNARD HEUVELMANS speculated that it might be a "marine saurian" of the same kind sighted by the German submarines *U-28* and *U-109* during World War I.

Source: Heuvelmans, *In the Wake of the Sea Serpents.*

Javan Eagle

In July 1997, members of a mountaineering team in East Java's Bromo Tengger Semeru National Park reported sighting a Javan eagle (*Spizaetus bartelsi*). (The same group also reportedly saw an "extinct" JAVAN TIGER.) Because the BIRD is officially extinct, Indonesia's Ministry of Forestry offered a reward

Though officially extinct, the Javan eagle is still occasionally seen by witnesses.

Do "extinct" tigers still survive on the island of Java?

of 3 million rupiahs ($356) for a photograph proving the eagle's survival. So far, the reward has not been collected.

Source: Karl Shuker, "Alien zoo." *Fortean Times* 106 (January 1998): 15.

Javan Rhinoceros   Ranked as one of the world's 12 most endangered species, the Javan RHINOCEROS (*Rhinoceros sondaicus*) once lived throughout Southeast Asia, but zoologists believed it was extinct outside of Java by the 1940s. That supposition was disproved in 1988, when Vietnamese hunters killed two specimens, whose remains were later identified by Dr. George Schaller of the New York Zoological Society. Schaller himself found rhinoceros tracks beside the Dong Nai River (75 miles northeast of Ho Chi Minh City), in February 1989, and estimated that 10-15 individuals might still survive in Vietnam. Hope had begun to fade a decade later, but conservationists were encouraged in May 1999, when a Javan rhino triggered an automatic camera in Cat Tien National Park, in Vietnam's central highlands. The resulting seven photographs proved beyond doubt that at least one member of the species still survived on the Asian mainland.

Source: Shuker, *The New Zoo*.

Javan Tiger   Yet another victim of mankind's depredation, the Javan TIGER (*Panthera tigris sondaica*) is one of those species presumably wiped from the Earth. Twelve living specimens were known in 1972, and with their deaths the subspecies became officially extinct. Authorities were startled, therefore, when a group of mountaineers allegedly sighted a tiger in July 1997, while hiking in East Java's Bromo Tengger Semeru National Park. (The same group also allegedly saw an "extinct" JAVAN EAGLE.) Spokesmen for the nation's Ministry of Forestry offered 3 million rupiahs ($356) for photos proving the tiger extant, but none have been produced so far. Indonesian researcher Didik Raharyono, involved in pursuit of Javan tigers since 1997, claims one personal sighting at Meru Betiri National Park and has collected hair samples formally identified by experts at the Indonesian Institute of Sciences as coming from a Javan tiger. An expedition mounted in October 2002 failed to locate the elusive CAT, but Ra-

haryono received tiger skin, teeth and whiskers from various locals and poachers, some of the items allegedly collected in 2002.

Source: "In search of the 'extinct' Javan tiger." *Jakarta Post* (30 October 2002); Karl Shuker, "Alien zoo." *Fortean Times* 106 (January 1998): 15; Karl Shuker, "Alien zoo." *Fortean Times* 168 (April 2003): 16.

Jeffreys Bay sea serpent   On 11 October 1912, four witnesses observed a SEA SERPENT from the beach at Jeffreys Bay, 60 miles south of Port Elizabeth, in South Africa's Cape Province. One of the observers, Robert Murray, was the 10-year-old son of Basutoland's financial secretary. Murray's mother penned the following account of the incident to her husband:

> On Friday last, Mr. Beckett, Mr. McKechnie and Mr. Eddie Nathan were fishing on the sandy beach near the Beach Hotel, Jeffreys Bay. Bobbie was with them. Suddenly they saw a black head in the waves, and Mr. McKechnie says he looked round to see where Bobbie was, as for a moment he thought it was he in the waves. Then the thing appeared again and they could see it was a sea-serpent 15 to 20 feet long, with a huge black and yellow head and enormous body. It was so close in they could see its eyes. Mr. Beckett tried to cast his line over it, but it cleared off as it saw him. The monster was rolling over and over in the waves and its big head was raised a full three feet above the surface. Bobbie was quite scared, and says that if Mr. Beckett had succeeded in catching the serpent he would have cleared for all he was worth for the hotel.

Long after the event, in 1960, Robert Murray claimed that his mother (not present on the beach) had greatly underestimated the animal's size. In fact, he said, it was 15-20 *yards* long, undulated vertically, and had reared its head "twice my own height or about 10 feet above the water." Furthermore, he declared:

> Against the yellow of its mouth when open, I could plainly see its black forked tongue darting in and out in the manner of any land serpent, of which I had seen many before that time. The body of the sea-serpent was about the thickness of a fully grown man but tapered towards the head to a neck of about eight inches in diameter.

BERNARD HEUVELMANS correctly noted that reptiles are incapable of vertical undulations, and he suggested that Murray's memory was incorrect on that point, as well as the creature's overall size. Heuvelmans further questioned whether any sane fisherman would cast his line at an animal 45-60 feet long, concluding that the witnesses had seen a large PYTHON swimming in the surf.

Source: Heuvelmans, *In the Wake of the Sea Serpents*.

Jehu Sands carcass   In April 1921, British newspapers reported the stranding of an unknown sea creature at Jehu Sands, 10-12 miles from Bombay, India. Unlike most GLOBSTERS washed ashore around the world, however, this beast survived on land for 48 hours, emitting pitiful cries until it finally expired. As described in print, the animal was 25 feet long and had a mouth 3 feet deep, lined with sharp teeth. Its skin was black, ribs clearly visible beneath. Its head resembled a human's, while the eyes were likened to those of an elephant. BERNARD HEUVELMANS and BEN ROESCH suggest that the creature was a short-finned pilot whale (*Globicephala macrorhynchus*), a cetacean species well known for beaching itself with fatal results. One drawback to that theory is its size, since *G. macrorhynchus* has a maximum recorded length of 17 feet 6 inches.

Sources: Heuvelmans, *In the Wake of the Sea Serpents*; Roesch, "A review of alleged sea serpent carcasses worldwide (Part Four —1907-1924)."

Jellyfish (Giant)   Jellyfish are found in a bewildering array of shapes, sizes and colors. One of the largest known to science, *Stomolophus nomurai*, was discovered in 1920, in the sea of Japan. Its bell may reach a width of 35 inches, with 15-foot tentacles, for an overall weight of 330 pounds. A jelly of similar size, *Chrysora achylos*, eluded discovery until 1997, despite its dark purple bell (three feet across) and 20-foot pink tentacles. Larger still is the lion's mane jellyfish (*Cyanea capillata*): a specimen recorded from Massachusetts Bay in 1865 had a bell seven feet in diameter, and trailing from it were 120-foot tentacles, for a tentacle spread of 247 feet! It would be comforting to think that *Cyanea* marks the limit of a drifting jelly's size, but that does not appear to be the case.

In the mid-1950s, diver Eric Russell was stalking a shark in the South Pacific, when the fish ducked into an underwater chasm. Resting on the lip of the cliff, Russell watched the shark swimming below him, then saw a huge dull-brown shape rising from the darkness further down. Russell described the creature as devoid of eyes and tentacles, but it was far from helpless. At first contact with the pulsing predator, the shark lapsed into convulsions and was drawn without resistance into the larger animal's gelatinous body. Apparently satisfied with its meal, the creature sank once more and vanished in the shadows.

In November 1969, while diving in the Atlantic Ocean about 14 miles southwest of Bermuda, skin divers Pat Boatwright and Richard Winer observed a huge jellyfish at 100-150 feet below the surface. They later estimated that the creature's pink-and-purple bell measured 50 to 100 feet in diameter. As it began to rise in their direction, Boatwright and Winer fled with all possible speed.

In January 1973, while sailing from Australia to the Fiji Islands, the 1,483-ton *Kuranda* met turbulent seas and was tossed by tumultuous waves. At one point, after the ship's bow was briefly submerged, it surfaced with a huge jellyfish draped across the deck, flailing monstrous tentacles in all directions. Captain Langley Smith described the pulsing mass as two feet deep, with tentacles at least 200 feet long; he estimated that the animal weighed 20 tons or more. One sailor snared by the tentacles suffered burns resembling those from hot steam, and he subsequently died. Unable to dislodge the monster, the *Kuranda* was at risk of floundering until its radio SOS brought help from a deep-sea salvage tug, the *Hercules*. Upon reaching the scene, crewmen aboard the *Hercules* sprayed the jelly with steam from two high-pressure hoses and thus dislodged it in time to save the *Kuranda*. Fragments of the creature were later analyzed in Sydney, where ichthyologists tentatively identified them as remains of *Cyanea*.

A final troubling case was reported from France in the late 1980s. Fisherman Henri Baiselle told authorities that he was swimming with his wife and two children in the Bay of Biscay, off Bordeaux, when a jellyfish the size of an automobile attacked and devoured the rest of his family. Police were skeptical, to say the least, and Baiselle was detained on murder charges until he passed a polygraph test.

Sources: "Giant jellyfish found off Japan." *The Australian* (28 November 2002); "Monster jellyfish." *Fortean Times* 169 (May 2003): 11; Karl Shuker, "Alien zoo." *Fortean Times* 112 (July 1998): 16; Shuker, "Alien zoo." *Fortean Times* 150 (October 2001): 21; Shuker, *From Flying Toads to Snakes with Wings*; Shuker, "Menagerie of mystery." *Strange Magazine* 20 (December 1998): 42; Sweeney, *Sea Monsters*.

Jersey Devil   It is sometimes difficult to say where fact and fiction meet in respect to this cryptid reported from southern New Jersey. The Jersey Devil's origins seem clearly mythical, yet more than 2,000 witnesses have claimed sightings of the creature over the past 270 years. In the standard legend, a woman named Leeds (or Shrouds) was cursed during pregnancy for practicing witchcraft (or insulting a minister) at Leeds Point (or Burlington, or Estellville). Her child was born deformed, complete with wings, cloven hooves and a tail, flapping off moments later to haunt the desolate New Jersey Pinelands. Witnesses to a local "flying monster" in the early 19th century included U.S. naval hero Stephen Decatur and Joseph Bonaparte, brother of Emperor Napoleon. An unknown MYSTERY MAULER slaughtered New Jersey livestock in the winter of 1840-41, and "devil" sightings continued from 1859 through 1899.

In 1903, folklorist Charles Skinner predicted that Jersey Devil encounters would cease in the 20th century, but a new rash of sightings proved him wrong in January 1909. Far from disappearing, the winged creature had expanded its range to include appearances in Delaware and Pennsylvania. Witnesses included policemen in Burlington and Camden, and the Rev. John Pursell

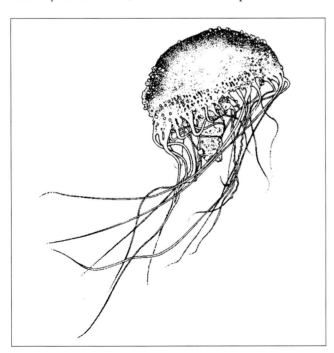

Reports of giant jellyfish have been logged since the 1950s.

This early sketch of the Jersey Devil depicts a strange composite creature.

of Pemberton. Nelson Evans, in Gloucester City, described the creature he saw in his yard one frigid January morning.

> It was about three feet and a half high, with a head like a collie dog and a face like a horse. It had a long neck, wings about two feet long, and its back legs were like those of a crane, and it had horse's hooves. It walked on its back legs and held up two short front legs with paws on them. It didn't use the front legs at all while we were watching...I managed to open the window and say, "Shoo," and it turned around and barked at me, and flew away.

The Jersey Devil subsequently vanished for 27 years, then resurfaced with a report of a "flying LION" seen at West Orange in 1926. One year later, a Salem taxi driver reported his encounter with an apelike creature resembling BIGFOOT. Confusion reigned thereafter, with hairy HOMINID reports in the 1930s and sightings of a "bloody-faced monster" at Gibbstown, in 1951. Authorities investigated various peculiar footprints, then declared the creature a HOAX. Phillip Smith disagreed, after he met the Jersey Devil walking down a Salem street in 1953. Four years later, in October 1957, conservation workers found a birdlike creature's skeletal remains in the Pine Barrens, but it proved to be a fake contrived for Halloween. Large birdlike tracks were found at Lake Atsion in 1960, and several witnesses sighted a creature resembling

a huge BIRD the following year. Slaughter of poultry and domestic animals resumed in Burlington County during 1966, while witnesses at Morristown encountered a "faceless, scaly creature with black hair." Lake Atsion produced more sightings in 1981 and 1987, the latter including a slaughtered dog and "strange tracks" around the carcass.

After another hiatus, sightings resumed in late 1995. Witness Sue Dupre was driving near Pompton Lake (northwest of Paterson) when she saw "a hopping animal with an ARMADILLO face" cross the highway in front of her car. Soon afterward, in mid-December, park ranger John Irwin met a strange creature in Wharton State Forest. Irwin's supervisor, Peter Gentile, filed this melodramatic report of the incident with the Park Ranger's Office:

> John drove along the narrow and lonely road that curved through the bleak darkness of the forest. He knew he was half-way there when he saw the Mullica River running next to him. But up ahead, in the shadows cast by his headlights, he noticed a large, dark figure emerge from the woods and move into the roadway. John, an experienced park service seasonal patrolman, thought the figure was a deer and slowed to let it cross. But as he got closer...the creature defiantly blocked the roadway. John had to stop his car to avoid hitting it. "This was like no deer I've ever seen," reported John. "It stood upright like a human, over six feet tall, and it had black fur that looked wet and matted. I didn't see any forelegs, either."
>
> John sat in his car only a few feet away from the monster. His initial shock soon turned to fear when the creature turned its deer-like head and stared through the windshield. But instead of gazing into the bright yellow glow of a deer's eyes, John found himself the subject of a deep glare from two piercing red eyes. The monster stood and glared for a few eternal minutes, as if it were contemplating some hellish decision. Then, suddenly, it turned and continued across the road, walking upright like a human.

Theories abound in the Jersey Devil's case. IVAN SANDERSON blamed the 1909 sightings on a scheme meant to depress local real estate values, and claimed he had found a set of fake feet used to make "devil" footprints in the snow. Later sightings have been variously explained as hoaxes, cases of mistaken identity, and sightings of various cryptids including Bigfoot, giant birds, and a creature resembling West Virginia's MOTHMAN.

Sources: Coleman, "Jersey Devil walks again"; Coleman, *Mysterious America*; Fort, *The Books of Charles Fort*; McCloy and Miller, *Phantom of the Pines*; Pontolillo, "An interpretation of the Jersey Devil."

Jervis Bay tracks Australian cryptozoologist REX GILROY reports that a set of "monster" tracks were found in 1942 at Jervis Bay, between Huskisson and Lambs Point on the coast of New South Wales. As described by Gilroy, the "finlike" prints were two feet wide and marked a trail where some unknown creature had left the surf, tramped across the sand, and then returned to the sea. In the absence of documentation, researcher Malcolm Smith and others question the report's validity.

Sources: Gilroy, "Australia's marine colossus"; Smith, *Bunyips & Bigfoots*.

Jetete Natives of the Chilean Andes report the existence of an unclassified flamingo species dwelling in the region, which they call Jetete. When questioned by ornithologists, they draw a clear distinction between the Jetete and Chile's three known flamingo species: the Chilean flamingo or *guaichete* (*Phoenicopteras chilensis*); the Andean flamingo or *tococo* (*P. andinus*); and James's flamingo or *chururo* (*P. jamesi*). Thus far, researchers have failed to observe the Jetete or obtain a specimen.

Source: Shuker, *The Lost Ark*.

Chilean witnesses describe the Jetete as a flamingo of unknown species.

Jezioro Zegrzynskie, Poland   In 1982, bathers on the shore of this man-made lake (18 miles north of Warsaw) saw a strange LAKE MONSTER rise briefly from the depths. They described it as 20 feet long, with a black head and long ears resembling a RABBIT'S. Ulric Magin suggested the creature might be a giant CATFISH, its barbels mistaken for ears, but the animal remains unidentified, and there have been no further reports to date.

Sources: Magin, "A brief survey of lake monsters of continental Europe"; Shuker, *From Flying Toads to Snakes with Wings*.

Jez-Tyrmak   This large unknown HOMINID reportedly dwells in Tibet, where residents distinguish it from the smaller YETI. Researcher IVAN SANDERSON reported that the creature's name translates as "the mountain one that scrambles using its hands," but Tibetans commonly interpret Jez-tyrmak as meaning "copper nails"—a reference to the color of the beast's fingernails. Aside from that distinctive feature (also found in GORILLAS and other primates whose nails are stained with juice from fruit or berries), the Jez-tyrmak is said to be covered in long black or gray hair. Variant names reported for the creature include Jelmoguz-jez-tyrmak, Dzezh-tyrmak and Zez tyrmak.

Source: Sanderson, *Abominable Snowmen*.

Jhoor   This unclassified 20-foot lizard of Bangladesh and northeastern India is said to enjoy a symbiotic relationship with the estuarine CROCODILE (*Crocodylus porosus*). Sightings are reported from India's Gir National Park, on the Katihar Peninsula (Gujarat State), and from near Sundarbans, Bangladesh.

Source: Fox, "The mysterious 'Jhoor.'"

Jigme Dorji National Park, Bhutan   An unnamed lake within this Bhutanese preserve is reportedly the home of an unidentified LAKE MONSTER. Witnesses include no less a personage than former king Jigme Dorji Wangchuck, who saw a large white creature swimming rapidly beneath the lake's surface, sometime in the late 1950s.

Source: Desmond Doig, "Bhutan." *National Geographic* 120 (September 1961): 384, 391-392.

Jimbra/Jingra   This unclassified primate, reported from the neighborhood of Lake Grace in Western Australia, is sometimes confused with the JINGARA of New South Wales and Queensland, on the far side of the continent. The creatures may be related, in fact, but links are impossible to prove while both remain unidentified. Aborigines in Western Australia report sightings of both male and female Jimbra, claiming that the short, dark APES are frequently aggressive and prone to attacking lone humans.

Source: Smith, *Bunyips & Bigfoots*.

Jingara   Confusion surrounds the identity of this unclassified Australian primate, reported from Queensland and New South Wales. A similarity in spelling prompts some authors to equate it with the Jingra or JIMBRA, an apelike creature of similar size allegedly found on the far side of the continent, in Western Australia. Further confusion is added by application of various alternate names for the Jingara, including Janjurrie, Jingera and Jongari. If this were not troublesome enough, the names Jingara and Jingera are also applied by aborigines to Egan Peak, a mountain in New South Wales where the much larger Yahoo or YOWIE has sometimes been sighted.

Semantic chaos notwithstanding, witnesses make clear distinctions between the YOWIE (man-sized or larger) and the Jingara, typically described as three feet tall and covered in dark hair, with a protruding muzzle like a bear's. In December 1999, witness Alan Bucholz saw one of the creatures near Gayndah, Queensland, and initially mistook it for a WALLABY until he noticed that it had no tail.

Sources: "Bear-like creature sighted." *Fortean Times*; Joyner, *The Hairy Man of South Eastern Australia*; Healy and Cropper, *Out of the Shadows*; Smith, *Bunyips & Bigfoots*; Smith, "Update on the Jongari."

Jogung   A confusion of names compounds the difficulty in pursuing an unclassified Australian APE or HOMINID. The Jogung is described as resembling an oversized GORILLA, 7 to 10 feet tall, covered with black or dark-brown hair. Some witnesses note the large genitals of male specimens and/or the pendulous breasts of females. The bipedal creature makes guttural sounds and emits a rank odor reminiscent of some reports involving BIGFOOT and the Florida SKUNK APE. Aborigines claim that the Jogung sometimes carries a club, which it uses to kill humans. The creature's tracks reveal splayed toes and measure up to 24 inches in length.

The Jogung enjoys a wide range, with reports on file from coast to coast, but here the confusion of names makes it difficult (if not impossible) to chart the creature's habitat. Some authors confuse it with Western Australia's much smaller JIMBRA or Jingra, while others mistake it for the 3-foot JINGARA of New South Wales and

Queensland. Other local names reported for the Jogung (perhaps erroneously) include Barmi birgoo and Illankanpanka (in Queensland); Pankalanka (Northern Territory), Kraitbull, Tjangara and Wolumbin (South Australia); and Lo-an (in Victoria). Further compounding the problem, the term Lo-an (or Lowan) is also used in Victoria to describe the Mallee fowl (*Leipoa ocellata*), a large BIRD known for its echoing call.

No attacks on humans by the Jogung have been logged in modern times, but occasional sightings continue. Prospectors Andy Hoad and Brett Taylor sighted a pair of the creatures near Lake Ballard, Western Australia in 1960, describing the male as nine-feet tall, while its female companion measured about seven feet. Retreating to their hut, the men found another apelike creature — this one 10 feet tall — in the process of wrecking the structure. Ten years later, in June 1970, mountaineers Ron Bartlett and Frank Sinclair met an 8-foot, foul-smelling Jogung at their camp near Mount Kosciusko, New South Wales. Brothers Vince and Trevor Collins were driving through the Great Sandy Desert of Western Australia, in 1977, when they saw a black gorilla leap from roadside shrubbery, brandishing a tree limb. Twelve years later, two carloads of off-road enthusiasts reported sighting a 13-foot club-wielding giant along Cooper Creek, between Birdsville and Maree, South Australia.

Sources: Gilroy, "Giants of the Dreamtime"; Gilroy, *Mysterious Australia*; Gilroy, "Mystery lions in the Blue Mountains."

Johan Hjort sea serpent   In 1960, the Norwegian oceanographic vessel *Johan Hjort* was charting a section of the Arctic Ocean, 60 miles north of Nordkapp, when crew members sighted a SEA SERPENT 500 to 600 yards from the ship. Biologist Finn Devold, from the Bergen Institute of Marine Research, described the incident.

> It looked like something standing up from the sea about a yard above the surface. I pointed at it and told Mr. Sune [the captain]; "What is that?" And when he discovered it he told the wheelman to turn the ship against it, and we moved against this obstacle about 200 metres and it sank down in the sea again, and when we arrived at the place we could see nothing.

> We were discussing what this was and it had a thickness about 20 centimetres [8 inches] I believe, and the height above the sea was about one yard. And it couldn't be a seal because I have seen so many seals before that time, and a seal has a shape like a bottle of champagne or something like that, and this was an even thickness from the head down to the sea board. I have never been sure of what we saw but it looks like a living creature…[I]t might be a piece of wood, but if it was we should have discovered it later.

Source: Heuvelmans, *In the Wake of the Sea Serpents.*

John H. Cordts sea serpent   On 31 August 1886, while navigating New York's Hudson River, Captain Conkling of the *John H. Cordts* recorded his sighting of a SEA SERPENT, reporting that "the head stood right up straight for a second or two, as if the animal wanted to breathe, then it sunk out of sight." Crewmen aboard the *LOTTA* saw a similar creature in the same vicinity, two days later.

Source: O'Neill, *The Great New England Sea Serpent.*

Jølstravatnet, Norway   This lake, in Norway's Sogn on Fjordane County, was once reputedly the home of a large LAKE MONSTER. According to legend the beast was dispatched in ancient times, when a wedding party sailing on the lake hung a silver ornament from the boat's railing to attract the creature. When the animal appeared, one of the crewmen struck it with a sword, severing its head.

Sources: Skjelsvik, "Norwegian lake and sea monsters"; Erik Knatterud, "Sea serpents in Norwegian lakes." http://www.mjoesormen.no.

Jucamari *see* **Ucumar**

Julyntha sea serpent   On 7 July 1960, passengers and crew aboard the charter boat *Julyntha* watched an unknown 70-foot creature swimming in the North Atlantic off Cape Ann, Massachusetts. Passenger Richard Laupot told a reporter for the *Gloucester Daily Times* that the animal "looked just like a SEA SERPENT… slithering along on the top of the water. It was grayish with dark rays and black sails on the top of it. It had a head like a gigantic SNAKE. We circled it for about 10 or 15 minutes." Laupot's wife told the paper, "The minute I saw it I knew exactly what it was…a sea serpent….It had these sails on top of it with yellow dots. Its head was like a dinosaur." Captain Ellis Hodgkins, commanding the *Julyntha*, did not share that certainty. "I have no idea what it was," he confessed. "I have never seen anything like it before in my life….It looked like a CAMEL half out of the water."

Source: O'Neill, *The Great New England Sea Serpent.*

Jumar   This unidentified ungulate, reported from Italy and southern France in the 16th and 17th centuries, is presumably extinct today. The creature apparently derived its name from the French term *jument* ("mare"), though various witnesses — including Neapolitan physicist Giambattista della Porta — described it as an impossible hybrid of bull and donkey. Georges, comte de Buffon, witnessed the dissection of two Jumar specimens in 1766 and pronounced them both small donkeys (*Equus asinus*). In the absence of physical remains, it is now impossible to identify the curious creature.

Sources: Georges, comte de Buffon, "De la dégénération des animaux," in *Œuvres complètes de Buffon.* Paris: Rapet, 1817-18; Giambattista della Porta, *Natural Magick.* London: T. Young and S. Speed, 1658.

Jungli-Admi *see* **Yeti**

Junjadee/Junjuddi   An unclassified primate or small HOMINID of Australia, the Junjadee adds further confusion to the subject of APES and/or "apemen" Down Under. As with Australia's other mystery primates, the creature is known by a bewildering variety of names across the continent: Bitarr, Brown Jack and Burgingin (in the Northern Territory); Dinderi (in Queensland); Net-net, Nimbunj and Nyol (in Victoria); Waaki, Winambuu and Yuuri (in New South Wales). Its general description — three to four feet tall, bipedal, covered with dark hair — suggests a creature similar to the JINGARA, though the Junjadee lacks the Jingara's pointed snout. Some Jingara footprints resemble those of a human child, while others have only three toes.

Aborigines sometimes attribute magic powers to the Junjadee, and claim that they protect lost children in the wild. They are less kindly toward adults, as Kempsey resident George Gray discovered in 1968, while camping out near Kookaburra, New South Wales. Gray woke to find a 4-foot hairy "dwarf" trying to drag him from his shelter. Despite its short stature and scrawny arms, the creature was strong enough to shake Gray violently, while its bristly gray hair and slick flesh prevented Gray from gaining a hold on his adversary. After several moments, the creature released Gray and fled, leaving Gray with a vivid impression of its apelike, copper-colored face. A similar tale of campers attacked in their sleep was related by Junjadee victim Nathan Moilan from the Great Dividing Range, west of Tully, Queensland.

Sources: Healy and Cropper, *Out of the Shadows*; Smith, *Bunyips & Bigfoots*.

Jurasek, Todd (n.d.)   American cryptozoologist Todd Jurasek is well known in Texas and Louisiana, where he was a charter member of the GULF COAST BIGFOOT RESEARCH ORGANIZATION (founded in February 1997) and he has participated in hunts for the elusive IVORY-BILLED WOODPECKER. In June 2002, Jurasek was a featured speaker at the GCBRO's conference in Conroe, Texas, where he presented a lecture on cryptic reptiles around the world. The following year, in July 2001, he traveled to Australia as part of a U.S. team collaborating with REX GILROY to seek evidence of the YOWIE'S existence.

Sources: Deseree Martinez, "The Believers." *Conroe* (TX) *Bulletin* (1 July 2002); Karl Shuker, "Alien zoo." *Fortean Times* 150 (October 2001): 20; "Cryptokeeper" website. http://www.cryptokeeper.com/ivory-search.htm; "More about GCBRO." http://www.gcbro.com/about.htm.

—— K ——

Kadimakara/Kadimurka   Aborigines apply these names to a supposed giant lizard with a horn on its forehead, said to inhabit marshes around Lake Eyre, South Australia. No modern sightings are on record, and some accounts suggest that the creature has been extinct since the Dreamtime (a mythic period comparable to the Biblical Eden). While native traditions describe the Kadimakara as reptilian, the most likely candidate is *Diprotodon optatum*, a 10-foot marsupial presumed extinct for some 6,000 years. Fossil remains of *Diprotodon* have been found near Lake Eyre, and others from Queensland bear tool marks suggesting the creatures were killed by ancient hunters.

Source: Patricia Vickers-Rich and Gerard Van Tets (eds.), *Kadimakara: Extinct Vertebrates of Australia*. Lilydale, Australia: Pioneer Design Studio, 1985.

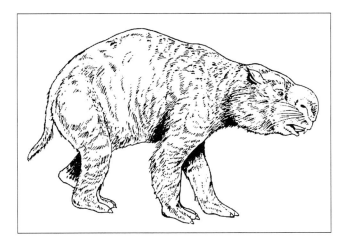

Bernard Heuvelmans thought Australia's Kadimakara might be a relict *Diprotodon*.

Kaha   A large, unclassified BIRD with silver plumage, reported from Tajikistan, the Kaha is mythologized to the point that its blood is said to cure blindness in humans. If the bird ever existed (sans medicinal properties), a dearth of modern sightings suggests that it is now extinct.

Source: Mirra Ginsburg, *The Kaha Bird: Tales from the Steppes of Central Asia*. New York: Crown, 1971.

Kaiapoi Tiger   On 18 July 1977, New Zealand 1YA Radio announced that a TIGER had been seen near Kaiapoi, on the South Island. The initial sighting dated from 10 July, when a local resident saw the big cat in her garden. Police initially discounted the report as a HOAX, until spoor and droppings of a large felid were found on 21 July, in the dunes at nearby Pines Beach. A full-scale search was then mounted, including armed men and spotters in a helicopter, but the hunt proved fruitless. Nonetheless, Inspector W.J. Perring told Sydney *Sun-Herald* on 24 July that he was "reasonably satisfied" an ALIEN BIG CAT had passed through Kaiapoi. Unsubstantiated local rumors claimed the tiger had escaped from a private menagerie and was later recaptured.

Source: Shuker, *Mystery Cats of the World*.

Kaipara Harbor sea serpent   On 12 January 1965, the pilot of a DC3 aircraft flying over New Zealand's North Island glimpsed a "stranded whale" in Kaipara Harbor, north of Helensville. The 100-foot object lay in approximately 30 feet of water, and a closer look suggested a metallic surface. New Zealand naval authorities declared that the harbor was inaccessible to submarines. Some Fortean authors treat this case as a sighting of a submerged UFO. An alternate explanation for the thing's metallic appearance might be sunlight reflecting on scales or wet skin. In either case, the object was never identified.

Source: Bord and Bord, *Unexplained Mysteries of the 20th Century*.

***Kaiserin Augusta Victoria* sea serpent**   At 6:30 a.m. on 5 July 1912, Captain Ruser and two other officers of the German ship *Kaiserin Augusta Victoria* saw an unidentified SEA SERPENT off Prawle Point, South Devon, England. Ruser noted in his log that the creature was 20 feet long and 12-18 inches in diameter, blue-gray on its back and white beneath. The animal seemed to be fighting an unseen opponent, thrashing the water violently with its tail. Though Ruser said the creature's form was unmistakably "reptilian," BERNARD HEUVELMANS concluded that it was probably a "monstrous EEL."

Source: Heuvelmans, *In the Wake of the Sea Serpents*.

Ka-Is-To-Wah-Ea   Seneca natives applied this name to a supposed aquatic cryptid of western New York. It may be synonymous with the MOSQUETO of Lake Onandaga, or may be equivalent to the generic term NAITAKA, applied to Canadian LAKE MONSTERS.

Source: Harriet Converse, "Myths and legends of the New York Iroquois." *New York State Museum Bulletin* 125 (1908): 113.

Kajanok Agdlinartok   The Kajanok Agdlinartok is a huge SEA SCORPION, the size of a boat, said to inhabit Greenland's LAKE NATSILIK. If such a creature were not threat enough, a giant FISH was also reported from the lake in 1954.

Source: "Water monsters: Greenland." *Fortean Times* 46 (Spring 1996): 29.

Kajanprati *see* **Bunyip**

Kakundakari   This unclassified primate or HOMINID reportedly inhabits the forested Kivu district, near the equator, in the Democratic Republic of Congo. Witnesses describe the animals as 2-3 feet tall, with dark hair covering the body, longer on the head and neck. A near-dead specimen was allegedly found by a hunter along the Lugulu River, in January 1957, and carried to a village near Kasese. Caged there, it recovered and was viewed by several dozen witnesses before it finally escaped. Years later, French researcher Charles Cordier found a small 4-toed footprint near a cave described by natives as the Kakundakari's lair. Decades of guerrilla warfare and deforestation do not bode well for wildlife in the DRC, and no reports of the Kakundakari have been published since the early 1970s.

Sources: Charles Cordier, "Animaux inconnus au Congo." *Zoo* 38 (April 1973): 185-191; Charles Cordier, "Deux anthropoides inconnus marchant debout, au Congo ex-Belge." *Genus* 29 (1963): 2-10.

Kalamalka Lake, Canada   British Columbia's Kalamalka Lake, located between Kelowna and Vernon, is reportedly the home of a 100-foot LAKE MONSTER. Five witnesses watched the creature for several minutes on 19 July 1978, noting that its fins were clearly visible. Based on the animal's great size, all five rejected suggestions that they had simply observed a large sturgeon (*Acipenser fulvescens*).

Source: Kirk, *In the Domain of the Lake Monsters.*

Kalanoro   Various Madagascan tribes agree on the existence of this unclassified primate, as researcher Raymond Decary reported in 1950, but they differ widely on descriptions of its attributes and habitat. Sakalava tribesmen, around Lake Kinkony, describe the Kalanoro as three feet tall, hairy, with 3-toed feet, inhabiting reed thickets on the fringes of lagoons. Natives at Lake Aloatra, however, insist that the Kalanoro are amphibious, in the nature of MERBEINGS. Other tribes separate them completely from the water. Betsileo tribesmen know the Kalanoro as forest dwellers, rarely more than two feet tall. The Bara tribe describes fleet-footed prowlers stealing food from villages in the Ankazoabo district. The Kalanoro of northern Madagascar reputedly live in caves and use their claws on humans who attempt to capture them. An element of sexual dimorphism may be involved, as some tribes appear to believe "their" Kalanoro are exclusively male or female. In the mid-1950s, BERNARD HEUVELMANS noted that some of the Kalanoro legends were "fantastic," but he noted that "they are found all over Madagascar, and it would be odd if they were utterly without foundation." Proposed Kalanoro "suspects" include relict specimens of giant lemurs *Archeolemur* or *Hadropithecus*, presumed to be extinct. Parts of the island nation remain unexplored today, including much of the Ambongo reserve and the Isalo mountains.

Sources: Coleman and Huyghe, *The Field Guide to Bigfoot, Yeti, and Other Mystery Primates Worldwide*; Heuvelmans, *On the Track of Unknown Animals.*

Kalooluk Lake, Alaska   Various books and Internet websites list this supposed Alaskan lake as a source of LAKE MONSTER reports, but none provide any dates or details of sightings. Extensive research reveals no such lake in Alaska. Presumably the listings are garbled references to KALULUKTOK LAKE.

Sources: Bord and Bord, *Unexplained Mysteries of the 20th Century*; Coleman, *Mysterious America*; Kirk, *In the Domain of the Lake Monsters.*

Kaluluktok Lake, Alaska   This lake, located at the head of the Kobuk River in northern Alaska's Arctic National Park, once allegedly harbored a giant FISH of ferocious appetite. In the early 20th century, an Inuit witness from Alatna claimed to have seen the creature devour a caribou and a man in a canoe. It was unclear whether both attacks occurred on the same occasion.

Source: Robert Marshall, *Arctic Village.* New York: Literary Guild, 1933.

Kamloops Lake, Canada   On 14 August 1996, witnesses Gordon Anderson and Mike Tarchuk used binoculars to watch an EEL-like creature swimming in this lake at Kamloops, British Columbia. They described the animal as mud-colored and 8-10 feet long. Despite its relatively small size, the thing three humps that surfaced for 3-4 seconds, then submerged before repeating the procedure.

Sources: Kirk, *In the Domain of the Lake Monsters*; Moon, *Ogopogo.*

Kanaima/Kenaima   This unclassified primate or HOMINID of Venezuela is said to reach the size of an adult human being. It may be identical to the MONO GRANDE of Venezuela and Colombia, and/or the SISEMITE of Guatemala. Aboriginal peoples sometimes invest the creatures with supernatural powers.

Source: Heuvelmans, "Annotated checklist of apparently unknown animals with which cryptozoology is concerned."

Kangaroo Man   On 24 December 1900, the *Daily Review* of Roseburg, Oregon published the following account of a strange HOMINID at large:

> The Sixes mining district in Curry [C]ounty has for the past 30 years gloried in the exclusive possession of a "KANGAROO man." Recently while Wm. Page and Johnnie McCulloch, who are mining there, went out hunting[,] McCulloch saw the strange animal-man come down to a stream to drink. In calling Page's attention to the strange being, it became frightened, and with CAT-like agility, which has always been a leading characteristic, with a few bounds was out of sight.
>
> The appearance of this animal is almost enough to terrorize the rugged mountain sides themselves. He is described as having the appearance of a man — a very good looking man — is nine feet in height with low forehead, hair hanging down near his eyes, and his body covered with a prolific growth of hair which nature has provided for his protection. Its hands reach almost to the ground and when its tracks were measured its feet were found to be 18 inches in length with five well formed toes.

When the creature surfaced again, in March 1904, the kangaroo allusion was discarded in favor of WILDMAN descriptions comparing it to "the very devil." On that occasion, William Ward fired several rifle shots at the beast, but his aim was defective. Today, most researchers consider the Kangaroo Man an early version of BIGFOOT or SASQUATCH.

Source: Green, *Sasquatch: The Apes Among Us.*

Kangaroo Valley Panther   Kangaroo Valley is a scenic area located 25 miles east of Tallong, New South Wales, near Australia's Moreton National Park. In 1968, local resident Harold McMahon reported to sightings of a large "black panther" on his property at Cambewarra Mountain, and 32 other witnesses soon joined the list. Four-toed pawprints measuring 5 × 5.5 inches were found and studied by naturalist Harry Butler, who reported that the tracks were "[d]efinitely not a dog print. This was made by a very big CAT, something about the size of a leopard." A cow vanished from David Sissens's farm at Barrengarry, with another pawprint left behind. Sightings of black cats spanned the next decade, but a twist was added in May 1978, when two local witnesses met a 6-foot, "fawny-gray" felid resembling a COUGAR (*Puma concolor*). A year later, in summer 1979, teenage hunter Peter Bruem sighted two cats—one black, one brown—lounging together in a gully. Some locals believe the cats are descendants of U.S. military mascots from World War II, but authors Paul Cropper and Tony Healy have uncovered newspaper reports of ALIEN BIG CATS prowling the area sporadically since 1909. Australian cryptozoologist REX GILROY claimed a sighting of the Kangaroo Valley panther in the early 1980s.

Source: Healy and Cropper, *Out of the Shadows.*

Kangaroos (Mislocated)

Kangaroos (Genus *Macropus*) are marsupials native to Australia, New Zealand and Papua New Guinea. In 1892, a group of U.S. businessmen debated mass importation of 'roos as an economic measure, to replace the dwindling herds of American bison but the scheme was never carried out. Still, the first in a long list of kangaroo sightings came only seven years later, and reports have continued to the present day. As with cases of mislocated ALLIGATORS, EMUS and other animals, authorities typically dismiss the creatures as escapees from an unnamed zoo or circus, while those institutions deny losing any specimens. The question remains moot, since the kangaroos are rarely apprehended. A partial list of mystery kangaroo sightings includes:

12 June 1899—A resident of New Richmond, Wisconsin reported a kangaroo in her yard around the same time a tornado swept through the district. Although a circus was in town, it had no kangaroos and none of its animals were missing.

"Phantom" kangaroos are reported from numerous sites in North America and Europe.

1900—Farmers around Mays Landing, New Jersey heard "screaming" in the night after a small kangaroo was seen in the area. Searchers followed strange tracks to a nearby swamp but could not find the animal.

January 1934—A "killer kangaroo" mauled pets and poultry around South Pittsburg, Tennessee. Reminded that kangaroos are vegetarians, the *Chattanooga Daily Times* replied: "There is absolutely no doubt about these facts, a kangaroolike beast visited the community and killed dogs right and left, and that's all there is to it." Some published accounts claim the "giant" creature "killed and ate" two police dogs.

January 1949—Bus driver Louis Staub reported a 5.5-foot kangaroo crossing the highway outside Grove City, Ohio.

1957-67—Residents of Coon Rapids, Minnesota (northwest of Minneapolis) reported numerous sightings spanning a decade. Several witnesses reported two kangaroos traveling together.

28 July 1958—Charles Wetzel saw a 6-foot kangaroo near his cabin, along the Platte River, outside Grand Isle, Nebraska. Other sightings soon followed at Endicott, Fairbury and Stanton, Nebraska.

26 July 1965—Bert Radar sighted a kangaroo on I-70, east of Abilene, Kansas.

15 August 1965—Jerry Condray reported a kangaroo northeast of Wakefield, Kansas.

Early 1967—William Shearer sighted a kangaroo crossing an open field at Puyallup, Washington.

Late May 1968—A kangaroo crossed the highway in front of a car near Monroe, Ohio.

3 August 1968—Witnesses reported a kangaroo on the campus of Michigan State University, in Lansing.

July 1971—Campus police vainly pursued another scholarly 'roo at Northwestern University, in Evanston, Illinois.

1 November 1971—Another sighting was recorded near Abilene, Kansas.

18 October 1974—Policemen Michael Byrne and Leonard Ciagi were left battered and embarrassed after they tried to "arrest" a kangaroo in a Chicago alley. Sightings in the Windy City continued through 15 November.

25 October 1974—An off-duty policeman reported a kangaroo at large in Plano, Illinois, 50 miles west of Chicago.

2 November 1974—Between 9:00 and 9:30 p.m., motorists in Plano and Chicago, Illinois reported near-misses with kangaroos. Experts deemed it impossible for one animal to cover 50 miles between the cities in a half-hour.

4-6 November 1974—Kangaroos were sighted at Plano, Millbrook and Lansing, Illinois.

12 November 1974—The phantom 'roo appeared at Rensselaer, Indiana. Two days later, it was seen in Carmel, moving on to a final Hoosier sighting at Sheridan, on 25 November.

14-17 July 1975—Kangaroos were twice seen in Decatur, Illinois, and a 5-foot specimen was sighted in a cornfield at DuQuoin, 100 miles farther south.

6 April 1976—Harry Masterson sighted a kangaroo at Rock Island, Illinois.

17 August 1976—Five policemen chased a kangaroo through the outskirts of Golden, Colorado before it escaped.

5 April 1978—Kangaroos returned to Wisconsin after a 79-year absence, with a sighting at Waukesha. At least eight more reports were logged in Waukesha County by 9 May. Cryptozoologist MARK HALL examined plaster casts of 6-inch footprints one specimen left behind.

24 April 1978—A witness photographed a large kangaroo in the woods near Menomonee Falls, Wisconsin. After viewing the photo, LOREN COLEMAN suggested that the animal might be a red-necked WALLABY (*Macropus rufogriseus*).

21 May 1978—A kangaroo surfaced in Eau Claire, Wisconsin, 185 miles from Waukesha.

31 May 1979—The kangaroo hunt went international, with a sighting in the Ontario suburb of Scarborough.

5 June 1979—Widely separated sightings in New Brunswick were recorded at Miramichi and at Douglasville (near the province's border with Maine).

September 1979—After kangaroo sightings in Concord, Delaware, authorities found a 6-inch lock of hair at the scene, with a quartet of 4.5-inch tracks.

1980—Reports of a kangaroo at large in San Francisco's Golden Gate Park sparked a fruitless search.

Early June 1981—Farmer Ray Ault was tending sheep near Cedar Fort, Utah when a large yellowish kangaroo bounded past the herd.

31 August 1981—Two kangaroos darted across a street in Tulsa, Oklahoma. One was struck and killed by a motorist who put it in the bed of his pickup truck. Several witnesses, including two police officers, saw the 3 foot 6 inch animal before the unnamed driver left the scene for parts unknown. Days later, another motorist narrowly avoided striking two 3-foot kangaroos at Owasso, Oklahoma. A Patagonian cavy (*Dolichotis patagonum*) was captured in Tulsa on 27 September, and while its point of origin remains unknown, the large rodent bears no resemblance to a kangaroo.

9 October 1981—Police and reporters chased a kangaroo around a Biltmore, North Carolina motel before it escaped.

1984—George Messenger sighted a 2-foot-tall creature that "looked like a small kangaroo" outside Bridgetown, Nova Scotia.

June 1984—A 6-foot kangaroo hopped across Highway 49 near Robertson, Tennessee.

23 September 1984—A motorist reported a kangaroo crossing I-94 near Detroit's Michigan Metropolitan Airport.

June 1986—Kangaroos bridged the Atlantic for a sighting of two 3-foot-tall specimens near Morange-Silvange, Moselle, France.

October 1986—Hugh MacLean reported a kangaroo sighting near Antigonish, Nova Scotia. Wildlife biologist Bob Bancroft found tracks resembling those of a 'roo.

January 1987—Further sightings were recorded at Cole Harbour and Eastern Passage, Nova Scotia.

31 May 1987—A mystery kangaroo returned to Scarborough, Ontario for another brief appearance.

10 July 1998—Residents of Raleigh, North Carolina reported a kangaroo hopping through their yards. Police failed to catch it, and no zoos reported any missing specimens.

4 August 1999—Lois Eckhart saw a kangaroo on her cattle ranch near Wellman, Iowa, watching as it "took off with a sort of a long, low hop." She filed no report until another sighting was broadcast from Ottumwa, on 25 August. Curators at the nearby Davis Zoo assured police that the animal was "definitely not" one of theirs.

October 2000—London police received four separate reports of a 6-foot kangaroo eating shrubbery and kicking domesting pets in Beckenham Place Park, Lewisham. Witnesses included several golfers, whom park manager Jim Horn described as "visibly distressed." Officers sent to investigate the sightings found tracks "which could be those of a kangaroo," but the beast eluded them.

December 2002—Crypto-researcher Chad Arment reported the claim of an unnamed witness who sighted a kangaroo or wallaby 2½-3 feet tall at an undisclosed location in Florida.

19 August 2003—Police at Wiener Neustadt, in southern Austria, scored a surprise capture after they cornered a kangaroo in a downtown parking garage. Efforts to identify the animal's presumed owner were fruitless.

September 2003—Police in Limburg, Belgium chased a kangaroo through fields outside of town, but failed to capture it.

15 October 2003—A kangaroo at large surprised motorists in Bosberg, Belgium, once more eluding police.

November 2003—Australian newspapers reported that kangaroos which escaped from a French zoological park in the early 1970s were thriving in Rambouillet Forest, west of Paris. Françoise Grangeon, mayor of Emance, told reporters, "Kangaroos have been part of our daily life for 20 years."

January 2004—CHUPACABRA researcher SCOTT CORRALES reported that residents of Santa Filomena, Chile were terrified of a "kangaroo-legged creature" prowling the outskirts of their village. Descriptions notwithstanding, the beast was a ferocious MYSTERY MAULER, seen "jumping with dogs in its mouth." While that behavior bore no resemblance to normal kangaroo activity, it mirrored the violence reported from South Pittsburg, Tennessee 70 years earlier.

Most zoologists refuse to consider the notion of kangaroos breeding and living wild across North America. It is simpler to blame each new sighting on a HOAX, a hallucination, or an "escape" from some private owner who is never identified. Even Loren Coleman, widely recognized as the premier authority on "phantom" kangaroos in the U.S., experienced a change of heart during two decades of research. In the first edition of his book *Mysterious America* (1983), Coleman treated kangaroo sightings as straightforward phenomena (albeit unexplained). Eighteen years later, in the new edition, he suggested that many (or most) North American sightings may involve, not kangaroos, but the elusive primates dubbed DEVIL MONKEYS.

Sources: Bord and Bord, *Unexplained Mysteries of the 20th Century*; Clark and Pear, *Strange & Unexplained Phenomena*; Coleman, "Caught on the hop"; Coleman, *Mysterious America*; "Florida 'kangaroo.'" *North American BioFortean Review* 4 (December 2002): 4-5; "Hunt for Flemish outback kangaroo." Expatica (16 October 2003); "Kangaroo mistaken for giant beaver." *The Australian* (20 August 2003); "Kangaroos run wild in France." *Sydney Morning Herald* (12 November 2003); Beastwatch UK, http://www.beastwatch.co.uk/; Scott Corrales, "'Kangaroo-legged' creature reported in Chile." http://www.rense.com/general48/leghtm.

Kano mystery snake   In late July 2001, a SNAKE of unknown species invaded Rijiyar Zaki village, near the northern Nigerian city of Kano. It reportedly bit at least 26 villagers, killing seven. Oddly, all of those bitten were women, and villagers claimed that only women could see the reptile. Traditional snake charmers claimed the serpent was "the same snake that terrorized Jangusa, a neighboring village," but no details were provided for that case. Nigeria is home to various venomous snakes, including the puff adder (*Bitis arietans*) and various cobras (*Naja* sp.), but speculation on the mystery reptile's identity is hopeless without a description.

Source: "Mystery snake invades village, kills 7." Reuters (3 August 2001).

Kansas River   Cryptozoologists LOREN COLEMAN and JOHN KIRK include this river on published lists of supposed aquatic cryptid habitats, but no dates or details of sightings are provided. Oddly, both also misplace the river in Missouri, though it is in fact confined to Kansas.

Sources: Coleman, *Mysterious America*; Kirk, *In the Domain of the Lake Monsters*.

Kappa   The Kappa ("reedbed man" or "river child") is a MERBEING of Japanese folklore that still surfaces occasionally in modern sightings. The amphibious creatures are typically described 3–4 feet tall, with a monkeylike head and pointed ears, 3-fingered hands and webbed 3-toed feet. Reports disagree as to whether the Kappa is covered in hair or scales, while some accounts refer to a "shell" on its back. Tourist flyers for Tona, in northern Honshū's Iwate Prefecture, warn tourists to be on the lookout for these "meddlesome water imps given to seducing maidens and eating horse livers." Elsewhere throughout their range, Kappas are also known as Kawachi, Kyuusenbou, Masunta, Mu Jima and Ningyo. Some reports describe them as aggressive toward humans, claiming they try to drown children. In November 1978, while fishing from a seawall at Yokosuka (north of Tokyo, in Kanagawa Prefecture), witnesses Makoto Ito and Toshio Hashimoto saw a frightening creature which they described as follows:

> It came out of the water. It just popped up from beneath the surface and stood there. It was not a FISH, an animal or a man. It was about three meters [9 feet 9 inches] in height and covered with thick, scaly skin like a reptile. It had a face and two large yellow eyes that seemed to be focused on us."

While authors LOREN COLEMAN and PATRICK HUYGHE present that incident as a Kappa sighting, the cryptid's size is roughly triple that reported for the average Kappa, and on balance it more closely resembles various LIZARD MEN reported from North America. A shrine in Kyūshū's Kumamoto Prefecture allegedly houses a Kappa's mummified hand, while the Matsuura Brewery, in Imari (Saga Prefecture, Kyūshū), displays a complete Kappa mummy. The latter specimen was found in a box during plant renovations, 50-odd years ago. So far, neither relic has been subjected to scientific study.

Sources: Coleman and Huyghe, *The Field Guide to Bigfoot, Yeti, and Other Mystery Primates Worldwide*; Catrien Ross, *Supernatural and Mysterious Japan*. Tokyo: Yenbooks, 1996; Kyoichi Tsuzuki, *Roadside Japan*. Tokyo: Aspect, 1997.

Kapre   The Kapre (or Xuĕ-rén) is a large primate or HOMINID reported from the Philippine islands of Luzon and Samar. Witnesses describe a creature resembling BIGFOOT or the TOK and KUNG-LU of Southeast Asia. Adults sometimes exceed eight feet in height and are "very GORILLA looking" except for their faces. They leave footprints twice the size of a human's and subsist on a diet including fruit, FISH, land crabs and rats. Some stories, as with Bigfoot and other unknown hominids, depict the creatures kidnapping human females. Others claim that Kapre sometimes exchange fish for cooked food in outlying villages. Spanish conquistadors allegedly clashed with Kapre in the 16th century, and the creature's name derives from the Spanish *kafre* ("Moor").

Sources: Karl Shuker, "Alien zoo." *Fortean Times* 122 (May 1999): 18–19; Bobbie Short, The Kapre of the Philippines, http://www.n2.net/prey/bigfoot/creatures/kapre.htm.

Kaptar   This unclassified HOMINID or WILDMAN of the Caucasus Mountains is well known to residents of Georgia, Azerbaijan and adjacent Russian territory (Dagestan). Kaptars generally match descriptions of the ALMAS reported from neighboring countries, standing 5–7 feet tall, covered in inch-long hair ranging from reddish-brown to gray or black. All have long arms, and the females have prominent breasts. The Kaptar's footprint typically measures 9–10 inches long, with splayed toes and a narrow heel. "Dwarf" Kaptars are also described in some sightings, chiefly from the southern Caucasus. In December 1941, while stationed 20 miles from Buinaksk, Dagestan, Lieutenant-Colonel V.S. Karpetyan of the Soviet Army Medical Corps was asked to examine strange "spy" captured in the nearby mountains. As Karpetyan described the event:

> I entered a shed with two members of the local authorities. When I asked why I had to examine the man in a cold shed and not in a warm room, I was told that the prisoner could not be kept in a warm room. He had sweated in the house so profusely that they had to keep him in the shed.
>
> I can still see the creature as it stood before me, a male, naked and bare-footed. And it was doubtlessly a man, because its entire shape was human. The chest, back, and shoulders, however, were covered with shaggy hair of a dark brown colour. This fur of his was much like that of a bear, and 2 to 3 centimeters [.75–1 inch] long. The fur was thinner and softer below the chest. His wrists were crude and sparsely covered with hair. The palms of his hands and soles of his feet were free of hair. But the hair on his head reached to his shoulders, partly covering his forehead. The hair on his head, moreover, felt very rough to the hand. He had no beard or moustache, though his face was completely covered with a light growth of hair. The hair around his mouth was also short and sparse.
>
> The man stood absolutely straight with his arms hanging, and his height was about the average — about 180 cm [5 feet 9 inches]. He stood before me like a giant, his mighty chest thrust forward. His fingers were thick, strong, and exceptionally large. On the whole, he was considerably bigger than any of the local inhabitants.
>
> His eyes told me nothing. They were dull and empty — the eyes of an animal. And he seemed to me like an animal and nothing more.

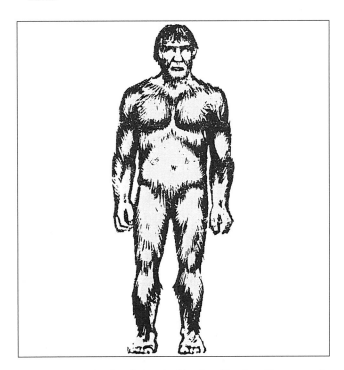

A Kaptar examined and sketched by Dr. Vazghen Karpetyan in December 1941 (*Pravda*).

As I learned, that he had accepted no food or drink since he was caught. He had asked for nothing and said nothing. While I was there, some water and then some food was brought up to his mouth; and someone offered him a hand, but there was no reaction. I gave the verbal conclusion that this was no disguised person, but a wild man of some kind. Then I returned to my unit and never heard of him again.

Karpetyan's description of the creature as a "giant" proves that size is relative. The Kaptar seen by V.K. Leontiev in July 1957, along Dagestan's Jurmut River, was closer to seven feet tall. Leontiev pursued and tried to shoot the creature, but it outran him and escaped. Two years later, in August 1959, veterinarian Ramazan Omarov met a male Kaptar in the Dagestan Caucasus. The following month, cryptozoologist MARIE-JEANNE KOFFMANN and a Russian companion glimpsed an albino Kaptar near Balakon, in northwestern Azerbaijan. Instead of snapping photos as agreed, however, Koffmann's aide opened fire with a pistol, whereupon the creature fled. BERNARD HEUVELMANS and BORIS PORSHNEV suggested that the Kaptar may comprise a relict population of NEANDERTAL MAN.

Sources: Bayanov, *In the Footsteps of the Russian Snowman*; Heuvelmans and Porshnev, *L'Homme de Néanderthal est Toujours Vivant*; Sanderson, *Abominable Snowmen*.

Karkotak Naag   In Nepalese folklore, the great SNAKE known as Karkotak Naag ("serpent king") inhabited the Kathmandu Valley until that vast lake was drained by a rival god, whereupon it retreated to a pond called Taudaha, four miles south of Kathmandu. Celebrants still visit Taudaha during certain festivals and dip into its waters to secure Karkotak Naag's blessing. No modern sightings of the creature are on record.

Source: Festivals, http://www.infonepal.com.np/festivals_shrawan.htm.

Katenpai *see* **Bunyip**

Kathlyn Lake, Canada   Kathlyn Lake (formerly Chicken Lake) lies north of Smithers, in northern British Columbia's Bulkley Valley. Native American folklore claims that a tribal princess was once seized by a serpent "larger than a canoe," whereupon tribesmen surrounded the lake with boulders and logs, set fires beneath the boulders, and rolled them into the lake. The LAKE MONSTER was thus boiled to death, along with the unfortunate princess. The treatment must not have been final, however, since another serpentine creature was sighted in 1934. Lake Kathlyn covers 420 acres, with a maximum recorded depth of 30 feet 10 inches. Some authors mistakenly call it Lake Kathlyn.

Sources: Garner, *Monster! Monster!*; Moon, *Ogopogo*.

Kaurehe/Kaureke *see* **Waitoreke**

Kavay   The Kavay is an amphibious predator reported from the Ankaizina Mountains of central Madagascar. Tsimihety tribesmen live in fear of the creature, which allegedly crawls from the water at night to attack unwary campers and tear out their eyes. BERNARD HEUVELMANS compared it to the fierce IEMISCH of South America, while granting that its violent reputation may be exaggerated.

Source: Heuvelmans, *On the Track of Unknown Animals*.

Kaweah sea serpent   In 1906, while steaming along the coastline of Tierra del Fuego, sailors aboard the Argentinean naval ship *Kaweah* saw a huge slab of ice drop from a seaside cliff into the water. Moments later, according to the ship's commander,

Lieutenant-Colonel Bevilaqua, a "strange and monstrous animal" raised its neck from the water near the same spot. Bevilaqua claimed the SEA SERPENT'S neck was 30 feet long, surmounted by a head resembling a horse's.

Sources: Jerome Clark, Calendar of Unsolved Mysteries (2001); Picasso, "South American monsters & mystery animals."

Kawekaweau   This unknown lizard of New Zealand's North Island is reported chiefly from the Waoku Plateau, near Gisborne. It resembles a GECKO, but grows much larger, with reported lengths of 2-6 feet and a body as thick as a man's forearm. Witnesses describe a serrated dorsal crest and red stripes running the length of the Kawekaweau's body. Some Maori folktales also claim the reptile has six legs, a mythical trait shared by the KUMI. A Maori chieftain reportedly killed a Kawekaweau in the Waimana Valley, sometime during 1870. More recently, witness Joe McClutchie claims to have seen the Kawekaweau twice, on nocturnal drives in the late 1960s and early 1980s. Between those sightings, in the 1970s, Neil Farndale was riding with friends after dark when their car struck and killed a 2-foot lizard, but they did not save the carcass. Some herpetologists think the Kawekaweau may represent a living population of the giant gecko (*Hoplodactylus delcourti*) discovered by Alain Delcourt in 1979, in the Marseilles Natural History Museum. Another long shot candidate is the tuatara (*Sphenodon punctatus*), a 2-foot lizardlike reptile presumably confined to several islands off the northeastern coast of New Zealand.

Source: Michel Raynal and Michel Dethier, "Lézards géants des Maoris: La verité derrière la légende." *Bulletin Mensuel de la Société Linnéene de Lyon* 59 (March 1990): 85-91.

Keating, Donald (1962–)   Ohio native Donald Keating's was 22 years old when a reading of JOHN GREEN'S *Sasquatch: The Apes Among Us* sparked an abiding interest in cryptozoology. The following year, Keating claimed a personal sighting of BIGFOOT in the Buckeye State, which prompted him to found the EASTERN OHIO BIGFOOT INVESTIGATION CENTER (also known as the Tri-State Bigfoot Study Group). He has published three books on unknown HOMINIDS, including *The Sasquatch Triangle* (1987), *The Eastern Ohio Sasquatch* (1989), and *The Buckeye Bigfoot* (1993). Since 1992, Keating has published a *Monthly Bigfoot Report*, and each year he hosts the country's largest Bigfoot conference in Newcomerstown, Ohio. His video documentary, *Sasquatch: The Mounting Evidence*, prompted *Bigfoot Times* to name Keating "Bigfooter of the Year" in December 1998.

Sources: Coleman and Clark, *Cryptozoology A to Z*; EOBIC website, http://www.angelfire.com/oh/ohiobigfoot/home.html.

Kéédieki   The Kéédieki is an unclassified HOMINID or WILDMAN, reported from the Verkhoyansk Mountains of Siberia's Sakha Republic. Based on eyewitness descriptions, it is similar (if not identical) to the ALMAS and CHUCHUNAA reported from other parts of Siberia. BERNARD HEUVELMANS and BORIS PORSHNEV suggest a relict population of NEANDERTAL MAN may inhabit that inhospitable region.

Source: Heuvelmans and Porschnev, *L'Homme de Néanderthal est Toujours Vivant*.

Keel, John Alva (1930–)   Influenced at an early age by the works of CHARLES FORT, John Keel went on to become one of the next generation's most widely-read Fortean authors. As a collector of anomalous events, Keel chronicled many reports of unidentified creatures, including the YETI, BIGFOOT, the THUN-

DERBIRD, SEA SERPENTS, LAKE MONSTERS and West Virginia's MOTHMAN. In his first book, *Jadoo* (1957), he claimed a personal Yeti sighting in Nepal. Keel differs radically from most cryptozoologists, however, in proposing a supernatural explanation for such sightings. Keel theorizes that "ultraterrestrial" gods (from an alternate reality beyond human knowledge) once ruled Earth, but left the planet following a prehistoric war with *Homo sapiens*. Interaction with the old gods continues, however, and thus explains a wide range of phenomena including "monsters," UFOs, "men in black," and so forth. Despite what some critics describe as "outrageous theories," Keel still deserves credit for compiling records of events and sightings found nowhere else. His other works of interest to cryptozoologists include *Strange Creatures from Time and Space* (1970), *The Mothman Prophecies* (1975), and *The Complete Guide to Mysterious Beings* (1994).

Sources: Clark and Pear, *Strange & Unexplained Phenomena*; Keel, *Jadoo*; Doug Skinner, "Lunch with Keel." *Fortean Times* 156 (April 2002): 34-35.

Kélékumba *see* Gnéna

Kellas Cat
In June 1984, a slender black wildcat was caught in a FOX snare on the grounds of Revack Lodge, near Grantown-on-Spey in the Scottish Highlands. It was a male, 3 feet 6 inches long, with a broad head, narrow muzzle, and canine teeth that extended over its lower lip when its mouth was closed. News of the catch quickly spread throughout Britain, but the specimen inexplicably vanished after it was delivered to a taxidermist for mounting. A Moray newspaper, the *Forres Gazette*, nonetheless headlined the story on 19 September, and another specimen surfaced two weeks later. This one, shot by Tomas Christie near Kellas, in January 1983, had been one of a pair. Photos of the mounted specimen were published, and cryptozoologist KARL SHUKER formally named it the "Kellas CAT," a label universally adopted since that time. Another male was killed in April 1985, 10 miles north of Revack Lodge, and it was sent to Di Francis (author of a 1983 volume on ALIEN BIG CATS in Britain) before finding its way to the British Museum. Yet another specimen was killed in October 1985, near Kellas, and the first live capture occurred near Redcastle on 28 February 1988. Di Francis subsequently obtained a pair of Kellas cats that produced a litter of kittens with curiously brittle bones (presumably the result of genetic defects). While Francis is convinced that Kellas cats represent a new species, others maintain that the animals are either melanistic specimens of Scottish wildcat (*Felis silvestris grampia*) or hybrids of wildcats and feral domestic cats (*F. s. catus*).

Sources: Francis, *My Wild Kellas Cats*; Shuker, *Mystery Cats of the World*.

Kellett sea serpent
In August 1923, the British ship H.M.S. *Kellett* was sent to survey part of the Thames estuary known as Black Deep, which had been closed to shipping since 1915. Arriving shortly after 9:00 a.m., the ship's crew was proceeding with the task at hand when Commander R.M. Southern saw a 6- to 10-foot serpentine neck rise vertically from the water, some 200 yards from the vessel. While Southern and Captain F.D.B. Haselfoot watched, the neck surface and submerged twice, remaining visible for 4-5 seconds each time. No camera was available, but Captain Haselfoot drew a rough sketch of the creature.

Source: Heuvelmans, *In the Wake of the Sea Serpents*.

Kempenfelt Kelly *see* Igopogo

Kenai Peninsula carcass
In October 1946, a large GLOBSTER washed ashore on southern Alaska's Kenai Peninsula. More than two decades later, without giving any further details, BERNARD HEUVELMANS identified the creature as a "Pacific grampus." He probably intended to describe Risso's dolphin (*Grampus girseus*)—a species of global distribution, also known as a grampus, gray grampus or whitehead grampus—but the "grampus" tag is also used for the much larger killer whale (*Orcinus orca*).

Source: Heuvelmans, *In the Wake of the Sea Serpents*.

Kènkob
The Kènkob were PYGMIES reported from Guinea and Sierra Leone in the early 19th century. Witnesses typically described dark-skinned people 3-4 feet tall, with the adult males lushly bearded. In 1818, French explorer Gaspard Mollien reported a village of Kènkob from the Guinea interior, describing them as great singers and excellent marksmen. Three decades later, Sigismund Kölle interviewed a tribal chief in Sierra Leone who described two pygmy tribes further inland, the Kènkob and the Bétsan. The absence of modern reports suggests that the tribes either died out or found a more remote habitat.

Sources: Gaspard Mollien, *Voyage dans L'Intérieur de L'Afrique, fait en 1818*. Paris: Mme. Ve Courcier, 1820; Sigismund Kölle, *Polyglotta Africana*. London: Church Missionary House, 1854.

Kent Big Cat Research
The Internet website for Kent Big Cat Research describes it as "the county's only investigation into reports and evidence of exotic CATS in the countryside." Founder Neil Arnold's stated goal is "to monitor behavioural patterns, diet, species and routes of these elusive animals." Rather than question their existence, Arnold "accepts them as a native species [*sic*] and hopes to bring the folklore into reality." He brands "those out there who attempt to monitor an entire nation of feline sightings" (such as the BRITISH BIG CAT SOCIETY) as "the current charge of the fright brigade." In Arnold's view:

> With a great number of so-called "big cat researchers" patrolling the country, in their inadequacy they are creating not only hysteria but also a myth. Each "hunter" wants his own quarry, not for the benefit of the animal, but for the benefit of themselves. Popularity, five minutes of fame and a bit of money lead the blind into a territory they know nothing about. Whilst these intrepid "researchers" investigate their sightings, not knowing the difference between a cat or dog print, they attempt to warn the public that these animals must not be cornered or they will turn aggressive. The fact is, it is the so-called "big cat researcher" who will harm the animal more than any country rambler or angler.

The *Kellett* sea serpent, after witness F.D.B. Haselfoot.

While Kent Big Cat Research observes and films ALIEN BIG CATS, its website — operating in conjunction with a site on paranormal phenomena, appears to say that the animals may be something more than flesh-and-blood creatures. As Arnold writes: "The mysterious felines [*sic*] of the area have been known to walk the same rural lanes and tranquil, dark valleys as the apparitions and wraiths."

Sources: Neil Arnold, "Kent Big Cat Research film and monitor lynx." *Farshores* (14 August 2002); Neil Arnold, "Kentish lynx watched for twenty minutes." *Farshores* (14 August 2002); Kent Big Cat Research, http://www.tudor34.freeserve.co.uk/KentBigCatResearch.htm.

Kent sea serpent In summer 1950, while swimming in the surf at Cliftonville, Kent, England, tourist John Handley saw the neck of a SEA SERPENT rise from the water less than 100 yards distant. He described the creature's head as two feet wide, with upright ears resembling a horse's. Another witness on the nearby beach confirmed Handley's description of the animal.

Source: Heuvelmans, *In the Wake of the Sea Serpents*.

Keshat An unclassified HOMINID or WILDMAN, the Keshat ("mountain man") is reported from the Caucasus Mountains in Russia's Adygey and Kabardin-Balkar Republics. Described as a 5-foot-tall biped, covered with brown hair, the Keshat differs little (if at all) from the KAPTAR reportedly found in the Dagestan Republic and neighboring Azerbaijan.

Source: Colarusso, "Ethnographic information on a wild man of the Caucasus."

Keshena Lake, Wisconsin Native American folklore names this 29-acre lake in Menominee County as the one-time abode of horned, serpentine LAKE MONSTERS, but no sightings are on file from modern times.

Source: Alanson Skinner and John Satterlee, "Folklore of the Menomeni Indians." *Anthropological Papers of the American Museum of Natural History* 13 (1915): 490–492.

Kheyak Another unclassified primate or HOMINID reported from Siberia, the Kheyak allegedly inhabits coastal mountains overlooking the Sea of Okhotsk, in Khabarovsk Territory. Its general description (6-7 feet tall, covered in dark hair) matches that of the more widespread CHUCHUNAA. Some local myths invest the creature with hypnotic powers.

Source: Bayanov, *In the Footsteps of the Russian Snowman*.

Khodumodumo The Khodumodumo ("gaping-mouthed bush monster") is a mysterious predator reported from South Africa in the early 20th century. In the 1920s, nocturnal attacks on livestock were reported from the Graff-Reinet region of South Africa's Eastern Cape Province. The Khodumodumo invaded numerous kralls (livestock pens) to snatch calves, goats and sheep, escaping over 6-foot fences with prey gripped in its jaws. Massed hunts failed to corner the beast, though farmers tracked its round pawprints with 2-inch claw marks clearly visible. The Khodumodumo's style and reputation echoed those of the ferocious NANDI BEAR, reported from Kenya and Uganda.

Source: Hichens, "African mystery beasts."

Khün Görüessü The Khün Görüessü is a reputed WILDMAN or unknown HOMINID reported from Mongolia and from China's Xinjiang Uygur Autonomous Region. Both regions have also produced ALMAS sightings, while China is home to the elusive YEREN. On balance, it seems likely that the various regional names refer to a single species of primate. Confusion with known animals also arises sometimes, as when the alleged pelt of a Khün Görüessü preserved at a Mongolian temple proved to be a bear's skin.

Source: Heuvelmans and Porshnev, *L'Homme de Néanderthal est Toujours Vivant*.

Khya *see* **Yeti**

Kianpraty *see* **Bunyip**

Kibambangwe Reports of this large, unclassified CAT surfaced from Uganda in the 1920s. Witnesses described the Kibambangwe ("snatcher") as roughly the size of a leopard (*Panthera pardus*) but dark in color, with "blackish markings" and small ears. Further confusion arises from the fact that Bantu natives sometimes use the same name for spotted hyenas (*Crocuta crocuta*). Game Warden Charles Pitman recalled a Kibambangwe that ravaged livestock herds in Bufumbira County and was never caught. In a separate case, two of the cats were reportedly killed after hunters tracked them to their lair in local lava caves, but the specimens were not preserved for study. Speculation on possible candidates ranges from melanistic leopards to oversized, abnormally dark-colored hyenas, but no recent reports are on file and the Kibambangwe's present status is unknown.

Sources: Charles Pitman, *A Game Warden Among His Charges*. London: Nisbet, 1931; Shuker, *Mystery Cats of the World*.

Kidoky This mystery primate or HOMINID of Madagascar is described as 4-5 feet tall, weighing 50-60 pounds. A shy forest-dweller, the Kidoky is covered in dark hair except for white marks bracketing its round and rather human face. Witnesses describe its mode of locomotion as a hopping run, and they recall its cry as a mournful *whoooo*. Witness Jean Pascou reported a jungle sighting in 1952. As with the KALANORO, some researchers think the creature may represent a relict population of giant lemurs, *Archeolemur* or *Hadropithecus*, which are presumed extinct.

Source: David Burney and Ramilisonina, "The *Kilopilopitsofy, Kidoky*, and *Bokyboky*."

Kigezi Turaco This disputed BIRD was briefly glimpsed by John Williams and other ornithologists during a visit to Uganda in the 1970s. Williams described it as green, with minor red markings on its wings. Skeptics suggest that Williams and company saw a Ruwenzori turaco (*Tauraco johnstoni*) and mistook it for an unknown species. The debate continues in print, forever unresolved unless a new specimen is collected. Williams named his bird for Uganda's Kigezi district where the sighting occurred (known today as Kabate District).

Source: John Williams, *A Field Guide to the Birds of East Africa*. London: Collins, 1980.

Kikiyaon The Kikiyaon of Senegal merges aspects of BIRD and demon in native folklore. Witnesses describe it as resembling a giant OWL, though some claim it is clothed in greenish-gray fur, rather than feathers. Sharp spurs protruding from its shoulders and a set of wicked talons add elements of Britain's OWLMAN and West Virginia's MOTHMAN. A deep-forest dweller, the Kikiyaon announces its presence with a cry that combines grunts and screams. Bambara natives fear it as an omen of death or bad luck and believe it can steal a human soul. Researcher Owen Burnham twice followed alleged Kikiyaon calls through the jungle, each time tracing the sounds to a specimen of Pel's fishing owl (*Scotopelia peli*), a well-known African bird that grows to a height of 25 inches.

Sources: Owen Burnham, "Kikiyaon the soul cannibal." *Encounters* 9 (June 1997); Shuker, "The secret animals of Senegambia."

Kikomba   This unrecognized primate or HOMINID, reported from the Kivu region of the Democratic Republic of Congo, allegedly shares its habitat with the equally elusive KAKUN-DAKARI. While the latter is normally described as 2-3 feet tall, the Kikomba is larger, sometimes exceeding five feet. Researcher Charles Cordier suggests that the two creatures may represent a single species with sexual dimorphism, the larger Kikomba representing males, while the Kakundakari are females. The Kikomba leaves footprints 8-12 inches long, notable for a second toe longer than its neighbors on either side. Various tribal names for the Kikomba throughout its range include Abamaánji, Tshingombé and Zaluzúgu. Author Jacqueline Roumeguère-Eberhardt suggests that the Kikomba also inhabits parts of Kenya 800 miles farther east.

Sources: Charles Cordier, "Deux anthropoïdes inconnus marchant debout, au Congo ex-Belge." *Genus* 29 (1963): 2-10; Heuvelmans, *Les Bêtes Humaines d'Afrique*; Roumeguère-Eberhardt, *Dossier X*.

Kilarney Lake, Canada   In 1885, a dynamite blast at this lake in New Brunswick allegedly forced a giant bullfrog (*Rana catesbeiana*) to the surface, where it was captured and put on display at the local Barker House Hotel. The specimen measured 27 inches long and tipped the scales at 42 pounds—a true giant, since the largest bullfrog on record measured eight inches and weighed 1 pound 4 ounces. In 1959, the creature's preserved body was donated to the York-Sudbury Historical Museum in Fredericton. No scientific study was performed on the remains until 1988, when a report from the Canadian Conservation Institute revealed the "Coleman frog" to be a HOAX. It was made of canvas, wax and paint, formally classified as "an amusing example of a colossal fake and deception."

Source: Joe Nickell, *Real-Life X-Files*. Lexington, KY: University Press of Kentucky, 2001.

Kilbrannon Sound sea serpent   At 7:00 p.m. on 28 July 1931, Dr. John Paton was bicycling with his daughter past Kilbrannon Sound, on Arran Island (off the west coast of Scotland), when he saw a curious object on the rocky shoreline. Believing it was a capsized boat, Paton stopped to get a closer look. As he later explained:

I had not gone more than a few yards when, to my astonishment, a head turned and looked at me from what I had thought to be the bow of the boat....I waved my daughter's attention to the creature, and made an effort to get as close as possible. The legs or flippers could not be observed, and I wanted to be sure of just what kind of extremities it had. I was disappointed, as the movement evidently frightened it, and it wobbled off the rock into the sea. It made off at a good pace, and left a considerable wake behind it.

The head was parrot-shaped—that is to say, that it had a kind of beak. It was of a rather light grey colour. The body was longer than that of a large elephant—of a similar colour, and just as shapeless. I am of opinion that although the head was small, and close to the body when I saw it, it is probable that the creature would be able to extend the head considerably....The head could be turned round so fully that there must have been rather a narrow neck between it and the huge body.

From Dr. Paton's description, BERNARD HEUVELMANS concluded that the creature he saw was a northern elephant seal (*Mirounga angustirostis*), which may exceed 11 feet in length.

Source: Heuvelmans, *In the Wake of the Sea Serpents*.

Kilchoan sea serpent   At 9:00 p.m. on 21 June 1965, while standing with her husband and a cousin on Mingary Pier, Kilchoan, (on Scotland's west coast), Lillian Lowe saw a SEA SERPENT swimming offshore. She watched the creature through binoculars until it submerged, and later described the experience as follows:

I saw what I thought to be a seal appear above the water, about a hundred yards offshore. Then, another hump appeared directly behind it and a few feet away. As it moved I came to the conclusion that the two humps belonged to one object. I said, "What's that?" My husband immediately sighted the creature but was silent. He said afterwards he was too amazed to speak. He could see a huge shape about forty feet long beneath the water, and after a few moments said, "a submarine I think." He then noticed what seemed to be legs or flippers paddling at the side of the body, creating a turbulence beneath the water. My cousin and I could only see the two humps moving steadily along and waited for a decision as to the identity of the creature, but all my husband could say was that he had never seen anything like it in his life. The two humps were very solid and dark and shiny, and the skin seemed to be like hide.

Mrs. Lowe rejected suggestions that she had merely seen a basking shark (*Cetorhinus maximus*), noting that she had seen many such FISH off the coast of Cornwall and none bore a resemblance to the Kilchoan creature.

Source: McEwan, *Mystery Animals of Britain and Ireland*.

Kildevæld, Denmark   This lake near Østerbro, in Denmark's København County, produced its first known LAKE MONSTER report in July 1986. Two strollers by the lake reported a dark object like a head and neck protruding three feet above the surface, moving back and forth across the lake while they watched.

Source: Bord and Bord, *Unexplained Mysteries of the 20th Century*.

Kilindini Monster   From December 1948 through February 1949, multiple witnesses reported a SEA SERPENT plying the waters between the Kenyan mainland and the island of Mombasa. Many sightings were logged from Mombasa's Kilindini Harbour, hence the nickname commonly applied to this still-unidentified creature. As note by BERNARD HEUVELMANS three decades later, Kenyan natives had long been familiar with the creature(s), but its "discovery" awaited a sighting by two Royal Air Force corporals at Christmas 1948. One of those witnesses, J. Somerville, told reporters, "It had a large flat gray head covered with scales, and what appeared to be horns sloping from its head. I saw a small portion of its back, which was about six feet in length." Within a week, 16 more European witnesses claimed sightings of the beast, including hotel proprietor E.C.A. Hynes on 9 February 1949. Four swimmers at Likoni saw the animal in late February, describing it as "the color of beer with a broad back rising 2_ feet from the water and three feet across." Skeptics insisted that the witnesses had merely seen an errant hippopotamus (*Hippopotamus amphibious*).

Source: Heuvelmans, *In the Wake of the Sea Serpents*.

Kilkerrin Bay sea serpent   In 1910, witnesses reported a SEA SERPENT with a 6-foot neck and a brown, hairy body from Kilkerrin Bay, on the coast of Ireland's County Galway. Regrettably, no further details of the creature's appearance or size are presently available.

Source: Bord and Bord, *Unexplained Mysteries of the 20th Century*.

Kilopilopitsofy   Madagascar's elusive Kilopilopitsofy ("floppy ears") is described as a nocturnal creature the size of a cow (without horns), clothed in dark skin with a pinkish tinge around its eyes and mouth, with fairly large ears that inspired its nickname. It lives near swamps and rivers, fleeing to the water when alarmed. Natives recognize its grunting call and claim the Kilopilopitsofy sometimes stuns adversaries with a defensive spray of urine. Despite its limited range, the Kilopilopitsofy is known by a variety of names, including Lalomena ("hippopotamus"), Omby-rano ("water cow"), Railalomena ("ancestor of the hippopotamus"), Tsomgomby and Tsy-aomby-aomby ("not cow cow").

In 1876, Madagascan tribesmen showed explorer Josef-Peter Audebert an alleged Kilopilopitsofy skin, which resembled the hide of an antelope. A century later, members of the Constant family were wakened from sleep by the creature's grunting sounds at Belo-sur-Mer, a remote fishing village on Madagascar's southwest coast. Zoologist David Burney visited the same village in summer 1998, with Madagascan archaeologist Ramilisonina, and interviewed multiple witnesses to the animal's present existence. One witness, Jean Pascou, selected a photo of a hippopotamus as the nearest likeness of the Kilopilopitsofy. Neighbors of the animal maintain that it does not eat human beings, but will charge and kill if cornered. Burney and Ramilisonina speculated that the Kilopilopitsofy may represent surviving specimens of *Hippopotamus lemerlei*, a dwarf Madagascan species presumed extinct, but they finally concluded that: "For the time being, at least, neither palæontology nor oral tradition can fully resolve the mystery, but both are clearly relevant to the discussion."

Sources: Burney and Ramilisonina," The *Kilopilopitsofy, Kidoky,* and *Bokyboky*"; Shuker, "Catch a kilopilopitsofy."

Kiltanya   This unknown HOMINID or WILDMAN reportedly inhabits the mountains of eastern Siberia, where it is best known for its protruding eyes and the 18-inch humanoid footprints it leaves behind. It thus shares territory with the KHEYAK, and indeed, the two names may refer to one creature, since the Kiltanya ("goggle-eye") is known by other descriptive names throughout Arctic range: Arysa ("plainsman"), Dzhulin ("sharp head"), Girkychavyl'in ("swift runner") and Teryk ("dawn man"). Each label captures some aspect of the Kiltanya's appearance or lifestyle.

Source: Shackley, *Still Living?*

Kilwa Masoko carcass   On 28 May 1975, Tanzania's *Daily News* reported that a fisherman named Mohammed Sefu had caught an unknown sea creature from the deepwater jetty at Kilwa Masoko. The unique beast had a large tongue but no teeth, sporting a beard, one ear, and a small horn on its head. If that combination was not strange enough, its only eye was on the creature's chest, while a sort of luminous "lamp" glowed from one flank. Its back was humped like a bovines, while two arms with five-fingered hands protruded from its chest. Farther back, its legs ended in feet with an uncertain number of toes. A photograph accompanied the press report, but the still-unidentified carcass disappeared without reaching the hands of any qualified zoologist.

Shuker: *From Flying Toads to Snakes with Wings.*

King Cheetah   On 14 October 1926, *The Field* published a letter from Major A.C. Cooper in Rhodesia (now Zimbabwe), concerning an unusual striped CAT, trapped in the Umvukwes Mountains, whose skin had been donated to the Queen Victoria Memorial Library and Museum by one Donald Frazer. Cooper described the animal as:

...a very stockily built leopard, with powerful limbs and a comparatively short thick tail. As against this there are the non-retractile claws of the cheetah, also the ruff round the neck, which is totally absent in the leopard. The background of the skin is the full yellow of the leopard, not the sandy yellow of the cheetah. The markings are like nothing on earth (note the longitudinal stripes down the back and shoulders)."

A photograph of the remarkable pelt accompanied Cooper's letter. Mammalogist Reginald Peacock studied the photo, finding no evidence of a ruff or non-retractile claws, and pronounced the cat an aberrant leopard (*Panthera pardus*). Cooper, meanwhile, continued his research in Africa and uncovered a second skin from the animal natives called Nsui-fisi ("leopard-hyena"). The second skin convinced Pocock, who named the cat *Acinonyx rex* ("king cheetah") in 1927. Twelve years later, Pocock changed his mind again, deciding that the specimens were merely normal cheetahs (*Acinonyx jubatus*) with aberrant pelage. The king was thus demoted to *A. j. var. rex.* Still, new skins emerged to challenge the final decree. Six were known by 1962, 13 by 1980, and 38 by 1987. Stranger yet, a number of those specimens came from mountain woodlands in Zimbabwe and South Africa, a habitat radically different from the grassy plains normally inhabited by cheetahs.

In 1979, Paul and Lena Bottriell launched a new study of the king cheetah, tracking down new pelts and filming the creature's range from a hot air balloon. Study of hairs from the new skins revealed that the cuticular scale pattern of king cheetah guard hairs resembled those of a leopard more closely than a normal cheetah's. In May 1981, a litter of cheetah cubs born to normal parents at Pretoria's National Zoological Gardens included one cub with "king" markings. Over the next six years, two more king cubs were born in captivity, while nine live specimens were caught in the wild. Scientists now believe that king cheetahs are spawned by a mutant allele that surfaces only in one small part of the hunting cat's range. In short, as KARL SHUKER observes, "the king cheetah is demonstrating evolution before our very eyes — the development within a specific range of a completely new race of cheetah, adapted not for daytime sprinting across open grasslands as its hunting mode but for nocturnal stalking through dense forests, where its more heavily patterned coat would provide it with excellent camouflage."

Sources: Bille, *Rumors of Existence*; Lena Bottriell, *King Cheetah*; Shuker, *Mystery Cats of the World.*

King Squirrel   In November 1998, an Indiana deer hunter met an unexpected creature on the outskirts of Crawford County's Hoosier National Forest. Accompanied by several playful squirrels, the beast was significantly larger and resembled a mink (*Mustela* sp.) or mongoose (*Herpestes* sp.). It made no attempt to harm the squirrels, but "interacted" with them as if engaged in silent communication. The hunter moved on in search of larger

An Indiana witness described the King Squirrel as resembling a mink.

prey, and his encounter was not published until December 2000. Its behavior earned the unknown animal the King Squirrel nickname from researchers Chad Arment and Brad LaGrange.

Source: Chad Arment and Brad LaGrange, "Crypto-varmints." *North American BioFortean Review* 2 (December 2000): 18-20.

Kingman County Lake, Kansas

This scenic lake is located within the Byron Walker Wildlife Refuge, near Kingman (30 miles west of Wichita). In late October 1967, the local newspaper reported claims that a 20-foot LAKE MONSTER had devoured a calf. The story was revived in August 1969, but no new sightings are on record.

Sources: Coleman, *Mysterious America*; *Kingman (KS) Leader Courier* (27 October 1967; 8 August 1969); Kirk, *In the Domain of the Lake Monsters*.

Kingstown Killer

This ALIEN BIG CAT killed livestock around Kingstown, New South Wales in 1956-57, while the EMMAVILLE PANTHER was hunting sheep in a nearby sector of Australia's New England region. Some researchers believe there was only one CAT at large in the region, while others suspect two or more. None were ever caught, and farmer Clive Berry (who lost 340 sheep to unseen predators) became convinced that the cats represented "something intangible."

Source: Healy and Cropper, *Out of the Shadows*.

Kinosoo

Kinosoo is the name applied by aboriginal natives to a supposed LAKE MONSTER inhabiting Cold Lake, on the Alberta-Saskatchewan border (Canada). The creature may be synonymous with NAITAKA, the generic cryptid described across western Canada in the 17th to 19th centuries, but while other Canadian bodies of water still produce "monster" sightings, Cold Lake seems presently inactive.

Source: *Weekend Magazine* (6 November 1976): 8.

Kinpélili/Kitikpili *see* Gnéna

Kipumbubu

The Rufiji River, in southern Tanzania, begins at Shuguli Falls and flows northeastward through Selous Game Preserve (the world's largest) before spilling into a vast mangrove forest (again, Earth's largest). Along its course, natives claim the Rufiji harbors a giant CROCODILE called Kipumbubu, which not only preys on villagers but sometimes also leaps from the water to seize prey from the decks of passing riverboats. Locals claimed the beast was still active in the early 20th century, but no recent sightings are reported from the river that hosts frequent rafting safaris.

Sources: Ronald Barker, *The Crowded Life of a Hermit* Nairobi: W. Boyd, 1942; Heuvelmans, *Les Derniers Dragons d'Afrique*.

Kirk, John III (1955–)

Vancouver journalist John Kirk's fascination with cryptozoology began in 1987, after two personal sightings of OGOPOGO, at British Columbia's Okanagan Lake. Two years later, with JAMES CLARK and PAUL LEBLOND, Kirk founded the BRITISH COLUMBIA SCIENTIFIC CRYPTOZOOLOGY CLUB (which he now serves as president, treasurer and editor). A parallel career in broadcast journalism has assisted Kirk in publicizing the BCSCC and its various endeavors. His first book, *In the Domain of the Lake Monsters*, was published in 1998. Companion volumes on BIGFOOT and DRAGONS are reportedly in progress.

Sources: Coleman and Clark, *Cryptozoology A to Z*; BCSCC website, http://www.cryptosafari.com/bcscc/index.htm.

Kitalargo *see* Lions (Spotted)

Kitanga

In the early 20th century, Embu natives of southeastern Kenya described a "LION-like forest cheetah" to Major Granville Orde-Brown. Orde-Brown never saw the CAT, which locals called Kitanga, but a similar cat was later reported from the forests of Senegal, where cheetahs (*Acinonyx jubatus*) are extremely rare. No specimens have thus far been collected for either locale.

Sources: Dower, *The Spotted Lion*; Shuker, *Mystery Cats of the World*.

Kitsilano Beach carcass

In early March 1941, a GLOBSTER washed ashore from English Bay onto Kitsilano Beach, Vancouver, British Columbia. Local reporters dubbed the carcass Sarah the Sea Hag, reporting that: "She had a large horse-like head with flaring nostrils and eye sockets; a tapering SNAKE-like body 12 feet long; and traces of long coarse hair on the skin." Some observers thought the remains belonged to CADBOROSAURUS, but biologists W.A. Clemens and Ian McTaggart-Cowan thought otherwise. On 5 March, Clemens told the press, "We're not sure if it is a basking SHARK [*Cetorhinus maximus*], but there is no doubt it is of the shark family." No more specific identification was ever released.

Source: LeBlond and Bousfield, *Cadborosaurus*.

Kitty Lawry sea serpent

On 9 July 1902, while passing Mark Island on the coast of Maine, Captain Chapman and Mate Drinkwater of the schooner *Kitty Lawry* observed "what appeared to be a huge SNAKE, going along at steamboat speed and turning its head from side to side as if taking a survey of the bay." No further description of the SEA SERPENT was provided.

Source: O'Neill, *The Great New England Sea Serpent*.

Kiushiu Maru sea serpent

At 11:15 a.m. on 5 April 1879, while passing nine miles off Cape Satanomisaki (at the southern tip of Kiushiu, Japan), officers aboard the Japanese steamer *Kiushiu Maru* beheld a strange spectacle. As Captain Davison later described the event:

[T]he chief officer and myself observed a whale jump clear out of the sea, about a quarter mile away. Shortly after it leaped out again, when I saw there was something attached to it. Got glasses, and on the next leap distinctly saw something holding on the belly of the whale. The latter gave one more spring clear of the water, and myself and chief then observed what appeared to be a large creature of the SNAKE species rear itself about thirty feet out of the water. It appeared to be about the thickness of a junk's mast and after standing about ten seconds in an erect position, it descended into the water, the upper end going first. With my glasses I made out the colour of the beast to resemble that of a pilot FISH.

The outcome of that titanic struggle was not seen, but BERNARD

Two views of the *Kiushiu Maru* sea serpent, based on eyewitness descriptions.

HEUVELMANS later concluded that the whale's adversary must have been a huge GIANT SQUID.

Source: Heuvelmans, *In the Wake of the Sea Serpents*.

Klamath Lake, Texas   Two books and various Internet websites list Klamath Lake, Texas as a source of LAKE MONSTER reports. None provides any sources or details of sightings, presumably because the lake itself does not exist. The authors may have been confused by ancient aboriginal reports from KLAMATH RIVER, in the Pacific Northwest.

Sources: Coleman, *Mysterious America*; Kirk, *In the Domain of the Lake Monsters*; Texas Lake Finder, http://www.tpwd.state.tx.us/fish/infish/regions/instate.htm

Klamath River   In the 18th and 19th centuries, Native Americans claimed that the Klamath River of southern Oregon and northern California was inhabited by cryptids known as "water dogs." No modern sightings are on file, and the creatures remain unidentified.

Source: Dixon, "Water monsters in northern California."

***Klaring* sea serpent**   Around 9:30 a.m. on 18 March 2001, two fishermen aboard the *Klaring* observed a SEA SERPENT in the Storfjorden, between Hareid and Sula in Norway's Møre og Romsdal County. They watched the large creature for two minutes in broad daylight, from a distance of 130-140 yards on a dead-calm sea. The *Klaring*'s captain, Terje Vestre, later told reporters that he was "rather pissed off that they did not let me know right away when they spotted the sea serpent, but I can understand that they were lost to the fascination of seeing the creature." Vestre trusted his crewmen, declaring that they had "seen all there is to see at sea" before the latest encounter. Ashore, stories circulated that six other fishermen had seen a similar creature, but no further details have been published.

Source: Erik Knatterud, Norwegian Sea Serpents, http://www.mjoesormen.no/norwegianseaserpents.htm.

Klato   Klato is the local nickname of a freshwater cryptid reported in the early 1940s from the Oyster River on Vancouver Island, British Columbia. Witnesses described the creature as 25 feet long and five feet in diameter, with a dark-colored back and orange underside. Its tail possessed two flukes, approximately six feet long. Swimming, it displayed 3-5 humps above the water's surface. Alternate names Klamahsosaurus, Klatomsaurus and Klematosaurus.

Sources: Garner, *Monster! Monster!*; Moon, *Ogopogo*.

Kleifarvatn, Iceland   In November 1984, Julius Asgeirsson and Olafur Olafsson were hunting BIRDS near this Icelandic lake, 20 miles south of Reykjavik, when they approached a pair of large boulders on the shore. To their amazement, the "boulders" came alive and revealed themselves as two horse-sized animals, racing boisterously up and down the beach. Asgeirsson and Olafsson watched from a distance of several hundred yards while the creatures cavorted, then plunged into the lake and swam out of sight. The two animals reportedly moved like dogs on land, but swam like seals. On shore, they left tracks resembling the hoof prints of a cow, but larger and with three toes, rather than two.

Sources: "Mystery creature in Icelandic lake." *Fortean Times* 43 (Spring 1985): 25; "On the beach." *ISC Newsletter* 3 (Autumn 1985): 10; Shuker, *From Flying Toads to Snakes with Wings*.

Knatterud, Erik (n.d.)   Norwegian cryptozoologist

Erik Knatterud lives in Hedmark County, near Lake Mjøsa, and was raised on tales of the resident LAKE MONSTER known as MJOSSIE. As an associate of JAN-OVE SUNDBERG, he has participated in GLOBAL UNDERWATER SEARCH TEAM expeditions in Sweden (September 1999), Scotland (March 2000) and Norway (August 2000). Knatterud maintains an Internet database of Norwegian aquatic cryptids (http://www.mjoesormen.no), and he also researches legends or sightings of unknown HOMINIDS throughout Europe. In 2002 he announced plans for a forthcoming book on MJOSSIE.

Sources: Karl Shuker, "Alien zoo." *Fortean Times* 156 (April 2002): 18; Shuker, "Alien zoo." *Fortean Times* 159 (July 2002): 17; Global Underwater Search Team, http://www.cryptozoology.st/.

Knobby   On 21 December 1978, 88-year-old Minnie Cook reported seeing a large, hairy biped at Carpenter's Knob, near Toluca, North Carolina (northern Cleveland County). She estimated that the HOMINID was six feet tall and weighed at least 200 pounds. That report prompted other locals to claim sightings dating from mid-summer. At nearby Casar, Sammy Price endured several nights of unearthly howling ("the awfullest scream you ever heard") from a creature that lurked in his yard, while brother Forest Price found one of his goats with its neck snapped. Those who heard the beast's cries compared them variously to a bull's roar and a "wailing in the night like a woman in pain." Several sets of tracks were found—though, oddly, never in conjunction with a sighting—but observers differed on their origin. "Wildlife protector" Lewis Barts identified the prints as bear tracks, while Daniel Cook claimed footprints "similar to those of an APE" were found at the mouth of a cave on Carpenter's Knob. Inevitably nicknamed Knobby, the creature was sighted at least 16 times by mid-January 1979, but it eluded mass searches and vanished as mysteriously as it had appeared.

Sources: Berry, *Bigfoot on the East Coast*; Bord and Bord, *The Bigfoot Casebook*; Jennie Palmer, "Bear or Bigfoot, Knobby's got 'em buzzin'." *Gastonia* (NC) *Gazette* (17 January 1979); Jennie Palmer, "Knobby: Where is he? What is he?" *Gastonia Gazette* (21 January 1979); Jennie Palmer, "Mystery creature still at large." *Gastonia Gazette* (19 January 1979); Robert Williams, "'Knobby': North Carolina's Bigfoot." *UFO Report* (September 1979): 24-27.

Koao/Koau   This unclassified flightless BIRD of Hiva Oa, in the Marquesas Islands (French Polynesia) is described as resembling a seagull-sized rail, with vestigial wings, bluish-purple plumage, with a yellow bill and legs. Thor Heyerdahl (of Kon-Tiki fame) was horseback riding on Hiva Oa in 1937, when he and a companion saw one of the birds run across his path and vanish in the undergrowth. Cryptozoologist MICHEL RAYNAL suggests that the Koao may be related to New Zealand's seldom-seen takahe (*Porphyrio mantelli hochstetteri*), perhaps a relict population of the flightless rail *P. paepae*, known from subfossil remains found on Hiva Oa. Ornithologists disagree on whether the birds are now extinct, or if a handful may survive in the Marquesas.

Sources: Heuvelmans, "Annotated checklist of apparently unknown animals with which cryptozoology is concerned"; Raynal, "The mysterious bird of Hiva-Oa."

Koddoelo   This ferocious predator of Kenya's Tana River region resembles the NANDI BEAR and South Africa's KHODU-MODUMO, both in general features and its aggressive temperament. Witness compare it to a giant BABOON, six feet long and nearly four feet tall at the shoulder, with a bushy mane, a prominent snout, long fangs and claws, an 18-inch tail. The Koddoelo

Kenya's Koddoelo resembles a giant baboon.

normally travels on all fours, but some accounts describe it walking on two legs. Accounts from the early 20th century describe it raiding sheep pens by night and charging at humans with no trace of fear. No recent reports are on file, suggesting that the creatures may have been exterminated or driven to seek more remote habitats.

Sources: Hobley, "Unidentified beasts in East Africa"; Charles Pitman, *A Game Warden Among His Charges*. London: Nisbet, 1931.

Koffmann, Marie-Jeanne (1919–)

A near-legendary figure in the field of unknown HOMINIDS, Marie-Jeanne Koffmann was born in Paris. In the 1930s, already a qualified surgeon, she moved to the Soviet Union as a political statement and worked in various Russian hospitals through World War II, mountaineering in her free time. Ironically, Dr. Koffmann was accused of spying for the French in 1948 and spent the next six years in a Russian labor camp. In 1958, she joined the first official expedition to seek unknown hominids in the Pamir Range, under Professor Kyril Stanjukovitch, and she later worked independently to investigate hundreds of "snowman" reports. In September 1959, Koffmann and a companion sighted a KAPTAR in Dagestan. The following year, she became an active member of the SOVIET SNOWMAN COMMISSION, prompting some medical colleagues to dub her "the Abominable Dr. Koffmann." She retired from medical practice in 1975, to spend much of her time on field work in the Caucasus Mountains. When the RUSSIAN SOCIETY OF CRYPTOZOOLOGY was founded, in 1987, Koffmann served as its first president. The collapse of Soviet communism and Russia's subsequent economic collapse forced Koffmann back to France in 1990. She is one of 17 honorary life members of the INTERNATIONAL SOCIETY OF CRYPTOZOOLOGY, hailed by author Myra Shackley as "the grande dame of the Caucasus ALMAS."

Sources: Norman, *The Abominable Snowmen*; Smith, *Strange Abominable Snowmen*; The grande dame of the Caucasus Almas, http://www.stgr-primates.de/dame.html; International Society of Cryptozoology, http://www.cryptozoologysociety.org/honorary.htm.

Kokako

The wattlebirds (*Callaeatidae*) are a small taxonomic family indigenous to New Zealand. Of three known species, one—the HUIA (*Heteralocha acutirostris*)—has been officially presumed extinct since 1906. Another, the tieke (*Philesturnus carunculatus*), survives in limited numbers on the North Island. The third species, the South Island's kokako or wattled crow (*Callaes cinerea*), is distinguished from the all-blue tieke by its orange-and-blue wattles. Last officially sighted in the 1960s, the kokako has been presumed extinct by many ornithologists for over three decades. Today, however, some researchers cherish hopes that it may yet survive.

A single kokako-type feather was found in the early 1990s, in a region of cut-over forest along the South Island's western coast, but contamination ruled DNA tests inconclusive. An unconfirmed sighting occurred near the same place, along the Glenroy River, in November 1996, encouraging searchers to believe Callaes kokakos might still be found in dense forests of the Grey and Maruia Valleys. In October 1997, Lloyd Robins recorded bird calls similar to the kokako's bell-like cry, near Murchison. The World Wildlife Fund and other groups financed an expedition in May 1998, led by ornithologist Rhys Buckingham, but deployment of automatic cameras and digital tape recorders failed to capture proof of surviving kokakos. Buckingham tried again in October 2000, with an expedition to Kahurangi National Park, but still the wattled crow remained elusive. Gold miner Des Gavin reported hearing the kokako's cry in February 2001, in an undisclosed region of South Otago, and he claimed to have found the bird's nest. Buckingham announced plans to interview Gavin and seek DNA tests on any feathers retrieved from the nest, but no further news of the kokako search had been released by press time for this volume.

Sources: Karl Shuker, "Alien zoo." *Fortean Times* 107 (February 1998): 14; Shuker, "Alien zoo." *Fortean Times* 142 (February 2001): 20; Shuker, "Alien zoo." *Fortean Times* 147 (July 2001): 17.

Kol-Bhalu

Mystery surrounds this cryptic canid, a seeming counterpart to the horned JACKAL of Sri Lanka, reported in the 1890s by several British residents in the Indian provinces of Guzerat, Kanara and Konkan. F.A. Hill was first to describe the beast, writing to the *Journal of the Bombay Natural History Society* in September 1893. He wrote:

The Kol-Bhalu is…generally described by natives …as a jackal, either old and toothless, mad, or in attendance on a TIGER or some other animal. I have also heard it positively asserted by some villagers that it is an old and toothless jackal which has developed horns….[O]n examination of two Kol-Bhalus which I killed at different periods, whilst in the very act of uttering their weird-like cry,…[b]oth were female jackals and bore the appearance of being extremely old, with short and almost hairless tails. The elder of the two had only a little short hair in patches on her body, and but one tooth in her head….The other had more hair, but it was very short and of a dirty appearance, and in her mouth were five or six teeth much broken and worn….It seems possible that the peculiar cry which earns for the jackal the name of Kol-Bhalu may be caused by the absence of teeth….

Similar stories, including eyewitness sightings, were reported to the same journal in June 1897, December 1897 and April 1898. None of the witnesses who glimpsed or shot supposed Kol-Bhalus made any reference to horns.

Source: Chad Arment, "Early notes on the Indian 'Kol-Bhalu.'" *North American BioFortean Review* 4 (March 2002): 19-24.

Kolor Hijau

Beginning in November 2003, women throughout Jakarta, Indonesia claimed that they were sexually assaulted in their homes by a curious half-human beast attired in green underwear. As fear of the night-prowler spread, journalists dubbed it Kolor hijau ("green underwear"), while police searched in vain for a culprit. Skeptics dismissed the claims as a case of mass hysteria, similar to Indian outbreaks involving the CRAWLING GHOST, MONKEY MAN and MUHNOCHWA, yet assaults reportedly continued.

Three Kolor hijau victims were finally identified in January 2004, after further attacks. The first incident allegedly occurred in Ciputat on 23 January, while a victim identified as Rosadah Jamin was sleeping with her husband and their 8-year-old daughter. She woke to find "a strange creature trying to tear my dress and scratch me with his claws. The creature was about 160 centimeters [5 feet 2 inches] tall, bald, with a flat face, a nose like a pig's snout, pointy ears, a paunch and hairy skin." Police took Jamin to Fatmawati Hospital in South Jakarta, where physicians opined that the scratches on her body "had not been made by human nails." A second assault was also reported on 23 January, this one on a resident of Pancoran Mas identified only as Sumiyati. Sumiyati woke to find herself under attack by "a half-pig, half-man creature wearing green underwear." She tried to fight the beast off, but fainted in the midst of the struggle. On 24 January, another Ciputat victim named Saripah told police that the Kolor hijau had attacked her the previous evening.

Ciputat police were frankly skeptical, announcing on 26 January that Saripah and Rosadah Jamin were suspected of filing false reports, a criminal offense bearing a penalty of 16 months in jail. Neither was charged, but authorities publicly branded them liars who craved public attention. Adrianus Meliala, a criminologist at the University of Indonesia, suggested that police might have good reasons for charging the women, "However, they must not do this just as an emergency measure to calm down the public or to stop the rumors spreading." On 28 January, Jakarta chief of detectives Mathius Salempang told reporters that two suspects had been jailed pending trial for one of the early rapes, committed at Bekasi in November 2003. The Kolor hijau, Salempang said, simply did not exist.

Sources: "Green-togged terror victims named suspects." *Jakarta Post* (26 January 2004); Evi Mariani, "Police arrest real suspects, not 'kolor hijau' in Bekasi attacks." *Jakarta Post* (28 January 2004).

Komandorskiye Islands sea serpent

In August 1962, the Soviet journal *Pirorda* (Nature) published an article by Dr. S.K. Klumov, of Moscow's Institute of Oceanology. In the piece, Klumov described a conversation he had in the 1950s with a harpooner named Evan Skripkin, concerning an unknown creature that had appeared "every year for several years running" near the Komandorskiye Islands (off the Kamchatka Peninsula). As Skripkin explained it to Klumov:

The creature always appears at the very same place, and we always see it at the same time: usually in the first half of July. The area is not far from Komandor, say 30 miles from or so south-east of there, in the Pacific. We run into it once or twice a year when we are whaling there. Of course it is no whale. We know whales: you can tell a whale by its appearance, its colour, its dorsal fin, and by the way it blows.

This thing doesn't blow, and it doesn't stick its head out of the water, but like [a] SHARK…it only shows the top part of its back. The back is enormous, very wide, and smooth, with no fins at all, and black in colour. It surfaces, does a roll, and plunges again. But it leaves a tremendous "trough." Only big sperm-whales leave as big a trough as that when they plunge. We haven't once been able to get close enough to this thing to get a shot at it, but we'd love to have a go with the harpoon gun, just to find out what it is….It's

a good 10 meters [32.5 feet] long, if I'm not mistaken, and I don't think my eye deceives me.

Dr. Klumov speculated that the creature might be a GIANT SQUID, while acknowledging that no black specimens of that cephalopod have yet been found.

Source: Dinsdale, *Monster Hunt.*

Kondlo/Inkondhlo

This unclassified BIRD or South Africa's KwaZulu-Natal Province is well known to Zulu tribesmen, if not to modern science. Natives include the glossy-black, turkey-sized bird in their diet whenever possible, reporting that it typically travels in flocks of 5-10 individuals, preferring grasslands as its habitat. Nor are Zulus the sole witnesses to the bird's existence. G.T. Court shot and ate several specimens in the Entonjaneni Hills, near Melmouth, between 1912 and 1914, later sighting a flock which he left unmolested in November 1960. Ornithologists differ on whether the Kondlo represents a new species of wildfowl (Order *Galliformes*), or if it may be a known species mistaken for new by uninformed witnesses.

Sources: G.T. Court, "Inkondhlo?" *African Wild Life.* 16 (1962): 81; G.T. Court, " 'Kondlo': A wild fowl." *African Wild Life* 16 (1962): 342; Shuker, "Gallinaceous mystery birds."

Kongamato

In the early 20th century, Frank Melland worked for the British colonial service in Northern Rhodesia (now Zambia) along the border with present-day Angola. His memoirs, published in 1923, recalled native reports of a flying creature called Kongamato ("breaker of boats") that hunted along certain local rivers. It was described to Melland as resembling "a lizard with membranous wings like a BAT." Further questioning produced information that Kongamato's "wing-spread was from 4 to 7 feet across, [and] that the general color was red. It was believed to have no feathers but only skin on its body, and was believed to have teeth in its beak: these last two points no one could be sure of, as no one ever saw a kongamato close and lived to tell the tale." When Melland displayed a drawing of a PTEROSAUR, "every native present immediately and unhesitatingly picked it out and identified it as a kongamato!" Melland's sources insisted that the reptile still existed, and he came away convinced that it had lived "within the memory of man." In closing, Melland wrote, "Whether it is scientifically possible that a reptile that existed in

African witnesses claim that the flying cryptid Kongamato resembles a prehistoric pterosaur (*William Rebsamen*).

the [M]esozoic age could exist in the climatic conditions of today I have not the necessary knowledge to decide."

G. Ward Price performed a similar experiment in 1925, upon hearing reports of a large, long-beaked "bird" that attacked humans in Rhodesian swamps. When Price confronted one of the animal's surviving victims with a picture of a pterosaur, the native screamed in fright. Three years later, Professor C. Wiman of Uppsala University dismissed all such stories out of hand, suggesting that African natives had derived a "legend of living Pterosaurians" from chance discovery of fossilized remains. That same year (1928) saw a published report from game warden A. Blayney Percival, in Kenya, declaring that:

[T]he Kitui Wakamba tell of a huge flying beast which comes down from Mount Kenya by night; they only see it against the sky, but they have seen its tracks; more, they have shown these to a white man, who told me about them, saying, he could make nothing of the spoor, which betrayed two feet, and an, apparently, heavy tail.

Around the same time, however, game warden Charles Pitman heard similar stories. In 1942 he wrote:

When in Northern Rhodesia I heard of a mythical beast which intrigued me considerably. It was said to haunt formerly, and perhaps still to haunt, a dense, swampy forest region in the neighbourhood of the Angola and Congo borders. Too look upon it is death. But the most amazing feature of this mystery beast is its suggested identity with a creature bat-bird-like in form on a gigantic scale strangely reminiscent of the prehistoric pterodactyl. From where does the primitive African derive such a fanciful idea?

Whatever its source, the "legend" also existed in Tanzania, as J.L.B. Smith ("father" of the COELACANTH) wrote in 1956.

The descendants of a missionary who had lived near Mount Kilimanjaro wrote from Germany giving a good deal of information about flying DRAGONS they believed still to live in those parts. The family had repeatedly heard of them from the natives, and one man had actually seen such a creature at night. I did not and do not dispute at least the possibility that some such creature may still exist.

Even before Smith's book went to press, in January 1956, J.P.F. Brown sighted two flying reptiles near Mansa, Zambia. He claimed they were approximately 4 feet 6 inches long, tails included, with wing spans around 3 feet 6 inches. The following year, a native man arrived at Mansa's hospital with a gaping chest wound, claiming that Kongamato had attacked him in the Bangweulu Swamp. Swedish cryptozoologist JAN-OVE SUNDBERG reports two sightings of flying reptiles in 1974–75, the first by two members of a British expedition in Kenya, the other by an American expedition in Namibia. ROY MACKAL led a team to Namibia in 1988, researching persistent reports of "flying SNAKES." Natives told Mackal that the cave-dwelling, featherless fliers had wingspans up to 30 feet. Mackal's group found OSTRICH bones scattered on rugged local hilltops, suggesting that some predator had carried the birds aloft, and one team member sighted a huge black-and-white creature in flight, albeit from a range of 1,000 feet. Most recently, in 1997, Kenyan exchange student Steven Romandi reportedly told KENT HOVIND that his village was plagued by creatures resembling pterosaurs, with 3- to 4-foot wingspreads, that sometimes opened graves because "their favorite food is decaying human flesh." That scavenging trait is also reported from Papua New Guinea, where natives call their flying cryptids ROPEN. Skeptics naturally balk at the notion of prehistoric reptiles or DINOSAURS surviving anywhere on Earth today. They suggest that

native witnesses (although presumably familiar with the wildlife of their homelands) have simply mistaken storks or other large birds for pterosaurs.

Sources: Gibbons and Hovind, *Claws, Jaws and Dinosaurs*; Heuvelmans, *Les Dernier Dragons d'Afrique*; Heuvelmans, *On the Track of Unknown Animals*; Frank Melland, *In Witchbound Africa*. London: Seeley, Service, 1923; "Museum director says there are no flying reptiles." *Rhodesia Herald* (5 April 1957); Charles Pitman, *A Game Warden Takes Stock*. London: J. Nisbet, 1942; G. Ward Price, *Extra-Special Correspondent*. London: George Harrap, 1957; "Pterodactyls seen near Northern Rhodesian river." *Rhodesia Herald* (2 April 1957).

Kon-Tiki sea creatures   On 28 April 1947, a small team of adventurers sailed from Callao, Peru aboard a balsa wood raft, the *Kon-Tiki*. Over the next 101 days, they silently traversed 4,300 miles of the Pacific Ocean to land at Raroia, Polynesia. Team leader Thor Heyerdahl later described their success in glimpsing many pelagic creatures rarely (if ever) seen by human beings.

The sea contains many surprises for him who has his floor on a level with the surface, and drifts along slowly and noiselessly. A sportsman who breaks his way through the woods may come back and say that no wild life is to be seen. Another may sit down on a stump and wait, and often rustlings and cracklings will begin, and curious eyes peer out. So it is on the sea too. We usually plough across it with roaring engines and piston strokes, with the water foaming round our bows. Then we come back and say there is nothing to see far out in the ocean.

As for the *Kon-Tiki*'s crew, Heyerdahl described their most remarkable encounter.

About two o'clock on a cloudy night, on which the man at the helm had difficulty in distinguishing black water from black sky, he caught sight of a faint illumination down in the water which slowly took the shape of a large animal. It was impossible to say whether it was plankton shining on its body, or if the animal itself had a phosphorescent surface, but the glimmer down in the black water gave the ghostly creature obscure, wavering outlines. Sometimes it was roundish, sometimes oval or triangular, and suddenly it split into two parts which swam to and fro underneath the raft independently of one another. Finally there were three of these large shining phantoms wandering round in slow circles under us. They were real monsters, for the visible parts alone were some five fathoms [30 feet] long....They were not whales, for they never came up to breathe.

Source: Thor Heyerdahl, *Kon-Tiki: Across the Pacific by Raft*. New York: Rand McNally, 1950.

Koolookamba   A mystery primate of West Africa, the Koolookamba is reported (under various regional names, including Itsena, N'tchego and Sipandjee) from Cameroon, Equatorial Guinea and Gabon. In the 1850s, French explorer Paul Du Chaillu shot a male specimen in southwestern Gabon, describing it as smaller than a male GORILLA (*Gorilla gorilla*) but stockier than a female of that species. Du Chaillu reported that the APE'S common name derived from its call ("kooloo, kooloo"). The skeleton of Du Chaillu's specimen is housed at the British Museum of Natural History, where experts still dispute its proper identification.

A possible female specimen of Koolookamba was captured alive in 1874, shipped to the Dresden Zoo from Loango, Republic of Congo. Some researchers thought it was a young female gorilla, while others classified it as a CHIMPANZEE (*Pan troglodytes*) or a chimp-gorilla hybrid (still unknown to science, either in captivity or in the wild). Today, some primatologists believe it was a bonobo (*Pan paniscus*), finally recognized as a separate species in

1933. Louis de Lassaletta reportedly shot a Koolookamba in 1954, in the Nsok district of Equatorial Guinea, but the kill brought science no closer to a final identification. In August 1998, Stephen Holmes went public with a 1993 WILDMAN sighting from Gabon, describing the creature he saw as bipedal, under five feet tall, and covered with reddish-brown hair. Local natives called the animal Sipandjee and described it as aggressive toward humans, though it did not attack Holmes. In 1967, W.C. Osman-Hill gave the Koolookamba a provisional scientific name, *Pan troglodytes koolokamba*, which recognized it as a subspecies of chimpanzee. KARL SHUKER suggests that the Koolookamba may represent a newly emergent species of chimpanzee, adapted to a mountainous habitat.

Sources: Cousins, "No more monkey business"; Steve Holmes, "Incident in Gabon." *Fortean Times* 113 (August 1998): 52; Heuvelmans, *Les Bêtes Humaines d'Afrique.*

Kootenay Lake, Canada   British Columbia's Kootenay Lake, located 110 miles east of Okanagan Lake (home of OGOPOGO), has produced LAKE MONSTER reports since October 1900, when Captain W.J. Kane of the steamer *Marion* sighted a 12-foot creature of "substantial bulk" paddling across the lake with stubby forelimbs. Around the same time, 12-year-old George Goudreau reported "something" that emerged at Crawford Bay and "indulged in a hearty meal" from a lakeside garbage pile. Searchers summoned by Goudreau found tracks in the mud, as of large web-toed feet. Young Goudreau told the press:

> The first I saw of it was on Monday [8 October]. I was standing outside of our house, and all at once the water began to splash awfully hard and then appeared a head and long body. I watched it for a few minutes, and then became afraid and ran into the house to tell them what I had seen. It appeared to be of a black and green color. About three feet of it was out of the water. It had four legs, each of which was ten inches long. I was awfully afraid of its jaws, as they seemed to be about that long (here the boy held his hands about a foot apart to show the scribe how long its vicious jaws were). I saw it at different times and different nights.

A neighbor, G.W. Sayer, also reported seeing the creature, which some presumed might be an ALLIGATOR. When that identity was suggested, however, "experts" instantly responded that no such reptile could survive cold Canadian winters. The beast was still alive in the early 1920s, though, when it was seen pursuing and devouring FISH, 10 miles from Nelson. A 1926 witness, W.J. Astley, thought the creature was a giant sturgeon (*Acipenser fulvescens*), while Alan Lean compared it to an oversize otter. An altogether different cryptid was seen by Naomi Miller in July 1937, while boating with her family near Kalso. Their motor died, and:

> Moments later we were aware of a ripple just ahead of the boat. A black head reared followed by at least one hump above the water some eight feet behind us. This weird creature swam between our boat and the shore to a position behind us. We sat hypnotized until the "Ogopogo" dived with a gurgling sound into the calm water....We do not know what we saw, but agree that it was longer than our 16 foot boat.

Source: Kirk, *In the Domain of the Lake Monsters.*

Korokombo *see* **Gnéna**

Kowi Anakasha *see* **Nalusa Falaya**

Kra-Dhan   The foul-tempered Kra-dhan ("great MONKEY") is described by witnesses in Vietnam as a large primate, reported from the highlands around Kon Tum and Jolong (where it is also called Bekk-Bok). Growing to a height around five feet, the Kra-Dhan makes a fierce opponent if encountered in the wild, and stories persist that one such creature killed a man near Kon Tum in 1943. LOREN COLEMAN and PATRICK HUYGHE suggest that the Kra-dhan's range may extend as far west as Nepal, where entomologist George Brooks and physician George Moore had a frightening encounter in June 1953, in the Gosainkund Pass, near Kathmandu. Seven or eight of the creatures surrounded Brooks and Moore, snarling and shrieking, until the two men scattered their assailants with pistol shots fired in the air. The Nepalese creatures had obvious tails, while reports from Vietnam include to reference to appendages.

Sources: Coleman and Huyghe, *The Field Guide to Bigfoot, Yeti and Other Mystery Primates Worldwide*; Sanderson, *Abominable Snowmen.*

Kraken *see* **Colossal Squid; Giant Squid**

Krantz, Grover S. (1931–2002)   Grover Krantz was born in Salt Lake City, grew up in Illinois, and returned to Utah with his family at age 10. He earned B.A. in anthropology from the University of Utah (1955), his M.A. from the University of California (1958), and his Ph.D. from the University of Minnesota (1971). A specialist in human evolution, Krantz taught at Washington State University from 1968 until he retired in the 1990s. His personal research on BIGFOOT began in 1963 and spanned the remainder of his life, during which time Krantz championed the PATTERSON FILM's authenticity and sparked controversy by insisting that a SASQUATCH should be killed to provide science with irrefutable proof of its existence. Critic PETER BYRNE called the plan "criminal and unnecessary," voicing concern that the first Sasquatch shot may be "the last one." Krantz responded bluntly to such arguments:

> If it's endangered, which I doubt, then it makes taking a specimen all the more important, because whatever is causing Bigfoot to become extinct is continuing. The government is going to pay no attention and do nothing to help unless you prove the animal exists. The only way to prove Bigfoot exists is to bring in a specimen. So the more endangered they are, the more critical it is to get that one specimen.

As for his critics, Krantz said, "You have to understand why people are taking a stand against shooting a Bigfoot. They know that once a specimen is brought in, the scientists will take over and the hunters are going to be pushed aside. They want to keep the mystery alive so they've got something going for them."

Such controversy notwithstanding, Krantz remained one of Bigfoot's most prominent advocates, suggesting that the creatures by represent a relict population of *GIGANTOPITHECUS*. In pursuit of his research, Krantz produced the first reconstructions of complete *Gigantopithecus* and *Meganthropus* skulls, as well as restoring various relics of *Homo erectus*. Krantz published eight books, including four on Bigfoot: *The Scientist Looks at Sasquatch* (1977, with Roderick Sprague), *The Scientist Looks at Sasquatch II* (1979, with Sprague), *Big Footprints* (1994) and *Bigfoot Sasquatch Evidence* (1999). His work was profiled in the 1999 documentary *Sasquatch Odyssey* (along with that of Byrne, RENÉ DAHINDEN and JOHN GREEN). Krantz died at home, of pancreatic cancer, on 14 February 2002.

Sources: Betts, "Wanted dead or alive"; Coleman, "Necrolog: Cryptocrypt"; Krantz, *Big Footprints.*

Krishna/Menx sea serpent   A regrettably vague SEA SERPENT report from the mid-19th century declares that two brigs of the Indian navy, the *Krishna* and *Menx*, were passing through the Strait of Malacca (between Malaysia and Sumatra) when an unknown creature 50-100 feet long swam between them, frightening the sailors on both ships. No further details of the sighting are available today.

Source: Heuvelmans, *In the Wake of the Sea Serpents*.

Krøderen, Norway   In the 19th and early 20th centuries, neighbors of this lake in Norway's Buskerud County reported sightings of a large-headed LAKE MONSTER that made sounds like a cow. No modern reports of the beast are on file.

Source: Skjelsvik, "Norwegian lake and sea monsters."

Krovatnet, Norway   The LAKE MONSTER reported from this body of water, near Ryfylke in Rogaland County, was allegedly decorated with yellow spots. The claims are impossible to verify, since no sightings have been logged in more than a century.

Sources: Kirk, *In the Domain of the Lake Monsters*; Skjelsvik, "Norwegian lake and sea monsters."

Krumbiegel, Ingo (1903-1992)   German mammalogist Ingo Krumbiegel wrote various articles on unknown creatures during his career, including the double-banded argus (described from a single feather in 1871), New Zealand's elusive WAITOREKE, and the Coje ya Menia ("WATER LION") of Angola. In the latter case, Krumbiegel was the first to suggest that the animal might be a surviving form of SABER-TOOTHED CAT. His classic volume on undiscovered animals, *Von Neueun und Unentdeckten Tierarten* (1950), preceded the work of BERNARD HEUVELMANS by five years, but it was not (as one Internet website contends) "the first ever cryptozoology book." Krumbiegel was one of 17 persons selected as honorary members of the INTERNATIONAL SOCIETY OF CRYPTOZOOLOGY.

Sources: Coleman and Clark, *Cryptozoology A to Z*; Ingo Krumbiegel, "Was ist der 'Löwe des Wassers'?" *Kosmos* 42 (1947): 143-146; International Society of Cryptozoology, http://www.cryptozoologysociety.org/honorary.htm.

Ksy-Giik   The Ksy-giik ("wild man") is an unclassified HOMINID or WILDMAN reported from Kazakhstan and Kyrgyzstan. In 1911-12, Russian anatomist Vitaly Khakhlov was assigned to Kazakhstan, where he collected eyewitness accounts of the Ksy-giik. One such creature was allegedly caught and described by his captor as follows:

> The "wild man" was a male, below average height, covered with hair "like a young CAMEL." He had long arms, far below his knees, stooped, with shoulders hunched forward; his chest was flat and narrow; the forehead sloping over the eyes with prominently arched brows. Lower jaw was massive without any chin; nose was small with large nostrils. The ears were large without any lobes, pointed back (like a FOX's). On the back of his neck was a rise (like a hound's). The skin on the forehead, elbows and knees hard and tough. When he was captured he was standing with his legs spread, slightly bent in the knees; when he was running he was spreading his feet wide apart awkwardly swinging his arms. The instep of the "wild man" resembled a human, but at least twice the size with widely separated fingers [*sic*]; the large toe being shorter than that of humans, and widely separated from the others. The arm with long fingers was like a human arm, and yet different.

Khakhlov submitted a formal report on the Ksy-giik to the Russian Academy of Imperial Sciences in 1913, proposing the scientific name *Primihomo asiaticus*, but Tsarist officials suppressed the document and ordered Khakhlov to say nothing more about it. BORIS PORSHNEV found the original report in 1959 and interviewed Khakhlov, while pursuing his own research into unknown hominids. Porshnev also uncovered two more Ksy-giik sightings from summer 1948, including the account of a Kazakh named Mad'yer, who allegedly killed a specimen in July, after it tried to kidnap his wife. Mad'yer kept one of the Ksy-giik's hands and later showed it to Russian geologist A.P. Agafonov, but Mad'yer was deceased when Porshnev heard the story in 1963, and his family denied any knowledge of the trophy. The other incident, in August 1948, involved a brief sighting by geologist M.A. Stronin along the Inyl'chek River, in Kyrgyzstan. As recently as August 2001, unidentified 18-inch footprints were found in the Alai Mountains, by a Kyrgyz soldier on border patrol.

Sources: "Bigfoot's footprints found in Kyrgyzia Republic." *Pravda* (29 August 2001); Heuvelmans and Porshnev, *L'Homme de Néanderthal est Toujours Vivant*; Sanderson, *Abominable Snowmen*.

Ktchi Pitchkayam/Tcipitckaam   Ktchi Pitchkayam ("great SNAKE") is a generic aboriginal term for LAKE MONSTERS throughout the eastern Canadian provinces of New Brunswick and Nova Scotia. As such, it is analogous to NAITAKA in the western half of the country. The name apparently does not refer to any particular cryptid.

Source: Gatschet, "Water-monsters of American aborigines."

Kting Voar *see* **Linh Duong**

Kuddimudra   This ferocious LAKE MONSTER reportedly inhabited certain water holes along the Diamantine River, in South Australia, through the early 20th century. Unlike most BUNYIPS, the Kuddimudra (or Coochie) was serpentine in form and sported a long mane of hair, thus more closely resembling certain SEA SERPENTS and freshwater cryptids of Europe and North America. It was said to prey on careless humans, dragging them into the water where it fed on them at leisure.

Source: George Farwell, *Land of Mirage*. London: Cassell, 1950.

Kul   The Kul is yet another unknown HOMINID or WILDMAN reported from the Arctic wastes of Siberia. Residents of the Yamal-Nenets Autonomous Province describe the creature as a hairy biped, 6-7 feet tall, with long arms and a pigeon-toed style of walking. Proximity and similarity of descriptions suggests that the Kul is identical to other Siberian hominids, including the ALMAS, CHUCHUNAA and KÉÉDIEKI.

Source: Bayanov, *In the Footsteps of the Russian Snowman*.

Kumi   Nineteenth-century witnesses described the Kumi as a large, unknown lizard inhabiting New Zealand's North Island. Most claimed the reptile was 5-6 feet long, though some reports made it as long as 12 feet. No lizards of comparable size are presently known in New Zealand, and suggestions that the Kumi witnesses may have seen a giant GECKO (*Hoplodactylus delcourti*) also fail to convince, since the largest (and only) known specimen measured two feet long. On balance, it seems likely that New Zealand once hosted (and may still support) a species of MONITOR LIZARD presently unidentified.

Source: James Hector, "On the Kumi." *Transactions of the New Zealand Institute* 31 (1899): 717-718.

Kung-Lu   The Kung-lu ("mouth man") is an unclassified primate or HOMINID reported from Myanmar, where it enjoys an unsavory reputation as a man-eater. All descriptions of the creature stress its large size, with some (perhaps exaggerated) stories placing its height around 20 feet. Vicious temperament aside, the Kung-lu generally conforms to descriptions of North America's SASQUATCH, and it strongly resembles the man-hunting TOK (or Taw) reported from Myanmar eastward, through Laos and Vietnam. IVAN SANDERSON noted that both the Kung-lu and Tok inhabit regions adjacent to habitats of the prehistoric ape GIGANTOPITHECUS, and he suggested that they may be identical to the form of YETI known to Sherpas as Dzu-Teh ("hulking thing").

Sources: Hassoldt Davis, *Land of the Eye.* New York: Henry Holt, 1940; Sanderson, *Abominable Snowmen.*

Kungstorn   In 1838, while playing with friends at Valais (in the French Alps), 5-year-old Marie Delex was snatched by an eagle that bore her away in full view of multiple witnesses. As later described by F.A. Pouchet in *The Universe* (1870): "Some peasants, hearing the screams, hastened to the spot but sought in vain for the child; they found nothing but one of her shoes on the edge of a precipice. It was not until two months later that a shepherd discovered the corpse of Marie Delex, frightfully mutilated, and lying upon a rock half a league [1.5 miles] from where she had been borne off." Nearly 100 years later, on 5 June 1932, 3-year-old Svanhild Hantvigsen was grabbed by a large BIRD under similar circumstances on the Norwegian island of Leka (Nord-Trøndelag County) and carried to a mountain slope 1.2 miles distant. There, searchers found the 42-pound child alive and unharmed, except for some rips in her dress. Other incidents of child-snatching by eagles were reported from Turkey in June 1937 and from Syria in February 1953.

Such attacks are commonly blamed on the Kungstorn ("king eagle"), a predator known in folklore throughout Europe. It is described as an eagle with a 6- to 7-foot wingspan, but researchers disagree on the bird's identity. Two candidates within that size range are the golden eagle (*Aquila chrysaetos*) and the endangered white-tailed eagle (*Haliaeetus albicilla*). Officially, eagles are incapable of lifting more than their own weight (about 12 pounds), an experiment conducted in 1940 found that a golden eagle with 4-pound weights tied to each leg "could hardly fly at all."

Artist's rendering of a Kungstorn abducting Marie Delex in 1838.

Nonetheless, reports of eagles snatching small children or dog-and-lamb-sized prey continue sporadically around the world.

Sources: Brookesmith, *Creatures from Elsewhere*; Rickard and Michell, *Unexplained Phenomena*; Shuker, "Big birds in Scandinavia"; Shuker, "'Big birds' update."

Kuperree   Aborigines of South Australia's Eyre Peninsula tell stories of a giant KANGAROO, called Kuperree, that was hunted to extinction by their ancestors within living memory. Scientists acknowledge the existence of a prehistoric kangaroo (*Macropus giganteus*) of the Late Pleistocene epoch, which grew approximately twice as large as extant kangaroos. *Macropus* presumably died out some 26,000 years ago.

Source: William Cawthorne, *Legend of Kuperree.*

Aboriginal folklore describes the Kuperree as a giant kangaroo.

Kurrea   This man-eating Australian LAKE MONSTER was reported from Boobera Lagoon, below Goodiwindi (New South Wales) during the 19th century. Like the KUDDIMUDRA of South Australia, the Kurrea deviates from the normal BUNYIP description, appearing to Aboriginal witnesses as a serpentine creature with an appetite for human flesh. No modern sightings are reported.

Source: Robert Mathews, *Folklore of the Australian Aborigines.* Sydney: Hennessey, Harper, 1899.

***Kurumba* sea serpent**   In mid-October 1939, soon after World War II began, Australian seaman Cecil Walters experienced a SEA SERPENT sighting which he kept secret for over four decades. As related by Walters in 1980, he was aboard the Australian naval oil tanker *Kurumba*, assigned to watch for submarines. Around 1:00 p.m. on the day in question, the *Kurumba* was northwest of King Sound, Western Australia (approximately 114° east latitude, 20° south longitude). With companion Jack Mack (later killed in action), Walters saw through his telescope a "huge animal" swimming four miles from the ship, at an estimated speed of 17 miles per hour. Its neck was elevated 10 feet from the surface and was the same diameter as an adult human's torso. Behind the upraised head and neck, two large "loops" or humps were visible, spaced about 30 feet apart. Overall, Walters estimated, the creature must have been at least 90 feet long. Its background color was the dull brownish-yellow of a dead leaf, sporting blotches of blue, green and yellow "like a multicoloured giraffe." The powerful telescope enabled Walters to see the animal's features, including a small ear set behind its eye. The creature's mouth remained shut, "but the jaws were constantly working and the tongue flicking in and out." In correspondence with author Malcolm Smith, Walters claimed to have photographed the creature through his telescope and later sent the photo to a relative (who recalled the picture, but lost it).

Source: Smith, *Bunyips & Bigfoots.*

Kussie Sightings of this supposed LAKE MONSTER at Lake Kussharo, on the Japanese island of Hokkaido, date from the early 1970s and continue to the present day. Kussie (or Kushii) is named after its lake, in the fashion of NESSIE, CHESSIE and others around the world. Witnesses describe the creature as dark in color, resembling a giant EEL up to 50 feet long; some reports also include ridges along the beast's back. On 2 September 1973, witness Toshio Komama snapped a long-range photograph that appears to show two unidentified animals swimming together.

Sources: "Japan's own sea serpent." *Newsweek* (11 August 1997): 8; Ronald Yates, "Old Nessie makes room for Kussie." *Chicago Tribune* (17 June 1976).

Kuwait carcass At 11:00 p.m. on 8 August 1997, Mohammed Yousef Obaid was fishing in the Persian Gulf near Al Fantas, Kuwait. He observed an object floating in the water near shore, initially mistaking it for a human corpse. Prodding the object with a stick, Obaid later said, "I was shocked to see that the creature, or whatever, had a strong resemblance to humans. I could see that the body was disintegrating but could distinctly spot the strange skull, remnants of eyes, ears and mouth, spinal cord and pelvis." The carcass fell into three pieces as Obaid hauled it ashore, whereupon he carried home the "skull" and attached spinal column, placing them in his freezer. News reports, accompanied by photographs, described the partial remains as five feet long, with a "big mouth, two nostrils, two eyes and two ears which jut out of the skull." Authorities showed no interest in the creature, and no scientific analysis was ever performed on the remains, but BEN ROESCH concluded from newspaper photos that the animal was probably a cownose ray (*Rhinoptera* sp.). If so, it marks the first time on record that a dead ray has been mistaken for a SEA SERPENT.

Source: Ben Roesch, "A mystery carcass off Kuwait." *Cryptozoology Review* 2 (Winter-Spring 1998): 6-7.

Kvalvatnet, Norway Norse folklore names this lake (near Beiarn in Nordland County) as the lair of a LAKE MONSTER, and large unidentified bones were reportedly found here, sometime in the early 20th century, but the fate of those relics is unrecorded and their owner remains unidentified. No modern cryptid sightings are on file.

Source: Eric Knatterud, Sea Serpents in Norwegian Lakes, http://www.mjoesormen.no.

Kvitseidvatnet, Norway Ancient records describe the LAKE MONSTER of this Norwegian lake, in Telemark County, as having a "head like a trough." Such a creature is difficult to visualize, and there are no recent sightings on file to encourage research.

Source: Skjelsvik, "Norwegian lake and sea monsters."

Kwanokasha *see* **Nalusa Falaya**

--- L ---

***La Décidée* sea serpent** On the afternoon of 25 February 1904, crewmen aboard the French gunboat *La Décidée* sighted a strange SEA SERPENT in ALONG BAY, on the coast of Vietnam. Lieutenant L'Eost described the incident as follows, in a letter to Rear-Admiral de Jonquières:

I first saw the back of the animal at about 300 yards, on the port bow, in the shape of a rounded blackish mass, which I took first for a rock and then, seeing it move, for a huge TURTLE 12 to 16 feet in diameter.

Shortly afterwards I saw this mass lengthen, and there emerged in succession, in a series of vertical undulations, all the parts of the body of an animal having the appearance of a flattened SNAKE, which I reckoned to be about a hundred feet long and the greatest diameter 12 to 16 feet. The animal having dived, I did not observe it again, my attention being distracted by handling the ship.

Details added by various crew members included black skin mottled with yellow patches, a raised head (grayish-white mixed with yellow), and jets of water spouting from the head. Witnesses disagreed on whether the creature's skin was smooth or rough and scaly.

Source: Heuvelmans, *In the Wake of the Sea Serpents.*

La Jolla, California sea serpent In November 1954, while fishing half a mile offshore from La Jolla (San Diego County), Grant King and Phil Parker met a creature which remains unidentified today. After watching the animal for 25 minutes, from a range of 50 feet, King said it had "a head and shoulders like a bull GORILLA and no face." Parker opined, "It wasn't a whale and it wasn't a sea LION. And it sure didn't look like a SNAKE."

Source: Heuvelmans, *In the Wake of the Sea Serpents.*

***La Lorraine* sea serpent** On 26 1904, passengers aboard the French liner *La Lorraine* observed a large SEA SERPENT in the North Atlantic, 560 miles west of Brest, France. The creature surfaced repeatedly, remaining visible for nearly an hour as it thrashed the surface into foam. Witnesses agreed that the animal's neck and head rose 12 feet from the water, revealing huge eyes and a pair of 20-inch horns atop its head, and that a long dorsal fin ran nearly the full length of its back. Estimates of the creature's length averaged 150 feet.

Source: "Eyes as big as saucers." *New York Tribune* (2 July 1904).

***La Meurthe* sea serpent** On 1 September 1889, sailors aboard the French transport *La Meurthe* met a SEA SERPENT in the Indian Ocean, off Madagascar. One witness thought it was an oversized SHARK, while several others said it had a shark's head on a more elongated body.

Source: Heuvelmans, *In the Wake of the Sea Serpents.*

***La Mutine* sea serpent** In the summer of 1893, officers and crew aboard the French gunboat *La Mutine* observed a long, black SEA SERPENT "swimming with vertical movements" in ALONG BAY, on the northern coast of Vietnam. No further details are available for this sighting, which was not reported publicly until 1922.

Source: Heuvelmans, *In the Wake of the Sea Serpents*.

Lac-à-la-Tortue, Canada Opinions differ on the nature of the LAKE MONSTER reported from Lac-à-la-Tortue (TORTOISE Lake), in Québec's Gatineau County. Some researchers believe the creature is a large muskellunge (*Esox masquinongy*), while others describe a much larger cryptid (up to 30 feet long), seen to race beneath the surface with breathtaking speed. The matter is complicated by a river system linking Lac-à-la-Tortue with eight other lakes in the county, including Lac Bitobi, LAC BLUE SEA, Lac-des-Cedres, Lac Desert, Lac Pocknock, Lac St. Clair, Lac Trent-et-un-Milles and Réservoir Baskatong. Collectively, the lake monsters of Gatineau County are sometimes called Horseheads. County residents once believed the Horse-heads also traveled on land, and sought to placate them by setting out saucers of cream.

Sources: Kirk, *In the Domain of the Lake Monsters*; Meurger and Gagnon, *Lake Monster Traditions*.

Lac Aylmer, Canada Québec's Lac Aylmer, 30 miles northeast of Sherbrooke, is said to be "bottomless." Like certain other lakes in North America and Europe, it surrenders drowning victims slowly, if at all. LAKE MONSTER reports from the region are no surprise, then, but they were late beginning, with a rash of reports in 1955-58. Witness Paul-Émile Grenier allegedly saw the creature three times in 1958, the first time glimpsed from his canoe. "I had the idea of shooting it with my carbine," Grenier told reporters, "but it was too far away and disappeared in the water. When it moved, a motorboat couldn't keep up with it. You could see the last fin, which cut through the water more quickly than a 100-horsepower motor." Sightings tapered off after 1958, and "virtual silence" has reigned since the last published sighting in 1970. Locals blame the Stratford Mine, which emptied waste into the lake throughout the 1950s, creating dangerous pollution and decreasing the FISH population. In the inter of 1976-77, witnesses at Lac Aylmer claimed a kind of "seal emerged from a hole, in an area where there was no ice," but details on the incident remain confused. A local newspaper, *La Tribune*, made a joke of it the following April Fool's Day, with a sham photo of the lakes "April-osaur."

Source: Meurger and Gagnon, *Lake Monster Traditions*.

Lac Bitobi, Canada *see* **Lac-à-la-Tortue**

Lac Blue Sea, Canada Lac Blue Sea, in western Québec, lies within a cluster of lakes reportedly inhabited by LAKE MONSTERS. From the 19th century to the present day, large serpentine creatures have been sighted in Lac Blue Sea, frequently appearing in the deep water off Point-à-Belcourt. Witness Olivier Garneau described his second sighting of the creature, in the 1940s, near Point-à-Belcourt.

> We were getting ready for fishing. I had a fishing rod about 16 feet long. Suddenly I heard it coming from the Île de Montigny. My wife was afraid. It seemed to me that if it made an arch, a 16-foot boat would have been able to pass underneath. It appeared to me to be grey, like FISH scales. It looked at me, its head almost folded back, like a horse.

Another local, Oscar Courchène, recalled his father's description of an animal sighted in the 1890s. "You could have passed a boat through it when it was making loops," he said. "It was about 30-35 feet long. They tried to shoot at it, but they never found it dead." According to old-timers, the creature(s) of Lac Blue Sea often traveled overland, to hunt in nearby LAC-DES-CÈDRES and LAC TRENTE-ET-UN-MILLES.

Source: Meurger and Gagnon, *Lake Monster Traditions*.

Lac Bowker, Canada Rumors of LAKE MONSTER activity are recorded from this small lake, near Richmond, Québec, but no dates or details of sightings are available. Locals believe Lac Bowker is connected to a nearby lake, Lac Rouche, by underground caverns, but no such passageways have been confirmed. Both lakes *are* fed by the Saint-François River, which also links other alleged "monster" lakes in the region.

Source: Meurger and Gagnon, *Lake Monster Traditions*.

Lac Breeches, Canada Lac Breeches, another "bottomless" lake located 30-odd miles southwest of Québec, was privately owned by a local fishing club until 1976, when the Parti Québecois came to power. LAKE MONSTER sightings began (or, at least, began to get published) after Lac Breeches was opened to the general public. Today, older fishermen describe a "thing of unbelievable length that would break their lines," but recent eyewitness sightings are scarce. In 1973, Navy divers explored an island in the middle of the lake, but they complained of "black mud in the water which hindered their observations."

Source: Meurger and Gagnon, *Lake Monster Traditions*.

Lac Brochu, Canada Around 1972, a witness named Geoffroy claimed to have seen a "prehistoric" LAKE MONSTER launch itself from the shore of this Québec lake (near RÉSERVOIR GOUIN) and swim beneath the surface at speeds exceeding 35 miles per hour.

Source: Meurger and Gagnon, *Lake Monster Traditions*.

Lac Brompton, Canada Longstanding traditions identify this Québec lake, 10 miles west of Sherbrooke, as the home of an unidentified LAKE MONSTER. Various witnesses describe the creature as "a round-backed whale" or an enormous FISH whose back resembles a capsized boat. Divers familiar with the lake complain of murky waters and 6- to 7-foot fish dwelling close to the bottom. In early June 1976, Pauline Robitaille saw an animal swimming in Lac Brompton which she described as follows:

> It was long, long, at least six feet, if not more, grey-coloured, and with an evil-looking head. You might have said it was a horse or something with a moustache. The snout was pointed and it had something like ears. It had three humps and a tail like a fish. The tail had two tips and it went quickly, like a whale. I saw it arch its back.

Two witnesses near the same spot, in June 1979, described the creature as "a kind of grey CAMEL in the water. The head was pointed and bearded. It was like a grey camel with humps."

Source: Meurger and Gagnon, *Lake Monster Traditions*.

Lac Commanda, Canada Visitors to this small Québec lake, near the village of Boileau in Argenteuil County, once reported finding a TURTLE on the shore "eight times the normal size reported in the region." Regrettably, no further information is available as to the species of turtle, the date of the sighting, or names of the witnesses.

Source: Meurger and Gagnon, *Lake Monster Traditions*.

Lac Creux, Canada   Locals report "water SNAKES" 8-10 feet long from this Québec lake, located north of Ottawa. Hunters sometimes shoot them, it is said, when the animals lift their heads above water, but no specimens have thus far been preserved.
Source: Meurger and Gagnon, *Lake Monster Traditions.*

Lac d'Alfeld, France   Huge FISH were reported from this lake, in the Haut-Rhin Department of France, during the 19th century. Though described as resembling trout, the creatures may in fact have been wels CATFISH (*Siluris glanis*), which attain acknowledged lengths of 15 feet. No modern reports are on file.
Source: Jean-François Variot, *Contes Populaires et Traditions Orales de l'Alsace.* Paris: Firmin-Didot, 1936.

Lac Decaire, Canada *see* **Lizzie**

Lac-des-Cedres, Canada *see* **Lac-à-la-Tortue**

Lac Deschênes, Canada   A serpentine LAKE MONSTER the size of a telephone pole was reported from this lake in 1879-80. No modern sightings are on file.
Source: Mackal, *Searching for Hidden Animals.*

Lac Desert, Canada *see* **Lac-à-la-Tortue**

Lac-des-Piles, Canada   Authors LOREN COLEMAN and JOHN KIRK include this Québec lake on published lists of LAKE MONSTER habitats, but neither provides any details of sightings.
Sources: Coleman, *Mysterious America*; Kirk, *In the Domain of the Lake Monsters.*

Lac La Belle, Wisconsin   Sightings of giant FISH and a serpentine LAKE MONSTER were reported from this lake, near Oconomowoc (Waukesha County) in the late 19th century. No modern reports of either cryptid are on file.
Sources: Garner, *Monster! Monster!*; "Western lake resorts have each a water monster." *Chicago Tribune* (23 July 1892).

Lac Maskinongé, Canada   Québec's Lac Maskinongé, located 50 miles north of Montréal, is named for its rich supply of muskellunge (*Esox masquinongy*). The lake's average depth is 82 feet, but underwater caverns of uncertain depth are reported. Divers sent to plumb those caverns note that the water is pitch-black below 40 feet, and some have been frightened by the size of FISH they met below. Reports of LAKE MONSTERS resembling floating logs may be explained by muskellunge of unusual size.
Source: Meurger and Gagnon, *Lake Monster Traditions.*

Lac Massawippi, Canada   Lac Massawippi, south of Sherbrooke, is a neighbor of Québec's Lac Memphrémagog, the reputed home of a LAKE MONSTER nicknamed MEMPHRÉ. Locals believe the two lakes are connected by uncharted tunnels, which may explain reports from Massawippi of oversized "FISH with cows' heads." Lac Massawippi is the deeper of the two lakes, with charted depths exceeding 1,200 feet, and the lake is reputed to harbor 7-foot sturgeon. As with certain other "monster" lakes, drowning victims rarely surface in Lac Massawippi, a circumstance which accentuates the lake's sinister reputation.
Source: Meurger and Gagnon, *Lake Monster Traditions.*

Lac Mégantic, Canada   Aboriginal LAKE MONSTER reports from Lac Mégantic, near Québec's border with Maine, apparently evolved into an April Fool's joke in a local newspaper. On 1 April 1980, journalist Guy Lavoie fabricated a story for the *Courrier de Frontenac*, describing the alleged discovery of a Nazi submarine from World War II, rusting on the bottom of the lake. Inspired by rumors of U-boats prowling the St. Lawrence seaway during World War II, Lavoie's story was meant as a joke, but certain local fishermen and divers apparently took the prank to heart, mounting expeditions to find the nonexistent sub. Reports of the phantom sub may, in turn, have fueled later cryptid sightings at the lake.
Source: Meurger and Gagnon, *Lake Monster Traditions.*

Lac Mékinac, Canada   Neighbors of this Québec lake, north of St.-Joseph-de-Mékinac, disagree on whether their resident LAKE MONSTER is a "big pike," a "really big SNAKE," or a "big grey beast" that defies simple description. Lac Mékinac is fed by the Mékinac River, in turn a tributary of the ST.-MAURICE RIVER that spawned "serpent" sightings in 1956. A vast underwater cavern, dubbed "the Devil's Hole," has not been successfully plumbed. A diving bell sent down to chart the cavern reportedly malfunctioned and failed in its quest.
Source: Meurger and Gagnon, *Lake Monster Traditions.*

Lac Pocknock, Canada *see* **Lac-à-la-Tortue**

Lac Rémi, Canada   Lac Rémi, in Québec's Argenteuil County, measures 984 feet long by 492 feet wide, but its small size does not rule out reports of LAKE MONSTERS. In this case, the creature is said to be a 6-foot, 220-pound northern pike (*Esox lucieus*), grown vastly out of proportion to its habitat and species. (Northern pike normally do not exceed 30 inches.) Some fisherman scoff at the story, but sporadic sightings continue.
Source: Meurger and Gagnon, *Lake Monster Traditions.*

Lac St. Clair, Canada *see* **Lac-à-la-Tortue**

Lac Saint-François, Canada   This Québec lake, lying southeast of Thetford Mines, is linked to neighboring LAC AYLMER by the Saint-François River. Reports of a local LAKE MONSTER date from 1957, when sightings peaked at Lac Aylmer, but reports continued into the 1980s, well after Lac Aylmer's cryptid had ceased to appear. The wife of Roger Roy, a rural mail carrier, described the animal she glimpsed with other witnesses, in 1979:

> We were very surprised. In the middle of the lake we saw an enormous back, and then we saw it go under. It was something alive, not a dead body; we could see the waves behind it, like a boat ploughing through the water. It was dark and wet. We were on the bridge of the River Sauvage, facing the larger part of the lake. It went very fast, like an upside-down boat, but longer and higher. We saw something like a fin above, which stretched from one end to the other. It was at least 15 feet [long], and disappeared like a big fat cable which went underwater. We didn't see the tail or the head, as if the FISH was swimming on its back.

Like other "monster" lakes of North America and Europe, Lac Saint-François is known as a lake where drowning victims rarely surface. Divers sent to recover one such victim, near the mouth of the River Sauvage, returned empty-handed with tales of "enormous fish" in the waters below. Some sketches of the creature vaguely resemble lake sturgeon (*Acipenser fulvescens*), but those fish rarely exceed five feet in length.
Source: Meurger and Gagnon, *Lake Monster Traditions.*

Lac Seul, Canada   Aboriginal folklore names this lake, northwest of Sioux Lookout in western Ontario, as an ancient abode of LAKE MONSTERS, but no modern sightings are recorded.
Source: "A brief survey of Canadian lake monsters." *INFO Journal* 39 (March-June 1981): 2-5.

Lac Simon, Canada   The "white SHARK" said to inhabit this lake, in Québec's Portneuf County, was apparently fabricated by supervisors at a Catholic summer camp (run by Brothers of Mary the Immaculate) to stop children from swimming without supervision. From that beginning, the tale spread by word of mouth and gained acceptance in some quarters, despite its inherent implausibility.

Source: Meurger and Gagnon, *Lake Monster Traditions.*

Lac Sinclair, Canada   Québec's Lac Sinclair, north of Hull in the Ottawa valley, is linked to LAC-À-LA-TORTUE and RÉSERVOIR BASKATONG by the River Gatineau, which feeds them all. In the summer of 1966, André Arsenault reported an unusual experience from the marshland nearby.

A friend and I penetrated the swamps, by way of a river, and came to a dead end with our motorboat. There, at the bottom of the river, which we could no longer navigate, amongst dead trees, moss and algae, we saw an object floating and wallowing in two or three inches of water. It was obviously a section of a cylinder; light browny yellow, 24 inches long and 10 inches in diameter. We raised it with an oar. It was heavy. It didn't have the texture of a FISH. And there were no fins. It was like a tube. You could say it was a clean-cut sausage, but what could have cut this piece? My friend, who was an habitual fisherman, had never seen anything like this. He said that it resembled part of an enormous serpent. Even the colour wasn't that of fish flesh. It couldn't have been there more than a week, because the flesh was still firm. If it was part of a serpent, like I think, it must have been an enormous one. In the same lake there were many small SNAKES and TORTOISES.

Source: Meurger and Gagnon, *Lake Monster Traditions.*

Lac Trent-et-un-Milles, Canada see **Lac-à-la-Tortue**

Lac Williams, Canada   A serpentine LAKE MONSTER 30-40 feet long and as thick as a flour barrel was reported from this Québec lake, southeast of Plessisville, in the early 1900s. No recent monster sightings are recorded, but in 1977 a fisherman landed a 6 foot 10 inch muskellunge (*Esox masquinongy*) at Lac Williams.

Source: Meurger and Gagnon, *Lake Monster Traditions.*

Lackagh Lake, Ireland   Lackagh Lake, in County Kerry, is not normally listed among Ireland's "monster" lakes, but it has produced one cryptid report all the same. In 1967, fisherman W.J. Wood sighted a 7-foot animal, yellow-brown in color, gliding beneath the surface of the water. No other accounts support the sighting, and it remains unexplained. A year before this sighting, Wood encountered another unidentified creature at LOUGH ATTARIFF.

Sources: Holiday, *The Dragon and the Disk*; McEwan, *Mystery Animals of Britain and Ireland.*

***Lady Rose* sea serpents**   Cryptozoologist PAUL LEBLOND reports that passengers and crew aboard the vessel *Lady Rose* glimpsed the SEA SERPENTS known as CADBOROSAURUS "on many occasions" in the 1960s, around Alberni Inlet on British Columbia's Tzartus Island. The only witness named is John Monrufet, and no further details are provided. LeBlond identifies his source as an untitled story from *Victoria Daily Colonist*, published on 2 February 1961.

Source: LeBlond and Bousfield, *Cadborosaurus.*

Lago Amadoier, Italy   Sightings of a large unidentified LAKE MONSTER have allegedly been reported from this Italian lake, but no further details are presently available.

Source: Magin, "A brief survey of lake monsters of continental Europe."

Lago Arenal, Costa Rica   In the early 1970s, fishermen reported a 98-foot LAKE MONSTER with a cowlike head plying the waters of Lago Arenal, in Costa Rica's Northern Zone. Those sightings were short-lived, but new cryptid reports began in July 2003, with claims of large CROCODILES inhabiting the lake. Witness José Quirós, operator of the Costa Rican Electricity Institute's hydroelectric plant at Lago Arenal, saw one of the reptiles sunning itself in the shallows near the plant's turbines. Employees at a popular lakeside restaurant also reported multiple sighting around their workplace. As waitress Maria Carazo told reporters in 2004, "The first time saw a crocodile four years ago, I pointed it out to people in the restaurant, but they said it was just a log. But then it turned and swam in the other direction. Logs don't do that." Local resident Joven Artavia, a 60-year-old veteran fisherman, dated his first crocodile sighting from 2002. Maria Mora, director of the regional Environment Ministry office, acknowledged receiving crocodile reports from Lago Arenal in 2002, but she did not investigate and claims no further sightings were reported to her agency. In January 2004, the San José *Tico Times* found more than a dozen witnesses who admitted seeing large reptiles in the lake. Officially, no crocodiles inhabit Costa Rica and no crocodilians of any sort are found in Lago Arenal. Two species found elsewhere in Central America are the American crocodile (*Crocodylus acutus*) and the common CAIMAN (*Caiman crocodilus*).

Source: Tim Rogers, "Crocodiles in Lake Arenal?" *Tico Times* (16-22 January 2004).

Lago Banyoles, Spain   In the 8th and 9th centuries, a DRAGON with armored flanks, tall spikes down its back, and a pair of useless vestigial wings reportedly terrorized neighbors of this lake in Catalonia. It fed on livestock, and several warriors dispatched to kill it disappeared without a trace. Emperor Charlemagne (800-814) sent troops to kill the monster, but they were likewise massacred. Different versions of the story end with the creature ultimately being killed, tamed, or simply disappearing of its own accord.

Source: Kirk, *In the Domain of the Lake Monsters.*

Lago Blanco, Argentina   In 1897, a farmer living near this lake in Chubut Province reported sightings of a long-necked reptilian LAKE MONSTER resembling a PLESIOSAUR. That report was among the stories that motivated Buenos Aires zoo director CLEMENTE ONELLI to organize an expedition to seek the elusive creatures in 1922.

Sources: Costello, *In Search of Lake Monsters*; Kirk, *In the Domain of the Lake Monsters.*

Lago Catemaco, Mexico   This lake, located in Mexico's Veracruz State, has a longstanding tradition of resident LAKE MONSTERS, sometimes described as giant CROCODILES. In 1969, a serpentine creature with two horns on its head reportedly crept ashore after nightfall, then fled back to the water when sighted by lakeside residents.

Source: Keel, *The Complete Guide to Mysterious Beings.*

Lago de Atitlan, Guatemala   Author JOHN KIRK includes this Guatemalan lake on a list of sites alleged to harbor LAKE MONSTERS, but he provides no details or description of the creature(s).

Source: Kirk, *In the Domain of the Lake Monsters.*

Lago de Nicaragua, Nicaragua JOHN KIRK offers this Central American lake as a reputed home of unidentified LAKE MONSTERS, but no details are provided. The listing is plausible, but no other available source presently supports it.
Source: Kirk, *In the Domain of the Lake Monsters.*

Lago di Como, Italy Persistent reports of a LAKE MONSTER from this body of water, in Italy's Lombardy region, received double confirmation with the capture of a large sturgeon (*Acipenser sturio*) in 1946, and the police interception of a contraband smuggler's submarine in 1947. Whichever was responsible for the local "monster" sightings, they have not been repeated.
Source: Mangiacopra, "The Lake Como monster."

Lago Esquel, Argentina A large, unidentified LAKE MONSTER was sighted by neighbors of this lake in 1956. Authorities did not appear to take the sightings seriously, but the witnesses remain convinced that they observed something extraordinary.
Source: Picasso, "South American monsters & mystery animals."

Lago Fagnano, Argentina In 1927, witnesses reported sightings of a large unknown creature from this lake in Tierra del Fuego National Territory. No serious investigation was pursued.
Source: Picasso, "South American monsters & mystery animals."

Lago Gutiérrez, Argentina Nearly four decades separates the two reports of LAKE MONSTERS from this lake, in Argentina's Río Negro Province. No details are presently available for the first report of a large unidentified cryptid, filed in 1938, but the second account is more specific. In 1976, witnesses claimed to have seen giant rays swimming in the lake—a double anomaly, since all known rays are pelagic.
Source: Picasso, "South American monsters & mystery animals."

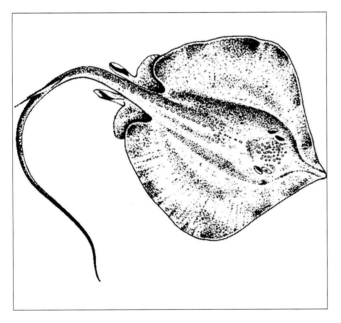

Giant rays were reported from Lago Gutiérrez in 1976.

Lago Lacar, Argentina As with Argentina's LAGO GUTIÉRREZ, this lake in Neuquén Province (near San Martin de los Andes) is said to harbor two distinct and separate LAKE MON-

STERS. One, the CUERO ("cowhide") is also shared with yet another two-monster lake, LAGO NAHUEL HUAPI. The second, reported in 1850, was an amphibious specimen of MERBEING.
Sources: Berta Koessler, *Tradiciones Araucanas.* La Plata, Argentina: Universidad Nacional de La Plata, 1962; Picasso, "South American monsters & mystery animals."

Lago Lolog, Argentina This lake in Argentina's Neuquén Province appears to harbor a LAKE MONSTER similar to the CUERO reported from LAGO LACAR and LAGO NAHUEL HUAPI. Witnesses describe the cryptid as sometimes resembling a log in the water, yet able to flatten itself into the shape of a cow's hide floating on the surface. On 17 January 1996, multiple witnesses reported an object like a large boulder cleaving the surface of the water and navigating under its own power.
Sources: Picasso, "South American monsters & mystery animals"; Tafur, "Mythical creatures in Argentine lakes."

Lago Los Angeles, Peru Early in 1974, witnesses reported sighting a silver LAKE MONSTER in this Peruvian lake. No more encounters with the surprising creature have been filed to date.
Source: "Silver lake monster in Peru." *Fortean Times* 4 (May 1974): 17.

Lago Maggiore, Italy This lake in Italy's Piedmont district is reportedly the home of a LAKE MONSTER with a head resembling a horse's. The description is familiar from other sites across Europe and North America, but no specific details on the sightings are presently available.
Source: Magin, "A brief survey of lake monsters of continental Europe."

Lago Nahuel Huapí, Argentina Argentina's Nequén Province may well hold the record for lakes with multiple LAKE MONSTERS in residence. In addition to LAGO LACAR and LAGO LOLOG, Lago Nahuel Huapí also boasts two distinct and separate cryptids. One, the CUERO ("cowhide") is shared with its sister lakes in the region, while another, dubbed NAHUELITO ("Little Nahuel") is described as a serpentine creature 15-20 feet long. And, as if this abundance of cryptozoological riches were insufficient, the lake also produced an alleged PTEROSAUR carcass (long since vanished) in the early 19th century.
Sources: Hans Krieg, *Als Zoologe in Steppen und Wäldern Patagoniens.* Munich: J.F. Lehmann, 1940; Magin, "Duck! It's a plesiosaur"; Picasso, "South American monsters & mystery animals."

Lago Pellegrini, Argentina A LAKE MONSTER resembling a PLESIOSAUR was reported from this lake, near Cinco Saltos in Río Negro Province, in the 1930s. No more recent sightings are on file.
Source: Hans Krieg, *Als Zoologe in Steppen und Wäldern Patagoniens.* Munich: J.F. Lehmann, 1940.

Lago Pueyrredón, Argentina In 1910, a reptilian LAKE MONSTER was reported from this lake in Argentina's Santa Cruz Province. No investigations were pursued, and the creature (if it existed) remains unidentified today.
Source: Picasso, "South American monsters & mystery animals."

Lago San Martín, Argentina In 1922, a Catalan journalist reported rumors of a LAKE MONSTER inhabiting this lake, in Santa Cruz Province. No further details are available, but author Peter Costello suggests the reporter confused Lago San Martín with a northern lake, San Martin de los Andes.
Source: Costello, *In Search of Lake Monsters.*

Lago Specchio di Venere, Italy   Wild, animalistic sounds in the night were reported from this lake on Isola di Pantelleria, Sicily, in July 1982, spawning rumors of a resident LAKE MONSTER. No actual sightings have yet been reported, nor have the cries been explained.

Source: Magin, "A brief survey of lake monsters of continental Europe."

Lago Titicaca, Peru   This large mountain lake, spanning the border between western Bolivia and southeastern Peru, has a long tradition of aboriginal LAKE MONSTER reports. Some witnesses describe a 12-foot animal resembling a seal or manatee, while others speak of a larger, long-necked creature resembling Scotland's NESSIE. A retired CIA agent claims to have photographed a cryptid at the lake, but no pictures have yet been released. Investigator Frank Stein collected eyewitness accounts of the creature(s) in 1994, while resisting facetious suggestions that he dub the animal "Titty."

Sources: "And an Altiplano Nessie.'" North-South: The Magazine of the Americas 4 (September-October 1994): 58; Bord and Bord, Unexplained Mysteries of the 20th Century.

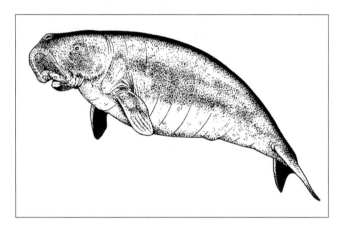

Some witnesses compare Lago Titicaca's cryptid to a manatee.

Lago Viedma, Argentina   In 1922, a Spanish journalist published rumors of a LAKE MONSTER inhabiting this lake, in Santa Cruz Province. Author Peter Costello pursued the matter but could find no actual reports of sightings through the early 1970s.

Source: Costello, In Search of Lake Monsters.

Lago Vintner, Argentina   A large, unidentified LAKE MONSTER was reported from this lake, in Chubut Province, in 1900. The dearth of later sightings and a lack of any meaningful investigation leave the mystery unsolved.

Source: Picasso, "South American monsters & mystery animals."

Laguna Iberá, Argentina   Native traditions suggest that a LAKE MONSTER once inhabited this body of water in Corrientes Province, but it is another without significant details.

Source: Hans Krieg, Als Zoologe in Steppen und Wäldern Patagoniens. Munich: J.F. Lehmann, 1940.

Laguna Origuere, Bolivia   Traditional LAKE MONSTER sightings give way to old native accounts of a giant FISH from this lake in eastern Bolivia. According to the tales on record from the Mojos Indians, Laguna Origuere's finny behemoth was fond of

capsizing boats. Whatever the creature may have been, it has not appeared in modern times.

Sources: Heuvelmans, "Annoted checklist of apparently unknown animals with which cryptozoology is concerned"; Alfred Métraux, "The native tribes of eastern Bolivia and western Matto Grosso." Bulletin of the Bureau of American Ethnology 134 (1942): 75.

Lake Ābaya Hāyk', Ethiopia   In the late 19th century, witnesses reported an unknown creature the size of an adult hippopotamus from this Ethiopian lake. It may in fact have been a hippopotamus (Hippopotamus amphibius), since that creature's broad range includes the eastern half of Ethiopia, but a shortage of details makes guesswork pointless.

Source: Maurice de Rothschild and Henri Neuville, "Sur un dent d'origine énigmatique." Archives de Zoologie Expérimentale et Générale 7 (15 October 1907): 333.

Lake Ainslie, Canada   Lake Ainslie, between Mabou and Scotsville in northeastern Nova Scotia, has produced multiple sightings of a brown or black LAKE MONSTER with a head resembling a horse's. In 1966, Carl Medcof suggested that local witnesses had really seen EEL-balls, occurring when masses of eels rise to the surface simultaneously. Such "balls" may be seven feet wide (if not larger), and could theoretically present the image of a larger animal's humped back. Still, witnesses who have sighted the local cryptid — including some who allegedly met the creature on shore — reject Medcof's explanation.

Sources: Garner, Monster! Monster!; King, In the Domain of the Lake Monsters; Carl Medcof, "Incidental records on behaviour of eels in Lake Ainslie, Nova Scotia." Journal of the Fisheries Research Board of Canada 23 (1966).

Lake Albacuytya, Australia   A large, dark-colored creature with a long neck was reported from this lake, in Victoria, during the late 19th century. Its description is unusual for Australia, matching reports of LAKE MONSTERS while diverging radically from the normal descriptions of Australian BUNYIPS.

Source: Smith, Bunyips & Bigfoots.

Lake Albert, Uganda/DRC   Lake Albert, spanning Uganda's western border with the Democratic Republic of Congo (formerly Zaire), reportedly contains more FISH than any other lake in Africa. Cryptozoologist JOHN KIRK includes it on a published list of African lakes spawning LAKE MONSTER reports, but he regrettably includes no details of sightings.

Source: Kirk, In the Domain of the Lake Monsters.

Lake Barombi Mbo, Cameroon   Sometime in 1948 or 1949, British soldiers and a group of native children reportedly saw two long-necked reptilian LAKE MONSTERS swimming in this lake, in southwest Cameroon. One creature had a "downward-pointing, spiny horn" on its head, from which the witnesses concluded that it must be male. Today, Lake Barombi Mbo suffers from effects of local deforestation and high-volume fishing, but no new sightings of large cryptids are reported.

Source: Averbuck, "The Congo water-dragon."

Lake Bathurst, Australia   The creatures known as BUNYIPS have been reported from various parts of Australia, in all shapes and sizes. The following report comes from witness E.S. Hall, in New South Wales.

One fine morning in November 1821, I was walking by the side of the marsh which runs into Lake Bathurst, when my attention was attracted to a creature casting up the water and making a noise, in sound resembling a porpoise, but shorter and louder: the head only was out of the water. At the distance I stood (about 100 yards) it had the appearance of a bull-dog's head, but perfectly black; the head floated about as though the animal was recreating itself; it cut up the water behind, but the quantity thrown up evinced neither strength nor bulk; it remained about five minutes, and then disappeared. I saw it at a greater distance afterwards, when it wore the same appearance.

One night my overseer placed a cart in the marsh, and in the morning got into it armed with a musket, very heavily charged with pieces of lead. The creature appeared at day-light, and the man fired; he saw the creature rise, and lie at full length on the reeds, about 5 feet long, but his shoulder was in such excruciating pain, from the recoiling of the musket, that he involuntarily shut his eyes from the agony, and when he opened them, the creature had just turned over and disappeared. Numbers of them have since been seen, but never shot at.

Source: Smith, *Bunyips & Bigfoots.*

Lake Burley Griffin, Australia

In April 2000, two men passing by this lake in Australia's Capital Territory witnessed a long wake on the surface, as if from the rapid passage of some large submerged object. Rumors abound, but no actual sightings of LAKE MONSTERS have yet been reported.

Source: "A monster in Lake Burley Griffin, Australia." *Cryptozoology Review* 4 (Summer 2000): 5-6.

Lake Burrumbeet, Australia

Fortean authors Colin and Janet Bord include this lake in Victoria (as Lake "Burrumbert") on a list of lakes supposed to harbor LAKE MONSTERS. No further details are provided, and while the lake in question may once have produced BUNYIP sightings, documentation remains as elusive as the creatures themselves.

Source: Bord and Bord, *Alien Animals.*

Lake Campbell, South Dakota

Lake Oahe is the largest lake in the Dakotas, spanning 150 miles from North Dakota's capital (Bismarck) to the capital of South Dakota (Pierre). Residents of Campbell County, South Dakota, sometimes call it Campbell Lake. In the early 1930s, Campbell County farmers suffered losses as an unseen MYSTERY MAULER preyed on their sheep and other domestic animals. Then, in 1934, a local witness claimed a four-legged reptilian creature resembling a DRAGON forced his tractor off the road, into a ditch. Large tracks reportedly led hunters to the shore of Campbell Lake, but the tantalizing story has no resolution, and some researchers view it as a HOAX.

Source: Keel, *The Complete Guide to Mysterious Beings.*

Lake Changhai, China

Lake Changhai ("Long Lake") is located in central China's Sichuan Province. On 12 October 1984, a scientist engaged in other business at the lake reported sighting a "miracle animal," which he described as 10 feet long, with a large body and a head resembling a horse's. Chinese authorities typically investigate such reports, but no further data is presently available from Lake Changhai.

Source: Bord and Bord, *Unexplained Mysteries of the 20th Century.*

Lake Charlevoix, Michigan

This large lake in Michigan's upper peninsula (Charlevoix County) produced a LAKE MONSTER sighting in 1895, when witnesses saw a green 30-foot cryptid basking in the sun near Gull Island. There appear to be no modern sightings of the animal.

Source: Nelson, "Sea serpents and hairy beasts."

Lake Chelan, Washington

Central Washington's Lake Chelan (Chelan County) stretches over 50 miles, from Stehekin in the north to Chelan in the south. With a maximum depth of 1,486 feet, it is the third-deepest lake in the U.S. On 21 December 1895, the *Seattle Times* reported a frightening event from Lake Chelan. According to that article, three travelers had stopped beside the lake, at a point called Devil's Slide, and one of them was bathing in the shallows when an unseen creature bit his leg and tried to drag him underwater. The man's companions pulled him clear:

…but what was their surprise to see the monster also emerge from the water firmly attached to the man's leg by its teeth. It was a horrid looking creature, with the legs and body of an ALLIGATOR and the head and restless eye of a serpent. Between its fore and hind legs, on either side, were large ribbed feathery looking wings. The tail was scaled but not barbed like that in the picture of the typical DRAGON. With the exception of the underpart of the throat and the tips of the wings, feet and tail, the creature was a beautiful white and its skin as soft as velvet. Knives, sticks and stones and everything else which were brought to bear upon the monster proved unavailing, and at last the ingenious travelers bethought themselves of heroic measure. They built a good fire and pulled the neck and belly of the beast, BIRD, or FISH across it, taking good care not to burn the leg of their comrade in the operation. After a while the scorching heat aroused the animal from its torpor. It began to move its body and to stretch out its leathery wings after the manner of a BAT, and suddenly flew into the air, still holding the man by the leg. After rising to a height of about 200 feet it took a "header" downward toward the lake, into which it plunged with a splash, burying itself and victim out of sight.

The article concluded with a report that local aborigines were panicked by the creature's appearance, fearing it might herald Earth's destruction. No other contacts with the strangely drowsy cryptid are on file.

Source: Garner, *Monster! Monster!*

Lake Clark, Alaska

Fortean authors Colin and Janet Bord include this 40-mile-long lake on a list of Alaskan sites alleged to harbor LAKE MONSTERS. No details are provided, but it may be worth noting that Lake Clark lies 30 miles north of Iliamna Lake, home "ILLIE," the state's most famous cryptid.

Source: Bord and Bord, *Unexplained Mysteries of the 20th Century.*

Lake Clinch, Florida

Cryptozoologists LOREN COLEMAN and JOHN KIRK include this Florida lake, near Frostproof (Polk County) on lists of alleged LAKE MONSTER habitats, but no further details are provided.

Source: Coleman, *Mysterious America;* Kirk, *In the Domain of the Lake Monsters.*

Lake Coeur d'Alene, Idaho

This lake in Idaho's Kootenai County appears on several published lists of U.S. lakes alleged to harbor LAKE MONSTERS, but no specific details are provided. The listings may refer to aboriginal legends, but guesswork is fruitless without further information.

Sources: Coleman, *Mysterious America;* Kirk, *In the Domain of the Lake Monsters.*

Lake Como, Colorado

Authors LOREN COLEMAN and JOHN KIRK list this lake, in San Juan County, among U.S. lakes allegedly inhabited by LAKE MONSTERS, but no details are furnished to support the claims.

Sources: Coleman, *Mysterious America;* Kirk, *In the Domain of the Lake Monsters.*

Lake Conway, Arkansas Fishermen at this lake in central Arkansas (Faulkner County) began reporting encounters with "strange finny monsters" in the early 1920s, but the cryptids did not make headlines until 1953. That spring, one angler allegedly hooked an 80-pound "freakish animal" on his trot line, but lost it as he hauled it in for a closer look. Another fisherman, casting for bass in shallow, reported seeing a strange head larger than a man's break the surface amid some shoreline weeds. The thing was hairless, with "dark brown FROG-like skin" and no visible eyes or ears. It understandably submerged when the man opened fire with a pistol. On 5 June 1953, another sighting was recorded at Brannon's Landing, where an unknown creature splashed around a fisherman's boat. The witness said, "It was a dark color, probably brown, marked by noticeable orange spots. Its neck was rounded and with little or no visible neck [*sic*]."

Sources: "Deep in the dark waters of Lake Conway lurks a terrible monster (or maybe not)." *Conway Log Cabin Democrat* (28 June 1974); Garner, *Monster! Monster!*

Lake Corangamite, Australia In 1872, a schoolteacher named D'Arcy shot several ducks near this lake in Victoria, but the current of Woordie Yallock Creek carried his prey into the middle of the lake. Without a boat, D'Arcy had no way to retrieve the ducks, but a stranger soon appeared, pushing a small punt on a cart. A quarter-century later, D'Arcy described what happened next.

> I told him if he would go for them he could have half. He did so, but while I was looking at him I heard him scream out and presently he capsized the punt and swam for his life into shore. When he got in, he could hardly stand, and told me that just as he was taking up the last duck, an animal like a big retriever dog, with a round head and hardly any ears, had come up close to the boat. He had such a fright he had capsized it.

D'Arcy himself never saw the creature, whose description as relayed is fairly typical for an Australian BUNYIP.

Source: Smith, *Bunyips & Bigfoots*.

Lake Creek Monster Grizzly Peak, in Colorado's San Juan Mountains, stands 10 miles northeast of Rico, on the boundary of Dolores and San Juan Counties. In the early 1880s, miners working in the area reported sightings of an unknown HOMINID they dubbed the Lake Creek Monster. Witnesses described the BIGFOOT-type creature as resembling a man, except for its coat of shaggy hair and uniquely long arms.

Source: Green, *Sasquatch: The Apes Among Us*.

Lake Decatur, Illinois Giant, mutated CATFISH the size of cows are said to dwell in the mud below a dam on this lake, in Macon County. Swimmers shy away from the area, but none of the creatures have yet been captured.

Sources: Coleman, *Mysterious America*; Troy Taylor, *Haunted Decatur Revisited*. Akron, IL: Whitechapel, 2000.

Lake DeSmet, Wyoming Aboriginal legends of a LAKE MONSTER in Lake DeSmet (six miles from Buffalo, in Johnson County) predate the arrival of white settlers in Wyoming. The creature was described as 30-40 feet long, with a mane or bony ridge along its back. In 1892, a settler named Barkey allegedly watched two of the animals paddling around the lake for 15 minutes.

Sources: Ella Clark, *Indian Legends from the Northern Rockies*. Norman, OK: University of Oklahoma Press, 1966; Edward Gillette, *Locating the Iron Trail*. Boston: Christopher, 1925.

Lake Dexter, Florida *see* **Astor Monster**

Lake Dulverton, Australia This Tasmanian lake, outside Oatlands, was the heart of a wildlife sanctuary in the 1930s. It dried up completely a half-century later, but locals revived it in the 1990s with a new dam, pumped-in water, and swarms of trout raised at a nearby hatchery. The real surprise, however, came on 4 January 2002, when residents sighted and photographed a long-necked LAKE MONSTER swimming in the middle of the lake. Tony Cawthorn, spokesman for Friends of Lake Dulverton, summed up the enigma when he told reporters, "People are pointing fingers everywhere, but it's a mystery how she got there." Sightings continued for roughly a week, but appear to have ceased since that time. Skeptics suggest the sightings may be part of a HOAX to recapture the lake's former glory with a touch of CRYPTOTOURISM. The published photos remain unexplained.

Source: Georgia Warner, "Dead lake's monster revival." *The Mercury* (10 January 2002).

Lake DuQuoin, Illinois This Perry County lake produced multiple LAKE MONSTER sightings from the summer of 1879 to 1968, when it was partially drained. No large creatures were found in the process, and reports have ceased since that time.

Source: Clark and Coleman, "American lake monsters."

Lake Elsinore, California *see* **Hamlet**

Lake Erie *see* **Bessie**

Lake Fegen, Sweden In 1969, a group of 20-plus witnesses watched a black, 12-foot cryptid paddling around this lake in Sweden's Jönköping County. Lake Fegen is 100 feet deep at its greatest depth.

Source: GLOBAL UNDERWATER SEARCH TEAM website, http://www.cryptozoology.st/.

Lake Furesö, Denmark A curious incident in February 1944 spawned rumors of a LAKE MONSTER inhabiting this lake, in Denmark's København County. Several residents observed violent splashing at a private pier, which briefly lifted a boat clear of the water and splintered several 1-inch wooden planks. The animal responsible for the disturbance was not seen and has not been identified.

Source: Bord and Bord, *Unexplained Mysteries of the 20th Century*.

Lake Geneva, Switzerland Old reports allude to a LAKE MONSTER inhabiting this lake, in Canton Vaud, but there seem to be no modern sightings on record.

Source: Magin, "A brief survey of lake monsters in continental Europe."

Lake Geneva, Wisconsin On 22 July 1892, two boys at Lake Geneva reported sighting a 100-foot serpentine LAKE MONSTER in the water. Locals subsequently claimed the animal had capsized several boats.

Source: Brown, *Sea Serpents: Wisconsin Occurrences of These Weird Water Monsters*; "Western lake resorts have each a water monster." *Chicago Tribune* (24 July 1892).

Lake George, Australia Sightings of a BUNYIP resembling a seal were reported from this lake, in New South Wales, during the 1830s. A century later, local Aborigines still believed that "a devil resembling a seal" inhabited the lake, but if so, it must have an escape route, since Lake George dries up completely during times of drought.

Sources: Healy and Cropper, *Out of the Shadows*; Smith, *Bunyips & Bigfoots*.

Lake George, New York *see* **Hippogriff**

Lake Hanas, China   FISH resembling titanic salmon allegedly inhabit this lake, in China's Xinjiang Uygur Autonomous Region. Biology teacher Xiang Lihao took his class to the lake in July 1985, and they observed a school of 60-odd giant fish swimming in the lake. Xiang described the fish as resembling taimen (*Huchio tainen*), a freshwater salmon that does not officially exceed six feet. These red monsters, however, measured 33 feet long by Xiang's estimate, with heads three feet wide and spiny dorsal fins. Six years later, in July 1988, a group of fishermen reported three similar fish, around 13 feet long.

Sources: "Giant fish reported in China." *ISC Newsletter*; Wen Jiao, "Does China have a Loch Ness monster?"

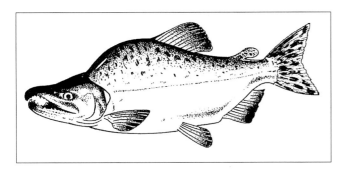

Chinese witnesses reported fish resembling giant salmon from Lake Hanas in 1985.

Lake Hindmarsh, Australia   In the early 20th century, witnesses reported a BUNYIP resembling a black pig floating on the surface of this lake, in Victoria. The creature was never identified.

Source: Smith, *Bunyips & Bigfoots*.

Lake Huron   Each of North America's Great Lakes has produced LAKE MONSTER sightings at one time or another. A large unknown creature was seen in Michigan's Thunder Bay, near Alpena, in June 1888. Four years later, in July 1892, witnesses reported a serpentine cryptid 60-75 long prowling the waters near Mackinac Island. More recently, in July 1975, a group of 10 unknown animals was seen swimming in the lake, offshore from Kincardine, Ontario. (Cryptozoologist JOHN KIRK describes that incident as the largest collective sighting of aquatic mystery creatures on record.) Another serpentine creature was seen on 25 June 1976, in Mackinac Strait and near Cheboygan, Michigan. In 1989, a tourist saw two animals resembling logs afloat, near Goderich, Ontario. As he watched, the creatures raised their heads above the surface, then began to swim across the lake at "tremendous speed."

Sources: Gardner, *Monster! Monster!*; Kirk, *In the Domain of the Lake Monsters*; "Loch Ness sea monsters spotted near Kincardine." London, Ontario *Free Press* (12 July 1975).

Lake Ishiku, Zambia   A reptilian LAKE MONSTER or giant SNAKE allegedly inhabits this lake, near Ndola, Zambia. No serious investigation of native claims has thus far been attempted.

Source: Dobney, "Myths and monsters."

Lake James, North Carolina   Lake James, 10 miles west of Morganton, lies equally in Burke and McDowell Counties, at the southern end of Lake James State Park. LAKE MONSTER reports from the district are uncommon, but in 1981 a group of fishermen reported sighting a dragonlike creature the size of an automobile.

Source: Mark Hall, "Lake monsters." *Wonders* 6 (March 1999): 11.

Lake Kanianka, Slovakia   Katie Sullivan's Internet website claims that LAKE MONSTER sightings were reported from this lake, near Bojnice Castle, in the 1990s, but no details or sources for the listing are provided.

Source: The Online Lake Cryptid Directory, http:/dive.to/lakemonsters.

Lake Katherine, Colorado   In August 1979, hikers Jerry Cross and Bill Hoppe reported sighting a 15-foot humpbacked animal swimming in this lake, in the Mount Zirkel Wilderness Area (Jackson County). The animal was black, they said, but no further details were forthcoming.

Source: *Denver Post* (19 October 1979).

Lake Katherine, Wyoming   Cryptozoologists LOREN COLEMAN and JOHN KIRK include this Wyoming lake on published lists of LAKE MONSTER habitats, but neither supplies any details. A possibility exists that both authors have confused this site with LAKE KATHERINE, COLORADO (scene of a cryptid sighting in October 1979), but that judgment remains speculative in the absence of further data.

Sources: Coleman, *Mysterious America*; Kirk, *In the Domain of the Lake Monsters*.

Lake Kegonsa, Wisconsin   Native Americans believed that a "vengeful and destructive" LAKE MONSTER inhabited this lake in Dane County, southeast of Madison, near Stoughton. Sightings were reported into the 1890s, but have seemingly ceased in modern times.

Sources: Brown, *Sea Serpents: Wisconsin Occurrences of These Weird Water Monsters*; Gardner, *Monster! Monster!*

Lake Kenosha, Connecticut   Cryptozoologist ROY MACKAL reports that a LAKE MONSTER was sighted on 11 November 1891, at this lake in Danbury, Connecticut. Unfortunately, no description is provided and no other source acknowledges the sighting.

Source: Mackal, *Searching for Hidden Animals*.

Lake Khaiyr, Siberia   In November 1964, members of a Soviet scientific expedition reported sighting an unidentified LAKE MONSTER in this lake in Siberia's Sakha Republic (150 miles inland from the Laptev Sea). Biologist Nikolai Gladikh was col-

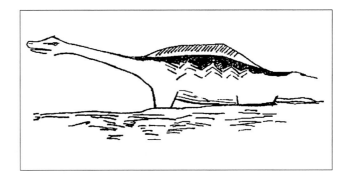

Siberia's Lake Khaiyr cryptid, based on eyewitness descriptions.

lecting water from the lake when he saw the creature on shore, apparently eating grass. He described the creature as having "a small head on a long shiny neck, an enormous body with bluish-black skin, and an upright dorsal fin." Other members of the party saw the animal later that day, "lashing the water with its long tail and sending out wakes all over the lake." Another expedition was announced for 1965, but no further reports have been published thus far.

Sources: Dinsdale, *Monster Hunt*; G. Rukosuyev, "The mystery of Lake Khaiyr." *Soviet Life* (June 1965): 41.

Lake Kök-köl, Kazakhstan *see* **Aidakhar**

Lake Koshkonong, Wisconsin Regrettable confusion surrounds the status of alleged LAKE MONSTER reports from Koshkonong Lake, located 27 miles southeast of Madison, Wisconsin. Author Betty Garner mentions a "very large water animal" seen at "Lake Koshkong" sometime in the 1890s, but she provides no further details. (There is no such lake in Wisconsin, but a Lake Kosh*long* exists in Ontario, Canada.) ROY MACKAL writes that 19th-century carp fishermen blamed the animal(s) for shredding their nets, while a farmer on the western shore claimed a monster had devoured several of his pigs. Meanwhile, the *Columbia Gazetteer of North America* reports that Lake Koshkonong was created in 1932, by erection of the Indian Lake Dam. In any case, while the lake sprawls over 10,460 square acres, it is nowhere more than seven feet deep. Skeptics suggest that any reports of "large animals" may refer to oversized pickerel (*Esox americanus*), while Mackal blames the incidents on "psychological bias."

Sources: Brown, *Sea Serpents: Wisconsin Occurrences of These Weird Water Monsters*; Garner, *Monster! Monster!*; Mackal, *Searching for Hidden Animals*; Columbia Gazetteer of North America, http://www.bartleby.com/69/64/K06664.html.

Lake La Metrie, Wyoming In September 1899, *Pearson's Magazine* published a short story titled "The Monster of Lake La Metrie." The tale follows two scientists to a fictional Wyoming lake, where they encounter a living PLESIOSAUR, coughed up from the depths by a recent volcanic eruption. After some sci-fi silliness involving brain transplants, a troop of cavalry arrives to kill the monster with a field gun. Author Ward Allen Curtis reportedly based his work on real-life reports of Rocky Mountain LAKE MONSTERS, but the story itself has no factual basis. It is all the more surprising, then, to find mythical Lake La Metrie included on lists of "monster" lakes published by cryptozoologists LOREN COLEMAN and JOHN KIRK.

Sources: Coleman, *Mysterious America*; Costello, *In Search of Lake Monsters*; Kirk, *In the Domain of the Lake Monsters*.

Lake Labynkyr, Siberia Since the 1950s, residents of eastern Siberia's Sakha Republic have reported LAKE MONSTER sightings from this lake, 500 miles southeast of LAKE KHAIYR on the Sordongnokh Plateau. Hunters claim the dark-gray animal with an "enormous mouth" devours dogs that leap into the water to retrieve fallen ducks. Dr. Sergei Klumov, writing for *Piroda* (*Nature*) in August 1962, speculated that the creature might be a large FISH or amphibian of unknown species. Expeditions from Russia and Estonia visited the lake in 1963 and 1964, respectively, but reported no sightings.

Source: Dinsdale, *Monster Hunt*.

Lake Ladoga, Russia Multiple sources cite this Russian

Lake La Metrie and its monster, shown here in an 1899 magazine illustration, are both entirely fictional.

lake as a source of LAKE MONSTER reports, but no dates or details of sightings are provided to facilitate further research.

Sources: Kirk, *In the Domain of the Lake Monsters*; The Online Lake Cryptid Directory, http://dive.to/lakemonsters.

Lake Leelanau, Michigan In the early 1800s, a dam was erected at the northern end of this Leelanau County lake (formerly known as Carp or Provemont Lake), thereby expanding its area to encompass neighboring marshland. A century later, in 1910, William Gauthier was fishing for perch on the lake when he sighted a protruding tree limb 5 feet tall and six inches in diameter. Deciding to tie up his boat, he approached the "tree" with rope in hand, only to see a pair of eyes pop open in a head near-level with his own. The creature, seemingly as startled as Gauthier, sank vertically out of sight and did not reappear.

Source: The Shadowlands, http://theshadowlands.net/serpent2.htm.

Lake Manitou, Indiana Before white settlers arrived on the scene, Native Americans believed this Fulton County lake (near Rochester) was inhabited by a devil ("manitou"). In July 1838, multiple witnesses reported sighting a 60-foot serpentine LAKE MONSTER swimming on the surface. One observer described the creature's head as resembling a cow's. Though relatively small — two miles long and half a mile wide at its widest point — Lake Manitou has never been plumbed to its bottom. The last effort, employing a 40-fathom line (240 feet) failed to determine its depth.

Sources: Garner, *Monster! Monster!*; Gatschet, "Water monsters of the American aborigines"; Donald Smalley, "The Logansport *Telegraph* and the monster of the Indiana lakes." *Indiana Magazine* 42 (1946): 249-267.

Lake Maquapit, Canada
Sightings of a medium-large unidentified animal have been filed from this New Brunswick lake in 1979. Skeptics insist the witnesses have simply seen an oversized snapping TURTLE (*Chelydra serpentina*).

Source: *Fredericton* (N.B.) *Gleaner* (8 September 1979).

Lake Maxinkuckee, Indiana
Authors LOREN COLEMAN and JOHN KIRK include this Indiana lake, near Curtis in southwestern Marshall County, on lists of supposed LAKE MONSTER habitats, but neither provides any details of actual sightings.

Sources: Coleman, *Mysterious America*; Kirk, *In the Domain of the Lake Monsters*.

Lake McGregor, Canada
This lake in eastern Alberta is an irrigations reservoir. In July 1945, a 12- to 14-foot long-necked animal was reported both from the lake itself, and from the nearby Saskatchewan River.

Sources: *Edmonton Journal* (8 July 1945); Garner, *Monster! Monster!*

Lake Mead, Nevada
Visitors to this lake, on southern Nevada's border with Arizona, have reported giant CATFISH in the water near Hoover Dam.

Source: Coleman, *Mysterious America*.

Lake Merritt, California
Lake Merritt, in downtown Oakland, was created in 1869 when the city dammed a 140-acre inlet of San Francisco Bay. It is maintained by lake keeper and marine biologist Dick Bailey, with a staff of dedicated volunteers. In December 2003, Bailey's monthly newsletter carried the following announcement:

Please don't feed the CROCODILE. He's big. He's blue. And he (she?) is in Lake Merritt. You can see it across the lake from the broken down dock by the Lake Merritt Hotel. First found trying to crawl up an old wall, it was recently noted out in deeper water. "Of course it is not an ALLIGATOR. They don't live in salt water. How he got here we haven't a clue. Maybe he swam in from the Berkeley shoreline.

An article in the *Oakland Tribune* described the beast as "6-feet-long with a large head and prominent nostrils and popping eyes. Its skin is rough and bumpy. Probably it has a tail and four short legs." Even so, the paper raised a question that it might be "a wild creation of human hands," planted in Lake Merritt by some unknown artist as a HOAX. That theory was borne out on Christmas Eve, when a group of student volunteers from St. Paul's School found a papier-mâché "carcass" floating near shore. "They propped it up against the [lake] wall where we first found it," Bailey reported. "We won't pull it out of the lake right away."

Source: Peggy Stinnett, "'Creature' discovered in Lake Merritt." *Oakland* (CA) *Tribune* (31 December 2003).

Lake Michigan
Lake Michigan is the only one of the Great Lakes lying entirely within U.S. territory. LAKE MONSTER reports have emerged from its waters for over a century, beginning in early August 1867, with sightings of a 40- to 50-foot serpentine creature by multiple witnesses, ranging from Evanston, Illinois to Michigan City, Indiana. Reporters for the *Chicago Tri-*

bune were impressed enough to write "that Lake Michigan is inhabited by a vast monster, part FISH and part serpent no longer admits of doubt." In 1892, unknown animals were reported swimming offshore from Muskegon and Petosky, Michigan. The 1890s also produced several reports of serpentine cryptids glimpsed from the Milwaukee, Wisconsin shoreline. Easily the most astounding story from that decade is the tale of the schooner *Cheney Ames*, allegedly wrecked by a huge serpent in the harbor at Muskegon, Michigan in July 1892. As described in the press, the ship was dashed against a pier in the harbor, without explanation, and a sailor dived in to assess the damage. Moments later, the man surfaced in a state of shock, "paralyzed" by something that "froze his blood and dried up his fountains of speech." The press detailed what he had seen:

Lodged between the wheel and rudder of that peculiarly constructed schooner, and coiled...several...times about the rudder was a serpent fully sixty feet in length. Its jaws, in which gleamed ferocious fangs, were distended and the gleaming bead-like eyes of the beast looked earnestly into the eyes of the sailor as he passed. The lower part of the body was yellowish pink and white, while the upper portion of the reptile was glossy black. The wheel had cut a gash in its side from which the blood spurted and discolored the water in the wake of the vessel.

Before the sailor could finish his story, the monster apparently freed itself and escaped. The ship's rudder, suddenly freed, caused the *Cheney Ames* to veer wildly across the channel, where it sank in shallow water. Subsequent investigation revealed that an hour before the accident, a large animal swimming like a "huge inverted corkscrew" had been sighted near the harbor by William Dixon, superintendent of the water department.

A new spate of sightings began on 21 June 1976, when the owner of the Four Seasons Motel at Point Nipigon saw an 18-foot serpentine creature entering Lake Michigan from the Straits of Makinac (communicating with LAKE HURON). Multiple reports of a similar beast were filed over the next week. Witnesses reported that the cryptid submerged any time a boat passed nearby.

Sources: Brown, *Sea Serpents: Wisconsin Occurrences of These Weird Water Monsters*; Garner, *Monster! Monster!*; Kirk, *In the Domain of the Lake Monsters*; Mark Hall, "Lake Michigan monsters." *Wonders* 2 (June 1993): 36-45; Mangiacopra, "Water monsters of the Midwestern lakes"; "Western lake resorts have each a water monster." *Chicago Tribune* (24 July 1892).

Lake Miminiska, Canada
Reports of a large "FISH-like serpent" issued from this lake in northern Ontario (west of Fort Hope, on the Albani River) during the early days of Canadian settlement. No more recent accounts are presently available.

Sources: Bord and Bord, *Unexplained Mysteries of the 20th Century*; Garner, *Monster! Monster!*

Lake Minchumina, Alaska
Lake Minchumina, north of Denali National Park, is Alaska's largest interior lake. Cryptozoologists LOREN COLEMAN and JOHN KIRK include it on published lists of North American LAKE MONSTER habitats, but neither provides any details of actual sightings.

Sources: Coleman, *Mysterious America*; Kirk, *In the Domain of the Lake Monsters*.

Lake Minnetonka, Minnesota
Lake Minnetonka ("big waters") lies three miles west of Minneapolis. On 19 April 1887, during construction of the Greys Bay Bridge, workers sighted a 30-foot serpentine LAKE MONSTER swimming below them. Five years later, on 24 July 1892, the *Chicago Sunday Tri-*

bune described an even more startling 30-foot monster, possessed of only "one green, blazing eye." That description follows:

...The few who have been at once privileged and horrified to behold this uncanny reptile describe it as of great length and of all the fantastic hues of Joseph's coat....

The lower part of its body is shaped like a TURTLE. This portion is flat and nearly round being some ten feet in diameter with a row of short stubby legs on each side, armed with long claws, like the turtle, alternating with other and much larger legs, which are found only among the batrachian species [frogs]. Overlapping this turtle body some five feet in front and twice that length behind writhe and twist the sinuous folds of the purely serpentine portion of this anomalous creature. It has no scales but is completely armored in a series of wart-like bunches as large as a man's head and varying color from white to black with all the intermediate shades of blue, purple, yellow and green.

It wears no mane, but tufts of hair of all imaginable colors occur at frequent intervals on every side from head to tail and below the wide jaws appears a long, bushy goatee of coarsest fiber. Its jaws are furnished with broad pointed teeth and in and out between these rows of glistening bone plays the red, bifurcated tongue with amazing swiftness. The monster's mode of propulsion is a curious cross between the ordinary snakelike natation and the awkward paddle of the turtle, but its speed is remarkable.

When suddenly and without premonition, the most horrible hybrid rises to the surface its vocal organs emit a peculiar noise, half-roar and half-scream and hiss which, added to the tumultuous lashing of the water with the restless tail, produces a most startling effect upon the ear.

Sources: Garner, *Monster! Monster!*; "Western lake resorts have each a water monster."

Lake Minnewanka, Canada

A "large FISH" with a long neck was reported from this lake in western Alberta (north of Canmore) in the early 20th century. The creature remains unidentified today.

Sources: Benedict, "The unknown lake monsters of Alberta"; Mabel Williams, *Through the Heart of the Rockies and Selkirks*. Ottawa: Canada National Parks Branch, 1924.

Lake Modewarre, Australia

In the 1830s, settler William Buckley recorded multiple sightings of BUNYIPS swimming in this Victoria lake (also known as Lake Werribee). As he recalled the animals 20 years later, "It [*sic*] seemed to be about the size of a full-grown calf, and sometimes larger; the creatures only appear when the river is very calm and the water smooth." Buckley never glimpses a Bunyip's head or tail, but claimed their backs were covered with dusky-gray feathers.

Source: John Morgan, *The Life and Adventures of William Buckley*. Hobart, Australia: A. MacDougall, 1852.

Lake Monona, Wisconsin

On 11 June 1897, Eugene Heath allegedly sighted a 20-foot serpentine LAKE MONSTER swimming across this lake, located at Madison, Wisconsin. Heath fired several gunshots at the creature, apparently without effect, before it submerged. Other witnesses reported sightings from at Tonywatha and Winnequah, on the lake's east shore. Years later, in the midst of dredging operations at Olbricht Park, a sand pump's allegedly jammed with large vertebrae thought to be the creature's. The whereabouts of those bones is unknown.

Sources: Brown, *Sea Serpents: Wisconsin Occurrences of These Weird Water Monsters*; Garner, *Monster! Monster!*; "What-is-it in lake." *Madison* (WI) *State Journal* (12 June 1897).

Lake Monroe, Florida

Authors LOREN COLEMAN and JOHN KIRK include this lake (at Sanford, in Seminole County) on lists of U.S. LAKE MONSTER habitats, but neither supplies any details of sightings.

Sources: Coleman, *Mysterious America*; Kirk, *In the Domain of the Lake Monsters*.

Lake Monsters

Throughout the world, hundreds of lakes and rivers are allegedly inhabited by large freshwater cryptids, collectively known as lake monsters. They are known from ancient folklore by a wide variety of names, including the Irish Péist or Piast, the Scottish Kelpie or "water horse," and the Scandinavian LINDORM or SKRIMSL. Each native tribe or nation of the New World had its own name for such creatures. In Australia, a bewildering cast of aquatic or amphibious cryptids are commonly lumped together as BUNYIPS.

Lake monster descriptions vary as widely as names and locations of sightings. Some appear to be giant FISH, while others are described as huge EELS or SNAKES. Oversized TURTLES and CROCODILES are seen on occasion. Some freshwater cryptids emulate classic SEA SERPENTS, with a display of multiple humps or coils on the water's surface. Others resemble PLESIOSAURS, with small heads mounted on long necks, attached to stout bodies equipped with flippers. Manes, horns, forked tongues and serrated spines have all been reported on various specimens. Their flesh is alternately smooth, rough, slimy, scaly, armored, furred or feathered. They range in size from 14 inches to 100 feet or more, and come in every color of the rainbow. Some have legs and crawl ashore from time to time, either to sunbathe or to feed. Some are aggressive, even man-eaters, while others flee at the first sight of human beings. Some honk, bark, hiss or bellow, but the great majority are silent save for thrashing placid waters into foam.

What are they?

No one knows, but numerous solutions are advanced by students of the global mystery. In some "monster" lakes, large fish, turtles or mislocated ALLIGATORS have been captured. Other locations are home to known species such as the Wels CATFISH (*Siluris glanis*), which may grow to 15 feet in length. Larger, more unusual cryptids require a greater stretch of the imagination, though. Some theorists suggest that prehistoric reptiles or mammals (such as the early cetacean ZEUGLODON) may have survived into modern times, but that notion fails to account for cryptids

Witnesses around the world describe lake monsters in various forms and sizes (*William Rebsamen*).

in lakes created long after such creatures were presumably extinct. ANTOON OUDEMANS believed that sea serpents and lake monsters all represented variations of one species, a giant long-necked seal he dubbed *Megophias*. Author Peter Costello proposed a similar creature, whose hypothetical physiology accounts for most details of NESSIE-type creatures, while answering objections that a reptile could not long survive in cold-water lakes. A few researchers, including F.W. Holiday and ROY MACKAL (in 1966), have suggested that some lake monster reports may involve large invertebrates on the order of a huge sea slug or a giant version of *Tullimonstrum gregarium* (known only from 6-inch fossils found in Illinois). In warmer climates — Africa, South America and Southeast Asia — Mackal and others argue for possible survival of large reptiles from the age of DINOSAURS.

Self-styled skeptics dismiss all such theories as flights of fantasy. They point to occasional HOAXES (as at SILVER LAKE, NEW YORK) to remind us of the obvious — i.e., that some supposed lake monsters are doubtless the product of some prankster's imagination. Some unknown creatures have been fabricated, or at least exploited, to promote a trend in CRYPTOTOURISM. All others, the nay-sayers insist, are readily explicable as cases of mistaken identity involving known species of fish, reptiles, BIRDS or mammals; or natural phenomena such as floating logs or mats of vegetation, ripples caused by wind or passing boats, and turmoil caused by underwater seismic activity. If lake monsters existed, they protest, surely some proof of their existence could be found.

But, then again, perhaps it has.

Since 1933, at least 15 different freshwater cryptids around the world have been captured in still photos, on movie film, or on videotape, with several photographed on multiple occasions. They include: BESSIE, CHAMP, CHESSIE, GUÀI WÚ, IGOPOGO, ISSIE, LIZZIE, MANIPOGO, MEMPHRÉ, MIGO, NESSIE, OGOPOGO, SELMA, STORSJÖODJURET, and the unnamed creature of LAKE DULVERTON, Tasmania. According to reports on file, unidentified animals have also been killed or captured in and around various lakes in Europe and the Americas, between Medieval times and 1914 (when an unidentified mammal was dragged from Lake Okanagan, in British Columbia). Critics maintain that all photos and videotapes are deliberate hoaxes, or else depict known objects on the water. As for carcasses and captives, none so far has been preserved for scientific study.

Freshwater cryptids covered in this volume are too numerous to list within a single entry. Readers will find them alphabetized by popular names, where applicable (e.g., Nessie, WEE OICHY, etc.), or by the name of their supposed habitat (e.g., LAKE ERIE, LOUGH REE, etc.).

Sources: Costello, *In Search of Lake Monsters*; Kirk, *In the Domain of the Lake Monsters*; Mackal, *Searching for Hidden Animals*; Meurger and Gagnon, *Lake Monster Traditions*; Shuker, *In Search of Prehistoric Survivors*.

Lake Murray, Papua New Guinea
In May 1995, a Seventh-Day Adventist missionary on New Britain, Papua New Guinea, claimed to have seen a large reptilian creature emerge from Lake Murray, casually browsing on plants along the lake's shore. The witness described a bipedal cryptid, resembling reconstructions of *Iguanodon*, a 30-foot DINOSAUR from the Early Cretaceous period (presumed extinct for some 80 million years).

Source: Gibbons, *Missionaries and Monsters*.

Lake Mweru, Zambia/DRC
This lake, spanning the border between Zambia and the Democratic Republic of Congo,

is 76 miles long and has a surface area of 1,900 square miles. The Luapula River flows through it, and the great Bangweulu Swamp lies nearby. Lake Mweru is one of several African lakes allegedly inhabited by the CHIPEKWE, a large reptilian creature resembling a DINOSAUR.

Sources: Heuvelmans, *Les Derniers Dragons d'Afrique*; Heuvelmans, *On the Track of Unknown Animals*.

Lake Natsilik, Greenland
This lake reportedly harbors two unidentified LAKE MONSTERS. One, reported from olden times, is described as a SEA SCORPION the size of a boat. The other, sighted by several witnesses in 1954, is apparently a huge FISH with a dorsal fin the size of a sail.

Source: "Water monsters: Greenland." *Fortean Times*.

Lake Norman, North Carolina
This lake, located 15 miles north of Charlotte, reportedly harbors giant CATFISH — and perhaps something else. In May 2002, local resident Matt Myers established an Internet website for the Lake Norman monster, which Myers calls "Normie." Over the next five months, the website scored 10,000 "hits" and received 21 reports of alleged eyewitness sightings. Descriptions of the creature(s) vary widely, including catfish 4-20 feet long; an unidentified dolphin-sized FISH; another with a "scabby-looking fin"; a "long, slender-looking SNAKE"; and a creature with a neck resembling a "large stick" thrust above the water's surface. Myers has expanded into sale of Normie souvenirs, representing the first expansion of CRYPTOTOURISM into cyberspace.

Sources: Mark Price, "Nessie has some local competition." *Charlotte (NC) Observer* (20 October 2002); LakeNormanMonster.com, http://monsterinthelake.com/norman/.

Lake Nyasa, Malawi
This African lake is rumored to support three different LAKE MONSTERS. In 1905, following a fierce storm at this African lake, explorer Hector Duff saw a large two-humped animal in a small inlet north of Nkhata Bay. Duff's native guides called the creature Dzimwé, claiming that it was commonly seen after storms, but a steamer captain later persuaded Duff that he had seen the bloated carcass of a dead hippopotamus. The lake's other cryptids, both unnamed, include a giant PYTHON and a strange animal sporting a zebra's head and a FISH'S tail.

Sources: Hector Duff, *African Small Chop*. London: Hodder and Stoughton, 1932; Heuvelmans, *Les Derniers Dragons d'Afrique*.

Lake of Bays, Canada
LAKE MONSTER sightings were reported from this Ontario lake, southeast of Huntsville, during 1946-48. Witnesses described a black NESSIE-type creature, with a long neck and humped back visible above the surface. The encounters occurred off the north point of Fairview Island and near Bigwin Island.

Sources: Garner, *Monster! Monster!*; Sanderson, "*Things.*"

Lake of the Ozarks, Missouri
This large lake, spanning four counties in central Missouri, reportedly harbors giant CATFISH, as well as a larger LAKE MONSTER with a 20-foot neck and humped back. Sightings of the latter, NESSIE-type creature date from 1935.

Sources: Jim Brandon, *Weird America*. New York: Dutton, 1978; Garner, *Monster! Monster!*; Vance Randolph, *Ozark Superstitions*. New York: Columbia University Press, 1947.

Lake of the Pines, Texas
This Texas lake, located 25 miles northeast of Longview, sprawls over parts of four counties

with a total surface area of 18,700 acres. Its maximum depth of 49.5 feet is sufficient to spawn reports of giant CATFISH, though none have been captured so far.

Source: Coleman, *Mysterious America.*

Lake of the Woods, Canada Ontario's aboriginal inhabitants described this lake, below present-day Kenora, as the abode of a serpentine LAKE MONSTER with antlers and a serrated ridge along its back. No modern sightings are on file.

Source: Chris Rutkowski, *Unnatural History.* Winnipeg, Canada: Chameleon, 1993.

Lake of the Woods, New York This lake, in Jefferson County, produced a spate of LAKE MONSTER sightings in the 1920s. Two witnesses who glimpsed the creature while boating, in 1929, described it as 20 feet long and "grayish tan, with a head not much bigger around than the neck or front loop of the body, but with a saw-tooth growth along its head and down the length of the neck or body, about six or seven feet." Three "arcs" or humps were clearly visible on the surface, before the animal submerged. Lakeside landowners reported drag marks on the bank, as if the creature sometimes pulled itself from the water.

Sources: Garner, *Monster! Monster!*; Sanderson, *"Things."*

Lake Onega, Russia This lake in the northeastern part of European Russia spans the borders of three political districts: Kareliya, Leningradskaya and Volgogradskaya. Katie Sullivan's Internet website lists Lake Onega as a source of LAKE MONSTER reports, but no details or sources are included with the listing.

Source: The Online Lake Cryptid Directory, http:/dive.to/lakemonsters.

Lake Ontario According to Native American legend, a great horned serpent emerged from Lake Ontario "2,200 years before the time of Columbus" and killed bystanders with its noxious smell. The first specific sighting of a LAKE MONSTER in the smallest of North America's Great Lakes was recorded in 1829, when two children allegedly saw a 20- to 30-foot serpentine creature near Grantham Township, Ontario (in Lincoln County). Six years later, in August 1835, a German science journal published a brief account of the cryptid. Witnesses in Kingston, at the mouth of the St. Lawrence River, logged their first sighting of the beast they nicknamed Kingstie in 1867. On 14 September 1881, the *Kingston Whig* reported that a "sportive creature" surprised passengers aboard the steamer *Gypsy*, en route from Ottawa to Kingston, "with its immense proportions, unsightliness and graceless pranks in the water." In 1882, a 50-foot animal resembling a giant EEL with a mane down its back was sighted offshore from Toronto. Six years later, passengers aboard the yacht *No Joke* were frightened by a similar creature near Kingston. In 1892, a married couple canoeing at Kingston were accosted by the animal and struck it over the head with an oar. Two Canadian physicians, Frank Bermingham and R.R. MacGregor, narrowly avoided a similar meeting with Kingstie in 1931, afterward describing its "fierce" eyes and skin covered with "warts or bunches." Witness John Alexander of Scarborough saw a 20-foot specimen off Toronto, in 1968. In the mid-1970s, officers of the Ontario Ministry of Natural Resources twice saw large unknown creatures basking on the shores of Prince Edward County. A 50-foot scaly, hump-backed animal was seen at Toronto in July 1978. The following month, a 25-foot gray-black cryptid with three humps was reported from Oshawa harbor, where witnesses dubbed it Oshawa Oscar. Not to be outdone, August witnesses at Beaverton christened their serpent Beaverton Bessie.

Sources: Garner, *Monster! Monster!*; Kirk, *In the Domain of the Lake Monsters.*

Lake Örekram, Norway Author JOHN KIRK includes this lake on a list of supposed LAKE MONSTER habitats, but his 24-page chapter on Norway's aquatic cryptids regrettably provides no details of sightings.

Source: Kirk, *In the Domain of the Lake Monsters.*

Lake Paika, Australia Two published accounts list this lake, in New South Wales, as a habitat of LAKE MONSTERS or BUNYIPS, but neither report provides any details of sightings.

Sources: Bord and Bord, *Alien Animals*; Kirk, *In the Domain of the Lake Monsters.*

Lake Patenggang, Indonesia Neighbors of this jungle lake, located southwest of Bandung, Java, reportedly treat their resident LAKE MONSTER with great reverence, burning opium on the lake shore to placate the beast. Various witnesses describe an 18-foot creature resembling a giant FISH, a huge TURTLE, or a long-necked PLESIOSAUR.

Sources: Shuker, *From Flying Toads to Snakes with Wings*; Shuker, *"Lesser known lake monsters."*

Lake Pocotopaug, Connecticut Author JOHN KIRK probably had this Middlesex County lake in mind when he included nonexistent "Lake Pocotopang, Massachusetts" on a list or alleged LAKE MONSTER habitats. In any case, the listing provides no details from which to proceed with research on the alleged cryptids.

Source: Kirk, *In the Domain of the Lake Monsters.*

Lake Quinault, Washington Native American folklore describes a LAKE MONSTER dwelling in this lake, at the northeast corner of the Quinault Indian Reservation in Gray's Harbor County, but no modern sightings are recorded.

Source: Albert Reagan and L.V.W. Walters, "Tales from Hoh and Quileute." *Journal of American Folklore* 46 (1933): 297, 324-325.

Lake Ripley, Wisconsin A large serpentine LAKE MONSTER was reported from this lake, in Jefferson County, during 1891. No more recent sightings are on file.

Source: Garner, *Monster! Monster!*

Lake St. Clair Lake St. Clair spans the border separating Michigan from Ontario, Canada. In 1948, passengers and crew aboard the cruise ship *City of Detroit III* reported sighting a 60-foot reptilian LAKE MONSTER in the middle of the lake. River access to LAKE HURON (northward) and LAKE ERIE (to the south) suggests that the creature may be identical with one of the various Great Lakes cryptids reported elsewhere.

Source: Nelson, "Sea serpents and hairy beasts."

Lake St. Martin, Canada Fortean authors Colin and Janet Bord include this lake, in central Manitoba, on a list of alleged LAKE MONSTER habitats, but no details of sightings are provided.

Source: Bord and Bord, *Unexplained Mysteries of the 20th Century.*

Lake Sakakawea, North Dakota North Dakota's largest lake, sprawling across three counties, was created by a dam on the Missouri River. Thus, while LAKE MONSTER reports are on file from local witnesses — it seems improbable that any ancient creatures inhabit these waters. Investigators suggest that the animals sighted may be large FISH, perhaps pallid sturgeon

(*Scaphirhyncus albus*) or paddlefish (*Polyodon spathula*). Sightings of 9-foot hairy HOMINIDS have also been reported from the forests of Lake Sakakawea State Park.

Sources: Bord and Bord, *Unexplained Mysteries of the 20th Century*; Hauck, *Haunted Places*; "Sakakawea monster." *Garrison* (ND) *Independent* (21 June 1979).

Lake Sary-Chelek, Kyrgyzstan
In 1962, Moscow radio reported sightings of a LAKE MONSTER from this lake, in the Tien Shan Mountains of what was then Turkestan. A Soviet biologist, Dr. Sergei Klumov, suggested that the witnesses had seen a flock of low-flying cormorants, and while he offered no factual support for that claim, no further sightings are on record from the area.

Sources: Costello, *In Search of Lake Monsters*; Dinsdale, *Monster Hunt*.

Lake Sentani, Indonesia
In World War II, while stationed in western New Guinea (now Irian Jaya, Indonesia), anthropologist GEORGE AGOGINO tossed a hand grenade into Lake Sentani, hoping to kill several FISH for his troop to eat. Among the finny casualties, a 12-foot SHARK bobbed to the surface, floating long enough for Agogino to draw a quick sketch before it sank out of sight. The shark was normal in appearance, but its presence in fresh water is anomalous. Subsequent reports suggest that 11-foot bull sharks (*Carcharhinus leucas*) may be found in Irian Jaya's Lake Jamoer. Another possibility is that Agogino's grenade may have mutilated a sawfish (*Pristis microdon*), found commonly in Lake Sentani. The sawfish may reach lengths of 19 feet, and removal of its unique serrated snout leaves a fish of sharklike appearance.

Sources: Heuvelmans, "Annotated checklist of apparently unknown animals with which cryptozoology is concerned"; Shuker, *From Flying Toads to Snakes with Wings*.

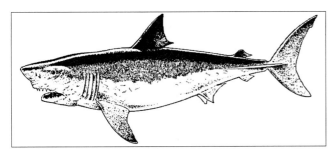

Witness George Agogino reported a shark from Lake Sentani in the 1940s.

Lake Sögne, Norway
Cryptozoologist JOHN KIRK includes this Norwegian lake on a list of alleged LAKE MONSTER habitats, as do Fortean authors Colin and Janet Bord. Unfortunately, neither publication offers any details of reported sightings.

Sources: Bord and Bord, *Unexplained Mysteries of the 20th Century*; Kirk, *In the Domain of the Lake Monsters*.

Lake Sor Sömna, Norway
Fortean authors Colin and Janet Bord, together with cryptozoologist JOHN KIRK, include this Norwegian lake on a published lists of supposed LAKE MONSTER habitats, but they provide no dates or details of reported sightings.

Source: Bord and Bord, *Alien Animals*; Kirk, *In the Domain of the Lake Monsters*.

Lake Superior
Like the rest of North America's Great Lakes, Lake Superior was known to aboriginal tribes as the home of a large LAKE MONSTER, and sporadic sightings have continued into modern times. On 3 May 1782, settler Venant St. Germain reported a brown-colored MERBEING that may have been a seal, swimming around Pie Island, in Ontario's Thunder Bay. Witnesses Van Dein and Angus Steinhoff reported a large serpentine creature swimming in Trout Bay, Michigan in 1932, while fishermen at Stannard Rock (a reef off the shore of Marquette County, Michigan) sighted a 20-foot FISH in July 1998. The largest fish known to inhabit Lake Superior is the lake sturgeon (*Acipenser fulvescens*), which reaches a maximum official length of nine feet. A photo snapped at Agawa Bay, Ontario allegedly depicts two serpentine creatures swimming offshore.

Sources: Richard Dorson, *Bloodstoppers and Bearwalkers*. Cambridge, MA: Harvard University Press, 1952; "Giant sturgeon in Lake Superior?" *Cryptozoology Review* 3 (Winter-Spring 1998): 6-7; Jay Gourley, *The Great Lakes Triangle* Greenwich, CT: Fawcett, 1977; Richard Lambert, *Exploring the Supernatural*. Toronto: McClelland and Stewart, 1955); Meurger and Gagnon, *Lake Monster Traditions*.

Lake Tahoe Monsters
On 7 September 1993, the supermarket tabloid *Weekly World News* published a story claiming that live DINOSAURS were roaming at large in the Sierra Nevada Mountains near Lake Tahoe, on the Nevada-California border. As detailed in that article and a subsequent videotape, the alleged discovery was made on 27 July 1993, by members of Frank Scharo's construction crew. While excavating soil at an undisclosed location, Scharo's team reportedly unearthed a large stone nodule that contained five football-sized eggs. Two of the eggs were destroyed when the nodule broke open, according to Scharo, while a third hatched on the spot and disgorged a foot-long reptilian creature that died moments later. Scharo and partner Camille Gardner thereupon took the eggs and carcass home, placing the reptile in their freezer, while the eggs were locked inside a steel shed. Various unnamed officials, they say, ignored their reports of the find. Three days later, on the morning of 30 July, Gardner found the couple's flock of chickens slaughtered in their coop, near the shed where a hole had been punched through one metal wall from the inside out.

The tale grows even more bizarre from there. One day after the chicken massacre, a certain Dr. Herbert McPlatten arrived at Scharo's home to examine the freezer carcass and remove it for further study. While "refusing to commit himself," McPlatten allegedly identified the creature as an embryonic *Allosaurus*, a 39-foot predatory relative of *Tyrannosaurus rex*, presumed extinct on Earth for some 140 million years. Scharo and Gardner, in a 25-minute videotape produced during 1994, speculated that *Al-*

Nevada's *Novusaur* and prey, based on descriptions from Frank Scharo and Camille Gardner.

losaurus had evolved over time into a pygmy mountain-dwelling form which they dubbed *Novusaur* ("new lizard"). Several television talk shows briefly hyped the story, but it has no ending. Nothing remains of the specimens allegedly unearthed in 1993, aside from photographs of Scharo clutching large eggs and a strange, small carcass. No trace survives on film or paper of the elusive "Dr. McPlatten," and despite Scharo's video reference to dinosaur sightings "spanning decades" around Lake Tahoe, no other reports were listed. Most observers now regard the episode as a short-lived HOAX for profit.

Source: *The Lake Tahoe Monsters* (videotape). Minden, NV: TTL Presentations, 1994.

Lake Tala, Australia   Fortean authors Colin and Janet Bord include this lake, in New South Wales, on a list of alleged BUNYIP or LAKE MONSTER habitats, but they provide no details of reported sightings. Cryptozoologist JOHN KIRK also lists the lake (as "Tarla") on a roster that includes no further information.

Sources: Bord and Bord, *Alien Animals*; Kirk, *In the Domain of the Lake Monsters*.

Lake Tanganyika   Lake Tanganyika is the second-largest lake in Africa and the fifth-largest on Earth. It measures 404 miles long from north to south, with an average width of 30 miles. Its mean depth is 1,853 feet, but deeper basins in the north and south plummet to 4,258 feet and 4,778 feet, respectively. (It is thus the second-deepest lake on Earth.) Four nations surround Lake Tanganyika, including Burundi, Tanzania, Malawi and the Democratic Republic of Congo. It is no surprise, therefore, that large LAKE MONSTERS have been periodically reported from this vast body of water. In 1914, witness M.V. Thierfelder allegedly watched a brown serpentine creature swimming offshore from Rumonge, Burundi. He claimed that the animal swam with a vertical undulating motion, revealing six humps above the water's surface, each 15 feet long and 9 feet high. From those calculations, Thierfelder estimated that the beast must measure between 111 and 168 feet long.

Sources: Heuvelmans, *On the Track of Unknown Animals*; O. Strack, "Auch in Tanganyikasee soll eine 'Nessie' leben!" *Das Tier* 9 (September 1963): 24.

Lake Taupo, New Zealand   This scenic lake near Waikato, on New Zealand's North Island, is a popular tourist destination. Australian cryptozoologist REX GILROY reported a large, unknown animal seen at the lake in May 1980, but no further details on the alleged sighting(s) are available.

Source: *Wellington* (N.Z.) *Dominion* (29 May 1980).

Lake Temiskaming, Canada *see* **Mugwump**

Lake Tiberias, Australia   In 1872, Joseph Barwick published the following account of his meeting with an unknown creature in Tasmania's Lake Tiberias, 20 years earlier.

> In the autumn of 1852 I was lying in ambush near Lake Tiberias for wild ducks. It was a fine moonlight night, when my attention was attracted by a commotion in the water some 15 yards from me among the debris of a fallen tree. I noticed a large animal which, after watching him for some time, I concluded must be a large [Tasmanian] devil. I fired at him, which caused him to flounder in the water. I saw he was seriously wounded and went to secure him, but when I got within 3 yards of him I saw to my surprise it was quite unlike any animal I ever saw before. His length appeared to be about 4ft. or 4ft. 6 inches, colour black, with a remarkable round bull dog like head, and what surprised me at the time was, instead of his making for the land he made for deep water.

Barwick was unable to reload his single-shot gun before the creature submerged, but he returned next morning with a friend and found quantities of 2-inch black, glossy hair at the scene. He also realized that the animal must have had very short legs, since the nearby water was only 15 inches deep, but only its back had been visible above the surface.

Source: Smith, *Bunyips & Bigfoots*.

Lake Toni, Russia   A giant SNAKE allegedly inhabits subterranean burrows around this lake in Siberia's Primor'ye Territory, emerging periodically to hunt and frighten local residents.

Source: Stonehill, "Giant serpents of the Russian Far East."

Lake Umanak, Greenland   A large, white LAKE MONSTER was reported from this lake in 1954. No further sightings have surfaced to date.

Sources: Bord and Bord, *Unexplained Mysteries of the 20th Century*; "Water monsters: Greenland." *Fortean Times* 46 (Spring 1986): 29.

Lake Vorota, Russia   In July 1953, while visiting this remote lake on Siberia's Sordongnokh Plateau (Sakha Republic), Soviet geologist V.A. Tverdokhlebov and a companion saw a shiny object floating 300 yards offshore. They first mistook it for an empty fuel drum, then watched in amazement as it came to life and swam rapidly toward the point where they stood. Scaling a nearby cliff for safety's sake, they studied the animal and later described it as follows: dark gray and 32 feet long, with a head 6 feet 6 inches wide, sporting light-colored patches on either side, with a slender 18-inch dorsal fin. The creature thrashed about the surface for some moments, raising "a cascade of spray," then submerged and did not reappear. Inhabitants of the nearest settlement, 75 miles away, claim Lake Vorota is inhabited by a "devil." Soviet scientist Sergei Klumov reported the sighting in August 1962, but no further accounts of the creature have surfaced to date.

Source: Dinsdale, *Monster Hunt*.

Lake Waubeau, Wisconsin   Three published books and at least two Internet websites include this supposed Wisconsin lake on lists of LAKE MONSTER habitats, although it does not exist. It seems likely that most of the authors confused the name of LAKE WAUBESA, although one (JOHN KIRK) lists *both* lakes separately.

Sources: Coleman, *Mysterious America*; Costello, *In Search of Lake Monsters*; Kirk, *In the Domain of the Lake Monsters*.

Lake Waubesa, Wisconsin   In summer 1922, a fisherman on this lake south of Madison (Dane County) was frightened by the sudden appearance of a dark-green EEL-like creature, 60–70 feet long, that held a reptilian head above the water as it swam. A short time later, other witnesses glimpsed the same animal from a cottage at Waubesa Beach. More sightings from various points on the lake were reported the following year.

Sources: Brown, *Sea Serpents: Wisconsin Occurrences of These Weird Water Monsters*; Garner, *Monster! Monster!*

Lake Wembo, Tibet   Tibet's Lake Wembo (sometimes spelled "Wenbu" or "Menbu") covers 310 square miles and has a maximum recorded depth of 300 feet. It is allegedly inhabited by a voracious long-necked LAKE MONSTER with a large head and a body the size of a house. Local villagers, herdsmen and officials of the Tibetan Communist Party claim the creature preys on yaks left grazing near the shoreline, seizing them in its jaws and dragging them into the lake. According to a June 1980 report in the

Peking Evening News, the animal is also blamed for the disappearance of a farmer, who vanished while rowing across Lake Wembo in a skiff.

Sources: Shuker, *From Flying Toads to Snakes with Wings*; Shuker, "Lesser known lake monsters."

Lake Willoughby, Vermont

In 1854, a travel writer reported that the surface of this lake in northern Vermont's Orleans County sometimes displayed violent agitation while the air above was perfectly still. Locals blame a resident LAKE MONSTER, citing the case of 12-year-old Stephen Edmonds, who reportedly killed a 23-foot SNAKE at Lake Willoughby in the early 1880s. Another story, from the 1950s, relates the accidental drowning of a sailor, home on leave, whose boat capsized near Mt. Pisgah. When the young man's body failed to surface, U.S. Navy divers allegedly went in search of his body. Instead of the corpse, however, they reportedly found the mouth of an underwater cave, inhabited by giant EELS as thick as telephone poles. Some versions of the story claim the divers allegedly photographed the eels, but no pictures were ever released. On 9 September 1986, Audrey Besse and her mother saw a serpentine cryptid swimming offshore from Westmore, at the lake's north end. Its back displayed two or three humps above the water.

Source: Citro, *Green Mountain Ghouls, Ghosts and Unsolved Mysteries.*

Lake Wingra, Wisconsin

Sightings of a LAKE MONSTER reported from Lake Wingra, in Madison, during the 1890s were apparently explained by the capture of a large snapping TURTLE (*Chelydra serpentina*).

Source: Brown, *Sea Serpents: Wisconsin Occurrences of These Weird Water Monsters.*

Lake Winnebago, Wisconsin

Wisconsin's Lake Winnebago ("Big Lake"), located in Winnebago County, appears on two published lists of supposed LAKE MONSTER habitats in North America. Unfortunately, neither list includes any details of reported sightings.

Sources: Bord and Bord, *Unexplained Mysteries of the 20th Century*; Coleman, *Mysterious America.*

Lake Worth Monster

In the summer of 1969, residents of Tarrant County, Texas reported frightening encounters with a "big white APE" around Lake Worth, six miles northwest of downtown Fort Worth. The first police reports of sightings were filed on 10 July, when John Reichert, his wife and four companions claimed a shaggy HOMINID had leaped from a tree and landed atop Reichert's car. The witnesses described it as "a cross between a man and a goat," covered in both fur and scales. Officers dispatched to the scene found nothing, but Reichert displayed a fresh 18-inch scratch on one side of his car, allegedly caused by the animal's claws. Amateur monster-hunters thronged the Lake Worth Nature Center after Reichert's story aired, and the creature appeared before 30-40 witnesses on 10 July. When sheriff's deputies arrived, the creature hurled an old tire at its pursuers and vanished into the woods. Observers described the bipedal beast as seven feet tall, weighing 300-500 pounds. One witness, Jack Harris, told reporters the creature uttered a "pitiful cry, like someone was hurting him. But it sure didn't sound human." Sporadic sightings continued into autumn, and local dress shop owner Allen Plaster snapped a fuzzy black-and-white photo of the creature which failed to solve the mystery. Witness Charles Buchanan logged the last known sighting of the Lake Worth monster on 7

November 1969. Subsequently, spokesmen for the Fort Worth Museum of Natural History claimed the witnesses had merely seen a common bobcat (*Felis rufus*). Rumors that police had captured pranksters with an ape suit remain unconfirmed. Speculation persists that the Lake Worth creature may had been an albino BIGFOOT or NORTH AMERICAN APE.

Sources: Bord and Bord, *The Bigfoot Casebook*; Blackman, *The Field Guide to North American Monsters*; Clark and Pear, *Strange & Unexplained Phenomena.*

Lakhatet *see* **Adlekhe-Titin**

Lakshir *see* **Adlekhe-Titin**

LaMonica, Richard (1953–)

Akron, Ohio native Richard LaMonica founded and maintains an Internet website titled Northeastern Ohio's Researchable Kryptids Accounts (NORKA). In LaMonica's own words: "My goals, in the field of Cryptozoology, are to be a part of the discovery of some of these missing and unknown creatures. I have a devout fondness for all things mysterious, and I hope to contribute what I know and have learned to these findings." Correspondents are invited to submit reports of BIGFOOT and other cryptid sightings within Ohio's borders.

Source: Northeastern Ohio's Researchable Kryptids Accounts, http://www.geocities.com/saqatchr/index3.html.

Längelmävesi, Finland

In 1945, a witness named Paasonen reported sighting a "water spirit" resembling an animate log in this lake, located in southern Finland. The description is typical of many LAKE MONSTERS sighted across Europe and North America.

Source: Jean Ferguson, *Les Humanoides*. Montréal: Lémac, 1977.

Langkawi carcass

In May 1996, Malaysian fishermen trawling near the northern island resort of Langkawi netted the 25-foot skeletal remains of an unknown sea creature at a depth of 175 feet. The crew took half an hour to lift the carcass aboard, then snapped photographs and threw it back into the sea, in fear that it might be a DRAGON. Spokesmen for the Malaysian Fisheries Department examined the photos and said they had "never seen anything like it." An unnamed Malaysian scientist allegedly analyzed tissue from the carcass and identified it as a killer whale (*Orcinus orca*), but no trace remains of that report and the source of his supposed sample remains problematic. KARL SHUKER examined one of the Langkawi photos, obtained from the *New Straits Times* in Kuala Lumpur and declared: "The teeth and vertebrae seem mammalian, yet the head seems reptilian. If it's a whale, the mouth seems unusually large. The remains would allow

Unnamed "experts" claimed the Langkawi carcass was a decomposed killer whale.

a marine biologist to identify it clearly had one studied it, but the detail in the photo is ambiguous."

Source: "Dragon, ahoy!" *Fortean Times* 89 (August 1996): 13.

Larrekeyah Point sea serpents   In the late 1940s, while walking on the cliffs at Larrakeyah Point (near Darwin, in Australia's Northern Territory), R.M. Richardson saw three large, black objects in the ocean below him. Each measured roughly 25 feet long, and Richardson initially thought they were logs, until all three began to move. Rushing down to the pier, Richardson saw one of the creatures raise its head as if to strike, before they swam away. Richardson described the animals as resembling tiger SNAKES (*Notechis scutatus*), a well-known venomous Australian species rarely exceeding five feet in length.

Source: Smith, *Bunyips & Bigfoots.*

Last Mountain Lake, Canada   This lake lies in a natural depression called Rowan's Ravine, part of a provincial park 50 miles northeast of Regina, Saskatchewan. In July 1964, multiple witnesses sighted a 30-foot LAKE MONSTER, shiny and dark, that "looked like egg-shaped groups attached together" when it swam.

Source: Garner, *Monster! Monster!*

Lau   In a 1923 study of the Nuer people, inhabiting the Upper Nile Province, British Deputy Governor H.C. Jackson wrote at some length about a creature called the Lau, resembling a huge SNAKE, that allegedly lived in swamps at the source of the White Nile.

> Various fantastic attributes attach to it, which may be mere embellishments on the part of the Nuer without necessarily disproving the existence of some hitherto unknown serpent of exceptional size.
>   Thus some say that it has a short crest of hair on the back of its head not unlike that of a crowned crane: others that it has long hairs, reminiscent of some of the mud-fish of the Nile, with which it entangles its unwilling victims and drags them into the river. In certain years, particularly during the rainy season, its belly is said to gurgle like the rumbling of an elephant....
>   The Nuer state that it inhabits holes in the banks of rivers or swamps, and spends most of its time in swamps. They are in mortal dread of it, and if they see the furrow in the ground that announces its presence, they run as fast as they can in the opposite direction. If a Nuer sees this serpent before it sees him, all is well, but if the serpent happens to sight even a large party of them first, all are expected to die....
>   There are so many stories of this creature from places as far apart as Bahr-el-Arab, Addar swamps, Bahr-el-Ghazal and Bahr-el-Zeraf, that it is difficult to dismiss the existence of some hitherto unknown serpent not unlike a gigantic PYTHON.

Captain William Hichens, pursuing the legend, procured a native carving of a Lau's head, which he photographed and published in the journal *Discovery* (December 1937). The complete skeleton of a Lau was allegedly retrieved from the Bahr al Zera‾f in 1914, but its bones were distributed among the Nuer as lucky charms, and no trace of it remains today. BERNARD HEUVELMANS, after reviewing various reports, suggested that the Lau and the LUKWATA of Lake Victoria are identical, "or at least animals of the same genus."

Sources: Hichens, "African mystery beasts"; Heuvelmans, *Les Derniers Dragons d'Afrique*; Heuvelmans, *On the Track of Unknown Animals*; Mackal, *A Living Dinosaur?*

Laughing Poparina   According to BIGFOOT researcher RAYMOND CROWE, this nickname is sometimes applied to unknown HOMINIDS in parts of Maryland. No further information on the nickname's origin is presently available.

Source: "Around the weird: Bizarre news briefs." *Wireless Flash News* (4 June 2002).

***Laura* sea serpent**   On 28 August 1817, while becalmed two miles offshore from Cape Ann, Massachusetts, sailors aboard the schooner *Laura* saw a SEA SERPENT that was subsequently dubbed *SCOLIOPHIS ATLANTICUS*. Captain Sewell Toppan and two of his sailors offered descriptions of the creature in sworn statements given before a justice of the peace on 30-31 August. As witness Robert Bragg recalled the incident:

> [A]bout 10 a.m. ... being on deck ... looking to windward, I saw something break the water, and coming very fast toward us....The animal came about 28 or 30 feet from us, between the vessel and the shore, and passed very swiftly by us; he left a very long wake behind him. About six inches in height of his body and head were out of the water, and I should judge about 14 or 15 feet in length. He had a head like a serpent, rather larger than his body and rather blunt; did not see his eyes; when astern of the vessel about 30 feet, he threw out his tongue about two feet in length, or nearly so, and let it fall again. He was in sight about ten minutes. I think he moved at the rate of 12 or 14 miles an hour; he was of a dark chocolate colour, and from what appeared out of water I should suppose he was about two and a half feet in circumference; he made no noise; his back and body appeared smooth; a small bunch on each side of his head, just above his eyes; he did not appear to be at all disturbed by the vessel; his course was in the direction for the Salt Islands; his motion was much swifter than any whale that I have ever seen, and I have seen many—did not observe any teeth; his motion was very steady, a little up and down. To this account I am willing to make oath.

Witness William Somerby corroborated Bragg's account, noting that the creature had eyes the size of an ox's and a light-brown tongue, which it "threw...backwards several times over his head, and let it fall again." Captain Toppan found the motion of the creature's head "sideways and quite moderate; the motion of the body, up and down.... I have been to sea many years and never saw any FISH that had the least resemblance to this animal."

Source: O'Neill, *The Great New England Sea Serpent.*

Lawas River, Malaysia   (*See illustration next page.*) In May 1985, witnesses sighted a cow-headed cryptid with a "big neck" and "eyes like lightbulbs" swimming in this river, in Sarawak State (Borneo). Some outsiders speculate that the creature was a dugong (*Dugong dugong*).

Sources: Bord and Bord, *Unexplained Mysteries of the 20th Century*; "Monster or mermaid?" *ISC Newsletter* 5 (Winter 1986): 9.

***Le Parseval* sea serpent**   In December 1886, passengers aboard the French dispatch-boat *Le Parseval* sighted a SEA SERPENT in the Red Sea. A quarter-century after the fact, witness Paul Cadiou recalled the incident as follows:

> I was on the bridge with the officer of the watch when I saw, emerging from the sea, a gigantic serpent resembling a "conger" with a flat head, and very dark in colour; the head and neck, curved as a swan swimming, must have measured five feet. It disappeared at the end of ten seconds; it swam on the port side, at our speed, which must have been nine knots [13.5 miles per hour]; others in the crew saw it besides me.

Source: Heuvelmans, *In the Wake of the Sea Serpents.*

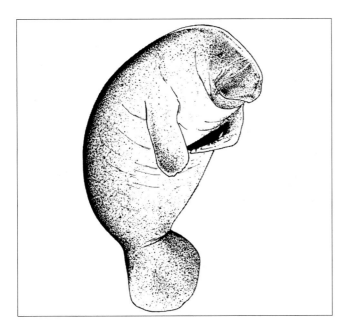

Some researchers believe the Lawas River cryptid is a dugong.

Le Seudre sea serpent   In 1878, sailors aboard the French ship *Le Seudre* saw an unidentified SEA SERPENT in the South Pacific, near New Caledonia (800 miles east of Australia). BERNARD HEUVELMANS considered the creature to be a specimen of his hypothetical "Merhorse."

Source: Heuvelmans, *In the Wake of the Sea Serpents.*

LeBlond, Paul H. (1938–)   Paul LeBlond is an oceanographer at the University of British Columbia in Vancouver and cofounder of the BRITISH COLUMBIA SCIENTIFIC CRYPTOZOOLOGY CLUB. He has conducted extensive field investigations and archival research on SEA SERPENTS, particularly the Pacific cryptid known as CADBOROSAURUS. In 1973, with John Sibert, LeBlond published a study of 30 sightings in Canadian waters between 1892 and 1969; two decades later, with coauthor Edward Bousfield, he published the first book devoted entirely to "Caddy." LeBlond's research led him to the conclude that at least three species of large pelagic cryptids still await discovery and classification.

Sources: Coleman and Clark, *Cryptozoology A to Z*; LeBlond and Bousfield, *Cadborosaurus*; LeBlond and Sibert, *Observations of Large Unidentified Marine Animals in British Columbia and Adjacent Waters.*

Leda sea serpent   On 20 August 1872, while traveling from Glenelg to Lochourn, Scotland aboard the cutter *Leda*, six passengers met a SEA SERPENT in the Sound of Sleat. Two of the witnesses, the Rev. John Macrae and the Rev. David Twopeny, later described the incident as follows:

> As we were getting the cutter along with oars we perceived a dark mass about two hundred yards astern of us, to the north. While we were looking at it with our glasses…another similar black lump rose to the left of the first, leaving an interval between; then another and another followed, all in regular order. We did not doubt its being one living creature; it moved slowly across our wake, and disappeared. Presently the first mass, which was evidently the head, reappeared, and was followed by the rising of the other black lumps, as before. Sometimes three appeared, sometimes four, five, or six, and then sank again. When they rose, the head appeared first, if it had been down, and the lumps rose after it in regular

order, beginning always with that next to the head, and rising gently; but when they sank they sank all together rather abruptly, sometimes leaving the head visible. It gave the impression of a creature crooking up its back to sun itself. There was no appearance of undulation; when the lumps sank, other lumps did not rise in the intervals between them. The greatest number we counted was seven, making eight with the head….The parts were separated from each other by intervals of about their own length, the head being rather smaller and flatter than the rest, and the nose being very slightly visible above the water; but we did not see the head raised above the surface…nor could we see the eye. We had no means of measuring the length with any accuracy, but taking the distance from the centre of one lump to the centre of the next to be six feet, and it could scarcely be less, the whole length of the portion visible, including the intervals submerged, would be forty-five feet.

The next day, reversing their journey, the clergymen were becalmed near Lochourn when the creature reappeared. This time, they wrote, it "showed itself in three or four rather long lines…and looked considerably longer than it did the day before; as nearly as we could compute, it looked at least sixty feet in length. Soon it began careering about, showing but a small part of itself, as on the day before." Later that day, the animal surfaced yet again near the island of Sandaig and "came rushing past us about a hundred and fifty yards to the south….It went with great rapidity, its black head only being visible through the clear sea, followed by a long trail of agitated water."

Source: Heuvelmans, *In the Wake of the Sea Serpents.*

The *Leda* sea serpent, based on eyewitness descriptions.

Leech Lake, Minnesota   John Aldrich and Richard Christman, manufacturers of electronic FISH-finders, were testing their newest model on this northern Minnesota lake (Cass County) in September 1976, when they scored "hits" on two 60-foot objects swimming at depths between 90 and 150 feet. Intrigued, Aldrich and Christman spent the next two days trolling with heavy downrigger equipment, but while the fish-finder tracked repeated sightings of the unseen creatures, their lures were ignored.

Source: Garner, *Monster! Monster!*

Lenny the Lizard   Canadians apply this nickname to a pint-sized cryptid reported from the Rouge River, east of Toronto. Though only 14 inches long, Lenny is nonetheless a striking vision, described by witnesses as a reptilian creature with purple ears and a bright blue tail.

Source: Garner, *Monster! Monster!*

Les Trois Lacs, Canada   Three small lakes comprise this composite body of water, located north of Asbestos, Québec. Local tradition has it that an "enormous FISH" once inhabited the lakes, hibernating in a nearby swamp during harsh winters. Some claim the fish was an overgrown muskellunge (*Esox masquinongy*), but it was never caught and sightings apparently ceased in the mid-20th century.

Source: Meurger and Gagnon, *Lake Monster Traditions.*

Lesser Sundas cat   Residents of Alor and Solor, two of the Lesser Sunda Islands (Indonesia) report the existence of an unclassified CAT distinguished by stubby knobs like horns above both eyes. British explorer Debbie Martyr collected reports of the still-unidentified animals during her search for the equally mysterious ORANG PENDEK.

Source: Shuker, "Blue tigers, black tigers, and other Asian mystery cats."

***Levant* sea serpent**   On 29 July 1827, passengers and crew aboard the sloop *Levant* met a SEA SERPENT in Vineyard Sound, off Gay Head (Martha's Vineyard), Massachusetts. Captain Coleman and others reported that they had "a very near and distinct view of the monster, and could not have mistaken it for any known species of FISH." Its description matched that of other New England pelagic cryptids, collectively labeled *SCOLIOPHIS ATLANTICUS*.

Sources: Heuvelmans, *In the Wake of the Sea Serpents*; O'Neill, *The Great New England Sea Serpent*.

Ley, Willy (1906–69)   German scholar Willy Ley studied paleontology and zoology at the Universities of Berlin and Koenigsberg before he published his first book of "romantic zoology," *The Lungfish and the Unicorn*, in 1941. Seven years later, it was revised and expanded for re-release as *The Lungfish, the Dodo and the Unicorn*. Reaching a wider audience on his second attempt, Ley shared his fascination for cryptozoological subjects with a global audience. Sequels included *Dragons in Amber* (1951), *Salamanders and Other Wonders* (1955), and *Exotic Zoology* (1959). The latter volume collected Ley's previous surveys of YETI, SEA SERPENTS and living DINOSAURS. His appeal to a popular audience paved the way for others, including BERNARD HEUVELMANS, in a decade before cryptozoology had a name of its own.

Source: Coleman and Clark, *Cryptozoology A to Z*; Heuvelmans, "The birth and history of cryptozoology."

Lickasjön, Sweden   In 1966, several members of the Hansson family reported a gray, 11-foot LAKE MONSTER swimming in this Swedish lake, near Motala in Östergötland County. Lickasjön has a maximum recorded depth of 55 feet.

Source: GUST website, http://www.cryptozoology.st/.

Li'kela-Bembe   In November 2000, WILLIAM GIBBONS and creationist lecturer Davie Woetzel penetrated the jungles and swamps surrounding Cameroon's Boumba and Loponji Rivers, seeking evidence of living DINOSAURS. As the first Westerners to visit the region, they collected native stories of an elephant-sized creature called Li'kela-bembe, said to possess a long neck, a snake-like head, and a powerful tail. When shown a range of pictures, including both extant and prehistoric animals, the tribesmen promptly selected pictures of sauropods as most closely resembling Li'kela-bembe. Gibbons and SCOTT NORMAN returned with a BBC television crew in February 2001, but their documentary failed to include any footage of Li'kela-bembe in the flesh. The description and name of the Cameroon cryptid are strikingly similar to those of MOKELE-MBEMBE, reported the Congo, further east.

Source: Karl Shuker, "Alien zoo." *Fortean Times* 146 (June 2001): 20.

Lilla Källsjö, Sweden   This lake, in Jämtland County, was the source of LAKE MONSTER reports during the 19th century. Locals often noted large waves on the lake with no wind to explain them, and the area was said to be "a 'stamping ground' for

Native witnesses in Cameroon describe the Li'kela-bembe as resembling a long-necked dinosaur (**William Rebsamen**).

ghosts and spooks." In 1863, 12-year-old Sven Anderson was fishing for perch on the lake when a creature resembling a huge bull surfaced 100 yards away, churning the water into foam and making "an awful noise." Adults investigating Anderson's report saw nothing, but they declared that quagmires surrounding the lake made it impossible for moose or livestock to reach open water.

Source: Bord and Bord, *Alien Animals*.

Lilla Värtan, Sweden   In 1913, witness M.O. Smith reported sighting an 80-foot serpentine LAKE MONSTER with 10 humps on its back, swimming across this lake in Sweden's Stockholm County.

Source: *Encyclopedia Universal Ilustrada Europeo-Americana* (Vol. 55). Madrid: Espasa-Calpe, 1930.

***Lily* sea serpent**   In October 1898, fishermen aboard the *Lily* encountered a strange SEA SERPENT off the coast of Stonehaven, Scotland. From a distance of 100 yards, the witnesses believed that they had found a capsized boat. When they had halved that distance, the animal raised its head (described as flatter than a whale's) and made off to sea. The *Lily*'s skipper, Alexander Taylor, reckoned the visible part of the creature was twice as long as his 31-foot boat, but he never saw the animal's tail and refused to guess its total length. The animal's hide was bluish, and its back had two dorsal fins set 20 feet apart, each the size and shape of a small boat's sail. Behind the second fin lay a hump resembling a CAMEL'S. BERNARD HEUVELMANS speculated that it might be a RHINOCEROS DOLPHIN, but its size far exceeds that reported for those cryptids.

Source: Heuvelmans, *In the Wake of the Sea Serpents*.

Lincoln Lynx *see* **Lindsey Leopard**

Lincolnshire sea monster   On 1 February 1743, *The London Magazine* published the following account from Cambridge University, of an unknown sea creature found alive in Lincolnshire:

A few days since an amphibious monster was brought hither, which has drawn the attention of the most curious of this University, who are unable to assign a proper name to it; some of our gentlemen call it a sea-lioness:

It was taken the 6th of last month at Fordike Wash in Lincolnshire, asleep on the sands: It was supposed to have followed a large shoal of herrings, and having overgorged itself, fell asleep, and was discovered by some fishermen, who immediately got some proper weapons and several bulldogs, by which means they took it.

It killed one of the best dogs in the county, and wounded four or five others; but lost one of its eyes in the engagement. It is bearded like a tyger, weighs 500 lbs, the fore feet are like a bear's, the hind like a fan, two feet wide when extended; its tail is like a neat's tongue; It is seven feet and a half long, and nine feet round. It is now alive and well, and made a present to the University, and as the sight of it is free, great numbers of people flock to see it.

TIM DINSDALE concluded that the "monster" in question was a bull sea lion, which appears to fit the description offered in all particulars.

Source: Dinsdale, *Monster Hunt.*

Lindorm
The Lindorm is a Scandinavian cryptid whose name derives from the Swedish *lind* ("flexible body") and *orm* ("worm" or "serpent"). In Medieval times, DRAGONS of northern Europe were commonly called Orms, and while the Lindorm fits the dragon mold in some particulars, it deviates radically in others. It is relatively small, described by witnesses as 10-28 feet long, with a body thickness equal to a large man's thigh. Unlike classic dragons, the Lindorm does not fly or belch fire. It is said to be black with a yellow underside; its head resembles a pike's (Family *Esocidae*), but with large eyes, small ears, and a forked tongue. (In short, not very like a pike at all!) Some specimens display a crest of mane. The tail, unlike that of a SNAKE or FISH, appears vestigial.

Another oddity in the Lindorm-dragon comparison is the frequency of Lindorm sightings reported from Sweden during the "rational" 19th century, when dragons were long since deemed mythical (or at least extinct) throughout the rest of Europe. Daniel Nilsson alleged grappled with a Lindorm in Sweden's Ulvehult Forest (near Odensö, Kronoberg County) in autumn 1826. In August 1869, Magnus Bergström claimed to have killed a Lindorm in Jönköping County, beside a lake: no overall dimensions were reported, but the creature's mouth was 11 inches wide, with fangs the size of a man's little finger. Farmer Johan Jonsson killed another Lindorm in Husaby Forest, Kronoberg County, in November 1878. Five years later, Kronoberg County sightings were reported from Hinneryd, Husaby Forest, Kalvsvik, Urshult, and from Skäggalösa Persgård estate. In 1883-85, researcher Gunnar Hyltén-Cavallius interviewed 48 Swedes who claimed Lindorm encounters over the past 60 years. No sightings are recorded for the 20th century, suggesting that whatever the Lindorm may have been, it is now either extinct or very rare.

Sources: Reidar Christiansen, *The Migratory Legends.* Helsinki: Suomalainen Tiedeakatemia, 1958; Rosén, "The dragons of Sweden"; Shuker, *Dragons: A Natural History.*

Lindsey Leopard
The Lindsey leopard is an ALIEN BIG CAT reported from Lincolnshire, England since 1995. Confusion of eyewitness descriptions is evident from the fact that some locals call the unknown animal the Lincoln LYNX. The great difference in size and appearance between a leopard (*Panthera pardus*) and a lynx (*Felis lynx*) suggests that Lincolnshire may harbor more than one exotic felid — or multiple breeding populations. A spate of sightings in 1995-96 included reports of large CATS in residential areas, even peering in the window of a home at Kingerby (in May 1996). Sightings continue to the present day, as evidenced by witness Chris Till's report from Laughton Forest (near Gainsborough) in July 2002, and motorist Rachael Wydrzynska's report

The Lindsey Leopard has been seen in Lincolnshire, England since 1995.

from Lincoln in March 2003. The cat seen by Wydrzynska bore little resemblance to a leopard. "It was the size of a largish dog," she told reporters, "but definitely moved like a cat with one bound from one side of the road to the other. It was gray and another thing that struck me was the speed with which it moved. I can't remember seeing a tail at the time but at one point it was only 10 meters [32 feet 6 inches] from the front of my bonnet." July 2003 brought fresh reports of a lynx, 18 inches tall at the shoulder, slaughtering 30-odd chickens at Collingham, between Lincoln and Newark. A man and dog pursued the cat, but it "shot off up a big willow tree" and disappeared.

Sources: "The missing lynx." *Lincolnshire Echo* (26 July 2003); Ben Rooth, "Big cat sighting resurrects legend of Lincoln lynx." *Lincolnshire Echo* (19 March 2003); Sieveking, "Watch out, big cat about"; "Walker revives leopard legend." *Lincolnshire Echo* (26 July 2002).

Linguin
This alleged living DINOSAUR of Borneo is known in the West only from a letter written by explorer PERCY FAWCETT to London's *Daily Mail* on 17 December 1919. After describing "relics of the Miocene age" said to survive in South America, Fawcett briefly mentioned the Linguin as "another such reptile as to whose existence there is locally no doubt entertained." Fawcett's letter was overlooked by cryptozoologists until KARL SHUKER uncovered it in 1995.

Source: Shuker, *In Search of Prehistoric Survivors.*

Linh Duong
In 1994, while visiting Vietnam's Ho Chi Minh City, German zoologist Wolfgang Peter saw a unique set of spiral horns in a street market stall and snapped several photographs. Subsequent consultation with colleagues around the world revealed that none had seen anything resembling the curious relic. Peter returned to Vietnam with zoologist Alfred Feiler and collected eight sets of the horns from various merchants. Conversations with hunters in the districts of Kon Tum, Dac Lac and Ban Me Thuot revealed that the animals were well known as Linh Duong ("holy goat"). Around the same time, zoologist Maurizio Dioli found similar horns in northern Cambodia's Mondulkiri and Rattanakiri Provinces, where the creature is called

Vietnam's Linh duong is known only from its antlers.

Kting Voar ("wild cow with vine-like horns"). Surprisingly, Diloli also discovered that a pair of Kting Voar horns had been donated to the Kansas Museum of Natural History in 1929, where they were classified as belonging to a young female kouprey (*Bos sauveli*).

By 1999, 20 sets of Linh Duong horns had been collected, but the animal itself remained elusive. A year later, the World Conservation Union declared it endangered, as a "precaution." Meanwhile, a French team of scientists led by Arnoult Seveau microscopically examined five sets of horns, declaring them to be "artificially deformed cow or buffalo horns—in short, a HOAX. DNA testing then proved that several Linh Duong relics were in fact the horns of cows or buffaloes. In 2001, a German report acknowledged that some Linh Duong trophies were "superficially embellished," but said it "remains unclear as to whether the horns were originally from cattle or another bovine taxon." An Eastern European report confused things further, asserting that phylogenetic analyses of 125 nearly-complete mitochondrial DNA sequences from Linh Duong specimens revealed the animal to be a valid species of buffalo, filling a gap between Asian buffaloes (*Bubalus*) and the African buffalo (*Syncerus*). Professor Robert Timm, working from separate samples in Kansas, likewise declares the Linh Duong a legitimate species. Clearly, the debate will not be resolved until a complete specimen is obtained—assuming that the holy goat exists.

Sources: Michele Hespe, "The dilemma of the horns." *Weekend Australian Magazine* (14-15 December 2002); Karl Shuker, "Alien zoo." *Fortean Times* 144 (April 2001): 22; Shuker, "Alien zoo." *Fortean Times* 149 (September 2001): 16.; Shuker, *The New Zoo*.

Lions (Melanistic)   While JAGUARS (*Panthera onca*) and leopards (*Panthera pardus*) produce melanistic cubs with fair regularity, no black morph of the lion (*Panthera leo*) has yet been verified. Still, in 1940 an experienced game warden claimed to have sighted a whole pride of jet-black lions in South Africa's Kruger National Park. (No further searches were conducted, and the sighting is unverified.) In 1975, a male lion cub was born at the Glasgow Zoo with a black chest and one black leg. Curators

subsequently mated the cub with his mother in hopes of producing black lions, but the female never conceived. In addition to African sightings, cryptozoologists LOREN COLEMAN and MARK HALL suggest that melanistic females may explain reports of male lions traveling with "black panthers" at various points around the U.S.

Source: Shuker, *Mystery Cats of the World*.

Lions (Mislocated)   Lions (*Panthera leo*) once ranged from Europe as far east as India, but today their range is officially limited to Africa. On any other continent, they rank as ALIEN BIG CATS whose presence in the wild must be investigated and explained. That geographic limitation notwithstanding, they continue to appear throughout the western hemisphere. The incidents in North America are typically explained as "escapes" from zoos or private menageries, but the official claims in that regard are rarely substantiated—and lion sightings in some surprising locations predate establishment of zoos and circuses in the New World. Some of the incidents on file include:

1700s—Folklorist Henry Shoemaker claims a maned lion was seen in the early 18th century, in New York County, New York.

1791—Farmers in Centre County, Pennsylvania complained that a huge CAT with a matted yellow-brown mane was killing and eating their livestock. The predation continued until 1797, when Peter Pentz killed two lions, male and female, in a cave on Bald Eagle Mountain (near present-day State College). Some accounts of the incident also mention three cubs.

July 1823—A brindle-colored cat of "great bulk," with "a most terrific front," escaped from hunters after being wounded at Russellville, Kentucky.

1836—Residents of Penobscot County, Maine, saw a male lion and heard its roars. The *Bangor Courier* reported that Maine's wild fauna included a huge maned cat known to native tribesmen as *lunkasoose*.

1868—Hunter Archie McMath killed an 11-foot lion in Lake County, California, after it had slaughtered several sheep and two young horses. The cat had a short mane, with black stripes on its shoulders and along its back.

Lions have been reported throughout North America since the early 18th century.

1901— Residents of Pocahontas County, West Virginia saw a large cat with long hair on its chest and belly, plus a tufted tail.

July 1917— Thomas Gullet, a butler at the Robert Allerton estate southwest of Monticello, Illinois was attacked by an "African lioness" while picking flowers. The beast was seen again on 15 July, nicknamed "Nellie" by the press. A maned male was seen near Decatur on 29 and 31 July, and sightings of one or both lions continued in central Illinois throughout that summer.

1 March 1941— A "panther," described by witnesses as a large maned cat of yellow-reddish color, was seen in western New Brunswick, Canada.

3-8 August 1948— A maned lion and a "black panther" were sighted by multiple witnesses at Elkhorn Falls and Richmond, Indiana (Wayne County). September brought reports of the same odd couple from neighboring Drake County, Ohio.

November 1950— One or more MYSTERY MAULERS, roaring like lions, killed 42 pigs, 12 chickens, four lambs and four calves in Peoria County, Illinois. The predators themselves were never seen.

12 November 1951— Lion sightings around Ceresco, Nebraska (Saunders County) launched a fruitless hunt for the elusive cat.

1953— New Brunswick residents reported sightings of two "African lionesses" traveling in company with a large black cat.

1 August 1954— Farmer Arnold Neujahr saw a lion two miles west of Surprise, Nebraska (Butler County), followed shortly by reports from Rising City, five miles to the south. Both towns are located 32 miles west of Ceresco.

1954— A "ragged-coated" lion was seen near a military base at Gagetown, New Brunswick. Authorities failed to locate the animal.

January 1958— A large maned cat was reported from Warrick County, in southwestern Indiana.

1959— A "miniature African lion" was blamed for the deaths of livestock and domestic pets in Lorain County, Ohio.

June 1960— Farmer Leo Dallaire saw a male lion on his property near Kapuskasing, Ontario. He described it as 5 feet long and 3 feet tall, with a prominent mane and a 4-foot tufted tail.

January-February 1961— A prowling lion killed chickens in Craig and Rogers Counties, Oklahoma. Rogers County Sheriff Amos Ward blamed a circus escapee, but the claim was not substantiated. A tourist in Craig County sighted the lion in March, followed closely by a report from two nurses at Eastern State Hospital (in Vinita) that they had seen the beast lurking in shrubbery on the hospital grounds.

1962— Sightings of a "lioness" in Huntington County, Indiana were accompanied by complaints of a big cat roaring.

July 1963— A "hairy" lion was seen prowling in company with a "black panther" around Joliet, Illinois. More sightings issued from the same area in August 1964.

20 October 1964— A hunting guide reported his encounter with a cat that looked "exactly like an African Lion" near McGundy Stream, New Brunswick.

May 1970— Six workmen in Winnebago County, Illinois saw a lion steal a bag of meat laid aside for pet dogs. They gave chase in a car, witness Tom Terry describing the cat as eight feet long, with a mane "like a regular lion." A large predator spooked local livestock in June and August, roaring in the night and leaving large pawprints along the Rock River's banks.

March 1971— Witness Howard Baldridge reported his meeting with a "small lion" twice the size of a domestic cat, near Centralia, Illinois. Baldridge insisted that except for its size, the animal precisely resembled lions he had seen on television.

1971— Lion sightings were logged from Croesbeck, Ohio.

September 1975— Witness reported a maned lion at large in Geauga County, Ohio (east of Cleveland).

1976— A farmer outside Alapaha, Georgia, J.H. Holyoak, opened fire with birdshot on a "half lion, half panther" that attacked his cattle. The wounded cat escaped into some nearby woods.

July 1976— "All sorts of people" in Tacoma, Washington, reported sightings of a large cat with "a shaggy black mane, light brown body, and a black tuft at the end of a long tail." Police launched a fruitless search for the beast.

1977— A maned lion attacked two dogs at Dierks, Arkansas (Howard County). Shortly thereafter, witnesses in the same area sighted a "black panther."

Autumn 1977— Police found a 2-month-old lion cub in Muscatine, Iowa. No owner was identified.

23 January 1978— A resident of Loxahatchee, Florida reported a lion wandering through her backyard. Authorities missed the cat, but determined that no animals were missing from the nearby Lion Country Safari.

10 November 1979— Multiple witnesses reported a lion at large in Coyote Hills Regional Park, at Fremont, California. Police officer William Fontes saw the cat in a county flood relief channel, but it eluded him. Days later, when the local owner of a chow puppy claimed his dog was to blame for the sightings, Officer Fontes replied, "The puppy in no way resembled the 300- to 400-pound animal observed in the flood control channel."

1982— While searching for EASTERN COUGARS, researcher Robert Downing was directed to a skeleton lying in a ditch near Rutherford, North Carolina. He sent the skull to the Smithsonian Institution, where mammalogists confirmed it as a specimen of *Panthera leo*. On the same trip, Downing heard stories of a lion shot by hunters in the Blue Ridge Mountains, sometime in the 1960s.

July 1984— A lion was sighted prowling at large in North Olmstead, Ohio (a Cleveland suburb). More sightings emerged from the vicinity of Dayton, 60 miles farther north, in November and December.

1985— A lion was seen wandering free near the Forth Worth (Texas) Zoo. Unable to locate the animal, police insisted that witnesses had actually seen a fluffy-eared Brittany spaniel.

1986— A maned lion and a large striped cat were reported by witnesses in the eastern Pennsylvania counties of Lackawana, Pike, Susquehanna and Wyoming. Searchers failed to capture the beasts.

June 1992— Police received multiple reports of a 7-foot maned cat in Mentor, Ohio (a Cleveland suburb). Witnesses vehemently rejected the official explanation that they had mistaken a "large golden retriever" for the King of Beasts.

June 1993— A rash of lion sightings emerged from Erie, Pennsylvania, after farmer Greg Havican reported a 150-pound male in his yard. The cat, blamed by Havican for recent disappearances of poultry on the farm, fled after Havican fired a shot in the air. It allegedly wore "a red collar with gold bells," but media bulletins confirm that no captive lions were reported missing in the state. Police called off their search on 3 June, despite new sightings of the cat, and it was never found.

1994— Witness saw and heard a roaring "African lioness" in southern Ohio's Clinton and Highland counties.

July 1995— Two separate groups of witnesses sighted an adult male lion near Cooper's Landing, on southern Alaska's Kenai Peninsula. State biologists were baffled and the cat presumably remains at large.

5 June 1996— Motorist Belen Gabb saw a "dirty beige" lion wandering across a Spokane, Washington golf course. Neighbors reported roaring in the night, but two days of mass searches failed to flush the cat from cover.

1998-99— An "African lioness" on the prowl was reported by residents of Juneau and Sauk Counties, Wisconsin.

September 2002— Within a span of three days, four adult lions weighing 600-800 pounds were shot around Quitman, Arkansas. Police could not explain how the animals "got loose," but neighbors blamed private menagerie owner Steve Henning—who insisted that none of his 11 lions was missing. Henning suggested that the cats had been released by some unidentified person who tried to give him several lions the previous week. Locals, meanwhile, remain tense. As Arvil Skinner told reporters, "Everybody is scared around here. People have to sit out with a high-powered rifle just to let their kids play in the yard. That's just how serious it is. It might be all right and it might not."

2 October 2002— Witnesses reported a lion at large in the forests of rural Carter County, Tennessee.

21 March 2003— Police in Warren, Michigan set traps in their vain search for a wandering "liger" (a lion-TIGER hybrid). The animal was caught on videotape, an apparent red collar around its neck suggesting an escaped pet, but it has so far eluded pursuers.

2 July 2003— Witness Caspar Lawson sighted a 400-pound lion in the Cincinnati suburb of Mason, Ohio. Authorities used helicopters and set traps in vain, as the cat slipped through their dragnet.

September 2003— Authorities in Van Buren Township, Michigan debated calling out the National Guard to help search for a lion reported by various residents. Police Sgt. Dennis Brooks had a near-miss with the cat on 18 September, after setting a baited trap. "Darned if the thing didn't show up," Brooks told reporters. "It walked all around the cage, stuck his head in the cage, looked around and then slowly walked away." More sightings followed, but the cat eluded hunters and troops were not called to pursue it.

2 November 2003— Florida police employed helicopters in a fruitless lion-hunt, after residents of Leesburg reported a 300-pound maned cat prowling the town's Stock subdivision. Authorities blamed the incident on a woman's garbled report of losing her "big cat," but that explanation failed to account for eyewitness reports of a lion at large.

Researchers LOREN COLEMAN and MARK HALL suggest that North American lion sightings may be explained by a relict population of *Panthera leo atrox*, an 11-foot predator that inhabited the western hemisphere from Alaska to northern South America from the Pleistocene epoch to relatively recent times. At the same time, they suggest that sightings of male lions with "black panthers" may be explained by the occurrence of melanistic females. Possible support for the theory of *P. l. atrox* survival comes from Latin America, where Spanish conquistadors reported lions in a 16th-century Aztec zoo, and Friar Johann Baegaert described two species of lions known in Mexico during his years in that country (1751-68). More recently, Peter Hocking has collected native stories a reddish-brown, short-maned cat the size of an adult lion, said to inhabit the Yanachaga Mountains of Peru's Pasco Department.

Sources: Bord and Bord, *Unexplained Mysteries of the 20th Century*; Karen Bouffard, "Van Buren Township stalks mystery cat." *Detroit News* (19 September 2003); Coleman, *Mysterious America*; Coleman, "Roaring at the mane event"; "Fourth lion shot in Cleburne County." Associated

Press (25 September 2002); Laura Goldberg, "Collar ID: Reports of a red-necked lion." *USA Today* (2 June 1993); Hocking, "Further investigation into unknown Peruvian mammals"; Paul Leightty, "'Liger' stalks Detroit suburb, police set traps." Reuters (22 March 2003); "Lion on the loose could be wild goose chase." WFTV-Orlando (3 November 2003); "Lion sighting reported in Mason." *Cincinnati Post* (3 July 2003); Kristin McAllister, "Lion in Warren?" *Dayton Daily News* (3 July 2003); Sheila McLaughlin, "Camera, search dog find no sign of lion." *Cincinnati Enquirer* (4 July 2003); Sheila McLaughlin, "Lion spotted lurking around rural area of Deerfield Twp." *Cincinnati Enquirer* (3 July 2003); Douglas Pils, "Ark. town on edge after lions killed." Associated Press (23 September 2002); Shuker, *Mystery Cats of the World*; Thomas Wilson, "African lion reportedly sighted roaming county's mountains." *Elizabethton* (TN) *Star* (3 October 2002); Thomas Wilson, "Student researches sightings." *Elizabethton* (TN) *Star* (23 October 2002).

Lions (Spotted)

The first known sighting of a spotted lion was reported from East Africa by Lieutenant Richard Meinertzhagen in 1903 (one year before Meinertzhagen discovered the Congo's giant forest hog). Overtime, reports were collected from six African nations, where the CATS are known by a variety of names: in Cameroon, they are Bung bung; in the Central African Republic, Bakanga; Ugandans call them Kiiseego, Kitalargo, Ntarargo or Uruturangwe; in Rwanda they are Ikimizi; in Ethiopia, Abasambo; and in Kenya, the spotted cats are Marozi.

Descriptions of the spotted lions vary regionally, as do names. The Bakanga has reddish-brown background color, dappled like a leopard. It barks like a dog and is aggressive toward humans. The Ikimizi, in keeping with its hunting grounds near the Virunga volcanoes, is chiefly gray with dark spots and a bearded chin. Uganda's Kiiseego is spotted like a hyena, but with a cat's long tail. It haunts the Ruwensori Range, where it preys on livestock and humans alike. One vicious specimen in Kinkizi County allegedly killed 100 persons, habitually bypassing goats and sheep to slay herdsmen and their children. The cat's grunting noises, followed by high-pitched shrieks, terrify rural natives throughout its range.

The most substantial reports of spotted lions have emerged from Kenya, where Marozis have been shot in the Aberdare Range and on the Mau Escarpment. In 1924, A. Blayne Percival killed a spotted lioness and her cubs in Kenya. Seven years later, game warden R.E. Dent saw four adults on Mount Kenya, near the headwaters of the Garcita River, between 10,000 and 11,000 feet.

Spotted lions are reported from at least six African countries (*William Rebsamen*).

Dent noted that all four were smaller and darker than average lions. A few months later, Dent's trappers snared a specimen but soon released it. In the 1930s, farmer Michael Trent shot a pair of spotted lions that raided his farm in the Aberdare Range, around 10,000 feet elevation. He preserved the skins, noting the male's sparse mane and the below-average size of both cats. No Kenyan sightings are on record since the 1930s, indicating that the cats may be extinct in that nation, but BERNARD HEUVELMANS remained optimistic enough in the 1980s to give them the provisional name *Panthera leo maculatus*. The coloration of spotted lions remains unexplained. Hybrid "leopons"—a leopard-lion mix—have been bred in captivity, but such pairings in the wild are very unlikely.

Sources: Dower, *The Spotted Lion*; C.A.W. Guggisberg, *Simba: The Life of the Lion*. Cape Town, South Africa: H. Timmins, 1961; Heuvelmans, "Annotated checklist of apparently unknown animals with which cryptozoology is concerned"; Shuker, *Mystery Cats of the World*; Wilhelm, Prince of Sweden, *Among Pygmies and Gorillas*. London: Gyldendal, 1923.

Lipata In 1932, French zoologist Albert Monard filed the following report concerning a giant CROCODILE reported by natives of northeastern Angola.

> 1. Its name is *lipata*, and not *libata* as my correspondent (A. da Paz) wrote. All the natives pronounce it the same way.
> 2. It exists only in the upper Tyihumbwe and in the Kasai [Rivers]; I have heard nothing of its presence in the Kuilo. Around Tyipukungu there are only two, one some six mile upstream from the other. Some natives say that there are three, others that there are many. Later we were told that the upstream *lipata*…had left its favourite haunt to settle even further upstream.
> 3. It is almost always hidden in the water; it does not appear on the surface except in the morning between nine and ten o'clock. Others say that you can see it in the evening before the sun goes down. All agree that it is very active when the rain falls, and that there is the best chance of seeing it then. It rarely comes out of the water; all the same we were shown some faint tracks made by the *lipata* on a little beach; they were too obliterated for us to make anything of them. On 1 September 1932, a man from Tyipukungu saw it sleeping on dry land around 9 or 10 a.m. The women on the Tyihumbwe who are in the habit of fishing on the river have almost all seen it at one time or another. They make a point of shouting before going into the water and this drives the beast away. As soon as it hears or is aware of man, it dives and disappears.
> 4. It attacks animals of all kinds—goats, pigs, cattle and even men—which it swallows in one mouthful. It will also eat crocodiles. The year before [1931], it took an ox and a goat belonging to the natives. This year it has taken nothing so far. Our correspondent knew of its existence in 1927 when he was on the way to Dala; the natives came and asked him for guns to kill it with, for it had just taken one of their cattle. Several *lipatas* have been killed. When the soma was a boy (which must have been 40 to 45 years ago), the natives set a trap after a *lipata* had taken three of their cattle. The animal took the bait and was killed. A white man who had shot a hippopotamus one evening came back in the morning to haul his quarry out of the water. He saw two *lipatas* eating its meat, and succeeded in killing one….The animal is said to be 13 to 20 feet long; like the crocodile, it has a serrated ridge of scales along its tail; its mouth is larger, its throat wider, and its eyes are closer together on the top of its head—an interesting detail.

Monard tried to kill a Lipata himself, by staking out a pig with a bag of arsenic tied to one leg, but the bait was ignored. ROY MACKAL speculates that the Lipata may be identical to the 50-foot MAHAMBA reported from the Congo, suggesting that both crea-

tures may be explained by survival of a relict crocodilian such as the 50-foot *Deinosuchus* (of the Late Cretaceous period) or *Ramphosuchus* (from the more recent Pliocene epoch).

Sources: Heuvelmans, *Les Derniers Dragons d'Afrique*; Heuvelmans, *On the Track of Unknown Animals*; Mackal, *A Living Dinosaur?*; Albert Monard, "Sur l'existence en Angola d'un grand reptile encore inconnu." *Bulletin de la Société Neuchâteloise de Sciences Naturelles* 57 (1932): 67-71.

Lithgow Panther This ALIEN BIG CAT of New South Wales, Australia (also known as Old Blackie) was first sighted in 1926. Witnesses describe a large black felid prowling the Gross Vale area, west of Sydney, and Lithgow resident Gayle Pound captured the animal on videotape in May 2001. Bagging the animal itself proved more difficult, however, as hunting parties sponsored by Sydney's Taronga Zoo and the National Parks and Wildlife Service returned from their quests empty-handed. As Gerald Martin, a member of Parliament, told the press in January 2002, "You name it, we tried it. The CAT has proved extremely elusive. It's as simple as that." A new rash of sightings around Lithgow in June 2002 included discovery of large pawprints and reports of the cat invading residential neighborhoods. Locals hoped that brushfires in October 2002 might have driven the cat away, but it returned once more in February 2003 and reportedly attacked a teenage boy three months later. That incident prompted authorities to compile a mass of reports spanning 77 years and plot the sightings on a map. Mayor Rex Stubbs of Hawkesbury told the press, "I believe there is enough evidence, including 89 sightings and 42 predation locations—as shown on our maps—to conclude a predatory animal of significant size exists within the Hawkesbury area. There's also reviews by independent experts of sites, photographs, footprints, scratch marks and witness statements. Efforts should be concentrated on determining a methodology to eliminate it." Less belligerent researchers hope some means may be found for humans and the cat(s) to peacefully coexist.

Sources: Len Ashworth, "'That cat' still creates stir." *Lithgow Mercury* (25 February 2003); Gail Knox, "Map tracks big cat." *Hawkesbury Gazette* (28 May 2003); "Lithgow Panther is back." *Victoria Herald Sun* (23 May 2003); "'Panther' hunt wound down." Australian Associated Press (23 January 2002).

Litledalsvatnet, Norway In ancient times, a large and vicious LAKE MONSTER was said to inhabit this lake, in Hordaland County. Locals lived in fear of the creature, which considered human beings tasty prey. Thankfully, no modern reports are on file.

Source: Skjelsvik, "Norwegian lake and sea monsters."

Little Brosna River, Ireland In ancient times, this river in County Offaly allegedly harbored an aquatic cryptid known as St. Abban's CAT. Today, it is unclear whether the reports described an ALIEN BIG CAT, a LAKE MONSTER, or some creature belonging entirely to mythology.

Source: Mary MacNickle, *Beasts and Birds in the Lives of the Early Irish Saints*. Philadelphia: The Author, 1934.

Little Murray River, Australia Most BUNYIP sightings date from the 19th century, but one of the most curious was recorded on 1 August 1947. That night, three men were passing the Little Murray River near Swan Hill, Victoria when they saw a black, 3-foot-long creature on the bank. Assuming it to be a wild pig, they ignored it and continued on their way. A month later, however, the same three men saw a similar creature swimming near the same spot. It moved against the river's current, raising a head and 9-inch-thick neck a foot above the surface. As it swam, the beast spouted water from its neck, the spray rising five feet in the air. When illuminated by a spotlight, the thing swam rapidly to shelter on the river's opposite bank and emitted a shrill whistle that "could be heard half a mile away."

Source: Smith, *Bunyips & Bigfoots*.

Little Red Men of the Delta

These unclassified primates (perhaps a species of NORTH AMERICAN APE) were initially described to IVAN SANDERSON by Tennessee resident James Meacham. Meacham's letter described an incident that allegedly occurred in 1957, while he was hunting near Jackson (Madison County).

> I would like to know if you can tell me anything about a creature that looks like a small APE or a large MONKEY that has hair the color of fur a reddish orange color. I saw such a creature when I was 15....Whatever it was did not have tail like a monkey but it did swing like one by its arms....
>
> I had a .22 caliber semiautomatic with me. I watched this thing for about 5 minutes so I have to believe it. I put fourteen .22 long-rifle shells into whatever it was. From where I was standing I couldn't have missed. We found 1 bullet in the tree trunk so 13 of them hit it. The part that sounds more impossible is that whatever it was, did not even move while 13 bullets went into it. If I had missed all 14 bullets would have gone into the tree trunk.
>
> ...We found a few hairs where I had shot, but nothing else except the bullet. There was not a trace of blood....Whatever it was did not even move till I headed for the tree. It traveled through those trees like an express train. I could hear the leaves rattle but could not see it.

Sanderson speculated that the creature might have been an escaped orangutan, though none was reported missing in the vicinity. Author Rosemary Guiley reports that the Little Red Men are also known in Kentucky, that they steal garments from clotheslines, "stay out of gunshot range and talk a lot," but her account must be regarded with some caution, since she mislocates the Meacham incident in Mississippi.

Sources: Guiley, *Atlas of the Mysterious in North America*; Sanderson, *Abominable Snowmen*.

Little Tennessee River, North Carolina

Various sources claim that aquatic cryptids have been reported from this river in far western North Carolina (Macon County), but none supply dates or details of sightings from which to continue research.

Sources Bord and Bord, *Unexplained Mysteries of the 20th Century*; Coleman, *Mysterious America*; Kirk, *In the Domain of the Lake Monsters*.

Livingston sea serpent

On 21 June 1908, passengers and crew aboard the steamer *Livingston* sighted a SEA SERPENT in the Gulf of Mexico, 50 miles north of Frontera (Tabasco State). The creature seemed to be sleeping on the surface as the ship came within 60 feet and stopped for 15 minutes to observe it. Witnesses estimated that the beast was "not less than 200 feet long...[and] about the diameter of a flour barrel in the center of its body, but not round." Its head was "approximately six feet long by three feet at the widest part. The color was dark brown and there were circles or rings near its tail." When the creature woke, startled, it swam away with its tail erect, making a noise like the rapid fire of a Gatling gun. On docking in New York, 20-odd witnesses signed sworn affidavits describing the incident.

Sources: Garner, *Monster! Monster!*; "200-foot sea serpent." *New York Times* (1 July 1908).

Lizard (Hairy)

Reptiles have no hair, yet a group of gold miners working on Papua New Guinea's Aikora River, near Mount Albert Edward, reported sighting hairy lizards on 17 April 1906. No specimens were captured, and most researchers believe the miners were confused by some small (perhaps unknown) rodent.

Source: Charles Monckton, *Last Days in New Guinea*. London: John Lane, 1922.

Lizard Men

Human-reptile hybrids have been a staple of Hollywood horror films since *The Creature from the Black Lagoon* hit theaters in 1954. Such animals should not exist in nature, but sporadic encounters with scaly HOMINIDS over the past half-century raise questions concerning our knowledge of inhuman nature. On 21 August 1955, while swimming in the Ohio River near Evansville, Indiana, Mrs. Darwin Johnson was grabbed and repeatedly pulled underwater by a clawed hand gripping her leg. She finally escaped, but her unseen attacker left a green palm stain on her knee, with deep scratches requiring medical treatment. In November 1958, motorist Charles Wetzel was terrorized by a reptilian creature that ambushed his car in near Riverside, California, gouging scratches in the windshield with its claws. Fourteen years later, in August 1972, three witnesses at THETIS LAKE, British Columbia, reported frightening encounters with a silver, scaly biped. One young man suffered cuts on his hand from sharp prongs on the manimal's head. Beginning in June 1988, dozens of persons in Lee County, South Carolina reported sightings of a 7-foot greenish-black creature around Scape Ore Swamp (near Bishopville). Biologists declared the plaster cast of one web-toed footprint a HOAX, and the bloody scales delivered to police by Kenneth Orr after a supposed clash with the monster proved to have come from a FISH. Orr, jailed for illegally packing a pistol, admitted fabricating the incident "to keep the legend of the Lizard Man alive." The initial sightings remain unexplained.

Lizard men have been seen in the U.S. and Canada (*William Rebsamen*).

Sources: Wayne Beissart, "On the lookout for 'Lizardman.'" *USA Today* (27 July 1988); Clark and Pear, *Strange & Unexplained Phenomena*; Coleman, "Other lizard people revisited"; Hauck, *Haunted Places*; "'Lizard man' facts." *Columbia* SC) *State* (15 August 1988); "Man admits 'Lizard Man' story a hoax." Associated Press (13 August 1988); Sieveking, "Lizard man."

Lizzie (Canada)

Lizzie is the nickname applied to a LAKE MONSTER allegedly inhabiting Lac Decaire, Québec. Descriptions of the unidentified creature generally conform to those reported from other Canadian lakes.

Source: "A brief survey of Canadian lake monsters." *INFO Journal* 39 (March-June 1981): 2-5.

Lizzie (Scotland)

Not to be confused with Québec's LAKE MONSTER of the same name, Scotland's Lizzie inhabits Loch Lochy, in the Highland district. A photographer claimed to have captured the creature on film in 1937, but skeptics insist the object depicted was a floating mass of vegetation. Eric Robinson and nine other witnesses watched Lizzie cavorting in the water,

250 yards offshore from Glenfintaig House, on 15 July 1960. Using binoculars, Robinson estimated that the light-colored creature measured 30-40 feet overall. As it rolled in the water, watchers noted "a fin or paddle on the side of its body." Fifteen years later, on the afternoon of 30 September 1975, five members of the Sargent family watched a black 20-foot creature for two minutes, from the highway near the Corriegour Lodge. On 13 September 1996, 16 witnesses at the same hotel saw a 12-foot cryptid with a "curved head" and three humps on its back swimming across the loch.

Sources: Costello, *In Search of Lake Monsters*; Dinsdale, *Monster Hunt*; "Good month for monster hunters." *Fortean Times* 95 (February 1997): 18; McEwan, *Mystery Animals of Britain and Ireland*.

Llamhigyn y Dwr   According to Welsh folklore, the Llamhigyn y dwr ("water leaper") once inhabited various rivers throughout Wales, lurking in ambush to devour any livestock that strayed too close to the water. It resembled a giant toad, but instead of powerful legs, it possessed a stout tail and wings. The creature's shrieking cry reportedly stunned domestic animals (and sometimes human beings), leaving them momentarily helpless as it sprang to the attack. No modern reports of the beast are on file.

Sources: John Rhys, *Celtic Folk-lore, Welsh and Manx*. London: Oxford University Press, 1901; Shuker, *From Flying Toads to Snakes with Wings*.

Llangorse Lake, Wales   Fortean authors Colin and Janet Bord include this lake, in the Powys district of Wales, on a list of supposed LAKE MONSTER habitats, but no details of any sightings are provided.

Source: Bord and Bord, *Alien Animals*.

Llyn Cowlyd, Wales   Welsh folklore names this lake, in the Conwy district, as the home of a fearful LAKE MONSTER. No modern reports are on file.

Source: Burton, *The Elusive Monster*.

Llyn Eiddwen, Wales   Ancient reports name this Welsh lake, in the Ceredigion district, as an abode of LAKE MONSTERS, but a dearth of modern sightings makes the tales difficult to evaluate.

Sources: Bord and Bord, *Alien Animals*; John Rhys, *Celtic Folklore*. Oxford: Clarendon, 1901.

Llyn Fanod, Wales   As with LLYN EIDDWEN, also located in the Welsh district of Ceredigion, folktales identify this lake as the former home of a fierce LAKE MONSTER. Locals report no modern sightings.

Source: John Rhys, *Celtic Folkore*. Oxford: Clarendon, 1901.

Llyn Farch, Wales   Yet another Ceredigion district lake with an ancient LAKE MONSTER tradition, Llyn Farch has produced no modern reports for cryptozoologists to investigate.

Sources: Bord and Bord, *Alien Animals*; John Rhys, *Celtic Folklore*. Oxford: Clarendon, 1901.

Llyn y Gadair, Wales   In the 18th century, a serpentine LAKE MONSTER reportedly attacked a swimmer in this lake, in the Gwynedd district of Wales, wrapping itself around his body before man and monster both sank out of sight.

Sources: Bord and Bord, *Alien Animals*; Marie Trevelyan, *Folk-lore and Folk-stories of Wales*. London: E. Stock, 1909.

Lo-An *see* **Jogung**

Lobizon   An unclassified WOLF or wild dog of Argentina,

The Lobizon is an unclassified wild dog of Argentina.

the Lobizon (or Almamula) is regarded by some superstitious people as a shape-shifting werewolf. It has a ferocious reputation and is invested with supernatural powers by native folklore. On 22 June 2000, members of the Gomez and Ovejero families claimed they were attacked by a Lobizon at Concepción del Bermejo, in northern Argentina. Armed with bricks and clubs, they pursued the animal, which "seemed to swell up and grow in size" when it got angry. Police took samples of the wounded creature's blood and hair, but no results have been announced. A week after the attack, authorities speculated that the culprit was a maned wolf (*Chrysocyon brachyurus*), a rare canid protected by law as an Argentine natural treasure.

Source: "Crying wolf in Argentina." *Fortean Times*.

Loch Achanalt, Scotland   Reports of LAKE MONSTERS in this Highland loch are traceable to a local storyteller, R.L. Cassie, who published various melodramatic accounts of alleged personal sightings in 1935-36. "Many of the animals seen…are of enormous size," Cassie wrote. "A hundred feet may be considered a mere minimum length." One whopper, whom Cassie dubbed Gabriel, allegedly measured 900 feet long — only 50 yards less than the loch's total length! No other source records cryptids from this loch, confirming that Cassie's accounts were a HOAX disguised as nonfiction reporting.

Sources: Cassie, *The Monsters of Achanalt*; Mike Dash, "Footnote to a footnote." *Fortean Times* 52 (Summer 1989): 66-67; Mike Dash, "Monsters of Achanalt." *Fortean Times* 177 (2003 Special): 48.

Loch Alsh, Scotland   This Scottish sea loch lies north of the Sound of Sleat, where passengers aboard the *LEDA* twice sighted SEA SERPENTS in August 1872. It also forms a passage between the North Atlantic (via Inner Sound) and LOCH DUICH, where large, unidentified sea creatures were seen in 1872 and 1886. All things considered, it is therefore no surprise that Loch Alsh produced a sighting of its own in 1893. The witness, Dr. Farquhar Matheson of London, was boating with his wife when he

…saw something rise out of the Loch in front of us — a long, straight, neck-like thing as tall as my mast. I could not think what it was at first. I fancied it might be something on land, and directed my wife's attention to it. I said, "Do you see that?" She said she did, and asked what it could be, and was rather scared. It was then 200 yards away and moving toward us.

Then it began to draw its neck down, and I saw clearly that it was a large sea-monster—of the saurian type. It was brown in colour, shining, and with a sort of ruffle at the junction of its head and neck. I can think of nothing to which to compare it so well as the head and neck of a giraffe; that is, it was not so much at right angles to it as a continuation of it in the same line. It moved its head from side to side, and I saw the reflection of the light from its wet skin.

…I saw no body—only a ripple of water where the line of the body should be. I should judge, however, that there must have been a large base of body to support such a neck. It was not a sea-serpent, but a much larger and more substantial beast—something of the nature of a gigantic lizard, I should think. An EEL could not lift up its body like that, nor could a SNAKE.

Source: Heuvelmans, *In the Wake of the Sea Serpents.*

The Loch Alsh sea serpent, after witness Farquhar Matheson.

Loch Assynt, Scotland   Lord Ellesmere of England published an article on this Highland loch's alleged LAKE MONSTERS in the early 1850s, including the account of two fishermen who met one of the beasts in 1837. It was gray and bristling with hair, its large eyes set in a head resembling a bulldog's. Lord Ellesmere reported that "[i]t was seen again soon afterwards on a small island in the Loch and is described as about the size of a stirk [young bull], but broader in the back, about three feet high, with four legs." Some years later, the Earl of Malmesbury declared them similar (if not identical) to the creatures found in Loch Arkaig (see ARCHIE).

Source: McEwan, *Mystery Animals of Britain and Ireland.*

Lochawe, Scotland   In the 16th century, fishermen avoided this lake in the district of Argyll and Bute, claiming that

it was inhabited by EELS as "big as ane horse with ane Incredible length." Many locals still believe the lake harbors an unknown LAKE MONSTER, referred to in Gaelic as *an Beathach mor Loch Abha.*

Sources: Costello, *In Search of Lake Monsters*; Holiday, *The Great Orm of Loch Ness.*

Loch Borralan, Scotland   The LAKE MONSTER reported from this Highland loch is said to be a man-eater, blamed by locals for the disappearance of two fisherman sometime in the distant past. According to the story, no trace of the sportsmen was discovered but their rods and some FISH they caught before disaster struck. Nearby, large hoofprints leading toward the water confirmed suspicions of a lurking predator at large.

Source: Harrison, *Sea Serpents and Lake Monsters of the British Isles.*

Loch Brittle, Scotland   This sea loch on the Isle of Skye's southern coast produced a SEA SERPENT report in 1917, after witnesses Ronald and Harry MacDonald reported sighting a long-necked creature rising from the depths.

Sources: Bord and Bord, *Alien Animals*; Gavin Maxwell, *Harpoon at a Venture.* London: Rupert Hart-Davis, 1952.

Loch Dochfour, Scotland   This small Highland lake is actually a northern extension of Loch Ness on the Caledonian Canal, used by migratory FISH to reach the legendary home of NESSIE. In 1995, two monster hunters claimed a sonar "hit" on a large, unidentified object near the lake's bottom.

Source: *CFZ Yearbook 1998.* Exeter, England: Centre for Fortean Zoology, 1998.

Loch Duich sea serpents   Multiple SEA SERPENT sightings were recorded from this sea loch, on the west coast of Scotland, between 1872 and 1886. The creature's first appearance, on 23 August 1972, occurred only two days after sightings were logged by passengers aboard the *LEDA*, less than three miles away. Boat-builder Alexander Macmillan was fishing from a boat at the mouth of the loch (and not far from neighboring LOCH ALSH), when he saw a large animal with three or four "half-rounds" on its back "rushing along in the sea." Like the traveling clergymen before him, Macmillan reported another meeting with the same creature or its twin on the following day (24 August). No details are presently available for the 1886 sighting, except that BERNARD HEUVELMANS listed it as occurring in summer.

Source: Heuvelmans, *In the Wake of the Sea Serpents.*

Loch Duvat, Scotland   In June 1893, witness Ewan MacMillan watched a shrieking LAKE MONSTER somewhat larger than a pony crawl ashore on the north side of this lake, on the Isle of Eriskay (Western Isles).

Sources: Bord and Bord, *Alien Animals*; John Campbell and Trevor Hall, *Strange Things.* London: Routledge and Kegan Paul, 1968.

Loch Eil, Scotland   This lake in the Scottish Highlands is an extension of LOCH LINNHE and shares that loch's tradition of LAKE MONSTER sightings. In 1962, author Denys-James Watkins-Pitchford described the following encounter with one of the lake's mysterious denizens:

I was watching some mallard paddling about among some weedy rocks at the end of a little promontory when there appeared out of the calm water exactly opposite me a large black shiny object which I can only compare with the blunt, blind head of an enormous worm.

It was, I suppose, some 50 yards from where I was standing, and it kept appearing and disappearing, not moving along, but rolling on the surface. The water was greatly disturbed all round the object. It had a shiny wet-looking skin, but the head (if head it was) was quite unlike a seal's and had no face, or nose, no eyes. It rose quite a long way out of the water, some three feet or more, before sinking back.

Sources: Dinsdale, *Monster Hunt*; Denys-James Watkins-Pitchford, *September Road to Caithness and the Western Sea*. London: Nicholas Kaye, 1962.

Loch Feith an Leothaid, Scotland This Highland loch is linked to LOCH ASSYNT and shares the larger lake's reputation for harboring LAKE MONSTERS. In the 1930s, witness Kenneth MacKenzie of Steen met a long-necked creature with a head resembling a deer's, when it rose from the water to peer across the stern of his boat. (Some published accounts of this incident refer to the lake as Loch Canish or Canisp.)

Sources: Costello, *In Search of Lake Monsters*; R. Macdonald Robertson, *Selected Highland Folktales*. Isle of Colonsay, Scotland: House of Lochar, 1961.

Loch Fyne, Scotland The LAKE MONSTERS reported from this loch, in the district of Argyll and Bute, generally conform to the long-necked NESSIE-type familiar from other Scottish lakes. One such "monstrous FISH" was reported in July 1570. Almost three centuries later, motorist Eustace Maxell was driving past Loch Fyne when he saw an offshore "sand bank" suddenly come alive and swim across the lake. Author Harold Wilkins describes a veritable war against the creatures of Loch Fyne, complete with at least one casualty, but his brief account lamentably lacks any dates.

A 30 foot monster, with girth of 30 feet, was washed ashore on Loch Fyne, Argyllshire. Fishermen swear that it is neither SHARK nor whale. Its head is in front of its mouth and two huge fins are well forward. The massive tail is powerful looking. The carcass lies in three feet of water at low tide. It is wondered if it is the monster rammed by the turbine steamer *King George V*, three weeks ago, or is the one shot with an explosive bullet, second week of June, off Inverary.

Sources: Harrison, *Sea Serpents and Lake Monsters of the British Isles*; McEwan, *Mystery Animals of Britain and Ireland*.

Loch Garget Beag, Scotland In 1938, witness Mary Falconer claimed to have seen 13 "water horses" run into this Highland lake and dive below the surface. No other modern reports of cryptid activity are on file from this site.

Source: R. Macdonald Robertson, *Selected Highland Folktales*. Isle of Colonsay, Scotland: House of Lochar, 1961.

Loch Garten, Scotland Ancient traditions of a predatory LAKE MONSTER surround this Highland loch, set in the midst of the Abernathy Forest. The creature was typically described as a cross between a horse and bull, with a huge head and jet-black mane. Legend has it that a local crofter once baited the creature with a lamb, tethered to a massive lakeside boulder. That night, a storm lashed the district, and morning's light revealed deep ruts where the boulder had been dragged into the loch. No subsequent monster sightings have been reported from Loch Garten.

Source: Harrison, *Sea Serpents and Lake Monsters of the British Isles*.

Loch Garve, Scotland Loch Garve, located near Strathpeffer in the Scottish Highlands, is yet another lake with longstanding LAKE MONSTER traditions. The local creature is supposed to have claimed at least two human victims in the distant past, but a dearth of modern sightings lets neighbors of the lake

rest peacefully. Notorious Highland yarn-spinner R.L. Cassie claimed a sighting at Loch Garve in 1935, during a busy year when cryptids surfaced wherever he looked.

Sources: Mike Dash, "Monsters of Achanalt." *Fortean Times* 177 (2003 Special): 48; Harrison, *Sea Serpents and Lake Monsters of the British Isles*.

Loch Glass, Scotland Witnesses reported a LAKE MONSTER from this Highlands lake in 1730, but no modern sightings are on file.

Source: Holiday, *The Great Orm of Loch Ness*.

Loch Hourn, Scotland Author Paul Harrison described this lake in Inverness County as "a wild and gloomy loch," befitting a site whose name translates as "Lake of Hell." A large LAKE MONSTER was sighted here in 1872, and again in 1934, when the four witnesses (including the Duke of Marlborough and three clergymen) described a 96-foot creature "with a flat and eyeless head, a black body which forged through the water, and, as it did so, raised its back in ridges which curved then flattened."

Sources: Dinsdale, *Monster Hunt*; Harrison, *Sea Serpents and Lake Monsters of the British Isles*.

Loch Laggan, Scotland Katie Sullivan's Internet roster of supposed LAKE MONSTER habitats includes this Scottish loch, located in Glen Spean, between Fort William and Kingussie. Unfortunately, no details or dates of sightings are provided.

Source: The Online Lake Cryptid Directory, http:/dive.to/lakemonsters.

Loch Laoghaire, Ireland In ancient times, this Irish lake was said to harbor a fire-breathing serpent. Celtic hero Finn of Fianna confronted the monster, and "in payment of what he suffered of its ravages he beheaded it with his weapons." No modern sightings of LAKE MONSTERS are recorded.

Source: Costello, *In Search of Lake Monsters*.

Loch Linnhe, Scotland This sea loch on the west coast of the Scottish Highlands has a long tradition of LAKE MONSTER sightings. In the 1890s, a large EEL-like animal with a mane was found dead at Corpach Lock, near Fort William, at the north end of the lake. Nearby, Loch Linnhe is linked to LOCH EIL, another source of occasional cryptid sightings. In the 1940s, Mrs. B.F. Cox saw one of Linnhe's long-necked creatures from a range of 20 feet, and witness Eric Robbins described another sighting in 1954. Ten years later, on 22 June 1964, a Mrs. Preston met another cryptid of the NESSIE type. Loch Linnhe's link to the ocean invites speculation concerning free access by SEA SERPENTS, and indeed, such a creature was seen at the loch's sea entrance, by passengers aboard the yacht *SHIANTELLE*, in 1887.

Sources: Harrison, *Sea Serpents and Lake Monsters of the British Isles*; Heuvelmans, *In the Wake of the Sea Serpents*; David James, "A fine weather monster." *The Observer* (27 December 1964).

Loch Lochy serpent *see* **Lizzie**

Loch Lomond, Canada Scottish influence is strong in the Canadian province of New Brunswick, thus accounting for the name of this lake—and also, perhaps, for its LAKE MONSTER traditions. Two published sources include Loch Lomond on lists of Canadian "monster" lakes, but neither provides any dates or details of sightings.

Sources: "A list of bodies of water in Canada reportedly inhabited by monsters." *INFO Journal* 45 (November 1984): 30-31; Bord and Bord, *Unexplained Mysteries of the 20th Century*.

Loch Lomond, Scotland   An atlas published in 1659 described this Scottish lake, in the district of Argyll and Bute, as the home of "FISH without fins" and a strange "floating island." In 1724, Alexander Graham of Duchray wrote, "in this Loch at the place where the River Enrick falls into it, about a mile west of the church of Buchanan, its [*sic*] reported by countrymen living there about, that they sometimes see the Hipotam or water-horse." On 22 September 1964, a Helmsborough butcher named Haggerty and his wife glimpsed a swimming creature's large humped back while driving past the lake. A short time later, crewmen aboard a passing freight train reported an object in Loch Lomond "bigger than a long boat and moving fast, just like a torpedo." Two more witnesses, a Mr. and Mrs. Maltman, saw a long-necked creature surface in the lake while they were camping near Luss, at Easter 1980. In 1997, Scottish researcher Nick Taylor reportedly captured one of the loch's elusive denizens on videotape. As described by author JOHN KIRK, "[t]he object is rather indistinct, but does not resemble any animal regarded as common in the realm of wildlife."

Sources: Costello, *In Search of Lake Monsters*; Dinsdale, *Monster Hunt*; Kirk, *In the Domain of the Lake Monsters*.

Loch Lurgainn, Ireland   Celtic folklore speaks of a "furious serpent" that once inhabited this lake, lamenting that "all that it destroyed of our host may not be told till distant doom." The creature was ultimately slain by a local hero, Finn of the Fianna.

Source: Costello, *In Search of Lake Monsters*.

Loch Maree, Scotland   This Highland loch, situated on a mountainous peninsula between Gruinard Bay and Loch Ewe, is renowned for sea trout fishing. It is also famous for tales of LAKE MONSTERS, accounting for its popular alternate name, Loch na Beiste. Local crofters once avoided the lake, from fear of its ferocious predators, and more recent sightings include familiar descriptions of creatures whose humped backs resemble capsized boats. In the 19th century, a landlord named Bankes became obsessed with the monster(s), spending a small fortune to empty the loch and fill it with lime, but the effort proved futile and Bankes became a public laughingstock.

Sources: Harrison, *Sea Serpents and Lake Monsters of the British Isles*; Whyte, *More Than a Legend*.

Loch Meiklie, Scotland   In ancient times, this Highland loch allegedly harbored a LAKE MONSTER, but no modern reports are on file.

Source: Gould, *The Loch Ness Monster and Others*.

Loch na Mna, Scotland   In 1873, while touring the Hebrides, Samuel Johnson and James Boswell collected the following tale of a deadly LAKE MONSTER from this loch on the small island of Rasay. As related by their guide:

He said there was a wild beast in it, a sea-horse, which came and devoured a man's daughter; upon which the man lighted a great fire, and had a sow roasted on it, the smell of which attracted the monster. In the fire was put a spit. The man lay concealed behind a low wall of loose stones, which extended from the fire over the summit of the hill, till it reached the side of the loch. The monster came, and the man with a red hot spit destroyed it. Malcolm [the guide] showed me the little hiding place, and the row of stones. He did not laugh when he told me the story.

Source: James Boswell, *The Journal of a Tour to the Hebrides with Samuel Johnson, LL.D.* London: Henry Baldwin, 1785.

Loch nan Dubhrachan, Scotland   In 1870, this loch on the Isle of Skye witnessed an unsuccessful attempt to capture a LAKE MONSTER. The local laird, MacDonald of Sleat, recruited men to drag the lake with a large net, while hundreds of neighbors turned out for an unexpected holiday featuring "more whiskey than at a funeral." The day's total bag was two pike, but spectators fled at one point, when the net snagged on some submerged object, mistakenly presumed to be the monster.

Source: Costello, *In Search of Lake Monsters*.

Loch Ness and Morar Project   In 1969, after receiving reports of a LAKE MONSTER known as MORAG in Loch Morar, the LOCH NESS INVESTIGATION BUREAU sent a team to study NESSIE'S most famous Scottish competitor. Sufficient evidence was found to justify full-time work at Loch Morar, whereupon a team of LNIB members volunteered to form the Loch Morar Survey. A new name was adopted in 1973, and scientific research continued until 1985, when the group disbanded.

Source: Campbell and Solomon, *The Search for Morag*; Harrison, *The Encyclopaedia of the Loch Ness Monster*.

Loch Ness Investigation Bureau   Known by various names over time, this organization was created in November 1961 as the Bureau for Investigating the Loch Ness Phenomena Limited, then formally incorporated on 20 March 1962 as the Loch Ness Investigation Bureau, a registered nonprofit charity. (Many media reports called it the Loch Ness *Phenomena* Investigation Bureau.) Early directors of the LNIB were David James, Richard Fitter, Peter Scott and Constance Whyte. In 1962-63, LNIB members stationed at the loch captured various unknown objects on film, but the indistinct quality of their films and photos made definitive analysis impossible. In 1970 the group changed its name again, to the more "serious sounding" Loch Ness Investigations, but dwindling funds forced LNI to close its doors two years later.

Sources: Harrison, *The Encyclopaedia of the Loch Ness Monster*; Mackal, *The Monsters of Loch Ness*.

Loch Ness Monster *see* **Nessie**

Loch Ness Monster Fan Club   Gary Campbell created this group in early 1996, upon learning that no organization existed to record his recent sighting of NESSIE. Campbell serves as president of the club with stated aims including: to serve as a first point of contact for persons interested in Nessie; to compile a comprehensive list of sightings; to put members in touch with others of similar interest or specialized expertise; and to serve as liaison between organizations of similar interest. Today, sightings of Nessie may be reported online, at the club's Internet website.

Sources: Harrison, *The Encyclopaedia of the Loch Ness Monster*; Loch Ness Monster Fan Club, http://www.lochness.co/uk/fan_club/.

Loch Oich, Scotland *see* **Wee Oichy**

Loch Pityoulish, Scotland   In ancient times, an albino LAKE MONSTER was said to inhabit the depths of this Highland loch. No modern sightings are recorded.

Source: R. Macdonald Robertson, *Selected Highland Folktales*. Isle of Colonsay, Scotland: House of Lochar, 1961.

Loch Poit na hI, Scotland   Medieval tales speak of LAKE MONSTERS inhabiting this loch on the Isle of Mull, but it would seem the animals did not survive to modern times.

Source: Antony Coxe, *Haunted Britain*. New York: McGraw-Hill, 1973.

Loch Quoich, Scotland Author Peter Costello identifies this Highland loch as one of the few Scottish lakes that have produced modern LAKE MONSTER sightings with no apparent link to ancient folklore. Three fishermen sighted one of the NESSIE-type creatures in the early 1930s, but they kept the incident secret for years, fearing ridicule. Several more sightings were collected by Dom Cyril Dieckhoff, of St. Benedict's Abbey.

Sources: Costello, *In Search of Lake Monsters*; Dinsdale, *Monster Hunt*; Whyte, *More Than a Legend*.

Loch Rannoch, Scotland Ancient tales of LAKE MONSTERS or "water horses" endure from this Perthshire loch, but no modern sightings maintain the tradition.

Source: John Macculloch, *A Description of the Western Islands of Scotland*. London: Hurst, Robinson, 1819.

Loch Scavaig, Scotland This large sea loch, located at the Isle of Skye's southern tip, was the scene of a SEA SERPENT sighting in the early 1900s. Sandy Campbell and John Stewart were fishing with a third companion from a skiff when Campbell saw:

an object rising out of the water about fifty yards to seaward of them. It was about a yard high when he first saw it, but, as he watched, it rose slowly from the surface to a height of twenty or more feet — a tapering column that moved to and fro in the air. Sandy called excitedly to the old men, but at first got only an angry retort to keep hauling the net and not be wasting time. At last Stewart looked up in exasperation, and then sprang to his feet in bewildered astonishment, as he too saw what Sandy was looking at. While this "tail" was still moving in the air they could see the water rippling against a dark mass below it which was just breaking the surface, and which they presumed to be the animal's body. The high column descended slowly into the sea as it had risen; and as the last of it submerged the boat began to rock on a commotion of water like the wake of a passing steamer. Steward was terrified; they dropped the net and rowed as fast as they could for shore.

Source: Heuvelmans, *In the Wake of the Sea Serpents*.

Loch Shin, Scotland In ancient times, this Highland loch allegedly harbored a yellow LAKE MONSTER with supernatural powers. According to tradition, one of the district's early Christian priests performed a human sacrifice to win the beast's cooperation in building a church. The superstitious trappings may disguise a real-life cryptid, but no modern sightings provide any further details.

Source: Harrison, *Sea Serpents and Lake Monsters of the British Isles*.

Loch Suainaval, Scotland A predatory LAKE MONSTER frightened neighbors of this loch, near Uig on the Isle of Lewis, in 1856. Local farmers threw lambs into the water, hoping to sate the creature's appetite and prevent it from raiding ashore. No sightings have been logged in modern times.

Source: Costello, *In Search of Lake Monsters*.

Loch Tay, Scotland A 14th-century map of Scotland described this Perthshire loch as the home of "FISH without fins," a "moving island," and "waves without wind." In 1965, multiple witnesses saw a large cryptid on shore, at the nearby FIRTH OF TAY.

Source: Costello, *In Search of Lake Monsters*.

Loch Treig, Scotland Medieval folklore identifies this Highland loch, below Ben Bevis, as the home of voracious LAKE MONSTERS. The stories were revived in autumn 1933, when B.N. Peech, an engineer in charge of a hydro-electric scheme at the lake, reported that some of his divers had sighted unknown creatures in the depths. Several workers left their jobs as a result of those reports.

Source: Costello, *In Search of Lake Monsters*; "Not the only monster: Hidden terrors of Loch Treig." *Aberdeen Weekly Journal* (19 October 1933).

Loch Urabhal, Scotland On 27 July 1961, schoolteachers Ian McArthur and Roderick MacIver were fishing at Loch Urabhal, near Achmore on the Isle of Lewis, when a LAKE MONSTER surfaced in shallow water some 45 yards away. The creature surfaced three times, then disappeared. As McArthur later told reporters, "It had a hump and there was either a small head or fin about six feet away from the hump. It swam like a dolphin but was much bigger." Loch Urabhal is landlocked, with no access from the sea.

Sources: Costello, *In Search of Lake Monsters*; Harrison, *Sea Serpents and Lake Monsters of the British Isles*; McEwan, *Mystery Animals of Britain and Ireland*.

Loch Vennachair, Scotland While touring Scotland in 1800, John Leyden reported that neighbors of Loch Vennachair (in the district of Stirling) "had been a good deal alarmed by the appearance of that unaccountable being, the water-horse (*Each Uisge*)." The animal was blamed for drowning several children as they crossed the lake, a few months prior to Leyden's visit.

Source: Costello, *In Search of Lake Monsters*.

Loch Warren, Scotland In 1923, while hunting at this Highland loch, a certain Colonel Trimble reported that a long-necked LAKE MONSTER emerged from the water and devoured his dog. No subsequent reports of the ferocious beast have surfaced, and the story's sole appearance in a French publication, four decades after the fact, may warrant skepticism.

Source: George Langelaan, *Les Faits Maudits*. Paris: Éditions Planète, 1967.

Loenvatnet, Norway On 18 July 1995, Gunnar Sveen reported a LAKE MONSTER sighting from this lake in Sogn og Fjordane County. He watched the creature — which he now calls "Loonie" — swimming on the surface for half an hour, describing it as a dark-colored animal with three humps, each approximately five feet long.

Source: Erik Knatterud, Sea Serpents in Norwegian Lakes, http://www.mjoesormen.no.

Long Island Sound sea serpents Multiple sightings of unidentified SEA SERPENTS were reported from New York's Long Island Sound during the 19th and 20th centuries. The first was reported on 3 October 1817, by witness James Guion, who saw a large serpentine creature "going with great rapidity up [the] sound" past Marmoneck Harbor. Two days later, at Rye-Neck, Thomas Herttell used a telescope to watch an animal with "a long rough dark looking body, progressing rapidly up sound [toward New York City] against a brisk breeze and a strong ebb tide." Some 40-50 feet of the beast's back was visible, described as "irregular, uneven, and deeply indented...creating a swell before him not unlike that made by a boat towed rapidly at the stern of a vessel." On 19 June 1818, an unknown pelagic giant was sighted off Sag Harbor, at the far end of Long Island from New York City. Six months later, on 17 December, a sea monster supposedly attacked the schooner *SALLY* off Long Island's coast, but most investigators now believe that case — and a dramatic woodcut illustration of the beast — to be a HOAX. A more believable sighting was logged by witnesses aboard the *ANNY HARPER*, who reported a sighting near the Connecticut shoreline of Long Island Sound in June 1890. By contrast, the keeper of the Stradford lighthouse was surely joking in September 1896, when he claimed to have sighted a 200-foot serpent with a neck like a ship's funnel raised 20 feet above the waves, sporting a green handlebar mustache. On 18 June 1913, an unknown creature with a head the size of a barrel was seen from a yacht off Rockaway Shoals. Finally, in 1929, a U.S. Coast Guard cutter met an unknown animal 20 miles off Montauk Point. As described by one of the officers aboard:

> I was on the bridge when I sighted something in the water about a half-mile off starboard bow. As it came nearer, I saw it was a strange creature with a long neck and a serpent-like head. It was moving through the water at about 10 to 12 knots [15-18 mph]. I called the helmsman and he summoned four or five men, all of whom started for a boat with the intention of launching it and capturing the creature. I immediately countermanded that intention because from what I could see of the creature's head and neck, it was quite apparent that it was big enough to swamp the boat. It eventually passed within about 200 yards of us and I could establish that the head was about 2 feet in diameter and was 8 to 10 feet out of the water. The front of its neck was very black and shiny like satin, glistening as if it had recently been under water. I could plainly see the wrinkles on the skin where the eye was turned toward the ship must have been two or three inches across.

Sources: Bord and Bord, *Unexplained Mysteries of the 20th Century*; Heuvelmans, *In the Wake of the Sea Serpents*; O'Neill, *The Great New England Sea Serpent*.

Long Pond, Canada

In 1967, a LAKE MONSTER resembling a 30- to 40-foot EEL was reported by witnesses from this Newfoundland lake, south of Gander.

Source: "A mari usque ad mari." *Fortean Times* 46 (Spring 1986): 44-51.

Loofs-Wissowa, Helmut (1927–)

Australian anthropologist and historian Helmut Loofs-Wissowa pioneered the study of Southeast Asian archaeology at Australian National University in Canberra. He also described himself as an "odd man out" in his profession, for espousing the belief that NEANDERTAL MAN has survived into modern times. Strongly influenced by the research and writings of BERNARD HEUVELMANS, Loofs-Wissowa began his own study of unknown HOMINIDS in 1960, collecting reports of "GORILLAS" from various regions of Vietnam and Laos. That research convinced him that a higher primate distinct from gorillas, CHIMPANZEES, orangutans and *Homo sapiens* exists today in Southeast Asia. In 1996, Loofs-Wissowa mounted an expedition to the Laotian-Vietnamese border, armed with photos and drawings of various great APES, Java Man (*Homo erectus*) and the MINNESOTA ICEMAN. Without exception, his native informants selected pictures of the Iceman as a likeness of the hairy bipeds reputedly found in their jungles. Asked what he would do if he encountered one of the creatures himself, Loofs-Wissowa replied, "I have no idea. I can't kill it, because it is another type of human. I can't experiment on it, because that would involve taking it out of the jungle. I would probably just let it be, hopefully after taking lots of photos." Today, Dr. Loofs-Wissowa is a retired Reader in Asian History and Visiting Fellow at ANU's Southeast Asia Centre.

Sources: Dmitri Bayanov, "Dr. Helmut Loofs-Wissowa." *Bigfoot Coop Newsletter* 17 (April 1997); Liz Tynan, "Neanderthals may live on as the yetis of the modern world." *ANU Reporter* (13 March 1996): 3.

Lophenteropneusts

These surprising invertebrates were first photographed in 1962, while oceanographers aboard the *Spencer F. Baird* were collecting information on deep-sea life in five trenches of the Southwest Pacific. Remote-control cameras snapped 4,000 photos of the sea bottom at hadal depths (below 20,000 feet), including pictures that captured these hitherto-unknown animals. Photos of long, coiled fecal strings on the ocean floor revealed small animals at the end of each string, measuring 2-4 inches long, with transparent bodies and a ring of anterior tentacles. Lophenteropneusts constitute a new species (and perhaps a new class). None have yet been collected for study.

Sources: Henning Lemche, "Hadal life as analyzed from photographs." *Videnskabelige Meddelser Dansk Naturhistorisk Forening* 139 (1976): 263-336; O.S. Tendal, "What became of Lemche's Lophenteropneust?" *Deep-Sea Newsletter* 27 (1998): 21-24.

Lost Lake, California

In August 2000, cryptozoologist LOREN COLEMAN interviewed Cynthia Fairburn concerning an incident that occurred at Lost Lake (north of Fresno, California) in 1971. As described by Fairburn, she and a friend were swimming in Lost River, at the point where it flows into Lost Lake, when they were frightened from the water by a giant CATFISH eight to ten feet long, lashing the surface of the water with a tail "at least two feet wide."

Source: Coleman, *Mysterious America*.

Lotta sea serpent

On 2 September 1886, sailors aboard the *Lotta* sighted a SEA SERPENT in New York's Hudson River, off Bearden Island. The encounter was brief, with Captain Hitchcock reporting that "the head stood right up straight for a second or two, as if the animal wanted to breathe, then it sunk out of sight."

Source: O'Neill, *The Great New England Sea Serpent*.

Lough Abisdealy, Ireland

Reported LAKE MONSTER sightings from this lough, in County Galway, date from the years of the Crimean War (1853-56), with witnesses describing a black, EEL-like predator some 35 feet long, which dined on sheep. In January 1914, a witness driving a horse cart past the lake sighted the creature slithering ashore. That summer, shortly before the outbreak of World War I, thre witnesses were driving past the lake when:

> ...suddenly they beheld a long black creature propeling itself rapidly across the lake. Its flat head, on a long neck, was held high, two great loops of its length buckled in and out of the water as it progressed. Obviously a SNAKE and a huge one. The three witnesses stared, doubtful of their own eyes at this amazing sight. The avenue is within a few yards of the water, so they were able to have a clear view of the mysterious monster.

Sources: Bord and Bord, *Unexplained Mysteries of the 20th Century*; Mackal, *The Monsters of Loch Ness*; McEwan, *Mystery Animals of Britain and Ireland*.

Lough Allen, Ireland

Ancient legends of a serpent chained to the bottom of this lake, in County Leitrim, may reflect real-life LAKE MONSTER sightings at some point in time, but no modern reports are on file to assist with research.

Source: Costello, *In Search of Lake Monsters*.

Lough Attariff, Ireland

Witness W.J. Wood filed the following report of his encounter with a LAKE MONSTER at this Irish lough, in County Cork:

> In 1966 in the month of June, I was fishing at Lough Attariff, a sixteen-acre lake in the hills between Clonakilty and Dunmanway. The sun was strong with a very light south-westerly breeze into

which I was fly-fishing with an expectant eye open for rising trout. Suddenly and quietly a long dark brown object surfaced at about a distance of 100 yards, facing directly towards me. It had the head of a well-grown calf and large glittering eyes almost at water level. The distance appeared to lessen and the creature's approach angle altered until it was parallel to me and about ninety yards distant. It seemed to be about ten to ten and a half feet long and protruded above the surface five or six inches. After about two minutes the animal submerged. A year later, Wood met another aquatic cryptid, this time at LACKAGH LAKE, 50 miles to the west of Lough Attariff.

Source: McEwan, *Mystery Animals of Britain and Ireland*.

Lough Auna, Ireland   Reports of a serpentine LAKE MONSTER have issued from this lake, in County Galway, since the late 19th century. In the 1890s, a woman cutting lakeside turf was frightened when one of the creatures came ashore, prompting her to drop her tools and flee. She reported that "its front appearance was something similar to a horse and it tailed off something like an EEL." Two later witnesses confirmed the resemblance to an eel, noting that the animal they saw was 30–40 feet long, with a bristly mane or fin on its back, and three or four humps undulating above the water's surface. Author F.W. Holiday went trolling for the creature with a net in 1969, but failed to haul it in. A decade later, in May 1980, Adrian O'Connell and a companion, retired Air Commodore Kort of the Netherlands Air Force, watched an unknown animal swimming 15 yards offshore. They reported that the creature's visible portion was five feet long and protruded a foot from the water.

Sources: Bord and Bord, *Unexplained Mysteries of the 20th Century*; McEwan, *Mystery Animals of Britain and Ireland*.

Lough Bray, Ireland   Ireland's County Wicklow boasts two Lough Brays, Upper and Lower, located in the Wicklow Mountains 10 miles southwest of Dublin bay. Lower Lough Bray is the larger of the two, and small at that, barely three-quarters of a mile long and one-half mile wide. Both lakes are something over 60 feet in depth. Unfortunately, witness "L.R." did not specify which Lough Bray he was visiting in spring 1963, when he and a friend saw:

a large hump like the back of a RHINOCEROS emerge from the water. Ripples spread out to each side of it and then a head something like a TORTOISE only many times bigger broke surface. It came up about three feet above the surface, moved slowly around and swam forward a few yards. As it did so the body was more clearly revealed, circular and not less than 10 or 12 feet in circumference. It was a dark greyish colour. Suddenly and silently the creature seemed to dive and smoothly vanished leaving an agitated swirl of water. We saw it for not less than three minutes.

Source: Dinsdale, *Monster Hunt*.

Lough Caogh, Ireland   Celtic folklore describes this lake in County Leitrim as the one-time lair of LAKE MONSTERS or "water horses." A young man reportedly captured one of the creatures and forced it to drag a plow through his fields for a time, before the animal rebelled and escaped to the lough, dragging its captor along to his death.

Source: Gibbons, *Missionaries and Monsters*.

Lough Carra, Ireland   Folklore names Lough Carra, in County Mayo, as the ancient abode of a "great serpent" that was ultimately slain by Celtic hero Finn of Fianna. The legend may be based on LAKE MONSTER sightings, but no modern reports are on file.

Source: Costello, *In Search of Lake Monsters*.

Lough Cleevaun, Ireland   Folktales identify this lough in County Wicklow as the ancient home of a dangerous LAKE MONSTER. Reports include the story of an English visitor who was warned against swimming in the lake, whereupon he tossed his dog into the water and watched it disappear forever in a swirl of foam. No modern sightings are on file to help cryptozoologists assess the early reports.

Source: Dinsdale, *Monster Hunt*.

Lough Crolan, Ireland   In the 1890s, an unidentified creature resembling a large EEL was reportedly stranded in a culvert linking Lough Crolan (in County Galway) to nearby Lough Derrylea. The animal was so repulsive that no one would approach it, leaving it to die and rot away. ROY MACKAL and F.W. Holiday visited the site in 1968 and determined that the creature may have been as large as 18 inches in diameter. It remains unidentified today. Witness Tom Connelly reported an animal resembling an oversized otter from Loch Crolan itself, in 1961. (The lake is also sometimes called Loch Gowlan.)

Sources: Holiday, *The Dragon and the Disk*; McEwan, *Mystery Animals of Britain and Ireland*.

Lough Cullaun, Ireland   Monster hunter ANTHONY SHIELS claims to have seen a LAKE MONSTER in this County Clare lough, displaying a 4-foot hump above the water's surface. Questions raised about Shiels's veracity in other cases makes this solitary sighting problematic.

Source: *Animals and Men* 10 (1997).

Lough Cullen, Ireland   In ancient times, this County Mayo lake was allegedly inhabited by a "great reptile" that terrorized the neighborhood, until it was killed by a Celtic hero named MacCumhail. No modern LAKE MONSTER sightings are reported from the lough.

Source: Costello, *In Search of Lake Monsters*.

Lough Derg, Ireland   Celtic folktales name this lough, in County Donegal, as the ancient lair of a LAKE MONSTER that swallowed 200 warriors before hero Finn of Fianna arrived to kill the beast and cut it open, thus liberating its still-living victims. Lough Derg ("Red Lake") takes its name from "this wonderful slaughter," but Finn apparently did not wipe out the lake's stock of cryptids. In the late 1960s, locals told investigator Lionel Leslie that "water horses" could still be seen in the lough from time to time.

Source: Costello, *In Search of Lake Monsters*.

Lough Dubh, Ireland   In March 1962, schoolmaster Alphonsus Mullaney was fishing with his son at on this lake, 13 miles east of Dunmore in County Galway, when he hooked some heavy object that snapped his fishing line. As Mullaney examined the broken line, his son screamed from the bank nearby, and Mullaney looked up to see a hideous creature splashing in the shallows.

It was not a seal or anything I had ever seen. It had, for instance, short, thick legs and a hippo face. It was as big as a cow or an ass, square faced, with small ears and a white pointed horn on its snout. It was dark grey in colour, and covered with bristles or short hair, like a pig.

The Mullaneys fled, returning shortly with an armed party of men, but the creature was gone and did not reappear. A spokesman for the National Museum offered reporters the vague opinion that "recently animals not native to these shores were found near Scotland and Ireland, such as TURTLES, indicating the possibility of climactic changes in the Atlantic." What this meant in regard to a landlocked lake is anyone's guess.

Sources: Costello, *In Search of Lake Monsters*; McEwan, *Mystery Animals of Britain and Ireland*; Shuker, *From Flying Toads to Snakes with Wings*.

Lough Eask, Ireland   A LAKE MONSTER of the long-necked NESSIE type was reported from this County Donegal lough for the first time in 1998.

Source: "This just in: Europe has a new monster." *American Way* (November 1998).

Lough Erne, Ireland   Celtic folklore identifies this 50-mile stretch of water, in County Cavan, as the hunting ground of a large "blue serpent," allegedly slain in ancient times by heroic Finn of Fianna. Whatever Finn killed, however, a serpentine creature of sorts was still plying the local waters in August 1999, when it frightened swimmer Claudia Westrich near Killykeen. A companion, Sean Walsh, took an indistinct photo of something in the river, but the animal escaped and remains unidentified. Following that incident, other locals came forward to describe encounters with a creature "up to eight feet long with a spikey head."

Sources: Costello, *In Search of Lake Monsters*; Harrison, *Sea Serpents and Lake Monsters of the British Isles*; "O'Nessie makes a splash." *Sunday People* (22 August 1999).

Lough Fadda, Ireland   Librarian Georgina Carberry was fishing with three friends at Lough Fadda, County Galway, in 1954, when she saw "a large black object which moved slowly, showing two humps. The head was about three feet out of the water, in one long curve. The mouth was open and set under the head like that of a SHARK. It was black in colour, and the skin was smooth. The whole body seemed to have movement in it." Carberry further described the animal as "wormy creepy" and remarked upon its "V-shaped tail." Lionel Leslie, a cousin of Winston Churchill, went hunting for the creature on 16 October 1965. With two witnesses present, including a clergyman, he detonated five pounds of plastic explosive in the lake, whereupon a large black object briefly surfaced, thrashing in the water, then sank out of sight again. In October 1967 Leslie returned to drag the lough with a 50-foot net, but storms foiled the hunt and he left empty-handed.

Sources: Costello, *In Search of Lake Monsters*; Harrison, *Sea Serpents and Lake Monsters of the British Isles*.

Lough Foyle, Northern Ireland   Celtic folklore names this lake, in County Londonderry, as ancient home of two huge serpents. The LAKE MONSTERS met their match after making a "fierce attack" on soldiers led by legendary hero Finn of Fianna, whereupon Finn killed them both. No modern sightings are on file.

Source: Costello, *In Search of Lake Monsters*.

Lough Geal *see* **Carabuncle**

Lough Glendalough, Ireland   Ancient folklore includes this lough, in County Galway, on a list of Irish lakes once inhabited by LAKE MONSTERS, but no modern sightings have been reported.

Sources: Bord and Bord, *Alien Animals*; Michael O'Clery *The Martyrology of Donegal: A Calendar of the Saints of Ireland*. Dublin: Irish Archaeological and Celtic Society, 1864.

Lough Graney, Ireland   Lady Augusta Gregory de-

scribed the LAKE MONSTER of Lough Graney, in County Clare, from an account received in 1920 of much earlier events.

> The lake down there is an enchanted place, and the old people told me that one time they were swimming there and a man had gone out into the middle and they saw something like a giant EEL making for him, and they called out "if ever you were a great swimmer show us now how you can swim to the shore." for they wouldn't frighten him by saying what was behind him. So he swam to the shore, and he only got there when the thing behind him was in the place where he was.

Source: Augusta Gregory, *Visions and Beliefs in the West of Ireland*. London: Putnam & Sons, 1920.

Lough Inagh, Ireland   According to Irish folklore, this lough in County Galway once harbored a LAKE MONSTER or "water horse," but no modern sightings sustain the legend.

Source: Nathaniel Colgan, "Field notes on the folklore of Irish plants and animals." *Irish Naturalist* 23 (March 1914): 53-64.

Lough Keel, Ireland   Fortean authors Colin and Janet Bord include this lough, in County Donegal, on a list of supposed LAKE MONSTER habitats published in 1981, but they provide no details of sightings. Curiously, the site was omitted from an expanded list of anomalous sites released by the same authors eight years later.

Sources: Bord and Bord, *Alien Animals*; Bord and Bord, *Unexplained Mysteries of the 20th Century*.

Lough Kylemore, Ireland   Cryptozoologist ROY MACKAL, together with authors Colin and Janet Bord, notes that LAKE MONSTER reports have been logged from this lake in County Galway, but no dates or details of sightings are furnished.

Sources: Bord and Bord, *Alien Animals*; Mackal, *The Monsters of Loch Ness*.

Lough Leane, Ireland   Celtic folklore names this lough in County Kerry as an ancient abode of LAKE MONSTERS. In August 1981, local resident Pat Kelly (who claimed psychic powers) allegedly photographed an unknown creature at Lough Leane and sent the photo to ANTHONY SHIELS. Skeptics note that the photo's provenance remains suspiciously obscure, and that it is virtually identical to a photo allegedly taken of MORGAWR five years earlier.

Sources: Chorvinsky, "The Lough Leane monster photograph investigation"; Harrison, *Sea Serpents and Lake Monsters of the British Isles*.

Lough Léin, Ireland   Irish folktales describe a dreaded "phantom" LAKE MONSTER inhabiting this lough, in County Killarney, before it was killed by Celtic hero Finn of Fianna. A dearth of modern sightings suggests that the harsh cure was effective.

Source: Costello, *In Search of Lake Monsters*.

Lough Looscanaugh, Ireland   Various sources note LAKE MONSTER sightings from this lough in County Kerry, but no dates or details are provided to facilitate further investigation. The listings may be based on folktales, but guesswork is futile.

Sources: Bord and Bord, *Alien Animals*; Holiday, *The Dragon and the Disk*.

Lough Major, Ireland   In late July 1963, three youths were fishing at this lough, in County Monaghan, when they were startled by "a monster, 8 to 10 feet long with two protruding tusks and a hairy head." One of the boys threw a stone at the creature, prompting it to rush their position on shore. They fled in terror, but returned next morning to discover that a dozen FISH abandoned on the bank had been reduced to scattered bones. Authorities suggested that the boys had seen a common otter, which they fervently denied. Another witness, Paddy Brady, then came forward to confirm the youths' description of the beast, which locals blamed for snatching fish from anglers' lines.

Sources: Dinsdale, *Monster Hunt*; Harrison, *Sea Serpents and Lake Monsters of the British Isles*.

Lough Mask, Ireland   This lough in County Monaghan has a long tradition of LAKE MONSTER sightings. As early as 1674, a predatory DOBHAR-CHÚ allegedly dwelled here and killed a local resident. Around the same time, during a drought that lowered the lake's water level, remains of an unidentified creature were reportedly found in a submerged cavern. In the late 19th and early 20th centuries, rumors circulated of an "Irish CROCODILE" inhabiting the lake. Witness A.R. Lawrence, of Tullamore, furnished the following account of a more recent sighting.

16 June 1963. Calm, sunny day. 9:15 a.m. Visibility clear. Object seen from shore of Inishdura Island. Range of 250 yards. As I stood on the boat slip looking northwest across the bay, I suddenly saw what appeared to be the head and tail of a large FISH close to the rocks. A second or so later, the movement was repeated in about the same place. Then there occurred another head and tail rise ahead (north-east) of the first two, followed by the same movement some yards further north-east.

I then realized I was watching two humps, one behind the other, moving forward slowly and regularly across the mouth of the bay. It seemed to me like the back of a very large EEL-like fish. I never saw the head or tail, but I would guess the humps were about five or six feet in length and the distance between them about eight or ten feet. The water through which the object traveled was only about three or four feet deep. It disappeared from my sight when a point on the island blocked my view.

Lawrence watched the animal for roughly 90 seconds, during which time it traveled some 250 yards. He estimated its height above water at 12–15 inches, describing the skin as smooth and black.

Sources: Dinsdale, *Monster Hunt*; Harrison, *Sea Serpents and Lake Monsters of the British Isles*; McEwan, *Mystery Animals of Britain and Ireland*.

Lough Melvin, Northern Ireland   This lake, in County Fermanagh, was formerly known as Lough Meilge. In ancient times, it allegedly hosted a serpentine LAKE MONSTER of great prowess, which was ultimately slain by Celtic hero Finn of Fianna. No modern cryptid sightings are reported.

Source: Costello, *In Search of Lake Monsters*.

Lough Muck, Ireland   A LAKE MONSTER was reported from this small lough, in County Donegal, during the late 19th century. The first witness, in 1885, was a young woman surprised by the creature while picking bog-bean in the shallows. She and later witnesses described a dark-colored animal that displayed two humps when swimming on the surface. Sporadic sightings apparently ended around 1894.

Sources: Costello, *In Search of Lake Monsters*; McEwan, *Mystery Animals of Britain and Ireland*.

Lough Murray, South Carolina *see* **Messie**

Lough na Corra, Ireland   In 1926, Mrs. A.V. Hunt of Tipperary described an experience from 1911, at this lake in County Mayo. Hunt was watching the lough with three companions one afternoon, below Croagh Patrick, when:

Suddenly the surface of the water was disturbed by a large black shape that rose and swam the length of the lake in what appeared to be a few moments. Other similar shapes appeared, and these weird things kept playing about, diving and swimming like a lot of seals. The lake is between two and three miles long and from the height on which we were, in comparison with the cattle, the creatures looked bigger than any house we could see; even with the aid of binoculars we could not distinguish any details at that distance....We called the men at work of the chapel to come and watch. After a short time the creatures disappeared, one by one, and the lake resumed its former tranquil appearance.

Sources: Costello, *In Search of Lake Monsters*; Harrison, *Sea Serpents and Lake Monsters of the British Isles*.

Lough Nahanagan, Ireland   Celtic folktales identify this lake, in County Wicklow, as the ancient home of a LAKE MONSTER or "water horse," but no modern sightings are on file.

Source: Robert Praeger, *Irish Landscape*. Dublin: Colin O. Lochlainn, 1961.

Lough Nahillion, Ireland   Cryptozoologist ROY MACKAL notes that LAKE MONSTER sightings have been filed from this lough in County Galway, but no dates or details are provided.

Source: Mackal, *The Monsters of Loch Ness*.

Lough Nahooin, Ireland   This small lake, near Claddaghduff in County Galway, measures roughly 100 yards long by 80 yards across at its widest point. In 1956, while passing by this lake, Michael Coyne saw a large, dark-colored animal swimming on the surface. At first, he thought it was a bullock, but a closer look showed him a large EEL-like creature at least 10 feet long, revealing a white belly as it rolled in the water. Twelve years later, on 22 February 1968, seven other members of the Coyne family met another cryptid at Lough Nahooin. They described it as 12 feet long, black and hairless, with an eel-like texture to its skin. At first, the creature raised a neck 12 inches in diameter, revealing a pale mouth but no visible eyes. When its head submerged, two humps appeared on the surface. Another witness, sheep farmer Thomas Connelly, met a strange animal ashore on 8 September 1968. He described it as black, larger than a donkey, with four stumpy legs. As Connelly watched, the creature slithered into Lough Nahooin and vanished. (Some accounts of this lake mistakenly call it Lough Claddaghduff.)

Sources: Harrison, *Sea Serpents and Lake Monsters of the British Isles*; Holiday, *The Dragon and the Disc*; Mackal, *The Monsters of Loch Ness*; McEwan, *Mystery Animals of Britain and Ireland*.

Lough Neagh, Northern Ireland   Ancient folktales name this lough, in County Antrim, as the one-time lair of a vicious LAKE MONSTER. Celtic hero Finn of Fianna reportedly killed the beast during his campaigns throughout the island.

Source: Costello, *In Search of Lake Monsters*.

Lough Ramor, Ireland   Celtic folktales claim that Lough Ramor (or Ramhuir), in County Cavan, once was home to a LAKE MONSTER "that surpassed the monsters of the world." Legendary hero Finn of Fianna allegedly killed the beast after a fierce battle in ancient times.

Source: Costello, *In Search of Lake Monsters*.

Lough Ree, Ireland   Legendary Celtic DRAGON-slayer Finn of Fianna allegedly killed a "fierce serpent" at this lough, in County Roscommon, but his valiant battle did not rid the site of its LAKE MONSTERS. Saint Mochua, a 6th-century abbot, reportedly invoked God's name to repel a creature that menaced a group of deer hunters, thus mimicking the Scottish confrontation between Saint Columba and NESSIE. On 18 May 1960, three Dublin clergymen were fishing from a boat on Lough Ree, when they sighted a strange animal 140 yards offshore from the lake's eastern bank. They described the creature in a report to the Inland Fisheries Trust.

> There were two sections above the water; a forward section of uniform girth, stretching quite straight out of the water and inclined to the plane of the surface at about 30°, in length about 18-24 inches. The diameter of this long leaning section we would estimate to be about 4 inches. At its extremity, which we took to be a serpent-like head, it tapered abruptly to a point.
>
> Between the leading and the following sections of this creature, there intervened about two feet of water. The second section seemed to us to be a tight, roughly semicircular loop. This portion could have been a hump or a large knob on the back of a large body under the surface that was being propelled by flippers. As to the dimension of this section, if a loop, we should say the girth of a large fifteen pound salmon; if, however, a round hump…we should put its base at about 18 inches….We would estimate the overall length of the two visible sections, measured along the surface from tip of snout to end of hump, at about 6 feet.
>
> The movement along the water was steady. There was no apparent disturbance of the surface, so that propulsion seemed to come from the well-submerged portion of the creature. There was no undulation of its body above the water. It was cruising at a very leisurely speed, and was apparently unconcerned about our presence.
>
> We watched it moving along the surface for a period of two or three minutes in a north-easterly direction. It was going towards the shore; then it submerged gradually, rather than dived, and dis-

Artist's conception of a May 1960 cryptid sighting at Lough Ree (*William Rebsamen*).

appeared from view completely. Another couple of minutes later it reappeared still following the same course….[I]t reached a point about 30 yards off shore, where it submerged and we saw it no more.

JAN-OVE SUNDBERG and two members of his GLOBAL UNDERWATER SEARCH TEAM visited Lough Ree with sonar gear in June 2001. They claimed "hits" on a large, unidentified submarine object, but the target was not sighted and remains unidentified.

Source: Dinsdale, *Monster Hunt*; "'Irish Nessie' noises studied." Reuters (9 July 2001); Kevin Smith, "Loch Ness hunters set sights on Irish monster." Reuters (13 June 2001).

Lough Rudraige *see* **Dundrum Bay**

Lough Shanakeever, Ireland   Sometime in 1954-55, when Patrick Canning went to fetch a donkey he had left out in the rain beside this lake in County Galway, he saw a "lovely black foal" circling the donkey as if about to attack it. A closer look revealed that the animal was not a horse, in fact, but an unknown creature with a long neck and no visible ears. At Canning's approach, the beast fled to the lough and disappeared into the water. Nearly a decade later, in 1963-64, witness Tommy Joyce was passing by the lake when he beheld a dark-gray creature swimming on the surface. Though he could not make out details, Joyce estimated the animal was 7 feet 6 inches long, resembling nothing he had ever seen before. A British soldier fishing at the lough reported another sighting in 1980. He described the creature lying on the surface, with small horns or eyes protruding from its head. Two years later, in June 1982, Tommy Joyce recorded his second sighting of the creature with its humped back visible above the water.

Sources: Harrison, *Sea Serpents and Lake Monsters of the British Isles*; Holiday, *The Serpent and the Disk*; McEwan, *Mystery Animals of Britain and Ireland*.

Lough Shandangan, Ireland   Celtic legends name this lough in County Clare as the ancient home of LAKE MONSTERS, but no modern sightings suggest that the creatures have survived.

Source: Meurger and Gagnon, *Lake Monster Traditions*.

Lough Swilly, Ireland   A ferocious LAKE MONSTER with

Saint Mochua defends Irish hunters against the beast of Lough Ree (*William Rebsamen*).

multiple eyes, dubbed Suileach, reportedly inhabited this lough in County Donegal during the 6th century. According to legend, it was dispatched by Irish saint Colum Cille.

Source: James MacKillop, *Oxford Dictionary of Celtic Mythology*. New York: Oxford University Press, 1998.

Lough Waskel, Ireland   In the late 1940s, a fisherman at this lake in County Donegal reportedly hooked some large animal and tried to reel it in, but he glimpsed only three feet of a brownish-gray back with cream-colored patches before the thing broke free and disappeared.

Source: Bord and Bord, *Unexplained Mysteries of the 20th Century*.

***Louisa Montgomery* sea serpent**   On 29 July 1879, sailors aboard the schooner *Louisa Montgomery* met a SEA SERPENT in the Gulf of St. Lawrence, near Pictou Island, between Prince Edward Island and the coast of Nova Scotia. Captain Samson, in charge of the vessel, reported that the creature was about 100 feet long and swam at seven knots (10.5 miles per hour).

Source: O'Neill, *The Great New England Sea Serpent*.

Loukusajärvi, Finland   In 1963, a white 6-foot creature with a body resembling a log and a head like a salmon's was reported from this Finnish lake.

Source: Meurger and Gagnon, *Lake Monster Traditions*.

Loveland Frog(s)   At 3:30 a.m. on 25 May 1955, while driving home from work along the Miami River near Branch Hill, Ohio (northeast of Cincinnati), Robert Hunnicut was startled to behold three strange creatures crossing the highway in front of his car. They were bipedal, but otherwise bore no resemblance to human beings: all were three feet tall, grayish, with bulging chests, repulsive faces with wide froglike mouths, and prominent wrinkles atop their bald heads. One carried a device that emitted sparks and filled the air with an unpleasant odor. The witness alerted police, but no trace of the creatures was found. Two months later, a motorist saw four small figures huddled on the bank of the Little Miami River in Loveland. No more sightings were reported until 1:00 a.m. on 3 March 1972, when a solitary specimen appeared before two patrolmen, crossing a road and leaping the guardrail in a rush to the Little Miami River. The policemen sketched the creature for posterity, describing it as four feet tall, frog-faced, bipedal and covered with leathery skin. In the wake of that incident, a local farmer also reported seeing one of the beasts, but the sightings thereafter ceased.

Sources: Blackman, *The Field Guide to North American Monsters*; Clark and Pear, *Strange & Unexplained Phenomena*.

***Lucy and Nancy* sea serpent**   On 18 February 1849, the *Boston Atlas* reported that passengers aboard the schooner *Lucy and Nancy* had sighted a SEA SERPENT in the Atlantic Ocean, near the mouth of Florida's St. John's River. Captain Adams described the creature as follows:

It lifted its head, which was that of a SNAKE, several times out of the water, seemingly to take a survey of the vessel, and at such times displayed the largest portion of its body, and a pair of frightful fins or claws, several feet in length.

Witnesses estimated that the animal was 90 feet long, and that its dirty-brown back was seven feet across at the widest point.

Source: Heuvelmans, *In the Wake of the Sea Serpents*.

Lukwata   Lake Victoria is the largest lake in Africa and the second-largest freshwater lake in the world (after LAKE SUPERIOR in North America). Its surface area (26,828 square miles) is larger than some African and European countries, despite a relatively modest depth of 270 feet. In 1902, Sir Harry Johnston, writing from Uganda, noted that:

There are…persistent stories amongst the natives that the waters of the Victoria Nyanza are inhabited by a monster (known to the Baganda as "Lukwata"). This creature, from the native accounts, might either be a small cetacean or a large form of manatee, or, more probably, a gigantic FISH. So far, however, only one European has caught a glimpse of this creature.

The witness in question was Sir Clement Hill, visiting Uganda in the first decade of the 20th century, reported that some unknown creature had tried to seize a native from the bow of a steam launch traveling from Kisumu to Entebbe. Hill saw only the animal's head, but he "was quite certain it was not a CROCODILE." There is no record of a manatee attacking humans, and BERNARD HEUVELMANS concluded that the Lukwata may be identical to the LIPATA reported from northeastern Angola. Neither, however, resembles the creature reported from Mohoru Bay by T.E. Cox and his wife, in late 1959. That animal was a more traditional LAKE MONSTER of the NESSIE type, 20-30 feet long, with a long neck, a reptilian head, and a stout body with two humps on its back.

Sources: Hichens, "African mystery beasts"; Heuvelmans, *Les Derniers Dragons d'Afrique*; Heuvelmans, *On the Track of Unknown Animals*.

Lummis's Pichucuate   Pichucuate is a Spanish term applied to various venomous SNAKES throughout Mexico and the U.S. Southwest. Unfortunately, ignorance confuses the issue, since the name is used not only for the cantil (*Agkistrodon bilineatus*) and lyre snake (*Trimorphidon tau*) in Mexico, but also for the harmless narrow-headed garter snake (*Thamnophis rufipunctatus*) in Arizona. Further compounding that confusion is the claim by Charles Lummis that he met *another* Pichucuate in Valencia County, New Mexico, on three occasions during 1889-1890. Lummis described a pencil-thin viper with a head the size of a man's fingernail, sporting horns above its eyes like a sidewinder's, with gray dorsal scales and a pink underside. The snake reportedly burrows in sand to ambush its prey, and delivers lethal venom despite its small size. No presently recognized species matches Lummis's description.

Sources: Arment, "Notes on Lummis's Pichu-cuate"; Charles Lummis, *The King of the Broncos, and Other Stories from New Mexico*. New York: Charles Scribner's Sons, 1897.

Lumut carcass   In February 2003, skeletal remains of "a big, unknown creature" were beached by the tide at Lumut, Brunei. A security guard found the bones on 16 February and notified police. According to media reports, the skeleton was 20 feet long, with "other small joint skeletal remains scattered about five feet away from each other," and "no one was able to make out what the creature was." Shreds of flesh still clung to some of the bones, near the tail. Investigators deduced that the remains had lain exposed for several days, since "a piece of the bone bore a signature, an indication that someone else had stumbled upon the remains and had left his mark." No result of the investigation has been published to date.

Source: Liza Mohd, "Skeletal remains of unknown creature found at Lumut beach." *Borneo Bulletin* (19 February 2003).

Lundevatnet, Norway   A serpentine LAKE MONSTER with eight or nine humps on its back was been reported from this lake, in Rogaland County, during the late 19th century. Witnesses claimed the creature swam faster than a rowboat.

Source: Skjelsvik, "Norwegian lake and sea monsters."

Lungfish (Giant)   Lungfish (Class *Dipnoi*) are FISH capable of breathing on dry land and propelling themselves with stubby fins resembling vestigial legs. Known species live in Africa, Australia and South America, but cryptozoologist ROY MACKAL has collected first-hand anecdotal evidence of 6-foot EEL-like specimens living in Vietnam. Thus far, none have been captured for study.

Source: Shuker, *Extraordinary Animals Worldwide.*

Lusca   Caribbean divers love to explore "blue holes," underwater pits plunging vertically for 200 feet or more through rock and coral around certain islands in the Bahamas and the Caicos Islands. The adventure is priceless, but it also comes with deadly risks attached. One peril recognized by native islanders is the Lusca, described as a giant cephalopod with 50-foot tentacles, said to inhabit blue holes and to emerge at night in search of prey along the surface. Legends speak of the Lusca as a man-eater, and it is sometimes blamed for disappearances of divers who fail to return from blue-hole excursions, but no specimen has yet been caught or photographed.

Sources: Palmer, "In the lair of the Lusca"; Wright, "The Lusca of Andros."

Caribbean divers fear a giant cephalopod known as the Lusca.

Lutz, John (1940–)   Baltimore resident John Lutz ranks among the most dedicated pursuers of surviving EASTERN COUGARS (*Puma concolor*). His fascination with the animals (presumed extinct throughout the eastern U.S.) dates from 1965, when his first story as a reporter for Baltimore radio station WFBR involved a COUGAR sighting near Gunpowder Falls, Maryland. The animal was never caught, but Lutz asked state police and other contacts to keep him informed of future sightings. In 1983, Lutz and wife Linda founded the Eastern Puma Research Network, distributing 25,000 "wanted" posters in 17 states. While supervising the Baltimore Department of Transportations truck di-

vision, Lutz still devotes 20 hours a week to his cryptozoology research. He has collected 5,300 reports of cougar sightings or tracks since 1983, in states east of the Mississippi River, and he has twice sighted cougars himself (in Tioga County, Pennsylvania and in Carroll County, Maryland). Lutz admits that wildlife officials "are more or less at odds with us," but he remains convinced that cougar breeding populations survive in the eastern U.S. "If they want to be seen, they will," Lutz told the *Baltimore Sun* in 2001. "If they don't, they won't. They're sly, they're sure, they're the most adaptable animals on earth. They're flesh and blood, and they do survive."

Source: Sandy Alexander, "Ignoring discouragement, Baltimore man continues his hunt for an elusive quarry." *Baltimore Sun* (4 February 2002).

***Lydia* sea serpents**   In late September 1827, Captain David Thurlo Jr. of the schooner *Lydia* claimed that he had harpooned a SEA SERPENT in the Atlantic, nine miles east of Mount Desert Island, Maine. According to Thurlo, he was fishing near the *Lydia* in a smaller boat when the creature appeared, and he cast a harpoon. The animal reared a sharklike head six feet out of the water, then fled with his harpoon and line. When Thurlo resumed fishing, a *second* creature surfaced, trailing him back to the schooner as Thurlo retreated. Thurlo described the animals as 65-80 feet long, dark-colored, with large visible scales. BERNARD HEUVELMANS dismissed the story as a HOAX.

Source: Heuvelmans, *In the Wake of the Sea Serpents.*

Lynx (Bulgarian)   The Eurasian lynx (*Lynx lynx*) officially became extinct in Bulgaria during World War II, but sightings continue to the present day. Given the increase in prey species since the 1950s, it would not be surprising to find that a small population of lynxes still survives in Bulgaria.

Sources: Nikolai Spassov, "Cryptozoology: Its scope and progress." *Cryptozoology* 5 (1986): 120-124.

Lynx reports continue from Bulgaria, although the cats are said to be extinct.

——M——

Maasie   On 6 August 1979, witnesses reported a 3-foot CROCODILE swimming in the Meuse River, near Ombret-Rawsa, Belgium. The animal was nicknamed Maasie, after the river's Flemish name (Maas), but it has not been seen again. In the absence of another explanation, authorities assume it was a pet released by some negligent owner.
Source: Bord and Bord, *Unexplained Mysteries of the 20th Century.*

Macarena Bear   Natives of the Serranía de la Macarena mountain range, in western Colombia, describe a local bear unknown to science, notable for its reddish-colored fur. No specimen has yet been collected for study, but mammalogists note that the Andes-dwelling spectacled bear (*Tremarctos ornatus*) displays various colors ranging from black to a dark reddish-brown in some individuals.
Source: Cryptzoology.com, http://www.cryptozoology.com/articles/mysterybears.php.

Macas Mole   In July 1999, cryptozoologist Angel Morant Forés found a mounted specimen of an unknown animal displayed in a shop at Macas, in Ecuador's Morona-Santiago Province. While he did not buy the animal, Morant took several photographs revealing a 15-inch animal with white fur and three brown stripes across its back, with webbed feet and a long snout like a mole's. Nothing is known of the animal's habitat or lifestyle, and no other specimen has yet been found. Ecuadorian zoologist Didier Sanchez later purchased the Macas specimen and suggested that it might be a water opossum (*Chironectes minimus*), altered by some unknown taxidermist to remove its pouch and otherwise reshape the beast's anatomy. KARL SHUKER, by contrast, proposes that it may represent an unknown species of insectivorous mammal.
Source: Karl Shuker, "Have trunk, will tantalize: A mystifying mammal from Macas." *Strange Magazine* 21 (Fall 2000), http://strangemag.com.

MacFarlane's Bear   On 24 June 1864, two Inuit hunters killed a large, yellow-furred bear near Rendezvous Lake, in Canada's Northwest Territories, located at 65° 52' north latitude and 127° 1' west longitude. The carcass was hauled to nearby Fort Anderson, where naturalist Roderick MacFarlane examined it three weeks later. The bear's skull and skin were preserved and sent to the Smithsonian Institution, where it was catalogued as an aberrant GRIZZLY BEAR and promptly forgotten. Another half-century passed before Dr. C. Hart Merriam noticed the remains, while making a definitive study of North American grizzlies. Merriam determined that the bear was, in fact, a new species, which he named *Vetularctos inopinatus* ("the unexpected, ancient bear"). No other specimens have been collected, but anecdotal reports from the turn of the last century refer to large off-white bears, resembling a grizzly-polar bear hybrid, allegedly known to natives of northern Canada and Alaska's Kodiak Island.
Sources: Bille, *Rumors of Existence*; Shuker, *From Flying Toads to Snakes with Wings.*

Machias Lake, Maine   On 9 December 1881, the *Aledo* (Illinois) *Democrat* published a short article claiming that a LAKE MONSTER had recently been seen at Machias Lake, in eastern Maine (Washington County). Unfortunately, the region surrounding Machias, Maine boasts at least five lakes named for the town, including Big, Little, Third, Fourth and Fifth Machias Lake(s). More than 120 years after the alleged sighting, it is impossible to tell which body of water produced the sighting.
Source: Coleman, *Mysterious America.*

Machrihanish carcass   On 2 October 1944, a "furry monster" washed ashore at Machrihanish, on western Scotland's Kintyre peninsula. As BERNARD HEUVELMANS described the beast, "It was 20 feet long, had huge eyes and feet, and crowds came and stared at it." Sadly, none of the gawking spectators were scientists, and the creature remains unidentified today.
Source: Heuvelmans, *In the Wake of the Sea Serpents.*

Mackal, Roy P. (1925–)   Following military service in World War II, Roy Mackal earned his B.A. from the University of Chicago in 1949, and completed his doctoral studies in 1953. He remained at the university for 37 years, as an associate professor of biochemistry, while conducting biochemical research that earned him global recognition. Mackal is also a skilled engineer, whose patented inventions include automatic parachutes and recovery systems for rockets, as well as a hydrogen generator used in weather balloons.
Mackal's cryptozoological research began in 1965, with his first expedition to Loch Ness. He served as scientific director of the LOCH NESS INVESTIGATION BUREAU from 1966 to 1972, and in 1967 recorded a personal sighting of NESSIE. On 10 August 1975, he joined ROBERT RINES, TIM DINSDALE and others to address Parliament on the subject of Scotland's most famous LAKE MONSTER. As the 1970s waned, Mackal focused on Africa's elusive MOKELE-MBEMBE. He led two expeditions in search of the alleged living DINOSAUR, in 1980 (with colleague JAMES POWELL) and 1981 (with MARCELLIN AGNAGNA and J. RICHARD GREENWELL). In 1988, Mackal returned to Africa, this time seeking KONGAMATO, the flying creature described by natives as resembling a Jurassic PTEROSAUR. Mackal was among the founding members of the INTERNATIONAL SOCIETY OF CRYPTOZOOLOGY, and served as vice president of that group from 1982 to 1996. His published books include *The Monsters of Loch Ness* (1976), *Searching for Hidden Animals* (1980), and *A Living Dinosaur? In Search of Mokele-Mbembe* (1987).
Sources: Clark and Pear, *Strange & Unexplained Phenomena*; Coleman and Clark, *Cryptozoology A to Z*; Harrison, *The Encyclopaedia of the Loch Ness Monster.*

Mackerle, Ivan (n.d.)   Czech cryptozoologist Ivan Mackerle has traveled widely in pursuit of cryptids on three continents. At various times, he has dived in search of NESSIE in the Scottish Highlands, stalked ALIEN BIG CATS in Britain, and searched for giant MONITOR LIZARDS in Australia. In 1990, while discussing his work at Loch Ness with a female student, Mackerle heard his first tales of the dreaded OLGOÏ KHORKHOI or Mongolian death worm, said to menace travelers in the vast Gobi Desert. Mackerle soon emerged as the top Western expert on that elusive creature, personally leading two expeditions to Mongolia in search of his quarry. And while he failed to bag (or even glimpse) the beast, Mackerle played a leading role in transmitting eyewitness reports to the West. Sadly, little of his original work is presently available in English, but Mackerle communicates to a larger audience via colleagues such as MICHEL RAYNAL and KARL SHUKER. Of the Olgoi khorkhoi, he insists, "The stories are true. This thing does exist. Too many people have seen it. Too many people have been killed by it for me to dismiss it as a fairy tale."

Sources: Randall Floyd, "Gobi Desert hides mysterious creature." Augusta (GA) Chronicle (31 January 1999); Shuker, *The Beasts That Hide from Man*; Ivan Mackerle, Olgoi-khorkhoi expeditions (Mongolia), http://perso.wanadoo.fr/cryptozoo/expeditions/olgoi_eng.htm.

MacKinnon, John Ramsay (1947–)   A British subject and the grandson of former prime minister James Ramsay MacDonald, zoologist John MacKinnon spent a year in Africa studying CHIMPANZEES and insects before completing his doctoral studies at Oxford University. Thereafter, MacKinnon spent most of his professional life in the Far East, including a 3-year study of orangutans in Borneo (1968–70) and extensive surveys of Asian wildlife. In 1970, while pursuing studies in Malaysia's Sabah State, MacKinnon discovered footprints of the unknown primate or HOMINID known to locals as BATÛTÛT. Two decades later, he was active in discovery of several new species from Vietnam's VU QUANG NATURE RESERVE. MacKinnon remains active with the Asian Bureau of Conservation and the World Wildlife Fund. His many publications include *In Search of the Red Ape* (1974), *Animals of Asia* (1975) and *Wild China* (1996).

Sources: Coleman and Clark, *Cryptozoology A to Z*; George Schaller, "On the trail of new species." http://www.nwf.org/international-wildlife/1998/newspeci.html.

Macquarie Harbor creature   On 20 April 1913, two prospectors named Oscar Davies and W. Harris saw an unidentified creature in the dunes abutting Macquarie Harbor, on Tasmania's west coast. Upon their approach, the beast fled out to sea. A newspaper report of the event, published on 6 July, described the creature in some detail.

> The characteristics are summarized as follows: It was 15 ft. long. It had a very small head, only about the size of the head of a KANGAROO dog. It had a thick arched neck, passing gradually into the barrel of the body. It had no definite tail and no fins. It was furred, the coat in appearance resembling that of a horse of chestnut colour, well groomed and shining. It had four distinct legs. It travelled by bounding—that is, by arching its back and gathering up its body so that the footprints of the forefeet were level with those of the hind feet. It made definite footprints. These showed circular impressions with a diameter (measured) of 9 inches, and the marks of claws, about 7 inches long, extending outwards from the body. There was no evidence for or against webbing....The creature travelled very fast. A kangaroo dog followed it hard in its course to the water, and in that distance gained about 30 feet. When first disturbed it reared up and turned on its hind legs. Its height, standing on the four legs, would be from 3 ft. 6 inches to 4 ft. Both men are quite familiar with seals and so-called sea-leopards that occur on this coast. They had also seen before and subsequently pictures of sea lions and other marine animals, and can find no resemblance to the animal that they saw.

BERNARD HEUVELMANS cited this creature as an example of his hypothetical "long-necked" SEA SERPENT, though the published description appears to refute that contention.

Sources: Heuvelmans, *In the Wake of the Sea Serpents*; Smith, *Bunyips & Bigfoots*.

Macro   On 2 May 1846, New Zealand governor George Grey wrote a letter to British zoologist J.E. Gray, in which he listed various known and cryptic animals described by Maori natives. Included on that list was:

> another new animal which they call a "Macro"; they say it is like a man covered over with hair, but smaller and with long claws; it inhabits trees and lives on BIRDS; they represent it as being strong and active, and state they are afraid of them. I hope in a few weeks to be able to visit the country (mountains covered with forests) which the animals live in, and as I am not afraid of them, I hope I shall send you one before long.

Sadly, nothing more was heard of this unclassified primate or HOMINID, and its identity remains a mystery. Some researchers consider it identical to the MAIROERO, but its size does not conform to descriptions of that alleged predatory man-snatcher. KARL SHUKER proposed, then discounted the brush-tailed possum (*Trichosurus vulpecula*) as a Macro candidate, leaving the cryptid's true identity unknown. Alternate names include Ngatimamaero and Ngatimamo.

Source: Shuker, *From Flying Toads to Snakes with Wings*.

Madagascar Mystery Cats   Madagascar, lying southeast of the African mainland in the Indian ocean, is officially devoid of native CATS. That scientific judgment, however, has not stemmed the flow of reports describing unknown felids. The first account, published by French author Paul Cazard in 1939, referred to cave-dwelling LIONS that preyed on smaller animals and human beings alike, terrorizing villages in the neighborhood of their mountain lairs. Cazard speculated that the predators might be relict SABER-TOOTHED CATS, but no evidence has yet been gathered to support his theory.

A smaller cat *has* been found on Madagascar, much more recently, but its classification remains undecided. First mention of this species came from author Ferdnand Mery in 1967, when he wrote:

> The Malagasy Academy possesses a specimen of a magnificent tabby cat, largest than a domestic cat. Details of its capture on Madagascar are uncertain, but of interest is that in the local Malagasy language, *pisu* = domestic cat, with *kary* used to denote "wild cats," even though wildcats do not officially exist on the island.

Luke Dollar, a U.S. researcher studying wildlife in northwestern Madagascar's Ankarafantsika National Park, has captured two of the felids, the latest (a pregnant juvenile) in spring 2003. The captive specimens closely resemble African wildcats (*Felis lybica*), but final classification awaits completion of DNA testing. No judgment had been rendered at press time for this volume.

Sources: Karl Shuker, "Alien zoo." *Fortean Times* 173 (September 2003): 18; Shuker, *Mystery Cats of the World*.

Madison Four Lakes, Wisconsin   Authors LOREN COLEMAN and JOHN KIRK include this supposed body of water on published lists of U.S. lakes with LAKE MONSTER sightings on file. No lake(s) by that name exist in the Badger State, but the capital at Madison *is* surrounded by four lakes: Lake Mendota, LAKE MONONA, LAKE WAUBESA and LAKE WINGRA. All four have produced "monster" sightings at various times. Lake Mendota's resident cryptid is nicknamed BOZHO, while Lake Wingra's proved to be a large TURTLE. Curiously, Kirk lists Madison's four lakes in addition to the nonexistent "Madison Four Lakes." Coleman omits Lake Wingra but includes Mendota, along with "Lake Monova" and "LAKE WAUBEAU" (also found on Kirk's list).

Sources: Coleman, *Mysterious America*; Kirk, *In the Domain of the Lake Monsters*.

Madrona Monster Lake Washington, east of Seattle, was once allegedly inhabited by an aquatic cryptid dubbed the Madrona Monster, after the Seattle suburb of Madrona, on the lake's west shore. Witnesses typically described the LAKE MONSTER as 75–100 feet long. Sightings were most common in July, but the beast appeared three times in February 1947, accompanied by "a sudden disturbance in the water followed by the violent surfacing of a tailless object." One witness that month described "a dark, crinkly backed object moving south in the lake." Madrona Beach resident Mary Barrie glimpsed the creature twice; on the second occasion, her gardener was present and opined that the object seen "was either a monster or a submarine." Seventeen years later, on the afternoon of 6 April 1964, Henry Joseph was boating with his wife and child at the northern tip of Mercer Island, when a large creature surfaced nearby. Joseph first mistook it for a 30-foot log, until it came alive and swam away. He later told reporters, "In my thirty years of [military] service, I've seen SHARKS, whales, blackfish, porpoises, and MANTA RAYS, but nothing like this."

Some say the mystery was solved on 5 November 1987, when an 11-foot white sturgeon (*Acipenser transmontanus*) washed ashore near Kirkland, Washington. JOHN KIRK reports that the FISH weighed more than 600 pounds and may have exceeded 100 years in age. The sturgeon was much smaller than any version of the Madrona Monster described by witnesses, but cryptid sightings have apparently ceased since its death.

Source: Garner, *Monster! Monster!*; Kirk, *In the Domain of the Lake Monsters*.

Maggot Maggot is the nickname applied to a supposed crustacean reported from Newfoundland, Canada during the mid-20th century. Witnesses described the 12-inch creature as resembling an American lobster (*Homarus americanus*), with 3-inch pincers, prominent fishlike eyes and three pairs of legs, but lacking the lobster's characteristic jointed tail. Its first appearance was

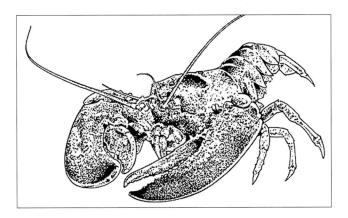

Was Newfoundland's Maggot simply a deformed lobster?

logged in fresh water, at Gander Lake, in the 1930s. In 1952, another specimen was allegedly seen at Swanger's Cove, on Bay d'Espoir. Skeptics maintain that various witnesses glimpsed normal lobsters and mistook them for some unknown creature.

Source: "A mari usque ad mare." *Fortean Times* 46 (Spring 1986): 44–51.

Magraner, Jordi (1967–2002) Spanish zoologist Jordi Magraner spent the last decade of his life pursuing the BAR-MANU ("big hairy one"), an unclassified primate or HOMINID reported from northwestern Pakistan. Encouraged by BERNARD HEUVELMANS, Magraner embarked on a tour of that country's rugged Chitral region during 1992–94, announcing the discovery of large humanoid footprints in the Shishi Kuh valley. On another occasion, Magraner and two European colleagues heard cries in the wild that "could have been made by a primitive primate voicebox." Magraner interviewed numerous Bar-Manu witnesses, reporting that several informants chose a picture of the MINNESOTA ICEMAN as a likeness of their local cryptid. Magraner's on-site research spanned 10 years, but he faced opposition in 2002, when his visa expired and he was served with orders to depart from Pakistan.

Magraner was planning to leave for Europe in September, but he never got the chance. On 2 August 2002, he was stabbed to death in the home he shared with 12-year-old servant Shamas-ur-Reham. In the wake of that crime, Pakistan's News Network International quoted police statements that Magraner "was residing illegally and was involved in some mysterious activities" involving "sophisticated communication equipment." Investigators further claimed that Magraner had visited neighboring Afghanistan and had dubious links." From that, they concluded that Magraner had "many foes and one of them might kill him for his alleged activities." At last report, the crime remained unsolved.

Sources: Loren Coleman, "Jordi Magraner (1967–2002)." Internet posted (5 August 2002); "Spanish zoologist found dead." News Network International (4 August 2002).

Mahamba Congolese natives describe the Mahamba as a giant CROCODILE, reputedly attaining lengths of 50 feet or more. Belgian explorer John Reinhardt Werner confirmed those stories in 1890, relating two personal encounters with crocodiles longer than his 42-foot A.I.A. steam launch. Six decades later, traveler Guy de la Ruwière reported a 23-foot crocodile with an abnormally long neck, seen in the Maika marshes, Democratic Republic of Congo. Africa's largest known crocodilian is the Nile crocodile (*Crocodylus niloticus*), with a record official length of 16 feet. The world's largest known species is the Indopacific (or saltwater) crocodile (*C. porosus*), with verified lengths of 23 feet and

African witnesses describe the Mahamba as a 50-foot crocodile.

recorded weights exceeding 2,200 pounds. Giants that they are, neither species matches the Mahamba for size, but three prehistoric crocodilian fits the bill quite nicely. The largest was *Rhamphosuchus*, a Pliocene monster 50–60 feet long, known from fossil beds in the Siwalik Hills of India. Next in size was 49-foot *Deinosuchus* (also known as *Phobosuchus*, "horror crocodile"), a late Cretaceous inhabitant of Texas. Another Cretaceous giant, *Sarcosuchus* ("flesh emperor crocodile"), lived in Niger, 700 miles northwest of the Mahamba's range, and exceeded 40 feet in length. As ROY MACKAL suggests, the survival of such prehistoric giants "would be a marvelously satisfying cryptozoological phenomenon"—and a nightmare for any human being who encountered such a creature in the wild.

Source: Mackal, *A Living Dinosaur?*

Maid of Judah sea serpent   At 11:00 a.m. on 20 November 1877, the vessel *Maid of Judah* encountered a SEA SERPENT while sailing off the coast of Australia, at 40°2' south latitude and 121°26' east longitude. The ship's chief officer described the incident as follows to the *Sydney Morning Herald*:

> [W]hile some of the hands were aloft they saw a very large serpent on the weather bow. The vessel passed close to it about forty yards off, and it appeared to be about the length of the vessel: the head of this object appeared to be sunk down out of sight, while a good part of the body and tail was to be seen quite plainly. It was of a browny green colour, and did not appear to have any motion at the time of the vessel passing. There was a fresh gale blowing at the time and a good deal of sea on, yet the thing was broadside on to the sea in curves, as if it was swimming, but the vessel was going faster and so I could not see if it had any motion.

Author Malcolm Smith suggests that the sailors were deceived by a giant chain of tunicates or salp, free-swimming pelagic invertebrates that sometimes form large floating colonies.

Source: Smith, *Bunyips & Bigfoots*.

Maipolina *see* **Water Tigers**

Mairoero   This unclassified primate or HOMINID of New Zealand has been reported since the 19th century. The first account, published in July 1844, noted accounts from the South Island as follows:

> Behind Totuki, [settlers] may explore the mountain dreaded by the natives, on account of its being the favourite residence of the *mairoero*. This is a wild man of the woods, strong, cunning, and mischievous, and addicted to running off with young people and damsels. His body is covered with coarse and long hair, which also flows down from the back of his head nearly to his knees. To compensate for this excessive quantity behind, his forehead is said to be bald. He was vividly described to us by a Maori who had seen one long ago, when he was a little boy, and was of opinion that "there is not a more fearful wild-fowl than your *mairoero* living."

In 1878, gold prospectors in the North Island's Coromandel Mountains reported encounters with hairy WILDMEN who carried clubs, stone knives and crude hatchets. Three decades later, in 1903, large humanoid footprints were found by miners in the Karangahake Gorge. More sightings from the Coromandel range were reported in 1952, 1963 and 1972 (the latter incident including discovery of four footprints measuring 14 inches long and 7 inches wide). More large tracks were found near Dusky Sound in 1974, and around Lake Manapouri (in the South Island's Fiordland National Park) in 1994.

Sources: Gilroy, *Giants from the Dreamtime*; Craig Heinselman, "Hairy *Mairoero*."

Makalala   During the 19th century, Wasequa tribesmen in Tanzania described the Makalala ("noisy") as a giant carrion BIRD, 7–8 feet tall when standing at rest. In the late 1870s, a certain Dr. Fischer reported that natives on Zanzibar had displayed to him a gigantic rib from the Makalala, measuring eight inches wide at its base and nearly one inch wide at the tip. The rib's length, strangely, was not recorded. Around the same time, French author Richard Chapelle reported that some Wasequa chiefs wore Makalala skulls as helmets, the great domes completely engulfing their heads. Native hunters allegedly trapped the birds by playing dead, then springing erect to strike with their spears when a Makalala landed to dine on their supposed corpses. KARL SHUKER suggests that the Makalala may represent a giant form of secretary bird (*Sagittarius serpentarius*), and in 1995 he proposed the scientific name *Megasagittarius clamosus* ("the noisy, giant secretary bird").

Source: Shuker, *In Search of Prehistoric Survivors*.

Malabar Mystery Cat   In 1912, a remarkable CAT was shot in the Malabar district of southwestern India, its pelt preserved and subsequently purchased by Holdridge Collins from G.A. Chambers in Madras. As Collins described the skin in 1915:

> The wide black portion, which glistens like the sheen of silk velvet, extends from the top of the head to the extremity of the tail *entirely* free from any white or tawny hairs.... In the TIGER, the stripes are black, of an uniform character, upon a tawny background, and they run in parallel lines from the center of the back to the belly. In this skin, the stripes are almost golden yellow, without the uniformity and parallelism of the tiger characteristics, and they extend along the sides in labyrinthine graceful curls and circles, several inches below the wide shimmering black continuous course of the back. The extreme edges around the legs and belly are white and spotted like the skin of a leopard....The skin is larger than that of a Leopard but smaller than that of a full grown Tiger.

Gerrit Miller Jr., curator of mammals at the Smithsonian Institution, concluded that the pelt belongs to a pseudo-melanistic leopard (*Panthera pardus*), presenting colors and patterns not seen in the normal melanistic specimens commonly called "black panthers." Whatever the truth of the matter, no other cat resembling the Malabar specimen has yet been reported.

Source: Shuker, *Mystery Cats of the World*.

Mala-Gilagé   In the 1850s, a French nobleman traveling in Africa collected native tales of the Mala-gilagé ("tailed men"), unclassified primates or small HOMINIDS said to inhabit territory south of the Chari River, in present-day Chad. Witnesses described the creatures as short in stature, with a full-body coat of hair over ruddy skin, longer hair on their heads, and a monkey-like tail. No other accounts of this alleged species exist.

Source: Stanislas, comte d'Escayrac de Lauture, *Mémoire sur le Sudan*. Paris: A. Bertrand, 1856.

Malagnira   Members of western Madagascar's Sakalava du Menabe tribe describe the Malagnira as a lemur smaller than the islands various mouse lemurs (*Microcebus* sp.), inhabiting the Tsingy de Bemaraha Nature Reserve. Without a type specimen, it remains unclear if the tribesmen are referring to a new species or one already known to science.

Sources: Nasolo Rakotoarison, et al. "Lemurs in Bemaraha." *Oryx* 27 (January 1993): 35–40; Shuker, *The Lost Ark*.

Malgomaj, Sweden   This lake, in Västerbotten County, has a maximum recorded depth of 355 feet. In 1917, witness Jonas

Lundberg reported a serpentine LAKE MONSTER 80–90 feet long swimming in the lake, with several humps displayed above the water's surface.

Source: Global Underwater Search Team, http://www.cryptozoology.st/.

Malpelo Monster   Isla de Malpelo is a mountainous island in the eastern Pacific, claimed by the Colombian government, located 314 miles west of Buenaventura, Colombia. Members of a naval outpost stationed there call Malpelo La Roca ("The Rock"). Its reefs teem with pelagic wildlife, allegedly including an unclassified species of deepwater SHARK dubbed the Malpelo Monster. Witnesses describe the FISH as 15 feet long, with large eyes and a dorsal fin located directly above the pectoral fins. Supposed photos of the shark(s), taken by divers, have thus far failed to resolve the mystery. Colombian biologist Sandra Bessudo opened an investigation in 2001, which had failed to identify the fish as of press time for this volume.

Source: *Sandra and the Unknown Shark* (2003), a 52-minute French documentary produced by Pierre Croimiaux and directed by Marie-Hélène Baconnet.

Mambu Mutu   Burundi natives dwelling near Lake Tanganyika and the Lukuga River live in fear of an aquatic cryptid they call Mambu Mutu ("crocodile man"), which they describe as half-man and half-FISH. Its strange appearance is frightening enough, but tribesmen maintain that the creature preys on human beings, killing them before it drinks their blood and eats their brains. Spanish researcher Angel Morant Fores speculates that the Mambu Mutu may be an African manatee (*Trichecus senegalensis*), although that inoffensive creature is a confirmed herbivore with no history of attacking humans. Another Spaniard, Carlos Bonet, suggests that the beast may be a "flat-skulled giant otter, a creature known in fact to drink blood." His source for that statement remains obscure, since the only known African otters (*Aonyx capensis* and *A. congica*) average four feet in length and tip the scales around 30–35 pounds. While they are carnivores, unlike the manatee, neither species is known to stalk humans.

Sources: Douglas Chapman, "The brain-eating crocodile man." *Strange Magazine* 17 (Summer 1996): 37; Karl Shuker, "Menagerie of mystery." *Strange Magazine* 15 (Spring 1995): 32–33.

Mamlambo   Xhosa tribesmen of South Africa's Eastern Cape Province describe the Mamlambo as an aquatic denizen of the Mzintlava River, near Mount Ayliff. Eyewitness accounts of this "half-FISH, half-horse" place its length at 67 feet, noting a head like a SNAKE'S or horse's, with eyes that shine green in the darkness. The Mamlambo is said to be a vicious predator, attacking human beings and devouring their brains. Natives blamed the creature(s) for nine deaths along the Mzintlava in the first quarter of 1997 alone. Local police called the deaths common drownings and explained post-mortem mutilations as the work of hungry crabs. Unconvinced, a group of local schoolteachers strongly disagreed, telling the *Cape Argus* newspaper, "We are not just ignorant, superstitious people. We are teachers. Educated. And we know that the monster is there. That is why we do not cross the river any more."

Sources: Kirk, *In the Domain of the Lake Monsters*; "Mamlambo on the loose." *Cape Argus* (17 May 1997).

Mammoths   The mammoths (*Mammuthus* sp.) were primitive elephants adapted to cold weather, whose range spanned Europe, North America and northern Asia during the Pleistocene

Witnesses claim that woolly mammoths have survived in parts of Asia.

epoch. They cut a striking figure with their long spiral tusks and the shaggy coats found in some species. *M. meridionalis* was likely the first to evolve, around 2 million years ago, in southern Europe. It stood 15 feet tall, a size equaled by *M. trogontherii* in northern Europe, but *M. trogontherii* boasted longer tusks (up to 17 feet in some male specimens). *M. columbi*'s range was limited to North America, where it reached a maximum height of 12 feet. Best known among these ancestors of modern elephants is probably the woolly mammoth (*M. primigenius*), which ranged over most of the northern hemisphere. It was the smallest mammoth, at nine feet tall, but its famous coat and fatty hump make it the typical mammoth for many researchers. A dwarf subspecies restricted to parts of Siberia, *M. p. vrangeliensis*, apparently peaked at 6 feet tall and weighed a mere 4,400 pounds.

Scientists are still uncertain as to when mammoths became extinct. Subfossil remains of frozen mammoths have been dated from 40,000 to 12,000 years old, and most scholars now grant that mammoths survived until 10,000 years ago, when human hunters hastened their demise. However, radiocarbon dating of bones, teeth and tusks, found on Siberia's Wrangel Island, prove that specimens of *M. p. vrangeliensis* survived at least to the year 2000 B.C., in historical times. Discovery of frozen, buried mammoths is undoubtedly responsible for widespread legends of giant moles, rats, or burrowing whales found among various peoples from Mongolia and Siberia to Alaska, but there are also three reports of live mammoth sightings on file from Russia and Thailand, between 1581 and 1984.

The first such sighting was recorded by Cossack chieftain Yermak Timofeyevich, who claimed a meeting with a large hairy elephant in Russia's Ural Mountains. The next, reported in 1918 and published in 1946, came from a hunter in Siberia's Yamal-Nenets Autonomous Province. While seeking game near the Obskaya Gulf, the hunter allegedly found oval footprints measuring 27 inches wide and 20 inches long, separated by a 13-foot stride. These he followed through the forest for several days, noting places where the beast's passage had broken tree limbs 10 feet off the ground. Finally, as he described:

One afternoon it was clear enough from the tracks that the animals weren't far off. The wind was in my face, which was good for approaching them without them knowing I was there. All of a sudden I saw one of the animals quite clearly, and now I must admit I really was afraid. It had stopped among some young saplings. It was a huge elephant with big white tusks, very curved; it was dark chestnut colour as far as I could see. It had fairly long hair on the hind-quarters, but it seemed shorter in front. I must say I had no idea that there were such big elephants. It had huge legs and moved very slowly. I've only seen elephants in pictures, but I must say that even from this distance (we were some 300 m [325 yards] apart) I could never have believed any beast could be so big. The second beast was around, I saw it only a few times among the trees; it seemed to be the same size.

On glimpsing his intended prey, the hunter realized that his rifle was inadequate for the task, and he quietly retreated. Nearly seven decades later and far to the south, Princess Rangsrinopadorn Yukol videotaped a peculiar elephant herd, glimpsed during a forestry survey of northern Thailand's Omkoi District of Chiang Mai in 1984. The princess claimed that the herd included 20–30 elephants, which she characterized as "Thai mammoths." Each, she said, was larger than a common elephant, with long tusks and shaggy hair on its back. Blurry still photos made from the videotape were released on 3 December 2000, with a claim from the princess that U.S. conservation workers had also seen the mammoths. (District chief Samarn Prangwacharakorn confirmed the royal sighting of 1984, stating that the herd included 27 "very wild" elephants.) A hunt for the mammoths was announced, then canceled on 7 December 2000, at the request of Thailand's Royal Forestry Department. Meanwhile, Prof. Naris Poompakphan of Kasetsart University examined the still photos and opined that the animals depicted were simply Asian elephants (*Elephas maximus*) that had failed to shed their juvenile hair.

Sources: Heuvelmans, *On the Track of Unknown Animals*; Karl Shuker, "Alien zoo." *Fortean Times* 145 (May 2001): 18–19.

Manapouri sea serpent

On 14 July 1891, passengers and crew aboard the steamer *Manapouri* saw a SEA SERPENT off East Cape, on the North Island of New Zealand. Witness Alfred Mathews, a surveyor, described the incident as follows:

The "monster" was also seen by the ship's officer in charge. It would from time to time lift its head and part of its body to a great height perpendicularly, and when in that position would turn its body round in a most peculiar manner, displaying a black back, white belly, and two armlet appendages of great length, which appeared to dangle about like a broken limb on a human being. It would then suddenly drop back into the water, scattering it in all directions. It had a flat head, and was about half a mile distant from the ship.

Source: Heuvelmans, *In the Wake of the Sea Serpents*.

Man-Beast of Darién

In 1920, a prospector named Shea allegedly shot a large unknown primate or HOMINID near Piñas Bay, in the Serranía del Sapo mountains of Panama's Darién Province. Shea described the creature as sixet tall, covered with black hair. Its feet were apelike in form, with the big toes protruding like thumbs. Shea estimated that the beast weighed some 300 pounds. As usual in such cases, the animal was not preserved or photographed.

Source: Richard Marsh, *White Indians of Darien*. New York: G.P. Putnam's Sons, 1934.

Mande Burung

This large, unclassified primate or HOMINID of northeastern India's West Garo Hills is described as a hairy biped resembling BIGFOOT or the Himalayan YETI. The most recent sightings were recorded in February 2002, when Nebilson Sangma and his brother allegedly saw one of the creatures on three consecutive days, feeding in a banana grove. The Sangmas also claimed to have seen the Mande Burung's forest lair. Local residents widely discounted the tale until another witness, Dipu Marak, videotaped the strange nest a few days later. (He did not see the creature.) Around the same time, a team of wildlife researchers found large humanoid footprints, 19.5 inches long, in the same area. Forestry officials maintain that the various witnesses have simply seen bears.

Source: Karl Shuker, "Alien zoo." *Fortean Times* (161): September 2002: 26.

Mangarisoaka

This unclassified ungulate of Madagascar's highlands is described as resembling a donkey with long, floppy ears. It also reportedly brays like an ass and possesses round hooves like a horse. Alternate names for the beast include Mangarsahoc ("beast whose ears hide its chin") and Tokatongotra. It is sometimes confused with the larger, amphibious KILOPILOPITSOFY ("floppy ears"). Proposed candidates for the Mangarisoaka include an unknown species of wild donkey or (less likely) a relict population of pygmy hippopotamus (*Hippopotamus lemerlei* or *H. madagascariensis*), presumed extinct for a millennium.

Source: Heuvelmans, *On the Track of Unknown Animals*.

Mangden

In the mid-1990s, zoologist John MacKinnon discovered a set of unique antlers in a box of unsorted bones collected from Vietnam's Pu Mat Reserve over the prior 30 years. (The same cache also yielded antler's from the country's legendary QUANG KHEM.) Vietnamese hunters identified the horns as belonging to the Mangden or black deer, but no further specimens have yet been obtained for study.

Sources: Eugene Linden, "Ancient creatures in a lost world." *Time* (20 June 1994): 56–57; Shuker, *From Flying Toads to Snakes with Wings*.

Mangehan sea serpent

In spring 1835, crewmen aboard the brig *Mangehan* saw a SEA SERPENT 10 miles off the eastern tip of Cape Cod, Massachusetts. Captain Shibbles, commanding the vessel, watched through a telescope raised a head the size of a barrel 7–8 feet above the water's surface. He also reported that "the neck had something that looked like a mane upon the top of it". One sailor claimed to have seen a similar creature earlier, off Gloucester, but the *Mangehan* sighting is the first report of a maned sea serpent in U.S. waters.

Sources: Heuvelmans, *In the Wake of the Sea Serpents*; O'Neill, *The Great New England Sea Serpent*.

Mangiacopra, Gary (1960–)

New England native Gary Mangiacopra has pursued cryptozoological research since his teens, enhanced in later years by a master's degree in biology. He is recognized today as one of North America's leading dracontologists, with numerous articles published on the subject of LAKE MONSTERS, SEA SERPENTS and the giant OCTOPUS. He speculates that some of the continent's aquatic cryptids, such as MANIPOGO, may be surviving ZEUGLODONS. In the 1990s, Mangiacopra broadened his studies to include ALIEN BIG CATS such as Connecticut's GLASTONBURY GLAWACKUS.

Sources: Coleman and Clark, *Cryptozoology A to Z*; British Columbia Scientific Cryptozoology Club,
http://www.cryptosafari.com/bcscc/manipogo.htm.

Manguruyú

South American explorer PERCY FAWCETT

described this unknown FISH as a large and toothless freshwater SHARK, said to devour animals and humans in the Río Paraguay. In 1998, researcher Mike Grayson suggested that the Manguruyú might be a giant sturgeon, though no such fish have ever been reported from the southern hemisphere. Cryptozoologist KARL SHUKER counters with the notion that Manguruyú sightings may refer to a species of giant CATFISH.

Sources: Mike Grayson, "The Fortean fauna of Percy Fawcett." *The CFZ Yearbook 1998*. Exwick, England: CFZ Publications, 1998; Shuker, "Close encounters of the cryptozoological kind."

Maningrida Monster

In 1972, two fishermen reported a SEA SERPENT sighting in the Arafura Sea, three-quarters of a mile offshore from Maningrida, Northern Territory, Australia. The witnesses described a serpentine animal 50–60 feet long, thrashing the surface for 15–20 minutes and emitting frightful moaning sounds. The creature's head was allegedly split into three sections, resembling a boat's propeller. A local newspaper, the Maningrida Mirage, referred to the beast as the "fabled Maningrida Monster," but researchers Paul Cropper and Malcolm Smith concluded that the sighting was a HOAX.

Source: Smith, *Bunyips & Bigfoots*.

Manipogo

Manipogo is the name applied to an alleged LAKE MONSTER inhabiting Canada's Lake Manitoba. Confusion arises when the name is also used for the supposed aquatic cryptids of Lakes Winnipeg and Winnepegosis, more properly called WINNIPOGO. All are named in imitation of OGOPOGO, from Lake Okanagan, but the Manipogo label is here applied solely to the cryptic inhabitant(s) of Lake Manitoba.

A huge lake, covering nearly 2,000 square miles, Lake Manitoba featured in aboriginal tales of large, serpentine creatures. In 1909, a trader for the Hudson's Bay Company sighted a 35-foot animal in the lake, its back protruding four feet above the surface. The next report came in 1935, from timber inspectors Charles Ross and Tom Spence. They described a creature with a small, flat head and a body resembling a DINOSAUR'S, covered in gray, wrinkled skin like an elephant's. Two decades later, in August 1955, four witnesses saw Manipogo near Graves Point. In 1957, Louis Belcher and Ed Nipanik saw a serpentine creature swimming along the lake's shoreline, while native guide Solomon Gleury reported a 30-foot creature roaring and diving. The year 1960 produced two mass-sightings. In the first case, on 24 July, 20 picnickers watched Manipogo surface, revealing its head and three distinct humps on its back. Three weeks later, on 9 August, a group of 17 witnesses saw three creatures resembling huge, dark-colored SNAKES swimming off aptly-named Manipogo Beach. Campers John Konefall and Richard Vincent snapped the first (and only) photograph of Manipogo pm 13 August 1962, near the mouth of the Waterhen River.

Those sightings, and the inconclusive photo, prompted two expeditions under zoologist James McLeod, but neither search produced hard evidence of Manipogo's existence. Still, sightings continue, including a 1987 report from members of the Allen family, who saw a large black creature swimming near their boat on Portage Bay. In 1997, rumors circulated that a 45-foot creature had been killed and smuggled away from Lake Manitoba, its remains either sold to a private collector for $200,000 or placed under guard by the Royal Canadian Mounted Police. Deluged by inquiries, spokesmen for the Mounties denied any knowledge of the incident, and their investigation yielded no further clues. A reward of 1 million dollars was offered for Manipogo's capture in March 2003, but frigid weather frustrated the organizers of "Festival Manipogo." The reward has not been collected.

Sources: Baumann, *Monsters of North America*; Katie Chalmers, "Manipogo remains a mystery." *Winnipeg Sun* (10 March 2003); Kirk, *In the Domain of the Lake Monsters*; Karl Shuker, "Menagerie of mystery." *Strange Magazine* 19 (Spring 1998): 22.

Mann Hill Beach carcass

In November 1970, a rotting GLOBSTER washed ashore at Mann Hill Beach, on the coast of Plymouth County, Massachusetts. It weighed 15–20 tons, and witnesses described it as resembling "a CAMEL without legs." Further analysis, however, proved the beast to be a decomposed basking shark (*Cetorhinus maximus*).

Source: Brookesmith, *Creatures from Elsewhere*.

Mannefjord, Norway

On 13 July 1867, a group of eight witnesses reported a LAKE MONSTER sighting from this body of water in Norway's Vest-Agder County. No modern sightings are on record.

Source: Skjelsvik, "Norwegian lake and sea monsters."

Manning River carcass

In 1952, the carcass of an unidentified creature was beached at the Old Bar entrance to the Manning River, near Taree, New South Wales, Australia. The precise date is unknown, and surviving reports do not indicate if the carcass was fresh or decomposed. Descriptions of the beast include a head resembling a calf's, but with a long ducklike bill. Two small "flaps" or fins were present, one on each side of the body, and it had a fan-shaped tail. The carcass measured 15 feet long and 8 feet 8 inches in circumference. Local residents suspected it was a dugong (*Dugong dugong*), but the Australian Museum's curator of mammals dismissed that possibility, since the record length of an adult dugong is 9 feet 6 inches. The curator, one Dr. Troughton, suggested that the creature was "some unusual form of whale," but he declined to examine the remains.

Source: Smith, *Bunyips & Bigfoots*.

Manta Rays (Unknown)

The manta (or devil) ray is the largest species of ray known to science. Nine subspecies were once recognized, but most zoologists now acknowledge only a single species, *Manta birostris*. The manta is a circumtropical species, found throughout the world within a range of 35 degrees above and below the Equator. It measures 4 feet wide at birth, and reaches a maximum disc width of 22 feet (though unverified

William Beebe was first to describe an unknown species of manta ray (*William Rebsamen*).

sightings of 30-foot specimens have been reported), with a record weight of 3,100 pounds. Color ranges from reddish-brown to black above, with white below. Although the manta's dark pigment is easily scuffed away, leaving uneven lighter patches, no specimens are known to bear symmetrical stripes.

That judgment notwithstanding, striped manta rays have been reported from the Pacific Ocean on several occasions. The first was seen by naturalist WILLIAM BEEBE on 27 April 1923, after it collided with his boat off Isla Genovesa in the Galápagos chain. Beebe described the ray as having white wingtips and symmetrical white markings on either side of its head. The following year, a specimen bearing two light V-shaped bands on its back was harpooned near Fanning Island (1,000 miles south of Hawaii), but its remains were not preserved for study. Another oddly-patterned specimen was seen off Ouvea, New Caldeonia in 1976. Thirteen years later, in December 1989, a German television crew filmed a manta resembling Beebe's description off the Pacific coast of Baja California. Finally, on 7 November 1999, a British Broadcasting Company team shot aerial footage of an unknown manta with white longitudinal bands on its wings, swimming along Australia's Great Barrier Reef.

Sources: Beebe, *Galápagos, World's End*; Sehm, "On a possible unknown species of giant devil ray, *Manta* sp."; Shuker, "Alien zoo." *Fortean Times* 131 (February 2000): 18–19; Biology of the Manta Ray, http://www.elasmo-research.org/education/topics/lh_manta.htm.

Mao-Rén   Residents of China's Hubei and Sichuan Provinces describe the Mao-rén ("hairy man") or Dà-mao-rén ("big hairy man") as an unclassified primate or HOMINID covered in reddish hair. The creature is bipedal, stands six feet tall, and leaves humanoid footprints. It is probably identical to the more familiar YEREN. A similar, if not identical creature is known in Kyrgyzstan as Mo-zhyn.

Source: Tchernine, *The Yeti*; Zhou, "The status of wildman research in China."

***Mapia* sea serpent**   On 11 February 1923, crewmen aboard the steamer *Mapia* saw a SEA SERPENT in the Indian Ocean, off the coast of Somalia, at 11° 50' north latitude and 57°37' east longitude. The ship's fourth officer, H.J. Van Nouhuys, described the incident as follows in the ship's log:

> I was on the starboard deck with the second officer, A. de Wild, when we were alerted by a violent blow on the water. It was so close to the port side of the ship that we could not see what it was nor exactly where it had happened. When we dashed to port we heard another violent splash (louder even than that made by a dolphin leaping out of the water) and we saw, some 30 yards away, a colossal sea-animal disappearing below the surface. It was about 6 feet thick, cylindrical, and as far as we could see it was 8 feet out of the water. It was shining, half light grey and half brown.

Source: Heuvelmans, *In the Wake of the Sea Serpents*.

Mapinguari   Mystery surrounds this Brazilian cryptid, described by most witnesses as a large primate or HOMINID, 5–6 feet tall and covered with long reddish hair. Some sightings are accompanied by large, humanoid footprints, while other witnesses report finding round "bottle" prints like those of the PÉ DE GARRAFA, and the two creatures are frequently confused. Some tales, like those describing unknown hominids from other regions, claim that the Mapinguari's feet point backwards. Others assert that the beast has only one leg, with which it hops from place to place. The Mapinguari is said to feed primarily on palm hearts and berries, knocking trees to the ground in search of its favorite

food, but it also has a reputation for killing cattle by means of ripping out their tongues. In 1930, a hunter named Inocêncio allegedly saw a Mapinguari after he became separated from his companions along the Río Uatumã. While spending the night in a tree, he heard terrifying cries in the jungle and soon glimpsed their source:

> Some forty yards away was a small clearing where a *samaumeira* had fallen and its branches had brought down other smaller trees. This was where the last cry had come from. Immediately afterwards there was a loud noise of footsteps, as if a large animal was coming towards me at top speed. When it reached the fallen tree it gave a grunt and stopped. Finally a silhouette the size of a man of middle height appeared in the clearing.
>
> It remained where it stood, looking perhaps suspiciously at the place where I was. Then it roared again as before. I could wait no longer and fired without even troubling to take proper aim. There was a savage roar and then a noise of crashing bushes. I was alarmed to see the animal rush growling towards me and I fired a second bullet. The terrifying creature was hit and gave an incredibly swift leap and hid near the old *samaumeira*. From behind this barricade it gave threatening growls so fiercely that the tree to which I was clinging seemed to shake....
>
> I looked to my gun again and fearing another attack, fired in the direction of the roaring. The black shape roared again more loudly, but retreated and disappeared into the depths of the forest. From time to time I could still hear its growl of pain until at last it ceased.

Nearly half a century later, a miner named Mário Pereira de Souza allegedly met a Mapinguari along the Río Jamauchím, in Pará State. The creature screamed and advanced on him with unsteady strides, emitting a foul odor. The same stench was noted by a witness near Alta Floresta (Mato Grosso) in the 1980s, but that Mapinguari sounded a "kind of whistle" as it stalked through the jungle. Two more sightings were reported in 1998, from Mato Grosso and Acre, each accompanied by a "weird" or "terrible" smell.

Longtime Mapinguari researcher DAVID OREN rejects the hominid hypothesis in favor of another candidate: the 20-foot, 3-ton Pleistocene ground sloth MEGATHERIUM. Oren reached his conclusion after interviewing 80 Mapinguari witnesses and seven hunters who claimed to have killed the elusive creatures. Others reject Oren's theory, insisting that the Mapinguari is a tropical version of SASQUATCH. Whatever it may be, its very name carries the power to frighten Brazilian natives. In the 1990s, Dutch zoologist Marc van Roosmalen reported that inhabitants of one village in Amazonas State had pulled up stakes after Mapinguari tracks were found in the nearby forest. In December 2001, David Oren told a British reporter, "It's still being sited regularly. Several people think they came face to face with the Devil in the forest." As if to emphasize that fact, CHUPACABRA researcher SCOTT CORRALES posted the following story various Internet newsgroups in April 2001:

> A Chupacabra-style bicho beast, called the Mapinguary, is running wild in Brazil's southernmost state of Rio Grande do Sul. An unknown beast in the state of Rio Grande do Sul attacked and killed two sheep and 25 chickens on a farm near Uruguiana, R.S.G., not far from Brazil' border with Argentina. The unidentified animal attacked and killed the sheep and then the chickens, one by one. The region is sparsely populated and lies very close to Argentina. Witnesses described the creature as a biped, 1.5 meters [4 feet 10 inches] tall, resembling a GORILLA with its anthropoid features and coarse black fur.

Sources: Axel Bugge, "Howling Amazon Monster Just an Indian Legend?" *Reuters* (18 December 2001); Axel Bugge, "Search for Amazon Mapinguari: Monster hunt or wild goose chase?" *Reuters* (10 January 2002); Scott Corales, "Mapinguary goes wild in southern Brazil." Internet post to Chupacabra newsgroup (26 April 2001); Heuvelmans, *On the Track of Unknown Animals*; Sanderson, *Abominable Snowmen*; Karl Shuker, "Alien zoo." *Fortean Times* 156 (April 2002): 18; Shuker, *In Search of Prehistoric Survivors*.

Mar del Plata sea serpents

In the 1980s, several witnesses reported SEA SERPENT sightings off the coast of Mar del Plata, Argentina. While most accounts described a traditional serpentine cryptid, one referred to "a cyclopean, smiling, and rather gelatinous CENTIPEDE."

Source: Picasso, "South American monsters & mystery animals."

Mara (Mislocated)

In early 1998, residents of rural Virginia reported encounters with a large unknown rodent, weighing 20–30 pounds, which moved by means of hopping like a RABBIT. Some witnesses compared the animals to BEAVERS, but without typical flat tail. KARL SHUKER suggests that the creatures may represent a naturalized population of mara or Patagonian cavy (*Dolichotis patagona*), a South American relative of the guinea pig and true cavy (*Dolichotis tschudii*) that grows to 29.5 inches in length. Maras are common in wildlife parks throughout the U.S., and escapees might establish themselves in a suitable climate. Indeed, during October 2003, neighbors of the Charlotte Metro Zoo near Rockwell, North Carolina reported creatures resembling "big rabbits on steroids" at large in residential areas. Two were reportedly shot by an unknown gunman, who fled the scene with their bodies. Zoo owner Steve Macaluso told reporters that his seven maras were accounted for, suggesting that the animals seen elsewhere were released by some unknown private collector.

Sources: Karl Shuker, "Alien zoo." *Fortean Times* 108 (March 1998): 17; Jonathan Weaver, "The troupe with Patagonian cavies is...." *Salisbury* (NC) *Post* (5 October 2003); Cavy Cousins, http://www.buddies.org/kvsource/cousins.html.

Mara River, Tanzania

Fortean authors Colin and Janet Bord include this African river on a published list of supposed LAKE MONSTER habitats, but no dates or details of sightings are provided.

Source: Bord and Bord, *Alien Animals*.

Marchlyn Mawr, Wales

Welsh folklore describes this lake, in Gwynedd, as the home of a DRAGON or LAKE MONSTER. No modern sightings are on file.

Source: Holiday, *The Dragon and the Disk*.

Margate carcass

On 1 November 1922, South African farmer Hugh Ballance told reporters of an epic battle he had witnessed off the coast of Margate, Natal. As he explained:

I saw what I took to be two whales fighting with some sea monster about 1,300 yards from the shore. I got my glasses and was amazed to see what I took to be a polar bear, but of truly mammoth proportions. The creature I observed to rear out of the water fully twenty feet and to strike repeatedly with what I took to be its tail at the two whales, but with seemingly no effect.

The struggle lasted three hours, while a crowd gathered on shore to watch. At last, the whales triumphed and swam out to sea, leaving their strange adversary floating dead on the surface. The story did not end there, however. The report continues:

That night the carcass drifted ashore on a beach near the aptly named Tragedy Hill. The body was colossal and spread out upon beaching, as do all large sea creatures without their natural element to support their bulk. It was 47 feet long, 10 feet wide and 5 feet high. It had a 10-foot-long tail, matched at the other end by a curious trunk-like appendage. "Where the head should have been," said Ballance, "the creature had a sort of trunk 14 inches in diameter and about five foot long, the end being like the snout of a pig." But the most astonishing feature of the monster, which could be seen clearly from the beach during the previous day's battle, was its impressive fur or hair covering, "eight inches long and exactly like a polar bear's, and snow white." There was no sign of any wound or blood stains. For ten days it lay there on the beach, attracting sightseers and flies, until the stench became intolerable. A team of 32 oxen failed to move it far and abandoned it near the water's edge, from where the night tide wafted it back into unknown depths.

Cryptozoologists from BERNARD HEUVELMANS to KARL SHUKER have been baffled by this creature's description, noting that the "furry" appearance seen in decomposing sharks and whales could not apply to an animal dead only 24 hours. CHARLES FORT sent queries to several South African newspapers but received no answers, whereupon he dismissed the report as "a foolish and worthless yarn."

Sources: Fort, *The Complete Books of Charles Fort*; Heuvelmans, *In the Wake of the Sea Serpents*; Michell and Rickard, *Living Wonders*; Shuker, "Bring me the head of the sea serpent!"

Mariana Trench sea serpent

On 20 September 2003, the Russian newspaper *Pravda* reported that Japanese marine biologists had achieved startling results from a deep-sea fishing expedition in the Mariana Trench, the deepest point in the Pacific Ocean. According to the article, a container filled with chum was lowered with a video camera to a depth of 4,750 feet in an effort to attract and film rare deep-water SHARKS. Some sharks were indeed attracted, but the report claimed they were soon dispersed by the advance of a huge unknown creature that allegedly measured 195 feet long. According to the GLOBAL UNDERWATER SEARCH TEAM'S Internet website, the Japanese scientists "still do not know what they saw, registered and filmed and not a single frame has been released." No bulletins have been forthcoming from Japan, and the *Pravda* report should be treated with caution, since Russia's former state newspaper has declined over the past decade into an organ of sensational tabloid journalism.

Source: Global Underwater Search Team, http://www.cryptozoology.st/.

Maribunda

Natives of Venezuela describe the Maribunda as a large primate resembling an oversized spider MONKEY (*Ateles* sp.), inhabiting rain forests along the Río Orinoco. Witnesses claim the animal is five feet tall, when standing erect. A similar name, *marimonda*, is applied to the white-bellied spider monkey (*A. belzebuth*), but the record height for that species is 3 feet 7 inches.

Source: Robert, Marquis de Wavrin, *Les Bêtes Sauvages de l'Amazonie et des Autres Régions de l'Amérique du Sud*. Paris: Payot, 1951.

Maricoxi

The Maricoxi are described by Brazil's Maxubi natives as hairy HOMINIDS or WILDMEN inhabiting the Mato Grosso jungles. In 1914, while exploring that region, PERCY FAWCETT twice encountered specimens who threatened him with crude bows and arrows. The first incident occurred as Fawcett's party was making camp, when Fawcett glimpsed a pair "large, hairy men with exceptionally long arms, and with foreheads sloping back from pronounced eye ridges, men of a very primitive kind, in fact, and stark naked." They fled when Fawcett shouted at them, but during the night Fawcett's party was haunted by sounds of horns in the forest, whose "sound was as eerie as the opening notes of some fantastic opera." The next day, Fawcett entered a small forest village:

> where squatted some of the most villainous savages I have ever seen. Some were engaged in making arrows, others just idled — great apelike brutes who looked as if they had scarcely evolved beyond the level of beasts.
>
> I whistled, and an enormous creature, hairy as a dog, leapt to his feet in the nearest shelter, fitted an arrow to his bow in a flash, and came up dancing from one leg to the other till he was only four yards away. Emitting grunts that sounded like "Eugh! Eugh! Eugh!" he remained there dancing, and suddenly the whole forest around us was alive with these hideous ape-men, all grunting "Eugh! Eugh! Eugh!" and dancing from leg to leg as they strung arrows to their bows. It looked like a very delicate situation for us, and I wondered if it was the end.

Fawcett resolved the stand-off by firing a pistol shot into the ground and scattering the Maricoxi. As his party left the settlement, "We were not followed, but the clamour in the village continued for a long time as we struck off northwards, and we fancied we still heard the 'Eugh! Eugh! Eugh!' of the enraged braves."

Source: Sanderson, *"Things."*

Marozi *see* **Lions (Spotted)**

Marsabit Swift   In 1980, ornithologists John Williams and Norman Arlott reported sightings of a large, unidentified swift from the Marsabit National Reserve, in Kenya's North Frontier Province. The BIRD was uniformly black, unlike other known swifts (Family *Apodidae*) on the African continent. To date, no specimen has been collected and skeptics suggest that witnesses actually saw a scarce swift (*Schoutedenapus myoptilus*), whose plumage is typically brown or gray.

Source: John Williams and Norman Arlott, *A Field Guide to the Birds of East Africa.* London: Collins, 1980.

Martin Lake, Canada   Several authors report that this lake, located in western British Columbia, has produced LAKE MONSTER reports. Unfortunately, none of the sources provide any dates or details of sightings.

Sources: Kirk, *In the Domain of the Lake Monsters*; Moon, *Ogopogo.*

Martin's False Potto   This prosimian species, never seen alive by Western eyes, is known only from two skeletons uncovered at Zurich University in April 1996. American mammalogist Jeffrey Schwartz was studying pottos [Family *Lorisidae*] preserved in Switzerland when he noticed that two of the specimens were clearly mislabeled. Collected in Cameroon, the skeletons had long tails, while true pottos have only rudimentary stumps, and variations in dentition also served to distinguish them from their apparent relatives. The new genus was named *Pseudopotto martini*, those some researchers still reject any distinction between the true and false pottos. The habits of Martin's false potto remain a complete mystery.

Sources: "Not a potto." *Scientific American* (April 1996): 18; Shuker, "Potty about pottos."

Martyn's Ape   This unknown APE or HOMINID was reported from Athelhampton, Dorset, England during 1978, around the same time the GHOST APE OF MARWOOD was sighted in Devon. Searches in both districts proved futile, as the creatures eluded pursuers and soon disappeared.

Source: Downes, "Born to be wild."

Marulan Tiger   Between 1927 and 1930, this ALIEN BIG CAT was blamed for raids on sheep herds in the southern highlands of New South Wales, Australia. Another large, striped CAT was active at nearby Tallong during the same time period. Most researchers consider the Marulan TIGER and the TALLONG TIGER to be identical.

Source: Healy and Cropper, *Out of the Shadows.*

Marx, Ivan Lee Sr. (1921–99)   Avid outdoorsman Ivan Marx served two years with the U.S. Navy during World War II, before returning to civilian life and his passion for hunting. He was a licensed bear-hunting guide and spent five years in Alaska, studying bears for the U.S. Fish and Wildlife Service, before earning a reputation as one of North America's most controversial SASQUATCH hunters. He claimed to have filmed BIGFOOT several times, but most cryptozoologists dismiss his cinematic efforts as obvious HOAXES.

Marx's pursuit of Bigfoot began in November 1958, when millionaire TOM SLICK employed Marx, ROBERT TITUMS and others to track the elusive HOMINID around Bluff Creek, California. Marx was also part of Slick's 1959 Pacific Northwest Expedition, which also included RENÉ DAHINDEN and JOHN GREEN, among others. In December 1969, Marx and many of the same investigators were involved in the Washington State investigation that produced casts of the BOSSBURG TRACKS. Marx unveiled his first alleged film of Bigfoot in 1971, and his footage entered theatrical release five years later, as *The Legend of Bigfoot*. John Green later wrote of those films:

> [I]t is second-hand information, but I am told that the son of a local man involved in the hunt had tried to tell people from the start that he knew where the movie was made, right on their ranch, but no one would listen to him. Finally someone did, and it turned out, as I verified for myself, that the creature in the movie was close to five feet in height, not 10, and that during the shooting of the film it stayed in one small area, although the cameraman had changed his position considerably to get different backgrounds....
>
> Please note that I do not say that Ivan faked that film, or the one of the white [S]asquatch in the snowstorm, or any other he has since then or may in the future emerge with. It is my considered opinion that the creature the film shows is a person dressed in black fur, and I know of nothing but Ivan's statement indicating that it is not.

On balance, Green considered Marx "the biggest, well, yarn-spinner, in California." Other critics were less kind, pointing out that the glowing "eyes" shown at one point in *The Legend of Bigfoot* were clearly a pair of automobile headlights. Criticism notwithstanding, Marx went on to claim more Bigfoot sightings and photographic evidence from Washington (1972) and Alaska (1973–75). Most of the material was movie footage, but Marx also published a curious still photo of an alleged Bigfoot perched on the edge of an Alaskan cliff. Marx faded into obscurity during the 1980s and he died of heart failure in California, following a lengthy illness, on 18 December 1999.

Sources: Coleman, *Bigfoot!*; Green, *Sasquatch: The Apes Among Us*; Guenette and Guenette, *The Mysterious Monsters.*

Mary sea serpent   On 9 July 1818, Captain Spark and the crew of the schooner *Mary* allegedly sighted a SEA SERPENT off the Massachusetts coast, near Jeffry's Ledge. They reported the creature swimming among 8–10 whales, whipping them with its tail like a cowboy driving cattle to market. BERNARD HEUVELMANS understandably dismissed the story as a HOAX.

Source: Heuvelmans, *In the Wake of the Sea Serpent.*

***Mary Hart* sea serpent**   At 8:00 a.m. on 17 June 1835, sailors aboard the brig *Mary Hart* reported a SEA SERPENT sighting eight miles of Chatham Light, on Cape Cod, Massachusetts. As Captain John Nichols described the incident, "We saw within a cable's length [720 feet] of us something lying in the water, resembling the shape of a SNAKE." The creature was black, some 40 feet long, and swam with its head above water "while its body bent with the waves of the sea."

Source: O'Neill, *The Great New England Sea Serpent.*

***Mary Lane* sea serpent**   On 4 August 1888, Captain Delory and several crewmen aboard the vessel *Mary Lane* saw a SEA SERPENT off Point Judith, Rhode Island, in Block Island Sound. It was the second sighting from the sound in a week, the other reported by sailors aboard the *SANFORD.* No details of the animal's description are available, beyond large size and a serpentine form.

Source: O'Neill, *The Great New England Sea Serpent.*

Mataperro   In January 2001, residents of Cala, in northern Colombia, reported the appearance of a MYSTERY MAULER they dubbed Mataperro ("dog killer"). Cala had already suffered a year-long series of animal killings blamed on the elusive CHUPACABRA, but the Mataperro seemed to be a very different creature. Witnesses described it as resembling a hump-backed dog, lead-gray in color, standing 20 inches tall. According to a local newspaper, witnesses "further stated that the predator generates some type of energy that affects human beings and must coincide with the energy it needs to levitate." That flight of fancy notwithstanding, searchers tracking the animal collected several clumps of unusual hair and made casts of strange pawprints at the site where two dogs were killed. The hair was submitted for scientific analysis, but no results of those tests were available when this volume went to press. On 26 April 2001, chupacabra researcher SCOTT CORRALES reported that the Mataperro had shifted hunting grounds to kill a dog in Calama, Chile. The carcass reportedly "showed signs of being mauled and stripped of the skin on its left side about the entire length of its body, from its back to its belly," yet its owner "did not find a single drop of blood in the animal's wounds, nor any blood spilled on the street around his dog."

Sources: Scott Corrales, "Mataperro strikes again in Calama, Chile." Internet posting to Chupacabra newsgroup (26 April 2001); "Mysterious animal leaves prints in La Banda." *La Estrella del Loa* (26 January 2001); "New Chupacabra evidence found." *La Estrella del Norte* (27 January 2001).

Mathews Range Starling   Witnesses in Kenya describe this unclassified BIRD as a starling with gray plumage, showing reddish feathers underneath its long tail. It is reported from high elevations in the Mathews Range. As yet, no specimen has been collected. Skeptics suggest a case of mistaken identification, perhaps involving the a female red-winged starling (*Onychognathus morio*), which has a gray head and reddish-brown primary feathers.

Source: John Williams, *A Field Guide to the Birds of East Africa.* London: Collins, 1980.

Matuyú   This large, unclassified primate or HOMINID of Brazil was described by 17th-century witnesses as bipedal, covered in dark hair, and roughly the size of an adult human being. As with other unknown hominids or WILDMEN around the world, some witnesses claimed that its feet are attached backwards.

Source: Simão de Vasconcellos, *Noticias Curiosas, y Necessarias das Cousas do Brasil.* Lisbon: I. da Costa, 1668.

Mau   Another mystery primate or HOMINID reported from Kenya, the Mau reportedly inhabits (and is named for) that country's Mau Escarpment. Native witnesses describe it as biped, roughly four feet tall, covered in black or reddish-brown hair. The Mau allegedly inhabit mountain caves, descending on occasion to raid cattle herds. Some accounts describe them using stones as primitive tools or weapons.

Sources: S.V. Cook, "The leprechauns of Kwa Ngombe." *Journal of the East Africa and Uganda Natural History Society* 20 (November 1924): 24; Roumeguère-Eberhardt, *Dossier X.*

Maui Mystery Cat   On 14 June 2003, Hawaiian press reports announced the presence of an ALIEN BIG CAT in the lower Olinda district of Maui. Eight sightings had been filed with the island's Invasive Species Committee since December 2002, reporting encounters with a 100-pound creature described as "cat-like, dark brown, with a large head and a long tail." While witnesses likened the CAT to a tan-colored COUGAR (*Puma concolor*), state wildlife biologist Fern Duvall opined that the beast "may be a leopard or JAGUAR" (both known for yellow pelts marked with black spots or rosettes). A clump of dark brown fur, recovered from the scene of a sighting on 9 June, conflicted with Duvall's hypothesis. Two large box traps were deployed, baited with meat, but they failed to catch the prowling felid. Locals were "very nervous" by late June, though no attacks on animals or humans were reported. A search of Olinda, completed on 25 June, revealed claw marks on trees, 4-inch pawprints, and the gnawed remains of several birds. "I believe it's for real," Duvall then told reporters. "There's something out there."

That judgment brought authorities no closer to their prey, however. New traps were laid, baited with chicken, and while one of the traps was demolished, hunters could not say if animals or human pranksters were to blame. The traps were dismantled on 8 July, and the hunt officially ended two days later, but Maui residents had not heard the last of their unwelcome visitor. On 15 July, wildlife officials blamed the cat for fatally mauling a 30-pound fawn. Big-cat expert Bill Van Pelt was borrowed from the Arizona Game and Fish Department three weeks later, but his high-tech hunt (including infrared cameras, recorded wildcat calls and "squeakers" that simulate wounded prey) proved fruitless. While maintaining that his goal was "to identify the animal, not capture it," Van Pelt saw nothing of the cat except some "deep and hefty" clawmarks on a guava tree. Before returning home, Van Pelt addressed a 50-person audience on 13 August, voicing his professional opinion that "there is a large cat in the area." Although uncertain, he declared that the cat was "probably" a cougar, jaguar (*Panthera onca*) or leopard (*Panthera pardus*). Another sighting on 25 August yielded two fresh pawprints but failed to provide a more precise description of the beast. New experts were imported in October, after five more sightings and the mauling of a local family's dog. They collected hair samples for DNA analysis, but no test results were announced prior to press time for this volume. While Maui residents settled in for a long siege, a spokesperson for the Invasive Species Committee, Mele Fong, voiced the question that preyed on their minds: "Who knows how long this could go on?"

Sources: "Evidence supports sightings of big cat on Maui." *Honolulu Advertiser* (25 June 2003); Timothy Hurley, "Bait changed as traps fail to catch big cat on Maui." *Honolulu Advertiser* (26 June 2003); "Hunt for large cat on Maui is called off." *Honolulu Star-Bulletin* (10 July 2003);

Timothy Hurley, "Big-cat search turns up marks high up on tree." *Honolulu Advertiser* (13 August 2003); Timothy Hurley, "Big-cat trapper coming to Maui." Honolulu Advertiser (10 October 2003); Timothy Hurley, "Expert says he's sure big cat is out there." *Honolulu Advertiser* (14 August 2003); Timothy Hurley, "Mystery cat on Maui suspected in dog attack." *Honolulu Advertiser* (10 September 2003); Timothy Hurley, "Officials look into possible attack by Maui mystery cat." *Honolulu Advertiser* (15 July 2003); Gary Kubota, "Arizona wildcat experts to assist Maui again." *Honolulu Star-Bulletin* (10 September 2003); Gary Kubota, "Expert says fur not best identifier of Maui creature." *Honolulu Star-Bulletin* (2 October 2003); "Residents on Maui spot large, catlike beast."

Mauke Starling

For many years, the prestigious British Museum maintained in its vast collection a mounted 7-inch BIRD labeled simply "The Mysterious Starling." While clearly a member of the starling family (*Sturnidae*), the mostly-brown specimen with a white breast and bronze tint to its head was unlike any other species known to science. Even its point of origin was unknown until 1986, when researcher Stors Olson examined the log of HMS *Blonde*, dating from 1825. On a voyage to Hawaii, the *Blonde* had stopped at Mauke, in the Cook Islands (east of Samoa), where ship's naturalist Andrew Bloxham collected the specimen. Despite that explanation, the bird remains a mystery, unseen (or, at least, unreported) by any other witness in the past 180 years.

Source: Bille, *Rumors of Existence.*

Mauretania sea serpents

In early 1934, during a Caribbean cruise, passengers and crew aboard the Cunard liner *Mauretania* reported three separate SEA SERPENT sightings. The first occurred on 30 January, a mile offshore from St. Eustatius Island (90 miles east of St. Croix). Witnesses described the animal as 65 feet long and 6 feet in diameter, further reporting that "45 feet of the body…could be seen in curves on the surface of the sea." Three days later, on 2 February, another unidentified creature was seen off La Guaira, near Caracas, Venezuela. This animal was 25 feet long, but descriptions of its wide mouth and lateral fins led BERNARD HEUVELMANS to pronounce it a MANTA RAY (*Manta* sp.). The third incident, in March, occurred 600 miles east of Nassau, in the Bahamas. That creature was described as 60 feet long, displaying four finned humps above the water's surface.

Source: Heuvelmans, *In the Wake of the Sea Serpents.*

Mauritius sea serpent

Sometime between 1693 and 1696, François Leguat and a companion caught a peculiar creature while fishing off the island of Mauritius, in the Indian Ocean. Leguat described the animal as follows:

It was a terrible serpent that weighed more than 60 pounds which we in our great innocence took for a lamprey or an EEL. This supposed eel seemed to us, in truth, most extraordinary, but the animal had fins, and we did not know there were such things as sea-SNAKES. Besides, we were so accustomed to discovering things that were new to us on land and sea, that the figure of this beast made us conclude nothing but that it was a species of eel that we had not seen before and which resembled a snake more than do the common eels. In fact it had the head of a snake or a CROCODILE, with long, sharp hooked teeth …but of quite a different size. This is a strange eel, we thought. What a monster! What terrible teeth!

BERNARD HEUVELMANS concluded from that description that the specimen was either a conger eel (*Conger* sp.) or a moray (*Muraenidae* sp.) of ordinary size.

Source: Heuvelmans, *In the Wake of the Sea Serpents.*

Mawas

The Orang Asli tribesmen of peninsular Malaysia describe this creature as a primate or HOMINID unknown to modern science. Its name is a Malay synonym for orangutan (*Pongo pygmaeus*), but that species is officially unknown on the Asian mainland, and the shaggy Mawas is considerably larger than a normal orangutan, reportedly standing 5–6 feet tall. Its shaggy coat may be black or brown, whereas the orangutan's hair is normally a reddish hue. Witness Liong Chong Shen saw two Mawas in his orchard, near Kampung Chennah, in December 1999. One was black, the other brown, prompting suggestions that the color variation may result from sexual dimorphism.

Sources: Hah Foong Lian, "Village abuzz over sighting of 'Mawa.'" *The Star* (2 January 2000); Healy and Cropper, *Out of the Shadows.*

Mayberry Monster

This unidentified creature reportedly visited Silver Run, Maryland (Carroll County, near the Pennsylvania border) in 1972. It was nicknamed for Mayberry Road, where the sighting occurred. Twenty years later, witness M.K. McDonnell described the animal as follows:

[W]e could see that it was big, covered in brown fur. The fur was wiry, like an Irish wolfhound. It took some steps on four legs, then suddenly stood like a man, which is what it reminded me of. It finished crossing [the road] on two legs and then leapt into the woods. I could hear it crashing through branches and dry leaves on the ground. Although I couldn't see it, I had the impression it ran off on all fours.

McDonnell noted that northern Maryland had experienced a rash of alleged BIGFOOT sightings around the time of this encounter.

Source: "The Mayberry monster." *Strange Magazine* 10 (Fall-Winter 1992): 16.

Mazinaw Lake, Canada

This Ontario lake, 30 miles east of Bancroft, is 300 feet deep and allegedly harbors a LAKE MONSTER blamed for at least one human fatality. No further details of the attack or subsequent sightings are presently available. Skeptics suggest that the "monster" is probably a large Atlantic sturgeon (*Acipenser oxyrhynchus*).

Source: Garner, *Monster! Monster!*

Mbielu-Mbielu-Mbielu

The Mbielu-mbielu-mbielu is yet another African cryptid said to resemble a living DINOSAUR, though of a kind very different from the long-necked sauropods. Witnesses describe this denizen of the Likoula River region, in the Republic of Congo, as sprouting large "planks" from its back, often coated with plant life resembling green algae. In 1980, a native witness interviewed by ROY MACKAL selected a picture of the 30-foot Jurassic reptile *Stegosaurus* as a likeness of the Congo's armored cryptid. A smaller stegosaur, the 16-foot *Kentrosaurus*, is

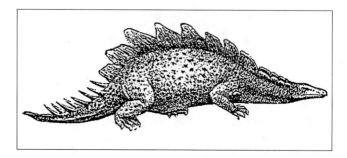

Descriptions of the Congo's Mbielu-mbielu-mbielu resemble a prehistoric *Stegosaurus*.

well-known from fossil beds in Tanzania (whereas *Stegosaurus* has thus far been found only in North America). Both species presumably vanished from Earth 144 million years ago.

Sources: Mackal, *A Living Dinosaur?*; Shuker, *In Search of Prehistoric Survivors.*

Mbilintu   The Mbilintu ("frightful unknown monster") is a large aquatic creature reported from various lakes and swamps in the African nations of Zambia, Tanzania and the Democratic Republic of Congo. German animal collector Carl Hagenbeck pursued rumors of the beast in the early 1900s, writing in 1909: "From what I have heard of the animal, it seems to me that it can only be some kind of DINOSAUR, seemingly akin to brontosaurus." It may be identical to the cryptid known elsewhere as MOKELE-MBEMBE or Isiququmadevu. In parts of its range, however, the Mbilintu is seemingly confused with a very different reptilian creature called CHIPEKWE.

Source: Shuker, *In Search of Prehistoric Survivors.*

Mborevisu   In the 1930s, South American author Narciso Colman claims that early Guarani tribesmen domesticated this huge, now-extinct quadruped, along with the Pleistocene *Glyptodon* and the MEGATHERIUM. Unfortunately, the Mborevisu's description is too vague to permit identification with any species known from the fossil record.

Source: Narciso Colman, *Nuestros Antepasados.* Paraguay: Editorial Guarani, 1937.

McClintock Lake, Canada   McClintock Lake lies in the southern Yukon Territory, midway between Teslin and Whitehorse (at 65°35' north latitude and 133°55' west longitude). In early January 1913, two unnamed trappers working near the lake discovered the apparent track of some large creature, 30 inches wide and deep enough to scrape the ground clear of snow. As reported in the *Dawson Daily News*, "[T]he earth beneath the snow where this trail was made was worn smooth, and where the body of the unknown creature had passed over logs and roots, they were scorched as though having been heated to the verge of taking fire."

The trappers gathered well-armed reinforcements and followed the trail for 12 miles, to a rocky canyon, where they finally lost the track without sighting its creator. "At various points," the newspaper claimed, "the monster body had been dragged around the base of giant trees and in such places the bark was torn away and the sulphurous odor was almost stifling." Subsequent reports described similar tracks found on two occasions in 1910, at McClintock Lake and east of Lake Marsh (some 40 miles farther west). Local Indian tribesmen also claimed that their ancestors had killed an animal resembling a DRAGON near Miles Canyon, "about 300 years ago." Several natives died in the struggle with that creature, "whose mouth was described as being similar to the intake of a thresher, except that the teeth were longer and closer together."

Sources: Benedict, "The dragons that stalked America"; "Monster animal is located in southern Yukon." *Dawson Daily News* (20 January 1913).

McGuire's Pond, New York   A LAKE MONSTER sighting was reported from this body of water at Forestport (Oneida County), in June 1893. No subsequent reports have surfaced, and some researchers now regard the incident as a HOAX.

Sources: Coleman, *Mysterious America*; Kirk, *In the Domain of the Lake Monsters*; Howard Thomas, *Folklore from the Adirondack Foothills.* Prospect, NY: Prospect Books, 1958.

McLeod, James (1946–)   Washington native James McLeod earned his bachelor's degree from the University of Washington in 1964, followed by a Ph.D. from Eastern Washington University in 1969. The following year, he accepted a teaching position at North Idaho College, where he remained through the 1990s as a professor of English, folklore, literature and religion. His interest in cryptozoology dates from 1983, when he read a brief account of the Idaho LAKE MONSTER known as PADDLER in LOREN COLEMAN'S *Mysterious America.* McLeod soon organized one of the North Idaho College Cryptozoology Club, one of the first such groups in the U.S. In 1984, he led the NICCC's "Cryptoquest" pursuit of Paddler at Lake Pend Oreille, and subsequently published *Mysterious Lake Pend Oreille and Its "Monster"* (1987). In that report, McLeod concluded that "about 98 percent of the sightings could be sturgeon" (*Acipenser transmontanus*).

Sources: Coleman and Clark, *Cryptozoology A to Z*; McLeod, *Mysterious Lake Pend Oreille and Its "Monster."*

***Mechanic* sea serpent**   On 18 May 1833, while fishing 20 miles off Cape Cod, Massachusetts, passengers aboard the schooner *Mechanic* sighted a floating object which they first believed to be a capsized boat. Witness Thomas Bridges explained:

> We, however, found the object to be alive, and soon saw very plainly that it was the SEA SERPENT. He came directly towards the vessel, and passed within 12 or 15 yards of us, going quite slowly so that we had an excellent view of him. He appeared to be about 80 feet long, judging from the length of our vessel....His color was rusty black — appeared at a distance to have a great many humps but as he came near, I rather thought it was only his undulating motion which gave that appearance....As he passed us, he turned his head a little on one side to look at us; he swam with his head out of the water. We saw him fairly, for more than half an hour — he was seen by all on board as well as myself — and the mate made an entry in the log book at the time.

Source: O'Neill, *The Great New England Sea Serpent.*

Mecheny   The Mecheny is a large primate or HOMINID reported from the Tyumen' Region of western Siberia. Witnesses describe it as a hairy biped resembling BIGFOOT, 6–7 feet tall, with broad shoulders, a barrel chest and no visible neck. Frequent sightings in the month of August promote speculation concerning possible migratory habits. Russian investigator Maya Bykova conducted extensive research on the Mecheny in 1987–88, collecting eyewitness reports that spanned four decades and reporting two personal encounters with the creatures. On the first occasion, 16 August 1987, Bykova was present when a Mecheny knocked on the window of a peasant family's rural cabin and a dog chased it away. Two months later, the dog was found dead, grossly mutilated by an unseen predator. On 22 August 1988, Bykova was visiting the same family when another Mecheny dropped by, permitting Bykova and her host to watch it for 75 minutes. Bykova had no camera to record the encounter. Other hominids reported from Siberia, perhaps identical to the Mecheny, include the ALMAS, CHUCHUNAA, KÉÉDIEKI, KHEYAK, KILTANYA, KUL, MIRYGDY, PIKELIAN, TUNGU and ZEMLEMER.

Source: Bayanov, *In the Footsteps of the Russian Snowman.*

Megalong Monster   This ALIEN BIG CAT raided livestock herds in the Megalong Valley of New South Wales, Australia during 1889. The creature left large, feline pawprints but eluded hunters and eventually left the region as mysteriously as it had arrived.

Source: Gilroy, "Giant mystery cats of Australia."

Megatherium   This giant ground sloth of the Pleistocene epoch measured 20 feet long and weighed up to three tons, resembling a huge bear more than its modern tree-dwelling descendants. A massive herbivore with three curved claws on each of its forefeet, the *Megatherium* could stand erect, balanced on its heavy tail, and browse from trees throughout its South American range (from Peru southward, through Bolivia and Argentina).

Although presumably extinct today, the *Megatherium* survived long enough to make contact with humans, a fact documented by rock paintings and other evidence uncovered by paleontologists. But could they have lived on in modern times, and might they still be ambling through some tropical forest today?

One explorer who thought so was Hesketh Prichard. He trekked over 3,000 miles through Argentina at the turn of the last century, seeking giant sloths, but came back empty-handed. Another believer is zoologist DAVID OREN, persuaded by years of investigation and interviews with close to 90 witnesses that the *Megatherium* and Brazil's elusive MAPINGUARI are identical. (Others disagree, insisting that the Mapinguari is an unclassified primate or HOMINID, on the order of BIGFOOT or the MONO GRANDE.)

Tehuelche tribesmen in Patagonia and neighboring Chile call their region's giant, slothlike cryptids Ellengassen or Succarath ("cloak skin"), names used interchangeably with the Spanish Lobo-toro ("WOLF bull"). Those creatures live in caves and snack from trees, the natives say, emitting wolflike howls when they encounter human beings. A similar creature, reported from Ecuador in the 1980s, was somewhat smaller than average, with an estimated 10-foot standing height. As recently as May 2001, Ohio geneticist John Lewis announced plans to track the *Megatherium* in South America, but no results of that endeavor have been aired to date.

Sources: "A century on and the adventure continues in hunt for the giant sloth." *Daily Express* (20 November 2000); "Giant ground sloth survival proposed anew." *ISC Newsletter* 12 (1993–96): 1–5; Marguerite Holloway, "Beasts in the mist." *Discover* 20 (September 1999): 58; Heuvelmans, *On the Track of Unknown Animals*; "Tristater searches for giant sloth." *Cincinnati Enquirer* (31 May 2001).

Mekong River   Southeast Asia's Mekong River winds along a course of some 2,600 miles, spanning the nations of Vietnam, Cambodia, Laos and Thailand. Neighbors of that tropic waterway claim that it harbors an aquatic DRAGON, ranging upward in length from 15 feet. Mottled brown, green and yellow like a coat of jungle camouflage, the creature is remarkable for its alleged nine nostrils. Skeptics suggest that giant CATFISH may be responsible for some Mekong sightings, but none have yet been caught to prove their case. British cryptozoologist Richard Freeman visited Thailand in October 2000, hoping to capture the beast on film for a television documentary, but the dragon failed to show itself on cue.

Sources: Peter Kann, "Vietnam journey." *Wall Street Journal* (10 November 1969); Karl Shuker, "Alien zoo." *Fortean Times* 141 (January 2001): 23.

Meldrum, D. Jeffrey (1958–)   As a native of the Pacific Northwest, born the same year BIGFOOT earned its famous nickname, Jeffrey Meldrum was familiar with unknown HOMINID reports from childhood onward. In 1989, he obtained his Ph.D. in physical anthropology from the State University of New York (Stony Brook), and thereafter specialized in primate foot mechanics. That training served him well in 1996, when he found and cast a series of SASQUATCH footprints in Washington's Blue Mountains, near Walla Walla. While serving as an associate professor of anatomy and anthropology at Idaho State University, and doubling as affiliate curator of vertebrate paleontology at the Idaho Museum of Natural History, Meldrum pursued his investigation of Sasquatch via footprints collected from 1960 through the 1990s.

Some researchers believe the giant ground sloth *Megatherium* may still survive in South America.

Anthropologist D. Jeffrey Meldrum.

His premise was simple: Despite scientific skepticism, "the footprints exist and warrant evaluation." After studying 100 casts and 50-odd photos of various prints, including the BOSSBURG TRACKS and footprints found at the site of the PATTERSON FILM, Meldrum concluded that Sasquatch anatomy differs significantly from that of human beings. Specifically, while human walking is characterized by "an extended stiff-legged striding gait with distinct heel-strike and toe-off phases," Bigfoot seems to use a very different mode of locomotion. As described in Meldrum's report:

[T]he Sasquatch appear to have adapted to bipedal locomotion by employing a compliant gait on a flat flexible foot. A degree of prehensile capability has been retained in the digits by maintaining the uncoupling of the propulsive function of the hindfoot from the forefoot via the midtarsal break. Digits are spared the peak forces of toe-off due to the compliant gait with its extended period of double support. This would be a efficient strategy for negotiating the steep, broken terrain of the dense montane forests of the Pacific and Intermountain West, especially for a bipedal hominoid of considerable body mass.

As for Bigfoot's flesh-and-blood reality, Meldrum says: "Given the scientific evidence that I have examined, I'm convinced there's a creature out there that is yet to be identified." At press time for this volume, Meldrum was at work on a companion volume to the Discover Channel's popular documentary *Sasquatch: Legend Meets Science* (2003).

Sources: Coleman and Clark, *Cryptozoology A to Z*; "ISU professor seeks to uncover truth about Sasquatch." *Idaho State Journal* (14 September 2002); Stefan Lovgren, "Forensic expert says Bigfoot is real." National Geographic News (23 October 2003); D. Jeffrey Meldrum, "Evaluation of alleged Sasquatch footprints and their inferred functional morphology," http://www.isu.edu/~meldd/fxnlmorph.html; personal communication with the author (1 February 2004).

Melville Island sea serpent   One day in June 1916, W.S. Arthur set off with Ned Baxter and five other companions to sail from Melville Island to Darwin, on the coast of Australia's Northern Territory. They had covered part of the 16-mile distance when they met an apparent SEA SERPENT. Arthur described the incident as follows:

I was steering with the big sweep oar, when Baxter shouted out to me, "What's that just astern there?" I turned sharply, thinking it was rocks when, to my surprise, and not more than 30 feet from me, appeared a huge head about 6 ft. out of the water, with five or six large parts of its body in a straight line with a division between each of them, reaching in all about 40 feet. As it came nearer, I lifted the blade of my oar as high out of the water as I could and tried to hit it on the head, which by this time was only a foot above the water. I missed hitting it, but felt a hard sudden jerk on my blade which nearly knocked me over the side. I grabbed the sheet of the sail, or I must have gone over. I looked around again, but could only see its wake windward to our boat. I found four teeth, three on one side and one on the other, broken off deeply in the ash oar. We extracted them from the oar and kept them as souvenirs, two of which are still in my possession.

It seems that the teeth were never examined by an expert on marine fauna, and while they may still exist, their whereabouts are presently unknown.

Source: Smith, *Bunyips & Bigfoots.*

Memegwesi   Algonquin tribesmen described the Memegwesi ("hairy-faced dwarf") as a kind of tailless primate, 3–4 feet tall, with short arms and bowed legs. Some early pictographs show the creatures interacting with human beings, and various legends describe them as tricksters, fond of playing pranks. According to Native American tradition, the creatures' range extended from Maine through northern Michigan, Wisconsin and Minnesota, northward to the Canadian provinces of Ontario, Manitoba and Saskatchewan. Some cryptozoologists speculate that the Memegwesi may be identical to the primates known as DEVIL MONKEYS or LITTLE RED MEN OF THE DELTA.

Sources: Frank Speck, "Myths and folk-lore of the Timiskaming Algonquin and Timagami Ojibwa." *Anthropological Series, Memoirs of the Geological Survey of Canada* 71 (1915): 82; John Roth, *American Elves.* Jefferson, NC: McFarland, 1997.

Memphré   Lake Memphrémagog ("beautiful waters") spans the U.S.-Canadian border, with 18 miles of its length in Québec and 14 miles in Vermont. Recorded sightings of its resident LAKE MONSTER, locally known as Memphré, date from 1816, when witness B. Merry and his wife saw a large creature the color of a "skinned sheep," possessing "12 to 15 pairs of legs." A poem published by Norman Bingham in 1850 described a "SEA SERPENT" patrolling the lake, devouring human prey. Four years later, Henry Wadleigh saw an animal resembling a log or capsized boat, peering above the water's surface with a head two feet wide. In 1891, William Watt described an animal 25–30 feet long, swimming with its head raised 3 feet above water.

The next recorded sighting, from October 1929, involved a local physician and two companions who saw Memphré on shore. The witnesses described it as resembling an ALLIGATOR, and they pointed out the tracks it left behind. In 1933, a dozen passengers aboard a cruise ship sighted an "elongated SNAKE-like FISH measuring over 50 feet in length and almost ten feet wide," swimming on the surface with an undulating motion. Two years later, while searching for the body of a drowning victim, scuba diver Max Leubker allegedly encountered several still-unidentified eels "6–8 feet long and as thick as a man's thigh." In 1939, a 30-foot creature resembling a dark, smooth-skinned EEL frightened five swimmers out of the lake. A much larger specimen appeared to witness Hector Guyon in the 1940s, near Green Point. A cousin of Guyon's, Noé Vien, also saw the creature, describing it as a very slender snake, brown or black in color, 150 feet long and only 12 inches in circumference.

Memphré took another hiatus after those sightings, and it may have had a make-over, as well. When it returned in 1972, witnesses described a 50-foot creature with a long neck and cowlike head, noteworthy for its large red eyes. Four years later, witnesses at Fitchbay described the beast as resembling "a seal with a long neck." Local witness Barbara Malloy, who claims three separate Memphré sightings, snapped a photo of the creature on 12 August 1983, while boating with her family. The rash of modern sightings prompted diver and historian Jacques Boisvert to compile an archive of Memphré reports, and to launch the INTERNATIONAL SOCIETY OF DRACONTOLOGY OF LAKE MEMPHRÉMAGOG. Sightings continue to the present, with reports of a 16-foot creature near Les Troi Soeurs Island in August 1997, and a 75-foot beast with a horselike head at Sergeant's Bay on 4 June 2000.

Memphré's story took a strange turn in May 2003, after Barbara Malloy claimed her fourth sighting of the creature. Two weeks later, she claimed legal ownership of Memphré's name under copyright statutes, warning merchants and journalists alike to refrain from any public mention of the beast without express permission. By that time, Malloy had organized her own International Dracontology Society at Newport, Vermont, competing with Boisvert's long-established group in Québec, and she threatened Boisvert with "$100,000 in civil fines" if he used Memphré's name. The tempest derailed attempts at a cross-border merger between Vermont's North Country Chamber and Québec's Northeast Kingdom Chamber, prompting Newport city spokesman Duncan Kilmartin to say that "Ms. Malloy has done more than any event or any other person in the last 30 years to introduce dissonance and disharmony between residents of the Eastern Townships and Vermont." When asked who had the right to utter Memphré's name, Kilmartin replied: "Anybody, anywhere, anyplace."

Sources: Miro Cernetig, "Monster of a border dispute looms over lake." *Toronto Star* (21 May 2003); "Film crew to begin work on Memphré documentary." *Caledonian-Record* (27 August 2003); Kirk, *In the Domain of the Lake Monsters*; Meurger and Gagnon, *Lake Monster Traditions*; Robin Smith, "Campaigns to own sea monster." *Caledonian-Record* (17 May 2003); Phillip Todd, "Lake monster tale takes a twist." *Montreal Gazette* (20 May 2003); Eileen Travers, "Merger dilemma: Who gets custody of lake monster?" *Montreal Gazette* (23 August 2003); "Woman recounts sighting of Memphremagog monster." *Caledonian-Record* (10 May 2003).

Mendelit *see* **Wobo**

Mendips Monster   This ALIEN BIG CAT of Somerset, England was stalked by a posse of armed farmers after it killed and mutilated ten ewes near Axbridge, in April 1998. Aside from the remains of its victims, however, no trace of the CAT was discovered.

Source: Sieveking, "Nothing more than felines."

Menehune   These unclassified primates or PYGMIES reportedly inhabit several of the Hawaiian Islands, with their greatest number concentrated on Kauai. Their name apparently derives from the Hawaiian *Manahuna*, once used to denote the lowest class in a hierarchical society. (The derivation of an alternate name, Nawao, is unknown.) They should not be confused with normal humans, however. Witnesses agree that the Menehune stand 2–3 feet tall and are covered in hair, which grows considerably longer on their heads. Low, protruding foreheads emphasize their simian appearance, though some folktales describe the Menehune's telepathic powers and their love of sports. A census of Kauai, conducted by King Kaumaulii, recorded 65 Menehune living in the island's Wainiha Valley. Some 250 years later, during World War II, Waimea schoolmaster George London and 65 of his pupils saw a group of Menehune playing near the local church. When the creatures noticed their human audience, they scattered and vanished, some scaling trees, while others ducked under the church's foundation. Examination of the property revealed no caves or tunnels, thus enhancing the Menehune's reputation for supernatural powers.

Sources: Coleman and Huyghe, *The Field Guide to Bigfoot, Yeti, and Other Mystery Primates Worldwide*; Katharine Luomala, "The Menehune of Polynesia and other mythical little people of Oceania." *Bernice P. Bishop Museum Bulletin* 203 (1951): 3–51.

Merbeings   Around the world and throughout history, most cultures have included legends of merbeings — aquatic or amphibious creatures often (but not always) described as human-FISH hybrids. Some were invested with supernatural powers and worshiped as gods, while others merely served as harbingers of good or bad fortune. The oldest on record is Ea, revered by Accadians around the Red Sea (also known as Oannes to the Greeks, Dagon among Hebrews, and Enki to ancient Sumerians). Phoenicians worshiped Derketo, a fish-tailed goddess of the eastern

Sailors have reported encounters with merbeings from ancient times through the 20th century.

Mediterranean, while Greeks and Romans kept their distance from aquatic Nereids. The Nix ("water man") was known from Germany northward into Scandinavia, where it shared territory with the Havmand ("sea man") of Denmark and Norway. Scotland and Ireland were visited by the seal-people called Selkies. Eastern Europe and Russia was the domain of the Rusálka ("mermaid") and Vodyany. Turkey's lecherous Silenus was a kind of amphibious satyr. The KAPPA ("river child") of Japan was a mischievous imp. In Africa, Lake Tanganyika's MAMBU MUTU ("crocodile man") terrorized natives, while the Mami Water was found in Ghana and Nigeria. The New World had merbeings of its own, including the Jipijkmak ("horned serpent people") and Sabawaelnu of eastern Canada; the Tchimose of British Columbia's Pacific coast; and the Unágemes ("spirit dwelling in the rock"), known to Passamaquoddy tribesmen in Maine. Farther south, the Mene Mamma ("mother of waters") was seen from the Caribbean to Argentina. Chile's Pacific coast harbored the Shompallhue ("lord of the waters"), an egg-headed, child-snatching creature who fathered the regions mermaids (Konilafquen).

Today, science explains most mermaid sightings as simple cases of mistaken identity, typically involving pinnipeds (seals and sea lions) or sirenians (dugongs and manatees). Various mermaids displayed through the ages in sideshows and museums were the product of deliberate HOAXES, including the "Tritons" manufactured by early Greek fishermen, the "Feejee Mermaid" touted by showman P.T. Barnum in the mid-19th century, and the "Jenny Hanivers" created by mutilating the egg cases of rays and skates (Suborder *Rajoidei*). Additionally, some humans are afflicted with the genetic disorder sirenomelia, which fuses limbs and gives the body a fishy or reptilian appearance. Explanations notwithstanding, sightings of merbeings have continued into modern times. Some of the milestones in their history include:

558 A.D. — An Irish fisherman named Boan allegedly netted Liban, a legendary mermaid, at Ollarbha, Northern Ireland.

887 — A supposed mermaid "whiter than [a] swan" washed ashore near Alba, on the Irish coast. Based on its recorded measurements — 195 feet long, with an 18-foot head and 7-foot nose — the creature was almost certainly a whale.

1118 — Irish fishermen reportedly captured two more mermaids, at Ossory and Port-Lairge.

1197 — Fishermen at Orford, Suffolk, England caught a merman whose beard and hairy chest more than compensated for his bald pate. The creature escaped soon afterward, then unaccountably returned for a voluntary 2-month sojourn at the castle of Sir Bartholomew de Glanville, before it once again fled to the sea.

1403—After the dikes at Edam, Holland ruptured, flooding nearby fields, a groups of women found a mermaid stranded in shallow water. They took it home and clothed it, after which it learned to spin cloth and "perform other pettie offices of women." Though kept alive in captivity for 15 years, the creature never spoke.

4 January 1493— Christopher Columbus, on his first visit to the New World, sighted "three sirens that rose high out of the sea, but were not as beautiful as they are represented." Most modern researchers believe Columbus was describing manatees (Family *Tricheridae*).

November 1523— A small mermaid from the Adriatic Sea was transported to Rome and placed on display. Observers described it as being the size of a 5-year-old child, built "like a man even to the navel, except the ears; in the other parts it resembled a fish." Author Peter Costello surmises that the creature was fabricated as a hoax.

1531— Another possible human creation, described as a "bishop-fish" (i.e., resembling a Catholic clergyman in ceremonial garb, but with a fish's tail) was reportedly caught on the Baltic coast of Poland.

1554— While leading an expedition to Argentina's Rio de la Plata, Spanish conquistador Juan Ortiz de Zarate reported that a merman had emerged from the river to attack a native woman.

1554— Another conquistador, Baltasar Ferreira, met a merbeing known to natives as Ipupiara on a beach near São Vicente, Brazil. After a brisk struggle, Ferreira killed it with his sword. The creature he described — hairy, with whiskers and tail fins — may well have been a seal or manatee, though local aborigines claimed the Ipupiara killed human prey by constriction.

1560— Fishermen reportedly caught seven merbeings off the coast of Ceylon (now Sri Lanka) and delivered them to a Jesuit physician named Bosquez. Dr. Bosquez dissected the creatures and found them anatomically similar to human beings.

Late 16th century— Anatomist Pieter Pauw dissected a merman captured on the coast of Brazil by agents of the Dutch East India Company. He described the creature as possessing a human head and torso, with a shapeless lower body. Several of its ribs and one hand (with webbed fingers) later found their way to Dr. Thomas Bartholin's "cabinet of curiosities" in Denmark.

17th century— A mermaid known to local natives as Pincoya was sighted near Ancaud, Chile.

15 June 1608— During explorer Henry Hudson's second voyage seeking the fabled northeast passage, two members of his crew saw a mermaid off the Russian coast, around 75° north latitude. They described it as of human size, with white skin, a woman's breasts and long black hair, and "the tail of a porpoise." Hudson noted that the creature was "close to the ship's side, looking earnestly at the men" before a wave "came and overturned her." Philip Gosse, a 19th-century naturalist, later said of this incident: "Whatever explanation may be attempted at this apparition, the ordinary resources of seal and walrus will not avail here. Seals and walruses must have been as familiar to these polar mariners as cows to a milkmaid. Unless the whole story was a concocted lie between the two men, reasonless and objectless, and the worthy old navigator doubtless knew the character of his men, they must have seen some form of being as yet unrecognised."

1610— Capt. Richard Whitbourne and other witnesses saw a mermaid in the harbor at St. John's, Newfoundland. The creature's upper body was smooth and white, while its hindquarters reminded Whitbourne of "a broad hooked arrow." It tried to climb aboard a boat occupied by several men, whereupon one struck it over the head with an oar.

1614— British mariner John Smith sighted a mermaid in the West Indies, initially mistaking it for a woman. He later described a creature with "large eyes, rather round, a finely shaped nose (a little too short), well-formed ears, rather too long, and her long green hair imparted to her an original character by no means unattractive." In fact, Smith had begun to "feel the first pains of love," until he saw that "from the waist the woman gave way to the fish!"

1632— Multiple witnesses reported a mermaid around Chiloé Island, in Chile's Gulf of Ancaud.

1652–53— An officer of the Dutch East India Company sighted two greenish-gray merbeings, male and female, swimming in Indonesian waters. Six weeks later, the same pair (or another) was seen by more than 50 witnesses near the same spot. Unfortunately, the description of that site, "near the islands of Ceram and Borneo," leaves much to be desired.

1667— Physician Thomas Glover saw a merman swimming in Virginia's Rappahannock River. The sleek-skinned, tawny creature he described standing upright in the water may have been a seal.

ca. 1670— A "Triton or Merman" tried to board the boat piloted by a Mr. Mittin (or Mitter) in Maine's Casco Bay. One of the men on board grabbed a hatchet and severed one of the creature's hands, "which was in all respects like the hand of a man." Thus wounded, the beast "presently sunk, dy[e]ing the water with his purple blood, and was no more seen."

1679— Spanish fishermen caught a supposed merman off the coast of Cadiz and brought him ashore. Their catch seemed human in most respects, but lacked nails on his toes and fingers, while revealing apparent scales on his back. The merman spoke a single word, "Lierjanes," which proved to be a Spanish village near Santandar. When he was transported there, locals identified the man as Francesco de la Vega, missing at sea and presumed drowned since 1657. Confronted with relatives, Francesco "showed no sign of affection or recollection, staring at them with chill fishy eyes, and receiving their embraces with cold indifference." He remained in the village until 1688, never speaking, then vanished again. Soon after his second disappearance, fishermen claimed they saw Francesco swimming in the Bay of Asturias, but he eluded pursuit.

1682— A "sea-man" was caught at Sestri, France and kept alive for several days, during which he refused food and drink while "weeping and uttering lamentable cries." Strangely, he was calmed for periods of time by sitting in a chair.

Late 17th century— Another French "sea-man" was shot and killed by a sentry at Boulogne. An account of the incident was published by Benoit de Maillet in 1748.

1 May 1714— While returning to France from a voyage to the East Indies, Samuel Fallours saw a bluish-gray "marine man" in the Gulf of Guinea, off the west coast of Africa. The creature wore "a sort of fisher's cap of moss on its head." It was most likely a West African manatee (*Trichechus senegalensis*).

1740— A merman was reportedly caught at Martinico, on the French coast. Benoit de Maillet described it as bearded and resembling the "sea-man" taken at Sestri in 1682..

10 August 1741— While passing Alaska's Shumagin Islands, naturalist Georg Wilhelm Steller recorded the first known sighting of STELLER'S SEA APE.

1774— A supposed mermaid from Greece, displayed in London, proved to be a fabrication concocted from the skin of a SHARK.

ca. 1790— While walking on the shore near Castlemartin, Dyfed, Wales, Henry Reynolds saw what he took for a teenage boy lolling in the surf. Drawing closer, he saw the creature's EEL-like tail, short arms, and brown streamers like ribbons sprouting from its scalp. The merman let Reynolds approach within 35 feet and remained where it was for an hour, before swimming out to sea.

1797— While strolling near Sandside Bay, on the Scottish coast, William Munro saw a creature resembling "an unclothed female," sitting on a rock that jutted out to sea, combing its shoulder-length brown hair. The mermaid's face was "of a natural form," while "the breasts and the abdomen, the arms and fingers [were] the size of a full-grown body of the human species." Moments later, the creature slid into the water and submerged. Munro reported the encounter 12 years later, after other mermaid sightings were logged from the same area.

13 October 1811— Farmer John McIssac saw a mermaid lounging on a seaside boulder, near Campbeltown, on Scotland's Kintyre Peninsula. It was 4–5 feet long, with a human torso and a reddish-green fish's tail "like a fan." After some two hours of "constantly, with both hands stroking and washing its breasts," the creature "tumbled clumsily into the sea." Witness Katherine Loynachan later reported an offshore sighting of the creature on 13 October, near the same place.

Summer 1814— A group of children saw what they mistook for a drowning woman, off the western coast of Scotland. Closer inspection revealed a mermaid of human appearance above the waist, whose hindquarters resembled "an immense large cuddy fish…in color and shape." The creature remained in view for two hours, "at times making a hissing noise like a goose."

15 August 1814— Two Scottish fishermen saw two merbeings swimming offshore from Port Gordon. The apparent male had dark skin, a wide mouth, and very long arms. His fair-skinned companion displayed prominent breasts.

May 1817— While crossing the North Atlantic, at 44° 6' west longitude, sailors aboard the vessel *Leonidas* saw a "strange fish," swimming with its human forequarters raised two feet out of the water. The encounter lasted for roughly six hours, during which the 5-foot creature repeatedly swam beneath the ship, appearing first on one side, then the other.

1830— A party of crofters cutting seaweed on Benbecula Island, in the Outer Hebrides, saw a mermaid "in the form of a woman in miniature" cavorting offshore. After the creature eluded pursuit, one member of the group threw a stone and struck it in the back. Several days later, the creature's body washed ashore two miles from the point of the first sighting. Sheriff Duncan Shaw reported that: "The upper part of the creature was about the size of a well-fed child of three or four years of age, with an abnormally developed breast. The hair was long, dark and glossy, while the skin was white, soft, and tender. The lower part of the body was like a salmon, but without scales." Villagers prepared a casket and buried the mermaid at Nunton, where its grave was pointed out to tourists through the early 1960s. No effort has been made to exhume and identify the creature.

July 1833— Three fishermen allegedly caught a 3-foot mermaid 30 miles off the coast of Yell, in the Shetland Islands. They kept the creature in their boat for three hours, then released it out of sympathy for its pitiful moaning. In affidavits sworn before a justice of the peace, they described the creature as having a woman's upper body, albeit with a face resembling a MONKEY'S, with 9-inch arms and a fish's tail (minus scales). Atop its head, the mermaid had "a few stiff bristles…extending down to the shoulders, and these it could erect and depress at pleasure, something like a crest."

1850— A mermaid was sighted in LAGO LACAR, ARGENTINA, near San Martin de los Andes in Neuquén Province.

1900— While retrieving stray sheep from a gully near Sandwood, Scotland, Alexander Gunn saw a human-sized mermaid with curly orange hair and aquamarine eyes. The creature's angry sounds convinced Gunn to leave it in peace.

1921— A classic mermaid, with a woman's upper body and a fish's tail, was sighted by fishermen near Dassen Island, off the coast of South Africa's Western Cape Province.

1934–35— While passing through the Strait of Magellan, a Scandinavian big-game hunter saw a mermaid with green hair and luminous eyes off the coast of Punta Arenas, Chile.

1937— Fishermen found a "very fair and beautiful" young man swimming off southern India's Malabar coast and brought him ashore, supposing he had fallen from some passing ship. On land, the youth refused to speak and "coiled his limbs about in the sand" until he saw an opportunity to flee, racing back to the water and vanishing under the surface.

1942–45— During service with the U.S. Navy in World War II, Rein Mellaart was stationed on Morotai Island, in the South Pacific. One day, he saw fishermen hauling in what he took for a shark, but which proved to be a mermaid. Above the waist, the creature "looked as human as any person you'd meet on the street," except for its six-fingered hands, while its tail was "exactly like a dolphin, with a double fin on the end." Moved when the mermaid "began to cry like a baby," Mellaart ran for help, but the creature was dead when he returned. Natives told Mellaart that the creatures were frequently hunted as food.

August 1949— Scottish fishermen reported a mermaid sighting off Craignure, on the Isle of Mull.

1950s— During renovation of a Japanese brewery in Saga Prefecture, a box was found containing the small, mummified remains of a supposed Kappa. The remains were displayed for several years, but surviving photographs have little value as evidence.

3 January 1957— While traveling by raft from Tahiti to Chile, a member of Eric de Bisschop's crew allegedly found a strange creature on deck, "standing up on its tail." As he approached, the animal knocked him aside and dived back into the sea, leaving the sailor with shiny fish scales on his hands.

1960–62— A mermaid resembling "a normal woman" was seen repeatedly around Kilconly Point, on the coast of County Kerry, Ireland.

March 1961— A series of mermaid sightings were reported from the Isle of Man, with witnesses including the mayor of Peel. In August, the Manx Tourist Board offered a reward for the capture of a live mermaid, which has not been collected.

1967— Widely separated mermaid sightings were reported from Victoria, British Columbia and from southern Borneo, Indonesia.

November 1978— Two construction workers at the U.S. Navy base outside Yokosuka, Japan claimed to have sighted a Kappa. Unlike most descriptions of those aquatic imps, however, the witnesses said the scaly, shell-backed creature was nearly 10 feet tall.

February 1985—Investigators collaborating with the INTERNATIONAL SOCIETY OF CRYPTOZOOLOGY obtained photographic proof that the RI, a merbeing reported from New Ireland, Papua New Guinea, is actually a dugong (*Dugong dugong*).

31 May 1985—Two children at Roque Saenz Peña, Argentina prevented one of the local merbeings (known as NEGROES-OF-THE-WATER) from abducting a younger child. Two days later, the same creature or its twin was reported harassing more children.

5 April 2001—Scientists in Ghana declared that they had identified the Mami Water as a West African manatee.

Researchers sometimes disagree on the traits common to merbeings, some discarding the half-man, half-fish description entirely to admit any amphibious cryptid of humanoid form. Authors LOREN COLEMAN and PATRICK HUYGHE, for example, include Madagascar's KALANORO, along with the LIZARD MEN seen in or near water at various points across the U.S. and Canada, and the predatory CHUPACABRA of Latin America.

Sources: Clark and Pear, *Strange and Unexplained Phenomena*; Coleman and Huyghe, *The Field Guide to Bigfoot, Yeti, and Other Mystery Primates Worldwide*; Costello, *The Magic Zoo*; Dinsdale, *Monster Hunt*; Gatschet, "Water-monsters of American aborigines"; "Ghanaian scientists unravel mystery mermaid's being." Panafrican News Agency (5 April 2001); Picasso, "South American monsters and mystery animals."

Mesna, Norway   This double lake, in Norway's Hedmark County, is properly divided into Nord-Mesma and Sud-Mesma ("north" and "south"). Local folklore claims that a large LAKE MONSTER was once seen crawling between the two bodies of water, but no modern sightings are on file.

Source: Erik Knatterud, Sea Serpents in Norwegian Lakes, http://www/mjoesormen.no.

Messie   Lake Murray, South Carolina lies west of Columbia, in northern Lexington County. It is 41 miles long, 14 miles wide, and has a maximum depth of some 380 feet. Recorded sightings of the LAKE MONSTER known as Messie date from 1933, the same year NESSIE first made international headlines from Scotland. (That coincidence explains the creature's alternate nickname: the Loch Murray Monster.) Sporadic reports continued over the next four decades, with the most dramatic recorded in 1973. Buddy and Shirley Browning were fishing with companion Kord Brazell, when a large creature surfaced and rushed toward their boat. It allegedly tried to clamber on board, but Buddy struck it with an oar and it submerged. State wildlife officials suggested that the "monster" might be an ALLIGATOR or large sturgeon, but the witnesses rejected that hypothesis. Buddy Browning told the press:

We noticed something coming out of the water at us. It attacked our boat! It wasn't an illusion, it wasn't an EEL or sturgeon. It was unlike anything I ever saw before, and I have been fishing Lake Murray for over 20 years. We never did ever figure out what it was. It was not an alligator. No! I know alligator when I see it! It was very aggressive...It was basically on top of the water where you could see it quite well.... I've never seen it since. I did come back that day. Kord and I came on back over here to the house and got the shotgun. We was going to go back after it and claim it! But we never did see it again.

In 1980, the local *Independent News* described Messie as "a cross between a snake and something prehistoric." Ten years later, South Carolina's Fish, Wildlife and Parks Department assigned biologist Lance Harper to collect reports of Messie. After he interviewed a dozen "reputable" witnesses, Harper strung nets around Lake Murray to collect fish samples, but some large object or creature tore gaping holes in the mesh. Marvin Corder, a retired Army general, claimed two sightings of Messie in the 1980s. As he described the cryptid: "This serpent-like creature is 40–60 feet long with the head and body resembling a snake, with a tail of an eel."

In October 1996, an anonymous caller told radio station WNOK-FM:

I was fishing on Shell Island, off of a friend's cove, and I saw a fin that was about two feet long come up. I thought it was a big bass, but I didn't know what it was, so I threw my line right out in front of it. It broke my rod in half and took it with it. All I had left was just the handle grip. That's all that was left. I didn't know what it was....All I know was it broke my rod in half. Just after that, I saw it roll, but that was it.

While some authors maintain that Messie sightings ended after 1997, such is not the case. In April 2000, Mary Shealey saw a creature resembling a capsized boat, swimming near Lake Murray Dam. She estimated that it was 30 feet long, while its back rose 10 feet above the surface. The following year, a swimmer claimed that Messie brushed against her in the water, noting that its skin was "very bumpy and sort of scaly-feeling."

Sources: Kirk, *In the Domain of the Lake Monsters*; The Loch Murray Monster, http://www.geocities.com/LochMurray/.

***Messir* sea serpent**   On 30 September 1888, passengers aboard the ship *Messir* saw a SEA SERPENT in the Red Sea, off the coast of Suakin, Sudan. Witness Zélie-Élisabeth Colvile described the incident as follows in her memoirs, five years later:

There was a great excitement, the crew rushing up to the side of the ship and eagerly pointing out something in the water. The Captain called us, and we hurried after him to see part of the body of some enormous sea-monster arching itself out of the water in a semi-circle, and only to be compared to a gigantic EEL. The crew called it *baten*; (Arabic word); but if it were not our friend the sea-serpent, it must have been some relative. The Captain told us he had seen it just before alongside the ship, some hundred feet long. The large portion we saw certainly led us to believe there must have been a deal more in the water.

BERNARD HEUVELMANS noted that the translation of *baten* depends on whether the "t" is hard or soft. In one case, the word simply means "whale," whereas the other meaning may be "belly" or "insides" (interpreted by Heuvelmans as meaning "animal from the deep belly of the seas").

Source: Heuvelmans, *In the Wake of the Sea Serpents*.

Metoh-Kangmi *see* **Yeti**

Mi-Chen-Po *see* **Yeti**

Michigan Bigfoot Information Center   Founder Wayne King describes the MBIC as "a grass roots group of Michigan residents pursuing studies into the SASQUATCH phenomena [*sic*]." Active since the late 1970s, the MBIC "seeks only to learn more about Bigfoot through non-threatening research, and is strictly against the idea of 'obtaining a specimen for science'....We are not trying to prove to the scientific community that Sasquatch exists, we are not seeking fame, publicity, or money by 'discovering' Sasquatch." The no-kill approach thus opposes claims by such researchers as GROVER KRANTZ and ROBERT TITUMS that only a type specimen will finally document BIGFOOT'S existence.

A measure of controversy has surrounded the MBIC since 1980, when author Kenneth Wylie publicly questioned the group's operations and ethics. Specifically at issue was the MBIC's solicitation of Sasquatch sightings, with a vow of confidentiality for those reporting encounters. As stated on the MBIC's website:

> Our "prime directive" is to protect the privacy of all those requesting it, who come forward with information on Sasquatch. First of all, because all such persons deserve their privacy, and secondly, because if we fail to preserve privacy we can expect many people will not share their knowledge and experiences with us.

Critics maintain that the group has not kept its promise. In 1982, Dr. Ron Westrum (of Eastern Michigan University's sociology department) wrote on the Internet: "I know of one case in which King promised confidentiality to witnesses, and then proceeded to give the details to the newspapers." Sadly, such controversy is as common to cryptozoology as to any other field of human endeavor. Michigan, meanwhile, remains a fertile ground for Bigfoot research, with sightings recorded since 1891.

Sources: Wylie, *Bigfoot: A Personal Inquiry into a Phenomenon*; MBIC website, *http://www.michiganbigfoot.org/links.html*; Ron Westrum comments in review of Wylie's *Bigfoot*, http://www.n2.net/prey/bigfoot/reviews/wylie.htm.

Miga   African natives describe the Miga ("water LION") as a ferocious aquatic predator, inhabiting various rivers in Guinea, the Central African Republic, and the Democratic Republic of Congo. It resembles a large FISH or cephalopod, with tentacles protruding from its head. The Miga reportedly lurks among rocks and attacks passing canoes, seizing their human occupants as prey. BERNARD HEUVELMANS suggested that the creature was a West African manatee (*Trichelus senegalensis*) straying beyond its normal range (Senegal and Angola), though manatees are not carnivorous and have no tentacles. Researcher Marc Micha proposed that the Miga's "tentacles" may be barbels of a giant CATFISH, while others suggest a possible freshwater OCTOPUS as the culprit.

Sources: Heuvelmans, *Les Derniers Dragons d'Afrique*; Raymond de Montrozier, *Deux Ans chez les Anthropophages ey les Sultans de Centre Africain*. Paris: Plon-Nourrit, 1902.

Migo   At 370 miles long, New Britain is the largest island in the Bismarck Archipelago, located off the northeastern coast of Papua New Guinea. On 1 February 1972, a Japanese newspaper (the *Mainichi Daily News*) reported that a LAKE MONSTER known as the Migo inhabited New Britain's Lake Dakataua, a body of water 1,410 feet wide and 30 feet deep, containing three small islands and a submerged volcano. Witness Shohei Shirai, head of the Pacific Ocean Resources Research Institute, described the Migo as resembling a mosasaur (a large marine reptile related to modern MONITOR LIZARDS, presumed extinct for some 65 million years). Twenty-two years later, in January 1994, cryptozoologist ROY MACKAL accompanied a Japanese television crew to Lake Dakataua, where photographers captured the Migo on film. That footage has never been aired, but copies were viewed by several researchers, including KARL SHUKER. His report described an "indistinct head," an apparent neck, and "a large flattened hump" that apparently propelled the creature. The Migo's vertical undulations prompted Mackal and Shuker to suggest that it might be a prehistoric ZEUGLODON (also proposed for such aquatic cryptids as OGOPOGO and CADBOROSAURUS, among others). Mackal subsequently changed his mind, after viewing a second videotape shot at closer range in summer 1994. Upon screening that footage, Mackal concluded that the Migo shown on-screen actually represented three Indopacific CROCODILES (*Crocodylus porosus*), captured for the first time in a mating ritual. Mackal's turn-around startled some other researchers and left them unconvinced.

Sources: Karl Shuker, "Alien zoo." *Fortean Times* 106 (January 1998): 15; Shuker, "New Britain's lake monster."

Mi-Gö *see* **Yeti**

Mihirung Paringmal   This large, flightless BIRD of Australia, significantly larger than an EMU, is known today from Aboriginal rock paintings Queensland and New South Wales. In Victoria, native folklore also claims the birds were still alive during the last period of volcanic activity, some 2,000–3,000 years ago. Two prehistoric candidates are known to science, but both presumably became extinct much earlier. One, *Dromornis stirtoni*, stood nine feet tall and weighed more than 1,300 pounds. It appeared in the Miocene fossil record (15 million years ago) and vanished in the Pleistocene (some 30,000 years ago). The smaller *Genyornis newtoni*, 6–7 feet tall, was also a more recent species, appearing in the Late Pleistocene and allegedly dying out around 26,000 years ago. In theory, then, neither bird should have had any contact with Australian Aborigines.

Sources: James Dawson, *Australian Aborigines*. Melbourne: G. Robertson, 1881; Patricia Vickers-Rich and Gerard Van Tets, eds., *Kadimakara: Extinct Vertebrates of Australia*. Lilydale, Victoria: Pioneer Design Studio, 1985.

Milford Haven sea serpent   On 6 March 2003, barmaid Lesley John was working at the Shipwright public house on the waterfront in Milford Haven, Pembrokeshire, Wales when she saw something unusual offshore. "I was standing at the bar and looking out towards the Haven," she told reporters. "At the side of the gun tower I saw something long and snakelike in the water. It was just after the ferry had left. There was white water, then a fin and something moving off." Four customers rushed outside with John to watch the creature. Witness Peter Thomas said, "I definitely saw a head and then the water splashed about 10 metres [33 feet] away. I sail my boat off Front Street and I have never seen anything like that before." Pub owner David Crewe arrived late on the scene, reporting: "All I saw was a tail disappearing into the water."

The Milford Haven sighting produced the predictable jibes against tipsy witnesses—"It makes you wonder what's in the beer," etc.—but John and company remained steadfast in their assessment of the creature they described as roughly the length of four or five cars parked end-to-end. Crewe offered a reward of £150 ($246) to anyone who could catch the creature alive. Two weeks after the initial report, local diver Len Bateman reported sighting a dolphin in the harbor and suggested that its unaccustomed presence might explain the SEA SERPENT sighting. Ron Watts, honorary curator of Pembroke's gun tower museum, had an even more prosaic explanation:

> There is a capsized, submerged rowing boat out there. When the ferry came in on the low tide, its bow thrusters and side thrusters would have pushed the rowing boat towards Port of Pembroke. It would have passed the gun tower by a few yards. When the ferry went out again after the tide turned, her bow props and starboard thrusters would have dislodged anything trapped in that area and sent it back out into the haven. I don't think there are any creatures out there we don't know about already.

Despite Watts's evident self-confidence, no such derelict boat had been found when this volume went to press, nor had the Milford Haven creature favored locals with another appearance.

Sources: "Dolphin solution to monster mystery?" *Western Telegraph* (18 March 2003); "Reward offered to net sea monster." *Western Telegraph* (13 March 2003); "Reward out for 'Milford Monster' spotted by pub's lunch customers." *Western Mail* (13 March 2003); "Welsh sea monster." *Fortean Times* 172 (August 2003): 27.

Milne   The only South American bear presently recognized by science is the spectacled bear (*Tremarctos ornatus*), a small species easily recognized by the yellow rings of fur around its eyes. They normally range along the Andes, from Venezuela to Peru, though specimens have been found as far afield as Panama and northern Argentina. Stories persist, however, of a much larger black bear, said to inhabit Peru's Gran Pajonal forest (Ucayli Department), where Campa tribesmen know it as the Milne. Explorer Leonard Clark was rafting through the Gran Pajonal, sometime in the 1940s, when he saw a Milne on shore, clawing open a rotten tree stump and feeding on the ants inside. A splash from one of Clark's oars startled the beast, whereupon it plunged into the river and tried to climb aboard Clark's raft. He shot the bear, but a school of PIRANHAS attacked the carcass before Clark could save it for study. Local natives later told Clark that the Milne was well known, together with another unnamed, red-furred bear reported from the lower Andes.

Sources: Leonard Clark, *The Rivers Run East*. New York: Funk and Wagnalls, 1953; Shuker, *From Flying Toads to Snakes with Wings*.

Milwaukee River, Wisconsin   In the early 1900s, a large serpentine cryptid was reported swimming in this Wisconsin river. Unfortunately, the sketchy accounts surviving today provide no further description and no clear location for the sightings.

Source: Garner, *Monster! Monster!*

Mindi   Australian Aborigines describe the Mindi as a large, nonvenomous SNAKE, 18–30 feet in length, inhabiting remote parts of South Australia and Victoria. It is said to ambush and devour EMUS, which it kills by constriction in the manner of a PYTHON. Legend imbues the reptile with supernatural powers, including the ability to kill with a glance and to spread disease among humans. Australia's largest known snake, the diamond python (*Morelia spilota spilota*), may reach 15 feet in length, but it naturally occurs only along the coast of New South Wales, far from the Mindi's reported inland domain.

Sources: Barrett, *The Bunyip and Other Mythical Monsters and Legends*; Whitley, "Mystery animals of Australia."

***Minerva* sea serpent**   In May 1821, sailors aboard the ship *Minerva* sighted a SEA SERPENT off the coast of Cape Ann, Massachusetts. Captain Crows, commanding the vessel, filed a report of the incident, but no details of the animal's description are presently available.

Source: O'Neill, *The Great New England Sea Serpents*.

Minhocão   The Minhocão ("giant earthworm") of South America is said to be a huge burrowing creature, up to 160 feet long and 16 feet wide, that leaves great furrows in its wake. In some accounts, it is said to be amphibious and a voracious hunter, dragging livestock under water when herds attempt to ford infested lakes or rivers. French scientist Auguste de Saint Hillaire was the first to inform Western readers of the Minhocão, in 1847, though the creature was already well known to aborigines and settlers ranging from Nicaragua to Uruguay.

Eyewitness accounts of the Minhocão span the last half of the 19th century. On a rainy night in 1849, one of the creatures plowed up the land surrounding a home owned by João de Deos, in Brazil's Parana State. Three years later, Lebino José dos Santos reported that a Minhocão had dug trenches deep enough to

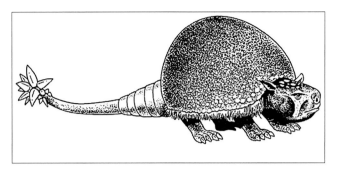

Is South America's elusive Minhocão a relict *Glyptodon*?

divert a tributary of the Ypanema River, in São Paulo State. Around the same time, a careless Minhocão allegedly trapped itself in a rocky cleft near Arapehy, Uruguay and died there. Observers claimed its skin was as thick as the bark of a pine tree, covered with scales like an ARMADILLO'S. In the early 1860s, Antonio José Branco found the land around his home near Curitibanos, Brazil (in Santa Catarina State) furrowed with trenches 10 feet wide and 2,600 feet in overall length, uprooting several large trees, which natives blamed on the Minhocão. Near the end of that decade, Francisco de Amaral Varella glimpsed a Minhocão on the bank of Brazil's Rio das Caveiras, six miles from Laje (Bahia State). He described it as short, but at least three feet thick, with a piglike snout. Not daring to attack it, he watched it plow furrows the width of its body before it vanished underground. Some weeks later, Varella and companion Friedrich Kelling found another Minhocão's tracks.

While no modern sightings of the Minhocão have been reported, suggesting that the creatures may be extinct, cryptozoologists still debate its possible identity. One candidate is the *Glyptodon*, a kind of prehistoric armadillo 10 feet long and 5 feet tall, that flourished in Argentina until 15,000 years ago. Though heavily armored, the *Glyptodon* was herbivorous and would not prey on livestock, even if it somehow learned to swim. BERNARD HEUVELMANS believed that depredations by giant ANACONDAS and/or relict ZEUGLODONS had confused the Minhocão's story. KARL SHUKER, in contrast, proposes a giant relative of the South American lungfish *Lepidoseren*, retaining the scales that its modern descendants lost during later stages of evolution.

Sources: Heuvelmans, *On the Track of Unknown Animals*; Shuker, *In Search of Prehistoric Survivors*.

Mi-Ni-Wa-Tu   Lakota tribesmen of North and South Dakota once described the Mi-ni-wa-tu ("river monster") as an aquatic cryptid inhabiting the MISSOURI RIVER. It was said to have a bison's body, covered in red hair, with a serrated ridge along its back and a flat tail resembling a BEAVER'S. A single horn protruded from its forehead, a trait reportedly shared with WHITEY (in Arkansas) and the cryptid(s) of WALGREN LAKE, NEBRASKA.

Source: J. Owen Dorsey, "Teton folk-lore notes." *Journal of American Folklore* 2 (1889): 133–139.

Minnesota Iceman   Depending on the reader's point of view (or prejudice), the 1960s sideshow specimen known as the Minnesota Iceman either proved the existence of unknown living HOMINIDS on Earth, or else it ranks among the most elaborate and convoluted HOAXES of all time. The tale began in 1967, when showman Frank Hansen began touring state and local fairs around the U.S. with a refrigerated truck, containing the icebound remains of an unidentified "What-is-It." According to

Hansen's ever-changing story in those days, the hairy, humanoid figure had been found by Russian sealers, Japanese whalers or Chinese fishermen, floating in a block of natural ice in the Sea of Okhotsk (between Russia's Kamchatka peninsula and the east coast of Siberia). Once salvaged, the Iceman somehow found its way to Hong Kong, where in turn it was purchased by an unnamed California millionaire. Said millionaire, in turn, either loaned or rented the creature to Hansen for a 2-year tour of North America.

In autumn 1967, Minnesota zoology student Terry Cullen saw the exhibit in Milwaukee, then proceeded to trail it across the Midwest, all the while striving in vain to interest various anthropologists in the creature. Finally, in late 1968, Cullen contacted IVAN SANDERSON, who asked a friend to examine the Iceman at the Chicago Stock Fair. Intrigued by the friend's report, Sanderson and colleague BERNARD HEUVELMANS drove to Hansen's farm at Rollingstone, Minnesota on 16 December 1968. Over the next two days, they examined the Iceman while making notes, sketches and photographs for future reference. As Heuvelmans summarized his findings:

> The specimen at first looks like a man, or, if you prefer, an adult human being of the male sex, of rather normal height (six feet) and proportions but excessively hairy. It is entirely covered with very dark brown hair three to four inches long. Its skin appears wax-like, similar in color to the cadavers of white men not tanned by the sun....The specimen is lying on its back...[T]he left arm is twisted behind the head with the palm of the hand upward.
>
> The arm makes a strange curve, as it were that of a sawdust doll, but this curvature is due to an open fracture midway between the wrist and the elbow where one can distinguish the broken ulna in a gaping wound. The right arm is twisted and held tightly against the flank, with the hand spread palm down over the right side of the abdomen. Between the right finger and the medius the penis is visible, lying obliquely on the groin. The testicles are vaguely distinguishable at the juncture of the thighs.

Heuvelmans and Sanderson both detected a strong odor of rotted flesh, escaping from one corner of the exhibit where its glass casket was cracked. They differed somewhat in descriptions of the Iceman's simian face. Sanderson thought the eye sockets were hollow, while Heuvelmans later wrote that he saw the left eye lying on the creature's cheek. From that, and an apparent stain of frozen blood behind the head, Heuvelmans surmised that the beast had been shot in the face, through its right eye, displacing the left and blowing out the back of its skull.

Though Hansen insisted that no articles on the creature should be published without prior approval from himself and the exhibit's unnamed owner, both Heuvelmans and Sanderson rushed into print with their findings. Heuvelmans published an article in Belgium, in February 1969, wherein he named the Iceman *Homo pongoides* ("apelike man"). Sanderson followed with a May 1969 magazine article in the U.S., dubbing Hansen's creature "the missing link." Before long, Hansen later claimed, he was contacted by a local sheriff and the FBI, both suspicious that the Iceman was a human murder victim. (The FBI denies any involvement in the matter.) To protect himself from prosecution, Hansen said, he returned the original specimen to its owner and replaced it with a model manufactured in Hollywood. The new exhibit, clearly advertised as "a fabricated illusion," went on tour with Hansen in 1969. A year later, Hansen confused matters further with a July 1970 magazine article claiming he shot the Iceman personally, when it attacked him during a 1960 hunting trip in Minnesota. The replica, he wrote, was created by sculptor Howard Ball in Jan-

uary 1967, with detail work on the body provided by colleagues of Hollywood makeup artist JOHN CHAMBERS. Hansen claimed he had toured with the model through 1967, then substituted the original in 1968, only to hide it again after Heuvelmans and Sanderson published their findings.

As if the matter were not confused enough, Sanderson later wrote (in October 1970) that he was aware of *five* Iceman replicas in circulation, including one built by John Chambers. He further claimed to have traced hair samples from the original specimen, collected when the Iceman was imported from Asia, "which turned up in a university in the [S]outh." (Sanderson did not produce the hairs, and the university was never identified.) In 1974, Heuvelmans revised his initial opinion of *Homo pongoides*, joining Russian hominologist BORIS PORSHNEV to assert that the Iceman constituted proof of NEANDERTAL MAN'S survival into modern times. Heuvelmans went on to speculate that Hansen had killed the creature during his military service in Vietnam, and that it might be a specimen of Southeast Asia's elusive NGUOI RUNG, smuggled back to the U.S. in a military casket. Primatologist JOHN NAPIER, though barred from viewing the Iceman itself, noted that photographs taken of Hansen's exhibit in April 1969 do not conform to descriptions of the creature penned by Heuvelmans and Sanderson, with respect to the teeth, feet and other morphological details. Napier finally concluded that the whole episode was a hoax, and that no "real" Iceman ever existed. Researcher MARK HALL suggests that the Iceman was a specimen of *Homo erectus*, presumed extinct for some 200,000 years, which he likens to the ALMAS or KAPTAR of Central Asia. All that can be said about this case today, with any confidence, is that the truth remains obscure.

Sources: Coleman, *Mysterious America*; Coleman and Clark, *Cryptozoology A to Z*; Frank Hansen, "I killed the ape-man creature of White-face." *Saga* (July 1970): 8–11, 55–60; Heuvelmans and Porshnev, *L'homme de Néanderthal est Toujours Vivant*; Napier, *Bigfoot*; Ivan Sanderson, "Bozo, The Iceman." *Pursuit* 3 (October 1970): 89; Ivan Sanderson, "Preliminary description of the external morphology of what appeared to be the fresh corpse of a hitherto unknown form of living hominid." *Genus* 25 (1969): 249–278; Ian Simmons, "The abominable showman." *Fortean Times* 83 (October-November 1995): 34–37.

Minnesota River, Minnesota   Sometime in the late 19th century, a 12-foot SNAKE was reportedly pulled from the Minnesota River by crewmen aboard a barge, passing the Minneapolis suburb of Eden Prairie. As soon as the snake was place on deck, it allegedly opened its mouth and disgorged a dozen smaller snakes. The reptiles' fate is not recorded, and its species is unknown. No snake of that size is known to live in North America.

Source: Morris Russell, *Uncle Dudley's Odd Hours*. Lake City, MN: Home Printery, 1904.

Miramichi Panther   In mid-December 2002, brothers Barry and Peter Campbell were driving to work at a cattle ranch five miles outside Miramichi, New Brunswick when they observed a large black CAT on property beside the highway. They stopped to watch the animal for 15 minutes, and later reported their "black panther" sighting to officers of the Miramichi Department of Natural Resources and Energy. Most "panthers" are melanistic specimens of leopard (*Panthera pardus*) or JAGUAR (*Panthera onca*), but neither are normally found in Canada. Barry Campbell believes he saw a black EASTERN COUGAR (*Puma con-*

Showman Frank Hansen with one version of his Minnesota Iceman.

color), although that species is presumed extinct in eastern North America and no melanistic COUGAR has ever been documented. No further sightings of the Miramichi Panther have thus far been reported.

Source: "Mysterious panther found in Miramichi." *New Brunswick Telegraph Journal* (24 December 2002).

Mirree-Ulla *see* **Bunyip**

Mirror Lake, Alaska   Confusion surrounds the source of LAKE MONSTER reports from Mirror Lake, near Chugiak, Alaska. Some accounts describe a creature with "the body of a man and the face of a beast," lurking in the algae-green waters to seize unwary human prey, while others present the tale as a ghost story. Some locals suggest that the legend was started by counselors at Camp Gorsuch, a nearby Boy Scout facility, either as a campfire tale or to discourage boys from unsupervised swimming.

Source: Eowyn Ivey, "Haunted houses, ghosts and Bigfoot... in Mat-Su? Oh my!" *The Frontiersman* (28 October 2002).

Mirygdy   Yet another unknown HOMINID or WILDMAN of Siberia, the Mirygdy ("broad shoulders") reportedly inhabits the far-eastern Chukotskiy Peninsula. Like BIGFOOT and other large primates found worldwide, it stands seven feet tall and has no discernible neck. Frigid weather makes it no surprise, perhaps, that the Mirygdy is seen mainly in summer. Its description matches those of other Siberian hominids, including the ALMAS, CHUCHUNAA, KÉÉDIEKI, KEYAK, KILTANYA, KUL, MECHENY, PIKELIAN, TUNGU and ZEMLEMER.

Source: Bayanov, *In the Footsteps of the Russian Snowman.*

Mishipizhiw   Despite the English translation of its Ojibwa name, the Mishipizhiw ("great LYNX") bears no resemblance to a CAT. Rather, it was described by 17th- and 18th-century tribesmen as a serpentine LAKE MONSTER inhabiting LAKE SUPERIOR and various other lakes throughout Ontario, Canada. Witnesses accounts of the creature include a serrated ridge along its spine and horns protruding from its head.

Source: Norval Morrisseau, *Legends of My People.* Toronto: McGraw-Hill Ryerson, 1977.

Misiganebic   In Algonquin folklore, the Misiganebic

("great serpent") was a large LAKE MONSTER with a head and mane resembling a horse's, found in various lakes throughout Wisconsin, Ontario and Québec. Sightings of large aquatic cryptids continue from bodies of water in all three areas to the present day.

Source: Muerger and Gagnon, *Lake Monster Traditions.*

Miss Waldron's Red Colobus Monkey   The African primate known as Miss Waldron's red colobus MONKEY (*Procolobus badius waldroni*) was officially discovered in December 1933, when researcher Willoughby Lowe collected eight specimens in the region of modern-day Ghana. Lowe named the species for a female traveling companion, Miss F. Waldron — and the monkeys promptly dropped from sight once more. No photographs of living specimens exist, and the last alleged live sighting occurred in March 1954, along the border of Ghana and Côte d'Ivoire. Determined searches for the monkeys during 1993–99 revealed no evidence of their survival, and Ohio State University anthropologist Scott McGraw formally declared the species extinct in 2000.

That verdict marked *P. b. waldroni* as the first primate to disappear from Earth in some 200 years, but it was not the final word. In 2001, McGraw received a monkey tail from Côte d'Ivoire, identified by DNA testing as belonging to *P. b. waldroni*. Later that same year, a complete skin was found in the possession of a hunter in southeastern Côte d'Ivoire. In early 2003, McGraw received a photo of a freshly killed specimen, also from war-torn Côte d'Ivoire. "This is the only known photograph of a Miss Waldron's red colobus," McGraw told reporters, "and it's dead. But everyone who knows anything about this primate says it's definitely a Miss Waldron's." McGraw went on to explain the monkey's importance:

When most of the forest is destroyed and the human population skyrockets and the most remote villages get shotguns, we can't expect to have a good number of these primates around. But if this monkey is extinct, then something has gone very, very wrong, as primates are pretty resilient. Its extinction may represent the beginning of a wave of extinctions which will make their way across this part of Africa. There could be a cascade of disappearances, including all of those animals that are dependent on high-canopy forests. Since there's very little canopy area left, this list could include forest elephants, leopards, CHIMPANZEES, and so on.

At press time for this volume, McGraw planned a new expedition to seek proof of the monkeys' survival in Ghana and Côte d'Ivoire.

Source: "New evidence suggests that monkey thought extinct still exists." Ohio State University press release (3 February 2004).

Mississippi River   It would be remarkable if North America's longest river (and fourth-longest in the world) had not spawned reports of aquatic cryptids at some point in history — and indeed, it has. As early as 1673, Menomini tribesmen in the region of present-day Wisconsin told explorer Jacque Marquette that the "Father of Waters" was infested with monsters, some resembling huge trees (with tentacles?), while others had heads resembling a TIGER'S. Two centuries later, in January 1878, a huge unknown creature reportedly attacked Captain Ed Baker's produce boat near Island 25, in the Mississippi's southern quarter. As described in the *Natchez* (Miss.) *Democrat* and the *Helena* (Mont.) *Independent*, the incident occurred on 9 January, and involved a remarkable beast. A newspaper report described the encounter as follows:

[A]s it neared the boat it suddenly veered to the right, striking the stern oar and knocking it overboard. John Caughlin and Dud Kelley alone remained on the roof, the balance of the crew taking refuge in the cabin. The monster came near enough to enable these two gentlemen to get a full view of him. They judged him to be sixty-five feet in length. His body was shaped like a SNAKE, his tail forked like a FISH and he had a bill like that of a pelican. His bill was fully six feet in length. He had a long flowing black mane like a horse. When he swam his head was eight feet above the water. It was a grand sight to see him move down the river.

The adventure was not without risk, however. At one point, Caughlin and Kelley maintained, the creature "lashed the water into foam with its tail, and spouted oblique streams of water forty feet high." Later, when Capt. Baker examined the barge, he found a sliver like ivory, allegedly from the animal's bill, embedded in the hull. Skeptical editors emerged from their interviews with Caughlin and Kelley to report: "We really think there is a big sea monster in the Mississippi River."

Sources: Garner, *Monster! Monster!*; Jacques Marquette, *Récit des Voyages et des Decouvertes du R. Père Jacques Marquette de la Comagnie de Jesus.* Albany, NY: Weed, Parsons, 1855.

Missouri River
Like the MISSISSIPPI RIVER, with which it shares a large drainage basing, the Missouri has produced its share of aquatic cryptid sightings. Aboriginal tribesmen of the Dakotas knew the MI-NI-WA-TU, a kind horned serpent that plied the broad waters before European settlers arrived, but sightings are not limited to olden times. In the summer of 1970, Ronald Haller was floating downriver near Fort Benton, Montana (Chouteau County), when a black FISH 6–8 feet long struck his boat with sufficient force to dent the fiberglass hull. Haller allegedly filmed the fish with a movie camera he carried, but the film has never been released.

Sources: Coleman, *Mysterious America*; Garner, *Monster! Monster!*

Mi-Teh *see* Yeti

Mitla
This unclassified quadruped of Bolivia's Río Madidi region was first described by explorer PERCY FAWCETT as "a black doglike CAT about the size of a foxhound." Despite two brief encounters with the Mitla, Fawcett could offer no further details of its appearance, and controversy surrounds the creature to this day. Cryptozoologist ROY MACKAL suggests that the beast may be a rare bush dog (*Speothos venaticus*), while KARL SHUKER proposes the even lesser-known small-eared dog (*Atelocynus microtis*). At the same time, however, Shuker does not rule out a felid candidate, recalling that some accounts of the elusive ONZA describe it as a "wolf-cat."

Sources: Mackal, *Searching for Hidden Animals*; Shuker, *Mystery Cats of the World.*

Mizokami, Kyle (n.d.–)
A Japanese-American writer based in San Francisco, Kyle Mizokami won renown in the mid-1990s as a "BIGFOOT folklorist," scouring North American archives for aboriginal legends referring to large, unknown HOMINIDS. Praised in equal measures for his humor and painstaking research, Mizokami established an Internet website devoted to sightings of Bigfoot and similar creatures. In 1997, Mizokami deviated briefly from his SASQUATCH studies, leading an expedition to California's Trinity Alps in search of reputed giant SALAMANDERS. Mizokami abandoned cryptozoology a year later, but his reputation followed him, causing some new acquaintances to view him as eccentric. In June 2001, Mizokami published a satirical piece on the subject, titled "The Scarlet B — Bigfoot Ruined My Sex Life."

Sources: Clark and Coleman, *Cryptozoology A to Z*; Kyle Mizokami, "The Scarlet B — Bigfoot ruined my sex life," *http://dir.salon.com/mwt/feature/2001/06/08/scarlet_b/index.html.*

Mjörn, Sweden
This lake, in Sweden's Västra Götaland County, has a maximum recorded depth of 150 feet. In July 1972, while fishing on the lake, Per Bengtsson and his son allegedly sighted a LAKE MONSTER several yards long and dark in color. While they watched, the creature dived and surfaced several times, then finally vanished from sight.

Source: Global Underwater Search Team, http://www.cryptozoology.st/.

Mjossie
Lake Mjøsa, in southern Norway's Hedmark County, produced its first LAKE MONSTER sightings in the late 14th century. Published accounts describe Mjossie (or the Mjoes Orm) as a "serpent of incredible magnitude" that rose from its submerged lair on summer nights, to prey on livestock. At other times, the beast "lift[ed] himself high above the waters, and roll[ed] himself round like a sphere" in displays that foretold the rise and fall of Norway's rulers. In 1522, a local hunter shot the Mjoes Orm with an arrow, through its eye, and killed it. When the massive carcass washed ashore, villagers burned it down to the bones. Those, in turn, lay on the shore for several years, until German traders allegedly hauled them away to parts unknown. Mjossie was not so easily eliminated, though. Years later, a farmer found another specimen lying with 30 feet of its dark-colored body on shore. He had time to observe a horselike head without visible ears, and to judge the body 18 inches thick, before the creature noticed him and fled back to the depths. Modern sightings are rare, and a 1995 expedition mounted to retrieve a sunken airplane saw no trace of aquatic cryptids.

Sources: Costello, *In Search of Lake Monsters*; Kirk, *In the Domain of the Lake Monsters*; Erik Knatterud, The Mjoes Orm, http://www.mjoesormen.no/themjoesorm.htm; Skjelsvik, "Norwegian lake and sea monsters."

M'ké-n'bé
Waci tribesmen of Benin describe the M'ké-n'bé a reptilian creature the size of an elephant, with a long neck and tail, inhabiting marshy tributaries of the Mekrou and Ouémé Rivers. Its description closely matches that of MOKELE-MBEMBE, an alleged living DINOSAUR reported from the Congo, and the very name M'ké-n'bé may be a contraction of that more famous cryptid's name. In 1959, animal collector W.T. Roth reported that his Waci guides refused to enter a swamp where they claimed a M'ké-n'bé was in residence.

Sources: "He have head for trunk." *Pursuit* 9 (January 1970): 16–17; Heuvelmans, *Les Derniers Dragons d'Afrique.*

Mlularuka
Natives of Tanzania claim that the Mlularuka is a dog-sized flying mammal, nocturnal in habits, that feeds on various fruits. Mangoes and pomegranates rank among its favorite foods, to the chagrin of farmers who produce those crops for market. Proposed Mlularuka include Lord Derby's scaly-tailed squirrel (*Anomalurus deribanus*), which may grow to lengths of 2 feet 6 inches, or an as-yet-unknown species of BAT.

Source: Hichens, "African mystery beasts."

Mmoatia
This unclassified primate of Ghana was reported for the first time in 1920. Akan tribesmen describe the Mmoatia ("little animal") as a small, hairy biped whose fur may range from white to red or black in color. It stands only one foot tall, on average, and emits a whistling cry. As in the case of many larger HOMINIDS around the world, the Mmoatia's feet are sometimes said to point backward.

Source: Allan Cardinal, *The Natives of the Northern Territories of the Gold Coast*. New York: E.P. Dutton, 1920.

Mngwa Natives of Tanzania's coastal forests describe the Mngwa ("strange one") as a CAT the size of a donkey, marked with gray stripes like a domestic tabby. The beast is also known as Nunda ("fierce animal"), a name that testifies to its cruel reputation as a man-eater. References to the Mngwa date back to the year 1150, when it was mentioned in a Swahili folk song. British settlers in the region (then called Tanganyika) dismissed the stories as fables until 1922, when the Mngwa revealed itself with a vengeance. Captain William Hichens, then serving as magistrate in the village of Lindi, described the event as follows:

It was common for native traders to leave their belongings in the village market every night, ready for the morning's trade; and to prevent theft and also to stop stray natives sleeping in the marketplace, an askari or native constable took it in turns with two others to guard the market on a four-hour watch. Going to relieve the midnight watch, an oncoming native constable one night found his comrade missing. After a search he discovered him, terribly mutilated, underneath a stall. The man ran to his European officer, who went with me at once to the market. We found it obvious that the askari had been attacked and killed by some animal — a LION, it seemed. In the victim's hand was clutched a matted mass of greyish hair, such as would come out of a lion's mane were it grasped and torn in a violent fight. But in many years no lion had been known to come into town.

Further investigation revealed two witnesses who had passed through the market place on the night of the killing. They had seen "a gigantic brindled cat, the great mysterious nunda which is feared in every village on the coast, leap from the shadows of the market and bear the policeman to the ground." Hichens posted more guards, but another askari was killed two nights later, with more gray hair found at the scene. Over the next month, similar killings occurred in other coastal villages, spreading terror among the natives. Poisoned bait was laid in vain, and hunting parties failed to find the predator before its rampage suddenly ended.

Hichens was also present in the 1937, when another series of attacks occurred around Mchinga. One of the victims in that spree was renowned big-cat hunter, who survived his wounds and told Hichen that his assailant was the Mngwa, neither lion nor leopard. As Hichens observed, "He had nothing to gain by telling me lies; on the contrary, as a hunter he depended for his livelihood on being absolutely truthful and trustworthy." Later still, hunter Patrick Bowen tracked the Mngwa's spoor after it struck a fishing village and made off with a small child. Brindled hairs were found at the scene, and Bowen said, "The spoor we were following appeared to be that of a leopard as large as the largest lion."

No living cat is known to match the Mngwa's description, but KARL SHUKER reminds us that prehistoric Africa harbored a felid known as *Panthera crassidens*, an ancestor to modern big cats that reached 11 feet 6 inches in length. Its fossils are known from Pleistocene deposits, and while the species is presumed extinct, it might serve as a model for the Mngwa if it had survived to modern times.

Sources: Heuvelmans, *On the Track of Unknown Animals*; Hichens, "African mystery beasts"; Shuker, *Mystery Cats of the World*.

Moa *Dinornis maximus*, known to New Zealand natives as the moa or roa-roa, was the tallest BIRD that ever lived on Earth. As many as a dozen smaller species also shared the islands, but *Dinornis* was the giant. At a height of 11 feet 6 inches, it towered over Madagascar's "elephant bird" (*Aepyornis titan*) and the fierce *Diatryma gigantea* of prehistoric Europe. Moas were thriving in New Zealand when humans discovered the islands, in the 10th century, but man's advent spelled doom for the flightless giants, as it did for so many other species. Between concerted hunting and destruction of their habitat for agriculture's sake, the moa was officially extinct by 1800.

Despite that verdict, sightings of the moa have persisted. Naturalist William Colenso first heard tales of living moas from North Island natives in summer 1838, and he spent the years collecting bones and other relics. That collection, and another cache compiled by the Rev. William Williams, were used to reconstruct the first moa skeletons for museums. Granted, those bones were fossilized, but newer relics have been found on the South Island, including mummified pieces of skin and relatively "fresh" feathers. In April 1850, a seal-hunter reportedly found moa bones still covered with flesh at Molyneux Harbor (South Island). Eleven years later, surveyors charting the territory between Riwaka and Takaka twice found fresh avian footprints, measuring 14 inches long and 11 inches across at the tips of the toes. In 1868, Sir George Grey interviewed Maori hunters who claimed to have seen seven small moas (and killed one of the birds) at Preservation Inlet. A

Artist's conception of Tanzania's ferocious Mngwa (***William Rebsamen***).

The fossil legs and pelvis of a moa reveal the bird's huge size.

trained zoologist claimed a live moa sighting on the South Island in 1960. Seven years later, a government naturalist emerged from the South Island's wooded Fjordland district to report discovery of "definite, concrete, fresh evidence of the continued existence of a small species of moa." An alleged sighting of two moas by German tourists, in May 1992, proved to be HOAX, but investigation continues on a lone-moa report, filed by three hikers from Craigieburn Forest Park on 20 January 1993. July 1999 marked the beginning of a proposed 5-year search for moas in Fjordland, led by researcher Keith Armstrong.

Sources: Heuvelmans, *On the Track of Unknown Animals*; Sanderson, *More "Things"*; Karl Shuker, "Alien zoo." *Fortean Times* 128 (November 1999): 18–19; Bruce Spittle, "Please tell me moa." *Fortean Times* 98 (June 1997): 54.

Moberly Lake, Canada
Moberly Lake is situated in the foothills of the Rocky Mountains, north of Chetwynd, British Columbia. Canadian cryptozoologist JOHN KIRK received his first report of LAKE MONSTER activity from Moberly Lake in 1989, when a local resident described encounters with a cryptid whose head resembles a horse's. Aboriginal tribesmen in the area had previously suppressed news of sightings, Kirk learned, out of fear the creature would be hunted and destroyed. Thus far, no further research at the lake has been attempted.

Source: Kirk, *In the Domain of the Lake Monsters*.

Mochel-Mochel
In the 1850s, Aborigines in the Darling Downs district of Queensland, Australia, were terrorized by a BUNYIP they dubbed Mochel-mochel, which reportedly ate all the FISH in the Condamine River and menaced human swimmers. White settler Thomas Downs saw the creature in Swan Creek, while driving a herd of wild horses back to his ranch. As he described the incident, 50 years later:

Much to my surprise I saw an animal in shape similar to a low set sheep dog, the colour of a PLATYPUS, head and whiskers resembling an otter, passing from the shallow water over a strip of dry land to the deep water. The back view of this creature's head was exactly like the bald head of a blackfellow.

In his memoirs, Downs also related the second-hand story of a swimmer who was so shocked by meeting the Mochel-mochel in the Condamine River that he suffered a seizure and died three days later. There was, however, no suggestion that the animal had actually attacked its unfortunate victim.

Source: Smith, *Bunyips & Bigfoots*.

Mocking Lake, Canada
Reports of a unknown LAKE MONSTER in Québec's Mocking Lake officially date from the late 1800s. Witnesses describe the creature(s) brown or black in color, 12–18 feet long and 2–3 feet wide, with a long, serrated dorsal fin.

Source: Garner, *Monster! Monster!*

Moehau Monster
In his 1978 survey of the SASQUATCH phenomenon, author JOHN GREEN briefly alluded to reports of the Moehau Monster, a supposed 7-foot HOMINID reported from New Zealand. Green dismissed the sightings as improbably, based on New Zealand's geographical isolation, but in fact sightings of hairy bipeds from that island nations span more than a century, beginning in the late 1870s.

Sources: Gilroy, *Giants from the Dreamtime*; Green, *Sasquatch: The Apes Among Us*.

Moffat Lake, Canada
Nestled in the Gatineau Hills of Québec's Pontiac Region, Moffat Lake has produced LAKE MON-STER sightings since the 1890s. As expected of a lake whose maximum recorded depth is 33 feet, the cryptids sighted are not of the giant class. One local resident described a typical specimen, seen by his father, as follows:

It was lying low in the water and looked like a tree trunk: big, round, and very black. It was about 15–20 feet long, but he saw only part of it. The head and the tail were under the water. As soon as he approached, it submerged itself. Another witness described his encounter with an unknown animal onshore, crossing a path beside the lake. It resembled "a big burnt log," which rose and "scuttled into the lake" (presumably on legs) as the witness approached. Researchers note that Moffat Lake is linked by rivers to two more Québec "monster" lakes, LAC AYLMER and LAC SAINT-FRANÇOIS, perhaps accounting for the episodic nature of local sightings.

Source: Meurger and Gagnon, *Lake Monster Traditions*.

Moha-Moha
On 8 June 1890, an Australian schoolteacher named S. Lovell was walking with six companions at Sandy Cape, on Queensland's Great Sandy Island, when they met a remarkable creature. Miss Lovett's description was published in the journal *Land and Water*, on 3 January 1891.

We have had a visit from a monster turtle fish. I send a sketch of it. It let me stand for half an hour within five feet of it. When tired of my looking at it, it put its large neck into the water and swept round seaward, raising its dome-shaped body about five feet out of the water, and put its twelve feet of fish-like tail over the dry shore, elevating it at an angle. Then, giving its tail a half twist, it shot off like a flash of lightning, and I saw its tail in the air about a quarter of a mile off where the steamers anchor.

It had neither teeth nor serrated jaw-bones. Native blacks call it "Moka, moka," and say they like to eat it, and that it has legs or fingers. I did not see its legs, as they were in the water. What I saw of it was about 27 ft. or 28 ft., but I think it must be 30 ft. in all. Whilst its head was out of water it kept its mouth open, and, as I could not see any nostrils, I fancy it breathes through its mouth. The jaws are about 18 in. in length; the head and neck greenish white, with large white spots on the neck, and a band of white round a very black eye and round upper and lower jaws. The body was dome-shaped, about 8 ft. across and 5 ft. high, smooth, and slate-grey in colour. Tail about 12 ft., the FISH part wedge-shaped, and fin of chocolate-brown. Then beautiful silver shading to white scales size of thumb nail.

The journal's editors supposed that Miss Lovell had seen a pig-nosed TURTLE (*Carettochelys insculpta*), native to Australia and Papua New Guinea. However, that species lives in fresh water, has no visible scales, and rarely exceeds 30 inches in length. Upon further inquiry, suggesting that she may have exaggerated the creature's size, Miss Lovell wrote:

The tail was over the dry shore for half an hour, so close to me that five footsteps would have enabled me to put my hand on it. The blacks, who had not seen it on the day I did, named it at once from my sketch, which must, therefore, be pretty accurate, and

Three views of the Moha-moha, after witness S. Lovell.

called it "Moha, Moha," and laughed and said, "Saucy Fellow, Meebee"— in English, "dangerous turtle." It is eight years since it attacked the black's camp. It can stand upright, and it put its legs on the shoulders of a powerful black, 6 ft. high, and knocked him down. That year it invaded their camp, and nearly caught one man by the leg. For months after the blacks camped inland.

Miss Lovell's companions signed an affidavit swearing to the accuracy of her description. A seventh witness, an Aborigine named Robert, further testified that he had seen the same creature ashore six days earlier. Despite that affidavit, BERNARD HEUVELMANS and other modern researchers generally regard the sighting as a HOAX.

Sources: Heuvelmans, *In the Wake of the Sea Serpents*; Smith, *Bunyips & Bigfoots.*

Mohán   From the 16th century onward, natives of Colombia have described this cave-dwelling primate or HOMINID as a muscular biped covered with black hair. It favors caverns close to lakes or rivers, and appears to be an avid swimmer. As in the case of other unknown hominids around the world, occasional assaults on human females are reported. In parts of its range, the Mohán is also known as Muan and Tigre Mono ("tiger monkey").

Source: "The Mohan." *Cryptozoology Review* 1 (Autumn 1996): 8.

Mohin-Goué   This large primate or HOMINID of Côte d'Ivoire resembles a CHIMPANZEE, but is described as aggressive toward humans. Like other unknown hominids around the world, the Mohin-goué allegedly kidnaps girls or women who enter its forest domain (between Buyo and Duékoué). A French hunter named Boisard saw one of the creatures in 1932, while crossing the Cavally River from eastern Liberia into Côte d'Ivoire. He described the Mohin-goué walking on all fours and using a stone to crush fruit. Strangely, despite its animalistic appearance, Boisard also claimed the creature was wearing a red loincloth. No reports of the Mohin-goué have been published since the late 1930s.

Source: Charles Levallée, "Encore les pygmées." *Notes Africaines* 4 (October 1939): 46–47.

Mokala *see* **Gnéna**

Mokele-Mbembe   Short of contact with extraterrestrial life forms, nothing could shock most scientists more profoundly than discovery of a living DINOSAUR. And while most scientists deem that event impossible, accounts of giant prehistoric reptiles tramping through the rain forests of Africa have been recorded since the 18th century, with reports ongoing to the present day.

The first known reference to Mokele-mbembe ("one who stops rivers") was published by a French missionary to west-central Africa, Abbé Lievain Bonaventure Proyart, in 1776. Proyart described the discovery of clawed footprints 3 feet wide and separated by a 7-foot stride, left by a creature "which was not seen but which must have been monstrous." Famed animal collector Carl Hagenbeck was the next to address such creatures in print, in 1909. His memoirs relate conversations with respected big-game hunters who described a "huge monster, half elephant, half dragon" inhabiting the Congo jungle. One informant referred to "some kind of dinosaur, seemingly akin to brontosaurus" (now *Apatosaurus*). In 1913, Capt. Freiherr von Stein zu Lausnitz was dispatched to survey Cameroon, emerging from the jungle with native reports of the river-dwelling Mokele-mbembe. Von Stein explained:

The animal is said to be of a brownish-gray color with a smooth skin, its size approximately that of an elephant, at least that of a

Africa's mokele-mbembe allegedly resembles a long-necked dinosaur (*William Rebsamen*).

hippopotamus. It is said to have a long and very flexible neck.... A few spoke about a long muscular tail like that of an ALLIGATOR. Canoes coming near it are said to be doomed; the animal is said to attack vessels and to kill the crews but without eating the bodies.

Six years later, on 23 December 1919, Capt. Leicester Stevens told British reporters that he was embarking for Africa to hunt the brontosaur at a location that remained "one of my secrets." Nothing came of the effort, despite its fanfare of publicity, but encounters of the prehistoric kind continued. In 1932, IVAN SANDERSON and GERALD RUSSELL were canoeing on the Mainyu River, in Cameroon, when they had a frightening experience:

When we were about in the middle of the mile-and-a-half-long winding gorge, the most terrible noise I have heard, short of an on-coming earthquake or the explosion of an aerial-torpedo at close range, suddenly burst from one of the big caves to my right.... Gerald tried to about-face in the strong swirling current, putting himself broadside to the current. I started to paddle like mad but was swept close to the entrance of the cave from which the noise had come. Thus, both Gerald and I were opposite its mouth; just then came another gargantuan gurgling roar and something enormous rose out of the water, turned it to sherry-colored foam and then, again roaring, plunged below. This "thing" was shiny black and was the *head* of something, shaped like a seal but flattened from above and below. It was about the size of a full-grown hippopotamus — this head, I mean.

Three years after that incident, witness Firman Mosomele saw a Mokele-mbembe with a neck 6–8 feet long, idling in the Likouala-aux-Herbes River near Epéna, Republic of Congo. In 1938, German explorer Leo von Boxberger collected more native tales of Mokele-mbembe, but his notes were lost in an attack by a hostile tribe. A group of PYGMIES allegedly trapped and killed a Mokele-mbembe at Lac Telé (Republic of Congo) in the late 1950s, afterward devouring its flesh, but everyone partaking of the meal reportedly died. A decade later, Congolese hunter Nicolas Mondongo saw a 30-foot specimen along the Likouala-aux-Herbes, between Bandéko and Mokengui.

Numerous cryptozoologists have tracked Mokele-mbembe through the Congo basin's forbidding swamps and jungles. JAMES POWELL made his first expedition in 1979, returning in early 1980 with ROY MACKAL. Mackal, in turn, came back in November 1981 with MARCELLIN AGNAGNA and J. RICHARD GREENWELL, representing the INTERNATIONAL SOCIETY OF CRYPTOZOOLOGY. Between those expeditions, in October 1981, HERMAN REGUSTERS and his wife claimed a sighting at Lake Telé. Though armed with a camera and tape recorder, they produced no concrete evidence. The audio recording failed to match the sounds of any known Congolese animal, but their photographs were overexposed and essentially worthless. Marcellin Agnagna had similar bad luck on 1 May 1983, while trying to film a Mokele-mbembe near Lac Telé: his movie camera was incorrectly set, and thus the film was ruined. WILLIAM GIBBONS made two visits to the Congo, in 1986 and 1992, but came back empty-handed. Journalist Rory Nugent claimed a sighting at Lake Telé in 1992, but the photos he published the following year were too blurry to substantiate his tale. The same was true of a 15-second videotape, shot by Japanese photographers flying over Lac Telé in September 1992. British researchers Adam Davies and Andy Sanderson led two Mokele-mbembe expeditions, in August 1998 and November 2000, without meeting the creatures. The most recent sighting to date, in February 2000, was reported by a village security officer from the Boumba River, near Molounda, Cameroon.

Inevitably, Mokele-mbembe has been the subject of at least one highly-publicized HOAX. When a supposed film of Mokele-mbembe aired on the television program *That's Incredible!* (1980–84), Roy Mackal investigated the claim and determined that the film had been made with a balsa-wood model "strapped to the shoulders of a very strong swimmer."

While confusion surrounds a number of large, reptilian cryptids reported from Africa — including the AMALI, CHIPEKWE, N'YAMALA and others — most descriptions of Mokele-mbembe resemble sauropod dinosaurs, herbivorous quadrupeds of the Mesozoic Era, instantly recognized by their long necks and tails. They ranged in length from 30 feet to more than 100 feet (the vast *Seismosaurus*, discovered in 1986), and most reached lengths of 50 feet or more. All are presumed to have died out by the end of the Cretaceous Period, some 65 million years ago. Alternate Mokele-mbembe suspects include the NDENDEKI, the giant TURTLE reported from Lake Telé, along with unknown species of giant IGUANAS (Family *Iguanidae*) or MONITOR LIZARDS (Family *Varanidae*). Skeptics insist that alleged Mokele-mbembe witnesses have simply exaggerated descriptions of such known animals as CROCODILES, elephants, and hippopotamuses.

Pygmy hunters reportedly killed a Mokele-mbembe at Lac Telé in the 1950s (*William Rebsamen*).

Sources: Dash, "Dinosaur caught on film?"; Davies, "I thought I saw a sauropod"; Heuvelmans, *Les Derniers Dragons d'Afrique*; Heuvelmans, *On the Track of Unknown Animals*; Sanderson, *More "Things"*; Shuker, "How dead are the dinosaurs?"; Shuker, *In Search of Prehistoric Survivors*.

Molonglo River, Australia

In 1886, a group of horsemen saw a BUNYIP as they were crossing the Molonglo River, south of Lake George, in New South Wales. They described the animal as "whitish in colour and about the size of a large dog; its face was like the face of a child." Despite that human resemblance, they panicked and drove the creature away with a volley of stones.

Source: Smith, *Bunyips & Bigfoots*.

Momo

Momo (short for "Missouri Monster") was an unknown HOMINID or NORTH AMERICAN APE reported from the neighborhood of Louisiana, Missouri (Pike County) during 1971–72. The first sighting was reported in July 1971, after two picnickers were frightened by a creature "half-APE and half-man," exuding a horrible odor. The beast fled after snatching a peanut butter sandwich and making a "little gurgling sound." Twelve months later, on 11 July 1972, three members of the Harrison family heard a shriek from their backyard and looked outside to find a hairy biped, smeared with blood, holding a lifeless dog beneath one arm. (A neighbor subsequently told police that his new dog had vanished.) Edgar Harrison scoured the nearby woods and found large, humanoid footprints atop Marzolf Hill. Momo sightings multiplied over the next two weeks, including a report from Cuivre River State Park. More tracks were found, but only one was submitted for scientific study: Lawrence Curtis, director of the Oklahoma City Zoo, deemed it a HOAX. Reports ceased thereafter, but memories of Momo were still vivid in April 2001, when J. RICHARD GREENWELL led members of the INTERNATIONAL SOCIETY OF CRYPTOZOOLOGY to interview local witnesses. They found a town divided over Momo's authenticity, while unknown thieves stole some of their equipment from a motel room. (It was returned, anonymously, after the police interrogated several local "characters.")

Sources: Baumann, *Monsters of North America*; Clark and Pear, *Strange & Unexplained Phenomena*; Coleman, *Mysterious America*; Coleman and Huyghe, *The Field Guide to Bigfoot, Yeti, and Other Mystery Primates Worldwide*; Brandy Warren, "Momo mystery rears its head once more in Louisiana, Mo." *Everyday Magazine* (2 May 2001).

Mongolian Death Worm *see* Olgoï-Khorkhoï

Monitor Lizards (Giant)

Monitor lizards (Family *Varanidae*) include the largest known lizard species on Earth. The Komodo dragon (*Varanus komodoensis*) takes top honors, with a record length of 10 feet. Other species of human size or larger include the crocodile monitor (*V. salvadori*), at 9 feet; the perentie (*V. giganteus*), at 8 feet 6 inches; the lace lizard (*V. varius*) and water monitor (*V. salvator*), both reaching 7 feet; Gould's monitor (*V. gouldii*) and Rosenberg's monitor (*V. rosenbergi*), at 6 feet 6 inches; the Bengal monitor (*V. bengalensis*), Gray's monitor (*V. olivaceous*) and Nile monitor (*V. niloticus*), all reaching 6 feet.

Those recognized lizards are impressive enough, but reports of much larger reptiles resembling giant monitors have been recorded from various parts of the world. The ARTRELLIA of Papua New Guinea allegedly grows to 26 feet, while lengths of 20–30 feet are claimed for the Australian MUNGOON-GALLI. Residents of northern India describe the BURU as a massive lizard, 11–14 feet long and boasting a 3-foot neck, while 20-foot monitors are reported from the Sundarbans (tidal forests at the mouths of the Ganges, in

India and Bangladesh). Africa's largest known lizard, the savanna monitor (*V. exanthematicus*), does not officially exceed 5 feet in length, yet a big-game hunter allegedly saw a lizard 10–12 feet long in the 1930s, near Ethiopia's border with Sudan. Skeptics maintain that Old World witnesses reporting giant monitors have merely glimpsed known species and exaggerated their proportions out of fear, or as a HOAX. It matters not that one encounter with the Mungoon-Galli was recorded by a herpetologist, and most involve hunters or natives well acquainted with the forms of local wildlife. At least those regions are inhabited by species known to walk the Earth. But what are we to make of giant lizard sightings in locations where no monitors should be?

In fact, reports of lizards rivaling (and frequently exceeding) the Komodo dragon's length have been recorded throughout Europe and the New World since the early 19th century. Those incidents include the following:

1810s— Early settlers in Ohio described a species of pink lizards 3–8 feet long infesting "Catlick Creek Valley," later identified by MARK HALL as Scippo Creek (Pickaway County). Some were said to boast horns like a cow's on their heads. A drought killed off the animals in 1820.

Late 19th century— Two boys fishing in a creek near Crosswicks, Ohio (Warren County) were attacked by a large "SNAKE with legs" that grabbed one youth and dragged him toward a nearby hollow tree. Adult bystanders saved the child, but the reptile slid into its hideout. Later, when a mob of 60 men returned and started cutting down the tree, the lizard emerged and ran away on its hind legs (a trait common to various monitors). Witnesses described the beast as 30–40 feet long, and 12 feet tall when standing erect. Its head was 16 inches wide, equipped with a long forked tongue like the Komodo dragon's. Its sturdy legs were 4 feet long, with 12-inch clawed feet. The lizard's scaly hide was black and white, with large yellow spots.

Late 1890s— A lizard "several yards long" was reported prowling around Ossum, France, where local folklore includes varied tales of large reptiles.

May 1935— Colorado native Myrtle Snow, three years old at the time, later claimed to have seen five "baby DINOSAURS" prowling near Pagosa Springs. Several months later, a farmer shot one of the reptiles. According to Snow, it was "about seven feet tall, was gray, had a head like a snake, short front legs with claws that resembled chicken feet, large stout back legs and a long tail." Snow further claimed to have seen a green specimen in 1937, lurking in a local cave, and later still (October 1978) she glimpsed another in the same vicinity.

August 1935— Hikers saw an 8-foot, green-and-yellow "DRAGON" in a forest near Monterose, Italy (north of Rome).

May 1939— Some 40 years after its last appearance, a giant lizard frightened berry pickers at Ossum, France.

July 1969— A resident of Forli, Italy claimed that he was chased by a 15-foot lizard with stout legs and "searing hot" breath.

1972— A prospector from Caracas, Venezuela reported sightings of a huge lizard resembling a Komodo dragon in the Galeras de El Pao region, sprawling over Cojedes and Guárico States.

June 1975— A farmer at Goro, Italy informed police of his encounter a 10-foot reptile he called "a snake with legs," whose body was "as thick as a dog." Officers found strange tracks at the scene, but did not see the creature.

July 1975— Several witnesses in Trimble County, Kentucky reported a 15-foot lizard prowling along Canip Creek. It resembled the earlier giant from Crosswicks, Ohio, including its red forked tongue and a black-and-white skin with "quarter-sized orange speckles over it." When startled, some observers claimed, the reptile rose and ran bipedally.

While skeptics dismiss all such sightings as hoaxes or exaggerated reports of known species (including escaped or abandoned monitors and IGUANAS in modern times), cryptozoologists examine other possibilities. Mark Hall suggests that the Scippo Creek "lizards" may, in fact, have been giant SALAMANDERS, perhaps relict specimens of *Matthewichnus caudifer* (known from Carboniferous fossil beds in Tennessee, presumed extinct for some 300 million years). Others note that a true giant monitor, *Meglania prisca*, walked the Earth as recently as one million years ago, reaching lengths up to 26 feet. Thus far, however, its fossils are known only from Australia.

Sources: Adrian Conan Doyle, *Heaven Has Claws*. London: John Murray, 1952; Arment, "Dinos in the U.S.A."; Bord and Bord, *Unexplained Mysteries of the 20th Century*; Mark Hall, *Natural Wonders*; Heuvelmans, *Les Derniers Dragons d'Afrique*; Silvano Lorenzoni, "More on extant dinosaurs." *Pursuit* 47 (Summer 1979): 105–109.

Monitor Lizards (Mislocated)

At least 46 species of monitor lizards (Family *Varanidae*) are presently known to science (some published reports claim "about 60"). Their normal range includes the Old World tropics, from Africa through southern Asia, to Indonesia, Australia, Papua New Guinea and the Philippines. None normally occur in Europe or the western hemisphere, but that has not prevented various species from appearing in many unexpected places. Those sightings (and captures) are typically explained in terms of escaped or abandoned pets, but authorities in Florida admit that breeding colonies of monitors exist within their state, and the same may well be true for other warm regions. Recent reports of monitors at large in North America include (but are not limited to) the following:

1960–70— Residents of British Columbia's Texada and Vancouver Islands reported multiple sightings of unknown 12-inch lizards that rose and ran on their hind legs when frightened (a trait common in monitors but unknown to recognized Canadian lizards).

1979— A Nile monitor (*Varanus niloticus*) was captured outside South Bay, Florida.

1981— Four boys in New Kensington, Pennsylvania pulled a "baby DINOSAUR" from a storm drain, then lost it when it squealed and ran away on its hind legs. They described the reptile as 2–3 feet tall when running erect, green in color, with a long tail. Subsequent sketches showed a crest atop its head, not found in monitors. Assuming that the crest was not invented, researcher Chad Arment suggests that the lizard may have been a green basilisk (*Basiliscus plumifrons*) imported from Central America as an exotic pet.

20 June 1981— A Nile monitor 6 feet 5 inches long was caught on a golf course at Royal Palm Beach, Florida.

Most monitor lizards found in the U.S. are probably escaped pets.

12 July 1981— A 5-foot Nile monitor weighing 30 pounds appeared at a private residence in Hypoluxo, Florida. Animal control officers captured it three days later.

14 July 1981— A resident of North Miami, Florida found a 5-foot Nile monitor inside the engine compartment of his car.

1982— Colorado residents filed the first of many reports describing large lizards dubbed RIVER DINOSAURS. Consistent descriptions portray large, long-necked reptiles with conical snouts, often seen running on their hind legs.

25 February 1984— A Nile monitor 6 feet long was shot at a pond in Findlay, Ohio.

1990— State authorities received their first report of a Nile monitor at large near Cape Coral, Florida.

July 1998— Two youths in Pueblo, Colorado reported sighting a lizard 3–4 feet long, green with black markings on its back and a yellow-orange underside. The reptile ran on its hind legs, holding its tail well off the ground. The boys allegedly snapped several photos of the creature in flight, but they were indistinct and may suggest a HOAX. (Another photo, showing 3-toed, 3-inch tracks could likewise be a fake.) Chad Arment contacted one of the witnesses in January 2000, seeking further evidence. Four months later, he received a photo of the young man posing with a rifle and a creature that appears to be an unknown, long-necked lizard 3–4 feet long. Suspecting that the beast might be a rubber model, Arment asked the hunter to try catching one of the lizards alive. The rest is silence.

August 2001— Sheriff's deputies searched in vain for a 5-foot monitor reported prowling the woods around Lake Lemon, in Brown County, Indiana. Various witnesses saw the reptile, but it eluded all capture attempts.

21 May 2003— A 4-foot Gould's monitor (*V. gouldii*) was sighted on a dairy farm in Marin County, California. Reptile rescue worker captured the lizard in early July, telling reporters, "I've had monitor calls from Marin to Sonoma (Counties). Often, you get them in the neighborhoods."

June-September 2003— Multiple witnesses reported sightings of a 9-foot lizard roaming the streets of Rabieh, a suburb of Beirut, Lebanon. Police dismissed the early reports, but changed their minds after the reptile dug up and partially devoured the carcasses of three horses. In the wake of that incident, authorities blamed an unnamed German suspect for illegally importing a Komodo dragon and releasing it before he left the country. The lizard was not captured.

July 2003— Biologists set traps for Nile monitors around Cape Coral, Florida, reporting that the Gulf Coast population of that species "has possibly reached the thousands." A total of 145 sightings had been recorded at Cape Coral alone, since the first report in 1990. A specimen 4 feet 5 inches long "and nowhere near full-grown" was trapped in September 2003. A 6.5-foot specimen was seen near the same location, but it eluded pursuers.

18 July 2003— Animal control officers caught a 3-foot savanna monitor (*V. exanthematicus*) in a residential neighborhood of Athens, Georgia.

Sources: Arment, "Bipedal lizards in North America"; Arment, "Dinos in North America"; Colette Bancroft, "Enter the dragons." *St. Petersburg* (FL) *Times* (26 September 2003); Bord and Bord, *Unexplained Mysteries of the 20th Century*; Coleman, *Mysterious America*; Alisa DeMao, "Big lizard pulls big surprise." *Savannah* (GA) *Morning News* (19 July 2003); "5-foot lizard eludes would-be captors in Brown County." *Indianapolis Star* (25 August 2001); "Fla. scientists try to trap giant lizards." *Washington Post* (18 July 2003); Carol Hunter, "N. Marin farmer shocked by 4-foot lizard." *Marin* (CA) *Independent Journal* (10 July 2003); "Komodo

caper, roo ruse." *Fortean Times* 178 (January 2004): 9; Karl Shuker, "Alien zoo." *Fortean Times* 166 (February 2003): 16; Kurt Van der Dussen, "Monitor lizard spotted near lake." *Bloomington* (IN) *Herald Times* (25 August 2001).

Monk Seal (Caribbean)

Modern science recognizes two living species of monk seals (Family *Monachinae*), the Mediterranean (*Monachus monachus*) and the Hawaiian (*M. schauinsland*). Christopher Columbus was first to meet the Caribbean species (*M. tropicalis*), when he ordered his crewmen to butcher eight of the "sea WOLVES" for meat in 1494, on the coast of Santo Domingo. The slaughter continued from that point onward, until the species was officially declared extinct in 1952. Five major scientific surveys have been carried out in the Caribbean since 1950, without finding any solid evidence of monk seal survival, but reported sightings persist to the present day. In 1997, a survey of 93 Haitian and Jamaican fishermen revealed that 16 claimed one or more monk seal sightings since 1995. Skeptics insist that the witnesses are mistaken, confused by sightings of other pinniped species.

Source: I.L. Boyd and M.P. Stanfield, "Circumstantial evidence for the presence of monk seals in the West Indies." *Oryx* 32 (1998): 310–316.

Monkey Man (India)

In April 2001, residents of Ghaziabad, India swamped police with calls reporting a wild APE or HOMINID roaming at large in the city. Sightings of the creature, dubbed Monkey Man by the press, soon escalated to include random attacks on people, either on the streets or in their homes. As the reports spread to encompass other towns and villages, police initially blamed "a man masquerading as a giant MONKEY." When sightings started in New Delhi, on 12 May, authorities declared that any citizen was free to shoot the Monkey Man on sight. The next day, 15 New Delhi residents were mauled within a 5-hour period, suffering injuries that ranged from bruises and scratches to deep "monkey bites." Rural police officials confidently told the *Hindustan Times* that Monkey Man was either "an extra-terrestrial or a remote-controlled robot." On 16 May, with two persons dead from injuries suffered while fleeing the creature, officers releases a sketch of Monkey Man, depicting a fierce-looking ape with long claws on its hands. A second sketch only made matters worse, planting a gold metallic helmet on the monster's head.

With such pronouncements from police in print, it came as no surprise that subsequent Monkey Man sightings included "an element of fantasy." On 26 May, authorities in Uttar Pradesh an-

Police sketches of India's Monkey Man, which sparked widespread panic in 2001.

nounced that they were charging "Hanuman, also known as the Monkey-Man and the Monkey Monster" with complicity in two accidental deaths. A reward of 75,000 rupees ($1,000) was offered to anyone who caught "Hanuman" on videotape, while a special police "flying squad" prepared to hunt the man-beast. Civilian theories on Monkey Man's identity covered the full range from an avatar of Hindu gods to an Indian version of BIGFOOT. Editors of the *New Statesman* suspected a cyborg or "bio-construct," advising worried readers that "You could cancel out its gymnastic abilities by throwing a pail of water on the motherboard on its chest, hidden beneath a layer of fake monkey fur." Russia's *Pravda* took the prize for fanciful reporting on 11 June, with a story headlined: "Monkey-Man Attacks Russian Airliner!" One week later, a "special crack team" of police in New Delhi reported that Monkey Man had never existed. The whole episode, they opined, was a case of mass hysteria that left 5 persons dead and another 75 injured.

That report notwithstanding, Monkey Man sightings resumed in late August 2001, with 10 attacks reported from Rupas, near Patna. A 6-month hiatus was broken in February 2002, as police hunted a simian prowler in the slums of Khanpur. July 2002 brought the panic back to New Delhi, where "a monkey-like machine" that "jumps and sparkles red and blue lights" attacked victims sleeping in the open. As in the case of the MUHNOCHWA, some authorities believed was "handled by anti-social elements to terrorize people." A 6-year-old boy plunged to his death from a roof, while fleeing Monkey Man on 23 July, and others sustained lesser injuries. Investigators ruled that most such injuries were accidental, suffered in flight from a mythical menace.

Sources: Chetna Banerjee, "Sucked into the madding crowd!" *The Tribune* (22 September 2003); John Chalmers, "Vigilantes scour Indian capital for monkey business." Reuters (18 May 2001); "Child dies as 'monkey man' sparks panic." *Gulf Daily7 News* (24 July 2002); "Indian police release pictures of Monkey man killer." *Ananova* (16 May 2001); Lalit Kumar, "DIG says 'shoot at monkeyman' as panic spreads." Times of India (13 May 2001); "Man, myth or monkey?" *Fortean Times* 148 (August 2001): 8–9; "Monkey madness." *Fortean Times* 149 (September 2001): 7; "Monkey-man attacks Russian airliner." *Pravda* (11 June 2002); "Monkey man scare grips eastern India." Agence France-Presse (21 July 2002); "'Monkey Man' Terrorises Indian Village." Agence France-Presse (24 July 2002); "Panic over monkey man in Ghaziabad." *Hindustan Times* (3 May 2001); "Police suspect 'monkey man' is alien or remote-controlled robot." *Ananova* (15 May 2001); Meghdoot Sharon, "Monkeyman creates scare in Khanpur." *Indian Express* (22 February 2002).

Monkey-Man (New Jersey)

Though unrelated to India's elusive cryptid (or mass hallucination) of the same name, New Jersey's Monkey-man allegedly frightened children at several Hoboken schools in the early 1980s. Police searched in vain for the hairy biped.

Source: "'Weird NJ' book flying off the shelves." Associated Press (26 January 2004).

Monkeys (British)

APES and monkeys are not native to the British Isles, but that scientific "fact" does not prevent sightings of unexplained primates in England. One such report came from St. David's, Pembroke, Wales in October 2002, when witnesses reported a monkey the size of a small dog "loping across fields at night with its tail standing up." Traps baited with bananas failed to snare the simian prowler, but it soon fled the district for parts unknown. Nine months later, in Norfolk, two "rogue monkeys" were reported at large, romping through gardens and screeching in a Northwold churchyard. Based upon descriptions

from eyewitnesses, Banham Zoo spokesman Gary Batters tagged the visitors as South American capuchins (*Cebus* sp.). As Batters explained to the press, "There is no reason why capuchins couldn't be sighted in Norfolk. Lots of people keep wild animals and they could escape or be deliberately released." Another report, from the West Norfolk Council, claimed that 12 marmosets had "gone missing" in Norwich, but no further details were provided. At press time for this volume, the elusive primates had not been apprehended or identified.

Sources: "Banana trap set for monkey on the loose." *The Western Mail* (19 October 2002); Isabel Cockayne, "The monkey puzzle spree." *Norfolk Eastern Daily Press* (29 August 2003); "Some simian stories." *Fortean Times* 168 (April 2003): 17; "Village's monkey puzzle." *Norfolk Eastern Daily Press* (28 August 2003).

Monkeys (U.S.)

Despite centuries of eyewitness reports describing various BABOONS, DEVIL MONKEYS, NORTH AMERICAN APES and other unclassified primates at large in the U.S., science recognizes no indigenous species of monkey or APE. It comes as no surprise, however, that reports continue to the present day. Only Florida admits to monkeys thriving in its swamps and forests, acknowledging that three primate species have taken root in breeding colonies. Asian rhesus monkeys (*Macaca mulatta*) were released deliberately near Silver Springs, in 1930, and today they are established in at least five counties, including Brevard, Broward, Lake, Marion and Monroe. Tourists are blamed for releasing vervet monkeys (*Chlorocebus aethiops*) in Broward County during the 1950s, thereby spawning two known colonies of "well over 120 animals" each. Squirrel monkeys (*Saimiri sciureus*) surfaced in the 1960s, when various small zoos and roadside tourist traps went out of business, and today they colonize at least six Florida counties, including Brevard, Broward, Collier, Dade, Marion and Polk. Statewide, the status of naturalized primate species is officially unknown, but no natural barriers prevent monkeys from expanding their range. Apopka, northwest of Orlando in Orange County, reported sightings of 3-foot-tall monkeys in 2000–01, and a rhesus monkey was captured alive at nearby Wekiwa Springs State Park in 2000.

While Florida sets an example for candor concerning naturalized species, it is not the only U.S. venue with exotic primates at large. In 1995, police in Gentry, Arkansas shot and killed a monkey of undetermined species after it panicked children on the playground of the Gentry Elementary School. Eight years later,

Exotic monkeys have established breeding colonies in at least eight Florida counties.

in July 2003, residents of Maynard, Massachusetts reported multiple sightings of a small monkey at large in their town. Scientists at Southborough's New England Regional Primate Center admitted that one of their squirrel monkeys had escaped on 11 July, but they insisted that the Maynard specimen "can't possibly be" their furry fugitive. In fact, they told reporters, "It's hard to know exactly how many monkeys are loose in central Massachusetts at any given time." Clearly, the same thing could be said for nearly any state in the U.S.

Sources: Alicia Caldwell, "Monkey see?" *Orlando* (FL) *Sentinel* (16 November 2003); Jules Crittenden, "Monkey business in Maynard." *Boston Herald* (1 August 2003); Brian Eastwood, "Maynard going bananas?" *Boston Herald* (31 July 2003); Jeff LeMaster, "Prowling primate spotted in Decatur." *Benton County* (AR) *Daily Record* (1 October 2003); Florida's Exotic Wildlife, *http://wld.fwc.state.fl.us/critters/exotics/exotics.asp.*

Mono Grande/Mono Rey Witnesses describe the Mono Grande ("big MONKEY) or Mono Rey ("king monkey") as a large arboreal primate, inhabiting a jungle range that sprawls over Venezuela, Colombia, Ecuador, Peru and Bolivia. It reportedly stands 5–6 feet tall, has no tail, and is sometimes aggressive toward humans, lobbing stones and wielding sticks as weapons. As with other unclassified primates and HOMINIDS worldwide, folktales depict the Mono Grande mating with humans. Some researchers equate the Mono Grande with DE LOYS'S APE, while others dismiss the latter cryptid as a HOAX. Archaeologist Pino Turolla allegedly sighted two large APES in the Venezuelan jungle, during 1968. Three decades later, British author Simon Chapman pursued the creature in vain. While he collected stories of a specimen displayed alive in Bolivia, and a skin obtained by unknown foreigners for DNA analysis, Chapman found no hard evidence to buttress those reports. He concluded that some Mono Grande sightings may involve spectacled bears (*Tremarctos ornatus*).

Sources: Chapman, *The Monster of the Madidi*; Heuvelmans, *On the Track of Unknown Animals*; Michael Shoemaker, "The mystery of the Mono Grande." *Strange Magazine* 7 (April 1991): 2–5, 56–60.

Monongahela sea serpent On 13 January 1852, crewmen aboard the whaling ship *Monongahela* alleged met a SEA SERPENT near the Marquesas Islands in French Polynesia (specifically, at 3° 10' south latitude and 131° 50' west longitude). Captain Seabury, commanding the vessel, urged his reluctant harpooners to pursue the creature as proof that such monsters existed. After a fearful chase, the beast was reportedly harpooned, whereupon a 16-hour struggle ensued, ending with the animal floating dead on the surface. As described by Captain Seabury:

> It was a male; the length 103 feet 7 inches; 19 feet 1 inch around the neck; 24 feet 6 inches around the shoulders; and the largest part of the body, which appeared to be somewhat distended, 49 feet 4 inches.

Seabury's crew allegedly butchered the serpent, finding that its skin concealed a 4-inch-thick layer of blubber, while its "oil was clear as water, and burnt nearly as fast as turpentine." As for the rest, he wrote:

> The heart I was enabled to preserve in liquor, and one of the eyes, but the head, notwithstanding it is cool, begins to emit an offensive odour; but I am so near the coast now that I shall hold on to it as it is; unless it is likely to breed a distemper.

No more was ever heard of the remarkable incident, and BERNARD HEUVELMANS deemed it "by far the greatest HOAX" en-

countered during his epic study of sea serpents. Still, he did confirm the *Monongahela*'s existence, and that of Captain Seabury, through records at New Bedford, Massachusetts. Strangely, no record of the vessel's fate remains, aside from a brief account published in 1959, claiming that the *Monongahela* had been found on the shore of Umak Island, in the Aleutians.

Sources: Frank Edwards, *Stranger Than Science.* New York: Ace Books, 1959; Heuvelmans, *In the Wake of the Sea Serpents*; Shuker, "Bring me the head of the sea serpent!"

Monster of Los Muermos On 1 July 2003, a large GLOBSTER washed ashore at Los Muermos, on the southern coast of Chile. The object, initially seen by sailors of the Chilean navy while they were examining the nearby carcass of a humpback whale (*Megaptera novaeangliae*), was 39 feet wide, weighed 13 tons, and defied easy classification. Elsa Cabrera, director of Santiago's Centre for Cetacean Conservation, told reporters, "We'd never before seen such a strange specimen. We don't know if it might be a giant squid that is missing some of its parts or maybe it's a new species." A day later, Cabrera suggested the creature might be a giant OCTOPUS, like the one washed ashore near St. Augustine, Florida in 1896. "We didn't see many tentacles, but from looking at pictures and descriptions of the 1896 animal and this one, the skin color and shape seem to match—a bit gray with bits of pink. We're all very impressed by its size, but it's going to take further study to know for certain what it is." Sergio Letelier, a researcher at Santiago's Museum of Natural History, analyzed samples of the flesh and weighed in with a contrary opinion on 7 July, telling the press: "It's not an octopus. I couldn't tell

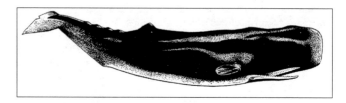

In 2003 scientists identified the Monster of Los Muermos as a decomposed sperm whale.

you what it is but it's not an octopus." Three days later, Letelier announced that the carcass belonged to a sperm whale (*Physeter macrocephalus*). "It has not been necessary to do DNA analysis in order to obtain identification," he said. "It was enough to find the dermal glands that belong only to this group."

Sources: "Chilean 'sea monster' to be sent to France." *Ananova* (3 July 2003); "Chilean experts say beached 'blob' a sperm whale." Reuters (11 July 2003); "Giant blob baffles marine scientists." BBC News (2 July 2003); "It's not an octopus, so what is 'the blob'?" ABC News (8 July 2003); Jeordan Legon, "Chilean scientists work to ID mysterious sea creature." CNN (2 July 2003); "The lesson of the 'Monster of Los Muermos.'" *Tierramerica* (8 August 2003); Mystery blob probe." *The Scientist* (9 July 2003); Jane Simon, "Beach blob baffles." *The Mirror* (4 July 2003).

Monster of Martin Mere In spring 2002, residents of Lancashire, England reported that a LAKE MONSTER the size of a compact car was attacking swans in Martin Mere, near Ormskirk. All of the BIRDS survived, but the assaults proved so frightening that swans temporarily deserted the lake. Jonathan Downes, of the Exeter-based Fortean Society, led a 4-man expedition to the lake, where they glimpsed "a very big FISH" on 25 July 2002. Further research disclosed that Francis Buckland, a local member of 19th-century Britain's Acclimatisation Society, allegedly released a wels CATFISH (*Siluris glanis*) into Martin Mere as part of the society's larger attempt to populate the British Isles with exotic species. Members of the European species may reach lengths of 15 feet 6 inches in the wild. "It is a lovely idea," Downes told reporters, "that the fish in Martin Mere is the same one that was introduced by Francis Buckland all those years ago. This is certainly possible, as they grow very slowly, and some can live for hundreds of years." No further efforts to identify or catch the lake's resident cryptid have been announced.

Sources: "Hunters on trail of mere monster." *Ananova.* (26 July 2002); Paul Matthews, "City's strange phenomena team are to go in search of the 'Monster of the Mere.'" *Exeter Express & Echo* (24 July 2002); "Monster hunters spot giant fish." BBC News (28 July 2002).

Monster of Pindray   This ALIEN BIG CAT was reported from the neighborhood of Pindray, in the Vienne Département of France, during the 1970s. Local searches failed to snare the animal, and it soon vanished from the area.

Source: Brodu and Meurger, *Les Félins-Mystère.*

Monster of the M25 *see* **Beast of Barnet**

Moolgewanke *see* **Bunyip**

Mooloolaba sea serpent   In November 1941, two Australian fishermen sighted a supposed SEA SERPENT offshore from Mooloolaba, Queensland (north of Brisbane). They described the animal as 60 feet long, noting that "Its body was marked with red and it had a red beard." Based on that description, naturalist Charles Barrett identified the creature as an oarfish (*Regalecus glesne*), although the record length for that species is roughly one-third the size described. Researcher Malcolm Smith believes the witnesses saw an unusually large oarfish and then exaggerated its size. BERNARD HEUVELMANS, meanwhile, was torn between the notion of a giant oarfish and a sighting of his hypothetical "mer-horse."

Sources: Heuvelmans, *In the Wake of the Sea Serpents*; Smith, *Bunyips & Bigfoots.*

Moore Reservoir, New Hampshire   Moore Reservoir (also called Moore Lake) is the fourth-largest body of water in Rhode Island, with a surface area of 3,500 acres. It lies near Littleton, below Moore Dam. On 20 May 1968, witnesses Richard Hansen, his wife, and companion Michael Stinchfield reported a luminous LAKE MONSTER floating in the reservoir, described as resembling a large ALLIGATOR. Strangely, some accounts of the incident report it as a UFO sighting.

Sources: Garner, *Monster! Monster!*; Richard Wolkomir, "The glowing 'thing' in Moore Lake." *Fate* 21 (November 1968): 32–36.

Moose (New Zealand)   Long rumored to exist in the lush tropical forests of New Zealand's South Island, moose are not currently recognized as living residents of the island nation (which lists two species of bats as its only native mammals). Three known subspecies of moose (*Alces alces*) are the Alaskan (*A. alces gigas*), the Canadian/North American (*A. alces americanus*) and the European (*A. alces machlis*). None naturally occur in the southern hemisphere, to the best of modern scientific knowledge, but New Zealand moose trackers explain the reported presence of a small breeding population by noting that hundreds of alien species were

DNA evidence indicates that naturalized moose survive in New Zealand.

imported by ill-conceived "acclimitization societies" around the turn of the last century, including some moose transported from Saskatchewan in 1909.

But have they survived?

Martin Boyce, professor of biology at the University of Alberta, believes the last transplanted moose died out in the New Zealand tropics in the 1950s. Still, he admits, "There have always been these rumors about moose down there. The moose of South Island are one of those fables that's been around for years." New Zealand biologist Ken Tustin disagrees and has devoted three decades to seeking what may be — if it still exists — the nation's largest mammal. Operating from Fiordland, using cameras triggered by motion and heat sensors, Tustin has obtained one grainy snapshot of a large creature standing beside two normal-sized deer, but he admits the photographic evidence is inconclusive.

Not so, Tustin insists, the evidence recovered in 2001 from Fiordland National Park, in the South Island's far-southwest corner. There, a clump of unfamiliar-looking hair was found by hunters and submitted for DNA testing to a government laboratory, with gratifying results. In July 2001 Tustin told reporters that the testing had removed all doubt, proving the hairs belonged to a moose and had come a living specimen, not a preserved trophy mount. "I was absolutely delighted," Tustin said. "I've been ridiculed [and] accused of falling for a HOAX, but I assure you it's no hoax."

Still, the moose itself remains elusive. "I've never actually clapped eyes on one," Tustin said. "Not yet, anyway. But I've always been sure they were out there. We still haven't caught a moose, but we're hopeful."

It promises to be no easy task, however. Even skeptic Martin Boyce notes that the area in question consists of "pretty dense bush.... [I]t's very wild with almost no roads and dense rain forest vegetation. It'd be very easy to hide a herd of moose in there." That said, Boyce maintains that there are "likely no more than a couple of dozen moose in the entire country."

New Zealand preservationists have urged the country's Department of Conservation to ban hunting of moose, should they exist, but others view the effort as redundant, since any *Alces* survivors have already dodged sportsmen for over half a century. As Ken Tustin observes, "The moose seem to be very capable of taking care of themselves."

Source: Chris Wattie. "New Zealander tracks down his country's version of Bigfoot." *National Post* (Toronto), 13 July 2001.

Moosehead Lake, Maine

Cryptozoologists LOREN COLEMAN and JOHN KIRK include this large lake (in Piscataquis County) on published lists of supposed LAKE MONSTER habitats, but they provide no dates or details of sightings.

Sources: Coleman, *Mysterious America*; Kirk, *In the Domain of the Lake Monsters*.

Morag

Morag is the supposed LAKE MONSTER of Loch Morar, located 70 miles southwest of Loch Ness in the Scottish Highlands. Loch Morar is smaller than Loch Ness, 14 miles long and 1.5 miles across at its widest point, but its depth plunges below 1,000 feet at a point between Meoble and Swordlands (making it Europe's deepest freshwater lake). Reported cryptid sightings at the loch date from 1887, with 34 recorded through 1981. Nearly half of those sightings (16) involved multiple witnesses. Descriptions of the creature(s) typically conform to those of NESSIE, including a neck 3–8 feet long and 1–5 dark humps visible above the water's surface. Eyewitness estimates of Morag's total length range from 8 to 40 feet, while colors run the gamut from yellowish gray to black. The most dramatic (or, at least, most violent) Morag encounter occurred on 16 August 1969, when the creature allegedly struck the stern of a speedboat driven by Duncan McDonnell and William Simpson. The impact knocked a kettle from the stove, prompting McDonnel to strike Morag with an oar, while Simpson opened fire with a rifle. The LOCH NESS INVESTIGATION BUREAU expanded its search to include Loch Morar in February 1970, with creation of the Loch Morar Survey (dissolved in the mid-1970s). Sporadic research continues at the loch. On 1 August 1996, scuba diver Cameron Turner found several large vertebrae in Loch Morar, at a depth of 60 feet, but they proved to be those of a deer. An indistinct photo of Morag exists, but its provenance is uncertain.

Sources: Coleman and Clark, *Cryptozoology A to Z*; Campbell and Solomon, *The Search for Morag*; Karl Shuker, "Menagerie of mystery." *Strange Magazine* 18 (Summer 1997): 24.

Morcegos

On one of his trips through the Brazilian jungle, sometime after his 1914 encounter with the legendary MARICOXI, explorer PERCY FAWCETT collected native tales of another unclassified HOMINID or WILDMAN known as the Morcegos ("BAT people"). Fawcett's informants described the Morcegos as nocturnal hunters who lived in earthen burrows or tunnels. Elsewhere across their range, the creatures were known as Cabelludos ("hairy people") or Tatus ("ARMADILLOS").

Source: Sanderson, *"Things."*

Morgan, Robert W. (1935–)

Ohio native Robert Morgan has spent most of his professional life in the film industry and in pursuit of unknown HOMINIDS. His interest in cryptozoology dates from 1957, when he glimpsed a creature he described as "a giant GORILLA" in Madison County, Wisconsin. Following his discharge from the U.S. Navy, Morgan pursued further research into the BIGFOOT phenomenon, and in 1974 he founded the AMERICAN ANTHROPOLOGICAL RESEARCH FOUNDATION with partner WILLIAM ERNST. Over the next quarter-century, Morgan and Ernst sponsored four American Yeti Expeditions in North America, along with 200-plus smaller field studies ranging from the Pacific Northwest to Florida and Central Asia. Morgan advocates a "no-kill" attitude toward SASQUATCH research, and he was instrumental in promoting passage of a Skamania County, Washington ordinance imposing a $10,000 fine for killing Bigfoot. In addition to numerous TV appearances and media interviews, Morgan was also the primary subject of a 1975 documentary film, *The Search for Bigfoot*. His own productions include *The Ultimate Legend Quest* (1992) and *The Bigfoot Pocket Field Manual* (1997). Morgan's 1996 audiotape, *Bigfoot: The Ultimate Adventure*, claimed to teach techniques (including meditation based on Native American rituals) that would "teach you how to come face-to-face with" Bigfoot. Morgan planned a Mongolian expedition to seek the ALMAS in 1999, but no further information on that project is presently available. His autobiography, *Soul Snatchers*, was published in 2003. At press time for this volume, Morgan still served as chief executive officer of the AARF and personally directed its American Yeti Expeditions subsidiary in search of the creatures Morgan calls Giant Forest People or FGs. His goal is stated on the AARF's Internet website:

> Morgan intends to select one specific area to personally concentrate his energies. There he will cultivate a resident FG family until they permit visitors so he can introduce other scientists to begin the acceptance without death process.

Sources: Coleman, *Bigfoot!*; Coleman and Clark, *Cryptozoology A to Z*; American Anthropological Research Foundation, http://www.true-seekers.org/.

Morgawr

Morgawr ("sea giant") is the local name applied to various SEA SERPENTS sighted off the coast of Cornwall, particularly those who visit Falmouth Bay. In 1876, one such creature was allegedly captured and killed. According to a brief report in the *West Briton* newspaper:

> The sea serpent was caught alive in Gerrans Bay. Two of our fishermen were afloat overhauling their crab-pots about 400–500 yards from shore, when they discovered the serpent coiled around their floating cork [buoy]. Upon their near approach it lifted its head and showed signs of defiance, upon which they struck it forcibly with an oar, which so far disabled it as to allow them to proceed with their work, after which they observed the serpent floating about near their boat. They pursued it, bringing it ashore yet alive for exhibition, soon after which it was killed on the rocks and most inconsiderately cast again into the sea.

The late 19th century produced two more sightings from Cornwall. On 11 October 1892, Rev, E. Highton saw a large serpentine creature swimming off the coast of Bude. Exactly one year later, witnesses watched another cryptid swimming at 25 miles per hour along Cornwall's northern coast, leaving a greasy trail on the water as seen with some pinnipeds.

Eyewitness descriptions of Cornish sea serpents are far from consistent. The creature sighted off Land's End in August 1906, by officers aboard the liner ST. ANDREW, reportedly had a head 18 feet long, with a huge mouth and teeth. A year later, some nondescript "huge sea monster" allegedly battled a lone fisherman in the Bristol Channel, making off with his oars and boat-hook. In 1926, two Falmouth fishermen netted a frightening creature while trawling three miles offshore. The beast escaped by ripping through their net, but the witnesses described it as 20 feet long, with an 8-foot tail and a "beak" 2 feet long by 6 inches wide. The animal had four scaly legs, and its broad back was covered with matted brown hair. A clump of that hair was submitted for study at the Plymouth Marine Biological Observatory, whose experts failed to identify it. Nearly a quarter-century later, in July 1949, Harold Wilkins and a friend saw "two remarkable saurians" resembling PLESIOSAURS, each 15–20 feet long, at the mouth of a creek near East Looe.

A sketch of Morgawr, after witness Sheila Bird.

Morgawr went on hiatus thereafter, until a new spate of sightings began around Falmouth in September 1975, continuing through January 1977. Most witnesses from that period agree that the creature was 15–20 feet long, with dark skin ranging from greenish-gray to black, a long neck and small head resembling a SNAKE'S, and prominent humps on its back. Some remarked on the beast's ugly face, while one claimed to have seen Morgawr eat an EEL. A rotting carcass stranded on Dungan Beach (Falmouth Bay) in February 1976 was dubbed the "Dungan DRAGON," but it proved to be a pilot whale (*Globicephala* sp.). On 5 March 1976, the *Falmouth Packet* published the first alleged photos of Morgawr, submitted by a correspondent known only as "Mary F." She claimed to have taken the pictures in February, at Trefusis Point, and went on to give her impressions of the animal:

> I'd say it was fifteen to eighteen feet long (I mean the part showing above the water). It looked like an elephant waving its trunk, but the trunk was a long neck with a small head on the end, like a snake's head. It had humps on its back which moved in a funny way. The colour was black or very dark brown, and the skin seemed to be like a sea-lion's....I did not like the way it moved when swimming.

While the photos revealed no obvious signs of fakery, and their subject resembled prior eyewitness accounts of Morgawr, they offered no hint of scale or proof of location. Appeals for Mary F. to identify herself have all proved fruitless, though she did send a second letter claiming that she sold the photo negatives to an unnamed American. Another supposed photo of Morgawr, also snapped in early 1976, was given to researcher ANTHONY SHIELS by a schoolboy known only as "Andrew."

Shiels soon came to dominate the search for Morgawr, in conjunction with three witches who tried to summon the beast via nude rituals. Shiels and his wife claimed a Morgawr sighting at Grebe Beach, in June 1976, but doubt has been cast on his role in the continuing investigation. Some critics state flatly that Shiels faked the "Mary F." photos or Morgawr, further charging that during the same period he faked sightings of the Cornish OWL-MAN. At best, his frequent references to witchcraft and magic opened the subject to further ridicule.

Morgawr sightings did not end in 1977. On 10 July 1985, four witnesses equipped with binoculars watched a large creature swimming off Portscatho. As Sheila Bird described the incident:

> [W]e were able to scrutinize the grey, slightly mottled creature closely and observe that there was either another hump at the base of its spine, or more likely that the muscular rhythms of the tail created the appearance of a hump. The tail seemed to be about as long as the body and the creature was an estimated seventeen to twenty feet in length. For several minutes we were able to observe this graceful creature, with its head held proudly as it glided swiftly and smoothly on the glassy surface of the water, illuminated in the clear evening sunlight....Suddenly the creature submerged; it did not dive, but dropped vertically like a stone without leaving a ripple, bubble or any trace of where it had been a moment before.

We watched hopefully for it to put in another appearance, but it had gone.

Another sighting was recorded on 26 July 1985, before Bird's report had been published. Fourteen years later, on 1 August 1999, museum employee John Holmes videotaped an unknown animal swimming with its neck raised above the surface of Gerrans Bay (scene of the alleged sea serpent capture in 1876). Holmes kept the tape secret until 2002, when he screened it for reporters and declared, "My pet theory is that it was a living fossil. I think that there is a group of plesiosaurs going around in the oceans of the world." The most recent reports of Morgawr were filed on 8 May 2002, when witnesses Dan Matthew and George Vinnicombe claimed separate sightings at Falmouth Bay on the same day.

Sources: Paul Berger, "Could marine creature be legendary dinosaur?" *Western Morning News* (3 July 2002); Paul Berger, "Westcountry's Nessie 'is probably a sunfish.'" *Western Morning News* (4 July 2002); Bord and Bord, *Alien Animals*; "Cornish beastie." *Fortean Times* 162 (October 2002): 7; Downes, "Whale of a time with a dragon"; Heuvelmans, *In the Wake of the Sea Serpents*; McEwan, *Mystery Animals of Britain and Ireland*; "Morgawr is back." *Fortean Times* 84 (December 1994-January 1995): 8.

Moses Lake, Washington

The first known sighting of a LAKE MONSTER from this Washington lake (in Grant County) was filed on 15 April 1982, after witness Cliff Johnson observed a large creature swimming between Marsh Island and the lake's shoreline. Johnson described the animal as reptilian, raising a head the size of a man's to peer above the water's surface. He further claimed that the beast was "far too large to be an ordinary SNAKE and was definitely not a FISH."

Source: Kirk, *In the Domain of the Lake Monsters*.

Mo-Zhyn *see* Mao-Rén

Mosqueto

Iroquois natives in New York once believed that a large reptilian LAKE MONSTER inhabited ONONDAGA LAKE (northwest of Syracuse, in Onondaga County). On at least one occasion, legends claim, the creature known as Mosqueto emerged from the lake and killed several tribesmen. No modern sightings of the creature are on file, but Onondaga Lake enjoyed a reputation for spawing smaller cryptids in the late 19th and early 20th centuries.

Sources: Coleman, *Mysterious America*; David Cusick, *Sketches of Ancient History of the Six Nations*. Lewiston, NY: The Author, 1827; *New York Times* (2 May 1882):2.

Mosvatnet, Norway

This lake, in Norway's Rogaland County, was once reportedly the home of an unidentified LAKE MONSTER. Witnesses described the creature as brown or black in color, with a head resembling a seal's and a ring of white around its neck. Sightings apparently ceased sometime in the 1920s.

Source: Skjelsvik, "Norwegian lake and sea monsters."

Mothman

Between November 1966 and November 1967, residents of western West Virginia reported multiple encounters with a bizarre winged creature that the media nicknamed Mothman. Most of the sightings occurred at Point Pleasant, where the animal appeared most often in and around an abandoned explosives dump known as the TNT Area. Descriptions of the Mothman varied, but most witnesses agreed that it stood 5–7 feet tall and was "much broader than a man," with a 10-foot wingspan and eyes that glowed red in the dark. It seemed to fly without flapping its wings, yet achieved startling speeds, several times keeping pace with cars driven at 70–100 miles per hour. Less agile on

Artist's conception of West Virginia's Mothman (*William Rebsamen*).

the ground, the creature stood erect at rest, but "waddled" when it walked. Its only sound was a shrill squeak, compared to rodents squealing or a "squeaky fan belt."

Mothman was seen at least 21 times during its 12 months of activity, by witnesses in West Virginia and neighboring Ohio. (Author JOHN KEEL claimed 26 sightings, including one each from Kentucky and Mississippi, but those cases deviated from the "norm" by describing giant BIRDS with little or no resemblance to Mothman.) Twelve of the 21 sightings involved multiple witnesses, and one of those described two Mothmen seen together. Sightings occurred both in daylight and at night. The last reported incident, in November 1967, came barely a month before Point Pleasant's Silver Bridge collapsed into the Ohio River on 15 December, claiming 46 lives. In retrospect, some local residents (and John Keel) appeared to believe that Mothman was a "specter of death," its appearances serving as "prophecies" of impending disaster. A subsequent film, *The Mothman Prophecies* (2002), made the alleged supernatural connection more explicit, with Richard Gere cast as investigative reporter "John Klein."

Various Mothman candidates proposed since 1966 include the sandhill crane (*Grus canadensis*), the turkey vulture (*Cathartes aura*), and a variety of native OWLS. Author MARK HALL also suggests an owl, but of the unclassified giant variety he dubs bighoot. Some accounts compare Mothman to Britain's OWLMAN, reported in 1976 (and dismissed by many critics as a HOAX). Other theories, spawned by Keel's reporting on the case, propose a link between Mothman and extraterrestrial spacecraft or a link to some parallel dimension. Whatever the truth, Mothman has passed

into folklore, commemorated by a 10-foot statue unveiled in Point Pleasant on 23 September 2003. The glowering figure, by sculptor Bob Roach, serves as a draw for incipient CRYPTOTOURISM. Mayor Jim Wilson speaks fondly of the tourists who have thronged Point Pleasant since 2002. "I don't care why they're coming," he told reporters, "as long as they're here. If they want Mothman, then we'll give them Mothman."

Sources: Bord and Bord, *Alien Animals*; Coleman, *Mothman and Other Curious Encounters*; Keel, *The Complete Guide to Mysterious Beings*; Keel, *The Mothman Prophecies*; Bob Rickard, "The Mothman special"; Stephen Schaefer, "'Mothman' sightings will continue." *USA Today* (23 January 2002); Chris Stirewalt, "Mothman lives." *Charleston* (WV) *Daily Mail* (23 September 2003).

Mount Airy Marauder *see* **Sykesville Monster**

Mount Meru, Tanzania   With an altitude of 14,978 feet, Mount Meru is the fifth-tallest mountain in Africa. In the late 1920s, while visiting an unnamed lake nearby, explorer Charles Stoneham reported finding tracks resembling those of a large CROCODILE. He did not glimpse the creature, but found their placement unusual, since no rivers fed the isolated lake.

Source: Charles Stoneham, *All Over Africa*. London: Hutchinson, 1934.

Mountain Boomer   In 1993, Texas UFO researcher Jimmy Ward reportedly collected tales from Brewster and Presidio Counties, describing a "giant lizard that walked on its hind legs and whose voice sounded like the roll of distant thunder." Based upon its noise and preference for roaming the foothills of Big Ben Ranch State Park, locals called their beast the Mountain Boomer. One witness interviewed by Ward claimed to have seen the creature eating road-kill, then fleeing as his vehicle approached. He described it as 5–6 feet tall, greenish brown, with small forelegs, stout hind legs, and a long tail carried parallel to the ground when it ran. Except for size, that description closely matches certain carnivorous DINOSAURS of the infraorder *Carnosauria*, including *Allosaurus* and *Tyrannosaurus*. Researcher Chad Arment found the resemblance too close for comfort, suggesting that the report(s) comprised a HOAX and noting that the Mountain Boomer nickname is sometimes also applied to the collared lizard (*Crotaphytus collaris*), a common species reaching 10–12 inches in length.

Source: Arment, "Dinos in the U.S.A."

Texas witnesses describe the Mountain Boomer as a large bipedal reptile.

Mourilyan Harbor sea serpent   In mid-August 1934, a SEA SERPENT allegedly visited Mourilyan Harbor, on the coast of Queensland, Australia. Strangely, while the incident is mentioned in various publications, no further details of the sighting have survived in print.

Source: Smith, *Bunyips & Bigfoots.*

Mourou-Ngou *see* **Water Leopard**

Mozambique Channel sea serpent   The Mozambique Channel lies between Madagascar and the African mainland. In August 1910, a French sailor (later captain) named Le Lièvre allegedly sighted a huge SEA SERPENT some 25 miles from the channel's southern entrance. Le Lièvre later claimed the animal was at least 200 feet long and as thick as a 190-gallon cask. BERNARD HEUVELMANS accepted the sighting as legitimate, but considered the description "rather exaggerated."

Source: Heuvelmans, *In the Wake of the Sea Serpents.*

Muan *see* **Mohán**

Muckross Lake, Ireland   Muckross Lake, in County Killarney, is one of Ireland's deepest lakes, with a charted depth of 244 feet. In August 2003, during an acoustic survey of the lake's Arctic char (*Salvelinus alpinus*) population, technicians from the National Parks and Wildlife Service reportedly scored sonar hits on "a huge mysterious mass the size of a whale." Though publicly acknowledged by official spokesmen, the object remains unidentified.

Source: "Whale-like mass found in Arctic." Islamic Republic of Iran Broadcasting News (19 August 2003).

Mud Lake, Arkansas   In spring 1897, residents of St. Francis County, Arkansas were reportedly bedeviled by a rowdy LAKE MONSTER that swam around Mud Lake, slapping the water's surface with its tail and emitting loud whistling sounds. At last, their aggravation reached a crisis point, as described in the *Forrest City Times* on 28 May:

A council of hardy natives was held and various means were suggested leading [to] the capture of what they termed the SEA SERPENT....[I]t was agreed, upon the urgent recommendation of an old salt who had seen service among the whalers way down in the Indian Ocean, to try the harpoon process. Two of these instruments were turned out of a plantation blacksmith shop, which equipped the attacking party for a hand to hand encounter. At the appearance of the monster, two boats were speedily manned and bore down upon the aquatic flounderer while he was seemingly enjoying his afternoon bath.

With great caution, the two boats neared the object of their murderous intention. So engrossed in his mode and mood of hilarity (churning the water and splashing it high in the air), the monster was unconscious of approaching danger till the deadly 'poons sunk deep into vital parts of his body.

Simultaneous with the strokes, which fastened the instruments into the flesh of the strange visitor, a desperate lunge was made for liberty and deeper water, which sped the boats over the surface of the glassy water at a terrific rate. The crews were determined and plucky and played out line and took up slack, as their swift and perilous cruise demanded.

After a 2-hour struggle, the creature died and was hauled ashore, where it measured 16 feet long and 8 feet around at the thickest part of its body. Those who manned the ropes described its weight as equal to "the largest ox." None present had ever seen anything resembling the beast, covered in scaly hide, whose long jaws boasted three rows of daggerlike teeth. As the *Times* ob-

served, "His FISH majesty had evidently lingered through a portion of the iron age as his exterior was decorated with two gigs and a hatchet." Several pieces of the creature were allegedly preserved (there whereabouts unknown today), while the rest was fed to hogs. Modern researchers disagree as to whether the 1897 report was a HOAX or a genuine account of some unknown creature's passing.

Sources: Garner, *Monster! Monster!*; "Rather fishy." *Forrest City* (AR) *Times* (28 May 1897).

Mud Lake, Utah   Authors LOREN COLEMAN and JOHN KIRK include this supposed Utah Lake on published lists of LAKE MONSTER habitats, but they provide no dates or details of sightings. According to Utah's Department of Environmental Quality, no such lake exists within the state. The listing may be a garbled reference to events reported from MUD LAKE, ARKANSAS in the late 19th century.

Sources: Coleman, *Mysterious America*; Kirk, *In the Domain of the Lake Monsters*; Utah Lakes and Reservoirs, http://www.waterquality.utah.gov/watersheds.lakes.htm.

Mudpuppies (Giant)   Mudpuppies (*Necturus* sp.) are a species of SALAMANDER native to the eastern United States. With the closely-related waterdogs, they are easily recognized by wing-like gills on each side of the head. The largest known species, *N. maculosus*, attains a maximum official length of 19⅛ inches, but sightings of much larger specimens have been recorded. In the early 1800s, Ohio settlers reported encounters with amphibious creatures, 6–7 feet long, inhabiting Scippo Creek (a tributary of the Scioto River in Pickaway County). The animals were pink and sported "horns" resembling those of a MOOSE, which might well described a much-enlarged mudpuppies gills.

Source: Shuker, *In Search of Prehistoric Survivors.*

Mudskipper (Glowing)   Mudskippers (*Periophthalmus* sp.) are curious FISH that spend much of their time (three-fourths by some estimates) on dry land, freely breathing air while they "walk" around on their fins. They are found over a wide range, from West Africa to Australia, Polynesia and Japan, but none are luminous — unless we accept a report filed from Indonesia in 1986. During that year, tropical agriculturalist Tyson Hughes allegedly saw an unknown specimen of mudskipper along the Ceram River, on the Indonesian island of Ceram. Unlike its relatives, this specimen pulsated with a red light in the darkness. Hughes failed to capture the fish, and no specimen has yet been collected to document his story.

Source: Karl Shuker, "Menagerie of mystery." *Strange Magazine* 16 (Fall 1995): 29.

Mugwump   Lake Temiskaming spans the border between Ontario and Québec (where it is known as Lac Témiscamingue). Its resident LAKE MONSTER, locally known as the Mugwump, has been sighted as recently as April 1979. Its description generally conforms to those of other aquatic cryptids in the region.

Source: Kirk, *In the Domain of the Lake Monsters.*

Muhalu/Mulahu   In the 1930s, Italian adventurer Attilio Gatti published native reports of an aggressive giant APE, called Muhalu or Mulahu, that inhabited the Ituri Forest (Democratic Republic of Congo). Witnesses described the beast as "exceptionally large," claiming heights of 7–8 feet. They also noted that the beast "walks erect habitually, and is covered with very dark, possibly black, fur, except for the face, where the hairs are white." In his pursuit of the Muhalu, Gatti allegedly found huge footprints and collected several long hairs (including some supposedly torn out by one of the creature's victims, an Australian photographer killed by the Muhalu during World War I). Researcher IVAN SANDERSON considered the Muhalu similar (if not identical) to the equally fearsome TANO GIANT. Reports that Gatti actually glimpsed the animal on one occasion are unverified.

Sources: Attilio Gatti, *Great Mother Forest*. London: Hoddard & Stoughton, 1936; Heuvelmans, *Les Bêtes Humaines d'Afrique*; Sanderson, *Abominable Snowmen*.

Muhlambela

In his 1948 memoirs, South African game warden Harry Wolhuter described the Muhlambela as an unknown species of venomous SNAKE, notorious for striking a human passerby from the branches of trees. Wolhuter claimed the reptile grew to lengths approaching 12 feet and featured a prominent crest on its head. Its most peculiar feature, however, was the bleating sounds it made. Snakes have no vocal cords, but the Muhlambela's description and habits generally conform to those of the equally mysterious CROWING CRESTED COBRA, widely reported throughout the southern half of Africa.

Source: Harry Wolhuter, *Memories of a Game-Ranger*. Johannesburg: Wild Life Protection Society of South Africa, 1948.

Muhnochwa

The Muhnochwa ("face scratcher") panic of 2002 ranks high among the most bizarre events in cryptozoological history. In early July, while parts of eastern India still echoed with reports of MONKEY MAN attacks, residents of nearby Uttar Pradesh found a new horror in their midst. Initially described as a "monster-man" who raked the faces of his victims with long claws, the Muhnochwa mauled 36 victims of various ages by 9 July. Inhabitants of 50 villages fled their homes or locked themselves inside, despite summer's broiling heat, while the unknown creature roamed abroad. By mid-August, descriptions of the Muhnochwa had altered to depict a nocturnal "flying sphere emitting red and blue lights." It was no less violent for being airborne, and some victims now sported burns on their faces and elsewhere. Two victims died from their wounds, with the official cause of death reported as "unknown." Riots flared, shops were burned, and a dozen persons were lynched by mobs that accused them of unleashing "the mysterious creature Muhnochwa."

Frustrated authorities tried in vain to explain the attacks. Deputy Inspector General of Police K.N.D. Dwivedi told reporters that the Muhnochwa was a "technologically developed special insect" 3–6 inches long, imported from Pakistan by "anti-national elements" seeking to topple the Indian government. Professor Ravindra Arora, at the Indian Institute of Technology-Kanpur, confidently blamed ball lighting caused by a pervasive drought. Meanwhile, Professor K.C. Pandey of Lucknow University identified the culprit *Schizodactylus monstruosus*, described as a rare and harmless insect "belonging to the grasshopper family." None of those solutions pacified the 10,000 rioters who stormed Barabanki's police station on 18 August, repelled by gunfire that killed one man and wounded 12 more.

As the furor spread to Madhya Pradesh, claiming another dozen victims, India's national intelligence agency deployed a investigative team of forensic scientists, physicists and electronic engineers. The squad examined 100 alleged Muhnochwa victims, reporting that 85 displayed various physical injuries. Ten of those were marked by "insect bites or scratches," while 10 more revealed indirect injuries (bruises, etc.) suffered while fleeing the mauler. Wounds among the other 65 remain officially unexplained, including three victims who reported grappling with Muhnochwa,

their palms scarred by hundreds of tiny gashes. While panicky villagers engaged in wholesale slaughter of squirrels and BATS to hyenas and WOLVES, Indian officials finally dismissed Muhnochwa as a product of mass hysteria.

Sources: "The face-scratcher." *Fortean Times* 164 (December 2002): 6–7; "Indian villagers blame UFO for attacks, but police blame insects." Associated Press (12 August 2002); "Lakhimpur muhnochwa is a rare grasshopper." *Times of India* (20 August 2002); Ian MacKinnon, "Panic spreads over face scratcher attacks." *The Scotsman* (24 August 2002); "Monster mania." *Fortean Times* 163 (November 2002): 7; Manjari Mishra, "Muhnochwa haunts Mayawati." *Times of India* (21 August 2002); "Muhnochwa terrorizes eastern UP." *India Express* (18 August 2002); Catherine Philp, "India calls in X-Files agents to unmask face-scratching alien." *The Times* (20 August 2002); Sharat Pradhan, "'Face-clawing monster' terrifies Indian state." Reuters (19 August 2002); "Shops gutted over 'muhnochwa' issue, 9 held in Uttar Pradesh." Press Trust of India (12 August 2002).

Muhuru

Peculiar confusion surrounds this supposed reptilian cryptid of Kenya, making it difficult (if not impossible) to identify. The first account of it was published by KARL SHUKER in 1998, relating an alleged sighting by missionary Cal Bombay and his wife. As told to Shuker by colleague WILLIAM GIBBONS, the Bombays were driving through the Rift Valley in 1963, en route to Nairobi, when they were forced to stop for a large "lizard" sunning itself on the roadway. They described the reptile as 9–12 feet long, dark gray in color, with a distinctive sail-like growth on its back. The beast moved on after 20 minutes, freeing the Bombays to proceed. Kenyan natives heard their story and identified the creature as Muhuru. Later, when interviewed by KENT HOVIND, the Bombays chose a drawing of the sail-backed *Dimetrodon* (a Permian reptile, presumed extinct for 225 million years) as a likeness of the Muhuru.

That story was strange enough, but Gibbons published his own account of the sighting in 2003, with certain significant changes. First, he placed the sighting in summer 1961, then altered the Muhuru's description to present a 9-foot reptile with a snakelike head, four stubby legs, and "diamond-shaped serrations about one-half of an inch to three inches in height running from the back of the creature's head to the tip of its tail." The story was illustrated with a painting by crypto-artist WILLIAM REBSAMEN, which bore no resemblance whatever to *Dimetrodon*. Thus, the initial riddle is compounded, leaving latter-day researchers to decide which (if either) description of the Muhuru they accept as accurate.

Sources: Gibbons, *Missionaries and Monsters*; Shuker, "From dodos to dimetrodons."

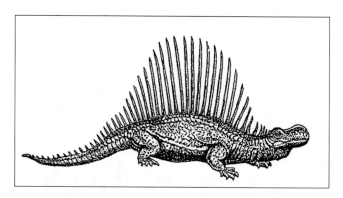

The Muhuru initially described by Cal Bombay resembled a prehistoric *Dimetrodon*.

Artist's conception of a rather different Muhuru (*William Rebsamen*).

Mulgewanke   This BUNYIP or MERBEING of Lake Alexandrina, South Australia was described by Aborigines as half-man and half-FISH, sporting a mop of reeds in place of hair atop its head. The creature's booming voice was often heard around the lake, into the early 19th century. No modern sightings are on file.

Source: Smith, *Bunyips & Bigfoots.*

Mulilo   Natives of Central Africa describe the Mulilo as a kind of giant, predatory worm or slug, jet-black in color, 6 feet long and 12 inches in diameter. As reported by W.L. Speight in 1940, tribesmen in Zambia and the Democratic Republic of Congo allegedly trap Mulilos by building cages lined with knife blades, baiting them with live poultry, and leaving them out overnight for the nocturnal creepers. When a Mulilo is caught and killed, pieces of its skin are worn by dancers in tribal fertility rituals. KARL SHUKER notes that the flesh of a worm or slug would hardly survive such handling. He proposes, instead, some unknown species of amphibian, perhaps one of the burrowing, legless caecilians (Order *Gymnophiona*). The largest known caecilian, from Colombia, is the 5-foot-long *Caecilia thompsoni.* Several smaller species inhabit the African continent.

Sources: Shuker, *From Flying Toads to Snakes with Wings*; Speight, "Mystery monsters in Africa."

Mullens, Rant (1896–?)   Twenty years before relatives of the late RAYMOND WALLACE claimed that he "invented" BIGFOOT at Bluff Creek, California in 1958, elderly ex-logger Rant Mullens issued a similar boast from Vancouver, Washington. Mullens approached the media in April 1982, claiming responsibility for one of the most famous incidents in the history of SASQUATCH research. According to Mullens, he and his uncle (George Ross) were on a fishing trip near Mount Saint Helens, in 1924, when they passed a miner's cabin and decided to frighten the strangers. Scaling a hill behind the cabin, Mullens and Ross rolled several boulders down the slope, then fled the scene. From that HOAX, Mullens said, evolved the tale of a battle between men and monsters at the site now called APE CANYON. Four years later, while cutting a trail near present-day Swift Reservoir, Mullens and several cohorts in the Forest Service "thought we would have a little fun." They whittled giant wooden feet and stamped huge footprints for their co-workers to find. Still at it three decades later, Mullens carved some of the big feet used by Ray Wallace to

fake casts in northern California. (Wallace admitted falsifying Bigfoot tracks with feet supplied by Mullens.) Cryptozoologists were unimpressed with the Mullens "confessions," noting that his sporadic pranks did not explain HOMINID footprints (much less eyewitness sightings) reported from six continents over a span of centuries. Researcher GROVER KRANTZ dismissed the Ape Canyon prank, if true, as a "particularly dumb hoax."

Sources: Coleman, *Bigfoot!*; "Logger says his big mouth is responsible for Bigfoot." *Bakersfield California* (4 April 1982).

Multi-State Bigfoot Research Roundtable   Organized in 2003, the MSBRR serves as a clearinghouse for BIGFOOT sightings and research across North America. The group's stated goal is to "research and investigate reports and activity by sharing ideas, information and expertise without barriers or limitations." Members are pledged to "cooperate and share in a manner that allows information to be forwarded quickly and easily to those who can work with it in the most efficient manner possible." A majority of identified members represent NORTHEASTERN OHIO BIGFOOT RESEARCH, including leaders Michael and Tammy Beckett. Others include Eric Altman, of the PENNSYLVANIA BIGFOOT SOCIETY; Maine-based cryptozoologist LOREN COLEMAN; William Dranginis, of VIRGINIA BIGFOOT RESEARCH; Mike Frizzell, of the Maryland-based Enigma Project; Mike George, director of the WESTERN NEW YORK BIGFOOT INVESTIGATION CENTER; RICHARD LAMONICA (of Northeastern Ohio's Researchable Kryptid Accounts); Jeff Lewis, of UTAH BIGFOOT INVESTIGATIONS; Robert Murdock, of the SASQUATCH INFORMATION SOCIETY; and Craig Woolheater, representing the TEXAS BIGFOOT RESEARCH CENTER. While it lasts, the MSBRR thus represents the first truly national organization committed to searching for SASQUATCH.

Source: Multi-State Bigfoot Research Roundtable, *http://www.msbrr. org/msbrr.html.*

Mummelsee, Germany   This lake, located in Germany's Baden-Württemberg State, reportedly harbored a LAKE MONSTER through the early decades of the 17th century. No modern sightings are recorded.

Source: Athanasius Kircher, *Mundus Subterraneus.* Amsterdam: J. Janssonium and E. Weyerstraten, 1665.

Mumulou   In the early 20th century, Ghari natives of the Solomon Islands told Western visitors stories of cave-dwelling primates or PYGMIES inhabiting several islands in the archipelago. On Guadalcanal, the elusive creatures were called Mumulou, while tribesmen on Maramasike simply dubbed them Mumu, and villagers on San Cristobal named them Kakamora. Witnesses typically described the Mumulou as dark-skinned and bearded, with long hair on its head and long nails or claws. It traveled with a kind of hopping motion, similar to that of MONKEYS. In the early 1920s, Charles Fox was exploring San Cristobal with a native party when he saw one of the creatures near a jungle river. It escaped, but left behind a half-eaten FISH and several small, wet footprints on the stony bank. No sightings have been logged since World War II, suggesting that the epic battles waged throughout the Solomons either annihilated the Mumulou or drove them deeper into hiding.

Source: Charles Fox, *The Threshold of the Pacific.* New York: A.A. Knopf, 1924; Heuvelmans, "Annotated checklist of apparently unknown animals with which cryptozoology is concerned"; "Is there an undiscovered people in central Guadalcanal?" *Pacific Islands Monthly* 20 (February 1950): 96; A.H. Wilson, "Guadalcanal's undiscovered people just another tale." *Pacific Islands Monthly* 20 (March 1950):7.

Mungoon-Galli   Australia's largest known lizard is the perentie (*Varanus giganteus*), a MONITOR LIZARD known to reach eight feet in length. That is still a good deal shorter than the world's record species, the Komodo dragon (*V. komodoensis*), but tales of much larger lizards have emerged from Australia since the 1830s. Timber cutters were the first to file reports of sightings from the Wattagan Mountains in New South Wales, where Aborigines knew the creatures as Mungoon-galli. Outlying ranches complain that the lizards sometimes eat cattle. In 1975, a group of hikers found large reptilian footprints and drag marks from a great tail on the fringe of the Wallangambe Wilderness, in the Blue Mountains of New South Wales. Two days after Christmas, that same year, a farmer near Cessnock, New South Wales saw a 30-foot monitor prowling on his land. The beast stood three feet off the ground on sturdy legs, its hide a mottled gray with dark stripes on the back and tail. Australian cryptozoologist REX GILROY went looking for giant monitors in Queensland, during June 1978, and while he failed to sight the Mungoon-galli, Gilroy found 30-odd reptilian footprints in a farmer's field, preserving one of them with plaster casts.

Such reports may be dismissed as fantasy or HOAXES, but the same cannot be said for a report filed by a veteran herpetologist. In early 1979, Frank Gordon was conducting field work in the Wattagan Mountains of New South Wales when he encountered an amazing reptile. Upon returning to his vehicle from several hours in the bush, Gordon noted what he thought to be a log lying nearby. When he started the engine, however, the "log" began crawling away, revealing itself as a huge monitor 27–30 feet long. A year later, while driving on the Bilpin Road (in the southern quarter of the Wallangambe Wilderness), a truck driver was startled by a 20-foot monitor crossing the highway in front of his vehicle. Skeptics insist that Mungoon-galli witnesses have simply exaggerated their encounters with larger-than-average perenties, but Gilroy offers another explanation. Australia once harbored a true giant monitor, *Megalania prisca*, that grew to lengths of 26 feet and weighed more than 1,300 pounds. Although presumed extinct since the Pleistocene epoch (about 1 million years ago), a relict population of such reptiles would explain Australia's sightings — and give hikers new reason to fear the Outback.

Sources: Gilroy, "Australia's lizard monsters"; Gilroy, "Giant lizards of the Australian bush"; Shuker, *In Search of Prehistoric Survivors*.

Herpetologist Frank Gordon encountered a Mungoon-galli in 1979 (*William Rebsamen*).

Munstead Monster   The Munstead Monster was an ALIEN BIG CAT reported from the region of Godalming, Surrey, England in September 1964. Though never captured, it left massive feline pawprints nearly six inches wide, which were preserved in plaster casts. Witnesses described it as resembling a COUGAR (*Puma concolor*), 5–6 feet long and 3 feet tall at the shoulder, capable of leaping over a 5½-foot fence.

Sources: Bord and Bord, *Alien Animals*; Sieveking, "Big cats in Britain."

Muntonkole   Luba tribesmen of the Central African Republic describe the Muntonkole as a large SNAKE that inhabits Lake Kisale. When seen on the surface, it is said to resemble a floating clay pot.

Source: William Burton, *Luba Religion and Magic in Custom and Belief*. Tervuren, Belgium: Musée Royal de l'Afrique Centrale, 1961.

Murung River Bear   As recently as the 1930s, Indonesian natives described this aggressive cryptid as an occasional visitor to the Kedang Murung River, in eastern Borneo. Large groups of the bearlike creatures reportedly gathered to feast on berries along the river banks. The beasts were accomplished swimmers, and sometimes attacked passing boats, inflicting serious (or fatal) wounds on human occupants. No recent sightings are on file.

Source: Leonard Clark, *A Wanderer till I Die*. New York: Funk and Wagnalls, 1937.

Musk Ox (Asian)   The musk ox (*Ovibos moschatus*) is a large, shaggy-haired bovid virtually unchanged from Pleistocene times. It inhabited most of the Earth's northern hemisphere before 10,000 years ago, when it presumably died out except in Arctic regions of Greenland and North America. That judgment notwithstanding, it appears that human beings interacted with the musk ox in Mongolia and Siberia much later than is commonly believed. In 1924, carvings of an animal resembling a musk ox were found on two silver plates dating from the first century B.C., removed from tombs in Mongolia's Noyon Uul Mountains. Twenty-four years later, several musk ox skulls scarred with apparent drill holes were unearthed on the Siberia's Taymyr Penin-

Did the Asian musk ox survive into historical times?

sula, dated between 1800–900 B.C. A subfossil musk ox skull was found in the same region, in 1984.

Source: Spassov, "The musk ox in Eurasia."

Mussie *see* **Hapyxelor**

Mutton Island sea serpent

On 5 May 1935, the light-house keeper on Mutton Island, off the coast of County Galway, Ireland, reportedly shot and killed a strange sea creature that had recently shredded several fishermen's nets. The beast measured 48 feet long and 28 feet in circumference at its thickest point, but was otherwise undescribed. No details of its disposal are recorded.

Source: Bord and Bord, *Unexplained Mysteries of the 20th Century.*

Myakka Photographs

On 29 December 2000, the Sarasota County (Florida) Sheriff's Department received a letter mailed seven days earlier. It read:

Dear Sir or Madam,

Enclosed please find some pictures I took in late September or early Oct. of 2000. My husband says he thinks it is an orangutan. Is someone missing an orangutan? It is hard to judge from the photos how big this orangutan really is. It is in a crouching position in the middle of standing up from where it was sitting. It froze as soon as the flash went off. I didn't even see it as I took the first picture because it was so dark. As soon as the flash went off for the second time it stood up and started to move. I then heard the orangutan walk off into the bushes. From where I was standing, I judge it as being about six and a half to seven feet tall in a kneeling position. As soon as I realized how close it was I got back to the house. It had an awful smell that lasted well after it had left my yard. The orangutan was making deep "woomp" noises, It sounded much farther away then [*sic*] it turned out to be. If I had known it was so close to the hedge roll [*sic*] as it was I wouldn't have walked up as close as I did. I'm a senior citizen and if this animal had come out of the hedge roll after me there wasn't a thing I could have done about it. I was about ten foot [*sic*] away from it when it stood up. I'm concerned because my grandchildren like to come down and explore in my back yard. An animal this big could hurt someone seriously. For two nights prior, it had been taking apples that my daughter brought down from up north, off our back porch. These pictures were taken on the third night it had raided my apples. It only came back one more night after that and took some apples that my husband had left out in order to get a better look at it. We left out four apples. I cut two of them in half. The orangutan only took the whole apples. We didn't see it take them. We waited up but eventually had to go to bed. We got a dog back there now and as far as we can tell the orangutan hasn't been back.

Please find out where this animal came from and who it belongs to. It shouldn't be loose like this, someone will get hurt. I called a friend that used to work with animal control back up north and he told us to call the police. I don't want any fuss or people with guns traipsing around behind our house. We live near I75 and I'm afraid this orangutan could cause a serious accident if someone hit it. I once hit a deer that wasn't even a quarter of the size of this animal and totalled [*sic*] my car. At the very least this animal belongs in a place like Bush [*sic*] Gardens where it can be looked after properly. Why haven't people been told that an animal this size is loose? How are people to know how dangerous this could be? If I had known an animal like this was loose I wouldn't have aprotched [*sic*] it. I saw on the news that MONKEYS that get loose can carry Hepatitis and are very dangerous. Please look after this situation. I don't want my backyard to turn into someone else's circus.

God Bless

I prefer to remain anonymous

The photos enclosed with the letter appeared to show an APE

of unknown size and species peering at the camera from behind a screen of palmettos. Sheriff's deputies initially dismissed the letter as a HOAX, but they passed it on to county animal control authorities. One of those officers, in turn, gave photocopies of the pictures to David Barkasy, owner of Sarasota's Silver City Serpentarium. Suspecting that the photos might depict Florida's elusive SKUNK APE, Barkasy alerted cryptozoologist LOREN COLEMAN to the breaking story. The sheriff's department created a file for the case on 18 January, regrettably stapling and otherwise damaging the original photos in the process. (Critics later claimed, falsely, that damage caused by file clerks in the sheriff's office proved the photos were fakes.) Barkasy traced the pictures to a Sarasota photo lab near Interstate Highway 75, where they were printed in December 2000. The lab's proprietor could not identify the customer who brought them in for processing.

There the matter rests, for now. Computer analysis of the photos shed no light on their authenticity, and while Coleman advises a wait-and-see attitude, publication of the pictures in February 2001 sparked a rash of speculation and debate ongoing to the present day. Various armchair analysts suggest that the grinning creature in the photos is a shaggy dog, a man in an ape suit, a cardboard cutout, a model of BIGFOOT, a computer-generated image, or an authentic Skunk Ape. No resolution is expected in the foreseeable future.

Sources: Coleman, *Bigfoot!*; "Myakka Skunk Ape photos." *Fortean Times* 145 (May 2001): 6; Mischa Vieira, "Tracking Myakka's wily Skunk Ape." *East County Observer* (12 July 2001).

Myllesjön, Sweden

Reports of a giant FISH or LAKE MONSTER resembling a floating log have emanated from this lake, in Blekinge County, since the 1920s. Roughly a decade later, after the beast had frightened several children from the lake, local residents sought to kill it. As Swedish artist Richard Svensson described the event to KARL SHUKER:

The local blacksmith made a hook the size of a ping-pong bat, a piece of board was made as a float, and a steel wire chosen as line and tied around a slim oak tree. A butcher donated a dead piglet for bait, and the entire contraption was hurled out into the lake. The next day the oak tree was found uprooted, bobbing about in the middle of the lake, where it stayed for a whole week until it sank. Nothing more happened and the monster was believed to be dead.

Sightings resumed in August 1962, however, whereupon 425 fishermen gathered to vie for a reward of 1,000 Swedish kroner ($130) offered for the creature's capture. (The largest fish caught was a 2.9-pound perch.) Three months later, another concerted effort was make to kill the beast. As Svensson told Shuker:

In November 1962, several large hooks were manufactures and baited with dead chickens and calves' heads. Most newspaper stories say that the efforts went resultless, but others claim that at least one of the calves' heads disappeared. During 1963, the diving log was seen again, and in September another fishing competition was held: now with the prize of 10,000 Swedish kroner [$1,300]. Again, it proved to be an uneventful event.

Sporadic sightings continued at Myllesjön through the 1970s, at least, but construction of a lakeside highway in 1996 seems to have doomed the creature that eluded so many sportsmen in decades past. A possible candidate for Myllesjön's hungry "log" is the wels CATFISH (*Siluris glanis*), a Eurasian species known to reach 15.5 feet in length.

Source: Shuker, *Mysteries of Planet Earth.*

Mysterious Beast   In the 1920s, while traveling in Paraguay, Royal Navy veteran C.W. Thurlow-Craig collected various native reports of a swamp-dwelling creature known simple as the Mysterious Beast. Witnesses described the animal as having a doglike head, with a body as thick as a horse's but twice as long, armed with a venomous barb on its tail. The creature was aquatic and lured its prey to the water, where it somehow created a whirlpool or suction to drag victims below the surface. Thurlow-Craig dismissed the tales as myths until it claimed a Welsh ranch hand named Thomas, sent to drive cattle across the Río Jacare (a tributary of the Río Paraguay). As described by Thurlow-Craig decades later, Thomas was swimming across the river when he "gave one yell of terror and disappeared in a huge swirl of water, thrown up by something very big indeed." Searchers armed with grappling hooks and dynamite failed to find any trace of the lost man's corpse.

Candidates for the attack included a large CAIMAN, the MANGURUYÚ (a supposed giant FISH), or the huge and toothless freshwater SHARK once described by explorer PERCY FAWCETT. Thurlow-Craig was prepared to forget the incident until 1930, when he personally drove a herd across the Río Jacare at the same place. As he described the incident in 1954:

[The] third and last sweep accounted for ten stragglers. As we were putting them over the last animal, a three-month-old calf that was swimming strongly behind its mother suddenly gave a great bawl, and was pulled under. I was within twenty yards of that calf, together with José and old Rufino, my foreman. We saw no fish, no ALLIGATOR, nothing but a great swirl of water.

Later, while exploring a marshy region known to natives as Swamp of the Beast, Thurlow-Craig discovered "a track such as I had never seen before, made by something either going into or coming out of the water, nearly 3 feet wide and about 6 inches pressed into the firm mud. It might possibly have been made by a great SNAKE, 35 feet long or thereabouts....[I]t had not been made by a big alligator, either, for there were no claw marks on either side. At that moment the mule took fright; and so did I....[W]e left that place!"

Source: C.W. Thurlow-Craig, *Black Jack's Spurs*. London: Curtis Brown Ltd., 1954.

Mystery Animal Research Centre of Australia
Australian native Sharon West was on vacation with her family in 1987, when she saw an ALIEN BIG CAT cross the highway in front of her car. That sighting launched her interest in cryptozoology and prompted her to create the Mystery Animal Association of Western Australia, renamed the Mystery Animal Research Centre of Australia in 1996. West describes the MARCA as a group "interested in proving the existence of at least two species of big cats and THYLACINES are roaming the mainland of Australia." At last report, its 60 members included residents of every Australian state and a few overseas. The group publishes a quarterly newsletter and maintains an active Internet website. When feasible, MARCA members pursue field investigations of new cryptid sightings, and reports are welcomed at the website.

Source: Mystery Animal Research Centre of Australia, http://www.webace.com.au/~pwest/marca/.

Mystery Maulers
Throughout recorded history, humans and their domesticated animals have been plagued by sporadic attacks from unidentified predators who strike and disappear at will, eluding hunters and avoiding traps, leaving eyewitnesses confused and frightened. Some of the killing sprees end with the death of a neighborhood dog or some recognized wild animal, but most cease as suddenly and mysteriously as they began. In many cases, the predators' behavior (drinking blood, eating only specific body parts, etc.) flies in the face of official explanations. Some such attacks are blamed on ALIEN BIG CATS, while other predators defy easy identification. An admittedly incomplete timeline of mystery mauler attacks worldwide includes the following:

774— Hundreds of people were killed by unidentified predators during the ASSYRIAN MONSTER INVASION, spanning modern-day Jordan, Syria and Iraq.

June 1764–June 1767— The BEAST OF GÉVAUDAN claimed more than 80 human victims in south-central France. A predator was finally killed, but its identity remains disputed.

May–September 1810— Scores of sheep were killed around Ennerdale, near the border between England and Scotland, by a predator that bit their throats and drank their blood, claiming 7–8 victims per night. A farmer knocked down by the creature described it as resembling a LION, while others compared it to a dog. The killing stopped after a dog was shot on 12 September.

January–April 1874— A similar vampire appeared in County Cavan, Ireland, killing up to 30 sheep per night. Again, throats were bitten and blood drained. Some farmers blamed the killings on WOLVES, though Ireland's last known wolf was shot in 1712. The spree continued despite the killing of two large dogs. At Limerick, several humans bitten by the unknown beast were confined to an asylum, "laboring under strange symptoms of insanity."

July–December 1893— A creature described as resembling a black dog, albeit with a blunt muzzle and longer-than-average tail, killed two women and a child around Trosna, in Russia's Orël Region. Hunters sought the beast in vain, though some reports claim that it vanished after eating poisoned bait.

October 1904— A night-prowling hunter killed sheep around Hexham, England. Locals claimed it was a wolf that had escaped from a private menagerie in Newcastle, 20 miles to the north, but massive hunts failed to locate the escapee.

November–December 1905— Vampiric predation resumed in England, this time at Badminton, South Gloucestershire. Sergeant Carter, of the Gloucestershire police, told the London *Daily Mail*: "I have seen two of the carcasses, myself, and can say definitely that it is impossible for it to be the work of a dog. Dogs are not vampires, and do not suck the blood of a sheep, and leave the flesh almost untouched." Nonetheless, reporters claimed that the killings stopped after a dog was shot on 16 December, or perhaps it was a JACKAL (as claimed by the *Bristol Mercury* three weeks earlier).

March 1906— A nocturnal hunter slaughtered sheep around Britain's Windsor Castle. Sentries fired at the creature but missed. On 18 March, the stalker surfaced at Guilford, 17 miles from Windsor, to kill 51 sheep in a single night.

October 1925— London's *Daily Express* (19 October) reported that some creature "black in colour and of enormous size" was butchering sheep around Edale, Derbyshire, "leaving the carcasses strewn about, with legs, shoulders, and heads torn off; broken backs, and pieces of flesh ripped off."

December 1925— An unidentified beast was shot while killing chickens at a farm near Greenwich, New Jersey. The Woodbury *Daily Times* (15 December) reported that it was "the size of a grown Airedale with black fur resembling Astrakhan. It...hopped kangaroo fashion. Its fore-quarters were higher than its rear and the latter were always in a crouched attitude. Its hind feet had four webbed toes. Its eyes were still open and very yellow and its jaw is neither dog, wolf, nor coyote. Its teeth are most curious, as the crushers in the lower jaw each have four prongs into which the upper teeth fit perfectly."

29 April 1938 — A resident of Columbus, Ohio reported an unknown creature gnawing on a bone in his backyard. He described the beast as "the size of a dozen CATS, head and feet large, fur gray with yellow stripes." Authorities could not identify its footprints.

1945–46 — Residents of Lebanon and Pottstown, Pennsylvania hunted in vain for a nocturnal creature that killed cattle and dogs. The prowler went unseen, but locals reported strange cries in the night, like a baby crying or a woman screaming.

July 1966 — Press reports described a fierce animal prowling the streets of Jessore, Pakistan, where it killed a young girl and injured two adults. Witnesses offered vague descriptions of the beast, while agreeing that it was not a TIGER or any other known denizen of the region.

March–August 1969 — Eyewitnesses and hunters quarreled over the identity of a predator that killed 800 sheep across Pennsylvania's Harrison, Lewis and Upshur Counties. The prowler killed by biting the throats of its victims, slaying up to 16 in one night. Vague descriptions of the beast placed its size somewhere between that of a FOX and a horse.

February 1974 — Farmers in Kenya's Mayanja district complained of widespread livestock depredation by a "new" beast described as a "combination of lion, leopard and dog." In fact, the region's last known lion was killed in 1954 and leopards are extremely rare. Government hunters failed to find the creature, prompting local rumors that the slaughter stemmed from sorcery or a plot by Ugandan refugees fleeing dictator Idi Amin.

January–March 1977 — Authorities in Jasper County, Mississippi searched in vain for a creature that invaded barns by night, ripping the ears from pigs. Witnesses described the beast as "slightly doglike," gray and black in color, six feet long and standing waist-high to a man, with a large head, small ears, and a shaggy tail.

April–December 1993 — Residents of Plovdiv, Bulgaria were terrorized by a creature that killed 16 persons, draining the blood from each. Scottiz Karpulsky was the first victim, attacked near dawn on 25 April while closing his nightclub. Karpulsky's widow told reporters, "Perhaps a big cat jumped on my husband from a window sill on the first floor and bit through his neck. I took an umbrella in my hand and ran towards the beast which was sucking his blood, then I ran away filled with panic." The stalker averaged two victims per month before it vanished. Police detective Igor Tolkov quoted a description gleansed from surviving witnesses: "It looks like a cat, but has huge sharp claws and glowing red eyes."

May–July 1995 — An unknown predator devoured 15 pet CATS around Gig Harbor, Washington. Authorities blamed coyotes (*Canis latrans*), but a hired trapper failed to snare the culprit(s).

October 1996 — An unidentified predator killed four children and ravaged livestock herds around Arment, Egypt (435 miles south of Cairo).

March 1997 — Roving packs of "wolflike desert creatures" attacked 23 people over 2 days, in the Cairo suburb of Qattamiya. Many attacks occurred on public streets, but in several cases the beasts invaded homes to maul their occupants. Police blamed wolves or coyotes, but the one creature beaten to death during a home invasion has not been publicly identified.

July 1999 — A peculiar predator killed dozens of pigeons and frightened human residents of Mafraq, Jordan, 62 miles north of Amman. Witnesses described it as resembling a cat, but with a small head and disproportionately large eyes, teeth and tail. The animal was reportedly caught on 25 July and delivered to a veterinarian for identification, but no further reports have been published to date.

December 2000 — Farmers hunted in vain for mysterious predator that killed 10 sheep around Belgium. Newspapers said the beast was "thought to be a wolf," but the nearest known wolf populations were found in Poland and Slovakia.

December 2002 — An unseen predator killed or carried off several family pets from a residential neighborhood of Hot Springs, Arkansas. In one attack, it killed an adult beagle and carried a second dog of similar size into the nearby woods. Efforts to trap the beast proved fruitless.

January 2003 — Residents of Rutland, Vermont walked in fear of an unknown animal that mauled two heifers and killed a dog, leaving its victims with "huge bite marks the size of two fists" and "claw marks like razor cuts" up to 1.5 inches deep. Veterinarians suspected a bear or EASTERN COUGAR (*Puma concolor*) at work, though cougars are officially extinct throughout the eastern U.S.

April 2003 — A farmer at Tarbert, England complained that some unknown creature had invaded his property, tearing the heads from chickens and peacocks while leaving their bodies intact.

May 2003 — Fifteen piglets were killed by some unidentified predator in an enclosed barn at Stanford on Soar, near Loughborough, North Leicestershire, England. All 15 suffered deep puncture wounds on each side of the neck, accompanied by scratches on one side. Only small amounts of flesh were eaten from the neck and shoulders.

May 2003 — Farmers in the Chilean village of Perquenco blamed "vampires or aliens" for the slaughter of 40 chickens in one night. Similar attacks on goats and other livestock throughout the Caribbean and Latin America are commonly attributed to the CHUPACABRA.

June 2003 — Hunters in Coventry, Rhode Island scoured the neighborhood for a 4-foot-tall creature resembling a bear, blamed for the mauling of a house cat. Despite its description, authorities insisted that the beast was a coyote.

September 2003 — Saunderstown, Rhode Island was the scene of further depredations, when witnesses Steven and Terry Kelly watched "a big, black creature" kill and mutilate a deer in their backyard. The Kelly's suspected a "black panther," while police again placed the blame on coyotes.

September–October 2003 — An unknown "mystery animal" killed cattle in Lamar County, Mississippi. Farmer Ashton Barefoot found one of his 1,000-pound cows dead after "something had caught it by the neck under the throat area and had eaten about 8 to 12 inches out the neck and flesh was eaten off the side of the head." Authorities blamed the attacks on "stray dogs," which have yet to be captured.

October 2003–February 2004 — An unidentified predator killed and mutilated at least two deer in Essex County, Massachusetts, while locals reported discoveries of strange tracks. Suspects include coyotes, LYNX, foxes, cougars, ABCs and fishers (*Martes pennanti*). In regard to fishers, animal control officer Jim Lindley noted, "The first deer had been dragged 50 to 100 yards. I don't see the fisher with that kind of strength. Is it a per mountain lion that someone turned loose or an exotic cat that was considered no longer cute by its owners? We're trying to figure out if it's something we can live with, or if we have to get it out for the sake of public safety."

Sources: Bord and Bord, *Unexplained Mysteries of the 20th Century*; Erin Emolock, "DEM says reported panther is really a coyote." *Providence* (RI) *Journal* (12 September 2003); Fort, *The Complete Books of Charles Fort*; Seth Harkness, "Wild animal attacks perplex residents, officials." *Rutland* (VT) *Herald* (11 January 2003); Mike Hellgren, "Hot Springs Animal Mystery Continues." KARK-TV (8 January 2003); Niles Jackson, "Killer beast eludes armed farmers." Associated Press (7 August 1969); Keel, *The Complete Guide to Mysterious Beings*; Alan Lupo, "New suspect joins wild lineup." *Boston Globe* (12 February 2004); "Mystery animal killing livestock." *Hattiesburg* (MS) *American* (22 October 2003); "Mystery beast kills ten sheep in Belgium." Reuters (22 December 2000); Trevor Ouellete, "Where in the world...?" *Fortean Times* 155 (March 2002): 48–49; "Shades of the sucker." *Fortean Times* 90 (September 1996): 16; "'Vampires or aliens' blamed for Chilean chicken slaughter." *Ananova* (14 May 2003).

Mystery Squids

The world's oceans hold many wonders in store for humanity, but two have already been glimpsed, in the form of squids unknown to science and as yet unclassified. The first, collected from Hawaiian waters and described in 1991, is known only from a single paralarval specimen whose adult form has never been seen. The solitary specimen measures only .76 inches long, but it is highly distinctive, with big eyes and a pair of unusually large lateral fins that account for its scientific name *Magnapinnidae* ("big fins"). Beyond that name, the squid's taxonomic family and genus remain unknown.

Another mystery squid, much larger than the Hawaiian specimen, has also been glimpsed at great depths and at scattered locations all over the planet, including the Atlantic, Indian and Pacific Oceans, and the Gulf of Mexico. None has yet been captured, though various oceanographers have seen and photographed specimens at depths below 3,000 feet. The deepest sighting came at 15,534 feet, in the western Atlantic off the coast of Brazil. Officially described for the first time in December 2001, the new mystery squid is known to reach 23 feet in length, but scientists find it more remarkable for its "strange looks and weird behavior." First, while other squids typically have eight arms and two much longer tentacles used for grasping prey, the new species has ten arms of identical length "with an elbow." (One report, perhaps garbled, referred to the creature's "20-foot-long spidery legs.") According to Michael Vecchione, of the U.S. National Marine Fisheries Service and the National Museum of Natural History, "The really long skinny arms are so much longer than the squid's body. We don't know of any cephalopod that has arms like that. This is well beyond a new species. New species are a dime a dozen. This is fundamentally different." Vecchione speculated that the long arms may function differently from those of other squids. "One of the animals bumped into the submersible and got tangled up in it. The animal seemed to have a problem letting go. It might go around waiting for small prey like crustaceans to stumble into it and get stuck — sort of like a living spider web."

Besides its unique appearance, the mystery squid also behaves strangely, in Vecchione's terms. "Whenever the submersible came up on one," he explained, "it was in a characteristic posture, floating vertically in the water with the arms spread out." (Squid normally swim backwards, in a "torpedo" shape, though they are also capable of forward motion.) Oceanographer William Sager, from Texas A&M University, added: "I had never seen anything like this creature. It just hung there, looking at us, as if suddenly seeing [a submersible] float up like a whale with lights was no big deal. We photographed and videotaped it for five to ten minutes, and when we got to shore, we went looking for someone who could identify it."

Thus far, that quest has been fruitless, though Vecchione speculates that the large squids may represent adult specimens of *Magnapinnidae*. As he explained, "All the juveniles came from the Pacific and they came from much closer to the surface — 200 meters [650 feet] from the surface. But it is not unusual for young to be near the surface and then go deeper as they mature." Formal conclusions await further study and the acquisition of an adult specimen. At press time for this volume, the mystery squid remained unclassified.

Sources: Maggie Fox, "Large squid baffles and amuses scientists." Reuters (20 December 2001); Shuker, "A supplement to Dr. Bernard Heuvelmans' checklist of cryptozoological animals"; "Strange sea creature spotted." Associated Press (21 December 2001); Richard Young, "Chiroteuthid and related paralarvae from Hawaiian waters." *Bulletin of Marine Science* 49 (1991): 162–185.

Mystic River, Massachusetts

An undated Internet posting from a correspondent identified only as "Antoinette S." describes a strange encounter with an unknown creature beside Boston's Mystic River. The account reads:

> While going by the river, we saw a strange creature (that to this day we cannot explain) crawl out of the water. It was about three to four feet long. It was black and looked like it was wearing a rubber suit. It was not human, but had arms and it reached out to us and made a strange noise. It had bulging bug eyes. After it made the noise and reached out to us, we screamed and ran. This creature was not human. I was curious and wanted to go back and see what it was, but my sister and her friend stopped me. We stopped by the police station to have them check it out since we had no idea what it was. But when we went back, there was no trace of anything. It was not our imagination because three of us saw it.

Source: Monsters, Monsters Everywhere, *http://paranormal.about.com/cs/creaturesweird/a/aa092903.htm*.

Mývatn, Iceland

This Icelandic lake produces occasional LAKE MONSTER sightings in the same pattern as those reported from other European and North American lakes. Some witnesses describe the creatures as resembling capsized boats on the water's surface, while others mention long necks and small heads raised in the manner of a periscope.

Source: Global Underwater Search Team, http://www.cryptozoology.st/.

—— N ——

Naden Harbour carcass

In July 1937, while opening the stomach of a sperm whale killed off British Columbia's Langara Island, flensers at Naden Harbour's whaling station discovered a curious creature. Despite some superficial damage from the whale's digestive fluids, the carcass was more or less intact. Three photos were taken of the animal, one preserved with a caption reading: "The remains of a Sperm Whale's Lunch, a creature of reptilian appearance 10 ft. 6 in. in length with animal like vertebrae and a tail similar to that of a horse. The head bears a resemblance to that of a large dog with features of a horse and the turn down nose of a CAMEL." Whaler Finn John, who witnessed the discovery, added that the animal "had a horselike head with large limpid eyes and a tuft of stiff whiskers on each cheek. Its long slender body was covered by a fur-like material, with the exception of its back, where spiked horny plates overlapped each other. It had skin-covered flippers and a spade-shaped tail, like a sperm whale."

A portion of the carcass was allegedly sent to the Nanaimo Biological Station, but no record of its arrival remains. Somehow, it appears to have reached Victoria's Provincial Museum instead. On 23 July 1937, the Vancouver *Province* ran an article on the discovery that read:

A theory advanced in Vancouver that portions of a marine mammal taken from the body of a sperm whale might have been part of a young SEA SERPENT which was an offspring of Victoria's famous CADBOROSAURUS was definitely exploded today by Francis Kermode, director of the provincial museum. Mr. Kermode said there was little doubt that the portion of a backbone, the piece of baleen and the portion of skin forwarded to the museum were pieces of a baleen whale, which he believes was of premature birth. The pieces were taken from a sperm whale caught at Naden Harbor in the Queen Charlotte Islands. The backbone is about six feet long.

As noted by researcher PAUL LEBLOND, Kermode was a controversial figure who started work at the museum in 1890, as a 16-year-old office boy and apprentice taxidermist, advancing to curator in 1904 without apparent benefit of any higher education. Indeed, his credentials are so spotty that a 1989 history of the museum declares that "one researcher has concluded that Kermode must have had a bonfire in the late 1930s, leaving in the files only those documents that showed him in a favourable mode." The museum's curator of mammals, Dr. Ian McTaggart-Cowan, was on vacation when the "sea oddity" arrived, and all traces of it had vanished by the time he returned, a few days later. Examining photos of the creature, McTaggart-Cowan freely admitted that it resembled no whale (or any other creature) he had ever seen. Years later, working from photos, Paul LeBlond calculated that the creature (draped across a 5-foot table and three packing crates, with the tail dangling over one end) actually measured between 11.5 and 12.5 feet long. The tail does not so much resemble a horse's, as it does the flippers of a seal. And it bears no resemblance whatever to a baleen whale (*Balaena* sp.).

Source: LeBlond and Bousfield, *Cadborosaurus*.

Nāga/Nāgaq

The Nāga is a giant SNAKE or DRAGON of Buddhist and Hindu mythology, but persistent reports suggest that a large reptilian creature known by the same name inhabits various remote parts of Southeast Asia. Most reports issue from territory along the Mekong River, but a similar creature, known as the Nāgaq or ULAR TEDONG ("buffalo snake") was said to inhabit the Tasek Bera and TASEK CHINI marshes, in Pahang State. In 1974, U.S. soldiers patrolling the Mekong in South Vietnam reportedly caught a 25-foot "Nāga FISH" that resembled an oarfish (*Regalecus glesnae*), although that species is pelagic and is not known to inhabit rivers.

Thailand has produced the most recent Nāga sightings. In 1992, Buddhist workmen at Phon Pisai, near the Laotian border, were confronted by a huge black snake while pulling down the ruins of an old monastery prior to erecting a new one. Three years later, Malinee Phisaphan was aboard a bus, crossing a bridge

near Nongkhai (northern Thailand), when she saw a black snake in the river below. She estimated it was 17 feet long and the same diameter as a soccer ball. (Several Asian PYTHONS reach or exceed that length, but none are black.) In 1997, a party of 30 witnesses walking along the Mekong bluffs near Phon Pisai saw a huge snake in the river below. One witness, Police Chief Suphat, estimated that the creature was 228 feet long, swimming with horizontal flexation typical of a reptile. Cryptozoologist Richard Freeman, representing the CENTRE FOR FORTEAN ZOOLOGY, visited Phon Pisai in October 2000 and interviewed various Nāga witnesses. He believed that Chief Suphat's size estimate was greatly exaggerated, perhaps resulting from a view of several snakes swimming in tandem or one large specimen leaving a dramatic wake. Freeman further determined that "Nāga bones" stored at the local police station were elephant's teeth, while a film of an alleged Nāga depicted a floating log. Finally, Freeman searched a cave where one local witness allegedly saw a Nāga 59 feet long in 1990. He found no snakes, but did uncover a population of luminous midge larvae, resembling the famous "glow worms" of New Zealand's Waitomo cave system (*Arachnocampa luminosa*) which had not been reported previously from Thailand.

Sources: Dinsdale, *Monster Hunt*; Freeman, "In the coils of the Naga"; "The Mekong Naga." *Fortean Times* 173 (September 2003): 71; Karl Shuker, "Alien zoo." *Fortean Times* 144 (April 2001): 23; Stewart Wavell, *The Lost World of the East*. London: Souvenir Press, 1958.

Nahuelito

LAGO NAHUEL HUAPI ("Lake of the TIGER'S Island") is located in the mountains of Argentina's Neuquén Province, near the Chilean border. The lake is 52 miles long and five miles across at its widest point, situated at 2,495 feet above sea level. The surrounding peaks soar to 7,875 feet and include some of Argentina's best ski slopes. Today, Lago Nahuel Huapi is a popular tourist destination, bounded on the south by San Carlos de Bariloche, a city of 100,000 inhabitants. It was not always so well known, however, and the lake's dark waters still conceal at least one tantalizing secret.

Reports of a resident LAKE MONSTER first reached European ears in April 1817, when two hunters named Milacsek and Shirdos collected native reports of a "strange animal" inhabiting Lago Nahuel Huapi. (The same hunters later claimed to have killed a flying animal resembling a PTEROSAUR as it emerged from a cave near the lake.) In April 1910, at the lake's Pass Coytrué inlet, George Garrett and his son saw "an object which appeared to be 15–20 ft. in diameter and perhaps 6 ft. above the water." Two British prospectors reported a similar sighting, a short time later, but the real furor did not erupt until 1922. In that year, American prospector Martin Sheffield informed zookeeper CLEMENTE ONELLI that he had seen an animal resembling a PLESIOSAUR in Lago Nahuel Huapi. Onelli mounted an expedition to find the creature, but his searchers returned empty-handed. Another expedition visited the lake in the 1950s, but it was largely ignored by the press and no record remains of its results.

Sightings of the creature locally known as Nahuelito ("little Nahuel," after the lake) continued through the remainder of the 20th century. On 16 February 1978, the mother of the Rev. Mauricio Rumboll saw the creature, swimming with its long neck raised 10 feet above the water's surface. More sightings were logged in the summer of 1979. Ten years later, in March 1989 local television aired footage of an indistinct large object moving in the lake. German journalist Esteban Bayer collected background information on Nahuelito, but he apparently confused the long-necked creature with another aquatic cryptid known as Cuero ("hide"), typically described as a flat-bodied bottom-dweller. Multiple witnesses saw Nahuelito in daylight, at close range, on 1 January 1994. Witness Paula Jacarbe claimed she could hear the animal breathing. Another member of the group, Jessica Campbell, reported two more sightings on a single afternoon in summer 1996. Other witnesses shared her encounter on that occasion, on the beach at Peninsula de San Pedro.

Sources: Jean-Jacques Barloy, *Les Survivants de L'ombre*. Paris: Arthaud, 1985; Costello, *In Search of Lake Monsters*; Kirk, *In the Domain of the Lake Monsters*; Hans Krieg, *Als Zoologe in Steppen und Wäldern Patagoniens*. Munich: J.F. Lehmann, 1940; "Local man lays claim to having caught sight of gigantic plesiosaur." *Toronto Globe* (6 April 1922); Magin, "Duck! It's a plesiosaur"; "Nahuelito: Creature story makes waves." *New Orleans Times-Picayune* (28 March 1989).

Naitaka   This generic name, translated as "lake demon," was applied by Okanagan tribesmen to various LAKE MONSTERS throughout western Canada. One

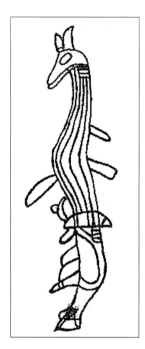

of several variant names, Na-ha-ha-itque, means "SNAKE in the water." Descriptions vary with time and place, but many of the animals described are large and serpentine in form, sometimes with heads resembling that of a horse. Today, better-known cryptids are commonly known by individual names such as OGOPOGO, MANIPOGO, and so forth.

Sources: Costello, *In Search of Lake Monsters*; Moon, *Ogopogo*.

Aboriginal artwork depicts the acquatic Naitaka.

Nalusa Falaya   Although its Choctaw name ("long black being") seems more suited to a LAKE MONSTER or SEA SERPENT, the Nalusa Falaya is an unclassified primate reported from the southern states of North America. Alternate names throughout its 19th-century range included Bohpoli ("thrower"), Hattak Chito ("big man"), Kowi Anakasha ("forest dweller") and Kwanokasha. The first refers to an alleged habit of pelting humans with sticks and stones, while the second might as easily refer to various BIGFOOT-type HOMINIDS such as the FOUKE MONSTER and the creatures reported from Louisiana's HONEY ISLAND SWAMP. Some modern cryptozoologists consider the Nalusa Falaya identical with NORTH AMERICAN APES and/or DEVIL MONKEYS.

Sources: Bigfoot: America's Ape?, http://www.ratsnest.net/bigfoot/skunkape.htm; Choctaw Legends and Stories, http://www.tc.umn.edu/~mboucher/mikebouchweb/choctaw/legends2.htm

Nampèshiu   Potawatomi tribesmen of Michigan and Wisconsin applied this generic term to LAKE MONSTERS found throughout those states in the 18th and 19th centuries. The term translates as "water panther," but the animal(s) bore no resemblance to Africa's WATER LEOPARD or the IEMISCH of South America. Instead, the Nampèshiu was described as serpentine, with bovine horns and a coat of yellowish fur.

Source: James Howard, "When they worship the underwater panther: A prairie Potawatomi bundle ceremony." *Southwestern Journal of Anthropology* 16 (1960): 217–224.

Nanauner   The Nanauner is an unclassified primate or HOMINID reported from southern Kenya. Native witnesses describe it as a large BIGFOOT-type biped covered in black hair (although one of its alternate names, Naibor, curiously translates as "the white"). A similar name (Nenaunir) is applied to the Masai tribe's god of storms, suggesting a possible overlap between mythology and descriptions of a real-life cryptid.

Sources: Heuvelmans, *Les Bêtes Humaines d'Afrique*; Roumeguère-Eberhardt, *Dossier X*.

***Nancy Hanks* sea serpent**   In 1898, brothers Albert and Robert Wass encountered a SEA SERPENT off the coast of Maine. Albert described the experience 35 years later.

> Robert and I were on board the A-1 copper-bottomed sloop *Nancy Hanks* bound from S.E. Rock Fishing Ground to N.E. Harbor about four or five miles southwest from Schoodic Point in the mouth of Frenchman's Bay, when a black object having the appearance of a ledge just awash, or a whale's back loomed up less than a quarter of a mile ahead. We could see and hear what appeared to be a spar buoy with its base held stationary, spanking its length on the surface of the water with a circular motion, at varying intervals of from two to five seconds.
>
> At first we thought it must be a whale being attacked by a thrasher or swordfish, but, on nearer approach, we were convinced that it was something different from what we had ever encountered. When we had reached a proximity of about 100 yards (and, believe me, that was close enough!), the monster straightened itself out to a form resembling a seventy-five-feet string of hogsheads. Whether the body was creased in sections or the color markings camouflaged it as such, I am not sure. It carried its head, which was like that of a horse, six feet higher than its body, the motion of swimming was like an EEL, and its speed, at least twenty knots [23 mph]. The absence of fins and the eel-shape of the tail settled all doubt that this could be any known type of whale.

Source: O'Neill, *The Great New England Sea Serpent*.

Nandi Bear   With the exception of Algeria's ATLAS BEAR, no bears are known from the African continent, though rumors and reports of their existence are found throughout recorded history. Greek author Herodotus, the "Father of History," described Libyan bears in the 5th century B.C. In 1668, Dutch merchant-explorer Olfert Dapper listed bears among the fauna of the Congo jungles. The first recorded European sighting of the East African cryptid known as the Nandi Bear was logged by British explorer Geoffrey Williams from Kenya, in 1905. Seven years later, after a new rash of sightings, Williams described the animal as follows:

> In size it was, I should say, larger than the bear that lives in the pit at the "Zoo" and it was quite as heavily built. The fore quarters were very thickly furred, as were all four legs, but the hind quarters were comparatively speaking smooth or bare....The head was long and pointed and exactly like that of a bear, as indeed was the whole animal. I have not a very clear recollection of the ears beyond the fact that they were small, and the tail, if any, was very small and practically unnoticeable. The colour was dark and left us both with the impression that it was more or less of a brindle, like a wildebeest, but this may have been an effect of the light.

In 1912, a Major Toulson glimpsed a strange beast near the same location, reporting that "it appeared to have long hair behind and it was rather low in front." The creature was 18–20 inches tall and ran with a shuffling gait. In March 1913, District Commissioner N.E.F. Corbett saw a creature covered with reddish-brown hair, "with a slight streak of white down the hind quarters, rather long from hock to foot, rather bigger than a

Some researchers believe the Nandi Bear is a large, aggressive hyena.

hyena, with largish ears." Around the same time, railroad workers in southern Kenya reported a creature that left rectangular 5-toed tracks, with clear evidence of claws. In fact, descriptions of the Nandi Bear — also known throughout Kenya and Uganda as Chemosit ("the devil"), Geteit, Kichwa mutwe and Shivuverre — vary so widely that Bernard Heuvelmans dubbed it "an East African proteus," suggesting that two different cryptids may be involved. One resembles a bear or very large hyena, while the other resembles a primate.

Wherever it is found, whatever it looks like, the Nandi Bear enjoys a vicious reputation. Around 1918, farmers in Kenya's Lumbwa district lost 67 sheep and goats to a MYSTERY MAULER who cracked their skulls and ate the brains within, still leaving 16 of its victims clinging to life when they were found. Local natives lived in fear of the beast, which also snatched children and sometimes even killed adult humans. Farmer Cara Buxton claimed the beast was later killed by native hunters and proved to be a large spotted hyena (*Crocuta crocuta*). In 1925, game warden Charles Hichens was sent to investigate the depredations suffered at another Kenyan village, where a night-prowling beast had snatched a 6-year-old girl from her hut and leaped with the child in its jaws over a fence 6 feet 6 inches tall. Hichens never saw the beast, but it returned one night to carry off his dog. Douglas Hutton shot two supposed Nandi Bears on the Chemomi tea estate, sometime in 1957–58, but the Nairobi Museum identified the animals as "giant forest hyenas." The shrieking Chemosit that chased engineer Angus McDonald around his hut near Kipkabus, Kenya in the early 1960s was seven feet tall, with an apelike face, capable of running either upright or on all fours.

Various suspects have been named as Nandi Bear candidates over time. Bernard Heuvelmans proposed an aardvark (*Orycteropus afer*) for some of the sightings, though it lacks the Nandi Bear's savage temperament and carnivorous appetite. LOREN COLEMAN and PATRICK HUYGHE suspect a kind of giant MONKEY, roughly coinciding with Heuvelmans's suggestion that a BABOON might be responsible for some of the attacks (though none known to science approaches the Nandi Bear's size). KARL SHUKER, meanwhile, proposed a relict population of short-faced hyenas (*Pachycrocuta brevirostris*), a LION-sized predator of the Pleistocene period presumed extinct for some 10,000 years.

Sources: Coleman and Huyghe, *The Field Guide to Bigfoot, Yeti, and Other Mystery Primates Worldwide*; Heuvelmans, *On the Track of Unknown Animals*; Charles Pitman, *A Game Warden Among His Charges*. London: Nisbet, 1931; Shuker, *From Flying Toads to Snakes with Wings*; Geoffrey Williams, "An unknown animal on the Uasingishu." *Journal of the East Africa and Uganda Natural History Society* 4 (1912): 123–125.

Nannup Tiger   Nannup, Western Australia is a wooded area located 175 miles south of Perth, between Busselton and Manjimup. Beginning in 1966, local ranchers were plagued by a MYSTERY MAULER they dubbed the Nannup TIGER, after its striped coat, although witnesses disagreed as to whether the beast was an ALIEN BIG CAT or a relict THYLACINE. Tom Longbottom logged one of the first sightings, describing the creature as follows:

It was about the size of a roo dog [dingo] with a big head, long body, heavy shoulders, long tail with brush on the last 12–14 inches or so. Some dark bands went around the body as well. Its eyes were not like dogs' eyes....The tracks were not dog tracks. We hear funny sounds at night like a choking or a soft barking which I'd say was him. Our dog...had a big fight in the roadway but he won't go out there any more. I don't blame him.

Longbottom reported that lambs and KANGAROOS alike fell victim to the nocturnal predator, found with their heads devoured but no other visible wounds. After a three-year hiatus, sightings resumed in spring 1970, with witnesses describing the creature(s) as "dark, striped, with a long tail, fast-moving and about the size of a big dog." Its 4-toed tracks, however, were considered "unusual" and not doglike. In October 1970, a full-scale weekend hunt was mounted by Nannup residents and officers of the Forestry Department, but HOAXERS intervened, distracting the searchers with a sheep shaved and painted to resemble a tiger. Still, the hunters found a lair supposedly occupied by their quarry and made plaster casts of its curious footprints nearby.

Sporadic sightings continued through the early 1970s. Three timber workers reported an encounter with a beast they called "a cross between a FOX, a dog and a CAT." Later, in November 1972, Joe and Freda Carmody watched the Nannup Tiger cross a rural highway, some 30–35 feet in front of their car. They described a "grand, upstanding creature" identical to thylacines depicted in old photographs. As Freda Carmody told reporters, "Both my husband and I are pretty keen on the bush and were both raised in the country, seeing enough dingoes and foxes to know what they look like." Alleged thylacine sightings continue in Western Australia, but hard proof of the animal's survival remains elusive.

Sources: Healy and Cropper, *Out of the Shadows*; "A tiger, by jingo!" *Brisbane Telegraph* (3 November 1971); Smith, *Bunyips and Bigfoots*.

Napier, John (1917–87)   British primatologist John Napier once served as director of the Smithsonian Institution's primate biology program. He also cultivated an avid interest in unknown HOMINIDS, including BIGFOOT and the YETI. Napier considered the PATTERSON FILM to be a HOAX, based on perceived discrepancies between the creature's apparent size and the evidence of tracks found at the California site where it was filmed. In February 1969, he learned of the MINNESOTA ICEMAN discovery from IVAN SANDERSON and attempted to obtain the specimen for scientific study, but his efforts proved fruitless and Napier concluded that this episode was also a hoax. Eight months later, though, discovery of the BOSSBURG TRACKS in Washington convinced Napier that Bigfoot must exist. Those footprints, from an apparently crippled SASQUATCH, led Napier to write in 1972:

It is very difficult to conceive of a hoaxer so subtle, so knowledgeable — and so sick — who would deliberately fake a footprint of this nature. I suppose it is possible, but it is so unlikely that I am prepared to discount it.

And if one Bigfoot existed, then by extension, there must be others. In closing, Napier noted, "I am convinced that the Sasquatch exists, but whether it is all that it is cracked up to be is another matter altogether. There must be *something* in northwest America that needs explaining, and that something leaves man-like footprints." Prior to his death in 1987, Napier was named an honorary member of the INTERNATIONAL SOCIETY OF CRYPTOZOOLOGY.

Sources: Coleman, *Bigfoot!*; Napier, *Bigfoot: The Yeti and Sasquatch in Myth and Reality.*

Narcissus sea serpent At 5:00 a.m. on 21 May 1899, soon after rounding Cape Falcon near Mers-el-Kébir, Algeria, sailors aboard H.M.S. *Narcissus* saw a 150-foot SEA SERPENT "apparently propelled by large fins, and lying very low in the water." In answer to skeptics, a Lieutenant Boothby replied:

> We saw some porpoises just after and their motion was not the same. You could see the porpoises jump or tumble over, but this creature lay steadily on the surface, gently gliding through the water…. The monster seemed to be propelled by an immense number of fins. You could see the fins propelling it along at about the same rate as the ship was going. The fins were on both sides, and appeared to be turning over and over. There were fins right down to the tail. Another curious thing was that it spouted up water [sic] like a whale, only the spouts were very small and came from various parts of the body.

Source: Heuvelmans, *In the Wake of the Sea Serpents.*

Narooma carcass On 15 April 1935, young brothers Keith and Joseph Thomson found a rotting carcass washed ashore near Narooma, on the coast of New South Wales, Australia. As described in the press:

> The animal was about eight feet long. It had a long, tapering, bony head. The lower jaw was studded with about 48 teeth, which were separated by half-inch gaps. Most of the teeth were missing from the top jaw. The eyes were set just behind the gape of the large mouth. There were two fins just behind the head, a large dorsal fin, and two horizontal fins at the end of the tail. The whole animal was covered with a smooth, leathery skin.

Most researchers today agree that the creature was some kind of dolphin, though no effort was made to preserve it or identify the species.

Source: Smith, *Bunyips & Bigfoots.*

Narrabeen Lakes, Australia Narrabeen Lakes is a northern suburb of Sydney, Australia, named for its waterways that serve as a focal point for recreation. The area has also produced some cryptid reports that defy easy classification, appearing neither as traditional BUNYIP nor LAKE MONSTER sightings. The first occurred at 1:15 p.m. on 3 April 1968, when Mabel Walsh and her nephew John were driving along Wakehurst Parkway. Off to one side of the road, they saw a strange creature standing in shallow water. As Mrs. Walsh described the animal:

> It was a bit over 4 feet tall, with dark grey, tough leathery skin, like an elephant's. It had small front legs and walked on its hind legs which were thick and round like an elephant's. It ambled out of the lake and ran into the scrub. It had a strange shuffling walk, but it was quite fast. It shocked me. It was a peculiar-looking thing. I've never seen anything like it. We saw it or only a few seconds….I didn't notice a tail or ears, but it had small eyes and smaller front legs or arms. Its head reminded me of an ant-eater's.

Its trunk was rigid, squared off at the end and stuck down and out at an angle.

Three years later, in April 1971, a party of children reportedly glimpsed a similar creature in the same area, but it eluded searchers and has not been seen again.

Sources: Smith, *Bunyips & Bigfoots*; *Sydney Mirror* (25 April 1971).

Narrow Lake, Michigan This lake, located in Eaton County, produced a LAKE MONSTER report on 2 September 1886, but no more recent sightings are on record.

Source: The Online Lake Cryptid Directory, http:/dive.to/lakemonsters.

Nart The Nart is an unclassified primate or HOMINID reported from the Caucasus Mountains of Georgia through the early 20th century. Its description generally matches that of SASQUATCH-type creatures, and it may be identical to similar cryptids reported from the same area, including the ABNAUAYU, DAV and TSKHISS-KATSI. Sometime in the 1920s, George Papashvily claimed a discovery of large humanoid bones in a cave near Gora Kazbek, but the evidence was not collected for study.

Source: George and Helen Papashvily, *Home, and Home Again.* New York: Harper and Row, 1973.

Nasnas/Nasua The Nasnas ("wild man") is an unknown HOMINID reported from the Pamir Mountains of Tajikistan, where it reportedly emulates other BIGFOOT-type cryptids by abducting human females as prospective mates. Peasants in the Vakhan region once allegedly returned the favor by hunting the Nasnas for food. The creature's description does not vary appreciably from other Pamir WILDMEN, including the ADAM-DZHAPAIS, DAV, FARISHTA, GOLUB-YAVAN, PARÉ and YABALIK-ADAM. The Nasnas name is apparently also used on occasion to describe a similar creature in Yemen.

Source: Bayanov, *In the Footsteps of the Russian Snowman.*

Natal sea serpents South Africa's Natal Province lies on the nation's east coast, incorporating the region sometimes called Zululand. Over time, it has produced some startling SEA SERPENT reports, beginning in 1922 with the still-unidentified MARGATE CARCASS of a creature resembling a giant polar bear, washed ashore after a 3-hour battle with whales offshore. The next report of an aquatic cryptid involves an apparent LAKE MONSTER, but as BERNARD HEUVELMANS noted, the lake in question (St. Lucia) is connected to the sea. A party of nine was night-fishing at the lake on 7 July 1933, when they observed what they believed to be a pair of hippopotamuses in the water. As witness George Court told the press:

> We all rose to get a better look at them. I took my field glasses to get a better view. To my amazement I saw floating in the calm water under a strong moon a long undulating dark body about 30 yards in length. The head and shoulders were similar to those of a hornless ox. The long body, which lay "S" shaped, appeared to be two feet broad. It was lying at right angles to the beach, and facing our camp. Mr. Esmonde-White had his field glasses on the creature also, and confirmed my opinion. Mr. Higgs, who has hunted hippo for forty years on this coast and had a pet hippo on his farm at one time, after looking through the glasses, said that hippo did not keep behind one another like that. They would also be making a noise….About 30 minutes later the creature disappeared by sinking beneath the surface of the lake, which at this spot averages about five feet deep.

Sea serpents returned to the headlines in Natal during April 1947, when several Merebank residents claimed to have seen a

60-foot specimen near Tiger Rocks, on the south coast. Bathers on the beach described "a flurry in the water and a black object about a mile from the shore." In late August, sailors aboard the *Harry Cheadle* reported a sighting at Durban. Tourists aboard the pleasure-cruiser *panther* also allegedly glimpsed a huge cryptid, though Bernard Heuvelmans dismissed that sighting as a HOAX. On 5 September 1947, witness J. Kennedy of Isipingo reported a creature with eyes "like red searchlights" that rose from the surf and "brayed like a hundred donkeys."

In January 1952, Gerald Pemberton and Nowell Udall reported a serpentine cryptid swimming in Ifafa lagoon near Umzinto, Natal. Seven years later, on 1 December 1959, fishermen aboard the CONGELLA reported sighting a school of 20 unknown creatures, each 30 feet long, offshore from Durban. Eight days later, Hans Greissing and Tom Evans were navigating the Maydon channel in a motorboat, when they met a creature which Greissing described as follows:

It looked like a wave—only it just shouldn't have been there. So we bore over to investigate. We were going pretty fast, and all of a sudden we found ourselves sliding over something. There was a bump, and our propeller, which fortunately was on a hinge, was whirled upwards out of the water. Then we saw the object below us. It was an enormous creature swimming just below the surface. We could not see the head or tail—only the central hump some 10 feet or so long. It was about 2½ feet wide and seemed to be grayish-white on top with black sides. There was no sign of any fin.

Dr. Heuvelmans made short work of the 1950s sightings in his classic study of sea serpents. In his judgment, Pemberton and Udall simply saw a PYTHON, the *Congella*'s crewmen met a pod of beaked whales, and the Greissing-Evans sighting involved a hippopotamus (albeit a rather strange one).

Source: Heuvelmans, *In the Wake of the Sea Serpents.*

Nawao *see* Menehune

Ndalawo
This mystery predator of Uganda was described by William Hichens in 1937 as "a fierce man-killing carnivore, the size and shape of a leopard, but with a black-furred back shading to grey below." Game warden Charles Pitman considered the beast a "partly melanistic leopard," retaining normal markings only the lower jaw and the extremities. The Ndalawo also deviates from normal leopard behavior by allegedly hunting in groups of three or four and emits a cackling sound reminiscent of hyenas. Ugandan natives insist that it is not a hyena, however, but something larger and more dangerous. A pelt from one specimen was allegedly procured sometime in the 1920s, but it was sent out of country before it could be examined.

Sources: Hichens, "African mystery beasts"; Shuker, *Mystery Cats of the World.*

Ndendeki
Natives inhabiting forests along the Likouala aux Herbes River, 35 miles from Lake Tele in the Republic of Congo, describe the Ndendeki as a giant TURTLE 13–16 feet in diameter. Africa's largest known turtle, the softshell (*Trionyx triunguis*), does not officially exceed three feet in length, though Congolese biologist MARCELLIN AGNAGNA sets the maximum size at 6 feet 6 inches. Earth's largest known living turtle, the leatherback (*Dermochelys coriacea*), may reach 7 feet 10 inches but is strictly a pelagic species. The largest known turtle of all time, *Archelon*, was a 12-foot marine reptile of the Late Cretaceous period (presumed extinct for at least 65 million years). Cryptozoologist ROY MACKAL suggests that the Ndendeki are oversized specimens of *T. triunguis*, further inflated by exaggeration in the telling.

Source: Mackal, *A Living Dinosaur?*

Congolese natives describe the Ndendeki as a giant turtle.

Ndesu/Nesu
This unclassified primate or HOMINID, reported from the Congo region in the 19th century, was described as a large, aggressive biped covered with dark hair. It had an evil reputation, purportedly rooted in its practice of stalking and devouring human beings. In that respect it mimics another Congolese hominid, the MULAHU, and the equally voracious ENGÔT of nearby Gabon.

Source: Paul Güssfeldt, Julius Falkenstein and Eduard Pechüel-Loesche, *Die Loango-Expedition.* Leipzig: P. Frohberg, 1907.

Neandertal Man
The proto-human species *Homo sapiens neanderthalensis* ("wise person from the valley of the River Neander") is named for the German valley where its first fossils were unearthed in 1856. Many other fossil sites have since been discovered from Gibraltar and North Africa through the Near East and central Asia. Neandertals (frequently spelled "Neanderthal") evolved around 250,000 years ago and flourished at the end of the Pleistocene Ice Age. Their bodies were relatively short and powerfully built, with large hands and joints, rather broad heads, flat noses and prominent brow ridges. Their brain capacity, often exceeding 1,400cc, was on average larger than that of modern *Homo sapiens*. The Neandertals' sophistication is revealed in well-developed tool technology and the apparent beginnings of organized religion, including displays of reverence for cave bears (*Ursus spelaeus*). Some anthropologists once believed that Neandertals interbred with more advanced migrants from Africa, but most rejected the notion, viewing the race as a side branch of the human family. In fact, analysis of skulls performed at the University of Zurich in 2001 indicates "separation of Neandertals and modern humans at the species level" that would have rendered such interbreeding impossible. Most scientists now believe Neandertals existed alongside *H. sapiens* for a time, then died out around 35,000 years ago because they were less adaptable to changing climate.

But *are* they extinct? Some researchers, including DMITRI BAYANOV, LOREN COLEMAN, BERNARD HEUVELMANS, PATRICK HUYGHE, BORIS PORSHNEV and IVAN SANDERSON have suggested that a relict population of Neandertals survives to the present day, thus explaining many reports of WILDMEN and unknown HOMINIDS around the world. Heuvelmans and Bayanov considered the MINNESOTA ICEMAN to be a Neandertal specimen. Sanderson found Neandertal footprints virtually identical to those of the GOLUB-YAVAN, while considering the ALMAS and KSY-GYIK other likely candidates. Coleman and Huyghe likewise include such cryptids as the NUK-LUK and WUDÉWÁSÁ among the latter-day Neandertals. Most mainstream scientists dismiss such speculation as unbridled flights of fantasy.

Sources: Coleman and Clark, *Cryptozoology A to Z*; Coleman and Huyghe, *The Field Guide to Bigfoot, Yeti, and Other Mystery Primates Worldwide*; Heuvelmans and Bayanov, *L'Homme de Néanderthal est Toujour Vivant*; "Neanderthals weren't human, say scientists." *Ananova* (1 August 2001); Shackley, *Still Living?*

Negroes-of-the-Water

These strange, amphibious primates or MERBEINGS are reported sporadically from Argentina, Paraguay and southern Brazil. Witnesses describe them as three feet tall or shorter, with bald heads and black skin covered by dark hair. Some accounts refer to webbed hands and feet. The creatures are nocturnal, and despite their preference for water, they sometimes climb trees. On 31 May 1985, two boys at Roque Saenz Peña, Argentina reportedly stopped one of the beasts from snatching a 5-year-old child. Several more sightings were reported from the area, on successive nights.

Sources: Coleman and Huyghe, *The Field Guide to Bigfoot, Yeti, and Other Mystery Primates Worldwide*; Picasso, "Infrequent types of Southern American humanoids."

Nekohebitori

News of this supposed Japanese cryptid reached the West in summer 2003, after New York resident David Nardiello returned from a 3-year teaching sojourn in Shinke-Cho, a small town near Osaka, on the island of Shikoku. One rainy night in May, while bicycling past a flooded rice paddy near his apartment building, Nardiello experienced a strange encounter. As he later told the *Long Island Press*, "I'm looking in the lake and I see this thing pop out. A white neck. And it's got two black eyes. And then it turns its neck to look at me. And it noticed me. And then, right as it noticed me-it started walking out. But it looked like it had CAT'S legs. It looked like maybe it was a lizard. It turns to look at me, then turns and takes out wings and starts to fly away. It must have gone almost 100 feet up in the air, out of nowhere. It sent shivers up my spine. I got the hell out of there." Moments later, safe in his apartment, Nardiello risked another glance outside. "I look out the window and I see it fly right by again," he said. "Really fast, too. Right up, close. [Its wings] looked like BAT'S wings. And its paws looked like a cat['s]—like the arms of a cat. It had a tail, too. [Its face] looked like a white SNAKE with black eyes. Like great-white-SHARK black eyes." A coworker subsequently identified the creature as a Nekohebitori ("cat snake BIRD"). Upon hearing the story, cryptozoologist LOREN COLEMAN speculated that the creature may be a variation of the KAPPA ("river child") familiar from Japanese folklore.

Source: Tristram Fox, "Paranormal P.I." *Long Island Press* (n.d., received via e-mail from Loren Coleman on 21 September 2003).

Nellie the Lion

Two months after the U.S. entered World War I, in July 1917, residents of central Illinois were frightened by reports of an ALIEN BIG CAT prowling around their community. The first reported witness/victim, butler Thomas Gullett, was attacked while picking flowers on the Robert Allerton estate, southwest of Monticello. Gullett escaped with only minor injuries, but his report of the assault by a CAT resembling a lioness (*Panthera leo*) spread panic throughout the area. Three hundred hunters scoured the countryside on 15 July, but the cat slipped past them to visit the Allerton mansion, a quarter-mile distant, where a housekeeper confirmed Gullett's description of the animal. Two days later, a pair of teenage boys glimpsed the cat beside the Sangamon River, east of Decatur, and searchers found 5-inch pawprints. Hysteria ensued, including several shooting incidents. (One shaky hunter fired on a car, whose headlights he mistook for the LION'S shining eyes.) Newspapers made light of the reports,

and dubbed the elusive cat Nellie, despite its fierce temper. On 29 July, two couples were driving between Decatur and Springfield when the cat charged their moving car. It seemed stunned by the collision, still sitting on the roadside when witness Earl Hill returned with police, but the cat then fled and evaded its pursuers in the dark. Farmer James Rutherford reported his encounter with a "large yellow, long-haired beast" two days later, but again the posse missed its prey. Nellie soon departed from the area, vanishing as mysteriously as "she" had come. Some researchers suggest the cat was a rare EASTERN COUGAR (*Puma concolor*), while others remain unconvinced. LOREN COLEMAN reports that *two* cats were seen in the area, but the witnesses he cites describe only one.

Sources: Clark and Coleman, "On the trail of pumas, panthers and ULAs"; Coleman, *Mysterious America*.

Nemesis sea serpent (185?)

Sometime in the 1850s, while en route to Rangoon through the Indian Ocean, the steamer *Nemesis* met a large reptile in the Indian Ocean. Passenger W.H. Marshall, former editor of the *Rangoon Chronicle*, described the incident in 1860.

> As the *Nemesis* was proceeding toward our destination, our attention was directed to an ALLIGATOR of enormous length, which was swimming along against the tide (here very strong), at a rate which was perfectly astonishing. I never beheld such a monster. It passed within a very short distance from us, its head and nearly half its body out of the water. I should think it could not have been less than five-and-forty feet long, measuring from the head to the extremity of the tail, and I am confident it was travelling at the rate of, at least, thirty miles an hour.

Alligators are not native to the Indian Ocean, nor do any known CROCODILES attain the size described by Marshall. Likewise, as observed by BERNARD HEUVELMANS, they do not swim at such speeds or with so much of their bodies above-water. Heuvelmans suggested that Marshall may have seen a surviving member of the *Thalattosuchia*, a family of FISH-tailed crocodilians from the Jurassic period, presumed extinct for at least 144 million years.

Source: Heuvelmans, *In the Wake of the Sea Serpents*.

Nemesis sea serpent (1900)

In 1900, passengers aboard the steamer *Nemesis* allegedly met a huge SEA SERPENT off Cape Naturaliste, Western Australia. Captain Laurence Thomson later published an account of the adventure in *Wide World Magazine* (March 1901), describing the creature as 300 feet long and three feet in diameter, raising its body from the water in three great arches while a long neck with a fin resembling a parasol scouted the surface. *Wide World*'s editors concluded that the creature "is, of course, nothing more than the gigantic OCTOPUS," but BERNARD HEUVELMANS dismissed it as a transparent HOAX, noting that the creature's undulations were "both mechanically and dynamically utterly impossible."

Source: Heuvelmans, *In the Wake of the Sea Serpents*.

Nepalese Dragon

The only report of this giant reptile to date was published by cryptozoologist WILLIAM GIBBONS in 2003, based on a second-hand report from the Rev. Resham Poudal, an Indian missionary to Nepal. The sighting occurred in 1980, at an undisclosed location. Poudal and several companions had camped overnight in a jungle clearing, beside a large "log" which surprised them next morning by sluggishly crawling away. As Poudal described the it:

> The animal was at least 40 feet in length, and about 5–7 feet in circumference. It was extremely well camouflaged and was a green-

Artist's conception of the Nepalese dragon reported by witness Resham Poudal in 1980 (*William Rebsamen*).

ish brown in color. Large armored scales protected the underbelly, and my informants tell me that the "DRAGON" moves very slowly — barely a foot or two per day. Its jaws were huge, and we were warned not to step directly in front of the creature, as it was capable of performing a powerful inhalation — sucking its prey (water buffalo) into its cavernous jaws from a distance of 10 or 15 feet. A six feet tall man could easily stand upright within its open jaws, which were enormous. Its eyes take on a greenish luminescent glow at night, a feature it uses to attract prey.

Sadly, none of Poudal's party came equipped with cameras, and since they feared to tackle the enormous creature, it was left to inch its way toward parts unknown. Gibbons notes that the reptile is legless, suggesting a giant SNAKE.

Source: Gibbons, *Missionaries and Monsters*.

Nepalese Tree Bear
In February 1983, while pursuing field work in Nepal's Barun Valley, near Mount Makalu, zoologists Robert Fleming and Daniel Taylor-Ide collected native reports of two bears allegedly residing in the area. One, the Himalayan black bear (*Ursus thibetanus*), was already familiar, but the other was unknown to science. Nepalese informants described it as an arboreal "tree bear," ultimately supplying several skulls whose teeth were consistently smaller than those of *U. thibetanus*. In early 1984, it was revealed that Kathmandu Zoo had an alleged tree bear specimen on display, captured sometime in 1982. With government permission, the bear was tranquilized and minute measurements were taken for a morphometric analysis. Further skulls were collected during 1984–85, but study of the specimens produced conflicting results. Some researchers now believe the Nepalese tree bear is nothing more than a juvenile form of *U. thibetanus*, while others (and most Nepalese natives) regard it as a distinct and separate species. Further study is needed to resolve the matter, but no new expeditions are currently planned.

Sources: "Evidence for new bear species in Nepal." *ISC Newsletter* 3 (Spring 1984): 1–3; "New Nepal bear now in doubt." *ISC Newsletter* 5 (Summer 1986): 11; Shuker, *From Flying Toads to Snakes with Wings*; Taylor-Ide, *Something Hidden Behind the Ranges*.

Nepean Island sea serpent
Nepean is a small, uninhabited island located south of Norfolk Island in the South Pacific (900 miles east of Australia). In 1870, Norfolk Island seaman John Adams described the following encounter with an unidentified SEA SERPENT:

On the 15th of October, 1870. wind S.E. and light, our boat being a mile off Nepean Island, and on the port tack, our look-out reported a calf (as the young whale is called) about a mile and a half distant on the lee bow. We accordingly kept off, and when about one hundred yards from the supposed calf, he said — "I cannot make out what it is; I have not seen a spout yet; but there is an animal of some sort, for his back is out of the water, and there is a wash there all the time." "Very well," was the answer; "Keep a sharp look out." On we went till within a few yards of the object, when the look-out exclaimed, "Look! it is a Sea Serpent!" And look we did. The boat shot within a yard of it, and there it was, a veritable Sea Serpent....When first seen, I suppose it must have been asleep, for its head was lying flat on the surface of the sea, and its body coiled up. The tail of the monster I saw plainly, hanging some three or four fathoms [18–24 feet] below the surface. When we came near it, the beast, if I may call it so, raised its head out of the water, looked at us, then slowly straightening himself, he very leisurely moved off, for it was not lying with its whole length on the surface, but, as nearly as I could judge, it must have been thirty or forty feet. It is of a reddish colour, about a foot or eighteen inches in diameter. We have been about the Island in boats almost every day when the weather's fine for nearly eighteen years, and have never seen anything like it before or since then.

Source: Heuvelmans, *In the Wake of the Sea Serpents*.

Neptune sea serpent
At noon on 3 January 1830, while traveling along the northern coast of Cuba from Matanzas to Havana, passengers and crew aboard the *Neptune* saw what they took for a ship stranded on a reef. As they drew closer, the "ship" was revealed as a "monster of dreadful proportions." As described by Captain Lopez:

It was 15 or 20 feet out of the water in an almost horizontal position, and it was surrounded by an innumerable quantity of FISH of various sizes, which swam in all directions, occupying a space of almost a mile around it. As we came nearer to this huge cetacean we saw it move its jaws, and a terrible noise like that made by a landslide was heard. A black fin, nearly 9 feet high and placed 60 feet from its mouth, slowly appeared. We could not judge the total length of this monster, as the tail did not appear above the surface of the water.

BERNARD HEUVELMANS concluded that the creature was, indeed, a whale — perhaps stranded and dying, with a caudal fin upraised and mistaken for a dorsal fin.

Source: Heuvelmans, *In the Wake of the Sea Serpents*.

Nerang River, Australia
In the early 1900s, Queensland residents living near the Nerang River were agitated by the appearance of a large BUNYIP in their midst. As old-timer W. Robin Smith told author Malcolm Smith in 1973:

The original story told of the bunyip somewhat resembling a horse [that] was claimed to have been seen on the Nerang-Camira Road about 70 years ago when the countryside was in a state of deluge. It was a shy creature and plunged into the Nerang River and was not heard of again for many years. Not until it was supposed to have been seen in the reputed "Bunyip Hole" at the lower end of the Merrimac Estate.

That belated reappearance provoked members of the local Nerang CROCODILE Club to burn the cryptid in effigy, on charges stealing publicity from their favorite reptile. The demonstration must have been effective, since no further sightings are on record. That said, Nerang *did* produce a YOWIE sighting in August 1978.

Source: Healy and Cropper, *Out of the Shadows*; Smith, *Bunyips & Bigfoots*.

Nesophontids   The nesophontids (Family *Nesophontidae*) were small insectivorous mammals, endemic to the Caribbean islands of Cuba, Haiti and Puerto Rico. Eight species were once recognized, but all were presumed extinct by the end of the 17th century. Zoologists were surprised, therefore, to find fresh nesophontid bone and tissue samples in barn owl pellets collected on Haiti, in 1930. The location suggests that any survivors must be Haitian nesophontes (*Nesophontes zamicrus*), but the find also encouraged speculation that relict populations may exist on other nearby islands.

Source: Shuker, *The Lost Ark*.

Ness Information Service   British NESSIE enthusiast Rip Hepple created this service in 1974, in response to dissolution of the LOCH NESS INVESTIGATION BUREAU. The NIS issued quarterly bulletins, aptly titled *Nessletters*, to subscribers worldwide. Its present status is uncertain, as research for this volume failed to locate any bulletins more recent than April 1997.

Source: Harrison, *The Encyclopaedia of the Loch Ness Monster*.

Nessie   The unknown creatures said to inhabit Loch Ness, collectively known as Nessie to enthusiasts worldwide, clearly rank with BIGFOOT and the YETI as "superstars" of cryptozoology. Loch Ness lies at the northern end of Scotland's Great Glen, a geologic fault bisecting the Highlands for some 300 million years. It is also part of the Caledonian Canal, linked to Inverness on the north and to Loch Oich (home of WEE OICHY) to the south. The loch is 24 miles long and roughly one mile wide, with a surface

Saint Columba rescues a swimmer from Nessie in the 6th century (*William Rebsamen*).

area of 21¾ square miles. It contains the greatest volume of fresh water in Britain, at an estimated 263 billion cubic feet. In addition to the Caledonian Canal, Loch Ness is fed by eight rivers and about 40 streams. Soundings taken in 1969, by the submersible *Pisces*, indicate that the loch is 975 feet deep. At any given time, Loch Ness contains an estimated 27 tons of FISH (chiefly salmon, trout and char). The loch's steep sides and peat-thick water limit rooted plants to the upper 10 feet of water, while greatly restricting underwater visibility.

Scottish historian Norton Newton claims that ancient Picts were the first humans to record sightings of Nessie, in prehistoric rock paintings of a creature commonly known as the Pictish Beast or Pictish Elephant. The first detailed sighting occurred sometime between A.D. 565 and 580 (accounts vary), when Irish missionary Saint Columba saw a "water monster" pursuing a swimmer at the mouth of the River Ness and called upon God's name to repel the creature. In the 1520s, witness Duncan Campbell saw "a terrible beast" come ashore, toppling trees and killing three men before it retreated, but some researchers claim the story refers to a different (unnamed) loch. Jimmy Hossack glimpsed Nessie in 1862, but no details of the sighting were recorded. In October 1871 or 1872, D. Mackenzie watched an animal resembling a log or capsized boat churning across Loch Ness. In summer 1885, Roderick Matheson reported "the biggest EEL I ever saw in my life," with "a neck like a horse with a mane." A year later, E.H. Bright and a cousin saw the creature emerge from woods on shore and "waddle" into the loch on four legs. Alexander Macdonald reported a huge SALAMANDER in the loch, in 1888. Multiple witnesses reported a "horrible great beastie" in 1895, while several persons saw the creature from Fort Augustus the following year. An unnamed Gypsy woman saw the creature ashore near Dores, sometime in the 1890s.

Sightings continued apace in the 20th century. Three witnesses sighted a moving hump like an upturned boat in December 1903. Four years later, John McLeod described an eel-like creature 30–40 feet long, swimming on the surface. In September 1909 (or 1912), five or six children saw a 20-foot creature, gray in color and with two short forelegs, burst from the woods and plunge into Loch Ness at Inchnacardoch Bay. In July 1914, Mrs. William Miller sighted the familiar "upturned boat"; her husband and James McGillvray saw the same creature nine years later, in May 1923. Between those sightings, James Cameron saw an "enormous animal" surface beside his boat (1916), and three witnesses surprised a long-necked, four-legged cryptid on shore (1919), describing it as "CAMEL-colored." The beast Alfred Cruickshank saw on shore in April 1923 was 20–25 feet long and 5–7 feet in diameter, "khaki green" in color, with four stout legs and large webbed feet. Mrs. Cumming McGillvray watched a moving hump the size of a horse's body for 10 minutes in August 1929. Ian Milne's sighting of 14 July 1930 was shorter, but he described a three-humped creature like "an enormous conger eel," swimming submerged at 16–17 miles per hour. Other undated sightings from the pre-1933 era included two more reports of the creature ashore and four more surface sightings by various locals.

The year 1933 witnessed construction of a new road on the south shore of Loch Ness, complete with blasting and felling of trees that offered passersby a much improved view of the loch. Sightings multiplied swiftly thereafter, though no two sources agree on how many persons have seen Nessie over the past three-quarters of a century. In 1976, ROY MACKAL wrote that "over the years there have been at least 10,000 known *reported* sightings at

Loch Ness but less than a third of those *recorded*." (In the same book, Mackal listed only 269 sightings.) David James, a founder of the LOCH NESS INVESTIGATION BUREAU, seemed to agree with those figures in 1981, claiming a total of 3,000 recorded sightings. A "thorough" survey by Ulrich Magin, in 1986, was more conservative, acknowledging about 600 sightings. Those reports include at least 26 sightings of cryptids on land (most recently on 22 February 1999) and at least 34 multiple-witness sightings since 1933. One of the stranger group sightings, reported in June 1933 by passengers aboard an airplane overflying the loch, described "a shape resembling a large ALLIGATOR, the size of which would be about 25 feet long by 4 feet wide." A surge of reports in 1996–2000 saw 64 sightings recorded. One of those, on 8 March 1996, involved two busloads of students en route to their school. Another, three months later, included 16 witnesses at the lochside Craigcarroch House Hotel. A lull followed, with only seven sightings reported in 2001–02. Sunday, 1 June 2003, set a new record for sightings, with three recorded at Fort Augustus in a single day.

Nessie is also the most photogenic cryptid on Earth, having been photographed, filmed and videotaped on numerous occasions since November 1933. At last count (in September 2003), there were at least 70 still photos, 31 motion picture films and three videotapes that purport to show Nessie in action. (Four other witnesses reported Internet sightings via live web cameras at Loch Ness, between June 1999 and August 2002.) Some have been explained away as showing natural phenomena (ducks, waves, floating logs, etc.), while others are obvious HOAXES. Some of the more dramatic (and still controversial) filmed evidence includes the following:

12 November 1933— Hugh Gray snapped Nessie's first photo at Foyers, apparently depicting a large body in the water.

1 April 1934— Dr. Kenneth Wilson took the SURGEON'S PHOTO, arguably the most famous Nessie photo of all time, frequently challenged by skeptics over the past seven decades.

29 May 1938— G.E. Taylor took the first color movie footage of Nessie, opposite Foyers. Analysts disagree on whether it shows a live animal feeding or a dead horse floating on the surface.

23 April 1960—TIM DINSDALE took his famous film of Nessie from a boat on the loch. Royal Air Force analysts reported that it depicts an "animate object" 12–16 feet long.

8 August 1972— Underwater footage, shot by members of a

Motorcyclist Arthur Grant met Nessie on land in August 1934 (*William Rebsamen*).

team led by ROBERT RINES, captured two frames depicting an apparent triangular (or rhomboid) flipper. The pictures prompted Rines and Peter Scott to christen Nessie *Nessiteras rhombopteryx*.

20 June 1975— The Rines team snapped more underwater photos, these capturing an apparent long-necked creature and a close-up of its head. The latter photo has been challenged as depicting a submerged tree stump, found and hauled to the surface in October 1987. The former remains unexplained, though ADRIAN SHINE believes it simply depicts shifting silt in the water.

21 May 1977— Two dramatic head-and-neck photos, allegedly taken from Urquhart Castle by self-proclaimed psychic ANTHONY SHIELS, reveal a creature closely resembling a DINOSAUR. Shiels, who claims he "conjured" Nessie to pose for the pictures, adamantly denies charges that the photos are fake.

16 July 2000— A "double-hump" photo was taken by Melissa Bavister opposite Boleskin House, on the loch's northern shore. Jim Cordiner, senior lecturer in photography at Glasgow's School of Building and Printing, declared that the picture shows a 25-foot object halfway across the loch. He further stated that the photo could not be a hoax, and ruled out such mundane explanations as a boat, reflection, shadow or wave. Skeptics predictably disagree.

May 2001— Strange photos taken near Invermoriston by James Gray, depicting a rather stiff "neck," were compared by one critic to pictures of a sports car's bumper. Gray likened the creature to a conger eel (*Conger* sp.). Strangely, while those pelagic eels are alien to fresh water, two were found dead on the loch's shore near Inverness, on 4 May 2001.

21 August 2002— More head-and-neck photos of an extremely thin-looking Nessie were snapped by tourist Roy Johnston. These photos bear some resemblance to those taken by James Gray in May 2001, and skeptics find them equally suspicious.

26 August 2002—A chance website visit by Andrew Whyley produced "the best underwater pictures of Nessie in 27 years." Andrews told reporters, "It moved all over the screen and seemed to have a purpose in its movement. The web cam refreshes every three seconds and I was able to get five shots over a minute or so."

16 September 2003— The CENTRE FOR FORTEAN ZOOLOGY announced receipt of "a remarkable piece of footage," taken at Loch Ness in April by an unnamed photographer. Results of the CFZ's analysis were pending at press time for this volume.

Nessie appears not only on film, but on sonar as well. Between December 1954 and July 2001, at least 53 different sonar "hits" on large unknown objects were recorded at Loch Ness, while submerged microphones recorded unexplained animal sounds in 1995 and 2000. One sonar hit, revealing two unidentified targets, coincided in time and place with the "flipper" film taken on 8 August 1972. On 19 June 1993, Nicholas Witchell's Project Urquhart team recorded hits on two large, submerged targets "that were definitely not shoals of fish." Producers of the *Nova* television program planned to debunk Nessie in 1997, but two large sonar contacts in the loch convinced them of the creature's existence. Three years later, sonic surveys of the loch recorded a series of piglike grunting noises whose frequency (747–751 hertz) matched sounds produced by elephant seals (*Mirounga angustirostris*), killer whales (*Orcinus orca*) and walruses (*Odobenus rosmarus*). On 1 July 2001, sonar prints taken aboard the *M.V. Nessie Hunter* revealed a serpentine shape with two dorsal humps.

Conversely, in July 2003, British Broadcasting Company producers declared that the negative results of their own sonar and satellite navigation surveys "proves Nessie does not exist." JAN-

OVE SUNDBERG and his colleagues in the GLOBAL UNDERWATER SEARCH TEAM dispute that finding, citing interviews with leaders of Kongsberg Simrad, which provided the BBC's gear. According to Erik Stenersen, the firm's product manager, Simrad gear cannot penetrate water below 325 feet and would not have enabled BBC technicians to scan the whole loch. "If they did," Stenersen said, "they used a technology we never heard about, but we are world-leading in this area." In fact, according to Kongsberg Simrad, the survey at Loch Ness was not a monster hunt at all, but rather "an acoustic survey…to provide a true baseline map of the loch floor and walls, a background against which other scientific data could be compared and put into context." Finally, according to the National Aeronautics and Space Administration, while "[i]nstruments on satellites in space, hundreds of kilometers above us can measure many things about the sea: surface winds, sea surface temperature, water color, wave height, and height of the ocean surface," they cannot track living organisms underwater.

Cryptozoologists, while unconvinced by the BBC verdict and other nay-sayers, still cannot agree on Nessie's true identity. Natural explanations for some of the sightings and photos include mirages; aquatic BIRDS; swimming deer; stray seals, whales, walruses, otters, eels or SHARKS; an escaped circus elephant hoisting its trunk above water; leaping fish; waves caused by wind or passing boats; all manner of flotsam from logs and mats of vegetation to dead livestock and naval mines; and a long series of hoaxes designed to promote CRYPTOTOURISM. Adrian Shine suggests that many surface sightings are produced by submarine currents, some pulsing as much as 130 feet high. In June 2001, Italian seismologist Luigi Piccardi proposed that Loch Ness is a kind of echo chamber for earthquakes, with subterranean rumbles producing ephemeral monsters topside, but spokesmen for the British Geological Survey dismissed the suggestion as "insupportable." Less commonplace theories on Nessie's identity include the following:

(1) Relict PLESIOSAURS, an early favorite based on descriptions of Nessie's long neck, were still championed by Robert Rines at the turn of the 21st century (though he fears that the creatures may now be extinct). Critics argue that plesiosaurs have been extinct for some 65 million years, and that no reptile could survive in Scotland's cold waters. Supporters of the theory note modern research on warm-blooded dinosaurs and suggest that plesiosaurs may have evolved to accommodate colder climates. Scrap dealer Gerald McSorley found a fossilized plesiosaur vertebrae at Loch Ness in July 2003, but spokesmen for the Museum of Scotland discounted the find. Paleontologist Lyall Anderson told reporters, "The fossil is definitely that of a plesiosaur—a very good example. And I believe Mr. McSorley when he says he found it where he did. But there's evidence to suggest it came from elsewhere and had been planted. The fossil is embedded in a gray, Jurassic-aged limestone. Rocks in the Loch Ness area are much older—they're all crystalline, igneous and metamorphic rocks." Museum spokesperson Hannah Dolby added: "Chances that the fossil originated where it was found are very slim….It was deposited there either by natural or artificial means. Borings on the fossil show it comes from a marine environment rather than a fresh water environment like the loch."

(2) A large, long-necked mammal presently unknown to science. ANTOON OUDEMANS proposed a giant long-necked seal to explain both SEA SERPENT and LAKE MONSTER sightings, later supported (at least provisionally) by researchers BERNARD HEUVEL-

MANS and Peter Costello. Other theorists have proposed a long-necked otter. Virtually any mammal would be better suited to the loch's cold waters than a reptile, but fossil records thus far fail to substantiate the existence of any such long-necked aquatic species.

(3) Large unknown amphibians, initially proposed by Roy Mackal in 1972. Once again, no such animals are known from the fossil record anywhere on earth, and the various arguments concerning cold-blooded reptiles in the loch apply equally to amphibians.

(4) Giant eels, suggested by various witnesses over the years. The European eel (*Anguilla anguilla*) does not officially exceed five feet in length, and the largest known pelagic conger barely doubles that size, but Bernard Heuvelmans suggested huge eels as one form of sea serpent, and some Nessie researchers believe that similar creatures live in Loch Ness. Reports of an 18-foot eel caught in an intake pipe at the Foyers hydroelectric plant on some unspecified date remain undocumented. In September 2003, RICHARD FREEMAN offered a new twist on this theory, claiming Loch Ness was inhabited by a family of eels 25–30 feet long, whose lives were prolonged to 100 years of more by "a bizarre freak of nature" that left them infertile. Three witnesses claimed a sighting of an eel 28–30 feet long near Dores, in January 2004, but researcher Steve Feltham identified the object as a black plastic discharge pipe from a nearby fish farm.

(5) Giant salmon, allegedly bred in the loch "years ago," now presumed extinct. Dennis Dickson raised this theory in June 2002, claiming that his family once tried to start a caviar business at Loch Ness, but succeeded only in breeding huge fish. Dickson suggested that sightings of Nessie actually involved the floating corpses of those salmon—which apparently vanish without a trace after bobbing briefly to the surface.

(6) Large invertebrates of various species. Prior to adopting his amphibian theory, Roy Mackal proposed (in 1966) that Nessie might be a huge, unknown species of sea slug (Superorder *Ophistobranchia*) that has adapted to live in fresh water. Two years later, F.W. Holliday proposed a giant version of *Tullimonstrum gregarium*, a 6-inch pelagic invertebrate from the Carboniferous period, presumed extinct for some 300 million years, whose fossils have been found in Illinois. In 1984, Anthony Shiels suggested an unknown giant cephalopod, which he helpfully dubbed *Dinoteuthis proboscideus*. Shiels speculates that the hypothetical creature's long proboscis might resemble a serpentine neck, if thrust above water, while the creature's rippling body could appear to have multiple humps.

(7) Twilight Zone Nessie, proposed by various theorists who pursue supernatural or extraterrestrial answers to the mystery of Loch Ness. Seven years before proposing his long-nosed cephalopod, Anthony Shiels veered in this direction with claims that he had summoned or "conjured" Nessie to pose for his camera. F.W. Holliday, in turn, abandoned his proposed giant invertebrate in 1973, claiming thereafter that Nessie was a supernatural DRAGON somehow linked to unidentified flying objects. In 1991, controversial researcher JON-ERIK BECKJORD suggested that "Space travelers could have come to Earth and lost some of their pets. This pet could have been Nessie, which has grown through the ages."

Sources: "A lot less monster." *Fortean Times* 165 (January 2003): 12; "Annual sightings of Loch Ness Monster hit a record low." *Inverness Courier* (2 January 2003); Will Barker, "Nessie is old eunuch eel." *The Sun* (22 September 2003); Burton, *The Elusive Monster*; Dash, "Status report: Lake monsters"; Costello, *In Search of Lake Monsters*; Dinsdale, *Loch Ness Monster*; Dinsdale, *Project Water Horse*; Harrison, *The Encyclopaedia of the Loch Ness Monster*; Holliday, *The Great Orm of Loch Ness*;

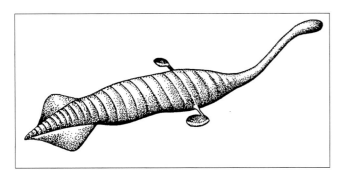

Author F.W. Holliday suggested that Nessie as a giant form of the prehistoric invertebrate *Tullimonstrum gregarium.*

"Loch Ness earthquake theory dismissed." BBC News (29 June 2001); "Loch Ness monster goes online." *Boston Herald* 11 June 1999); "The Loch Ness moaner." *Fortean Times* 84 (December 1994-January 1995): 8; Mackal, *The Monsters of Loch Ness*; Calum Macleod, "Were Picts the first to spot Nessie?" *Inverness Courier* (5 January 2004); McEwan, *Mystery Animals of Britain and Ireland*; "Nessie dorsa." *Fortean Times* 101 (August 1997): 18; "Nessie-hunter explains away 'mystery' creature." *Inverness Courier* (16 January 2004); "Nessie makes new waves." *Fortean Times* 150 (October 2001): 16–17; "New Nessie sightings." *Fortean Times* 123 (June 1999): 21; James Owen, "Loch Ness sea monster fossil a hoax, say scientists." *National Geographic News* (29 July 2003); "Record day for Nessie sightings." *Inverness Courier* (6 June 2003); "Whole loch of sightings going on." *Fortean Times* 91 (October 1996): 8; Witchell, *The Loch Ness Story*; "BBC survey in Loch Ness is a hoax." Global Underwater Search Team, *http://www.cryptozoology.st/*.

Nestor sea serpent   In September 1876, officers and crew aboard the steamer *Nestor* met an unidentified SEA SERPENT between Malacca and Penang. Captain Webster described the experience under oath on 18 September.

> On September 11, at 10:30 a.m., fifteen miles north-west of North Sand Lighthouse, in the Malacca Straits, the weather being fine and the sea smooth, the captain saw an object which had been pointed out by the third officer as "a shoal!" Surprised at finding a shoal in such a well-known track, I watched the object, and found that it was in motion, keeping up the same speed as the ship, and retaining about the same distance as first seen. The shape of the creature I would compare to that of a gigantic FROG. The head, of a pale yellowish colour, was about twenty feet in length, and six feet of the crown were above the water. I tried in vain to make out the eyes and mouth; the mouth may, however, have been below water. The head was immediately connected with the body, without any indication of a neck. The body was about forty-five or fifty feet long, and of an oval shape, perfectly smooth, but there may have been a slight ridge along the spine. The back rose some five feet above the surface. An immense tail, fully one hundred and fifty feet in length, rose a few inches above the water. This tail I saw distinctly from its junction with the body to its extremity; it seemed cylindrical, with a very slight taper, and I estimate its diameter at four feet. The body and tail were marked with alternate bands of stripes, black and pale yellow in colour. The stripes were distinct to the very extremity of the tail. I cannot say whether the

The *Nestor* sea serpent, after Captain Webster.

tail terminated in a fin or not. The creature possessed no fins or paddles so far as we could perceive. I cannot say if it had legs. It appeared to progress by means of an undulatory motion of the tail in a vertical plane.

The ship's surgeon, Dr. James Anderson, added: "It was apparently of a gelatinous (that is, flabby) substance. Though keeping up with us at the rate of nearly ten knots an hour [11.5 mph], its movements seemed lethargic. I saw no legs or fins, and am certain that the creature did not blow or spout in the manner of a whale. I should not compare it for a moment to a SNAKE. The only creatures it could be compared with are the newt or frog tribe." Since frogs have clearly visible legs and no tails, BERNARD HEUVELMANS concluded that Captain Webster meant to call the beast a giant tadpole, rather than a frog. Dr. Andrew Wilson suggested that it was a GIANT SQUID (*Architeuthis*), but Heuvelmans correctly notes the apparent absence of tentacles and the striped color scheme unknown to any specimen of giant squid thus far observed.

Source: Heuvelmans, *In the Wake of the Sea Serpents.*

Net-Net *see* Junjadee

New Aberdour sea serpent
Sometime in 1894 or 1895, H.C. Birnie and his father were walking on the beach at New Aberdour, Aberdeenshire, Scotland, when they saw "a long SNAKE-like thing" stretched out between the surf and some rocks on the shore. At their approach, the creature slithered back into the water and vanished. A dozen years later, Birnie saw another SEA SERPENT, this time while serving as a junior officer aboard H.M.S. *CAMPANIA*.

Source: Heuvelmans, *In the Wake of the Sea Serpents.*

New Caledonia sea serpents
New Caledonia is a French dependency in the South Pacific, some 750 miles east of Australia and 800 miles northwest of New Zealand. Several SEA SERPENTS were sighted in nearby waters during the 20th century, with the first appearing in Nouméa harbor on 22 September 1923. Two native women saw the creature, "whose head stuck out about 30 feet, [and] looked like a sea horse with a crest running well down its back. It also spouted water and emitted sounds like rifle shots. Eight days later, three witnesses saw the beast two miles offshore from Nouméa, between Mâitre Isle and Tabou. They described it rising repeatedly from the water "like a lighthouse," sometimes showing two "branches" as if head and tail were raised together, while it "frequently spouted a jet of vapor." From that description, BERNARD HEUVELMANS concluded that the witnesses had seen "a homeric duel" between his hypothetical "Merhorse" and a GIANT SQUID.

The next report, six years later, was filed by R. Reynell Bellamy, who described his experience as follows:

> In September 1929 I was living in a remote corner of the French South Sea Island of New Caledonia, and there one day in a shallow, sandy bay close to my plantation I was privileged to see a great sea-SNAKE. My attention was first taken by a dark object moving in the water about two or three hundred yards from shore; I pointed it out to my wife, saying it must either be a TURTLE or a dugong, with which those waters abound. But even as we looked, a third dark spot appeared above the surface, travelling immediately behind the first; then yet more of these humps broke water and at the same time the first one uprose, revealing a typical snake's head supported on the usual serpentine neck and form.
>
> On seeing this we realized immediately that we were looking at a giant water-snake, and we shinned up a tree overlooking the

beach, where I could have a better view of the creature. It was now swimming obliquely across the bay, and from my vantage-point could observe the animal completely, both above and below the water, which was as clear as crystal. It swam in a leisurely manner, with the head upheld some four or five feet above the surface, while behind it, coil upon coil of its great length kept protruding out of the water; its head was darting to and fro as though searching for something, then, on sighting a shoal of mullets, it plunged after them at great speed, and finally disappeared amongst them amid a deal of splashing and a shower of frantically jumping fishes.

At the time I estimated the reptile as being about sixty feet long, and, as having a head about the same size as a Newfoundland dog, but when, some weeks later, one of my hunting dogs, in pursuit of a deer, swam across the bay and in the very same spot as that in which we had observed the sea-serpent, I saw at once that I had originally much under-estimated its size.

Some time afterwards someone suggested that what I had taken for a sea-serpent might in reality have been a school of porpoises swimming one behind the other, the leader along with its head above the water; also it was argued water-snakes do not swim in the manner I described. Since then I have watched carefully many of the smaller sea-snakes — usually about three or four feet long, which are very numerous in the sea around New Caledonia, and which in swimming made exactly the same movements as did their larger relative.

That claim notwithstanding, no snake is physically capable of flexing its spine in vertical curves as described by Bellamy. Still, Bernard Heuvelmans made allowances for Bellamy's mistake, concluding that he had seen a large unknown mammal, rather than a reptile. Little can be made of Bellamy's references to other cryptid sightings around New Caledonia, including two alleged sightings off Nouméa (see NEW HEBRIDES SEA SERPENT below), since he supplied no dates and Heuvelmans could find no independent corroboration of the incidents.

Twelve years later, in the final year of World War II, Arthur Féré and six companions glimpsed another unknown creature while boating across Ouengho Bay, near Canala, on a clear morning. Féré later recalled:

As we were going into Ouengho Bay we all saw a a strange shape, sticking up above the water. At first we thought it was a tree with a large branch pointing towards the sky, because it remained quite immobile….The presence of this drifting object intrigued us very much, so we made for it. As we approached, we began to see a sort of big head followed by a black neck, marked with yellow. It reminded us of a giraffe. Following the neck, we could make out a big long shape just below the surface of the sea. We went on approaching. When we were about 200 yards away, it suddenly came to life and dived, raising a big plume of water. Our reaction was to put the helm about and make for land. I must admit we were all very frightened.

In 1946, it was reported that M. Routier of the Geological Mission of the French Institute of Oceania visited Féré at Canala, bearing "a photo of an identical animal caught in the China Sea," but the photo remains elusive and no record of any such capture presently exists.

Source: Heuvelmans, *In the Wake of the Sea Serpents*.

New Caledonian Owlet Nightjar

This dark-colored BIRD with mottled plumage (*Aegotheles savesi*), the largest known nightjar (Family *Aegothelidae*), was once endemic to New Caledonia. The only preserved specimen was caught in 1880, after it entered a house through the bedroom window. No more were ever collected, and the species is presumed to be extinct. Still, a local hunter claimed to have shot one in 1970 (no evidence was pro-

duced), and two birdwatchers claimed a brief sighting in 1998.

Sources: Bille, *Rumors of Existence*; Birding-Aus, http://menura.cse.unsw.edu.au:64800/1998/11/msg00339.html.

New England Sasquatch Research Center

The NESRC appears to be a one-man operation run by researcher Bill Green from his home in Bristol, Connecticut. An Internet website notes that Green began collecting SASQUATCH reports in 1987. He solicits sighting reports without respect to their location and offers a free newsletter in return for a self-addressed, stamped envelope.

Source: Bigfoot 2001, *http://www.maxpages.com/bigfoot2001*.

New England sea serpent

At 7:45 a.m. on 25 July 1899, passengers and crew aboard the ocean liner *New England* observed a SEA SERPENT off the coast of Newfoundland, at 45° 37' north latitude and 58° 9' west longitude. Newspaper reports described the creature as a "great lizard" whose "carinated back" rose six feet above the ocean's surface. As reported in the *Gloucester Times and Cape Ann Advertiser*:

The Captain said that his attention was called to an object off the starboard bow, which he first made out to be a ship's boat or part of a derelict. He bore two points out of his course to ascertain just what the object was, believing it might be a wreck with some poor sailors in need of assistance. The steamer approached to within about 40 feet of the object, which still had the appearance of a submerged wreck. Suddenly a thin stream of water was thrown in the air and the animal — for it proved to be one — moved off at right angles to the ship, going through the water at an eight knot clip [9 mph]….

Its head was visible for only a few seconds when it raised it from the water to gaze unconcernedly at the big ship as she approached. The neck was elongated and the head hooded. The captain did not say it was a sea serpent, but acknowledged it was the strangest animal he had ever seen in his 40 years' experience at sea….One of the saloon passengers said that he believed it was a giant sea lizard.

Source: O'Neill, *The Great New England Sea Serpent*.

New Harbor mystery fish

In August 1880, Captain S.W. Hanna caught a large unknown FISH at New Harbor, Maine. The serpentine creature was 25 feet long and 10 inches in diameter at its thickest point. It had a flat head, whose upper portion extended very slightly above a small mouth filled with sharp teeth. Two small pectoral fins were positioned behind the gill slits, with a triangular dorsal fin on the same axis. A final curious fin was found at the end of its tail. The fish was dark-colored above, and dirty-white below. Rather than preserve the unique specimen, Hannah discarded it as "a streak of ill-luck rather than good business, having torn my nets very badly and otherwise bothering me in my business." Cryptozoologists BERNARD HEUVELMANS and KARL SHUKER suggest that the fish may represent a new species of frilled SHARK, though the known species (*Chlamydoselachus anguineus*) rarely exceeds six feet in length. BEN ROESCH disagrees, proposing a new species of large, elongate bony fish.

Sources: S.W. Hanna, "Description of an eel-like creature taken in a net at New Harbor, Maine, in 1880." *Bulletin of the U.S. Fish Commis-

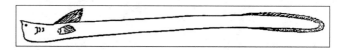

The New Harbor mystery fish, as sketched by S.W. Hanna in 1880.

sion 3 (1883): 407–410; Heuvelmans, *In the Wake of the Sea Serpents*; Roesch, "A review of alleged sea serpent carcasses worldwide (Part One — 1648–1880)"; Shuker, "The search for monster sharks."

New Hebrides sea serpent

In September 1929, while attempting to defend his claims of a SEA SERPENT sighting at New Caledonia, witness R. Reynell Bellamy described several other sightings reported from the South Pacific. One of those involved a planter on the island of Epi, in the New Hebrides group (now Vanuatu) that lies 300 miles northeast of New Caledonia and 600 miles west of Fiji. Sadly, Bellamy provided no names or dates, but he described the incident as follows:

I know personally, a planter from Api [*sic*], in the New Hebrides group, who, when he was once becalmed in his recruiting schooner, saw close alongside his vessel a huge SNAKE about eighty feet long. The reptile raised its head about twelve feet out of the water to look at the schooner in which it appeared to be most interested, but finally swam off without attempting to molest the craft. The native boys aboard were immensely excited at the creature's appearance, but said that they had known of its existence before; the planter described its colour as being yellow and brown running into not very well-defined stripes; and it had, he stated, at the back of its head a soft mane of very coarse hair.

Reptiles are hairless, a fact that prompted BERNARD HEUVELMANS to list the Epi cryptid as a specimen of his theoretical "Merhorse," an unknown pelagic mammal.

Source: Heuvelmans, *In the Wake of the Sea Serpents*.

New Quay sea serpent

In late August 1963, while walking along the cliffs at New Quay, Wales, Mr. P. Sharman observed a strange animal in a cove 100 feet below. The creature resembled a PLESIOSAUR, black in color and 30–40 feet long, with a long neck and small head, four flippers and a short tail. Several seals fled the cove as Sharman watched, though the larger animal did not pursue them. Curiously, Sharman said, "After I had watched the thing for a few minutes I realized there was a remote possibility that I was looking down upon a floundering basking SHARK [*Cetorhinus maximus*]. This seemed more and more probable, so I left the area." In fact, however, while basking sharks may die and decompose to resemble a long-necked plesiosaur, the stout-bodied FISH bear no resemblance to prehistoric reptiles while alive.

Source: McEwan, *Mystery Animals of Britain and Ireland*.

New River Inlet carcass

In spring 1885, the rotting carcass of a large sea creature was stranded at New River Inlet, Florida (near Fort Pierce, in St. Lucie County). As luck would have it, the president of the U.S. Humane Society, the Rev. Gordon of Milwaukee, was visiting the area when the carcass was discovered. Author J.B. Holder described what happened next.

While lying at anchor in New River Inlet the flukes of the anchor became foul with what proved to be a carcass of considerable length. Mr. Gordon quickly observed that it was a vertebrate, and at first thought it was probably a cetacean. But, on examination, it was seen to have features more suggestive of saurians. Its total length was forty-two feet. Its girth was six feet. The head was absent; two flippers, or fore-limbs, were noticed, and a somewhat slender neck...six feet in length. The carcass was in a state of decomposition; the abdomen was open, and the intestines protruded.

The striking slenderness of the thorax as compared to the great length of body and tail very naturally suggested to Mr. Gordon, whose reading served him well, the form of some of the great saurians whose bones have so frequently been found in several localities along the Atlantic coast. No cetacean known to science has such a slender body and such a well-marked and slender

Eyewitness sketch of the carcass stranded at New River Inlet, Florida in 1885.

neck….[A]ppreciating the great importance of securing the entire carcase, Mr. Gordon had it hauled above the high-water mark, and took all possible precautions to preserve the bones until they could be removed….He counted without the possible treacherous hurricane; the waters of the "still-vexed Bermoothes," envious of their own, recalled the strange waif.

Florida's only hurricane of 1885 struck on 23–24 August, which hardly qualifies as "spring." Still, the carcass was lost in some manner, leaving researchers to speculate on its identity. BERNARD HEUVELMANS speculated that it may have been a whale SHARK (*Rhincodon typus*), while BEN ROESCH suggests the smaller basking shark (*Cetorhinus maximus*). Either might decompose to present a "reptilian" form, but in the absence of physical evidence, the question can never be definitively answered.

Sources: Heuvelmans, *In the Wake of the Sea Serpents*; Roesch, "A review of alleged sea serpent carcasses worldwide (Part Two — 1881–1891)."

New South Wales carcass

Next to nothing is known about this creature, reportedly found in autumn 1959. It goes unmentioned in the standard texts on SEA SERPENTS, and the single source available fails even to identify the precise location of its discovery along the coast of New South Wales, Australia. The partial remains were found in a FISH trap and hauled ashore, where they were reportedly photographed (though the photos have not survived). The carcass measured 18 feet 6 inches, and while our anonymous source reports that "the vertebrae belong to a SHARK, without a doubt," no further evidence or information is available.

Source: Dubious Globsters, *http://www.geocities.com/capedrevenger/dubiousglobsters.html*.

New Zealand mystery cats

New Zealand's only native mammals are two species of BATS; all others (with the possible exception of the elusive WAITOREKE) have been introduced by man in relatively recent times. It was all the more surprising, therefore, when a rash of ALIEN BIG CAT sightings were reported in summer 1977 — and not merely one CAT, at that. On 8 July, the *New Zealand Herald* reported that security officer Graham Stevens had seen an adult LION at large in Mangere, an Auckland suburb. Police were summoned and searched the neighborhood in vain. The owner of a visiting circus was questioned and insisted that none of his cats had escaped. Ten days later, a TIGER was sighted at Kaiapoi, with reports continuing over the next two weeks. Again, police searched for the cat without result, but Inspector W.J. Perring pronounced himself "reasonably satisfied" that a large cat had visited the region. It was never caught, though rumors suggested that an unnamed private owner had retrieved his wandering pet. No further sightings of either big cat are on record.

Source: Shuker, *Mystery Cats of the World*.

New Zealand sea serpents

In addition to multiple GIANT SQUID carcasses stranded on its shores, the island nation of New Zealand has also produced some intriguing SEA SERPENT reports. In 1891, crewmen aboard the *MANAPOURI* and the *ROTOMAHANA* reported sightings off the North Island's coast. BERNARD

HEUVELMANS lists another North Island sighting in 1897, but regrettably provided no further details. The first on record from the South Island was described by witness C. Howard Tripp, in a letter dated 16 September 1904:

> About 6 years ago I was getting into the 8 a.m. train at Timaru, New Zealand, when, what at first appeared to be a sooty albatross, seemed to drop on to the sea with a great splash about 500 yards from me. The sea was calm, but the sun was slightly in my eyes. However, as I had never seen an albatross come down in that way before and disappear below the surface, I watched the spot, and soon saw it come up again, and then saw it was not an albatross, but the tail of some fish, as it had a long, thin body attached to it. It came down again with a great splash, disappeared and went up again, and then disappeared entirely. I should say that the body attached to the tail was about eighteen inches in diameter by the tail, and thickened to two feet or more about 12 to 16 feet from the tail, which was about the height it came up above the sea. I was naturally immensely surprised and struck by what I saw, so continued to watch, and a few seconds after the final disappearance of the tail I saw a most distinct serpent's head come out of the water about 50 yards from where the tail had disappeared; it came out with about 10 or 15 feet of body all of a uniform thickness of about 3 or 4 feet, seemed to look round, and then disappeared, and I never saw it again. Where I saw it was shoal water of about three fathoms [18 feet] and on the edge of a dolerite reef. It might have been a bottle-nosed whale, and I might have been deceived by the sun being slightly in my eyes, but my first impression at the time was, and still is, that it was a serpent-like creature. Subsequently I heard that the serpent had about two days previously been seen about 10 miles south of Timaru, and the movements I saw corresponded with the description I had read of a serpent being seen off the coast of the North Island of N.Z. about a year previously.

Tripp's report was followed on 10 May 1899 by a sighting from the barque *OPANA*, involving a 40-foot creature described as "an immense shark." A much larger cryptid was reportedly seen in the early 1930s, by Captain J. Munroe, off New Zealand's North Cape. Munroe described the creature as serpentine, 150 feet long, and as thick as a steamer's smokestack.

Source: Heuvelmans, *In the Wake of the Sea Serpents*.

Newcastle Harbour sea monster

On 17 November 1891, a government diver was working on moorings in Newcastle Harbour, New South Wales, Australia. While thus engaged at a depth of 29 feet, he noticed a shadow passing and glanced up to determine its source. According to a local newspaper:

> As it came closer he perceived a huge sea monster fully 30 ft. long, with a bulldog-shaped head, sharp piercing eyes, and a savage mouth. It seemed to be extremely flat, with two large fins flapping, and swam along quietly, but determinedly.

The diver swiftly made his way topside, and the creature surfaced while he was describing it to his coworkers. Two boats pursued it, their occupants stabbing the animal several times with boathooks before it submerged and escaped. On 5 December, a similar creature returned to the harbor, where it was harpooned and dragged ashore. It proved to be a sunfish (*Mola mola*) 12 feet wide, 9 feet long, and weighing 1.5 tons. Three days later, a second, slightly smaller specimen was caught in the harbor. While journalists maintained that the first FISH caught was the "monster" seen in November it did not match the reported dimensions.

Sources: "Another sea monster in the harbour: Captured and on exhibition." *Newcastle Herald* (7 December 1891); "Sea monster in the harbour." *Newcastle Herald* (18 November 1891); "The sea monster's mate

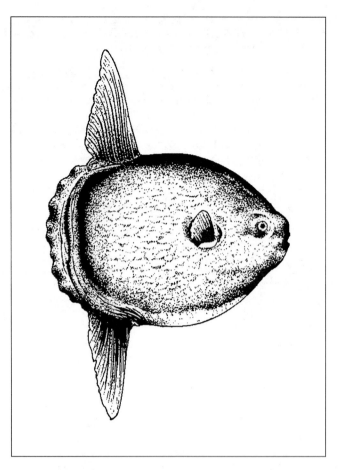

The "sea monster" harpooned at Newcastle Harbor in December 1891 proved to be a large sunfish.

captured: Together in life and death." *Newcastle Herald* (8 December 1891).

Newfoundland sea serpents

As with New Zealand, the Canadian province of Newfoundland has produced both multiple GIANT SQUID strandings and reports of unidentified SEA SERPENTS in its coastal waters. The first pelagic cryptid sighting was reported by witness W. Lee as occurring at Cape Breton "many years before 1819." (BERNARD HEUVELMANS somehow settled on 1805.) Lee described a creature 200 feet long, dark green in color, swimming with "flexuous hillocks." Researcher Constantin Samuel Rafinesque-Schmaltz later wrote that Lee's creature "appears to be the largest on record, and might well be called *Pelamis monstrosus*; but if there are other species of equal size, it must be called then *Pelamis chloronotis*, or Green-back Pelamis."

Most of the other Newfoundland sightings were logged by witnesses on shipboard, from the *SILAS RICHARDS* (1826), the *ROBERTSON* (1834), the *HATTIE F. WALKER* (1886), the *NEW ENGLAND* (1899) and the *CORINTHIAN* (1913). In May 1932, the sea cast up the carcass of a still-unidentified "huge beast with a pointed snout and sharp teeth and looking very like a SNAKE." Two more reports issued from Newfoundland in August 1936. The first, published on 19 August, described an encounter off Port au Port, near Stephenville on the Gulf of St. Lawrence:

> The Newfoundland natural resources department announced today [that] fishermen on the west coast of Newfoundland had reported a second appearance of what they said was a 150-foot sea

Sea serpents have been sighted off Newfoundland's shores since the early 19th century.

monster. The department said fishermen at Portauport [*sic*] sent messages to the department last week saying the reported monster had scared boats away from fishing grounds in that vicinity.

Two days later came another report from St. John's, presumably describing the same creature.

Newfoundland fishermen told vivid — but unconfirmed — tales tonight of a sea monster on the west coast that stuck its head 60 feet out of the water and snorted blue vapor from its nostrils. Sharp-eyed fishermen produced a collective picture of the monster like this: At least 200 feet long and 18 feet in diameter, eyes as big as an enamel sauce pan and spaced two feet apart; a mane larger than that of any horse. The fishermen even claimed the monster was so big it set up waves that rocked fishing boats, and for days no boat dared venture to sea.

The most recent Newfoundland sighting, as of press time for this volume, was recorded by fishermen at FORTUNE BAY in May 1997.

Sources: Heuvelmans, *In the Wake of the Sea Serpents*; O'Neill, *The Great New England Sea Serpent*.

Ngani-Vatu   This giant BIRD on Fiji, in the South Pacific, was alleged to attack and carry off human prey. No sightings have been reported since the 19th century. It is unknown whether the creature was entirely mythical, or if some real-life creature inspired the original stories.

Source: Johannes Anderson, *Myths and Legends of the Polynesians*. New York: Farrar and Rinehart, 1931.

Ngarara   Maori natives of the 19th century described New Zealand's Ngarara as a large lizard with a serrated dorsal crest and prominent teeth. It reportedly lived in riverside caves, emerging to hunt a mixed bag of prey. Possible candidates include the tuatara (*Sphenodon punctatus*) and the giant GECKO (*Haplodactylus delcourti*), though neither officially exceeds two feet in length. The Ngarara was said to be considerably larger.

Source: Margaret Orbell, *The Natural World of the Maori*. Dobbs Ferry, NY: Sheridan House, 1985.

Ngatimamaero/Ngatimamo *see* **Macro**

Ngend   Bantu tribesmen in Cameroon describe the Ngend as a primate larger than a GORILLA, which travels with equal ease through treetops and on the ground. No such APE is known to science, and skeptics suggest that the creature is mythical, per-

haps concocted from garbled accounts of gorillas found in the Congo rain forests.

Source: R.P. Galopeau, "Un animal fabuleux du Cameroun: Le 'Ngend." *Notes Africaines* 25 (January 1945): 6–7.

Ngoima   This mystery BIRD of the Congo is described as resembling an eagle, with a wingspan of 10–13 feet, with legs and talons the size of a strong man's hand and forearm. Witness André Mouelle described it to ROY MACKAL as dark brown to black, with lighter shadings underneath its wingtips. The Ngoima inhabits forests, where it preys on goats and MONKEYS. Mackal compares it to another fierce raptor, the Guanionien ("leopard of the air"), described by explorer Paul du Chaillu in 1870. That bird allegedly carried off human infants, and blinded with its talons any hunters who approached its nest. Mackal identifies the Guanionien as the martial eagle (*Polemaetus bellicosus*), whose average wingspan is seven feet. While granting that an unusual specimen might attain 10 feet, however, Mackal admits that a 13-foot wingspan must represent either an exaggeration by witnesses of "a very rare exception." Another problem with the match, however, is that martial eagles rarely (if ever) share the Ngoima's supposed forest habitat. The Congo's next-largest raptor, and a certified forest-dweller, is the crowned eagle (*Stephanoaetus coronatus*), but its maximum acknowledged wingspan is 5 feet 6 inches.

Source: Mackal, *A Living Dinosaur?*

Ngoloko   Natives of Kenya describe this unclassified primate or HOMINID as a SASQUATCH-type biped, eight feet tall and covered with dark hair, remarkable for its foul body odor. It may display curiosity toward humans, as noted in a report from the late 19th century. A group of Swahili tribesmen were tapping rubber trees when one of their number saw a Ngoloko "stalking" the group — or perhaps merely observing them — and shot it with an arrow. The wounded creature fled, but soon collapsed. Witness Heri wa Mabruko later claimed that the beast's hands had only a thumb and one finger each, the fingers tipped with claws 2–3 inches long. The feet, by contrast, had three toes and large prehensile "thumbs." Assuming that the hands were not deformed or damaged in some way, they may have evolved in the manner described. (Members of the Vadoma tribe, inhabiting Zimbabwe's Zambezi Valley, have two-toed feet resembling lobster's claws. They were photographed and examined for the first time in September 1969.) Researchers LOREN COLEMAN and PATRICK HUYGHE consider the Ngoloko identical to the Congolese KIKOMBA and MULAHU, though neither of those are alleged to share the Ngoloko's curious hands and feet.

Sources: Coleman and Huyghe, *The Field Guide to Bigfoot, Yeti, and Other Mystery Primates Worldwide*; Heuvelmans, *Les Bêtes Humaines d'Afrique*; George Nicholas, "2-toed Zambezi tribe apparently real." Copley News Service (14 September 1969); Tchernine, *The Yeti*.

Ngoroli *see* **Water Leopard**

Nguma-Monene   Cryptozoologist ROY MACKAL calls the Nguma-monene ("great boa") Africa's most mysterious reptilian cryptid — no small statement on a continent where natives have reported more than half a dozen animals resembling living DINOSAURS. This one, in fact, resembles nothing known to science, either from the distant past or modern times. Witnesses describe the Nguma-monene as a huge lizard, serpentine in form, attaining lengths of 130–195 feet, with a serrated ridge along its spine. Despite their name for the creature, natives insist that the Nguma-monene is not a SNAKE, but rather a vastly elongated quadruped. In 1961, the eldest sister of Congolese official Michel Zabatou watched for 30 minutes as a specimen "much larger" than a PYTHON swam slowly upstream along the Motaba River. Ten years later, in November 1971, missionary Joseph Ellis was en route to a village Bible class on the Motaba when he met a 30-foot Nguma-monene, also in the water. Neither specimen approached the epic sizes claimed by tribal witnesses, but both were more than twice the size of Earth's largest known lizard (*Varanus komodoensis*). And indeed, except for the ridge on its spine, the Nguma-monene bears a striking resemblance to Africa's Nile MONITOR LIZARD (*Varanus niloticus*).

Sources: Gibbons, *Missionaries and Monsters*; Mackal, *A Living Dinosaur?*

Artist's conception of Joseph Ellis's 1971 encounter with the Nguma-monene (*William Rebsamen*).

Nguoi Rung   The Nguoi Rung ("forest man"), also called Kh? trâu ("big MONKEY") or Briaou, is an unclassified primate or HOMINID reported from the area once known as Indochina (now including Vietnam, Cambodia and Laos). Witnesses describe it as bipedal, 5–6 feet tall, and covered in hair that ranges from reddish to gray or black in color. Like SASQUATCH and other unknown hominids, the Nguoi Rung have a reputation for abducting humans on occasion, and also reportedly break into houses at night to take food. In a region cursed by war for half a century, the Nguoi Rung had its share of run-ins with soldiers and officials of various nations. U.S. sentries fired on a night-prowling "APE" at Cam Ranh Bay, in 1967, but the creature escaped, leaving only blood traces and humanoid footprints behind. Four

years later, Ai Thi tribesmen captured two Nguoi Rung that were raiding their FISH traps near Dak Lak. A team of scientists and soldiers from Duc My reportedly came to examine the captives, then shaved and dressed them before driving them off to parts unknown. By 1974, reports of Nguoi Rung were so common that North Vietnamese General Hoang Minh Thao requested a scientific expedition to the region south of Kon Tum, but no creatures were found. Vietnamese cryptozoologist DAO VAN TIEN has collected information on the creatures since 1963 and published his findings (albeit still without a specimen) in 1990. Reports continued through that decade, and HELMUT LOOFS-WISSOWA chronicled sightings in the Laotian highlands, in 1996.

Sources: "Ape story lingers." *Army Reporter* (27 April 1970); Coleman and Huyghe, *The Field Guide to Bigfoot, Yeti, and Other Mystery Primates Worldwide*; Dao Van Tien, "Wildman in Vietnam." *Tap Ci' Lâm Nghiêp* 6 (1990): 39–40; Heuvelmans and Porschnev, *Le'Homme de Néanderthal est Toujours Vivant*; "Vietnamese zoologists investigate wildman reports." *ISC Newsletter* 11 (1992): 9–10.

Nhang   Although its name translates as "CROCODILE" from Old Persian, the Nhang was described in ancient accounts as a creature half reptile and half seal, which infested certain rivers throughout Armenia, Iran and Turkey. Human beings were reportedly included in the amphibious predator's diet. Until such time as further evidence is obtained, the most likely explanation involves exaggerated and mythologized reports of the Nile crocodile (*Crocodylus niloticus*).

Source: Mardiros Ananikian, *Armenian Mythology*. Boston: Archaeological Institute of America, 1925.

Niagara River   The Niagara River is 35 miles long and forms the natural link between LAKE ERIE and LAKE ONTARIO. As both of those lakes have are said to be inhabited by LAKE MONSTERS, so the river has also produced its share of aquatic cryptid sightings. Unknown creatures ranging from 12 to 50 feet long have been sighted sporadically in the Niagara River since 1878, with the most recent account dating from the late 1970s. In that incident, tourists Don and Shirley Benware saw a dark, smooth-skinned creature swimming near Navy Island, trailing a broad wake behind it.

Source: Whalen, "Monster in Niagara River?"

Nichols Lake, Michigan   On 23 May 1972, a visitor to this lake (in Newaygo County) allegedly sighted a 30-foot LAKE MONSTER, swimming with its head and neck raised six feet above the water's surface. This appears to be the lake's only sighting of record.

Source: The Online Lake Cryptid Directory, http:/dive.to/lakemonsters.

Nicola Lake, Canada   Nicola Lake lies six miles northeast of Merritt, British Columbia. Aboriginal people believed the lake was inhabited by one of the LAKE MONSTERS known throughout western Canada as NAITAKA, but no modern sightings are on record.

Source: James Teit, *The Thompson Indians of British Columbia*. New York: American Museum of Natural History, 1900.

Nightgrowler   Residents of Australia's Goldsborough Valley (south of Cairns, Queensland) gave this name to an unseen nocturnal prowler in autumn 1995. Those who heard its deep, ferocious snarls remain convinced that it was not a dingo or any other canid, but rather some type of ALIEN BIG CAT. Thus far, no actual sightings are on record.

Source: Karl Shuker, "Alien zoo." *Fortean Times* 104 (November 1997): 15.

Nighthawk Lake, Canada

Fortean authors Colin and Janet Bord include this Ontario lake, near Timmons, on a list of supposed LAKE MONSTER habitats, but the provide no dates or details of sightings.

Source: Bord and Bord, *Unexplained Mysteries of the 20th Century.*

Nightingale Reed Warbler

This elusive BIRD, *Acrocephalus luscinia astrolabii*, is known to science only from two specimens collected by a French expedition in the 1930s. Unfortunately, the careless collectors did recall which Pacific island yielded the birds, and their present status is a mystery.

Source: Bille, *Rumors of Existence.*

Nikaseenithuloonyee

Aboriginal inhabitants of Alaska describe this pelagic cryptid as a sometime visitor to Cook Inlet, southwest of Anchorage. Witnesses describe it as resembling an oversized ALLIGATOR, though Alaska's cold waters are presumably inhospitable to reptiles. The creature (if it exists) may correspond to the hypothetical "marine saurian" described by BERNARD HEUVELMANS in 1968.

Source: Bill Vaudrin, *Tanaina Tales from Alaska.* Norman, OK: University of Oklahoma Press, 1969.

Nimbunj *see* Junjadee

Ninki Nanka

West African natives describe the Ninki Nanka as an aquatic cryptid inhabiting various rivers in Gambia, Guinea and Senegal. Witnesses offer a composite description of the creature, said to have a long neck, a head resembling a horse's (but with horns), and a body resembling a CROCODILE'S. Estimates of the animal's length average 30 feet. In 1935, Thomas Dalrymple interviewed native witnesses in Gambia and reported their claim that the Ninki Nanka resembled pictures they had seen of a model DINOSAUR.

Source: Chris Moiser, "Ninki Nanka: The dragon of the Gambia." *Animals and Men* 24 (2001).

Niños-Mono

South American legend has it that these small bipeds, covered entirely with dark hair, are mentally retarded children abandoned to live in the jungle by heartless parents. A more likely explanation is an unclassified species of primate or small HOMINID. Reports of the Niños-Mono have been filed from Bolivia, Chile, Colombia and Peru.

Source: Picasso, "South American monsters & mystery animals."

Nirivilu/Ngarrafilu

Argentina's Araucanian natives described the Nirivilu as a huge river-dwelling creature that combined qualities of a SNAKE and a WOLF. No modern reports are on file, but it may be identical to one of various LAKE MONSTERS or giant snakes reported from other parts of the continent.

Sources: Gregorio Alvarez, *El Tronco de Oro.* Nuequén, Argentina: Pehuen, 1968; Picasso, "South American monsters & mystery animals."

Nittaewo

The Nittaewo ("one who has nails) or Vanara ("man of the woods") is an unclassified primate of Sri Lanka, reported in various reports from the 19th century onward. Sri Lanka's Veddah tribesmen described the Nittaewo as a race of PYGMIES, 3–4 feet in height (with females smaller than the males), covered in thick reddish fur, with short arms and long claws on their fingers. The Nittaewo reportedly have no language and use no tools or weapons, but their cunning allowed them to evade periodic Veddah hunting parties. Primatologist W.C. Osman Hill suspected that the Nittaewo were a lost tribe of Negrito aborigines, while BERNARD HEUVELMANS suggested an anthropoid APE such as the pygmy siamang (*Symphalangus klossi*). IVAN SANDERSON ranked them among his hypothetical "proto pygmies" as an undiscovered species. Other cryptozoologists suggest the possible isolation and survival on Sri Lanka of *Homo erectus*.

Sources: Heuvelmans, *On the Track of Unknown Animals*; Hill, "Nittaewo, an unsolved problem of Ceylon"; Nevill, "The Nittaewo of Ceylon"; Sanderson, *Abominable Snowmen*; Spittel, "Leanama, land of the Nittaewo"; Spittel, "Legend of the Nittaewo."

No Man's Friend Pond, Georgia

Despite its name, No Man's Friend Pond (near Adel, in Cook County) is actually a densely-wooded swamp. Humans easily get lost there, and the eerie terrain seems perfect for a "monster" habitat. In fact, various books and Internet websites list the "pond" as a source of LAKE MONSTER reports, but none provides any details of sightings.

Sources: Bord and Bord, *Unexplained Mysteries of the 20th Century*; Coleman, *Mysterious America*; Kirk, *In the Domain of the Lake Monsters*; Georgia Place Names, http://www.kenkrakow.com/gpn/n.pdf.

Noidore sea serpent

In the early 1920s, British trader Ernest Davies lived in the South Pacific's Tuamotu Archipelago (which includes Tahiti). Years later, he described a SEA SERPENT encounter that he experienced one evening, while lounging on the poop deck of the schooner *Noidore*. Davies heard a rippling sound some 40 yards away and:

> Gazing in that direction, I saw a queer-looking black form approaching the vessel. It came up in a leisurely sort of way and, after rubbing itself against our side, reared itself almost to the height of the main deck. I was never so surprised, or more scared in my life. The head of this weird visitant was shaped not unlike that of a horse; it had greenish eyes, and an expression that to me was malignant in the extreme. The three natives, who had spotted the thing as soon as it first appeared, were stiff with fright....The monster, sea-serpent or whatever you like to call it, surveyed us for a moment or two, and then dropped back into the water and leisurely went off.
>
> The natives were not in a fit state to discuss the matter that night. They believed it was an evil spirit. But old natives to whom I related the incident the next morning were not particularly interested. I then discovered that the sea-serpent, if such it was, is fairly often seen in those parts. A short time afterwards I heard from a reliable source that a sea-serpent had been cast up by a tidal wave on a reef some distance off. It measured fifty-three feet in length, and had a girth of twelve feet.

Sadly, no further information is available on the case of the stranded creature, and Davies's source remains unknown.

Source: Heuvelmans, *In the Wake of the Sea Serpents.*

Noreen sea serpent

On 3 September 1957, crewmen aboard the scalloper *Noreen* observed a unidentified creature 120 miles east of Georges Bank, near Nantucket, Massachusetts. The boat's cook, 20-year Navy veteran Joseph Bourassa, described the event to the *New Bedford Standard Times*:

> At 4:25 p.m. today a strange object was seen surfacing off the starboard quarter about 100 yards from the ship. He had a peculiar look about him. He had a large body and a small ALLIGATOR-like head. The neck seemed to be of medium size, matching the size of the head. The body was shaped somewhat like a seal. There was a mane of bristly hair or fur which ran down the middle of the head.
>
> He would surface the upper part of his body and glide out of the water with the lower part of his body remaining submerged. The portion of his body which was visible measured about forty

feet in length. We estimated his weight to be between thirty-five and forty tons overall.

At no time did the whole body show. He stayed on the surface no longer than forty seconds at a time. You could hear the heavy weight of his upper body when he dove below, creating a splash and a subsequent wake. He surfaced four times in twenty minutes, during which we were trying to stay clear of him. The captain changed course to steer away from him and the queer fellow surfaced on our starboard beam.

We changed course again and he then rose off our starboard bow, keeping his same distance from us. The Captain ordered the drags be brought in. Once the drags were on deck, the Captain turned the boat and steamed at full speed to the west, away from the queer fellow….

Another peculiar thing about him as that when he'd surface he would turn his head looking toward us and it seemed to us he was playful and curious. Another point was that on the upper part of his body there were two flippers, similar to those of a seal. The weather was clear and visibility was good. The sea was rough and sloppy. The wind was coming from the west-southwest at about 30 miles an hour.

Seven years later, on 17 May 1964, the same newspaper recalled the *Noreen* sighting in a series of reports on Massachusetts sea serpents. That summary of the incident described a creature "whose alligator head rose 26 feet in the air," a startling deviation from Bourassa's original report (which contained no reference to a long neck). In 1968, BERNARD HEUVELMANS speculated that a careless journalist had transformed a neck 2 feet 6 inches long into a 26-foot whopper, but Bourassa's description simply referred to a neck of "medium size." Twenty years after the incident, author Gary Mangiacopra obtained a brief statement from the *Noreen*'s captain, Robert Smith, who said: "It was a strange looking creature different from the usual SHARK, or whales, porpoise, swordfish, etc., we often see every trip. It didn't spout like a whale and seemed to stay on the surface of the water most of the time just gliding along with us."

Sources: Heuvelmans, *In the Wake of the Sea Serpents*; O'Neill, *The Great New England Sea Serpent*.

Norfolk Gnasher

This ALIEN BIG CAT of Norfolk, England created a stir in 1997, with at least 54 sightings reported between July and December. Norfolk's representative in Parliament called for an official investigation, but nothing came of the plea. Local police hunted the CAT in vain.

Sources: "Annual cat-alogue of sightings." *Fortean Times* 128 (November 1999): 6; Sieveking, "Big cats in Britain."

Norman, Scott T. (1964–)

California native Scott Norman was 30 years old when a co-worker introduced him to HERMAN REGUSTERS, lately returned from a search for the Congo's elusive MOKELE-MBEMBE. That conversation, followed by further research, fired Norman's imagination on the subject of living DINOSAURS and cryptozoology in general. Norman began construction of his Internet website (Cryptozoological Realms) in July 1996, and the next year found him networking with various researchers, including WILLIAM GIBBONS, WILLIAM REBSAMEN and KARL SHUKER (whose website he designed). As a fellow "young Earth" creationist, Norman worked well with Gibbons and Rebsamen, assisting Gibbons with plans for future field expeditions.

Source: Cryptozoological Realms, *http://www.cryptozoologicalrealms. com/*.

Norman sea serpent

On the evening of 17 July 1875, sailors aboard the steamer *Norman* spied a SEA SERPENT in Cape Cod Harbor, off Plymouth, Massachusetts. The creature seemed to be chasing a swordfish. As described by Captain Garton:

The head of the monster was raised at least ten feet above the ocean, but remained stationary only for a moment, as it was almost constantly in motion; now diving for a moment, and as suddenly reappearing to the same height. The submarine leviathan was striped black and white, the stripes running lengthways, from the head to the tail. The throat was pure white, and the head, which was extremely large, was full black, from which, just above a lizard-shaped head, protruded, an inch or more, a pair of deep black eyes, as large as ordinary saucers. The body was round, like a FISH-barrel, and the length was more than one hundred feet. The motion was like that of a caterpillar, with this exception: that the head of the SNAKE plunged under the water, whereas the head of the worm merely crooks to the ground.

Passengers aboard the steamer *Roman*, passing from Boston to Philadelphia around the same time, saw the same creature, but strangely reported it fleeing the swordfish.

Sources: Heuvelmans, *In the Wake of the Sea Serpents*; O'Neill, *The Great New England Sea Serpent*.

North American Apes

In the early 1960s, cryptozoologist LOREN COLEMAN coined the name North American Ape (often shortened to NAPE) for a group of unclassified primates described by witnesses across the continent, typically smaller than SASQUATCH-type HOMINIDS and lacking the tails seen on most DEVIL MONKEYS. As previously noted, reports of large APES resembling GORILLAS have been logged from various parts of the U.S. since the 19th century, but NAPES are generally smaller. They may be identical to cryptids described in other accounts as LITTLE RED MEN OF THE DELTA and/or the SKUNK APE. Various researchers disagree on whether some larger cryptids — including the FOUKE MONSTER, KNOBBY, OLD SHEFF and others — should be treated as NAPES or classified with BIGFOOT. Footprints may settle the debate, as hominids typically leave tracks resembling a human's, while NAPES display the opposed big toe common to gorillas, CHIMPANZEES (*Pan troglodytes*) and similar primates.

Although such reports are commonly dismissed as involving "escaped" primates from unnamed zoos or circuses, evidence suggests that NAPES preceded the arrival of white settlers on the continent. Aboriginal stone carvings at Rock Creek, Illinois depict various familiar animals in addition to apelike "footprints with the great toes turned at right angles." Likewise, early settlers in Allen County, Kentucky named a wooded valley near present-day Scottsville "Monkey Cave Hollow" because of its simian inhabitants. In the 1960s, Harold Holland of Scottsville wrote to IVAN SANDERSON:

About 20 years ago one old man who had moved from this area but returned for a final visit to his home, told me that when he was a boy of about 7 or 8 years, he saw the carcass of the last "MONKEY." He stated that a hunter came by his father's house and displayed the dead beast. He said that he could not recall exactly what it looked like (after all it had been 80 years

Do North American apes explain some hominid sightings? (*William Rebsamen*).

or thereabouts) but that the creature had hands and feet "like a person" and was about the same size he was himself, had no tail and was covered with brown hair.

More recent incidents include the following:

16 August 1926: According to the *New York Times*, one J. Blanchard, night watchman for the New Jersey Power and Light Company's plant in Booton, captured an ape by knocking it down from a power line with a wooden pole. Then, on 18 August, the *Times* reported that an escaped chimpanzee had gratefully surrendered to its keeper at Booton the previous day (17 August), after fleeing the Rockaway zoo and swimming across the Rockaway River. (Primatologists deny that chimps can or do swim.) As noted by Loren Coleman, it seems very strange that two apes should be caught in the same New Jersey town within 48 hours.

Summer 1941: The Rev. Marsh (or Lepton) Harpole was hunting along Gum Creek (near Mount Vernon, Illinois) when he saw a creature resembling a BABOON perched in a nearby tree. The beast jumped down and approached him, whereupon Harpole struck it with his gun barrel. When that failed to repulse the aggressive animal, Harpole fired over its head and the beast ran away. Local residents reported wild cries in the night for several months thereafter, but hunters failed to locate the ape.

August 1960: The Rev. E.C. Hand sighted a creature locally known as a BOOGER along Walnut Creek, near Clanton, Alabama. A search was mounted, but the hunters found only "giant ape" footprints. One print, preserved in a cast, was "about the size of a person's foot but looking more like a hand."

Spring 1962: Loren Coleman, with brothers Bill and Jerry, found a single 10-inch footprint with a fully opposed big toe in a dry creek bead near Decatur, Illinois. This incident prompted Coleman to coin the NAPE name.

June 1962: Residents of Trimble County, Kentucky were frightened by a 6-foot creature described as "not quite a dog, a panther or a bear." The beast walked upright, with long arms hanging to its knees. It allegedly killed a calf and was blamed for the disappearance of several more animals.

Spring 1966: The morning after Eulah Lewis reported an apelike creature prowling around near her trailer in Brookville, Florida, investigators discovered rounded footprints with "one big toe stuck out to the side like a thumb on the hand."

1967–70: A farmer at Calumet, Oklahoma reportedly fed a "chimpanzee" for three years, but failed in all attempts to capture it. In December 1970, an unseen creature raided a henhouse at El Reno (12 miles southeast of Calumet) and left a strange handprint on the door. The print was seven inches long and five inches wide. Lawrence Curtis, director of the Oklahoma City Zoo, examined the "deformed" print and could not identify it, though he pronounced it similar to a primate's.

September 1968: Witnesses at Hamburg, Arkansas reported sightings of "a thing that looks like a man but has a gorilla head."

August 1971: Following Skunk Ape sightings in Florida's Big Cypress Swamp, rabies control officer Henry Ring was dispatched to look for evidence. Ring reported that he "found nothing but a bunch of strange tracks, like someone was walking around on his knuckles"—exactly the way great apes move.

25 April 1973: Henry McDaniel and his wife saw a creature resembling a gray monkey, with short arms and pink eyes, outside their home at Enfield, Illinois. When they fired at it with a gun, the animal covered 50 feet in three leaps. The next local sighting described an unknown 3-legged beast. On 6 May, four witnesses saw an apelike animal 5–5.5 feet tall standing in the doorway of an abandoned barn outside Enfield.

July 1975: While passing through the Turkey Creek district near Lockridge, Iowa, Wendell and Gloria Olsen observed a bushy-tailed apelike creature on a deserted farm. Three months later, on 3 October, Herbert Peiffer saw a shaggy 5-foot animal near Turkey Creek. It walked on all fours, but rose on its hind legs to approach him, whereupon Peiffer fled. Hunters failed to find the beast, but they discovered apelike footprints and some partially eaten turkeys.

July–September 1978: At least 11 witnesses reported sighting an apelike animal around Ottosen, Iowa (Humboldt County). Estimates of its size varied widely, but the first witnesses described it as a "short, hair, apelike animal with fangs and deep-set eyes."

June 1980— Two Massachusetts men canoeing on a small lake called The Nip (near Bridgewater) glimpsed a small apelike creature walking on an island. They landed to search for the beast, but found nothing.

18 October 1987: A creature resembling an ape was seen at Honeybrook Township, Pennsylvania. Sixteen days later, on 3 November, a local resident shot a monkey weighing 50 pounds, covered in reddish-brown fur. Police failed to trace the animal's origin, and experts at the University of Pennsylvania School or Veterinary Medicine could not identify its species.

Early 1990s: A witness in Harrison County, Indiana reported sighting a 4-foot-tall primate of "light tan/cream color" that "used its front arms/legs to propel itself" in a manner "between a dog and an ape."

30 January 2002: Four witnesses saw a black, shaggy apelike creature about five feet tall, running through the woods near Lake Monroe, Indiana (outside Bloomington). The animal ran on all fours and left 5-inch tracks. Thirteen months after the sighting, a former anthropology professor, retired from Indiana University since the 1970s, denounced the sighting as a HOAX, claiming he had found deer and dog hair "deliberately planted" at the scene. No evidence was produced to support the aged "expert's" conclusion.

1 October 2003: Arkansas newspapers announced that "a large animal believed to be an ape or a monkey" had been seen three times around Decatur during late September. Spokesmen for a nearby animal park, Wild Wilderness Drive-Thru Safari in Gentry, reported no escapes. Reports of the creatures size and color varied, and it had not been captured at press time for this volume.

17 October 2003: Television broadcasts from Knoxville, Tennessee described a veritable siege around LaFollette, as locals hunted a 3-foot-tall "monkey or chimpanzee" blamed for killing CATS and dogs in residential neighborhoods. Eyewitness reports described an animal with long arms, "bottom teeth about two and a half inches long," and "gray-looking in front, [while] the rest of his body looks dark brown." Three days later, new reports claimed more than 100 pets missing and presumably devoured by a primate "perhaps weighing 400 pounds." Rumors claimed the beast had escaped from a traveling circus, but the Campbell County sheriff's office had no reports of fugitive apes. By 22 October, reporters had begun to call the beast a Skunk Ape, linking it to Florida's MYAKKA PHOTOGRAPHS. A short-term rush of CRYPTOTOURISM ensued, while university biologists denied that any primate would devour cats and dogs. A goat was found slaughtered and partially eaten on 10 November, followed three days later by an Internet posting from Loren Coleman, reporting rumors that the predator had been shot and killed by local police. A story in the *LaFollette Press* refuted those tales on 14 November, announcing that "the alleged animal is still on the alleged loose," where it remained at press time for this volume.

An undated Internet report suggests that NAPES may also be found in Canada. Ian Harper was riding his bicycle near Lake Scugog, Ontario in broad daylight when he saw a neighbor's dog pursuing a strange creature. As Harper described the animal: "It was about three feet tall, with long willowy arms and a large head. My first thought [was that] it was a big white monkey." At Harper's approach, the thing emitted "a very loud sub-sonic grunt or blast" that frightened boy and dog alike into flight.

Science recognizes no indigenous North American primates, so various explanations have been advanced to explain NAPE sightings. One involves the escape or release of domestic pets. Florida authorities acknowledge that breeding colonies of squirrel monkeys (*Samiri sciureus*) have been established in Marion County since the 1950s, and in two other counties since the 1970s, but those small monkeys with prominent tails do not explain sightings of much larger, tailless specimens. Other researchers suggest that chimpanzees may have reached the U.S. aboard slave African slave ships, anytime between the 17th and 19th centuries, in addition to those theoretically fleeing zoos and circuses. Loren Coleman believes that NAPES may represent a relict population of *Dryopithecus*, a European primate known from Miocene fossils, presumed extinct for some 9 million years. He further suggests that the apes learned to swim, expanding through North America along the Mississippi River and its tributaries. Most primatologists and anthropologists dismiss the notion out of hand, but Roderick Sprague, at the University of Idaho, has praised Coleman's tireless research. Still, Sprague notes that the total lack of fossil evidence for *Dryopithecus* in North America "is a weak point in an otherwise well developed argument."

Sources: Berry, *Bigfoot on the East Coast*; Bord and Bord, *The Bigfoot Casebook*; Bord and Bord, *Unexplained Mysteries of the 20th Century*; Clark and Pear, *Strange & Unexplained Phenomena*; Coleman and Clark, *Cryptozoology A to Z*; Gibbons, *Missionaries and Monsters*; Green, *Sasquatch: The Apes Among Us*; Cliff Hightower, "Missing cats leave animal control officer wondering." *Knoxville* (TN) *News Sentinel* (21 October 2003); Bob Hodge, "Campbell beast out of season." *Knoxville* (TN) *News Sentinel* (26 October 2003); Brad LaGrange, "Primates in Harrison County, Indiana?" *North American BioFortean Review* 1 (April 1999): 13; Jeff LeMaster, "Prowling primate spotted in Decatur." *Benton County* (AR) *Daily Record* (1 October 2003); Susan Sharp, "Monkey madness continues." *LaFollette* (TN) *Press* (14 November 2003); Cryptozoology, *http://www.pararesearchers.org/Cryptozoology/crypto3/crypto3.html*

North American Science Institute

Confusion surrounds the origins of this organization, which surfaced publicly for the first time on 23 October 1997, announcing a "research alliance" with the BIGFOOT FIELD RESEARCERS' ORGANIZATION. Jeff Glickman, an Oregon forensic scientist, was named as executive director, while Todd Deery identified himself as the NASI's research director. The only other member publicly identified was LOREN COLEMAN, named as "one of the first Research Board members." The group's maiden press release described it as "a nonprofit organization which serves as an institutional home for scientific and educational projects related to the BIGFOOT phenomenon." Meanwhile, a separate Internet listing identified the NASI as the successor to DANIEL PEREZ's Center for Bigfoot Studies. The NASI's primary goal was described as the creation of "a single central repository [that] will enable researchers to

more quickly and accurately identify habitats and migration routes should the phenomenon originate from an unclassified animal species."

One month after its first public bulletin, the NASI released a report on the PATTERSON FILM, attempting to discover if the SASQUATCH depicted in that film was a human being in an APE suit or an unclassified animal. The report hinged on calculation of chest measurements, concluding that the figure's chest had a circumference of 82.98 inches. From that, in turn, the NASI estimated its weight at 1,957 pounds, and thus concluded that it could not be a man. Based on those calculations, Bigfoot must spend 4–8 hours per day consuming food equivalent to 15,600 calories. Conflicting reports from Coleman state that the study cost $40,000 or $75,000, but no financial statement was included with the report. If any further bulletins were published by the NASI, they have not survived, and the group's website is no longer active.

Sources: Coleman, *Bigfoot!*; Coleman and Clark, *Cryptozoology A to Z*; North American Scientific Institute, huisam.150m.com/Athens_P3/wbs.html; The People Behind Cryptozoology, http://www.ncf.carleton.ca/~bz050/homepage.cp.html.

North Carolina Bigfoot Investigations

Organized in 2003, North Carolina BIGFOOT Investigations announced its creation with the launch of an Internet website soliciting HOMINID sighting reports throughout the Tarheel State. No officers were identified at press time for this book, and the website link for new members was "on hold temporarily."

Source: North Carolina Bigfoot Investigations, http://groups.msn.com/NCBigfootInvestigations/entrypage.msnw.

North Saskatchewan River, Canada *see* Pink Eye

North Shrewsbury River, New Jersey

Various authors include this Monmouth County river on published lists of supposed aquatic cryptid habitats, but none to date provides any dates or details of sightings.

Sources: Bord and Bord, *Unexplained Mysteries of the 20th Century*; Coleman, *Mysterious America*; Kirk, *In the Domain of the Lake Monsters*.

Northeastern Ohio Bigfoot Research

According to its Internet website, this group is a nonprofit organization seeking "to prove the existence of BIGFOOT in Ohio and across the globe." Members are committed to a "no kill" philosophy, convinced that "studying Bigfoot in its natural untouched habitat with no harm is the best way to understand this creature," and it offers cooperation only to others who share that position. Group founders are listed as Michael and Tamara Beckett, with Jeff Weingart and family. The NOBR's website includes an online newsletter, a schedule of forthcoming events, information on Ohio SASQUATCH sightings, and contacts for researchers throughout North America.

Source: Northeastern Ohio Bigfoot Research, *http://www.neobfr.org/*.

Northern California Bigfoot Organization

This group first drew media attention in May 1999, following a series of BIGFOOT reports in Trinity County, California. Robert Everett, a 64-year-old Navy veteran and self-identified director of the NCBO, told reporters, "This is the time of year they start to move." Internet listings place the NCBO's headquarters at Hyampom, California, but no other members are identified. The last public mention of the NCBO came in 2000, when Everett launched an abortive campaign for local political office. Everett died on 11 October 2003, leaving the future of his group uncertain. The NCBO had no website at press time for this volume, and its present status is unclear.

Sources: "Bigfoot returns to Trinity County." *Redding* (CA) *Record Searchlight* (20 May 1999); Robert Everett obituary, *Redding* (CA) *Record Searchlight* (17 October 2003); Jim Schultz, "Modine, Everett vie for Trinity board job." *Redding* (CA) *Record Searchlight* (3 November 2000).

Northwest League for the Protection of Sasquatch

In the 1970s, alarmed by reports of hunters seeking to kill BIGFOOT, a group of state employees in Olympia, Washington organized the Northwest League for the Protection of SASQUATCH. Thirty years later, ex-member Caroline Feiss described the group as "an excuse to get together, drink some wine and concoct fun." Between drinks, Feiss recalled, "We decided Bigfoot needed legal protection, first under the state and then under the Endangered Species Act. The first was easy. Jim Dolliver [a future state Supreme Court justice] and Ralph Munro [later Washington secretary of state] helped create a proclamation declaring the Sasquatch to be the Washington state monster. The proclamation was read on the Capitol steps with a band, crowds of people and great speeches." The national effort failed, however, since federal authorities require a type specimen for listing under the Endangered Species Act. "That proved our undoing," Feiss told the *Seattle Times*. "The Northwest League disbanded soon afterwards."

Source: "Creation of a state monster." *Seattle Times* (23 December 2002).

Norton Mere, England

Reports of a lurking LAKE MONSTER emerged from Shropshire, England in May 1973, after three visitors to this lake reported seeing a large wake on the surface with no visible cause. Searches were organized, but they proved fruitless. The incident remains unexplained.

Source: "And now...a monster in the Midlands." *Fortean Times* 2 (January 1974): 13–14.

Norwegian sea serpents

Norway may have produced more SEA SERPENT sightings than any other country on Earth, as well as the oldest on record. Erik Walkendorf, the Archbishop of Trondheim penned the first reference to sea serpents in a public letter two years before his death, when he wrote to Pope Leo X in 1520: "The smallest of them are 60 feet long and 10 feet thick. The squarish head is longer than the body. They are grey of colour and are only seen when the air is clear and the sea is calm; they are greedy creatures that kill people."

Indeed, early accounts of Norse sea serpents emphasize their conflict with mankind. The serpent of Ellinggård inlet (in Østfold) raided dairy herds and proved impervious to bullets, until one brave farmer brained it with an oaken club and took one of its vertebrae for use as a milking stool. Another terrorized fishermen on Brekkestad Bay (in Sør Trøndelag) until blacksmith Jørn Hovde mounted a spiked ram on his boat and gored the creature to death. A similar ram was used at Sørøya, west of Hammerfest, to kill a serpent that invaded the Sandøyfjord. More fishermen were trapped at sea near Brynilen, in the Tysfjord, while a serpentine cryptid circled their boat for two days. The serpent of Ofotfjord proved more timid, fleeing at the first approach of boats, while another at Store Latøya chased fishing boats ashore. Åsmund Ørekvam fashioned a long-handled axe to fight the serpent of Ørekvam (in Hordaland), but stopped short of actual contact. Johannes Furuberg fired a gun into the mouth of a serpent that menaced him in the Bjornefjord, and it vanished in a swirl of

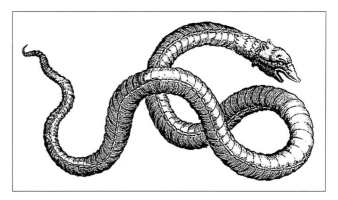

Norwegian sea serpent reports date from the early 16th century.

bloody water. In the Boknafjord, at Ølensundet, locals watched a great serpent battle one of three "sea horses" that invaded its territory, turning the sea red with blood. The sea horse killed its rival, but suffered grievous wounds in the struggle.

Another high-ranking Scandinavian clergyman, Olaus Magnus, fled his native Sweden for Italy during the Reformation, and there published his highly-detailed map of northern lands in 1539, replete with drawings of terrible sea monsters. His later *History of the Nordic People* (1555) would wait 103 years for an English translation, which included the following passage:

> They who in Works of Navigation, on the Coasts of Norway, employ themselves in fishing or Merchandise, do all agree in this strange story, that there is a Serpent there which is of vast magnitude, namely 200 feet long, and moreover 20 feet thick; and it is wont to live in Rocks and Caves toward the Sea-coast about *Berge[n]*: which will go alone from his holes on a clear night, in Summer, and devour Calves, Lambs, and Hogs, or else he goes into the Sea to feed on Polypus, Locusts, and all sorts of Sea-Crabs. He hath commonly hair hanging from his neck a Cubit [16 inches] long, and sharp Scales, and is black, and he hath flaming shining eyes. The SNAKE disquiets the shippers, and he puts up his head on high like a pillar, and catcheth away men, and he devours them; and this hapneth not, but it signifies some wonderful change in the Kingdom near at hand; namely that the Princes shall die, or be banished; or some Tumultuous Wars shall presently follow.

Historian Jonas Ramus offered another glimpse of the great serpent in his history of pagan Norway, *Nori Regnum* (1689): "Anno 1687, a large Sea-snake was seen by many people at Dramsfiorden; and at one time by eleven persons together. It was in very calm weather; and so soon as the sun appeared, and the wind blew a little, it shot away just like a coiled cable, that is suddenly thrown out by sailors; and they observed that it was some time in stretching out its many folds."

The 18th century brought reports of three sea serpent carcasses stranded on Norwegian shores. BERNARD HEUVELMANS suggests that the first, at Kobberveug (1720), was probably a GIANT SQUID, but the others at Amund and Karmen Island (sometime before 1753) remain unidentified today. In late August 1746, while traveling to Trondheim, Lorentz de Ferry met a sea serpent near Molde. As he described the incident in a sworn affidavit five years later, he was reading a book on deck when:

> Suddenly I noticed mumbling voices among my 8 oarsmen, and I noticed that the course had been shifted to off the shore. I asked for an explanation and was answered that the sea serpent had been straight ahead. Even if the men looked a bit frightened, I at once ordered the course to be turned back towards land to head for the mysterious creature. The sea serpent passed in front of us, and

again I ordered the boat to turn to get closer to the creature. But the sea serpent swam faster than we were able to row, so I raised my flintlock gun loaded with pellets and shot at the animal who immediately dived a short distance away. We moved over to the spot where the serpent had last been seen. It was easy to find due to the calm weather. The water was thick with blood, may be a pellet or two had hit it. In vain we rested a while on the oars to see if it surfaced again. The sea serpent looked like this: The head was held two feet above the water and had the same shape as a horse's head. Its colour was sort of greyish, and the snout was quite black. The eyes were very big, and a long, white mane hung from the neck into the water. The body was very thick. 7–8 humps were visible, and we estimated a 6 feet distance between each hump.

Erik Pontoppidan, the bishop of Bergen from 1747 to 1764, devoted much time to the study of pelagic cryptids and related much of their local history in his two-volume *Natural History of Norway* (1752–53). As Pontoppidan advised his readers, "I have been among those who have doubted the reality and the existence of the sea serpent, but at last my doubts were refuted by solid evidence." In fact, he noted, "Hundreds of our finest sailors and fishermen have been eyewitnesses to the sea serpent. I have met a lot of people from our fjords in the north, and they were able to confirm my questions, and their descriptions of the animal is the same. Some who has come here for trading purposes regard these questions as superfluous as questions whether cods or whales exist." There were, however, some regional variations in sea serpent morphology. Pontoppidan observed: "Those on our coast differ likewise from the Greenland Sea-Snakes, with regard to the skin, which is as smooth as glass, and has not the least wrinkle, but about the neck, where there is a kind of mane, which looks like a parcel of sea-weeds hanging down to the water." The serpents' appearance was also seasonal. "This sea creature dwells in the deep except for July and August which is its playing time. It surfaces when the sea is dead calm, but sinks back when the slightest stir ripples the surface."

Some of Pontoppidan's sightings were very recent. In 1745, he wrote, "A fisherman met a long, big and strange animal north of Bergen. It came swimming towards his boat and got so close that the waves hit the boat before the animal submerged and was gone. This was not unlike a Sea-calf [seal] as to the fore-part, and had furred skin. The body was broad and big as a vessel of 50 lasts burthen; and the tail, which seemed to be about six fathoms [36 feet] long, was quite small and pointed at the end." Five years later, another fisherman "who had been so close to it that he actually had been able to touch its smooth skin, told that sometimes these animals are said to raise the head out of the water and snatch one of the crew from a boat. I do not know if this is true, as it is quite uncertain whether it is a fierce predator or not." Another account, consigned to a footnote, read: "There is a report, but not altogether to be depended upon, that some peasants at Sundmœr have catched a Snake lately in a net, which was three fathoms [18 feet] long, and hag four legs: this must somewhat resemble a CROCODILE. The peasants ran away frightened, and left the Snake to do the same."

Governor Benstrup observed a sea serpent in 1753 and sketched it for Pontoppidan, adding a note that "this creature does not, like the EEL or Landsnake, taper gradually to a point, but the body, which looks to me as big as two hogsheads, grows remarkably small at once just where the tail begins." In 1767, Knut Leem's *Description of the Sami people of Finnmark* included reference to a cryptid "about 240 feet long, with black eyes and a head the

size of a whale head, but of shape like a serpent. Its neck is narrower than the main body, and it has got long light grey hair hanging down on both sides of the neck like the mane of a horse. The back is also light grey, but the belly is rather whitish. It is most often seen in dead calm weather, with many coils that partly shows above the surface, partly hidden in the water. People are afraid of this nasty sea creature, and stays away if possible when it is around."

On 28 July 1815, five men in a sailboat met a serpent in the Romsdalsfjorden, which swam "by the help of ten fins on the front part of the body." When it was close enough, witness J.C. Lund fired at the beast's large head with a flintlock musket and thus caused it to retreat. Heuvelmans notes 22 Norwegian sightings between 1827 and 1848, the first involving five witnesses near Drøbak in August 1827. Lars Johnöen, a fisherman at Smölen, claimed multiple sightings of serpents 30–40 feet long, with heads and manes resembling those of a horse. Residents of Kristiansund regarded their 114-foot serpent as a regular summertime visitor, favoring calm days and submerging when the wind blew. On 13 July 1867, eight witnesses saw a sea serpent at Mandsfjord, on Norway's southern coast. They described it as 90–120 feet long, with two "protuberances" on its head, showing 10–12 humps on the water's surface.

Sightings continued as the 19th century drew to a close. On 16 August 1885, a 100-foot serpent with a "flat scaly head" and 17 visible humps menaced a boatload of boys returning to the mainland from Rödöy Island. Seven years later, on 23 September 1892, five peasants working on the Suldal watched a creature 18–20 feet long, resembling a capsized boat and leaving a wake like a steamer's behind as it passed. In 1894, fishermen at Ersvika (south of Hammerfest) lost three days work while two aggressive serpents patrolled their coastal waters, forcing them to stay on shore.

The new century's first sighting was recorded at Oslofjord, on 4 August 1902, by 11 passengers aboard the yacht *TONNY*. Six years later, a Dutch tourist at Sognefjord watched an animal resembling a huge white-bellied eel rise four times from the water, then submerge. In 1910, E.R. Eliassen and his father logged the northernmost sighting to date, while boating near Ingøy Island, north of Rolvsøy. As Eliassen described the creature, seen from 50 yards:

A long neck, with a small head on it, rose 5 — or possibly even 6 — feet above the water. Behind the neck was a long hump, of about the same length. Astern of this the body was submerged for a short distance, but then rose again in the form of a larger hump — suggesting that those portions of it which remained hidden under the surface must be of great size.

In June or July 1914, a serpent visited Bogen on the Ofotfjord, west of Narvik. Witness W.E. Parkin described the creature:

What met my gaze was an object sticking out of the water at an angle of approximately 45°. It appeared, from where I was, to be about five or six feet out of the water. Behind it was a gap, and then several regular humps. The largest number I counted at one time was seven, and the smallest five.

During World War II, a group of Finnøy fishermen saw a sea serpent beached at Vegglandet, in the Sagfjord, but it plunged into the sea and vanished as their boat drew closer. The next sighting, in 1961, was logged by passengers aboard the oceanographic vessel *JOHAN HJORT*. A 19-year hiatus was broken in August 1980, when an unknown creature showed three humps above the surface near Gressviktangen. Two years later, on 7 August 1982, four witnesses at Søgne saw a similar gray-black creature, revealing three humps with a yard of open water between them. On 1 June

The Ingøy Island sea serpent, after witness E.R. Eliassen.

1999, Arnt Helge Molvær was walking along the fjord near Ålesund when he saw a large creature in the water. He estimated it was 81–98 feet long and five feet in diameter, with a square dorsal fin 12–16 inches high. He watched the beast through binoculars before running home for his video camera. Upon his return, some 40 minutes later, the creature was still present and Molvær captured it on tape, while it nosed around a floating whale carcass. After Molvær's tape was aired on television, several other witnesses came forward with recent sightings from the same area. Norway's most recent sighting (as of press time for this volume), was recorded at Storfjorden (southwest of Ålesund) by fishermen aboard the *KLARING* on 18 March 2001.

Sources: Heuvelmans, *In the Wake of the Sea Serpents*; Erik Knatterud, Norwegian Sea Serpents, *http://www.mjoesormen.no/norwegianseaserpents.htm*.

Nottawasaga Bay, Canada

In June 1938, a LAKE MONSTER of "uncanny speed" was seen by several witnesses, swimming off Wasaga Beach, in Nottawasaga Bay (at the southern end of Georgian Bay, Ontario). Some witnesses compared it to a seal, while others claimed it "churned the water like an ocean liner." Georgian Bay, in turn, is linked at several points to LAKE HURON, with access to the North Atlantic via the St. Lawrence River. Aquatic cryptids of varying sizes and descriptions have been sighted in all the Great Lakes and various connecting rivers over the past 200 years. There is likewise no reason why a wandering pinniped may not have visited Nottawasaga Bay or its adjoining waters.

Sources: Garner, *Monster! Monster!*; Richard Lambert, *Exploring the Supernatural*. Toronto: University of Toronto Press, 1967.

Nottingham Lion

Shortly after 6:00 a.m. on 29 July 1976, milkmen David Bentley and David Crowther were startled by the appearance of an ALIEN BIG CAT at Tollerton, four miles southeast of Nottingham, England. Both witnesses described the CAT as an adult lioness (*Panthera leo*), complete with the typical tuft at the end of its tail. Police toured nearby villages with loudspeakers, warning local residents to stay indoors, and a Clipstone farmer reported large pawprints found on his property. Armed officers accompanied by tracking dogs and a helicopter searched the region for a week, in vain, though sporadic sightings continued outside the main path of the hunt. In all, 65 witnesses claimed LION sightings, but police responding to their calls found nothing, nor were there any reports of predation. Still, Inspector John Smith told the press on 4 August, "We are almost totally convinced it is there." Two days later, police spokesmen changed their tune, declaring that the lion was simply an unidentified "large dog"—which had likewise slipped through their clutches.

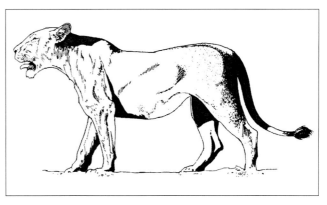

Residents of Nottingham, England sighted a lioness in 1976.

Witnesses who saw the cat were not persuaded by the press release.

Sources: Bord and Bord, *Alien Animals*; McEwan, *Mystery Animals of Britain and Ireland*; "The Nottingham lion saga." *Fortean Times* 18 (October 1976): 25–26; Shuker, *Mystery Cats of the World*.

Nova Scotia sea serpents

The province of Nova Scotia has produced a fair number of Canadian SEA SERPENT reports since the early 19th century. The first on record was logged from Halifax harbor on 15 July 1825, when multiple witnesses watched a 60-foot creature with a body the size of a tree trunk writhing in the water, displaying eight humps or coils. Throughout most of the performance, its head was held three feet above the water's surface. Eight years later, on 15 May 1833, Captain W. Sullivan and four other members of a Canadian rifle brigade saw a creature in Mahone Bay which they described as a "common SNAKE" 80 feet long, black streaked with white, holding its head six feet above the water as it swam. In August 1845, a 100-foot creature was seen swimming offshore from Merigomish, on the northern coast by "two intelligent observers." British author Charles Lyell described the incident as follows:

One of the witnesses went up a bank in order to look down upon it. They said it sometimes raised its head (which resembled that of a seal) partially out of the water. Along its back were a number of humps or protuberances, which, in the opinion of the observer on the beach, were true humps, while the other thought they were produced by vertical flextures [*sic*] of the body. Between the head and the first protuberance there was a straight part of the back of considerable length, and this part was generally above water. The colour appeared black, and the skin had a rough appearance.

The animal was seen to bend its body almost into a circle, and again to unbend it with rapidity. It was slender in proportion to its length. After it had disappeared in deep water, its wake was visible for some time. There were no indications of paddles seen. Some other persons who saw it, compared the creature to a long string of fishing-net buoys moving rapidly about.

In the course of the summer, the fishermen on the eastern shore of Prince Edward's Island, in the Gulf of St. Lawrence, had been terrified by this sea monster, and the year before, October 1844, a similar creature swam slowly past the pier at Arisaig, near the east end of Nova Scotia, and, there being only a slight breeze at the time, was attentively observed by Mr. Barry, a millwright of Pictou, who told Mr. Dawson he was within 120 feet of it, and estimated its length at sixty feet, and the thickness of its body at three feet. It had humps on the back, which seemed too small and close together to be bends of the body.

The body appeared also to move in *long undulations*, including many of the smaller humps. In consequence of this motion, the head and tail were sometimes both out of sight, and sometimes both above water, as represented in the annexed outline, given from memory. The head...was rounded and obtuse in front, and was never elevated more than a foot above the surface. The tail was pointed, appearing like half of a mackerel's tail. The colour of the part seen was black.

St. Margaret's Bay, on the southern coast, also attracted its share of sea serpents. In the summer of 1846, schoolmaster James Wilson and a companion sighted an object offshore which they first took for a string of buoys on a long net. Moments later:

They...perceived the object to be a large Serpent, with a head about the size of a barrel, and a body in proportion, with something like a mane flowing down its neck. It carried its head erect, with a slight inclination forward....Wilson thinks the animal was from about seventy to one hundred feet in length. Its color seemed to be a sort of steel-gray.

Three years later, in summer 1849, another pelagic cryptid appeared to four fishermen on South West Island, just outside the mouth of St. Margaret's Bay. The four bravely launched a boat and drew close enough to observe a creature 60 feet long and as thick as an 80-gallon cask. The Rev. John Ambrose later summarized their description of the animal:

It was proportioned like an EEL, i.e. tapering tapering towards the extremities, with no caudal fin perceptible, but one very high fin, or row of spines, each about an inch in diameter at the base, erected along its back, serving indeed for a dorsal fin, like the folding fin of the *Thynnus vulgaris*, or albicore [sic]. This spinal erection seemed to occupy about one third of its length, each end of it being about equi-distant from the Serpent's extremities; and at a distance, somewhat resembling, in size and appearance, the sail of a skiff. The animal's back was covered with scales, about six inches long and three inches wide, extending in rows *across* the body, i.e., the longer diameter of the scale being in the direction of the circumference of the body. The colour of the back was black. The men had no opportunity of seeing the belly, but what the Americans would call "a smart chance" of becoming acquainted with the inside of it; for the creature, perceiving the boat, raised its head about ten feet above water, turned towards it, and opened its jaws, showed the inside of its mouth red in colour and well armed with teeth about three inches long, shaped like those of a cat-fish. The men now thinking it high time to terminate the interview, pulled vigorously for shore, followed for some distance by the snake, which at length gave up the chase and disappeared.

BERNARD HEUVELMANS also refers in passing to a carcass stranded at St. Margaret's Bay sometime "before 1864" and found by "a lady," but he includes no source for the report and provides no further information. It remains, like his effort to identify the creature, a tantalizing question mark.

On 6 March 1947, Charles Ballard of Sydney wrote to IVAN SANDERSON, describing his encounter with an unknown creature at Sydney Harbor (eastern Nova Scotia). While driving from Sydney to North Sydney, Ballard had seen an 80-foot creature swimming 350 feet offshore, traveling at 5–7 miles per hour. It was, he wrote:

Eel-shaped, practically a gigantic eel, big around as a ten gal. keg...no part of it over a foot under water, and undulations along the body...like a small eel I have seen swimming in brooks, but there would be one or two undulations coming up out of the water for 6 or 8 feet and the upper part of the undulations would come 4 or 5 feet out of the water. No fins, just a BIG eel.

A rather different cryptid—a pure-white TURTLE 45 feet long—was reported by crewmen aboard the *Rhapsody* from Nova

Scotia's southern coast in June 1956. Fortean authors Colin and Janet Bord report three sightings from Cape Sable Island in July 1976, but they describe only one. Keith Ross and his son Rodney were anchored in fog off Pollock's Ledge, several miles offshore, when a 50-foot creature surfaced and swam past their boat. Rodney said:

I never seen CROCODILES other than on television, but its head was sort of like that coming out of the water. Peaked at the top, with a big wide mouth. Its neck was full of things that looked like gigantic barnacles. Its eyes were in sockets but popped out of the side of its head, and it had two tusks maybe two or three feet long and four inches or so round....I didn't think it was a whale. Not with a head like that and those tusks.

Nova Scotia's most recent sighting, as of press time for this book, was recorded by a fisherman at Cape Breton in June 2003.

Sources: Bord and Bord, *Unexplained Mysteries of the 20th Century*; Heuvelmans, *In the Wake of the Sea Serpents*.

Novianuk Lake, Alaska In 1959, a LAKE MONSTER resembling ILLIE (the giant FISH of Iliamna Lake) was reported from this lake, in Alaska's Katmai National Park.

Source: Gil Paust, "Alaska's monster mystery fish." *Sports Afield* (January 1959): 54, 66.

Nowata Monster Nowata County, in northeastern Oklahoma, has a history of HOMINID sightings dating from 1915, when a resident of Wann encountered a creature 5–6 feet tall that "stood with its arms stretched out. It was about four feet wide in the chest, and hairy all over. It was like a bear or something, but it stood up like a man." That creature may have been more frightened than the witness, for it did not reappear until late July 1974. John and Margie Lee logged multiple sightings of a creature resembling SASQUATCH on their farm, near Watova, over a two-week period. The animal reportedly "played games" with the Lees, leaving an empty bucket in the doorway of their barn each night, no matter how the Lees attempted to conceal the pail around the premises. Soon, the nocturnal prowler became a nuisance, peering in windows, ransacking the barn, and stealing a neighbor's chickens. Deputy sheriffs Buck Field and Gilbert Gilmore were called to Watova and saw the creature, firing several shots in the darkness, but they found no evidence that it was wounded. In September 1975 the beast (or its twin) surfaced at Noxie, north of Nowata, where several farmers fired on it without effect. One witness there reported two creatures together. The Noxie visitors left 3-toed footprints and smelled "like rotten eggs or sulfur." Sporadic sightings around Nowata County were reported through mid-1980.

Sources: Bord and Bord, *The Bigfoot Casebook*; Bord and Bord, *Unexplained Mysteries of the 20th Century*; Rife, *Bigfoot Across America*.

Nsanga This giant reptile, resembling a smooth-skinned CROCODILE of huge proportions, reportedly inhabits Zambia's Bangweulu Swamp. Confusion arises from the fact that Bantu tribesmen also use the name Nsanga for the tiger fish (*Hydrocynus vittatus*), but they draw a clear distinction between that 40-inch finny predator and the creature that devours hippos. Explorer Paul Graetz obtained strips of a supposed Nsanga's hide on Mbawala Island, in 1909, but the samples were not preserved for study. In 1958, BERNARD HEUVELMANS suggested that the Nsanga might be an unknown species of large MONITOR LIZARD, but 20 years later he revised that opinion and proposed an aquatic species of SABER-TOOTH CAT. Some authors apparently confuse the Nsanga and EMELA-NTOUKA, a supposed living DINOSAUR reported from Zambia and neighboring countries.

Sources: Paul Graetz, *Im Motorboot quer durch Afrika*. Berlin: Braunbeck und Gutenberg, 1913; Heuvelmans, *Les Derniers Dragons d'Afrique*; Heuvelmans, *On the Track of Unknown Animals*.

Nsanguni   Apparently unrelated to the NSANGA, this aquatic cryptid of Zambia's Luanshya River is described by natives as a giant SNAKE. Lamba tribesmen blamed the Nsanguni for flooding and other fatal mishaps that occurred during excavation of the Roan Antelope copper mine, in the late 1920s. No recent sightings are recorded.

Sources: Clement Doke, *Lamba Folk-Lore*. New York: American Folk-Lore Society, 1927; F. Spearpoint, "The African native and the Rhodesian copper mines." *Journal of the Royal Africa Society* 36 (July 1937): 3–8.

Ntambo Wa Luy   Although its name translates as "water lion," the Ntambo wa luy described by Congolese natives bears no resemblance to a CAT. Witnesses describe it as 25–30 feet long and five feet tall at the shoulder, weighing an estimated two tons. A long horn sprouts from its head, and the creature's clawed, 3-toed tracks measure 16 inches long and eight inches wide. The Ntambo wa luy is at home on land or in water, and sometimes attacks hippopotamuses, goring them fatally with its horn. In short, descriptions of this animal from the Democratic Republic of Congo match most particulars of the EMELA-NTOUKA, a supposed living DINOSAUR known in surrounding countries. Explorer Gabriel Becker reported the creature's distinctive tracks in the 1950s, from the DRC's Kasai-Occidental region.

Source: Heuvelmans, *Les Derniers Dragons d'Afrique*.

Ntarargo *see* **Lions (Spotted)**

N'Tchego *see* **Koolookamba**

Ntonou   Malinke tribesmen of Côte d'Ivoire once described the Ntonou as a primate or small HOMINID covered in hair, with a short tail. Even those who thought of it as human agreed that the Ntonou was extremely primitive, lacking tools and knowledge of fire, but the creatures still allegedly mingled with more advanced tribes and sometimes fathered hybrid offspring (some of whom allegedly had tails). Local natives generally agree that the species was extinct by the early 1900s.

Source: Frantz de Zeltner, "Notes sur la sociologie soudanaise." *L'Anthropologie* (1908): 217, 222–228.

Nuk-Luk   This unclassified HOMINID or WILDMAN, dubbed Nuk-luk ("man of the bush") or Nakani ("bad Indian"), reportedly inhabits the ill-reputed Nahanni Valley in Canada's Northwest Territories, where several trappers and prospectors vanished or were murdered in the first half of the 20th century. (Those victims found were typically decapitated.) Two sightings were recorded in spring 1964, the first in April, when multiple witnesses glimpsed a bearded "man-shaped figure" on a butte at the junction of the Liard and South Nahanni Rivers. Two months later, two witnesses at Fort Simpson saw a similar creature. Where the first specimen had been naked, however, the second wore a skirt of apparent moose skin, with ankle-high boots, and carried a club. Researchers LOREN COLEMAN and PATRICK HUYGHE report stories of similar "bushmen" across the Yukon territory and into Alaska. They suggest that the creatures may comprise a relict population of NEANDERTAL MAN.

Source: Coleman and Huyghe, *The Field Guide to Bigfoot, Yeti, and Other Mystery Primates Worldwide*.

Nunkse Lee Kwala   Swedish cryptozoologist JAN-OVE SUNDBERG was the first to publish Native American accounts of this playful SEA SERPENT, said to inhabit the waters around British Columbia's Hornby Island. Based on its demeanor, description and habitat, we may safely assume that the creature is identical to CADBOROSAURUS.

Source: Global Underwater Search Team, http://www.cryptozoology.st/.

Nyalmo/Nyulmo   This unclassified primate or HOMINID of southern Tibet, Nepal and northern Bangladesh is described by witnesses as a ferocious predator, 13–20 feet tall, which preys on mountain sheep and yaks (with an occasional human being thrown in for variety). BERNARD HEUVELMANS believed the creatures represent a relict population of *GIGANTOPITHECUS*, and while he considered them distinct from the YETI, he suggested they might be identical to the TOK, KUNG-LU and shan-tu reported from Southeast Asia.

Sources: Heuvelmans, "Annotated checklist of apparently unknown animals with which cryptozoology is concerned"; Heuvelmans, *On the Track of Unknown Animals*.

Nyama *see* **Gnéna**

N'yamala   Natives of Gabon describe the N'yamala ("mother of canoes") as a large amphibious reptile inhabiting the Ngounié and Ogooué Rivers. Witnesses report that the creature exceeds 30 feet in length and weighs as much as an adult elephant. The N'yamala's most striking feature is its long neck, comparable in size and form to that of a sauropod DINOSAUR. In fact, when herpetologist JAMES POWELL visited the region in 1979, tribesmen selected a picture of the dinosaur *Diplodocus* as a likeness of the N'yamala. In that respect, it precisely resembles the Congo's MOKELE-MBEMBE, and cryptozoologist ROY MACKAL considers the two creatures identical. Natives informed Powell that the N'yamala is a vegetarian, but they insist that it also attacks and kills hippopotamuses on sight.

Sources: Heuvelmans, *Les Derniers Dragons d'Afrique*; Mackal, *A Living Dinosaur?*; Mackal, *In Search of Hidden Animals*.

Nyaminyami   Natives of Zimbabwe believe that the Zambezi River is protected by a "river god" called Nyaminyami, which possesses a FISH'S head and a SNAKE'S body. In 1957–58, Nyaminyami was blamed for a series of accidents suffered by workmen on the Zambezi, during construction of the Earth's largest manmade dam. That structure measures 132 miles long and 24 miles thick. It also created Lake Kariba, an "inland sea" spreading over 3,600 square miles of former wilderness. Despite the several incidents, Nyaminyami was not sighted during construction of the dam, and no recent reports are on file.

Source: Frank Clements, *Kariba: The Struggle with the River God*. New York: G.P. Putnam's Sons, 1959.

Nycker/Nykur   This LAKE MONSTER of Scandinavia has been reported from Sweden's Lake Mälaren (Stockholm County), as well as from various lakes in Iceland. Swedish reports date from 1652, and farmers feared the creature in Iceland as late as 1850. Danish author Eggert Olafsson, in his book *Travels in Iceland* (1772), described the Nykur as "an aquatic horse which…resides in the deepest of their freshwater lakes." The creatures sometimes mated with mares to produce foals of "ticklish or delicate disposition," prone to throwing riders who made them enter water. Descriptions of the creature(s) generally conform to those of other aquatic cryptids throughout Scandinavia, but no modern sightings are recorded.

Sources: Jerome Clark's Calendar of Unexplained Mysteries, 2001;

Costello, *In Search of Lake Monsters*; Benjamin Thorpe, *Norse Mythology*. London: Edward Lumley, 1851.

Nykkjen   Norway's Myrkevatn, in Møre og Romsdal County, is a mountain lake also known to local inhabitants as Svartevatn ("Black Lake"). Dark waters are coupled with a long history of LAKE MONSTER sightings, involving a maned creature whose back resembles a capsized boat. Myrkevatn also reportedly harbors a Nøkk ("water man"), described as a bearded MERBEING. One of the creatures was sighted by farmer Kari Ivarsdotter in 1938, but no more recent sightings have been published.

Source: Meurger and Gagnon, *Lake Monster Traditions*.

Nzefu-Loï   Cryptozoologists differ widely on possible explanations for the Nzefu-loï ("WATER ELEPHANT"), an amphibious cryptid reported from the Lualaba River between Bukama and Kaniamba, in the Democratic Republic of Congo. Natives describe the Nzefu-loï as having a body the size of a hippopotamus, a long neck, short ivory tusks, and a tail resembling a horse's. On occasion, it is said to kill (but never eat) the hippos that share its domain. In general terms (tusks and tail aside), it thus resembles the Congo's MOKELE-MBEMBE, but BERNARD HEUVELMANS suggested that the creature may be a mammal. He did not believe the Nzefu-loï represented the aquatic form of Africa's elusive PYGMY ELEPHANT, but rather proposed a relict population of *Dinotherium*, a Pleistocene elephant presumed extinct for some 100,000 years. Twenty years later, Heuvelmans also conceded that some reports of the Nzefu-loï might refer to a WATER LEOPARD, perhaps a surviving SABER-TOOTHED CAT. Other researchers propose that the animal may be a form of living DINOSAUR.

Sources: Heuvelmans, *Les Derniers Dragons d'Afrique*; Heuvelmans, *On the Track of Unknown Animals*.

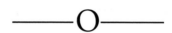

Oaxaca carcass   In his book *Secret Cities of Old South America*, Harold Wilkins describes a remarkable incident from the mid-17th century.

> In the year 1648, there appeared on the *playa* (beach) of Santa Maria del Mar, Oaxaca [on the Pacific coast of southern Mexico], a dreadful monster which, on the flood tide of the sea, was thrown up on the waves. Its bulk was great and appeared to the eye like a reef. The folk of the pueblo, 200 paces away from where it was, saw it at break of day, and were so terrified that they were on the point of quitting their houses. It moved and swayed slowly on the sands, and on the second day the motion was less. On the third day it was motionless. In eight days a bad smell arose from the huge carcase, and the fold saw BIRDS swoop down from the sky and dogs began to eat the putrefying flesh. Convinced thereby that the monster was dead, the people plucked up courage to approach it. They found it to be 15 varas long [41 feet 7 inches],and upon the sand it exceeded two varas [5 feet 6 inches] high. Its pelt was remarkable, of a red colour, like that of a cow. Its ears lacked folds (*cangilones*). It had two fore-feet, and its tail was like a pillar, being so oily and greasy, and stinking so much that not even the dogs could eat it. A shoulder-blade, shaped like a fan, was jointed, and a third of a vara [8.5 inches] in diameter. Its rib was the width of an eighth [?] and two varas long. The tail, or caudal extremity, reached to the shoulder blade and formed very singular buttocks.

It is difficult to assess this report, 350 years after the fact, and a reviewer criticized Wilkins for offering his readers "a wealth of jumbled information and misinformation, guesses and probabilities." BERNARD HEUVELMANS and BEN ROESCH concluded that the animal described was probably a whale, though Heuvelmans punctuated his guess with a question mark, and Roesch acknowledged that "the reddish skin color is somewhat strange." Likewise, cetaceans are not typically known for their "very singular buttocks."

Sources: Heuvelmans, *In the Wake of the Sea Serpents*; Roesch, "A review of alleged sea serpent carcasses worldwide (Part One —1648–1880)"; Harold Wilkins, *Secret Cities of Old South America*. New York: Library Publishers, 1956.

***Oceanic* sea serpent**   On 11 August 1880, Captain Thomas Brocklehurst met an unidentified SEA SERPENT in the North Pacific. He later described the incident in terse language, as follows:

> 1880, August 11th. Sea smooth! Ther. 58. hot sun at noon. Lat. 48.37 [north], Long. 180 [west]. crossing from Japan to San Francisco. Sitting alone on poop of steamer *Oceanic* at noon, looking at flying FISH, saw a long serpent in water 1 or 2 feet below surface, alongside the vessel, thought length 40 feet, circumference 2 to 4 feet, pale yellow colour, dark line on back and on ribs, head a little bigger than body, could not see any fins, saw it for 5 or 6 minutes, and then mentioned it to friends on board.

Source: Heuvelmans, *In the Wake of the Sea Serpents*.

Ochokochi *see* **Abnauayu**

Oconomowoc Lake, Wisconsin   This lake in Waukesha County has a tradition of Native American LAKE MONSTER sightings from the early 19th century, but no details are presently available. Presumably, whatever creatures may have once inhabited the lake are now extinct.

Source: Brown, *Sea Serpents: Wisconsin Occurrences of These Weird Water Monsters*.

Octopus (Freshwater)   All known cephalopods are marine animals, and octopuses require higher salinity levels in water than do squid. Nonetheless, over a span of 57 years, seven encounters with octopuses in fresh water were reported from various points in North and South America. The incidents include:

11 January 1946—Six octopuses, the largest weighing 20 pounds, were pulled from the North Branch of the Blackwater River, near Morgantown, West Virginia. All died en route to Thomas High School, where they were examined by science teacher Mary Colabrese and photographed by local reporters.

1955—Two boys reportedly caught an octopus with 2-foot tentacles in a creek near Grafton, West Virginia (Taylor County). It died soon after delivery to a local dog-catcher.

30 January 1959—A gray octopus was reported crawling onto a bank of the Licking River near Covington, Kentucky.

8 April 1966—Three children were attacked by a 35-inch octopus in a creek at Rivera, Uruguay. Local authorities speculated (somewhat illogically) that the animal was carried to that point "by flooding from rains."

11 July 1970— Mangled pieces of an octopus were found in the pipes of a slaughterhouse pumping station at Quemú-Quemú, in Argentina's landlocked La Pampa Province. No explanation for the discovery was advanced.

15 October 1990— Two workers at San Miguel de Tucumán, Argentina (at the foot of the Andes, 300 miles from the nearest ocean) reportedly found a live octopus "under the ground." Again, the incident remains unexplained.

19 November 1999— A dead octopus was found on fossil beds beside the OHIO RIVER, at Jefferson, Indiana. No sign of decomposition was noted by examiners, who disagreed on whether it was a bumblebee two-stripe octopus (*Octopus filosus*) or a Caribbean armstripe octopus (*O. burrys*). Both are sold through aquariums to private owners.

1 December 2003— Fisherman John Mazurek caught a live octopus which he found clinging to the gate of a dam at LAKE CONWAY, ARKANSAS. Spokesmen for the Arkansas Game and Fish Commission speculated that the octopus was dumped by an unknown private owner when it grew too large for an aquarium. News reports did not identify the species.

In addition to those specific incidents, three Oklahoma lakes have longstanding traditions of large, lurking cephalopods blamed for various drownings and disappearances of swimmers. The sites include Lake Oolagah (Rogers County), Lake Tenkiller (Cherokee County), and Lake Thunderbird (Cleveland County). No captures are recorded from any of the Oklahoma Lakes. Despite official skepticism, a possibility of freshwater cephalopods is suggested by the acknowledged existence of a small frehswater JELLYFISH (*Craspedacusta sowerbii*), reported from 44 U.S. states since 1991. The most recent specimen was captured in a pond near Grand Island, Nebraska on 7 September 2003.

Sources: Arment and LaGrange, "A freshwater octopus?"; "Displaced critters." *Doubt* 48 (1955): 341; "Illinois Fisherman Catches Octopus at Lake Conway." Associated Press (4 December 2003); "More details needed." *Doubt* 16 (1946): 242; Tracy Overstreet, "Freshwater jellyfish found in Nebraska." *Grand Island* (NE) *Independent* (14 September 2003); Picasso, "South American monsters & mystery animals"; Lake and River Monsters, http://www.angelfire.com/bc2/cryptodominion/lakebeasts.html.

Octopus (Giant) In March 2002, the largest octopus on record was dredged up by a fishing trawler in the South Pacific, off New Zealand's remote Chatham Islands. The specimen was incomplete, badly damaged in transit, but it still weighed 134 pounds, with a mantle length of 27 inches and a total length of 9 feet 4 inches. Steve O'Shea, a marine biologist with the National Institute of Water and Atmospheric Research, told reporters that the living creature must have been "the size of a fully mature male GIANT SQUID." O'Shea estimated that it might have weighed 165 pounds, with a total length exceeding 13 feet (for a radial spread approaching 30 feet). The surprise was compounded by acknowledgement that the species, *Haliphron atlanticus*, was previously unknown in the Pacific. Its next largest competitor, the Pacific species *Enteroctopus dofleini*, may officially exceed a radial spread of 20 feet and 100 pounds in weight.

Impressive as they are, those recognized cephalopod giants pale in comparison to other monsters reported from the Atlantic and Pacific Oceans. On 30 November 1896, a huge GLOBSTER was beached near St. Augustine, Florida. Local physician DeWitt Webb photographed and measured the mutilated carcass, which was 20 feet long, 5 feet wide, and 4 feet high, with an estimated weight of 5 tons. The stumps of five arms radiated from a pink-

Giant cephalopods pose a possible threat to humans (*William Rebsamen*).

ish-gray, pear-shaped body; nearby, a severed tentacle measured 28 feet long and 8 inches thick. A storm dragged the rotting carcass back to sea in January 1897, but it beached again further south, where Webb hauled it ashore with a team of horses. A sample of the thing's tough flesh was sent to cephalopod specialist Addison Verrill, at Yale University. Verrill initially identified the carcass as a giant squid, then changed his mind and declared it a new species, which he christened *Octopus giganteus*. The ink was barely dry on that pronouncement, though, when Verrill re-

The probable remains of a giant octopus, beached at St. Augustine, Florida, in 1896.

versed himself and declared the object a spermaceti tank from the head of a sperm whale (*Physeter catedon*). Thankfully, another sample from the carcass was preserved at the Smithsonian Institute, and this has been subjected to further analysis over time. Tests performed by Joseph Gennaro (1963) and ROY MACKAL (1986) indicated that the sample was connective tissue similar to that of an octopus; a third test by Sidney Pierce (1994) named the material as collagen, thus supporting the sperm whale hypothesis. The question is thus unresolved, though whales do not possess tentacles such as that found on the Florida beach.

Adventure writer Harry Riesberg muddied the waters further with a series of articles and books pretending to describe violent encounters between deep-sea salvage divers and an unknown species of giant octopus. His first offering, published in *Mechanix Illustrated* (February 1939), included supposed photos of a diver battling a huge octopus in waters off the coast of Cuba. He later recycled the story, relocating the battle to waters off Peru, the Bahamas, and so forth. In each case, the photographs published depicted divers posed with a fake, inflatable octopus.

The Riesberg HOAX notwithstanding, other reports of giant octopuses bear examination. Those on file include:

1928— While stationed with the U.S. Navy at Pearl Harbor, Hawaii, Robert Aiken sighted a group of six huge octopuses off the coast of Oahu. He estimated that each specimen had a radial spread approaching 40 feet. Aiken returned to the site with a film crew in July 1936, but the outcome of that venture is unknown.

Spring 1941— While transporting aviation fuel from Maine to Louisiana, crewmen aboard the USS *Chicopee* met a giant octopus off the east coast of Florida, midway between St. Augustine and Fort Lauderdale. Thirty years later, witness John Martin informed FORREST WOOD that he first saw an object on the ocean's surface "which could not be readily described." Martin first mistook it for a floating mass of kelp, but a closer look left no doubt as to the beast's identity. As described by Martin, "The coils of its arms were looped up like huge coils of manila rope. However, the coils were over 36 inches in circumference." He estimated that the creature's mantle was 30 feet wide, with arms of equal length "coiled but moving slowly."

1950— Diver Madison Rigdon saw an octopus "the size of a car" attacked by SHARKS off Oahu's Lahilahi Point (near Makaha). He described the creature's tentacles as 30 feet long, with suckers as big as dinner plates.

1950— Fisherman Val Ako sighted an even larger octopus lounging on a reef off Hawaii's Kona Coast. He estimated that its tentacles were 75 feet long, with suckers the size of automobile tires.

1984— Bermudan fisherman John Ingham blamed a giant octopus for interfering with his livelihood. On 29 August, Ingham lost an 8-foot-square prawn trap to some unseen predator, as he was reeling it in from the sea bed. Five days later, he lost a 6-foot-square trap, snapped from its cable at a depth of 1,800 feet. On 19 September, while laying more traps, Ingham's boat — the *Trilogy*— was towed for one-third of a mile by a creature that printed a 50-foot-high pyramidal shape on sonar.

Sources: Coleman and Huyghe, *The Field Guide to Lake Monsters, Sea Serpents, and Other Mystery Denizens of the Deep*; "Giant octopus blamed for deep sea fishing disruptions." *ISC Newsletter* 4 (Autumn 1983): 1–6; "Giant octopus dredged up off New Zealand." Reuters (27 March 2002); Kim Griggs, "Giant octopus puzzles scientists." BBC News (28 March 2002); Mackal, "Biochemical analysis of preserved *Octopus giganteus* tissue"; Mangiacopra, "More on *Octopus giganteus* Verrill: A new species of cephalopod." *Of Sea and Shore* 6 (Spring 1975): 3–10, 51–52; Plaskett,

"Plumbing the depths"; Michel Raynal, "Octopus hoax." *Fortean Times* 163 (November 2002): 52; Raynal, "The case for the giant octopus"; Raynal, "Debunking the debunkers of the giant octopus"; Harry Rieseberg, "Octopus, terror of the deep." *Mechanix Illustrated* 21 (February 1939): 42–44; Nick Sucik, "Just when you thought it was safe to go snorkeling: Hawaii's giant octopuses." *North American BioFortean Review* 2 (December 2000): 11–17; "Terrors from the deep." *Fortean Times* 56 (Winter 1990): 14; Addison Verrill, "A gigantic cephalopod on the Florida coast." *American Journal of Science* 4 (January 1897): 79; Addison Verrill, "Additional information concerning the giant cephalopod of Florida." *American Journal of Science* 4 (February 1897): 162–163; Addison Verrill, "The supposed giant octopus of Florida: Certainly not a cephalopod." *American Journal of Science* 4 (April 1897): 355–356.

Ødegårdskilen, Norway

This lake, in Norway's Østfold County, reportedly harbors a LAKE MONSTER resembling a large floating log, distinguished by its prominent tongue. Modern sightings are rare, and the lake receives little attention even from Scandinavian cryptozoologists.

Source: Skjelsvik, "Norwegian lake and sea monsters."

Odenwald Beast

This generic term was applied to an ALIEN BIG CAT sighted at various points throughout the German state of Hesse in 1989. Eyewitnesses agreed that the CAT(s) resembled a black panther (actually a melanistic leopard, *Panthera pardus*). The first sighting occurred at Odenwald, in August, followed by an October report from Heubach. The hectic days of 1–2 November 1989 brought more reports of sightings from Fürth, Lindenfels, Steinbach and Winterkasten. Hunts were organized without result, aside from discovery of a few large pawprints, and no livestock predation was reported.

Source: Magin, "The Odenwald beast."

Oggy

On 8 April 2002, an anonymous message was posted to the forum section of the Ogston BIRD Club's Internet website. According to the unnamed writer, he/she had made a remarkable sighting that morning, at the Ogston Reservoir in Derbyshire, England. Around 5:00 a.m., the author was allegedly watching gulls circle the reservoir, when two dark humps broke the water's surface, each 6 feet long and some 18 inches high. The message went on to describe a creature whose flesh looked slimy "like the skin of an EEL, similar in colour too — but whatever it was was far too large to be an eel." Veteran NESSIE-hunter Steve Feltham gave the elusive cryptid its current nickname, while professing a desire to seek more information at the reservoir. Thus far, no further sightings have been publicized.

Source: Karl Shuker, "Alien zoo." *Fortean Times* 164 (December 2002): 18.

Ogopogo

One of North America's most famous LAKE MONSTERS resides in Okanagan Lake, on the Pacific slope of the Rocky Mountains in British Columbia. Before the arrival of European settlers, aboriginal people knew the creature as NAITAKA, a generic term applied to freshwater cryptids throughout western Canada. White missionaries reached the area in 1860, and John MacDougal lost a team of horses in the lake that same year, pulled under by some unseen force that never released them. The first Anglo witnesses reported sightings from the lake in 1872. Encounters with the creature have been fairly constant ever since, but it did not receive its modern nickname for another half-century. In 1924, singer Davy Burnaby popularized a song titled "The Ogo-Pogo," and H.F. Beattie wrote a parody to fit Naitaka two years later. The name caught on, and the *Vancouver Daily Province* declared Ogopogo the creature's "official" name on 24

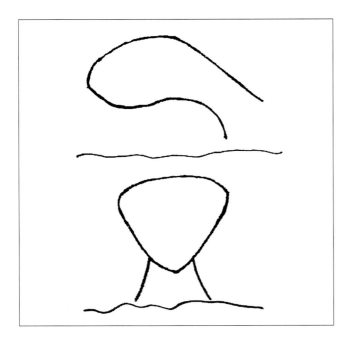

An eyewitness sketch of Ogopogo from the 1950s.

August 1926. A dozen years before that christening, in 1914, a strange GLOBSTER washed ashore at Okanagan Lake. It measured 5–6 feet long and weighed 400 pounds. It had a round head, blue-gray skin, stout flippers and a broad tail. An amateur naturalist identified the creature as a manatee (*Trichechus* sp.), normally native to tropical seas and rivers, but author Peter Costello disputes that view, suggesting that it was an Ogopogo whose long neck had been severed or rotted away. With the remains forever lost, the question must remain unanswered.

Eyewitness descriptions of Ogopogo are remarkably consistent with those of other cold-water cryptids ranging from Canada to Europe, virtually interchangeable with descriptions of NESSIE in Scotland. Estimates of size vary from 20 to 70 feet, with the average around 50 feet. (A bus driver watched four small animals swimming 50 feet from shore, in February 1948. In 2000, a local security guard claimed to have seen three juvenile specimens "with their embryonic sacs still attached.") Ogopogo's hide is smooth, reported in various shades of dark blue, green, gray and black. When seen above water, its head is often compared to a horse's, held at right angles to the 5- to 10-foot neck; some witnesses describe a pair of stubby horns atop the head. As with Nessie and others, Ogopogo sometimes shows its back above the surface, resembling an overturned boat. On other occasions, a series of humps or arches are reported, ranging in number from 2 to 14. Some witnesses describe a forked tail, which may in fact refer to flukes like a cetacean's. Whatever its method of locomotion, the creature makes good time. In May 2001 it allegedly outpaced a boat traveling at 30 miles per hour, and faster speeds have been reported.

Scarcely a year has passed without multiple sightings since Ogopogo was christened in 1926. Sightings by multiple witnesses are common, including those reported by five yachtsmen (August 1926); by 30 carloads of travelers (September 1926); by two visiting families (July 1949); by 16 persons on a bus (June 1950); by another party of 15 (July 1954); by 30 parishioners at a church picnic (July 1962); by 15 cannery employees (July 1967); by 30 witnesses at a lakeside campground (February 1978); by 50-odd

tourists at Blue Bird Bay Resort (August 1980); by four members of the BRITISH COLUMBIA SCIENTIFIC CRYPTOZOOLOGY CLUB (July 1989); and by members of a documentary film crew (April 2002).

In addition to hundreds of eyewitness sightings, Ogopogo has also been photographed or filmed on at least 14 occasions over the past four decades. Eric Parmenter snapped the first known photo in 1967, followed by Arthur Folden's short segment of 8mm film in August 1968. Edward Fletcher took five snapshots of Ogopogo from the Westbank Yacht Club in August 1976. Longtime researcher ARLENE GAAL was next, with a photo of the creature's wake in May 1979. Ten weeks later, a tourist from Alberta shot three minutes of movie film at Peachland Hill. Larry Thal captured 10 seconds of Ogopogo on film in August 1980, while Eugene Boiselle made the first hazy videotape in September 1982. Cryptozoologist JOHN KIRK took one minute of videotape from Mission Hill in May 1987. Ken Chaplin caught Ogopogo on video in July 1989, while Arlene Gaal joined him to take more video footage and snapshots from the same location five days later. In August 1989, John Kirk taped Ogopogo's distant gliding hump for nearly 25 minutes. Paul DeMara captured three video sequences of unexplained surface disturbances on 24 July 1992. Michael Zaiser snapped five photos of a 40-foot long-necker in February 1996. Most recently, on 18 April 2002, Ogopogo obligingly surfaced for a film crew shooting a documentary on older sightings. The resultant 90-second film clip reveals a dark hump passing through the water, with "something sideways, something strange" on top.

As one of a half-dozen cryptids possessing "star appeal," Ogopogo has inspired a trend of CRYPTOTOURISM around Lake Okanagan. This, in turn, prompts critics to dismiss all sightings as the product of crass publicity stunts, but blithe dismissal of the photos, films and videotapes is more difficult — and no amount of modern hype explains the many sightings logged before Ogopogo became a media sensation.

Sources: Costello, *In Search of Lake Monsters*; Gaal, *Beneath the Depths*; Gaal, *In Search of Ogopogo*; Gaal, *Ogopogo*; "Lake monster is movie's star." *Fortean Times* 136 (August 2000): 20; Kirk, *In the Domain of the Lake Monsters*; "Lake monsters status report." *Fortean Times* 102 (September 1997): 28–31; McLean, *Ogopogo: His Story*; Moon, *Ogopogo*; Karl Shuker, "Alien zoo." *Fortean Times* 144 (April 2001): 22; Shuker, "Alien zoo." *Fortean Times* 145 (May 2001): 22.

Ogua   Ogua is the local name applied to an alleged freshwater cryptid reported from the Monongahela River outside Rinesville, West Virginia (Monongalia County). Witnesses disagree radically on the creature's appearance, some describing a 20-foot FISH with a 6- to 8-foot dorsal fin, while others refer to a reptilian head and long tail (either flat or serpentine). Local legends claim the Ogua comes ashore at nightfall and lies in wait along forest trails, to ambush deer and drag them to the lake.

Source: Cain, "Ogua: The Rinesville river monster."

Ohio Bigfoot Research and Study Group   Headquartered in Cincinnati, the OBRSG is, in its own words, "dedicated to the study of SASQUATCH in and around the state of Ohio"—although, curiously, spokesman George Clappison lists a residential address in Baltimore, Maryland. Sightings from Ohio are solicited, with a promise of confidentiality for all witnesses unless privacy is expressly waived. As Clappison explains the group's methods and philosophy:

The Ohio Bigfoot Research and Study Group is not a big game hunting club and does not have as its goal to bring in a dead

Sasquatch for the scientific establishment to examine. No firearms are carried into the field during on-site investigations. It is the opinion of the Ohio Bigfoot Research and Study Group that Ohio supports a population of previously unknown primates.

Documentation of this phenomenon is viewed as a primary function. Whether these elusive creatures are limited to the same natural constraints as the rest of the animal kingdom, or whether there are other aspects involved, is not known at this time.

Source: OBSRG website, http://users1.ee.net/pmason/obrsg.html.

Ohio Bigfoot Research Team

The OBRT—described on its Internet website as "Forever growing!"—apparently consists of four related individuals: Bill, Joe, Jon and Richard Etterling. The team does not stint on sensational claims, as revealed on the Web:

We have discovered a great percentage of BIGFOOT information that scientists use around the world today. All the information you view on our site is factual. We are all willing to take lie detector test just to prove we are right!

Throughout the years, we have had many sightings, found a large percentage of Bigfoot sign, and we have had many other occurrences that turns out [sic] to be important information.

All members of the Obfrt have actually been sworn into truth. We do not tell lies nor do we support those that do, so what you see, is what we have found and we are behind that 100%.

An archive of sightings is offered online, with this proviso: "We try to make it EASY to understand the creature, however this can be very hard because it isn't easy to understand!"

Source: OBRT website, http://get-me.to/bigfoot.

Ohio Bigfoot Search Group Club

The OBSGC is a two-man effort, consisting of founders Dallas Gilbert and Wayne Burton. Gilbert was drawn to BIGFOOT research by two personal sightings, the first in 1996. The present "club" was founded after Burton telephoned Gilbert "and he told me of the things he had seen over in Kentucky and we both decided to try and get the creature on film." By 2000, Gilbert was prepared to announce on his Internet website:

I feel like we have amassed an incredible amount of data about bigfoot, along with many photographs, and a video that is not released to the public as of yet. Nor will it be, because I don't wish to go down the same road that many others have with their own photographs and videos.

Gilbert's website does, however offer "a few photographs that you can judge for yourself as to the reality of Bigfoot's existence."

Source: OBSGC website, http://www.angelfire.com/co4/OBSC/info.html.

Ohio/Pennsylvania Bigfoot Research Group

Organized in 1978, the OPBRG has as its stated goal "to research, seek, and investigate the BIGFOOT phenomenon in Ohio and Pennsylvania in an objective, scientific manner to find the truth." In soliciting eyewitness reports, the group's Internet website observes:

We estimate that only a few percent of witnesses contact or tell someone about their experience. It is very important to relate any and all information to us to allow us to: further investigate, log the information, correlate and build scientific data, find conclusions, and obtain evidence of the creature. We conduct all our research in a benign manner and have no intentions of injuring the creature. All of your information, personal and locations, will be kept strictly confidential.

Source: Ohio/Pennsylvania Bigfoot Research Group, http://members.tripod.com/sasquatchsearch/.

Ohio River

In early July 1893, witnesses at Parkersburg, West Virginia (in Wood County) reported a serpent 8–15 feet long swimming past their settlement, in the Ohio River. Details are vague beyond references to the reptile's large head. It was apparently bound for parts unknown and did not return.

Source: *Pittsburgh* (PA) *Post* (8 July 1893).

Oh-Mah *see* Bigfoot

Oil Pit Squid

On 15 November 1996, workers at General Motors Delphi Plant No. 9 in Anderson, Indiana (Madison County) discovered small "squid-like" creatures swimming in the toxic effluvium of a used-oil pit. The startled employees reportedly caught one specimen in a jar and placed it in the plant office for safekeeping, they returned to their task of cleaning up the facility. Three months later, on 26 February 1997, state environmental management authorities received an anonymous complaint of "illegal hazardous waste activity" at the Delphi plant, including "unusual growth" in the oil pit. Investigators arrived on 7 March to inspect the site, but no creatures were found in the pit, and the captive specimen had meanwhile vanished. The mystery remains unsolved.

Sources: Ken de la Bastide, "Creature in Plant 9 pits." *Anderson* (IN) *Herald Bulletin* (4 March 1997); Swartz, "Mystery of the oil pit squids."

Okauchee Lake, Wisconsin

Located in Waukesha County, Okauchee Lake produced reports of a 6-foot, 90-pound FISH in the 1880s. Ten years later, an immense "serpent" was also sighted in the lake. Neither creature was ever captured or identified, but sightings ceased before the turn of the 20th century.

Sources: Garner, *Monster! Monter!*; "Western lake resorts have each a water monster." *Chicago Tribune* (24 July 1892).

O'Keefe's Lake, Canada

In 1883, a LAKE MONSTER sighting was reported from O'Keefe's Lake, on Prince Edward Island, but most researchers now dismiss it as a HOAX.

Source: Frank MacArthur, *Legends of Prince Edward Island*. Charlottetown, Canada: H.M. Simpson, 1976.

Okoboji Lake, Iowa

On 23 June 2001, while visiting this lake in Dickinson County, three witnesses observed an unidentified LAKE MONSTER rise from the water and scrape against the dock where they were standing. One witness specifically recalled the creature's head as a "very good-sized oval or sphere," larger than a bowling ball. The animal's hide was dark green or blue, and had no visible scales.

Source: Shadowlands, http://theshadowlands.net/sightings.htm.

Old Blackie *see* Lithgow Panther

Old Man of Monterey Bay

This affectionate nickname belongs to a SEA SERPENT sighted occasionally during the 1930s, in central California's Monterey Bay. Eyewitness descriptions varied so widely that it is difficult to believe a single creature was responsible for all the sightings. Various witnesses compared the animal's upraised head to that of a bull, a SNAKE, an elephant, a giraffe, a horse, a duck, a human being and an APE. Reports from the early 1930s refer to the creature's long neck, while later accounts emphasize its hulking body. In 1938, crewmen aboard the fishing boat *Dante Alighieri* sighted a 30-foot FISH-tailed animal whose massive head featured an old man's face with huge eyes and a gaping sickle-mouth. A year later, fishermen aboard the *Santa Anna* prodded a log floating on the surface, only to discover that it was a seal-like animal "50 times the size of a sea elephant." The prodding incident may have incensed the Old Man, since it vanished thereafter and has not returned.

Sources: Martin, "Sea monsters"; Reinstedt, *Mysterious Sea Monsters of California's Central Coast.*

Old Mill Pond, New Jersey

Cryptozoologist ROY MACKAL reports that a LAKE MONSTER was sighted in Old Mill Pond, near Trenton, on 1 March 1975. Unfortunately, as Mackal observes, no further research has been done on the case to date, and no details of the sighting are available. The area remains, as Mackal says, "virgin territory" for cryptozoologists.

Source: Mackal, *Searching for Hidden Animals.*

Old Ned

This venerable LAKE MONSTER of Lake Utopia, New Brunswick (Charlotte County) was initially reported by a crew of lumberjacks working near St. George, in 1856. Twelve years later, dynamite charges set off in the lake brought a large animal to the surface, but it survived the explosions and rifle fire from shore, diving once again to the depths. On 3 August 1868, an unidentified creature was allegedly killed on land, between Lake Utopia and nearby Pasamaquoddy Bay. It was subsequently displayed in a traveling show, flyers for which described the beast as 28 feet long and 13 feet in diameter, with legs 5 feet 4 inches long and a huge mouth 5 feet 6 inches wide. Unfortunately, no records remain of the carcass's fate.

Whatever it was, Old Ned returned four years later, for a string of sightings that compared it to a DRAGON, a giant TURTLE, and a "huge black rock." Average eyewitness estimates pegged the creature's size at 60 feet long and 10 feet wide. A smaller animal, 10–15 feet long, with a back protruding 1–2 feet above water, was seen in the lake by four witnesses on 9 July 1982. Explanations advanced for the sightings include floating logs, swimming deer, river otters, and a variety of large native FISH.

Sources: Garner, *Monster! Monster!*; E.J. Russell, "The monster of Lake Eutopia." *Canadian Illustrated News* (30 November 1872).

A portrait of Old Ned prepared by B. Kroupa in 1872.

Old Sheff

In August 1869, an unknown primate or HOMINID resembling a GORILLA spread panic among the residents of the Arcadia Valley in Crawford County, Kansas. Farmers blamed the animal for knocking down their fences, releasing livestock to pillage cornfields. A mob of 60 citizens pursued the creature on one occasion, to no avail. A witness named Trimble described the creature:

> It has so near a resemblance to the human form that the men are unwilling to shoot it. It is difficult to give a description of this wild man or animal. It has a stooping gate, very long arms with immense hands or claws; it has a hairy face and those who have been near it describe it as having a most ferocious expression of countenance; generally walks on its hind legs but sometimes on all fours. The beast or "what is it?" is as cowardly as it is ugly and it is next to impossible to get near enough to obtain a good view of it.

Sources: Bord and Bord, *The Bigfoot Casebook*; Coleman, "Gorillas in the midst."

Old Yellow Top

Since 1923, Cobalt, Ontario (near the border with Québec) has produced reports of a BIGFOOT noted for its blond "mane," earning the nickname Yellow Top. The first account, published in the North Bay *Nugget* on 27 July 1923, described the meeting of two prospectors with "the PreCambrian Shield Man." Witness Lorne Wilson said, "It sure was like no bear that I have ever seen. Its head was kind of yellow and the rest of it was black like a bear, covered with hair."

The creature's next appearance, reported by two witnesses from the Cobalt Mining Camp, occurred in April 1946. The passage of 23 years apparently entitled Yellow Top to become *Old* Yellow Top, and newspaper reports alluded to a previous sighting in 1906 or 1907, without providing details. A third sighting, reported by 27 miners en route by bus to work at Cobalt Lode on 4 August 1970, nearly ended in tragedy when bus driver Aimee Latreille swerved to avoid striking Old Yellow Top in the road. This time, newspaper accounts of the incident explained that "[t]he story started back in the early 1900s when a group of construction workers claimed to have seen the creature." Old Yellow Top seems to have gone on hiatus since his near-miss with death in 1970, with no further sightings reported.

Sources: Green, *Sasquatch: The Apes Among Us.*

Oldeani Monster

The term "monster" is frequently used — and abused — in reference to cryptids, and rarely more so than in the case of the inoffensive reptile dubbed the Oldeani Monster. On 25 February 1962, naturalist Peter Scott and two companions caught a large, unidentified chameleon in Tanzania's Ngorongoro Conservation Area, near Oldeani Peak. The lizard was brown, with small red spots and horizontal stripes along its flanks, sporting a small horn on its nose. Scott took the lizard back to England, where it died after 18 months in captivity. Herpetologists who examined the creature failed to identify it, and the preserved remains were subsequently lost. Scott believes the lizard represented a new species of chameleon, which he provisionally named *Chamaeleo oldeanii*, but the loss of the type specimen barred formal recognition, and no more specimens have yet been found. KARL SHUKER suggests that Scott's find may have been another rare chameleon, *Bradypodion uthmoelleri*, found in the same vicinity during 1938 and never seen again.

Sources: Peter Scott, *Travel Diaries of a Naturalist.* London: Collins, 1983; Shuker, "Here be dragons."

Olentangy River, Ohio

Ohio's Olentangy River flows some 60 miles, from a point near Galion (Crawford County) in the north to Columbus in the south. The 22-mile stretch between Delaware and Worthington is officially a "scenic" river, and university scientists study ecology in the surrounding Olentangy River Wetland Research Park. With so many eyes on the river and its surrounding territory, the one-time-only appearance of a large cryptid is all the more surprising and mysterious. Still, on 4 April 1982, a group of Columbus police and firefighters sighted a large animal resembling a hippopotamus in the Olentangy. The animal eluded pursuit and has not been seen again.

Source: "Aquatic animal puzzles Ohioans." *ISC Newsletter* 1 (Spring 1982) 9.

Olgoï-Khorkhoï   The first Western mention of this cryptid from Mongolia's vast Gobi Desert was published in 1926, by Roy Chapman Andrews. While engaged in the American Museum of Natural History's Central Asiatic Expedition, in the early 1920s, Andrews was warned to beware of the Olgoï-khorkhoï ("intestine worm"), said to be a large fossorial invertebrate. The creature would not bite, Andrews was told, but when unearthed it spat acidic venom that maimed or killed on impact. Andrews never met the creature, but stories persist to the present day, including vague accounts of a scientist killed when he prodded an Olgoï-khorkhoï with a metal rod.

Three Czech expeditions were mounted to find the "Mongolian death worm" in the 1990s, but all of them returned empty-handed. Proposed explanations include a giant earthworm, some species of burrowing SNAKE (perhaps a new variety of spitting cobra), and an unknown creature with shocking powers akin to the electric EEL.

Sources: Roy Andrews and Henry Osborn, *On the Trail of Ancient Man.* New York: G.P. Putnam's Sons, 1926; Karl Shuker, "Menagerie of mystery." *Strange* 16 (Fall 1995): 31–2, 48; Shuker, "Meet Mongolia's death worm"; Shuker, "Menagerie of mystery." *Strange* 18 (Summer 1997): 53–54.

Some researchers speculate that the Olgoï-khorkhoï may be an unknown venomous snake.

Olitau   In 1932, while hunting along a mountain stream in Cameroon, GERALD RUSSELL and IVAN SANDERSON were dive-bombed by a large winged creature resembling a giant BAT. Russell fired at the animal with a shotgun, but he apparently missed. Sanderson described it as "a black thing the size of an eagle. I had only a glimpse of its face, yet that was quite sufficient, for its lower jaw hung open and bore a semicircle of pointed white teeth set about their own width apart from each other." The animal returned near sundown, flying in the opposite direction. Natives of the region called the creature Olitau and regarded it with sufficient dread to abandon their jungle camp in darkness, at mention of its name.

Africa's largest known bat is the hammer-headed fruit bat (*Hypsignathus monstrosus*), and since that species is notoriously timid, BERNARD HEUVELMANS suggested that the Olitau might be a flying reptile, on a par with Kenya's KONGAMATO. Sanderson, meanwhile, believed that he had met a giant bat unknown to science, which has yet to be identified.

Sources: Heuvelmans, *On the Track of Unknown Animals*; Sanderson, *Investigating the Unexplained*; Shuker, "A belfry of crypto-bats."

Ivan Sanderson believed the Olitau was a giant bat unknown to science.

Olo-Banda *see* **Bir-Sindic**

Omak Lake, Washington   Aboriginal tribesmen believed that a LAKE MONSTER inhabited this lake in Washington's Okanogan County, on the present-day Colville Indian Reservation. No modern sightings are on record, however, and it should not be confused with British Columbia's Lake Okanagan, home of the extremely active OGOPOGO.

Source: Walter Cline, "Religion and world view," in Leslie Spier (ed.), *The Sinkaietk or Southern Okanagon of Washington.* Menasha, WI: George Banta, 1938.

On Niont   Aboriginal inhabitants of present-day Ontario, Canada once described the On Niont as a LAKE MONSTER found in various bodies of water throughout the province. It was described to 17th-century Jesuit missionaries as being large and serpentine in form, with a horn protruding from its skull. No sightings are on record from European settlers in the region, and none at all from modern times. At this remove, it is impossible to say if the On Niont was wholly legendary, or if the native traditions were based on actual cryptid encounters.

Source: S. Paul Ragueneau, "Relation of what occurred in the mission of the fathers of the Society of Jesus in the Huron country, in New France, in the years 1647 and 1648," in Reuben Thwaites (ed.), *The Jesuit Relations and Allied Documents.* Cleveland: Burrows Brothers, 1898.

Onça-Canguçu   During an expedition to Brazil's Mato Grosso State in 1996–97, Dutch zoologist Marc van Roosmalen collected reports of a large unclassified CAT from natives in the

Rio Aripuanã district. They described the Onça-canguçu (Portuguese for "big-headed JAGUAR") as a jet black cat with a white collar and a tufted tail-tip. Van Roosmalen speculates that the cat may represent a black species of jaguar (*Panthera onca*). Natives promised him a skull and pelt from an Onça-canguçu in 2001, but at last report van Roosmalen was still waiting.

Source: Karl Shuker, "Alien zoo." *Fortean Times* 139 (November 2000): 22.

Onelli, Clemente (1864–1924)

Italian naturalist and paleontologist Clemente Onelli moved to Argentina in the early 1890s and participated in the survey work conducted to resolve boundary disputes between Argentina and Chile in 1897. While engaged in that task, he collected reports of reptilian LAKE MONSTERS from Patagonia that fired his imagination, prompting Onelli to suggest that ancient PLESIOSAURS might survive in remote jungle lakes. A decade later, Onelli heard the story of a huge unidentified carcass, allegedly found near the RIO TAMANGO in 1902. Finally, while serving as director of the Buenos Aires Zoo in 1922, he received an account from a U.S. prospector in the Chebut Territory of Patagonia, describing a swan-necked reptile

Clemente Onelli sponsored a search for a living *Plesiosaurus* in 1922.

dwelling in a local lake. A second report from the same area, this one back-dated to 1913, inspired Onelli to launch a full-scale expedition, departing Buenos Aires on 23 March 1922. Hampered by terrain, logistic difficulties, and complaints from Argentina's Society for the Protection of Animals, the expedition was officially declared a failure on 26 April. Onelli remained convinced of the creatures' existence, but he lacked official support for further investigations. He died in Buenos Aires on 20 October 1924.

Source: Costello, *In Search of Lake Monsters*; Proyecto Ameghino — Clemente Onelli, www.argiropolis.com.ar/ameghino/biografias/one.htm.

Onondaga Lake, New York

Oneida tribal folklore claims that Onondaga Lake, located on the northwest side of Syracuse, New York, was once inhabited by a huge LAKE MONSTER called the MOSQUETO, which rose from the depts to kill many tribesmen. No modern sightings of that creature are recorded, but the lake more recently enjoyed a strange reputation for spawning marine animals of uncertain origin. On 28 April 1882, a 6-foot seal weighing 100 pounds was shot and killed at the lake. Locals speculated that the seal had come from LAKE ONTARIO, via the Oswego River. Roughly a decade later, local fishermen caught an odd-looking specimen identified as a sargassum fish or mousefish (*Histrio pictus*), native to the Gulf of Maine. In December 1902, two Atlantic short-finned squids (*Illex illecebrosus*) were hooked from Onondaga Lake in separate incidents. Dr. John Clark, writing to *Science* on 12 December, observed: "There are salt springs near Lake Onondaga [*sic*]: so perhaps there is, in the lake, a sub-stratum of salt water." CHARLES FORT dismissed

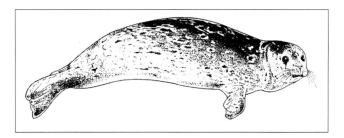

A seal was shot at New York's Onondaga Lake in 1882.

the notion of separate salt-and freshwater layers in the lake, each harboring different life forms like floors in a hotel, and no evidence of such a phenomenon has yet been produced from Onondaga Lake. Another "expert," one Professor Ortmans of Princeton University, recalled that fishermen sometimes use squid as bait, suggesting that two specimens may have escaped into the lake. That theory overlooks the fact that bait squid are normally dead, and it fails to address the other anomalous creatures pulled from Onondaga Lake.

Source: Fort, *The Complete Books of Charles Fort*.

Onyare

Mohawk tribesmen of the 17th-century identified the Onyare as a large, horned serpent, said to inhabit the St. Lawrence River in the neighborhood of modern-day Caughnawaga, Québec. No modern sightings or reports from European settlers are on record.

Source: Gatschet, "Water-monsters of American aborigines."

Onza

The confusion surrounding this Latin American CAT begins with its name. *Onza* is Spanish for "ounce," apparently derived from the Latin *luncea* ("LYNX"). In Spain, it is used to describe the cheetah (*Acinonyx jubatus*), while in Central and South America it is applied to a variety of well-known cats, including the ocelot (*Leopardus pardalis*) in Guatemala, the jaguarundi (*Herpailurus yaguarondi*) in Colombia and Venezuela, and in Portuguese (*onça*), the JAGUAR (*Panthera onca*) of Brazil. Further north, however, in Mexico's Sierra Madre Occidental, the Onza has long been described as a mystery cat resembling a COUGAR (*Puma concolor*), but smaller and more aggressive. The Mexican Onza sometimes displays faint stripes on its shoulders, and a dark stripe down its back, with stripes or spots on the inside of its legs.

Mexico's ancient Aztec inhabitants called the Onza *cuitlamiztli*, regarding it as a species distinct from both cougar and jaguar. Spanish conquistadors noted the Onza's ferocious courage, extending to vigorous battle with armed men and their hunting dogs. Hunter Joseph Shirk killed a female Onza in March 1938, on La Silla Mountain, but he discarded its remains and photos of the carcass seemed to depict an ordinary cougar. Longtime researcher Robert Marshall furnished a supposed Onza's skull to J. RICHARD GREENWELL in the 1980s, and two more skulls were soon obtained for testing. Then, in February 1986, Greenwell obtained a complete specimen from Sinaloa's San Ignacio District, shot by hunters on 1 January. That carcass was dissected, and DNA tests were performed on the tissue, but another decade passed before the results were published in *Cryptozoology* (1996). According to those tests, the Sinaloa cat was a common cougar, identical in all respects to normal specimens from North America.

Sources: Carmony, *Onza!*; Dratch, et al., "Molecular genetic identification of a Mexican Onza specimen as a puma (*Puma concolor*)"; Marshall, *The Onza*; "Onza specimen obtained: Identity being studied." *ISC Newsletter* 5 (Spring 1986): 1–6.

Oogle-Boogles

Waterton Lakes, despite its plural name, is a single body of water spanning the international boundary between Montana (Glacier County) and Alberta, Canada. Its southern tip lies in Montana's Waterton Glacier International Peace Park, while two-thirds of the lake is found north of the border, in Alberta's Waterton Lakes National Park. Borders notwithstanding, local residents on both sides of the line agree that Waterton Lakes hosts a thriving colony of aquatic cryptids, known collective (and facetiously) as Ooogle-Boogles. Most reports describe long-necked creatures with cowlike heads, and humped backs visible above the surface. Multiple accounts refer to smaller "baby monsters" matching the general description of their elders.

Sources: Garner, *Monster! Monster!*; Sanderson, "*Things.*"

Opana sea serpents

On 10 May 1899, while sailing 100 miles southeast of New Zealand in the Coral Sea, Captain John Martin, aboard the barque *Opana*, observed three SEA SERPENTS. The creatures appeared hourly, the first one measuring about 40 feet from dorsal fin to tail. Martin remarked that the first specimen had "a large piece off its fin near the top," and concluded, "I thought it was an immense SHARK." In fact, as BERNARD HEUVELMANS noted, the notched dorsal fin is characteristic of basking sharks (*Cetorhinus maximus*), and it is likely that Martin glimpsed three such creatures — or saw the same one three times.

Source: Heuvelmans, *In the Wake of the Sea Serpents.*

Operation Appalachia

Operation Appalachia is an informal network of researchers founded by Eric Altman (in Pennsylvania), Mike Frizzell (in Maryland) and Ron Schaffner (in Ohio). While primarily concerned with BIGFOOT sightings, the group also pursues any other cryptid sightings reported from the Appalachian Mountains of eastern North America. Ohio researcher DONALD KEATING maintains the group's Internet website, accepting eyewitness reports and membership applications. Other identified associates include Marcus Adams and Tim Arcilesi (Maryland), Mark Bylsma (Florida), Denny Calisti (Pennsylvania), Trish Cameron (Massachusetts), Rick Fisher (Pennsylvania), Mike George (New York), John Marshall and Sarah Weiler (Ohio), Larry Wells (North Carolina), and Kenny Young (Kentucky).

Source: Operation Appalachia, http://www.angelfire.com/oh/ohio-bigfoot/OA.html.

Operation Big Cat

One of several British groups dedicated to tracking ALIEN BIG CATS, Operation Big Cat focused primarily on Norfolk sightings. Founder Bob Engledow helmed the effort from his home in Sprowstown, collecting 55 eyewitness sightings in 2001 and almost 70 the following year. Most of the CATS sighted in Norfolk were described as LYNXES (*Felis lynx*), COUGARS (*Puma concolor*) or black panthers (actually melanistic leopards, *Panthera pardus*). As Engledow told reporters in December 2002, "Our fear continues for the safety of the people of Norfolk in the event of a man-eater becoming established here. Should one of these animals pose a threat to human life at some future date, we need to know where to search for it. The animal should then be captured and placed in captivity for its own protection and ours." Sadly, poor health forced Engledow to retire from the hunt in January 2003, at age 60, and Operation Big Cat closed its files. At his last press conference, Engledow said, "It has been great fun and we have met all sorts of interesting people. We have really enjoyed it. But the BRITISH BIG CAT SOCIETY has started to notice Norfolk now and we will leave it up to them."

Sources: "A puma just ran across my path." *Norwich Evening News* (25 July 2002); "Big Cat Bob hangs up his binoculars." *Norwich Evening News* (31 January 2003); "Big cat sightings reach nearly 70." *Norwich Bulletin* (23 December 2002); Sieveking, "Big cats in Britain."

Orang Bati

The Orang Bati ("flying man") is an enigmatic creature reported from the neighboring islands of Ambon and Ceram, Indonesia. Witnesses describe it as 4–5 feet tall, with ruddy skin and black, leathery wings. Some descriptions include a long tail or allude to the nocturnal flier's eerie, wailing call. It allegedly roosts in dormant volcanoes, including Mount Kairatu on Ceram, and soars by night to feed on poultry, livestock, and the occasional human being. Indonesian authorities dismiss the creature as a myth, while cryptozoologists debate the possible existence of an unknown giant BAT.

Sources: Gibbons, *Missionaries and Monsters*; Shuker, "Is Batman alive and well and living on the island of Seram?"

Orang Dalam

This unknown primate or HOMINID of Malaysia generally matches U.S. descriptions of BIGFOOT, ranging from 6 to 10 feet tall, emitting foul odors, and leaving humanoid footprints 16–19 inches long. Sometimes the tracks reveal only four toes, a trait mirrored in various reports of NORTH AMERICAN APES. The creature's common Malay name means "man of the interior." Alternate names throughout its jungle range include Hantu jarang gigi ("thin-toothed demon") and Kaki besar ("big foot"). Some researchers contend that the Orang Dalam and the generally smaller ENSUT ENSUT represent a single unclassified species. Sightings have been fairly constant since the 1950s. A discovery of large four-toed tracks was reported from Cape Tanjun Piai, in Johor State, in January 1995.

Sources: Coleman and Huyghe, *The Field Guide to Bigfoot, Yeti, and Other Mystery Primates Worldwide*; Stephens, "Abominable Snowmen in Malaysia"; Shuker, "A Malaysian man-beast."

Orang Ekor

Yet another mystery primate of Malaysia, the Orang Ekor ("tailed man") may represent an unknown species of MONKEY, a folklore tradition of primitive jungle-dwelling people, or a mixture of both. In any case, no reports of "people" with tails have been recorded from the region since the late 19th century.

Source: Walter Skeat and Charles Blagden, *Pagan Races of the Malay Peninsula*. London: Macmillan, 1906.

Orang Gadang

Indonesia's Orang Gadang ("big man") is said to be a 10-foot forest-dwelling HOMINID, who leaves 24-inch manlike footprints. Unlike Malaysia's ORANG DALAM and North America's BIGFOOT, however, witnesses maintain that the Orang Gadang has only sparse hair on its body (though the hair atop its head grows long and wild). Sightings have been reported from the western part of Borneo and neighboring Sumatra. While frequently mentioned in connection with Indonesia's ORANG PENDEK, the Orang Gadang should not be confused with that smaller, hairy biped.

Sources: Dammerman, "De nieuwontdekte Orang Pendek"; Pijil, "De Orang Pendek als Sneeuwman."

Orang Gugu *see* Orang Pendek

Orang Kubu

The first known reference to this unclassified Indonesian primate or HOMINID appeared in 1818, in the form of a brief description from traveler William Marsden. Marsden distinguished between the Orang Kubu and another hairy forest-dwelling species, the orang gugu, but provided no meaningful details on either. Thirty years later, U.S. adventurer Walter Gibson (later special advisor to the king of Hawaii), glimpsed one of the man-sized creatures on Sumatra, describing it as "covered with hair, that looked soft and flowing….[T]he mouth was wide, lips protruding, and chin formed no part of the hairy face; yet it was pleasantly human in its expression." Local natives told Gibson the Orang Kubu "were brutes, they had no worship, no marriage, no law, no clothing, no idea of its use; they were the accursed of Allah, companions of djins on earth; fit only to be beasts of burden." The description left Gibson to speculate, rhetorically:

> Was this then some lower grade of human being, some connecting link between man and beast, more human than orang utan, or CHIMPANZEE; and less so than Papuan or Hottentot? I could not say so from what I saw, nor from all the strange stories I heard. But that beings of well made human form, covered with hair, almost without speech, and living on raw food, dwell in the caves and tree tops of the forests of Sumatra, are facts that are well established.

Source: Walter Gibson, *The Prison of Weltevreden.* New York: J.C. Riker, 1855.

Orang Letjo *see* Orang Pendek

Orang Minyak

The Orang Minyak ("oily man") is an aggressive unknown HOMINID or primate reported from peninsular Malaysia. Natives of the region claim that this large, hairy biped attacks rural villages by night and carries off young women. One such incident allegedly occurred on 29 September 1965, but villagers were able to repel the creature with machetes. Nearly four decades later, in September 2001, reports emerged from Malaysia that residents of Kuala Kedah village (in Kota Star district) had briefly captured an Orang Minyak, but the animal allegedly escaped, leaving villages so frightened that they mobbed and beat its careless captor. A possibility of overlap exists between reports of the Orang Minyak and the larger ORANG DALAM, said to inhabit the same vicinity.

Sources: "Man attacked in 'oily man' case." *The Malaysia Star* (23 September 2001); Norman, *The Abominable Snowmen.*

Orang Pendek

While several unknown HOMINIDS or primates are more famous than Sumatra's Orang Pendek — including BIGFOOT, the YETI, and Australia's YOWIE — this relatively modest candidate for "missing link" seems most likely to have its existence confirmed in the foreseeable future. Native knowledge of the Orang Pendek ("short man" or "little man") predates the arrival of European explorers, and the creature is known by various names across its range, including Atu Pandek, Orang Gugu, Orang Letjo ("gibbering man"), Sedapa and Sindai. Its possible existence was initially reported to the West in 1818, when William Marsden — the British Secretary in Resident on Sumatra — sent a brief description to the Admiralty. Edward Jacobson reported the first discovery of small, humanoid footprints almost a century later, in August 1915. A Dutch settler named Van Herwaarden provided the best description to date, in 1924, writing that the animal:

> …was also hairy on the front of its body; the color there was a little lighter than on the back. The very dark hair on its head fell to just below the shoulder blades or even almost to the waist. It was fairly thick and very shaggy. The lower part of its face seemed to end in more of a point than a man's; this brown face was almost hairless, whilst its forehead seemed to be high rather than low. Its eyes were frankly moving; they were of the darkest color, very

Skeptics claim the Orang pendek is simply a misidentified orangutan.

lively, and like human eyes. The nose was broad with fairly large nostrils, but in no way clumsy…. Its lips were quite ordinary, but the width of its mouth was strikingly wide when open. Its canines showed clearly from time to time as its mouth twitched nervously. They seemed fairly large to me; at all events they were more developed than a man's. The incisors were regular. The color of the teeth was yellowish-white. Its chin was somewhat receding. For a moment, during a quick movement, I was able to see its right ear, which was exactly like a little human ear. Its hands were slightly hairy on the back. Had it been standing, its arms would have reached to a little above its knees; they were therefore long, but its legs seemed to me rather short. I did not see its feet, but I did see some toes which were shaped in a very normal manner. The specimen was of the female sex and about five feet high. There was nothing repulsive or ugly about its face, nor was it at all apelike.

Two Orang Pendek bodies were allegedly discovered in the 1940s, and a hunter claimed to have captured a live specimen in 1954, but no such specimens were ever produced. John MacKinnon found a trail of 5-inch footprints in remote Ulu Segama National Park (Sabah Province), in 1969, and reported, "The toes looked quite human, as did the shapely heel, but the sole was both too short and too broad to be that of a man and the big toe was on the opposite side to what seemed to be the arch of the foot." British author Deborah Martyr found similar tracks in 1989 and sent a plaster cast of one footprint to the Indonesian National Parks Department, but it was lost. Over the next nine years, Martyr led several

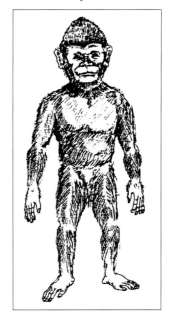

Eyewitness sketch of the Orang pendek.

more expeditions into the Karinci Region, discovering more footprints and twice sighting the creatures herself (in 1994 and 1998).

The most auspicious evidence to date was collected in September 2001, by a three-man team including Alan Davies, Andrew Sanderson and Keith Townley. At a point between Mount Kerinci and a lake called Gung Tujah, the searchers found two long strands of yellow-orange hair dangling from a bush, beside a fresh footprint. They took the hairs as evidence and photographed the track. At the suggestion of KARL SHUKER, Davies sent the hairs for DNA analysis at Deakin University in Melbourne, Australia, while the photos went to primatologist Colin Groves in Canberra. In February 2003, Dr. Hans Brunner announced that was unable to match the Orang Pendek hairs to samples taken from a human being and from various known mammals of Sumatra. "So far," Brunner said, "I have found that the two hairs which I have are different from any species which I have compared them with. If nothing comes which looks like the same I would have to say there could be an animal that we do not yet know about." Dr. Groves declined to release his findings on the footprint photographs until Brunner completed all possible tests on the hairs, but he told Andrew Sanderson to expect "good news." Five months later, on 18 July 2003, Brunner formally declared that the hairs matched no animal presently known to science. An August 2003 press release confirmed that the Orang Pendek footprints were also "unique."

Sources: Nigel Burton, "Northeast adventurer set to prove abominable snowman exists." *Northeast Echo* (4 September 2002); "Creature features." *Fortean Times*; Dammerman, "The Orang Pendek or ape-man of Sumatra"; (4 September 2002); Heuvelmans, *On the Track of Unknown Animals*; "Man-beast hunts in the Far East." *Fortean Times*; Paul Mcmillan, "Explorer finds key to Yeti mystery." *Evening Chronicle* (9 August 2003); Martyr, "An investigation of the *Orang-Pendek*, the 'short man' of Sumatra"; "Me and my Yeti." *Manchester Online* (19 July 2003); Sanderson, *Abominable Snowmen*; Karl Shuker, "Alien zoo." *Fortean Times* 154 (February 2002): 20–21; "Tests being carried out on 'yeti' hair." *Ananova* (4 September 2002); Van Herwaarden, "Een ontmoeting met een aapmensch." *De Tropische Natuur* 13 (1924): 103–106.

Orange Eyes   Orange Eyes is the nickname applied to a BIGFOOT-like creature (or NORTH AMERICAN APE) reported sporadically from Ohio. Witnesses agree that the creature's luminescent eyes are its most striking feature, even if descriptions otherwise reveal dramatic variations. One observer described the animal as "11-foot-tall, hairy, [and] completely orange." Fifteen-year-old Larry Abbot, who met the creature near Point Isabel in autumn 1968, described it as 10 feet tall, with massive 4-foot shoulders, covered in light brown hair. "The thing put me into sort of a trance," Abbot said. "I couldn't talk. Maybe it was just fright, but I couldn't open my mouth." Other sightings of Orange Eyes were reported from New London in August 1973, and from Alliance in March 1977.

Sources: Blackman, *The Field Guide to North American Monsters*; Bord and Bord, *The Bigfoot Casebook*; Cohen, *The Encyclopedia of Monsters*; Coleman, "The colour of mystery."

Orange Mound Monster   In 2002, a night-prowling MYSTERY MAULER invaded the Orange Mound neighborhood of Memphis, Tennessee, reportedly emerging from the woods to slaughter CATS and dogs, dropping their mutilated carcasses along the nearby railroad line. By October 2003, when officers of the Tennessee Wildlife Resource Agency and the Shelby County Environmental Office began investigating residents' complaints, rumors claimed that a WOLF or EASTERN COUGAR was at large. In fact, no one had seen the Orange Mound Monster, but locals heard its shrill nocturnal cries. "It's real loud," Lori Armour told reporters. "I mean it makes a ringing in your ear and it shakes the whole brick house." Neighbor Helen Williams said, "We are scared to come out at night." Authorities were unimpressed. Wildlife officer Andy Tweed opined, "It just looks like a coyote

problem right now. It may be something larger than that but we haven't found evidence it." At press time for this book, the mystery was still unsolved, the creature unidentified.

Sources: Christine Connolly, "Orange Mound mystery." WREG-TV, Memphis (28 October 2003); Anna Hartman, "Mysterious creature terrorizes neighbors." WMC-TV, Memphis (23 October 2003).

Orel Panther   On 12 August 1893, *The Field* published a brief item on the appearance of an ALIEN BIG CAT in Russia. It read:

> For some days past a panther, which escaped from the grounds of a landed proprietor who had a fancy for keeping wild animals, has been at large in the province of Orel, Russia [200 miles south of Moscow], to the terror of the villagers. The panther has already killed six persons; and although repeated *battues* have been organised by various sportsmen of the district, they have not succeeded in slaying the beast.

From that grim but straightforward beginning, the Orel Panther affair soon devolved into chaos. Eyewitness descriptions of the predator varied widely, including reports that the "panther" resembled a LYNX, a WOLF and a TIGER. A follow-up piece in *The Field* (19 August) described the creature as "the height of a wolf, of a yellow colour, with a blunt muzzle. His tracks are round, like a wolf's, about 3½ in. in diameter, but the claws imprint pointed tracks." Soldiers stalking the beast indiscriminately slaughtered animals including dogs, hens and a hapless striped hog. No further mention was made of the animal's wealthy owner, and the beast was never caught — though a report published in December 1893 claimed it vanished into woodlands beyond the River Vetebet after eating two poisoned sheep carcasses.

Source: Shuker, *Mystery Cats of the World*.

Oren, David Conway (n.d.)   A renowned ornithologist born in the U.S., David Oren went to Brazil in 1977, working for the Emilio Goeldi Museum in Belém while completing his Harvard doctorate. He soon heard legends of the jungle-dwelling MAPINGUARI, but dismissed them as simple myths. The weight of anecdotal evidence changed his mind in 1984, and Oren began his long personal search for the creature which remains elusive to this day. In 1994, Oren published a Goeldi Museum monograph proposing the giant Pleistocene ground sloth *MEGATHERIUM* as a Mapinguari candidate, further suggesting that the creature may have survived into historic times — or even to the present day. Oren's multiple expeditions have collected evidence that a journalist summarized in 1999 as including "a clump of hair, several fecal samples from different areas, and some casts of footprints." A second paper, published in 2001, included interviews with seven Amazon hunters who claim to have killed Mapinguaris, plus 80 more reports of eyewitness encounters. Many of Oren's colleagues dismiss his quest as Quixotic, but none doubt his conviction. As explained by former Harvard classmate Kent Redford, "David has chosen to devote his life to the animals and plants of the Amazon. So in a sense his conviction in the existence of Mapinguari has as much to do with seeking a powerful symbol for the need to conserve the Amazon as it does with his conviction that this animal really exists. I think that part of the passion he exhibits toward this search is, in fact, passion toward a search for the ongoing survival of the Amazon rain forest." In 2001, Oren moved to Brasilia and a new post with the U.S.-based Nature Conservancy, an environmentalist group.

Sources: "Bigfoot in the Amazon." *Whitley Strieber's Unknown Country* (7 January 2002); Marguerite Holloway, "Beasts in the mist." *Discover*

20 (September 1999): 58; Karl Shuker, "Alien zoo." *Fortean Times* 156 (April 2002): 18.

Orkney Islands sea serpents

The Orkney Islands, off the northern coast of Scotland, have produced three SEA SERPENT sightings and four alleged strandings since the early 19th century. The first and most famous case, that of the STRONSAY BEAST in 1808, is discussed in a separate entry. The next local incident involved a live sighting off the coast of Stenness, sometime during 1819–20, dramatized by Sir Walter Scott in *The Pirate* (1822):

> The Sea-SNAKE was also known, which arising out of the depths of Ocean, stretches to the skies his enormous neck, covered with a mane like that of a warhorse, and with its broad glittering eyes, raised mast-head high, looks out, as it seems, for plunder or for victims.

Another carcass beached at Kirkwall, in 1894. Details are unavailable, but BERNARD HEUVELMANS concluded that the remains belonged to a basking SHARK (*Cetorhinus maximus*). In August 1910, while duck-hunting with two relatives from a boat near the Skerries of Work in Meil Bay, W.J. Hutchinson saw several whales leaping from the water offshore, apparently pursued by a large animal whose head and neck rose repeatedly above the surface. The frightened hunters steered away from the beast and watched it submerge after five minutes in view. They described it as brown, with a head resembling that of a horse or CAMEL.

Nine years later, in August 1919, another strange creature made multiple appearances between Brims Ness and Tor Ness. The first sighting was logged by fishermen on 5 August, followed by a report from vacationing lawyer J. Mackintosh Bell a few days later. Bell was boating with with friends around 9:30 a.m., when several fisherman called his attention to an animal riding the waves nearby.

> I looked, and sure enough, about twenty-five to thirty yards from the boat, a long neck as thick as an elephant's fore-leg, all rough-looking like an elephants hide, was sticking up. On top of this was the head which was much smaller in proportion, but of the same colour. The head was like that of a dog, coming sharp to the nose. The eye was black and small, and the whiskers were black. The

An Orkney sea serpent, after witness J. Mackintosh Bell.

neck, I should say, stuck about five to six feet, possibly more, out of the water.

Two more rotting carcasses were stranded separately during January 1942, at DEEPDALE HOLM and HUNDA. Heuvelmans — again without providing details — dismissed both as the remains of stranded basking sharks. A local naturalist, J.G. Marwick, disagreed with respect to the former specimen and dubbed it *Scapasaurus*, reporting in the *Orcadian* of 5 February 1942 that he considered it "one of a species considered extinct many ages ago — a marine saurian in fact."

Sources: Dinsdale, *Monster Hunt*; Heuvelmans, *In the Wake of the Sea Serpents*; McEwan, *Mystery Animals of Britain and Ireland*.

Orme's Head sea serpent

At 3:00 p.m. on 3 September 1882, a SEA SERPENT appeared off the coast Caernarvonshire (northern Wales), before a group of impeccable witnesses (including a lawyer and a justice of the peace). The tourists were standing on Llandudno pier, facing the sea, when they sighted the creature near Little Orme's Head, proceeding toward the Great Orme. The account of one witness, F.T. Mott, was published in *Nature* on 25 January 1883.

> It is estimated to have been fully as long as a large steamer; say 200 feet; the rapidity of its motion was particularly remarked as being greater than that of any ordinary vessel. The colour appeared to be black, and the motion either corkscrew-like or SNAKE-like, with

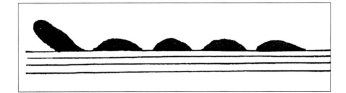

The Orme's Head sea serpent.

> many vertical undulations. Three of the observers have since made sketches from memory, quite independently of the impressions left on their minds, and on comparing these sketches, which slightly varied, they have agreed to sanction the accompanying outline as representing as nearly as possible the object which they saw. The party consisted of W. Barfoot, J.P. of Leicester, F.J. Marlow, solicitor, of Manchester, Mrs. Marlow, and several others.

Source: Heuvelmans, *In the Wake of the Sea Serpents*.

Ormsjøen, Norway

This lake, in Norway's Hordaland County, once allegedly boasted an Orm ("worm" or DRAGON) bristling with spikes, which allegedly surfaced on one long-ago occasion to terrorize members of a wedding party in their boat. Today, only the name remains, leaving researchers at a loss to separate fact from myth.

Source: Skjelsvik, "Norwegian lake and sea monsters."

Orontes sea serpent

A curious SEA SERPENT sighting from the West Indies occurred in the spring of 1873 but was not published for another three decades, until retired naval commander Reginald Yonge sent an extract from the log-book of H.M.S. *Orantes* to the *Illustrated London News*. That entry read:

> March 20, 1873, 3:15 a.m. — Air pump rod carried away. Stopped engines 7:20 a.m. As Captain Perry and myself were walking on the upper bridge we saw something, which first attracted my attention through being white, rise gradually out of the water, and remain stationary for a few seconds. It was the head of an immense monster, and in shape looked for me very much like an EEL'S

head. It rose about 5 ft. out of water, but what was its length under water I could not see. The ship was drifting toward it. I ran down into the chart house for a rifle and while getting it (as the Captain afterwards told me) the head had gradually sunk and risen again close to the ship—almost so close as to touch it, and the Captain had a still better view of it. It appeared not to appreciate the vicinity of the ship as it turned leisurely, sinking at the same time, and swam away in a south-westerly direction, rising to the surface once or twice when the Captain had a shot at it with the rifle I had brought him, after which we saw the FISH no more. It was seen also by Flemming, quartermaster, and Ransom, signal-man, from the lower bridge, and by Lieutenant Lang, from his cabin port, aft, who said that his attention was drawn to it when it first rose by hearing it make a snorting noise. It is considered by those who saw it to be about forty feet in length. The back of the head was black, the throat and belly white, and the eye white and set well back. A few others saw it, but the troops and ship's company being at breakfast, there were not many people on deck.

In a letter mailed with the log-book extract, Yonge added more details of the sighting.

At the time we had just come through the Mona Passage, between San Domingo and Puerto Rico, in the West Indies. The weather was beautifully fine. Latitude, about 20 deg. N.; longitude, 70 deg. W.

The Captain is now Admiral John Laisne Perry, whose name, I am glad to see, is still in the Navy Lit (retired). The First Lieutenant, Lang, is William Metcalfe Lang, now a retired Admiral.

I remember well when the late Admiral Sir Rodney Abundy, Commander-in-Chief at Portsmouth, inspected the ships on April 16 following. He took me and questioned me as to this marine monster of which I had made a rough sketch at the time. And I have no doubt that there is some record of it now at the Admiralty if the *Orontes'* old log still exists.

I believe that I must have considerably under-estimated the height to which the monster's head rose above water—for I do not think that I should have so distinctly seen it if it had been only five feet. However I have left it as I originally wrote it down in my journal.

Source: Heuvelmans, *In the Wake of the Sea Serpents.*

Orpheus Island sea serpent   In 1934, while scouting locations for an Australian travel documentary, film producers Pierce Mack and Robert Steele sighted a SEA SERPENT near Orpheus Island, off the northern coast of Queensland. Steele described the creature as "twenty-five feet long, a snakelike head with fins on either side, a tail more like an EEL than a snake, the body about twelve inches in diameter, no particular fangs or tongue showing, and the body an impressive lime-green tinged with brown around the fins." They followed the animal for a quarter-mile, as it kept pace with their boat and several times raised its head above the surface. Unfortunately, Mack and Steele had no cameras aboard when the incident occurred.

Source: Smith, *Bunyips & Bigfoots.*

***Osborne* sea serpent**   On 2 June 1877, crewmen aboard the yacht *Osborne* encountered a strange SEA SERPENT off Cape Vito, on the northern coast of Sicily. Commander Hugh Pearson sent a report of the incident, signed by three of his officers, to British Admiral Sir George Elliott, which read:

On the evening of that day, the sea being perfectly smooth, my attention was first called by seeing a ridge of fins above the surface of the water, extending about thirty feet, and varying from five to six feet in height. On inspecting it by means of a telescope, at about one and a-half cables' distance, I distinctly saw a head, two

flappers, and about thirty feet of the animal's shoulder. The head, as nearly as I could judge, was about six feet thick, the narrower, about four to five feet, the shoulder about fifteen feet across, and the flappers each about fifteen feet in length. The movements of the flappers were those of a TURTLE, and the animal resembled a huge seal, the resemblance being strongest about the back of the head. I could not see the length of the head, but from its crown or top to just below the shoulder (where it became immersed), I should reckon about fifty feet. The tail end I did not see, being under water, unless the ridge of fins to which my attention was first attracted, and which had disappeared by the time I got a telescope, were really the continuation of the shoulder to the end of the object's body. The animal's head was not always above water, but was thrown upwards, remaining above for a few seconds at a time, and then disappearing. There was an entirely [*sic*] absence of "blowing" or "spouting." I herewith enclose a sketch (A) showing the view of the "ridge of fins," and (B) of the animal in the act of propelling itself by its two fins.

After printing Pearson's story, *The Times* of London suggested that the creature had been forced to surface by a volcanic eruption in the Gulf of Tunis, two weeks earlier. No evidence exists to support that assertion.

Source: Heuvelmans, *In the Wake of the Sea Serpents.*

Two eyewitness sketches of the *Osborne* sea serpent.

Oscar   Residents of Crow Wing County, Minnesota apply this affectionate nickname to an alleged LAKE MONSTER sighted in Big Pine Lake, in 1971. The creature remains unidentified, though some locals suggest it may be a large sturgeon. With a maximum depth of 18 feet, Big Pine Lake could scarcely conceal a cryptid of much greater size.

Source: Garner, *Monster! Monster!*

Osensjøen, Norway   Local traditions assert that this lake, in Hedmark County, was once inhabited by a serpentine LAKE MONSTER, but no sightings have been filed in modern times.

Source: Skjelsvik, "Norwegian lake and sea monsters."

Oshawa Oscar *see* **Lake Ontario**

Osodrashin *see* **Yeti**

Osoyoos Lake   Osoyoos Lake spans the international border between British Columbia and Washington State (Okanogan County). Its northern section lies in the midst of Canada's only desert, and as a warm-water lake it defies Canadian LAKE MONSTER tradition. Still, on 4 August 1923, Osoyoos produced a report of what may be Canada's largest aquatic cryptid. Six youths were boating at the north end of the lake that afternoon, when they saw a 100-foot "whale" rise from the depths and race toward them, frightening them thoroughly before it dived and disappeared.

Sources: Kirk, *In the Domain of the Lake Monsters*; Moon, *Ogopogo: The Okanagan Mystery.*

Ossie

Ossie is the nickname applied to a 50-foot SEA SERPENT with square dorsal fins, sighted by fishermen off the coast of Carvarvon, West Australia between May and July 1999. The name is presumably a combination of the slang term "Aussie" (for Australian) and the nicknames given to various well-known aquatic cryptids around the world, including NESSIE (at Loch Ness), ISSIE (in Japan's Lake Ikeda), and Tahoe TESSIE (from Lake Tahoe, on the California-Nevada border). Unlike LAKE MONSTERS, however, Ossie was not constrained by physical boundaries and it has not returned since the spate of initial sightings in 1999.

Source: "Other cryptozoology news." *Cryptozoology Review* 4 (Summer 2000): 8.

Ossun Lizard

Since February 1893, residents of Ossun-ez-Angles, in the French Pyrenees, have reported sporadic encounters with a green lizard 5–6 feet long, sporting a prominent fleshy dewlap. No reptile matching that description — and no lizard of that size — is presently known to exist in Europe. French police mounted a futile search for the creature after a sighting in May 1939. Suggestions that the creature seen on each occasion is an escaped pet IGUANA (*Iguana iguana*) plainly ignore the time span involved.

Source: Philippe Janvier, *Le Monde Étrange des Reptiles*. Paris: Albin Michel, 1973.

Ostman, Albert (1893–1969)

In the summer of 1924, lumberjack Albert Ostman embarked on a prospecting trip to British Columbia, in search of gold. While camping near Toba Inlet (70 miles northwest of Vancouver), Ostman was allegedly kidnapped one night by a powerful intruder who scooped him up, sleeping bag and all, in the middle of the night. The unseen abductor carried him for miles, finally depositing Ostman in a sort of box canyon, where Ostman was stunned to find that he had been snatched by BIGFOOT. In fact, four of the creatures confronted him, later described by Ostman as "a family, old man, old lady and two young ones, a boy and a girl." The "old man" stood eight feet tall, while his apparent spouse measured seven feet and weighed (by Ostman's estimate) between 500 and 600 pounds. The animals were not aggressive, but searched through Ostman's belongings and ate some of his food. Though armed with a rifle, Ostman hesitated to fire, believing that his weapon might only enrage the creatures. After two days in captivity, Ostman fed the "old man" a can of snuff, then escaped when the tobacco made his captor ill. Ostman went public with his story in 1957, and his first-person account of the experience appears in various books. Skeptics dismiss the story as an old-timer's "tall tale," while cryptozoologists remain divided on the subject of Ostman's credibility.

Albert Ostman claimed he was kidnapped by a Sasquatch family in 1924.

Sources: Green, *Sasquatch: The Apes Among Us*; Sanderson, *Abominable Snowmen*.

Ostrich (Mislocated)

The flightless ostrich (*Struthio camelus*) is officially the largest living BIRD on Earth, reaching a maximum 8-foot height and weighing up to 300 pounds. Native to Africa, ostriches are today raised for slaughter on ranches throughout the world, and their occasional escape typically explains sightings in locations where they do not normally occur. Still, police in central Norway's Nord Trondelag region could not explain the reported appearance of an ostrich at large on 9 July 2002. Motorists Hallvard and Annie Aasen saw the bird dash across a rural highway and disappear into the forest, reporting the encounter to authorities at their next stop. Police informed the media that no one in Nord Trondelag had reported a missing pet ostrich, and the district has no ostrich farms. Ornithologist Jostein Sandvik told the newspaper *Tronder Avisa* that the Aasens had actually seen a crane. "It runs the same way as an ostrich," Sandvik said, "and cannot fly at this time of year due to its feathers changing." Unconvinced, Annie Aasen told reporters, "I could not believe my own eyes, but I am sure about what we saw. At first we wondered if it really was an ostrich, but it ran in front of us for so long that in the end we had no doubts about it."

Source: "Couple shocked by ostrich in middle of Norway." *Anananova* (10 July 2002).

Otepää, Estonia

During the 16th century, residents of this town in Valga County reportedly sacrificed cattle at a nearby lake, to placate a ravenous LAKE MONSTER. The practice has thankfully been abandoned, and no modern reports of the beast are on file. At this remove, it is impossible to judge whether the animal ever existed, or the sacrifices were based on unfounded superstition.

Source: Oskar Loorits, *Grundzüge des Estnischen Volksglaubens*. Lund, Sweden: Carl Bloms, Boktryckeri, 1951.

Ottawa River, Canada

Cryptozoologists LOREN COLEMAN and JOHN KIRK include Ontario's Ottawa River on published lists of North American lakes and rivers allegedly inhabited by large aquatic cryptids, but neither provides any details or descriptions of the creature(s).

Sources: Coleman, *Mysterious America*; Kirk, *In the Domain of the Lake Monsters*.

Oudemans, Antoon Cornelius, Jr. (1858–1943)

Antoon Oudemans Jr. was born at Batavia, Holland, into a family of scientists and scholars. As a child, he grew interested in natural history and pursued that field throughout his life. Although he ultimately specialized in ticks and mites, Oudemans also nurtured a passion for study of SEA SERPENTS. He published his first article on the subject in November 1881, while still a student at the University of Utrecht, suggesting that the great pelagic cryptids might be surviving specimens of a "PLESIOSAUR-shaped ZEUGLODON." (In fact, the mammalian zeuglodon bore no resemblance to a reptilian plesiosaur.) Soon after his graduation in 1885, Oudemans was chosen to serve as director of the Royal Zoological and Botanical Gardens at The Hague. There, he continued painstaking research on sea serpent reports and revised his opinion of the creature's identity. His magnum opus on the subject, *The Great Sea Serpent* (1892), reviewed 187 credible accounts and concluded that the unknown creature was a giant long-necked seal, which Oudemans dubbed *Megophias*. Oudemans resigned his director's post in 1895, to pursue a long career of teaching, research and writing. When NESSIE first made headlines in 1933, Oudemans proposed that Loch Ness was inhabited by a land-

Antoon Oudemans made this sketch of Nessie based on eyewitness descriptions.

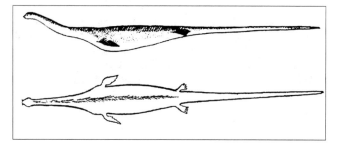

Oudemans also sketched *Megophias*, his archetypal sea serpent.

A sketch of Cornwall's Owlman, after various eyewitnesses.

locked form of *Megophias*. In retrospect, the primary weakness of his theory lay in a refusal to believe there might be more than one aquatic cryptid at the root of sea serpent and LAKE MONSTER reports. Oudemans died before completing a sequel to *The Great Sea Serpent.*

Sources: Coleman and Clark, *Cryptozoology A to Z*; Heuvelmans, *In the Wake of the Sea Serpents.*

Ouokolo *see* **Gnéna**

Oûuahi This strange unclassified primate of South America has been reported from jungle areas of Brazil, Colombia and Venezuela. Not to be confused with the equally enigmatic DE LOYS'S APE or MONO GRANDE of the same vicinity, the Oûuahi (allegedly named for its whooping cry) is described as covered with auburn hair, possessed of blue-gray eyes beneath a thick brow ridge. The tailless creature's limbs are distinctive: its forearms are noticeably shorter than the upper arms, and its thighs are longer than its shins. When walking erect, the Oûuahi moves with a rolling gait, walking on the outsides of its feet. No specimen has yet been collected from any point in its substantial range.

Source: Roger Courteville, *Avec les Indiens Inconnus de l'Amazonie.* Paris: Amiot, Dummont, 1951.

Owlman On 17 April 1976, while on vacation with their parents at Mawnan (in Cornwall, England), young sisters June and Vicky Melling allegedly sighted a large "BIRD-man" hovering over the spire of a local church. Three months later, on the night of 3 July, two 14-year-old girls reported seeing the same creature, at the same location. Witness Sally Chapman later told ANTHONY SHIELS:

> It was like a big OWL with pointed ears, as big as a man. The eyes were red and glowing. At first I thought it was someone dressed up, playing a joke, trying to scare us. I laughed at it, we both did,

then it went up in the air and we both screamed. When it went up you could see its feet were like pincers.

Companion Barbara Perry recalled the thing's "nasty owl-face with big ears and big red eyes. It was covered in grey feathers. The claws on its feet were black. It just flew straight up and disappeared in the trees."

Two more girls on holiday, the Greenwood sisters, saw the "bird" on 4 July 1976. Jane Greenwood told reporters, "It was in the trees standing like a full-grown man, but the legs bent backwards like a bird's....It has red slanting eyes and a very large mouth. The feathers are silvery gray and so are his body and legs. The feet are like big black crab's claws." Other sightings, all by girls, were reported from the neighborhood of Mawnan Church in June and August 1978. Author Graham McEwan reports that a similar creature frightened four young men near Sandling Park (in Hythe, Kent) on 16 November 1963.

Questions surround the role of veteran prankster Tony Shiels in the Owlman sightings of 1976–78. Interviewed in 1985, Shiels claimed to be "baffled" by the sightings and described the several witnesses as honest. Twelve years later, he told author Jon Downes that he (Shiels) had "invented" Owlman, but Downes "obviously (and quite rightly) did not believe me." In 2002, Shiels speculated publicly that the incidents involved a clever HOAX, but he claimed no responsibility. A more prosaic theory suggests that the Mawnan witnesses may have seen a Eurasian eagle owl (*Bubo bubo*), which stand four feet tall at rest, with a 6-foot wingspan.

Sources: McEwan, *Mystery Animals of Britain and Ireland*; Shiels, "That owl devil moon"; Shiels, "The owling."

Owls (Giant) Owls are predatory BIRDS found throughout the world in various sizes. The largest known species on Earth, the eagle owl (*Bubo bubo*), may have a 6-foot wingspan and hunts prey ranging in size from RABBITS to FOXES and fawns. The largest known species in the Western Hemisphere is the great horned owl (*Bubo virginianus*), with an official maximum wingspan of 4 feet 7 inches. Such birds are impressive, but they pale to insignificance beside accounts of truly giant owls, standing four feet or taller at rest, with wingspans reported as 10–12 feet. In the 18th and 19th centuries, Native Americans described huge owls (sometimes called "flying heads") ranging over a wide territory from New Jersey, through Ohio, West Virginia and the Ozark Mountains, into southern Texas. Their prey allegedly included lambs, calves and children. Cryptozoologist MARK HALL has dubbed the creature Bighoot and proposed it as an explanation for West Virginia's MOTHMAN sightings of 1966–67. An Ohio witness claims to have

Giant owls are reported from North America and Europe.

sighted a 10-foot owl on two occasions during 1982–83, at Rocky Fork Lake (Highland County), but the exaggerated size suggests confusion with an even larger flying cryptid, the THUNDERBIRD. In England, reports of a similar creature (dubbed OWLMAN) panicked Mawnan residents in the 1970s. On 19 July 2002, an Internet posting from "MoonSeeker" claimed that "enormous" owls had staged daylight attacks on several cropdusting aircraft around Veliki Popovac, a Serbian town in the Mlava River valley. Attacks on cattle and sheep were likewise reported. In a passage redolent of supermarket tabloid journalism, the Serbian newspaper *Glas* cited an unnamed veterinarian's opinion that "this event is being caused by increasingly powerful solar radiation due to the destruction of the ozone layer." No substantiation of the Serbian attacks has been produced to date.

Sources: Joseph Bruhac, *Stone Giants and Flying Heads.* Trumansburg, NY: Crossing, 1979; Mark Hall, "Bighoot — The giant owl." *Wonders* 5 (September 1998): 67–79; Hall, "Bighoot — The giant owl." *Wonders* 6 (2001): 4–5; Hall *Thunderbirds!*; Shuker, "A giant owl and a giant hyrax…?"; "Large owls attack aircraft." (19 July 2002) The Black Vault, http://www.blackvault.com/.

Øyvatna, Norway Located in Norway's Buskerud County, this lake was once allegedly the home of a LAKE MONSTER notable for its large eyes and head resembling a calf's. Once again, as with other Scandinavian lakes, sightings have waned or ceased altogether in modern times.

Source: Skjelsvik, "Norwegian lake and sea monsters."

Ozark Howler The Ozark Howler is a prime example of a cryptozoological HOAX. The "creature" broke cover in April 1998, with Internet reports of an initial sighting near Branson, Missouri. Alleged witness Fred Sprout claimed to have seen the beast, which he described as a most unusual "CAT," 10–12 feet long and 4 feet tall at the shoulder, with two curved horns atop its head. Nickname notwithstanding, the Howler hardly made a sound — but there was someone laughing in the shadows. KARL SHUKER reported the alleged sighting in July 1998, predicting it would prove to be a hoax, and subsequent research by LOREN COLEMAN traced the charade to its author, a still-unidentified college student.

Source: Loren Coleman, "Mysterious world." *Fate* 51 (September 1998): 10–11, 70; Karl Shuker, "Alien zoo." *Fortean Times* 112 (July 1998): 17; Shuker, "Alien zoo." *Fortean Times* 114 (September 1998): 18.

Ozenkadnook Tiger In 1968, Rilla Martin of Melbourne, Australia snapped a unique photograph of a curious beast near Ozenkadnook, Victoria. The photo shows a creature with a head resembling a dog's, whose foreparts seem to have white stripes on black pelage, while the hindquarters and tale are white. KARL SHUKER believes the TIGER's stripes are shadows cast by bushes in the photograph, but that diagnosis brings us no closer to resolving the still-unknown creature's identity.

Source: Shuker, *Mystery Cats of the World.*

P

Pablo Beach sea serpent Swimmers at Pablo Beach, Florida (renamed Jacksonville Beach in 1925) reportedly saw a SEA SERPENT swimming offshore in 1891. BERNARD HEUVELMANS listed the incident in his classic 1968 survey of pelagic cryptids and included a melodramatic sketch of bathers fleeing a veritable DRAGON in the surf, but he unfortunately did not write a single line about the incident. Based on the illustration alone, it may well have been HOAX.

Source: Heuvelmans, *In the Wake of the Sea Serpents.*

Pach-an-a-ho (*See illustration on next page.*) The Pach-an-a-ho is a giant BIRD of Yakima Indian folklore, whose aboriginal name is variously translated as "crooked beak" or "rough-looking bird." In 1997, a Native American party visiting a U.S. museum reportedly identified the fossil remains of *Diatryma gigantea*, a 7-foot flightless bird of the early Eocene epoch, as Pach-an-a-ho. Officially extinct for 40 million years, Diatryma cannot have interacted with human beings to produce even a "racial memory" — unless it survived far beyond its presumed date of extinction. A similar situation prevails with the legendary VOUROUPATRA of Madagascar.

Source: Karl Shuker, "Alien zoo." *Fortean Times* 103 (October 1997): 15.

Yakima tribesmen describe the giant bird Pach-an-a-ho as resembling a prehistoric *Diatryma gigantea.*

Pacifique **sea serpent**   On 19 June 1923, a radio officer aboard the French vessel *Pacifique* saw a SEA SERPENT in the South Pacific, while sailing from Éfaté (in the New Hebrides) to New Caledonia. The officer, M. Martin, described the experience:

> On 19 June we had left Port-Vila for Nouméa and had just rounded Cap les Pins on the south of Lifou Island. It was about four o'clock in the afternoon, and the weather was magnificent. About 100 yards away at 30° on the starboard bow, there was a considerable movement in the sea. I saw a strange animal raise its head, neck and beginning of its body out of the water. This happened in a flash. Near me Seamen Picot, Cardot, Cointreau and Viale were working at painting a boat. "Did you see that animal?" I asked them. At the same moment it emerged a second time, and we all five saw it very clearly, but this time it did not dive with a splash but sank slowly down.

Martin description of the creature was vague, beyond comparing its color to "a new cork" and insisting that it bore no resemblance to a whale beyond its great size. One of the other seamen described the visible neck as equal in thickness to the boiler-room's air shaft, topped by a conical head.

Source: Heuvelmans, *In the Wake of the Sea Serpents.*

Packda   The Packda ("big APE") was described by 19th-century witnesses as an unclassified primate inhabiting the heavily forested mountains of Palawan Island, in the Philippines. Whether the creature still survives is presently unknown, since the last account of it existence dates from the years of U.S. military occupation following the Spanish-American War.

Source: Dean Worcester, *The Philippine Islands and Their People.* New York: Macmillan, 1899.

Paddler   Despite long habitation by Native Americans and a continuous white presence since Thompson's trading post was established in 1809, the supposed LAKE MONSTER of Lake Pend Oreille, Idaho did not appear until August 1944, when a sighting was reported at Farragut Naval Training Station. More sightings of Paddler (as locals call the creature) were logged in the 1970s, and a group of boaters reported a large gray object outpacing

their craft in May 1985. Around the same time, U.S. Navy spokesmen made their first admission that new torpedoes and submarine sonar devices are sometimes tested at Lake Pend Oreille. Researcher James McLeod believes the Navy "invented" Paddler as a cover for their secret tests and to discourage tourism around the lake. In November 1996, Commander Rick Schulz, head of the Navy's David Taylor Acoustic Research Center near Bayview (at the south end of the lake), told the Spokane (Washington) *Spokesman-Review*, "I think that is definitely false. But I can't say that in the past an employee sitting at the bar didn't lean over to a buddy and say, 'Hey, did you know...?', that sort of thing."

Sources: Huyghe, "Deep secrets"; McLeod, *Mysterious Lake Pen Oreille and Its "Monster"*; "Navy monster?" *Fortean Times* 98 (June 1997): 18.

Paint River, Michigan   In 1922, two residents of northern Michigan's Iron County reported sighting a "SEA SERPENT" in the Paint River. They described the creature as long and dark in color, with a head larger than a bucket, revealing six humps as it swam upstream with undulating motions.

Sources: Coleman, *Mysterious America*; Guiley, *Atlas of the Mysterious in North America*; Sanderson, *"Things."*

Pal Rai Yuk   Inuit natives of Alaska describe the Pal Rai Yuk as a large and dangerous aquatic creature frequenting the coastal waters of Nunivak Island, seen more rarely in the open sea. The creature has a head resembling a SNAKE'S, typically viewed when the Pal Rai Yuk raises its neck 7–8 feet above water's surface. On rare occasions when the creature's tail is seen, a flipper is displayed. When Dr. John White, with the Field Museum of Natural History, interviewed Nunivak Island natives concerning the Pal Rai Yuk, he heard varied accounts of the beasts killing hunters and kayakers. A similar creature is known on tiny King Island, 400 miles farther north in the Bering Strait, where the Inuit call it Tizheruk. ROY MACKAL suggests that the Pal Rai Yuk may be a form of giant, long-necked seal, similar to the animal proposed by some cryptozoologists as a LAKE MONSTER.

Source: Mackal, *Searching for Hidden Animals.*

Pallid Sailfin   This deep-sea FISH has been seen only once, when WILLIAM BEEBE descended in a bathysphere to depths of 2,500 feet off Bermuda, in the early 1930s. Beebe described it as two feet long, torpedo-shaped in the manner of a barracuda, with small eyes, a large mouth, and a long diaphanous pectoral fin. Unlike many fish that Beebe met at great depths, the pallid sailfin was not luminous. He named it *Bathyembryx istiophasma*, but no type specimen has yet been collected to formalize that identification.

Source: Beebe, *Half Mile Down.*

Palmyra Fish *see* **High-Finned Whales**

Paltry Beach carcass   On 29 July 2001, fisherman Ed Hodder discovered a large carcass stranded on Paltry Beach, 12 miles west of St. Bernard's, Newfoundland. Media reports described the rotting body as 22 feet 8 inches long, weighing 3–4 tons, and "covered in coarse white hair the length of an average man's hand." No head was discernible, and while the creature had "what appears to be a skeletal structure consisting of a backbone and ribs," observers found it "impossible to tell which end is which." There was "only a suggestion of limbs," more specifically "flaps of flesh on either side [that] could just as well be ears as fins." One veteran fisherman pronounced it "the Loch Ness monster," while Hodder quipped, "Maybe it's a whale turned inside out." Wayne King, representing the Newfoundland Department of Fisheries and Oceans, told reporters on 2 August, "We're pretty well sure it's not some strange sea creature. I can say I have seen whales dead before and certain SHARKS. It's similar. Given the fact that it is so severely decomposed, it's just a job to positively identify what species of whale or shark it is." Cetologist John Lien of Memorial University left his options open, declaring "If you don't know, the easiest thing is to say it's a sea creature. We all think the ocean is an intriguing place. It's quite exciting." DNA tests were reportedly scheduled, but at press time for this volume no final verdict had been rendered on the animal's identity.

Sources: Ryan Cleary, "'Monster' beached." *The Telegram* (1 August 2001); Barb Sweet, "'Monster' likely whale or shark: DFO." *The Telegram* (2 August 2001).

Paluxy tracks

In 1908, a flood on the Paluxy River uncovered curious tracks in a limestone bed near Glen Rose, Texas (Somervell County, southwest of Dallas-Fort Worth). Local resident Ernest Adams discovered the footprints, but they were largely ignored until the late 1930s, when Roland Bird arrived to study them for the American Museum of Natural History. Bird reported that some of the fossil tracks were clearly made by DINOSAURS of the Cretaceous period, roughly 100 million years ago, but others resembled the imprints of human feet. Granted, at 15–20 inches long and eight inches wide they were not *normal* footprints, but Bird detected heels and insteps in the proper places for humanoid tracks. Proponents of the Biblical creation story and "young Earth" theology (asserting that the planet is less than 7,000 years old) hailed the Paluxy tracks as "proof" that men and dinosaurs had shared the landscape prior to Noah's flood, around 4000 B.C. In fundamentalist eyes, the oversized "human" tracks at Paluxy also verified Old Testament references to GIANTS. Creationist film-maker Stan Taylor summarized the religious case in 1973, with his documentary *Footprints in Stone*.

Still, evolutionary scientists largely ignored the Paluxy tracks until 1980, when Ohio computer programmer Glen Kuban made the first of several trips to study the footprints. In 1982, Kuban noted faint color patterns in the shape of dinosaur toes extending from the "human" tracks. Later that year, the American Humanist Association funded the first true scientific expedition to examine the Paluxy tracks. Team members John Cole, Laurie Godfrey, Ron Hastings and Steven Schafersman examined the footprints, discovering that different minerals had filled in portions of various dinosaur tracks and then petrified to give them a humanoid appearance. Other "human" tracks at the site were simple products of erosion, while a few were plainly chiseled out by persons unknown to support the creationist case. Subsequent discovery of dinosaur tracks outside Clayton, New Mexico confirmed that sediments may "sculpt" animal tracks and give them a radically different appearance. Leading creationists were invited back to Paluxy and reviewed the evidence, with the result that *Footprints in Stone* was soon withdrawn from circulation. Even now, however, some extreme fundamentalists still tout the Paluxy tracks as "evidence" of a mythical "young Earth," and a few sell casts of the footprints for profit.

Sources: Philip Kitcher, *Abusing Science: The Case Against Creationism*. Cambridge, MA: MIT Press, 1982; John Wilford, "Fossils of 'man tracks' shown to be dinosaurian." *New York Times* (17 June 1986).

Pamba

Africa's LAKE TANGANYIKA ranks among the world's most impressive lakes. With a surface area of 12,350 miles, it is the continent's second-largest lake, and the seventh-largest on Earth. It is also the second-deepest in the world (4,800 feet) and has the third-largest volume of water (after the Caspian Sea and Russia's Lake Baikal). It comes as no great surprise, therefore, that Lake Tanganyika has also spawned reports of LAKE MONSTERS, which Swahili tribesmen call Pamba. In 1912, famed animal collector Carl Hagenbeck met a French naturalist, lately returned from Lake Tanganyika, who reported encounters with "amphibious animals, of gigantic size, similar in various ways to the elephant, the RHINOCEROS and the hippopotamus." Hagenbeck offered a lucrative reward for proof of such a creature, but he died in April 1913 with his hopes still unfulfilled. Lake Tanganyika, incidentally, is linked to other African lakes by a system of rivers whose waters reportedly harbor the beast called CHIPEKWE, said to resemble a living DINOSAUR. Further confusion derives from the fact that Pamba is also the name applied to a large perchlike FISH, the lates (*Lates angustifrons*), that inhabits Lake Tanganyika and grows to 6 feet 6 inches in length.

Sources: Heuvelmans, *On the Track of Unknown Animals*; Speight, "Mystery monsters of Africa."

Pangboche Hand

Throughout the Himalayas, various Buddhist lamaseries historically have preserved certain relics (scalps, skin, body parts) allegedly belonging to the sacred YETI. Some of those objects are admittedly manmade, existing simply to *represent* the creature known to millions of outsiders as the ABOMINABLE SNOWMAN, but an air of mystery surrounds other relics. And none is more mysterious than the Pangboche hand.

Nepal's Pangboche lamasery lies south of Mount Everest and 175 miles east of Kathmandu. There, Buddhist holy men once preserved both a supposed Yeti scalp and a near-skeletal hand. The latter object was unknown to Western researchers before 1958, when members of an expedition sponsored by Texas oilmen TOM SLICK and F. Kirk Johnson Jr. discovered the existence of the Pangboche hand and another preserved at the Makalu lamasery. Neither institution would permit removal of the objects, but Makalu's lamas permitted PETER BYRNE to photograph and X-ray their mummified "hand." British primatologist W.C. Osman Hill examined those photos and X-rays, finally deciding that the bones belonged to either a WOLF or snow leopard. After advising the Slick-Johnson team to focus their attention on the Pangboche hand, Osman Hill hatched a plot with Byrne to obtain more solid evidence. He provided Byrne with several bones from a human hand, suggesting that a covert switch might furnish the team with proof of the Yeti's existence.

Back at Pangboche in early 1959, Byrne persuaded the lamas to grant him privacy while he examined the hand. Within moments, he removed several pieces from the relic and wired human bones in their place. On 3 February, Byrne wrote to Slick:

I shall not go into details here of how we got the thumb and the phalanx of the Pangboche hand. The main thing is that we have them, and that the lamas of the monastery *do not know* that we have them. Because they do not know it is of the utmost importance that there is [*sic*] no news releases on this or any publicity for some time....The Pangboche hand is still complete, as far as the lamas are concerned. It still has a thumb and an index proximal phalanx. What they do not know, and what they *must never know*, is that the thumb and the p. phalanx at present on the hand are human ones, which we switched.

Hollywood film star James Stewart, a friend of oilman Johnson, was recruited to smuggle the bones from Nepal to Europe in his luggage. Osman Hill received the relics on 20 February 1959, and six days later wrote: "This proves from examination of the thumb and phalanx to be human." Zoologist Charles Leone performed serological analysis on skin fragments from the digits (DNA testing was unknown at the time) and reached inconclusive results. The tissue did not come from a human, GORILLA or other known primate; neither was it from a bear, cow, goat, horse or pig. Frederick Ulmer, curator of mammals at the Philadelphia Zoo, wrote to Slick in March 1959 that the Pangboche metacarpals "are considered massive even for a mountain gorilla. Metacarpals are extremely wide and flat on top. Hand is massive." Anthropologist Stanley Garn, meanwhile, found that "the relative lengths of segments of digits to the metacarpals is somewhat out of order for the normal man." Osman Hill's opinion of the Pangboche hand evolved over time. By July 1959, he thought the bones belonged to some unknown primate. A year later, he told IVAN SANDERSON the hand might be a relic of NEANDERTAL MAN. Another researcher, anthropologist GEORGE AGOGINO told author Gardner Soule:

I did notice that the hand had very flat metacarpals, far flatter than is normally expected in a human being, but something which is very characteristic of the giant anthropoids. Many people who have examined this hand feel that it is a human hand with very primitive characteristics. It is so close to the border line it could be a non-human hand with very advanced characteristics and still be little different than it is currently. I do not feel that this hand is a normal human hand at all. The flat metacarpals, particularly in the top surface, just do not occur among human beings very often, if at all. Feel at the back of your own hand. It his highly characteristic, however, of all the giant anthropoids.

Such verdicts were decidedly unwelcome in some quarters. In 1960–61, Sir Edmund Hillary led a Himalayan expedition that included several military officers, anxious to spy on Chinese military forces in Tibet. Along the way, Hillary stopped at several lamaseries to heap ridicule upon their Yeti relics. At Pangboche, Hillary pronounced the famous hand "essentially a human hand, strung together with wire, with the possible inclusion of several animal bones." He made no effort to identify the animal(s) in question, while pretending that the mystery was solved. Two decades later, celebrity naturalist Marlin Perkins discarded even that qualifier, writing simply that the Pangboche hand "turned out to be human." In fact, no researcher since early 1959 had seen the hand in its original condition, nor were any aware of Byrne's switch until the latter 1980s. In 1991, producers of the television program *Unsolved Mysteries* sent part of the Pangboche hand's original skin (preserved by Osman Hill in 1959) for analysis at the University of California's biomedical laboratory. The resultant verdict deemed it "near human" but otherwise unidentified. Further tests were planned, but the hand vanished from Pangboche in 1992, presumably taken by thieves. Its fate and final destination are unknown.

Sources: Clark and Pear, *Strange & Unexplained Phenomena*; Coleman, "Not so abominable now"; Coleman, *Tom Slick and the Search for the Yeti*; Marlin Perkins, *My Wild Kingdom*. New York: E.P. Dutton, 1982; Sanderson, *Abominable Snowmen*; Soule, *Trail of the Abominable Snowman*.

Panguitch Lake, Utah

Scenic Panguitch Lake, located in the Dixie National Forest (southwestern Garfield County), takes its name from the Paiute word for "big FISH." Aboriginal folklore alludes to inhabitants much larger than the lake's famous trout, but no sightings are on record since white settlers arrived in 1873.

Source: The Online Lake Cryptid Directory, http:/dive.to/lakemonsters; History of Panguitch Lake, http://www.panguitchlake.net/history.shtml.

Pankalanka *see* Jogung

Paradise Parrot

The paradise parrot (*Psephotus pulcherrimus*) was an unusually colorful, medium-sized parrot native to the border region between Queensland and New South Wales, Australia. Once moderately common, living in pairs or small family groups, the BIRDS nested near ground level in hollowed-out termite nests and similar places, feeding primarily (if not exclusively) on grass seeds. The parrot's plumage mingled aqua, black, brown, turquoise and scarlet hues. Human incursions on the parrot's habitat, including livestock overgrazing and land clearance by fire, drastically reduced the birds numbers through the late 19th century and early 1900s. Many experts thought the parrot extinct by 1915, and the last confirmed sighting was recorded on 14 September 1927. Subsequent searches found no evidence of survivors, but once again, as in so many other cases, unconfirmed sightings have continued to the present day. The Queensland Parks and Wildlife Service launched a formal but unconventional search in October 2000, seeking not the birds themselves, but rather a species of moth known to feet on the parrot's droppings. The search was unsuccessful.

Source: Karl Shuker, "Alien zoo." *Fortean Times* 140 (December 2000): 23.

Parainen Island sea serpent

In June 1978, a SEA SERPENT was sighted by multiple witnesses on Parainen, largest island in the Turunmaa Archipelago, offshore from Turku, in southwestern Finland. Descriptions of the unknown creature generally conformed to those of other large pelagic cryptids reported through the ages from Scandinavian waters.

Source: Bord and Bord, *Unexplained Mysteries of the 20th Century*.

Paré/Peri

This unclassified HOMINID or WILDMAN of Central Asia features in the folklore of Iran, the Caucasus Mountains of Russia and the Pamirs of Tajikistan. Its territory thus overlaps that of the ALMAS, DAV and KAPTAR, which may be identical. A curious historical footnote concerns the alleged use of Parés as subhuman soldiers during the Avestan age (ca. 600–300 B.C.)

Source: Heuvelmans and Porshnev, *L'Homme de Néanderthal est Toujours Vivant*.

Parkers Cove carcass

On 17 September 2002, a decomposing carcass washed ashore at Parkers Cove, near Annapolis Royal, Nova Scotia. Media reports described the creature as 32 feet 6 inches long, with "a long neck and a small skull." Grant Parker, who discovered the remains, told reporters, "I believe this is the remnant of an animal from times gone by." Two scientists from Halifax, Chris Harvey-Clark and Andrew Hebda, thought otherwise, pronouncing the remains those of a basking SHARK (*Cetorhinus maximus*).

Sources: Kevin Cox, "N.S. townspeople see monster in carcass of basking shark." *The Globe and Mail* (18 September 2002); "Experts dismiss town's sea monster claims." *Ananova* (19 September 2002).

Parker's snake

For the best part of a quarter-century, herpetologists have debated the identity of an unclassified venomous SNAKE, said to inhabit the Western Province of Papua New Guinea. Fred Parker was the first to report its existence, in 1982, with descriptions of three human fatalities inflicted around Wipim during 1972–73. The victims were all children, who died more swiftly than expected from the bite of any known snake on the island. Parker described the snake as a 6-foot aquatic species, with smooth scales and a relatively short tail. Despite its deadly reputation among New Guinea natives, no specimen has yet been killed or captured.

Source: Fred Parker, *The Snakes of Western Province*. Port Moresby: Papua New Guinea Department of Lands and Environment, 1982.

Partridge Creek Monster Reports of animals resembling living DINOSAURS typically emerge from some tropical wilderness, but this rare exception comes from the Klondike region of northwestern Canada's Yukon Territory. It first saw light in April 1908, when alleged eyewitness George Dupuy published his story in the French journal *Je Sais Tout*. The tale began in 1903, when James Butler and Tom Leemore were tracking three large moose near Clear Creek, 100 miles east of Dawson. The hunters were ready to fire, when their quarry suddenly bolted in panic. When they reached the spot, Butler and Leemore found the impressions of a huge animal pressed into the swampy ground. Those tracks included a furrow 30 feet long, 12 feet wide and 2 feet deep, flanked by clawed footprints 5 feet long and 2.5 feet wide, trailing drag marks from a tail 10 feet long and 16 inches wide. The men followed those tracks to a deep gully known as Partridge Creek, where the trail abruptly ended.

Following that aborted adventure, Butler and Leemore made their way to a trading post on Armstrong Creek, home to the Rev. Pierre Lavagneux, where Butler had agreed to meet George Dupuy for a hunting expedition. Though initially skeptical, Dupuy agreed to join the others in a renewed search for the yet-unseen Partridge Creek monster. Accompanied by the Rev. Lavagneux and several Indians, the hunters returned to Partridge Creek and were setting up camp when a shattering roar sent them scrambling for their rifles. Moments later, they saw an animal 50 feet long, black in color, with a horn on its snout and gray bristles like those of a wild boar sprouting from its hide. The creature walked on all fours at first, then reared onto its hind legs before roaring again and retreating into the ravine. The Rev. Lavagneux compared the animal to *Ceratosaurus*, a Jurassic relative of *Tyrannosaurus rex*, known from fossil remains since 1883 and presumed extinct for at least 140 million years.

Dupuy published the story only after receiving a letter from the Rev. Lavagneux, dated 25 December 1907, which described another sighting of the animal. According to that letter, Lavagneux and 10 of his Indian parishioners had seen the beast on Christmas Eve, racing through the snow with a full-grown caribou

Witness George Dupuy described the Partridge Creek monster as resembling a *Ceratosaurus*.

clamped in its jaws. As KARL SHUKER notes, the Yukon's frigid winter landscape (with temperatures of -45°F on the day of Lavagneux's alleged sighting) should be fatal even for a dinosaur that somehow sprouted hair. No other sightings of the Partridge Creek Monster are recorded, and the case appears to be a HOAX on par with the lone sighting of Papua New Guinea's ROW.

Sources: George Dupuy, "Le monstre de 'Partridge Creek.'" *Je Sais Tout* 39 (15 April 1908): 403–409; Shuker, *In Search of Prehistoric Survivors*.

Pascagoula River, Mississippi Various published sources include this river, in southeastern Mississippi, on lists of supposed aquatic cryptid habitats. Those listings seem plausible enough, since the Pascagoula flows into the GULF OF MEXICO, but none of the authors provide any dates or details of sightings.

Sources: Bord and Bord, *Unexplained Mysteries of the 20th Century*; Coleman, *Mysterious America*; Kirk, *In the Domain of the Lake Monsters*.

Passaic Falls, New Jersey Authors LOREN COLEMAN and JOHN KIRK include Passaic Falls, at Peterson, New Jersey (Passaic County) on published lists of supposed LAKE MONSTER habitats. Unfortunately, neither provides any dates or details of sightings. The listings apparently are not garbled references to a pair of ALLIGATORS found in the Passaic River on 11 September 1933, since Coleman treats that case separately in his text.

Sources: Coleman, *Mysterious America*; Kirk, *In the Wake of the Sea Serpents*.

Passenger Pigeon The story of the passenger pigeon (*Ectopistes migratorius*) is a cautionary tale for environmentalists worldwide. The 16-inch BIRDS, with blue-gray dorsal plumage and cinnamon-pink undersides, were once the most abundant birds on Earth, so numerous in North America that their passage literally blocked out the sunlight, filling the air with a thunder of beating wings. In the early 1800s, one flock observed in transit between Indiana and Kentucky measured one mile wide and 240 miles long. The arrival of white settlers and their firearms proved disastrous for the passenger pigeon, as millions were wantonly blasted from the sky for food and "sport." Ohio hunter Press Southworth claimed dubious honors by shooting the last confirmed wild specimen on 24 March 1900. Fourteen years later, on 1 September 1914, the last captive specimen died at Cincinnati's Zoo and the species was officially extinct.

That avian holocaust, however, has not prevented sporadic sightings around the eastern U.S. In October 1907, West Virginia resident A.B. Elbon allegedly sighted a flock of 500 passenger pigeons at Elk Mountain, but his report went unconfirmed. Robert Wright claimed a close-range sighting of two birds on 10 June 1929, near Munising in Alger County, Michigan. Three months later, Dr. Philip Hadley and a companion saw a lone passenger pigeon in the same region of Michigan's upper peninsula. Faced with skepticism, Hadley insisted that he recognized the bird from specimens seen in his youth, and he went on to document several more alleged sightings. Two more encounters were reported in 1965, from Homer, Michigan and Park Ridge, New Jersey. Skeptics insist that witnesses have been deceived by glimpses of mourning doves (*Zenaida macroura*) or band-tailed pigeons (*Columba fasciata*), and cryptozoologist KARL SHUKER agrees that passenger pigeon survival is unlikely, since the birds' mating ritual involved massed gatherings in large flocks. In Shuker's view, the scattered stragglers missed by gunmen could not have rallied or adapted their instinctive behavior in time to save the species from extinction.

Sources: Bille, *Rumors of Existence*; Errol Fuller, *Extinct Birds*. Ithaca, NY: Cornell University Press, 2001; Philip Hadley, "The passenger pigeon." *Science* 71 (1930): 187.

Pathfinder Reservoir, Wyoming

While some Wyoming lakes have LAKE MONSTER traditions dating from the 19th century, the sole report to date from Pathfinder Reservoir (40 miles southwest of Casper) is of much more recent vintage. In 1983, two visitors reported seeing a large FISH of unknown species, with two humps visible on its back. No further sightings are on record, and the incident remains unexplained.

Source: *Casper Star-Tribune* (7 April 1983).

Patterson Film

Ex-rodeo cowboy Roger Patterson's life changed forever in December 1959, when he picked up a copy of *True* magazine and read an article on SASQUATCH by IVAN SANDERSON, titled "The Strange Story of America's ABOMINABLE SNOWMAN." Instantly captivated by the BIGFOOT mystery, Patterson created the Northwest Research Association (based at his home in Yakima, Washington) and in 1966 published a book titled *Do Abominable Snowmen of America Really Exist?* The following year, he began work on a documentary film about Bigfoot, working with a friend, Robert Gimlin. In September 1967, while Patterson and Gimlin were searching the forests around Mount Saint Helens, Patterson's wife Patricia took a call from friends in Willow Creek, California. There, in the same region where Bigfoot had earned his famous nickname nine years earlier, contacts described the recent discovery of HOMINID footprints in three different sizes, suggesting a possible Sasquatch family. Patterson and Gimlin swiftly agreed to shift the location of their search.

In preparation for the California trip, Patterson rented a Kodak 16mm movie camera, described in various reports as either a K-100 or a K-200 model. When he had not returned the camera by 18 October, its owner filed a complaint with local police. Two days later, Patterson and Gimlin were riding on horseback through the Six Rivers National Forest, following a rocky creek bed. As they rounded a large pile of logs, the men suddenly beheld a large Sasquatch, clearly female from its pendulous breasts, standing nearby in the open. Patterson reached for his camera, stowed in his left saddle bag, while his horse shied and fell to the ground. Gimlin, meanwhile, drew his .30–06 rifle and held it ready to fire if the creature attacked. With camera in hand, Patterson started filming from a range of 112 feet, while running toward the Sasquatch. At 81 feet he stumbled and fell, then resumed filming as the creature retreated into the forest. Further progress on foot was arrested when the Sasquatch turned to stare at Patterson. He later told GROVER KRANTZ, "It looked at me with such an expression of contempt and disgust, that I just stayed right there." Or, as he told JOHN GREEN, "You know how it feels when the umpire tells you, 'One more word and you're out of the game'? That's the way it felt." He kept filming, though, until his camera ran out of film with the Sasquatch 265 feet away. Before the film ran out, Patterson exposed 952 frames.

What happened next remains a source of controversy. Various published accounts claim that both men followed the creature for 30 feet, 150 feet or three miles before losing its trail in the woods. Gimlin, in a November 1967 radio interview, denied any pursuit, saying simply that Patterson remained afoot at the scene while he (Gimlin) "watched her until she went up the road about 300 yards, and she went around a bend in the road and that was the last I seen of her." The Sasquatch left a series of 10 large footprints, 14.5 inches long and 6–9 inches wide (again, reports differ). Patterson allegedly filmed the tracks, but that film has been lost. He also made plaster casts of at least two footprints. Researcher Lyle Laverty visited the scene and photographed the tracks on 21 October. Tracker and taxidermist ROBERT TITMUS arrived eight days later and made casts of all 10 footprints, later reporting that four showed "clear evidence" of prior casting when he reached the scene. (Patterson insisted that he made only two casts on 20 October.) Titmus also followed the creature's trail and reported evidence that it had stopped 125–150 yards from the scene of the encounter, to watch its pursuers from hiding. (Titmus also told Krantz that the initial confrontation occurred at a range of 25 feet, but that estimate fails to mesh with the other evidence.)

Only a handful of scientists agreed to view the film, and most of those quickly denounced it as a fake. The movie screened in various small-town theaters around the Pacific Northwest, while Patterson grew increasingly discouraged. Over the next four years, increasingly short of cash while he waged a losing fight against Hodgkin's disease, Patterson sold various rights in the film to different investors. Around 1970, word came from a contact in Thailand that a Sasquatch-type creature was held captive at a remote Buddhist monastery. Patterson planned an expedition with Krantz to see the creature, spending most of his savings before he learned the report was a HOAX. Patterson died soon after that final disappointment, in 1972.

Meanwhile, the controversy surrounding his film lived on. In 1969, John Green showed the film to Ken Peterson, a senior executive at Disney Studios, who said that his special-effects could not produce a fake monster of such quality. Two years later, RENÉ DAHINDEN showed the film to a pair of experts in the biomechanics of human locomotion, Dmitri Donskoy in Moscow and Donald Grieve in London. Donskoy opined that the film showed

The Patterson film, depicting an alleged female Sasquatch, remains shrouded in controversy after four decades.

a massive animal, in no sense human, whose stride was more efficient than a human's. Grieves rendered a split decision: if the film was made at 24 frames per second, he reported, its subject could be a man in an APE suit, walking rapidly; if filmed at 18 frames per second, however, it "exhibits a totally different pattern of gait" from any human being. Therein lay a problem, for Patterson's rented camera had *two* speeds. While he normally filmed at 24 fps, Patterson claimed that sometime after his Bigfoot encounter, he found the camera set at 18 fps (perhaps from his fall on 20 October). That raised a further problem, though, because the camera in question had no 18 fps setting: its listed speeds were 24 and *16* feet per second. Years later, Grover Krantz obtained a statement from Kodak that their camera settings were approximate and might be off by 10 percent. Krantz himself ran tests with one camera that filmed at 19 fps while set at 16 fps.

The film's speed is crucial to determining the subject's height. Patterson estimated that the creature he filmed was seven feet tall. Tests performed by Krantz and others showed that subject size varied radically with increasing film speed. At 16 fps, the creature in Patterson's film would stand between 7 feet 4 inches and 8 feet six inches; at 18 fps, its height could range from 5 feet 9 inches to 7 feet 4 inches; while at 24 fps it would be a puny 3 feet 8 inches to 4 feet 2 inches. Krantz (and most others) finally settled on a height around 6 feet 7 inches, which coincided with the creature's 81.5-inch stride. Russian researchers DMITRI BAYANOV and Igor Bourtsev, reporting in 1972, agreed that the film was most likely exposed around 16 fps. (In the process, Bayanov nicknamed the female Sasquatch "Patty," after Patterson's surname.) Primate biologist JOHN NAPIER, though convinced of Bigfoot's existence, raised a loud voice of dissent. While admitting that he "could not see the zipper" of an ape suit, Napier maintained that either the film or Patty's footprints (and perhaps both) were faked.

Trouble dogged the film after Patterson's death. Yakima businessman Albert DeAtley Jr. loaned Patterson money to fund a documentary in 1967, thus becoming a partner in Bigfoot Enterprises. The loan was unpaid in 1970, when Patterson's terminal illness was diagnosed, and DeAtley wrote the debt off, giving his share to his brother-in-law. Gimlin sued DeAtley and Patricia Patterson for his share of the proceeds in 1975, and the case was settled out of court for an undisclosed amount. In 1991, Nevada private investigator Clyde Reinke spoke to Bigfoot researcher Peter Guttilla, claiming that Patterson had faked his film while "on the payroll" of American National Enterprise (ANE), a production company that released several nature films in the 1970s. Reinke claimed that he "signed Patterson's checks," though none ever surfaced. He also named three ANE employees who allegedly helped fake the movie, and that ANE "made millions" from the film. Guttilla interviewed the men and reported that Reinke's leads were "dead ends." In fact, Patterson had negotiated with ANE for use of his film in a documentary titled *Bigfoot— Man or Beast*, but that occurred in 1971 and marked his only contact with the studio.

Meanwhile, Canadian investment counselor Chris Murphy approached René Dahinden (owner of still-photo rights in the film), offering to serve as his promoter/manager. They worked together for a time, until Murphy launched a series of unauthorized publications, including claims that computer enhancement of the film showed several Sasquatch "babies" lurking in the trees behind Patty. Dahinden then severed all ties to Murphy, while Murphy schemed to discredit the film publicly. He was not alone in that

effort, as the 20th century drew to a close. Major attacks on the Patterson film in the past decade include:

Summer 1996— Mark Chorvinsky, a magician and editor of *Strange Magazine*, published claims that Hollywood monster-maker JOHN CHAMBERS designed an ape suit for Patterson in 1967. The story, cited as "common knowledge" in Tinsel Town, still circulates despite a total lack of evidence and explicit denials from Chambers in 1997.

August 1998— In a program on Bigfoot, producers of the *X-Creatures* series blatantly misquoted Robert Gimlin, claiming that he "now believes the film may be a hoax" perpetrated by Patterson without his knowledge. In fact, as Gimlin told the press in 1999, "I was there. I saw it. The film is genuine."

December 1998— Fox Television aired a program titled *World's Greatest Hoaxes*, including the Patterson film in that genre. The "evidence" included repetition of Clyde Reinke's discredited charges (with Reinke now billed as a "former ANE executive"), and UFO researcher Karl Korff's assertion that primates do not have a crease down their backs such as Patty displays on film. (In fact, they all do. It is a standard piece of primate anatomy, marking the juncture of large back muscles.) Korff identified insurance agent Jerry Romney as "the man in the suit," but no supporting evidence was offered and Romney denied any role in the film's production.

January 1999— A news report by Joseph Rose quoted Sasquatch researcher CLIFF CROOK's claim that a metallic object resembling "a belt buckle" is visible on Patty in digitally-enhanced frames of the Patterson film. Chris Murphy did his best to publicize that claim. Controversial researcher JON-ERIK BECKJORD soon chimed in with claims that he saw a "metal tube" on Patty's arm. To date, no other viewers of the film have spotted these or any other anomalous objects dangling from the creature's body.

February 1999— Washington attorney Barry Woodard announced that an unnamed client from Yakima donned an ape suit to portray Patty in 1967. Now, Woodward told reporters, the man wished to sell his story and planned a lawsuit to recover the costume. Woodard claimed that his client had passed a polygraph test and said, "We anticipate that we will be telling the full story to somebody rather quickly." The rest is silence.

November 2001— Internet posters launched a new round of claims that "digitized" versions of the film reveal several juvenile Sasquatches, including one in Patty's arms (apparently invisible to the naked eye). Within 24 hours, a self-described financier of the project admitted, "It is possible that I have been the victim of a hoax being perpetrated by the person supposedly involved in digitizing the Patterson film." No more is heard of the "exciting breakthrough."

November 2002— Following the death of notorious Bigfoot hoaxer RAYMOND WALLACE, his family declared that Wallace "told Patterson where to go" in October 1967. Within hours, media sources distorted the initial (unsupported) claim and aired reports that Wallace's wife donned an ape suit to portray Patty. Thus far, no evidence supporting any of the Wallace claims has been revealed.

April 2003— LOREN COLEMAN returned from London with news that "definitive proof is in the works" to show that Patterson faked his film. He noted that "[t]his could be earth-shaking, if it pans out." In fact, those airing the claims proved to be Karl Korff and others involved in the December 1998 Fox-TV broadcast. "Full details" were promised in a forthcoming book, with a preview scheduled for 20 October 2003, but that date passed without revelations.

September 2003— Mary Gwinn, book reviewer for the *Seattle Times*, announced publication of a new book written by Mill Creek, Washington author Greg Long. Entitled *The Making of Bigfoot: The Inside Story*, Long's tome allegedly "delivers the skinny on Roger Patterson," whose "footage was exposed as a hoax last year [*sic*]." Still, at its belated release in summer 2004, Long's book produced no proof of a hoax, relying instead on hearsay "evidence," backed by a strident e-mail campaign, which failed to persuade veteran researchers.

1 March 2004— Greg Long appeared on Jeff Rense's syndicated radio show, promoting his "explosive new exposé." Long identified Washington resident Bob Heironimus as "the Man Who Wore the Bigfoot Suit" for Patterson, while denouncing Bob Gimlin as an active accomplice to the hoax. The still-missing costume was allegedly created by one Philip Morris, whom Long described as "an expert in GORILLA suits" and "the only one in the U.S. who was making gorilla suits for the public in 1967." Heironimus confessed the hoax and hired attorney Barry Wood in 1999, Long claimed, because he felt that Patterson had cheated him of proceeds from the film. No proof of that claim was forthcoming, in print or otherwise, and promises of a big-budget TV production based on Long's book remained unfulfilled at press time for this volume.

Sources: Bayanov, *America's Bigfoot: Fact, Not Fiction*; Byrne, *The Search for Bigfoot*; Clark and Pear, *Strange & Unexplained Phenomena*; Coleman, *Bigfoot!*; Coleman and Clark, *Cryptozoolgy A to Z*; Mary Gwinn, "Down times, good times." *Seattle Times* (14 September 2003); Krantz, *Bigfoot Sasquatch Evidence*; Roger Knight e-mail message (7 January 2004), http://www.bigfootforums.com; Jeff Rense interview with Greg Long (1 March 2004), http://www.soundwaves2000.com/rense/archives.html.

Patuxent River, Maryland

In 1933, witnesses reported a "DRAGON" swimming in the lower reaches of this Maryland river. No detailed description of the creature has survived, but the sighting occurred near the Patuxent's confluence with Chesapeake Bay, where a SEA SERPENT known as CHESSIE is sometimes reported, and 20-odd miles from the alleged habitat of another aquatic cryptid dubbed POTOMAC PATTY. It may be that sightings of all three creatures involve the same animal, or members of the same species. Alternatively, mislocated ALLIGATORS have also been seen in Maryland's rivers on several occasions.

Source: Alain Dessaint (ed.), *Historical Tours through Southern Maryland Today*. La Plata, MD: Southern Maryland Today, 1983.

Pauca Billee

In 1868, the *Naturalist's Note Book* published the following brief report from a correspondent known only as "R.B.W.":

A nondescript animal, said to be a flying CAT, and called by the Bhells *pauca billee*, has been shot by Mr. Alexander Gibson, in the Punch Mehali [India]. The dried skin was exhibited at the last meeting of the Bombay Asiatic Society. It measured 18 inches in length, and was quite broad when extended in the air. Mr. Gibson, who is well known as a member of the Asiatic Society and a contributor to its journal, believes the animal to be really a cat, and not a BAT or flying-FOX, as some contend.

No other record of the Pauca Billee exists, and the fate of its preserved skin is impossible to trace after so much time has elapsed. (See also CATS [WINGED].)

Sources: R.B.W., "Flying cat." *Naturalist's Note Book* 5 (1868): 318; Shuker, *From Flying Toads to Snakes with Wings*.

Pauline sea serpent

On 8 July 1875, sailors aboard the barque *Pauline* witnessed an extraordinary spectacle in the South Atlantic, while sailing 20 miles off Cap São Roque, Brazil. Captain George Drevar described the event in his log.

The weather fine and clear, wind and sea moderate. Observed some black spots on the water, and a whitish pillar, about thirty feet high above them. At the first glance I took all to be breakers as the sea was splashing up fountain-like about them, and the pillar a pinnacle of rock, bleached with the sun; but the pillar fell with a splash, and a similar one rose. They rose and fell alternately in quick succession, and good glasses showed me it was a monstrous SEA-SERPENT coiled twice around a large sperm-whale. The head and tail parts, each about thirty feet long, were acting as lever, twisting itself and victim round with great velocity. They sank out of sight aboutevery two minutes, coming to the surface still revolving; and the struggles of the whale and two other whales, that were near, frantic with excitement, made the sea in their vicinity like a boiling cauldron; and a loud and confused noise was distinctly heard. This strange occurrence lasted some fifteen minutes, and finished with the tail portion of the whale being elevated straight in the air, then waving backwards and forwards, and lashing the water furiously in the last death struggle, when the body disappeared from our view, going down head foremost to the bottom, where no doubt it was gorged at the serpent's leisure; and that monster of monsters may have been many months in a state of coma, digesting the huge mouthful. Then two of the largest sperm-whales that I have ever seen moved slowly thence towards the vessel, their bodies more than usually elevate out of the water, and not spouting or making the least noise, but seeming quite paralyzed with fear; indeed, a cold shiver went through my own frame on beholding the last agonizing struggle of the poor whale that had seemed as helpless in the coils of the vicious monster as a small BIRD in the talons of a hawk. Allowing for two coils round the whale, I think the serpent was about 160 or 170 feet long, and 7 or 8 feet in girth. It was in colour much like a conger-EEL; and the head, from the mouth being always open, appeared the largest part of its body.

Far from lying comatose, however, the same SEA SERPENT or its twin appeared once more to the *Pauline*'s crew only five days later. As Captain Drevar described the event, "At seven a.m., July 13, in the same latitude, and some eighty miles east of San Roque, I was astonished to see the same or a similar monster. It was throwing its head and about 40 feet of its body in a horizontal position out of water as it passed onwards by the stern of the vessel." Drevar surmised that a white stripe painted on the *Pauline*'s hull "might have looked like a fellow-serpent to it, and, no doubt attracted its attention. As I was not sure it was only our free board it was viewing, we had all our axes ready, and were fully determined, should the monster embrace the *Pauline*, to chop away for

The *Pauline* sea serpent battles a sperm whale.

its backbone with all our might, and the wretch might have found that for once in its life that it had caught a Tartar."

The animal did not attack, however, and the *Pauline* sailed away intact. A similar battle was viewed four years later, near Japan, by sailors aboard the *KIUSHIU MARU*, and while BERNARD HEUVELMANS believed the whale's opponent in the latter contest was a GIANT SQUID, he concluded that the *Pauline*'s crew had seen a monstrous eel.

Source: Heuvelmans, *In the Wake of the Sea Serpents*.

Pé de Garrafa   The Pé de Garrafa ("bottle foot") is a supposed primate or HOMINID of Brazil's rain forests, so called because its round footprints resemble the mark of a bottle pressed into soft earth. Some legends claim the creature only has one leg, but most accounts agree on its ferocious nature. When seen, the Pé de Garrafa (also known throughout its range as Kubê-rop and Pelobo) is described as five feet tall and covered in dark hair, sometimes roaring fiercely. Various witnesses have confirmed the existence of such odd tracks, noting that they swerve off-course to avoid obstacles, but their author remains elusive. BERNARD HEUVELMANS compared the round prints to a series of "Devil's hoofmarks" found in snow across Devon, England on the morning of 9 February 1855 and still unexplained to this day. He did not propose that one cryptid had leapt from England to Brazil, however. Rather, Heuvelmans proposed "a meteorological origin as Dr. Maurice Burton has suggested might be the cause…though no meteorologist has been able to put forward a phenomenon that would explain them." In fact, James Rennie *did* suggest "freakish air currents" as the cause of Devon's snowy hoofprints, but wind would hardly produce deep, round impression in soil or mud.

Sources: Heuvelmans, *On the Track of Unknown Animals*; Rui Prado Mendonça Jr., "Pé de Garrafa." *Caça e Pesca* (December 1954).

Peak Panther   This ALIEN BIG CAT has been reported from the Peak district of Derbyshire, England since the mid-1980s. Witnesses describe a classic "black panther," 4–5 feet long, with a glossy coat, drooping tail and small ears. A mass police search around Hayfield, in 1989, failed to corner the CAT, and it was seen on two successive days at Chapel-en-le-Firth, by witness Dennis Morley, in January 1994. The second time, Morley declared, the cat appeared to have a RABBIT in its mouth. More sightings from the region were logged in 1998.

Sources: Sieveking, "Beasts in our midst"; Sieveking, "Nothing more than felines."

Pedal Fish   In September 1995, while fishing at a lake near Guaracai, Brazil (northwest of São Paulo), Paulino Clemente hooked a curious 5-inch specimen with only one gill, barbels like a CATFISH, and small legs sprouting from its sides. Aside from its strange appearance, the FISH caught Clemente's attention by living more than 15 minutes out of water. Biologist Angela Pereira Garcia examined the specimen and declared that it was not a mutant, nor did it belong to any known species. The fish's legs, Pereira found, were fully articulated. "It is not a case of a defective fin," she said, "but of a useful component, since there is a membrane between the toes." Pereira surmised that the fish relied on air to live, and may have left the water to breathe at frequent intervals. Thus far, no other specimens have been collected.

Source: "Fish caught walking underwater." *Fortean Times* 86 (May 1996): 40.

Pedmore Puma   This ALIEN BIG CAT of Britain's West Midlands (also called the Beast of Belbroughton and the Cadley Cat) has been sighted repeatedly since the turn of the 21st century. The first sighting of a "wildcat" was logged in July 2000, and four months later it was blamed for injuries suffered by a Belbroughton pony. Sightings then ceased until autumn 2002, when a large CAT resembling a COUGAR (*Puma concolor*) was seen at Cradley and Halesowen. Curiously, the next cat reported by witnesses around Pedmore and Cradley, between 15 January and 5 February 2003, was jet-black. Unnamed "experts" speculated that the cat could be a cougar, leopard (*Panthera pardus*) or jaguar (*Panthera onca*), though melanistic cougars are unknown to science. Inspector Geoff Tomkins of the Dudley South Police cautioned locals to avoid contact with the animal(s), while adding that "it does appear it's fairly timid and keeps away from people." The *Stourbridge News*, meanwhile, offered to purchase any photos of the creature snapped by amateur big-game hunters.

Source: "Big cat shock for car driver." *Express & Star* (25 January 2003).

Peel Street Monster   During the winter of 1933–34, residents of Peel and Brickkiln Streets in Wolverhampton, England were terrorized by a creature resembling a giant rat, which attacked and bit several small children and snapped at the throat of one adult pursuer. On 18 January 1934, 17-year-old George Goodhead saw the "miniature monster" lurking in a vacant lot on Brickkiln Street. As he later described the experience, "I went and saw a queer animal, far too big for a rat, leaping towards a child about five year[s] old. I shouted and the thing turned on me. It crouched, its eyes bulging, then it leaped like lightning." Snatching up a handy brick, Goodhead brained the creature, after which a crowd of locals gathered and stomped it to death. A parade of naturalists, taxidermists and veterinarians examined the animal, but none were able to identify more than its gender (male). Within 24 hours of Goodhead's adventure, a female "monster" was found dead in the same general area, this one identified as a female coatimundi (*Nasua nasua*), a South American relative of the raccoon with no known history of aggression toward humans. Rumors of a basement-breeding "monster" colony prompted hectic searches, but no more unusual creatures were found, and the female coati was absolved of any link to the rampage when locals learned that its carcass had been discarded by a traveling circus. The Peel Street predator remains unidentified.

Sources: The Peel Street Monster Hunt, http://www.westmidlands.com/millennium/1900/1925–1949/1934.html.

Pegrand Lake, Nevada   Multiple books and Internet websites include this supposed Nevada lake on lists of alleged LAKE MONSTER habitats, but none provide any dates or details of alleged sightings. Strangely, while the rumors must have started somewhere, extensive research reveals no such lake in Nevada (or anywhere else, for that matter). Perhaps some early author garbled the name of PYRAMID LAKE, while others listed the name without checking their sources.

Sources: Bord and Bord, *Unexplained Mysteries of the 20th Century*; Coleman, *Mysterious America*; Kirk, *In the Domain of the Lake Monsters*; Nevada Lakes, http://www.parksandtourism.net/dir/Nevada_Lakes/index.shtml; USGS, http://waterdata.usgs.gov/nv/nwis/current/?type=lake.

Peninsula Python   In 1944, this large SNAKE of indeterminate species visited the Cuyahoga River valley, between Cleveland and Akron, Ohio. The first sighting was logged on 8 June, when farmer Clarence Mitchell reported an 18-foot serpent crawling through his cornfield. Mitchell made no attempt to kill or capture the reptile, whose sinuous track was as wide as an auto tire. On 10 June, John and Paul Szaly found similar tracks on their farm, but no snake was seen. Two days later, Mrs. Roy Vaughn summoned firefighters after the snake invaded her chicken coup and devoured a hen, but the culprit escaped before help arrived. Rumors circulated that a carnival truck had crashed in the region two years earlier, presumably releasing a captive PYTHON, but herpetologists could not explain a tropical snake's survival through two Ohio winters, and extensive research by LOREN COLEMAN failed to document the accident. Zookeepers in Cleveland and Columbus offered rewards for the snake, if captured alive, but their money was safe. A mass search around Kelly Hill, on 25 June, failed to corner the reptile, but it surfaced two days later, to frighten Pauline Hopko and scatter her terrified milk cows. On 29 June, Mrs. Ralph Griffin met the snake in her backyard, reporting that it reared up cobra-like, five feet off the ground. Scattered sightings continued along the Cuyahoga into early autumn, but posses were always too late or too slow to catch up with the snake. Whether it froze that winter in some unknown lair or crawled away to find a warmer climate, the Peninsula Python did not reappear in Ohio.

Sources: Robert Bordner, "The Peninsula Python: An absolutely true story." *Atlantic Monthly* 176 (November 1945): 88–91; Coleman, *Mysterious America.*

Penistone Panther

This ALIEN BIG CAT derived its name from Penistone Road in New Mill, Yorkshire, England, where it was sighted for the first time on 16 April 1996. Scattered sightings continued through September of that year, with witnesses including Eric Vawser, former chairman of the Penistone Conservative Association. Some locals and reporters also called their resident prowler the Beast of Broomhill. A 3-foot-long decomposed felid carcass found at Cat Hill, near Barnsley, proved to be a large domestic CAT.

Source: Sieveking, "Watch out: Big cat about."

Pennock Island sea serpent

Pennock Island lies at the southern end of Alaska's Alexander Archipelago, near Ketchikan. On 8 May 1947, Lauri Carlson and a companion were rowing around the island's north point when a strange animal suddenly surfaced, 25 feet away from their small boat. Carlson described the creature's head as resembling a cow's only smaller. It was mounted on an 8-inch neck, and when the animal submerged seconds later, a line of fins resembling a serrated crest was visible along its back. The witnesses declined to guess its length. BERNARD HEUVELMANS noted the animal's resemblance to descriptions of the SEA SERPENT known farther south as CADBOROSAURUS.

Source: Heuvelmans, *In the Wake of the Sea Serpents.*

Pennsylvania Association for the Study of the Unexplained

The PASU was founded in September 1981, by Greensburg residents Stan Gordon and George Lutz, recruiting 35 members by May 1982. Gordon was already well known among UFO researchers, active in that field since age 13 (in 1965), but the group also pursued reports of SASQUATCH-type HOMINIDS and other cryptids sighted throughout Pennsylvania. The PASU ceased operation in November 1993, but Gordon moved on to serve as a consultant with the Paranormal Society of Pennsylvania.

Sources: Marcia Dunn, "Association investigates unexplained." *Las Vegas Review-Journal* (14 May 1982); Paranormal Society of Pennsylvania, *http://home.supernet.com/~rfisher/contact.html.*

Pennsylvania Bigfoot Society

Greensburg, Pennsylvania native Eric Altman's fascination with BIGFOOT began at age 10 and broadened into active research four years later, inspired by a meeting with Stan Gordon (director of the PENNSYLVANIA ASSOCIATION FOR THE STUDY OF THE UNEXPLAINED). In 1999, Altman joined Steve Anderson and Henry Benton to create the Pennsylvania Bigfoot Society. Altman currently serves as the group's director and doubles as a consultant on SASQUATCH phenomena for the Paranormal Society of Pennsylvania. The PBS sponsors an annual East Coast Bigfoot Conference, featuring guest speakers and discussions of sightings reported from the eastern U.S. Membership dues are $20 per year, or $30 for a family membership, which includes subscription to the quarterly *Keystone Sasquatch Report.* The PBS also maintains an active Internet website where sightings may be reported. In February 2003, after a Crawford County sighting, members searched the woods around Guy Mills but found no evidence. Still, Altman remains optimistic. "I'm 95 percent sure they are real," he told reporters in November 2003. "I have seen footprints in the snow and mud. I have talked with hundreds of witnesses who obviously are shaken up by what they have seen. I think there is something out there. What we are trying to do is prove it or disprove it."

Sources: Scott Westcott, "Does Bigfoot live in Pennsylvania's woods?" *Erie* (PA) *Times News* (16 November 2003);Pennsylvania Bigfoot Society, *http://www.pabigfootsociety.com/*; Paranormal Society of Pennsylvania, *http://home.supernet.com/~rfisher/contact.html.*

Pensacola sea serpent

Pelagic cryptids are rarely described as aggressive toward humans, but a first-person story published in *Fate* magazine (May 1965) cast the SEA SERPENT in a different light. The report, titled "Escape from a Sea Monster," was written by 19-year-old college student Edward Brian McCleary and professed to describe an attack that claimed four human lives. Cryptozoologist TIM DINSDALE investigated the report and received the following letter from McCleary in July 1965:

On the 24th of March, 1962, off the coast of Pensacola, Florida, a "skin-diving" accident occurred. I was the lone survivor of the five on the trip. We were in an Air Force rescue raft bound for a sunken ship a few miles off the coast. When the storm cleared, we were in a dense fog, therefore not knowing our position or the direction of the shore. We, or rather I was later informed, were 5 miles out. After sitting for about an hour, we began to hear strange noises, rather like the splashing of a porpoise or other large fish [*sic*]. Accompanying the noise was a sickening odor like that of dead FISH. The noise got closer to the raft and it was then we heard a loud hissing sound. Out in the fog we saw what looked like a long pole, about 10 feet high, sticking straight up out of the water. On top was a bulb-like structure. It bent in the middle and went under. It appeared several more times getting closer to the raft each succeeding time. Many people, at this point, do not understand why we abandoned the raft....

What happened to us is that we became terror stricken; in an open raft in a March fog miles off the coast with an unknown terror lurking near us. The wisest thing to do would have been to stay in the raft, but we were too terrified to think clearly. Now that I am safe I still wonder if I should have stayed.

After we were in the water we became split up in the fog. From behind I could hear the screams of my comrades one by one. I got a closer look at the thing just before my last friend went under. The neck was about 12 feet long, brownish-green and smooth looking. The head was like that of a sea-TURTLE, except more elon-

Artist's conception of the Pensacola sea serpent attack described by Edward McCleary (*William Rebsamen*).

gated, with teeth (I am not positive of this. It looked as if there were teeth on the gums.) I did not see any fins, although there appeared to be what looked like a dorsal fin when it dove under for the last time. Also, as best I am able to recall, the eyes were green with oval pupils.

I finally made it to the ship, the top of which protruded from the water, and stayed there for most of the night. Early that morning I swam to shore and was found by the rescue unit.

Fact or fiction? Dinsdale seemed inclined to accept the story as true, while BERNARD HEUVELMANS suspected a HOAX (or at least exaggeration on McCleary's part). Only one person knows the final truth, and McCleary was untraceable at press time for this volume.

Sources: Dinsdale, *Monster Hunt*; Heuvelmans, *In the Wake of the Sea Serpents*.

Pentland Skerries sea serpent   The Pentland Skerries are four small, uninhabited islands found in the eastern Pentland Firth, midway between Scotland's northernmost tip and the Orkney Islands. On 9 September 1937, the *Orcadian* newspaper published the report of John R. Brown, occasional lighthouse keeper, concerning a SEA SERPENT he observed near the islands. Brown's story read:

It was about noon when we were working down at the landing at the East End that on chancing to look out to sea I noticed the sea breaking white as on a submerged rock. As I knew there were no rocks in that particular spot, I watched for a little and presently a great object rose up out of the water — anything from 20 to 30 feet and at an angle of about 45°. It was round-shaped and there appeared to be a head on it, but as it was about half a mile from the shore I could not be sure.

I called the attention of the other two men but unfortunately before they got their eyes on the spot it had disappeared again, though both of them saw the foam it had made. We watched for a considerable time but it never appeared again.

I have seen what fishermen call a killer whale's [*Orcinus orca*] fin rise high out of the water, often, but the fin of a Killer resembles the sail of a boat and is easily recognized whereas this object was definitely round-shaped.

Source: Dinsdale, *Monster Hunt*.

Penwith Puma   This ALIEN BIG CAT of Cornwall, England made its first appearance in the Trevaylor Woods, near Penwith, in November 1999. That said, it was hardly the first CAT to

trouble residents of Cornwall, where the BEAST OF BODMIN MOOR has long been a notorious visitor.

Source: Sieveking, "Nothing more than felines."

Pepson Island sea serpent   On 11 March 1952, the Agence France-Presse released the following news bulletin through media outlets in Tokyo, Japan.

A SEA-SERPENT 50 feet long and 3 feet thick is at present being hunted by Korean zoologists. This monster is said to live on Pepson Island, 15 miles off Pusan [South Korea], where it is believed to have eaten an 18-year-old girl last year. Korean scientists are preparing special electrical instruments with which they hope to catch it.

Regrettably, no further reports on this intriguing case were published, and the outcome of the hunt (if it ever occurred) remain unknown.

Source: Heuvelmans, *In the Wake of the Sea Serpents*.

Perez, Daniel (1963–)   California native Daniel Perez became fascinated with SASQUATCH at age 10, after viewing a film on the FOUKE MONSTER, *The Legend of Boggy Creek*. Six years later, he founded the still-active Center for BIGFOOT Studies and published the first issue of the *Bigfoot Times* newsletter. Though employed full-time as an electrician, Perez remains a self-described "super active investigator" and claims that he has "been to more alleged Bigfoot filming sites than anyone in the world." In 2002, he visited Russia and interviewed several renowned hominologists, including DMITRI BAYANOV, Igor Bourtsev, Vadim Makarov and Mikhail Trachtengerts. Perez has published three books on Sasquatch, including *The Bigfoot Directory* (1986), *Big Footnotes: A Comprehensive Bibliography Concerning Bigfoot, the Abominable Snowman and Related Beings* (1988), and *Bigfoot at Bluff Creek* (1994). At press time for this volume, he was reportedly writing another book on the PATTERSON FILM.

Sources: Coleman and Clark, *Cryptozoology A to Z*; Center for Bigfoot Studies, http://www.bigfoottimes.com; Daniel Perez, My Russian Trip, Bigfoot Encounters, *http://www.n2.net/prey/bigfoot/articles/perez_russia.htm*.

Perth sea serpent   In October 1900, officers and crew aboard the *Perth* reportedly saw a SEA SERPENT in the Indian Ocean off Fremantle, Western Australia. *Wide World Magazine* reported that the creature's description "confirmed every detail" of a creature sighted from the *NEMESIS* that same year, but the report was otherwise vague and the magazine gave the *Perth*'s captain different names (Campbell and Grant) in successive issues. BERNARD HEUVELMANS treated the case as a possible HOAX.

Source: Heuvelmans, *In the Wake of the Sea Serpents*.

Perugia Marsh Monster   In 1933–34, reports of a vaguely-described "water monster" issued from marshlands surrounding Perugia, Italy (100 miles north of Rome). Those marshes are linked to the sea by the TIBER RIVER, which encouraged speculation on the advent of a misdirected SEA SERPENT, but no further reports have been filed from the region.

Source: Bord and Bord, *Unexplained Mysteries of the 20th Century*.

Peruvian Wildcat   Witnesses describe this unclassified CAT as roughly the size of a domestic cat, with tabby coloring and canine teeth above average length. It reportedly inhabits montane forests in Peru's Cuzco Department, along the Río Urubamba, and allegedly breaks the established behavioral pattern of all other New World cats by forming packs of 10 or more to hunt BIRDS and small rodents. (Similar stories are told in Guyana of the much larger WARACABRA TIGER.) Piro tribesmen also claim that ocelots (*Felis pardalis*) and jaguarundis (*F. yagouaroundi*) sometimes join these hunting packs to comb the jungles for prey, though the notion sounds fanciful.

Source: Hocking, "Large Peruvian mammals unknown to zoology."

Peter Pond Lake, Canada *see* Puff

Pewaukee Lake, Wisconsin
Several sightings of a large, green LAKE MONSTER were reported from this Waukesha County lake in the 1890s, but no modern reports are on file.

Sources: Brown, *Sea Serpents: Wisconsin Occurrences of These Weird Water Monsters*; Garner, *Monster! Monster!*; Mackal, *Searching for Hidden Animals*.

Philomel sea serpent
On 14 October 1879, sailors aboard the British ship H.M.S. *Philomel* met an unfamiliar animal in the Red Sea's Gulf of Suez. As the ship's commander described the creature:

When first observed it was rather more than a mile distant on the port bow, its snout projecting from the surface of the water, and strongly marked ripples showing the position of the body. It then opened its jaws, as shown in the sketch, and shut them again several times, forcing the water from between them as it did so in all directions in large jets. From time to time a portion of the back and dorsal fin appeared at some distance from the head. After remaining some little time in the above-described position, it disappeared, and on coming to the surface again, it repeated the action of elevating its head and opening the jaws several times, turning slowly from side to side as it did so.

On the approach of the ship the monster swam swiftly away, leaving a broad track like the wake of a ship, and disappeared beneath the waves.

The colour of that portion of the body that was seen was black, as was also the upper jaw. The lower jaw was grey round the mouth, but of a bright salmon colour underneath (like the belly of some kinds of lizard) becoming redder as it approached the throat. The inside of the mouth appeared to be grey with white stripes, parallel to the edges of the jaw, very distinctly marked. These might have been rows of teeth, or some substance resembling whalebone. The height the snout was elevated above the water was at least fifteen feet, and the spread of the jaws quite twenty feet.

BERNARD HEUVELMANS speculated that the creature was "a large whale of known species," but he offered no specific candidates. Author Charles Gould, meanwhile, speculated that it might have been a giant FISH, somehow related to the small deep-sea dweller *Eurypharynx pelecanoides*.

Source: Heuvelmans, *In the Wake of the Sea serpents*.

Philomena sea serpent
On 18 August 1912, Boston fishermen aboard the *Philomena*, commanded by Captain John McKinnon ("one of the best known mackerel killers on the coast") reportedly fought and slew a SEA SERPENT off Cape Porpoise, Maine. A front-page story in the *Gloucester* (Mass.) *Daily Times* described the event six days later.

A small school of mackerel in the seine boat were pulling in the seine when a commotion was noticed among the FISH, and the sea serpent, which had evidently been under the seine, made its appearance alongside the boat to the alarm and disgust of the crew, who had never seen anything like it before....[I]t became entangled in the seine, tearing it to pieces, and then started off at a 2.40 gait with the boat, seine and everything in tow, all the mackerel estimated at about 40 barrels, getting away.

Seeing that something was wrong, the fishing steamers *Victor*

and *Ethel*, which were fishing in the same location, came to the assistance of the *Philomena*'s men and a pretty stiff fight ensued, the combined crews of the three steamers joining in the attack on the serpent, knives, boat hooks, clubs and anything that came handy being used.

At last one of the *Philomena*'s men armed with a knife a foot long reached a vital spot, and after a great splashing the serpent succumbed. Capt. McKinnon describes the sea monster as being from 50 to 60 feet in length, its body which resembled in size and shape an immense tree trunk being black with rough skin covered with barnacles. It had what the fishermen call a hammer head and an immense fin on the back resembling a leg of mutton sail and nearly as large.

The skipper was afterwards sorry that he did not tow the serpent into port, but with a badly exhausted crew and a wrecked seine he concluded it best to cut him adrift. Called "Big Ben" by the fishermen, and dreaded by them so much that they invariably pulled up stakes when he put in an appearance, he has been seen every summer along the coast for many years, although its existence has been doubted by many.

Needless to say, McKinnon's tale did nothing to resolve such doubts, though he confirmed the story as accurate two decades later. Whatever the truth of the matter, "Big Ben" or his offspring continued to appear off the New England coast for 80-odd years after the *Philomena*'s rare adventure.

Source: O'Neill, *The Great New England Sea Serpent*.

Phoenix sea serpent
In March 1840, Captain Samuel Fears of the schooner *Phoenix*, en route from Gloucester to Boston, saw a broken mast floating in Massachusetts Bay. Planning to haul it aboard for salvage, Fears was shocked when the "mast" raised its head and rudely thrust out a long tongue. The SEA SERPENT dived and vanished seconds later, leaving only a vague impression of its massive size.

Source: O'Neill, *The Great New England Sea Serpent*.

Pi *see* Yeti

Piasa
In Native American folklore, the Piasa was a giant predatory BIRD with a taste for human flesh. Illinois chief Ouatoga and 20 warriors allegedly cornered and killed the monster (or one of them), and their victory was commemorated in a petroglyph overlooking the Mississippi River near present-day Alton, Illinois. The first European explorer to see the cliff painting, on 1 August 1673, was Father Jacques Marquette. His journal, published in 1681, described the Piasa as 30 feet long and 12 feet tall, with a deer's head and antlers, a man's face with a TIGER'S beard, red eyes, the wings and talons of a raptor, and a long tail like a FISH'S that encircled the body. The whole monstrous picture was painted in three colors: red, black and bluish-green. Marquette estimated the painted creature's wingspan at 16–18 feet.

No reliable sketch of the Piasa petroglyph remains, and the original no longer exists, a victim of erosion, random target practice by settlers, and a quarrying operation that shattered the cliff face in 1856. Herbert Forcade painted a new version of the creature on bluffs overlooking Alton's West Broadway in 1924, but that in turn was leveled in the 1960s. A 3-ton metal replica stood on Norman's Landing, 2 miles west of Alton, from 1983 to 1995. The latest version, painted by volunteers of the American Legends Society in 1998, now serves as the centerpiece of Piasa Park (opened in 2001).

What (if anything) was the Piasa? In 1877, author Perry Armstrong speculated that the legend may have been founded on tribal memories of a relict PTEROSAUR, an idea studied and accepted by some later cryptozoologists. Others, including MARK HALL, suspect that the Piasa may represent the predatory THUNDERBIRD described in other aboriginal legends. In any case, as KARL SHUKER observes, preparation of the original petroglyph involved a substantial investment of time and energy for the artists, a labor unlikely if the Piasa had been a wholly imaginary monster.

Sources: Perry Armstrong, *The Piasa, or The Devil Among the Indians.* Morris, IL: E.B. Fletcher, 1877; George Priest, *The Great Winged Monster of the Piasa Valley: The Legend of the Piasa.* Dallas: The Author, 1998; Shuker, *In Search of Prehistoric Survivors.*

Pig Man

The Pig Man is a southern equivalent of BIGFOOT or SASQUATCH, said to inhabit southeastern Georgia's Okefenokee Swamp. Local residents sometimes distinguish between this shaggy biped and the similar SKUNK APE or BOOGER Man, both likewise reported from the swamp, but any difference seems to lie in regional jargon, rather than physical distinctions.

Source: Michelle Delio, "Having a gas in Okefenokee Swamp." Wired News, *HTTP://WWW.WIRED.COM/NEWS/ROADTRIP/0,2640,61284,00.HTML.*

Pigfoot

In summer 2002, residents of Greenwich Township, New Jersey (Cumberland County) reported sightings of a 600-pound hog with 3-inch tusks roaming the streets of their community and its surrounding woods. Police were repeatedly summoned, but the porcine prowler vanished each time before they arrived, making officers feel "like they were looking for a ghost." Public appeals to the hog's unknown owner went unanswered, and authorities reported that the region had no swine farms. By autumn, the elusive porker had been nicknamed Pigfoot, and a dogcatcher warned locals that since the animal had not been castrated, it "could not only be amorous but also aggressive." Sharon Kiefer met Pigfoot while walking her dogs one morning. "It was pretty scary," she told reporters afterward. "It must have been lying flat. When we rounded the bend, it started rising up out of the woods. I know I screamed loudly. Its ears are the size of a football, and they bend inward and they are real furry. It's white, like a ghost pig or something. It ran as fast as my dogs. Now that's scary." Pigfoot's luck ran out on 12 December 2002, when it visited the Hancock Harbor Marina, on the Cohansey River. Marina owner Scott Gifford and two companions lassoed the hog, then wrestled it into a small fenced yard. "It was a battle all the way," observer Martin Morse told reporters. "He was bucking and squealing." Still, by the following day, Gifford declared, "He's a gentle as a lamb. You can walk up to him and feed him an apple." As for Pigfoot's ultimate fate, a spokesperson for Cumberland County's Society for the Prevention of Cruelty to Animals said, "Best-case scenario, he'll be re-

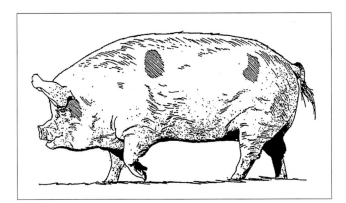

New Jersey's Pigfoot proved to be a large stray hog.

turned to wherever he escaped from." At press time for this volume, Pigfoot's owner had not been identified.

Sources: Adam Fifield, "New Jersey's mystery hog captured." *Philadelphia Inquirer* (13 December 2002); "Pig Foot sightings have Cumberland County town hog wild." Associated Press (12 December 2002); Luis Puga, "Residents beware the Greenwich pig." *The Press of Atlantic City* (12 December 2002); Brian Uzdavinis, "Pigfoot captured at Hancock Harbor." *The Press of Atlantic City* (14 December 2002).

Pikelian

The Pikelian is an unclassified HOMINID reported from the Magadan Region of Siberia. Natives there describe the creature as a large, omnivorous, cave-dwelling biped, covered entirely in grayish-brown hair. Aside from its regional name, there is little (or nothing) to distinguish the Pikelian from other unknown hominids across Siberia, including the ALMAS, CHUCHUNAA, KÉÉDIEKI, KHEYAK, KILTANYA, KUL, MECHENY, MIRYGDY, TUNGU or ZEMLEMER.

Source: Bayanov, *In the Footsteps of the Russian Snowman.*

Pink Eye

This aquatic cryptid, reported from the North Saskatchewan River in Alberta, Canada, derives its name from eyewitness descriptions of its pink or red eyes. The animal made its first appearance in April 1939, pursuing Chief Walking Eagle as he crossed the river near Rocky Mountain House. The chief described his assailant as 50 feet long, with an elephant's girth. Three years later, on 22 July 1942, some boys swimming in the river were startled when a "floating log" came alive, thrashing the water with a long, muscular tail. Around the same time, author JOHN KIRK reports that a creature resembling OGOPOGO was sighted, swimming downstream with six smaller (presumably juvenile) specimens. No sightings are on record since that final incident.

Sources: Benedict, "The unknown lake monsters of Alberta"; Kirk, *In the Domain of the Lake Monsters*; "River 'monster' sends swimmers scrambling." *Calgary Herald* (24 July 1942); "Rocky Mountain terror." *Calgary Herald* (27 July 1942); "Water monster scares Indians at Rocky Mountain House." *Calgary Herald* (29 April 1939).

Pink-Headed Duck

The pink-headed duck (*Rhondonessa caryophyllacea*), identified in 1790, once inhabited India and adjoining regions of Bangladesh, Myanmar and Nepal. Its common name derived from the male's distinctive pink head, with a lighter grayish-pink in females. As with the DODO, the PASSENGER PIGEON and so many other species, the arrival of white settlers spelled disaster, and the ducks were hunted to presumed extinction by 1936. Speculation on its possible survival persists, however, and a specimen was definitely shot at Manroopa Lake, in India's Bihar State, on 27 January 1947. The hunter who killed it, L.P. Singh, claimed several more sightings at Manroopa Lake during 1948–49, but the ducks managed to stay out of range. Game warden K.L. Mehtra claimed two sightings of a male specimen in Haryana State, south of Simla, in February 1960. Four decades later, in 1998, Tibetan forestry reported a sighting 100 miles south of Lhasa, near the border of Bhutan. British researchers Peter Gladstone and Charles Martell explored the area but found no evidence of surviving pink-headed ducks.

Sources: Errol Fuller, *Extinct Birds.* Ithaca, NY: Cornell University Press, 2001; Rory Nugent, *The Search for the Pink-Headed Duck.* Boston: Houghton Mifflin, 1991.

Pinky

Florida's St. Johns River is sometimes called "the American Nile." It is one of the few U.S. rivers that flow northward, meandering from Brevard County's Lake Hell 'n' Blazes (in SKUNK APE territory) through a chain of lakes and swamps before it broadens and veers eastward to meet the sea at Jacksonville, 310 miles from its headwaters. Beginning in the 1950s, Jacksonville newspapers carried reports of a large, unknown creature lurking in the St. Johns. A decade later, while bow hunting along the river, biology student Mary Lou Richardson and two companions glimpsed an amphibious beast with a flat head and relatively short neck, later compared by IVAN SANDERSON to a donkey-sized DINOSAUR. Four other groups of tourists reported sightings the same afternoon, and inquiries revealed that the animal was well known to local residents.

Still, the creature excited little comment outside Florida and did not win its now-famous nickname until May 1975, when five boaters near the river's mouth encountered a startling specimen. Witness Dorothy Abram compared the thing to "a dinosaur with its skin pulled back so all the bones were showing...[and] pink, sort of the color of boiled shrimp." Its head was the size of a human's or larger, sprouting knobby, snail-like horns or antennae. Its eyes were dark and slanted, while flaps resembling fins or gills dangled below the 3-foot neck. Companion Brenda Langley agreed with Abram's general description, adding that the creature reminded her of a DRAGON. Newspapers dubbed the animal Pinky, and so it remains, though earlier accounts made no apparent reference to color.

Sanderson and MARK HALL suggest that Pinky is a relict dinosaur, with Hall proposing *Thescelosaurus*, an 11-foot bipedal reptile that lingered in North America to the late Cretaceous period (65 million years ago). KARL SHUKER suggests that a more likely candidate may be an unknown giant SALAMANDER, perhaps related to Japan's *Megalobatrachus japonicus* (attaining lengths of 5 feet 6 inches). Other possibilities, proposed by skeptics, run the full gamut from floating logs to manatees (*Trichechus manatus*) and Atlantic sturgeons (*Acipenser oxyrhynchus*).

Sources: Coleman, "The colour of mystery"; Mark Hall, "Pinky, the forgotten dinosaur." *Wonders* 1 (December 1992): 51–59; "New monster haunting river called 'Pinky.'" *Arkansas Gazette* (12 June 1975); Steve Reudiger, "Pink 'sea monster' lurks in river, rattles fishermen." *Jacksonville Times-Union* (16 May 1975); Sanderson, "The five weirdest wonders in the world"; Shuker, *In Search of Prehistoric Survivors*.

Piranha (Mislocated)

Piranhas rank among the Earth's most notorious FISH. Ten species are recognized, divided into four genera. All are native to warm lowland rivers and lakes of South America, east of the Andes, where they hunt in schools and have a reputation for devouring much larger animals in gruesome feeding frenzies. Adults of various species range from 6 to 24 inches long, with colors running a gamut from yellow and red through steel-gray, blue and near-black. Piranhas are renowned for their bulldog profile and bristling teeth, but they are also frequently mistaken for their inoffensive relatives, the pacus (*Colossoma* and *Piractus*). The species most commonly exported for aquariums is the red-belly piranha (*Pygocentrus nattereri*). Various U.S. states, from California to Texas and Florida, ban private ownership of piranhas, and several other nations have followed suit, but legal restrictions have not stopped the fish from surfacing in at least 13 states since the 1970s. Stateside captures of piranha in the wild include:

Florida— One fish taken from a borrow pit linked to Snapper Creek in Miami (1974); one piranha caught at Lake Mabo, Boca Raton, prompting authorities to kill all fish in the lake with rotenone (4 April 1979); one specimen pulled from a canal west of Fort Lauderdale, in Broward County (date unknown); reports of piranha pulled from the Tamiami Canal (1969–79) are unconfirmed.

Hawaii— Piranhas were initially reported from Wahiawa Reservoir, on Oahu, in June 1992, but the first specimen (a mature female) was caught eight months later (23 February 1993).

Indiana— A 2.5-pound piranha was caught at Griffy Lake, near Bloomington (July 2001).

Massachusetts— A 5-inch piranha was taken from Lexington Reservoir, Middlesex County (3 August 1981); a 5.7-inch specimen was caught at Island Grove Pond, in Abingdon (August 1984); one piranha was caught in a pond near Westminster (22 July 1985); another was found in Horn Pond, at Woburn (summer 1993).

Michigan— A piranha was found dead on the shore of an unnamed lake near Ann Arbor (1977).

Minnesota— A single specimen was taken from Duban Lake, in Rice County (July 1993); another was caught at Simley Pond, in Dakota County (August 1998).

Ohio— One piranha was pulled from the Rocky River near London, Madison County, with a second specimen observed but not captured (August 1975).

Nebraska— A 12-inch specimen was caught at Harlon County Lake, in Republican City (September 1987); three more piranhas were found, near death from cold, in the Lincoln County drain near North Platte (January 2000).

Oklahoma— A 6.6-inch piranha was found dead in Theta Pond, on the campus of Oklahoma State University in Stillwater (12 November 1993).

Pennsylvania— According to the U.S. Geological Survey, "one, or possibly more reports came from an unspecified locality or localities" in the 1980s.

Rhode Island— Media reports describe a piranha caught in the Flat River Reservoir, at Coventry Center (summer 1991).

Texas— A 5-inch piranha weighing 119 grams was taken from the Boerne City Reservoir, in Kendall County (1991).

Virginia— A piranha was caught at Indian Lake, a borrow pit near Virginia Beach (22 August 1987).

All piranhas found in U.S. waters are assumed to be deliberate releases from private aquariums, but there is no obvious reason why the prolific fish should not be able to reproduce in warm climates. Indeed, reports indicate that the proprietors of a Florida amusement park established a small breeding colony of black piranha (*Serrasalmus rhombeus*) in an outdoor pond. Wildlife officials list the impact of piranha introduction in the U.S. as "unknown," but the discovery of even one such fish commonly produces panic in small towns. Specimens caught in Alabama and California, initially identified as piranhas, have thus far proved to be look-alike pacus on closer examination.

Outside the U.S., piranhas have been caught in China, England, France and Russia. The fish were introduced to China's Dalian Ocean Amusement Park in 1985, but subsequent private purchases caused official alarm. While no releases have been publicized, the Chinese government banned further imports of piranhas in December 2002, imposing fines equivalent to $6,250 on violators. Two piranhas were pulled from the Garonne River, in France, during 1991. Five years later, two more adults measuring 14 and 18 inches were caught at Lac de la Ganguise, a French holiday resort 30 miles southeast of Toulouse. Despite the number of misplaced piranha caught to date, Russian fisherman Boris Belov is apparently the only human casualty. In June 2000, he was bitten by a specimen he hooked from Staraya Surka Lake, near the village of Polyana Surskovo in the Volga region. Belov froze the fish and gave it to authorities, who imposed a local ban on swimming. On 17 February 2004, a 4-inch red-belly piranha fell onto the deck of a Thames riverboat at Dagenham, East London. The freshly-killed fish was apparently dropped by a seagull flying overhead.

Sources: Bord and Bord, *Unexplained Mysteries of the 20th Century*; "China bans flesh-eating piranha fish." Beijing Times (28 December 2002); Pat Hurst, "'Man-eating' piranha drops in on a Thames barge." *The Scotsman* (19 February 2004); "I think I've got a bite." Fortean Times 93 (December 1996): 11; "Seriously out of place." Fortean Times 141 (January 2001): 7; Bethany Swaby, "Strange fish caught at Griffy Lake." *Bloomington* (IN) *Herald Times* (11 July 2001); Caribe Amarillo, *http://www.angelfire.com/biz/piranha038/rhombeus.html*; USGS, *HTTP://CANAL.ER.USGS.GOV/QUERIES/SPFACTSHEET.ASP?SPECIESID=429*.

Piranu   This name was generically applied during the 19th and early 20th centuries to freshwater cryptids reported from various rivers across the pampas region of central Argentina. Eyewitness descriptions of the Piranu resembled those of LAKE MONSTERS familiar from parts of North America and Europe, with a head resembling a horse's and large, soulful eyes. In that respect, at least, the Piranu bore no likeness to Argentina lake creatures resembling PLESIOSAURS, reported from scattered locations during the same time frame.

Source: Juan Ambrosetti, *Supersticiones y Leyendas.* Buenos Aires: La Cultura Argentina, 1917.

Pitt Lake Dragons   Pitt Lake lies 10 miles northeast of Burnaby, British Columbia, in the crowded southwest corner of the province. At first glance, it seems an unlikely hunting ground for cryptozoologists, but in fact it has produced reports of two distinct and separate cryptids. One, the PITT LAKE GIANT, is considered separately. The other is reportedly a species of large, unidentified lizards reaching lengths of five feet or more, sporting horns on their heads. Hikers Warren and Sharon Scott claim to have met the reptiles in June 1973, capturing several small (presumably juvenile) specimens while avoiding the larger ones. Warren says he sent one of the lizards, preserved in alcohol, to the Simon Fraser University's biology department, but no reply was forthcoming. When the story went public in March 1978, the university denied ever seeing the lizard. JOHN KIRK notes that the Scott's have since "disappeared," and their tale remains impossible to verify. Skeptics insist that the story is either a HOAX or an exaggerated description of the Pacific giant SALAMANDER (*Dicamptodon tenebrosus*), which reaches a maximum length of 11 inches. Suggestions that the Scotts met a group of mislocated ALLIGATORS are likewise unconvincing, since the "DRAGONS" reportedly inhabited a woodland valley *near* Pitt Lake, but clearly separated from the water.

Sources: "Is a lost world waiting to be found near Pitt Lake?" *Vancouver* (B.C.) *Province* (12 May 1978); Kirk, *In the Domain of the Lake Monsters*; Shuker, *From Flying Toads to Snakes with Wings*.

Pitt Lake Giant   Thirteen years before stories of the PITT LAKE DRAGONS first made headlines, residents of southwestern British Columbia were already familiar with another cryptid said to inhabit the region. Witnesses describe the Pitt Lake Giant as shaggy HOMINID 10–15 feet tall, with long arms and a massive torso. Its 4-toed footprints surpass the average BIGFOOT'S in size, measuring up to 24 inches long and 12 inches wide. On 28 June 1965, prospectors Ron and Loren Welch allegedly followed a set of those tracks through the woods near Pitt Lake to a smaller icebound lake, where they sighted the creature itself. They managed to draw a sketch of the beast before it turned and walked away into the forest.

Sources: Green, *On the Track of the Sasquatch*; Green, *Sasquatch: The Apes Among Us*; Hunter and Dahinden, *Sasquatch*.

***Planet* sea serpent**   On 7 September 1839, sailors aboard the schooner *Planet* met a SEA SERPENT while en route from Sag Harbor to Kennebec, Maine. While 30 miles offshore from Seguin, Captain David Smith and his men had a "distinct view" of the creature, as it passed within 40 feet of the ship. As later described in the press:

> They could see his whole length. His color and shape were very nearly like a black SNAKE, without anything that looked like fluke or fins. Most of the time he had his head out of the water four or five feet. He was as long as the schooner, about 70 feet, and his body appeared as large as a barrel, but smooth — nothing like bunches on his back, as some have described him. They were probably deceived by his undulatory or wriggling motion in swimming, his back appearing above the water at regular distances.

Captain Smith had a harpooner on board, but he spared the creature's life in knowledge that he lacked the lines required to haul it ashore.

Source: O'Neill, *The Great New England Sea Serpent*.

Platypus (Pelagic)   The platypus (*Ornithorhyncus anatinus*) is an amphibious montreme (egg-laying mammal) native to eastern Australia and the island of Tasmania. It is instantly recognizable for its ducklike bill, webbed feet, and tail resembling that of a BEAVER. It also possesses a venomous spur on its hind legs that may be used in self-defense. Adult males typically measure 18–24 inches in length. These creatures are unusual enough, but cryptozoologist BOBBIE SHORT has collected an even stranger report of an apparent pelagic platypus sighted in coastal waters near Mountain Point, Alaska (south of Ketchikan). The witness,

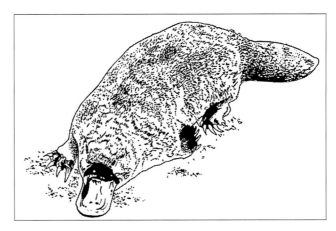

Witnesses report a marine platypus from the Alaskan coast.

described as "an experienced commercial fisherman," said the creature — observed in shallow water for about one minute — was six feet long, dark in color, with an obvious "bill" and webbed feet. No mention was made of a tail, but the witness "stated categorically that it was not a known species of seal." A pelagic, cold-water platypus three times the size of the largest known Australian specimen surely qualifies as a mysterious "unknown."

Source: "Marine platypus." *North American BioFortean Review* 3 (2000): 10–11.

Plesiosaurs   The plesiosaurs (Order *Plesiosauria*) were marine reptiles of Jurassic and Cretaceous periods (213–65 million

Plesiosaurs came in various shapes and sizes, from the long-necked *Elasmosaurus* to ferocious *Kronosaurus*.

years ago). Contemporaries of the DINOSAURS, they are not classified as members of that order. Plesiosaurs are recognized by their long-necked form, described by 19th-century paleontologist Dean Conybeare as "SNAKES threaded through the bodies of TURTLES." Known species ranged from 7 feet 6 inches (*Plesiosaurus*) to 46 feet long (*Elasmosaurus*), and swam with four flippers, two on either side of the body. A superfamily of pliosaurs evolved from plesiosaurs, with shorter necks and massive heads, ranging in length from 15 feet (*Macroplata*) to 42 feet (*Kronosaurus*).

Almost from the moment their first fossils were discovered, in the 19th century, relict plesiosaurs have been proposed to explain sightings of various long-necked SEA SERPENTS and LAKE MONSTERS. The SURGEON'S PHOTOGRAPH of Scotland's NESSIE emphasized the resemblance to a plesiosaur, and while skeptics argue that reptiles could not survive in cold-water lakes or seas, debate over reptilian evolution and theoretical warm-blooded dinosaurs leaves the question open. (As late as 2001, investigator ROBERT RINES remained convinced that Nessie was, in fact, a plesiosaur.) Tropical climates offer a more hospitable habitat for large reptiles (assuming any survived into historic times), and zoologist CLEMENTE ONELLI organized an expedition to seek surviving plesiosaurs in Argentina, during the early 1920s. None were found, but occasional sightings continue, with reports of the long-necked creature known as NAHUELITO filed from Patagonia in 1989.

One of the most surprising plesiosaur reports comes not from South America or Africa, but from England. Esteemed British author Harold Wilkins was strolling with a friend along a creek near East Looe, Cornwall, at 11:30 a.m. on 5 July 1949, when he met "two remarkable saurians." The creatures were 15–20 feet long and precisely resembled museum reconstructions of plesiosaurs, with "bottle-green" heads. "What was amazing," Wilkins noted, "was their dorsal parts: ridged, serrated, and like the old Chinese pictures of DRAGONS. Gulls swooped down towards the one in the rear, which had a large piece of orange peel on its dorsal parts." Wilkins and his friend swiftly retreated, leaving the reptiles to deal with the gulls on their own.

Through the years, many "long-necked" carcasses or GLOBSTERS have been stranded on beaches throughout the world, sometimes hailed as the remains of plesiosaur-type "prehistoric monsters." Thus far, most of those subjected to scientific testing have proved to be basking SHARKS (*Cetorhinus maximus*), which often decompose to offer the appearance of a long neck and small, reptilian head.

Sources: Costello, *In Search of Lake Monsters*; Keel, *The Complete Guide to Mysterious Beings*; Magin, "Duck! It's a plesiosaur"; Shuker, *In Search of Prehistoric Survivors*.

Plumper* sea serpent On 10 April 1849, the *Illustrated London News* published a letter from an unnamed officer of the British naval ship H.M.S. *Plumper*, describing an encounter with a SEA SERPENT some three months earlier. It read:

On the morning of the 31st December 1848, in lat. 41° 13' N. and long. 12° 31' W., being nearly due west of Oporto [Portugal], I saw a long black creature with a sharp head, moving slowly, I should think about two knots [2.3 miles per hour], through the water, in the north westerly direction, there being a fresh breeze at the time, and some sea on. I could not ascertain its exact length, but its back was about twenty feet if not more above water; and its head, as near as I could judge, from six to eight. I had not time to make a closer observation, as the ship was going six knots [7 mph] through the water, her head E. half S., and wind S.S.E.

The creature moved across our wake towards a merchant barque on our lee-quarter, and on the port tack. I was in hopes she would have seen it also. The officers and men who saw it, and who have served in parts of the world adjacent to whale and seal fisheries, and have seen them in the water, declare they have neither seen nor heard of any creature bearing the slightest resemblance to the one we saw.

There was something on its back that appeared like a mane, and, as it moved through the water, kept washing about; but before I could examine it more closely, it was too far astern.

RUPERT GOULD later examined the *Plumper*'s log, confirming its location and the sighting of a merchant ship on the date in question, but the record contained no mention of unknown animal. Still, BERNARD HEUVELMANS accepted the sighting as genuine, though lamentably vague on details.

Source: Heuvelmans, *In the Wake of the Sea Serpents*.

Po di Goro, Italy A 10-foot "SNAKE with legs," black in color, was reported from this lake, in Italy's Emilia-Romagna district, on 27 June 1975. The animal was never caught, but local "experts" insisted that it must be an "escaped CROCODILE." As to where the elusive reptile theoretically escaped from, the rest is silence.

Sources: Bord and Bord, *Unexplained Mysteries of the 20th Century*; Edoardo Russo, "Meanwhile in Italy: The Goro monster." *Pursuit* 35 (Summer 1976): 62.

Pollyanna* sea serpent In late May 1930, Captain Cecil Moulton and 22 sailors aboard the schooner *Pollyanna* allegedly met a SEA SERPENT off Georges Bank, Massachusetts. A local newspaper described the creature as "a 150-foot something with a head like a horse and poised above a smooth sea…like a huge EEL, moving at least 10 knots [11.5 miles per hour] and never casting an eye on the schooner. It disappeared to the westward still going strong when last seen. The thing was a greenish-black with a buff underbody and about the size of a gasoline drum through its middle." Unnamed "old-timers" reportedly dismissed the sighting as a mistake involving a school of porpoises.

Source: O'Neil, *The Great New England Sea Serpent*.

Ponik Lake Pohénégamook, located almost on the border between Canada and Maine, has been called "the Loch Ness of Québec." Its cryptic denizens are not the most famous Québecois LAKE MONSTERS— that honor still belongs to CHAMP, of Lake Champlain — but the creature(s) known as Ponik have appeared sporadically since the 1870s. An unnamed lumberjack reportedly glimpsed one of the animals in 1874, and a short time later, farmer Benôit Levasseur "saw something 25–30 feet long plunge twice, and then it was lost in the water." Alex Bélanger saw the beast in 1900, and many hunters subsequently tried to shoot Ponik from canoes, all in vain. Around 1913, a logging boss named Noë Ducharme went fishing for Ponik with specially-made hooks, but his bait (meat and cheese) disappeared each time while the hooks snared nothing.

After those early showings, Ponik faded from view until May 1957, when Philippe Gagné and his wife saw a 15-foot creature with a fishlike head splashing in the adjacent St.-François River. A short time later, the Rev. J.-Leopold Plante, of St.-Éleuthère, saw "a long overturned canoe crossing the lake, leaving a wake behind." In 1958, the Québec Department of Game and Fisheries sent Vadim Vladykov to investigate recent sightings. Vladykov interviewed witnesses, creating a composite of a brown or black creature 12–35 feet long, with a serrated ridge or fin along its back. Sadly, Vladykov's report vanished from government files in 1960, after he left Québec for the University of Ottawa. Sightings continue to the present day, including multiple reports in 1976–77 of a black animal 20–25 feet long, with a three humps on its back. A sonar trace of Ponik, 25 feet long and swimming 25 feet below the surface, was obtained in summer 1977. The "overturned canoe" description echoed in another sighting from November 1979, while the most recent report (from 3 August 1998) described a 25-foot creature with a long, high dorsal fin.

Proposed explanations for the sightings at Lake Pohénégamook run the gamut from outright HOAXES to mistakes involving floating logs, mislocated seals, swimming deer or moose, and wandering Atlantic sturgeon (*Acipenser osyrhyncus*). Sturgeon are not native to the lake, but Vadim Vladykov reported that several local residents had released captive FISH in the lake, hoping to launch a local caviar industry. The fish may live 50–55 years, and grow quite large: a 14-foot specimen was caught in New Brunswick, in 1924. The sturgeon's back also presents a serrated appearance that might seem reptilian to some observers, but veteran fishermen around Lake Pohénégamook insist that they are not deceived by any normal fish, regardless of its size. The mystery endures.

Sources: Mangiacopra, "Canada's La Bête du Lac"; Meurger and Gagnon, *Lake Monster Traditions*; Thomas Pawlick, "Québec's answer to the Loch Ness monster." *Harrowsmith* 4 (January 1980); Nick Thomas, "'Something' (maybe) lurks in the depths of a Quebec lake." *Wall Street Journal* (17 November 1977).

Pontsticill Puma   Details concerning this ALIEN BIG CAT of Wales are regrettably sparse. Sightings were reported in the 1990s, with a farmer at Mid Glamorgan who saw the beast from 12 feet away describing it as 3 feet long and "sleek."

Source: "Catalogue of Wales' weird cats." BBC News (26 August 2000).

Poomoola   In the first half of the 19th century, a BIGFOOT-type HOMINID known as Poomoola reportedly inhabited forests around Mount Katahdin, in northern Maine's Baxter State Park. Legends claim that the creature subsisted on FISH, which it devoured alive. It also allegedly killed Indians, while avoiding white settlers, and thus earned the alternate nickname "Injun Devil."

Source: Green, *Sasquatch: The Apes Among Us.*

***Poonah* sea serpent**   In December 1878, the British liner *Poonah* was en route from England to India, via the Suez Canal and Red Sea, when passengers aboard reportedly saw a SEA SERPENT. The only witness to report the sighting was a certain Mrs. Turner, wife of a Calcutta banker, who could not recall if the ship was anchored off Suez (in the Red Sea) or Aden (in the Gulf of Aden) when the incident occurred. From that vague beginning, a friend of Mrs. Turner, Robert Greg, described the event to ANTOON OUDEMANS as follows:

She says it almost exactly resembled the marine animal seen by the officers of the OSBORNE, 2 June 1877, of Sicily, only it had no flippers (being motionless); and she saw both the head and 7 or 8 fins

The *Poonah* sea serpent.

on the back, all at the same time in a line. She cannot remember exactly how many dorsal fins there were, but they were large, slightly curved back and not all the same size. She did not notice any eyes or mouth, seeing it for such a short time, and being so much surprised at its size and a glimp [*sic*]. The head looked 4–6 feet in diameter, like a large tree trunk say at 150 feet. The head was very glumsy [*sic*] and thick, and very like the butt end of a cannon, as shown in Lieut. Haynes['s] drawing…and without the flippers, which at once very strongly reminded her of the animal she saw. The colour was nearly black like a whale. The whole length appeared considerable, perhaps as long as a ordinary tree, or moderate sized ship! The fins were very large.

Source: Heuvelmans, *In the Wake of the Sea Serpents.*

Pope Lick Monster   Pope Lick Creek flows through wooded terrain in Jefferson County, Kentucky, 15 miles east of Louisville. In the 1940s and early 1950s, hikers and campers in this area reported sightings of a creature sometimes described as a "GOATMAN"— i.e., a hairy biped with a head resembling a goat's. Later researchers stress the beast's resemblance to a BIGFOOT-type HOMINID or NORTH AMERICAN APE, including an incident wherein Boy Scouts were routed from their camp by an unseen, howling assailant who pelted them with stones. A short independent film about the creature, titled *Legend of the Pope Lick Monster*, may be viewed at the Louisville Public Library. No recent encounters with the beast are on file, but members of the GULF COAST BIGFOOT RESEARCH ORGANIZATION note that sightings have been logged from other parts of the Jefferson Forest and throughout Kentucky at large.

Source: Gulf Coast Bigfoot Research Organization http://gcbro.com/.

Popobawa   Since the early 1970s, island residents of Zanzibar and neighboring Pemba have been terrorized by sporadic attacks from a winged home invader called Popobawa, who mauls (and sometimes rapes) the occupants of selected houses. The first assaults occurred on Pemba in 1972, around the time that Zanzibar's chief minister was assassinated. Victims claimed the Popobawa was humanoid in form, with one eye, batlike wings, and sharp claws. Some claimed it could speak, and ordered them to confess their ordeal publicly or face further torment. Panic ensued as self-proclaimed Popobawa victims, including several men, announced that they had been attacked and sodomized in their homes after nightfall. Still, the anxiety faded after a few weeks — then resumed in the 1980s, with a new rash of assaults. Another lull was broken in April 1995, when the Popobawa appeared on Zanzibar to claim more victims. Rumors spread that the creature assumed human form in daylight, and a mentally unbalanced suspect was lynched after he confessed to staging the attacks. No further outbreaks have been reported since May 1995, and while Zanzibar's main hospital treated numerous alleged Popobawa victims for various injuries, skeptics still insist that the incidents were nothing more than mass hysteria.

Source: "Dwarf batman terrorises Zanzibar." *Fortean Times* 86 (May 1996): 11.

Pori *see* **Gnéna**

Pornic Panther   ALIEN BIG CATS are less common in France than in Britain, but they still appear from time to time. This one prowled the neighborhood of Pornic, in Brittany, during the mid-1980s. As with most ABCs before and after, it eluded searchers and finally vanished as mysteriously as it first appeared.

Source: Campion-Vincent, "Appearances of beasts and mystery-cats in France."

Porshnev, Boris Fedorovich (1905–72)   Arguably the most influential Russian cryptozoologist of all time, Boris Porshnev was educated as a historian with special interest in the origins of mankind. In the 1950s, he broadened that interest to include reports of unknown HOMINIDS in Soviet territory, including the ALMAS, KAPTAR and others. Porshnev was instrumental in founding the SOVIET SNOWMAN COMMISSION to investigate such reports, marking the first true national effort to solve a cryptozoological mystery. In 1958–59, despite Cold War tensions, TOM SLICK and other foreign researchers visited the Soviet Union to share information with Porshnev and his colleagues. In the 1960s, Porshnev visited Georgia to investigate the story of ZANA, the captive female ABNAUAYU who allegedly bore several children from human fathers. As Porshnev described the experience, "From the moment I saw Zana's grandchildren, I was impressed by their dark skin and negroid looks. Shalikula, the grandson, has unusually powerful jaw muscles, and he can pick up a chair, with a man sitting on it, with his teeth." Porshnev was thus convinced that NEANDERTAL MAN had not become extinct in prehistoric times, but lingered to the present day. Colleague DMITRI BAYANOV explained the essence of the theory:

> According to Porshnev, something very fundamental which happened with the rise of modern man was speech, or human language. In terms of evolution its acquisition was so rapid and recent that our non-speaking ancestors simply had no time to disappear under the pressure of their garrulous descendants. Thus, the existence of WILDMEN is not a fortuity but a necessity.

Porshnev's government sponsors were not always pleased with his theories. In fact, they suppressed his monograph on Zana and Neandertal survival (though 180 copies reportedly survive, somewhere in Russia). Encouraged by the PATTERSON FILM and the MINNESOTA ICEMAN, still Porshnev parted company with cryptozoologists who devoted themselves entirely to the search for a type specimen. In 1967 he wrote:

> The public is much taken by the illusion that the 'snowman' problem can only be solved by a sensational breakthrough. A single 'proof' will be obtained and submitted: here you are! No, the process of science is more modest and more majestic. In its course knowledge is accumulated and deepened, new information is added to old information, and its overall reliability is increased. A single sensation won't work if only because any sensation can be questioned: photographs and films can be faked, while a live specimen can be declared a rare pathological case, a freak of nature.

Porshnev persevered, and in his last years wrote a book with BERNARD HEUVELMANS detailing his theory of Neandertal survival. Sadly, he died two years before the work was published as *L'Homme de Néanderthal est Toujours Vivant* (1974).

Sources: Coleman and Clark, *Cryptozoology A to Z*; Dmitri Bayanov, "A hominologists view from Moscow, Russia." Bigfoot Co-op, *HTTP://COOMBS.ANU.EDU.AU/~VERN/WILDMAN/BAYANOV.TXT*; Occultopedia, *http://www.occultopedia.com/a/almas.htm*.

Port Royal sea serpent   On 20 April 1850, the *Illustrated London News* relayed a story from South Carolina, claiming that a 150-foot SEA SERPENT had surfaced in Port Royal Sound on 15 March. Instead of retreating to the Atlantic when sighted, the creature allegedly entered the Broad River and swam upstream until it was stranded near Beaufort. There, a firing squad of frightened citizens reportedly killed it with volleys of gunfire — and then, apparently, left the carcass unexamined until it somehow disappeared. BERNARD HEUVELMANS dismissed the story as a HOAX.

Source: Heuvelmans, *In the Wake of the Sea Serpents*.

Portsmouth sea serpent   On 30 July 2002, a party of friends from was enjoying the sun and surf at Teddy's Beach, Rhode Island when the day suddenly "turned into a nightmare that most only witness in the movies." According to a report of 1 August in the Fall River (Massachusetts) *Herald News*, the fun and frolic was shattered by screams from Rachel Carney, swimming some distance offshore. "I was deep out in the water and kept hearing this hissing sound. Then I saw its head come up showing me its big teeth. It kept rolling while it was swimming and knocking into my feet. I just froze." Carney's fiancé, Dennis Vasconcellos, swam to her rescue, hauling her toward shore. As he described the animal, "This thing was big. I mean its head was almost the size of a basketball. I just kept backing in to shore, but it was looking at me and hissing. The other people around there were pulling their kids out of the water." Witnesses told the *Herald News* that the serpentine creature was "about 15-feet long, with four-inch teeth, greenish-black skin and a white belly." Ed Baker, spokesman for the University of Massachusetts-Dartmouth's Center for Marine Science and Technology could shed no light on the beast's identity beyond suggesting that "a tropical animal" may have been swept northward by warm ocean currents. Baker noted that a PIRANHA had recently been caught at Coventry, Rhode Island, while an ALLIGATOR was "on the run" in Lincoln.

Source: Greg Miliote, "Sea creature spooks swimmers." *Herald News* (1 August 2002).

Portuguese sea serpent   In March 1849, a British Royal Navy commander named Nolloth reportedly sighted a SEA SERPENT in the Atlantic, off the coast of Portugal. Unfortunately, as noted by BERNARD HEUVELMANS more than a century later, this is one of the rare British reports for which no further details were recorded, lacking details as basic as Nolloth's first name and the name of his ship. No description of the creature is available.

Source: Heuvelmans, *In the Wake of the Sea Serpents*.

Poskok   This unclassified venomous SNAKE of eastern Europe was first described to the English-speaking world by author Maurice Burton in 1959. The information came, in turn, from a resident of Sarajevo, Bosnia, named M.F. Kerchelich, who wrote:

> We have in Yugoslavia a dreaded specimen of jumping snakes called locally "poskok," meaning "the jumper"…found mainly in Dalmatia along the east coast of the Adriatic and the mountainous regions of Hercegovina [sic] and Montenegro. In fact, there exists an island near Dubrovnik called "Vipera," which is a well-known breeding place of "the jumper." The average size of this snake is between 60 and 100cm [23–39 inches] though considerably larger specimens were seen. The colour seems to vary, according to environment, from granite grey to dark reddish brown. The snake is dreaded for its poison and aggressiveness when disturbed, though it will usually hide on approach of man.…I can vividly remember three cases of meeting the "poskok," the first was in Montenegro, when on a trip I stopped the car to stretch my legs.

It was lying in the middle of the road, some 100 metres [325 feet] ahead of the car, sleeping in the sun. After watching it for some time it must have felt my presence, curled up and jumped into a dry thorn bush at the kerb of the road and disappeared. The jump was at least 150cm [4 feet 10 inches] long and 80–90cm [31–35 inches] high. On the second occasion, I was driving a jeep in southern Dalmatia and, coming round the corner, I could just see a snake about to cross the road. The car must have frightened it and quite suddenly it jumped at the front mudguard and was killed by the rear wheel. The third time I met a "postok" was when I was fishing a small stream in Croatia and leaning against a dry tree trunk. Suddenly I noticed a hissing sound above me, and, having been warned of snakes, scrutinised my surroundings very carefully. It took me quite a time to discover that one of the dry branches was not a branch at all but a "poskok" watching me intently.... All three specimens I have seen were not more than 3 to 4cm [1.2–1.6 inches] in diameter at the thickest part.

No snake known to science can jump in the manner described by Kerchelich. In 1996, herpetologist John Cloudsley-Thompson suggested that the Poskok was in fact the western whip snake (*Coluber viridiflavus*). KARL SHUKER notes, however that the normal distribution of *C. viridiflavus* is limited to the northwestern portion of the former Yugoslavia, while several related species of similar appearance are found throughout the Poskok's supposed range. All the whipsnakes are slender and swift, aggressive when cornered or handled, but none can jump like the Poskok and none are venomous. While the Poskok's existence remains unproved, NATO troops assigned to war-torn Bosnia were warned in advance to beware of snakes that could jump six feet in the air.

Sources: Burton, *More Animal Legends*; Shuker, "Sarajevo's jumping snake."

Potomac Patty   This name is applied to any of several aquatic cryptids seen in the Potomac River of Maryland, Virginia and the District of Columbia. In 1978, former CIA employee Donald Kyker was lounging on his porch at Bay Quarter Shore, in Heathsville, Virginia when he saw an unknown creature swimming 75 yards offshore. Kyker described the animal as having "a 25–30 foot long sleek body, dark gray, 8 inches in diameter and about to move [*sic*] at 7 to 8 miles per hour." Kyker summoned two neighbors, Howard and Myrtle Smoot, who also saw the beast. Subsequently, three more of the creatures swam by, one of them longer than the Smoots' 36-foot porch. Howard Smoot reportedly shot one of the smaller creatures, whereupon all three submerged. Neighbor C. Phillip Stemmer confirmed the second sighting, telling reporters that the animals moved "like self-propelled logs. They weren't just three somethings floating there. They were moving faster than the water. They were making waves." Some researchers treat Potomac Patty as identical to CHESSIE, a SEA SERPENT reported from nearby Chesapeake Bay.

Source: Bord and Bord, *Unexplained Mysteries of the 20th Century*.

Potsdam sea serpent   A SEA SERPENT report which cryptozoologist BERNARD HEUVELMANS considered to of "great importance" was filed in 1910 by F.W. Van Erp, third officer of the Dutch steamer *Potsdam*. It read as follows:

On 13 December 1910, at one o'clock in the afternoon in 49° 20' N. latitude, 24° 8' W. longitude, at the changing of the watch, we saw a strange FISH on the starboard, a little ahead of the beam. From close to, it seemed to us to be shaped like a gigantic SNAKE, 120 to 130 feet long, and about 2 feet in diameter. It was moving very fast. From time to time the head was raised almost perpendicularly out of the water, up to a height of 8 or 10 feet; it remained in this position for some time and then disappeared again. These

two movements went with a considerable splashing of water that rose to about 20 feet, while the tail stirred up the water no less violently (the tail was flat and wide in shape, with a forked end). One could also see one bend in the body. The colour was dark grey above and white below, which was very clearly marked on the head. The animal was watched for about three minutes.

Heuvelmans considered the report crucial, despite what he deemed great exaggeration of the creature's length, because the tails of long-necked pelagic cryptids are rarely observed. Heuvelmans concluded that the "forked" tail "must really be its outspread webbed hind-feet." His reason for ruling out possible flukes, such as those of cetaceans, was left unexplained.

Source: Heuvelmans, *In the Wake of the Sea Serpents*.

Powell, James H., Jr. (n.d.)   Texas native James Powell Jr. earned his B.A. from Columbia University and an M.S. from Texas Technical University (Lubbock) before proceeding to study herpetology at the University of Colorado. His field work focused more specifically on CROCODILES, first in Yucatán and Belize, later in the South Pacific and Africa with the Crocodile Specialist Group of the International Union for Conservation of Nature and Natural Resources. In 1960, Powell read BERNARD HEUVELMANS'S classic text, *On the Track of Unknown Animals* (1958), and was captivated by the chapters on supposed living DINOSAURS in Africa. Powell planned an expedition to the Congo in 1972, but diplomatic red tape delayed the trip by four years and diverted him to Gabon. There, his interviews with natives convinced Powell that a local cryptid called N'YAMALA was similar, if not identical, to the more famous MOKELE-MBEMBE. (Powell also sought evidence of the OLITAU, reported by IVAN SANDERSON in the 1930s, but without success.) Back in the U.S., Powell joined forces with cryptozoologist ROY MACKAL to plan a new African expedition for 1980. While that effort likewise failed to reveal a living sauropod, Powell's rigorous investigations mark him, in Mackal's words, as "a cryptozoologist par excellence."

Sources: Mackal, *A Living Dinosaur?*; Mackal, *Searching for Hidden Animals*.

Powsaswop   Aboriginal tribesmen applied this name to a large aquatic creature found in Canada's Saskatchewan River. No descriptions of the beast survive today, an no modern sightings are on record. Powsaswop was most likely a regional name for NAITAKA, the LAKE MONSTER common in native folklore throughout western Canada.

Source: Bord and Bord, *Alien Animals*.

Powys Beast/Puma   This ALIEN BIG CAT made its first appearance at Churchstone, Powys, Wales in September 1980, described by the nurse who saw it as resembling a LYNX (*Felis lynx*). A month later, farmer Michael Nash lost four sheep at Llangurig, the animals clawed and bitten in a manner not resembling typical dog attacks. On 23 October, Nash found a 5-inch pawprint outside his barn and heard strange snoring sounds from within. Police were summoned and surrounded the barn, keeping watch through the night, but when they entered next morning, the barn was empty. Experts who examined the pawprint, noting its oval shape and four visible claw marks, pronounced it unlike that of any CAT known to science. The Powys Beast has not been seen again.

Source: Shuker, *Mystery Cats of the World*.

Prah Sands carcass   On 7 June 1928, the rotting carcass of a long-necked sea creature washed ashore at Prah Sands, in

Cornwall, England. Speculation on a possible SEA SERPENT stranding was cut short when experts examined the remains and identified the creature as a basking SHARK (*Cetorhinus maximus*).

Source: Heuvelmans, *In the Wake of the Sea Serpents*.

Pretoria Phantom Leopard   While leopards (*Panthera pardus*) are found in the northern portion of South Africa, they rarely encroach on that nation's interior—and none are known to dwell around the administrative capital at Pretoria. It was all the more surprising, then, when residents of Pretoria's Faerie Glen neighborhood reported a "spotted thing," presumed to be a leopard, prowling their residential streets on 2 November 2002. More sightings were logged over the next seven days, including one report of the CAT seen with a RABBIT-sized "something" in its mouth, and several dogs went missing in the area. Police initially dismissed the sightings as HOAXES or practical jokes, then searched in vain for the elusive cat. The search acquired new urgency with a report that some unseen predator had killed eight antelopes on

Urban leopard sightings frightened residents of Pretoria, South Africa, in 2002.

a nature reserve near the city. Chris Conradie, terrain manager for the reserve, suspected a female leopard with two or three cubs was to blame for the raids, but traps set for the hunters remained empty. Deon Cilliers, project manager at De Wildt Cheetah Breeding Project, suggested that a caracal (*Felis caracal*) might be the culprit, but Conradie insisted that the smaller cat could not consume the volume of meat devoured during a 24-hour time frame. Whatever the prowler's identity, reported sightings ceased after the game reserve attacks, and the "phantom" predator vanished.

Sources: Eagan Williamson, "Pta's phantom beast a killer." *News 24* (15 November 2002); Eagan Williamson, "There is a leopard in my street." *News 24* (9 November 2002).

Priam sea serpent   In 1879, while traveling aboard the Holt Blue Funnel liner *Priam*, Dr. C.H. Caldicott allegedly saw a SEA SERPENT in the Indian Ocean. Caldicott did not report the sighting until 1953, at which time he described a creature of uncertain length, showing its head and "six to eight arches" above the water's surface. "The coils were about ¼ mile away," he wrote, "but there was no mistaking what they were."

Source: Heuvelmans, *In the Wake of the Sea Serpents*.

Princess Charlotte sea serpent   In his classic 1968 study of SEA SERPENTS, cryptozoologist BERNARD HEUVELMANS reports that the captain of the steamer *Princess Charlotte* sighted the cryptid known as CADBOROSAURUS sometime in 1932–33, while sailing between Vancouver, British Columbia and Victoria, on Vancouver Island. Unfortunately, no further details were provided and the sighting is omitted from a 1995 treatment of "Caddy" by PAUL LEBLOND and Edward Bousfield.

Sources: Heuvelmans, *In the Wake of the Sea Serpents*; LeBlond and Bousfield, *Cadborosaurus*.

Princess Joan sea serpent   In 1933, Captain Arthur Slater of the steamer *Princess Joan* affixed his signature to a list of witnesses who claimed sightings of the British Columbian SEA SERPENT subsequently dubbed CADBOROSAURUS. BERNARD HEUVELMANS noted the incident in 1968 without providing details, but it is omitted from the list of "Caddy" sightings compiled by PAUL LEBLOND and Edward Bousfield in 1995.

Sources: Heuvelmans, *In the Wake of the Sea Serpents*; LeBlond and Bousfield, *Cadborosaurus*.

Princess sea serpent (1856)   On 4 October 1856, the *Illustrated London News* published the following extract from the log of the *Princess*, detailing Captain A.R.N. Tremearne's encounter with a SEA SERPENT off the coast of South Africa:

> Tuesday, July 8, 1856. Latitude accurate 34° 56' S.; Longitude accurate 18° 14' E. At one p.m. saw a very large FISH, with a head like a walrus, and twelve fins, similar to those of a black fish, but turned the contrary way. The back was from 20 to 30 feet long; also a great length of tail. It is not improbable that this monster has been taken for the great sea-serpent. Fired and hit it near the head with rifle-ball. At eight, fresh wind and fine.

The "black fish" mentioned is the orca or killer whale (*Orcinus orca*). Tremearne's sketch of the creature reveals 12 lateral fins, each curved toward the head.

Source: Heuvelmans, *In the Wake of the Sea Serpents*.

The *Princess* sea serpent (1856), after A.R.N. Tremearne.

Princess sea serpent (1875)   SEA SERPENTS of a particular description appeared so frequently off the New England coast during the 19th century that they were christened with the collective name SCOLIOPHIS ATLANTICUS. One such sighting occurred in July 1875, in Nahant Bay, Massachusetts. Witnesses aboard the yacht *Princess* included the Rev. Arthur Lawrence, Francis Lawrence and his wife, Mary Fosdick, Albion Reed and Robert Reed. A few days after the incident, the Rev. Lawrence wrote the following account:

> On the 30th of July, 1875, a party of us were upon the yacht *Princess*, and while sailing between Swampscott and Egg Rock, we saw a very strange creature. As nearly as we could judge from a distance of about one hundred and fifty yards, its head resembled that of a TURTLE or SNAKE, *black above and white beneath*. It raised its head from time to time some six or eight feet out of the water, keeping it out from five to ten seconds at a time. At the back of

The *Princess* sea serpent (1875), from eyewitness descriptions.

the neck there was a fin, resembling that of a black-fish [*Orcinus orca*], and underneath, some distance below its throat, was a projection which looked as if it might have been the beginning of a pair of fins or flippers, like those of a seal. But as to that, we could not be sure, as the creature never raised itself far enough out of the water to enable us to decide. Its head seemed to be about two and a half feet in diameter. Of its length we could not judge, as only its head and neck were visible. We followed it for perhaps two hours. It was fired at repeatedly with a Ballard rifle, but without apparent effect, though one ball seemed to strike it. It was seen and watched by the whole party upon the yacht.

In response to questions from the Boston Society of Natural History, the Rev. Lawrence wrote, "I should suppose it to be one of the saurian family. It seemed to me to be neither a FISH, snake, nor turtle. If such a thing as an ichthyosaurus is extant, I should think this creature to be one of the same family."

Sources: Heuvelmans, *In the Wake of the Sea Serpents*; O'Neil, *The Great New England Sea Serpent*.

Privateer sea serpent

On 5 August 1879, while sailing in the Atlantic 100 miles west of Brest, France, Captain J.F. Cox of the British ship *Privateer* reportedly saw a SEA SERPENT. Cox later said, "It was like a great EEL or SNAKE, but as black as coal tar."

Source: Heuvelmans, *In the Wake of the Sea Serpents*.

Proctor Valley Beast

Bonita, California is a town of some 13,000 inhabitants, located southeast of San Diego. Ten miles east of Bonita, rural Proctor Valley has the reputation of a small-town lover's lane — and as the habitat of a BIGFOOT-type HOMINID that sometimes lurches from the darkness to interrupt the groping of impassioned teenagers. Skeptics dismiss the reported sightings as HOAXES or hysterical reactions to an urban legend, and while rumors that the beast once killed a youth appear to be unfounded, reports of fresh encounters with the Proctor Valley Beast circulated through San Diego County as recently as August 2003.

Source: Chris Moran, "Monster legend alive and well in south county." *San Diego Union-Tribune* (24 August 2003).

Protector sea serpent

In his biography of Commodore Edward Preble, author James Fenimore Cooper describes an encounter with a SEA SERPENT in July 1779, when Preble (then an 18-year-old ensign on the American warship *Protector*) was engaged in a campaign against a British base on Penobscot Bay, Maine. Cooper wrote:

It was while thus employed, that an incident occurred to Preble, that is worthy of being recorded, more especially since subsequent events have confirmed its truth. Preble related the affair substantially as follows: The *Protector* was lying in one of the bays on the eastern coast, which has been forgotten, waiting the slow movements of the squadron. The day was clear and calm, when a large serpent was discovered outside the ship. The animal was lying on the water quite motionless. After inspecting it with the glasses for some time, Capt. Williams ordered Preble to man and arm a large boat, and endeavor to destroy the creature; or at least to go as near to it as he could....The boat thus employed pulled twelve oars, and carried a swivel in its bows, besides having its crew armed as boarders. Preble shoved off, and pulled directly towards the monster. As the boat neared it, the serpent raised its head about ten feet above the surface of the water, looking about it. It then began to move slowly away from the boat. Preble pushed on, his men pulling with all their force, and the animal being at no great distance, the swivel was discharged loaded with bullets. The discharge produced no other effect than to quicken the speed of the monster, which soon ran the boat out of sight.

There is no question that in after-life, Preble occasionally mentioned this circumstance, to a few of his intimates. He was not loquacious, and probably saw that he was relating a fact that most persons would be disposed to doubt, and self-respect prevented his making frequent allusions to it. When it is remembered that Preble died long before the accounts of the appearance of a similar serpent, that have been promulgated in this country, were brought to light, it affords a singular confirmation of the latter. Preble stated it as his opinion, that the serpent he saw was from one hundred to one hundred and fifty feet long, and larger than a barrel.

Source: James Fenimore Cooper, *Lives of Distinguished American Naval Officers*. Philadelphia: Carey & Hart, 1846.

Provincetown carcass

In his classic 1968 survey of SEA SERPENT sightings and strandings, BERNARD HEUVELMANS lists a carcass beached at Provincetown, Massachusetts in 1939. No further information on the case was provided, but recent Internet searches suggest that the stranding actually occurred in January 1937, and that the remains were identified as those of a basking SHARK (*Cetorhinus maximus*).

Sources: Heuvelmans, *In the Wake of the Sea Serpents*; Basking Shark, http://octopus.gma.org/fogm/Cetorhinus_maximus.htm.

Przewalski's Horse

This wild horse (*Equus ferus prezewalskii*) is related to the European tarpan, with some authors suggesting the two may in fact be identical. Discovered in the 1870s by Nikolai Mikhailovich Przhevalsky, a Russian explorer and geographer, the species represents the only extant wild horse that, in its purebred state, is not descended from domestic horses. Przewalski's horse is smaller than most domestic horses (weighing under 700 pounds), dun-colored, with a large skull and bulging forehead, sporting an upright crest of dark hair on its head and neck, and a dark dorsal stripe linking the mane to a dark tail. These horses once ranged from western Mongolia to China's northern Xinjiang Province, where wild stallions sometimes mated with mares from domestic herds. While many specimens survive in zoos around the world, the last purebred Przewalski's horse — a mare called "Orlitsa" — was captured in 1947. Some sources list the horse as officially extinct in the wild, though others simply call it rare. Scientists reported sighting a group of seven in 1966, and a small population may survive in Mongolia's Altai Mountains. In the 1990s, United Nations Development Program researchers laid plans for reintroduction of Przewalski's horse to its former range, but no word on the effort's progress is presently available. The great question, as MATTHEW BILLE suggests, is whether the new herds, if and when they arrive, will "find any old friends waiting to greet them."

Source: Bille, *Rumors of Existence.*

Pterosaurs (Living)

Pterosaurs were the first group of vertebrates to take up flying as a way of life. The order's earliest members were accomplished flyers by the Late Triassic period (190 million years ago, 70 million years before the first known BIRD), and various species endured through the Late Cretaceous (65 million years ago). Known species ranged in size from *Anurognathus*, with a 1-foot wingspan, to *Quetzalcoatlus*, at 39 feet (some reports say 51 feet). *Pteranodon*, with a 23-foot wingspan, also boasted a great bony crest on the back of its head, familiar to viewers of various science-fiction films. Although contemporaries of the DINOSAURS, pterosaurs are not classified as members of that order. The first pterosaur fossils were found in Germany, in 1784, and the first known report of a living specimen surfaced 72 years later. According to the *Illustrated London News* of 9 February 1856:

A discovery of great scientific importance has just been made at Culmout [Haut Marne, France]. Some men employed in cutting a tunnel to unite the St. Dizier and Nancy Railways, had just thrown down an enormous block of stone by means of gunpowder, and were in the act of breaking it to pieces, when from a cavity in it they suddenly saw emerge a living being of monstrous form.

This creature, which belongs to the class of animals hitherto considered to be extinct, has a very long neck, and a mouth filled with sharp teeth. It stands on four long legs, which are united together by two membranes, doubtless intended to support the animal in the air, and are armed with four claws terminated by long and crooked talons. Its general form resembles that of a BAT, differing only in its size, which is that of a large goose. Its membranous wings, when spread out, measure from tip to tip three me-

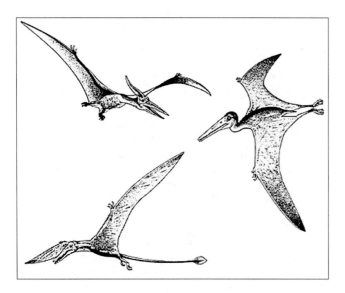

Prehistoric flying reptiles appeared in many diverse forms.

Reports of living pterosaurs have been filed around the world in modern times (*William Rebsamen*).

tres twenty-two centimetres [10 feet 6 inches]. Its color is a livid black; its skin is naked, thick and oily; its intestines only contained a colorless liquid like clear water. On reaching the light this monster gave some signs of life, by shaking its wings, but soon after expired, uttering a hoarse cry. This strange creature, to which may be given the name of a living fossil, has been brought to Gray, where a naturalist well versed in the study of paleontology, immediately recognized it as belonging to the genus *Pterodactylanas*, many fossil remains of which have been found among the strata which geologists have designated by the name Lias. The rock in which this monster was discovered belongs precisely to that formation the deposit of which is so old that geologists date it more than a million years back. The cavity in which the animal was lodged forms an exact hollow mold of its body, which indicates that it was completely enveloped by a sedimentary deposit.

No other record exists of this revolutionary discovery, and we may safely dismiss it as a journalist's practical joke until such time as the preserved remains may reappear from the cryptozoological Twilight Zone. The British-French charade has not dissuaded other witnesses from filing reports of live pterosaurs, however, with incidents continuing to the present day. In addition to sightings of the creature known in Africa as KONGAMATO and the ROPEN of Papua New Guinea, reported elsewhere in this volume, some of those accounts include:

19th century— Two hunters named Milacsek and Shirdos allegedly shot a sort of reptilian pelican outside a cave at Lago Nahuel Huapi, Argentina (home of the LAKE MONSTER known as NAHUELITO). Reports differ as to the creature's final disposition. German author Hans Krieg claims the hunters took only its head, and discarded that after three days; Krieg concludes the animal was nothing more than a flying steamerduck (*Tachyeres patachonicus*), though that familiar bird bears no resemblance whatever to a pelican. Another German scribe, Ulrich Dunkel, asserted that the beast was delivered to Santiago's National Museum of Natural History (established in 1830), but was lost during one of Chile's recurring civil wars, sometime prior to 1891.

1907— Members of the Austrian von Trappe family settled at Momella, in present-day Tanzania, and established a cattle ranch. Margarete von Trappe soon heard stories from local natives of flying reptiles that lived on nearby Mount Meru, descending at night to hunt on the surrounding plains.

1947—A witness identified only as J. Harrison allegedly saw five pterosaurs flying in a V-formation near Manaus, Brazil. He described the animals as having flat heads, long necks and beaks, ribbed wings resembling brown leather with a 12-foot span, and no apparent feathers.

May 1961—A New York businessman flying his small private plane over the Hudson River Valley claimed he had been "buzzed" by a "big bird" that behaved "like a fighter plane making a pass." A closer look revealed that his assailant was "a damned big bird, bigger than an eagle. For a moment I doubted my sanity because it looked more like a pterodactyl out of the prehistoric ages."

Early 1960s—A couple driving through California's Trinity National Forest glimpsed the silhouette of a huge "bird" soaring above their vehicle. They estimated the creature's wingspan at 14 feet and described it as resembling a pterodactyl more closely than a normal bird.

July 1969—Two men boating on Lake Dewey, in Michigan's Sisters Lakes region, were startled when "everything turned black" as a huge winged creature flew overhead. The beast had leathery skin without feathers, and one witness sketched it in the form of a pteranodon.

1970—A soldier stationed in Vietnam's central highlands (near Pleiku) saw a "big bird" flying 20 feet above his head in broad daylight. Its wingspan was 12 feet or more and "[i]t was black and yellow, with the beak similar to the pterodactyl species."

1 January 1976—Two girls, 14-year-old Jackie Davis and 11-year-old Tracey Lawson, reported an unearthly flying cryptid from Harlingen, Texas. As described by the children, the "horrible-looking" creature was black, five feet tall, with a "GORILLA-like" face, red eyes, and a stout 6-inch beak that uttered shrill cries. It landed in a freshly plowed field, 100 yards from the girls, where adults found 3-toed tracks, eight inches long, pressed 1.5 inches into the soil. (A 170-pound man was reportedly unable to produce footprints as deep, despite repeated attempts.)

1 January 1976—Within hours of the Harlingen incident, Dr. Berthold Schwarz reported an equally strange encounter at Great Notch, New Jersey. "I wouldn't have thought anything of it," Schwarz said, "except that it was so huge and its wings didn't seem to be flapping much at all. But what disturbed me most was that it was so white, even as dark as it was. How could it have been so white? Unless—I know this sounds ridiculous—it was luminous."

7 January 1976—The action switched back to Texas, when Alvérico Guajardo heard something heavy strike his mobile home at Brownsville. Stepping outside, he saw a black, 4-foot-tall animal with folded batlike wings, red eyes and a long beak. Squeaking high-pitched cries, it backed into the shadows atop Guajardo's roof, then apparently flew away.

11 January 1976—Two men on a ranch outside Poteet, Texas, saw a 5-foot "bird" standing atop a water tank. At their approach, it vaulted aloft without seeming to flap its wings.

14 January 1976—On hearing strange, rustling sounds outside his Raymondville, Texas, home, Armando Grimaldo stepped outside at 10:30 p.m. and was attacked by a large, batlike creature 5–6 feet tall, with a 10- to 12-foot wingspan and sharp claws on its feet. After wrenching free of the beast with torn clothing, Grimaldo observed its apelike face, red eyes, and dark leathery skin. Unlike the other witnesses, however, he claimed the thing had no visible beak.

16 January 1976—Dean and Libby Ford reported a "big black bird" flying near Brownsville, Texas. Later, browsing through a book on paleontology, they identified the creature as a pteranodon.

18 January 1976—Sightings of an identical creature were reported by witnesses at Olmito and San Benito, Texas.

21 January 1976—Francisco Magallanez claimed a similar bat-winged, red-eyed creature attacked him near Eagle Pass, Texas. Fortean authors Colin and Janet Bord note "doubtful features" to his story but provide no details.

24 February 1976—Three elementary school teachers at San Antonio claimed that a huge "bird" with a 15- to 20-foot wingspan swooped low over their cars as they were driving. Witness Patricia Bryant told reporters, "I could see the skeleton of this bird through the skin or feathers or whatever, and it stood out black against the background of the gray feathers." Later, using an encyclopedia to identify the creature, all three identified it as a featherless pteranodon.

1983—Three women on a farm near Thermal, California, followed their barking dog until they met a 6-foot winged, featherless creature. Its body was "very muscular, like a man," with leathery skin like an elephant's and long claws on its toes. Furthermore, its "head was the shape of a pterodactyl [*sic*] with red bulging eyes and protruding bone in the front and back of its head." As the dog and women approached, it flew away on "wings so big you could hear them flap in the wind."

14 September 1983—Ambulance driver James Thompson had a clear view of "a large bird-like object" as it flew over Highway 100 near Los Fresnos, Texas (near the Mexican border). Thompson said, "Its tail was what caught my attention. I expected him to land like a model airplane. That's what I thought he was, but he flapped his wings enough to get above the grass....It had a black or grayish rough texture. It wasn't feathers. I'm quite sure it was a hide-type covering....I just watched him fly away." The creature's body was 8–10 feet long, with a wingspan of 5–6 feet. It had a hump on the back of its head, a short neck, and a pouch at its throat like a pelican's. In retrospect, Thompson called it "a pterodactyl-like bird."

Summer 1986—Three hunters in the Asteroussia Mountains near Pirgos, Crete, reported a batlike flying reptile with a beak like a pelican's and large claws on fingerlike protrusions from leathery wings. It was dark gray in color and made a loud flapping noise as it flew overhead.

November 1993—A couple stopped at a highway rest area near Lusk, Wyoming, noticed a strange animal standing in a nearby field. One witness said, "It stood—my estimate is about 5 feet tall, husband estimates 6 feet. It was greenish gray and appeared to be a pterodactyl. We sat by the side of the road for about 20 minutes watching this thing. It sat and flexed and stretched its wings, each of which were as long as its body was tall. It also turned its head several times, looking out across the field. We stayed as long as we could and we did stop again on our return trip home, but the thing was gone."

Date unknown—An couple was swimming in the pool at their apartment complex in Altus, Oklahoma, when a man-sized flying creature landed on a nearby fence. They later described it as "brown and leathery looking" with "reptilian features." Personnel at nearby Altus Air Force Base acknowledged that "there were a few reports of the thing each year but no one knew what it was. The best explanation they could offer was that it's something that comes out of the desert."

Skeptics insist that all such sightings are either cases of mistaken identity (involving storks, vultures, etc.) or deliberate HOAXES.

And it must be admitted that some recent pterosaur accounts were clearly false. An alleged pteranodon photo taken by "witness" Billy Meier in 1996 proved to be a snapshot of a painting by Czech artist Zdenek Burian, published in numerous books since the early 1960s. Four years later, an alleged photo of Civil War soldiers posed with a dead pterosaur and uncovered by researcher "Derek Barnes" was Hollywood publicity stunt for the TV series *Freaky Links* (see Appendix C). In January 2002, Internet reports of "dinosaur-birds" found living atop a Venezuelan plateau and discovered by "Dr. José Ramos-Pajaron" of Caracas University likewise proved false. KARL SHUKER found that no professor existed, while SCOTT CORRALES revealed that the name Pajaron means "big bird" in Spanish.

Sources: Bord and Bord, *Alien Animals*; Bord and Bord, *Unexplained Mysteries of the 20th Century*; "Dinosaur photograph." *Fortean Times* 91 (October 1996): 57; Ulrich Dunkel, *Abenteur mit Seeschlangen*. Stuttgart: Kreuz-Verlag, 1961; "Flying critter." *North American BioFortean Review* 3 (2000): 10; Heuvelmans, *Les Derniers Dragons d'Afrique*; Heuvelmans, "Lingering pterodactyls"; Heuvelmans, *On the Track of Unknown Animals*; "Is this a pterodactyl." *Fortean Times* 134 (June 2000): 21; Keel, *The Complete Guide to Mysterious Beings*; Hans Krieg, *Als Zoologe in Steppen und Wäldern Patagoniens*. Munich: J.F. Lehmann, 1940; John Michell and Robert Rickard, *Living Wonders*. London: Thames and Hudson, 1982; A. Blayney Percival, *A Game Ranger on Safari*. London: Nisbet, 1928; Ron Schaffner, "Recently obtained anecdotal accounts of 'big birds' and 'pterosaurs.'" *North American BioFortean Review* 9 (December 2002): 6–15; Karl Shuker, "Alien zoo." *Fortean Times* 158 (June 2002): 21; J.L.B. Smith, *Old Fourlegs: The Story of the Coelacanth*. London: Longmans, Green, 1956; Thanassis Vembos, "A prehistoric flying reptile?" *Strange Magazine* 2 (1988): 29; "What Billy Meier-Saur." *Fortean Times* 98 (June 1997): 54; Did Pterosaurs Survive Extinction?, *http://paranormal.about.com/library/weekly/aa061702a.htm.*

Puff   Peter Pond Lake lies in northwestern Saskatchewan, Canada, 200 miles north of North Battleford. The lake is 40 miles long and 14 miles wide, with a surface area of 302 square miles. In the 1970s, it was said to harbor an amphibious LAKE MONSTER called Puff (after the popular 1960s song "Puff the Magic Dragon"). Puff is known only from two brief sightings, in 1977 and 1979. In the first case, witnesses described a reptilian creature crawling out of the water, but a search by officers of the Royal Canadian Mounted Police revealed nothing. The latter report, by the Rev. Raymond LeMay, summarized eyewitness accounts of a similar animal entering the lake from dry land. No other sightings are on file.

Source: Kirk, *In the Domain of the Lake Monsters*.

Pukau   Members of the Saiap Dusuns tribe, residing in the Sabah district of northern Borneo claimed by Malaysia, describe the Pukau as hybrid of pig and deer, armed with a sharp tongue that it uses to defend itself if disturbed. No such animal is recognized from the island, but KARL SHUKER notes that a similar creature—the wild pig known as babirusa (*Babyrousa babyrussa*)—inhabits neighboring Celebes and several smaller Indonesian islands. In fact, the babirusa ("deer pig") fits the Pukau's description in all particulars, from its long and slender legs to its curved tusks that might be mistaken for a "sharp tongue." While no babirusa are known to inhabit Borneo, transitory land bridges are thought to have linked Borneo with Celebes and other nearby islands during the Pleistocene period, granting "alien" animals a ready means of access.

Source: Shuker, *In Search of Prehistoric Survivors*.

Pumina *see* **Python (Giant)**

Pyar-Them *see* **Yeti**

Pygmies (Unknown)   Every culture on Earth has legends of "little people," typically described as much smaller than normal humans but otherwise closely resembling *Homo sapiens*. Some are described as extremely primitive, living in burrows or building rude shelters from sticks and foliage, while others (fairies, leprechauns, etc.) are sometimes invested with magical powers. Our task is to separate mythology and superstition from hard evidence and determine whether any such diminutive people lived in the past or may still exist today.

Aside from victims of dwarfism or other genetic abnormalities, the smallest known people on earth are Pygmies, defined as a human subpopulation in which an average height of five feet or less is an inherited trait. Pygmy populations presently exist in central Africa, Malaysia, the Philippines, Papua New Guinea and India's Andaman Islands. Ancient Greek and Roman authors penned realistic descriptions of short-statured races quite different in appearance from modern Pygmies, but those reports are now widely dismissed as mere legends. It is more difficult to discount the 19th-century discovery of a "pygmy graveyard" near Sparta, Tennessee, where skeletons corpses were found interred in graves two feet long, 14 inches wide and 18 inches deep. One of the skeletons unearthed, apparently that of an adult human, reportedly measured 2 feet 10 inches in length. Doubters maintain that the remains were those of dwarves or normal persons dismembered and buried in pet-sized graves for no apparent reason.

More recently, on 1 October 2002, a boy named Julio Carreño made a startling discovery while vacationing with his parents near

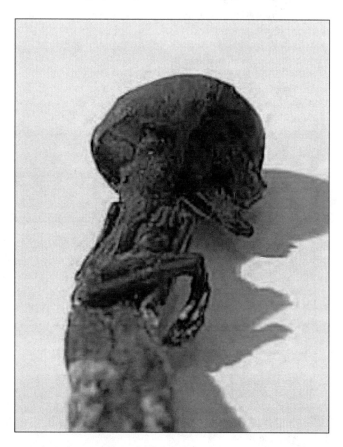

Less than three inches tall, this humanoid creature was found in Chile, in October 2002.

Concepción, Chile. Poking around under some bushes, Carreño found a tiny humanoid creature 2.8 inches long, with a disproportionately large head and long fingers. The thing sipped water but would take no food, appearing in a moribund condition. "When we found it," Armando Carreño later told reporters, "it was able to open its eyes. Then a few days later, once we had returned to Santiago, it opened its eyes one more time. It never opened them again. There was something peculiar about that; when we thought it was already dead, the body was still warm, and it stayed warm for a long time. I always thought that a dead body was supposed to be cold." Soon after final death, the body shriveled into a mummified state. Veterinarian Pedro Katán could not identify the creature, and while tabloid newspapers suggested extraterrestrial origins, biologists at the University of Chile thought it might be the premature fetus of some forest animal, perhaps a feral CAT. DNA tests were scheduled to identify the creature, but no results have been announced so far. Photos of the tiny corpse, published around the world, have failed to elicit an identification.

Sources: "A pygmy graveyard in Tennessee." *Scientific American Supplement* 1 (1876): 259; Heuvelmans, *Les Bêtes Humaines d'Afrique*; "Humanoid from Chile." *Fortean Times* 166 (February 2003): 7; Ley, *Exotic Zoology*; S.G. Morton, "Pigmies in the Mississippi River valley." *Proceedings of the Academy of Natural Science of Philadelphia* 1 (November 1841): 125–126.

Pygmy Brown Bear

In 1992, Peter Hocking collected several reports of an unknown brown bear, smaller than average, inhabiting Peru's Yanachaga National Park (Pasco Department). The witnesses were park rangers, familiar with wildlife in the park, who clearly distinguished the bear they had seen from the well-known spectacled bear (*Tremarctus ornatus*). In one case, they had observed one of the pygmy bears raised in captivity by a private owner. Skeptics note that *T. ornatus* is the only bear recognized in South America, suggesting that the rangers were deceived by glimpses of specimens below normal size.

Source: Hocking, "Further investigation into unknown Peruvian mammals."

Pygmy Elephant

Two species of African elephant are presently acknowledged by science. The adult male bush elephant (*Loxodonta africana*) stands between 9 feet 9 inches and 13 feet at the shoulder, while females are somewhat smaller. Adult males of the forest elephant (*L. cyclotis*) are shorter, ranging from ranging from 7 feet 9 inches to 9 feet 9 inches at the shoulder (with females smaller still). Since the 19th century, however, stories of a forest-dwelling pygmy elephant have set hunters combing the jungles for a species of pachyderms as yet unclassified.

In 1904, Baron Maurice de Rothschild purchased a curious elephant tusk in the marketplace of Addis Ababa, Ethiopia. The tusk matched no known species of elephant, measuring roughly two feet along its curve, with a rounded tip, flat sides along most of its length, and five natural grooves at the bottom. A year later, animal collector Carl Hagenbeck captured an apparent pygmy elephant near Ndjolé, in Gabon, transporting it to Germany. Zoologist Theodore Noack examined the specimen, called "Congo," and declared it a subspecies of African elephant, which he called *Loxodonta africana pumilio*. Congo was sold to the Bronx Zoo, where it reached a 6-foot height before it died in 1915.

Meanwhile, in June 1907, a traveler named Le Petit claimed to have sighted several pygmy elephants along the Congo River, and later reported a second encounter with five specimens near Lake Mai-Ndombe, in what was then the Belgian Congo. In 1911, a Lieutenant Franssen of the Belgian army shot an elephant that measured 5 feet 5 inches tall, sporting 2-foot tusks. Two years later, a settler in the neighborhood of Léfini displayed a piece of thick hide, covered with bristly red hair, to naturalist Hans Schomburgk, reporting that it came from the local "river elephant." (Some stories of the pygmy elephant suggest that it pursues an amphibious lifestyle.) Henri Schouteden proposed a new scientific name for the species in 1914, calling it *Loxondonta fransseni*. More sightings were reported from Gabon in 1923 and 1926, and two pygmy elephants were captured in the Congo's Uelé region. One measured 4 feet 8 inches at the shoulder, while the other stood 4 feet 3 inches, both having "long and stout tusks almost touching the ground."

Pygmy brown bears are reported from Peru.

Reports of miniature pachyderms emanate from Africa and Asia.

More evidence accumulated after World War II. On 11 March 1948, an adult male was shot at Aloombé, on the coast of Gabon between Libreville and Port-Gentil. Though clearly old, it measured only 6 feet 4 inches tall. In January 1955, François Edmond-Blank led an expedition to Cameroon, hoping to capture a specimen for the University of Copenhagen. He returned empty-handed, despite claims of having penetrated dense marshland to find a group of 12 elephants, none of whom stood more than six feet tall. In September 1957, one Captain Chicharro met a herd of 21 pygmy elephants near the Rio Benito in Equatorial Guinea, and he killed an adult measuring 6 feet 6 inches at the shoulder. German animal collector Ulrich Roeder obtained a dead specimen in Cameroon, during the 1970s; its tusks measured 2 feet 5 inches long, and Roeder placed its age at 16–18 years. Hans-Jurgen Steinfurh subsequently filmed three pygmy elephants beside the Yobe River, in the Central African Republic. All bore the tusks of adults, though none was taller than 5 feet 6 inches at the shoulder. In May 1982, former West German ambassador Harald Nestroy photographed a group of pygmy elephants in the Likouala region, Republic of Congo. Comparison to a great egret (*Egretta alba*) shown in one photo revealed that the tusked adults were no more than five feet tall. Finally, a dead female specimen was found by L.P. Knoepfler at a PYGMY village in Gabon, also in the 1980s. The elephant was 5 feet 3 inches tall, and the full-term fetus in its womb proved that the specimen was a mature adult.

Despite such evidence, most zoologists still reject the pygmy elephant as a separate species, contending that the individuals killed, captured and photographed to date are merely stunted specimens of *L. cyclotis*. BERNARD HEUVELMANS deviated from the view of most cryptozoologists, suggesting that pygmy elephants may not be pachyderms at all, but rather relict deinotheres (presumed extinct since the Pleistocene period). KARL SHUKER, building on reports of small, amphibious "water elephants," has suggested the possibility of surviving *Moeritherium*, the Late Eocene "dawn elephant" that roamed North Africa 36–34 million years ago.

Surprising news on pygmy elephants emerged from Borneo's Sabah State on 6 September 2003, with an announcement from Malaysia's Wildlife and National Parks Department and the Worldwide Fund for Nature. Spokesmen declared that DNA testing and other examinations performed on Borneo's elephant population (cut off from interbreeding with their fellow Asian elephants since the 17th century) proved the island's pachyderms to be a new and distinct subspecies. In addition to being smaller than their mainland ancestors, the Borneo pygmies have larger ears, longer tails and straighter tusks. Various media reports placed the Borneo pygmy elephant population somewhere between 100 and 2,000 individuals. The debate over pygmy elephants in Africa continues.

Sources: Bille, *Rumors of Existence*; "Borneo elephants reclassified as new subspecies." Associated Press (6 September 2003); Heuvelmans, *On the Track of Unknown Animals*; Alex Kirby, "Borneo's elephants gain recognition." BBC News (6 September 2003); "New evidence supports existence of pygmy elephant." *ISC Newsletter* 9 (Spring 1990): 1–6; "New pygmy elephant photos indicate separate species." *ISC Newsletter* 11 (1992): 1–3; Shuker, *In Search of Prehistoric Survivors*.

Pygmy Gorilla   Between 1847 and 1876, all GORILLAS (*Gorilla gorilla*) collected by scientific institutions came from a restricted area in Central Africa, around the Gabon Estuary. In 1877, a curious specimen was collected from much farther south. It was a female, smaller than any known gorilla, with variations in skeletal structure, musculature, and longer hair on the back. French zoologists Edmond Alix and Aimé Bouvier identified as a separate species of pygmy gorilla (*Gorilla mayéma*). Robert Hartmann disagreed, contending in 1885 that the specimen was simply a young female gorilla. Walter Rothschild took a different view in 1905, reporting that the animal was "a very large APE of the group of *Simia vellerosus* Gray, and not a gorilla at all." The original type specimen disappeared from the Paris Museum before Daniel Elliot published his *Review of Primates* in 1914, but Elliot applied the *G. mayéma* label to three other specimens (a male, female and juvenile) found at Frankfurt's Senckenberg Mu-

Bernard Heuvelmans proposed that the Pygmy Elephant might be a relict *Deinotherium*.

Primatologists debate the existence of a pygmy gorilla species in Africa.

seum. At the same time, Elliot created a new genus (*Pseudogorilla*) for the pygmy gorilla, thus placing it midway between gorillas and CHIMPANZEES (*Pan troglodytes*). Four decades later, primatologist Colin Groves concluded that Elliot's Frankfurt "pygmies" were merely young specimens of *G. gorilla*. He therefore declared that *G. mayéma* never existed as a separate species, though the original specimen is unavailable for comparison. Most zoologists presently deny the existence of pygmy gorillas.

Sources: Groves, "The case of the pygmy gorilla"; Heuvelmans, *Les Bêtes Humaines d'Afrique*; Heuvelmans, *On the Track of Unknown Animals*.

Pygmy Rhinoceros
Kroo tribesmen in Liberia claim that a RHINOCEROS unknown to science inhabits the forests of their homeland. Animal collector Hans Schomburgk initially believed they were referring to the large black boars of eastern Liberia, but the Kroo insisted that the rhino was a separate species and Schomburgk finally accepted their stories, though he never found the beast. BERNARD HEUVELMANS described the elusive creatures as pygmies, while reporting that they were supposedly the size of elephants. Aquatic habits are alleged, and some reports suggest that the unknown rhinos may also be found in Cameroon, Gabon, and certain portions of the Congo basin. Cryptozoologist ROY MACKAL suggests, albeit with reservations, that the forest-dwelling rhino may be the same creature known in the Congo's Likouala region as EMELA-NTOUKA, often described as a living DINOSAUR. Its designation as a "pygmy" in various texts remains unexplained.

Sources: Heuvelmans, "Annotated checklist of apparently unknown animals with which cryptozoology is concerned"; Heuvelmans, *On the Track of Unknown Animals*; Mackal, *A Living Dinosaur?*

Pyramid Lake, Nevada
Paiute shamans believed this lake, northeast of Reno in Washoe County, was inhabited by a demon in the form of a great serpent, which left footprints on the lake bed that were visible in clear weather. No sightings have been reported since the early 19th century.

Sources: Hubert Bancroft, *The Native Races of the Pacific States of North America*. New York: D. Appleton, 1876; King, *In the Domain of the Lake Monsters*.

Pythons (Giant)
While most herpetologists agree that the ANACONDA (*Eunectes murinus*) is the world's largest known SNAKE in terms of weight, Southeast Asia's reticulated python (*Python reticulatus*) currently holds the world record for length. The *Guinness Book of World Records* cites a specimen killed by villagers on Celebes (Indonesia) and measured by a civil engineer at 32 feet 9.5 inches, but no evidence exists and the Wildlife Conservation Society's standing reward of $50,000 for a snake 30 feet or longer remains unclaimed. The largest specimen ever found in captivity was a female reticulated python named Colossus, held at the Pittsburgh Zoo, which measured 28 feet 6 inches and tipped the scales at 320 pounds. (A specimen 21 feet 10 inches long was killed in Malaysia, in September 1995, while trying to swallow a man it had killed.)

Africa's largest known snake, the rock python (*Python sebae*), reportedly grows to 25 feet, and larger specimens have been reported (though never confirmed). In 1929, Arthur Loveridge measured a "fresh" python skin at 30 feet, but he acknowledged that the living snake was likely 5–6 feet shorter. Three years later, Mrs. Charles Beart shot a specimen outside a Congolese school that reportedly measured 32 feet 2¼ inches. In 1958, elephant hunter K.H. Krofft reportedly shot a 23-foot python in Rhode-

sia (now Zimbabwe), and found a 6-foot CROCODILE in the snake's stomach. Nonetheless, in 1962, herpetologist V.F. FitzSimons wrote that "it is most unusual nowadays to find a snake exceeding 20 feet, while the average length can be put at 13 to 15 feet."

Still, as with the anaconda, stories of *much* larger pythons still circulate throughout Asia and Africa. The NĀGA may be one such reptile, and natives of Central Africa describe a gigantic python known to them as Pumina. Roman legionnaires in Africa reportedly met huge snakes on at least two occasions. A 45-foot python was allegedly captured in Ethiopia and shipped off for display at Alexandria. A 120-foot monster dubbed the "earth shaker" was also supposedly killed and skinned by Roman troops, with a loss of several soldiers in the process, but the disposition of its hide is not recorded. Another true monster, 130 feet long, was allegedly killed by Congolese tribesmen in 1932, but "the snake was made into stew for the natives before a reliable measure could be taken."

Beside such behemoths, the specimen photographed in 1959 seems almost puny. Colonel Remy Van Lierde, a Belgian military helicopter pilot, was patrolling the Congo's war-torn Katanga district, 60 miles northwest of Kumina, when he spied a huge snake below him and snapped a photograph. The picture is black-and-white, but Van Lierde described the snake as dark brown or green on top, with a white underside. He estimated its length at 40–50 feet, with a head three feet long and two feet wide. On noticing the helicopter, the snake raised its head 10 feet off the ground and poised as if to strike. Analysis of the photo, based on Van Lierde's presumed 500-foot altitude, seems to confirm his estimates of the creature's size. Skeptics suggest, however, that he may have flown considerably lower, while others insist that the photo is a fabricated HOAX.

Cryptozoologists were naturally excited on 29 December 2003, when the Indonesian newspaper *Republika* announced that a reticulated python 49 feet long, weighing nearly 1,000 pounds, was on display at a small zoo in Curugsewu, Java. According to the zookeeper, a local named Rohmad, the snake — dubbed Fragrant Flower — measured 62 feet when captured in mid-2002, but "four meters [13 feet] reportedly had to be severed after a rotten deer was found undigested in its stomach." Rohmad did not explain how the python had survived that radical procedure, but he de-

Remy Van Lierde snapped this photograph of an alleged giant python in the Belgian Congo, in 1959.

clared that it was now "rather fussy about its food," subsisting on a diet of four dogs per month. "We have given it dogs of various colors but this snake didn't want to eat them," Rohmad added. "It only wants to eat fierce brown dogs." When herpetologists arrived to measure Fragrant Flower in early January 2004, they found a healthy specimen with no apparent signs of amputation. While it wriggled and resisted, the examiners determined that it measured 21–22 feet long.

Sources: "Indonesia park puts world's longest snake on show." Reuters (30 December 2003); Chris Mattison, *The Encyclopedia of Snakes*. New York: Facts on File, 1995; "Python tries to swallow man." *Fortean Times* 85 (March 1996): 12; "World's largest snake caught." Associated Press (29 December 2003); Here We Are in Africa, *http://www.pythons.net/larges-nake3.html*; Mysterious creatures, *http://www.theshadowlands.net/creature.htm#congo*.

Pythons (Mislocated)

Pythons rank among the more popular exotic pets in the U.S. and Europe, and various non-endangered species are readily available at countless pet shops, reptile shows, and from countless other sources. Inevitably, some escape or are deliberately released by their owners when they grow uncomfortably large or care becomes more expensive than anticipated. Such escapes or releases presumably explain most encounters with pythons at large in abnormal habitats, although the presumed owners are rarely identified. Questions linger in some cases, though, including that of Pennsylvania's elusive PENINSULA PYTHON and the 15-foot Burmese python (*Python molurus bivittatus*) found dead in a canal at Birmingham, England in January 2003. In February 2004, campers shot and killed a 15-foot Burmese python at an old mining pit outside Mulberry, Kansas.

Southern Florida is one place where naturalized pythons appear to have put down roots and established breeding colonies. Tales of giant SNAKES have emerged from the Everglades for centuries, and pythons of various species have been sighted or extracted from the swamp since the early 1980s. State biologists estimate that 1,000 pythons escaped to the wild when their owners' homes were destroyed by Hurricane Andrew in 1992, while countless others may have been deliberately released. Other large constrictors, including BOAS and ANACONDAS, are listed among the 276 species of exotic reptiles, amphibians, BIRDS and mammals whose escapes are registered with the Florida Fish and Wildlife Conservation Commission. Still, authorities warn against unnecessary panic, and herpetologist Joe Wasilewski told the press in 2002, "I'd stake my reputation that they're not going to be chasing people." No python nests or eggs have yet been found in the wild. However, as Everglades park biologist Skip Snow told the *Miami Herald*, "The interesting thing about these snakes is they do adapt to a fairly wide range of habitat conditions. What we will probably find is that they're quite capable of making a go at it."

Sources: Curtis Morgan, "Invasion of the Everglades: Giant snakes have a new hangout." *Miami Herald* (22 December 2002); Joe Noga, "Campers find 15-foot python in local strip pit." *Pittsburg* (KS) *Morning Sun* (24 February 2004); Steve Swingler, "15-foot python dead in canal." *Birmingham Evening Mail* (23 January 2003).

Qattara Cheetah

The cheetah (*Acinonyx jubatus*) is not normally found in Egypt, but reports of pale specimens with unusually thick coasts have emerged from that nation's Qattara Depression since the early 1960s. A Bedouin tribesman reportedly captured one of the CATS in 1967, and pug marks resembling those of a cheetah were found in the region on at least two occasions, in the 1990s. Skeptics argue that the cats — if they exist at all — comprise an isolated population which has undergone minor changes in pelage and coloration.

Source: Amman, "Close encounters of the furred kind."

Qoqogaq

Described by Inuit natives of Alaska as a huge white bear, the Qoqogaq has passed into legend with some decidedly un-bearlike features — notably a skull five feet wide and ten powerful legs! Said to roam the northwestern part of Alaska, between Point Barrow and Cape Prince of Wales, the Qoqogaq might be dismissed as simple folklore were it not for a sighting in 1913. In that year, Inuit tribesmen trekking eastward from Point Barrow reportedly heard a large creature swimming beneath them, under a thick layer of ice. An inadvertent sound from one of the hunters caught the beast's attention, and its massive head burst upwards through the ice. As reported by the witnesses, only luck and fast sled dogs save them from being devoured.

Source: Diamond Jenness, "Stray notes on the Eskimo of Arctic Alaska." *Anthropological Papers of the University of Alaska* 1 (May 1953): 5–13.

The Qattara cheetah is a supposed Egyptian subspecies.

Quagga

The Quagga was a variant form of zebra, formally named *Equus quagga* in 1788, by Johann Gmelin. Unlike its well-known relatives, the creature was light brown in color, with brown stripes showing only on the head, neck and shoulders. As MATTHEW BILLE notes, it "looked rather like the Creator's rough draft for the zebra." Once found throughout much of South Africa and southern Namibia, the Quagga was hunted to apparent extinction around 1875. The last captive specimen died at the Amsterdam Zoo on 12 August 1883. Still, as BERNARD HEUVELMANS noted in 1986, occasional Quagga sightings are still reported from Namibia. Since 1986, the South African Museum's Quagga Project has attempted to revive the species through selective breeding. The effort has produced 32 foals since 1988, with the first specimen displaying proper Quagga stripes and background coloration born in November 1991. Work on the project continues.

Sources: Bille, *Rumors of Existence*; Heuvelmans, "Annotated checklist of apparently unknown animals with which cryptozoology is concerned"; Turnbull, "Back from the dead?"

Quang Khem Described by native hunters in Vietnam's Pu Mat district as a "slow-running deer," the Quang Khem remains formally unclassified today, although biologist Nguyen Ngoc Chinh collected a skull from the region in 1994. Other Quang Khem skulls were found in a separate shipment dispatched to Hanoi, and DNA testing performed on the specimens at Copenhagen University confirmed that the creature's genetic profile matches no other animal presently known to science. The Quang Khem is described as a primitive deer, whose short antlers resemble horns on a Viking helmet. The search for a living specimen continues in Pu Mat, located slightly to the north of Vietnam's famous VU QUANG NATURE PRESERVE.

Sources: Linden, "Ancient creatures in a lost world"; Karl Shuker, "Menagerie of Mystery." *Strange Magazine* 15 (Spring 1995): 30.

Queanbeyan River, Australia Located near a town of the same name in New South Wales, Australia, the Queanbeyan River reportedly hosted a BUNYIP in the late 19th century. The Rev. John Gale published the following account in 1927, when he was 95 years old:

I myself, when duck-shooting along the banks of the Queanbeyan River, saw rise, a hundred yards or so ahead of me, a bog dog-like amphibian, which (apparently seeing me) plunged beneath the water and I saw it no more. Other credible persons had seen the like in the same river near town, and reported their observations.

Source: Gale, *Canberra: History and Legends*.

Queen Eleanor sea serpent In the spring of 1912, third mate A.F. Rodger saw an unidentified SEA SERPENT from the steamer *Queen Eleanor*, while passing Cape Matapan, at the southern tip of mainland Greece. He recalled the incident years later, in correspondence with a team of BBC radio broadcasters, and described it as follows:

The creature was on a parallel course to us and going at about the same speed, and it remained visible enough for our Chief Engineer to go down to his cabin, bring up his rifle, and take a shot at it. Whether he hit it or not I do not know, but it then disappeared. It appeared to us to be the commonly reported eel-like creature having no distinct head but the long neck and two coils or humps behind the neck.

Since EELS do not, in fact, possess "long necks," the radio hosts requested further details. Rodger replied that he had observed the creature for roughly five minutes, during which it was:

Distant about 1 cable, approximate length laterally about 30 feet, diameter about 18 inches. Colour what we soon after learned to know as camouflage. I cannot be certain about undulations but I can remember seeing underneath the coils as it was on our port side with the sun, of course, to starboard. I still favour its having

been a giant eel or sea-snake though I know none of that length has ever been reported.

Source: Heuvelmans, *In the Wake of the Sea Serpents*.

Queensland carcass On 19 March 1883, the *New Zealand Times* reported that decomposed remains of a 40-foot sea monster had been found on a Queensland, Australia beach and transported to Rockhampton for study. The GLOBSTER boasted an 8-foot snout "in which the respiratory passages are yet traceable" and an "enormous" hip bone. Scientists of the day were baffled by the carcass, but BERNARD HEUVELMANS and BEN ROESCH later suggested that the creature was a whale of indeterminate species. Even granting that the "snout" may have been rolled-up rotting flesh, however, the giant hip bone remains enigmatic. No marine mammal has a prominent pelvis, and the vestigial pelvic bones of whales are completely detached, atrophied to 12 inches or less in large adults.

Sources: Heuvelmans, *In the Wake of the Sea Serpents*; Roesch, "A review of alleged sea serpent carcasses worldwide (Part Two—1881–1891)."

Queensland sea serpents Following the MOHA-MOHA incident of June 1890, reports of SEA SERPENTS fell into disfavor along the coast of Queensland, Australia. Crewmen aboard the *BAWEAN* reported a sighting off Brisbane, in July 1925, but matters rested until 1934. Multiple sightings were recorded in August of that year, by witnesses in Bowen, Mourilyan and Townsville. The most detailed account was filed by Oscar Swanson, later published in the *Victorian Naturalist*. According to Swanson, he was fishing with his son Harold and a third party, William Quinn, offshore from Townsville on 18 August 1934. Soon after launching their motorboat, they saw four dark objects in the water beyond the Fairway Beacon, midway between Townsville and Magnetic Island. The boat closed to 150 yards before the creature "submerged, going down like a submarine, sinking slowly." Swanson continues:

Then we thought it would come at us, and we turned to make for the Beacon, which has a ladder to the top on which a lamp is lit. We were wishing that we were in a speed boat. We stowed the little fellow up forward under the bit of decking we had, and hoped for the best. I might mention that the sea at this time was smooth as glass. After about five minutes the monster arose again in the same place (coming up just like a submarine). We were about three-quarters of a mile past the Beacon; on reaching it we caught hold of the ladder and watched to see what movements the monster would make. After waiting half an hour and seeing no movements, excepting the head swaying from side to side, as if watching us, we decided to make back to town, get rid of the boy, and get a camera, as it looked as though the monster would stop there all day. On reaching the jetty wharf, I rang Mr. Jim Gribbard, subeditor of the *Townsville Bulletin*, who picked up a press photographer, Mr. Ellis, and armed with two cameras, we once more set out (without the boy).

By the time they returned, however, the creature had vanished. Swanson drew a sketch of the creature, showing a raised head and three trailing humps, all covered with scales. He also provided this further description:

You will see, by the rough sketch submitted, what the monster was like. The head rose about 8 feet out of the water, and resembled a huge TURTLE's head; the mouth remained closed. The head was about 8 feet from the back of the head to the front of the mouth, and the neck was arched. The color was grayish-green. The eye (we could only see one, being side one) was small in comparison to the rest of the monster. The other part in view was three curved humps about 20 feet apart, and each one rose from 6 feet in the front to a little less in the rear. They were covered with huge scales about the size of saucers, and also covered in barnacles. We could not get a glimpse of the tail, as it was under the water.

Subsequent reports indicate that a similar creature was seen the week prior to Swanson's encounter, at Mourilyan Harbor, where it trailed a fishing launch for 50 yards and made loud noises. A week after Swanson's sighting, three witnesses at Bowen described a 30-foot creature with a body like "a huge armoured hose," raising its turtlelike head eight feet above water. Three fishing parties near Townsville reported sightings that same day (around 25 August), with one witness telling reporters: "Its head resembled a huge turtle more than anything else, and was slightly arched. Farther along three smaller dark objects were seen, giving the appearance of a Monster of the sea with a series of humps." Crewmen aboard the *TRENTBANK* and the *REHATA* soon reported sightings from the same area.

The 1934 sightings were all but forgotten, and World War II was underway, when two fishermen sighted a 60-foot serpentine creature near Mooloolabak, north of Brisbane. Sight unseen, local experts pronounced it an oarfish (*Regalecus glesne*), although that fish's maximum acknowledged length is 21 feet. BERNARD HEUVELMANS accused the Mooloolabak witnesses of exaggeration—yet he still listed their creature as a possible specimen of unknown "super eel" in his 1965 compilation of serpent reports.

Sources: Dinsdale, *The Leviathans*; Heuvelmans, *In the Wake of the Sea Serpents*.

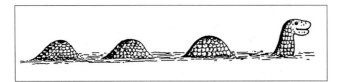

A Queensland sea serpent, after witness Oscar Swanson.

Queensland Tiger

The first report of an Australian TIGER was filed in 1705, by an agent of the Dutch East India Company at Batavia, on the coast of Western Australia. Reports still issue from throughout the continent Down Under, but their greatest concentration is in Queensland, hence the name most frequently applied to this unknown creature even when it surfaces in other districts. A bullock driver met the animal north of Cardwell, Queensland in 1864, but its first public notice outside Australia came seven years later, when the Zoological Society of London published an account from Cardwell police magistrate Brinsley Sheridan. He described the beast as follows:

It was lying camped in the long grass and was as big as a Native Dog (dingo); its face was round, like that of a CAT, it had a long tail, and its body was striped from the ribs under the belly with yellow and black. My dog flew at it, but it could throw him. I fired my pistol at its head; the blood came. The animal then ran up a leaning tree. It then got savage and rushed down the tree at the dog and then at me. I got frightened and came home.

Sightings continue to the present day, with over 100 collected by naturalist Janeice Plunkett between 1970 and 1973. Witnesses typically describe a creature four to five feet long (including tail) and 18 inches high at the shoulder. Its coarse-haired coat is usually tan or light gray, with black stripes encircling the body and tail. Fond of tree-climbing and savage when cornered, the

Artist's conception of a Queensland tiger, based on eyewitness descriptions (*William Rebsamen*).

Queensland tiger feeds on WALLABIES and smaller game, but also kills livestock on occasion.

Numerous Queensland tigers were reportedly killed in the early 20th century. A Kuranda resident reported in 1910, "Most of the tiger cats which I have killed were about four feet long and of fawn color, with black stripes running across the body, which was fairly long, unlike an ordinary cat." A hunter from Tiaro, after killing one in 1915, said the animals were "slightly taller and heavier built than a domestic cat, with a large head and strong shoulders. Also striped rings around the body. This specimen had a young one on each teat, approximately ten in all." The last publicized killing of a specimen occurred in 1932, in the Cardwell Range. Researchers Paul Cropper and Tony Healy suggest that the Queensland tiger is now extinct, killed off by poison bait earmarked for dingoes or from eating equally poisonous South American cane toads. Recent sightings, however, have persuaded author REX GILROY that a small population still survives.

Australia has no native cats, and while it is theoretically possible that some exotic species was introduced to the Outback, three alternative suspects are usually cited as candidates for the true Queensland tiger. One, the marsupial "LION" (*Thylacleo carnifex*), is presumed extinct today but may have survived in Australia as late as 10,000 years ago—and perhaps more recently. The Tasmanian THYLACINE, another marsupial listed as extinct, has been also been nominated, but its doglike head and paws bear no resemblance to the Queensland tiger's, while its stripes are only on the back. Finally, the spotted-tailed quoll (*Dasyurops maculatus*) is a kind of marsupial weasel which averages three feet six inches in length. While sometimes dubbed the "tiger quoll" or "tiger cat," this creature lacks the size and fearsome temperament of a typical Queensland tiger. Furthermore, its dark coat with head-to-tail vivid white spots bears no resemblance to the striped "cat" described by witnesses.

Sources: Healy and Cropper, *Out of the Shadows*; Heuvelmans, *On the Track of Unknown Animals*; Shuker, *Mystery Cats of the World*; Smith, *Bunyips & Bigfoots*.

Querqueville sea serpent

On the afternoon of 25 or 26 January 1934, the captain of tugboat *117* sighted a large, unidentified creature swimming rapidly some distance off the breakwater at Querqueville, France (west of Cherbourg). The witness described a horselike head, raised above the waves before the animal submerged. When it resurfaced, 150 yards further on, the beast revealed a long neck "like a CAMEL'S."

One month later, on 28 February, a fisherman found a strange carcass beached at Querqueville. It measured 20 feet overall, including what appeared to be a 3-foot neck, and its diameter at the thickest point was five feet. Fifty yards away from the carcass, a pile of entrails was found, described in press reports as including the animal's kidneys, lungs and peritoneum. Dr. Georges Petit, dispatched from the Paris Museum, arrived to examine the carcass on 1 March. His report follows:

> Washed up on the tide, it now appeared as a shapeless mass, greyish in colour, which one might have taken at first for a rock if it had not extended in front in the spinal column, somewhat stripped of flesh, and the bare whitish skull.
>
> I realised at once that it was not a marine mammal, as had been supposed, but a plagiostomous fish of the Selachian order.
>
> With the help of those who had seen the animal soon after it was washed up, I pieced together its general appearance. The first dorsal [fin] still survived, mutilated; I could see where the second dorsal, the ventrals and the much smaller anal had been, though they were entirely missing, and work out the shape of the caudal and separate the pectorals. Some fifty yards from the carcase I was able to examine pieces of the intestines which still had the spiral valvula characteristic of the Selachians and a reddish lobulate gland, which had been variously called an ovary and a pancreas, but which was actually the spleen. And I removed, to bring to the Museum, several "exhibits" such as the skull and the anterior part of the vertebral column.
>
> After my observations of the carcase, my belief is that the Querqueville "monster" must be a basking shark (*Cetorhinus maximus* Gunn). The *exact* identification of a shark is of course impossible without the teeth or the spicules on the skin. With this animal we had no data upon which to base exact measurements nor any specimen with which to compare the skull.

Before leaving Querqueville, Dr. Petit also questioned the skipper of tug *117* and concluded that the man had seen a large basking shark swimming offshore. BERNARD HEUVELMANS accepted Petit's diagnosis on the carcass but rejected his finding in regard to the January sighting, since the tug's captain specifically recalled a long neck and no dorsal fins. Heuvelmans therefore declared, "I find it hard to believe that the two events really have anything to do with one another," and he ranked the January creature as a specimen of his hypothetical "long-necked" sea serpent.

Sources: Heuvelmans, *In the Wake of the Sea Serpents*; Shuker, "Bring me the head of the sea serpent!"

Quickfoot   An unknown APE or HOMINID, dubbed "Quickfoot" by the press, was reported from West Lothian, Scotland in November 1995. Witness David Colman was driving with his wife and three children through Knock Forest, in the Bathgate Hills, when he glimpsed a 6-foot manlike, hairy creature

The hairy hominid known as Quickfoot was reported from Scotland in 1995 (*William Rebsamen*).

running on a forest path beside the road. (Colman estimated its speed at an improbable 70 miles per hour, hence the media nickname.) On noticing Colman's vehicle, the creature stopped and snarled, then fled into the woods. Colman noted that "It seemed angry that we had disturbed it." The date of Colman's sighting is unclear, but he admitted to reporters that "It has taken me a long time to speak about this."

Source: "Quickfoot sighted in Scotland forest." *Fortean Times.*

Quinault Lake, Washington   Aboriginal folklore identifies this 4-mile-long lake, in Grays Harbor County, as the traditional home of a predatory LAKE MONSTER. No modern sightings are recorded.

Source: Albert Reagan and L.V.W. Walters, "Tales from the Hoh and Quileute." *Journal of American Folklore* 46 (1933): 297, 324–325.

Quinkin   An unclassified HOMINID reported from northern Queensland, Australia, the Quinkin is probably identical to the creature more commonly called Yahoo or YOWIE. Aboriginal cave paintings found on the Cape York peninsula depict a traditional giant named Turramulli, identified in legend as a Quinkin, whose description tallied in most respects with that of the Yowie — i.e., a hulking, hairy figure who slept in caves and roamed at night in search of human prey or KANGAROOS. Unlike most Yowies, however, Turramulli had only three fingers per hand and three toes on each foot, all tipped with long talons.

Source: Healy and Cropper, *Out of the Shadows.*

—— R ——

Rabbits (Giant)   While giant rabbits are typically dismissed as the stuff of *Alice in Wonderland* fantasy, reports of oversized specimens have been filed from Australia, England, Ireland and the United States. Proposed explanations vary with the lo-

cale, but no specimens have yet been collected, and the sightings remain unexplained.

From Australia, BERNARD HEUVELMANS reports that gold prospectors in the remote Outback have reported sighting rabbits up to nine feet long, sometimes dubbed BUNYIPS. Naturalist Ambrose Pratt speculated that the witnesses may have encountered relict specimens of *Diprotodon optatum*, the largest known marsupial, presumed extinct on Earth for at least 6,000 years. Another prehistoric candidate is *Palorchestes azatel*, a horse-sized marsupial weighing as much as a ton, with a tail and hind legs resembling those of a KANGAROO, which permitted it to sit upright and graze on low-hanging branches. Christine Janis has proposed a third suspect, from the extinct kangaroo subfamily *Sthenurinae.*

In 1947, 5-year-old Karl Pflock met a truly startling specimen in a hay field behind his Campbell, California home. He described the creature as "a huge rabbit—giant ears, eyes like saucers, and *at least* six feet tall." Pflock and the animal fled in opposite directions, with the cryptid vanishing into a nearby orchard. "When I ran into the house and to my mother for comfort," Pflock recalled, 46 years later, "she pooh-poohed everything, of course, patted me on the head, told me not to fret. All I'd seen was an overfed jackrabbit. But I knew better, and still do."

The creature glimpsed by Michael O'Regan in Ireland, also circa 1947, was of more modest size. He mistook it for a large dog at a range of 40 yards, "then realized that its gait was neither that of a dog nor of a FOX." When he closed the distance to 20 yards and saw the animal in profile, O'Regan realized it was "the biggest hare I'd ever seen." Though armed with a rifle, he spared the beast's life, and later described the sighting to his brother, who opined that he had seen "a mountain hare" (*Lepus timidus*). That explanation hardly satisfied, though, since *L. timidus* reaches a maximum length of 24 inches, tipping the scales at no more than nine pounds.

Two other reports of giant rabbits are on file from Hampshire and Surrey, in England. Eyewitness descriptions agree in each case, referring to rabbits the size of large dogs, gray in color, hopping in the normal manner of a rabbit's locomotion. One account, from witness Gary Cook of East Worldham, adds the detail of floppy ears "that almost reach the ground." Witnesses Bruce and Dan Woolley fail to mention ears in their report, but a pub-

Reports of giant rabbits are a global phenomenon.

lished suggestion that they really saw a stocky muntjac deer failed to convince the Woolleys of their error.

Sources: Heuvelmans, *On the Track of Unknown Animals*; "Megabunnies." *Fortean Times* 163 (November 2002): 52; Karl Pflock, "Lepus giganticus?" *Fortean Times* 169 (May 2003): 52.

Rabbits (Pink)   For over a quarter-century, since the mid-1970s, residents of northeastern Scotland have reported sighting rabbits in flamboyant and most unnatural colors, including pink, ginger-red and bright orange. Experts initially suggested that the rainbow rabbits were offspring of a chance mating between wild rabbits and escapees from some exotic menagerie, but proliferation of sightings through the late 1990s seems to indicate a local breeding population. The rabbits clearly exist, but the cause of their bright and widely-varied hues has yet to be explained.

Source: Karl Shuker, "Alien zoo." *Fortean Times* 110 (May 1998): 17.

Rakshi-Bompo *see* **Yeti**

Randsfjorden, Norway   This lake, in Norway's Oppland County, has a long tradition of LAKE MONSTER reports, but no sightings have been reported in modern times. The dearth of modern sightings suggests that the cryptids (if they ever existed) are now extinct.

Source: Erik Knatterud, "Sea serpents in Norwegian lakes," http://www.mjoesorman.no.

Raritan Bay carcass   On 15 June 1822, New York newspapers reported that a sea monster 30 feet long and 18 feet in circumference had been harpooned and hauled ashore at Middleton Point, on New Jersey's Raritan Bay. The beast had six rows of teeth and its liver reportedly yielded three barrels of oil. It was subsequently placed on public display as the "Leviathan or Wonderful SEA-SERPENT," but French zoologist Charles-Alexandre Lesueur identified the creature as a basking shark (*Cetorhinus maximus*).

Source: Heuvelmans, *In the Wake of the Sea Serpents.*

Rassic   Rassic is the name applied by locals to a supposed LAKE MONSTER inhabiting Sweden's Lake Råsvalen, in Örebo County. Sightings date from 1914, when witness Karl Gustavsson reported a 12-foot FISH in the lake. Eight decades later, in the summer of 1987, a 15-foot creature resembling a log was seen swimming near the Kalmarslund Recreation Center. Members of the GLOBAL UNDERWATER SEARCH TEAM visited Lake Råsvalen in November 1997, plumbing its 100-foot depths with hydrophones, and leader JAN-OVE SUNDBERG later claimed to have recorded strange underwater sounds.

Source: GUST website, http://www.cryptozoology.st/.

Rat-tail (Giant)   Science recognizes 285 pelagic species of rat-tail or grenadier FISH (Family *Macrouridae*). The largest known species, the giant grenadier (*Albatrossia pectoralis*), attains a maximum official length of five feet. Nonetheless, a 6-foot rat-tail was reported from Bermuda in the 1930s, and a 10-foot specimen was sighted in the Gulf of Mexico in the late 1960s. Both sightings occurred in deep water, and no specimens exceeding the known limits of *A. pectoralis* have yet been collected.

Source: Soule, *Mystery Monsters of the Deep.*

Rauflovatnet, Norway   Rauflovatnet, in Nord-Trøndelag County, is another of Norway's many lakes with old traditions of LAKE MONSTER sightings. Once again, unfortunately, no detailed descriptions have survived, and sightings seem to have ceased in the late 19th century.

Source: Skjelsvik, "Norwegian lake and sea monsters."

Raynal, Michel (1955–)

French native Michel Raynal worked as a physicist and chemist for ten years prior to his employment as a senior manager for France Télécom. In cryptozoology, Raynal is best known for his extensive bibliographical research, and for his authorship of several dozen published articles.

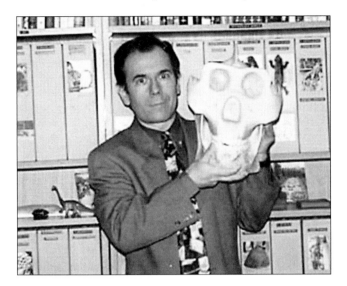

French cryptozoologist Michel Raynal with the skull of *Gigantopithecus.*

He also operates an Internet website, the Virtual Institute of Cryptozoology, and has prepared a multimedia program on the subject for the Cité des Sciences et de l'Industrie of La Villette (Paris).

Source: Virtual Institute of Cryptozoology, http://perso.wanadoo.fr/cryptozoo/.

Rebsamen, William Murphree (1964–)

Arkansas native William Rebsamen may be fairly described as the Renaissance man of cryptozoology. His interest in unknown animals was sparked by *The Legend of Boggy Creek* (1972), a film depicting the FOUKE MONSTER. As a teenager, Rebsamen studied under famous wildlife artist Susan Morrison and Sea World muralist Robert Walters, subsequently earning a bachelor's degree in fine art from the Kansas City Art Institute. As an artist, Rebsamen first worked with Ducks Unlimited, then established his own popular line of Pet Portraits.

A longstanding interest in cryptozoology and a desire to educate the public on its authenticity prompted Rebsamen to begin painting cryptids. His original artwork illustrates various publications of LOREN COLEMAN, WILLIAM GIBBONS, SCOTT NORMAN and KARL SHUKER (and the present volume). In addition to painting, Rebsamen has produced a 40-minute CD entitled *Music Inspired by Cryptozoology*, with instrumental tracks including "Bigfoot is Watching" (spoken segments by Loren Coleman), "Happy Little Sauropod," "Into the Depths" (spoken segments by William Gibbons), and "Into the Heart of Darkness." Rebsamen describes his music as "Jazz Fusion/Electronica meets Pink Floyd or Alan Parsons."

Crypto-artist William Rebsamen at work.

In 2002, Gibbons's website listed Rebsamen as vice president of Creation Generation, a religious organization that carries out cryptozoological expeditions while preaching the dangers of evolutionary theory.

Sources: William Rebsamen Gallery, http://www.rebsamen-wildlife.com/index.html; Creation Generation website, http://www.kingkongvsgodzilla.com/chupa/; personal communication with the author (29 June 2003).

Red Cedar Lake, Wisconsin

The first report of a LAKE MONSTER in Red Cedar Lake (Jefferson County, 25 miles east of Madison) was filed by a fisherman in 1891. The witness described a large, undulating form, but could not say if it had been a FISH or reptile. Other locals soon came forward with reports of sightings, adding details that included a large head, overall length approaching 50 feet, and a serrated ridge along the creature's back.

Unsubstantiated rumors claimed the cryptid passed at will through an underground channel connecting Red Cedar Lake to Lake Ripley, but no such channel was found. Skeptics suggested that the creature was a HOAX, designed to boost sales of lakefront property. In any case, sightings dwindled over time and have not been repeated since the turn of the 20th century.

Sources: Brown, *Sea Serpents: Wisconsin Occurrences of These Weird Creatures*; Costello, *In Search of Lake Monsters.*

Red-Eye

BIGFOOT researcher Rick Berry reports that the first accounts of an unknown HOMINID in South Carolina date from the turn of the 20th century, when a hairy biped known as Red-Eye frightened residents of Black River, in Lee County. Unfortunately, no details or sources are provided, and various published surveys of the Bigfoot phenomena (including Berry's) begin their lists of specific South Carolina sightings in the 1970s.

Source: Berry, *Bigfoot on the East Coast.*

Red-Headed Cat

Sometime in the mid-1990s, "a couple of years" before 1998, a large unidentified CAT was reportedly shot by hunters in (or "near") Jackson County, Tennessee. The shooters allegedly photographed their kill, but then suppressed the photos in fear of prosecution for killing an endangered species. The animal was described as "cheetah-like in form, but [with] a blood-red head and paws, a red line running from the back of its head to its tail (which was also red), and a golden-brown body patterned with black stripes and spots. The pelt, supposedly preserved and hidden in one hunter's basement, has yet to be recovered, despite ongoing investigations by KARL SHUKER and Tennessee investigator Scott McNabb.

Sources: Karl Shuker, "Menagerie of mystery." *Strange Magazine* 19 (Spring 1998): 23; Shuker, "Menagerie of mystery." *Strange Magazine* 20 (December 1998): 39.

Red Horse Lake, Canada   A supposed LAKE MONSTER was reported from this Ontario lake, near Lyndhurst, in the 1970s. A witness, frightened by the creature near Cold Spring Bay, described it as 60–80 feet long, greenish-black in color, with a head resembling a horse's.

Source: Shadowlands website, http://theshadowlands.net.

Red River, Canada   Witnesses reported sightings of an unidentified reptilian creature from this Manitoba River (south of Winnipeg) in August 1940. The creature resembled an ALLIGATOR or CROCODILE, but it was never captured and soon disappeared.

Source: "A brief survey of Canadian lake monsters."

Red Wolf   A MYSTERY MAULER reported from the Vienne Department of central France, this creature attacked livestock in the early years of the 19th century. Witnesses who stalked the predator in vain said it resembled a wolf, except for its striking red fur. Its size presumably ruled out a FOX as the culprit. All attempts to kill or capture the prowler were futile, but it ultimately vanished as mysteriously as it came.

Source: Henri Ellenberger, "Le monde fantastique dans le folklore de la Vienne." *Nouvelle Revue des Traditions Populaires* 1 (1949): 407–435.

Redondo Beach Merman   In May 1935, crewmen aboard a fishing boat sighted a strange creature three miles offshore from Redondo Beach, California. The witnesses described it as a "merman" 10–12 feet long, with a human face framed by dark hair and a beard. They particularly noted the creature's broad forehead and shiny eyes. As the fishermen lowered a skiff to pursue the cryptid, it vanished underwater with a flash of its fishy tail. Reports of MERBEINGS are normally dismissed as mistaken sightings of sirenians (manatees or dugongs), but

California fishermen encountered a strange merbeing in 1935.

none are native to the California coast, and it seems unlikely that experienced fishermen would mistake a common seal for a 12-foot bearded man-FISH.

Source: Bord and Bord, *Unexplained Mysteries of the 20th Century.*

Redwood, California sea serpent   In July 1955, while walking along the beach near Redwood, California, Joseph Korhummel saw an apparent SEA SERPENT splashing in the water a short distance offshore. Korhummel climbed some nearby rocks to get a better view, observing a greenish-brown serpentine creature with a dorsal fin set close behind its head. He described the animal as 16–18 feet long and one foot in diameter.

Source: Keel, *The Complete Guide to Mysterious Beings.*

Regnaren, Sweden   This lake in Sweden's Gävelborg County, with a maximum depth of 90 feet, has produced sporadic reports of a nondescript LAKE MONSTER. Locals also describe occasional sightings of "hoop SNAKES," mythical reptiles known the world over for seizing their tails in their mouths and rolling downhill to escape enemies.

Source: GUST Website, http://www.cryptozoology.st/.

Regusters, Herman A. (n.d.)   Electronics engineer Herman Regusters was employed as a consultant to the National Aeronautics and Space Administration's Jet Propulsion Laboratory in Pasadena, California during 1980, when he read reports of ROY MACKAL'S first attempt to find MOKELE-MBEMBE, a supposed living DINOSAUR in the Congo region of Africa. One of hundreds who contacted Mackal that year, seeking a role in his next expedition, Regusters offered to contribute various pieces of high-tech equipment, including satellite tracking gear to facilitate the search. After a meeting in Chicago, Mackal accepted Regusters's offer and provisionally named his new effort the Mackal-Regusters Likouala Expedition. Problems arose on 10 June 1981, after Regusters held a press conference in Los Angeles and distributed fliers containing "at least as dozen errors," including references to nonexistent Congo ALLIGATORS and head-hunters. Regusters dismissed Mackal's objections as "nit-picking" and printed T-shirts emblazoned with a logo for the "Mackal-Regusters Dinosaur Trek." Their final falling-out came in July 1981, when Regusters rejected a contract prepared by Mackal and Texas sponsor Jack Bryan. Mackal ultimately went to Africa with J. RICHARD GREENWELL, a colleague from the INTERNATIONAL SOCIETY OF CRYPTOZOOLOGY, while Regusters launched an independent expedition with his wife.

The Regusters African Congo Expedition began on 7 September 1981 and ended on 9 December. Despite various logistics problems, the team reached Lac Télé, in the Republic of Congo with 28 native bearers. Subsequently, Regusters and wife Kim claimed a sighting of Mokele-mbembe, observed through binoculars while swimming in the lake. Regusters said the beast "appeared to have a slender neck about 6 feet long, a small head and about 15 feet of back." Although he did not see the creature's body or tail, he pegged its total length at 30–35 feet and declared that "[i]t certainly was much larger than an elephant." On another occasion, unidentified growling sounds were recorded, presumed to be the giant creature's call. Regusters emerged from the jungle with 23 rolls of film, all but one frame over-exposed or damaged in transit. The sole photograph depicts a dark-colored object of unknown size breaking the lake's surface. Also retrieved were footprint casts and fecal samples, likewise unidentified. Skeptics dismiss the single photo as a picture of a swimming elephant and note that none of the team's native guides saw the creature in question. Reguster published a report which read, in part:

It is the overwhelming conclusion of the participants of this expedition that some unidentified type of animal inhabits the Lac Tele vicinity and possibly exists throughout the entire forest region of the Likouala. It would seem unreasonable to suppose that the various accounts of sightings and of related incidents are being fabricated for the purpose of amusing or accommodating a few investigators. In addition, much added weight is given by the testimony of high government officials who have nothing to benefit through such distortions. The majority of the invalid data is being generated by the designs and self-interest of foreign investigators. Among these is the continued promotion of forest-dwelling PYGMIES as a source of invalidatable information, in a region where it has been established that, at this date, any such people remaining are inaccessible.

The final comment was presumably a jibe at Mackal, whose 1981 expedition employed several "inaccessible" pygmies as guides. A dozen years after his foray to the Congo, Regusters met SCOTT NORMAN and described the Lac Télé adventure, thus prompting Norman to launch his own career in cryptozoology.

Sources: Mackal, *A Living Dinosaur?*; Cryptozoology.com, *http://www.cryptozoology.com/cryptids/mokele.php*; Mokele-Mbembe, *http://www.geocities.com/Area51/Cavern/7270/mokele.html*; Mokele-Mbembe: Last of the Dinosaurs?, *http://www.angelfire.com/falcon/megaraptor/mokele-mbembe.htm*.

Reinsvatnet, Norway
In the mid-16th century, a LAKE MONSTER was allegedly killed at Klype, on the shore of this lake in Norway's Rogaland County. The large, unidentified creature was shot after it became stuck in a narrow lakeside pass, then it was buried beneath a cairn of stones. No further cryptid sightings have emerged from the region.

Sources: Costello, *In Search of Lake Monsters*; Skjelsvik, "Norwegian lake and sea monsters."

Repstadvatnet, Norway
Located near Søgne, in Vest-Agder County, this Norwegian lake was reputedly inhabited by a LAKE MONSTER in the 18th century. Witnesses described the creature as serpentine in form, with a flowing horselike mane on its neck. No sightings of the cryptid have been logged in modern times.

Sources: Costello, *In Search of Lake Monsters*; Kirk, *In the Domain of the Lake Monsters*; Skjelsvik, "Norwegian lake and sea monsters."

Réservoir Baskatong, Canada see Lac-à-la-Tortue

Réservoir Gouin, Canada
Located in western Québec, near the Ashuapmushuan Provincial Reserve, Réservoir Gouin reportedly harbors an unidentified LAKE MONSTER. Unfortunately, no description of the creature is available, and no eyewitnesses are publicly identified.

Sources: Coleman, *Mysterious America*; Kirk, *In the Domain of the Lake Monsters*.

Reuss River, Switzerland
DRAGON sightings were reported sporadically from the Reuss River, in Canton Luzern, during the 15th and 16th centuries. Reports coincided with flooding of the lake at Luzern, as when a "great and horrible dragon-worm" was seen from a bridge spanning the Reuss in 1468. Other sightings were reported in 1480 and 1566, but none are on file from modern times.

Sources: "Eel be back," *Fortean Times*; Alois Lütolf, *Sagen, Bräuche, Legenden aus den fünf Orten Luzern, Uri, Schwyz, Unterwalden und Zug*. Luzern: J. Schiffmann, 1862.

Dragons allegedly inhabited Switzerland's Reuss River in Medieval times.

Rexbeast
In January 2004, Australian cryptozoologist REX GILROY announced his "discovery" of a giant HOMINID surpassing the YOWIE in stature. As described by Gilroy, the mountain-dwelling creature — which he called Rexbeast, since its "original name seems lost" — stands 10 feet tall and is well known among Aborigines in eastern Australia. The Rexbeast is not only huge, in Gilroy's estimation, but it also makes and uses stone "megatools" weighing 33–44 pounds, several of which Gilroy claims to have collected in his travels. Nor is the Rexbeast extinct, since Gilroy and wife Heather claim discovery of fresh footprints, 35 inches long and 19.5 inches wide, found along the Tuross River, New South Wales, in 2001. Gilroy announced plans for a full-scale Rexbeast hunt in winter 2004–05, planned in collaboration with two unnamed U.S. BIGFOOT researchers.

Source: Blue Mountains UFO Research Club, *http://www.internetezy.com.au/~mj129/monthly_meetings_january2004.html*.

Reynolds Lake, Kentucky
In the latter 1960s, this small lake near LaGrange, Kentucky (Oldham County) spawned reports of a giant SNAKE on the prowl. An early witness, in 1965, described the reptile as "about two feet around, with the biggest head you ever saw, and large beady eyes." Locals claimed the snake had devoured most of the lake's FISH and FROGS, while some accused it of stalking barnyard animals. The last reported sighting came in 1968, when the animal frightened a fisherman from Tennessee, grabbing his catch and his expensive fishing gear.

Sources: "More and more." *Fate* 16 (December 1965): 22; Kentucky's Aquatic Cryptids, *http://www.geocities.com/cryptidwrangler/kycryptids2.html*.

Rhinoceros (African one-horned)
Two species of rhinoceros are known to inhabit the African continent south of the Sahara Desert: the black rhinoceros (*Diceros bicornis*) and the white rhinoceros (*Ceratotherium simum*). Both feature two horns on their snouts, and while no one-horned African rhino is recognized by science, scattered reports of such a creature have been logged over a wide range, including Chad, Sudan, Ethiopia and Somalia, southward through Mozambique and northern portions of South Africa. A 12th-century gold-plated carving, excavated at the Mapungubwe archaeological site in South Africa's Northern Province, clearly depicts a one-horned rhino. Live sightings apparently ended in the 19th century, leaving cryptozoologists to speculate on the creature's identity. Suggested explanations include mistaken sightings of a known rhinoceros who had some-

how lost one horn; a congenital deformity that sometimes prevents growth of a posterior horn in white rhinos; and the former existence of an unknown one-horned species in Africa, now presumed extinct.

Sources: Fulgence Fresnel, "Sur l'existence d'une espèce unicorne de rhinocéros dans la partie tropicale de l'Afrique." *Comptes Rendus de l'Accademie des Sciences* 26 (1848): 281; Elizabeth Voigt, *Mapungubwe: An Archaeological Interpretation of an Iron Age Community.* Pretoria: Transvaal Museum, 1983.

Reports of a one-horned African rhinoceros date from the 12th century.

Rhinoceros Dolphin Most cryptids never earn a scientific name, making it all the more unusual when an unconfirmed species has two. The RHINOCEROS Dolphin is one such rarity, sighted initially in October 1819, by naturalists Joseph Gaimard and Jean-René Quoy. Gaimard and Quoy were traveling from the Hawaiian islands to Australia when they sighted a school of unknown dolphins near Palmyra Atoll, at 5° 52' north latitude, 162° 6' west longitude. The animals were roughly 10 feet long, with spotted black-and-white upper bodies. Each had two dorsal fins, with the unusual second fin close to the head, curved backward like a rhino's horn. In 1824, still without a type specimen in hand, Gaimard and Quoy named the species *Delphinus rhinoceros.* Another sighting was recorded in April 1856, when residents of Cornwall, England saw two specimens swimming with a school of common dolphins (*D. delphus*) in Lantivet Bay. In 1991, Michel Raynal suggested that the elusive cryptid might be a new beaked whale, instead of a dolphin. Accordingly, he named the species *Cetodipteros rhinoceros.* Despite two Latin names, the rhinoceros dolphin remains unrecognized by modern science.

Sources: Jean-René Quoy and Joseph Gaimard, *Voyage autour du monde.* Paris: Pillet Aîné, 1824; Raynal, "Do two-finned cetaceans really exist?"; Shuker, *From Flying Toads to Snakes with Wings.*

Rhinoceros Whale Another two-finned mystery cetacean, not to be confused with the RHINOCEROS DOLPHIN, was glimpsed for the first time by Italian naturalist Enrico Giglioli. Professor Giglioli was circumnavigating the Earth aboard the *Magenta* when he made his sighting on 4 September 1867, in the South Pacific some 1,000 miles west of Chile. The animal resembled a baleen whale, with greenish-gray dorsal coloration and grayish-white beneath. Giglioli pegged its length at 60 feet, noting the presence of two erect dorsal fins, situated about 6.5 feet apart.

In 1870, Giglioli named his discovery *Amphiptera pacifica,* al-

though its existence has yet to be recognized. A second possible sighting occurred in October 1898, when fishermen aboard the *Lily* saw a similar creature off the coast of Stonehaven, Scotland. The witnesses described that whale as 68 feet long, with 20 feet between its twin dorsal fins. Nine decades later, on 17 July 1983, passengers aboard a sailboat in the Mediterranean, between Corsica and France, allegedly sighted a whale with two dorsal fins, a trapezoidal head, and a white underside.

Sources: Raynal, "Do two-finned cetaceans really exist?"; "Scared by a sea serpent," London *Daily Mail* (10 October 1898); Shuker, *From Flying Toads to Snakes with Wings.*

Rhône sea serpent (1905) On 13 April 1905, while returning from Chile to France, Captain P. Guillou of the *Rhône* sighted a SEA SERPENT at 52° south latitude and 75° west longitude. As he described the incident:

I saw sticking up some twenty yards away in our wake and 5 feet above the water, the head of an animal which I cannot compare to anything but those which used to decorate the prow of Viking ships and the big junks of the Niger....The animal seemed startled. All I saw was the head and neck which followed the undulating movements of the body, which seemed to me to be long. It made off at a considerable speed.

Source: Heuvelmans, *In the Wake of the Sea Serpents.*

Rhône sea serpent (1964) One afternoon in late May or early June 1964, Jacques Borelli was fishing near the mouth of the Rhône River, west of Marseille, when he saw a SEA SERPENT offshore. As he later described the incident to BERNARD HEUVELMANS:

I was spinning for mackerel with my son in a slight chop, when, looking astern, we suddenly saw, about a hundred yards away, a shoal of mackerel leaping as if they were being chased. Then there appeared a sort of beam, light chestnut, cylindrical in shape and with a rounded end. This "beam" of which the part out of the water must have measured 6 feet in length and about a foot in diameter, was sloping forward and moved without our being able to see any wake at that distance, then it disappeared after about 30 seconds.

Source: Heuvelmans, *In the Wake of the Sea Serpents.*

Rhum sea serpent Rhum is an island located 17 miles off the west coast of Scotland, in the Sea of Hebrides. One summer afternoon in the early 1900s, while fishing from a small boat offshore, two residents of Rhum were startled "when they saw an object about thirty feet in height moving to and fro out of the sea. The day was fine and hot, and they thought they could see the body in the water waving at speed towards them." Frightened of the SEA SERPENT, they fled to shore at once and were not pursued.

Source: Heuvelmans, *In the Wake of the Sea Serpents.*

Ri Global traditions of MERBEINGS include reports of encounters with human-FISH hybrids from every continent, throughout recorded history. One such elusive cryptid, the Ri of Melanesia, has been positively identified through the diligent efforts of cryptozoologists. In November 1979, while observing Barok natives on New Ireland, Papua New Guinea, anthropologist Roy Wagner collected reports of the Ri and logged a personal sighting at Ramat Bay of "something large swimming at the surface in a broad arc toward the shore." Four years later, in June 1983, Wagner returned to New Ireland with a party that included J. RICHARD GREENWELL, of the INTERNATIONAL SOCIETY OF CRYPTOZOOLOGY. On 5 July, at Nokon Bay, Wagner and Greenwell

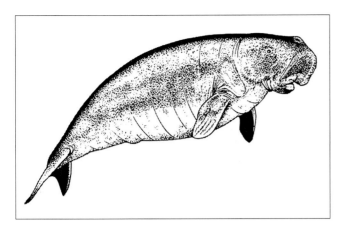

New Ireland's elusive Ri was identified as a dugong in the 1980s.

observed a Ri swimming offshore and snapped several photos that revealed a dark object rising above the water's surface. In February 1985, an expedition led by Thomas Williams and sponsored by the Ecosophical Research Association visited Nokon Bay aboard the diving boat *Reef Explorer*. There, on 10 February, a Ri was sighted and photographed underwater, establishing its identity as a dugong (*Dugong dugong*).

Sources: Wagner, "The *Ri*: Unidentified aquatic animals of New Ireland, Papua New Guinea"; Wagner, et al., "Further investigations into the biological and cultural affinities of the Ri"; Williams, "Identification of the Ri through further fieldwork in New Ireland, Papua New Guinea."

Richilieu River, Canada   Details are scarce concerning the "siren" reportedly killed in this Québec river, east of Montreal, in 1672. Some researchers believe it may have been an errant seal, lost after entering the St. Lawrence seaway.

Source: Charles Bécard and Marc de Villiers du Terrage, *Les Raretés des Index, "Codex Canadiensis": Album Manuscrit de la Fin du XVIIe Siècle Contenant 180 Desins Concernant les Indigènes, Leurs Coutumes, Tatouages, la Faune et la Flore de la Nouvelle France.* Montreal: Éditiones du Boutton d'Or, 1974.

Richmond Beast   The Richmond Beast is a reputed ALIEN BIG CAT, sighted in recent years around Richmond, North Yorkshire, England. The latest report of the creature (at press time for this volume) was filed from East Sheen, where a large feline pawprint was found in a homeowner's garden, in mid-September 2002. Local authorities were skeptical, despite thousands of similar reports all over the country. Investigators noted that there is no zoo in the vicinity, and no large exotic animals are registered with the Richmond Council, as required by law.

Source: "Is there a Richmond beast?" *Richmond and Twickenham Times* (20 September 2002).

Rideau River, Canada   In 1881, while traveling from Ottawa to Kingston, passengers aboard the steamer *Gypsy* allegedly sighted a large serpentine creature swimming in this Ontario river. No other sightings are on record from the Rideau, which links the Ottawa River to Lake Ontario.

Source: Bord and Bord, *Unexplained Mysteries of the 20th Century.*

Rimi   The Rimi is an unclassified primate or HOMINID reported from mountainous regions of eastern Nepal and Tibet. Witnesses describe the creature as 7–9 feet tall, covered in black hair, with prominent teeth. Its name translated from Tibetan as "mountain man," and while locals take care to distinguish Rimi from the more famous YETI, the two cryptids may be identical. In

1953, Lama Chemed Rigdzin Dorje Lopu claimed to have seen two mummified Rimis, one at Tibet's Racaka Monastery, the other at an undisclosed location. Neither specimen has yet been located by outside researchers.

Sources: Heuvelmans, *On the Track of Unknown Animals*; Shuker, *In Search of Prehistoric Survivors.*

Rines, Robert H. (1923–)   Arguably the most famous Loch Ness researcher aside from TIM DINSDALE, Robert Rines grew up on tales of NESSIE but disregarded them for the first 46 years of his life, refusing to accept the possible existence of the "monster." In those days, Rines was a world-renowned patent attorney, a physicist and engineer whose groundbreaking work on sonar helped find the *Titanic*. That changed in 1969, after Rines attended a lecture by cryptozoologist ROY MACKAL. Impressed by the evidence of Nessie's existence, Rines — then president of the ACADEMY OF APPLIED SCIENCE (AAS) — offered his professional assistance to the LOCH NESS INVESTIGATION BUREAU.

Rines visited Loch Ness for the first time in September 1970, but his team's effort to draw Nessie out with sexual attractants failed. The next year he tried sonar, and while that effort also proved fruitless, Rines and his wife saw Nessie surface in Urquhart Bay, on 23 June 1971. Thirty years later, Rines described the experience for CBS News.

> I didn't want to stop looking at what I could not believe. There in the middle of the Loch is the back of what, when we put the telescope and the binocs on it, looked like a giant elephant's back, and as we looked at it, we had 10 minutes, Scott. This isn't a fleeting kind of thing. We had 10 minutes. This lumbering thing turned around, gave us the wonderful spectacle of coming right back in front of us and submerged.

Encouraged by that sighting, Rines returned to Loch Ness in 1972 with sonar and underwater cameras, which he mounted off Temple Pier, in Urquhart Bay. There, on 8 August, a series of pictures were snapped that included the famous "flipper photo," alleged to reveal part of Nessie's anatomy. Skeptics dismissed the photo as meaningless, but it convinced Rines that his search would ultimately lead him to a living PLESIOSAUR.

Back at the loch in 1975, Rines secured two more remarkable underwater photos on 21 June, including the renowned (or notorious) "gargoyle head" picture presumed by some observers to depict Nessie's face, and a "full body" shot that appears to show a long-necked creature passing by the camera's lens. Critics subsequently claimed discovery of a twisted log on the loch's muddy bottom that matches the "gargoyle" face to near perfection, but controversy endures — and Rines was not discouraged by the doubters.

Full-time teaching duties at the Massachusetts Institute of Technology barred Rines from field work, but AAS members returned to Loch Ness with sonar equipment in 1976, 1978 and 1980, recording "hits" that remain unexplained. Rines himself returned to the loch in 1984, but no further contacts with Nessie were recorded. In 1991, Rines and the AAS briefly engaged in the pursuit of BIGFOOT, mounting motion-sensitive cameras at an Oregon site selected by PETER BYRNE, but without result. In 1997, Rines and Charles Wyckoff returned to Loch Ness, to film a documentary sponsored by the *Nova* television series. While their sponsors hoped to debunk Nessie, Rines recorded two large sonar contacts that convinced the producers of Nessie's existence.

In June 2001, while accompanied by cameras from the CBS News program *60 Minutes II*, Rines sighted and photographed a peculiar stationary object on the loch's bed near the mouth of

Urquhart Bay, at a depth of 333 feet. Rines described the object as resembling "a decaying or a decayed carcass and vertebrae and things of this sort" that resembled what "paleontologists have told us we might expect to see after many years of rotting." When Rines returned with equipment to retrieve the "carcass" in 2002, however, it could not be found.

Sources: Harrison, *Encyclopaedia of the Loch Ness Monster*; "Monster Hunter," *60 Minutes II* (24 July 2002); Rines, "Summarizing a decade of underwater studies at Loch Ness"; Rines, et al., "Activities of the Academy of Applied Science related to investigations at Loch Ness, 1984"; Wyckoff, et al., "An unmanned motion-sensitive automatic infrared camera tested in a Pacific Northwest quest for possible large primates."

Ringsjøen, Norway   Neighbors of this lake, in Norway's Hedmark County, reported sightings of a large LAKE MONSTER during 1868. Witnesses described the cryptid as possessing a horselike head and prominent white teeth. No modern reports are on file.

Sources: Kirk, *In the Domain of the Lake Monsters*; Skjelsvik, "Norwegian lake and sea monsters."

Río Beni, Bolivia   In the early 1880s, a 36-foot scaly animal was reportedly killed along this river of northern Bolivia. Its remains were sent to La Paz for study, but their fate is unknown. Surviving descriptions say the creature had a doglike head, with two smaller "heads" sprouting from its back.

Source: "A Bolivian saurian." *Scientific America* 49 (1883): 3.

Rio de Janeiro sea serpent   In February 1958, an unknown SEA SERPENT frightened residents and travelers in the vicinity of Rio de Janeiro, Brazil. Witness Walter Ferreira de Rocha described the creature as "a monster with a giraffe's neck, a hump on the back and a long tail. A local fisherman who met the beast at sea, Amaldo Serapio Jesús, initially mistook it for a sea lion, but quickly changed his mind. "When I came closer," Serapio told reporters, "I saw that it was a monstrous green serpent with a head as big as a barrel. I at once made for the coast and gave up fishing for the rest of the day." Another fisherman, Mario de Castro Abreu, claimed the animal rivaled a whale in length. Police armed with dynamite and automatic weapons swarmed Rio Bay in search of the creature, and one patrol allegedly fired upon it, on 10 February. No further sightings were reported after that incident.

Source: Heuvelmans, *In the Wake of the Sea Serpents*.

Río Guaviare, Colombia   This river of eastern Colombia reputedly hosts large aquatic cryptids, but no descriptive details are available. Cryptozoologist JOHN KIRK, author of the only English-language source referring to the creatures, makes matters worse by misplacing the river in Brazil.

Source: Kirk, *In the Domain of the Lake Monsters*.

Río Magdalena, Colombia   In 1921, travelers along this river in northern Colombia reported a brief encounter with a large reptile resembling a prehistoric *Iguanodon* (presumed extinct since the early Cretaceous period, 100 million years ago). No evidence remains of the incident, which was apparently the only sighting of an alleged DINOSAUR from this region.

Source: Shuker, *In Search of Prehistoric Survivors*.

Río Marañón, Peru   In the early 20th century, Indians of northern Peru claimed this river was the home of a large, herbivorous reptile resembling a DINOSAUR. No reports of the creature have been filed in the period since World War II.

Witnesses described the Río Magdalena cryptid as resembling a prehistoric *Iguandodon*.

Source: Leonard Clark, *The Rivers Ran East*. New York: Funk and Wagnalls, 1953.

Rio Mármore, Brazil   In 1931, while exploring the Mato Grosso jungles of Brazil, Swedish adventurer Harald Westin encountered a 20-foot reptile on the bank of the Rio Mármore. He later described it as gray in color, with four legs and red eyes set in a head resembling that of an oversized ALLIGATOR. Westin fired his rifle at the creature, with no apparent effect. Unfazed, the beast passed on into the forest, while Westin fled in the other direction.

Source: Shuker, *In Search of Prehistoric Survivors*.

Rio Paraguaçu, Brazil   In 1995, a party of geology students investigating quartz deposits in the Sinorca Mountains of eastern Brazil (Bahía State) sighted two strange reptilian creatures along the Rio Paraguaçu, where it passed through the plain of Orobo. They described the animals as 30 feet long, 6-foot necks and 8-foot tails. If true, the report would seem to corroborate other accounts of Brazilian animals resembling DINOSAURS, including a description offered by explorer PERCY FAWCETT in 1911.

Source: Shuker, *In Search of Prehistoric Survivors*.

Rio Paraguai, Brazil   Cryptozoologist JOHN KIRK reports that unknown aquatic creatures have been seen along this river, in Brazil's Mato Grosso State, but he provides no description or source for the claim. The alleged creature may be identical to MANGURUYÚ, a giant FISH reported from the river's southern branch in Paraguay; alternatively, Kirk may have confused the two rivers, since his list of "monster" sites includes none for Paraguay.

Source: Kirk, *In the Domain of the Lake Monsters*.

Rio Paraná, Brazil   Author JOHN KIRK attributes cryptid sightings to this river in Brazil's Goias State without providing sources or descriptions. His claim is thus impossible to analyze, but it may be a mistaken reference to the CAA-PORA, an unknown HOMINID or primate reported from the same region.

Sources: Kirk, *In the Domains of the Lake Monsters*; Picasso, "South American monsters and mystery animals."

Rio Putumayo, Brazil   Investigator JOHN KIRK offers no details or sources while listing this river in Brazil's Amazonas

State as a source of aquatic "monster" reports. The claim is thus impossible to analyze.

Source: Kirk, *In the Domain of the Lake Monsters.*

Rio Tamango, Argentina In 1902, while serving with the Boundary Demarcation Commission assigned to settle a border dispute between Chile and Argentina, a Norwegian engineer named Vaag allegedly found the carcass of a large, unidentified reptile beside the Rio Tamango. At the same place, Vaag reported finding tracks on the river bank which he thought might belong to a second creature of similar size. The remains were not preserved for study, but Dr. CLEMENTI ONELLI of the Buenos Aires Zoo later cited the case as evidence that PLESIOSAURS still lived in South America.

Source: Costello, *In Search of Lake Monsters.*

Rio Trombetas, Brazil Details and sources are lacking from author JOHN KIRK'S report that this river, in the northern part of Brazil's Pará State, has produced aquatic "monster" sightings. Without further information, no analysis is possible.

Source: Kirk, *In the Domain of the Lake Monsters.*

River Dinosaur Since 1982, witnesses in around Colorado have reported encounters with a fleet-footed reptile popularly dubbed the "River DINOSAUR." Reports describe the creature as three feet tall, with a 2-foot tail, a long neck, conical snout, and armlike appendages in place of traditional forelegs. Witnesses agree that the animal walks and runs exclusively on its hind legs, being sighted most often in close proximity to streams or ponds. Herpetologists note that MONITOR LIZARDS match the creature's general description, and that they frequently run on their hind legs while using their long tails for balance.

Source: Karl Shuker, "Alien zoo." *Fortean Times* 166 (February 2003): 16.

River Gudenå, Denmark In September 1943, Danes living near this river (in Viborg County) were troubled by a 6-foot aquatic SNAKE unknown to the region. One person attacked by the aggressive reptile tried to defend himself with a stick, then fled in fear. The spate of sightings was short-lived, and the creature has not returned.

Source: Bord and Bord, *Unexplained Mysteries of the 20th Century.*

River Ribble, England In June 1999, while walking their dogs through Preston, Lancashire, Edwin and Sheila Smith saw a strange creature rise from the nearby River Ribble. As Sheila described the incident:

From quite a distance up the river, I cannot say just how far, I saw a very tall thin object protruding from the water. At that point I was only casually glancing and joked to my brother, "Look, the Loch Ness monster," and we thought no more of it.

Nevertheless I kept my eye on it, and as we walked on — we were gradually getting closer to it — I was still trying to make out what it could be, my thoughts being that it was probably a tree or the branch of a tree stuck in the river. Then just about thirty seconds later as we drew level with it, this thing just completely submerged into the river. It created a cascade of ripples, it even made the dogs curious, and we were nearly speechless.

Stephens described the uplifted object as dark brown, four feet long and one foot in circumference, with no visible head. No other reports have been filed from the region.

Source: Harrison, *Sea Serpents and Lake Monsters of the British Isles.*

River Shannon serpents Irish folklore speaks of "shin-ing serpents" in the River Shannon, and sightings have continued into modern times. In July 1922, with Ireland's civil war in full fury, multiple witnesses saw a large serpentine creature swimming in the river below Limerick. Another sighting of a similar, further downstream, was logged in 1933. Perhaps significantly, LOUGH REE on the River Shannon also has a longstanding tradition of "monster" reports.

Sources: Costello, *In Search of Lake Monsters*; McEwan, *Mystery Animals of Britain and Ireland.*

River Ticino, Italy In 1934, a large horse-headed animal was sighted in this northern Italian river, near the point where it spills into LAGO MAGGIORE (on the Swiss-Italian border). Since the lake also enjoys a tradition of similar sightings, it is reasonable to assume that the animal sighted was a wandering LAKE MONSTER. The Ticino also extends for some distance beyond Lago Maggiore, into southern Switzerland, thereby providing hypothetical cryptids with an opportunity for travel.

Source: Magin, "A brief survey of lake monsters of continental Europe."

Roa-Roa *see* **Moa**

Robert Ellis sea serpent In October 1805, while sailing through the Welsh Menai Strait, passengers and crew aboard the *Robert Ellis* allegedly saw "a strange creature like an immense worm" swimming after the ship. Worse lay in store, as described in a published account of the incident:

It soon overtook them, climbed on board through the tiller-hole, and coiled itself on the deck under the mast. The people at first were dreadfully frightened, but taking courage they attacked it with an oar and drove it overboard. It followed the vessel for some time but a breeze springing up, they lost sight of it.

BERNARD HEUVELMANS, in his classic compilation of SEA SERPENT reports, suggested that the creature may have been a giant EEL — or that the incident may have been fabricated as a HOAX.

Source: Heuvelmans, *In the Wake of the Sea Serpents.*

Robertson sea serpent On 22 June 1834, officers aboard the Scottish vessel *Robertson* saw an unusual SEA SERPENT off the southern coast of Newfoundland, Canada. At first, they mistook the creature for a capsized boat, then realized it was alive. Captain Neill described the beast as follows:

Immediately above the water its eye was seen like a large deep hole. That part of the head which was above water measured about twelve feet [high], and its breadth or width twenty-five feet. The snout or trunk was about fifty feet long, and the sea occasionally rippled over one part, leaving other parts quite dry and uncovered. The colour of the parts seen was green, with a light and dark shade; and the skin was ribbed, as represented in the sketch.

From the description and drawing, BERNARD HEUVELMANS concluded that the creature was a rorqual whale (Family *Bal-*

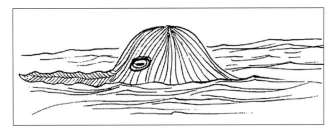

The *Robertson* sea serpent, sketched by Captain Neill.

aenopteridae) floating belly-up, and that its "eye" was in fact a fatal throat wound. Other authors have suggested that it was a giant OCTOPUS.

Source: Heuvelmans, *In the Wake of the Sea Serpents.*

Rock Lake, Washington

Rock Lake is located in eastern Washington's Whitman County, 25 miles southwest of Spokane. LAKE MONSTER reports date from 1835, when an Indian war party fleeing from U.S. troops was allegedly attacked and slaughtered by a large beast from the lake. Sporadic sightings have continued into modern times, exacerbated by the fact that drowning victims rarely surface in this cold-water lake. Suggested explanations for the sightings include a school of sucker FISH swimming in tandem, and the possibility that large sturgeons inhabit the lake. However, as researcher JOHN KIRK observes, "[S]ome people consider a sturgeon lurking in an inland lake equally as mysterious as the possibility of a monster existing there."

Sources: Kirk, *In the Domain of the Lake Monsters*; Charles Skinner, *Myths and Legends of Our Own Land.* Philadelphia: Lippincott, 1896.

Rocky

Rocky is the nickname locally applied to a LAKE MONSTER inhabiting Rock Lake, Wisconsin (Jefferson County). Sightings date from 1867, when a witness named R. Hassam speared the creature in some lakeside rushes, then found he "could no more hold it than an ox." In August 1882, Rocky interrupted a rowing race on the lake, frightening contestants and filling the air with "a most sickening odor." One witness likened the animal to "a huge dog," while others described a head raised three feet above water, with "huge jaws" gaping a foot or more. Curiously, Rock Lake spawned another unsolved mystery a century after those incidents, when divers found the crumbling remains of several large pyramids on the lake's muddy bottom. Rocky's home should not be confused with ROCK LAKE, WASHINGTON—also a source of unexplained cryptid reports.

Sources: Brown, *Sea Serpents: Wisconsin Occurrences of These Weird Water Monsters*; Frank Joseph, *The Lost Pyramids of Rock Lake.* St. Paul, MN: Galde, 1992.

Rocky River, Australia

On the night of 11 December 1853, a traveler camped beside the Rocky River, near South Australia's Mount Remarkable, heard splashing sounds from a nearby waterhole. Approaching the site, he glimpsed a dark shape in the moonlight, swimming toward shore. At sight of the man and his horse, the creature turned away and submerged. The witness described it as a BUNYIP 15–18 feet long, with a large head, a neck like a horse's, and a thick coat of bristly hair.

Source: Smith, *Bunyips and Bigfoots.*

Rodrigues Island Solitaire

Rodrigues Island is part of the Mascarene group, located east of Madagascar in the Indian Ocean. An 18th-century visitor to the island penned a description of an endemic BIRD, forgotten until the document was discovered in a Parisian archive, in 1825. It read:

> The solitaire is a large bird, which weighs about forty or fifty pounds. They have a very big head, with a sort of frontlet, as if of black velvet. Their feathers are neither feathers nor fur; they are of a light gray colour, with a little black on their backs. Strutting proudly about, either alone or in pairs, they preen their plumage or fur with their beaks and keep themselves very clean. They have their toes furnished with very hard scales, and run with quickness, mostly among the rocks, where a man, however agile, can hardly catch them. They have a very short beak, of about an inch in length, which is sharp. They nevertheless do not attempt to hurt anyone, except when they find someone before them, and when

hardly pressed try to bite him. They have a small stump of a wing which has a sort of bullet at its extremity, and serves as a defense. They do not fly at all, having no feathers to their wings but they flap them and make a great noise with their wings when angry and the noise is something like thunder in the distance. They only lay, as I am led to suppose, but once in the year, and only one egg. Not that I have seen their eggs, for I have not been able to discover where they lay. But I have never seen but one little one alone with them, and if any one tried to approach it, they would bite him severely. These birds live on seeds and leaves of trees, which they pick up on the ground. They have a gizzard larger than a fist, and what is surprising is that there is found in it a stone the size of a hen's egg, of oval shape, a little flattened, although this animal cannot swallow anything larger than a small cherrystone. I have eaten them; they are tolerably well tasted.

Subsequent fossil and subfossil remains, found in caves on Rodrigues, confirmed the bird's existence and it was recognized by science as *Pezophaps solitarius.* That recognition came to late to save it from apparent extinction at human hands, but sporadic sightings suggest the possibility of a few surviving specimens at large. François Leguat reported sightings of a similar bird on nearby Réunion Island, which he named *Ornithaptero solitaria*, but ROY MACKAL notes a total absence of subfossil or fossil remains from Réunion to support Leguat's account.

Sources: Mackal, *Searching for Hidden Animals*; Masauji, *The Dodo and Kindred Birds.*

Roesch, Ben S. (1980–)

Precocious Canadian cryptozoologist Ben Roesch began publishing a respected journal, *The Cryptozoology Review*, when he was 16 years old. He is presently a university student in Toronto, majoring in marine biology (with special focus on SHARKS) and general zoology. While his journal has ceased publication, Roesch uses his spare time to maintain an Internet website titled Taking a Hard Look at Cryptozoology. He is credited with identifying the eleventh specimen of megamouth shark (*Megachasma pelagios*), caught at Cagayan de Oro, in the Philippines, on 21 February 1998.

Sources: Coleman and Clark, *Cryptozoology A to Z*; Taking a Hard Look at Cryptozoology, http://www.ncf.carleton.ca/~bz050/Home-Page.cryptoz.html.

Rohrwolf

The Rohrwolf of Austria and Hungary is another of those rare cryptids graced with two different scientific names, though its identity and modern-day existence still remain in doubt. Witnesses described it as resembling a WOLF, but significantly smaller. Hungarian scientist M. Mojsisovics consid-

Europe's Rohrwolf is an unidentified canid.

ered it a diminutive subspecies of gray wolf (*Canis lupus*) and so named it *C. l. minor* in 1887. Five decades later, in 1938, Gyula Éhik proposed that the Rohrwolf was actually a larger subspecies of golden JACKAL (*Canis aureus*), and thus he renamed it *C. a. hungaricus*. Examination of museum specimens has so far failed to resolve the controversy, though most authorities favor Mojsisovics's classification. Further study is hampered by the fact that Rohrwolves apparently became extinct sometime in the early 20th century.

Sources: Eugen Nagy, "Der ausgerottete ungarische Rohrwolf (*Canis lupus*) war kein Schakal (*Canis aureus*)." *Säugetierkundliche Mitteilungen* 4 (1956): 165–167; Eduard-Paul Tratz, "Ein betrag zum kapitel 'Rohrwolf' *Canis lupus minor* Mojsisovics, 1887." *Säugetierkundliche Mitteilungen* 6 (1958): 160–162.

Rombovatnet, Norway

This Norwegian lake, in Nordland County, lies in a region of near-pristine wilderness, some 1,463 feet above sea level. Local Laplanders frequently pass through the region with herds of reindeer, but one season the animals balked at camping near the lake. Curious herdsmen reportedly found the carcass of an unidentified 21-foot creature rotting on a nearby sandbank, and they promptly left the area. Sadly, no details are available as to the date of that incident or what became of the carcass. Coincidentally (or otherwise), Rombovatnet is located six miles west of Sandnesvatnet, another Norwegian lake known for reports of a LAKE MONSTER called the VASSTROLLET ("water troll").

Sources: Kirk, *In the Domain of the Lake Monsters*; Erik Knatterud, "Sea Serpents in Norwegian Lakes," http://mjoesormen.no.

Rømmie

Rømmie is the nickname applied to a LAKE MONSTER reported from Lake Rømsjøen (formerly Rømmen), near the Swedish border in Norway's Østfold County. Reports filed since the 18th century describe a dark-colored animal between 15 and 50 feet long, with a head like a calf's and a body resembling a log. It swims with undulating motions, but has also (rarely) been reported on dry land. Witnesses disagree on whether it has legs or fins. A mass sighting was recorded on 20 September 1976, when school bus driver Asbjørn Holmedal and 15 students watched a 30-foot creature swimming between the lake's shore and Bjørnøya Island. In the 1990s, Rømskog's town council offered a reward of 10,000 Norwegian Kroner ($1,400) for Rømmie's capture, but the bounty has not been collected. The most recent reported sighting, from 2001, involved a local witness who saw the creature on shore and watched it slide into the lake. While academic experts dismissed such reports as sightings of "gas-filled logs," members of the GLOBAL UNDERWATER SEARCH TEAM (GUST) visited the lake with sonar equipment in June 2002. On the second day of the search, team leader Espen Samuelsen told reporters, "Already on the first night, we registered a sound that we at first thought was coming from a canoe. But no canoe appeared and the sound suddenly stopped after 30 seconds. We think this is a previously unidentified animal." No further evidence was found, but GUST leaders remain hopeful that some future expedition may yet identify Rømmie.

Sources: Costello, *In Search of Lake Monsters*; Samuelsen, "In search of the Norwegian Nessie"; Skjelsvik, "Norwegian lake and sea monsters."

Ropen

Late in 1999, cryptozoologist WILLIAM GIBBONS reported discovery of a "new" cryptid, the Ropen ("demon flyer"), reported from parts of Melanesia. Gibbons based his report on information obtained from two unnamed missionaries in Papua New Guinea, who described a large flying reptile said to frequent lakes and mountain caverns. In early 2001, Gibbons provided KARL SHUKER with a more detailed report, claiming that natives of the region actually recognized *two* flying cryptids.

The first — identified by Gibbons as the "true" Ropen — is apparently restricted to Rambutyo (or Rambunzo), a small island off the east coast of Papua New Guinea; and to Umzoi, a somewhat larger island lying between Papua New Guinea and New Britain. Witnesses describe the animal as reptilian, with a 3- to 4-foot wingspan, long jaws filled with teeth, and a slender tail tipped with a diamond-shaped flange. In fact, its description precisely matches reconstructions of *Rhamphorhynchus*, a PTEROSAUR presumed extinct since the end of the Jurassic period, 144 million years ago. Local natives and their missionary spokesmen claim this Ropen is a cave dweller, so attracted by the smell of rotting flesh that it sometimes attacks funeral parties. It also loves FISH, and snatches them from native boats while the fishermen cower in fear.

A much larger species of Ropen — properly called Duah (again, "demon flyer") by the aborigines it terrorizes. The Duah/Ropen reportedly boasts a 20-foot wingspan and a bony crest on its head, thus becoming a dead-ringer for *Pteranodon*, a Pterosaur of the Cretaceous period (144–65 million years ago). Gibbons reports that one of his anonymous missionary sources saw the Duah circling over a New Guinea lake in 1995, and that another minister (likewise unidentified) saw one of the cryptids "more recently," resting in a mountain cavern. Witnesses claim the Duah's underside occasionally glows at night, flashing as if the luminescence is a voluntary function.

It is tempting to dismiss the Ropen out of hand, based on the sources sited thus far, since Gibbons openly promotes living DINOSAUR reports as "proof" of a religious "young Earth" doctrine (dismissing evolutionary theory as "a lie," while insisting that Earth is no more than 6,000 years old). Second-hand reports from anonymous clergymen, frankly, to not inspire confidence. That said, it is worth noting that the Ropen closely resembles descriptions of KONGAMATO, a flying reptile reported from Africa since the 1920s. Karl Shuker has also investigated the Ropen, producing another source with no sectarian agenda.

Specifically, Shuker uncovered a letter sent to the journal *Ancient American* in 2000, by Minnesota resident Robert Helfinstine. In that letter (and in a subsequent conversation with her-

New Guinea's predatory Ropen resembles a living pterosaur (*William Rebsamen*).

petologist Mark Bayless), Helfinstine described a 1994 expedition to Papua New Guinea, wherein a group of U.S. scientists (including Dr. M.E. Clark, formerly of Illinois University) collected native testimony on the mainland Ropen/Duah, its glowing belly, and its reputed habit of digging up graves to feed on decayed human flesh. One odd tale, related by Helfinstine, described a native's encounter with a sleeping Ropen. The man deftly tied one of the creature's legs to a log, but his efforts roused the animal, which instantly flew away with the log trailing behind it.

Another correspondent, Brian Irwin, provided Shuker with more Ropen data in September 2001. On a visit to Papua New Guinea that summer, Irwin had personally interviewed various natives concerning the Ropen, recording details of their personal encounters with the beast. Inhabitants of Rambutyo told Irwin that Ropens were common in the 1970s, with two or three often seen flying together at night, but their numbers had thinned to the point that only solitary specimens were now reported. On nearby Manus Island, a school headmaster told Irwin that he had once seen a Ropen perched in a tree on Goodenough Island. A policeman and other locals reported sightings on Umoi during Irwin's visit to that island, reporting that it lived atop Mount Bel, but Irwin failed to glimpse the creature himself.

Sources: Karl Shuker, "Alien zoo." *Fortean Times* 133 (April 2000): 20; Shuker, "Alien zoo." *Fortean Times* 142 (February 2001): 21; Shuker, "Flying graverobbers."

Rosa sea serpent Regrettably, few details are available for this report of a SEA SERPENT sighted in the North Sea. The trawler *Rosa* was 10 miles southeast of Montrose, on the east coast of Scotland, when crewmen saw the animal, sometime in the summer of 1905. Witnesses said the creature raised its head five or six feet above the water's surface, prompting BERNARD HEUVELMANS to speculate that it might be a specimen of his hypothetical "long-necked" sea serpent.

Source: Heuvelmans, *In the Wake of the Sea Serpents*.

Rosshire Lioness This ALIEN BIG CAT was reported in the mid-1970s from the Rosshire district of western Scotland. Its popular name derives from eyewitness descriptions of a large CAT resembling an African lioness (*Panthera leo*), but the same description might as easily have fit a COUGAR (*Puma concolor*). Precise identification is impossible, since the cat was never photographed or captured.

Sources: Rickard, "The Scottish 'lioness'"; Rickard, "The Scottish lions."

Rothschild's lobe-billed bird of paradise This mysterious BIRD is one of six distinctive species (Family *Paradisaeidae*) described from solitary specimens collected by hunters from Papua New Guinea in the 19th century. Initially christened *Loborhamphus nobilis*, it was dismissed by Erwin Stresemann, in 1930, as a simple hybrid of known species. Today some ornithologists believe Stresemann's judgment was hasty, but the bird remains elusive and may be extinct.

Source: Fuller, *The Lost Birds of Paradise*.

Rotomahana sea serpent On 1 August 1891, officers and crew aboard the steamer *Rotomahana* spied a SEA SERPENT off the coast of New Zealand. The ship's chief officer, Alexander Kerr, described the incident as follows:

On Saturday morning last, August 1st, about 6:30 o'clock, we were off Portland Light, between Gisborne and Napier. I was on deck looking over the weather side, to see if I could see the land, when

I saw the object, whatever it was, rise out of the water to the height of about 30 ft. Its shape was for all the world like a huge conger EEL, with the exception that it had two large fins that appeared to be about 10 feet long. The creature was nor more than 100 yards away at the outside, and I should estimate its girth at between ten and twelve feet. I could not see its back as it was coming straight toward the steamer, but its belly and fins were pure white. The creature's head did not appear to be particularly definite, the neck running right up into the head the same as that of a large eel. It was broad daylight at the time, and the sun was shining clearly. When it went beneath the water it did not fall forward like a FISH that is jumping, but drew itself back as if with a contortion. I only saw it the once which was the last time it rose ....As to its length I could give no opinion, but as the creature rose some 30 ft. out of the water I should imagine there were still two-thirds of it in the water, but that is only my supposition.

Quartermaster Peter Nelson agreed that "The fins seemed to be about 10 ft. long, and were situated about 20 ft. from the head. The tips of the fins were about touching the water. Where the fins joined the body the latter seemed to bulge out. I did not see the fins the first time it rose, but I saw them each time afterwards. The belly and the fins were pure white. I saw the back part. It was the colour of an eel."

Source: Heuvelmans, *In the Wake of the Sea Serpents*.

Rotsee, Switzerland Ancient reports from this lake, in Canton Luzern, describe it as the home of two distinct LAKE MONSTERS—or perhaps one creature capable of changing its appearance. In 1599, local residents were panicked when a huge serpent or DRAGON emerged from the lake to bask on shore. Later reports described a creature resembling a log or wooden beam adrift on the surface, which may have been the serpent once again or another cryptid altogether. The question remains unanswered, and no modern sightings are on file.

Source: Johann Cysat, *Beschreibung dess Berühmbten Lucerne-oder 4.Waldstätten Sees*. Luzern: David Hautten, 1661.

Row Sometime in the 1930s, while honeymooning in the trackless Sterren Mountains of New Guinea, Charles and Leona Miller allegedly discovered a previously unknown cannibal tribe called the Kirrirri. Those fierce man-eaters unaccountably welcomed the young white couple, and Leona soon noticed an odd tool used by tribal women to crack coconuts. It resembled the tip of an elephant's tusk, 18 inches long and weighing 20 pounds. When questioned, the Kirrirri explained that the object was a horn collected from a giant reptile they called Row (after its roaring call). Tribesmen then led the Millers on a two-day hike to reach a swamp where the Row made its home. There, the couple supposedly met and filmed a 40-foot creature resembling a DINOSAUR.

The film (perhaps predictably) showed nothing when developed later, but the Millers provided a remarkable description of the Row in two subsequent books. They claimed the beast was measured 40 feet overall, with a long neck and tail, a beak like a TURTLE'S, a bony collar behind its head, and a line of triangular plates on its back. The Row's "horn" proved to be a long spike at the tip of its tail. If all this were not amazing enough, the huge creature also rose on its hind legs to graze from trees.

Skeptics rightly questioned why the Millers' two books on New Guinea, published in 1939 and 1941, contained no photos of the Row or its severed horn in the Kirrirri village. The couple's credibility was not enhanced when subsequent research failed to locate any trace of the Kirrirris themselves. Finally, BERNARD

HEUVELMANS noted that the Row displayed a surrealistic blend of physical traits from three unrelated groups of dinosaurs: the general long-necked form of a diplodocid, the beak and bony frill of a ceratopcid, and the dorsal plates of a stegosaurid. On balance, the Row was almost certainly a HOAX.

Sources: Heuvelmans, *On the Track of Unknown Animals*; Charles Miller, *Cannibal Caravan*. New York: Lee Furman, 1939; Leona Miller, *Cannibals and Orchids*. New York: Sheridan House, 1941; Shuker, *From Flying Toads to Snakes with Wings*.

Royal Saxon sea serpent

In late July 1829, while passing southwest of the Cape of Good Hope, officers aboard the *Royal Saxon* met a SEA SERPENT in the Indian Ocean. No description of the creature has survived, but the sighting was confirmed by Captain Petrie and Dr. R. Davidson, superintending surgeon of the Nagpore Subsidiary Force.

Source: Heuvelmans, *In the Wake of the Sea Serpents*.

Ruffed Cat

In 1940, while traveling alone on a trip to collect Mexican mammals, IVAN SANDERSON visited an unnamed village in the Sierra de Nayarit mountains of Nayarit State (on the Pacific coast, northwest of Guadalajara). Surveying pelts collected by the villagers, Sanderson noted one unique CAT skin he could not identify. It measured six feet from nose-tip to the base of a relatively short tail, which added another 18 inches to the pelt's overall length. Sanderson observed that "[t]he legs appeared to have been rather long compared to, say, a house-cat or a puma." The paws, still attached, were disproportionately large and possessed bright-yellow claws. The pelage was predominantly brown, with wavy stripes of alternate light and dark brown on the flanks, while the lower legs were nearly black. A stripe down the back was also dark brown, as was the creature's tail. Behind the cat's shoulders, thick hair grew forward to create a prominent ruff. Sanderson purchased the skin, with a smaller one resembling the first, then moved on to Belize, where he placed his specimens in storage. Tragically, a flood wiped out the lot before they could be studied further, and no similar skins have been found to date.

Source: Sanderson, "More new cats?"; Shuker, *Mystery Cats of the World*.

Rugaru

This name — variously translated from the Lakota language as "big hairy man" or "man of the mountains" — is sometimes used by various Aboriginal tribes of Canada, Minnesota and North Dakota to describe BIGFOOT or the resident NORTH AMERICAN APE. Variant forms of the name throughout that range include Rugarau and Ruugaru, traced by some linguists to the French-Cajun *loup-garou* ("werewolf"). That supernatural connection prompts some researchers to dismiss the Rugaru as a purely mythical creature, but Bigfoot researchers note that the term is equally applied in modern times to the elusive flesh-and-blood cryptid.

Source: Peter Matthiessen, *In the Spirit of Crazy Horse*. New York: Viking, 1991.

Rukh Balu

The Rukh Balu ("tree bear," in Nepalese) is said to inhabit wooded valleys of the Makalu-Barun National Park in eastern Nepal. Witnesses describe it as a black, mostly arboreal bear weighing an average 150 pounds. Locals allege that the creature builds complicated nests above ground, in the branches of trees, sometimes descending to raid corn fields around harvest time. No type specimens have yet been collected, but the Rukh Balu has still been graced with two different scientific names. In 1869, Thomas Oldham graced it with the label *Selenarctos ar-* *boreus*; 124 years later, Daniel Taylor-Ide named the elusive creature *Ursus nepalensis*. Taylor-Ide's research, in 1983–84, included interviews with villagers in the Barun Valley, who insist that their homeland harbors two distinct species of bear, the Asiatic black bear (*Ursus thibetanus*) and a smaller arboreal species. Taylor-Ides collected 11 skulls of the latter, noting that its molars and premolars are smaller than those of *U. thibetanus*, but critics assert that the skulls belong to juvenile Asiatic black bears. The issue clearly will not be settled without collection of a complete specimen.

Sources: "Evidence of a new bear species in Nepal." *ISC Newsletter* 3 (Spring 1984): 1–3; Taylor-Ide, *Something Hidden Behind the Ranges*.

Russell, W.M. "Gerald" (1911–79)

A native New Yorker, Gerald Russell attended Cambridge University in England (1928–31), where he became close friends with classmate IVAN SANDERSON. In 1932, Russell joined Sanderson as a member of the Percy Sladen expedition to Africa, where they experienced two remarkable encounters with still-unidentified cryptids. First, on the Mainyu River in the British Cameroons (now Cameroon), they encountered a creature known to natives of the region as MOKELE-MBEMBE, which Sanderson described as follows:

> When we were in the middle of the mile-and-a-half-long winding gorge, the most terrible noise I have heart, short of an on-coming earthquake or the explosion of an aerial-torpedo at close range, suddenly burst from one of the big caves to my right....I started to paddle like mad but was swept close to the entrance of the cave from which the noise had come. Thus, both Gerald and I were opposite its mouth; just then came another gargantuan gurgling roar and something enormous rose out of the water, turned it to sherry-colored foam and then, again roaring, plunged below. The "thing" was shiny black and was the *head* of something, shaped like a seal but flattened from above to below. It was about the size of a full-grown hippopotamus — this head, I mean.

Having survived that close encounter with the unknown, Russell and Sanderson had another surprise two months later, when they were buzzed by a kind of giant BAT, known locally as OLITAU, in the Assumbo Mountains.

Undaunted by those adventures, Russell joined the William Harkness Asiatic Expedition to Tibet in 1933–34, pursuing and collecting specimens of giant panda (*Ailuropoda melanoleuca*). In 1939 he volunteered for service with Britain's Royal Navy, later seeing combat in the Mediterranean and during the D-Day Normandy landings. After World War II, Russell visited China in pursuit of the rare golden takin, but his quest was foiled by the advance of Communist troops. In 1954, he was among the leaders of the London *Daily Mail*'s expedition to find the YETI in Nepal. There, he collected eyewitness reports and alleged Yeti droppings, putting his experience to good use four years later as a member of TOM SLICK'S expedition to Nepal. On that trip, Russell and his Sherpa guide reportedly sighted a Yeti in the Arun Valley. Poor health regrettably forced Russell to abandon the Slick expedition before it concluded, but he lived for another 21 years in New York, writing and producing films about his worldwide expense as an animal collector.

Sources: Coleman, *Tom Slick and the Search for the Yeti*; Coleman and Clark, *Cryptozoology A to Z*; Sanderson, *More "Things."*

Russian Society of Cryptozoologists

Organized sometime after the collapse of the Soviet Union, this organization (also sometimes called the Russian Society of Cryptozoology) is headquartered at Moscow's Darwin Museum, on Vavilova

Street. Its founder and original president was famed HOMINID researcher MARIE-JEANNE KOFFMANN, whose longtime pursuit of the ALMAS prompted the group's first major field expedition in 1992. Koffmann was succeeded as president by Vadim Makarov, who published a comprehensive Russian-language *Atlas of the Snowmen* in 2002.

Sources: Michael Trachtengerts, "Yeti and us." *Russian Hunter's Newspaper* 16 (18 April 2001); Vadim Makarov website, http://almas.ru/eng/news/Atlas_e.htm; Primates: Almasty 92, http://www.stgr-primates.de/newfindings.html.

Ruys's Bird of Paradise   This is another of the six controversial species (Family *Paradisaeidae*) described from solitary specimens collected in Papua New Guinea during the 19th century. As with the others, its exact date and location of collection are unknown. The species was named *Neoparadisea ruysi*, but Erwin Stresemann subsequently discounted it as a hybrid of known species, in 1930. More recently, some ornithologists have defended its classification as a unique species, but no more specimens have yet been found, and many researchers assume the BIRD is now extinct.

Source: Fuller, *The Lost Birds of Paradise*.

Ryukyu Kingfisher   The Ryukyu kingfisher (*Halcyon miyakoensis*) is — or was — a 9½-inch marsh-feeding BIRD with a long beak, cinnamon-colored head and underside, a blue-green back, and brownish-black wings. The only known specimen, residing today in a Tokyo museum, was reportedly collected in 1887, on Miyako Island in the Ryukyu chain (south of Japan). Introduction of rats allegedly drove the birds to extinction, but some researchers question whether sparse reports of the kingfisher's discovery are accurate, nurturing hope (however faint) that it may yet survive on some remote Pacific island.

Sources: Bille, *Rumors of Extinction*; Errol Fuller, *Extinct Birds*. New York: Facts on File, 1987; Guy Montfort, *Rare Birds of the World*. London: William Collins & Sons, 1988.

S

Saber-Tooth Cats   Between the Oligocene and Pleistocene epochs, 40 million to 100,000 years ago, Earth was inhabited by several species of ferocious felids armed with fangs much longer than any found in modern terrestrial predators. Those aptly-named saber-teeth ranged over most of the planet, and some apparently co-existed with primitive humans. The earliest saber-tooth CAT was *Eusmilus*, an 8-foot Oligocene hunter whose fossils have been found in France and across North America from Wyoming to the Dakotas. *Megantereon* was next in line, flourishing from India and Africa through Europe and North America in the Late Pliocene and Early Pleistocene (3-2 million years ago). Around the same time, a marsupial saber-tooth, *Thy-lacosmilus*, prowled the grasslands of Argentina. *Homotherium* covered most of the world, from Java and China to Europe and North America, during the Pleistocene epoch. Short-tailed *Smilodon* appeared in the Late Pleistocene, with subspecies *S. fatalis* and *S. populator* ranging over North and South America, respectively.

Some of those hunters may have sampled human flesh along with that of prehistoric megafauna, but mainstream science insists that they are all long gone, driven to extinction by one or another of various factors. Still, reports persist of apparent saber-toothed cats surviving into historic times, and even to the present day. Human contact with saber-teeth would explain the Cro-Magnon carving of a SCIMITAR CAT unearthed in the French Pyrenees, in 1896. Surviving saber-teeth, perhaps adapted to an amphibious lifestyle, may also solve the riddle of WATER LEOPARDS reported from Africa and the Argentinean YAQUARU. Reports of "mutant JAGUARS" with grotesquely long fangs persist from different parts of South America. As recently as 1994, witness Roberto Gutierrez reported seeing a saber-toothed cat in northern Mexico, though details of the sighting are elusive.

Sources: Karl Shuker, "Alien zoo." *Fortean Times* 117 (December 1998): 19; Shuker, *Mystery Cats of the World*.

Sachayoj *see* **Ucumar**

Sacramento River, California   Northern California's Sacramento River has produced diverse cryptid reports for more than a century. In 1891, witnesses glimpsed the "head of a gigantic lizard" in the river, near Woodland. In 1939, herpetologist George Myers claimed that a SALAMANDER 25–30 inches long — roughly five times the official maximum size of the state's largest known species — had been pulled from the river at some unspecified point. Although he allegedly examined the amphibian, Myers did not preserve it, and skeptics dismiss his claim as a HOAX. Six decades later, at 1:15 a.m. on 14 August 1999, Paul Roberts was walking his dog along the river, in downtown Sacramento, when he heard splashing below and allegedly saw a snakelike creature 20-30 feet long. As he later wrote to *Fortean Times* magazine:

***Smilodon* is the most familiar of several prehistoric saber-tooth cats.**

Artist's conception of a cryptid reported from the Sacramento River in 1891 (*William Rebsamen*).

It looked like it was doing something out of water with its body, causing the loud splashing noise. When I threw rocks at it, it instantly made the sound of submerging. At one point, when we were at the edge of the river and my dog was lapping the water, it edged close to us. I took my dog and backed away.

The creature did not follow, and no further sightings are on record from its waters, either of giant reptiles or amphibians.

Sources: Gibbons, *Missionaries and Monsters*; George Myers, "Asiatic giant salamander caught in Sacramento River." *Copeia* 2 (June 1951); Paul Roberts, "River serpent." *Fortean Times* 128 (November 1999): 52.

Sacramento sea serpent On 30 July 1877, officers and crew aboard the vessel *Sacramento*, en route from New York to Melbourne, met an unidentified SEA SERPENT in mid-Atlantic, at 31° 59' north latitude and 37° west longitude. Helmsman John Hart described the creature to reporters three months later, on arrival in Australia:

It had the body of a very large SNAKE; its length appeared to me to be about fifty feet or sixty feet. Its head was like an ALLIGATOR'S, with a pair of flippers about ten feet from its head. The colour was or a reddish brown. At the time seen it was lying perfectly still, with its head raised about three feet above the surface of the sea, and as it got thirty or forty feet astern, it dropped its head.

BERNARD HEUVELMANS noted that the only known sea-going crocodilian, the Indo-Pacific or saltwater CROCODILE (*Crocodylus porosus*), is one-third the size of the *Sacramento* creature at maturity and normally resides 10,000 miles from the region of the sighting. Still, he accepted the report as legitimate and listed the beast as a specimen of his hypothetical "marine saurian."

Source: Heuvelmans, *In the Wake of the Sea Serpents*.

Saddle Lake, Canada Between 1974 and 1995, an estimated 100 witnesses reported sightings of an unidentified LAKE MONSTER from this lake, located 100 miles northeast of Edmonton, Alberta. The creature is typically described as serpentine in form, 8-18 feet long, with a head resembling a horse's and a hairy torso. Occasional reports include short ears or horns on the animal's head. The sheer volume of sightings makes this one of Canada's most active "monster" lakes in recent times.

Source: Garner, *Monster! Monster!*

Saguaro Lake, Arizona This manmade lake lies in the heart of the Tonto National Forest, 10 miles northeast of Mesa,

Arizona. LOREN COLEMAN reports that giant CATFISH up to nine feet long have been sighted in deep water below the dam at the west end of the lake.

Source: Coleman, *Mysterious America*.

St. Andrew sea serpent In August 1906, officers aboard the transatlantic liner *St. Andrew* sighted a SEA SERPENT as they were rounding Land's End in Cornwall, England. Witnesses saw 18 feet of the creature's body visible on the surface. As one later told the New York *American*, "The jaws were armed with great fin-like teeth, and the body would probably be about 5 feet in circumference." Based on the vague description, BERNARD HEUVELMANS (while accepting the report as legitimate) could not decide if the animal represented his hypothetical "long-necked" sea serpent or the "super-EEL." The creature does not conform to typical descriptions of the Cornish sea serpent known as MORGAWR.

Source: Heuvelmans, *In the Wake of the Sea Serpents*.

St. Andrew's Bay sea serpent One afternoon in late March 1943, Thomas Helm and his wife were boating on St. Andrew's Bay, Florida, south of Panama City, when they observed a SEA SERPENT in the Gulf of Mexico. Their first view of the creature came at 4:00 p.m., when they saw "a head about the size of a basketball on a neck which reached nearly four feet out of the water" moving toward their 17-foot boat. As Helm further described it:

The entire head and neck were covered with wet fur which lay close to the body and glistened in the afternoon sunlight. When it was almost beside our boat the head turned and looked squarely at us. My first thought was that we were seeing some kind of giant otter or seal… but this was not the face of an otter or seal. As a youngster I had run a trapline and knew mink and otter full well….The head of this creature, with the exception that there was no evidence of ears, was that of a monstrous cat. The face was fur covered and flat and the eyes were set in the front of the head.

Helm said the creature's fur was chocolate-brown, its eyes gleaming black and the size of a silver dollar. Beneath its flattened nose they saw a "mustache of stiff black hairs with a downward curve on either side." Suddenly, the beast vanished in a swirl of water and did not reappear. Helm waited 19 years to publish his account, stressing that the thing he saw could not have been a pinniped. "Seals and sea lions," he wrote in 1962, "have long pointed noises and the eyes are set on the sides of the head like those of a squirrel or rat. The creature my wife and I saw had eyes which were positioned near the front of its face like those of a cat."

In 1968, BERNARD HEUVELMANS opined that the animal might be a juvenile specimen of his hypothetical "maned merhorse, a sea-foal as it were." Presumably, the mane would flourish only in adulthood, since Helm saw none on his specimen. The creature's flat face poses a problem, though, since most witnesses agree that the "merhorse" has a long head resembling that of a horse.

Sources: Helm, *Monsters of the Deep*; Heuvelmans, *In the Wake of the Sea Serpents*.

St. Croix River The St. Croix River marks a portion of the border between Maine and New Brunswick, flowing from St. Croix southward to Passamaquoddy Bay. On 10 August 1903, fishermen at Bayside, New Brunswick reported an unknown creature swimming in the river. They described it as having a large head, with green eyes and two sets of fins that propelled it through the water.

Source: Bord and Bord, *Unexplained Mysteries of the 20th Century*.

St. Croix sea serpent   On 2 October 1909, passengers and crew aboard the steamship *St. Croix* sighted a SEA SERPENT off the coast of Santa Barbara, California. Witnesses described the creature as resembling a 60-foot EEL, with a body as thick as a man's. Cryptozoologist PAUL LEBLOND includes the report on a published list of CADBOROSAURUS sightings, although Santa Barbara lies some 450 miles south of Caddy's normal range.

Source: LeBlond and Bousfield, *Cadborosaurus*.

Saint François-Xavier sea serpent   On 18 March 1925, Captain Raoul Jaillard of the French steamer *Saint François-Xavier* sent the following letter to his superior officer:

> Sir, I am sending you a little sketch drawn at several minutes after the apparition of the famous SEA-SERPENT. The second captain, the second lieutenant, the radio officer and the third engineer are unanimous in confirming the following lines:
>
> On 2 February 1925 while on passage from Nouméa to Newcastle, the ship making 10 knots [11.5 mph.], at 18:30 hours [6:30 p.m.] abeam of Port Stephens on the east coast of Australia, two masses like TURTLES' shells were seen floating 30 feet from the ship on the starboard bow.

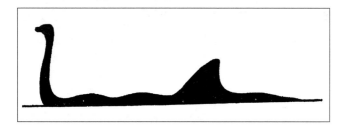

The *Saint François-Xavier* sea serpent, after witness Raoul Jaillard.

> Abeam of the engines there rose a big head like a CAMEL'S head, on a long flexible neck having a great similarity to a swan's neck. The height of the neck was about eight feet. The body, as thick as the big Bordeaux barrels, formed a chain of five loops; on the fourth loop, an aileron as on SHARKS of large dimensions, measuring 5 feet in height and in width at the base. The aileron seemed to be black in colour; the colour of the animal was dirty yellow, the skin smooth without appearance of scales.
>
> As it passed astern of the ship and was abeam of the starboard screw, the animal's head began to move backwards and forwards, which led us to think it had been touched by the blade of the screw; its movement seemed hindered and was not at all like the little SNAKES near the coast.
>
> The animal was visible *for fifteen minutes*, no optical illusion is possible. For, besides the testimony of the Europeans, the Blacks from New Caledonia serving as seamen on board, the Annamite boys and Chinese stokers all gave one cry: "There's the DRAGON!" The Chinese even made an offering to it.
>
> As night falls very quickly at that time we could not give other details, being one and all fairly taken aback by this fantastic apparition.

Jaillard's sketch of the creature revealed four humps, rather than five "loops," with a tall fin on the third. BERNARD HEUVELMANS concluded that the creature was a specimen of his hypothetical "long-necked" sea serpent.

Source: Heuvelmans, *In the Wake of the Sea Serpents*.

Saint Helena manatee   In 1655, while visiting the South Atlantic island of Saint Helena, British traveler Peter Mundy found a 10-foot "sea lion" beached and dying near Chappell Val-

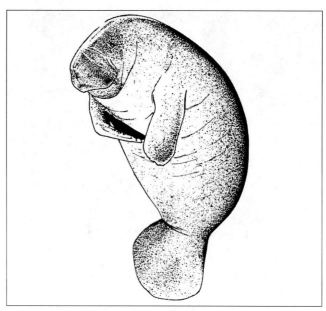

Is the Saint Helena Manatee extinct today?

ley. Year-round inhabitants of the island also killed large creatures they called "sea cows" for their meat and oil, but the animals were never plentiful and the last known specimen was slain in 1810. Although the case is now impossible to prove, cryptozoologists speculate that the creatures may have represented an unclassified, now-extinct species of sirenian (manatee or dugong), or perhaps an elephant seal (*Mirounga leonina*).

Sources: Richard Lydekker, "On the supposed former existence of a sirenian in St. Helena." *Proceedings of the Zoological Society of London* (20 June 1899): 796-798; Shuker, "Hoofed mystery animals and other crypto-ungulates, Part III." *Strange Magazine* 11 (Spring-Summer 1995): 25-27, 48-50.

Saint Helena sea serpents   The island of Saint Helena is a British dependency located in the South Atlantic, some 1,000 miles off the coast of Angola. It is most famous as the prison were Napoléon Bonaparte spent his final days, but cryptozoologists know Saint Helena for a series of SEA SERPENT sightings reported from its waters in the 1850s. The first incident was reported in 1854, by a Dutch sea captain named De Weerdt, but no details of the creature's description have survived, beyond a reference to its horselike mane. An unnamed captain of a Lamport and Holt steamer reported another sighting in 1856. On 12 December 1857, officers aboard the *Castilian* met an large, unidentified creature northwest of the island. Six weeks later, yet another unknown animal was reported by Captain Suckling, piloting the *CARNATIC* between Saint Helena and Cape Town, South Africa. Based on its mane, BERNARD HEUVELMANS considered the first creature a specimen of his hypothetical "merhorse," but he reached no conclusion on the other three sightings.

Source: Heuvelmans, *In the Wake of the Sea Serpents*.

Saint-Jean-des-Monts carcass   On 24 December 1961, the rotting carcass of a supposed SEA SERPENT washed ashore at Saint-Jean-des-Monts, Vendee, France. Despite its outward resemblance to a prehistoric PLESIOSAUR, examination of the remains soon proved the creature was a basking shark (*Cetorhinus maximus*).

Source: Heuvelmans, *In the Wake of the Sea Serpents*.

St. Lawrence River, Canada   In addition to a legendary cryptid called the ONYARE, described by early Mohawk tribesmen, Québec's St. Lawrence River also produces reports of oversized EELS around Rivière Ouelle.

Sources: Gatschet, "Water-monsters of American aborigines"; Roger Martin, *L'Anguille*. Montreal: Leméac, 1980.

St. Lucia Estuary sea serpent   On 7 July 1933, farmer George Higgs led a fishing party to St. Lucia Estuary, a lake connected to the sea in South Africa's KwaZulu-Natal Province. In addition to his four children and two Zulu servants, Higgs was accompanied by G.P. Court, L. Esmonde-White, and Jack Nicolas. That night, in camp, the party was roused by the activity of what they took for hippos in the lake. As Court later told the press:

> We all rose to look at them. I took my field glasses to get a better view. To my amazement I saw floating on the calm water under a strong moon a long undulating dark body about 30 yards in length. The head and shoulders were similar to those of a hornless ox. The long body, which lay "S" shaped, appeared to be two feet broad. It was lying at right angles to the beach, and facing our camp. Mr. Esmonde-White had his field glasses on the creature also, and confirmed my opinion. Mr. Higgs, who has hunted hippo for forty years on this coast and had a pet hippo on his farm at one time, after looking through the glasses, said that hippo did not keep behind one another like that. They would also be making a noise....About 30 minutes later the creature disappeared by sinking beneath the surface of the lake, which at this spot averages about five feet deep.

Source: Heuvelmans, *In the Wake of the Sea Serpents.*

St. Lucie River, Florida   Florida is not without its share of cryptids, including various LAKE MONSTERS and unknown inhabitants of various rivers. In May 1975, Mrs. Dimiter Stoyanoff reported sighting a 30-foot cryptid, brownish-gray in color, as it swam along the North Fork of the St. Lucie River, in St. Lucie County. The reported size, if accurate, rules out a normal ALLIGATOR.

Source: Salkin, "Mysterious water monsters of North America."

St. Margaret's Bay carcass   Mystery surrounds the stranding of an unidentified GLOBSTER at St. Margaret's Bay, Nova Scotia, east of Halifax, in the mid-19th century. BERNARD HEUVELMANS reports that the carcass was found by an unnamed woman, sometime prior to 1864, but no further details are presently available.

Source: Heuvelmans, *In the Wake of the Sea Serpents.*

St. Margaret's Bay sea serpent   In 1912, three witnesses reported a SEA SERPENT sighting from St. Margaret's Bay, in Kent, England. They described a creature with a "long sinuous black body," swimming rapidly by means of vertical undulations until a ship rounded the headland, whereupon the beast submerged.

Source: Heuvelmans, *In the Wake of the Sea Serpents.*

St. Marys River, Michigan   A brief flurry of aquatic cryptid sightings emerged from this Michigan river, below Sault Ste. Marie, in 1892. Most researchers now regard the incident as a HOAX, though nearby LAKE HURON has also produced several LAKE MONSTER reports.

Source: "Western lake resorts have each a water monster." *Chicago Tribune* (24 July 1892).

St.-Maurice River, Canada   Québec's St.-Maurice

River, a tributary of the ST. LAWRENCE RIVER, links several lakes renowned for LAKE MONSTER reports. It is no surprise, then, that the St.-Maurice also has a tradition of "critter" and "serpent" sightings. Locals claim that cryptids hide in various submerged caverns, and a "big SNAKE" was seen in the river, from the Grand-Piles heights, in 1956.

Source: Meurger and Gagnon, *Lake Monster Traditions.*

Saint-Quay-Portrieux sea serpent   In summer 1911, François Gélard and his two sisters saw a SEA SERPENT off Saint-Quay-Portrieux in Saint-Brieux Bay (Breton, France). Nearly a quarter-century later, Gélard described the incident as follows:

> We were just finishing lunch, and it was about one o'clock in the afternoon, when my sister, Madame Ollivier, cried, "Look, there's a dog swimming!" Near where my sister pointed my attention was first drawn to a small sailing yacht, then I saw, between the boat and the shore, nearer to the coast, the animal she was pointing at, and which I assumed, without looking closely, was a dog belonging to some member of the crew. However, it came closer to us, and I could not help being surprised at the speed with which it swam and the length of its neck raised above the waves.
>
> I looked at this strange swimmer with some ship's binoculars I had, and I saw at once that it had nothing in common with a dog. Nor was there anything else I could compare it with, and the only thing I could think of then that was at all like what I could see of its body, i.e. its head and neck, was the head and neck of a giraffe.
>
> Its course, however, had brought it facing me, and I could then make out another strange peculiarity of its structure. This was a sort of black dome or hump, which appeared some distance behind its neck. My complete ignorance about the shape of the rest of the body under the water, and my inclination to assume that it was like that of a huge snake, led me to think that this spherical hump was just a coil of its body appearing. But I was surprised to see that this hump seemed fixed in the wake like that of a ship's prow, which the animal's neck left, and that it followed its every movement.
>
> The rest of the body was entirely under the water, but not very deep and marked by a great disturbance on the surface. At a distance from the head which seemed to me to be at least 30 feet, a great churning of the water marked the position of its caudal fins, which must have been the chief means of propulsion.

After the creature had proceeded for 100 yards or so along the coast, another identical animal joined it and the pair swam out to see, where they were soon lost to sight. BERNARD HEUVELMANS considered the incident a positive sighting of his hypothetical "long-necked" sea serpent.

Source: Heuvelmans, *In the Wake of the Sea Serpents.*

***Saint-Yves* sea serpent**   In October 1913, Captain Jean-Marie Le Pennec of the vessel *Saint-Yves* reported a SEA SERPENT sighting while en route from Stavanger to Paimpol, France. He described the creature as 30 feet long, with a cigar-shaped body and a mouth filled with prominent teeth. BERNARD HEUVELMANS concluded that the animal was "an ordinary cetacean," but declined to speculate on its species.

Source: Heuvelmans, *In the Wake of the Sea Serpents.*

***Saladin* sea serpent**   On 12 March 1870, Captain Slocum and sailors aboard the American schooner *Saladin* met a SEA SERPENT in the Caribbean. A report in the *Pall Mall Gazette* sketched the creature as follows:

> It is described as being 100 feet in length, its body measuring forty and its tail sixty feet. The most curious feature about it was an immense body of hard gristly matter, twelve feet in height, forty feet in width, with the same length, entirely void within, forming a

large bladder-shaped balloon, which, filled with air, buoyed the serpent on the water. This oval buoy had regular ridges, running from the apex or head (for this bladder preceded the body of the fish) to where it joined the main body. These ridges extend fore and aft at intervals of four inches, with a regular height of two inches, and gave to the surface the appearance of the network of a balloon. The bladder portion was elastic and yielded to the movement of the sea; it was two inches thick, but of a hard, dense, impenetrable character, and would resist knife or bullet. On each side of this floating dome were two heavy paddles, each five feet long, by which the monster made progress. The fish proper, which was but an appendage tailed on to this blown-up bladder, consisted of a heavy fishy substance, with brown sides; and about ten feet from the dome were two eyes, one on either side of a large horn. From this point the fish tapered on to a forked tail of material as heavy and hard as iron. Captain Slocum declares that the tail would weigh 100lb. to the cubic foot, and the forks of the tail stood horizontally in the water, but submerged four feet, the rest of the monster "sitting lightly on the ocean wave."

While deeming the published description "quite incomprehensible," BERNARD HEUVELMANS concluded that the *Saladin's* crew had in fact seen a dead whale floating belly-up on the surface, its abdomen distended by internal gasses. He explained the "horn" as the cetacean's extruded penis, flanked by barnacles mistaken for "eyes."

Source: Heuvelmans, *In the Wake of the Sea Serpents*.

Salamanders (Giant)

Salamanders are amphibians that superficially resemble lizards. Modern science recognizes 9 families, divided into 60 genera and 358 living species. Three species of "giant" salamanders are presently known, including the hellbender (*Cryptobranchus alleganiensis*) of eastern North America, the Chinese giant salamander (*Andrias* [or *Megalobatrachus*] *davidianus*), and the Japanese giant salamander (*A. japonicus*). The official record length for a hellbender is 29⅛ inches, while the Asian species may reach lengths of 5 feet 2 inches. By contrast, the Pacific giant salamander (*Dicamptodon ensatus*) does not officially exceed 6⅝ inches in length, but reports of much larger specimens have emerged from northern California's Trinity Mountains.

Attorney Frank Griffith was the first to file such a report, in the 1920s. While hunting deer at the head of the New River, near Salmon Mountain in Trinity County, Griffith peered into a small unnamed lake and allegedly saw five huge salamanders, 5-9 feet long. Griffith claimed that he caught one on a baited hook, but it was too heavy for him to drag it from the water. In 1939, her-

petologist George Myers examined a much smaller giant, 25-30 inches long, that was pulled from the SACRAMENTO RIVER. Twelve years later, he wrote, "The animal was a fine *Megalobatrachus* (unquestionably identified generically by its closed gill openings), in perfect condition." Strangely, Myers did not preserve the specimen, and he could not explain its leap from Asia, beyond suggesting that "a Californian *Megalobatrachus*…would not be zoo-geographically surprising." In January 1960, Vern Harden allegedly dragged a salamander 8 feet 4 inches long from a remote lake in the Trinity range, but a blizzard forced him to release the creature after taking hasty measurements.

Such stories have inspired various hunters to search for California's giant amphibians over the past half-century, but all have returned from the quest empty-handed. In 1948, biologist Thomas Rogers made four treks into the Trinity Alps without glimpsing one of the giants. Brothers Bernard and John Hubbard mounted two expeditions in 1958-59, then announced in 1960 that they had "definitely established" the existence of giant salamanders in the Trinity Alps. A new expedition was planned, but never materialized. Later that year, Texas millionaire TOM SLICK diverted members of his latest BIGFOOT expedition to search for giant salamanders, but they found none and denounced the effort as a "silly side trip." September 1960 witnessed yet another expedition, led by three California zoology professors. Thomas Rodgers, seemingly embittered by his own failures, denounced that effort as a bungled attempt by "boy scouts" who allegedly "mistook logs for salamanders." The team allegedly found a specimen of *D. ensatus* measuring 11.5 inches, but no proof was forthcoming and the official record for that species stands. "It is hoped," Rodgers wrote, "that this evidence will kill any rumors about any giant salamanders (much less *Megalobatrachus*) in the Trinity Mountains of California." KYLE MIKOZAMI mounted the most recent search to date, in 1997, and was likewise unsuccessful.

Sources: Coleman, "Promises of giants"; George Myers, "Asiatic giant salamander caught in the Sacramento River." *Copeia* 2 (June 1951); Thomas Rodgers, "Report of giant salamander in California." *Copeia* 3 (September 1962).

Sally sea serpent

On 17 December 1819, a ferocious SEA SERPENT allegedly attacked the schooner *Sally*, off the coast of LONG ISLAND, New York. No record of the incident survives in newspaper accounts, but a 19th-century engraving depicts the beast as a veritable living DINOSAUR, with a gaping maw and two fins like cherub's wings behind its head. BERNARD HEUVELMANS dismissed the case as a HOAX, and author J.P. O'Neill omits it entirely from her exhaustive history of New England sea serpents.

Sources: Heuvelmans, *In the Wake of the Sea Serpents*; O'Neill, *The Great New England Sea Serpent*.

Salstern, Sweden

This lake, in Sweden's Östergötland County, has a maximum recorded depth of 75 feet. Sightings of a serpentine LAKE MONSTER were recorded in the 19th century, but no modern reports are on file.

Source: Global Underwater Search Team, http://www.cryptozoology.st/.

Saltie

Saltie is the nickname applied to a SEA SERPENT reported from the Baltic Sea, off the coast of Saltsjöbaden, Sweden (near Stockholm) in the early 20th century. The first sighting at the fashionable resort was logged in April 1904, by post office clerk Axel Nilsson. Karl Johansson, a local boat builder, saw the creature a month later. An army lieutenant named Hernlund

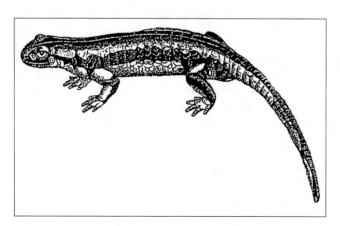

Giant salamanders have been sighted in northern California.

glimpsed a similar beast in August 1905, showing three humps above the waves. In October 1906 the witnesses included Victor Ankarcrona, Grand Huntsman to the Court of Sweden and a close friend of King Oscar II. He described a creature 60-80 feet long, with a large head resembling a TURTLE'S, moving with a wormlike motion that enabled it to match a motorboat's speed. Emil Smith and his wife saw large, dark-gray mass in May 1909. In September 1913, Saltie collided with Nils Österman's speedboat near Vaxholm, then returned two months later for a sighting by Count Axel Cronheim. Einar Oberg reported two 6-foot creatures swimming together, in July 1920, off the coast of nearby Svenskär (Västernorrland County).

Sources: Heuvelmans, *In the Wake of the Sea Serpents*; Global Underwater Search Team, http://www.cryptozoology.st/.

Salvaje   The Salvaje ("savage") is an unclassified primate or HOMINID known to aboriginal peoples from Chiapas State in southern Mexico through Venezuela and Colombia. Witnesses describe the creatures as bipedal, 3-5 feet tall, and covered with reddish hair. As in so many other hominids or WILDMEN covered in this volume, the Salvaje allegedly kidnaps human females on occasion and is said to walk on "backwards" feet. The beasts emit piercing cries like a human in distress, but they seem to lack coherent speech. A Venezuelan hunter named Fernando Nives claimed a sighting of three Salvajes in 1980, while stalking game along the Río Orinoco, 25 miles north of Puerto Ayachuco. Five years later, a construction worker at Puerto Ayachuco saw one of the creatures while he was bulldozing a new road through the forest. A bush pilot in the same area found pigeon-toed humanoid footprints on his dirt airstrip in 1988, estimating that their maker weighed 80-100 pounds.

Sources: Coleman and Huyghe, *The Field Guide to Bigfoot, Yeti, and Other Mystery Primates Worldwide*; Fabio Picasso, "More on the Mono Grande mystery." *Strange Magazine* 9 (Spring-Summer 1992): 41, 53.

Samdja *see* **Yeti**

Samoan carcass   In 1974, while visiting American Samoa, Australian tourist Joseph Elkhorne found the 3-foot carcass of an unknown creature lying on a beach. He snapped three photos of the curious remains, and then forgot about them for nearly three decades, until the pictures and negatives surfaced during a bout of house-cleaning. Thus reminded, he gave copies of the photos to a marine biologist in Melbourne and e-mailed others to a second scientist (and relative by marriage) in Portugal. Neither expert could identify the animal, and their best guesses as to its identity diverged radically. In Melbourne, it was regarded as possibly "some sort of sea bird," while Elkhorne's contact in Portugal suspected it was a Portuguese man-o-war (a large species of JELLYFISH). In fact, neither diagnosis seems satisfactory on closer inspection, since the carcass had no feathers and none of the man-o-war's trademark tentacles. The mystery remains unsolved, presumable forever.

Source: Joseph Elkhorne, "Sea creature." *Fortean Times* 142 (February 2001): 53.

San Clemente Monster   San Clemente Island lies 60 miles off the coast of southern California, in the Gulf of Santa Catalina. It is best known in recent history as the favored retreat of disgraced ex-President Richard Nixon, but the waters surrounding San Clemente also produced a series of SEA SERPENT sightings in the first half of the 20th century. The San Clemente Monster made its first appearance sometime between 1914 and

1919, racking up a list of witnesses that included the era's top-ranking stars of big-game fishing. Ralph Bandini, secretary of the local Tuna Club (America's first big-game fishing organization) recorded several accounts of the creature, including a description from one of his own crew members concerning a beast with "eyes as big as plates," before he glimpsed the animal himself in September 1920. On that occasion, while fishing a mile west of Mosquito Harbor, Bandini experienced a sighting that he later described as follows:

All of a sudden I saw something dark and big heave up. I seized my glasses. What I saw brought me up straight! A great columnar neck and head, I guess that is what it was, lifting a good 10 feet. It must have been five or six feet thick. Something that appeared to be a kind of mane of coarse hair, almost like fine seaweed, hung dankly. But the eyes — those were what held me! Huge, seemingly bulging, round — at least a foot in diameter! We swung toward it....Then, even as I watched through the glasses, the Thing sank. There was no swirl, no fuss....Just a leisurely, majestic sinking — and it disappeared, about a quarter of a mile away.

Bandini later saw the creature twice more in the same area, but never again at such close range. George Farnsworth, president of the Tuna Club, described the beast in similar terms:

Its eyes were 12 inches in diameter, not set on the side like an ordinary FISH, but more central. It had a big mane of hair about two feet long. We were within a hundred feet of it before it went down. This was no sea elephant. It was some kind of mammal, for it could not have been standing so long unless it was.

Other Tuna Club officers and big-game fishing stars who reported sightings of the San Clemente Monster included Joe Coxe, Jimmy Jump, and millionaire George Thomas III. Most agreed that the beast was seen most often between San Clemente and Santa Catalina Island. The last known sighting was recorded on 8 June 1953, when a crew of nine professional fishermen led by Sam Randazzo saw a creature with a 10-foot neck, 5-6 feet thick, whose eyes were "cone-shaped, protruding, and about a foot in diameter." Eyewitness descriptions of the beast were so similar, in fact, that author J. Charles Davis II observed (in 1954): "It is almost as if a recording had been made and each man played the same record. Now please bear in mind, because I think this is important, that these men were all interviewed separately and none of them knew that I had talked to anyone else about the San Clemente Monster!"

Source: Heuvelmans, *In the Wake of the Sea Serpents*.

San Francisco sea serpents   In his classic tabulation of SEA SERPENT sightings, published in 1968, BERNARD HEUVELMANS reported that an unknown marine creature had been sighted at San Francisco in 1935. Sadly, no further details were available and no other sources to date have reported the case. Half a century later, on 5 February 1985, two witnesses driving past San Francisco Bay allegedly sighted a 60-foot serpentine beast in the water, apparently chasing seals. They described the creature as dark green in color, fading to a shade of cream on the underside.

Sources: Bord and Bord, *Unsolved Mysteries of the 20th Century*; Heuvelmans, *In the Wake of the Sea Serpents*.

San Miguel de Padrone, Cuba   In summer 1971, residents of this Cuban town reported a black LAKE MONSTER with horns atop its head inhabiting a nearby lagoon. No recent sightings of the creature are on file.

Source: "San Miguel lagoon's monster rumor grows." *Columbus* (OH) *Dispatch* (23 August 1971).

Sanderson, Ivan Terence (1911–73)

A native of Edinburgh, Scotland, Ivan Sanderson spent part of his childhood on his father's game preserve in Kenya, before earning master's degrees in botany, geology and zoology. In the 1930s, he led expeditions into some of the Earth's most remote and forbidding locales, collecting specimens and native tales of exotic creatures that soon filled a series of popular books. (In the process, he also experienced personal encounters with cryptids including MOKELE-MBEMBE and the OLITAU.) Sanderson's zoological titles include *Animal Treasure* (1937), *Caribbean Treasure*(1939), *Animals Nobody Knows* (1940), *Living Treasure* (1941), *Animal Tales* (1946), *Living Mammals of the World* (1955), *Follow the Whale* (1956), *The Monkey Kingdom* (1957), *The Continent We Live On* (1961), *The Dynasty of Abu* (1962), *The Natural Wonders of North America* (1962), *Ivan Sanderson's Book of Great Jungles* (1965) and *The USA: This Treasured Land* (1966).

In the 1940s, Sanderson launched a series of articles in the *Saturday Evening Post* that cemented his credentials in cryptozoology, including essays on SEA SERPENTS and living DINOSAURS. During the 1950s and 1960s, while appearing frequently on television talk shows with exotic animals, Sanderson penned articles for other magazines on subjects including BIGFOOT and LAKE MONSTERS. His 1961 treatise on unidentified HOMINIDS, *Abominable Snowmen: Legend Come to Life* remains unrivaled in the field despite the passage of four decades since its publication. Other Sanderson volumes of interest to cryptozoologists include "*Things*" (1967), *More "Things"* (1969) and *Investigating the Unexplained* (1972). In 1965, Sanderson founded the SOCIETY FOR THE INVESTIGATION OF THE UNEXPLAINED, and served as its leader for the remainder of his life. Three years later, with BERNARD HEUVELMANS, he investigated the case of the MINNESOTA ICEMAN, pronouncing it a genuine specimen of cryptic hominid.

That confusing episode, still hotly debated, caused some critics to dismiss Sanderson as a gullible eccentric. Their jibes escalated when Sanderson produced two controversial books on unidentified flying objects. In the first volume, *Uninvited Visitors* (1967), he proposed that UFOs might be sentient atmospheric life forms; the second, *Invisible Residents* (1970), proposed that some UFOs were piloted by members of an advanced undersea civilization existing side-by-side with terrestrial humans. Cancer claimed Sanderson's life on 19 February 1973. His autobiographical work *Green Silence: The Making of a Naturalist* was published posthumously, in 1974.

Sources: Clark and Pear, *Strange & Unexplained Phenomena*; Coleman and Clark, *Cryptozoology A to Z*.

Sanderson's Worm

Cryptozoologists are not always required to travel far from home in their search for unknown animals. In 1971, IVAN SANDERSON and his wife saw a long worm-like creature, pinkish-orange in color, slithering along the bottom of a deep pond on their New Jersey farm. Unequipped to catch it at the time, they later returned to the site, but never saw the thing again.

Source: Mark Hall, "Sobering sights of pink unknowns." *Wonders* 1 (December 1992): 60-64.

Sandewan

In summer 1997, during a visit to Zimbabwe's Chizazira National Park, British zoologist Carina Norris discovered a strange trail of apparent blood spots leading to a nearby cliff, where they abruptly ended. Her guide explained that such trails are characteristic of the Sandewan, an elusive creature inhabiting rocky ground. The "blood" trails were typically composed of discrete drops, and were not smeared as if a wounded animal had dragged itself along the ground. "Common sense" explanations for the strange trails include BIRD droppings or splotches of fruit juice left behind by MONKEYS, though neither accounts for the Sandewan's straight and orderly trail. In native mythology, Norris learned, the person who captures a Sandewan and gives it to a tribal chief earns rich rewards, but no hunter within living memory had accomplished that feat. She surmised that the creatures must be small, since the trail she followed passed beneath low-hanging bushes without disturbing their leaves, but no satisfactory candidate has yet been proposed.

Source: Karl Shuker, "Menagerie of mystery." *Strange Magazine* 20 (December 1998): 37-38.

Sandmen *see* **Squattam's Growlers**

Sandwell Valleygator

Bromwich, in Britain's West Midlands, is the hometown of cryptozoologist KARL SHUKER, but it had produced no reports of mysterious creatures until March 1999, when an unknown predatory reptile dubbed the Sandwell Valleygator or Sandwell Snapper appeared in Swan Pool. The first sighting was recorded on 30 March, when fisherman Mike Sinnatt watched a "marvelously shaped piece of wood" come alive and attack a goose floating on the water's surface. Within 24 hours, a dozen more reports of aggressive reptilian quadrupeds were filed by visitors to the pond. Skeptics initially dismissed the reports as premature April Fool's Day pranks, but members of the Sandwell Council were sufficiently concerned to close the pond during Easter Bank Holiday (3-6 April). Within a week of the pond's reopening to swimmers, a North American snapping turtle (*Chelydra serpentina*) was caught at Swan Pool, but Sandwell Council spokesmen denied that it was the elusive Valleygator. More than two years later, a second snapping turtle was dragged from the pond, this one 2 feet 5 inches long and weighing 20 pounds. It remains to be seen whether Swan Pool has any more secrets to yield.

Sources: Karl Shuker, "Alien zoo." *Fortean Times* 155 (March 2002): 22; Shuker, "Beware — valleygator!"

Sanford sea serpent

On 30 July 1888, three crewmen aboard the tug *Sanford* saw "an immense monster…swimming rapidly" across Block Island Sound, offshore from Watch Hill, Rhode Island. The SEA SERPENT swam with "his head elevated some six feet and showing a long back-fin, which projected for many feet above the surface."

Source: O'Neill, *The Great New England Sea Serpent*.

Sans Peur sea serpent

On 22 January 1888, while sailing past Travancore at the southernmost tip of India, passengers aboard the yacht *Sans Peur* observed a large SEA SERPENT from a

The *Sans Peur* sea serpent, after witness Florence Caddy.

distance of 200 yards. It measured roughly the length of the yacht. Witness Florence Caddy described it as:

> a large luminous serpentine form, which rose slowly out of the water in two large curves (like two arches of a low bridge), letting me see distinctly the large diaper pattern marked on the flattened silvery sides of a huge SNAKE.

Caddy further recalled that the animal's most striking features were "the flatness of its sides, its silvery luminousness, [and] its bridge-like curves in gentle but decidedly vertical motion." From that description, and despite its great size, curators at London's Natural History Museum concluded that the creature was an oarfish (*Regalecus glesne*) swimming on its side.

Source: Heuvelmans, *In the Wake of the Sea Serpents*.

Sansandryi   Diola tribesmen of Senegal once described the Sansandryi as a large primate or small HOMINID inhabiting forests along the Casamance River. As many other unclassified primates are said to have "backwards" feet, so the Sansandryi allegedly walks backwards in an effort to confuse pursuers. It has no speech or knowledge of tools, but allegedly steals rags from human settlements on occasion to make crude garments. No reports of the Sansandryi have been recorded since the early 1900s, suggesting that the creatures may now be extinct.

Source: Maclaud, "Notes anthropologiques sur les Diola de la Casamance." *L'Anthropoogie* (1907): 67, 81.

Sansavatnet, Norway   Neighbors of this Norwegian lake, in Rogaland County, once claimed that it harbored a 200-foot LAKE MONSTER. No modern sightings of the creature(s) are recorded.

Source: Skjelsvik, "Norwegian lake and sea monsters."

***Santa Clara* sea serpent**   On 30 December 1947, the U.S. Hydrographic Department received a message from the passenger liner *Santa Clara*, en route from New York City to Colombia, stating that the ship had struck a SEA SERPENT at 34° 34' north latitude and 74° 7' west longitude (118 miles east of Cape Lookout, North Carolina). As chief mate William Humphreys later described the incident, the ship was sailing on a calm sea in broad daylight when:

> Suddenly [Third Mate] John Axelson saw a snakelike head rear out of the sea about 30 feet off the starboard bow of the vessel. His exclamation of amazement directed the attention of the other two mates to the Sea Monster, and the three watched it unbelievingly as in a moment's time it came abeam of the bridge where they stood and was then left astern. The creature's head appeared to be about 2½' across, 2' thick and 5' long. The cylindrically shaped body was about 3' thick, and the neck about 1½' in diameter. As the monster came abeam of the bridge it was observed that the water around it, over an area of 30 or 40 feet square, was stained red. The visible part of the body was about 35' long. It was assumed that the color of the water was due to the creature's blood and that the stem of the ship had cut the monster in two, but as there was no observer on the other side of the vessel there was no way of estimating what length of body might have been left on that side. From the time the monster was first sighted until it disappeared in the distance astern it was thrashing about as though in agony. The Monster's skin was dark brown, slick and smooth. There were no fins, hair or protuberances on the head, neck, or visible parts of the body.

A HOAX was discounted, since the Grace Line imposed a $500 fine on officers who filed false log entries. Christopher Coates, of the New York Zoological Society's aquarium, opined that the creature injured by the *Santa Clara* was an oarfish (*Regalecus

The ***Santa Clara* sea serpent**, sketched from eyewitness descriptions.

glesne), although that FISH is noted for its prominent fins and the spiny ridge running from head to tail along its back. BERNARD HEUVELMANS suggested that the beast was, in fact, either a giant EEL or a specimen of his hypothetical "long-necked" sea serpent.

Source: Heuvelmans, *In the Wake of the Sea Serpents*.

Santa Cruz carcass   In May 1925, a rotting carcass washed ashore near Santa Cruz, California. The creature measured 36 feet 6 inches, much of that length consumed by a long neck ending in a head described as larger than an adult human being. Its eyes were tiny by comparison, and it reportedly had a flat bill resembling a duck's. Examination of the skeleton identified the creature as a specimen of Baird's beaked whale (*Berardius bairdii*), but the long "false neck" remains unexplained.

Source: Dubious Globsters, http://www.geocities.com/capedrevenger/dubiousglobsters.html.

***Santa Lucia* sea serpent**   Sometime in the early 1930s, Captain Walter Prengel of the Grace liner *Santa Lucia* reported a sighting of the SEA SERPENT known as CADBOROSAURUS off the coast of Vancouver Island, British Columbia. Editor Archie Wills, of the *Victoria Daily Times*, noted the incident in a list of sightings without specific dates. Authors PAUL LEBLOND and Edward Bousfield omit the sighting from their later study of "Caddy."

Sources: Heuvelmans, *In the Wake of the Sea Serpents*; LeBlond and Bousfield, *Cadborosaurus*.

Santer   An ALIEN BIG CAT reported from North Carolina in the 1890s, the Santer was described as large and gray, with stripes resembling those of a TIGER. The first sightings, accompanied by predation of domestic pets and livestock, were reported in Iredell County between August and October 1890. The CAT then seemingly went on hiatus until 1897, when it resurfaced in neighboring Yadkin County, moving eastward into Wilkes County in 1899. Hunters scoured the countryside in vain. When similar incidents occurred in Iredell County during May 1934, locals claimed the MYSTERY MAULER was a descendant of the original Santer. Once again, their efforts to trap it proved fruitless, but the predator vanished as mysteriously as it had come.

Source: Angelo Capparella III, "The Santer: North Carolina's own mystery cat?" *Shadows* 4 (January 1977): 1-3 and *Shadows* 4 (February 1977): 1-3.

Sapo de Loma   The Sapo de Loma ("toad of the hill") is described by witnesses as a large, unclassified amphibian inhabiting various wooded valleys of the Andes Mountains in Peru and Chile. It is reportedly large enough to prey on BIRDS and rodents, while exuding a potent venom to defend itself from larger animals. Science recognizes 116 species of poison-arrow frogs (Family *Dendrobatidae*) from South America, but the largest is barely two inches long at maturity.

Source: Shuker, *From Flying Toads to Snakes with Wings.*

Sasa An unclassified BIRD once reported from the Fijian islands of Kandavu and Viti Levu, the Sasa is now believed to be extinct. Natives described it as a ground-dwelling bird, roughly the size of a chicken, with speckled plumage. KARL SHUKER suggests that it may have been a megapode (Family *Megapodiidae*), whose number includes brush turkeys and scrub hens still extant in Australia and on various Pacific islands. Like the rumored Sasa, megapodes build mounds of soil to incubate their eggs, making their nests vulnerable to humans and various other predators.

Source: Shuker, "Gallinaceous mystery birds."

Sasabonsam Ashanti natives in Ghana describe the Sasabonsam as a flying creature 5-6 feet tall, with a 20-foot wingspan, a humanoid face with long teeth, an emaciated body, and short legs with peculiar feet (sometimes described as facing backward). At a glance, it appears to resemble the cryptids known as MOTHMAN in the U.S. and OWLMAN in Britain, but while those creatures have eluded all pursuers, a Sasabonsam was allegedly killed and photographed in the early 20th century. That event reportedly occurred in February 1918, when a tribesman named Agya Wuo found a Sasabonsam sleeping in a hollow tree and killed it, carrying the body to his village. District Commissioner L.W. Wood allegedly viewed and photographed the creature on 22 February, reporting that its skin was speckled black and white, with scaly ridges above the eyes. In the 1930s, researcher Joseph Danquah obtained an Ashanti carving of the Sasabonsam, and he later located L.W. Wood. Wood confirmed his presence in Ghana during 1918, but strangely claimed he "was not sure" if he had photographed the remarkable creature killed by Agya Wuo. BERNARD HEUVELMANS concluded that the Sasabonsam was a species of giant BAT, known elsewhere in Africa as OLITAU or KONGAMATO, but skeptics maintain that the creature is wholly imaginary.

Sources: Joseph Danquah, "Living monster or fabulous animal?" *West African Review* 10 (September 1939): 19-20; Heuvelmans, *Les Derniers Dragons d'Afrique*; Shuker, "A belfry of crypto-bats."

Sasquatch Prior to 1958, the large HOMINIDS or NORTH AMERICAN APES commonly called BIGFOOT were known by a variety of aboriginal names, from Atahsaia (among Zuni tribesmen) to Yayaya-ash (among Modocs). In the Pacific Northwest, where "classic" Bigfoot sightings are most common, many native names began with "S," including Saskehavis, Sokqueatl, S'oq'wiam, Sossq'tal and Susquatch. In April 1929, Canadian journalist J.W. Burns merged and Anglicized those names, coining the catch-all term Sasquatch to describe the forest giants. Thus, it is not an "Indian" name, as often claimed in print, but rather an attempt to make the native names more palatable for white readers. Today, the names Sasquatch and Bigfoot are synonymous, applied without regard for the location of specific sightings.

Sources: J.W. Burns, "Introducing B.C.'s hairy giants." *Macleans* (1 April 1929): 9; American Indian Names for Bigfoot, http://www.cherokeefox.com/Bigfoot_names.html.

Sasquatch Information Society No background information is presently available on this Seattle-based Internet clearinghouse for data concerning BIGFOOT. The society's website names no officers or members, and while it provides links to

Canadian journalist J.W. Burns coined the name Sasquatch for unknown hominids in 1929 (*William Rebsamen*).

groups or individual researchers across the U.S., some of the links were outdated and nonfunctional at press time for this volume. The SASQUATCH sightings database includes reports from coast to coast, and baseball caps with a group logo are offered for sale, but the page on "Events" was blank, suggesting that the society is either inactive or exists only as the cyberspace equivalent of a paper organization.

Source: Sasquatch Information Society, http://www.bigfootinfo.org/.

Sasquatch Investigations of Mid-America Oklahoma City resident Hayden Hewes, better known as the director of the International UFO Bureau, founded this early BIGFOOT research group sometime in the early 1980s. The group, if such it truly was, received its first and only national publicity in April 1982, after 15-year-old Billy Parry reported a SASQUATCH sighting near Vici, Oklahoma. Dark hairs found at the scene were sent to Hewes, who told reporters on 14 April, "The hair sample looked very interesting. At this point, we cannot confirm what kind of animal it came from." Hewes said the evidence was being forwarded to the Oklahoma State Bureau of Investigation for analysis, but no results were ever published. At the time, Hewes seemed optimistic, declaring, "I feel it's just a matter of time before a Bigfoot is captured alive." Today, while the SIMA is still listed as active on various Internet websites, no links are provided and the group appears to be defunct.

Sources: "Red-brown-haired, smelly creature puzzling experts." *Indianapolis Star* (12 April 1982).

Sasquatch Unlimited *see* **Texoma Bigfoot Research and Investigation**

Sat-Kalauk   Native folklore in Myanmar identifies the Sat-kalauk as a mysterious vampire CAT. Its favorite prey is the Sambar deer (*Cervus unicolor*), which it reportedly kills by springing onto the deer's back, biting its neck and drinking its blood. Vampirism is unknown among cats, and evidence from the 1950s suggests that the Sat-kalauk may not be a felid at all. In 1954, a supposed Sat-kalauk was caught near Myatkina and upon examination proved to be a yellow-throated marten (*Martes flagivula*), a mustelid related to weasels and WOLVERINES.
Source: U Tun Yin, "Miscellaneous gleanings on wild life in Burma." *Burmese Forester* 4 (1954): 24-27.

Savannah River, Georgia   Cryptozoologists LOREN COLEMAN and JOHN KIRK include this Georgia river on published lists of supposed aquatic cryptid habitats, but they provide no dates or details of sightings.
Source: Coleman, *Mysterious America*; Kirk, *In the Domain of the Lake Monsters*.

Sawtooth Dolphin *see* **Holadeira**

Say-Noth-Kai   Salish tribesmen of British Columbia once applied this name generically to various LAKE MONSTERS and SEA SERPENTS. It is the regional equivalent of NAITAKA and similar names coined for aquatic cryptids by aboriginal tribes throughout North America.
Source: Kirk, *In the Domain of the Lake Monsters*.

Scarborough sea serpent(s)   On 10 June 1930, Australian newspapers carried the following item from Scarborough, New South Wales:

Four men fishing off Bellambi claim that they came in contact with a SEA SERPENT 30 feet long, and with a mouth large enough to take in their boat and its occupants! The party comprised J. Lin, A. Gray, R. Wiley and G. Richardson. One of the number noticed what he took to be a piece of wreckage, and gave the order to pull closer to it. When within about twenty feet, the monster raised its neck and head about six feet out of the water, they say, and roared something like a seal. The party pulled away, and the monster followed for half a mile. Then they made for the beach and safety.

David Stead, an expert in Australian marine fauna, first opined that the creature was a GIANT SQUID (*Architeuthis*), but changed his mind upon hearing that its head was nearly 6 feet wide, with an 8-foot mouth resembling a pelican's. It must, Stead then decided, have been a piked rorqual (*Balaenoptera rostrata*).

Two days after the initial sighting, three witnesses atop a Scarborough cliff saw another unknown creature — or the same one — swimming past Bellambi Reef. They described the beast as "about 80 or 90 feet long, of dark greyish color and with a frightfully ugly head" that arched above the waves on a long, serpentine neck. Clearly, this was no whale, and Stead returned to his first diagnosis, branding it a giant squid. Four decades later, BERNARD HEUVELMANS wrote of that pronouncement, "I can only suppose it had a date with the Bellambi whale and was waving a tentacle to say 'Here I come!' or cocking a snook at the crowd on the beach."
Sources: Heuvelmans, *In the Wake of the Sea Serpents*; Smith, *Bunyips & Bigfoots*.

Schomburgk's Deer   An impressive ungulate once endemic to Thailand's Chao Phrya Basin, Schomburgk's deer (*Cervus schomburgki*) was initially described in 1863. Its handsome chocolate-brown hide and the male's ornately branched antlers, including as many as 33 points, made it so attractive to hunters that it was driven to presumed extinction in the 1930s. Thailand's last known wild specimen was shot in September 1932, while the last captive specimen — kept at a temple in Samut Sakhon Province — was killed by a drunken villager six years later. In February 1991, United Nations agronomist Laurent Chazée found a pair of the deer's distinctive antlers at a medicine shop in Laos. The proprietor, when questioned, claimed that the deer had been shot in a neighboring province, during 1990. Thus far, no Laotian population of *C. schomburgki* has been confirmed.
Source: Gerard Schroering, "Swamp deer resurfaces." *Wildlife Conservation* (December 1995): 2.

The "extinct" Schomburgk's deer may still survive in Southeast Asia.

Schwarzsee, Switzerland   Swiss folklore identifies this lake as the one-time lair of a LAKE MONSTER known as a "water horse" or "sea-bull." No modern sightings of the creature(s) are recorded.
Source: Werner Manz, "Volksglaube und sage aus dem Sarganserland." *Schweizerisches Archiv für Volkskunde* 25 (1925): 229-238.

Scimitar Cat   In 1896, archaeologists discovered a stone carving from the Paleolithic period in a grotto at Isturitz, in the French Pyrenees. The statuette measured 6.5 inches long, and while its lower legs were broken off, the subject was still recognizable as some species of CAT. Only a photo of the carving now remains, since the original was lost, but it still fuels controversy in the ranks of zoologists and paleontologists. Specifically, its deeply-curved lower jaw brought to mind an extinct SABER-TOOTHED CAT, *Homotherium latidens*, also known as the scimitar cat. Available evidence suggests that the scimitar cat resembled a giant LYNX, with its oversized canine teeth flattened and razor-edged for slicing, unlike the conical fangs seen on most saber-teeth. Before discovery of the Isturitz carving, scientists believed the scimitar cat had been extinct in mainland Europe for some 200,000 years, but dating of the statuette suggests survival for an additional 165,000 years, at least. Skeptics maintain that the unknown Cro-Magnon artist simply botched his depiction of a cave LION (*Panthera leo spelaea*), which certainly survived until some 40,000 years ago. In March 2000, fishing vessel *UK33* trawled a partial lower jaw of *H. latidens* from the North Sea's floor southeast of the Brown Banks. Radiocarbon analysis dated the bone at 28,000 years old, roughly the same age as the Isturitz statuette.

Source: Karl Shuker, "Alien zoo." *Fortean Times* 174 (October 2003): 28; Shuker, *Mystery Cats of the World*.

Scoliophis Atlanticus

Scoliophis atlanticus ("Atlantic humped SNAKE") was the scientific name proposed by the Linnaean Society of New England for a SEA SERPENT seen repeatedly off the Massachusetts coast during 1817-19. At least 33 sightings were reported by Bay State witnesses during that span, with 7 more from coastal waters of Maine and New York. The name was selected after two boys found a 3-foot-long black, hump-backed snake at Loblolly Cove, near Cape Ann, Massachusetts. The reptiles lumpy spin reminded observers of the humps displayed by its large supposed relative at sea, hence the name selected. A four-page diagnosis of the captured snake concluded:

> On the whole, as these two animals agree in so many conspicuous, important and peculiar characteristics, and as no material difference between them has yet been clearly pointed out, excepting that of size, the Society will probably feel justified in considering them as individuals of the same species, and entitled to the same name, until a more close examination of the great Serpent shall have disclosed some difference of structure, important enough to constitute a specific distinction.

French zoologist Ducrotay de Blainville disagreed, suggesting that the Massachusetts specimen was simply a deformed common black snake (*Colubris constrictor*). He wrote: "I have no doubt that this individual is in a quite abnormal condition; perhaps after receiving a number of blows in its youth, the injured parts remained damaged and were unable to grow, at least in a regular manner, while those which were unaffected went on moving as they should, and were able to develop fully." French-American naturalist Constantin Samuel Rafinesque-Schmaltz subsequently renamed the New England sea serpent *Megophias* ("big snake").

Source: Heuvelmans, *In the Wake of the Sea Serpents*.

An early 19th-century artist's depiction of *Scoliophis atlanticus*.

Scottish Big Cat Society

Founded by Ayrshire resident MARK FRASER in 1999, the Scottish Big Cat Society conducts field investigations of ALIEN BIG CAT sightings and maintains an active website for discussion of evidence supporting their existence. Various disputes arose in 2002-03, between Fraser's organization and a rival group—the SCOTTISH BIG CAT TRUST—which were aired on the Internet and seemingly are unresolved today. Spokesmen for the SBCT accused Fraser of "deliberately attempting to cause confusion by pretending that his website is run by this organisation." Fraser replied, naming two of the Trust's leaders as disgruntled defectors from his pre-existing organization. Regrettably, such personal conflicts are as common in cryptozoology as in any other field of human endeavor, but research proceeds in spite of distractions. Fraser's group collaborates on various investigations with the BRITISH BIG CAT SOCIETY.

Source: Scottish Big Cat Society, http://www.scottishbigcats.co.uk/.

Scottish Big Cat Trust

Created as "an informal investigative and discussion group" pursuing reports of ALIEN BIG CATS, this group was organized in June 2001 by former members of MARK FRASER'S SCOTTISH BIG CAT SOCIETY. Reasons for the split remain controversial, despite repeated airings on the Internet. In April 2002, the dissidents laid claim to Fraser's original name, then abandoned it in June to become the Scottish Big Cat Trust. A year later, on 23 June 2003, the SBCT was formally recognized as a tax-exempt charity. Its website includes details of some 1,300 ABC sightings in Scotland, and members reportedly collaborate on research projects throughout Britain, the U.S. and Africa. In autumn 2003, identified members of the SBCT executive council included: president Ben Wills, residing in North Carolina, selected for his "refreshingly non-European view" of ABCs; John Murray of Glasgow, treasurer and scientific officer; George Markie, secretary and an ABC witness at Fife, in May 2002; Fran Lockhart, sightings coordinator; Reuel Chisolm, press officer; Christina Kéroualle-Smith, publications officer; Phil Crosby, boasting two ABC sightings in Aberdeenshire; retired policeman George Redpath; Allan Paul, employed with the Ministry of Defense; journalist Ralph Barnett; and veterinarian Mick Orsi, assigned to examine remains of animals allegedly killed by ABCs in Scotland.

Source: Scottish Big Cat Trust, http://www.bigcats.org/abc/index.html.

Scottish Bride sea serpents

On 23 November 1869, the captain and crew of the bark *Scottish Bride* reported a sighting of two SEA SERPENTS 60 miles east of Delaware Bay, at 38°16' north latitude and 74°9' west longitude. The larger of the creatures was 25 feet long, covered with scales like a CROCODILE'S, with a large, flat head. The other, only a few feet long, was presumed to be a juvenile specimen.

Sources: "The old 'fishy' story." *New York Herald* (30 November 1869); O'Neill, *The Great New England Sea Serpent*.

Scottish sea serpent

Sadly, no specific date or location is available for the 19th-century SEA SERPENT sighting reported by a friend of Sir Walter Scott, somewhere along the Scottish coast. BERNARD HEUVELMANS notes that the incident occurred before 1821, and he lists the creature as a specimen of his hypothetical "merhorse." It was doubtless that incident that inspired Scott to write in *The Pirate* (1822):

> The Sea-SNAKE was also known, which arising out of the depths of Ocean, stretches to the skies his enormous neck, covered with

a mane like that of a war-horse, and with its broad glittering eyes, raised mast-head high, looks out, as it seems, for plunder or for victims.

Source: Heuvelmans, *In the Wake of the Sea Serpents.*

Scott's Dolphin   On 4 February 1968, while passing through the Strait of Magellan, naturalist Peter Scott observed a school of Commerson's dolphins (*Cephalorhyncus commersonii*) swimming alongside his ship. Among the familiar cetaceans, he also glimpsed two peculiar specimens with brown backs and white undersides, which fit the description of no known dolphins. Author Darren Naish suggests that Scott actually saw black dolphins (*C. eutropia*) and mistook their dark-gray coloration for brown.

Sources: Darren Naish, "Cryptocetology: The page 254 story." *Animals and Men* 8 (January 1996): 23-29; Peter Scott, *Travel Diaries of a Naturalist.* London: Collins, 1983.

Scrag Whale   Early settlers at Nantucket, Massachusetts reported that a peculiar whale visited their harbor for three consecutive days, sometime in the 1670s. By the time a local blacksmith fashioned the settlement's first harpoon, the creature had left and was seen no more. Witnesses called it a scrag whale, meaning lean or bony, a term typically reserved for whales found in the final stages of starvation. In 1725, based on those accounts and subsequent sightings at sea, British naturalist Paul Dudley described the scrag whale as "nearly akin to the fin-back [or rorqual, Family *Balaenopteridae*], but instead of a fin on its back, the ridge of the after-part is scragged with half a dozen knobs or knuckles." In 1777, Johann Erxleben formally named the species *Balaena gibbosa*, but others disagreed, suggesting that scrag whales were either mutilated rorquals or juvenile northern right whales (*Eubalaena glacialis*). Today, it is generally accepted that they represented a rare North Atlantic population of gray whales (*Eschrichtius robustus*) that were hunted to extinction by the mid-19th century.

Sources: Mark Carwardine, *Whales, Dolphins and Porpoises.* New York: DK Publishing, 1995; Shuker, *From Flying Toads to Snakes with Wings.*

Sea Dog   According to Haida tribesmen of British Columbia, this fantastic amphibious creature once inhabited the waters surrounding Moresby Island, in the Queen Charlotte Islands. A strange hybrid of various species, the Sea Dog (or Tsemaus) was a quadruped that also boasted wings, a dorsal fin and razor-sharp tusks. No modern sightings of the fearsome creature are recorded.

Source: Moon, *Ogopogo.*

Sea-Fern sea serpent   In October 1954, Captain Barney Armstrong of the *Sea-Fern* reported his encounter with a SEA SERPENT off the coast of Newport Beach, in southern California (Orange County). Armstrong claimed the creature was a "sickly green" and pegged its weight at 20 tons. *Fate* magazine summarized Armstrong's account of the incident:

"We were coming in at about 4:30 p.m. when I spotted the thing sticking out of the water about four feet," he said. He throttled down and circled it. The head was round, thorny, and seemed to have a kind of horn, like a cornucopia, hanging. Its mouth was two feet across.

Strangely, while Armstrong said the creature only had one eye, passenger Orrel Reed Jr. insisted that it had two. Despite a tradition of sea serpent sightings in the area, including the SAN CLEMENTE MONSTER, BERNARD HEUVELMANS dismissed the *Sea-Fern* report as a HOAX.

Source: Heuvelmans, *In the Wake of the Sea Serpents.*

Sea of Galilee Monster   A large reptile resembling a CROCODILE was sighted by several witnesses in Israel's Sea of Galilee, during July 1993. No crocodilians are presently indigenous to the region, and the sightings remain unexplained. No recent reports of the creature are on file.

Source: Loren Coleman, "Sea of Galilee monster." *Strange Magazine* 12 (Fall-Winter 1993): 28.

Sea Scorpions   Eurypterids, dubbed sea scorpions because of their long tails with a spinelike appendage at the tip, were among the largest and most fearsome predators found in early prehistoric oceans. Closely related to modern arachnids (scorpions and spiders), they appeared during the Ordovician period, 500 million years ago, and flourished for 250 million years, until the last know species vanished in the Permian times. Their fossils are found on all continents and display such remarkable preservation that their external structure is the best known of any extinct animal. The smallest species was barely 4 inches long, but the largest exceeded 6 feet 6 inches. And while modern scientists are confident that no eurypterids survive today, reports from different regions of the Earth suggest they may be wrong. Examples include:

LAKE NATSILIK, GREENLAND— Folklore relates that this lake was once inhabited by "boat-sized" sea scorpions. No recent sightings are reported, and the aquatic arachnids seem to have yielded their domain to giant fISH.

11 March 1959— While diving off Miami Beach, Florida, Bob Wall entered a submarine cave and encountered a creature vaguely resembling a giant lobster. Newspaper reports dubbed the animal SPECS, for its protruding eyes. Cryptozoologist MARK HALL suggests that it may have been a living eurypterid.

12 February 1989— Remote-control cameras employed by a scientific expedition in the South Pacific photographed an unknown creature in the Peru Trench, at a depth of 13,616 feet. It was 2.5 inches long and had five pairs of jointed appendages. The first pair seemingly served as antennae; the second pair was very long and carried high above the body; and the last three pairs were legs used

Do prehistoric sea scorpions survive in modern times?

to propel the animal along the ocean's floor. Observers remarked on the creature's strong resemblance to a tailless whip scorpion (Order *Amblypygi*), but those arachnids are terrestrial and chiefly desert dwellers.

Sources: Shuker, *In Search of Prehistoric Survivors*; Hjalmar Thiel and Gerd Shriever, "The enigmatic DISCOL species: A deep see pedipalp?" *Senckenbergiana Maritima* 20 (October 1989): 171-175; "Water monsters: Greenland." *Fortean Times* 46 (Spring 1986): 29.

Sea Serpents

Since the first time human beings built a humble boat or raft and ventured out to sea, mariners have reported encounters with large, unknown creatures commonly lumped together under the name of sea serpents. Early navigational maps were decorated with fantastic sketches of DRAGONS at sea, imprinted with the warning: "Here be monsters." Many of the beasts described were neither serpentine nor reptilian in form, but the early name endures — and reports continue to the present day. Some coastal regions log so many sightings that their resident cryptids earn familiar nicknames: CADBOROSAURUS (or Caddy) in British Columbian waters; Cornwall's MORGAWR; the SAN CLEMENTE MONSTER of southern California; or Java's ZEE-GANGSA.

Over the past three centuries, some real-life "monsters" of the sea have been identified, and thus some early sightings were explained. Today we recognize that many sea serpent reports from antiquity (and stranded GLOBSTERS, too) involved whales, GIANT SQUIDS, large SHARKS of various species, MANTA RAYS, and the like. Still, much remains unknown about the oceans and their wildlife. Marine biologist Jesse Ausubel declared, in October 2003, that "some 95 percent of the ocean is still unexplored biologically." It is a bold zoologist indeed who dares repeat Georges Cuvier's rash dictum of the 19th century and claim that no large species wait to be discovered in the ocean depths.

From the early 19th century onward, cryptozoologists have labored to identify and classify sea serpents. In 1817, the Linnaean Society of New England proposed the name *SCOLIOPHIS ATLANTICUS* ("Atlantic humped SNAKE") for a hump-backed creature seen repeatedly off the coast of Massachusetts. Naturalist Constantin Samuel Rafinesque-Schmaltz soon countered with the generic name *Megophias* ("big snake"), retained by ANTOON OUDEMANS in 1892, when he climaxed a study of 162 sea serpent reports by naming the elusive creature *Megophias megophias*. At the same time, however, Oudemans recognized that many characteristics attributed to sea serpents (hair, manes, whiskers, vertical flexure of the spine, etc.) are seen only in mammals. Thus, while clinging to the reptilian name, Oudemans confidently announced that the sea serpent was a long-necked seal with a serpentine tail, reaching lengths of 50-100 feet.

Later researchers faulted Oudemans for insisting that one species of cryptid accounted for all sea serpent sightings, as well

Reptiles are physically incapable of the vertical undulations performed by many "sea serpents."

as reports of LAKE MONSTERS such as NESSIE and OGOPOGO. In fact, descriptions of pelagic cryptids from around the world were too diverse for any one-size-fits-all approach to be acceptable. BERNARD HEUVELMANS was the first to propose a comprehensive system of classification, in 1968, after reviewing 587 sea serpent sightings reported from 1622 to 1966. Of that number, he dismissed 56 reports as HOAXES; 52 as "certain or probable mistakes"; 9 as "incomprehensible, unclassifiable or very suspect"; and 121 as "vague and therefore doubtful." From the remaining 349 reports, Heuvelmans concluded that nine species of large cryptids occupy the oceans of the world. They include:

Long-necked: The most common, with at least 82 sightings, these creatures are described as large mammals (probably pinnipeds) with long, flexible necks, sometimes compared by witnesses to a CAMEL or giraffe. Rolls of body fat alter descriptions of the creature's body. Some witnesses describe short horns on the head, which Heuvelmans believed are "probably erectile tubes arising round the nostrils." They enjoy wide distribution, with reports from every corner of the Earth.

Merhorses: The next most common, with at least 71 recorded sightings, best known for descriptions of their flowing manes, huge eyes and whiskers. These mammals reportedly attain lengths of 60-100 feet, including a "medium to long" neck, and they swim by means of rapid vertical undulations. Global distribution rivals that of the Long-necks, with heaviest concentrations around British Columbia (Caddy), the British Isles and Scandinavia.

Many-humped: With 59 sightings, this mammal is named for the numerous humps displayed along its back, presenting a false impression of vertical undulation when it swims on the surface. IVAN SANDERSON suggested that the humps, in fact, may be air sacs that provide stability in the water and an oxygen reserve for deep dives. Reported lengths range from 60-115 feet, and the creatures are said to swim at surface speeds of 25-45 miles per hour. Heuvelmans believed this species represented an archaic cetacean, similar to the ZEUGLODON, as evidences by its bilobate tail fins and occasional reports of a dorsal fin on its back. Distribution is apparently restricted to the Atlantic Ocean and the Gulf of Mexico.

Super-otters: Next in line, with 28 sightings, these creatures are precisely what the name suggests — vastly elongated otters, with reports of lengths ranging from 65 to 100 feet. At close range, the skin is often described as wrinkled or hairy. Teeth are visible when the creature opens its mouth. Reports come only from the North Atlantic, concentrated along the coasts of Norway and Greenland.

Many-finned: This peculiar species, with 26 sightings, apparently reaches lengths of 60-70 feet and sports a head resembling that of a seal or walrus, but its signature characteristic is the row of prominent fins lining each side of its body behind a short neck. Witnesses describe 4-12 fins on a side for these animals. Their skin is smooth, resembling tanned leather, and supported in places by large dermic plates or scales. Color is typically described as gray, with dirty-yellow patches. Global distribution includes a heavy concentration in the South China Sea, with scattered reports from Australia, the east coast of Africa, and the southeastern United States.

Super-EELS: Giant eels account for 23 probable sightings, while another 41 reports of "ambiguous periscopes" vexed Heuvelmans throughout his study. He could not decide if they represented long-necks swimming on the surface or super-eels briefly rising from the depths. Unlike his other categories, Heuvelmans claimed that there are "certainly several different species" of giant eels,

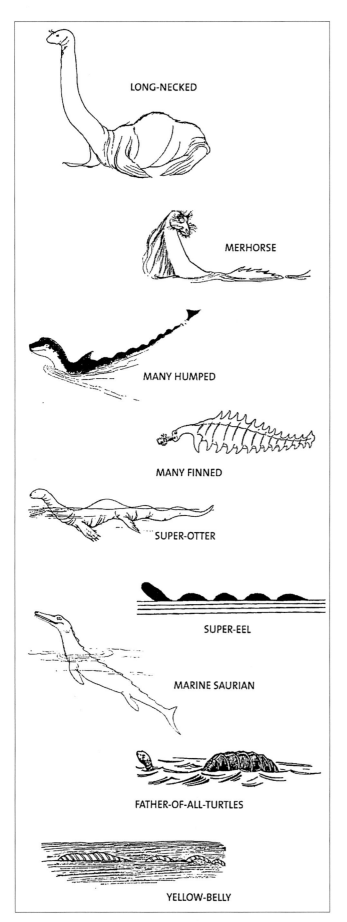

LONG-NECKED

MERHORSE

MANY HUMPED

MANY FINNED

SUPER-OTTER

SUPER-EEL

MARINE SAURIAN

FATHER-OF-ALL-TURTLES

YELLOW-BELLY

"perhaps even different genera belonging to unrelated groups." That may explain their widespread distribution, from the Mediterranean and South Atlantic to Melanesia and the Chinese coast.

Marine saurians: True reptiles are these, resembling oversized CROCODILES at sea. In fact, Heuvelmans believed that they represent relict thalattosaurs, early ancestors of the crocodilians presumed extinct since the Triassic period, 213 million years ago. Alternative candidates might be the mosasaurs, members of a successful but short-lived aquatic offshoot from the MONITOR LIZARDS, known from Cretaceous fossil beds. The nine sightings on record range from the Atlantic and Caribbean to the Bay of Bengal.

Yellow-bellies: With six sightings, this creature is the only one named for its color, specifically a bright yellow underside with a black stripe along the spine and black transverse bands on its sides. With reported lengths of 60-100 feet, these creatures have large, flat heads and flattened fusiform bodies, with long tapering tails. Witnesses sometimes compare them to giant tadpoles, and Heuvelmans could not determine if they represent a fish or an amphibian. Sightings have thus far been confined to tropical waters of the Indian Ocean and South Pacific.

Father-of-All-TURTLES: The rarest creatures on Heuvelmans's list, with only four sightings, giant turtles have nonetheless surfaced from Indonesia to Newfoundland. Heuvelmans proposed a small relict population of the Cretaceous sea turtle *Archelon*, known from fossils to reach a length of 12 feet.

Subsequent attempts to classify sea serpents have borrowed heavily from the groundbreaking work of Oudemans and Heuvelmans. In 1973, after analyzing 30 Cadborosaurus sightings or strandings reported between 1892 and 1969, researchers PAUL LEBLOND and John Sibert proposed a simplified list of three sea-serpent species. The most common resembled Heuvelmans's long-necker, with the addition of a flowing mane. A second species had much in common with Heuvelmans's merhorse, retaining huge saucerlike eyes, though stripped of its mane. A third, uncommon species vaguely resembled Heuvelmans's many-humped creature, though it emerged as more serpentine, with a serrated dorsal fin and a head resembling a sheep's. LeBlond and coauthor Edward Bousfield modified that classification in 1995, asserting that one species of cryptid was responsible for most Caddy sightings.

Meanwhile, cryptozoologist GARY MANGIACOPRA proposed his own system of classification in a series of articles published in *Of Sea and Shore*, during 1976-77. After reviewing 64 reports from the 19th century, Mangiacopra proposed the following four species of sea serpents:

Dorsal-finners: Seen primarily along the eastern coast of North America, this species reaches lengths of 70-100 feet, with diameters of 9-15 feet. Color ranges from green to brown above, with a yellow underside. The head resembles that of a FROG or ALLIGATOR, up to 15 feet in length, with 5-foot jaws sporting 6-inch teeth. A large dorsal fin gives the species its proposed name.

Horn Heads: Reported chiefly from the North Atlantic, this apparent reptile reaches lengths of 25-60 feet, sprouting horns from its skull and serrated protrusions on its back. The hide is scaly, and some witnesses describe the tail as forked. The creature's head is round or oval, flat on top, and some two feet wide. Adults have been seen with their young on occasion, and this species sometimes spouts water, thus drawing attention to itself.

Left: Bernard Heuvelmans described nine supposed species of unknown marine cryptids (**Bernard Heuvelmans**).

Maners: Sharing much in common with Heuvelmans's mer-horse, this species reaches lengths of 15-50 feet, with a serpentine body and a long head resembling that of a horse of SNAKE. A 10-foot neck is decorated with a flowing mane, and sometimes with a kind of beard. Distribution, once again, is limited to the North Atlantic.

Multicoiled: Similar in concept to Heuvelmans's many-humped sea serpent, this presumed species from the North Atlantic reaches lengths of 20-100 feet. Its long and relatively slender body travels by means of undulations that present an impression of coils or humps. Reports of multiple dorsal fins may also explain sightings of the many-finned variety. Some witnesses report a hissing or whistling sound, as of venting steam, which may be caused by the creature's breathing.

The latest revision of sea serpent classification was published in 2003 by LOREN COLEMAN and PATRICK HUYGHE. Their list of 14 aquatic cryptids includes 4 freshwater species — the Giant BEAVER, Mystery MONITOR, relict DINOSAURS and Mystery SALAMANDER— but the other 10 appear primarily in marine habitats. They include:

Classic sea serpents: A species of global distribution, reaching 100 feet or more in length, including Cadborosaurus, CHESSIE, and most of the North Atlantic serpents ranging from Scandinavia to New England.

Waterhorse: Combining elements of Heuvelmans's long-necker and merhorse, this species presumably reaches 40-100 feet in length. Examples listed include the *CORINTHIAN*, *HILARY*, SAN CLEMENTE MONSTER and *VALHALLA* sea serpent, as well as lake monsters Nessie, CHAMP, MORAG, OGOPOGO and NAHUELITO.

Mystery cetacean: Presented as a class, rather than a species, mystery cetaceans include all unknown whales and dolphins sighted worldwide through the years. Coleman and Huyghe also include GAMBO, the still-unidentified creature stranded on Gambia's Bungalow Beach in June 1983.

Giant SHARK: The authors cautiously nominate *CARCHARODON MEGALODON* as the most likely candidate for sightings of huge unknown sharks in various seas.

Mystery MANTA: Initially sighted by WILLIAM BEEBE in 1923, this marine cryptid is the one of the few thus far captured on film.

Great sea CENTIPEDE: At 30-60 feet in length, this species embodies Hevelmans's many-finned sea serpent. The CON RIT of Vietnam's ALONG BAY and the *NARCISSUS* sea serpent of 1899 are offered as examples.

Cryptid chelonian: This category, corresponding to Heuvelmans's Father-of-all-turtles, covers all reports of giant aquatic turtles (as opposed to TORTOISES), whether found in salt or freshwater. Examples specifically sited include the MOHA-MOHA, dismissed by Heuvelmans as a hoax, and the creature seen by witnesses aboard the *ANNIE E. HALL*.

Mystery sirenian: The only species included by the authors in this category is STELLER'S SEA COW, presumed extinct for over 200 years.

Giant OCTOPUS: Last but certainly not least, Coleman and Huyghe include a huge cephalopod as their final marine cryptid, citing reports from the Caribbean and Florida's Atlantic coast.

Although Bernard Heuvelmans suffered ridicule from mainstream scientists for his imaginative classification of sea serpents, his 1968 study remains the most comprehensive to date and is the only survey of the 20th century to treat sea serpent sightings as a global phenomenon. New sightings recorded since 1968, and rediscovery of older reports that eluded Heuvelmans, have done little to challenge his original assessments.

Sources: Coleman and Huyghe, *The Field Guide to Lake Monsters, Sea Serpents, and Other Mystery Denizens of the Deep*; Heuvelmans, *In the Wake of the Sea Serpents*; LeBlond and Bousfield, *Cadborosaurus*; LeBlond and Sibert, *Observations of Large Unidentified Marine Animals in British Columbia and Adjacent Waters*; Mangiacopra, "The great unknowns of the 19th century"; Oudemans, *The Great Sea-Serpent*.

Séah Malang Poo   This large, unclassified CAT prowls Thailand's Khao Sok National Park, living and hunting among the region's karst limestone mountains. Witnesses describe its stocky build, with a coat of alternating brown and black stripes. One specimen was reportedly shot and skinned in the 1930s, its pelt dispatched to Thailand's national museum, but no further information on that evidence has yet been disclosed.

Sources: Shuker, "Blue tigers, black tigers, and other Asian mystery cats." *Cat World* 214 (December 1995): 24-25.

Searle, Frank E. (n.d.)   Arguably the most controversial NESSIE researcher of all time, Frank Searle moved to Loch Ness in June 1969 or 1970 (accounts differ), soon after retiring from the British army with a captain's rank. He lived first in a tent near Dores, then moved to a trailer at Lower Foyers which he turned into a souvenir shop dubbed the Loch Ness Information Centre. Between October 1972 and July 1974, Searle produced a series of dramatic Nessie photos, widely denounced as fakes by a majority of researchers. Three witnesses who allegedly shared one sighting with Searle could not be found for comment, and Searle withheld his photo negatives from would-be analysts. Two photos, said to reveal Nessie's neck and tail respectively, were apparent cut-and-paste productions using a picture of a DINOSAUR taken from a common postcard. Criticism notwithstanding, in 1976 Searle published a dramatic account of his quest, titled *Nessie: Seven Years in Search of the Monster*.

A year later, in February 1977, Searle was joined at Loch Ness by Belgian researcher Lieve Peten, who served as his "assistant monster huntress" through March 1979. Peten never glimpsed Nessie, but she helped Searle turn out a quarterly newsletter beginning in April 1977. Predictably, critics found the publication filled with "very little positive data and rather more self-publicizing propaganda." Peten also crewed a pair of observation boats with Searle, the *Seeker* and *Seeker II*. Following Peten's return to Belgium, Searle continued publishing his newsletter through December 1983. He left Loch Ness in 1985, for parts unknown. In retrospect, Lieve Peten remains convinced of Nessie's existence, but she now reserves judgment "on any photograph taken by anybody at all, since anything can be faked." Critic Stuart Campbell is more outspoken, declaring that "Frank is a charlatan, a HOAXER who after all these years believes in his own fraudulent pictures and cock-and-bull stories."

Sources: Harrison, *The Encyclopaedia of the Loch Ness Monster*; This Nessie is Too Good to Be True, http://www.bahnhof.se/~wizard/cryptoworld/index224a.html; Loch Ness — The Facts, http://www.geocities.com/Area51/Vault/9054/nessie.*html*.

Secretary Bird (Philippines)   The secretary BIRD (*Sagitarius serpentarius*) is an African species, known for its crest, size (4 feet tall, with a 7-foot wingspan), and preference for eating SNAKES. Officially, except in zoos, it does not exist outside of sub-Saharan Africa, but French naturalist Pierre Sonnerat described a very similar bird seen during a visit to the Philippines in 1771-72. Sonnerat's bird was not identical to its African cousin, however. He reported that the feathers comprising the lower portion of the Philippine specimen's crest were longer than those in

Witnesses report an unknown species of secretary bird from the Philippines.

the upper portion, exactly reversing the pattern seen in Africa. Likewise, while the central tail feathers are longest in *S. serpentarius*, Sonnerat claimed the outer feathers of his specimen's tail were longer. Both traits, in fact, are found in the Philippine eagle (*Pithecophaga jefferyi*), formally described in 1896, and many researchers now believe that Sonnerat sighted that species, rather than a misplaced secretary bird. KARL SHUKER, meanwhile, notes that secretary birds were deliberately introduced onto the West Indian island of Martinique in 1832, to eradicate venomous snakes, and he suggests that something similar may have transpired in the Philippines.

Source: Shuker, "All new talon show."

Sedapa *see* Orang Pendek

Seealpsee, Germany
Ancient legends maintained that this German lake, in Bayern State, was the lair of a slumbering DRAGON whose awakening might prove disastrous for local residents. The story suggests a tradition of LAKE MONSTER sightings, but no modern reports are on file.

Source: Karl Reiser, *Sagen, Gebräuche und Sprichwörter des Allegäus*. Kempten, German: J. Kesel, 1902.

Séhité
These unclassified primates or HOMINIDS of Côte d'Ivoire are described by Guéré tribesmen as diminutive bipeds covered with long reddish hair. Tradition has it that they traded goods with rural villagers until the 1930s, when the Séhité retreated farther into the jungle. A native aide to French zoologist André Ledoux reported a sighting in 1947, and the same year allegedly saw one of the creatures shot by an elephant hunter near Toulépleu. The disposition of its carcass is unknown. IVAN SANDERSON considered the Séhité similar, if not identical to, the AGOGWE of East Africa.

Sources: Heuvelmans, *On the Track of Unknown Animals*; Sanderson, *Abominable Snowmen*.

Seileag/Shiela
While NESSIE and MORAG remain the most famous of Scottish LAKE MONSTERS, many other lochs besides Ness and Morar produce occasional cryptid sightings. Reports from Loch Shiel, in the Highland district, have been recorded since 1874, when witnesses glimpsed a fast-moving creature with

three humps on its back. A similar report was filed in 1905, by four passengers aboard the local mail steamer *Clan Ranald*. Three visible humps were confirmed in 1911, by two men who watched the creature through a telescope. In 1926, Ranald MacLeod and a companion watched one of the beasts crawl ashore at Sandy Point, noting its long neck, broad head, wide mouth and seven "sails" on its back. Overall, MacLeod estimated, Seileag was longer than the *Clan Ranald*. Other local witnesses agreed that the creature, like Nessie, sometimes left the loch to crawl on land. Sandie MacKellaig tried to shoot one of the beasts from his small boat, in the early 1930s, but his aim was poor. Witnesses at Glenfinnan, on the loch's northern tip, reported sightings in the 1950s and in 1979. A tourist named G.B. Gordon claimed to have photographed Seileag in 1991, but the picture's authenticity is still hotly debated. As recently as 9 June 1998, a sighting was reported from the stylish Glenfinnan House Hotel.

Sources: Costello, *In Search of Lake Monsters*; Whyte, *More Than a Legend*; Zarzynski, "'Seileag': The unknown animal(s) of Loch Shiel, Scotland."

Selbusjøen, Norway
Ancient LAKE MONSTER traditions surround this lake, in Norway's Sør-Trondelag County, but it is not among the country's active "monster" lakes.

Source: Erik Knatterud, Sea Serpents in Norwegian Lakes, http://www.mjoesormen.no.

Selma/Seljora
The Norwegian lake Seljordsvatnet, in Telemark County, has produced LAKE MONSTER sightings since 1750. In summer of that year, local resident Gunleid Andersson-Verpe was rowing from Ulvneset to Nes when he was "attacked by a sea horse" which proved "so obstinate that the boat overturned." Andersson-Verpe escaped without injury, but henceforth boaters on the lake armed themselves with axes and pikes. The first clear description of the creature now dubbed Selma came from Capt. Hans Klokkarstogo, master of a paddle-wheeler that plied the lake in the 19th century. Klokkarstogo and other witnesses described a serpentine beast with the head and mane of a horse, and a tail like that of a FISH. In 1880, Bjorn Bjørge and his mother claimed to have killed a 3-foot lizard which they believed was a juvenile lake monster. The carcass lay beached for several weeks, but villagers refused to approach it and the animal was never identified.

Sightings of Selma (or Seljora) continued throughout the 20th century. In summer 1918, Karl Karlsson glimpsed the beast while fishing from a bridge at Sandnes. Two years later, Eivind Fjodstuft was fishing at Sinnesodden Point when he saw an animal resembling a huge black CROCODILE, 50-65 feet long, emerge from the lake and climb a nearby cliff face. When he mustered nerve to approach it, the creature scrambled back to the water and quickly submerged. Over the next three decades, multiple witnesses reported sightings of hump-backed cryptids in the lake, with size estimates ranging from 13 feet to 175 feet in length. In May 1963, witness Torje Lindstøl saw a long-necked creature with a head resembling a deer's, swimming 150 feet offshore from Svarvaren. Three months later, Walter Berg saw a 30-foot animal resting on Seljordsvatnet's surface.

Investigators have mounted expeditions to the lake since September 1969, when brothers Alf and Arne Thomassen donned scuba gear to search underwater. At one point, they found deep grooves in the lake bed, as if some heavy object had been dragged along the bottom at a depth of 50 feet. Six months later, Arne Thomassen returned to mount underwater cameras equipped with echo sounders around Sinnesodden Point, and while the cameras were triggered several times, the resultant photographs showed nothing. Dentist Rolf Langeland saw Selma in summer 1975, estimating its length at 98-163 feet, and he returned with 10 companions the following year, to mount a 2-week vigil christened Operation Summerbird. One member of the team reported two sightings of Selma, but the photographs he snapped were inconclusive. Arne Thomassen also returned in 1976, descending with powerful lights to a depth of 98 feet, where he once again found large, unexplained drag marks on the lake's floor.

The most persistent researchers at Seljordsvatnet have been Swedish cryptozoologist JAN-OVE SUNDBERG (who coined Selma's nickname) and his GLOBAL UNDERWATER SEARCH TEAM (GUST). During their first expedition, in July 1977, Sundberg's crew recorded sonar hits on large submerged objects, moving within 30 feet of the team's boat. On 7 July, the sonar tracked three such objects moving underwater on parallel courses. The group also reported multiple surface sightings of a "torpedo-shaped" object 10-16 feet long. Back at the lake in July 1978, Sundberg glimpsed an unknown creature with a "lizard-like" head 10-12 inches long, raised 12-16 inches above the water on a slender neck. He shot two rolls of 8mm movie film, but the evening darkness prevented him from capturing the beast on celluloid. The GUST team returned in August 1998 and August 2000, each time recording sonar hits and underwater sounds like "a cross between a snorting horse and an eating pig." On 8 August 2000, crew member ERIK KNATTERUD claimed a surface sighting of Selma, but the creature submerged before he could photograph it.

Tourist sightings at Seljordsvatnet have continued in tandem with ongoing investigations. Fisherman Bjarne Haugstol saw a creature with three humps on its back, in July 1986. Six years later, Erik Nordseth shot 20 seconds of videotape on an unknown object 10-15 feet long, cruising the surface at a speed of 8-14 miles per hour. Kari Aakre and her family saw three of the animals swimming in tandem near Seljord, in July 1995. The most recent sighting, as of press time for this volume, was reported by a local resident who saw two large animals "chasing each other" on 23 July 2003.

Sources: "International team to search Norwegian lake for 'sea serpent.'" Agence France-Presse (25 February 1998); Kirk, *In the Domain of the Lake Monsters*; Jonathan Tisdall, "Seljord serpent spotted again." *Aftenposten Nettutgaven* (24 July 2003); Erik Knatterud, Sea Serpents in Norwegian Lakes, http://www.mjoesormen.no.

Sémé An unclassified primate or HOMINID of northern Gabon, the Sémé is described by Bantu tribesmen as a tailless biped, 2-3 feet tall and covered in reddish-orange hair. The hair on its head is unusually long, sometimes falling to its waist. Curiously, for an APE, the Sémé is said to herd wild forest hogs, and its humanoid footprints are sometimes allegedly found in conjunction with hog tracks. BERNARD HEUVELMANS suggested that tales of the Sémé derived from confusion of red colobus MONKEYS (*Pilocolobus* sp.) with forest-dwelling PYGMIES in Gabon.

Source: Heuvelmans, *Les Bêtes Humaines d'Afrique*.

Senegal Dolphin In 1971, zoologist Willem Mörzer Bruyns announced the discovery of a new dolphin species, seen in great numbers along the coast of Senegal. He described the cetaceans as six feet long, with brown backs and white undersides. Significantly, they lacked the spots typically found on bridled dolphins (*Stenella attenuata*), also known as pantropical spotted dolphins. Critics say Mörzer Bruyns was hasty in proclaiming a new species, noting that marked variations in color and spotting are found in *S. attenuata*, both geographically and individually.

Sources: Heuvelmans, "Annotated checklist of apparently unknown animals with which cryptozoology is concerned"; Willem Mörzer Bruyns, *Field Guide of Whales and Dolphins*. Amsterdam: Tor, 1971.

Senegal Stone Partridge The stone partridge (*Ptilopachus petrosus*) is a colorful game BIRD of medium size, weighing up to 1.7 pounds, that inhabits rocky mountain gorges throughout a broad territory ranging from Africa to Central Asia. In Senegal, witnesses report an apparent subspecies, as yet unclassified, that is distinguished by its smaller size, spotted head, paler breast, and a preference for dense forest undergrowth rather than the open ground preferred by the nominate species. Its existence remains to be confirmed.

Source: Shuker, "Gallinaceous mystery birds."

Serpent Lake, Minnesota Despite its name, this Minnesota lake, located south of Crosby in Crow Wing County, has no tradition of LAKE MONSTER sightings. In fact, its Ojibwa name — meaning "SNAKE" — was applied in reference to a tribesman exiled there for adultery. The predictable confusion is compounded by a 30-foot statue of a serpent in Crosby, and by proclamation of the surrounding countryside as Serpent Park.

Source: Nick Sucik, "Solving a lake monster myth." *Cryptozoology Review* 4 (Summer 2003): 3.

Serranía del Moroturo, Venezuela In the late 1970s, LAKE MONSTER sightings emanated from an unnamed lake outside this Venezuelan city, in Lara State. While some claim the creature resembled a DINOSAUR, skeptics suggest that it may be a large ANACONDA.

Source: Silvano Lorenzoni, "More on extant dinosaurs." *Pursuit* 47 (Summer 1979): 105-109.

Setesdahl, Norway Norse folklore describes this lake in Aust-Agder County as the lair of a ferocious LAKE MONSTER, but it has produced no modern sightings.

Source: Skjelsvik, "Norwegian lake and sea monsters."

Seton Lake, Canada Seton Lake, located east of Lillooet, British Columbia, is allegedly the home of sturgeons (*Acipenser* sp.) far exceeding record lengths for those impressive FISH. Locals claim that specimens 22-28 feet long have been seen in the lake, but none of those whoppers have yet been landed to prove the case.

Source: "Meanwhile, in Yakutia." *Fate* 20 (June 1967): 22-24.

Sevier Lake, Utah Authors LOREN COLEMAN and JOHN KIRK list this lake, in Utah's Millard County, as a source of LAKE MONSTER reports. Those listings are presumably based on a vague report published in the *Decatur (IL) Republican* on 10 June 1873, but that account is suspect. Utah historian Jay Hammond notes that Sevier Lake has been "usually dry" since settlers began diverting water from the Sevier River for irrigation purposes, from the late 1850s onward. Most maps also show the lake as dry, though some sources describe it as an intermittent salt lake.

Sources: Coleman, *Mysterious America*; Kirk, *In the Domain of the Lake Monsters*; Jay Hammond, Sevier Lake, http://www.media.utah.edu/uhe/s/sevierlake.html.

Shamanu Once the smallest of the WOLVES on Earth, the Japanese wolf (*Canis lupus hodophilax*) disappeared as prey populations dwindled in the 18th and 19th century, until the last known specimen was killed in January 1905. Still, reports of unknown wolflike canids emerge from the islands of Honshū and Kyūshū, with a heavy concentration around Honshū's Chichibu-Tama National Park. On 14 October 1996, photographer Hiroshi Yagi snapped 19 close-range pictures of a Shamanu in the park. Nine months later, on 8 July 1997, Satoshi Nishida took 10 photos of a female specimen on Kyūshū. Skeptics suggest that Shamanu witnesses have either seen feral dogs (*Canis familiaris*) or rare descendants of interbreeding between dogs and Japanese wolves prior to 1905.

Source: Karl Shuker, "Alien zoo." *Fortean Times* 107 (February 1998): 15.

Shān Gui   The Shān gui ("mountain monster") is a large unclassified primate or HOMINID, once reported from southern China and northern Vietnam. In parts of China it is also known as Shān da-rén ("big man of the mountain"), and in Vietnam as Shan tu. Chinese poet Qu Yuan wrote a poem about the Shān gui in the third century B.C.E., but no modern reports are on file. It seems safe to suggest that the creature is identical to China's YEREN and the Vietnamese TOK or NGUOI RUNG.

Source: Zhou Guoxing, "The status of wildman research in China."

Sharks (Freshwater)   Sharks are FISH belonging to the superorder *Selachii*, subdivided into 8 orders and 30 families. They are found worldwide, ranging in size from 8 inches long to more than 40 feet. They are normally saltwater creatures, though one subspecies of bull shark (*Charcharinas nicaraguensis*) has adapted to fresh water, inhabiting Central America's largest lake, Lago Nicaragua. Bull sharks (*C. leucas*) have also been reported from Lake Jamoer in Irian Jaya, Indonesia. Additionally, the river sharks (Genus *Glyphis*) are known to swim far upstream in various rivers of tropical Asia. They include the critically endangered Ganges river shark (*Glyphis gangeticus*); the Bizant river shark (*Glyphis* species "A"), known only from two specimens collected in Queensland, Australia; the Borneo river shark (*Glyphis* species "B"), known from two specimens collected in the 1890s and in March 1997, respectively; and the New Guinea river shark (*Glyphis* species "C"), described from five jaws and two juvenile specimens lost since their collection.

Do actual freshwater sharks exist outside of Nicaragua? Scientists remain skeptical, but evidence continues to accumulate, suggesting that some sharks may thrive — or at least survive — far

Unidentified freshwater sharks are reported from several locations worldwide.

from their normal oceanic habitat. Modern reports of mislocated sharks include the following:

Early 1900s— Explorer PERCY FAWCETT described huge toothless sharks inhabiting the Rio Paraguay, in Brazil. Today, some researchers believe Fawcett encountered a species of giant CATFISH.

1940s—GEORGE AGOGINO reported a 12-foot shark in Lake Sentani, Irian Jaya (the Indonesian half of New Guinea). Skeptics suggest that it may in fact have been a largetooth sawfish (*Pristis microdon*), which inhabits the lake and reaches lengths of 19 feet.

14 July 1968— A 4-foot, 20-pound shark of undisclosed species was pulled from Rivieres des Prairies, a river adjacent to Montreal-Nord, Québec. Presumably, it reached that location from the North Atlantic, via the St. Lawrence River.

July 1976— Two young fishermen caught a 3.5-foot sand shark (*Charcharius taurus*) in the Dallas suburb of Arlington, Texas, some 200 miles from the nearest salt water.

18 August 1977— A shark of unknown species, 25 inches long and weighing 10 pounds, was caught at East Lynn Lake, in landlocked West Virginia's Wayne County.

Late June 1978— A dead shark was found in the water-intake pipe of a Detroit, Michigan factory, apparently drawn from LAKE ERIE. No further description of the fish is presently available.

5 June 2000— At 1:30 a.m., passersby alerted police to a stranded shark thrashing at the intersection of Argyle and Carunna Streets, in central Glasgow, Scotland. The fish was dead when officers arrived. Its presence on the pavement remains unexplained.

13 December 2001— Media reports announced that a 6-foot shark of undisclosed species had been found lying on the pavement of a rural Alabama highway "250 miles from the nearest body of salt water." No further details were forthcoming.

5 September 2002— A 4-foot tope shark (*Galeorhinus galeus*) was found dead on an island in the River Dearne at Barnsley, South Yorkshire, England. To reach that point, the fish must have traveled 60-odd miles upstream from its normal North Sea habitat. The manner of its stranding, in the middle of an island footpath, was not explained.

Sources: Bord and Bord, *Unexplained Mysteries of the 20th Century*; "Not from round these parts." *Fortean Times* 170 (June 2003): 15; "Seriously out of place." *Fortean Times* 141 (January 2001): 7; Karl Shuker, "Alien zoo." *Fortean Times* 105 (December 1997): 16; Cryptid fish, http://www.angelfire.com/bc2/cryptodominion/fish.html; Lago de Nicaragua, http://nd.essortment.com/lagodenicaragu_rbxb.htm; *Shark News* 9 (June 1997), http://www.flmnh.ufl.edu/fish/organizations/ssg/sharknews/sn9/shark9news11.htm.

Sharlie   Payette Lake, in western Idaho's Adams County, is seven miles long and 3,900 feet deep, surrounded by majestic mountains at 5,000 feet above sea level. Rumors of a LAKE MONSTER in residence date from the 1920s, when loggers and railroad construction workers claimed sightings of large unknown creatures, but the first national reports emerged in summer 1944. During July and August of that year, more than 30 witnesses reported sightings of the beast locals dubbed Slimy Slim. On 21 August, *Time* magazine published the following description from witness Thomas Rogers, auditor of a respected business firm in Boise:

> The serpent was about fifty feet away and going five miles an hour with a sort of undulating motion....His head, which resembles that of a snub-nosed CROCODILE, was eighteen inches above the water. I'd say he was thirty-five feet long.

Overnight, Payette Lake experienced a spurt of CRYPTO-

TOURISM, and sporadic sightings of hump-backed, long-necked creatures continued through the early 1950s. In 1954, the *Payette Lakes Star* sponsored a contest to give Slimy Slim a new name, and the prize went to Virginia resident Lee Tury for Sharlie (as in, "Vas you dere, Sharlie?"). Sightings were less frequent over the next two decades, but Sharlie played a strong return engagement June 1977. Three residents of McCall glimpsed the creature while dining on the patio of a local café, witness Linda Palmer reporting that Sharlie was 30-40 feet long, swimming with its humped back elevated 3-4 feet above the lake's surface. Around the same time, Doug Crowther and Cathleen Millburn were fishing at Cougar Bay when a 3-humped creature broke the surface near their boat.

Sources: Garner, *Monster! Monster!*; Kirk, *In the Domain of the Lake Monsters*; Mangiacopra, "Sharlie: A preliminary report on possible large animals in the Payette Lakes of Idaho."

Sharpe's Lobe-billed Riflebird

Another of the six "lost" BIRDS of paradise (Family *Paradisaeidae*) reported from Papua New Guinea in the 19th century, Sharpe's lobe-billed riflebird (*Loboramphis ptilorhis*) was widely dismissed as a hybrid specimen in 1930. Still, some ornithologists and cryptozoologists believe it may constitute a genuine species. None have been reported for well over 100 years, and the birds may now be extinct.

Sources: Fuller, *The Lost Birds of Paradise*.

Sharypovo, Russia

In November 1991, the Russian news agency Tass reported that a 21-foot SNAKE, green and with a sheeplike head, had been sighted swimming in an unnamed lake near this city, in Siberia's Krasnoyarsk Territory. No further information is presently available on this intriguing cryptid.

Sources: Kirk, *In the Domain of the Lake Monsters*; "Snake with sheep head is spotted in a lake." *Baltimore Sun* (21 November 1991).

Shatt al Arab River, Iran

In his definitive 1975 study of dangerous animals, author Roger Caras includes the following brief and tantalizing item:

From Teheran comes a report of a diminutive black FISH in the Shatt al Arab River. It reputedly has killed 28 people with a venomous bite. Death is said to be swift. No other information is presently available. (No other fish is known to have a venomous bite, and this report is at least suspect.)

In fact, at least one fish *does* have a venomous bite. The black-line fangblenny, found in the Red Sea and its northern gulfs, Suez and Aqaba, injects venom from grooved teeth in its lower jaw. It also qualifies as diminutive, with a maximum recorded length of 2.5 inches, but it does not inhabit fresh water and no human fatalities have ever been reported. Cryptozoologist KARL SHUKER suggests two other possible candidates, both found in the Shatt al Arab River, but finally dismisses both from the running. One, the naturalized species *Heteropnestes fossilis*, is variously known as the stinging CATFISH, the Indian catfish, and the Asian stinking catfish. It reaches lengths of 4-21 inches and is blackish in color, but its nonlethal venom is channeled through spines in its pectoral fins. Another sometime denizen of the Shatt al Arab is the long-tailed moray EEL (*Thyrsoidea macrura*) whose bite is either venomous or highly infectious from bacteria found in its mouth. Again, however, no human fatalities are known, and with maximum lengths approaching 12 feet the moray could not be mistaken for a tiny fish.

Source: Shuker, "Fins, fangs and poison."

Sherwood Forest Thing

England's Sherwood Forest, in Nottinghamshire, is most famous as the scene of Medieval clashes between Robin Hood and the wicked Sheriff of Nottingham, but the dawn of a new millennium brought hunters to the region for a very different reason. In 2002, reports emerged from Sherwood of an 8-foot, red-eyed hairy HOMINID prowling the forest and frightening hikers. Chris Mullins, of nearby Loughborough, organized a Beastwatch club to collect reports of the creature, hypothetically linked to ancient accounts of WILDMEN in Europe and the British Isles. "While having some reservations myself," Mullins told the *Evening Post*, "I believe it's feasible. WILDMEN could still exist in our time. Notts and Derbyshire are known for their underground caves and catacombs, explored and unexplored, and the woods could conceal a lot."

Source: "Some thing in the woods." Evening Post (28 November 2002).

Shiantelle sea serpent

On 30 July 1887, while cruising on the yacht *Shiantelle*, J.A. Harvie Brown and Prof. Matthew Heddle saw a SEA SERPENT off the coast of Shuna, Argyll, Scotland. Prof. Heddle, a geologist, later described the creature as follows:

I set down the length at from 60 to 65 feet. There was a very low flat head like a large skate, say 4½ feet...[and]...ten "hummocks" increasing in bulk and altitude toward the central one....The thing I saw appear three times—first time end on was a worthless observation, except that on this occasion the whole was *rushing* through the water. On the other two occasions there was hardly any forward motion at all. The whole disappeared at the same moment, and reappeared also at the same moment....The disappearance and reappearance were both without the *least* splash; but at the moment of disappearance the second time *the foremost two of the last three hummocks coalesced into one*.

Harvie Brown, meanwhile, reported that:

I counted with the binoculars twelve or perhaps thirteen humps at almost perfectly regular distances the one from the others. The first of these humps appeared to be moving rapidly through the water across the line of vision, and to be breaking and spraying water, and the other eleven or twelve (I had only time to count them once) maintained all their relative positions with one another and collectively with the first, *yet* did not appear in themselves to me to move, though slight ripples of water were visible, nearly throughout the whole length. The whole disappeared and reappeared at least four times to me, apparently simultaneously or almost so throughout its length. When last it was seen, it was moving on a course almost parallel to the shore, which shore runs N.E. or thereby. The distance from the ship at which time I first saw it, and from that time to its final disappearance was estimated by me at about half a mile by eye (but this may have been an over-estimate of distance).

Despite that observation, Brown then proceeded to dismiss the creature as "a tide-rip or tidal-wave," an explanation already discounted in Prof. Heddle's detailed analysis of the animal's movements.

Source: Heuvelmans, *In the Wake of the Sea Serpents*.

Shiashia-Yawá

Native hunters in Ecuador describe the Shiashia-yawá as a jungle CAT midway in size between the JAGUAR (*Panthera onca*) and the ocelot (*Leopardus pardalis*). It averages 4.5 feet in length, but its most distinctive characteristic is white background pelage, covered with closely-packed solid-black spots. Skeptics explain Shiashia-yawá reports as occasional sightings of an albino jaguar.

Source: Cryptid Felids, http://www.angelfire.com/bc2/cryptodominion/felids.html.

Shiels, Anthony Nicol (n.d.) British subject Anthony ("Doc") Shiels is a professional psychic and magician whose role in cryptozoology has been controversial, to say the least. Long interested in reports of SEA SERPENTS and LAKE MONSTERS, Shiels contends that aquatic cryptids are paranormal creatures subject to summoning via telepathy and/or witchcraft. With his wife, Shiels claimed a sighting of the Cornish creature known as MOR-GAWR in June 1976, but they had no corroborating witnesses or evidence. The following month, Shiels was on hand to interview young witnesses who claimed sightings of the winged creature OWLMAN, also in Cornwall—a coincidence that prompted some critics to accuse him of staging a HOAX. On 17 November 1976, accompanied by David Clarke of *Cornish Life*, Shiels saw Morgawr again, this time from Parson's Beach at Mawnan. Both men snapped photographs, but a malfunction of Clarke's camera left his negatives double- and triple-exposed. Shiels's photos were little better, since his camera lacked a long-distance lens.

No such failure of technology occurred on 21 May 1977, when Shiels visited Urquhart Castle at Loch Ness. Before the trip, he later claimed, Shiels had engaged a group of psychics to conjure NESSIE from the depths, and Scotland's most famous cryptid appeared on schedule, posing for two remarkable photos with its long neck raised above the water. Snapping the pictures was one thing; keeping them safe was, however, another. Photo-journalist David Benchley made a glass copy negative enlargement of one photo, apparently showing the back of Nessie's head, and printed several of the copies for newspaper publication. Shiels, meanwhile, allegedly mailed the original negative to a fellow magician in Boston, only to have it vanish from the envelope in transit. Back at home, Shiels himself dropped and smashed the glass negative, leaving only Benchley's prints of the photo in existence today.

His other negative, showing Nessie face-on toward the camera, was submitted via TIM DINSDALE to the Royal Photographic Society for analysis. Society president Vernon Harrison found no evidence of trickery, concluding that while the photo might be faked, it seemed "very unlikely." Author Colin Bord also studied the photos and declared:

> If these pictures are faked, I cannot detect how it was done. Such fakes certainly could not be called "crude." If they were produced by double exposure or superimposition they would need the services of a skilled laboratory staff and have to be the work of a skilled and well-equipped photographer. Having met the man, I do not think that either his photographic equipment…or his knowledge of photo techniques are up to it. The alternative is that he took a boat out into the loch with a buoyant life-size model

Sketches of the Cornish sea serpent Morgawr, after witness Anthony Shiels.

aboard, popped it into the water, went ashore, photographed it twice in such a way that it changed shapes between shots, and went out again to retrieve it. All this on an afternoon in May at a famous tourist attraction. I find it simpler to believe in the existence of water monsters.

Critics counter with the arguments that (a) no landmarks are visible in Shiels's photos to prove where the pictures were taken, and (b) that as proprietor of the Fortean Picture Library, renting copies of the photo for publication at prices ranging from $60 to $200, Bord might conceivably have personal motives for promoting the pictures as genuine.

Shiels faced more heat in August 1981, after self-proclaimed psychic Pat Kelly sent him a photo of an alleged lake monster, reportedly snapped at LOUGH LEANNE in Ireland's County Kerry. Skeptics noted that the creature shown in that photo bore a striking resemblance to that depicted in two photos of Morgawr, allegedly taken in February 1976 by still-unidentified photographer "Mary F." While denying any trickery, Shiels seemed to contradict his own previous view of supernatural lake monsters in 1984, when he suggested that Nessie might be a giant, long-nosed cephalopod unknown to science, which Shiels dubbed *Dinoteuthis probsocideus*. In 1991, researcher Mark Chorvinsky accused Shiels of faking the "Mary F." Morgawr photos; two years later, in April 1993, Chorvinsky also named Shiels as the prime suspect in a photographic fraud at Lough Leane. For the record, Shiels stands by his denials of participating in a hoax of any kind.

Sources: Mark Chorvinsky, "The Lough Leane monster photograph investigation." *Fate* 46 (March 1993): 31-35 and (April 1993): 31-34; Mark Chorvinsky, "The 'Mary F.' Morgawr photographs investigation." *Strange Magazine* 8 (Fall 1991): 8-11, 46-49; Harrison, *The Encyclopedia of the Loch Ness Monster*; Harrison, *Sea Serpents and Lake Monsters of the British Isles*; McEwan, *Mystery Animals of Britain and Ireland*; Shiels, "Surrealchemy vs. cryptozoology."

Shine, Adrian J. (1950–) Self-taught naturalist and one-time London printer Adrian Shine has spent more than a quarter-century researching the ecology of Scotland's Loch Ness and Loch Morar, reputed homes of the famous LAKE MONSTERS known as NESSIE and MORAG. He assumed leadership of the Loch Ness and Morar Project in 1974, issuing a series of reports on research at both lochs over the next nine years, and has devoted himself to Loch Ness full-time since 1984. In the 1970s, Shine designed and built his own one-man submersible, dubbed "Machan," which may now be seen at the Official Loch Ness Exhibition in Drumnadrochit. He has been instrumental in organizing and leading the best-known expeditions to Loch Ness, including Operation Deepscan (1987, employing sonar), Project Urquhart (1992, including computer enhancement of various films and photos), and the Rosetta Project (1994, preparing a timeline "calendar of events" with cores taken from the loch's bed). At the dawn of a new millennium, Shine designed Drumnadrochit's Loch Ness 2000 Exhibition, and he remains active in support of research at the loch.

Shine's opinions on Nessie and Morag have fluctuated over time. In 1976 he wrote:

> The theme of our…work at Morar has been that there still existed within the British Isles unexplored regions of considerable size, from which have come reports of large unknown creatures, the study of which was outside the scope of the usual apparatus of limnology…. Our main objective remains unchanged however. If British naturalists through some faith in human testimony from the

Scottish lochs pursue a fiction, then at worst we may be embarrassed but if we ignore a fact then we may be given cause to be ashamed.

In January 1994, Shine opined that most of the 4,000-odd Nessie sightings on record involved the wakes of passing boats. His new "favorite theory" for any leftover sightings involved a "lovelorn Baltic sturgeon" (*Acipenser sturio*) trapped in Loch Ness while searching for a mate. Four months later, members of his Loch Ness Project publicized the story of an alleged HOAX surrounding the 1934 SURGEON'S PHOTO of Nessie. In January 2000, Shine himself faced hoax allegations after press reports disclosed that he was breeding a large sturgeon at Drumnadrochit. "This is a bit embarrassing," he said, "and I would rather that there is not too much publicity about the fish. It is all part of an experiment I am conducting — the fish occasionally breaks the surface in the summer and is spotted by visitors and we are recording their description of what they see." Gary Campbell, president of the LOCH NESS MONSTER FAN CLUB, replied: "It's no wonder that he doesn't want any publicity. This experiment has the worst overtones of pseudo science that have been seen at Loch Ness for years. What happens when the fish grows too big for the pond? It might be unfair to suggest that the fish may end up in the loch, be spotted and then be caught, thus proving Mr. Shine correct all along, but the coincidences are a bit much to take."

Sources: Harrison, *The Encyclopaedia of the Loch Ness Monster*; "Loch Ness monster could really be lost Baltic sturgeon." Associated Press (2 January 1994); Official Loch Ness Monster Fan Club, http://www.lochness.co.uk/fan_club/news.html; Loch Ness 2000, http://www.loch-ness-scotland.com.

Shiru

The Shiru are unknown primates or small HOMINIDS of the Andes, reported from Colombia and Ecuador. Naturalist Claus Oheim related the following information on the species in the 1940s:

The so-called *Shiru*, I have heard of from Indians and a few white hunters on both sides of the Andes, but decidedly more so on the eastern slopes, where vast mountainous areas are still quite unexplored, and rarely if ever visited. All reports describe the Shiru as a small (4-5 feet) creature, decidedly hominid, but fully covered with short, dark brown fur. All agreed that the Shiru was very shy, with the exception of one Indian, who claimed having been charged after having missed with his one and only shot from a muzzle loading shotgun, a weapon still used by the majority of Indians, along with the blowgun. These reports were rather sober and objective, and in no way tinged with the colorful imagination, into which Latin-Americans are prone to lapse.

IVAN SANDERSON classified the Shiru as "proto-PYGMIES," along with such cryptids as the AGOGWE and SÉHITÉ of Africa, and the ORANG PENDEK of Sumatra.

Source: Sanderson, *Abominable Snowmen*.

Shooter's Hill Cheetah

In July 1963, sightings of an ALIEN BIG CAT resembling a cheetah (*Acinonyx jubatus*) frightened residents of Woolwich, southeast London. The first report was filed by trucker David Back, who stopped his vehicle at Shooter's Hill on the A207, at 1:00 a.m. on 18 July, to help what he thought was an injured dog. A closer look revealed his mistake, as a large spotted cat fled into the night. Police were summoned, and a pair of officers reported a "large golden animal" had leapt across the hood of their car. At dawn, a concentrated search was launched, including 126 police officers, 30 soldiers from nearby Woolwich Barracks, and 21 tracking dogs, but the beast eluded its pursuers and vanished without a trace.

Witnesses reported a cheetah from southeast London in 1963.

Sources: McEwan, *Mystery Animals of Britain and Ireland*; Shuker, *Mystery Cats of the World*.

Short, Bobbie (1954–)

California native Bobbie Short is a registered nurse whose fascination with cryptozoology dates from 8 September 1985, when she personally glimpsed a 7-foot SASQUATCH on a hiking expedition through Trinity National Forest. That experience inspired prodigious research, including a visit to the Philippines, where Short obtained native descriptions of the HOMINID known as KAPRE.

Short is a member of the BRITISH COLUMBIA SCIENTIFIC CRYPTOZOOLOGY CLUB, the INTERNATIONAL SOCIETY OF CRYPTOZOOLOGY, RAYMOND CROWE'S Western Bigfoot Society, and the San Diego Zoological Society. In 1997, she served briefly on the NORTH AMERICAN SCIENCE INSTITUTE'S research board, when that group analyzed the PATTERSON FILM. At her San Diego home, Short created a priceless archive of BIGFOOT literature, research data and other material, including a collection of filed and footprint casts compiled by investigator ROBERT TITMUS. Unfortunately for researchers, those items were lost in October 2003, when Short's home was destroyed by wildfires that swept through southern California.

Sources: Coleman and Clark, *Cryptozoology A to Z*; Loren Coleman, message posted to Bigfoot Internet newsgroup (29 October 2003).

Shuker, Karl P.N. (1959–)

Born at Bromwich, in Britain's West Midlands, Karl Shuker dates his fascination with cryptozoology from 1972, when he received a copy of BERNARD HEUVELMANS'S classic work *On the Track of Unknown Animals* as a birthday gift. Determined to investigate life's mysteries, he enrolled at the University of Leeds and there obtained his B.A. with honors in zoology, followed by a Ph.D. in zoology and comparative physiology from the University of Birmingham. A 1979 diagnosis of insulin-dependant diabetes limited Shuker's capacity for field work but did nothing to fetter his imagination. Today, he is globally recognized as an author and researcher on all aspects of animal life and unexplained phenomena, the heir apparent to Heuvelmans himself.

At press time for this volume, Shuker's published books include *Mystery Cats of the World* (1989), *Extraordinary Animals Worldwide* (1991), *The Lost Ark* (1993), *Dragons: A Natural History* (1995), *In Search of Prehistoric Survivors* (1995), *The Unexplained*

Dr. Karl Shuker with the fossil skull of a saber-tooth cat.

(1996), *From Flying Toads to Snakes with Wings* (1997), *Mysteries of Planet Earth* (1999), *The Hidden Powers of Animals* (2001), *The New Zoo* (2002) and *The Beasts That Hide from Man* (2003). He has also served jointly as a consultant/ contributor to anthologies including *Man and Beast* (1993), *Secrets of the Natural World* (1993), *Almanac of the Uncanny* (1995), the *Guinness Book of Records* (1997– present), *Mysteries of the Deep* (1998), *Guinness Amazing Future* (1999) and *Monsters* (2001). He further serves as a contributing editor and cryptozoological columnist for various magazines, including *Fate*, *Strange* and *Fortean Times*. Shuker appears frequently on radio and television, and is a consultant for BBC's quiz show *Mastermind* and the Discovery Channel's series *Into the Unknown*.

He is a scientific fellow of the Zoological Society of London, a fellow of the Royal Entomological Society, and a member of the INTERNATIONAL SOCIETY OF CRYPTOZOOLOGY. In his rare free moments, Shuker indulges his passion for motorcycles, vintage rock'n'roll, wildlife postage stamps, quizzes and travel. In November 2001, he won £250,000 on the British (original) version of the world's most popular TV quiz show, *Who Wants to Be a Millionaire?*

Sources: Coleman and Clark, *Cryptozoology A to Z*; Dr. Karl P.N. Shuker, http://members.aol.com/karlshuker/.

Shunka Warak'in

The Shunka warak'in ("carrying off dogs") is described by aboriginal tribesmen along the U.S.-Canadian border as a large quadruped known to snatch dogs and to cry like a human when wounded. The first published account of

the creature appeared belatedly in 1977, describing a specimen shot in the 1880s, near southern Montana's Madison River. As author Ross Hutchins described the event:

> One winter morning my grandfather was aroused by the barking of the dogs. He discovered that a wolflike beast of dark color was chasing my grandmother's geese. He fired his gun at the animal but missed. It ran off down the river, but several mornings later was seen again at about dawn. It was seen several more times at the home ranch as well as at other ranches ten or fifteen miles down the valley. Whatever it was, it was a good traveler....
>
> Those who got a good look at the beast described it as being nearly black and having high shoulders and a back that sloped downward like a hyena. Then one morning in late January, my grandfather was alerted by the dogs, and this time he was able to kill it. Just what the animal was is still an open question. After being killed, it was donated to a man named Sherwood who kept a combination grocery and museum at Henry Lake in Idaho. It was mounted and displayed there for many years. He called it "*rindocus*."

While a photograph survives, the whereabouts of that specimen is presently unknown. Still, recent sightings suggest that the Shunka warak'in may still exist. In July 1991, several witnesses reported an animal resembling a hyena running at large in the Alberta Wildlife Park near Legal, Alberta. Cryptozoologist MARK HALL has also uncovered reports of modern-day sightings in Illinois, Iowa and Nebraska. LOREN COLEMAN suggests that the creature may be a relict *Borophagus*, a hyenalike canid found in Pleistocene North America and now presumed extinct. Other prehistoric candidates include the Miocene bear-dogs (Family *Amphicyonidae*) and *Chasmaporthetes ossifragus*, a hyaenid that occupied North America as recently as 10,000 years ago.

Sources: "The Alberta hyena." *Fortean Times* 61 (February-March 1992): 9; Coleman, "Hunting hyenas in the US"; Coleman and Clark, *Cryptozoology A to Z*.

Shuswaggi

Lake Shuswap lies 65 miles north of Kelowna, British Columbia, at the northern end of the Okanagan Valley. Like the larger Okanagan Lake, Shuswap is allegedly inhabited by LAKE MONSTERS known collectively as Shuswaggi, Shoosy or Sicopogo, while aboriginal tribesmen call it Ta-zama-a or Tazum-a ("water bear"). A native hunter reportedly killed a Ta-zama-a in 1904 and sold its pelt at Enderby, 15 miles to the south. The skin is unavailable today, but those who saw it claimed that the creature rivaled a GRIZZLY BEAR in size, with 4-inch-long hair and 12-inch feet resembling those of a mole.

More recent witnesses describe a very different creature, resembling a giant EEL 20-30 feet long, jet black, showing multiple humps as it swims on the surface. Two sightings were reported from the lake in July 1948, and another in 1953. Strangely, the witnesses in the latter case—Bert Hanna and Don Leady—changed their story several days after the fact, to claim they had seen a "white seal." (An albino freshwater pinniped, found nearly 200 miles from the nearest ocean, would constitute a marvel in itself.) Nine years later, in August 1962, Oregon tourist Richard Medley saw Shuswaggi from the lake's south shore, describing a dark hump 6-8 feet long that protruded 18-20 inches from the water. On 3 June 1984, Linda Griffiths and her three children a 25-foot creature that showed seven low humps on the surface.

Sources: Kirk, *In the Domain of the Lake Monsters*; Moon, *Ogopogo*; Shuker, *From Flying Toads to Snakes with Wings*.

Shuyak Island carcass

In July 1951, a large rotting carcass washed ashore on Alaska's Shuyak Island, north of Kodiak Island at the mouth of Cook Inlet. No details are available today, but most researchers assume that the creature represented some species of whale.

Sources: Heuvelmans, *In the Wake of the Sea Serpents*; Dubious Globsters, http://www.geocities.com/capedrevenger/dubiousglobsters.html.

Siemel's Mystery Cat   Known only from a single pelt, this still-unclassified CAT was shot in the Mato Grosso jungle by Brazilian hunter Sacha Siemel, sometime in the first quarter of the 20th century. The cat had a stocky build and fawn-colored pelage, with brown spots and a darker stripe along the spine. No other like it has been catalogued, before or since. Siemel believed it was the product of cross-breeding between a COUGAR (*Puma concolor*) and a JAGUAR (*Panthera onca*). Such hybrids have allegedly been bred in captivity, though proof remains elusive, and experts suggest that such a pairing in the wild is extremely unlikely.

Source: Shuker, *Mystery Cats of the World*.

Sierniki, Poland   In the 19th century, stories circulated through this Polish city that a nearby stream harbored a large SNAKE with a head resembling a goat's. No sightings of the alleged creature have been recorded in more than 100 years.

Source: Otto Knoop, *Sagen der Provinz Posen*. Berlin: H. Eichblatt, 1913.

Sika Deer   The sika deer (*Cervus nippon*) is an ungulate native to East Asia, resembling a small elk (*C. elaphus*) in appearance. Wild populations may be found in West Virginia, where the species was privately introduced in 1916, but it is not known to live in any other U.S. state. On 9 October 2003, a sika deer was struck and killed by a hit-and-run driver in Belpre, Ohio. Neighbors quickly dressed the carcass for meat, while state wildlife authorities puzzled over its origin. George Foreman, wildlife officer for Athens County, speculated that the deer may have escaped from a local game farm, now defunct, or that it was released by private owners. Ohio has no laws restricting ownership of exotic animals, which sometimes escape or are freed by their negligent owners.

Source: Dave Payne Sr., "Exotic sika deer killed on Belpre road." *Marietta* (OH) *Times* (10 October 2003).

***Silas Richards* sea serpent**   On 16 June 1826, passengers and seamen aboard the New York packet *Silas Richards* saw a SEA SERPENT off George's Bank, south of Newfoundland. Passenger William Warburton later wrote to a business colleague: "The humps on the back resembled in size and shape those of a dromedary." In fact, that particular species of CAMEL (*Camelus dromedarius*) has only one hump, while Warburton's sketch of the creature he saw boasts 11, prompting BERNARD HEUVELMANS to rank it as a specimen of his hypothetical "many-humped" sea serpent.

Source: Heuvelmans, *In the Wake of the Sea Serpents*.

***Silkworth* sea serpent**   One moonlit night in the summer of 1884, while en route to Québec, the captain and crew of the vessel *Silkworth* sighted a SEA SERPENT in the Gulf of St. Lawrence. No description of the creature remains, beyond a statement that its head resembled that of a conger EEL (*Conger* sp.).

Source: O'Neill, *The Great New England Sea Serpent*.

Silver Lake, Massachusetts   Authors LOREN COLEMAN and JOHN KIRK include this lake, in Middlesex County, on published lists of supposed LAKE MONSTER habitats. No dates or details of sightings are included in either account.

Sources: Coleman, *Mysterious America*; Kirk, *In the Domain of the Lake Monsters*.

Silver Lake, New York   America's most notorious LAKE MONSTER of the 19th century surfaced for the first time at Silver Lake, in western New York's Wyoming County, on the night of 13 July 1855. At 9:00 o'clock that evening, six local fishermen were "frightened most out of their senses" by a creature they claimed was 80–100 feet long, rising from the depths and swimming toward their boat. Breathless newspaper reports soon spread the story far and wide. A local Indian named John John told reporters that his people had long been aware that a creature "as big as a flour barrel" lived in Silver Lake. Charles Hall and his family logged a sighting on 27 July, describing the beast's calflike head, 3-foot neck, and tall dorsal fin.

A stampede of CRYPTOTOURISM ensued, as hunters and gawkers flocked to the small towns surrounding Silver Lake. In nearby Perry, a Vigilance Society was organized to watch for stray monsters and police the rowdy newcomers. A dozen witnesses reported sightings on 1 August 1855, prompting the *New York Times* to declare that "the existence of a monster fish or serpent species in the quiet waters of Silver Lake was established beyond reasonable doubt, if indeed there had been room for doubt in the past week." A watchtower was built at the lake's north end, with sentries on duty around the clock. In September, a group of local businessmen joined forces as The Experiment Company, raising $1,000 for a bid to catch the beast alive. Still, it remained elusive and seemed to dislike the uproar. Sightings tapered off through winter and ceased entirely by mid-1856.

The Silver Lake creature was nearly forgotten by 19 December 1857, when Perry's main hotel, the Walker House, burned to the ground. Sifting the ashes, firefighters were shocked to find the charred remains of a 60-foot monster, built from wire and canvass. Under interrogation, hotel owner A.B. Walker and accomplice Truman Gillett confessed to building the model and submerging it in Silver Lake with weights attached, then causing it to surface periodically by means of air pumped through a buried pipeline from a giant pair of bellows. Locomotion was achieved with ropes, dragging the monster to and fro. Walker had hatched the scheme to boost his failing hotel business, then retired the beast to his attic when the risk of discovery became too great.

Thus was the great "sea serpent" of Silver Lake deflated — almost. Nearly 150 years after the fact, author Joe Nickell took issue with the HOAX scenario. While not denying the Walker-Gillett fraud, Nickell cited earlier reports of unknown creatures seen in Silver Lake, suggesting that the pranksters merely capitalized on an existing tradition of cryptid sightings. In place of a bona fide monster, Nickell suggested a northern river otter (*Lutra canadensis*) as the animal seen and misidentified by early witnesses.

Sources: Keel, *The Complete Guide to Mysterious Beings*; Mackal, *Searching for Hidden Animals*; Joe Nickell, *Real-Life X Files*. Lexington, KY: University Press of Kentucky, 2001.

***Silvery Wave* sea serpent**   One of the most outlandish SEA SERPENT reports ever filed comes from alleged witness J. Cobbin, of Durban, South Africa. He described the creature, supposedly seen from the deck of the *Silvery Wave* on 30 December 1871, as follows:

He was at least one thousand yards long, of which about one third appeared on the surface of the water at every stroke of his enormous fan-shaped tail, with which he propelled himself, raising it high above the waves, and arching his back like a land-SNAKE or a caterpillar. In shape and proportion he much resembled a cobra, being marked by the same knotty and swollen protuberance at the back of the head on the neck. The latter was the thickest part of the serpent. His head was like a bull's in shape, his eyes large and glowing, his ears had circular tips and were level with his eyes, and his head was surrounded by a horny crest, which he erected and depressed at pleasure. He swam with great rapidity and lashed the sea into a foam, like breakers dashing over jagged rocks. The sun shone brightly upon him; and with a good glass I saw his overlapping scales open and shut with every arch of his sinuous back like the rainbow.

Between that grandiose description and the fact that Cobbin claimed the behemoth as his *third* sea serpent sighting, BERNARD HEUVELMANS felt safe in dismissing the tale as a HOAX.

Source: Heuvelmans, *In the Wake of the Sea Serpents.*

Silwane Mazzi   Only one account of the Silwane mazzi (Bantu for "unpleasant water animal") has been recorded from South Africa's KwaZulu Natal Province, and that may be considered suspect. In 1937, Aleko Lilius allegedly saw a large scaly creature resembling a DINOSAUR, which left a trail of 3-toed tracks between the Mofolozi River estuary and the nearby ocean. The footprints were 16 inches long and 13 inches wide, separated by a 4-foot stride. Lilius published his story seven years later, admitting that he had seen a tribal witch doctor make similar tracks in the sand with a carved wooden foot. Skeptics also noted that the name Silwane mazzi is applied by many Bantu-speaking natives to the common CROCODILE. Nonetheless, IVAN SANDERSON was sufficiently impressed to suggest that Lilius had seen a living hadrosaur (Family *Hadrosauridae*), one of the "duck-billed" dinosaurs that flourished during the Cretaceous period.

Sources: Aleko Lilius, "I saw the monster of Umfolozi Lake." *True* (July 1944): 20-23, 92-94; Ivan Sanderson, "That forgotten monster: Old three toes." *Fate* 20 (December 1967): 66-75.

Simcoe Kelly *see* **Igopogo**

Sinkhole Sam   In the 1950s, residents of Inman, Kansas were fascinated and appalled by tales of Sinkhole Sam, a giant SNAKE or EEL said to inhabit a flooded pit outside this Harvey County town, northeast of Hutchinson. Alleged witnesses said the creature was 15 feet long and 21 inches in circumference. Rumors suggested that it had emerged from some deeper cavern when his lair was flooded. Talk of Sam faded with time, and no recent encounters are reported.

Source: Beccy Tanner, "Sasquatches? Sea serpents? They're here in Kansas." *Wichita Eagle* (18 December 2000).

Sint-Holo   Early Chickasaw tribesmen described the Sint-holo as large aquatic SNAKE, commonly found in various lakes and rivers of northern Mississippi and western Tennessee. The creatures reputedly lived in caves, emerging to hunt prey that sometimes included human beings.

Source: John Swanton, "Social and religious beliefs and usages of the Chickasaw Indians." *Annual Report of the Bureau of American Ethnology* 44 (1928): 251.

Sipandjee *see* **Koolookamba**

Sirrush   In 1902, archaeologist Robert Koldewey unearthed the main ceremonial entrance to the ancient city of Babylon, near present-day Baghdad, Iraq. Dating from the 6th century B.C.E., the gate was erected by King Nebuchadnezzar II and decorated with carvings of various animals. The king's personal Cuneiform

Ivan Sanderson proposed that Africa's Silwane Mazzi was a relict *Hadrosaurus.*

inscription on the gate reads, in part: "Fierce bulls [*rimi*] and DRAGONS [*sirrushu*] I put onto the gateyard and thus supplied the gates with such overflowing rich splendor that all humanity may view it with wonderment." Researchers believe the carved bulls represent aurochs (*Bos primigenius*), a 10-foot-long species ranging from Europe through North Africa to India between Pleistocene times and the early 17th century. But if the *rim* (singular of *rimi*) truly existed, what was the Sirrush, with its long legs and tail, scaly hide, and a tall horn rising from its forehead?

Professor Koldewey ventured a guess in 1918, writing: "If a creature like the *sirrush* existed in nature it would belong the order of Dinosauria and the sub-order of Ornithopods. The iguanodon of the Cretaceous layers of Belgium is the closest relative of the dragon of Babylon." That suggestion, hinting that a 30-foot DINOSAUR presumed extinct for some 100 million years had modeled for carvings made in historical times, was nothing short of astounding. Scriptural support for Koldewey's theory is found in the Old Testament apocryphal book *Bel and the Dragon*, penned as an addendum to the *Book of Daniel* during the 2nd century B.C.E. That account, discarded by clerical editors who compiled the "true" Bible centuries later, described Nebuchadnezzar II maintaining a dragon alive in the Babylonian Temple of Bel (from the Arimaic *baal*, or "lord").

Timing aside, one major problem with Koldewey's selection of a Sirrush candidate is the fact that *Iguanodon* possessed no horns. Other prehistoric reptiles fit the bill, however, including *Tsintaosaurus*, a 33-foot member of the duckbilled dinosaurs (Family *Hadrosauridae*), whose Late Cretaceous fossils, found in China, reveal a slender horn like a UNICORN'S protruding from the skull. Another duckbill, 30-foot *Lambeosaurus* from North America, had two bony growths on its head, including a backward-pointing horn and a tall rectangular crest pointing forward. Both were herbivores, but there were also several large carnivores that sported horns of various sizes. Their number included *Baryonyx*, a 20-foot predator from Early Cretaceous Europe; *Proceratosaurus*, a 15-foot hunter from Europe's Jurassic period; and the larger *Ceratosaurus*, a 20-foot carnivore known from Jurassic fossil beds in North America.

Sources: Dougal Dixon et al., *The Macmillan Illustrated Encyclopedia of Dinosaurs and Prehistoric Animals.* New York: Collier Books, 1988; Heuvelmans, *On the Track of Unknown Animals.*

Sisemité   The Sisemité is yet another unknown primate or HOMINID of Latin America, reported at various times and with different regional names from the montane forests of southern Mexico, Guatemala, Honduras, Nicaragua and Belize (where the creatures are portrayed in ancient Mayan carvings). Mayan tribesmen knew it as Qetcux ("abductor"), and other local names throughout the creature's range include Chichimeque, Itacayo, Sirpi and Suinta. From different accounts spanning generations, the Sisemité appears to be a tropical version of BIGFOOT. Author George Gordon described it as follows, in a 1915 article on Guatemalan folklore:

> There is a monster that lives in the forest. He is taller than the tallest man and in appearance he is between a man and a MONKEY. His body is so well protected by a mass of matted hair that a bullet cannot harm him. His tracks have been seen on the mountains, but it is impossible to follow his trail because he can reverse his feet and thus baffle the most successful hunter. His great ambition, which he has never been able to achieve, is to make fire. When the hunters have left their camp fires he comes and sits by the embers until they are cold, when he greedily devours the charcoal and ashes. Occasionally the hunters see in the forest little piles of twigs which have been brought together by El Sisemite (also called Sisimici) in an unsuccessful effort to make fire in imitation of men. His strength is so great that he can break down the biggest trees in the forest. If a woman says a Sisemite, her life is infinitely prolonged, but a man never lives more than a month after he has looked into the eyes of the monster. If a Sisemite captures a man he rends the body and crushes the bones between his teeth in great enjoyment of the flesh and blood. If he captures a woman, she is carried to his cave, where she is kept a prisoner.

IVAN SANDERSON classified the Sisemité as a "neo-GIANT," along with such hominids as the SASQUATCH, TOK and MAPINGUARI, suspecting that all might represent relict populations of *GIGANTOPITHECUS*.

Source: Sanderson, *Abominable Snowmen*.

Sisiutl   Sisiutl ("sea-wolf") is yet another name applied by aboriginal peoples to the SEA SERPENTS frequently seen along the coast of British Columbia. The creatures were described as serpentine in form, with horns or crests atop their heads. Some accounts also referred to dorsal fins and/or a pair of flippers that propelled the Sisiutl through the water. Some of those characteristics agree with modern descriptions of CADBOROSAURUS, reported from the same region.

Source: Michael Swords, "The Wasgo or Sisiutl: A cryptozoological sea-animal of the Pacific Northwest coast of the Americas." *Journal of Scientific Exploration* 5 (1991): 85–101.

Sister Lakes Monster   Rumors of a shaggy monster lurking in the swamps of Cass County, Michigan date from 1962, but the creature first made headlines two years later, in spring 1964. That May, fruit pickers fled their jobs in the orchards around Sister Lakes (misspelled "Silver Lakes" in some accounts), after several witnesses reported encounters with a 9-foot HOMINID with luminous eyes. Gordon Brown and his brother saw the beast cross a road in front of their truck on 9 June, then followed it into the woods. A closer look revealed it as "a cross between a GORILLA and a bear," prompting the men to retreat at high speed. Farmers John and Evelyn Ultrup reported multiple encounters with a 500-pound creature that chased their dogs and once pursued Evelyn herself on "great thundering feet" that made the ground quake.

After three teenage girls saw the creature on 11 June, Sister Lakes experienced a rush of CRYPTOTOURISM, with hundreds of would-be monster hunters flocking to the area. Local merchants took full advantage of the situation, announcing Monster Sales, selling monster-hunting kits and placing Monster Burgers on the menu at a local café, but the Sister Lakes Monster was seen no more. Today, some researchers consider its visitation the first recorded appearance of MOMO.

Sources: Bord and Bord, *The Bigfoot Casebook*; Coleman and Huyghe, *The Field Guide to Bigfoot, Yeti, and Other Mystery Primates Worldwide*.

Sivatherium   The *Sivatherium* was a prehistoric ancestor of modern giraffes (Family *Giraffidae*) that more closely resembled a MOOSE. Standing seven feet tall at the shoulder, the stout-bodied males of this species sported huge branching antlers atop their skulls, with a smaller pair of conical horns directly above their eyes. Sivatheres ranged from North Africa across Asia to sub-Himalayan India during the Pliocene epoch, while a close relative (*Libytherium*) also roamed North Africa. Paleontologists once believed that sivatheres became extinct before human beings appeared on Earth, but evidence suggests that they may have survived into historic times. Specifically, creatures resembling sivatheres are depicted in 8,000-year-old Saharan petroglyphs, as well as Egyptian and Syrian figurines displayed at the British Museum. In 1927-28, while excavating the Sumerian city of Kish in central Iraq, archeologists found a bronze chariot-ring bearing the figure of an ungulate with large antlers, dated from approximately 2750 B.C.E. Skeptic David Reese, writing in 1990, noted that a portion of that figure's broken antlers were recovered in 1977, and that they more closely resemble the horns of a Persian fallow deer (*Dama dama mesopotamica*). Still, most authorities now concede that sivatheres shared the planet with humans, though the date of their final extinction remains in dispute.

Sources: Edwin Colbert, "The enigma of *Sivatherium*." *Plateau* 51 (1978): 32-33; David Reese, "Paleocryptozoology and archeology: A sivathere no longer." *Cryptozoology* 9 (1990): 100-107.

Skaha Lake, Canada   Skaha Lake lies five miles south of Okanagan Lake, in British Columbia. The unknown creatures sighted there over the past half-century thus dwell almost literally in the shadow of OGOPOGO, Canada's best-known LAKE MONSTER. The two lakes are connected by the Okanagan River and a manmade channel, each large enough to theoretically permit passage of some good-sized animal in either direction. It is somewhat surprising, therefore, that the first cryptid sighting at Skaha Lake was not reported until 1950, when two witnesses reported a large, unidentified beast in the water. (Ogopogo had been seen in Okanagan Lake a few days earlier.) Another Skaha sighting was recorded in August 1953, followed by a 35-year hiatus until the next report, in 1988. On that occasion, pilot Graeme Merrick had just taken off from Penticton's airport, skimming over the nearby lake, when he saw three large creatures emerge side-by-side from beneath a shoreline shelf. One of the animals was roughly 30 feet long, while the other two were slightly smaller. Merrick's sighting provoked speculation on flooded underground caverns connecting the two neighbor lakes, but no evidence has yet been produced to support the idea.

Sources: Gaal, *In Search of Ogopogo*; Kirk, *In the Domain of the Lake Monsters*.

Skaholt, Iceland   In the mid-18th century, Danish author Eggert Olafsson toured Iceland, collecting stories from various archives and informants. One story he relayed dated from 1595, when a group of parishioners leaving a church in Skaholt were startled by a "monstrous creature, as high as a house," diving into a nearby river. Witnesses described the beast as having a head like a seal's, but tall spikes jutting from its back spoiled any further resemblance to a pinniped.

Source: Jerome Clark, *Calendar of Unexplained Phenomena*, 2001.

Skaket Beach carcass   In December 1964, a decomposing GLOBSTER washed ashore at Skaket Beach, near Orleans, Massachusetts (on Cape Cod). The creature had a skull the size of a raccoon's, connected to the body by a 4-foot neck, and also sported a long, slender tail. One local journalist compared it to a prehistoric "pterodactyl," though he doubtless meant a PLESIOSAUR. In any case, analysis of the remains identified the creature as a basking shark (*Cetorhinus maximus*) in the advanced state of decomposition that often imparts a reptilian form.

Sources: Heuvelmans, *In the Wake of the Sea Serpents*; Dubious Globsters, http://www.geocities.com/capedrevenger/dubiousglobsters.html.

Skegness sea serpents   The 1960s produced multiple SEA SERPENT sightings along the coast of Skegness, Lincolnshire, England. The first report was filed on 7 August 1960, after five witnesses from Wainfleet watched a creature passing offshore from Gibraltar Point. Ray Handsley and his wife described the object as 10-12 feet long, resembling "a long black line on the surface" and "traveling along the edge of the deep water" at an estimated 40-50 miles per hour. Their son believed it was a submarine, while witness Vera Digby compared the thing to a 9-foot torpedo traveling "a foot above water." To that, Ray Handsley replied, "It had no superstructure. It looked perfectly flat. The curious thing was that there was no wake after it." Another witness, Pauline North, also believed it was a submarine, until the object took wing and she realized it was a flight of wild ducks (*Melanitta nigra*) skimming the surface.

Reporters were thus embarrassed by their early accounts of the "Skeg-Ness Monster," but sea birds would not explain the sighting reported from nearby Chapel St. Leonards by George and May Ashton, in October 1966. While strolling on the beach, they saw "something like the Loch Ness monster" swimming less than 100 yards offshore. As George Ashton told the press:

It had a head like a serpent and six or seven pointed humps trailing behind. At first I thought it was a log but it was traveling at about 8 mph and going parallel to the shore. We watched it for some time coming from the direction of Chapel Point until it disappeared out of sight towards Ingoldmells. I just didn't believe in these things and tried to convince myself it was a flight of birds just above the water. I even thought of a miniature submarine but after watching it for some time I knew it couldn't be. There as no noise. It just skimmed through the water.

Publication of that sighting prompted Skegness resident John Hayes to describe his own experience of several weeks earlier, when he was cycling through Winthorpe and heard a "loud crack" at sea. As described in the *Skegness Standard*:

He looked towards the sea and saw a "huge dark shape" about 500 yards out, moving at about 20 mph and leaving a wake behind it. He did not report the sighting at the time as he thought it might be a whale or some other identifiable creature. The *Standard* report last week prompted him to reveal his information however. "I still believe there are things which have yet to be discovered," says Mr. Hayes.

Source: Heuvelmans, *In the Wake of the Sea Serpents*.

Skerray Beast   Between 1973 and 1979, residents of Sutherland in northern Scotland reported sightings of an ALIEN BIG CAT they called the Skerray Beast. Many of the encounters occurred in broad daylight, with some near sites where sheep were killed and partially devoured. Veterinarians who examined the sheep attributed their wounds to a feline predator, but organized hunts in the region failed to bag the creature(s).

Source: "Scottish puma: Saga or farce?" *Fortean Times* 34 (Winter 1981): 24-25; Animals, http://www.geocities.com/SoHo/Cafe/1614/Celtwicc/CELTS/CELTS04.HTM.

Skiff Lake, Canada   In late July 1887, a 30-foot LAKE MONSTER was allegedly sighted in Skiff Lake, 45 miles west of Fredericton, New Brunswick. No modern sightings of the creature are recorded.

Source: Charles Skinner, *Myths and Legends Beyond Our Borders*. Philadelphia: Lippincott, 1899.

Skodje, Norway   Neighbors of this lake, in Norway's Møre og Romsdal County, reported sightings of a 20-foot LAKE MONSTER with a head and flowing mane resembling a horse's in the 19th century. The last report was apparently filed in the late 1860s.

Source: Skjelsvik, "Norwegian lake and sea monsters."

Skookum Cast   Minor controversy surrounds this Native American term and its early application to the unclassified HOMINIDS commonly known as BIGFOOT or SASQUATCH. As used by the Chinook tribe of northwestern Oregon, *skookum* simply meant "powerful," and was combined with other words to complete an idea. In 1867, surveyor F.W. Brown recorded accounts of large humanoid creatures around Mt. Rainier, Washington which were dubbed Skookum Quash ("powerful terror"). Modern researchers Henry Franzoni and Mike George further maintain that Skookum was itself a Chinook name for Sasquatch, while the neighboring Quinault tribe of coastal Washington called the creatures Skukum. A tantalizing legacy of early man-beast encounters survives to the present in such place names as Skookum Lake, Oregon and Skookum Creek, Washington. In fact, Franzoni cites no less than 214 Skookum place names, scattered throughout the Pacific Northwest from Oregon and Washington, through Idaho, British Columbia and Alaska.

At one such place, Skookum Meadow in southwestern Washington's Gifford Pinchot National Forest, 13 members of the BIGFOOT FIELD RESEARCHERS ORGANIZATION prepared to meet Sasquatch on its home turf in September 2000. Armed with night-vision goggles, infrared cameras, sound equipment and a sexual attractant concocted from human and GORILLA scents, the team pitched camp on 16 September. Generous portions of scent were applied to trees surrounding the camp, while "mud traps" were baited with fruit and the crew played recordings of a supposed Bigfoot call taped in 1999. Soon, they heard answering cries from the forest, described by leader Richard Noll as sounding "sort of like a high-pitched scream by a woman, trailing off to a gurgle." On 22 September, fruit was missing from two of the "traps," but no footprints were found. The third mud-wallow bore a deep impression, as if some large animal had paused to rest there. The body print was photographed and preserved with 325 pounds of Hydrocal B-11 casting material, capturing the outline of a large humanoid figure's left arm, buttocks, hip, thigh, testicles, ankles and heels.

Reactions to the Skookum cast were predictably mixed. Richard Noll declared the evidence "consistent with an animal that can use its forelimbs as leverage separate from the hind limbs in raising its body from a sitting position." Anatomist/anthropologist JEFFREY MELDRUM saw markings on the cast consistent with the dermal ridges found on human soles, deeming the imprint "evidence that justifies objective consideration." Skeptic CLIFF CROOK maintained that the cast revealed impressions from the belly of a kneeling elk, to which longtime researcher JOHN GREEN replied:

Some of the holes in the mud, not readily identifiable in that form, turned out to be beautiful prints of huge, humanlike heels, complete with hair patterns on the Achilles tendon — good enough to cause the author of a text on primate anatomy to reverse a long-held opinion as to the existence of the Sasquatch. And those poor fools who have found the cast completely convincing include several people with relevant doctorates and careers, one of them considered by many to be the greatest field zoologist of our time. Primatologists at the Smithsonian Institution, on the other hand, have said they will not look at the cast even if someone drives clear across the country to show it to them. Who are the scientists and who are the believers?

Other votes of confidence for the Skookum cast's authenticity came from zoologist LeRoy Fish, anthropologist GROVER KRANTZ, and cryptozoologist LOREN COLEMAN. Even Benjamin Radford, editor of the debunker's journal *Skeptical Inquirer*, was led to remark that the cast, if authentic, was "arguably the most significant find in the past two decades."

Sources: Coleman, *Bigfoot!*; American Indian Names for Bigfoot, http://www.cherokeefox.com/Bigfoot_names.html.

Skrimsl Skrimsl ("monster") is a generic name applied to aquatic cryptids in Iceland. While sometimes used for SEA SERPENTS seen in coastal fjords, the term more frequently describes LAKE MONSTERS reported from various freshwater sites. Chief among the island's "monster" habitats is the Lagarfljót, a river of northeastern Iceland that stretches over 85 miles, including a flooded glacial valley 21 miles long and 350 feet deep, properly known as Lögurinn Lake. Some locals call the Lagarfljót cryptid(s) Lagarflótsormurinn ("serpent of the Lagarfljót), while the unknown denizens of Skoradalsvatn and other Icelandic lakes are simply known as Skrimsls.

The first report of a Skrimsl was recorded in summer 1345, when the *Icelandic Chronicle* noted "a wonderful thing in the Lagarfljót which is believed to be a living animal. At times it seems like a great island, and at others, there appeared humps...with water between them. No-one knows the dimensions of the creature, for none saw its head or tail, consequently there is no certainty as to what it was." Four centuries later, in 1749-50, three witnesses reported a creature "the size of a large vessel" traveling along the Lagarfljót at high speed. More sightings were recorded in 1819 and 1860, when British traveler Sabine Baring-Gould recorded the following description:

The Skrimsl measures 46 feet long, the head and neck are 6 feet, the body 22 feet and the tail 18 feet, according to the estimate of farmers on the shore of the lake. The monster was seen the day before we arrived at Grudd, by the farmer of the place. His story and description of the FISH were so remarkable that we instituted inquiries which resulted in our hunting out several individuals who had seen the monster. On one occasion it was observed by three farmers who reside on the shore of the lake, two of whom I met and questioned on the subject. One of these men produced a sketch of the creature, which he made whilst it was floating on the surface of the water for half-an-hour.

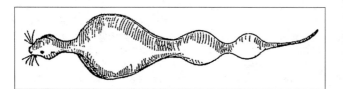

An eyewitness sketch of Iceland's Skrimsl.

Baring-Gould also reported that a large GLOBSTER was beached along the Lagarfljót in 1860, where a certain Dr. Hjaltalin examined the remains and failed to identify them, beyond noting that the bones were "quite different from a whale's."

Skrimsl sightings are not confined to olden times. In November 1984, two of the creatures were seen in Kleifervatn, a lake in southwestern Iceland. Witnesses described them as black, with "horse-like characteristics" and the capability to come ashore, where they frolicked on the beach. That report varied substantially from earlier Skrimsl descriptions, including a reference to hoofprints in the sand, and JOHN KIRK suspects that HOAXERS tampered with the scene, thus compromising the whole incident. Be that as it may, when residents of Egilstaddir on the Lagarfljót celebrated their town's 50th anniversary in 1997, a prize was offered for the best photograph of a Skrimsl. Many were submitted, some of them obvious fakes, but others left contest organizer Gundmundir Steingrimsson puzzled and intrigued. A teacher and his pupils from the school at Hallormsstadarskóli reportedly watched a Skrimsl in the Lagarfljót for 25 minutes, one afternoon in 1985, and produced another photograph. Thus far, none of the photos have been published.

Sources: Costello, *In Search of Lake Monsters*; Dash, "Status report: Lake monsters"; Kirk, *In the Domain of the Lake Monsters*; "The Lagarfljót monster and other water beasts." *Daily News from Iceland* (28 May 1999).

Skunk Ape This large, foul-smelling HOMINID or NORTH AMERICAN APE is Florida's version of BIGFOOT, and while the mal-

Artist's conception of a surprise encounter with Florida's skunk ape (*William Rebsamen*).

odorous nickname is sometimes applied to creatures seen in states ranging from Georgia to Arkansas and Tennessee, it is best known as a Florida phenomenon. Various accounts claim sightings of the beast(s) by fishermen and trappers prior to World War II, perhaps as early as the 1920s, but the earliest published report dates from 1942, when a witness named Isaac claimed a tall ape-like creature leaped onto the running board of his vehicle, south of Branford in Suwannee County, and thus rode a half-mile while peering in the driver's window. Five years later, a 4-year-old girl in Lakeland reported a hairy creature standing in her family's backyard. In spring 1957, two hunters claimed that a large ape with glowing eyes invaded their camp, in the Big Cypress Swamp.

Sightings multiplied rapidly from the mid-1960s onward, with at least 135 reports filed between 1963 and 1979. While hairy hominids were seen all over Florida, the main hot spots were Brooksville, in Hernando County (31 sightings); the Elfers-Port Richey area of Pasco County (9 reports); and Ochopee, on the western fringe of the Big Cypress Swamp. A peculiar pocket of sightings also emerged from the neighborhood of Cayo Pelau, in Charlotte County, where one fisherman claimed he saw "families" of hairy bipeds wading between islands. Many witnesses describe the creatures' horrid body odor, comparing it to sulfur, rotten eggs or stale urine. Descriptions of Skunk Apes vary widely in size, from CHIMPANZEE-sized dwarves to broad-chested giants 7-9 feet tall. In some cases, dogs attack the beasts on sight, but other accounts claim that trained hunting dogs will not follow their scent. Footprints sometimes accompany the sightings, with the largest to date measuring 17.5 inches long and 11.5 inches wide. Many of those reveal an opposed big toe, common to apes, but others are described as manlike. Several Floridians claim to have fired on Skunk Apes, including highway patrolman Robert Hollemeyal on 9 January 1974, but thus far the creatures seem impervious to bullets.

Skunk Ape sightings waned after 1985, until a brisk resurgence 12 years later. On 18 July 1997, a busload of foreign tourists glimpsed one of the animals outside Ochopee. Three days later, local fire chief Vince Doerr saw a large primate crossing the road near his home and snapped a blurry long-distance photograph of some dark object in a grassy field. Three more reports were filed from the Ochopee region by mid-August, including the account of naturalist James McMullen, who met a 7-foot, 50-pound primate while stalking COUGARS in the Everglades. Ochopee resident David Shealy, fascinated with the Skunk Ape since a childhood sighting at age 10, spent eight months staking out his own backyard before he shot a roll of 27 photos on 8 September 1998. Critics dismissed that incident as a HOAX, but new controversy erupted in early 2001, with publication of the now-famous MYAKKA PHOTOGRAPHS, in Sarasota County. Shealy sought public funding for a Skunk Ape expedition, but Ochopee's Tourist Development Council rejected his bid on 31 May 2002, with a letter that read in part:

> If such an animal does reside in the Everglades, it serves the tourist promotion business interest best as an legend and would lose its tourist value if an expedition was funded and returned with less than credible proof. Then again, if it was found and harmed in any way, the resulting backlash from the animal's rights contingent would be total.

In February 2003, Shealy dropped another bombshell, claiming that an amorous Skunk Ape had invaded his Trail Lakes Campground, frightening female tourists with its foul odor and "an erection measuring more than 12 inches long." On 14 June 2003, Shealy hosted a Skunk Ape Festival at the campground, crowning marine biologist Michelle Maynard as the first "Miss Skunk Ape" while 75 celebrants enjoyed beer and barbecue. Three months later, Shealy and Maynard led a television crew into the swamp, taping a Halloween episode for the PBS program *New Florida*, but the Skunk Ape failed to appear for his close-up. While Florida journalists acknowledge Shealy as the "most high-profile Skunk Ape expert" in the business, critics generally dismiss his media events as publicity stunts.

Sources: Berry, *Bigfoot on the East Coast*; Bord and Bord, *The Bigfoot Casebook*; Coleman, *Mysterious America*; Green, *Sasquatch: The Apes Among Us*; Jerry Hill, "Stories of 'skunk apes' are dubious." *Bradenton* (FL) *Herald* (9 July 2002); Kelly Icardi, "Skunk Ape Festival honors man who first celebrated creature." *Naples* (FL) *Daily News* (16 June 2003); Keel, *The Complete Guide to Mysterious Beings*; Dan Meek, "Skunk Ape is skunked." *Everglades Echo* (9 July 2002); Rife, *Bigfoot Across America*; "Skunk Ape Flashings Arousing Attention In Everglades." *Wireless Flash* (12 February 2003); Elizabeth Wendt, "Miami PBS station films skunk ape-seeking expedition." *Naples* (FL) *Daily News* (2 September 2003).

Slagnässjön, Sweden

In the summer of 1965, Ivar Anderson and a companion were dragging this Blekinge County lake in an effort to retrieve a lost fishing net. While so engaged, they hooked some unseen object underwater that began to drag their boat across the lake. Anderson's companion, an experienced horse-breaker, shouted that he had "a beast on the drag" that was "ten times stronger" than the average wild horse. The wild ride continued for several minutes, then ended with a great swirl of water on the surface as the unseen animal broke free. Strangely, there seems to be no tradition of LAKE MONSTER sightings from Slagnässjön, and it is not listed among the lakes investigated by Sweden's native GLOBAL UNDERWATER SEARCH TEAM.

Source: Bord and Bord, *Alien Animals*.

Slaguggla

In August 2000, correspondent Michael Sewell informed KARL SHUKER of a supposed giant OWL inhabiting the Scandinavian Arctic. Known in Swedish as Slaguggla ("strike owl"), for its aggressive temperament, the BIRD allegedly possessed a 10-foot wingspan and was capable of lifting reindeer calves. Two months later, John Kahila contradicted that report

Scandinavian witnesses describe the Slaguggla as a giant owl.

with the announcement that Slaguggla is the Swedish name for the Ural owl (*Strix uralensis*), whose record 4-foot wingspan is impressive, but still far short of gigantic.

Sources: Karl Shuker, "Alien zoo." *Fortean Times* 139 (November 2000): 23; Karl Shuker, "Alien zoo." *Fortean Times* 141 (January 2001): 23.

Slal'i'kum
British Columbia's Chilliwack tribe used this term of unknown meaning to describe a LAKE MONSTER inhabiting Cultus Lake and its feeder streams in the Fraser Valley. Witnesses described the Slal'i'kum as 14 feet long on average, with a 4-foot head and neck, a long tail, and short legs resembling a BEAVER'S. Like many other aboriginal cryptids, the Slal'i'kum seems to have vanished with the advent of the 20th century. Authors LOREN COLEMAN and PATRICK HUYGHE report alleged sightings from Cultus lake in the 1990s, but no further dates or details are provided.

Sources: Coleman and Huyghe, *The Field Guide to Lake Monsters, Sea Serpents, and Other Mystery Denizens of the Deep*; Oliver Wells, *The Chilliwacks and Their Neighbors*. Vancouver, B.C.: Talonbooks, 1987.

Slaven's Pond, Ohio
Another cryptid known from only a single sighting is the creature reported from Slaven's Pond, in Bainbridge, Ohio. Witness Joe Roush allegedly saw the animal in 1953, describing it as 6-8 feet long. Otherwise, his description was lamentably vague, and no further reports were forthcoming. It seems unlikely that the small pond could conceal an animal of any size for very long.

Source: "Joe Roush's sea serpent." *Fate* 7 (March 1954): 10-11.

Slick, Thomas Baker Jr. (1916–62)
The life of amateur cryptozoologist Tom Slick has all the trappings of an Indiana Jones adventure film. Born at Clarion, Pennsylvania on 6 May 1916, he was originally named Thomas Bernard Slick, after his father's partner in the oil business, but a bitter falling out between the men subsequently prompted Slick's parents to rename him Thomas Baker Slick Jr. Slick's millionaire father died in 1930, whereupon Bernice Slick married her late husband's current partner, Charles Urschel. Three years later, Urschel was kidnapped by George ("Machine Gun") Kelly's gang in Oklahoma City, released after payment of $100,000 ransom. Kelly's arrest in Memphis was a major media event in 1933, including (false) reports that he coined the term "G-men" to describe FBI agents.

Raised on stories of his father's travels in the Far East, Tom Slick harbored an insatiable appetite for adventure. In August 1937, with three classmates from Yale University, he visited Loch Ness to search for NESSIE and interviewed eyewitnesses of Scotland's most famous LAKE MONSTER. Failing at that, Slick founded multiple scientific research groups, including the Foundation of Applied Research (1941), the Institute of Inventive Research (1944) and the Southwest Research Institute (1947). His interest was drawn back to cryptozoology in 1954, by the London *Daily Mail*'s fruitless attempt to find a YETI in the Himalayas. In May 1956, Slick initiated correspondence with Irish-born Yeti researcher PETER BYRNE, and that December found them charting an expedition of their own, with support from the San Antonio Zoo.

The Slick Yeti Reconnaissance of 1957 lasted barely five weeks, from 14 March to 18 April, but it proved to be an adventure in itself. In Nepal, Slick cheated death by inches in a mountain bus crash, then went on to interview multiple Yeti witnesses. His team found three separate sets of alleged Yeti tracks, including one set

Texas millionaire Tom Slick spent years tracking the Yeti and other cryptids (*William Rebsamen*).

in mud from which footprints were cast and preserved. The group also found curious droppings and strands of unidentified hair, but that evidence vanished after its delivery to the Delhi Zoo in India. A panel of experts, including GEORGE AGOGINO, disagreed on whether the footprints Slick cast had been made by an unknown species of giant panda or an "exceedingly unusual" primate.

In either case, it was enough to keep Slick interested in pursuing the Yeti and other unclassified cryptids. He next teamed with Texas oilman F. Kirk Johnson to finance the first Slick-Johnson Snowman Expedition, spanning 16 weeks between February and June 1958. The new team included Peter Byrne and his brother Bryan, W.M. ("GERALD") RUSSELL, photographer George Holton and Swiss mountaineer Norman Dhyrenfurth. In April, the team's Sherpa guides claimed two sightings of a small Yeti in the Chhoyang River valley, while Dhyrenfurth discovered a supposed Yeti cave and bed near Dudh Kosi. Yeti relics preserved at various monasteries were also examined. Slick's team photographed two alleged Yeti scalps, preserved at the Pangboche and Thyangboche, in addition to a pair of mummified Yeti hands. The "hand" preserved at Makalu proved to be a snow leopard's foreleg, but the PANGBOCHE HAND proved more intriguing and was marked for further study. Evidence collected on his first two Nepalese expeditions propelled Slick toward a startling conclusion about the Yeti:

> From discussions with the natives, as well as from previous reports, we believe that there are at least two types of APE-like animals in this area and perhaps three or more types. The large type is known as Yeti.

BERNARD HEUVELMANS and IVAN SANDERSON were persuaded by Slick's argument, and altered their theories accordingly. Meanwhile, the 1959 Slick-Johnson Snowman Expedition forged ahead without fanfare, intent on collecting physical evidence. Peter Byrne managed to steal part of the Pangboche Hand, smuggling it back to the U.S. with help from actor James Stewart, while other members of the team collected samples of supposed Yeti droppings. Analysis of the feces brought mixed results: one batch apparently came from an herbivore, while another donor was omnivorous. George Agogino thought the droppings he analyzed came from a "hungry wolf," while Heuvelmans found the eggs of an unknown parasite in another sample. "Since each species of animal has its own parasites," he concluded, "this indicates that the host animal is also equally an unknown animal."

While that search was proceeding in Nepal, Slick pressed investigations on other cryptozoological fronts. In Sumatra, he sponsored an expedition under Swiss animal collector Peter Ryhiner, to find the cryptic primate known as ORANG PENDEK. Regrettably, the footprints Ryhiner found impressed in jungle mud turned out to be a bear's. Press reports from the period also refer to Slick-funded expeditions in Papua New Guinea, but no details are presently available about that quest. In Alaska, meanwhile, Slick hired local hunting guide Lyle Aylesworth to search for ILLIE, the giant fish or LAKE MONSTER of Iliamna Lake that Aylesworth first sighted in September 1942. Once again the effort was fruitless, his money wasted.

Autumn 1958 put BIGFOOT in the news from Northern California, and Slick soon turned his eyes in that direction, launching his Pacific Northwest Expedition in 1960. "If the creature is what it appears to be," Slick opined, "its capture could be one of the most important scientific events of all time." In addition to the Byrne brothers, this effort gathered SASQUATCH hunters RENÉ DAHINDEN, JOHN GREEN, ROBERT TITMUS, IVAN MARX and others. Some would remain comrades for the rest of their lives, while others fell apart in bitter quarrels, but for the moment they were allies. Some bridled at the "wasted side trip" when Slick dispatched them to seek giant SALAMANDERS in the Trinity Mountains, but they soon returned to Bigfoot's trail. In 1961 the effort expanded to British Columbia, with Slick providing rifles and sending Titmus through a crash course in embalming at a Washington hospital. All seemed to feel that SASQUATCH might be waiting for them around the next bend, but it was not to be.

On 6 October 1962, Slick and his pilot died when their small aircraft crashed or exploded near Dell, in southwestern Montana's Beaverhead County. Published accounts differ on Slick's destination, the weather, and the cause of the crash. Some persons close to Slick blamed sabotage, but their case cannot be proved. René Dahinden later summarized the aftermath of Slick's demise:

> The Pacific Northwest Expedition ended abruptly in 1962....All of Slick's records concerning the Sasquatch had been sent to his research institute in San Antonio. This material has never been traced and it has been speculate that Slick's family and/or associates, embarrassed by his participation in the hunt, were quick to get rid of anything smelling of involvement.

In 2000, spokesmen for 20th Century Fox announced plans to produce a feature film based on Slick's life. According to the press release, Oscar-winner Nicholas Cage had been cast to play the title character in *Tom Slick: Monster Hunter*. A release date in 2002 was predicted, but at press time for this volume the film remained as elusive as the creatures Slick hunted for most of his life.

Sources: Coleman, *Tom Slick and the Search for the Yeti*; Coleman and

Clark, *Cryptozoology A to Z.*; Green, *Sasquatch: The Apes Among Us*; Hunter and Dahinden, *Sasquatch.*

Slieve Mish Lough, Ireland   Irish legends name this lough, in County Kerry, as the ancient home of a fierce LAKE MONSTER, but no modern sightings are on file.

Source: R.I. Best and Osborn Bergin, *Lebor na Huidre: Book of the Dun Cow*. Dublin: Royal Irish Academy, 1929.

Slimy Caspar   In the 1950s, 20-odd residents of New Hamburg, in southeastern Ontario, complained to police about a reptilian creature that emerged from the nearby Nith River and left 3-toed tracks in the soil of various adjacent farms. Witnesses included New Hamburg's treasurer and chief of police, who described the animal as a greenish-brown lizard of sorts, weighing approximately 50 pounds. Despite a vow to bag the beast dead or alive, the chief tracked it in vain. Dubbed Slimy Caspar — or simply The Thing — New Hamburg's unwelcome prowler eventually disappeared without a trace. All lizards and crocodilians known to science have five toes; the only SALAMANDER with fewer than four toes per foot is the olm (*Proteus anguinus*), a fossorial albino species found in Yugoslavia and northern Italy, whose record size does not exceed 12 inches.

Sources: Garner, *Monster! Monster!*; Sanderson, *"Things."*

Slimy Slim *see* **Sharlie**

Slow Lorises (Unknown)   The slow loris (*Nycticebus coucang*) is a prosimian whose range stretches from northern India through Southeast Asia to the Indonesian archipelago. Adult specimens are 12-16 inches long, with large eyes ringed in brown fur, light-colored pelage marked by a brown stripe down the spine, and a vestigial stump of a tail. Despite some variations in color, they are readily distinguished from other primates in their normal habitat. Over the past 116 years, however, sightings and supporting evidence have suggested the possible existence of two variant species or subspecies.

The first was captured alive near Lunglei, in eastern India's Mizoram Territory, in December 1899. The creature resembled a slow loris, but its coat was white, marked by a black stripe down the back and dark triangular patches around each eye. It also possessed a long bushy tail, never seen before in *N. coucang*. The animal was photographed and publicly displayed, but its ultimate fate is unknown and no similar specimens have yet been collected. Nonetheless, KARL SHUKER felt confident enough to propose the scientific name *Nycticebus caudatus* in 1993. A year later, in December 1994, another abnormal slow loris was seen at an animal market in Hanoi, Vietnam. The witness in this case was Douglas Richardson, assistant curator of mammals at the London Zoo. He described a primate resembling *N. coucang*, but larger and lighter than normal in color. Richardson did not purchase the specimen, and its status remains unconfirmed.

Sources: Shuker, *From Flying Toads to Snakes with Wings*; Shuker, *The Lost Ark.*

Small-Headed Flycatcher   Nearly two centuries after its formal description, the small-headed flycatcher (*Sylvania microcephala*) inspires controversy among scientists and amateur birdwatchers. Two of America's most famous ornithologists, John Audubon and Alexander Wilson, filed conflicting claims of first discovering the bird in rural New Jersey. Wilson published a detailed description in 1812, based on a specimen he shot in the swamps of southern New Jersey, during April of 1810 or 1811. Audubon countered with a claim that he found the species near

Louisville, Kentucky in 1808, and went to his grave claiming Wilson had stolen his discovery. Today, some ornithologists believe the flycatcher—noted for its general olive color, with brown wings and tail over a dull-yellow breast—never existed at all. Instead, the skeptics claim, both Audubon and Wilson were deceived by immature specimens of some recognized species, claiming new discoveries in a bid for personal glory. In support of that contention, critics note that no other specimens have been found since 1812. Peter Dunne, director of the New Jersey Audubon Society's Cape May Bird Observatory, disagrees with that assessment, observing that skeptics have yet to produce another known bird resembling the small-headed flycatcher. As he told the press in September 2003, "There is no foundation for the conclusion they mistook it for another species. I think there were probably species in North America that were extinct before they were documented. The same thing is going on now in the rain forests of South America."

Source: Richard Degener, "An avian mystery hatches in Cape May County." *Press of Atlantic City* (29 September 2002).

Smith Lake, Georgia

Cryptozoologists LOREN COLEMAN and JOHN KIRK include this lake on published lists of alleged LAKE MONSTER habitats. However, an exhaustive search of available sources reveals no such lake in the state of Georgia.

Source: Coleman, *Mysterious America*; Kirk, *In the Domain of the Lake Monsters*; Guide to Georgia Lakes, http://www.sportsmansinfo.com/Pages/lakes.htm; Roadside Georgia, http://roadsidegeorgia.com/links/outdoors/lakes.

Snake River, Idaho

The Snake River marks roughly half of Idaho's border with Oregon. On 22 August 1868, a 20-foot cryptid with fins or wings was seen swimming in the river past Olds Ferry, near Weiser, in southwestern Washington County. Thus far, no return visits have been noted.

Sources: Federal Writers' Project, *Idaho Lore*. Caldwell, ID: Caxton Press, 1939; Garner, *Monster! Monster!*

Snakes (Flying)

Around the world, most cultures have ancient traditions that include accounts of flying snakes or DRAGONS. In Mexico, the Aztecs worshipped a huge winged serpent called Quetzalcoatl, which later lent its name to the largest known PTEROSAUR (*Quetzalcoatlus*). In the 5th century B.C.E., Herodotus (the "father of history") penned the following account of his visit to the Nile Delta, south of present-day Bupullus, Egypt:

> I went once to a certain place in Arabia to make enquiries regarding the winged serpents. A winged serpent shaped like a snake, with wings not feathered, but covered with a leathery-like skin similar to those of a BAT. Vipers are found in all parts of the world, but winged serpents are nowhere seen except in Arabia. If they could increase as fast as their nature would allow, impossible would it be for man to sustain himself on the earth.

Unlike most dragon sightings, though, reports of flying serpents have continued into modern times, emerging from far-flung venues. Some countries reporting these creatures include:

Bulgaria: In summer 1947, while walking along a rural path, Izzet Göksu encountered three snakes ranging in length from three to six feet. Startled by her appearance, the reptiles allegedly unfolded wings and flew 6-9 feet off the ground, disappearing into the forest nearby.

France: Sometime in 1930-31, a green flying snake six feet long frightened a woman passing through the forest near La Bollène-Vésubie, in the Alpes-Maritimes Department. She had only a

Flying snakes have been reported worldwide throughout recorded history.

brief glimpse of the creature, but clearly described it as a winged serpent.

Namibia: In January 1942, native workers abandoned the Esterhuise sheep ranch near Keetmanshoop, after their employer ignored their reports of a large winged snake menacing the flocks. Deprived of workers, the rancher sent his son to guard the sheep while they grazed. That evening, when the youth failed to return, an armed party went in search of him. They found 16-year-old Michael Esterhuise unconscious and carried him home, where he lay groggy and incapable of speech for three days. Upon recovering, the boy described a huge flying snake—perhaps 25 feet long, with a wingspan equal to its length—that had swooped from a rocky hillside to land amongt his sheep. The snake had smelled like "burned brass," and the shock of its appearance rendered him unconscious. Armed with dynamite, a hunting party returned to the site and blasted a cave where the creature was thought to reside. After the blast, they heard a moaning sound from within, followed by silence.

South Africa: In 1985, witness Marcus Oarum reported an encounter with a large winged snake, which he met in the Drakensburg Mountains. Three years later, searchers thought they had found a flying snake's skull, but the broken relics proved to be pelvic bones from an OSTRICH (*Struthio camelus*).

Wales: During the first half of the 19th century, a large population of aggressive winged snakes allegedly inhabited the woods around Penlline Castle, north of Cowbridge. They were finally exterminated to prevent their raids on local poultry flocks, but scattered reports of similar reptiles continued for some years thereafter, generally describing animals that lived near waterfalls and used the heights to swoop upon their prey.

No winged reptiles are known to exist on Earth today. Pterosaurs, the last true reptilian fliers, presumably died out some 65 million years ago, though reports of Africa's KONGAMATO and Papua New Guinea's ROPEN challenge that point of common knowledge. Asia boasts three reptiles capable of gliding when they leap from trees, but none is capable of sustained flight. Two are lizards, the so-called flying dragon (*Draco volans*) of Indonesia and Kuhl's GECKO (*Ptychozoon homalocephalus*) of Southeast Asia, both equipped with flaps of skin along their abdomens that can be spread to form rudimentary wings as they leap from tree to tree. Borneo's 5-foot golden tree snake (*Chrysoplea ornata*) flattens its body when it leaps into space, sometimes gliding 50-65 feet between takeoff and landing. None of those species are found in Europe or Africa, and none approach the size of flying snakes reported from Namibia, leaving the mystery unsolved.

Sources: Gibbons, *Missionaries and Monsters*; Izzet Göksu, "Flying snakes in Bulgaria." *Fortean Times* 78 (December 1994-January 1995): 57; Mackal, *Searching for Hidden Animals*; Shuker, *From Flying Toads to Snakes with Wings*.

Snakes (Giant)

Snakes (Suborder *Serpentes*) are legless reptiles found on every continent except Antarctica. At press time for this volume, science recognizes 11 families, subdivided into 47 genera and 2,389 species. Different species range from 6 inches long at maturity to 20-odd feet. ANACONDAS and PYTHONS are the acknowledged giants of the serpent world, and while natives of tropical regions describe other huge serpents — including the BU-RIN and the SUCURIJÚ GIGANTE — no one yet has collected the Wildlife Conservation Society's standing reward of $50,000 for a snake that measures 30 feet or longer. Still, new sightings are reported regularly, often from locations where no "common" giant snakes should normally be found. Some of those sightings include:

1873 — New York residents reported 30-foot snakes from the marshy "drowned lands" around Lake Champlain, suggesting a possible link to the LAKE MONSTER locally known as CHAMP.

1897 — An unidentified 16-foot snake, more than doubling the length of any recognized U.S. species, was killed at Lock Springs, in Missouri's Daviess County.

1919 — Hikers reported a 40-foot snake lurking around Broad Top Mountain, in Huntingdon County, Pennsylvania. Sporadic sightings have persisted through the years, with locals claiming the snake(s) hibernate in abandoned coal mines during winter.

1933 — Sightings of a snake 15-18 feet long were reported from Holdredge, in Nebraska's Phelps County.

1939 — Workers employed by the Civilian Conservation Core reported huge snakes from the Hockomock Swamp, near Bridgewater, Massachusetts. Three decades later, in 1970, an 8-foot common boa (*Constrictor constrictor*) native to South America was killed by vehicles while crossing a road in the same area.

Summer 1944 — Neighbors of Ohio's Cuyahoga River searched in vain for a giant snake dubbed the PENINSULA PYTHON.

9 June 1946 — While horseback riding near his home at Kenton, Ohio, Orland Packer met a snake of unknown species that he later described as 8 feet long and 4 inches thick. The reptile struck Packer, biting through his boot and breaking his ankle, then bit his horse for good measure before vanishing into the woods.

July 1946 — Members of the Willard Tollinger family saw a 20-foot snake coiled in a shallow stream near Flat Rock, in Bartholomew County, Indiana. Pigs and other domestic animals were reported missing from the area throughout that summer.

1950 — Witnesses sighted a 25-foot snake of unknown species outside Wewoka, in Seminole County, Oklahoma.

1952 — An unidentified 18-footer was reported from Fort Wayne, Indiana.

Huge snakes of unknown species are reported worldwide.

1958 — A resident of Massachusetts told author JOHN KEEL that he had encountered a giant snake the previous year, while hunting with a friend at an unnamed location. The man claimed he was riding in a Jeep when a small animal darted across the road in front of him, followed closely by a snake "as big around as a truck tire." Though moving swiftly, the reptile took several seconds to clear the road. The frightened hunters did not pursue it.

1959 — Residents of Albertville, in northern Alabama's Marshall County, reported a 30-foot snake in the vicinity.

1962 — Witnesses sighted a 28-foot snake near Hazel, Kentucky, on the Tennessee border in Calloway County.

Summer 1970 — "Big" snakes of unknown species were seen at Alloy and Orihuela, in the Alicante district of Spain.

July 1973 — Spanish sightings continued, with reports of a "giant" snake seen near Acueche, in Cáceres Province.

October 1978 — Eileen Blackburn nearly crashed her car when she met a huge snake on Interstate Highway 15, 2.5 miles south of Cascade, Montana. She told reporters: "It was between 20 and 30 feet long and its coils were at least three feet across. It covered my side of the freeway. It was standing, with its head up, and it was taller than the hood of my car. I tried to slow down and I'm sure I hit it or it struck at the car because it hit high on the left-hand side of my car. It appeared to be a sort of gray-white in color with a tan strip. It had a flat head that came down to a point and the head was wider than the body. The body was about six inches in diameter at its widest point, and, from the way it stood and the shape of its head, it looked like a cobra." Police Chief Earl Damon acknowledged similar reports from other motorists, but he found nothing when he visited the scene.

1982 — A hog farmer in southeastern Texas reported a snake more than 25 feet long prowling around his property. On one occasion, he thought he had killed the reptile, but it later returned to snatch one of his pigs.

1984 — Siberian miners reported a 30-foot snake crossing the road one morning, while they were en route to the Nikolayevskiy mines in Primor'ye Territory. Similar accounts from the region speak of snakes 15 feet and longer.

July 2000 — Reports of a 30-foot snake emerged from Little River County, in southwestern Arkansas. Wedia Landsell saw the reptile several times at a pond on her property, normally appearing at dawn or dusk. Locals reported the snake devouring prey that ranged in size from frogs to cranes and herons.

In addition to those specific reports, undated sightings of very large snakes have been collected by MARK HALL and others. Those cases include a 120-foot snake allegedly killed by French soldiers near Bénoud, Algeria; a 30-foot reptile "spotted like a rattlesnake," seen outside Nashville, Tennessee; an alleged 60-footer seen at Vincennes, Indiana; a 40-foot specimen reportedly killed at Fredonia, Kansas; and a 20-foot specimen killed in a barn at Loudonville, Ohio. Apparently, none of the serpents allegedly killed were preserved for scientific study or identification. Hall lists a total of 17 giant snake sightings across the U.S. between 1940 and 1995, but his roster includes some creatures normally treated as LAKE MONSTERS.

Sources: Bord and Bord, *Unexplained Mysteries of the 20th Century*; Coleman, *Mysterious America*; Dinsdale, *Monster Hunt*; Mark Hall, "Giant snakes." *Wonders* 6 (2001): 8-9; Keel, *The Complete Guide to Mysterious Beings*; Paul Stonehill, "Giant serpents of the Russian Far East." *Strange Magazine* 13 (Spring 1994): 29.

Snåsavatnet, Norway

This lake, in Nord-Trøndelag County, has an ancient tradition of LAKE MONSTER sightings, which have continued sporadically into modern times. In 1984, witnesses reported an object resembling a submarine crossing the lake.

Sources: Skjelsvik, "Norwegian lake and sea monsters"; Erik Knatterud, Sea Serpents in Norwegian Lakes, http://www.mjoesormen.no.

Snezhniy Chelovek *see* Yeti

Snow Worm   In spring 1978, California researchers Corey Rudolph and Douglas Trapp were camped in southern California's San Gabriel Mountains, seeking evidence of local BIGFOOT activity. While traversing the snowy high desert one morning, they found a wormlike creature wriggling along the bank of a small creek. When they picked up the animal, it coiled into a ball resembling "some sort of wire." As Trapp described the creature 22 years later:

> [T]he skin was smooth, but it was very stiff, and could not be forced to re-coil. Its body was maybe 5 mm [_ inch] in diameter and about 9 inches long when fully outstretched. It was brown in color, and its head was an abrupt stump with what looked like the ball from a ball[point] pen at the end. It had no eyes or anything, just a wire-like body with a ball-pen mouth. In fact, we weren't even sure it was a mouth at all. It also had no apparent anus.

Trapp took the animal home and kept it alive in a plastic bowl for three months, without feeding it, before he returned to the original capture site and released it. In the meantime, he scoured libraries and telephoned several "worm experts," without matching the creature to any known species. He reported the discovery in 2001, suggesting that the elastic creature be named the Rudolph-Trapp Snow Worm, but classification remains impossible without a type specimen in hand.

Source: Douglas Trapp, "The California 'snow-worm.'" *North American BioFortean Review* 1 (April 1999): 18.

Socastee Monkey   Since the early 1980s, reports of a rogue MONKEY at large have sparked debate around Socastee, South Carolina. Located five miles west of Myrtle Beach, in Horry County, Socastee produced its first simian sighting in 1982, when

Unknown monkeys have been seen around Socastee, South Carolina, for over two decades.

local zookeeper Kathleen Furrell claimed that she saw a capuchin monkey (*Cebus* sp.) cavorting in her driveway. After taking stock of her own animals, Furrell determined that none were missing and reported her encounter to authorities. No action was forthcoming, and local animal control officers dismiss the tales as unfounded rumors. Wildlife experts likewise suggest that small primates could not survive South Carolina's cold winters, but sightings persist to the present day.

Source: David Klepper, "Fact or fiction?" Myrtle Beach (SC) Sun News (23 July 2002).

Society for Cryptozoological Organisms and Physical Evidence
Little information is available concerning this group, once based in Cincinnati, Ohio. In 2001, director Denise Richards claimed 90 members, all "interested in the study, sharing of information and new theories on the topic of BIGFOOT." She added: "We dabble in other organisms like the SKUNK APE and other cryptids, but Bigfoot is our main focus." Free membership and a quarterly newsletter were promised, along with facilities for reporting Bigfoot encounters via the Internet. Additionally, Richards and SCOPE claimed affiliation with three other organizations: the Ohio, Indiana and Kentucky Bigfoot DNA Research Center; the International Skunk Ape and Bigfoot DNA Research Group; and the Tri-State Speleological Society. None of those groups were apparently active at press time for this volume.

Source: S.C.O.P.E. New, http://skunkape.veryweird.com/.

Society for the Classification of Unknown Great Apes
Bill McClintock was listed as executive director of the SCUGA in June 2001, when the group was profiled by an Internet magazine primarily concerned with software issues. He claimed more than 2,000 members nationwide, all dedicated to pursuit of unknown HOMINIDS, while defining SCUGA as a group that "is not interested in HOAXES, unsubstantiated reports, fake footprints, or anything else that makes BIGFOOT research a laughing stock. We believe that if there is an unclassified species of great APE in the forests of the [N]orthwest, it should be properly characterized zoologically." To that end, he maintained a sightings database, attempting to analyze trends while separating wheat from chaff. McClintock specifically disavowed any connection to "the more popular aficionado groups such as [the] BIGFOOT fiELD RESEARCHERS ORGANIZATION." Because such groups "list anything and everything, no matter what joker reports it," McClintock said, "it's impossible to glean anything statistically useful out of their databases." As for SCUGA, its status was uncertain at press time for this volume. All Internet searches led back to the Web address of two defunct Bigfoot groups in Cincinnati, Ohio.

Source: Brian Dunning, "On the trail of Sasquatch." *ISO FileMaker Magazine* (June 2001), http://www.briandunning.com/browse/browse0601.shtml.

Society for the Investigation of the Unexplained
Founded by IVAN SANDERSON in 1965, the SITU was America's premier Fortean research organization over the next decade. Its members investigated a wide variety of incidents and sightings, ranging far beyond the bounds of cryptozoology to include UFOs, hauntings and other paranormal phenomena. The SITU's journal, *Pursuit*, published many articles on BIGFOOT, living DINOSAURS, GLOBSTERS, SEA SERPENTS and similar topics. The group survived Sanderson's passing in 1973, but it faded from view by the end of that decade and is now defunct.

Sources: Coleman, *Bigfoot!*; Keel, *The Complete Guide to Mysterious Beings.*

Society Island Parrot   The Society Islands are part of French Polynesia, in the South Pacific. The group comprises the Leeward and Windward Islands, two clusters of volcanic and coral islands spanning some 450 miles of ocean, with a total land area of 650 square miles. The Leeward Islands include Bora-Bora, Huahine, Maiao, Manuae, Maupihaa, Maupiti, Motu One, Rai'atea, Tahaa, and Tupai. The Windward Islands include Mehetia, Moorea, Tahiti and Tetiaroa. Only 8 of the 14 islands are presently inhabited by humans. Capt. James Cook named the Society Islands in 1769. On another voyage, five years later, members of his crew captured two specimens of a colorful BIRD, dubbed the Society Island parrot. Sadly, no details as to where the birds were found has survived, and there is no Society Island per se. No other members of the species have been seen by Western eyes, and speculation on their continued survival endures to the present day.
Source: Bille, *Rumors of Existence.*

Soderica Lake, Croatia   Croatia's only "monster" lake, located near Koprivnica, produced a sighting of an unknown long-necked creature similar to NESSIE in autumn 1999. Two local fishermen reported the encounter, which has not been repeated.
Source: Shadowlands Sea Serpent Page, http://theshadowlands.net/serpent.htm#croatia.

Sogpa *see* **Yeti**

Somenos Lake, Canada   Various sources list this small lake, on southeastern Vancouver Island near Duncan, as a source of LAKE MONSTER reports. Unfortunately, no dates or details of sightings are provided.
Sources: Bord and Bord, *Unexplained Mysteries of the 20th Century*; "A brief survey of Canadian lake monsters." *INFO Journal* 39 (March-June 1981): 2–5; Kirk, *In the Domain of the Lake Monsters.*

Somerset Panther   Police in Somerset, England were placed on alert in March 2003, after a resident of Puriton, near Bridgwater, reported a "black panther" sighting on 17 March. The witness described a jet-black ALIEN BIG CAT roughly the size of a Labrador retriever, and she claimed to have snapped several photos which have yet to be published. While increasing patrols in the area, authorities took a wait-and-see attitude. "If we get a lot more sightings in the same area," a police spokesman told reporters, "then it would be something we would actively investigate further."
Source: "Police alert after 'big cat' sighting." BBC News (17 March 2003).

Sonkala *see* **Gnéna**

Søråsjøen, Norway   A vaguely-described LAKE MONSTER was once reported from this lake in Hedmark County, where witnesses claimed it was grayish-black in color and approximately one foot in diameter. No clear impression of its length or other salient details has survived, and no recent sightings are recorded.
Source: Skjelsvik, "Norwegian lake and sea monsters."

Sordolik Bay sea serpent   A rare SEA SERPENT sighting from the Black Sea was reported in spring 1952, when witness Vsevolod Ivanov allegedly saw a bizarre creature 82–98 feet long swimming in Sordolik Bay, near Planerskoye in the Ukraine's Crimean Republic. According to Ivanov, the huge animal was brown on top, with a white underside. It had a head resembling a SNAKE'S and swam snake-fashion in the water, but also coiled itself into a ball and floated idly on the surface.
Source: Maya Bakova, "Black Sea serpents." *Fortean Times* 51 (Winter 1988–89): 59.

South Carolina Cryptozoological Society   Founded in 2003, the SCCS is a creation of successful cryptofiction author D.L. Tanner (see Appendix D). The group held its first conference in November 2003, at South Carolina's Greenville Technical College, speakers including LOREN COLEMAN and MARK HALL. With cryptid reports on file that include BIGFOOT, MESSIE, the SOCASTEE MONKEY and sightings of giant amphibians in GOOSE CREEK LAGOON, the Palmetto State offers cryptozoologists no shortage of research opportunities.
Source: The Cryptofiction World of Author D.L. Tanner, http://webpages.charter.net/dltanner/sccs.html.

South Pond, Canada   Newfoundland's South Pond lies near Crescent Lake, home of the supposed LAKE MONSTER popularly known as CRESSIE. In the 1980s, while investigating a drowning at South Pond, divers from the Royal Canadian Mounted Police reported sightings of giant EELS with bodies as thick as a man's thigh. Thus far, no specimens have been obtained and the eels remain unidentified.
Source: Kirk, *In the Domain of the Lake Monsters.*

South Saskatchewan River, Canada   In early June 1949, Parker Kent and members of his family allegedly saw an unknown creature swimming in the South Saskatchewan River near Medicine Hat, in southeastern Alberta. The witnesses claimed it was 5–8 feet long, covered with fur, and had a head resembling an ALLIGATOR'S. A Calgary newspaper report dubbed the creature Agopogo, either a pun on OGOPOGO or a careless misspelling of that famous LAKE MONSTER'S popular name. No further sightings are on file.
Source: "Newspaperman sees Agopogo." *Calgary Herald* (9 June 1949).

Southern Oregon Bigfoot Society   This SASQUATCH research organization was founded by Matthew Johnson, a veteran woodsman who describes himself as "very persistent in finding the answer to the existence of BIGFOOT." Johnson maintains an active Internet website and leads weekend expeditions in search of unknown HOMINIDS or evidence supporting their existence. Other identified members of the SOBS include co-founder and U.S. Navy veteran Ray Rosa; forest firefighter Roger Amos; wildlife biologist and author Bill York; private school administrator Doug Thomas; auto mechanic Kevin Jones; Internet webmaster Matt Haverly; retired Coast Guard search-and-rescue officer Joe Wolff; and "official camp cook" Ron Dean. The group claims discoveries of "interesting evidence," but reveals no specifics.
Source: Southern Oregon Bigfoot Society, http://www.sobsresearch.org/.

Soviet Snowman Commission   For whatever reason, the governments of various foreign countries including Russia, China and Vietnam have historically shown more interest in research concerning unknown HOMINIDS than have the "free" Western nations. An example of that interest was the so-called Soviet Snowman Commission, more properly termed a Commission of the Academy of Sciences of the USSR. To this day, despite the thawing of East-West relations and the collapse of Russian communism, little is known of the Snowman Commission's work beyond the fact that it was organized in 1958 to collect and analyze evidence of unknown hominids reported from Soviet territory, including the ALMAS, KAPTAR and others spanning a range broad range from the Caucasus Mountains to Siberia. Identified members of the group include DMITRI BAYANOV, MARIE-JEANNE KOFFMANN, BORIS PORSHNEV, and Dr. A.A. Mashkovtsev and Dr. P. Smoline. LOREN COLEMAN reports that the commission communicated with Texas millionaire TOM SLICK in 1958-59, assisting his search for the YETI, but relations must have been strained inasmuch as Slick's team also collaborated with the Central Intelligence Agency. The commission apparently dissolved sometime during the 1960s.

Sources: Coleman and Clark, *Cryptozoology A to Z*; Shackley, *Still Living?*; The Grand Dame of the Caucasus Almas, http://www.stgr-primates.de/dame.html.

Specs   On 11 March 1959, scuba diver Bob Wall was employed as a tourist guide for passengers aboard the glass-bottomed boat *Comrade II*, cruising in shallow water two miles offshore from Miami Beach, Florida. His job that day was to point out coral formations and other underwater sights for the customers topside. Midway through the performance, Wall encountered a strange creature that frightened him out of the water and into the boat. He described it as 5 feet 6 inches long, tailless, with 8 hairy legs that hoisted it 3 feet off the ocean floor. Its head featured two short antennae and eyes two inches wide mounted on slender stalks (from which its nickname derives). KARL SHUKER suggests that Wall was spooked by a large spiny lobster (*Panulirus argus*), but that species rarely reaches reach two feet in length. Wall, meanwhile, insists that the creature he saw was no known crustacean or cephalopod.

Source: Shuker, *In Search of Prehistoric Survivors*.

Sperillen, Norway   A serpentine LAKE MONSTER 50 feet long, sporting a prominent mane on its neck, was seen in 1893, as it emerged from nearby woods and rushed into this lake. No further sightings were reported by neighbors of Sperillen, in Norway's Buskerud County.

Source: Erik Knatterud, Sea Serpents in Norwegian Lakes, http://www.mjoesormen.no.

Spiders (Giant)   Giant spiders have featured in numerous science-fiction and horror films since the 1950s, lumbering across movie screens in pursuit of humans reduced to the size of insects. In reality, the largest spider known to science is the Goliath bird-eating tarantula (*Theraphosa blondi*) of South America, with a body 3.5 inches long and a maximum 13-inch legspan. Two other Brazilian tarantulas, *Grammostola mollicoma* and *Lasiodora parahybana*, may achieve 10-inch legspans. An even larger species, *Megarachne servinei*, is known from Carboniferous fossil beds in Argentina, where specimens have been found with legspans exceeding 20 inches. Still, those hairy predators do not approach the size of fictional arachnids — but disturbing reports from Africa and the Pacific speak of truly monstrous spiders lurking in tropical forests. Cryptozoologist WILLIAM GIBBONS obtained the following account from Margaret Lloyd, concerning an experience reported by her parents:

Mr. and Mrs. R.K. Lloyd were on a motoring "honeymoon" in the Belgian Congo [now the Democratic Republic of Congo] in 1938 when they spotted a large object crossing the jungle trail ahead of them. At first they took it to be a large jungle cat or a sizeable monkey walking on all fours. As they drew closer, the creature turned

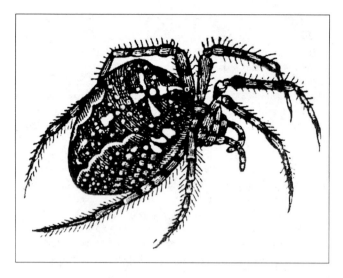

Reports of giant spiders emanate from Africa and Papua New Guinea.

out to be a gigantic spider! Mrs. Lloyd let out a piercing scream while her husband attempted to pull his camera from its case. Unfortunately, his hands were shaking so much from the excitement of the encounter that he missed his chance completely. The spider continued on its way into the jungle at the same steady pace, seemingly unfazed by the wheezing Ford convertible that almost ran it over.

According to the Lloyds, the creature was quite enormous — with legs close to three feet in length!

Another frightening encounter occurred in the 1940s, some 6,000 miles farther east. Australian researcher Peter Hynes reported the case in 2001, based on conversations with a female acquaintance. According to that story, the informant's father was a soldier in the Australian army, fighting Japanese invaders along the Kokoda Trail in Papua New Guinea's central highlands, circa 1943-45. One afternoon, while seeking a place to relieve himself in the jungle, the soldier crouched beside a spider's web that stretched 10-15 feet in each direction. Glancing higher, he was horrified to find a huge spider dangling within a foot of his face. He described the arachnid as jet-black, with a body "the size of a small dog or puppy." Its stout, hairy legs were proportionately shorter than those of the "dinner plate tarantulas," displaying "more bulk than spread." The frightened soldier "backed out of there *very* slowly and carefully," but he recalled that close encounter for the rest of his life.

Source: Chad Arment, "CZ conversations: Giant spiders." *North American BioFortean Review* 3 (October 2001): 28-29.

Spinifex Man   This large unknown primate or HOMINID of Western Australia takes its name from the region's tough spinifex grass. It resembles the more famous YOWIE, described as a hairy biped reaching heights of 10 feet, but its 2-toed footprints bear little resemblance to the Yowie's tracks. Peter Muir found a trail of those odd prints near Laverton, in early September 1970. Skeptics suggest that the tracks belong to naturalized OSTRICHES (*Struthio camelus*), which have been imported to Australia as livestock since the early 20th century.

Source: "The Abominable Spinifex Man." *Pursuit* 13 (January 1971): 9-10.

Spirit Lake, Canada *see* **Wasgo**

Spirit Lake, Iowa Authors LOREN COLEMAN and JOHN KIRK include this Iowa lake, in Dickinson County, as a source of LAKE MONSTER reports, but no dates or details of any sightings are revealed.

Source: Coleman, *Mysterious America*; Kirk, *In the Domain of the Lake Monsters*.

Spirit Lake, New York Various sources claim that LAKE MONSTER sightings have been reported from this lake, in Genesee County, but published accounts provide no dates or details.

Sources: Garner, *Monster! Monster!*; Alfred Hulstrunk, "Assorted ghosts, ghouls and goblins of New York State." *Binghamton* (NY) *Press* (14 August 1977).

Spirit Lake, Washington Spirit Lake lies at the northeastern base of Mt. Saint Helens, in Skamania County. Local aborigines once claimed that the lake was inhabited by a LAKE MONSTER whose head resembled that of a bear. No modern sightings of the creature are on file.

Source: Paul Kane, *Wanderings of an Artist Among the Indians of North America*. Toronto: Rasmussen Society, 1925.

Spofford Lake, New Hampshire Spofford Lake lies 10 miles west of Keene, in southwestern New Hampshire's Cheshire County. Sometime in the early 1980s, a scuba diver was searching the lake's bottom when he paused to rest on what he took to be a sunken log. At first contact, however, the "log" came alive and slithered away, revealing itself as a gray, 20-foot-long SNAKE or EEL. Around the same time, another diver reported meeting vaguely-described "monsters" in nearby DUBLIN LAKE.

Source: Craig Heinselman, "A lake monster in New Hampshire?" *North American BioFortean Review* 4 (March 2002): 14.

Spotted Bushbuck This small African antelope is known only from a single incomplete skin, collected in Liberia during the late 19th century and preserved at Berlin's Humboldt University Museum of Natural History. Its common name derives from the spots that cover its hide. No scientific name has been assigned.

Source: Heuvelmans, "Annotated checklist of apparently unknown animals with which cryptozoology is concerned."

Spottsville Monster On 9 February 1977, the Owensburg, Kentucky *Messenger-Inquirer* reported that residents of Spottsville, in Henderson County, had sighted a BIGFOOT-type HOMINID sometime in late 1975. Sadly, no further details were forthcoming, and on-site investigation by researcher Michael Polesnek failed to illuminate the matter.

Sources: Bord and Bord, *The Bigfoot Casebook*; Green, *Sasquatch: The Apes Among Us*.

Spring Lake sea serpent On 22 September 1895, Willard Shaw was lounging with friends and family on the porch of his home in Spring Lake, New Jersey when they saw a SEA SERPENT passing offshore. The witnesses later agreed that it was 75-100 feet long, with a head resembling that of an ALLIGATOR, which it held 6 feet above the water's surface while swimming. Shaw estimated the beast's speed at 40 miles per hour, achieved by swimming with a series of vertical undulations.

Source: "Was it a sea serpent?" *New Haven* (CT) *Evening Register* (24 September 1895).

Sproat Lake, Canada Located on British Columbia's Vancouver Island, west of Port Alberni, Sproat Lake is 14 miles lone and one mile wide. Its tradition of LAKE MONSTER sightings dates from the 19th century, but no modern reports are on file.

Source: Kirk, *In the Domain of the Lake Monsters*.

Sqrats "Sqrats"— the unlikely offspring of mixed breeding between *squirrels* and *rats*— have allegedly been seen in various cities across the U.S., with scattered reports spanning several decades. Authorities dismiss such tales as urban myths, and zoologists note the improbability (if not outright impossibility) of such a pairing, but occasional sightings continue. The most recent to date, from New York City, involved a rash of alleged Sqrat sightings in spring 1999.

Source: Karl Shuker, "Alien zoo." *Fortean Times* 130 (January 2000): 18.

Squattam's Growlers Prior to introduction of the SKUNK APE label to describe BIGFOOT-type creatures in Florida, unknown HOMINIDS were known by a variety of nicknames in Dade County. The most common term, of unknown origin, was Squattam's Growlers, though Seminole tribesmen knew the creatures as Sandmen and commercial fishermen sometimes called them Buggers (a variation of BOOGER).

Source: Green, *Sasquatch: The Apes Among Us*.

Sraheen Lough *see* **Glendarry Lough**

Stafford Lake, California Persistent tales of a LAKE MONSTER inhabiting Stafford Lake, north of San Francisco in Marin County, were validated after a fashion when the lake was drained in August 1984. On 23 August, workers found a white sturgeon (*Acipenser transmontanus*) thrashing in a shallow pool. The fish measured 6 feet 5 inches long and tipped the scales at 125 pounds. It was transported to San Francisco's Steinhart Aquarium, where it died on 28 August 1984.

Sources: "'Sea monster' dead." *Las Vegas Sun* (29 August 1984); "Sea monster found alive." *Las Vegas Sun* (24 August 1984); "Stafford Lake monster caught." *ISC Newsletter* 4 (Winter 1985): 8.

State Line Pond, Connecticut In May 2003, residents of Tolland County, Connecticut claimed that a 20-foot PYTHON inhabited State Line Pond, a lake two miles northwest of Stafford. The story originated with nocturnal fishermen who claimed encounters with the giant SNAKE, prompting state police to seek help from Connecticut's Department of Environmental Protection. Animal control officer Michael Hurchala visited the lake in daylight and reported sighting four snakes, all normal-sized black rat snakes ((*Elaphe obsoleta obseleta*) common throughout the eastern U.S. Hurchala claimed one of the snakes he saw was "maybe seven feet" in length, a foot longer than the maximum accepted length for that species.

Source: Rick Guinness, "'State Line Pond monster' likely a black snake." *Manchester* (CT) *Journal Inquirer* (23 May 2003).

Steller's Sea Ape German naturalist George Wilhelm Steller ranks among the first Arctic explorers. His great voyage aboard the *Saint Peter*, commanded by Vitus Bering, culminated in disaster when the team was shipwrecked on Bering Island, on 28 November 1741, but Steller's diaries survived and were published for the first time in 1751, a decade after his death. Those diaries included the following description of a remarkable creature seen 260 miles south of Kodiak Island, in the Gulf of Alaska (around 52° north latitude and 155°west longitude). Steller described the incident as follows:

> On August 10 we saw a very unusual and unknown sea animal, of which I am going to give a brief account since I observed it for two whole hours. It was about two Russian ells [5 feet] in length; the head was like a dog's, with pointed erect ears. From the upper and lower lips on both sides whiskers hung down which made it

look almost like a Chinaman. The eyes were large; the body was longish round and thick, tapering gradually towards the tail. The skin seemed thickly covered with hair, of a gray color on the back, but reddish white on the belly; in the water, however, the whole animal appeared entirely reddish and cow-colored. The tail was divided into two fins, of which the upper, as in the case of SHARKS, was twice as large as the lower. Nothing struck me more surprising than the fact that neither forefeet as in the marine amphibians nor, in their stead, fins were to be seen.

Steller likened the creature to a legendary animal called *Simia marina danica* (Danish sea MONKEY), depicted in Konrad Gesner's *Historia Animalium* of 1558. He tried to shoot the animal, thus to obtain a specimen, but both shots missed and it fled out of range, though it was later seen "several times at different places of the sea."

Based on Steller's description, various scientists proposed formal names for the creature. Johann Walbaum called it *Siren cyodephala* (1792); George Shaw proposed *Trichechus hydropithecus* (1800); and Johann Illiger suggested *Manatus simia* (1811). Still, no more was seen of Steller's sea ape until June 1965, when Miles Smeeton reported a sighting four miles off the northern coast of Atka, in the Aleutian Islands. Smeeton described an animal the size of a sheep, covered in reddish-orange hair, with a drooping mustache. Skeptics, including Steller's biographer Leonhard Stejneger, insist that Steller mistook a juvenile northern fur seal (*Callorhinus ursinus*) for an unknown mammal. Cryptozoologist ROY MACKAL has proposed a more intriguing solution, suggesting that Steller glimpsed an immature specimen of some yet-unknown long-necked pinniped, perhaps related to the leopard seal (*Hydrurga leptonyx*).

Sources: Bille, *Rumors of Existence*; Mackal, *Searching for Hidden Animals*; Miles Smeeton, *The Misty Islands*. London: George Harrap, 1969.

Steller's Sea Cow   In the winter of 1741-42, while shipwrecked on Bering Island in the Komandorski chain, between Kamchatka and the Aleutians, German naturalist George Steller encountered another Arctic creature previously unknown to science. Unlike STELLER'S SEA APE, however, some of these animals were killed and dissected, providing a more detailed view of their anatomy. The largest of sirenians, related to dugongs and manatees, the creatures were described as follows by A.E. Nordenskjöld:

> Steller's sea cow...was of a dark-brown color, sometimes varied with white spots or streaks. The thick leathery skin was covered with hair which grew together so as to form an exterior skin, which was full of vermin and resembled the bark of an old oak....The head was small in proportion to the large thick body, the neck short, the body diminishing rapidly behind the short fore-leg terminated abruptly without fingers or nails, but was overgrown with a number of short thickly placed brush-hairs; the hind-leg was replaced by a tail-fin resembling a whale's. The animal wanted teeth, but was instead provided with two masticating plates, one in the gum, the other in the under jaw. The udders of the female, which abounded in milk, were placed between the fore-limbs.

By the time Nordenskjöld penned those lines in 1881, Steller's sea cow had been officially extinct for 113 years. The last confirmed specimens were killed in 1768, though Bering Island hunters claimed to have slain more in 1780. Polish naturalist Benedykt Dybowski believed the species survived as late as 1830, and two Bering Island residents claimed a sighting of a solitary specimen in 1854. Russian fishermen reported a sea cow stranded at Siberia's Gulf of Anadyr in 1910, but the claim was not investigated. Four

Sightings of Steller's sea cow persist, although it is presumed extinct (*William Rebsamen*).

decades later, in the early 1950s, Russian harpooner Ivan Skripkin claimed that sea cows visited the waters off Bering Island each July. Later still, in July 1962, crewmen aboard the Russian whaler *Buran* reported six sea cows feeding in a lagoon near Siberia's Cape Navarin. In 1976, a fisherman named Ivan Chechulin claimed he had met a sea cow at Anapkinskaya Bay, south of Cape Navarin, and that the creature let him touch it. Still, without a specimen to prove the case, most scientists insist that Steller's sea cow is a phantom of the Arctic seas, long since extinct.

Sources: Bille, *Rumors of Existence*; Heuvelmans, *In the Wake of the Sea Serpents*; Mackal, *In Search of Hidden Animals*; Raynal, "Does Steller's sea cow still survive?"

Steller's Sea Raven   The last cryptid described by German naturalist George Steller, while he was shipwrecked on Bering Island in the bleak winter of 1741-42, was a white cliff-dwelling BIRD resembling a cormorant (*Phalacrocorax* sp.), which Steller called a sea raven. No other witness has described the bird to date, but researchers still speculate about its possible identity. Candidates proposed thus far include the pigeon guillemot (*Cephus columba*) with white winter plumage, a species of Pacific sandpiper called the surf bird (*Aphriza virgata*), and some as-yet-unknown species of white cormorant. As with STELLER'S SEA APE, the riddle is insoluble until such time as a specimen is collected.

Source: Shuker, *Mysteries of Planet Earth*.

Stensjön, Sweden   This Swedish lake, located in Östergötland County, has a maximum depth of 40 feet. In the 1930s, local residents reported a 30-foot LAKE MONSTER dwelling there, but no modern sightings are on file.

Source: Global Underwater Search Team, http://www.cryptozoology.st/.

Stinson Beach sea serpent   On 31 October 1983, five construction workers employed by California's Department of Transportation reported a SEA SERPENT sighting off Stinson Beach, in Marin County. After watching the creature through binoculars, the witnesses agreed that it was dark in color, 100 feet long, and had humps on its back. An estimated 100 sea birds and two dozen sea lions followed the beast as it swam parallel to the coastline. Witness Mark Ratto told reporters, "The body came out of the water first. There were three bends, like humps, and they rose straight up. Then the head came up to look around."

Sources: "'Sea serpents' seen off California coast." *ISC Newsletter* 2 (Winter 1983): 9-10; "Serpent sighted off California coast." Associated Press (3 November 1983).

Store Le, Sweden

Giant CATFISH are reported from this lake, in Västra Götland County. The European wels catfish (*Siluris glanis*) reaches an acknowledged length of 15 feet 6 inches, though no specimens have yet been caught or verified from Store Le.

Source: Erik Knatterud, Sea Serpents in Norwegian Lakes, http://www.mjoesormen.no.

Storevatn, Norway

A LAKE MONSTER 27-30 feet long, resembling a capsized boat with fins, was reported from this lake near Askøy, in Norway's Hordaland County, through the early 20th century. No recent sightings are recorded.

Source: Skjelsvik, "Norwegian lake and sea monsters."

Storsjöodjuret

Storsjöodjuret ("Storsjö monster") is the supposed LAKE MONSTER of Lake Storsjön, in Sweden's Jämtland County. It is uncertain when the creatures first rose from the lake's 300-foot depths to reveal themselves. Dr. Peter Olsson, who undertook the first systematic study of Storsjöodjuret in 1898-99, traced the initial sighting to 1820. A century later, in 1996, Sten Rentzhog — president of the Östersund Society for the Scientific Investigation of Lake Storsjön — claimed to have hundreds of sightings on file, dating back to 1635. Be that as it may, no published eyewitness accounts of Storsjöodjuret presently predate the second decade of the 19th century.

A local farmer filed what seems to be the earliest report in 1820, claiming that a large creature had chased his boat near Funäs, at the south end of the lake. In the early 1830s, a housepainter announced his sighting of "the Storsjön leviathan." Aron Anderson and several other witnesses saw the beast near Hackås in 1839, noting its resemblance to a red-gray horse with a flowing white mane. On 19 July 1855, four farmers saw a 25-foot animal as wide as a rowboat swimming offshore from Sanne. Three years later, Erik Isaksson saw a large beast resembling a capsized boat, off Östersund. In 1863, J. Bromee and his family sighted a crea-

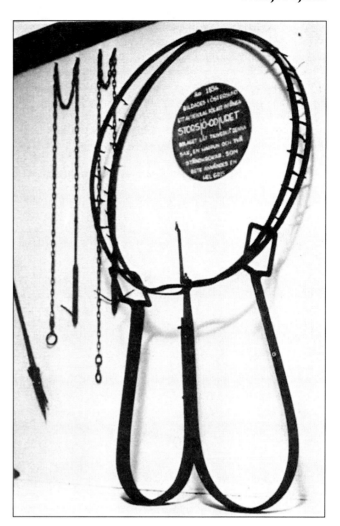

This trap, built for Storjöodjuret in 1895, failed to snare its intended prey.

A sketch of Storsjöodjuret, based on eyewitness reports.

ture with four short legs thrashing in the waters near shore, between Billsta and Hackås. As it fled their approach, the beast revealed 10-12 humps above water. In summer 1868, a witness saw Storsjöodjuret swimming at "arrow speed" near Åssjön, north of Östersund. More sightings were reported from Billssa in autumn 1870, near Kjalsmarsundet in summer 1873, and again from Åssjön in August 1889 and autumn 1892. Sisters Karin and Marta Olsson were washing clothes near Ås, in October 1893, when Storsjöodjuret appeared and frightened them out of their wits. Climbing a nearby tree, they watched it raise a doglike head atop a neck 8-9 feet long, trailed by a 14-foot body with two forefeet or flippers visible. King Oscar II contributed money in 1894, when amusement-park proprietor Maria Helin formed a company to catch the beast, but Storsjöodjuret remained at large, appearing 10 more times during 1896-99.

As at other active "monster" lakes, sightings from Lake Storsjön continued into the 20th century. Witnesses Anders Berqvist and Jonas Hansson saw a 2-humped creature swimming past Myrviken on 14 July 1931. A 9-foot animal with prominent ears, rolling eyes and a slavering tongue frightened Anna Rham at Åssjön, on 12 August 1947. Carina Johnsson snapped the first known photographs of Storsjöodjuret near Brunfloviken, on 10 August 1983. Eleven months later, on 18 June 1984, a supposed embryonic cryptid was found washed ashore, later delivered to the Jämtland Museum where it remains unidentified. Gun-Britt Widmark captured one of the creatures on videotape, while boating with a party of senior citizens off Östersund, on 20 July 1996. While swimming near Tippskar Island on 8 August 1997, Elin and Cecilia Hemreus met a creature with a horselike head, a 6-foot neck, and large scales resembling armored plates on its back. A new century of sightings dawned in July 2000, when a woman at Brunflo saw a creature 20–25 feet long, "golden with a blackish back," swimming 90 feet offshore. JAN-OVE SUNDBERG and his GLOBAL UNDERWATER SEARCH TEAM have conducted studies at Lake Storsjön, but without thus far collecting any concrete evidence to identify Storsjöodjuret.

Sources: Costello, *In Search of Lake Monsters*; Dash, "Status report: Lake monsters"; Dinsdale, *Monster Hunt*; Kirk, *In the Domain of the Lake Monsters*; "Monster machinations." *Fortean Times* 92 (November 1996): 18.

Straits of Messina sea serpents
BERNARD HEUVELMANS reports that a SEA SERPENT was seen in the Straits of Messina, separating Sicily from Italy, in 1953. No further information is available on that case, but another cryptid was seen nearby, by tourists spear fishing off Grillone (near Copanello, in the Calabrian province of Catanzaro) in August 1958. That creature was described as resembling an oversized moray EEL (*Muraenidae* sp.). After comparing that testimony to other sightings from the region, Heuvelmans concluded that "[t]he only sort of sea-serpents normally to live in the Mediterranean seem to be a sort of giant moray."

Source: Heuvelmans, *In the Wake of the Sea Serpents*.

Strathyre Lynx
In March 2003, two separate witnesses reported sightings of a large black CAT with lynxlike pointed ears, seen prowling through Strathyre Forest in the Scottish Highlands. Local wildlife author Bridget MacCaskill told the *Stirling Observer*, "I have checked fairly carefully the descriptions given to me and have seen droppings that could belong to a large feral cat, but it is most certainly not a LYNX. They are no longer native to this country. The cat is not a threat to humans, it would flee a mile." Despite that judgment, and similar opinions offered by other experts, researchers involved in pursuit of ALIEN BIG CATS noted that three lynxes were killed around Inverness in 1927. More recently, a northern lynx (*Felis lynx*) was shot at SUFFOLK, England in 1991, after killing 15 sheep, and another was captured alive outside London in May 2001.

Source: Lesley Pollock, "Something stirring in Strathyre." *Stirling Observer* (31 March 2003).

Strömstad sea serpent
In early March 1939, Edwin Hansson and several companions reportedly sighted a 16-foot SEA SERPENT off the coast of Strömstad, in eastern Sweden. They described the creature as gray in color, flashing a mouthful of teeth and growling as their boat approached. BERNARD HEUVELMANS notes that the general appearance and behavior conform to that of a pinniped, though he leaves the question of its species unresolved.

Source: Heuvelmans, *In the Wake of the Sea Serpents*.

Stronsay Beast
In September 1808, John Peace was fishing on the coast of Stronsay (formerly Stronsa), in the Orkney Islands, when he found a large carcass beached and surrounded by sea birds. His first impression was that of a creature with a long, thin neck and tail, a head no larger than a seal's, a bristling mane

on the neck, and several pairs of legs or fins. Peace soon fetched George Sherar, who helped him measure the carcass as "exactly fifty-five feet in length from the hole in the top of the skull…to the extremity of the tail." Another observer, Thomas Fotheringhame, obtained the same result by measuring "from the junction of the head and neck, where there was the appearance of an ear, to the tail." Sherar subsequently signed an affidavit in which he swore:

> That the length of the neck was exactly fifteen feet, from the same hole to the beginning of the mane: That he measured also the circumference of the animal as accurately as he could, which was about ten feet, more or less; and the whole body, where the limbs were attached to it, was about the same circumference: That the lower jaw or mouth was awanting; but there were some substances or bones of the jaw remaining, when he first examined it, which are now away: That it had two holes on each side of the neck, beside the one on the back of the skull: That the mane or bristles were about fourteen inches in length each, of a silvery colour, and particularly luminous in the dark, before they were dried: That the upper part of the limbs, which answers to the shoulder-blade, was joined to the body like the shoulder-blade of a cow, forming part of the side: That a part of the tail was awanting, being incidentally broken off at the extremity; where the last joint of it was bare, was an inch and a half in breadth: That the bones were of a gristly nature, like those of a halibut, the back-bone excepted, which was the only solid one in the body: That the tail was quite flexible, turning in every direction, as he lifted it; and he supposes the neck to have been equally so from its appearance at the time: That there were either five or six toes on each paw, about nine inches long, and of a soft substance: That the toes were separate from each other, and not webbed, so far as he was able to observe; and that the paw was about half a foot each way, in length and in breadth.

Fotheringhame observed that "the skin seemed to be elastic when compressed, and of a greyish colour, without any scales: it was rough to the feeling, on drawing the hand over it, towards the head; but was smooth as velvet when the hand was drawn toward the tail." He further noted that "a part of the bones of the lower jaw, resembling those of a dog, were remaining at that time, with some appearance of teeth, which were soft, and could be bent by the strength of the hand."

William Folsetter, a local farmer, found the beast's stomach lying detached outside its body and later recalled "that it was about four feet long, and as thick as a firkin [a container equal to ¼ the volume of a barrel], but flatter: That the membranes that formed the divisions, extended quite across the supposed stomach, and were about three sixteenth of an inch in thickness, and at the same distance from each other, and of the same substance, as the stomach itself: That the section of the stomach, after it was opened, had the appearance of a weaver's reed: That he opened about a fourth part of the supposed stomach which contained nothing but a reddish substance, like blood and water, and emitted a fetid smell."

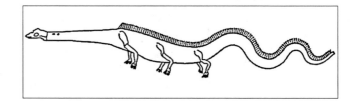

The Stronsay carcass, based on eyewitness descriptions.

Dr. John Barclay, after examining the Stronsay remains, proposed that the creature belonged to a new genus, which he named *Halsydrus* ("sea snake"), and he further suggested that "as it evidently appeared to be the Soe-Ormen described above half a century ago" by Norwegian author Erik Pontoppidan, its specific name should be *Halsydrus pontoppidani*. A more detached review of the evidence, including rough or bristly skin and pliable "gristly" bones, indicates that the Stronsay Beast was almost certainly a decomposed SHARK—but of what species?

The largest shark presently known to science, the whale shark (*Rhincodon typus*), is known to reach lengths exceeding 50 feet, but it steers well clear of cold seas. The basking shark (*Cetorhinus maximus*) is a more likely candidate, but the Stronsay Beast exceeds the record length for that species by almost 40 percent. That discrepancy prompted BERNARD HEUVELMANS and KARL SHUKER to suggest that it might represent a still-unknown species of giant shark. BEN ROESCH is more conservative in his analysis, preferring the notion of a truly gigantic basking shark to the prospect of a whole new species.

Sources: Heuvelmans, *In the Wake of the Sea Serpents*; Roesch, "A review of alleged sea serpent carcasses worldwide (Part One —1648-1880)"; Shuker, "Bring me the head of the sea serpent!"

Stump Pond, Illinois

Stump Pond is located on the Perry County fairgrounds in Du Quoin, Illinois. Reports of a LAKE MONSTER inhabiting the pond date from summer 1879, when a fisherman named Paquette claimed an unseen animal had passed him by with speed enough to rock his boat. In July 1880, two miners allegedly saw a green 12-foot snake as thick as a telephone pole swimming toward shore. Sporadic sightings continued until 1968, when the pond was partially drained and its fish were removed. Some large CATFISH were found, the largest weighing 30 pounds, but nothing bigger was revealed. Nonetheless, some witnesses still insist that a much larger animal once appeared in the pond or rocked their boats on its surface.

Sources: Coleman, *Mysterious America*; "The monster of Stump Pond." *Fate* 18 (January 1965): 24-25.

Sturgeon Bay, Wisconsin

Local legends claim that a hairy "serpent" once snatched two sisters from Sturgeon Bay, in Wisconsin's Door County, but no details of the alleged incident are available. Sketchy accounts omit even the date of the supposed attack, and no one seems to know if the LAKE MONSTER came from Green Bay, to the west, or from nearby LAKE MICHIGAN.

Source: Frank Joseph, *The Lost Pyramids of Rock Lake*. St. Paul: Glade, 1992.

Stuysfjordhylen, Norway

Norse folklore described this lake, in Vest-Agder County, as the one-time lair of a strange LAKE MONSTER. The 18-foot creature allegedly resembled a floating log or beam, with slits for eyes and a forked tail. No modern sightings are on file.

Source: Skjelsvik, "Norwegian lake and sea monsters."

Succarath *see* **Megatherium**

Sucurijú Gigante

Brazilian witnesses describe the Sucurijú gigante ("giant boa") as huge amphibious SNAKE of the Amazon River and its tributaries. Some researchers consider it identical to the giant ANACONDA reported in various accounts, but others—including BERNARD HEUVELMANS and TIM DINSDALE—regarded it as a distinct and separate species. Lorenz Hagenbeck, one-time director of the Hamburg Zoo and a firm believer in the huge reptile's existence, compiled descriptions of a reptile bear-

ing no resemblance to an anaconda: dark chestnut brown in color, mottled dirty-white underneath, with huge luminous eyes, measuring 130 feet long and 30 inches in diameter, tipping the scales around 5 tons. A priest in Brazil, Father Victor Heinz, met the great snakes twice, describing his first encounter as follows:

> During the great floods of 1922, on May 22 at about 3 o'clock to be exact, I was being taken home by canoe on the Amazon from Obidos; suddenly I noticed something surprising in midstream. I distinctly recognized a giant water-snake at a distance of some 30 yards…. Coiled up in two rings the monster drifted quietly and gently downstream. My quaking crew had stopped paddling. Thunderstruck, we all stared at the frightful beast. I reckoned that its body was as thick as an oil-drum and that its visible length was some 80 feet. When we were far enough away and my boatmen dared to speak again they said that the monster would have crushed us like a box of matches if it had not previously consumed several large capybaras.

Father Heinz reported that another Sucurijú gigante was killed some time later, a day's march south of Obidos, on the shore of Lago Grande de Salea. Hunters caught it in the act of swallowing an adult capybara (*Hydrochaeris hyrdochaeris*), and they found four more of the 4.5-foot, 140-pound rodents inside the snake's stomach. On 29 October 1929, Father Heinz met another reptilian giant on the Amazon, while traveling to Alemquer around midnight. Approaching from the opposite direction, Heinz saw two blue-green lights like the navigation lights of a steamer, but his native crew recognized the object as "*una cobra grande.*" Heinz continued:

> Petrified, we all watched the monster approach; it avoided us and recrossed the river in less than a minute, a crossing that would have taken us in calm water ten to fifteen times as long. On the safety of dry land we took courage and shouted to attract attention to the snake. At this very moment a human figure began to wave an oil-lamp on the other shore, thinking no doubt, that someone was in danger. Almost at once the snake rose on the surface and we were able to appreciate clearly the difference between the light of the lamp and the phosphorescent light of the monster's eyes. Later, on my return, the inhabitants of this place assured me that above the mouth of the Piaba there dwelt a *sucurijú gigante.*

Portuguese merchant Reymondo Zima, navigating the Rio Ja-

Victor Heinz meets the Sucurijú gigante (*William Rebsamen*).

munda with his wife and son on 6 July 1930, had a similar frightening encounter. As he described it later:

> Night was falling when we saw a light on the right bank. In the belief that it was the house I was looking for I steered towards the light and switched on my searchlight. But then suddenly we noticed that the light was charging towards us at an incredible speed. A huge wave lifted the bow of the boat and almost made it capsize. My wife screamed in terror. At the same moment we made out the shape of a giant snake rising out of the water and performing a St. Vitus's dance around the boat. After which the monster crossed this tributary of the Amazon…at fabulous speed, leaving a huge wake, larger than any of the steamboats make at full speed. The wave hit our 13m [42-foot] boat with such force that at every moment we were in danger of capsizing. I opened my motor flat out and made for dry land. Owing to the understandable excitement at the time it was not possible for me to reckon the monster's length. I presume that as a result of some wound the animal lost one eye, since I saw only one light. I think the giant snake must have mistaken our searchlight for the eye of one of his fellow snakes.

A Franciscan priest, Father Protesius Frickel of Oriscima, reported that he saw a Sucurijú gigante during one of his trips along the Rio Trombetas. It was lying in the water with its head on shore, and Frickel boldly disembarked to approach within 20 feet of the beast. "It's eyes," he later wrote, "were as large as plates." Father Heinz also recounted one last report of a monster snake, occurring 12 weeks after Reymondo Zima's adventure:

> On 27 September 1930, on an arm of water that leads from Lake Mauricania to the Rio Iguarapé, a Brazilian named João Penha was engaged in clearing the bank to make it easier for the TURTLES to come up and lay their eggs. At a certain moment, behind one of those floating barriers made of plants, tree-trunks and tangled branches, against which steamers of 500 tons often have to battle to force a passage, he saw two green lights. Penha thought at first it was some fisherman who was looking for eggs. But suddenly the whole barrier shook for 100m [325 feet]. He had to retreat hurriedly for a foaming wave 2m [6 feet 6 inches] high struck the bank. Then he called his two sons, and all three of them saw a snake rising out of the water pushing the barrier in front of it for a distance of some 300m [975 feet] until the narrow arm of water was finally freed of it. During all this time they could observe at leisure its phosphorescent eyes and the huge teeth in its lower jaw.

Sources: Dinsdale, *Monster Hunt;* Heuvelmans, *On the Track of Unknown Animals.*

Sudd Gallinule

The gallinules or swamphens (*Porphyrio* sp.) are wading birds related to the rails and coots (Family *Rallidae*), which inhabit swampy terrain. They are characterized by dark iridescent plumage and red bills tipped with yellow. They are found worldwide, including several species in Africa, but at least one species may have passed unnoticed by modern science. Witnesses in the Sudd region of southern Sudan claim encounters with a nocturnal species of gallinule which has yet to be verified or formally described.

Source: Shuker, "A supplements to Dr. Bernard Heuvelmans' checklist of cryptozoological animals."

Sūet-jùen *see* Yeren

Suez carcass

In early January 1950, a badly decomposed carcass was beached at Suez, on the Red Sea. Despite early speculation that it might be a SEA SERPENT, the creature was soon identified as a specimen of Bryde's whale (*Balaenoptera edeni*).

Source: Heuvelmans, *In the Wake of the Sea Serpents.*

Suffolk sea serpents

Unidentified SEA SERPENTS were twice reported off the coast of Suffolk, England in the 1930s. The first sighting, in June 1931, involved three witnesses but was not reported until December 1933, apparently from fear of ridicule. On the day in question, Sibyl Armstrong was walking with her governess and cook, at Thorpeness, when they saw a large animal swimming rapidly, parallel to the coast, some 400 yards offshore. It displayed two large humps above the surface, plus a head roughly three times the size of a human's. The witnesses estimated its total length at 50-60 feet. Armstrong later said, "If one had not known the length of the body in the water behind, one would have thought it a colossal BIRD."

Seven years later, on 21 October 1938, Suffolk fishermen William Herrington and Ernest Watson were casting their nets near the South Barnard buoy, off Southwold, when some unknown creature raised its large head 40 yards from their boat. The beast towered over them briefly, then made off "at a terrific speed," estimated at 35 miles per hour. Retreating swiftly to shore, Herrington and Watson described the animal as gray in color and 60 feet long, with a humped back like a CAMEL'S.

Sometime in the 1950s, a "peculiar FISH" was caught by fishermen off the coast of Orford Ness, Suffolk. Witness Mildred Nye described the creature to TIM DINSDALE in January 1962, as follows:

> I saw it on a motor-lorry, of the kind with no sides. The body took up the length of the lorry and the tail hung down over the end and trailed in the dust. I was told it measured 17 or 18 feet. The tail was as long as the body; it was shaped like a cow's tail and had a bunch of webbed fingers at the end that formed a fan shape, when I spread them out. It had four large flappers, two on each side, like hands, each finger larger than mine and webbed in-between. The

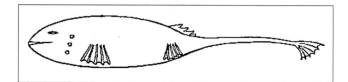

The Orford Ness carcass, after witness Mildred Nye.

fingers were boned, evidently, because I could not bend them. The eyes were small and shut with two lids; top and bottom — and another across the corner….Three holes like inset pipes, big enough to take my walking stick which I poked into them….A small frill of fins where the tail joined the body. I was told that the Curator of the [local] Museum came out by car to see the thing and could not place it at all. I did not hear — indeed, could not find out — what eventually happened to it.

Nye's sketch of the creature reveals a creature that Dinsdale compared to a "gigantic tadpole," and which resembles nothing presently known to science.

Source: Dinsdale, *Monster Hunt;* Heuvelmans, *In the Wake of the Sea Serpents.*

Suldalsvatnet, Norway

Residents of Norway's Rogaland County once reported LAKE MONSTER sightings from this body of water, describing a creature that frequently resembled a capsized boat on the surface. Its skin was sleek grayish-brown, and its pointed head sported large eyes. Skeptics blame the incidents on mats of rotting vegetation rising from the lake's bottom. As with many other Scandinavian lakes, no recent sightings are on file.

Source: Skjelsvik, "Norwegian lake and sea monsters."

***Sultan* sea serpent** In 1909, officers and crew aboard the steamer *Sultan* reportedly met a SEA SERPENT in the China Sea. Captain Harbord, commanding the vessel, later described the beast for *Wide World Magazine*: "The length of the creature would be fifty feet, and from the top of its back to the water would be seventeen to eighteen feet. It was of great bulk. The body was light brown in colour."

Source: Heuvelmans, *In the Wake of the Sea Serpents*.

***Sumatra* sea serpent** Sometime in October or November 1877, officers aboard the vessel *Sumatra* allegedly saw a SEA SERPENT in the Red Sea, offshore from Mocha, Yemen. Sadly, they did not record any description for the creature—a lapse made doubly curious by the fact that Captain Anderson, commanding the ship, had seen another large marine cryptid in 1861, while piloting the *DELTA*.

Source: Heuvelmans, *In the Wake of the Sea Serpents*.

Sumatran Hummingbird According to modern science, hummingbirds (Family *Trochilidae*) are found only in the western hemisphere, where the smallest species—and the smallest living BIRD on Earth—is recognized as the 2.24-inch bee hummingbird (*Mellisuga helenae*) of Cuba. It was no small surprise, then, when Otto and Nina Irrgang reported sightings of a new species roughly half that size, from the Indonesian island of Sumatra. The Irrgangs allegedly sighted the tiny birds twice during 1957-58, including one incident where an insect-sized specimen hovered within a foot of their faces. They described the bird as 1.5 inches long, with a striped yellow back and brown underside. No recognized Indonesian bird precisely matches that color pattern, and the smallest known birds on Sumatra measure 3.5 inches at maturity. Some skeptics believe the Irrgangs were deceived by an unidentified flying insect, while others dismiss their reports as a HOAX.

Source: Coleman, *Tom Slick and the Search for the Yeti*.

Summerland sea serpent In December 1950, Opal Lambert glimpsed a SEA SERPENT while working at the post office in Summerland, California, in southern Santa Barbara County. "I was stamping Christmas cards," she told reporters, "when I looked up and saw it swimming in circles about 200 yards from shore." Lambert claimed the creature's head and neck rose four feet above the water's surface, then submerged after roughly 10 minutes.

Source: Heuvelmans, *In the Wake of the Sea Serpents*.

Sumske Dekle The Sumske dekle ("forest girls") were once described as female HOMINIDS or WILDMEN of Croatia, where they sometimes adopted rude trappings of primitive civilization and were capable of mating with humans. How that might transpire is not entirely clear, since the creatures were described as wild and inarticulate, covered with black or red hair. It may be that circumstances similar to those surrounding ZANA in Georgia arose from time to time, but no specific cases are recorded and no alleged hybrid offspring are known. A typical sighting from 1870 involved the brothers Paurovic´, surprised one night by a Sˇumske dekle while sleeping in a stable at Severovac. The creature fled when they awoke, and the brothers gave chase without success, having no explanation for what they planned to do if they had caught their visitor. It seems peculiar that no male specimens are described, since both genders are required to perpetuate the species. Perhaps the Sumske dekle were female specimens of the widespread ALMAS or KAPTAR. In any case, they apparently fell prey

to man's violence, since Croatian sightings ceased entirely after World War I. Elsewhere in Eastern Europe, similar creatures have been called Divi-te (in Bulgaria), Divozenky (Czechoslovakia), Dziwo-zony (Poland), and Divji moz (Slovenia).

Source: Zvonko Lovrencevic, "Creatures from the Bilorga in northern Croatia," in Markotic and Krantz, *The Sasquatch and Other Unknown Hominoids*, pp. 266-273.

Sunda Islands Horned Cat While pursuing her long search for the ORANG PENDEK, Deborah Martyr also collected native descriptions of an unknown felid species said to inhabit Alor and Solor, in Indonesia's Lesser Sunda Islands. Witnesses describe the animals as similar in size and form to domestic CATS, but with short horns protruding from above each eye. No serious effort has yet been made to collect a type specimen.

Source: Shuker, "Blue tigers, black tigers, and other Asian mystery cats."

Sundberg, Jan-Ove (1947–) Swedish journalist Jan-Ove Sundberg has devoted his full-time attention to cryptozoology since 1997, when he founded the GLOBAL UNDERWATER SEARCH TEAM to investigate reports of LAKE MONSTERS. His efforts began modestly and close to home, with investigation of STORSJÖODJURET, the cryptid said to inhabit Sweden's Lake Storsjön. From that beginning, Sundberg soon expanded his program to include expeditions in Norway, Scotland and Ireland. In 2001 he roused controversy with announcement of plans to trap NESSIE, prompting angry reactions from locals at Loch Ness and supernatural curses from self-styled "King of the Witches" Kevin Carlyon. Some critics charged that Sundberg's on-camera confrontations with Carlyon trivialized the Loch Ness investigation, reducing the quest to a farce, and while Sundberg abandoned his trapping plans, he remained committed to identifying Nessie. On 19 March 2002, Sundberg was rushed to a hospital in Motala, Sweden, suffering from a critical condition described in various reports as diabetic neuropathy and/or a tumor on his spine. Rescued by "aggressive surgery," Sundberg emerged from rehabilitation with plans for another Loch Ness expedition in 2005. Meanwhile, he charted investigations for nearby Swedish lakes and worked with audio experts at the Fauna Communications Research Institute to enhance supposed recordings of the Norwegian cryptid known as SELMA. As Sundberg explained in a July 2003 interview, "In the years to come we will concentrate our search to Lake Seljordsvatnet, Norway, where I think we have our best chance to prove a family of unknown creatures. With the right team, the right sponsors and the right agenda it's now only a matter of time before we can prove that cryptids do exist."

Sources: Global Underwater Search Team, http://www.cryptozoology.st/; Lois Wickstrom, "Interview with Jan-Ove Sundberg, July 22, 2003." Nessie's Grotto, http://www.simegen.com/writers/nessie/jan4.htm.

Sundsbarmvatnet, Norway While LAKE MONSTER sightings from many Scandinavian lakes are relegated to ancient folklore, the same cannot be said of Sundsbarmvatnet, in Norway's Telemark County. A large aquatic animal, generally conforming to descriptions of those from other lakes across the country, was last seen there on 25 July 1976.

Source: Erik Knatterud, Sea Serpents in Norwegian Lakes, http://www.mjoesormen,no.

***Suntrana* sea serpent** In late April 1947, while operating the tugboat *Suntrana* on behalf of the Juneau Lumber Company, Lou Baggnon and his wife saw a SEA SERPENT in Security Bay, on Alaska's Kuiu Island (56°52' north latitude, 134°20' west longitude). Both witnesses agreed that the creature "had a flat, goggle-eyed head and was looping along through the water" with a series of vertical undulations.

Source: Heuvelmans, *In the Wake of the Sea Serpents.*

Surgeon's Photograph

On the morning of 19 April 1934, London gynecologist Robert Kenneth Wilson and companion Maurice Chambers were en route to a hunting excursion at Inverness, Scotland, when Wilson stopped his car beside Loch Ness, two miles north of Invermoriston. After an all-night drive, he needed rest. Wilson later described what happened next:

> I had got over the dyke and was standing a few yards down the slope and looking toward the loch when I noticed a considerable commotion on the surface some distance out from the shore, perhaps two or three hundred yards out. I watched it for perhaps a minute or so and saw something break the surface. My friend shouted: "My God, it's the Monster!" I ran the few yards to the car and got the camera and then went down and along the steep bank for about fifty yards to where my friend was and got the camera focused on something which was moving through the water. I could not say what the object was as I was far too busy managing the camera in my amateurish way.

Wilson made four exposures before the creature disappeared, then drove on to Inverness and delivered his photo plates to George Morrison, at Ogston's pharmacy, for developing. Two of the plates were blank, a third revealed the now-famous profile of NESSIE'S head and neck poised above the water, and the fourth captured the creature as it was nearly submerged. Against Morrison's advice, Wilson sold the best photo's copyright to the London *Daily Mail*, which published it for the first time on 21 April. (The dates are important, since later reports falsely claim that Wilson snapped his photos on 1 April, as an "obvious" April Fool's Day joke.) Morrison kept the second photo's negative and subsequently lost it, after making prints. The "sinking" shot would not be found again and published for another 20 years.

Over the next six decades, controversy swirled around the famous "surgeon's photograph" of Nessie. Skeptics universally conceded that Dr. Wilson was a man of unquestioned integrity, but they insisted that his photo showed a bird or otter bobbing on the surface of Loch Ness. TIM DINSDALE, PAUL LEBLOND and others reached a contrary conclusion, concluding from analysis of the photo that Nessie's visible neck must be at least four feet long. There the matter rested until March 1994, when two members of

Dr. R.K. Wilson snapped this famous photograph of Nessie in April 1934.

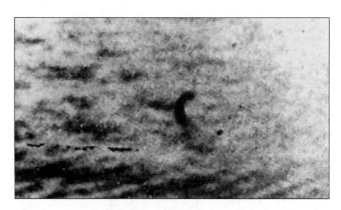

Debunkers ignore the second Wilson photograph, showing the alleged "model monster's" head in a very different posture.

ADRIAN SHINE'S Loch Ness Project, Alastair Boyd and David Martin, claimed to have proof that the famous photo was a HOAX.

Their story, in brief, was this: Sometime in 1991, 88-year-old Christian Spurling, variously named in press reports as a "photographer" or "modelmaking enthusiast," had confessed to faking the surgeon's photo in conjunction with his stepfather Marmaduke Wetherell, stepbrother Ian Wetherell and Maurice Chambers. Together, they had sculpted a 12-inch model of Nessie from "plastic wood," affixed it to a toy submarine, and with a 35mm Leica camera as it floated in a small Loch Ness inlet. After printing that photo, the jokers photographed the print with a quarter-plate camera and sent Dr. Wilson — now demoted from a man of impeccable honesty to a "veteran practical joker" — to have it developed in Inverness. Spurling died in November 1993, and was thus unavailable for questioning when Boyd and Martin broke their story four months later, roughly timed to coincide with the 60th anniversary of the famous photo's first publication.

In order to evaluate the "hoax" report — which swept the media in 1994 and is today uncritically accepted as established fact — some background is required. Marmaduke Wetherell was a self-proclaimed big-game hunter who wangled support from the *Daily Mail* for a Nessie-stalking expedition in December 1933. As one source at the *Daily Mail* later recalled:

> Wetherell promised us results before he had even left for Scotland. We took it all as a bit of a joke; I don't think anyone involved with the press of that era really understood the seriousness of the situation. People went Nessie-crazy. We received dozens of letters complaining about Wetherell — not him personally, but the "big game hunter" bit. Our readers actually thought that he was going to track it down, kill it and drag it back to Fleet Street. It was a great shame that things turned out as they did. I am sure the big-game hunter was only living up to his title: playing a big game.

On 23 December, Wetherell declared that he had found Nessie's footprints beside Loch Ness. On 4 January 1934, experts at the British Museum completed their analysis of Wetherell's two footprint casts and announced that both came from the right-rear foot of a hippopotamus, presumably a mounted specimen. (They were eventually matched to an umbrella stand.) It is unknown to this day whether Wetherell planted the tracks himself, but he was certainly embarrassed by exposure of the hoax. Ten days later, Wetherell claimed to have seen Nessie himself on 15 January, from the deck of the motorboat *Penguin*. No one else aboard saw the creature, but Wetherell's sponsors at the *Daily Mail* accepted his report that Nessie was a large gray seal (*Halichoerus grypus*) and nothing more. The expedition was dissolved, and Wetherell soon resigned from the Royal Geographical Society. If we believe Christian Spurling, the episode left Wetherell hungry for revenge, seeking to embarrass the very journalists who had mocked him in print.

But why, if payback was the game, would Wetherell and all of his accomplices but Spurling take the secret to their graves? The answer to that question may reside somewhere within a text on aberrant psychology — but it is only relevant if Spurling told the truth in 1991. And as it happens, there is ample evidence that he did not. Among the points ignored by journalists who covered Spurling's story, we must note the following:

(1) While Spurling's statement is frequently described as a "deathbed confession," he lived for at least two years after giving his statement to Boyd and Martin. We may rightly question why the hoax report was published only after Spurling's death, when he could not be cross-examined, and why the two "detectives" allowed various authors to claim that they "got the truth out of [Spurling] not long before his death." Any suggestion of an old man "clearing his conscience" at death's door is both inaccurate and deliberately misleading.

(2) The claim that Wetherell and company snapped their photo in a small Loch Ness inlet is plainly false. The surgeon's photo normally displayed in print is cropped from the larger original, which plainly shows a shoreline in the background. Wherever it was taken, the picture certainly was not staged in an inlet or backwater channel. Boyd and Martin's failure (or refusal) to identify the supposed inlet furthermore suggests, in journalist Richard Smith's words, "an unfortunate double standard of evidence."

(3) The *second* Wilson photo, revealing Nessie in a very different posture, is habitually omitted from accounts of Spurling's confession. Its existence effectively disproves the claim that a rigid model was used in the first photograph — and, in fact, Spurling himself apparently had no knowledge of the second photo's existence. When questioned about it, the *Ness Information Service Newsletter* reveals, "Christian was vague, thought it might have been a piece of wood they were trying out as a monster, but [was] not sure."

(4) Published claims that Dr. Wilson "gave only one interview after taking the photograph [*sic*]" and/or that he "retreated" from his original description of the incident are patently false. His testimony remained consistent from 1934 until his death in 1969.

(5) Various accounts describe the clockwork submarine as either 14 or 18 inches long. While small wind-up toys of that sort certainly existed in 1933-34, an exhaustive review of antique toy catalogs reveals none in the size range described by Spurling.

(6) Finally and decisively, research by KARL SHUKER and others has revealed that "plastic wood," the patented medium allegedly used by Spurling to concoct his Nessie model, did not exist in April 1934. Regardless of the motives behind his story or its long-delayed publication, the event could not have occurred as described.

On balance, the motives of Spurling, Boyd and Martin are less important than the media's reaction to their tale. Once again, as in the 1990 exposé of THREE-TOES and the coverage of BIGFOOT hoaxer RAYMOND WALLACE in 2001, we find "objective" reporters on every continent abandoning any semblance of critical thinking to take Spurling's tale at face value. Some went further still, inserting fabrications of their own. Stephen O'Meara, writing for *Omni* magazine in December 2000, states falsely of Tim Dinsdale's 1960 film that "when the Royal Air Force analyzed the film,

they concluded only that something, probably a motorboat, was moving in the water." In fact, as noted elsewhere in this volume, the RAF's analysts said the exact *opposite* of what O'Meara claims. They ruled out boats of any kind, surface or submarine, and concluded that Dinsdale's film depicted "an animate object."

Sources: Dinsdale, *Loch Ness Monster*; "Fake in the lake." *People* Patrick Huyghe, "Not necessarily Nessie." *Omni* 16 (September 1994): 78-79; LeBlond and Collins, "The Wilson Nessie photo: A size determination based on physical principles"; Stephen O'Meara, "The Loch Ness monster: Anatomy of a hoax." *Odyssey* 9 (December 2000): 20-24; Shuker, *In Search of Prehistoric Survivors*; Richard Smith, "The classic Wilson Nessie photo: Is the hoax a hoax?" *Fate* 48 (November 1995): 42-44.

Surrey Puma The panic engendered by this ALIEN BIG CAT of southern England during 1964-66 truly began in 1955, when a woman walking her dog near Abinger Hammer, Surrey, met a large CAT resembling a COUGAR (*Puma concolor*) crouched over the remains of a half-eaten calf. Four years later, a motorist passing Preston Candover in Hampshire saw "an enormous great cat padding across the road and into trees on the other side. It did not look like any domestic cat or dog, but was rather like a cross between the two. It had a cat's head and a short neck and was the size and colour of a yellow [L]abrador. Its tail was fairly long and its coat roughish-looking." Later that year, a taxi-driver at Aldershot claimed he saw a LION leap over a hedge outside Tweezledown Racecourse. Ernest Jellett saw "something like a big-cat" prowling near the Heathy Park Reservoir, on 16 July 1962. During the winter of 1962-63, a large cat paid repeated nocturnal visits to Bushylease Farm, between Crondall and Ewshot, Hampshire.

The predator returned to Bushylease on 30 August 1964, mauling a 450-pound bull. Officials from the Ministry of Agriculture blamed the wounds on barbed wire, while a local veterinarian believed a living predator was responsible. The barbed-wire theory was discarded on 7 September, when the first of many 5_-inch feline pawprints were found at a riding stable in Munstead. The cat slaughtered a deer at Cranleigh, Surrey on 23 September, and two policemen glimpsed it at Stoke Poges on 12 No-

The Surrey puma ranks among Britain's most famous cryptids.

vember. More sightings were reported from Nettlebed, Oxfordshire in November and from Ewhurst, Surrey in mid-December 1964. Hunts were organized throughout the region, but with no result. Authorities had 362 sightings on file by August 1966, when former police photographer Ian Pert snapped a picture of a large cat passing by a house in Worplesdon, Surrey, but the creature in the photo may have been a feral domestic cat.

While the Surrey Puma dropped out of headlines in 1967, KARL SHUKER notes that strange cryptid sightings resumed during 1971-73, including multiple reports of a supposed "black panther" in the area. Other unknown animals reported during that time frame included large cats in various shades of brown and a dog-sized creature described as possessing a long tail, large feet, and "an ugly cat-like face." None was ever captured or identified.

Sources: McEwan, *Mystery Animals of Britain and Ireland*; Shuker, *Mystery Cats of the World*.

Sutherland sea serpent

During September 1873, a SEA SERPENT appeared three times off the coast of Sutherland, in northern Scotland. The first sighting occurred on 16 September, while Lady Florence Gower and a companion were riding in a carriage along the seashore, eight miles east of Dunrobin. Gower vaguely described the creature as a long, large animal, while her friend thought it might have been a wave. The next day, a physician named Souter saw the beast from his home in Golspie, as it swam near shore. He claimed it was 40-50 feet long and raised

The Sutherland sea serpent, after witness James Joass.

its neck 4 feet above the water's surface. (Still a skeptic, he told his family at breakfast, "If I believed in sea serpents, I should say I have seen one this morning.") The final witness, the Rev. James Joass of Golspie, was an amateur archeologist. He learned of the first two sightings on 17 September, before glimpsing the creature himself. As he later described that occasion to a friend:

> Next day at noon [18 September], on a calm sea, I saw through a glass, about a half mile out, a floating object, which was certainly part of some sort of beast, dead or basking. It drifted along with the tide, and suddenly disappeared near the curing shed. At no time did it raise itself higher than when first seen. Colour brown and light yellow; apparent size seen, about 8 ft. or 10 ft. It was watched for half an hour, and two sketches made here.

Despite the lack of detail in his report, Joass opined that the creature, when finally identified, would prove to be a prehistoric PLESIOSAUR.

Source: Heuvelmans, *In the Wake of the Sea Serpent*.

Suwarro Atoll carcass

Suwarro is the southernmost atoll of the Northern Cook Islands (Polynesia). In spring 1899, sailors aboard the *Emu* were passing Suwarro when they saw a 60-foot carcass floating on the surface of the ocean. They hauled a portion of the body ashore for closer examination, reporting that

the 3-foot-long head resembled that of a horse, with only two teeth in the lower jaw. The remaining skin was brown and covered with hair. The creature's ribs were 2.5 feet long, attached to a spine 4 inches in diameter. Most researchers now believe the carcass belonged to a beaked whale (Family *Ziphiidae*), though the species remains uncertain.

Source: Heuvelmans, *In the Wake of the Sea Serpents*.

Svartsjön, Sweden

Sometime in the 1860s, witnesses Kalle Gustavsson and Adolf Tancred allegedly saw a serpentine LAKE MONSTER 15-20 feet long basking near a stream that feeds this lake, in Dalarna County. They said the creature was brown, with horns on its head and a flowing mane on its neck. No modern sightings are recorded from Svartsjön.

Source: Global Underwater Search Team, http://www.cryptozoology.st/.

Svarttjärn, Sweden

One of Sweden's more recent LAKE MONSTER sightings was reported from this lake, near Varmdolandet in Stockholm County, in 1933. Witnesses offered familiar descriptions of an animal resembling a capsized boat on the lake's surface. Size was not specified, but Svarttjärn's maximum recorded depth of 15 feet precludes any giant cryptids.

Source: Global Underwater Search Team, http://www.cryptozoology.st/.

Swan Lake, Michigan

Tucked away in the heart of upper Michigan's Hiawatha National Forest, 52-acre Swan Lake produced a curious LAKE MONSTER report on 15 August 1946. Investigators reported that the animal seen swimming in the lake that afternoon was actually a cow.

Source: "No such animal." *Doubt* 17 (1947): 260.

Sykesville Monster

Sykesville, Maryland lies 20 miles northwest of Baltimore, in Carroll County. Sightings of an unknown BIGFOOT-type HOMINID in the area date from the late 19th century, when author Jesse Glass Jr. recorded encounters with the so-called Apple Creature. More reports were logged in 1944 and 1958, when a woman reported that her dogs attacked a large ape-like beast, and that one of them died in the struggle. In 1959, a police officer saw the creature crossing a highway and called for it to halt. When it approached him, the patrolman fired his pistol with no apparent effect, then fled the scene. The next reports date from 1968, including a claim that two policemen were trapped in their car when the Sykesville Monster attacked them. Sporadic sightings continued through the early 1970s, with a concentrated spate of reports in May and June 1973. Thirty-odd witnesses in that "flap" agreed that the creature was 7-8 feet tall, weighing 350-400 pounds. After a 5-year hiatus, sightings resumed in 1978, expanding to include reports from Mount Airy, some 15 miles farther west. Residents there dubbed their unwelcome visitor the Mount Airy Marauder, but it did not stay for long. Summer 1979 found the beast back in Sykesville. Willard McIntyre reportedly fired on the creature in spring 1982, but the gunplay did not discourage a series of summer appearances in Patapsco Valley State Park. Dennis Volkman claimed to have videotaped a hairy biped in the park on 2 September 1986, and local sightings continued through 1987.

Source: Berry, *Bigfoot on the East Coast*.

Syrian Ostrich *see* Arabian Ostrich

Sysladobsis Lake, Maine

Nine-mile-long Sysladobsis Lake, located some 20 miles east of Burlington, Maine, sprawls over portions of Hancock, Penobscot and Washington Counties.

In the mid-19th century, local residents claimed the lake was occupied by an 8-foot SNAKE with a head resembling a dog's. No modern sightings of such creatures have been reported.

Source: Charles Skinner, *Myths and Legends of Our Own Land.* Philadelphia: Lippincott, 1896.

Table Rock Lake, Missouri
This lake, in southern Missouri's Stone County, was created when engineers dammed the White River in 1957. Like nearby Branson, Table Rock Lake is a modern tourist attraction, but it still produces reports of CATFISH 5-6 feet long. Some locals claim the elusive giant FISH are "as big as Volkswagens," but proof remains elusive. Bill Anderson, a biologist for the Missouri Department of Conservation, argues that the lake's depths are devoid of oxygen between October and December each year, but colleagues admit that the Table Rock dam "acts as a nutrient sink" for aquatic wildlife.

Source: Wright Thompson, "In pursuit of the giant catfish." *Kansas City Star* (6 July 2003).

Tabourie Lakes sea serpent
Tabourie Lakes is a town on the coast of New South Wales, Australia (south of Wollongong). In early February 1931, Walter Roots was fishing in the Tasman Sea from some seaside rocks at Tabourie Lakes, when he saw a SEA SERPENT offshore. The *Moss Vale Post* described his experience on 6 February.

> The animal, Mr. Roots said, was of a reddish-brown colour and was from 25 to 30 feet long. It had a head resembling a pig and just behind the head were two floppy arms. The body was similar to a huge barrel and the tail was vertical, like a ship's rudder. Most surprising features were the creature's eyes, which were protruding and appeared to be as large as saucers, and its teeth, which were sabre-like and fully six inches long. Mr. Roots says that the animal dived into the water and rose with a FISH in its jaws. The fore part of its body was lifted about five feet from the water and, swaying from side to side, the animal bit the fish in half and after chewing the portion dived after the other, bringing it to the surface and eating it also.

Though alarmed by the animal's sporadic emission of sounds "like the loud grunt of a pig," Roots watched it for 25 minutes until it swam out to sea. Two companions missed the show, but they later confirmed that Roots was visibly upset when he rejoined them.

Source: Smith, *Bunyips & Bigfoots.*

Tag
Tag is the supposed LAKE MONSTER of Tagai Lake, British Columbia (near Prince George). The lake is horseshoe-shaped, 35-40 feet deep except for one point where the bottom plummets to 150 feet. Fishermen have long described an unknown creature 10-12 feet long, briefly glimpsed in the water, including witness Phil Streifel's sighting of a black "something" swimming submerged in August 1976. Cryptozoologist JOHN KIRK suggests that the creatures are white sturgeons (*Acipenser transmontanus*), known to inhabit the system of rivers that feeds Tagai Lake.

Source: Garner, *Monster! Monster!*; Kirk, *In the Domain of the Lake Monsters.*

Tahitian Red-billed Rail
This small, black-and-white BIRD with a red beak and pink legs is known to science only from a painting made by naturalist George Forster, while he circled the globe with Captain James Cook in the 19th century. On the strength of that painting and Forster's description alone, the bird was named *Rallus pacificus*, but no specimen was ever collected and the species was deemed officially extinct in 1775. That judgment notwithstanding, Tahitian natives claim the birds—variously known to islanders as eboonaa, oomnaa and tevea—survived on the island of Mehetia well into the 20th century.

Source: Bille, *Rumors of Existence.*

Taiyuan sea serpent
In summer 1907, while crossing the Celebes Sea, a lookout aboard the steamer *Taiyuan* saw an object ahead which he took for a floating log. The ship changed course to avoid a collision, but as it drew closer, third officer S. Clayton realized the object was alive. He later wrote:

> Almost abreast now and no longer foreshortened, was stretched an enormous writhing serpent of fabulous size. Yet monstrous as it was, its proportions were as fine as our English Grass SNAKE, though the head may have been more angular and more boldly outlined. The creature so far as I could see, appeared to be a perfect replica of a land snake. It was at least seventy feet long, having a girth corresponding to its length for a snake. It was of a rather dark cane colour, (of course, I saw none of the underside) having uneven dark brown patches or figuring such as one might expect to find joined by concatenation on closer inspection. Its convolutions were not vertical as many illustrations used to depict them, but horizontal on a plane of the surface of the water: the serpent being just submerged only. Apart from its writhing motion I could gather nothing about its propulsion....It did not seem to panic at the very close proximity of the ship; but continued steadily along our side, its course being exactly opposite to ours. I have wondered if it could have been a PYTHON of staggering dimensions, something on the lines of the S. American ANACONDA, but far larger, crossing between the islands. Indeed, my private opinion of the serpent's length has always been eight feet, but I state it here as seventy purposely to err on the side opposed to exaggeration.

While the movements described by Clayton clearly indicate a reptilian physiology, no snake known to science attains even half of the *Taiyuan* SEA SERPENT'S reported length.

Source: Heuvelmans, *In the Wake of the Sea Serpents.*

Tallong Tiger
This ALIEN BIG CAT, also known as the Marulan TIGER, slaughtered sheep throughout the Southern Highlands of New South Wales, Australia from 1927 to 1930. Hunters failed to stop the CAT(S), and while no firm description was ever compiled, the references to a tiger suggest the cat's pelage was striped. Tigers (*Panthera tigris*) are not native to Australia, but the THYLACINE, a marsupial predator presumed extinct since the 1930s, did have a striped coat. After 1930, the predation abruptly ceased until "the cats came back" in 1968, for a new round of slaughter blamed on the KANGAROO VALLEY PANTHER.

Source: Healy and Cropper, *Out of the Shadows.*

Tanacth/Thanacth This strange cryptid of 16th-century India was described as a large, tailless primate resembling a TIGER in form and size. Witnesses claimed the Tanacth possessed a humanoid face and hands, with black hair on its head and tawny fur covering the body, while its hind feet resembled those of a big CAT. A specimen was reportedly captured and transported to the Middle East, where French traveler André Thevet saw it in the early 1570s. No modern reports of the Tanacth are on file.

Source: André Thevet, *Cosmographie Universelle*. Paris: L'Huilier, 1575.

Taniwha Maori natives describe the Taniwha as a kind of LAKE MONSTER inhabiting caves and swamps along the Waikato and Whanganui Rivers, on New Zealand's North Island. Witnesses describe the beast as resembling an oversized CROCODILE, but some also believe it serves as a guardian of various local landmarks, armed with supernatural powers to repel despoilers. At times, it was thought to act more directly, tipping canoes and devouring their occupants. In November 2002, Taniwha believers from the Ngati Naho tribe found themselves in conflict with highway engineers along the Waikato, north of Wellington. Tribal elders warned that the Taniwha might curse the project if it proceeded, resulting in needless traffic deaths. Maori spokesperson Brenda Maxwell further complained that engineers were "willing to trample on our culture" to cut highway costs. "Get away from the swamp," she warned. "It's as simple as that." Construction resumed after brief negotiations, and the Taniwha failed to make an appearance, but some tribesmen still blamed the creature(s) for mishaps along the highway. Meanwhile, some optimistic promoters suggested that the Taniwha might become a draw for CRYPTOTOURISM, as NESSIE has in Scotland, and OGOPOGO in British Columbia. At press time for this work, no steps had yet been taken to cash in on the Taniwha controversy.

Sources: Jan Corbett, "Transit and the taniwha." *New Zealand Herald* (9 November 2002); T.W. Downes, "Maori mentality regarding the lizard and *Taniwha* in the Whanganui River area." *Journal of the Polynesian Society* 46 (1937): 206-224; Louisa Herd, "Don't be timorous about our beastie." *New Zealand Herald* (14 January 2003); "Hunting the taniwha—and Maori." *Sunday Star-Times* (4 February 2003); Ainsley Thomson, "Work to resume near one-eyed taniwha." *New Zealand Herald* (8 November 2002).

Tanjil Terror Few details are available concerning this ALIEN BIG CAT, reported from the vicinity of Tanjil, Victoria (Australia) in the first half of the 20th century. Unlike some other predators, described by witnesses as resembling LIONS (*Panthera leo*) or COUGARS (*Puma concolor*), the Tanjil Terror remains a tantalizing blank. No descriptions of it have survived, beyond its reputation for ferocity.

Source: Healy and Cropper, *Out of the Shadows*.

Tanna Dove In 1774, a single specimen of previously unknown dove was caught on Tanna Island, Vanuatu (in the South Pacific). The brown-backed BIRD with a reddish-orange breast was named *Gallicolumba ferruginea*, and that is the end of its story. No other specimen has ever been procured, or even seen by Western eyes. Its present status is unknown.

Source: Bille, *Rumors of Existence*.

Tano Giant In 1911, author Louis Bowler published the following account of a large, unclassified primate or HOMINID described by natives as the Tano Giant:

Far away in the primeval forests of the Upper Tano, in the Gold

Coast Colony [present-day Ghana], a strange tale is told by the natives of a wild man of the woods, who would appear from the description given to be a white APE of extraordinary stature and human instinct. The natives who live in the village near to the haunts of this freak of nature are terrified out of their wits. They barricade their doors at night, and place boiled plantains and cassava on the jungle paths leading into the village to propitiate him and appease his hunger. They declare he comes to the village at night, and only runs when fire is thrown at him. The women especially are almost scared to death, and go in a body to their plantain farms. It appears that two women while gathering plantains were confronted by this creature. One he seized and flung over his shoulder carrying her off; the other ran screaming with fright back to the village. No trace of the other woman has been found. Several children have been taken by this creature, their mutilated bodies found with the whole of their heads devoured.

The hunters and women who have seen this animal describe him as "past all man" in size; his arms they describe as thick as a man's body; his skin "all the same as a white man," with black hairs growing thereon. The hands have four fingers but no thumb, the head is flat, and, as they describe it, "left small for big MONKEY head," meaning that it was very near or like a large monkey's head. They say the mouth "was all the same as monkey with big teeth sticking out, and he carries a skin of a bush cow," which the natives say "he carries for cloth when small cold catch him," meaning he wraps himself up in it when feeling cold. A hunter tried to shoot him, but he smashed the gun and broke both the hunter's arms. Many other incidents are related of this terror of the Upper Plains.

Source: Louis Bowler, *Gold Coast Palaver*. London: John Long, 1911.

Tantanoola Tiger Between 1893 and 1895, a MYSTERY MAULER known as the Tantanoola TIGER raided farms around Tantanoola, South Australia, killing as many as 50 sheep per night. A local schoolteacher told authorities the creature had invaded his kitchen, then fled when he entered the room, declaring, "It was a tiger." Another frightened witness described the beast as "grinning, yellow and gleaming with satin stripes." The killing spree ended on 21 August 1895, after Tom Salt shot a night-prowling creature at Mt. Salt (18 miles from Tantanoola), but the mystery remains. The animal was stuffed and mounted in a glass case at the Tiger Hotel—but what was it? Some who viewed it described a "strange-looking dog," while others claimed the predator was an "Assyrian WOLF," allegedly stranded when the ship *Helena* sank nearby. As late as 1957, aged pioneer Alf Warman viewed the animal and exclaimed, "That's my dog," claiming he raised the bloodhound-deerhound mix from a puppy in the late 1880s, then gave it to friends in South Australia. All who saw the stuffed animal agree that it had no stripes. A curious footnote to the story involves rustlers David Bald and Robert Edmondson, who began stealing sheep around Tantanoola soon after Tom Salt shot his strange specimen. Sometimes, Bald and Edmondson left pools of blood behind, to blame the "tiger" for their crimes, remaining at large until they were caught in the act, in December 1910. In retrospect, some researchers believe the actual predator may have been a THYLACINE, while others blame an ALIEN BIG CAT.

Sources: Healy and Cropper, *Out of the Shadows*; Smith, *Bunyips & Bigfoots*.

Tantawanglo Tiger During the 1930s and 1940s, an ALIEN BIG CAT preyed on livestock around Tantawanglo, New South Wales, Australia. Researchers Paul Cropper and Tony Healy note that the region has a long history of diverse cryptid sightings, spanning the period from 1821 to the 1990s. Aside from the alleged TIGER, local residents have also reported sightings of black panthers, THYLACINES, and YOWIES.

Source: Healy and Cropper, *Out of the Shadows*.

Tapir Tiger   This unclassified CAT of Ecuador is described by witnesses as gray in color, six feet long, standing four feet high at the shoulder, with paws notably larger than those of a JAGUAR (*Panthera onca*). Its favorite prey is said to be TAPIRS. Witness Juan Bautista Rivadeneira allegedly sighted a specimen along the Río Morona in 1969. Ecuadorian natives consider the Tapir TIGER a distinct and separate species from the melanistic jaguar.

Source: Cryptid Felids, http://www.angelfire.com/bc2/cryptodomin-ion/felids.html.

Tapirs (Unclassified)   Tapirs (Family *Tapiridae*) are ungulates found in tropical regions of both hemispheres. They are the most primitive of Earth's large mammals, having change little in the past 20 million years. As odd-toed mammals (perissodactyls), tapirs are related to horses and RHINOCEROSES, but they more closely resemble pigs or anteaters. Four species are known to science, all of them presently endangered. The Malayan tapir (*Tapiris indicus*) is the largest known species, attaining 800 pounds in weight. The three Latin American species include Baird's tapir (*T. bairdii*), the Brazilian tapir (*T. terrestris*) and the mountain tapir (*T. pinchaque*). Some sources suggest, however, that other species may still be undiscovered.

In 1924, an officer in the Royal Dutch-Indian Army, K. Brevet, captured two unusual tapirs near Babat, Sumatra (Indonesia). Both were entirely black, whereas the Malayan tapir typically has a white "saddle" on its back and flanks. Both specimens died in captivity, and attempts to crossbreed them with normal Malayan tapirs failed. While some researchers viewed the two captives as melanistic specimens of *T. indicus*, Dutch zoologist K. Kuiper nonetheless classified them as a distinct subspecies in 1926, naming them *T. indicus* var. *brevetianus*. Unfortunately, no other black tapirs have been seen or collected in Asia over the ensuing eight decades. Meanwhile, in 1996-97, Dutch zoologist Marc van Roosmalen briefly glimpsed what he believes to be a new species of tapir in the Rio Madeira region of Brazil's Amazonas State. He was unable to capture a specimen on either occasion, and the new species remains unconfirmed.

Sources: Laurie Goering, "Amazon primatologist shakes family tree for new monkeys." *Chicago Tribune* (11 July 1999); K. Kuiper, "On a black variety of the Malay tapir (*Tapirus indicus*)." *Proceedings of the Zoologi-

cal Society of London* (July 1926): 425-426; The Tapir Gallery, http://www.tapirback.com/tapirgal/.

Tartar sea serpent   In 1892, near Bermuda, two officers aboard the British naval ship *Tartar* sighted a SEA SERPENT in the Atlantic Ocean, near Bermuda. They agreed to keep the incident a secret, "having due regard to the skepticism of the British public," and witness H.L. Fleet did not report the sighting until 1922, by which time he had retired from the Royal Navy as an admiral.

Source: Heuvelmans, *In the Wake of the Sea Serpents*.

Tasek Chini, Malaysia   This lake in Malaysia's Pahang State is allegedly inhabited by a LAKE MONSTER or giant SNAKE analogous to the NĀGA of Buddhist and Hindu mythology. Scientific expeditions have visited the lake, apparently without result. Tasek Chini is also a popular tourist resort, famous for the lush growth of lotus flowers that cover the lake's surface from June through September. A similar giant reptile, known as ULAR TEDONG, was said to inhabit Pahang's Tasek Bera through the early 1960s, but industrial pollution in that area has killed off most aquatic wildlife.

Sources: Dinsdale, *Monster Hunt*; Heuvelmans, "Annotated checklist of apparently unknown animals with which cryptozoology is concerned"; Kirk, *In the Domain of the Lake Monsters*.

Tasmanian Carcasses   Over a period of 119 years, between 1878 and 1997, the beaches of Tasmania yielded four carcasses of sea creatures whose identities remain speculative, at best. The first is known only from vague descriptions of its long, serpentine body, but BERNARD HEUVELMANS concluded (90 years after the fact) that it was probably a stranded oarfish (*Regalecus glesne*). He may have been correct, but the case is now impossible to prove.

In August 1960, rancher Ben Fenton and two of his employees were rounding up cattle near Sandy Cape, on Tasmania's west coast, when they found a large GLOBSTER on the beach. The hulking mass of tissue measured 17 feet 11 inches by 19 feet 6 inches, and weighed an estimated 5-10 tons. Fenton's party left the object where it was, but tides gradually moved it northward over the next 19 months. It was March 1962 before word of the globster reached Hobart, Tasmania and a scientific team was dispatched to examine the mass. Dogs and horses shied from its acidic smell, but the zoologists reported no clear evidence of decomposition. Instead, they found the mass covered with rubbery, hairy skin, lacking a head or any bones, with:

> five gill-like, hairless slits on each side of the front. There were also four large hanging lobes in front, with a smooth gulletlike orifice between the centre pair. The rim of the hind part of the creature had many cushiony flanges, each carrying a single row of sharp, pencil-like spines.

The cream-colored flesh could not be cut with a knife, but an axe severed various slabs for laboratory study. (The crude dissection was also filmed, but the film has been lost.) Strangely, no report was forthcoming, and a second team was sent on 16 March to retrieve further samples. Most of the object was gone by that time, but the inspectors described what remained:

> When laid out flat, the material was eight feet long, three feet wide, and ten inches thick.... It consists throughout of tough, fibrous material loaded with fatty or oily substances....The material did not contain any bones, spines, or other hard structures....[T]he hair-like material of the exposed surfaces was merely a consequence of desiccation and leaching of fat-filled fibrous material.

Unknown tapirs are reported from Brazil and Sumatra.

Initially, the analysts thought it was blubber, but tests revealed that the flesh consisted mainly of collagen, the primary component of connective tissue. The final report states merely that it comprised "a decomposing portion of a large marine animal." Bruce Mollinson, leader of the original investigative team, then announced that his tests had ruled out "a whale, seal, sea elephant, or squid." What, then, was left?

That nagging question echoed in November 1970, when Ben Fenton announced his discovery of another Tasmanian globster, 30 miles south of Temma. Reporters photographed another "hairy" mass of tissue on the beach, this one measuring 9 feet 8 inches by 3 feet 11 inches. This time, no scientists were willing to visit the scene or collect samples, preferring to ignore the find completely.

Tasmania's west coast was graced again in December 1997, this time by a globster stranded at Four Mile Beach, north of Zeehan. Conflicting reports described the mass as 12-20 feet long, 4-6 feet wide, and 3 feet high at the end loosely termed its "head." Several "flipper-like arms" were described and depicted in photographs snapped by the press. Local scientists offered the standard explanation from afar, declaring that the mass was "most likely" whale blubber, but Wildlife Service biologist Irynej Skira frankly told reporters, "We have no idea what it is." Tissue samples were taken for DNA testing, "to determine which species of whale was responsible," but no results of those tests had been published as of press time for this volume.

Sources: Dinsdale, *Monster Hunt*; "Mystery blob found in Tasmania." *Fortean Times* 109 (April 1998): 21; Ben Roesch, "Other cryptozoology news." *Cryptozoology Review* 2 (Winter-Spring 1998): 11-12; Smith, *Bunyips & Bigfoots*.

Tasmanian Devils (Mislocated)

The Tasmanian devil (*Sarcophilus harrisii*) is a carnivorous marsupial, roughly the size of a small dog. As implied by their common name, the creatures are officially restricted to the island of Tasmania, though fossil evidence shows that they once ranged over most of eastern Australia. Most zoologists insist the "devils" were hunted to extinction by Aborigines and dingoes (*Canis familiarus* var. *dingo*) before the 18th-century arrival of European settlers, but significant evidence to the contrary has been available for over a hundred years.

In 1855, a traveler known only as "Cambrian" found Tasmanian devils living in the provinces of New South Wales, Victoria and Western Australia. Forty years later, a breeding colony was reported from Lake Albert, New South Wales. A live specimen

was captured at Toobarac, Victoria in 1912, and another was caught in western Victoria 60 years later. Two more were killed by Victoria motorists in separate incidents, in 1991. A female specimen was caught alive at Balga, Western Australia in 1997. Thus far, most Australian zoologists have chosen to ignore the 19th-century reports, while maintaining that all latter-day specimens found on the mainland must be escapees from private collectors or animal smugglers. Private importation to the mainland is presently illegal.

Sources: Cambrian, "Notes on the natural history of Australasia." *Melbourne Monthly Magazine* 1 (1855): 95-101, 164-169, 360-362; "In search of Tassie devils." *Hobart Mercury* (19 August 2001); Karl Shuker, "Alien zoo." *Fortean Times* 109 (April 1998): 16.

Tatus *see* **Morcegos**

Tatzelwurm

The Tatzelwurm ("clawed worm," in German) is a large unclassified lizard encountered by witnesses throughout Europe's Alps. Observers describe it as a thick-bodied reptile, 1-4 feet long, with a blunt head, short legs and a stout tail. Many reports describe it as aggressive and venomous, some branding the lizard a prodigious jumper, while others claim that it wriggles along with only two legs. The Tatzelwurm's deadly reputation was enhanced in 1779, when climber Hans Fuchs died of a heart attack after meeting two specimens near Salzburg, Austria. A Swiss photographer named Balkin produced the only photo of a Tatzelwurm in 1934, but critics brand it a HOAX, employing a ceramic FISH.

A year before that incident, zoologist Jakob Nikolussi named the lizard *Heloderma europaeum*, and by so doing drew a tentative link to Earth's only known venomous lizards, the desert-dwelling Gila monster (*H. suspectum*) and Mexican beaded lizard (*H. horridum*). Reports of Tatzelwurm sightings continued into the 1990s, and two naturalists found the skeleton of a still-unidentified lizardlike creature in the Alps near Domodosola, Italy, in 1990.

Sources: Heuvelmans, *On the Track of Unknown Animals*; Magin, *Trolle, Yetis, Tatzelwürmer*.

Artist's conception of the elusive Tatzelwurm.

Do Tasmanian devils exist on Australia's mainland?

Some researchers believe the Tatzelwurm is an unknown legless lizard.

Tautphaus Park, Idaho Sometime in the early 1900s, a LAKE MONSTER was reported from an unnamed lake in this park, at Idaho Falls (Bonneville County). No further description is presently available, and no more recent sightings are on record.

Source: Coleman, *Mysterious America.*

Tavelsjön, Sweden This lake, in Sweden's Västerbotten County, has a maximum depth of 75 feet. It has no longstanding tradition of LAKE MONSTER reports, but witnesses reported a large creature resembling a capsized boat on 23 July 1943. That sighting appears to be the only incident on record.

Source: Global Underwater Search Team, http://www.cryptozoology.st/.

Taylor, Daniel Scott, Jr. (1940–) A former U.S. Navy submariner, Daniel Taylor designed and built the *Viperfish*, a yellow one-man mini-sub with on-board sonar, and brought it to Scotland in 1969, under auspices of the LOCH NESS INVESTIGATION BUREAU. He logged no sightings of NESSIE at the loch, but Taylor did report a strange event on one dive, which he described to the *Glasgow Herald* as follows:

I was about 130 feet down when I suddenly found that the bottom had been stirred up. I thought at first it must have been my own prop wash and I stayed there for a few minutes. Then I found I was facing up the slope and not down. An ordinary FISH could not have turned a two-ton submarine right round, and there were no currents. Something might have been sitting there and left in a hurry when it heard me coming. Unfortunately I did not have my forward sonar search going at the time.

Taylor left Scotland convinced that he had experienced a near-miss with Nessie. At home in South Carolina, he assured reporters that the LAKE MONSTER'S existence was "pretty well established. Not just one — probably between 20 and 50." While some observers claimed that his *Viperfish* inspired the Beatles song "Yellow Submarine," Taylor planned a return match at the loch. In October 1998 he announced plans to build a 30-ton, 4-man submarine called *Nessa*, fast enough to pursue fleeing cryptids and armed with a lance to collect tissue for DNA testing. The *Nessa*'s price tag ranged from $250,000 to $500,000 in various reports, financed by sale of Taylor's home, and while he planned to search Loch Ness again in summer 1999, unspecified setbacks have thus far prevented Taylor from realizing his dream. As of press time for this volume, he had not received permission for a new hunt from Scotland's Department of Agriculture and Fisheries, and Taylor's Nessa Project website is currently inactive.

Sources: Harrison, *The Encyclopaedia of the Loch Ness Monster*; Dave Moniz, "$500,000 dream: Inventor hunts for Scots' legend." *Christian Science Monitor* (20 October 1998); Loch Ness Monster, http://www.yowiehunters.com/crypto/reports/loch_ness_monster.htm.

Ta-Zum-A *see* **Shuswaggi**

Tchimose This amphibious primate or MERBEING of British Columbia was described by Lillooet tribesmen as having a humanoid face and two tails. It was also aggressive, sometimes tipping canoes and attacking their occupants. Researchers LOREN COLEMAN and PATRICK HUYGHE consider it identical to the reptilian "gill man" reported from THETIS LAKE in August 1972, further linking the Tchimose to accounts of the predatory CHUPACABRAS and the HOMINIDS reported from Louisiana's HONEY ISLAND SWAMP.

Sources: Coleman and Huyghe, *The Field Guide to Bigfoot, Yeti, and Other Mystery Primates Worldwide*; James Teit, "Traditions of the Lillooet Indians of British Columbia." *Journal of American Folklore* 25 (1912): 287-371.

Tcinto-Saktco Aboriginal tribesmen described the Tcinto-saktco ("long-horned serpent") as a reptilian creature with deerlike antlers, inhabiting various lakes and rivers throughout Alabama. No modern sightings are on record, but various other aquatic cryptids (including the MI-NI-WA-TU, WHITEY and the LAKE MONSTERS of WALGREN LAKE, NEBRASKA) are also said to have horns on their heads.

Sources: Mackal, *Searching for Hidden Animals*; John Swanton, "Religious beliefs and medical practices of the Creek Indians." *Annual Report of the Bureau of American Ethnology* 42 (1928): 473-672.

Tcipitckaam *see* **Ktchi Pitchkayam**

Teggie Llyn Tegid (or Lake Bala) is located in northern Wales, near the town of Gwynedd. The lake is 4 miles long and 250 deep at its deepest point. During World War I, Royal Navy officers reportedly stocked the lake with seals, imported for submarine detection experiments, and while none supposedly remain, LAKE MONSTER reports at Llyn Tegid date from the mid-20th century. Locals call their resident cryptid Teggie (or Anghenfil), and provide conflicting descriptions that frustrate attempts to identify the creature(s). Grocer John Rowlands glimpsed Teggie in the 1970s, describing an 8-foot-long creature whose head was the size and shape of a soccer ball. Soon after that sighting, lake warden Dewi Bowen reported a beast resembling a CROCODILE, but with two long humps on its back. More recently, in March 1995, brothers Andrew and Paul Delaney saw a small-headed NESSIE-type creature raise its long neck 10 feet above the surface of the lake. That report earned Teggie its first international media coverage. In autumn 1995, a Japanese film crew visited Llyn Tegid and hired a mini-submarine once used to explore Loch Ness, but they failed to catch Teggie on film. British researcher Nick Taylor had better luck in 1997, producing a videotape of the creature that remains controversial to this day. Some viewers believe the green animal depicted is too far out in the lake to be HOAXED, while others claim the beast looks "plastic" or man-made. Additional questions were inspired by Taylor's remarkable luck, viewing Teggie a few short months after he videotaped another unknown creature at LOCH LOMOND, Scotland.

Sources: Kirk, *In the Domain of the Lake Monsters*; Karl Shuker, "Teggie and the Turk"; "Teggie and other beasts of Bala." *Fortean Times* 82 (August-September 1995): 14.

Teh-Lma *see* **Yeti**

Tému The Tému ("short") is an unclassified primate or HOMINID reported from forested regions around Robertsport, Liberia. Vai tribesmen describe the creatures as hairy bipeds smaller than an average human, with prominent noses and a mane of longer hair on their heads (presenting the appearance of a beard). The Tému makes whistling sounds that some witnesses interpret as a means of communication.

Source: Heuvelmans, *Les Bêtes Humaines d'Afrique.*

Tenby sea serpent In March 1907, British newspapers reported that a crew of fishermen from Tenby, Wales, had seen "a monster FISH 200 feet long" while trawling in the English Channel. Strangely, although the creature supposedly had "four fins as big as sails," published accounts still maintained that "its general appearance was that of a SEA-SERPENT." Sixty years later, BERNARD HEUVELMANS concluded that "unless its dimensions have been very much exaggerated it sounds more like a HOAX."

Source: Heuvelmans, *In the Wake of the Sea Serpents.*

***Terrapin* sea serpent** In June 1896, officers and crew aboard the *Terrapin* sighted a SEA SERPENT in New Brunswick's St. Andrews Bay. Captain Brooks, commanding the vessel, reported the incident, but no detailed description of the creature has survived.

Source: O'Neill, *The Great New England Sea Serpent*.

Terror of Tedburn This ALIEN BIG CAT was reported from the neighborhood of Tedburn, Devon, England in the 1970s. Like most other such creatures, it evaded capture and remains unidentified today.

Source: Moiser, *Mystery Cats of Devon and Cornwall*.

Terror of Trods This ALIEN BIG CAT takes its popular name from the Roxby Trods, a sector of open land between Roxby and Winterton, in North Lincolnshire, England. Sightings date from December 2003, with witnesses agreeing that the CAT resembles a "black panther," roughly equal in size to a large dog. At nearby Brigg, police received a motorist's report that he had seen a large black cat pouncing on some smaller animal in a roadside field. On 4 January 2004, a hiker found large pawprints near the abandoned Cringlebeck Farm, outside Roxby, and while the tracks were photographed, no positive identification had been published prior to press time for this volume.

Sources: "'Big cat' warning." *Scunthorpe Telegraph* (29 December 2003); "Did trod prowler leave a mark?" *Scunthorpe Telegraph* (5 January 2004).

Teslin Lake, Canada This large Canadian lake, spanning the Yukon's border with British Columbia, produced a LAKE MONSTER report in June 1977. Witness Menno Bosma was fishing with two friends in daylight when he saw a dark-colored creature with black spots showing 25-35 feet of its back above the lake's surface. When Bosma approached in his boat for a closer look, the animal submerged and disappeared. No further sightings are on record.

Source: Kirk, *In the Domain of the Lake Monsters*.

Tessie Witnesses describe this supposed LAKE MONSTER of Lake Tahoe (on the California-Nevada border) as a brown, hump-backed creature 12-25 feet long. Legends of the beast, including Washoe tribal tales, have circulated since the 19th century, but most published sightings date from the mid-1980s. Police officers Kris Beebe and Jerry Jones glimpsed Tessie in June 1982, while they were water-skiing at Lake Tahoe. Other sightings with multiple witnesses were recorded in June 1984 and April 1985, and a tourist filmed Tessie in 1986. A scientific expedition to Lake Tahoe in 1984 reported "inconclusive" results. Andrew Navarro saw Tessie in 1991 and described it as follows to author JOHN KIRK:

The first thing that I saw was water shooting out of the lake, like when a whale blows water out of its blow hole. Then I saw the surface of the waterbeing disturbed by something underneath. This was followed by a hump of a brown creature which came out of the water. It moved around in a circle for a while and then it was gone. The movement of the creature was up and down, not side to side like a SNAKE.

Kirk himself visited Lake Tahoe in 1988 and observed "a number of strange waves in the lake that could not be explained as naturally occurring phenomena." Skeptics suggest that Lake Tahoe may be inhabited by one or more white sturgeon (*Acipenser transmontanus*), though no such FISH have been caught in the lake and their nearest confirmed habitat is the SACRAMENTO RIVER, 75 miles away. A Tahoe Tessie Museum, located at King's Beach, promotes CRYPTOTOURISM for visitors who tire of gambling at nearby Stateline, Nevada.

Sources: Kirk, *In the Domain of the Lake Monsters*; "Lake Tahoe monster filmed." *Fortean Times* 46 (Spring 1986): 25; McCormick, *The Story of Tahoe Tessie*.

Texas Bigfoot Research Center Organized in 1999, the Dallas-based TBRC is a self-described "team of highly motivated people," united "to undertake one of the most daunting tasks of the new millennium: the classification of the largest living primate as yet unknown to man." Its leaders regard the Lone Star SASQUATCH as "a sub-species of BIGFOOT inhabiting the forested regions of Texas." As detailed on the TBRC's Internet website, the group's goal is:

to venture into the study, observation and documentation of these animals' behavioral patterns in their natural habitat. Our research is conducted in a "totally benign" fashion, and in the least intrusive way possible. Our goal is not the killing of a specimen, but the study of living animals in their natural habitat. Our goals reach beyond the task of the taking of a specimen, to the providing of pertinent information about these animals behaviors to mainstream science.

Members of the TBRC pursue those goals via use of motion-sensitive infrared cameras, audio recordings of alleged Bigfoot calls, "and other methods which have yet to be disclosed." Director Craig Woolheater has been fascinated with Bigfoot since childhood, and claims a personal sighting near Alexandria, Louisiana on 30 May 1994. Husband-wife researchers Gino and Lori Napoli serve the TBRC as director of field operations and lead photographer, respectively. Honorary members include JOHN BINDERNAGEL and Arkansas resident Smokey Crabtree, best known for his writings about the FOUKE MONSTER.

Source: Texas Bigfoot Research Center, http://www.texasbigfoot.com/.

Texoma Bigfoot Research & Investigation Formerly known as SASQUATCH Unlimited, the TBRI is a small BIGFOOT research group based in northeastern Texas. Leader David Holley solicits eyewitness reports through his Internet website, regardless of the incident's location. Unlike various "no kill" research groups throughout the U.S., Holley and the TBRI seek "to provide the specimen which will prove [Bigfoot's existence] beyond all doubt."

Source: Texoma Bigfoot Research & Investigation, http://www.ratsnest.net/texoma/.

Teyu-Yagua The Teyu-Yagua ("alligator JAGUAR") was once described as an amphibious reptile resembling a DINOSAUR, inhabiting various lakes and rivers of Argentina. A ferocious predator, it included human beings in its diet whenever possible. On one occasion, in 1631, a Teyu-Yagua allegedly destroyed a fleet of canoes and devoured dozens of Guayrenos Indians. No modern report of the voracious creature are on file.

Sources: Anibal Cambas, *Leyendas Misioneras*. Misiones, Argentina: El Eco de Misiones, 1938; Picasso, "South American monsters & mystery animals."

Thasos sea serpent In spring 1916, while approaching the Greek island of Thasos, a party of sailors and fishermen experienced an alarming incident. A half-century later, witness E. Plessis described it as follows to BERNARD HEUVELMANS:

Coming from Salonica we were coasting along the west of Thasos when I saw on the starboard beam a periscope...heading in exactly the reverse direction. This periscope stood 5 to 6 feet out of the water, and moved at great speed, about 10 or 12 knots [12-14 mph]. I gave the "submarine warning." But we looked like a peaceful neutral fishing-boat, and the periscope did not alter course and seemed to disdain us. Several days afterwards the chief of the Naval Staff at Salonika...reprimanded me for giving the "submarine warning" when he was certain there were no German submarines in the area....I should add that the speed of this periscope was impossible, for neither the German submarines nor ours could do 6 knots [7 mph] submerged. I had forgotten this adventure when your [book] brought it to mind.

Plessis had recently read the French edition of Heuvelmans's book on SEA SERPENTS, and in retrospect decided that the "periscope" he saw had been an unknown creature's head and neck. Heuvelmans concluded that Plessis had seen a specimen of his hypothetical "long-necked" pelagic cryptid.

Source: Heuvelmans, *In the Wake of the Sea Serpents.*

Thetis Lake, Canada   While most Canadian LAKE MONSTERS conform to descriptions of similar creatures reported from Europe and the U.S., the beast sighted at Thetis Lake, British Columbia was described as a "gill man" or "cousin of the creature from the Black Lagoon" (see Appendix B), conforming to reports of LIZARD MEN from other locations. Witnesses Robin Flewellyn and Gordon Pike reported the first sighting of a scaly 5-foot-tall biped on 19 August 1972, and Flewellyn suffered a cut on his hand from one of six razor-sharp spines protruding from the creature's scalp. Police were still investigating that incident four days later, when Mike Gold and Russell Van Nice saw the thing on the opposite lake shore. They described it as having a "human" body covered with silver scales, large ears, the face of a "monster," and "a point sticking out of its head." Cryptozoologists LOREN COLEMAN and PATRICK HUYGHE consider the Thetis Lake creature a specimen of the aquatic primate known to Canadian natives as TCHIMOSE, further suggesting that it may be similar to the predatory CHUPACABRAS.

Sources: Coleman and Huyghe, *The Field Guide to Bigfoot, Yeti, and Other Mystery Primates Worldwide*; Kirk, *In the Domain of the Lake Monsters.*

The Thing   In summer 1993, during a night dive from the Anse Chastanet dive resort at Soufrière, St. Lucia, Felix Voirol saw a segmented worm the size of a moray EEL (Family *Muraenidae*). The creature—latter dubbed "The Thing"—vanished into a crevice of the reef on contact with light. Subsequent reports allege that photos have been taken of similar worms, but they have not been published. KARL SHUKER reports that partial specimens (all lacking heads) have been collected, but they remain unidentified today. Dr. Susan Marsden, an expert in polychaete worms at McGill University (in Montréal), suggests that The Thing may represent an unknown species of rock worm (Family *Eunicidae*) or members of a known species afflicted with gigantism.

Sources: Ben Roesch, "'The Thing': A cryptic polychaete of St. Lucia." *Cryptozoology Review* 1 (Summer 1996): 12-19; Shuker, "A supplement to Dr. Bernard Heuvelmans' checklist of cryptozoological animals."

***Thingvalla* sea serpent**   On 10 December 1886, crewmen aboard the Danish steamer *Thingvalla* and pilot boat No. 11 met a SEA SERPENT in the North Atlantic, 30 miles off Nantucket, Massachusetts. Captain Laub, commanding the *Thingvalla*, described the creature as a "queer whale," but James Hanman (skipper of the pilot boat) insisted that it was no cetacean known in that 19th-century whaling port.

Source: O'Neill, *The Great New England Sea Serpent.*

Thomas, Lars (1960–)   Danish ichthyologist Lars Thomas graduated from the University of Copenhagen in 1986, as a specialist in FISH morphology. His interests are not limited to ocean life, however, and a fascination with cryptozoology dating from his teens has led Thomas around the world in pursuit of various cryptids. In 1990, he led a team of six Danish students to Cornwall, England, seeking the elusive BEAST OF EXMOOR. While his party failed to sight that ALIEN BIG CAT, Thomas received a fecal sample collected by researcher Nigel Brierly, which contained hairs from a COUGAR (*Puma concolor*). Over the next decade, Thomas investigated mystery CATS in his native Denmark, searched for STORSJÖODJURET in Sweden, sought traces of the SISEMITÉ in Belize, and conducted an 18-month investigation of various cryptids in Australasia. While some of his findings have been published in English-language journals, most of Thomas's work is presently available only in Danish.

Sources: Coleman and Clark, *Cryptozoology A to Z*; Cornish Big Cats, http://www.scottishbigcats.co.uk/nigelsresponse.htm.

Thompson's Lake, Illinois   Authors LOREN COLEMAN and JOHN KIRK include this lake, near Havana (Mason County) on published lists of supposed LAKE MONSTER habitats, but no dates or details of sightings are offered.

Sources: Coleman, *Mysterious America*; Kirk, *In the Domain of the Lake Monsters.*

Thorskafjord, Iceland   An aquatic cryptid described as resembling "a large boat floating keep uppermost" was frequently reported from this fjord, on Iceland's northern coast, during the 19th century. Locals also claim that one of the creatures known as SKRIMSL came ashore in 1819, leaving tracks behind it on the beach.

Source: Costello, *In Search of Lake Monsters.*

Three-Toes   Three-toes is the name coined by IVAN SANDERSON for amphibious cryptids who left their curious tracks on beaches from Australasia to Argentina and New England. In each case, a creature possessing two large, 3-toed feet apparently left the ocean and waddled around on land, leaving footprints in mud and sand. The prints averaged 18 inches in length, and the beast(s) walked with a whopping 6-foot stride. In South Africa, where Zulu tribesmen called the creator of the tracks Silwane manzi, a tribal witch doctor was summarily executed for trying to mimic the tracks in an apparent HOAX. Witness Aleko Lilius photographed the creature's tracks and collected native eyewitness descriptions of an animal resembling a huge CROCODILE adapted for bipedal walking. Lilius himself had a near-miss with the predatory reptile, arriving in time to photograph a heap of feces that included many FISH bones. Seven years later, Lilius published an article describing another set of 3-toed tracks, this trail leading to mangled human remains.

The most famous spate of Three-toes sightings occurred in 1948, at Clearwater, Florida. Between February and October of that year, the creature(s) left numerous tracks on Florida beaches and river banks, the trails stretching from 100 yards to a mile in length. At least a dozen witnesses reported sightings of the beast itself, at different times. Two pilots from a local flying school, John Milner and George Orfanides, saw it swimming in eight feet of clear water, 200 feet off the shore of Hog Island. They described the animal as 15 feet long, with a "very hairy body, a heavy blunt head and back legs like an ALLIGATOR but much heavier. The tail [was] long and blunt." Two tourists, boating at Tarpon

Springs, saw a creature "having a head like a RHINOCEROS but with no neck. It sort of flowed into its narrow shoulders. It was gray and covered with short thick fur. It had short, very thick legs and huge feet, and from its shoulders hung two flippers. It didn't run into the water, or dive in; it sort of slid in half sidewise."

Ivan Sanderson carried out his own Florida investigation in 1948, filing a 53-page report with the New York *Herald Tribune* and the National Broadcasting Company. His study included detailed measurements of 3-toed footprints averaging 13.5 inches long and 11 inches wide on flat ground, separated by a stride ranging from 31 to 60 inches. More critical, in light of later claims, is the fact that the footprints altered in size over varied terrain, ranging from a minimum of 9.87 inches long to a maximum length of 13.5 inches. Where the creature scaled embankments, its feet were plainly flexed, leaving clawed toe prints with no trace of a heel. The prints were also impressed to different depths, depending on the soil's moisture and consistency. At one point, where the prints measured three-quarters of an inch deep, Sanderson noted: "We were unable to make any impression on this [soil] by stamping or even by throwing a 35-pound lead model of the imprints down upon it from a height of three feet." From his calculations and eyewitness interviews, Sanderson concluded (somewhat surprisingly) that the Florida Three-toes was probably a giant penguin, similar in form to *Palaeondyptes antarcticus*, a 7-foot creature whose fossils are found in New Zealand.

Fifteen years after Sanderson's death, in June 1988, Florida residents Tony Signorini and Al Williams approached the *St. Petersburg Times* with a claim that they had faked the 3-toed tracks in 1948. Together, they had fabricated a pair of 30-pound iron boots in the form of a DINOSAUR'S track, which Signorini allegedly donned to tramp along various beaches. Displaying the fake monster feet, Signorini explained, "I would just swing my leg back and forth and give a big hop. The weight of the feet would carry me. They were heavy enough to sink down in the sand." In 2000, author Mike Dash reported: "The boots per-

fectly matched the plaster cast of prints taken on Clearwater beach, proving that the affair was a hoax."

Or, was it?

As with the SURGEON'S PHOTO of NESSIE in 1934 and the claims of BIGFOOT hoaxer RAYMOND WALLACE in 2002, reporters eagerly swallowed Signorini's story, blaring it to every corner of the Earth and ridiculing Ivan Sanderson in the process. Mike Dash was typical, writing:

> The whole ridiculous business still retains the power to baffle. The principal puzzle is how a naturalist of Sanderson's standing could have allowed himself to be taken in by what was really a rather crude deception. When the tracks were found it was observed that they seemed to have been made by a jointless, flat-bottomed foot, and, while their size may have suggested that they were made by something much taller than a man, the distance between each print was not much more than a single human stride.

In fact, the "hoax" reports (and Dash's summary in particular) leave several glaring questions unanswered, while coping with others through shameless fabrication. Even ignoring the dozen witnesses who reported encounters with unidentified creatures along Florida's coast in 1948, we are left with multiple inconsistencies. First, the tracks were *not* all flat-bottomed and jointless, as claimed by Dash. Sanderson described multiple occasions when the feet were clearly bent, as noted above, showing no trace of heel in soft earth. It should be obvious that cast-iron feet cannot vary in size from one print to the next, but the Florida tracks routinely did so. Likewise, the image of Tony Signorini "hopping" to achieve a 5-foot stride in 30-pound boots (without smearing the prints) is absurd. Finally, the hoax scenario fails to explain how Signorini's boots produced _-inch impressions in packed sand where Sanderson and company could make no imprint with lead casts five pounds *heavier*, hurled at the ground from a height of three feet. On balance, while there seems to be no doubt that Signorini and Williams may have faked some 3-toed tracks in 1948, their responsibility for *all* such tracks found over an 8-month span is by no means established.

Sources: Dash, *Borderlands*; Jan Kirby, "Clearwater can relax: Monster is unmasked." *St. Petersburg Times* (11 June 1988); Bob Rickard, "Florida's penguin panic." *Fortean Times* 66 (December 1992-January 1993): 41-43; Sanderson, *More "Things."*

Thunderbird   Many cultures throughout the world feature legends of predatory BIRDS large enough to prey on human beings or much larger animals. One such creature, the North American Thunderbird, was apparently known to aboriginal tribes from Alaska to the Gulf of Mexico, under various names. Inuit carvings depict huge birds snatching whales from the sea, a trait confirmed by legends from the Pacific Northwest. Large prey, including killer whales (*Orcinus orca*), moose and caribou were allegedly grabbed without difficulty in the Thunderbird's powerful talons, then dropped over rocky mountain crags to effect a quick kill before feeding. Primitive rock art across the U.S. and Canada commemorates native encounters with huge birds that sometimes swept humans away to their mountaintop nests, from which only the bravest warriors ever managed to escape. Reported sightings by Amerindian witnesses continued into the late 19th century — and, indeed, reports of giant birds continue throughout North America to the present day.

Several Thunderbird candidates have been proposed by cryptozoologists. The largest known U.S. bird, the California condor (*Gymnogyps californianus*), is clearly too small, with a maximum acknowledged wingspan of 9 feet 4 inches. Candidates from pre-

Ivan Sanderson concluded that Florida's Three-toes was a giant penguin.

history include the largest flying bird known to science, *Argentavis magnificens*, a vulture of Late Miocene Argentina, presumed extinct for some 5 million years. *Argentavis* stood 5-6 feet tall at rest and weighed 158 pounds, soaring aloft with a wingspan of 23-25 feet. Two smaller relatives from North America, *Teratornis incrediblis* and *T. merriami*, boasted wingspreads of 19 and 12 feet, respectively. A long-shot reptilian candidate from Late Cretaceous North America, *Quetzalcoatlus*, was the largest known PTEROSAUR, with a 39-foot wingspan. That prehistoric reptile is named for Quetzalcoatl, the legendary flying serpent of the Aztecs.

Sources: James Deans, "The Thunder-bird." *American Antiquarian and Oriental Journal* 7 (1885): 357-358; Arlene Fradkin, *Cherokee Folk Zoology: The Animal World of a Native American People, 1700-1838.* New York: Garland, 1990; Hall, *Thunderbird!*; Alanson Skinner, "The Algonkin and the Thunderbird." *American Museum Journal* 14 (1914): 71-72.

Thunderbird Photo   The 40-year pursuit of this artifact, said to prove the existence of the legendary THUNDERBIRD (or something equally remarkable) is a classic case study in the frustration suffered by cryptozoologists. The story begins, in fact, with an article published in the Tombstone (Arizona) *Epitaph* on 26 April 1890, which read:

A winged monster, resembling a huge ALLIGATOR with an extremely elongated tail and an immense pair of wings, was found on the desert between Whetstone and Huachuca mountains last Sunday by two ranchers who were returning home from the Huachucas. The creature was evidently greatly exhausted by a long flight and when discovered was able to fly but a short distance at a time. After the first shock of amazement had passed the two men, who were on horseback and armed with Winchester rifles, regained sufficient courage to pursue the monster and after an exciting chase of several miles succeeded in getting near enough to open fire with their rifles and wounding it. The creature then turned on the men, but owing to its exhausted condition they were able to keep out of its way and after a few well directed shots the monster partly rolled over and remained motionless. The men cautiously approached, their horses snorting in terror, and found that the creature was dead. They then proceeded to make an examination and found that it measured about 92 feet in length and the greatest diameter was about 50 inches. The monster had only two feet, these being situated a short distance in front of where the wings were joined to the body. The head, as near as they could judge, was about 8 feet long, the jaws being protruding about half way from the head. They had some difficulty in measuring the wings as they were partly folded under the body, but finally got one straightened out sufficiently to get a measurement of 78 feet, making the total length from tip to tip about 160 feet. The wings were composed of a thick and nearly transparent membrane and were devoid of feathers and hair, as was the entire body. The skin of the body was comparatively smooth and easily penetrated by a bullet. The men cut off a portion of the tip of one wing and took it home with them. Late last night one of them arrived in this city for supplies and to make the necessary preparations to skin the creature, when the hide will be sent for examination by the eminent scientists of the day. The finder returned early this morning accompanied by several prominent men who will endeavor to bring the strange creature to this city before it is mutilated.

The desert DRAGON never arrived in Tombstone, and the sensational story — including total anonymity of all concerned — has the feel of a belated April Fool's HOAX. It might have rested there and been forgotten, but for author Jack Pearl. In the May 1963 issue of *Saga* magazine, Pearl published an article describing an

A hoax version of the Thunderbird photograph, purporting to show a pterodactyl killed by Civil War soldiers.

incident from 1886, wherein the *Epitaph* allegedly "published a photograph of a huge BIRD nailed to a wall. The newspaper said it had been shot by two prospectors and hauled into town by wagon. Lined up in front of the bird were six grown men with their arms outstretched. The creature measured about 36 feet from wingtip to wingtip."

Pearl's article raised several issues. First, he described the slaying of a giant bird, rather than a much larger reptile. Second, he placed the event four years ahead of the *Epitaph*'s famous dragon story, suggesting either an error or two distinct and separate events. (The desert dragon goes unmentioned in Pearl's story.) It was the description of a photo, however, that caused the greatest furor. *Epitaph* staffers received countless queries about the supposed Thunderbird photo, finally scanning back issues in vain for any such picture. If the photo existed, it must have been published somewhere else. Pearl was clearly mistaken, at least on that point.

Rumors concerning the Thunderbird photo still circulate widely in Fortean circles. Several researchers, including JOHN KEEL, insist that they have seen the picture, but none recalls exactly where or when. One story claims that IVAN SANDERSON displayed the photo on an unnamed television program in the 1960s, then lost it and spent the rest of his life seeking another copy. Searches of various men's magazines and newspaper archives led to similar dead-ends. Author Larry Thomas claims to have seen the photo in 1980, in a book of Old West photographs whose title he's forgotten, though the picture "burned itself into my mind's eye, and I feel that its accuracy is quite high." (His sketch of the alleged photo reveals a dozen men holding a lifeless bird of indeterminate species, wings outstretched to 20 feet or more.) KARL SHUKER suggests that various researchers have confused their memory of a photo showing African hunters with a dead stork, widely published in the 1960s and early 1970s. Various photos have been faked along the way, by obvious cut-and-paste techniques or more sophisticated Internet technology, but the "real thing" (if it ever existed) remains elusive.

Sources: Bord and Bord, *Alien Animals*; Mark Chorvinsky, "The search for the Thunderbird photo continues." *Strange Magazine* 15 (Spring 1995): 44; Clark and Pear, *Strange & Unexplained Phenomena*; Hall, "Thunderbirds are go"; Harry McClure, "Tombstone's flying monster." *Old West* (Summer 1970): 2; Jack Pearl, "Monster bird that carries off human beings." *Saga* (May 1963): 29-31, 83-85; Larry Thomas, "The search for the Thunderbird photo." *Strange Magazine* 18 (Summer 1997):

34-35; Shuker, *In Search of Prehistoric Survivors*; Shuker, "The search for the Thunderbird photo continues."

Thylacine   The thylacine (*Thylacinus cynocephalus*) was a doglike marsupial predator, native to the Australian island of Tasmania. Its name derives from the Greek *thylakos* ("leather pouch"), but the animal's striped coat made "Tassie TIGER" a more popular nickname among settlers (who also dubbed it the "zebra wolf," "tiger-wolf" and "hyena"). Despised for their killing of sheep, thylacines were ruthlessly hunted from the 1820s onward. The Van Dieman Land Company offered a bounty for "tiger" pelts in 1830, followed by the Tasmanian government in 1888. Over the next 21 years, before the bounty system was repealed, at least 2,898 thylacines were slaughtered in Tasmania. The last confirmed shooting occurred in May 1930, and three years later, Elias Churchill trapped the last known wild specimen in the Florentine Valley. Hunting of thylacines was banned by law in July 1936, but the move came too late. The last known specimen on Earth died two months later, after negligent keepers left it exposed to inclement weather at the Hobart Domain Zoo.

After the fact, some Tasmanian settlers regretted the thylacine massacre. In 1937, public officials proposed the establishment of a wildlife refuge in southwestern Tasmania, and two expeditions were launched in 1937-38 to find any surviving thylacines. Both parties reported numerous thylacine tracks, but no living animals were found. Still, sightings continue on Tasmania to the present day, accompanied by occasional discovery of tracks. Researcher Steven Smith collected 315 thylacine sightings on Tasmania between 1936 and 1980, of which he judged 103 to be "good." Paul Cropper and Tony Healy raised the number beyond 400 sightings by 1994, with half of those involving multiple witnesses. Several photos of a supposed thylacine were snapped from a helicopter near Birthday Beach, in 1957, but the pictures were inconclusive. Several Tasmanian hunters claim to have trapped or shot thylacines between 1948 and 1953, but no evidence of their illegal actions was preserved.

While Tasmanian researchers cast their nets for a living thylacine, more witnesses claimed sightings of the Tassie tiger on mainland Australia. It is known that thylacines once inhabited the island continent: a mummified carcass was found in Western Australia, in 1966, and thylacine fossils surfaced in South Australia during August 2001. Still, scientists presume that the creatures died out sometime between 1000 B.C. and 1788 A.D., killed off by aboriginal huntsmen and their imported dingoes. That official

Sightings of the "extinct" thylacine continue throughout Tasmania and mainland Australia.

verdict, however, does not prevent thylacines from appearing to numerous witnesses. By 1994, Cropper and Healy had collected some 500 sightings, spanning the continent and six decades. Witness Rilla Martin photographed an apparent thylacine near Goroke, Victoria in 1964. Twenty years later, Kevin Cameron snapped two photos of another specimen near Yoongarillup, Western Australia. (All photos taken to date are disputed by skeptics.) In August 2003, an inquiry conducted under Australia's Freedom of Information Act revealed 20 sightings reported from parkland within 13 miles of downtown Sydney. Wildlife biologist Nick Mooney told reporters that same year, "I still get occasional sighting reports by people I implicitly trust. They're subjective but still compelling." Government officials, meanwhile, compare thylacine reports to sightings of Elvis Presley and brand the phenomenon a "mass sociogenic illness." In May 2002, scientists at Sydney's Australian Museum announced their plan to clone thylacines, using DNA extracted from a cub preserved in alcohol since 1866. (Melbourne DNA expert Janette Norman promptly dismissed the scheme as "fantasy.") Cryptozoologists, meanwhile, remain hopeful that live thylacines may yet be discovered in the wild. Some believe relict thylacines may explain a number of Australia's ALIEN BIG CAT sightings, such as the case of the TANTANOOLA TIGER.

Sources: Beresford and Bailey, *Search for the Tasmanian Tiger*; Simon Bevilacqua, "Credible sightings keep hopes alive." *The Mercury* (6 July 2003); Bille, *Rumors of Existence*; Cropper and Healy, *Out of the Shadows*; Douglas, "The thylacine: A case for current existence on mainland Australia"; "Extinct Australian tigers 'alive and well.'" *Ananova* (18 August 2003); Tanya Giles, "Tigers lurk in the suburbs." *Sydney Herald Sun* (19 August 2003); Guiler, *Thylacine*; Wayne Miller, "Tasmanian tiger clone a fantasy: scientist." *The Age* (22 August 2002); Luke Sayer, "Tassie tiger alert after reported bush sighting." *The Mercury* (21 June 2002); Slee, *The Haunt of the Marsupial Wolf*; Smith, *Bunyips & Bigfoots*; "Tassie tigers 'as likely as Elvis.'" ABC News (20 August 2003); "Thyla seen near CBD?" *Sydney Morning Herald* (18 August 2003); "Thylacine fossil in SA could 'rewrite history.'" Australian Associated Press (28 August 2001).

Tianchi Lake, China *see* **Guài Wù**

Tiber River, Italy   In the 6th century, a DRAGON whose body resembled a huge beam of wood was allegedly seen near Rome, during a flood on the Tiber. No further information on the sighting is available today.

Source: Gulielmus Durantis, *Rationale Divinorum Officiorum*. Augsburg, German: Günther Zainer, 1470.

Tigelboat   In November 1975, the Antara News Agency announced that native villagers in Kalimantan (Indonesian Borneo) had captured a curious quadruped known as the Tigelboat. As described in the report, this creature had a TIGER's body, the legs of a goat and clawed feet of a chicken, with a "leonine" neck, a cow's ears, a goatlike beard, and a trunk resembling an elephant's. It was kept alive briefly in a jail cell at Tenggarong, but it died and was disposed of without scientific examination. Nonetheless, KARL SHUKER has offered a reasonable suggestion for the creature's identity, proposing a juvenile specimen of Malayan TAPIR (*Tapirus indicus*). Although presumed extinct on Borneo for some 10,000 years, *T. indicus* may yet survive in some remote corner of the jungle island. Young specimens are striped (perhaps reminding untrained observers of a tiger), relatively slender legs, a mane of sorts, bovine ears and an abbreviated trunk.

Sources: Shuker, *From Flying Toads to Snakes with Wings*; Shuker, *In Search of Prehistoric Survivors*.

Tigers (Blue)

In September 1910, Methodist missionary Harry Caldwell experienced a startling encounter with a most unusual CAT in the Futsing region of southeastern China's Fujian Province. Between sermons, Caldwell was also a veteran big-game hunter who bagged dozens of tigers (*Panthera tigris*), but the specimen he saw that afternoon was unique in his experience. Fifteen years later, Caldwell described it as follows:

> The markings of the animal were marvellously beautiful. The ground colour seemed to be a deep shade of maltese, changing into almost deep blue on the under parts. The stripes were well defined, and so far as I was able to make out similar to those of a tiger of the regular type.

Beauty notwithstanding, the Rev. Caldwell was prepared to kill the beast when he spied two children in his line of fire and resisted the urge. Writing of the experience in 1925, Caldwell claimed a second sighting of the creature and noted other reports of blue tigers from the same part of China (amplified in 1986 by BERNARD HEUVELMANS).

Sources: Roy Andrews, "The trail of the blue tiger." *North American BioFortean* Review 6 (May 2001): 80-91; Caldwell, *Blue Tiger*; Heuvelmans, "Annotated checklist of apparently unknown animals with which cryptozoology is concerned"; Shuker, *Mystery Cats of the World*.

China allegedly harbors blue tigers (*William Rebsamen*).

Tigers (Melanistic)

Feline melanism occurs most often in tropical species, especially the leopard (*Panthera pardus*) and JAGUAR (*Panthera onca*), whose melanistic specimens are commonly known as "black panthers." Curiously, no melanistic tiger (*Panthera tigris*) has yet been documented by science, but reports

Though undocumented by science, melanistic tigers are reported from various Asian countries (*William Rebsamen*).

of black tigers have emerged from Asia since the 18th century. In 1772, British artist John Forbes painted a black tiger shot in southwestern India and displayed in his presence. An accompanying note from Forbes explained that:

> It was entirely black yet striped in the manner of a Royal-Tyger, with shades of a still darker hue, like the richest black, glossed with purple. My pencil is very deficient in displaying these mingled tints; nor do I know how to describe them better than by the difference you would observe in a black cloth variegated with shades of rich velvet.

That painting was sold to an unknown owner in 1965, and is presently unavailable for study. Fourteen years after Forbes produced it, an "all-black Tiger from the East Indies" was allegedly displayed at the Tower of London, but again, no evidence remains. In 1844, another black tiger (this one from Java) was reportedly displayed at London's St. James's Church, en route to the court of Napoléon Bonaparte. Two years later, naturalist C.T. Buckland reported that a black tiger had slaughtered cattle and at least one human being in India's Chittagong Hills (present-day Bangladesh). Buckland saw that CAT, after a villager killed it, and he described it as follows:

> It was a full-sized tiger, and the skin was black, or very dark-brown, so that the stripes showed rather a dark black in the sunlight, just as the spots are visible on the skin of a black leopard ….No doubt was expressed about the animal being a black tiger.

Unfortunately, that specimen was so far decomposed by the time Buckland saw it, that the skin could not be preserved. Hunters reported a black tiger from southern India's Cardoman Hills, in September 1895, but it escaped. Forest ranger T.A. Hauxwell claimed to have wounded a black tiger in Myanmar, during 1914, but the animal escaped and was not recovered. Another dead specimen, likewise badly decomposed, was reported from the Lushai Hills of Assam (India) in 1928. A "black tiger" captured near Dibrugarh, India on 4 September 1936, proved on closer examination to be a melanistic leopard. A chocolate-brown tiger skin was allegedly displayed at a British commissioner's home in Betul, India, in 1937, but it too has been lost. In 1952, a huge black tiger raided cattle herds at a remote Indian village. Natives described the beast as 20-24 feet long, and while authorities found large pug marks, they never saw the animal itself.

Despite those disappointments, evidence exists that tigers sometimes appear with very dark coats. One such was born to normal parents in the early 1970s, at the Oklahoma City Zoo. Director Warren Thomas described the cub to KARL SHUKER as having:

> a normal ground color, but considerable darkening over the shoulders, down both front legs, over the pelvis, and encompassing both back legs. The darkening was essentially the same coloring as the stripes. Over the areas of darkening, the stripes were only partly visible.

Sadly, the cub was killed by its mother soon after birth, but its body was preserved in formalin and verifies the published description. Between 1961 and 1988, four separate reports of tigers with uniform brown coats emerged from the Similipal Tiger Reserve, in eastern India's Orissa State. In October 1997, cryptoartist WILLIAM REBSAMEN informed Shuker that he had seen a photo of a black tiger, some 20 years earlier, in a book about the Ringling Brothers Circus. (The search continues for that volume, its title presently unknown.) A month after that revelation, Shuker learned of two more quasi-melanistic specimens from Lala Singh, chief research officer at the Similipal Reserve. One was a tigress killed in self-defense at Podagad, in July 1993; the other was a skin confiscated from a hunter and delivered to India's National Museum of Natural History in February 1993. As described by Singh, "The major peculiarity in the body colouration was that the coat had a black background with tawny stripes on the back, and white stripes on the ventral side."

Sources: S.R. Sagar and L.A.K. Singh, "Tiger without stripes." *Indian Forester* 115 (1989): 277-278; Shuker, "Black is black...isn't it?"; Karl Shuker, "Menagerie of mystery." *Strange Magazine* 19 (Spring 1998): 23, 54; Shuker, *Mystery Cats of the World*; Singh, *Born Black: The Melanistic Tiger in India.*

Tigers (Mislocated)

Tigers are the largest CATS in Asia, found in various subspecies from Siberia through the Indian subcontinent and Southeast Asia to Sumatra, Indonesia. Five subspecies are currently known to exist. They include the Bengal tiger (*Panthera tigris tigris*), found in India, Nepal, Bangladesh, Bhutan and Myanmar; the Siberian (or Amur) tiger (*P. t. altaica*), of Siberia, northeastern China and North Korea; the South China tiger (*P. t. amoyensis*), with 20-30 wild specimens surviving in central and eastern China; the Indochinese tiger (*P. t. corbetti*), found in southern China, Myanmar, Cambodia, Laos, Vietnam and peninsular Malaysia; and the Sumatran tiger (*P. t. sumatrae*), confined to Sumatra. Three other subspecies are presumed extinct, though certain evidence suggests they may survive. Those include the BALI TIGER (*P. t. balica*), the CASPIAN TIGER (*P. t. virgata*), and the JAVAN TIGER (*P. t. sondaica*).

Tigers found living wild outside their normal range qualify as ALIEN BIG CATS, and reports are more common than skeptics care to admit. Locations with reports of mislocated tigers on file include the following:

Afghanistan— Afghan natives blamed U.S. servicemen for releasing ferocious Pisho Palang ("tiger cats") on the Shomali plains north of Kabul, in August 2003. One Kabul magazine headlined the story with a claim that "in Shomali, dangerous animals are eating people." As the story spread, multiple sightings and vicious attacks were reported. U.S. authorities denied the rumors, claiming any tigers found in Afghanistan must have crossed the mountains from neighboring China. No specimens have yet been produced for study, but alleged witness Mohammed Yakob insisted, "Before this new Army came here, we didn't have these cats."

Australia— Reports of large, striped cats have been filed from various parts of Australia since the 19th century. Those covered elsewhere in this volume include the JAMBEROO TIGER, the MARU-

Tiger sightings beyond the cats' normal range remain unexplained.

LAN TIGER, the TALLONG TIGER, the TANTANOOLA TIGER and the TANTAWANGLO TIGER. Some researchers believe that Australian tiger reports may in fact represent sightings of surviving THYLACINES or marsupial LIONS (*Thylacoleo carnifex*), presumed extinct for some 10,000 years.

Borneo— While tigers are officially restricted to the Indonesian island of Sumatra, persistent reports suggest that the cats may also inhabit Borneo. Live sightings have occurred as recently as 1995, and various natives possess tiger skins, skulls and teeth which allegedly came from specimens killed on the island.

New Zealand— The KAIAPOI TIGER was seen by witnesses in July 1977, but it eluded police despite extensive searchers.

South Korea— The last confirmed sighting of a Bengal tiger in present-day South Korea was recorded from the Daedok Mountains of Gyeonggi Province, in 1921. Still, Australian soldiers reported contact with one or more "huge" tigers during 1952, and native researcher Lin Sun-nam has pursued the quest for tigers since 1996. At one point, Lin found claw marks on a tree which he believes to be a tiger's, and in February 1998 he found tiger-like pug marks on a snowfield in the remote Hanbuk Mountains. Lin regularly sets out dead RABBITS as bait and plays recordings of a male tiger's mating call over loudspeakers in the wild, thus far without result.

United States— Tiger sightings in the U.S. are commonly blamed on mistaken identity of "escapees" from zoos and circuses, although the latter cats are rarely captured and their presumed owners typically remain anonymous. In fact, alleged tiger encounters predate the Revolutionary War. A partial list includes the following reports:

1767— A large striped cat was seen in Pepin County, Wisconsin.

1823— A tiger was seen in Logan County, Kentucky.

1890— Tiger reports were filed from Iredell and Tyrrell Counties, North Carolina.

1897— The same tiger or its twin visited Wilkes and Yakin Counties, North Carolina.

1899— Witnesses in Wilkes County quarreled over whether their latest feline prowler was a tiger or a "black panther."

January 1963— A cat described as "black with stripes" was seen in Champaign County, Illinois.

1967—A tiger and a lion were reported in separate sightings from Connecticut.

1970s—An alleged tiger made repeated appearances around Rockcastle County, Kentucky. Hunters failed to track it down.

1977—Tiger reports emanated from Marlington, West Virginia.

1986—Witnesses in four Pennsylvania counties (Lackawana, Pike, Susquehanna and Wyoming) reported sightings of an adult tiger and a maned lion.

23 May 1993—Employees at an AT&T facility in Miami Township, Ohio (Greater Dayton) videotaped a tiger seen prowling near their workplace. Police acknowledged that the video revealed "a large cat" weighing 300-400 pounds. Searches proved fruitless, and meat laid out as bait went untouched.

27 January 1999—Police responded to reports of a tiger prowling through Jackson Township, New Jersey. Four hours later, the cat was seen in nearby woods, and officers killed it that night, after attempts to tranquilize it failed. All 26 tigers at two local menageries were accounted for, and police never traced the cat's presumed owner. A necropsy revealed that the tiger had eaten nothing for several days.

6 April 2001—Residents of Medina Township, Ohio reported a tiger at large, but authorities were skeptical, insisting the beast was merely "a Savannah wildcat…about the size of a small dog," which had escaped from its owner. Whatever its identity, at last report the cat remained at large.

October 2002—Rumors circulated that "a baby Bengal tiger" had been killed by traffic on Interstate 40 in Oklahoma, but no further information is presently available.

Sources: Bille, *Rumors of Existence*; Coleman, *Mysterious America*; Robyn Dixon, "Afghan 'tiger cat' claws at U.S. image." *Los Angeles Times* (10 August 2002); "Korean tigers." *Fortean Times* 173 (September 2003): 71; Erik Meijaard, "The Bornean tiger: Speculation on its existence." *Cat News* 30 (Spring 1999): 12-15; Karl Shuker, "Alien zoo." *Fortean Times* 168 (April 2003): 16; Shuker, *Mystery Cats of the World*; Shuker, "Tracking a Turkish tiger"; Christine Sima, "'Tiger' on loose is more like kitty, a caretaker says." *Medina* (OH) *Gazette* (6 April 2001); Smith, *Bunyips & Bigfoots*; "Tiger terror." *Strange Magazine* 15 (Spring 1995): 38; "Wild animals on the run." *Fortean Times* 127 (October 1999): 20.

Tigre de Montagne

TIGERS (*Panthera tigris*) are not native to Africa, though natives of Chad, Senegal and the Central African Republic describe a mountain-dwelling striped CAT larger than a LION (*Panthera leo*), which they call Tigre de Montagne or Coq-ninji (both translating as "mountain tiger"). In addition to red fur with white stripes, the cats are said to be tailless and to have extremely long fangs. French hunting guide Christian Le Noël collected reports of the cats in the 1960s, and once heard loud roaring from a mountain cave, which his native identified as the warning cry of a mountain tiger. Subsequently, the tracker identified a picture of the SABER-TOOTHED CAT *Machairodus* (presumed extinct for at least 2 million years) as a likeness of the Tigre de Montagne.

Sources: Shuker, *In Search of Prehistoric Survivors*; Shuker, *Mystery Cats of the World*.

Tigre Mono *see* **Mohán**

Tikis River, Philippines

On 5 November 2001, members of the Aeta tribe sighted five unidentified creatures swimming in the Tikis River near Mount Pinatubo, on Luzon. The animals were jet black in color and varied substantially in size: one was described as seven feet long and three feet wide, while another was

"the size of a jeep." No heads or tails were visible above water, but the brief glimpse frightened villagers away from their normal fishing area. Sightings continued into January 2002, but with no clearer view of the bashful beasts.

Sources: Tonette Orejas, "Strange creatures alarm Aeta tribesmen." *Philippine Daily Inquirer* (14 January 2002); Karl Shuker, "Alien zoo." *Fortean Times* 157 (May 2002): 21.

Tilford Lynx

LYNX sightings in Surrey, England date from the 1760s, when a CAT the size of a spaniel dog was reported at large in the county. The Tilford Lynx is a more recent visitor, sometimes confused with (if it is not in fact identical to) the SURREY PUMA. Today it is widely acknowledged that specimens of northern lynx (*Felis lynx*) live wild in Britain. An adult specimen was shot near Beccles, Suffolk in 1991, after it killed 15 sheep over a two-week period.

Sources: Rickard, "The 'Surrey Puma' and friends"; Sieveking, "Big cats in Britain."

Tim the Yowie Man *see* **Bull, Tim**

Tingstäde Trask, Sweden

This marshy lake, on northern Gotland (a large island off the east coast of Sweden), has a maximum recorded depth of 10 feet. That has not prevented it from generating LAKE MONSTER reports, however. In July 1976, witness Henry Bendegard reported sighting an unknown 6-foot animal swimming in the lake. He described its most noteworthy feature as a round head.

Sources: Kirk, *In the Domain of the Lake Monsters*; Global Underwater Search Team, http://www.cryptozoology.st/.

Tinicum Cat

This wildcat of Pennsylvania has been reported sporadically since the early 19th century. Burrel Lyman shot two long-tailed "bobcats" near Roulette (McKean County) sometime before 1840, and three more specimens were caught by C.H. Shearer at Irish Gap, in 1857-58. Six decades later, during 1919-21, a pair of strange wildcats disturbed Bucks County residents with their nocturnal shrieking. Hunter Tunis Brady trapped and killed a male specimen near Tinicum Township, on 16 January 1922, and delivered it to game warden Warren Fretz at Doylestown. Fretz had the CAT mounted, but the specimen has long since disappeared. Observers in the 1920s agreed that it was neither a bobcat (*Lynx rufus*) nor a feral domestic cat (*Felis silvestris catus*), but suggested that it might represent a European wildcat (*F. s. silvestris*) introduced in colonial days. Lynn Wycoff trapped a wildcat with a foot-long tail near Wharton, in September 1951, and while the animal lived for a time in captivity, it was never tamed. After three months, Wycoff reported, "It is a big cat now. Nobody can tell me that it is a bobcat. Their color lightens as they grow older but this animal's color has not changed." Author Robert Lyman later reported that "Hundreds of persons saw the captured animal but nobody seemed to know what it was. All agreed that it was a nasty tempered, snarling beast."

Sources: Chad Arment, "More odd 'wildcat' reports." *North American BioFortean Review* 4 (2000): 41; Robert Lyman Sr., *Amazing Indeed! Strange Events from the Black Forest*. Coudersport, PA: Potter Enterprise, 1973; Henry Shoemaker, *Felis Catus in Pennsylvania?* Altoona, PA: Times Tribune Co., 1922.

Tinnkjødnet, Norway

Norse folklore tells us that this lake, in Vest-Agder County, once harbored a LAKE MONSTER with a mane on its neck like a horse's. No modern sightings of the creature(s) are recorded.

Source: Costello, *In Search of Lake Monsters*.

Tinnsjøen, Norway   An ancient tradition of LAKE MONSTER sightings surrounds this lake in Telemark County, but no modern reports are on file.

Source: Erik Knatterud, Sea Serpents in Norwegian Lakes, http://www.mjoesormen.no.

Tirichuk/Tirisuk   Inuit natives once described this aquatic cryptid as a denizen of Alaska's Buckland and Noatak Rivers. It was said to be reptilian and serpentine in form, though some accounts included four legs and long feelers or tentacles used to capture prey (including human beings).

Sources: Blackman, *The Field Guide to North American Monsters*; Edwin Hall, *The Eskimo Storyteller*. Knoxville: University of Tennessee Press, 1975; Chester Lucier, "Buckland Eskimo myths." *Anthropological Papers of the University of Alaska* 2 (May 1954): 215-233.

Titmus, Robert (1918-97)   California native Robert Titmus was an expert woodsman from his youth, skilled at hunting and taxidermy. His first brush with cryptozoology occurred in June 1942, while working on construction of a wartime highway in Alaska. Titmus was aboard a boat passing through the Wrangell Narrows, southeast of Petersburg, when he glimpsed on shore a "giant of a creature, built like a big, overly-muscled man." Half a century later, speaking to J. RICHARD GREENWELL, Titmus estimated that the creature was 7-8 feet tall and weighed 1,000-1,400 pounds. "It was very big and very heavily muscled," Titmus recalled. "But I just flatly refused to believe what I was looking at."

At the time, Titmus had no knowledge of the HOMINID known as SASQUATCH. Sixteen years later, his interest in the creature was revived after a friend found large, humanoid footprints at Bluff Creek, California. That incident resulted in the cryptid being nicknamed BIGFOOT, and Titmus was instantly captivated by the mystery. As he later told Greenwell, "I was wondering, you know, what in the world could be leaving tracks like this, and suddenly I thought to myself: 'Well, you damned fool, you *saw* one of these things up in Alaska in 1942.' That's when the connection came to me."

Titmus henceforth devoted his life to searching for Bigfoot throughout the Pacific Northwest. In November 1959, Titmus found new tracks in California which persuaded millionaire TOM SLICK to launch his first Bigfoot expedition. A second Slick expedition took Titmus to British Columbia in 1961, and he continued the search in Canada after Slick's death, the following year. A short time later, Titmus claimed a sighting of three "unidentified bipedal creatures" climbing a cliff on the British Columbian coast. When he ran out of money, Titmus started a taxi cab business at Kitimat, using his profits to finance the hunt. Though he became a Canadian citizen, Titmus continued to follow Sasquatch wherever its huge footprints led. In October 1967, he rushed to the California site where the PATTERSON FILM was produced, and Titmus found enough fresh evidence to convince him the film was legitimate. Constantly afield despite chronic pain from a 1962 back injury, Titmus discovered Bigfoot tracks at various points in California and Canada over the last 30 years of his life. Shortly before his death, Titmus agreed with GROVER KRANTZ that a Sasquatch must be killed to provide skeptical scientists with a type specimen. "You bring it in, and then dump it on his damned desk," Titmus said. "That's what it will take."

Sources: John Green, "Bob Titmus, 1918-1997." *ISC Newsletter* 12 (1993-1996): 6-7; J. Richard Greenwell, "Interview: Bob Titmus." *ISC Newsletter* 12 (1993-1996): 1-6.

Tjangara *see* **Jogung**

Tlanúsi   Cherokee tribesmen of the 19th century described the Tlanúsi as a large SNAKE or giant leech, said to inhabit Hiwassee Creek near the site of present-day Murphy, North Carolina (Cherokee County). No modern sightings of any similar cryptid are on file.

Source: Gatschet, "Water-monsters of American aborigines."

Tnata   The Tnata was a BUNYIP reported from the Edwards River in New South Wales, Australia during the 19th century. Witnesses described it as having the head and neck of an EMU, with a mane and tale like those of a horse, and flippers like a seal's. The creature supposedly dined on crayfish and laid its eggs in PLATYPUS nests. No modern reports of the Tnata are on record.

Sources: Bord and Bord, *Alien Animals*; Whitley, "Mystery animals of Australia."

Tok/Taw   The Tok ("mouth") is described by natives of Southeast Asia as a large primate or WILDMAN that raids jungle villages for livestock and occasional human prey. Some superstitious folk impute supernatural powers to the creatures, regarding them as werewolves, but cryptozoologists treat them as unclassified HOMINIDS. Researcher IVAN SANDERSON considered the Tok identical to the KUNG-LU, and drew strong parallels with the Himalayan YETI known as Dzu-Teh. Sanderson's informants, including several Americans who visited the region prior to escalation of the Vietnam War, reported that the Tok (or Taw) was said to prey exclusive on thin people, while shunning fat ones.

Two reports from European witnesses describe the Tok's ferocity. In 1951, French agent Jean-Pierre Delaine was visiting an Indochinese village near the present-day border between Laos and Thailand, when two Toks entered the village by night and abducted a girl. Delaine fired at one of the 9-foot hairy kidnappers, perhaps wounding it, and then was nearly killed when the second viciously attacked him. Spared when his pistol discharged in the struggle and frightened off his assailant, Delaine joined a search party that found the girl's body next morning, surrounded by humanoid footprints, most of the flesh gnawed from her head and arms. Nine years later, while visiting the Lahu tribe on Myanmar's border with Thailand, British official Harold Young was present when a solitary Tok (or Taw) killed another young woman and fled into the night. William Young, the son of Baptist missionaries in Myanmar, was lucky by comparison. In the 1950s, he twice grappled with Toks that broke into his parents' bungalow, but each time the creature fled without resistance, leaving Young with strands of shiny black hair in his fists.

Sources: Christopher Dane, *The Occult in the Orient*. New York: Popular Library, 1974; Norman, *The Abominable Snowmen*; Sanderson, *Abominable Snowmen*.

Tokandia   This unclassified primate of Madagascar is described by witnesses as primarily arboreal, though it sometimes descends to the ground and moves on all fours, sometimes hopping. Its call allegedly resembles a human cry. BERNARD HEUVELMANS speculated that it might represent an unknown species of lemur.

Source: Heuvelmans, *On the Track of Unknown Animals*.

Toké-Mussi *see* **Bigfoot**

Tokolosh   Natives of Mozambique, South Africa and Zimbabwe commonly invest this unclassified primate or HOMINID with human qualities and/or supernatural powers. Witnesses commonly describe the Tokolosh as 3-4 feet tall, resembling a BA-BOON with hair longer than usual. Some accounts credit the creatures with powers of speech and describe them wearing animal skins as clothing. Tokoloshes are widely accused of mischievous acts and sometimes serve as scapegoats in cases of alleged adultery. No specimen of Tokolosh has yet been collected, but the creature retains its place as a kind of pint-sized African bogeyman.

Sources: Heuvelmans, *Les Bêtes Humaines d'Afrique*; Mkhululi Titi, "Woman claims Tokoloshe invasion." *East London Daily Dispatch* (2 October 1998); "Weird hobgoblin has Africans scared." *Durban Daily News* (29 March 1960).

Tompondrano   The Tompondrano ("Lord of the Sea") was once identified by Madagascar natives as a kind of SEA SERPENT that frequented waters surrounding their island home. Witnesses described the creature as 70-80 feet long, marked with longitudinal stripes in various colors, known to swim by means of vertical undulations. French traveler Georges Petit allegedly sighted a specimen south of Toliara, Madagascar on 21 January 1926, while sailing with a crew of native fishermen. Petit's companions regarded the phosphorescent beast as a harbinger of calamity.

Source: Georges Petit, *L'Industrie des Pêches à Madagascar: Faune des Colonies Françaises.* Paris: Mart G. et Colon, 1930.

Tongan Giant Skink   The Kingdom of Tonga (also called the Friendly Islands) consists of some 150 South Pacific islands, 36 of which are inhabited by humans. Most of the islands have active volcanic craters, while a minority are coral atolls. French scientist Jules Sébastien César Dumont d'Urville led a 3-year expedition to Polynesia in 1926-29, and his team spent a month at Tonga (20 April-21 May 1827), during which time they collected two specimens of a new lizard species. The lizards were skinks (Family *Scincidae*), the larger of them 12.7 inches long. The

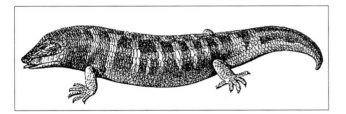

Cash rewards have thus far failed to produce new specimens of Tonga's giant skink.

species was named *Tachygyia microlepis*, but no other specimens have yet been found. Herpetologists generally considered it extinct, a victim of imported CATS and rats, until three unconfirmed sightings sparked a renewed search in 1985. Biologist John Gibbons offered a $100 reward for specimens of *T. microlepis*, commonly dubbed "the gray ghost," but that bounty has yet to be claimed.

Source: Ienich and Zug, "*Tachygyia*, the giant Tongan skink: Extinct or extant?"

Tongue-Eater   This bizarre creature was described for the first time on 14 August 1997, by *Deutsche Presse Agentur*, a German-language newspaper in Managua, Nicaragua. Witnesses in Boaca Province described the beast as "part turkey, part CAT," alleging that it attacks cows and humans alike, ripping out the victims' tongues and drinking their blood. The Tongue-eater's mode

of attack distinguished it from the predatory CHUPACABRAS, which is not known to remove the tongues of its prey. No further accounts of the creature(s) have been published since 1997.

Source: Douglas Chapman, "Here comes the 'Tongue-eater.'" *Strange Magazine* 19 (Spring 1998): 37.

Tonmawr Cat   In November 1981, residents of Tonmawr, Wales reported a large gray CAT of unknown species prowling the vicinity. Witness Steven Joyce snapped a long-distance photo of the animal which sadly revealed no details of its appearance. A short time later, however, Joyce photographed two smaller cats taking bait from his garden. Local politician Howell Britton claimed to have seen the small cats with the larger one, suggesting that they were its cubs. Analysis of the latter photos suggested that the cats were domestic tabbies, but researcher Di Francis documented the existence of a larger cat when she visited Tonmawr and photographed a jet-black specimen four feet in length. Francis returned to the village in 1982, after a new spate of sightings, and took casts of a 5-inch pawprint found in mud, clearly revealing four claw marks.

Sources: Francis, *Cat Country*; Shuker, *Mystery Cats of the World.*

***Tonny* sea serpent**   At 3:30 p.m. on 4 August 1902, 11 passengers aboard the sailing yacht *Tonny* saw a SEA SERPENT at the mouth of Oslofjord, Norway. The yacht's owner, the Rev. Hans Davidsen, described the incident as follows:

We soon saw that it was an unknown sea-animal moving at — so far as we could judge — about 4 *mil* an hour [16 mph]. It was one or two cables away from us. From time to time, three big humps showed on the surface, and three of us also saw the creature's head, oblong in shape and, as we reckoned, about 3 feet long. The humps formed a continuous series and were dark in color, with a shining surface. They seemed to be at least 2 feet in diameter. Seen from the side, the animal's motion seemed to be undulating. It is impossible to give an exact estimation of the creature's length. From what we saw the head and the three visible humps were certainly 20 feet long altogether. From the distance between the head and the humps, and the length and thickness of the latter, the total length must have been about 60 feet. We all saw that the humps were joined, and could not belong to a series of creatures swimming in line. Because of its great speed, the animal left a broad wake behind it. We did not see foam, but we all noticed that the front part of the body raised a considerable wave. The head was held near the surface in a slightly oblique position. One of the passengers thought he saw a fin on the creature's back. We watched it for five to ten minutes with the naked eye and through powerful binoculars.

Source: Heuvelmans, *In the Wake of the Sea Serpents.*

Too   German naturalist Hans Schomburgk was the first European to report this East African cryptid, described by native witnesses as resembling a black pygmy bear. The Too remains elusive, but some researchers now believe it represents a melanistic ratel (*Melivora capensis*), the fierce badgerlike animal found over much of the African continent. Large ratels may be 2 feet 6 inches long and are known for their aggressive temperament.

Source: Hans Schomburgk, *Wild und Wilde im Herzen Afrikas.* Berlin: E. Fleischel, 1910.

Toongie   Natives of Papua New Guinea describe the Toongie as a huge lizard inhabiting the Fly River region. While boating on the river with a native companion in 1960, Jesuit missionary Henry LeClerc reportedly sighted a Toongie sunning itself on a log near the water. LeClerc's guide refused to land the boat in the reptile's presence, but LeClerc returned alone to the site that evening. The lizard was gone, but LeClerc measured the 30-foot log and claimed that the lizard was of equal length. It resembled an oversized MONITOR (Family *Varanidae*), but was more than twice the length of the largest known lizard on Earth (*Varanus komodoensis*). Other reports of the Toongie compare it to a long-necked sauropod DINOSAUR.

Source: Gibbons, *Missionaries and Monsters.*

Toor-Roo-Don *see* **Bunyip**

Toplitzsee, Austria This lake in Steiermark State, 40-odd miles east of Salzburg, is said to be the resting place of treasure looted by Nazis during World War II. More recently, a 49-foot LAKE MONSTER allegedly bit through a video cable submerged in the lake by British contractors. Two divers from the Royal Aquanautic Society were menaced by the creature, but escaped unharmed to shore. Author JOHN KIRK reported the incident in 1998, but he failed to cite a source and no further details of the supposed attack are recorded. This appears to be the only sighting of the creature Kirk dubs the "Toplitz Terror."

Source: Kirk, *In the Domain of the Lake Monsters.*

Torfinnsvatnet, Norway Ancient tradition names this lake, in Hordaland County, as the abode of a LAKE MONSTER possessing "a DRAGON's head, a large mouth, and limbs like a CROCODILE." No modern sightings of the creature are on file.

Source: Costello, *In Search of Lake Monsters.*

Torneträsk, Sweden This lake, in Norbotten County, ranks as Sweden's deepest with a maximum recorded depth of 510 feet. Sightings of unidentified LAKE MONSTERS resembling capsized boats date from the early 20th century. Several members of the Stockel family observed one such animal, 50-65 feet long, while boating near Salmi on 20 July 1981.

Source: Kirk, *In the Domain of the Lake Monsters.*

Tortoises (Giant) Tortoises (Family *Testudinidae*) include any wholly terrestrial TURTLES except the box turtles (Genus *Terrapene*). Ten genera are recognized, divided into 41-50 living species (expert opinions differ). Twelve large species are known from the Galapagos Islands, with the best-known giant (*Geochelone nigrita*) reaching lengths of 4 feet 3 inches. The Aldabra tortoise (*G. gigantea*) is next in size, with a maximum recorded length of 3 feet 4 inches. An intermediate giant, the 4-foot-long Malagasy tortoise (*G. grandidieri*), has been presumed extinct since the 19th century, but native testimony suggests that it survived on Madagascar until the 1940s (if not later).

Sources: Raymond Decary, *Le Faune Malgache, son Rôle dans les Croyances et les Usages Indigènes.* Paris: Payot, 1950; Carl Ernst and Roger Barbour, *Turtles of the World.* Washington, DC: Smithsonian Institution Press, 1989.

Touraco (Unknown) The touracos [Family *Musophagidae*] are brightly-colored African soft-billed BIRDS. Twenty-three species are recognized today, but at least one more may exist. In the 1970s, three respected ornithologists glimpsed an unrecognized green specimen with small red patches on its wings, flying at large in southwestern Uganda's Impenetrable Forest. Skeptic Jonathan Kingdon, a recognized expert on African wildlife, doubts that a new species exists. Instead, he suggests that his three colleagues were deceived by brief glimpses of the red-winged Ruwenzori touraco (*Tauraco johnstoni*). Resolution of the debate awaits collection of a specimen.

Sources: John Williams and Norman Arlott, *A Field Guide to the Birds of East Africa.* London: Collins, 1980; Shuker, "A supplement to Dr. Bernard Heuvelmans' checklist of cryptozoological animals."

Tōya-Ko, Japan On 17 February 1978, the newspaper *Hokkaido Shimbun* reported a LAKE MONSTER sighting from this lake on the northern Japanese island of Hokkaido (not Kyūshū, as reported in some accounts). Witnesses at Bentenjima watched the creature for 10 minutes, reporting that it showed three humps above the surface while swimming partly submerged.

Source: Kirk, *In the Domain of the Lake Monsters.*

Tran Hong Viet (1942–) Vietnamese zoologist Tran Hong Viet began his investigation of the unknown Asian HOMINID called NGUOI RUNG in 1977. Over the next five years he collected eyewitness accounts of the creature, and in 1982 cast an unidentified humanoid footprint on the slopes of Chu Mo Ray, near the Cambodian border in the Sa Thay District of Vietnam's Kontum Province. The print measured 11 inches long by 6 inches wide. A decade later, in November 1992, Professor Tran collected and identified the first remains of a previously unknown ungulate, the saola (*Pseudoryx nghetinhensis*) from the VU QUANG NATURE RESERVE. In 1996, Tran was featured on a television special concerning the Nguoi Rung, produced by the Japanese Fortean Information Society. A year later, he was named to serve as director of the VIETNAM CRYPTOZOIC AND RARE ANIMAL RESEARCH CENTER. In 1998 the Vietnamese government furnished Tran with a grant to publish his research on the country's resident WILDMAN.

Sources: Coleman and Clark, *Cryptozoology A to Z*; Nguoi Rung: mythical or missing ape, http://coombs.anu.edu.au/~vern/wildman.html.

Tranquebar Beast On 8 January 1973, the *Hindu*, an Indian newspaper, reported that fishermen had captured a strange beast in the sea off Tranquebar, Madras. The creature was described as three feet long, covered in orange scales, with a pointed nose like an anteater's. When brought ashore, it proved able to run on land as well as it could swim. KARL SHUKER notes the animal's slight resemblance to a pangolin (*Manis* sp.), while observing correctly that none of the seven known pangolin species are either orange or amphibious. The Tranquebar beast remains unidentified.

Source: Shuker, *From Flying Toads to Snakes with Wings.*

Transcaucasian Cat In 1904, reports emerged from Transcaucasia (a Russian district south of the Caucasus Mountains, in present-day Georgia and Azerbaijan) of a CAT formerly unknown to science. Russian zoologist C. Satunin named the animal *Felis daemon*, based on his study of two mounted specimens, three skins and three skulls preserved at the St. Petersburg Academy of Sciences. The specimens ranged from 36-45 inches in length, tails included, with color varying from reddish-brown to black with red tinges. Other scientists rejected Satunin's identification of a new species, insisting that his specimens represented feral domestic cats. Cryptozoologist KARL SHUKER, meanwhile, suspects that the Transcaucasian cat may be related to Scotland's elusive KELLAS CAT.

Source: Shuker, *Mystery Cats of the World.*

Tratratratra/Trétrétrétré This unknown primate of Madagascar was reported by French traveler Etienne de Flacourt in 1658 and thereafter vanished from the public record. Flacourt described it as a round-faced creature the size of a 2-year-old child, with ears resembling a human's, apelike feet with opposed big toes, and a short tail. It was said to be a solitary animal, named for the sound of its chattering call. Speculation on its possible identity generally refers to various species of giant lemurs, all presumed to be extinct.

Source: Heuvelmans, *On the Track of Unknown Animals.*

Trauko/Tranco   The Trauko is an unclassified primate or HOMINID reported from southern Chile, where natives describe it as a mountain-dwelling counterpart of North America's BIG-FOOT. Human trespassers on the Trauko's turf are sometimes pelted with stones, and Araucanian tribesmen blame the elusive cryptid for those attacks.

Sources: Gregorio Alvarez, *El Tronco de Oro.* Buenos Aires: Editorial "Pehuén," 1968; Alejandro Chionetti, *Mundos Paralelos.* Buenos Aires: Cielosur, 1979; Picasso, "South American monsters & mystery animals."

Traverspine Gorilla   This unknown large primate or HOMINID derives its name from the Traverspine River in Labrador, Canada, where it was seen sporadically over two decades beginning in the late 19th century. Although described as a GORILLA, commonly reported under bark or rotten logs for food, the bipedal creature left strange two-toed footprints measuring 12 inches long, pressed deeply into soft earth. It visited the Michelin homestead, near Goose Bay, during two consecutive winters prior to the outbreak of World War I, frightening children and eluding the hunters who followed its tracks. Cryptozoologists differ as to whether the beast was a SASQUATCH or NORTH AMERICAN APE, though its peculiar tracks fit neither of those cryptids.

Sources: Clark and Pear, *Strange & Unexplained Phenomena;* Lionel Leslie, *Wilderness Trails in Three Continents.* London: Heath Cranton, 1931; Elliott Merrick, *True North.* New York: Charles Scribner and Sons, 1933.

Trelquehuecuve *see* **Cuero**

Trentbank sea serpent   In September 1934, crewmen aboard the cargo ship *Trentbank* saw a SEA SERPENT off the coast of Mackay, Queensland. The creature matched descriptions provided in August, by several witnesses at Townsville.

Source: Heuvelmans, *In the Wake of the Sea Serpents.*

Tresco sea serpent   On 30 May 1903, sailors aboard the cargo steamer *Tresco* allegedly saw a SEA SERPENT in the Atlantic Ocean, 90 miles off Cape Hatteras, North Carolina. Second officer Joseph Grey first saw a disturbance in the water, which proved to be a school of 40-odd SHARKS fleeing as if from some unseen danger. An hour later, crewmen spied an object resembling a derelict boat on the surface, and the *Tresco* moved closer to look for survivors. As it approached, however, "A might and horrible head came out of the water, surmounting a tall, powerful neck that had the thickness and strength of a cathedral pillar." Grey later told *Wide World Magazine* that the creature "looked for all the world like some fantastic Chinese DRAGON become a living reality; or a page from a scientific work picturing some ancient saurian monster, neither reptile nor beast wholly, but both in part." It was 100 feet long and eight feet wide, with a humped back and high dorsal fin, propelled through the water by lateral fan-shaped fins. Grey went on:

> There was something unspeakably loathsome about the head, which was five feet long from nose to upper extremity. Such a head I never saw on any denizen of the sea....Underneath the jaw there seemed to be a sort of pouch, or drooping skin....The nose, like a snout upturned, was somewhat recurved....I can remember no nostrils or blow-holes. The lower jaw was prognathous, and the

lower lip was half projecting, half pendulous. Presently I noticed something dripping from the ugly lower jaw. Watching, I saw that it was saliva, of a dirty drab colour.

Grey went on to say that the creature was toothless, except for two "very long and formidable molars...like a walrus's tusks." Its red eyes "carried in their dull depths a sombre baleful glow, as if within them was concentrated all the fierce menacing spirit that raged in the huge bulk behind." Strangely, the malevolent beast did not attack, and BERNARD HEUVELMANS concluded that Grey's story "stinks to high heaven as a HOAX."

Source: Heuvelmans, *In the Wake of the Sea Serpents.*

Trilobites   Trilobites (Class *Trilobata*) rank among the most successful of Earth's organisms. They were among the first Cambrian arthropods, appearing in the fossil record some 590 million years ago, and they thrived in various forms (8 orders and 32 families) over the next 350 million years, finally dropping from sight in the Permian Period (about 200 million years ago). *Homo sapiens*, by contrast, is a relative flash-in-the-pan, with barely 4 million years on Earth. Since their first discovery in 1698, scientists have pondered the riddle of trilobite extinction. Today, some go further still, and question whether the durable invertebrates may still be living somewhere in the ocean depths.

Author WILLY LEY was the first to publish claims of a living trilobite, in 1948. According to that report, a live specimen was caught in 1830, dredged up from a depth of some 7,200 feet, but the story proved to be false on all counts. (In fact, the animal was netted at a lesser depth and only *resembled* a trilobite. It was a new species of crab, dubbed *Serolis trilobitoides.*) Later, in 1967, zoologist Ralph Buchsbaum informed ROY MACKAL that recent photographs of the Pacific Ocean's floor revealed fresh tracks resembling fossilized trilobite trails found in Canada. Mackal studied the evidence, concluding that trilobite survival to the present day was "improbable," but "not impossible." The Pacific tracks remain unexplained, and the search for their author continues.

Sources: Ley, *The Lungfish, the Dodo, and the Unicorn;* Mackal, *Searching for Hidden Animals.*

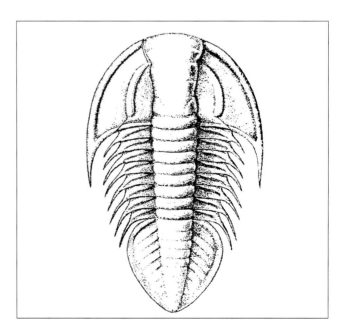

Do prehistoric trilobites survive at great ocean depths?

Trinity River, California   Members of the aboriginal Wintun tribe once claimed this river (in Trinity County) was inhabited by a fiercer "water panther." Descriptions of the creature are vague, and do not specifically resemble the IEMISCH of South America or Africa's WATER LEOPARD. It is possible that early witnesses had seen one of the giant SALAMANDERS reported from this region through the 1960s.

Source: Dixon, "Water monsters in northern California."

Tri-State Bigfoot Study Group *see* **Keating, Donald**

***Tropper* sea serpent**   On 20 March 1906, Captain Rathbone of the vessel *Tropper* reported a SEA SERPENT sighting near Dungeness, Kent, England. The 50-foot creature was dead when he saw it, floating half-submerged in the Strait of Dover. Aside from its length and serpentine form, Rathbone noted the beast's white stripes and small ears. Six decades later, BERNARD HEUVELMANS considered the sighting legitimate but could not identify the animal as belonging to any known species.

Source: Heuvelmans, *In the Wake of the Sea Serpents*.

Trusthorpe sea serpent   On 4 November 1966, the *Skegness Standard* newspaper published a letter from R.W. Midgley, recalling a summer vacation he spent at Trusthorpe, Lincolnshire, England in 1937 or 1938. Midgley was walking along the sea-wall one morning, when:

> probably no more than 400 yards from the water's edge, I saw what can only be described as a sea monster. No head was visible, but I saw quite clearly what appeared to be four or five half-links of a partly submerged, huge SNAKE-like body. It disappeared after about five minutes. I am quite certain I had not witnessed a school of porpoise, dolphin or the like.

Source: Heuvelmans, *In the Wake of the Sea Serpents*.

Tshenkutshen   Witnesses describe this unclassified CAT of Ecuador as being the size a JAGUAR (*Panthera onca*), with a humped back and widely variable coloration. Some are black, while others display a white coat with black spots, but all apparently boast distinctive stripes on the chest in red, yellow, black and white (thus explaining the popular nickname "Rainbow TIGER"). A hunter named Policarpio Rivandeira allegedly bagged a specimen in 1959, at Cerro Kilamo, but no trace of it remains today.

Source: Cryptid Felids, http://www.angelfire.com/bc2/cryptodominion/felids.html.

Tsinquaw   The Tsinquaw is an unidentified LAKE MONSTER said to inhabit Cowichan Lake, on British Columbia's Vancouver Island. Aboriginal descriptions of the creature acquired new urgency in October 1959, when fisherman Abe Johnson hooked an unseen behemoth that towed his boat around the lake for several hours, before his line snapped. A year later, sportsmen J. Curtis Watson set trap lines in a fruitless attempt to catch the Tsinquaw, though eight tourists sighted the beast in broad daylight on 11 September 1960. Those witnesses described the Tsinquaw as 12 feet long, with an elongated head, vaguely resembling a porpoise. More recently, in 1995, Jaz Jazlowiecki and three companions saw a blackish-gray animal at Cowichan Lake, swimming at 5-10 miles per hour with two humps visible above the surface. When they started their motor to leave the scene, the creature submerged and did not reappear.

Sources: Kirk, *In the Domain of the Lake Monsters*; Moon, *Ogopogo*.

Tskhiss-Katsi   The Tskhiss-katsi ("goat man") is an unclassified primate or HOMINID of Georgia's Caucasus Mountains.

Its range and description are virtually identical to those of the ABNAUAYU, ALMAS, DAV and NART. Cryptozoologists BERNARD HEUVELMANS and BORIS PORSHNEV theorized that the Tskhiss-katsi might represent a relict population of NEANDERTAL MAN.

Source: Bayanov, *In the Footsteps of the Russian Snowman*; Heuvelmans and Porshnev, *L'Homme de Néanderthal est Toujours Vivant*.

Tsongomby   The Tsongomby is yet another unclassified primate reported during modern times from the island of Madagascar. BERNARD HEUVELMANS considered it an unknown species of lemur, suggesting in 1986 that it may now be extinct.

Source: Heuvelmans, "Annotated checklist of apparently unknown animals with which cryptozoology is concerned."

Tsy-Aomby-Aomby *see* **Kilopilopitsofy**

Tua Yeua   The Tua Yeua ("big thing") is an unclassified primate or HOMINID reported from Thailand and southern Myanmar since the 19th century. London mammalogist William Blanford described it in 1891, based on sightings by British travelers, as a bipedal creature covered in dark red fur. Sometime later, an army captain named Bingham received a dead female specimen from native hunters and described it in detail to Dr. Boonsong Lekagul, a physician and onetime secretary general of Thailand's Association for the Conservation of Wildlife. The creature's skeleton was saved, then subsequently lost before it could be examined by qualified scientists. Eyewitness descriptions of the Tua Yeua have prompted some cryptozoologists to speculate that it may be identical to China's elusive YEREN. It does not, however, match descriptions of Indonesia's ORANG PENDEK.

Sources: William Blanford, *The Fauna of British India: Mammalia*. London: Taylor and Francis, 1891; Jeffrey McNeely and Paul Spencer, *Soul of the Tiger*. New York: Doubleday, 1988; Bigfoot Encounters, http://www.n2.net/prey/bigfoot/creatures/kubu.htm.

Tuckerbill Swamp, Australia   In 1929-30, a bizarre BUNYIP was reported from Tuckerbill Swamp, near Leeton, New South Wales. According to the stories told by witnesses, this unique beast had two heads, one positioned at each end of its body, thus permitting it to swim in alternate directions on a whim. Longevity was not among its qualities, however, and no modern sightings are on file.

Source: Smith, *Bunyips & Bigfoots*.

Tufi Mariner Shark   This unclassified species of SHARK is described by residents of Papua New Guinea as closely resembling a tiger shark (*Galeocerdo cuvier*), except for a black triangular patch on the anterior lobe of its pectoral fin. The Tufi Mariner is also smaller than the average tiger shark, 6-7 feet long

The Tufi Mariner resembles a familiar tiger shark.

versus the adult tiger's 12-14 feet. BEN ROESCH suggests that witnesses may have misinterpreted markings on juvenile tiger sharks, but he admits that the reported capture of several identical specimens weakens that theory.

Source: Ben Roesch, "The 'Tufi Mariner.'" *Cryptozoology Review* 3 (Summer 1998): 5.

Tumbata *see* Bunyip

Tunatpan *see* Bunyip

Tungu The Tungu is yet another unclassified primate or HOMINID of Siberia, reported from forested areas of the Gydanskiy Peninsula, southward through the Nadym and Taz regions. Its description generally matches those of other Siberian cryptids, including the ALMAS, CHUCHUNAA, KÉÉDIEKI, KHEYAK, KILTANYA, KUL, MECHENY, MIRYGDY, PIKELIAN and ZEMLEMER.

Sources: Bayanov, *In the Footsteps of the Russian Snowman*; Shackley, *Still Living?*

Turtle Lake Terror Turtle Lake, located 50 miles east of Lloydminster, Saskatchewan, Canada, boasts a tradition of LAKE MONSTER sightings dating from the early 19th century. Local aborigines described a "big FISH" dwelling in the lake, but modern-day witnesses speak of a long-necked creature 25-30 feet long, displaying a fin and three humps when it swims on the surface. Its head is sometimes likened to that of a dog, horse or pig. Dubbed the Turtle Lake Terror, this cryptid apparently delights in frightening bathers and shredding fishermen's nets. On at least two occasions, two of the creatures were seen swimming together. Speculation on the Terror's identity ranges from an oversized sturgeon (*Acipenser fulvescens*) to a relict PLESIOSAUR.

Sources: "Canadian 'monster lakes' in the news." *ISC Newsletter* 1 (Summer 1982): 5-6; Garner, *Monster! Monster!*; Kirk, *In the Domain of the Lake Monsters*.

Turtles (Giant) Turtles (Order *Chelonia*) are ancient reptiles that evolved into a shelled form more than 200 million years ago. Today, 244 living species are recognized by science, divided into 13 families and 75 genera. Those living entirely on dry land are known as TORTOISES (Family *Testudinidae*), and are considered elsewhere in this work. The remainder, except for box turtles (Genus *Terrapene*), spend much of their time in or around water, and sea turtles (Families *Cheloniidae* and *Dermochelyidae*) come ashore only to lay their eggs. The largest living turtle known to science is the Pacific leatherback (*Dermochelys coriacea*), which averages 6-7 feet in length. The largest known freshwater turtle is the narrow-headed softshell (*Chitra indica*), with a record length of 45 inches. The largest North American species is the alligator snapper (*Macroclemys temminckii*), with a record length of 31.5 inches and confirmed weights exceeding 300 pounds.

Those records notwithstanding, sightings of much larger turtles still issue from land and sea, around the world. Indiana residents report encounters with the BEAST OF 'BUSCO, and another huge specimen was allegedly sighted when workmen drained a swamp near Black Oak, Indiana in July 1950. Congo natives speak of the huge NDENDEKI, while reports of giant turtles inhabiting Hoàn Kiem Lake, in the heart of Hanoi, Vietnam date from 1428 and have continued to the present day. The urban lake was choked with garbage in December 1996, when a large and apparently ancient turtle surfaced before multiple witnesses, swimming within six feet of shore. Its head was the size of a soccer ball, with peeling skin, and observers estimated its width at some 40 inches. The turtle was videotaped on 23 March 1998, but expert viewers of

the tape could not agree on its identity. Some believed it was a narrow-headed softshell turtle, while others cast their vote for the smaller Sinhoe's softshell turtle (*Rafetus swinhoei*), with a maximum official length of 13 inches. Professor Ha Dinh Duc, of Hanoi National University, considers it a new species, which he has named *Rafetus hoankiemensis*. A reptilian egg, two inches long and one inch in diameter, was found on the lake's shore in April 2000, but attempts to incubate it proved futile. In October 2003, Bronx Zoo reptile curator John Behler told the media, "We know next to nothing about this species or its habitat requirements, other than the fact that it is extremely rare and is presumably on the brink of extinction." A month later, Vietnamese researchers and members of the U.S.-based Wildlife Conservation Society announced plans to visit lakes in Thanh Hoa Province, 100 miles south of Hanoi, where other giant turtles have been reported but never confirmed.

At sea, reports of giant turtles have exceeded anything yet seen on land. BERNARD HEUVELMANS, in his 1968 study of SEA SERPENTS, reported seven cases in which witnesses described the cryptids they had seen as massive turtles. Five of those are covered elsewhere in this volume, including the creatures seen by passengers aboard the *NESTOR* (1876), the *ANNIE L. HALL* (1883), the *VALHALLA* (1905), the *CERAMIC* (1932) and the *Rhapsody* (1956). A sixth sighting was reported from Back Bay, Bombay (now Mombai, India) in October 1921. The anonymous witness was sailing a small boat and described the cryptid seen as follows:

> The upright neck stood some 10 feet, I should say, perpendicularly from the sea surface, tapering very slightly towards the head. The diameter of this column appeared to be about 18 inches near the water. It seemed to be covered with large scales and, in colour, was a light olive green at the back, shading off to a dirty yellow in front. The head was like that of a gigantic tortoise, or turtle, but any body to correspond with that head and neck would be, at least, fifty feet long, I should judge.

Heuvelmans believed that judgment accurate only if the creature was serpentine in form, whereas he thought a turtle with a 15-foot body might support a 10-foot neck. Finally, he was unable to decide if the unnamed witness had seen a turtle or a PYTHON swimming at sea.

The last sighting of a supposed giant turtle recorded by Heuvelmans occurred off Soay, western Scotland, on 13 September 1959. Witnesses James Gavin and Tex Geddes were boating when they saw the creature, which Gavin described as follows:

> At the waterline the body was 6 to 8 feet long. It was hump-shaped rising to a centrally-placed apex about two feet high. The line of the back was formed by a series of triangular-shaped spines, the largest at the apex and reducing in size to the waterline. The spines appeared to be solid and immobile — they did not resemble fins. I got only a lateral view of the animal but my impression was that the cross section of the body was roughly angular in shape. Apart from the forward glide I saw no movement.
>
> The neck appeared to be cylindrical and, at a guess, about 8 ins. in diameter. It arose from the water about 12 ins. forward of the body. I could not see where they joined; about 15 to 18 ins. of neck was visible. The head was rather like that of a tortoise with a SNAKE-like flattened cranium running forward to a rounded face. Relatively it was as big as the head of a donkey. I saw one laterally placed eye, large and round like that of a cow. When the mouth was opened I got the impression of large blubbery lips and could see a number of tendril-like growths hanging from the palate. Head and neck arose to a height of about two feet. At intervals the head and neck went forward and submerged. They would then reemerge, the large gaping mouth would open (giving the im-

pression of a large melon with a quarter removed) and there would be a series of very loud roaring whistling noises as it breathed. After about five minutes the beast submerged with a forward diving motion — I thought I saw something follow the body down. It later re-surfaced about a quarter of a mile further out to sea and I then watched it until it disappeared in the distance (I have since heard that the crews of two lobster boats, fishing north of Mallaig, have also seen this animal — much to their consternation).

Heuvelmans finally listed a "father-of-all-turtles" (named for a legendary Sumatran reptile) among his nine hypothetical sea serpent species, but he considered it "very rare" and accepted as "probable" only four of the sightings presented in his text. The Bombay sighting he dismissed as "dubious," while the *Rhapsody* and Soay sightings were rejected for their occurrence in cold-water regions that Heuvelmans deemed unsuitable for a reptile. Three years later, in August 1971, a leatherback turtle weighing 1,500 pounds was caught near Mallaig, Scotland. Veteran NESSIE-hunter TIM DINSDALE viewed it briefly, but the creature was

Survival of the prehistoric turtle *Archelon* may explain sightings of giant turtles at sea.

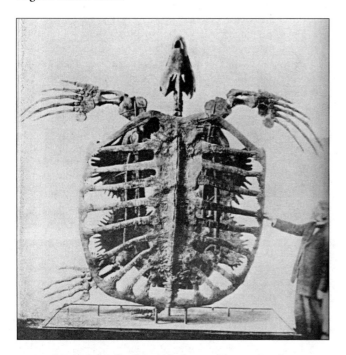

An *Archelon* fossil reveals the turtle's massive size.

shipped out to some unknown cannery before he could interest zoologists in retrieving it.

Two giant turtle sightings overlooked by Heuvelmans were recorded in September 1494 and March 1955. Witnesses in the first case included navigator Christopher Columbus, who (with other members of his crew) saw a whale-sized turtle swimming off the coast of the present-day Dominican Republic. On 8 March 1955, while drifting on a raft in Colombia's Gulf of Urabá, L. Alejandro Velasco saw a yellow turtle some 14 feet long (or twice the length of the record leatherback). Heuvelmans suggested that the father-of-all-turtles represents a relict population of *Archelon ischyros*, a Late Cretaceous sea turtle that measured 16 feet long and 12 feet wide, tipping the scales at an estimated 11,000 pounds.

Sources: Dinsdale, *Project Water Horse*; Carl Ernst and Roger Barbour, *Turtles of the World.* Washington, DC: Smithsonian Institution Press, 1989; Heuvelmans, *In the Wake of the Sea Serpents*; Mackal, *A Living Dinosaur?*; "Monsters of the deep." *Fortean Times* 100 (August 1997): 6; Magin, "In the wake of Columbus's sea serpent"; Margie Mason, "Group moves to save endangered turtle." Associated Press (3 November 2003); Karl Shuker, "Alien zoo." *Fortean Times* 113 (August 1998): 18.

Twin Lakes, Massachusetts   In April 1890, a 25-foot "water SNAKE" was reported from this site, in the Berkshire Hills. The area had no previous tradition of LAKE MONSTER sightings, nor did the creature subsequently reappear.

Source: Charles Skinner, *Myths and Legends of Our Own Land.* Philadelphia: Lippincott, 1896.

Twin Lakes Reservoir, Colorado   Twin Lakes Reservoir is Colorado's largest glacial lake. It lies near Leadville, at the foot of Mount Elbert (the state's highest peak). The lake sprawls over 1,700 acres, with a maximum depth of 70 feet. In 1939, several members of the Gerardi family allegedly saw a LAKE MONSTER with "a DINOSAUR's head" swimming in the lake, but their sighting was not widely reported for another 40 years. No recent sightings are on file.

Sources: *Denver Post* (17 June 1979); Twin Lakes Reservoir, http://www.ohwy.com/co/t/twinlkre.htm.

Two-Tongues   A report published in May 1979 described this "ultra-mysterious" Malaysian mammal as a 200-pound quadruped with dark fur and large eyes set in a head resembling a raccoon's. If that description was not strange enough, the report went on to say that the creature had two tongues, visible inside a mouth with teeth resembling those of both human and CAT. It was fond of bananas but never drank water, instead absorbing moisture through its skin. KARL SHUKER speculates that the report may be a much-exaggerated description of a Malay badger (*Mydaus javanensis lucifer*), but a specimen is clearly required to solve this riddle.

Source: Shuker, *From Flying Toads to Snakes with Wings.*

***Tyne* sea serpent**   On 20 April 1920, while traveling between Casablanca and Rio de Janeiro, crewmen aboard the Royal Mail packet *Tyne* saw a SEA SERPENT in the South Atlantic, at 1° 30' north latitude and 28° west longitude. Third officer Thomas Muir first thought the creature's neck was a spar sticking out of the water, then realized his mistake when he observed the beast through binoculars, keeping pace with the *Tyne* at 14 miles per hour. Muir later recalled:

It was clearly a creature of some description, and the head, like an umbrella handle, turned and looked at the ship, then the creature closed in towards us to a distance of about 400 yards. It kept speed

The *Tyne* sea serpent, after witness Thomas Muir.

with the ship, and appeared to be looking at us. For roughly five minutes it travelled parallel with us, then the neck curved over like a swan, and it dived out of sight. At the time I wondered what the body was like, there being considerable spray behind the neck, with flashes of dark body like a whale; but I was not sure whether it was a long sinuous body like a SNAKE, or rounded like a whale.

Source: Heuvelmans, *In the Wake of the Sea Serpents.*

Tyrifjorden, Norway

This lake, in Norway's Buskerud County, was once reportedly the home of a LAKE MONSTER prone to appearing on the eve of perilous times. Ivar Weil, writing in a Norse geographical journal, described the harbinger of doom as ranging from 7–26 feet long. No modern reports of the beast are on file.

Sources: Costello, *In Search of Lake Monsters*; Skjelsvik, "Norwegian lake and sea monsters."

Tzartus-Saurus

This SEA SERPENT is named for Tzartus Island, in Vancouver Island's Barkley Sound (British Columbia), where it was said to be a frequent visitor in the late 19th and early 20th centuries. Witnesses described it as 40–60 feet long and ser-

pentine in form, with a head resembling a horse's. On balance, it seems likely that the Tzartus-saurus is identical to CAD-BOROSAURUS.

Source: Moon, *Ogopogo.*

Tzuchinoko

Mentioned in various Japanese manuscripts dating from the 13th century onward, the Tzuchinoko ("child of the straw bat") is described by witnesses as a short, squat-bodied SNAKE with short horns above its eyes and an abbreviated, slender tail. Various witnesses, including a veteran snake-hunter named Tokutake, draw a clear distinction between the Tzuchinoko and the more familiar Halys viper (*Agkistrodon halys*). Tokutake claimed to have captured two specimens, in 1969 and 1971, but he killed and ate the reptiles without submitting them for study. Other reports of kills and captures dating back to 1938 likewise have yielded no tangible evidence. A witness named Kawano allegedly photographed a Tzuchinoko at Yoshino (east of Osaka) in 1968, then lost the film before it was developed. On 21 May 2000, a farmer cutting grass at Yoshii (in Okayama Prefecture) reportedly killed "a snake-like creature with a face resembling the cartoon cat Doraemon" and buried its remains. On learning of the incident, officials from the Yoshii Municipal Government reportedly dug up the snake and delivered it to Prof. Kuniyashu Satoh at Kawasaki University of Medical Welfare. Incredibly, the professor dismissed the creature as "a kind of snake," without any more detailed identification. Its whereabouts is presently unknown, but the incentive for a Tzuchinoko's capture increased dramatically thereafter, when Yoshii mayor Ryuichi Arashima offered ¥20 million ($175,461) for a live specimen, vowing to increase the bounty by ¥1 million ($8,733) for each year the creature remained unidentified.

Sources: Dethier and Dethier-Sakamoto, "The *Tzuchinoko*, an unidentified snake from Japan"; Heuvelmans, "Tzuchinoko, a 'Tatzelwurm' from Japan"; Shuker, "Loco for a Tzuchinoko."

—U—

U-28 sea serpent

Even cryptids sometimes fall prey to the folly of mankind's fratricidal wars. A case in point was recorded in 1915, by Captain Georg Günther Freiherr von Forstner, commanding the submarine *U-28* in the second year of World War I. His account of a SEA SERPENT sighting, published 18 years later in the *Deutsche Allgemeine Zeitung*, reads:

On 30 July 1915 our *U 28* torpedoed the British steamer *Iberian* (5,223 tons) carrying a rich cargo in the North Atlantic. The steamer, which was about 600 feet long, sank quickly, the bow sticking almost vertically into the air, towards the bottom a thousand fathoms or more below. When the steamer had been gone for about 25 seconds, there was a violent explosion at a depth which was clearly impossible for us to know, but which we can reckon, without risking being far out, at about 500 fathoms [3,000 feet]. A little later pieces of the wreckage, and among them a gigantic sea-animal, writhing and struggling wildly, were shot out of the water to a height of 60 to 100 feet.

At that moment I had with me in the conning tower my officers of the watch, the chief engineer, the navigator, and the helmsman. Simultaneously we all drew one another's attention to this won-

der of the seas. As it was not in Brockhaus nor in Brehm we were, alas, unable to identify it. We did not have the time to take a photograph, for the animal sank out of sight after 10 of 15 seconds....It was about 60 feet long, was like a CROCODILE in shape and had

The *U-28* sea serpent, based on eyewitness descriptions.

four limbs with powerful webbed feet and a long tale tapering to a point.

That the animal should have been driven up from a great depth seemed to me very understandable. After the explosion, however it was caused, the "underwater crocodile," as we called it, was shot upwards by the terrific pressure until it leapt out of the water gasping and terrified.

BERNARD HEUVELMANS later speculated that Capt. Forstner must be mistaken either on the time lapse or the depth involved, since the *Iberia* could scarcely have sunk at speeds approaching 85 miles per hour, to reach a depth of 3,000 feet in 25 seconds. Far from being an abyssal creature, then, Heuvelmans suggests that it was swimming relatively near the surface—as any air-breathing reptile would certainly do.

Source: Heuvelmans, *In the Wake of the Sea Serpents.*

U-109 sea serpent   Three years after officers of the German submarine *U-28* logged their encounter with a 60-foot reptile in the North Atlantic, fellow countrymen aboard the *U-109* met an even larger specimen in the North Sea. The sighting was logged at 10:00 p.m. on 18 July 1918, with World War I still raging in Europe. Captain Werner Löwisch, commanding the *U-109*, described the 100-foot creature as having "a long head, jaws like a CROCODILE'S and legs with very definite feet." This cryptid escaped without injury and was not seen again. The *Bremer Nachrichten* published Löwisch's account in 1933.

Source: Heuvelmans, *In the Wake of the Sea Serpents.*

Ucluelet, Vancouver sea serpent   In November 1947, fisherman George Saggers reported a SEA SERPENT sighting off Ucluelet, on Vancouver Island's Barkley Sound. Saggers may have seen the creature commonly known as CADBOROSAURUS, although his description—published six months later in *Fate* magazine, revealed discrepancies from "Caddy's" typical appearance. The Saggers report read, in part:

Suddenly I had the funniest feeling. A sort of shiver went up and down my spine, and I had a feeling that I was being watched. Immediately I looked all around.

On my port side, about 150 feet away, was a head and neck raised about four feet above the water, with two jet black eyes about three inches across and protruding from the head like a couple of buns, staring at me.

It just didn't look real. I've never seen anything like it. The head seemed to be the same size as the neck, about eighteen inches through and of a mottled color of gray and light brown....

After it looked at me for one full minute, it turned its head straight away from me, showing the back of its head and its neck. It appeared to have some sort of a mane, which seemed like bundles of warts rather than hair. It looked something like a mattress would, if split down the middle allowing rolls of cotton batting to protrude. The color of the mane was dark brown.

Curiously, Saggers sighted his creature days after a mysterious 40-foot carcass was hauled ashore at EFFINGHAM, on the west coast of Vancouver Island. The identity of that creature remains in dispute today. In April 1962 another strange carcass was beached at Ucluelet, this one 14 feet long with "a head like an elephant." Some observers believe the remains were those of an elephant seal (*Mirounga leonina*).

Sources: Heuvelmans, *In the Wake of the Sea Serpents;* LeBlond and Bousfield, *Cadborosaurus;* Saggers, "Sea serpent off Vancouver."

Ucumar   An unknown HOMINID reported from the Andean regions of Bolivia, Peru and Argentina, the Ucumar is known by a variety of regional names, including Ucu, Ucamari, Ukamar-zupai, Jucamari and Sachayoj. Witnesses typically describe the creature as a half-man, half-bear, covered in long black hair. It is bipedal and leaves humanlike footprints, averaging 17 inches long. A reputed cave-dweller, the Ucumar is said to dine on honey and wild fruit, but some reports call it a kidnapper of children and women (the latter allegedly snatched for breeding purposes). A specimen was reportedly killed at Charcas, Bolivia in 1549, while another was said to be captured alive in 1917, at Tucumán, Argentina. A report published by Friar Pedro Simon, in 1963, described the slaying of a hermaphroditic Ucumar by Venezuelan soldiers. That creature allegedly measured 4.8 meters (15 feet 7 inches) tall, but the date was not recorded and its corpse was not preserved. Reported sightings continued through the early 1960s around Calilegua village in Jujuy, Argentina. Skeptics who deny the existence of unknown hominids suggest that Ucumar reports may result from rare encounters with a spectacled bear (*Tremarctos ornatus*).

Sources: Chapman, *The Monster of the Madidi;* Latapi, "Ucumar, the Argentinian Yeti"; Picasso, "South American monsters & mystery animals."

Uelmansee, Germany   This lake, located in the state of Rheinland-Pfalz, was once reputedly the home of giant FISH. Two specimens appeared in the late 18th century, locals say, following the death of an Uelman family heir. If true, that sighting and others like it are probably explained by the presence of Wels catfish (*Siluris glanis*), which may attain a length of 16 feet.

Source: Philipp Wirtgen, *Die Eifel in Bildern und Darstelungen.* Bonn: A. A. Henry, 1866.

Ufiti   An unclassified primate reported from Malawi, the Ufiti (or Fireti) made its first dramatic public appearance in November 1959, when a large black APE was seen watching road construction workers at Nkhata Bay, on the western shore of Lake Nyasa. Observers described the animal as 5 feet 6 inches tall, weighing perhaps 150 pounds. Witness J. Leonard Goodwin snapped photographs of the creature in February 1960, but while some accounts claim those photos "clearly show" a female CHIMPANZEE (*Pan troglodytes*), the matter is far from settled. A report from the *Rhodesia Herald,* dated 7 February 1960, read:

An eminent Rhodesian zoologist, Mr. R.H.N. Smithers, of the National Museum, was able, even from the poor pictures available, to point out several unusual features. He said:

"From the statements I have heard from Nyasaland [now Malawi], the animal would at first appear to be a chimpanzee. There are, however, two facts that do not support this contention. The animal has a distinctly muzzle-like face, while the chimpanzee has a flat 'pushed in' type of face. Secondly, the animal is, as far as I can recollect, more than a thousand miles from where it should be if it was a chimpanzee. The beast is obviously not a BABOON, even though it has a baboon-like face, as baboons have tails and are not black in colour. In addition, a baboon does not have this animal's posture and bearing. Then there is the enormous size of the animal, which does not agree with either the chimpanzee or the baboon." Mr. Smithers said it was most unlikely that the animal was of a new species, and added that, if better photographs could be obtained as well as plaster casts of the feet, it would probably be possible to identify it.

In fact, a subsequent report claimed that footprint casts *were* made, revealing "three toes and a large thumb." Strangely, despite that description which fits neither humans nor any known primate, the same report asserted that Ufiti's footprints "are said to be more human than animal." A subsequent bulletin, dated 17 March 1960, only heightened the confusion.

> Nyasaland's rain-forest monster, Ufiti, has been identified as a new sub-species of chimpanzee by two game experts from the Rhodes-Livingston Museum.
>
> Mr. B.L. Marshall and Mr. C. Holliday, who are keeping the creature under almost daily observation, have not yet been able to obtain any photographs. Ufiti remains as elusive as ever, vanishing as soon as she is approached, and thick bush and poor light add to the difficulties of getting clear pictures.
>
> Ufiti, who is believed to be in season, has returned to her favourite observation point at the Limpasa Bridge after an absence of about a fortnight. The Chief Conservator of Forests, Mr. R.G.M. Willan, who is touring the area, was among several people who saw the creature when it reappeared near the road on Tuesday.
>
> The two game experts, who are collecting photographs and other forms of visible evidence, hope to arrange a bigger expedition to explore the whole rain-forest area.
>
> It is unlikely, however, that any scientific expedition will be allowed to capture Ufiti for closer examination until it can be established that more of the creatures exist in the rain-forest.

Naturalist IVAN SANDERSON waxed eloquent in dissecting that press release, noting its manifest contradictions (no photos vs. a collection of photos; an "elusive" creature under "almost daily observation." etc.), and concluded that Ufiti could not be a chimpanzee after all. Further research uncovered a series of similar sightings from Malawi and Portuguese East Africa (now Mozambique) in 1952-53. In Mozambique, the creature was known as Firete. Witnesses there reported unknown apes in black and gray, suggesting possible sexual dimorphism.

An alleged Ufiti specimen, dubbed "Ogo," was caught in March 1964, and shipped to England's Chester Zoo. It died on 23 April of a parasitic lung infection, and no report on its identity is presently available. Stranger still, reported sightings from Malawi apparently ceased with Ogo's capture.

Sources: "Camera captures unknown ape," *Popular Science Monthly*; Heuvelmans, *Les bêtes humaines d'Afrique*; Hill, "The Ufiti: The present position"; Sanderson, *Abominable Snowmen*.

Ui-Go *see* Yeti

Uktena

A legendary North Carolina LAKE MONSTER, whose Cherokee name means "keen-eyed," the Uktena apparently was not confined to any specific body of water in the Tarheel State. Witnesses to its appearance described a serpentine creature, dark in color, with lighter rings or spots decorating its body. The beast's forehead was notable for protrusions variously described as horns, antlers, or a diamond-shaped crest. Some accounts claimed the Uktena was venomous.

Sources: Arlene Fradkin, *Cherokee Folk Zoology*. New York: Garland, 1990); James Mooney, "Myths of the Cherokee." *Annual Report of the Bureau of American Ethnology* 19 (1900): 297-300.

Ulak/Uluk

This unclassified mountain-dwelling primate or HOMINID of Central America is typically described as five feet tall, tailless, and covered with black hair. Its name, in the Sumo Tawahka dialect, is variously interpreted as "MONKEY monster" or "big wild man." The Ulak is reported from the Montañas de Colon in Honduras and from Nicaragua's Cordillera Isabella, where local variations on its common name include Uluk and Wulasha. A feature shared by the Ulak and various other tropical hominids is the claim that their feet "point backwards." In the

Ulak's case, that description is sometimes broadened to include a claim of "backwards teeth."

Source: Eduard Conzemius, "Ethnographical survey of the Miskiro and Sumu Indians of Honduras and Nicaragua." *Bulletin of the Board of American Ethnology* 106 (1932): 168.

Ular Tedong

Regarded by some as identical to the NĀGA of India and Thailand, these large "golden serpents" or "buffalo snakes" were once said to inhabit the Tasek Bera, a remote lake in central Malaysia's Pahang State. Explorer Stewart Wavell went looking for the creatures in 1951 and collected native testimony describing large SNAKES that were gray in their juvenile state and gold-colored as adults. The Ular Tedong also sported small, soft horns on top of its head. Wavell failed to spot the animal, but his memoir of the hunt includes mention of an eerie close encounter at the Tasek Bera.

> A single staccato cry from the middle of the lake chilled my blood with fear. It was a snort: more like a bellow — shrill and strident like a ship's horn, and elephant's trumpet, and sea-lion's bark all rolled into one. I was momentarily petrified then frantically switched on the recorder and waited for the next cry — but it never came.

A party of Royal Air Force personnel reportedly sought to observe the Ular Tedong in 1962, but again the searchers returned empty-handed. Cryptozoologist KARL SHUKER surmised that the beast might be a relict elasmosaurus, believed extinct since the Late Cretaceous period, but the theory is unlikely to be tested. In June 2002 Shuker reported that the Tasek Bera had essentially been destroyed by encroaching palm-oil plantations and rampant weeds, transforming the mysterious lake into "little more than a cesspool."

Sources: Dinsdale, *Monster Hunt*; Shuker, *In Search of Prehistoric Survivors*; Shuker, "R.I.P. Tasek Bera"; Wavell, *The Lost World of the East*.

Umfuli sea serpent

On 4 December 1893, Captain R.J. Cringle and other officers of the Natal Line steamer *Umfuli* encountered a SEA SERPENT off Rio de Oro, while approaching the Cape of Good Hope at latitude 21° 41' north and longitude 17° 30' west. They observed the creature for 30 minutes, after which the ship's mate, C.A.W. Powell, logged the following report:

> 5:30. Sighted and passed about 500 yards from ship a Monster FISH of the Serpent shape, about 80 ft. long with slimy skin and short fins at about 20 feet apart on the back and in cir[cumference] about the dimension of a full sized whale. I distinctly saw the fish's mouth open & shut with my glasses. The jaw appeared to me about 7 feet long with large teeth. In shape it was just like a Conger EEL.

Capt. Cringle sketched the creature and supplied this additional account.

> When we first saw it, I estimated that it would be about 400 yards away. It was rushing through the water at great speed, and was

The *Umfuli* sea serpent, after witness R.J. Cringle.

throwing water from its breast as a vessel throws water from her bows. I saw full 15 ft. of its head and neck on three several occasions....The body was all the time visible....The base, or body, from which the neck sprang, was much thicker than the neck itself, and I should not, therefore, call it a serpent. Had it been breezy enough to ruffle the water, or hazy, I should have had some doubt about the creature; but the sea being so perfectly smooth, I had not the slightest doubt in my mind as to its being a sea-monster.... This thing, whatever it was, was in sight for over half an hour. In fact, we did not lose sight of it until darkness came on.

Capt. Cringle suffered much embarrassment after the sighting. As he later observed, "I had been told that it was a string of porpoises, that it was an island of sea-weed, and I do not know what besides. But if an island of sea-weed can travel at the rate of fourteen knots [21 miles per hour], then I give in, and confess myself deceived. Such, however, could not be." On balance, Cringle said, "I have been so ridiculed about the thing that I have many times wished that anybody else had seen that sea-monster rather than me."

Source: Heuvelmans, *In the Wake of the Sea Serpents.*

Unicorn   The root of myths surrounding the horned (sometimes magical) horses known as unicorns is uncertain. Researcher Peter Costello believes they originated with Greek historian, physician and traveler Ctesias, writing around 380 B.C. The relevant passage from his work reads:

There are in India certain wild asses which are as large as horses, and larger. Their bodies are white, their heads dark red, and their eyes dark blue. They have a horn on the forehead which is about a foot and a half long. The dust filed from this horn is administered in a potion as a protection against drugs. The base of this horn, for some two hand-breadths above the brow, is pure white; the upper part is sharp and of a vivid crimson; and the remainder, or middle portion, is black. Those who drink of these horns, made into drinking vessels, are not subject, they say, to convulsions or to the holy disease [epilepsy]. Indeed, they are immune even to poisons if, either before or after swallowing such, they drink wine, water, or anything else from these beakers. Other asses, both the tame and the wild, and if fact all animals with solid hoofs, are without the ankle-bone and have no gall in the liver, but these have both the ankle bone and the gall. This ankle-bone, the most beautiful I have ever seen, is like that of an ox in general appearance and size, but it is as heavy as lead and its colour is that of cinnibar through and through. The animal is exceedingly swift and powerful, so that no creature, neither horse nor any other, can overtake it.

Unicorn sightings persisted through the mid-19th century.

Aristotle (384-322 B.C.) subsequently described *two* kinds of unicorn, dubbing them "the Indian ass and the Oryx," but he was clearly wrong about the latter, since the Arabian oryx (*Oryx leucoryx*) has two horns. Unicorns are mentioned nine times in the Bible, but most scholars now concede that the original text refers to an extinct form of wild ox, the Aurochs (*Bos primigenius*)—which also had two horns.

Unicorn sightings, while rare, continued from Roman times until the mid-19th century. Julius Caesar, writing in the first century A.D., described a one-horned stag inhabiting the Erzgeberg region of southern Germany. A group of pilgrims led by Felix Fabri saw a large one-horned animal near Egypt's Mount Sinai, on 20 September 1483. Twenty years later, Lodovico de Varthema reported single-horned cattle from the port city of Saylac, Somalia.

Jesuit priest Jeronimo Lobo claimed that unicorns were "common" throughout Ethiopia in 1630; three decades later, a party of Portuguese sailors in Ethiopia confirmed Lobo's report. Pioneer Olfert Dapper, in 1673, noted unicorns from the forests of present-day Maine, along the Canadian border. John Campbell, in South Africa, reported that natives had killed a "real unicorn" with a 3-foot single horn in 1820. Fulgence Fresnel, the French consul at Jiddah, Saudi Arabia, reported in April 1843 that another unicorn resembling a wild bull with "elephant's legs" had been killed in eastern Chad.

Common suspects in the unicorn mystery include various species of RHINOCEROS, antelope and wild donkey. Spiral tusks from the Narwhal (*Monodon monceros*) were often advertised as unicorn's horns before 1638, when Ole Wurm proved they belonged to an Arctic cetacean. Other explanations may include genetic mutations in ordinary species, injured animals with one horn missing, or unicorns "manufactured" by HOAXERS. In the late 20th century, several homemade "unicorns" were found in the United States, typically goats with horns surgically grafted to their foreheads, enlisted as props at Renaissance fairs and the like. As late as December 2002, a shipment of alleged unicorn bones was delivered to New Zealand's Auckland Museum, where experts determined that the bones came from a cow or water buffalo.

Sources: Beer, *Unicorn: Myth and Reality*; Costello, *The Magic Zoo*; Freeman, *The Unicorn Tapestries*; Radca, *Historical Evidence for Unicorns*; Shephard, *The Lore of the Unicorn*; "'Unicorn' bones in unmarked shipment." *Dominon Post* (11 December 2002).

Unktehi/Unktéxi   Said to inhabit the MISSOURI RIVER, its tributaries and connected lakes, the Unktehi was described by Sioux tribesmen as a kind of DRAGON, serpentine in form but walking on four legs, sporting a large horn on its head and spikes on its tail. It was sometimes blamed for flooding along the Missouri, but modern researchers doubt the creature was ever seen by living humans. Instead, they suggest, the stories arose from accidental discovery of dinosaur fossils in the Badlands and Black Hills of South Dakota.

Sources: Richard Erdoes and Alfonso Ortiz, eds. *American Indian Myths and Legends.* New York: Pantheon, 1984; Gatschet, "Water monsters of American aborigines."

Urisee, Austria   This lake, in Austria's Tyrol district, was said to harbor a large unidentified beast in the 19th century. A dearth of modern sightings indicates that the creature (if it ever existed) is now extinct.

Source: "Seeschlange," in Hanns Bächtold-Stäubli, ed. *Handwörterbuch des deutschen Aberglaubens.* Berlin: W. de Gruyter, 1930.

Urnersee, Switzerland   This Swiss lake, located in Canton Schwyz, was the scene of a dramatic LAKE MONSTER sighting on 25 August 1976. On that day, a group of witnesses watched a long-necked creature, described as 20 to 25 feet long, bellowing like a cow as it surfaced three times near Brunnen. The excitement soon turned to embarrassment, however, when the producers of a Swiss television program admitted launching a model monster in the lake. For once, eyewitnesses had underestimated a creature's size, since the model measured 60 feet.

Source: Magin, "A brief survey of lake monsters of continental Europe."

Uruguayan sea serpent   In January 1824 a traveler from Boston reportedly sighted a SEA SERPENT in the South Atlantic, 60 miles off the coast of Uruguay. The witness reported his sighting to an early cryptozoologist, Professor Benjamin Siliman, on condition that his anonymity be preserved. Unfortunately, no details of the sighting have survived.

Source: Heuvelmans, *In the Wake of the Sea Serpents.*

Usan sea serpent   In 1849, fishermen at Usan, Scotland caught what they believed to be "a young SEA SERPENT" and delivered it to the secretary of a local museum. As described in the *Montrose Standard*:

> The animal, whatever it may be called, is still alive, and we have just been favoured with a sight of it; but whether it really be a young sea-serpent or not, we shall leave to those who are better acquainted with Zoology than we are to determine. Be it what it may, it is a living creature, more than 20 feet in length, less than an inch in circumference, and of a dark brown chocolate colour. When at rest its body is round; but when it is handled it contracts upon itself, and assumes a flattish form. When not disturbed its motions are slow; but when taken out of the water and extended, it contracts like what a long cord of caoutchouc [rubber] would do, and folds itself up in spiral form, and soon begins to secrete a whitish mucous from the skin, which cements the folds together, as for the purpose of binding the creature into the least possible dimensions.

Zoologist Edward Newman identified the creature as a specimen of *Gordius marinus*, a marine nemertean worm now known as *Lineus longissimus*. It commonly reaches lengths of 16-33 feet, and BERNARD HEUVELMANS suggests that large specimens may exceed 100 feet in length.

Source: Heuvelmans, *In the Wake of the Sea Serpents.*

Utah Bigfoot Investigations   This organization's Internet website describes it as "a group of select individuals" committed to "networking information and resources to compile data used as a collective group to determine whether BIGFOOT is Fact or Fiction." The only identified members are founder Jeff ("Storm") Lewis and Mark Woody, who respectively claim 15 and 25 years of experience in pursuit of unclassified HOMINIDS. Based in Salt Lake City, the UBI concerns itself primarily with Utah sightings, with corresponding interest in reports from neighboring states. Woody explains his interest in the chase: "I love a mystery, and the possibility of large hominids amongst us, demands serious, unbiased research and investigation. To think there is

nothing to all the evidence and eyewitness testimony, or to ignore all the evidence pointing to a large primate, in North America, would be the height of hubris."

Source: Utah Bigfoot Investigations, http://www.cal-company.com/utahbigfootinvestigations/.

Utah Lake, Utah   Utah's second-largest lake, located south of Salt Lake City in Tooele County, produced its first LAKE MONSTER reports before white settlers invaded the Great Basin. Ute tribesmen spoke of "water babies" haunting the lake, and claimed that a nameless monster once swallowed a warrior near Pelican Point. Isaac Fox was the first known white witness, in 1864, sighting a 25- or 30-foot reptilian beast on the lake's north shore. According to Fox, the monster had dark eyes and a doglike head. It allegedly pursued him on land, then retreated to the water and joined a second creature in the lake before submerging. A second witness from 1864, Henry Walker, claimed the animal resembled "a large SNAKE…with the head of a greyhound." Two years later, a pair of men cutting hay near the north end of the lake saw a yellow creature with black spots, menacing them with a forked, flicking tongue. In 1868, two more witnesses described the animal's doglike head and "wicked-looking black eyes."

Descriptions of the Utah Lake creature were not always consistent, however. In 1871, Mormon bishop William Price and two fellow travelers, passing along the lake's western shore, saw a 60-foot snake whose upper body, raised six feet above the surface, resembled a length of stovepipe. Nine years later, while boating on the lake, young Willie Roberts and George Scott beheld a "small animal" resembling a deer or beaver, swimming toward their boat. As it drew closer, the beast raised a "huge" head like that of an ALLIGATOR, snapping 3-foot jaws and roaring like a LION, chasing them toward shore with a series of "savage gestures." Salt Lake City's *Deseret News*, reporting the incident, asked, "Does the Smithsonian know of this terror?"

Evidence supporting the existence of an unknown creature in the lake was reported in 1870, when a group of Springville fishermen hauled in a large skull with a five-inch tusk protruding from its lower jaw. Unfortunately, no analysis of the skull was performed and its fate — like the identity of Utah Lake's cryptid(s) — remains unknown. Reports from the lake have apparently ceased since World War II, when U.S. Steel established a local plant that polluted the water.

Sources: Arave, "Mythical beasts lurk in 5 Utah lakes"; Bagley, "Maybe there is a monster in Utah Lake."

Uyan   An unknown HOMINID or APE reported from Malaysia, the Uyan is described is three feet tall and covered with dark hair over tan or brownish skin. It is bipedal, and occasional reports describe individuals accompanied by domesticated dogs. A Malaysian naturalist, David Labang, tried to capture a Uyan in the 1980s, searching in Perang State (25 miles west of Kuala Lumpur), but he failed to sight or snare a specimen.

Source: Jeffrey McNeely and Paul Wachtel, *Soul of the Tiger*. New York: Doubleday, 1988.

———— V ————

Vaal River, South Africa   The Vaal River is a northern tributary of South Africa's larger Orange river. From Sterkfontein Beacon, near Breyten (Mpumalanga Province), it flows 750 miles

southwest to its confluence with the Orange near Douglas. A plateau river with a shallow bed, the Vaal's middle section comprises most of the Free State's northern provincial boundary. A portion of the river, confined by the Vaaldam, offers fishing and other recreational activities. An unidentified "monster" allegedly dwells in that part of the Vaal, described as a giant lizard that sometimes emerges to cross nearby roads. In April 1965, Constable James Padenenski told reporters, "We receive a report about every 30 days. People demand that the police do something. If that lizard is really out there and I ever see it, you'll see me moving in the other direction."

Source: Warren Smith, *Strange Monsters and Madmen.* New York: Popular Library, 1969.

Valhalla sea serpent In December 1905, while engaged in an expedition of scientific discovery, passengers aboard the yacht *Valhalla* sighted an unidentified SEA SERPENT in the South Atlantic, fifteen miles out from the mouth of Brazil's Rio Parahiba. One of the witnesses, naturalist E.G.B. Meade-Waldo, described the encounter.

> On Dec. 7th, 1905, at 10:15 a.m., I was on the poop of the "Valhalla" with Mr. [M.J.] Nicoll, when he drew my attention to an object in the sea about 100 yards from the yacht; he said, "Is that the fin of a great FISH?"
> I looked and immediately saw a large fin or frill sticking out of the water, dark seaweed-brown in colour, somewhat crinkled at the edge. It was apparently about 6 feet in length, and projected from 18 inches to 2 feet from the water.
> I got my field-glasses on to it (a powerful pair of Goerz-Triëder), and almost as soon as I had them on the frill, a great head and neck rose out of the water in front of the frill; the neck did not touch the frill in the water, but came out of the water in *front* of it, at a distance of certainly not less than 18 inches, probably more. The neck appeared about the thickness of a slight man's body, and from 7 to 8 feet was out of the water; head and neck were all about the same thickness.
> The head had a very turtle-like appearance, as had also the eye. I could see the line of the mouth, but we were sailing pretty fast, and quickly drew away from the object, which was going very slowly. It moved its head and neck from side to side in a peculiar manner: the colour of the head and neck was dark brown above, and whitish below — almost white, I think.

Meade-Waldo added further details in a letter to cryptozoologist RUPERT GOULD, stating:

> It made a wave as it went along, and *under* water behind the neck I could see a good-sized body. As we drew ahead we could see it swing its neck from side to side as it lashed the sea into foam.
> The eye and the edge of the neck had a turtle-like appearance to us both. We were so astonished at the time that we could neither of us speak! We then visited (late) Lord Crawford [owner of the yacht], and he said he would stop the yacht if it was any use; but we decided as we were making about 14 knots [21 miles per hour] it would not be much use.

The *Valhalla* sea serpent, after witness M.J. Nicoll.

M.J. Nicoll, himself a zoologist, sketched the creature and provided his own account.

> This creature was an example, I consider, of what has been so often reported, for want of a better name, as the "great sea-serpent." I feel sure, however, that it was not a reptile that we saw, but a mammal. It is, of course, impossible to be certain of this, but the general appearance of the creature, especially the soft, almost rubber-like fin, gave one this impression.

Gould, for his part, suspected the creature was a giant TURTLE, comparable to the MOHA-MOHA. Thirty years later, BERNARD HEUVELMANS cast another dissenting vote, listing the animal as a specimen of his hypothetical "super EEL."

Source: Heuvelmans, *In the Wake of the Sea Serpents.*

Valley River, North Carolina Descriptions are sadly lacking for the "water monster" said to inhabit this river in far western North Carolina (Cherokee County). It may, in fact, be identical to the creatures reported from the LITTLE TENNESSEE RIVER, spanning Graham and Swain Counties.

Sources: Bord and Bord, *Unexplained Mysteries of the 20th Century;* Coleman, *Mysterious America.*

Valleygator *see* **Sandwell Valleygator**

Vangsmjøsa, Norway Located in Oppland County, this Norwegian lake produced several LAKE MONSTER reports in the early 20th century. Around 1910, multiple witnesses described a large "serpent" swimming in the lake, displaying five or six humps and raising its head above the surface on a long, slender neck. No recent reports are on record.

Sources: Erik Knatterud, "Sea serpents in Norwegian lakes." http://www.mjoesormen.no; Skjelsvik, "Norwegian lake and sea monsters."

Vangsvatnet, Norway Another Norwegian lake once said to host a LAKE MONSTER, Vangsvatnet was supposedly dammed by its resident to the point of overflowing at some unspecified point in the distant past. Local residents allegedly distracted the creature with bright brass ornaments and lured it away. It apparently did not return, since no modern reports suggest any unknown fauna in the lake.

Source: Erik Knatterud, "Sea serpents in Norwegian lakes." http://www.mjoesormen.no.

Varmints A slang corruption of the term "vermin," this label is used throughout the United States for unwanted predatory animals (bobcats, coyotes, etc.). In cryptozoology, the term has been historically applied to a variety of unknown animals across the U.S., including ALIEN BIG CATS and various MYSTERY MAULERS. Because of the term's diverse and widespread use, no typical "varmint" description is available.

Source: Predator Defense Institute, "Varmint hunting." http://pdi.enviroweb.org/varmints.htm.

Vasitri An unknown HOMINID reported from Orinoco River valley in Venezuela, the Vasitri ("big devil") is described as a manlike figure covered in dark hair. Natives of the region claim the Vasitri builds crude huts and is carnivorous, sometimes including human beings in its diet. The creature also reportedly kidnaps women from time to time, for breeding purposes. An early account of the creature, published by Baron Alexander von Humboldt in 1825, claims that a woman snatched from San Carlos lived with her Vasitri captor for several years and bore its hairy children.

The Vasitri is an unknown hominid reported from Venezuela (*William Rebsamen*).

The tale, although reversed, is reminiscent of stories surrounding ZANA, an ABNAUAYU reportedly captured in the nation of Georgia during the mid-19th century.

Sources: Alexander von Humboldt, *Personal Narrative of a Journey to the Equinoctial Regions of the New Continent, during the Years 1799-1804.* London: George Bell, 1900 [reprint]; Sanderson, *Abominable Snowmen.*

Vasstrollet   The Vasstrollet ("water troll") is a LAKE MONSTER said to reside in Lake Sandnesvatnet, on Hamarøy Island, in Norway's Nordlund County. The first modern report was filed in 1910, after nocturnal boaters collided with a dark-colored animal 15 to 20 feet long. Regular sightings (mostly in summer) continued from that point onward, though the creature seldom made headlines outside the immediate area. Local resident Karl Sandnes described a sighting 60 years after the first report.

> On a fine summer's evening in 1970 I was sitting in my cabin, which is right by the lake. It was still light outside and completely calm. Suddenly I saw something that surfaced by a small point on the other side of the lake. It was an object that looked like an upside-down boat and it swam for some 300 meters on the surface before it dived and vanished. Shortly thereafter it surfaced again. It swam rather quickly, faster than you could row a boat, and it made great waves.

An expedition to Lake Sandnesvatnet collected numerous sighting reports in autumn 1972, but it failed to identify the Vasstrollet. JAN-OVE SUNDBERG has also investigated the creature, though his GLOBAL UNDERWATER SEARCH TEAM has yet to give Lake Sandnesvatnet concentrated attention. The sightings — and the mystery — continue.

Source: Kirk, *In the Domain of the Lake Monsters.*

Västjuten, Sweden   Västjuten Lake, located in Sweden's Östergötland County, was the scene of a DRAGON sighting in 1899. The slithering creature, possibly a form of unidentified LAKE MONSTER, has not reappeared since its debut, leaving the matter unresolved.

Source: Jan-Ove Sundberg's GUST Zoology website. http://www.bahnhof.se/~wizard/cryptoworld/index33.htm.

Vättern, Sweden   Another Swedish source of LAKE MONSTER reports, Lake Vättern lies in Västra Götaland County. Sight-

ings are more frequent here than in some Scandinavian locations, and a tourist claims to have photographed the resident cryptid near Hjo in August 1972, but the resultant print was inconclusive at best.

Source: Jan-Ove Sundberg's GUST Zoology website. http://www.bahnhof.se/~wizard/cryptoworld/index33.htm.

Veado Branco   While exploring Brazil's Rio Aripuanã region in 2000, zoologist Marc van Roosmalen collected native accounts of the Veado Branco, an unclassified mazama deer said to be midway in size between the country's two known species (*Mazama americana* and *M. gouzazoubira*). The search for a type specimen continues, as of last report, without success.

Source: Karl Shuker, "Alien zoo." *Fortean Times* 139 (November 2000): 22.

Ved   A form of WILDMAN or WUDÉWÁSÁ, the Ved reportedly lived in northern Croatia's Bilogora Mountains prior to World War I. Although described as tall, hairy HOMINIDS in the general pattern of BIGFOOT and YETI, the Ved were allegedly civilized enough to build houses and fashion rough clothing. Stories of their collaboration and friendship with humans smack of mythology. No accounts of Ved being killed in the Great War have so far been uncovered, but sightings apparently ceased with the outbreak of hostilities in 1914.

Sources: Lovrencevic, "Creatures from the Bilogora in northern Croatia"; Markotic and Krantz, *The Sasquatch and Other Unknown Hominids.*

Vélé   The Vélé are an alleged race of PYGMIES said to inhabit forests on the Fiji Islands. They are typically described as hairy, with conical heads and a penchant for lobbing small clubs at unlucky humans. BERNARD HEUVELMANS considered them "largely mythologized," but acknowledged the possibility of undiscovered primates on the islands. The most recent publicized sighting occurred in July 1975, when a group of eight Vélé were seen by children at the Lautoka Methodist Mission School on the island of Viti Levu.

Sources: *Fiji Times* (19 July 1975); Heuvelmans, "Annotated checklist of apparently unknown animals with which cryptozoology is concerned."

***Venetian* sea serpent**   On 20 June 1888, officers of the steamer *Venetian* sighted an unknown SEA SERPENT off the Massachusetts coast, "northward of Georges Shoals and about 190 miles from Boston." No clear description of the creature was provided, but the *Venetian*'s captain, one Mr. Muir, later told reporters, "It was unlike any animal I ever saw. It couldn't have been a SHARK. It certainly was not the back of a whale, although we had seen plenty of whales for two days."

Source: O'Neill, *The Great New England Sea Serpent.*

Venice, California carcass   Cryptozoologist JOHN KEEL reports that a strange carcass washed ashore at Venice, California in December 1955. It was described as serpentine in form, 16 feet long and 14 inches in diameter, "complete with fins and a snakish head." The carcass weighed 800 pounds, but no further details are presently available.

Source: Keel, *The Complete Guide to Mysterious Beings.*

Venus Lake   Located on Isola de Pantelleria, an Italian-owned island midway between Sicily and Tunisia, Venus lake produced a spate of LAKE MONSTER rumors in July 1982. No creature was seen, but "strange" sounds issued from the lake on several consecutive nights, thus spawning fears of a resident cryptid.

Source: Bord and Bord, *Unexplained Mysteries of the 20th Century.*

Veo   Reports of this unidentified creature issue from Rintja, a small island in the Lesser Sunda chain, between Flores and Komodo. Rintja natives say the Veo is "as big as a horse," with a long head, scaly back and flanks, fur underneath, and large claws on its feet. The animal's distinctive cry, mostly heard around sundown, sounds like "hoo-hoo-hoo." Though normally inoffensive, feeding primarily on ANTS, termites and beached shellfish, the Veo will rear up and strike with its talons if threatened, size making it a formidable opponent.

Stature aside, descriptions of the Veo closely match the pangolin (or scaly anteater), a creature native to Africa and Asia. Although the largest living pangolin, Africa's *Manis gigantea*, rarely exceeds five feet in length, a larger species (*M. paleojavanicus*) inhabited the Greater Sunda islands of Borneo and Java during the Pleistocene epoch (2 million to 10,000 years ago). Fossil remains prove that *M. paleojavanicus* sometimes grew beyond eight feet in length, and while it is officially extinct today, Czech cryptozoologist Jaroslav Mares suggests that a relict population may still survive in the Lesser Sundas.

Source: Mares, *Svet Tajemnych Zvírat*; Shuker, "A scaly tale from Rintja."

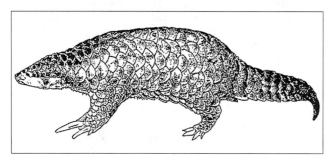

Witnesses claim that the Veo resembles a giant pangolin.

Vietnam Cryptozoic and Rare Animals Research Center
Following repeated discoveries of new ungulates in the 1990s, captured in the rain forest of Vietnam's VU QUANG NATURE PRESERVE, the country's government decreed that a broad inventory of Vietnam's fauna should be undertaken without further delay. Accordingly, the Vietnam Cryptozoic and Rare Animals Research Center was established in May 1997, at the Teachers Training College-Vietnam National University, in Hanoi. Professor TRAN HONG VIET, chairman of the university's zoology department, was named director of the center. Despite the widespread damage inflicted by nearly four decades of warfare, new discoveries continue from Vu Quang and elsewhere in the country, encouraging further exploration.

Source: Coleman and Clark, *Cryptozoology A to Z*.

Viitna, Estonia   Located in Lääne-Viru County, Viitna stands near a lake which has produced multiple reports of hairy yellow FISH. Thus far, the creatures (if they exist) remain unidentified.

Source: Oskar Loorits, *Grundzüge des estnischen Volksglaubens*. Lund, Sweden: Carl Bloms Boktryckeri, 1951.

Villa Gesell sea serpents   The Argentine coastal town of Villa Gesell produced several strange SEA SERPENT sightings during the 1980s. While the creatures seen were typically described as serpentine, one specimen was said to be "a cyclopean, smiling, and rather gelatinous centipede."

Source: Picasso, "South American monsters & mystery animals."

Villa Rico carcass   On 25 December 1996, a strange carcass washed ashore on Villa Rico beach, at Claveria, in the Philippine province of Masbate. It measured 26 feet long and was described as EEL-like, with a head resembling a TURTLE'S. Though nearly skeletal, the carcass retained fins. Observers noted that it had no ribs, and that the skull appeared to have a blowhole similar to a cetacean's. Researchers who examined photos of the carcass and samples of the creature's flesh could not identify it, finally settling on a vague conclusion that it may have been a "dolphin-like fish." A missionary at Davao City, Ken Sandberg, suggested that the creature might be a PLESIOSAUR, thus supporting his religious belief in a "young Earth" no more than 6,000 years old. BEN ROESCH, after viewing newspaper photographs of the carcass, pronounced it a decomposed basking shark (*Cetorhinus maximus*). The alleged blowhole, possessed by no fish, remains unexplained.

Sources: "Is sea 'monster' a plesiosaur?" *Philippine Star* (1 March 1997); Roesch, "Another 'sea serpent' carcass." *Cryptozoology Review* 2 (Winter-Spring 1998): 7-8.

***Ville de Lisbonne* sea serpent**   In 1847, officers and crewmen of the Portuguese ship *Ville de Lisbonne* reportedly sighted a sea serpent during one of their Atlantic voyages. Captain Juan Alphonso Zarco y Capeda is named as the ship's commander in one brief newspaper report, but the story is sadly devoid of any further details. BERNARD HEUVELMANS considered the report a HOAX.

Source: Heuvelmans, *In the Wake of the Sea Serpents*.

***Ville de Rochefort* sea serpent**   On 21 April 1840, while crossing the Gulf of Mexico, passengers aboard the French ship *Ville de Rochefort* observed an unknown SEA SERPENT. The ship's commander, Captain d'Abnour, reported that the creature was like a

> long chain of enormous rings, resembling a number of barrels linked together, and in form very like the back of a silkworm.... As the ship approached...we presently saw the extremity of an enormous tail, longitudinally divided into two sections, white and black. This tail appeared to wind itself up, and repose on a part of the object itself. Then, at the other extremity, we saw a membrane rising to the height of about two metres from the water, and inclining itself at a considerable angle upon the mass (without leaving it, however): and this led me to conjecture that the monster before us was provided with an apparatus for the purpose of respiration, like the lampreys. At last we perceived something like an antenna rising from the water, to the great height of nearly eight metres [26 feet], terminated by a crescent at least five meters [16 feet 3 inches] from one extremity to the other.

BERNARD HEUVELMANS correctly noted that lampreys have no breathing "membrane" that rises above water. He suggested that Captain d'Abnour may have observed a large whale — or perhaps the rare sight of a whale locked in combat with a GIANT SQUID.

Source: Heuvelmans, *In the Wake of the Sea Serpents*.

Virginia Bigfoot Research
Virginia BIGFOOT Research is embodied in the person of Manassas resident William Dranginis, whose interest in unknown HOMINIDS sprang from an undated personal sighting in Culpepper County. Dranginis and two friends, one of them a U.S. federal agent, were scouring the local woods for Civil War relics when a large hairy biped sprinted through the trees in front of them. As Dranginis later described the beast, "I have never seen such massive shoulder muscles, the whole body was built for speed and agility ....I think the creature deliberately ran in front of us to draw our attention from what

was following behind it. What it was we will never know. It could have been family unit or its mate. But this creature took a big chance by running directly in front of us." Dranginis claims discovery of several SASQUATCH-type footprints in various sizes, but his deployment of motion-activated microphones and video cameras have thus far failed to capture evidence of any cryptid activity. He remains committed to nonviolent field research, explaining: "I really want to look into the eyes of one of these animals. Maybe then I can get on with my life. This has been a time consuming and costly hobby for me but I wouldn't trade it for the world!"

Source: Virginia Bigfoot Research, http://www.virginiabigfootresearch.org/html/main.php.

Vojmsjon Lake, Sweden

Located in Västerbotten County, Vojmsjon is one of 19 Swedish lakes that have produced LAKE MONSTER reports. The creatures sighted here, when described at all, resemble others from the region (and around the world) in their shared resemblance to a capsized boat.

Source: Kirk, *In the Domain of the Lake Monsters.*

Vondel sea serpent

At 10:00 a.m. on 8 September 1907, officers of the Dutch ship *Vondel* observed a SEA SERPENT in the Indian Ocean, at latitude 8° 30' north, longitude 67° 15' east. Captain C.S. Visser prepared two sketches of the creature and logged the following report.

> At irregular intervals the beast several times raised its head above the water and then let it fall noisily on the surface. The first two times the animal was seen it also showed its tail, which appeared and disappeared at almost the same time as the head. As the monster was seen head on and from a fairly considerable distance, certainly more than a mile, the head and tail seemed very close together, and it was not possible to judge the animal's length; there is likewise little that can be said exactly about the other dimensions. The other times that the animal rose out of the water, only the head was visible and was watched until it was so far away that observation was impossible. The colour of the head and tail was black.

Sixty years later, BERNARD HEUVELMANS suggested that the creature's "tail" was probably a dorsal fin. He considered the *Vondel* cryptid an unknown fISH, similar to one seen from the yacht *VALHALLA* in 1905.

Source: Heuvelmans, *In the Wake of the Sea Serpents.*

The *Vondel* sea serpent, after witness C.S. Visser.

Vopnafjöđur, Iceland

Iceland's Lake Vopnafjöđur produced two LAKE MONSTER sightings on 13 February 1963, when a black, hump-backed animal twice surfaced before witnesses. It remains unidentified, and no more recent sightings have yet come to light.

Source: Bord and Bord, *Unexplained Mysteries of the 20th Century.*

Vouroupatra/Vorompatra

A large flightless BIRD reported from Madagascar, the Vouroupatra was typically described as larger than an OSTRICH and laid eggs the size of a football. Etienne de Flacourt, the first French governor of Madagascar, reported the Vouroupatra as extant but elusive in 1658. Eyewitness sightings ceased in the mid-19th century, and no source claims that the bird is still living today. The Vouroupatra candidate most often proposed is *Aepyornis maximus*, a prehistoric "elephant bird" which reached 10 feet in height and weighed nearly 1,000 pounds. A fearsome predator, *Aepyornis* relied on speed to run down its prey — which may well have included early human inhabitants of Madagascar. *Aepyornis* eggs measured more than one foot long and equaled 150 hen's eggs in volume, ranking as the largest known single cells. Multiple *Aepyornis* eggs in a subfossil state were found on Madagascar in the 19th century, strengthening the case for its survival into fairly recent times.

Sources: Etienne de Flacourt, *Histoire de la grande isle Madagascar.* Paris: G. de Luyne, 1658; Heuvelmans, *On the Track of Unknown Animals*; Strickland, "Supposed existence of a giant bird in Madagascar."

Vu Quang Nature Reserve

After centuries of foreign occupation and 30 years of unrelenting warfare (1946-75), it might be supposed that no cryptids could survive in Vietnam, but thankfully, that supposition is mistaken. In fact, the Vu Quang Nature Reserve — located in the Annamite Mountains of Vietnam's Quang Tri Province — has produced a series of delightful surprises for zoologists since the early 1990s. Although Quang Tri suffered intensive bombing during the U.S. war in Vietnam, Vu Quang remained relatively unscathed, a concentration of dense mountain rain forest surrounded by protective cliffs. It is, in some respects, the very model of Sir Arthur Conan Doyle's *Lost World.*

Vu Quang gave up its first secret in 1992, with discovery of the saola or Vu Quang ox, in fact a robust muntjac deer. It was unknown to science until Dr. John MacKinnon found three pairs of strange horns in the homes of local hunters. By year's end, more than 20 specimens were collected, including three complete skins, and DNA analysis validated the saola's status as a new species (*Pseudoryx nghetinhensis*). Several live specimens were captured between 1994 and 1998, but they soon died in captivity. Others have been photographed in the wild with remote-control infrared cameras.

Vietnam's Vu Quang Nature Reserve produced many discoveries in the 1990s, including three species of muntjac deer.

In 1994 a larger muntjac was discovered in Vu Quang, formally *Megamuntiacus vuquangensis* ("giant muntjac of Vu Quang"). Three years later, searchers spotted a dwarf specimen, known to locals as *sam coi caoong* ("deep-forest deer"). Eighteen skulls were collected by hunters in subsequent months, resulting in the creature's 1998 formal identification as *Muntiacus truong-sonensis* (Truong Son muntjac, after the mountains where it lives). During the same period, zoologists in Vu Quang discovered a new species of CATFISH (*Crossocheilus*) and Dr. MacKinnon discovered horns belonging to an ungulate the locals call MANGDEN ("black deer"), which remains formally unclassified today.

Vu Quang was not the only source of remarkable Vietnamese discoveries in the 1990s. In 1994, a few miles to the north, the Pu Mat district yielded relics of another unknown deer called QUANG KHEM by local hunters. The same year witnessed discovery of a spiral-horned ungulate known to Vietnamese as *linh duong* ("holy goat"), now formally identified as *Pseudonovibos spiralis*. A third discovery for 1994 was the capture of a female *tua* (a forest-dwelling goatlike ungulate) in central Vietnam's Thua Thien-Hue Province. Because that specimen was immature, its status as

a new species remains in dispute. The remarkable year 1994 closed with December's revelation of a giant cream loris, formerly unknown to science, at Hanoi's animal market. Of 12 large, new mammals discovered in the 20th century, 7 were found in Vietnam.

That rash of zoological discoveries prompted creation of the VIETNAM CRYPTOZOIC AND RARE ANIMALS RESEARCH CENTER in May 1997. Professor TRAN HONG VIET was appointed director of the project and retains that post today. Discoveries logged since the Center's creation include another small deer, the Pu Hoat muntjac (1998), and a JAVAN RHINOCEROS, long believed extinct in Vietnam, photographed at Cat Tien National Park in 1999.

Sources: Karl Shuker, "Alien zoo." *Fortean Times* 106 (January 1998): 14-15; Shuker, "Alien zoo." *Fortean Times* 127 (October 1999): 18; Shuker, "Menagerie of mystery." *Strange Magazine* 15 (Spring 1995): 30-31; Shuker, "Menagerie of mystery." *Strange Magazine* 16 (Fall 1995): 30-31; Shuker, "Menagerie of mystery," *Strange Magazine* 18 (Summer 1997): 52; Shuker, "Menagerie of mystery," *Strange Magazine* 19 (Spring 1998):20-21; Shuker, *The New Zoo*; Shuker, "Wild Kthing, I think I love you."

W

Waab   The Waab is an unclassified primate or HOMINID reported from Sudan. Witnesses describe a tall bipedal creature covered in red hair, but Sudanese folklore also claims that the Waab has no joints anywhere in its body, which should logically render it immobile. That feature, and occasional claims of the Waab's fluency in various human languages, incline most researchers to regard it as a mythical being. Rewards offered for the capture of a Waab in 1950 failed to produce a specimen for study.

Sources: "Jointless *Waab* of African Sudan: One of the world's fabulous creatures." *National Geographic News Bulletin* (25 April 1950); "Reward for a Waab." *Western Folklore* 9 (1950): 387-388.

Waaki *see* **Junjadee**

Waa-Wee   This name was applied to an Australian BUNYIP inhabiting Midgeon Lagoon, 16 miles north of Nerrandera, New South Wales, in the latter 19th century. In April 1872, three witnesses heard a "sound as of a body rushing rapidly through the water, making a noise as loud as that caused by a North Shore steamer." One of those present described what happened next.

> We stood still, deeply interested, and watched the approach of the animal, which having, as we presumed, lately risen to the surface, was evidently not aware of our presence. It came on with great swiftness until it was scarcely 30 yards from the edge of the lagoon, when it appeared suddenly to catch sight of us, and stopped instantly.
>
> It lay on the water then perfectly still, and I had a splendid view of a creature that surprised me more than anything I had ever seen in my life. The animal was about half as long again as an ordinary retriever dog; the hair all over its body was jet-black and shining, its coat was very long, the hair spreading out on the surface of the water for about five inches and floating loosely as the creature rose and fell by its own motion. I could not detect any tail, and the hair about its head was too long and glossy to admit of my seeing its eyes; the ears were well marked.

The Waa-wee remained in place for 30 minutes, then swam off

and submerged with no sign of alarm. The witness offered a £20 reward for its corpse, £50 if the thing was captured alive, but the cash was never claimed.

Sources: Healy and Cropper, *Out of the Shadows*; Smith, *Bunyips & Bigfoots*.

Wabash River, Indiana   In the early 1890s, two women from Huntington, Indiana (15 miles southwest of Fort Wayne) reported an unidentified creature swimming in the Wabash River, south of town. They described it as having the head of a LION, and a stout tail that whipped the water into froth.

Source: Charles Skinner, *Myths and Legends of Our Land*. Philadelphia: Lippincott, 1896.

***Wacouta* sea serpent**   On 10 July 1902, while entering Sydney Harbor on Cape Breton Island, Nova Scotia, the yacht *Wacouta* reportedly found its way blocked by a 200-foot SEA SERPENT. Witnesses included the yacht's owner, U.S. railroad tycoon J.J. Hill, and members of his crew.

Source: O'Neill, *The Great New England Sea Serpent*.

Wading River, New York   Authors LOREN COLEMAN and JOHN KIRK list this river, near the Long Island town of the same name, as a source of aquatic cryptid reports. Unfortunately, neither account provides any dates or details of sightings in the area.

Sources: Coleman, *Mysterious America*; Kirk, *In the Domain of the Lake Monsters*.

Waheela   Inuit natives and occasional trappers describe the Waheela as a snow-white wolf, much larger than normal WOLVES (*Canis lupus*), inhabiting the Arctic regions of Alaska and Canada's vast Northwest Territories, including the ill-famed Nahanni Valley. IVAN SANDERSON recorded the experience of a hunter (identified only as "Frank") who allegedly met and wounded a Waheela in the Nahanni, sometime in the 1940s or 1950s. Frank described the creature as 3½ feet tall at the shoulder, with a broad head, shaggy white coat and comparatively short legs. Another friend of Sanderson's, photographer Tex Zeigler, reported sightings of Waheela from the Alaskan tundra. LOREN COLEMAN subsequently uncovered a much earlier report, from Indiana University's historical archives, concerning three trappers who met a Waheela near an unnamed lake in northern Michigan. Descriptions of the Waheela bear a resemblance to the Midwest's wolflike SHUNKA WARAK'IN. Some researchers believe the creatures may be relict specimens of bear-dog (Family *Amphicyonidae*), presumed extinct in North America for some 5 million years.

Sources: Sanderson, "The dire wolf"; Shuker, *In Search of Prehistoric Survivors.*

Waimarama carcass   On 10 January 1951, a curious 30-foot skeleton washed ashore on the remote Waimarama coast near Hastings, New Zealand. Observers reported that the creature's skull was 3.5 feet wide and featured a protruding 3-foot tusk. Journalists speculated that the animal might have been killed and cast ashore by submarine earthquakes, but debate surrounding its resemblance to a prehistoric monster ended one day later, when zoologists K.E. Crompton and W.M. Moore identified the bones as those of a BEAKED WHALE (*Berardius bairdii*), declaring that its "tusk" was the whale's pointed snout. In the wake of that announcement, witness F.O. Bryce recalled sighting a similar cetacean in Polorus Sound, on 3 January, but the whale she saw was only half the size of the Waimarama carcass. Though such whales are rare in New Zealand's coastal waters, it seems that at least two visited the area in January 1951.

Source: Peter Hassall, "50 years ago this month." *Fortean Times* 142 (February 2001): 18.

Waitoreke   Tales of a mysterious aquatic creature have emerged from New Zealand since the late 18th century. Sailors under Captain Cook sighted a CAT-sized, bushy-tailed animal at Dusky Sound in May 1773, while an 1844 expedition to Lake Wanaka reported contact with BEAVERS. Four years later, Walter Mantell reported that Maori natives called the creatures Waitoreke ("spurred one who dives into water") or Kaurehe. One tribal source told Mantell there were two kinds of Waitoreke, one land-dwelling and the other amphibious. He also explained —

> that the length of the animal is about two feet from the point of the nose to the root of the tail; the fur grisly (*sic*) brown, thick short legs, bushy tail, head between that of a dog and a cat, lives in holes, the food of the land kind is lizards, of the amphibious kind, FISH — does not lay eggs.

Maori sources also denied that the Waitoreke had a pouch, thus ruling out marsupial candidates. Thirteen years later, in June 1861, biologist Julius von Haast sighted tracks of the creature, resembling those of a European otter (*Lutra lutra*) along the South Island's Ashburton River. Though largely ignored by science for the past 145 years, the Waitoreke continues to appear sporadically. Grassmere resident A.E. Trapper reported six sightings between 1890 and 1921, on various fishing expeditions, including one observation of two Waitorekes together in 1912. Other sightings were reported from various locations in 1936, 1957, 1968, 1971 and 1973. Most researchers believe the Waitoreke is an otter, and author G.A. Pollock goes so far as to identify the subspecies as *Lutra lutra barang*, known throughout Southeast Asia and Indonesia. Malcolm Smith, meanwhile, suggests that the creature may be something else entirely — an unknown, indigenous New Zealand

New Zealand's Waitoreke may be an unclassified otter.

mammal whose discovery would be, as Smith notes, "the zoological discovery of the century."

Sources: Heuvelmans, *On the Track of Unknown Animals*; G.A. Pollock, "The South Island otter: A reassessment." *Proceedings of the New Zealand Ecological Society* 21 (1974): 57-61; Smith, *Bunyips & Bigfoots.*

Wakandagi   (*See illustration on next page.*) Aboriginal Sioux tribesmen applied this name to an aquatic cryptid found in the MISSOURI RIVER. Traditional descriptions of the animal(s) include antlers and hooves, with a powerful tail used in swimming. The Wakandagi may be identical to the unknown creatures reported from the Missouri in modern times.

Sources: Garner, *Monster! Monster!*; Gatschet, "Water monsters of American aborigines."

Walchensee, Germany   In the 19th century, neighbors of this lake in Bayern State reported that a LAKE MONSTER inhabited its depths. Some who saw the creature described it as a "giant whale," while others claimed it was serpentine in form. No modern sightings are on file.

Sources: Friedrich Panzer, *Bayerische Sagen und Bräuche.* Munich: C. Kaiser, 1855; Johann Sepp, *Altbayerischer Sagenschatz zur Bereicherung der Indogermanischen Mythologie.* Munich: E. Stahl, 1876.

Waldagi   (*See illustration on next page.*) Aboriginal Australians describe the Waldagi as a doglike animal distinct and separate from both domestic dogs (*gunjar*) and dingoes (*moran*). It reportedly inhabits the Kimberley Mountains of Western Australia, and eyewitness accounts make it clear that the Waldagi is not considered a "spirit animal," but rather represents a flesh-and-blood creature as yet unclassified by science. Researcher Erich Kolig suggests that it may be a surviving form of mainland THYLACINE.

Sources: Erich Kolig, "Aboriginal man's best foe?" *Mankind* 9 (December 1973): 122-123; Shuker, *Mystery Cats of the World.*

Walensee, Switzerland   In the 19th and early 20th centuries, witnesses reported a FISH the length of tree trunks from this lake, in Switzerland's Canton Sankt Gallen. The sightings probably involved wels CATFISH (*Siluris glanis*), which may grow to 15 feet in length.

Source: Werner Manz, "Volksglaube und sage aus dem Sarganserland." *Schweizerisches Archiv für Volkskunde* 25 (1925): 229-238.

Walgren Lake, Nebraska   Walgren Lake (formerly Alkali Lake) is located south of Hay Springs, Nebraska, in Sheridan County. Local LAKE MONSTER reports date from the 1880s, when a predatory creature allegedly rose from the lake to prey on

Australians consider the elusive Waldagi a canid species distinct from the wild dingo pictured here.

livestock. The most detailed description was furnished in 1922 or 1923 (accounts vary), by duck hunter J.A. Johnson. According to that report:

> The animal was probably forty feet long, including the tail and head, when raised in alarm as when he saw us. In general appearance, the animal was not unlike an ALLIGATOR, except that the head was stubbier and there seemed to be a projection like a horn between the eyes and the nostrils. The animal was built much more heavily throughout than an alligator. Its color seemed a dull gray or brown.
>
> There was a very distinctive and somewhat unpleasant odor noticeable for several moments after the beast had vanished into the water. We stood for several minutes after it had gone, hardly knowing what to do or say, when we noticed several hundred feet out from the shore a considerable commotion in the water.

Roy Mackal suggests that Walgren Lake's "monster" is a misplaced elephant seal.

> Sure enough the animal came to the surface, floated there a moment…lashed the water with its tail, suddenly dived and we saw no more of him.

Johnson claimed that he could name 40 other witnesses to the creature's existence. Author Betty Garner perceives a resemblance between Johnson's animal and WHITEY, a cryptid reported from the White River in Arkansas, and she furthermore describes both as "gigantic penguin type of monsters," though Johnson's description bears no resemblance to a BIRD of any kind. Cryptozoologist ROY MACKAL, meanwhile, surmised that Walgren Lake's cryptid might be an elephant seal (*Mirounga leonina*) that made its misguided way to Nebraska along the MISSISSIPPI RIVER. How it would then travel another 175 miles westward across the plains of the Cornhusker State is unexplained. LOREN COLEMAN suggests that this creature and other "horned" lake monsters may comprise a relict population of hadrosaurs, "duck-billed" DINOSAURS presumed extinct since the Late Cretaceous period (65 million years ago).

Sources: Coleman, "Telling horny stories"; Garner, *Monster! Monster!*; Guiley, *Atlas of the Mysterious in North America*; Hall, "'Horrors' from the Mesozoic"; Mackal, *Searching for Hidden Animals*; Swatek, "Nebraska's famous lake monster."

Walker Lake, Alaska   LAKE MONSTERS resembling ILLIE (of Alaska's Lake Iliamna) have reportedly been seen at Walker Lake, located east of Kobuk, on the southern fringe of the Endicott Mountains. Speculation on the identity of Alaska's aquatic cryptids ranges from giant FISH or landlocked whales to "something left over from prehistoric times." Thus far, none have been captured on film or in the flesh.

Source: Garner, *Monster! Monster!*

Wallabies (Mislocated)   Wallabies are marsupial relatives of the KANGAROOS, virtually indistinguishable from their larger "cousins" except in size. Some 25 species are native to Australia, New Zealand and Papua New Guinea, but breeding colonies of naturalized wallabies have also been established in various parts of Britain over the past century. A Peak District colony of red-necked wallabies (*Macropus rufogriseus*) numbered 60-odd individuals in the late 1930s, but its numbers have declined dramatically and no confirmed sightings are on record since 1995. Elsewhere in Britain, however, the exotic hoppers appear to be thriving. A sampling of recent sightings includes:

1970s— A private landowner introduced wallabies to Inchconnachan (one of 23 islands in LOCH LOMOND, SCOTLAND) as part of a planned wildlife park. The scheme was later abandoned, along with the wallabies, who increased their number to 40 over the next three decades.

May 1996— Multiple wallaby sightings around Gloucester, England began on 9 May with a report a 3-foot specimen from Parkwood Crescent, Hucclecote. Over the next five days, three sightings were logged in Barnwood. Police inquiries found no animals missing from nearby zoos, and authorities acknowledged a colony living wild on Cannock Chase. A hotline established by Citizens Wallaby Watch received no new sightings in June.

5 June 1998— A tourist reported a 4-foot wallaby grazing along the A27 highway near Arundel, West Sussex. Multiple sightings from the same area had been recorded in recent years, although "wildlife experts" insist that harsh winters will kill off the animals. Sussex police wildlife liaison officer WPC Linda Batsleer told reporters, "We reckon there is a group of at least six living in area."

Thriving wallaby populations exist in Great Britain.

20 March 2000— A motorist filed the latest of several wallaby sightings from Dorset, this one reporting an animal in the woods near Lyme Regis. Police had a veterinarian on alert, armed with a tranquilizer gun, but the creature(s) remained at large.

January 2002— Twelve months of kangaroo sightings climaxed when zoologist Trevor Smith captured a wild wallaby at High Wycombe, Buckinghamshire.

May 2002— A wallaby crashed into the basement flat of Tony and Jean Meeghan in Henley-on-Thames, Oxfordshire. The Meeghans initially thought a burglar had ransacked their home, but DNA tests on blood found at the scene proved the vanished culprit was a wallaby.

June 2002— Motorist Jane Martin reported that an animal resembling "a kangaroo in full flight" had passed her car on a busy highway at Lower Assenden. On 2 June, a dead wallaby was found along the M40 motorway near Stokenchurch, Buckinghamshir. Newspaper reports alleged that "mobs of wallabies are believed to live with herds of deer on nearby estates in the Chilterns."

August 2002— Eyewitness reports suggest that Loch Lomond's island wallabies have made their way to the mainland. A boatman for the Luss Estates, on the loch's eastern shore, reported two sightings in recent weeks, while a truck driver nearly struck a wallaby on the highway. Authorities announced the presence of "another large colony" in the Lake District.

Sources: "Dorset's roaming wallaby keeps a jump ahead." Carlton TV Teletext (21 March 2000); Michelle Fleming, "'Kangaroo' find sparks mystery." *Bucks Free Press* (4 June 2002); "The hopper." *Fortean Times* 90 (September 1996): 17; Kay Jardine, "Wandering wallabies take shore leave." *Glasgow Herald* (22 August 2002); Karl Shuker, "Alien zoo." *Fortean Times* 101 (August 1997): 17; "Wallaby shock for tourist." *Chichester Observer* (6 June 1998); "Wayward wallabies roam Old Dart." *Canberra Times* (15 June 2002).

Wallace, Raymond L. (1918-2002)

When Ray Wallace died on 26 November 2002, at age 84, few outside his immediate family in Centralia, Washington took notice. That changed 10 days later, with a rash of stories in the media claiming that Wallace had "invented the legend of BIGFOOT" in 1958. Overnight, the

report traveled worldwide, embroidered and distorted as it made the rounds. Suddenly, the late Ray Wallace had vaulted from obscurity to become what journalists once called a "nine-days' wonder"—though his story would endure far longer. *Sports Illustrated* ran the tale on 20 January 2003, and Dan Rather recycled it three months later on CBS News, as if Wallace had just passed away.

In essence, the story was this: Nine days after Wallace expired, members of his family approached the media, declaring that Wallace had used large wooden feet to fake SASQUATCH tracks around Bluff Creek, California in 1958, resulting in newspaper reports that coined the Bigfoot nickname. Furthermore, the family said, Wallace and his brother Wilbur had ranged far and wide, planting tracks with fake feet of various sizes across the Pacific Northwest. According to his kin, Wallace had also fabricated APE suits and faked photos of Bigfoot. In 1967, it was claimed, he directed monster-hunter Roger Patterson to the site near Bluff Creek where the PATTERSON FILM captured Sasquatch on celluloid. Summing up, son Michael Wallace told reporters, "Ray L. Wallace was Bigfoot. In reality, Bigfoot just died."

As the story traveled, it began to mutate. On 6 December 2002, the Associated Press reported: "Michael Wallace said his father called the Patterson film 'a fake' but claimed he'd had nothing to do with it. But he said his mother admitted she had been photographed in a Bigfoot suit, and that his father 'had several people he used in his movies.'" One day later, across the Atlantic, *The Scotsman* alleged: "Mr. Wallace later persuaded his wife to dress up in a MONKEY suit for 'Bigfoot' photographs, and he told Roger Patterson, a rodeo rider, to set up his camera to film the famous footage…which supposedly showed the creature walking up the hillside." Meanwhile, a television broadcast in Pocatello, Idaho claimed that Wallace's kin "say they still have pieces of the costume that was worn in the film." (None were produced.) The *Glasgow Daily Record* of 7 December asserted that the Patterson film displayed "the wife of a building company boss in a monkey suit." Even the motive for Wallace's trickery varied over time and distance. Nephew Dale Wallace told the *Vancouver Province* (8 December) that "He did it for the joke and then he was afraid to tell anyone because they'd be so mad at him." A day later, elderly ex-logger John Auman grabbed the spotlight with a claim that the original Bluff Creek prank "wasn't intended as a prank to revive the legend of Bigfoot. Wallace left the giant footprints around construction equipment parked in the woods to scare away vandals who had been targeting the vehicles."

Cryptozoologists were chagrined by the media's eager acceptance of claims that Wallace had "invented" Sasquatch more than 150 years after the first recorded sighting by a white settler in North America. In fact, Wallace's reputation for spawning HOAXES was well known among Bigfoot researchers from the 1960s onward. JOHN GREEN had frequent contact with Wallace, whom he dubbed "a great bullshit artist." In February 1967, Wallace wrote to Green, claiming that he had found an "ape cave" on Mount Saint Helens and "made some of the nicest casts of those…apes tracks that I have ever saw." Later, in October 1969, Wallace wrote to Willow Creek's *Klam-ity Kourier*:

> Big Foot used to be very tame, as I have seen him almost every morning on the way to work…. I would sit in my pickup and toss apples out of the window to him. He never did catch an apple but he sure tried. Then as he ate the apples I would have my movie camera clipping off more footage of him. I have talked to several movie companies about selling my movies which would last for three hours. The best offer I've had so far is $250,000.

No film ever appeared, but Wallace kept up a prolific correspondence, constantly elaborating on his lies. On 24 May 1978, he wrote to researcher Dennis Gates:

> I just want to inform you Big Foot hunters that Big Footed creatures are people, they speak a language. I could tell you more about the Sasquatch or Bigfoot than anyone else....I made ten thousand feet of movies of the Big Foots before I told Roger Patterson where to go....I could take you to a cave in Northern California where the Big Foots live in a very rich gold mine cave. Did you know that TOM SLICK bought Big Foot skeletons for many years and turned them over to the Pentagon in Washington, D.C.?....I have talked to the Big Foots many times. They didn't understand me and I didn't understand them, but their brown eyes told the story that they are very sad because the bear hunters are killing all their people.

A year later, in April 1979, Wallace spun a tale for John Green of a time when "all the Big Foots were killed and hauled down the Klamath River in a tug boat and out into the ocean 12 miles to where was a small ship anchored in international waters and frozen into a block of ice and then transported to Hong Kong and sold, so now there aren't any more left in northern California." Still, Wallace offered photos to Green in December 1984 and January 1989, but none were ever delivered. Cryptozoologist LOREN COLEMAN has advertised nationally for any Bluff Creek photographs or footprint casts from 1958 or 1967 that match Wallace's collection of phony footgear, but thus far none have been disclosed. On 21 January 2003, the Willow Creek-China Flat Museum offered $100,000 to "anyone who can demonstrate how the 'Bigfoot' tracks that were observed in the Bluff Creek valley in northern California in 1958 and later could have been made by a human or humans"— and again, the rest is silence.

Sadly, the global media's performance in the Wallace case rivaled the 1994 feeding frenzy surrounding the Loch Ness SURGEON'S PHOTOGRAPH. The issue, finally, is not whether Ray Wallace faked any particular Sasquatch film or footprint. Instead, we must question the speed with which "skeptical" journalists suspend disbelief, swallowing a confessed hoaxer's claims without even a pretense of research, and regurgitating threadbare lies as an exposé of Final Truth.

Sources: David Carkhuff, "Bigfoot feat: Remarkable hoax looms large in Grant County family's history." *Blue Mountain Eagle* (25 December 2002); Coleman, *Bigfoot!*; Ian Dow, "Legend of Big Fib." *Glasgow Daily Record* (7 December 2002); John Green correspondence to Bigfoot Internet newsgroup (9 December 2002); John Hubbell, "Bigfoot backers mourning." *San Francisco Chronicle* (7 December 2002); Franz Lidz, "Bigfoot: 1958-2002." *Sports Illustrated* (20 January 2003); "Mythchief." *Ottawa Citizen* (10 December 2002); "Vandal-control new angle in Wallace hoax claim." Associated Press, (9 December 2002).

Wallowa Lake, Oregon   Legends of the early Nez Perce tribe name Wallowa Lake, south of Joseph in northeastern Oregon's Wallowa County, as the traditional home of a predatory LAKE MONSTER. White settlers later spun their own tales, including claims that the lake has no bottom and, more recently, that its bed is littered with numerous vehicles sunk while driving on its frozen surface during winter. Sightings of large "sea creatures" in Lake Wallowa have continued sporadically to the present day, prompting the county chamber of commerce to organize a Monster Observation and Preservation Society in the 1980s. Members of a scuba-diving team called the Atomic Ducks have plumbed the lake's depths each August since 1997, but none has yet reported an encounter with the cryptid(s).

Source: Rick Swart, "Atomic Ducks dive for 'treasure' at Wallowa Lake." *Wallowa County* (OR) *Chieftain* (21 August 2003).

Wally   Walling Pond is a flooded gravel pit located at the corner of 16th and McGilchrist Streets in Salem, Oregon. It seems an unlikely venue for a "monster," but that did not prevent local fishermen from spinning tales of Wally, a giant FISH said to inhabit the pond. From the early 1990s onward, various anglers described their near-misses with Wally, a few reporting glimpses of its massive body at the surface, while most simply went home with severed lines. By the turn of the new millennium, some locals openly referred to Wally as "Salem's Loch Ness monster." Al Bruno was a typical Wally-stalker, claiming to have hooked and lost the mythic fish "at least 20 times" between 1995 and 2003. Another angler, Tony Corner, told the *Salem Statesman*, "When he hit, you knew it was big. I've hooked into him, and there's no turning him. It was like you hooked onto the bumper of a truck." Joe Linn finally landed Wally on 22 July 2003, after several other failed attempts. The creature proved to be a sturgeon (*Acipenser fulvescens*) 4 feet 4 inches long. Authorities could not explain how the non-native fish found its way to Walling Pond.

Source: Henry Miller, "Walling Pond legend landed." *Salem* (OR) *Statesman* (31 July 2003).

Walrus Dog   Inuit natives of western Alaska describe the Walrus Dog (or Az-i-wû-gûm-ki-mukh-'ti) as an aquatic predator larger than an adult walrus, which preys on FISH and seals but stands guard over walrus colonies along the Bering Strait, slapping the water with its sharp-edged tail to signal approaching danger. Nineteenth-century witnesses agreed that the Walrus Dog was black, but differed as to whether it was clothed in fur or scales. Some also claimed its tail was armed with spikes, which it used to deadly effect if cornered by humans. Its call was said to be a high-pitched whistling sound. No living creature known to science matches the Walrus Dog's description, and the handful of DINOSAURS who come closest were neither aquatic nor (presumably) suited to Alaska's Arctic climate.

Sources: Diamond Jenness, "Stray notes on the Eskimo of Arctic Alaska." *Anthropological Papers of the University of Alaska* 1 (May 1953): 5-13; Edward Nelson, "The Eskimo about Bering Strait." *Annual Report of the Bureau of American Ethnology* 18 (1896-97): 442-443.

Wa-Mbilikimo   This unknown primate or HOMINID, reported from the neighborhood of Kenya's Mount Kilimanjaro, is described by witnesses as 3-4 feet tall, covered in dark hair, with shoulder-length hair on its head. Its description is similar to that of Tanzania's AGOGWE, the WATU WA MITI of Mozambique-Zimbabwe, and the KAKUNDAKARI reported from the Democratic Republic of Congo. BERNARD HEUVELMANS suggested that the creatures may represent a relict population of australopiths.

Source: Heuvelmans, *Les Bêtes Humaines d'Afrique*.

Wanganui carcass   In early October 1997, a rotting GLOBSTER washed ashore at Wanganui, on the southwestern coast of New Zealand's North Island. A CNN report of 14 October described it as 8-10 feet long, whitish, covered with hair, foul-smelling, with "large, paddle-like tentacles." Local zoologists identified the remains as part of a sperm whale (*Physeter macrocephalus*).

Source: "Recent cryptozoology news." *Cryptozoology Review* 2 (Autumn 1997): 5.

Wangul *see* **Bunyip**

Wanjilanko   An unclassified big CAT reported from the Casamance Forest of southern Senegal, the Wanjilanko is described as reddish in color with lighter stripes, boasting unusually long fangs and a negligible tail. Native tradition maintains that the Wanjilanko stalks and kills LIONS (*Panthera leo*). Cryptozoologist KARL SHUKER and others suggest that the creature may represent a relict population of prehistoric SABER-TOOTHED CATS.

Source: Shuker, "The secret animals of Senegambia."

Waracabra Tiger Native of Guyana describe this unidentified CAT as resembling a common JAGUAR (*Panthera onca*), though it size and color varies. The cats also differ from jaguars by reportedly hunting in packs, which make them all the more dangerous to jungle travelers or tribesmen. The common name derives from high-pitched call of the waracabra bird (better known as the gray-winged trumpeter, *Psophia crepitans*), whose call is similar to the cat's shrieking cry. Author Charles Barrington Brown was first to describe the mysterious cats, in 1876, repeating the advice of his Indian guides that "they were small and exceedingly ferocious TIGERS; that they hunted in packs, and were not frightened by camp fires or anything except the barking of dogs." While Brown's party was crossing the Curiebrong River, "a shrill scream rent the air from the opposite side of the river, not two hundred yards above our camp, and waking up echoes in the forest, died away as suddenly as it rose. This was answered by another cry, coming from the depths of the forest, the intervals being filled up by low growls and trumpeting sounds, which smote most disagreeably upon the ear. Gradually the cries became fainter and fainter, as the band retired from our vicinity, till they utterly died away." Brown's frightened companions declared that a pack of Waracabra Tigers might include as many as 100 individuals.

Author Everard im Thurn declared, in 1883, that he had found three witnesses to the Waracaba Tiger's existence, but he deemed at least one of the reports greatly exaggerated. In place of an unknown species, im Thurm suggested that the cats might simply be COUGARS (*Puma concolor*), glimpsed traveling through the forest as a family unit. Henry Kirke offered another account of the cats in 1898, reporting that: "There is a mysterious beast in the forest called by the native Indians the 'waracabra tiger.' All travellers in the forests of Guiana speak of this dreaded animal, but strange to say, none of them appear to have seen it. The Indians profess the greatest terror of it. It is said to hunt in packs (which tigers never do), and when its howls awake the echoes of the forest, the Indians at once take to their canoes and wood skins as the only safe refuge from its ravages."

Zoologist Lee Crandall, likewise, heard many reports of the Waracaba Tiger in Guyana, but could find no one who admitted seeing the creatures. From that, he concluded that the "tiger" was not a cat at all, but rather the nocturnal bush-dog (*Speothos venaticus*), which prowls South American jungles in packs after nightfall. The secretive bush-dog's range extends from Panama southward to Paraguay, spanning the continent from Colombia and Peru through Brazil.

Sources: Charles Brown, *Canoe and Camp Life in British Guiana.* London: E. Stanford, 1876; Lee Crandall, *A Zoo Man's Notebook.* Chicago: University of Chicago Press, 1966; Henry Kirke, *Twenty-five Years in British Guiana.* London: Kegan, Paul, Trench, 1883; Shuker, *Mystery Cats of the World.*

Warialda Cougar This ALIEN BIG CAT has been reported from the neighborhood of Warialda, New South Wales, Australia since the early 1960s. Witnesses describe it as a sandy-colored felid resembling a New World COUGAR (*Puma concolor*), drawing a clear distinction between this cat and the jet-black EMMAVILLE PANTHER sighted 60 miles farther east during the same time frame. Cougars are not native to Australia, but may have been introduced as pets or Allied military mascots during World War II.

Source: Healy and Cropper, *Out of the Shadows.*

Warrigal/Waregal Witnesses describe the Warrigal of New South Wales, Australia as an ALIEN BIG CAT resembling a maned adult LION (*Panthera leo*). In April 1945, a party of hikers saw four Warrigals crossing Cedar Valley, in the Blue Mountains. Ten years later, in October 1955, reports of a shaggy-maned lion prompted extensive armed searches Wentworth Falls and the Blaxland-Glenbrook region, but no cats were seen. A large cat reportedly slaughtered sheep around Penrith in 1972, and three hunters fired on a supposed lion in the same area, five years later, but the animal escaped unharmed. The following year, Australian cryptozoologist REX GILROY claimed to have found large, fresh

Australian witnesses describe the Warrigal as resembling an "African" lion.

pawprints in a cave near Medlow Bath. In 1988, more tracks were found by a party of campers near Hampton, west of Katoomba, where cattle had recently been mauled. Gilroy suggests that the creatures may comprise a relict population of marsupial lions (*Thylacoleo carnifex*) presumed extinct in Australia for some 10,000 years. Others propose the more mundane explanation of a lion escaped from an unidentified zoo or private menagerie.

Sources: Gilroy, "Giant mystery cats of Australia"; Gilroy, "Mystery lions in the Blue Mountains"; Shuker, *In Search of Prehistoric Survivors.*

Wasgo The Haida Indians of British Columbia describe the Wasgo ("sea wolf") or Sisiutl as a combination SEA SERPENT and LAKE MONSTER. In the 19th century, it was reported from the Pacific Ocean and Hecate Strait, surrounding the Queen Charlotte Islands, and from Spirit Lake, near the village of Skidegate (on Graham Island). As described by witnesses and depicted in native carvings, the Wasgo was serpentine in shape, with large eyes and flippers.

Source: Swords, "The Wasgo or Sisiutl."

Washington Bigfoot Research Group According to this group's Internet website, the WBRG was created "when individual Bigfoot researchers with ongoing research efforts in the state of Washington came together with a combined 75 years of experience in the field of SASQUATCH research." The initial impetus came from Jim Knapp, affectionately dubbed the group's "old man," who worked with Roger Patterson's brother in 1967, when the PATTERSON FILM was produced. Knapp passed the story on to son Ronald, and subsequently bought him a copy of Patterson's book, *Do Abominable Snowmen of America Really Exist?* A few years later, Ron's younger brother reported a BIGFOOT sighting from Washington's Blue Mountains, confirming the family fascination with cryptozoology. Other identified members of the WBRG include Ron Madden, a wilderness tracker who claims a Sasquatch sighting near Yakima, and co-founder Fred Bradshaw, who allegedly sighted the creatures four time between 1985 and 2000. On the last occasion, Bradshaw videotaped the retreating Bigfoot, but Ron Knapp admits that the images are "difficult to distinguish."

Source: Washington Bigfoot Research Group, http://www.w-b-r-g.com/home.html.

Washington State Sasquatch Search Group

This organization's Internet website describes it as "Washington State's *leading* SASQUATCH research organization," a suggestion of the rivalry among groups ostensibly committed to the same goals. The WSSSG was created on 5 January 1998, by veteran big-game hunters Jerry Felton and Andrew Peterson, who run the group today as co-directors. Membership figures are confidential, but Felton and Peterson claim to run "the largest Sasquatch e-mail discussion list on the Internet" (Sasquatch@egroups.com), with some 450 subscribers. They also offer a "researcher referral system," with cyberlinks to BIGFOOT investigators nationwide. While the WSSSG's achievements are difficult to quantify, it operates on a positive note: "We believe with good data, modern technology and our own ideas we will provide certain 'discovery' of this mysterious creature called Sasquatch."

Source: Washington State Sasquatch Search Group, http://www.angelfire.com/wa/sasquatchsearch/.

Washipi

These unknown primates of northern Argentina's Grand Chaco region have been mythologized by local natives to the status of "little people" on a par with elves or leprechauns. In fact, eyewitnesses describe MONKEY-faced, stout-bodied creatures covered with dark hair, standing between 1 foot 6 inches and three feet tall, producing gruff sounds that bear no resemblance to human speech. The Washipi are diurnal grazers, reportedly subsisting on a diet of fruit, nuts and honey.

Source: John Roth, *American Elves*. Jefferson, NC: McFarland, 1997.

Wasson, Barbara (1927-98)

Oregon BIGFOOT investigator Barbara Wasson Butler, known more commonly by her maiden name, earned her B.A. in psychology in 1948, from the University of California at Berkeley. While employed at clinical work in Missouri, she earned her M.A. in psychology from Washington University (in St. Louis). Wasson subsequently moved to Oregon and there maintained a private counseling practice, while her spare time was consumed pursuing Bigfoot reports throughout the Pacific Northwest. Her self-published book, *Sasquatch Apparitions: A Critique on the Pacific Northwest Hominoids* (1979), analyzed the hunt for Bigfoot psychologically and spared no criticism of rival researchers whose personal quarrels (in Wasson's opinion) retarded the objective scientific search for SASQUATCH. Cancer claimed Wasson's life on 9 October 1998.

Sources: Coleman and Clark, *Cryptozoology A to Z*; Wasson, *Sasquatch Apparitions*.

Water Bull

This legendary LAKE MONSTER of the British Isles appears to be a smaller and more amiable version (perhaps a juvenile form) of the "water horse" reported from various Scottish lochs in ancient times. Generally described as the size of a milk cow or smaller, the Water Bull possessed no horns, but otherwise resembled a short-legged bull. Witnesses reported a variety of colors, ranging from black, through brown and red to white. In myth, the creatures sometimes mated with dairy cows and thus improved their quality of milk, but other stories mark the Water Bull as a harbinger of bad luck and disease. No modern sightings are on file, suggesting that the creatures (if they ever existed) are now extinct.

Sources: John Campbell, *Superstitions of the Highlands and Islands of Scotland*. Glasgow: J. MacLehose and Sons, 1900; Robert Robertson, *Selected Highland Folktales*. Edinburgh: Oliver and Boyd, 1961.

Water Cattle

Lake Socho-nor, in Outer Mongolia, is named for the cryptids known as Water Cattle (*socho*) that once allegedly inhabited its depths. Local natives believed the lake was created by a deluge similar to Noah's flood in the Bible, poured out as divine wrath against the inhabitants of a lost ancient city, while the gods spared their innocent cattle by making the creatures amphibious. Legends aside, there is a noteworthy resemblance between the Mongolian Water Cattle and the WATER BULLS reported from ancient Scotland. Although Socho-nor reportedly dried up during a drought in the mid-19th century, local farmers still claimed to see the tracks of Water Cattle on its banks in the early 1930s.

Source: Henning Haslund, *Men and Gods in Mongolia*. New York: E.P. Dutton, 1935.

Water Elephant

In June 1907, while traveling along the Congo River near its junction with the River Kassai, a traveler named Le Petit glimpsed a strange animal swimming with only its head visible above water. Le Petit's native guides identified the creature as a Water Elephant, and he subsequently saw five specimens together in the swampy land between Lake Tumba and Lake Mai-Ndombe (in the present-day Democratic Republic of

Small aquatic elephants are reported from Africa and Thailand.

Congo). This time, Le Petit shot one of the animals, but his porters were unable to retrieve its body from the marsh. Le Petit described the creatures as 6–8 feet tall at the shoulder, with 4-toed feet, relatively short legs, and hairless skin resembling that of a hippopotamus (but darker in color). The animals had long, ovoid heads, with ears similar in shape to those of an African elephant but proportionately smaller, 2-foot trunks, and no tusks. Their necks were also roughly twice as long as a normal elephants, presenting the appearance of a giant TAPIR. Babuma tribesmen told Le Petit that Water Elephants spend daylight hours in water, emerging at night to graze on the shore. Author R.J. Cunninghame published Le Petit's description in 1912, but no more sightings were reported until early 2003, when a helicopter pilot reported sighting a herd of "strange elephants" at Lake Tumba. WILLIAM GIBBONS planned an expedition to the DRC for mid-2003, accompanied by a French film crew, but no further word on the effort was available at press time for this volume.

Meanwhile, word of an altogether unexpected Water Elephant emerged from Southeast Asia in May 2003. A Bangkok newspaper, *The Nation*, reported on 2 May that restaurateur Direk Siangthaen had obtained the carcass of "a rare small animal similar in appearance to an elephant" from sources at Mae Sot, Myanmar (Burma). The truly miniature animal reportedly measured three inches tall and five inches long, tipping the scales at a mere 300 grams. Direk claimed the animal was caught in a mountain pond and died after a week in captivity. "I believe it really is a water elephant, because every part of the animal is similar to a normal elephant," he told reporters. "And I was also told that when it was alive its bellows were similar to those of an elephant." According to Direk, X-rays taken at a Burmese hospital (but unavailable for study in Bangkok) revealed a skeleton "similar to that of a full-sized elephant."

The Bangkok specimen remains unidentified at press time for this volume, and has not been placed on public display. As for Central Africa's larger Water Elephant, cryptozoologist KARL SHUKER suggests a relict population of prehistoric proboscids, perhaps *Moeritherium* (the "dawn elephant") or the larger *Phiomina*, both found in Africa through the early Oligocene epoch, some 30 million years ago.

Sources: "Dead 'water elephant' turns up in Mae Sot. *The Nation* (2 May 2003); Heuvelmans, *On the Track of Unknown Animals*; Karl Shuker, "Alien zoo." *Fortean Times* 165 (January 2003): 20; Shuker, *In Search of Prehistoric Survivors*; Shuker, *The Unexplained*; "Water elephant 'has no place in traditional culture.'" *The Nation* (5 May 2003).

Water Leopard/Lion/Panther

Throughout central and eastern Africa, natives speak of large, ferocious CATS that dwell in water, launching their surprise attacks on prey from lakes and rivers, dragging their prey into submerged caves where they feed at leisure. The animals are known throughout their range by many names, usually translating into English as some variation of Water Leopard, Water LION, or Water Panther. Common features include large size, extremely long fangs, and aggressive temperament. Some of the creatures described far exceed the size of any known cat, past or present, and details of certain descriptions suggest confusion with larger reptilian cryptids resembling living DINOSAURS. Nations reporting these aquatic felids include the following:

Angola: The Coje ya Menia ("water lion") allegedly inhabits the Cuango and Cuanza Rivers and their tributaries. Natives describe the cats as somewhat smaller than a hippopotamus. They reportedly kill hippos, but strangely do not eat the carcasses.

Central African Republic: Cats known variously as Dilali ("water lion"), Mourou-Ngou ("water leopard"), Ngoroli ("water elephant"), Mamaimé and Nze ti Gou lurk in various rivers and lakes. The maned Dilali is typically five feet long and three feet tall at the shoulder (though some allegedly grow as large as a horse). They kill CROCODILES and hippos but do not eat them. Favored prey includes FISH and human beings. The Mourou-N'gou hunts in pairs along the Bamingui, Bangoran, Gribingui, Iomba, Kotto, Koukourou, Mbari and Ouaka Rivers. Another maneater, it measures 8–12 feet long, with stripes or dappled spots on brownish fur. Old military records at Ndélé confirm that such a creature tipped a boatload of French-African soldiers in 1910, afterward seizing one man and dragging him under the water. Lucien Blancou told a similar story in 1936, of human victims taken from Dogolomandji, 20 miles southeast of the Gribingui. A specimen was reportedly caught in a fishnet, on the Bangoran in 1950, but its fate is unknown. A fisherman on the Bamingui claimed one of the cats nearly tipped him from his boat in February 1985. The 10-foot Ngoroli, said to kill hippos and crocodiles along the Vovodo River, should not be confused with the peaceable WATER ELEPHANT of the Congo.

Chad: Both the Dilali and Morou-N'gou reportedly dwell here, as well as in the Central African Republic. In 1912, while stationed on the Ouham River in southern Chad, German Lieutenant Naumann of Ulm offered a reward for one of these reputed maneaters, but he got not takers. Reports of hippos slashed by an unknown assailant issued from the Chari River region in 1920 and again in 1970.

Democratic Republic of Congo: Depending on their location, aquatic felids here are variously known as Ntambo wa luy ("water lion"), Simba ya Mai ("water lion"), or Nze ti Gou ("water panther"). The Ntambo wa Luy is sometimes confused with a larger reptilian neighbor. Native descriptions indicate that supposed juvenile specimens are reddish-brown in color, resembling the aquatic cats found elsewhere in Africa, while presumed "adults" are black and measure up to 26 feet long, leaving 16-inch, 3-toed footprints. Both versions of the beast are said to prey on hippos, moving swiftly on both land and water.

Kenya: Natives of this East African nation call their aquatic felids Dingonek, Ndamathia and Ol-Maima. Most specimens have spotted coats and may sometimes be found basking on river banks. In 1907, big-game hunter John Jordan fired at one such specimen along the Migori River, near Lake Victoria, but the beast submerged and disappeared. Jordan claimed that its clawed

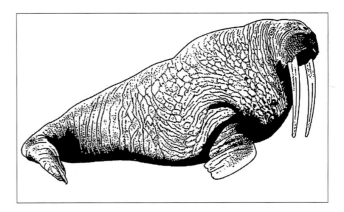

Karl Shuker suggests that Africa's water leopard may be an unknown creature resembling a walrus.

pawprints were as large as a hippo's tracks. Native reports of black, scaly specimens 14–18 feet long, dragging thick tails behind them, apparently refer to a different (reptilian) cryptid.

Sudan: The large-fanged Nyokodoing generally conforms to the descriptions of amphibious cats from neighboring countries.

Tanzania: Kenya's southern neighbor also harbors the predatory Dingonek.

What are these mysterious creatures? In 1947, German author Ingo Krumbiegel suggested a relict population of SABER-TOOTHED CATS, found over most of the Earth between the Oligocene and Late Pleistocene epochs. BERNARD HEUVELMANS agreed with that suggestion, speculating that prehistoric cats may have evolved to seek shelter in submerged lairs. KARL SHUKER, by contrast, suggests the existence of an unknown walruslike creature in Africa, supported by cave paintings found in South Africa's Orange Free State and a 1952 report from John Hunter that Ituri Forest pygmies chose pictures of a walrus as the likeness of a local predatory cryptid.

Sources: Heuvelmans, *Les Derniers Dragons d'Afrique*; Heuvelmans, *On the Track of Unknown Animals*; Shuker, *Mystery Cats of the World*; Shuker, "Operation Mourou N'gou." *Strange Magazine* 15 (Spring 1995): 33.

Water Panther *see* Greers Ferry Lake, Arkansas

Water Tigers

As Africa produces widespread reports of WATER LEOPARDS, so tales of Water TIGERS have long emanated from various nations of South America. And as in Africa, debate continues with regard to the creatures' true identity. Some of the confusion is spawned by reports of a creature known as IEMISCH (and many other names) throughout a range spanning parts of Argentina, Brazil, Chile, Guyana, Uruguay and Venezuela. Though sometimes called a water tiger, described by witnesses as a fierce aquatic predator the size of a COUGAR (*Puma concolor*), the Iemisch is regarded by most cryptozoologists as an unknown species of giant otter. Another fierce amphibian, reported from Argentina and neighboring Paraguay, is the YAQUARU, sporting huge fangs or tusks and a woolly coat, sometimes growing as large as a donkey. As with the Iemisch, some witnesses claim the Yaquaru bears a stronger resemblance to an otter than a CAT. When those cryptids are removed (at least provisionally) from the equation, we find reports of Water Tigers emanating from the following South American nations:

Argentina: Explorer Manuel Palacio reported that cave paintings from Lago Posadas (Santa Cruz Province) depict SABER-TOOTHED CATS stalking long-nosed creatures that resembled *Macrauchenia*, known from Pleistocene fossils.

Brazil: Natives of Amapá State, in the Serra de Tumucumaque region, report encounters with the Aypa, an aquatic felid with a head and neck like a JAGUAR (*Panthera onca*), extremely long fangs, and a coat of glossy fur or "scales."

Colombia and Ecuador: In 1950, a French sailor named Picquet told author Peter Matthiessen that the jungles of both these nations were inhabited by "a rare striped cat not quite so large as a jaguar and very timid, which is possessed of two very large protruding teeth." Picquet claimed to have seen one such animal himself. The story led Matthiessen to speculate that "the sabertoothed tiger, like the cougar, had long ago established itself here in a smaller subspecies and had thus survived the Ice Age extinction of its North American ancestor." In 1989, Juan Bautista Rivadeneira glimpsed a rather different Water Tiger at the mouth of Ecuador's Río Jurumbaino. He described it as black, with short legs and a tail like a cow's.

French Guiana: The Maroni River and its tributaries reportedly harbor a 10-foot predator known as Maipolina or Popoké, armed with tusks like those of a walrus and clawed feet resembling an anteater's. Witnesses describe a fawn-colored animal with a white belly, short fur, drooping ears and large eyes reminiscent of a TAPIR'S. In October 1962, a boy drowned in the Maroni at Maripasoula, and locals blamed the Maipolina when his partially-devoured corpse was found. The same elusive predator was blamed for six other violent deaths in recent years, around Maripasoula, Benzdorp and Wacapeu.

Paraguay: In 1975, hunters killed a "mutant jaguar" at an uncertain location. Zoologist Juana Acavar examined the cat and speculated that it might be a surviving *Smilodon*, a Pleistocene saber-tooth known from fossils in North America and Argentina.

Indeed, many cryptozoologists now suspect that saber-toothed cats may have survived the Ice Age in various parts of Latin America. KARL SHUKER argues that Yaquaru and Maipolina may even represent a single species, with a display of sexual dimorphism (with the larger, shaggy-coated Yaquaru the male).

Sources: Bernard Heuvelmans, *On the Track of Unknown Animals*; Picasso, "South American monsters & mystery animals"; Shuker, *Mystery Cats of the World*.

Waterbobbejan

The Waterbobbejan ("water BABOON") is a supposed unknown primate or HOMINID reported since the 1880s from South Africa. Native traditions of this creature predate the arrival of European settlers, but aborigines are not the only witnesses. In 1965, two youths reported a sighting on the Leeufontein plantation, located between Swartruggens and Koster, in the country's North-West Province. They described the animal as a baboon six feet tall, covered in sandy-reddish hair. Baboons known from the region (*Papio cynocephalus*) reach a maximum height of 2 feet 6 inches, while other native primates are smaller still.

Source: Hall, "Rumble in the jungle."

Wattleless Guan

This unidentified BIRD, reported from Peru's Yanachaga National Park (Pasco Department), is said to resemble the wattled guan (*Aburria aburri*), but without the fleshy wattle characteristic of that species. Native witnesses describe its plumage as jet-black.

Source: Hocking, "Further investigation into unknown Peruvian mammals."

Watu Wa Miti

The Watu Wa Miti ("men of the trees") are unclassified primates or HOMINIDS reported from Mozambique and Zimbabwe. Native traditions describe them as aggressive and violent toward humans, with some legends claiming the creatures are spirits of a bygone race killed off by war and famine. At 4–5 feet tall, covered with dark hair, the Watu Wa Miti may well be synonymous to the creatures known elsewhere in Africa as AGOGWE, KAKUNDAKARI and WA-MBILIKIMO.

Sources: Heuvelmans, *Les Bêtes Humaines d'Afrique*; Heuvelmans, *On the Track of Unknown Animals*; Sanderson, *Abominable Snowmen*.

Wava E. sea serpent

On 26 August 1948, four passengers set out from York, Maine to Gloucester, Massachusetts aboard the cabin cruiser *Wava E.* Those on board included the boat's owners, Harold and Wava Robie, and two friends, Deering and Edna Roberts. Around 11:00 a.m., soon after passing New Hampshire's Isle of Shoals, the four travelers saw what they took for a reef in water that should have been at least 100 feet deep. Stopping to check their charts, they were surprised to see the "reef" submerge, then surface astern of the boat with three humps visible above water, rapidly swimming away. As Deering Roberts later told historian Edward Snow, "All four of us saw a SEA SERPENT that August day in 1948. It was an awesome spectacle that left us very quiet and thoughtful for some time afterward."

Source: O'Neil, *The Great New England Sea Serpent*.

Weatherford Monster   Weatherford, Texas (20 miles west of Fort Worth, in Parker County) reputedly harbors a creature so mysterious that no two witnesses can readily agree on a description. Most sightings emanate from the vicinity of 1,210-acre Weatherford Lake, but the cryptid is not a LAKE MONSTER. It appears on land, described by some observers as a hairy HOMINID resembling BIGFOOT, while others claim it travels on all fours. An Internet website devoted to the mystery reports that "a few people have even said that this creature is mainly hairless, and resembles a giant ARMADILLO." Still other accounts compare the creature to a huge bull with luminous eyes, sometimes breathing fire. Native Americans compound the riddle further, with ancient stories of a legendary spider-man. In the early 1970s, two local monster-hunters produced plaster casts of the creature's alleged footprints, resembling the tracks of a giant CROCODILE. Skeptics dismissed the episode as a HOAX, while the curious absence of a right-hand forward track earned the creature such nicknames as "South Paw" and "Lefty." Sporadic sightings continue to the present day, and the unknown beast earned its first mention in the local *Weatherford Democrat* on 16 January 2000.

Source: The Monster of Weatherford, TX, http://www.geocities.com/legendary_spider_man/weatherford.htm.

Wee Oichy   Scottish highlanders use this affectionate name for the supposed LAKE MONSTER of Loch Oich, although the creature was feared in times past. ANTOON OUDEMANS uncovered the following tale in 1934 and took it for an accurate account of true events.

> Tradition has it that many years ago some children residing at Inchlaggan were playing on the loops of the Garry at this spot when a huge "beiste" in the shape of a deformed pony appeared on the bank of the river. Curious to learn whether the creature was not a real pony, on which they could enjoy a ride, the children went up to it, and, the story has it, that they found the "beiste" so docile that one of them ventured on its back. No sooner had the child done so than the "beiste" plunged into the pool with the rider at the same time carrying with it a child clung to its mane. No trace was ever found of the bodies thus mysteriously drowned.

A river connects Loch Oich to Loch Ness (home of NESSIE), and some researchers believe unknown creatures may swim back and forth between the two lochs. In the mid-1930s, investigator J.W. Herries discovered several witnesses who had seen an animal in transit, reporting:

> I interviewed three young men who had seen this object making its way from Loch Ness to Loch Oich. Afterwards I saw the lock keeper at Loch Oich, who had a close-up view. His daughter called his attention to a strange animal in an almost land-enclosed bay close to their house. He went out and saw swimming about an animal six feet long, something like an otter, but much larger. He told his daughter to bring his gun; but before she could do so, the stranger had submerged. He was knowledgeable about the water and its denizens, but could liken what he had seen to nothing in his previous experience.

In 1960, Professor Angus Ross of Edinburgh University suggested that the creatures in Loch Oich and Loch Ness were misplaced GIANT SQUIDS. A year later, on 8 July 1961, the Scottish

Daily Express published a photo of Wee Oichy that proved to be journalistic HOAX.

Source: Costello, *In Search of Lake Monsters*.

Weisse Elster, Germany   During the 19th century, reports of a giant FISH emanated from this lake in Germany's Sachsen-Anhalt State. The creature was never caught, but other German lakes and rivers are known to be inhabited by wels CATFISH (*Siluris glanis*), which attain a maximum official length of 15 feet 5 inches.

Sources: Robert Eisel, *Sagenbuch des Voigtlandes*. Gera, Germany: C.B. Griesbach, 1871; August Witzschel, *Sagen aus Thuringen*. Vienna: W. Bräumüller, 1866.

Wejuk   French explorer Samuel de Champlain heard native tales of Wejuk ("wet skin") when he visited the region in 1609, but the first known sighting by a European settler was not recorded for another 150 years. In 1759, during the French and Indian War, soldiers led by Major Robert Rogers were returning from an attack on the St. Francis Indians, when the met a strange creature south of Lake Champlain's Missiquoi Bay (on the Vermont-Québec border). A soldier named Deluth described the beast as resembling "a large black bear, who would throw large pine cones and nuts down upon us from trees and ledges." On balance, the animal sounds less like a bear than a SASQUATCH-type HOMINID or NORTH AMERICAN APE.

Source: Citro, *Green Mountain Ghosts, Ghouls and Unsolved Mysteries*.

West Hawk Lake, Canada   Manitoba's deepest lake, located near the provincial border with Ontario, produced occasional LAKE MONSTER rumors during the 19th century. Today, the lake is used extensively by scuba divers who appreciate its pristine waters. Resort lodges line the lake's wooded shores, but despite so much tourist activity, no modern cryptid sightings are on file and West Hawk Lake is generally omitted from published lists of Canadian "monster" lakes.

Source: Chris Rutkowski, *Unnatural History: True Manitoba Mysteries*. Winnipeg" Chameleon, 1993.

West Wycombe monster   In February 2001, residents of West Wycombe, Buckinghamshire, England reported the appearance of "a Loch Ness monster" in flooded fields outside town. The first sighting, on 14 February, was logged from the George and Dragon Hotel, prompting skeptics to suggest that local entrepreneurs had invented the creature to promote CRYPTOTOURISM. Australian bartender Steve Burdett denied charges that he had invented the beast. "I was walking back from the pub when I first saw it," he told reporters. "We don't have monsters like that in Oz." Mary Marshall, operator of the Village Store on High Street, sold out her first issue of greeting cards printed to celebrate the creature's arrival. "I think he is wonderful," Marshall declared. "It's good to have a male version of the Loch Ness monster." No explanation of the cryptid's gender was forthcoming, and sightings have apparently ceased.

Source: Matthew Harris, "Mystery creature at West Wycombe." *Bucks Free Press* (20 February 2001).

Western Bigfoot Society   *see* **Crowe, Raymond**

Western New York Bigfoot Investigation Center   Based in Newfane, New York (Niagara County), the WNYBIC was founded in January 2000. Its Internet website describes the group as "dedicated to a non-hostile approach to investigating the

BIGFOOT phenomenon," and lists reported sightings from 28 New York counties. No officers or members are identified, but prospective "affiliate researchers" are invited to apply for membership free of charge. The group's interest in Bigfoot extends beyond New York, as does its membership. The WNYBIC apparently supports itself by selling SASQUATCH footprint casts and other curios. Affiliate researchers are required to: (1) have a strong interest in the Bigfoot phenomenon; (2) be willing to spend time both in the field and interviewing witnesses; (3) help the group seek out local sighting reports; and (4) submit copies of research results.

Source: The Western New York Bigfoot Investigation Center, http://wnybic.freeyellow.com/.

Wewiwilemitá Manetú

Shawnee tribesmen described the Wewiwilemitá Manetú as a giant SNAKE inhabiting various Ohio lakes and rivers. An alternate aboriginal name for the LAKE MONSTER, Msí Kinépikwa, translates into English as "great reptile." In modern times, Ohio witnesses have reported aquatic cryptids from CHARLES MILL LAKE, LAKE ERIE, the OLENTANGY RIVER and SLAVEN'S POND.

Source: Gatschet, "Water-monsters of American aborigines."

Whe-Atchee

Aboriginal tribesmen described the Wheatchee as an evil female monster inhabiting Lake Steilacoom, south of Tacoma, Washington (Pierce County). No modern cryptid sightings are recorded, and Lake Steilacoom is normally omitted from published lists of Washington's "monster" lakes.

Source: Haunted Places — Washington State, http://www.horrorfind.com/haunted/places/statewashington.html.

Whidbey Island carcass

Whidbey Island lies in the heart of Puget Sound and is the largest of several islands in Washington's Island County. Surrounding waters have produced many SEA SERPENT sightings over the past 125 years, most describing a creature popularly known as CADBOROSAURUS or Caddy. On 29 September 1963, island resident Ruth Cobert found a 25-foot decomposing carcass stranded on the coastline south of Sunset Beach. The creature's skull measured 20 inches long and resembled that of a horse. Its spine was six inches in diameter where it joined the skull, tapering to two inches at the tail. Dr. A.D. Welander, at the University of Washington's Fisheries Department, studied newspaper photos of the carcass and declared it a basking shark (*Cetorhinus maximus*). No tests were performed on the actual remains.

Source: LeBlond and Bousfield, *Cadborosaurus*.

Whiskered Swift

Witnesses from various locations in Africa and Asia describe this unclassified BIRD as a swift (Family *Apodidae*) with pale gray markings resembling whiskers around its beak. While undiscovered species of birds certainly exist, some skeptics insist the witnesses in question have merely seen known swifts carrying feathers or some other nesting material in their beaks.

Source: Phil Chantler, *Swifts: A Guide to the Swifts and Treeswifts of the World*. New Haven, CT: Yale University Press, 2000.

White Demon

Cryptozoologist JOHN GREEN reports the case of "a huge, light-colored upright creature" seen lurking around an abandoned Richland, Washington gravel pit in the summer of 1966. Several youths claimed to have fired on the BIGFOOT-type creature, which they called the White Demon, but aside from high-pitched screams it seemed impervious to bullets.

Source: Green, *Sasquatch: The Apes Among Us*.

White Thing

In the early 1930s, residents of northwestern Georgia's Floyd County were agitated by reports of an albino forest-dwelling cryptid called the White Thing, sighted first around the Sanders farm. Though never clearly seen, mainly heard crying in the woods at night, the beast was typically described as being "big, bad and dangerous like a white panther or something even worse." Fifty years after the fact, Frank Sanders confessed in print that he and a group of childhood playmates had fabricated the story after glimpsing a white OWL on his family's property. Their aim was juvenile amusement, designed to "add a little spice to their rather dull humdrum lifestyle." As rumors spread, though, the HOAX briefly took on a life of its own, then faded as all hoaxes must, when the jokers outgrew their charade.

Source: Frank Sanders, "'The white thing.'" *Tullahoma* (GA) *News* (25 September 2003).

Whitey

The White River travels some 155 miles as the crow flies, spanning two states from Texas County, Missouri to its meeting with the Arkansas River east of Nady (Desha County, Arkansas). Its north and south forks are separated by Norfolk Lake, on the Arkansas-Missouri border. Local Quapaw Indians told early settlers about a "moving island" in the river, known to vanish and appear at will, and the first recorded sighting of the cryptid known as Whitey dates from 1850. Whitey's particular affinity for Newport, Arkansas begins with the Civil War, when the creature allegedly rammed and sank a Confederate riverboat carrying a precious gold shipment. The creature surfaced off Newport again in 1890, but another 47 years elapsed before Whitey made headlines again.

New sightings began in summer 1937, including reports from some of Newport's most prominent merchants. An outlying farmer, Bramlett Bateman, claimed the creature was a frequent visitor to his stretch of shoreline. Neighbors accused him of fabricating tales to lure visitors (an early form of CRYPTOTOURISM), and the charge so angered Bateman that he swore out the following affidavit on 22 September 1937:

> I, Bramlett Bateman, state under oath, that on or about the first of July 1937, I was standing on the bank of the White River about one o'clock and something appeared in the river about 375 feet from where I was standing, somewhere near the east bank of said river. From the best I could tell, from the distance, it would be about 12 feet long and 4 or 5 feet wide. I did not see either head or tail, but it slowly rose to the surface and stayed in this position some five minutes. It did not move up or down the river at this particular time but afterward on many different occasions I have seen it move up and down the river, but I never have, at any time been able to determine the full length or size of said monster.
>
> Some two weeks ago, from this date, September 22nd, 1937, I saw the same thing upstream about 200 yards from where it made its first appearance. On the last day that I saw the monster it was in the current of the river. Before it was always seen in the eddy. There is no question in my mind whatever but that the monster remains in this stretch of river.

Altogether, Bateman later claimed, he saw Whitey more than 100 times in 1937-38. Thereafter, the beast vanished from Newport again until June 1971. The first new witness claimed that Whitey had "a smooth kind of skin, but it looked as though it was peeling off. Maybe they were scales." When that report was published, fisherman Ernest Denks acknowledged a sighting the previous week. He said:

> The thing I saw must have weighed at least 1,000 pounds. It looked like something that came from the ocean. It was gray, real long, and had a long pointed bone protruding from its forehead.

On 28 June, Cloyce Warren snapped an indistinct photo of a 30-foot creature with a spiny back that "looked like something prehistoric." Witness Lloyd Hamilton took another photo of a "great, big, huge, spiny-backed monster," but his color film was ruined when a local journalist developed it as black-and-white. On 5 July, two men found large tracks on Towhead Island, surrounded by water more than 100 feet deep. The clawed, 3-toed footprints measured 14 inches long and eight inches wide. Sheriff Ralph Henderson examined the tracks, but acknowledged a possible HOAX. On 21 July 1971, monster-hunters Joey Dupree and Ollie Ritcherson claimed Whitey had surfaced beneath their boat, lifting them out of the water. Aging Bramlett Bateman chimed in with a claim that he had seen Whitey "lots of times" that summer. According to Bateman, it "looked just like it looked when I saw it in '37 and '38."

At that point, the Newport Chamber of Commerce devised a scheme to profit from Whitey's return. Diver Charles Brown was hired to search the river bottom at a point where journalists and TV crews would have to pay for access to the water. Brown found nothing, but Whitey surfaced near Jacksonport in June 1972, where R.C. McClaughlen's family watched it thrash the surface for five minutes. By then, the state legislature had passed a resolution declaring that:

> The part of the White River in Arkansas from a southern point at Old Grand Glaize, Arkansas, to a northern point near Rosie, Arkansas, is the natural habitat of the White River Monster, and that this part of the White River be set aside and known henceforth as "White River Monster Sanctuary and Preserve," and that it is unlawful to molest, kill, trample or harm the White River Monster while in its native habitat.

Theories abound concerning Whitey's identity. Some researchers suspect a giant CATFISH, while IVAN SANDERSON suggested an oversized ALLIGATOR. Author Betty Garner proposed a huge penguin, comparing Whitey to the horned cryptid of WALGREN LAKE, NEBRASKA (though penguins have no horns or spikes). Cryptozoologist ROY MACKAL proposed that both creatures were misplaced elephant seals (*Microunga leonina*).

Sources: Baumann, *Monsters of North America*; Garner, *Monster! Monster!*; Mackal, *Searching for Hidden Animals*.

Wihwin

In the 19th century, Mískito tribesmen of Central America described the Wihwin as an amphibious creature vaguely resembling a horse with prominent fangs. It reportedly inhabited Caribbean coastal waters off Honduras and Nicaragua, sometimes coming ashore in the summer for reasons unknown.

Source: Hubert Bancroft, *The Native Races of the Pacific States of North America*. New York: D. Appleton, 1875.

Wildmen

Every culture spawns tales and legends of Wildmen (and Wildwomen), near-human creatures that lurk on the fringes of civilization or hide in some trackless wilderness, emerging at odd times to interact with people (often to the detriment of both). ENKIDU, in the Sumerian *Epic of Gilgamesh*, was such a creature. The Greeks and Romans knew them as satyrs and fauns. Early Anglo-Saxons dubbed them WUDÉWÁSÁ ("wood man"), while Medieval artists captured their shaggy, snarling likeness in paintings and sculpture. Marco Polo returned from his travels with stories of men who had tails. Queen Mary's Psalter, a 14th-century document now preserved in the British Library, includes a sketch of a Wildman trapped by hunting dogs. When Europeans "discovered" the New World, Wildmen were already there, appearing in guises that cannot be explained with simple reference

to the nearest Indian tribe. A brief review of American Wildmen includes the following:

18th century— Delaware tribesmen in Ohio warned white settlers about hairy denizens of the forest, advising that "they had to leave out food for the wild ones of the woods to keep the peace."

1784— *The Times* of London published an article describing the capture of a shaggy HOMINID by aborigines at Lake of the Woods (in present-day Ontario, Canada).

23 April 1793— A report from the Western Territories (in present-day North Carolina) described sightings of Wildmen "between twelve and fifteen feet high, and in shape resembling a human being, except the head, which is in equal proportion to the body and drawn in somewhat like a tarapin [*sic*]; its feet are like those of a negroe [*sic*], and about two feet long, and hairy, which is of a dark dun color; its eyes are exceedingly large, and open and shut up

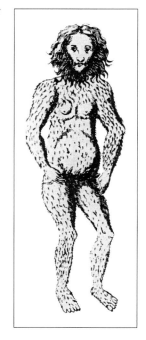

Reports of hairy wildmen date from the earliest recorded history.

and down its face; the hair of its head is about six inches long, stands straight like a negroe's; its nose is what is called Roman." Several such beasts were reported, some allegedly shot while attacking settlers (who called the things YAHOO).

30 August 1818— Residents of Ellisburgh, New York sighted "an animal resembling the Wild Man of the Woods," covered with hair, that stooped forward when running and left wedge-shaped footprints

1829— A 13-foot-tall Wildman was reportedly cornered and killed in a Georgia swamp.

1830s— A "wild child" was frequently seen around (and in) Indiana's Fish Lake (in present-day LaPorte County) and near Bridgewater, Pennsylvania. The latter animal "had the appearance of a child seven or eight years old though somewhat slimmer and covered entirely by hair." Its quasi-human features did not prevent hunters from trying to shoot the "child," but it eluded them.

1834— A "wild man of gigantic stature" surfaced in eastern Arkansas, with sightings in Greene, Poinsett and St. Francis Counties. The thing lingered for nearly two decades and was seen many times. The last recorded sighting, in March 1851, was reported by two Greene County hunters who saw the Wildman chasing some cattle. Newspapers speculated that "he was a survivor of the earthquake disaster which desolated that region in 1811."

13 May 1849— A trapper called One-Eye Bascomb glimpsed a "strange critter" in swamps near present-day Eagletown, Oklahoma. His description generally conformed to other Wildman sightings.

2 January 1855— A hairy, manlike creature 18 inches tall was reportedly captured at Waldoboro Maine, the incident reported four months later by a newspaper in Washington. The Wildman's fate is unknown.

1856— A "wild man" reportedly ambushed a horseman riding near the Arkansas-Louisiana border, dragging the man from his horse, scratching and biting him before it mounted up and rode away.

1860s — A shaggy, 7-foot "Giant of the Hills" was frequently seen in the Ouachita Mountains of Arkansas, said to live in caves along the Saline River. Sometime after 1865, local settlers captured the beast, dressed it in clothes, and housed it in the Benton jail. The "wild man" reportedly escaped and was recaptured, but no further details are available.

Late 1860s — Residents of the Arcadia Valley (Crawford County, Kansas) reported frequent encounters with a "wildman or GORILLA" which they nicknamed OLD SHEFF.

Late 1860s — Trackers in northern Nevada pursued a manlike "object" seen carrying a club and a dead RABBIT.

September 1869 — A hunter stalking game east of Davenport, Iowa saw an ugly, sandy-haired "wild boy" catching and eating fiSH from a river.

1870 — A "wild man" was seen but eluded capture in Crow Canyon, near California's Mount Diablo (Contra Costa County). Searchers found 13-inch footprints where the thing had walked.

June 1870 — Hunters following "very large barefoot tracks of a human being" captured a "wild man" in Frontier County, Nebraska. They relieved him of a heavy club and briefly detained him while providing food. As reported at the time, "None could tell by his language to what nationality he belonged, nor where he came from or stayed." The prisoner was soon released, whereupon a local scribe declared, "Nothing more was seen of him for several years. A large skeleton was found in a canyon near Moorefield, which we supposed to be the remains of the Wild Man, who must have died unwept and alone."

1878 — The Metropolitan Theater of Louisville, Kentucky exhibited a creature billed as the "Wild Man of the Woods," allegedly captured in Tennessee. Advertisements described it as 6 feet 5 inches tall and covered with fish scales. Most researchers today dismiss the incident as a HOAX.

October 1879 — Two hunters in Vermont's Green Mountains met a "wild man" they described as "about five feet high, resembling a man in form and movement, but covered all over with bright red hair, and having a long straggling beard, and very wild eyes." They fired on it, producing "fierce cries of pain and rage," then dropped their guns and fled.

Early 1880s — A hunter named Jack Dover saw a 7-foot "wild man" picking berries near Happy Camp, California (Siskiyou County).

1885 — Hunters reported a hairy "man" eating flesh from a deer in the Cascade Mountains, near Lebanon, Oregon.

August 1893 — A large "wild man" frightened residents of Rockaway Beach, on Long Island, New York.

January 1894 — Multiple witnesses reported a 6-foot "wild man" armed with a club, prowling the woods around Dover, New Jersey.

29 August 1895 — The *Daily Press* reported that a "wild man" had seized a traveler's horse, killed the animal and dragged it away in "Delamere County," New York. No such county exists.

April 1897 — A "wild man" was seen repeatedly in woods around Stout, Ohio.

December 1904 — Four hunters spied a young "wild man" with "long matted hair and a beard" near Horne Lake, on Vancouver Island (British Columbia). The creature fled at high speed through "impenetrable" brush.

March 1908 — The *Vancouver Province* reported a recent disturbance from Bishop's Cove: "A monkeylike wild man who ap-

pears on the beach at night, who howls in unearthly fashion between intervals of clam digging, has been the cause of depopulating an Indian village....The Indians say that they have tried to shoot it but failed."

1951 — A woman hiking along the Eel River (north of Eureka, California) allegedly met a red-eyed, hairy creature "with the strangest-looking fangs that I have ever seen." She later told IVAN SANDERSON, "However, the strangest thing [was that] he had on clothes. They were tattered and torn and barely covered him, but they were still there."

1971 — Residents of Lawton, Oklahoma sighted a tall, hairy figure dressed in clothes several sizes too small. Witnesses remarked on the being's ability to jump 12-15 feet in a single bound.

What are these creatures? Hermits are often proposed as suspects, and some such do exist. The "wild man" captured by residents of Pulaski County, Arkansas in December 1875 turned out to be a transient lunatic, described in newspaper accounts as "the wildest, greasiest, ugliest-looking, half-clad specimen of humanity it was ever our lot to behold." Modern cryptozoologists explain many Wildman sightings with reference to BIGFOOT or NORTH AMERICAN APES. BERNARD HEUVELMANS, MARK HALL and others suggest that Wildman sightings around the world may be explained by relict populations of primitive prehumans, such as NEANDERTAL MAN or *Homo erectus*, long since presumed extinct.

Sources: Bord and Bord, *The Bigfoot Casebook*; Coleman, *Mysterious America*; Shackley, *Still Living?*

Williams, Autumn (1973–)

BIGFOOT researcher Autumn Williams was born in Washington on 20 October 1973, the sixth anniversary of the PATTERSON FILM. Her childhood was spent in the shadow of Mount Rainier, where she reports that her family "had repeated encounters with SASQUATCH creatures." That experience sparked a lifelong fascination with unknown HOMINIDS and prompted her to launch an Internet website (OregonBigfoot.com) in 2000. Williams describes the project as "a mixture of my fascination for Sasquatchology and my love for statistics and computers," and she maintains that website under its original title, despite a recent move to Minneapolis. As Williams explains her work, "My area of expertise is long-term witnesses. I am fascinated by rural families who claim ongoing encounters similar to what my own family experienced." That interest was reflected in fall 2003, when Williams emerged before a national audience as the database/web programmer and host of *Mysterious Encounters*, broadcast by the Outdoor Life Network.

Cryptozoologist Autumn Williams, with a footprint cast of Oregon's Sasquatch.

Sources: Autumn Williams, personal communication (4 October 2003); Oregon Bigfoot.com, http://www.oregonbigfoot.com/index.php.

Williams Lake, Canada Williams Lake, in British Columbia's Cariboo Mountains, is said to be inhabited by a LAKE MONSTER resembling the more famous OGOPOGO.

Source: Moon, *Ogopogo*.

Williams Lake, Michigan Located north of Oakland-Pontiac International Airport, in the Detroit suburb Waterford, Michigan (Oakland County), this small lake produced a curious cryptid report in 1973. The witnesses, a teenage couple, were parked the lake when a creature resembling a huge lizard allegedly charged their car, leaving dents and scratches in the bodywork. No other sightings of the aggressive reptile have thus far been recorded. Fortean authors Colin and Janet Bord list the incident as a LAKE MONSTER sighting, though no evidence exists that the creature came from or returned to the water.

Sources: "A chronology of Michigan creatures." *Michigan Anomaly Research* 1 (Winter 1980): 4; Bord and Bord, *Unexplained Mysteries of the 20th Century*.

Williamson, Gordon (1936-2003) Greenwich native Gordon Williamson earned a degree in zoology from King's College and worked as a science officer on whaling ships while completing his Ph.D. thesis on cod stocks off the Newfoundland Bank. Trained as a teacher in Edinburgh, Williamson taught school until 1965, then resumed his career as a marine biologist in the Far East (where he wrote the definitive guide to squid and OCTOPUS species of Hong Kong). Back in Scotland by 1972, Williamson continued teaching, then pioneered CRYPTOTOURISM by launching the first minibus tours of Loch Ness and environs. Though not a believer in NESSIE, he examined videotape of an unidentified creature swimming near Castle Urquhart and published a paper suggesting that some "monster" sightings were attributable to seals in the loch. While conducting his tours, Williamson continued marine research on EELS and consulted with various international experts. Severe head injuries from a traffic accident in 2000 led to Williamson's death in March 2003.

Source: "Tour guide who did not believe in Nessie." *Inverness Courier* (7 April 2003).

Williamsport Monster In early 1909, reports of a monster at large circulated around Williamsport, in Pennsylvania's Lycoming County. One witness signed an affidavit describing the beast as "a BIRD possessing powerful wings and the body of a horse." Another who allegedly glimpsed the creature lost his job as a late-night streetcar driver, after he abandoned his car and passengers to seek refuge in a saloon. Chickens were slaughtered, with hoof prints reminiscent of the JERSEY DEVIL found at the scene. Sightings ended after well-armed residents announced their intention of killing the creature on sight. More than four decades later, in June 1953, local banker Fred Heim announced that he and two friends had invented the beast as a HOAX. Heim worked as a reporter for the *Williamsport News* in 1909, and he allegedly conceived the plot after his editor told him to "go out and see what you can stir up." With companions Albert Bubb and John Knight, Heim said he used "a deformed horseshoe with ends broken off" to create strange footprints, then pointed them out to passersby. The rest, according to Heim, was simply a case of mass hysteria. The slaughtered chickens remain unexplained.

Source: "Canadian excitement stirs ghost of 'monster' that local residents saw in '09." *Williamsport (PA) Sun* (18 July 1953).

***Wilson* sea serpent** In early June 1818, sailors aboard the brig *Wilson* allegedly sighted a large object drifting offshore from Cape Henry, Virginia. A boat was lowered to inspect what they first mistook for a capsized ship, then recognized as a 190-foot SEA SERPENT. Reviewing the case 150 years later, BERNARD HEUVELMANS found it "most suspicious" that the creature allowed humans to approach and view it at leisure, without fleeing or attacking. He finally dismissed the sighting as a HOAX.

Source: Heuvelmans, *In the Wake of the Sea Serpents*.

Winambuu *see* **Junjadee**

Wingecarribee River/Swamp, Australia Australian author William Hardy Wilson, writing in 1920, claimed to have examined courthouse records at Berrima, New South Wales, that described reports of BUNYIP sightings along the nearby Wingecarribee River. The stories were told by escaped prisoners, who allegedly met the creatures while fleeing from Berrima's jail (constructed in 1839). Unfortunately, the records have long since been lost, and Wilson provided no details or dates for the sightings. Researchers Paul Cropper and Tony Healy add that Wingecarribee Swamp (near Moss Vale) "was, for many years, reported to be the home of a fearsome bunyip." No modern sightings are on file, however, prompting Cropper and Healy to suggest that the creature was a misguided seal, whose access from the sea was blocked by construction of the Warrangamba Dam.

Sources: Healy and Cropper, *Out of the Shadows*; Smith, *Bunyips & Bigfoots*.

Winnipogo A measure of confusion surrounds this alleged LAKE MONSTER of Manitoba, Canada. Named in the style of British Columbia's OGOPOGO, Winnipogo is said to inhabit both Lake Winnipeg and neighboring Lake Winnepegosis. It is not alone, however, and some authors insist on calling all of the province's aquatic cryptids MANIPOGO—a name initially coined for large, unknown animals sighted in Lake Manitoba. It may, furthermore, be identical to the creature known by aboriginal tribesmen as NAITAKA (a name applied to lake monsters throughout Canada before European settlers arrived).

That said, Winnipogo has produced some dramatic sightings in its own right. In April 1918, while shooting ducks at Fuller Bay, on Lake Winnepegosis, Oscar Frederickson claimed that some submerged creature lifted a large block of ice in the shallow water near shore. In 1935, witnesses C.F. Ross and Tom Spence allegedly sighted an animal resembling a DINOSAUR, with a single horn on the back of its head, near the northern end of Lake Winnepegosis. Around the same time, Oscar Frederickson found a curious bone on the lake's north shore, 20 miles from Burrow's Landing. The relic was later lost in a fire, but not before Frederickson carved a wooden model of it, six inches long and three inches in diameter. Three decades later, he displayed the replica to Dr. James MacLeod, chairman of the Zoology Department at the University of Manitoba and an active student of Manitoba's aquatic cryptids. MacLeod cautiously described the carving as a "good copy" of a vertebra from "an animal long extinct or thought to be." A visit to the site of Frederickson's find revealed no more remains, but photos of the carving were published in August 1961, accompanied by MacLeod's sketch of the prospective donor (resembling a ZEUGLODON).

Sources: Coleman and Clark, *Cryptozoology A to Z*; Costello, *In Search of Lake Monsters*; Eber, "The scientific search for a prehistoric monster"; Mackal, *Searching for Hidden Animals*.

Winooski River, Vermont Various authors include the Winooski River (northwest of Burlington) on lists of lakes and rivers with resident cryptids, and while one claims sightings from the 20th century, no dates or details are provided. Through the 1960s, the Winsooki was badly polluted by chemicals and other waste from various mills and factories. It has greatly improved since the 1970s, but any unknown animals probably died or fled to cleaner waters in the 19th century.

Sources: Bord and Bord, *Unexplained Mysteries of the 20th Century*; Coleman, *Mysterious America*; Kirk, *In the Domain of the Lake Monsters*.

Winsted Wildman

The unknown HOMINID or primate draws its name from Winsted, Connecticut (Litchfield County), though its original sightings were logged farther north, around Colebrook. There, in the winter of 1892, a tall, hairy biped reportedly stole chickens and a RABBIT from a farmer's coop, leaving footprints in the snow as it fled blasts of gunfire. Two years later, the same beast or its twin chased a man through the woods near Colebrook. Hunters tracked it to a cave in the side of a nearby mountain, stretching chains across the entrance, but they found the chains broken next morning. In the summer of 1895, John Hall saw a BIGFOOT-type creature cross the road in front of his wagon, while riding near Colebrook. A short time later, on 17 August, Riley Cooper was frightened by a shouting, hooting WILDMAN while picking berries near Winsted. Several published accounts describe another incident from August 1895, wherein a shaggy monster killed and carried away Peter Thomas's horse in "Delamere County, New York." Unfortunately, no such county exists in the Empire State: there is a Dela*ware* County, and a town called Delmar near Elsmere (below Albany), but the unusual report of a wildman attack remains impossible to verify.

Author H. Haden Blackman reports that Winsted Wildman sightings "continued with a fair amount of frequency for the next century," leading to "an incredible surge" of reports in 1972. (One case is cited, from July.) Other sightings allegedly occurred in July 1974 and in October 1989, when Blackman says the creature wandered onto a shooting range near Bristol (16 miles southeast of Winsted). Strangely, none of those incidents are recorded in any of the standard Bigfoot texts. Blackman cites no sources, and the quality of his reportage on other cryptids does not inspire confidence.

Sources: Berry, *Bigfoot on the East Coast*; Blackman, *The Field Guide to North American Monsters*; Bord and Bord, *The Bigfoot Casebook*.

Winthorpe sea serpent

One night in early summer 1966, while cycling past the Derbyshire Miner's Centre at Winthorpe, Lincolnshire, England, John Hayes heard a "loud crack" from the nearby sea and stopped to look offshore. As the *Skegness Standard* described the event in October 1966:

> He looked towards the sea and saw a "huge dark shape" about 500 yards out, moving at about 20 m.p.h. and leaving a wake behind it. He did not report the sighting at the time as he thought it might be a whale or some other identifiable creature. The "Standard" report last week [of another SEA SERPENT sighting] prompted him to reveal his information however. "I still believe there are things which have yet to be discovered," says Mr. Hayes.

Source: Heuvelmans, *In the Wake of the Sea Serpents*.

Wisconsin sea serpent

In July 1888, while approaching the mouth of the Hudson River, officers aboard the *Wisconsin* sighted a SEA SERPENT 30 miles offshore from Sandy Hook, New York. According to the ship's doctor and purser, the unknown animal was green and measured at least 60 feet long.

Source: Heuvelmans, *In the Wake of the Sea Serpents*.

Wiwiliámecq'

Although its name translates as "snail" in English, Algonquin tribesmen described this LAKE MONSTER of Boyden Lake, Maine (Washington County) as a horned serpent 30-40 feet long, typically found behind waterfalls. Some versions of the legend transform the Wiwiliámecq' into a SEA SERPENT, plying the coastal waters of neighboring New Brunswick, Canada. No modern sightings are on record from Boyden Lake.

Source: Gatschet, "Water-monsters of American aborigines."

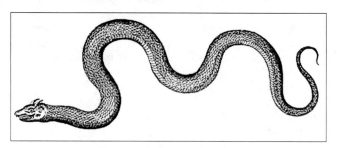

Aboriginal folklore describes the Wiwiliámecq' as a huge horned serpent.

Woadd-El-Uma

This unknown HOMINID or MERBEING of Sudan reportedly inhabited the Nile River valley through the mid-19th century. Natives of the region described the Woadd-el-uma ("son of the mother," in Arabic) as an amphibious species, man-sized and covered in brown or red hair. The lake- and marsh-dwelling creatures sometimes came ashore to feed on fruit, typically a few days before the Nile's seasonal floods. In June 1832, traveler Joseph Russegger found a set of strange footprints, identified by his guide as a Woadd-el-uma's, near the third cataract of the Nile. The tracks emerged from the river, skirted Russegger's camp, then returned to the water. Russegger described the 10-inch footprints as possessing four long toes and a fully opposed big toe (like the track of an APE). The prints lay three feet apart and were angled at 70 degrees from the direction of travel, prompting Russegger to conclude that the creature traveled by hopping.

Source: Joseph Russegger, *Reisen in Europa, Asien und Afrika*. Stuttgart: E. Schweizerbart, 1849.

Wobo

TIGERS (*Panthera tigris*) are not native to Africa, yet reports of ferocious striped CATS have been logged from the East African nations of Ethiopia and Sudan. In Ethiopia, the unclassified creatures are called Wobo (by the Amhara people) and Mendelit (in the Tigre district). Across the border in Sudan, they are referred to as Abu Sotan. In the 19th century, Ethiopian witnesses described the Wobo as larger than a LION (*Panthera leo*), with black stripes on yellow-brown or gray-brown pelage. A Wobo pelt was allegedly displayed in the cathedral at Eifag through the early 1860s, but its fate is unknown and skeptics suggest that it was a tiger skin imported from Asia. In 1868, Theodor von Heuglin reported that the Abu Sotan inhabited rocky mountains near Sudan's River Rahad, where natives described large cats marked with black stripes or blotches.

Source: Shuker, *Mystery Cats of the World*.

Wokolo/Woukolo see Gnéna

Woldingham Lion

This ALIEN BIG CAT of East Surrey, England was sighted by witness Anne Stanette in 1978. Stanette later described the incident as follows to author Graham McEwan:

The Woldingham Lion appeared in Surrey, England, during 1978.

While I was out riding in Grangers Woods, Woldingham, in May 1978, I saw what I believe to be a LION rush across the road in front of me. It ran from the Oxted side into thick bushes on the opposite side. It was about ten to twelve yards from me. It was a beige/light brown colour and had a small head in comparison with the rest of its body. (It had no shaggy mane.) Its back legs seemed more muscly than the front. I saw it sideways on. It did not move as a dog does.

As noted by McEwan, the CAT described by Stanette more closely resembles a COUGAR (*Puma concolor*) than a lion (*Panthera leo*). Male lions are maned, while females are not noted for small heads.

Source: McEwan, *Mystery Animals of Britain and Ireland.*

Wolds Panther

This ALIEN BIG CAT of Lincolnshire, England has been sporadically reported since 1997, when motorist Lee Mansi reported a large black CAT crossing the highway near Wragby. The following year, Charlie Sutton told reporters that he saw a panther dash across the road near a picnic ground in Willingham Woods. In 2001, a sighting was logged near the Louth Golf Club. John Brown was driving through Scamblesby when the cat crossed his path, in July 2002, and a resident of Baumber saw it sniffing around her chicken coops soon afterward. In January 2003, Rob Barnes confronted the beast in his driveway, at Langton. Three months later, in Ludford, Christine Tye described the cat she saw as "black with a long black tail" and "a gray face like a puma." Sightings multiplied so rapidly thereafter, that the *Skegness Standard* offered a £100 reward for an authentic photo of the animal. That bounty remained uncollected at press time for this volume, but sightings continue. On 2 July 2003, a hiker claimed to have found the cat's lair outside Louth, and while reporters found piles of pheasant feathers strewn nearby, no panther was at home when they arrived. Jayne Elliott, writing for the *Louth Leader*, told her readers, "We have spoken to some wild cat experts who do believe that pumas and black panthers could live in the Wolds." Nine days after the Louth sighting, Sandy Richardson of Hemingby found "a great big black thing" lurking in a backyard trailer. Richardson collected dark hairs at the site, which the *Louth Leader* submitted for DNA analysis. The result, published on 15 October 2003, indicated that the creature was "a wild cat belonging to the leopard [*Panthera pardus*] family. Sandy

Richardson received the *Leader's* £100 reward for evidence authenticating the beast's existence.

Source: "It really is out there!" *Louth Leader* (15 October 2003); "Man 'finds' big cat's lair." *Horncastle News* (2 July 2003); "More sightings add to Wolds panther mystery." *Horncastle News* (13 August 2003); "'Wolds beast was in my caravan'—claim." *Horncastle Today* (10 September 2003)

Wolf Deer

Two sightings, reported 20 years apart, provide the only record of this strange cryptid, allegedly combining features of a canid and an ungulate. In 1951, Mrs. Lawrence Laub was startled to meet an animal resembling "a cross between a wolf and a deer" on her farm outside Calumet, Oklahoma (Canadian County). Its feet were "huge pads," and it had small ears, long hair over its body, and a bushy tail. She threw a stick at the creature, but it refused to be stampeded, ambling away in its own good time. Other locals reported "strange" tracks in the neighborhood, but no one else sighted the odd hybrid creature.

Two decades later and 450 miles farther north, H.H. Christensen and D.R. Clark were driving through Yellow Medicine County, Minnesota, when they met an "odd-looking deer" along Florida Creek, eight miles from Canby. Clark stopped the car and got out to confront the animal, waving his arms and shouting. When the beast ignored him, Clark drew a gun and fired several shots in the air, but the "deer" simply walked a short distance away and lay down. Clark refrained from killing the strangely placid animal, and saw it for the last time as he drove away.

Source: Jerome Clark, "A message from Magonia." *Fortean Times* 8 (February 1975): 5-6.

Wolf Pond, Pennsylvania

In September 1887, residents of Franklin County, Pennsylvania reported a serpentine cryptid, 30 feet long and six inches in diameter, from the vicinity of Wolf's Pond. It was described as green, with yellow rings. Sketchy accounts of the sighting make it impossible to say if the animal was a LAKE MONSTER or a giant SNAKE seen on land.

Sources: Garner, *Monster! Monster!*; Charles Skinner, *Myths and Legends of Our Land.* Philadelphia: Lippincott, 1896.

Wolumbin *see* Jogung

Wolverhampton Puma

In July 1980, while walking along an abandoned railroad line between Aldersley and Compton, Wolverhampton, England, a schoolteacher saw a large animal appear from the woods 50 yards ahead. Convinced that he had seen a COUGAR (*Puma concolor*), the witness reported his sighting to Michael Williams, superintendent at the Dudley Zoo. Williams visited the scene with the zoo's chief curator of CATS, and they saw the animal two miles from the scene of the first sighting. As Williams described the incident:

It disappeared, and then we heard BIRDS mobbing something in the thick cover and an animal emerged onto the track about 300 yards in front. It was a large animal which had a round head, was level across the back, had a heavy tail held low, and when it turned to look at us was very narrow. Everything about it was cat-like but we couldn't get nearer than about 300 yards....If we could find proof that a puma had escaped within a reasonable area of Wolverhampton then I would have said that we had seen it. No such escapes were reported, however, and the cat has not been seen again at Wolverhampton, though cougars and other ALIEN BIG CATS are sighted frequently throughout England.

Source: McEwan, *Mystery Animals of Britain and Ireland.*

Wolverines (Mislocated)

Wolverines (*Gulo gulo*) are the world's largest known mustelids, reaching lengths of four feet, standing 18 inches tall at the shoulder, and tipping the scales at 60 pounds. While their natural range stretches from continental Europe across Siberia to North America, they are unknown to the British Isles — or were, until early 1992. Between February 1992 and August 1992, six wolverine sightings were logged around Letterston, Wales. Local farmer Lawton Watts twice saw wolverines on his land before a pair of 70-pound lambs were slaughtered by an unseen predator in September 1992. Four more lambs were torn apart in May 1995.

By that time, sightings had spread to Exmoor, England, where naturalists Trevor and Endymion Beer saw two wolverines in January 1994. A month later, John Cobbett reported a wolverine stalking RABBITS near St. Audries, Somerset. In summer 1994, a wolverine was reportedly struck and killed by a car outside Wembworthy, Devon. London photographer Joanne Crowther saw the carcass but did not snap a photo at the time. Other sightings in 1994 were reported from Pembroke National Park, from Somerset's Quantock Hills, and from South Moulton (on the edge of Dartmoor). Still, no specimens have been collected, and KARL SHUKER notes persistent rumors that two binturongs (*Arcticitis binturong*), 4.5-foot-long wolverine look-alikes, were released on Exmoor in the 1970s.

Sources: Sieveking, "Big cats in Britain"; Shuker, "Who's afraid of the big bad wolverine?"

Wolverines have been sighted in Britain since 1992.

Wolves (Surviving)   The gray wolf (*Canis lupus*) is the largest wild canid known to science. It was also once the Earth's most widely distributed mammal, inhabiting most of the northern hemisphere above 15° north latitude. Exterminated in Britain by the 17th century and hunted to extinction over much of their North American range in the 19th and early 20th centuries, gray wolves maintain fair numbers today in Alaska and parts of Canada. In the 48 contiguous United States, only Minnesota hosts a significant wolf population, with an estimated 1,200 individuals. About 35 members of the subspecies *C. l. lycaon* survive in Michigan and Wisconsin, while approximately 30 members of *C. l. iremotus* are known to live in the Pacific Northwest. Elsewhere in the U.S., the subspecies *C. l. baileyi* is officially extinct, its numbers whittled to 10 reported survivors in Mexico. Despite those losses, however, witnesses around the U.S. and the United Kingdom continue to report sightings of wolves or wolflike creatures in areas where they should not exist. Some examples include:

1975 — Angry farmers in Jasper County, Mississippi reported that an unidentified wolflike predator was raiding hog farms, bit-

ing the ears from one pig after another. In March 1977, authorities hunted in vain for an identical MYSTERY MAULER at Jackson, Mississippi.

Spring 1978 — A "doglike animal, larger than a FOX, tan with a long dark tail" attacked a pony at Prestonburg, Kentucky, leaping on its victim's back and biting at the pony's neck before it was driven away. The pony was severely injured.

1982 — Two cattlemen driving near Cheyenne, Oklahoma met a curious animal along the highway. Alex Inman said, "It was bigger and broader than a dog would be. Its head pretty much sat down on its shoulders, and it walked on four legs." Companion George Springer declared, "It was not fuzzy or furry, but slick-haired, like a pig. It was kind of smooth moving. It didn't bounce any. It was pretty heavy, and had a pretty big body." When the men honked their horn, the animal wandered out of sight at a leisurely pace.

27 July 1994 — Jerry Coleman and four companions saw a large "wild dog," three feet tall at the shoulder, crossing a field north of Elgin, Illinois.

August 2000 — While hunting in the Clashindarroch Forest of Aberdeenshire, Scotland, Conrad Sheward claimed a sighting of a gray wolf at 120 yards. "Initially," he said, "I thought it was a huge fox. It was grey with a whitish tail, but it was too big for a fox."

Fall 2002 — Randy Worker shot a gray wolf near Henry, Illinois, in Marshall County, on 29 December 2002. The animal's identity was confirmed by DNA tests in July 2003. Although the gray wolf is protected by law throughout the U.S., no charges were filed against Worker, who apparently believed that he was shooting a coyote (*Canis latrans*).

15 December 2002 — A hunter stalking coyotes shot and killed a 100-pound male gray wolf near Spalding, Nebraska, marking the state's first confirmed wolf sighting in 90 years.

June 2003 — After an ear-tagged wolf from Wisconsin was shot in eastern Indiana, other residents reported sightings to the press and to authorities. One Ripley County farmer claimed sightings

Wolf sightings persist in many regions where the animals are deemed extinct.

of at least four wolves around his property, including one trapped and killed by a neighbor.

24 August 2003— Witness Doudley Tolley saw a wolf on his farm near Stoke Abbott, Dorset, England. "When it was 15 yards away from me," he told reporters, "I could see it was a wolf. It was dark grey, taller than a large Alsatian [German shepherd], with spindly legs, not as thick set as an Alsatian. It looked at me as though it was thinking, 'Shall I go back or shall I go through the hedge?' It was unhurried. It was a beautiful animal in very good condition."

1 November 2003— Irene Carruthers met two large gray wolves while walking on a path near her home at Carlisle, Scotland. As she described the creatures to police, "They were grey and white and had long legs. They were nothing like domestic dogs and they were absolutely stinking."

November-December 2003— Several residents of Oxford, Connecticut reported wolf sightings. Witness Malcolm Major photographed one of the creatures on 26 December, but the resultant photo was not clear enough to permit positive identification.

January 2004— Mike and Kyle Ushka photographed a canine cryptid near Southbury, Connecticut. While their photos were clear, controversy surrounds the depicted subject. Skeptics insist that the animal captured on film is a wolf-dog hybrid, crossbreeding of which is banned by law in Connecticut.

As for the wolves or wolflike creatures who survive their close encounters with humanity, various explanations are advanced in different quarters. One possibility, as with the EASTERN COUGAR, is that gray wolves still survive in numbers and in places unacknowledged by "experts." Another theory is that witnesses alleging wolf sightings have been misled by dogs, coyotes or foxes. Yet another offers hybrid animals as a solution, either a wolf-coyote mix or the more likely "coy-dog." One such predator was killed at Williamsburg, Virginia on 1 October 1977, after several years of terrorizing local livestock.

Sources: Bord and Bord, *Unexplained Mysteries of the 20th Century*; "Family reports sighting wolf." *Zwire* (14 January 2004); Jeff Lampe, "Henry hunter's mystery prey was rare gray wolf." *Peoria* (IL) *Journal Star* (25 July 2003); George McLaren, "Wolves are out there, say some Hoosiers." *Indianapolis Star* (17 September 2003); Stephen Meredith, "Wolves spotted in a villager's garden." *News and Star* (20 November 2003); Phil Potter, "'Extinct' animals may not be gone." *Evansville* (IN) *Courier Press* (5 October 2003); "Sighting of a wolf reported." *Bridport & Lyme Regis* (England) *News* (29 August 2003); "Wolf shot near Spalding is Nebraska's first in 90 years." *Lincoln* (NE) *Journal Star* (28 March 2003); Beastwatch UK, http://www.beastwatch.co.uk/.

Wood, Forrest G. (1919-92)

Indiana native Forrest ("Woody") Wood graduated from Earlham College in 1940 and subsequently served with the U.S. Army Air Corps during World War II. Discharged from military service in 1945, he earned a master's degree in marine biology from Yale but left the doctoral program for employment with the American Museum of Natural History on Bimini, in the British West Indies. From there, Wood moved on to work as curator at Marine Studios (later Marineland) in Florida (1951-63), and in various scientific capacities for the U.S. Navy (1963-84). Wood's fascination with pelagic cryptids included research on the alleged giant OCTOPUS stranded at St. Augustine, Florida in 1896. He traced a sample of the creature's tissue to the Smithsonian Institution and, with biologist Joseph Gennaro, obtained an analysis that convinced him of the huge cephalopod's existence. With Gennaro, Wood published a report on the creature in *Natural History* (March 1971), but he fumed

when editors inserted a melodramatic subtitle: "Stupefying Colossus from the Deep!" In 1982, Wood was a founding member of the INTERNATIONAL SOCIETY OF CRYPTOZOOLOGY, and he served on the ISC's board until failing health compelled his resignation. Shortly before his death, ISC leaders named Wood the group's first American honorary member. Wood died on 17 May 1992, and his ashes were scattered at sea.

Source: J. Richard Greenwell, "Forrest G. Wood, 1919-1992." *ISC Newsletter* 2, no. 1 (1992): 5-6.

Woodbury Water Witch

Little is known of this Vermont LAKE MONSTER, aside from the fact that it reportedly inhabits Woodbury Lake (Washington County). The first published reference to it appeared in *Vermont Life* (winter 1975), with a brief statement that "this reclusive amphibian, whose length has been estimated at anywhere up to 12 feet, generally lurks half-submerged in...quiet parts of Woodbury Lake. While precise descriptions vary, a number of sightseers agree the Water Witch has a scaly body, a web-like tail and sports a forklike antenna...just above two large recessed eyes."

Source: Citro, *Ghosts, Ghouls and Unsolved Mysteries*.

Woofin Nanny

In the summer of 1966, a still-unidentified MYSTERY MAULER attacked pets and livestock around Greensboro, North Carolina. Media reports indicated that the slain animals were drained of blood, apparently through puncture wounds resembling fang marks. Witnesses who glimpsed the predator described it as resembling a large, shaggy CAT. Despite attempts to hunt or trap it, the creature eluded all pursuers. The origin of its peculiar nickname remains obscure.

Sources: Farnum Gray, "Armed men staked out to await 'Woofin Nanny.'" *Winston-Salem* (NC) *Journal and Sentinel* (12 July 1966); Farnum Gray, "'Woofin Nanny' has mamas on edge." *Winston-Salem* (NC) *Journal and Sentinel* (9 July 1966).

Woolly Cheetah

In 1877, London Zoo director Philip Sclater announced the acquisition of a highly unusual CAT from South Africa. As described by Sclater, the immature male specimen generally resembled a cheetah (*Acinonyx jubatus*):

> ...but is thicker in the body, and has shorter and stouter limbs, and a much thicker tail. When adult it will probably be considerably larger than the Cheetah, and is larger even now than our three specimens of that animal. The fur is much more woolly and dense than in the Cheetah, as is particularly noticeable on the ears, mane and tail. The whole of the body is of a pale isabelline colour, rather paler on the belly and lower parts, but covered all over, including the belly, with roundish dark fulvous blotches. There are no traces of the black spots which are so conspicuous in all of the varieties of the Cheetah which I have seen, nor of the characteristic black line between the mouth and eye.

Sclater provisionally named the woolly cheetah *Felis lanea*. A year later, he learned that a second specimen was preserved at the South African Museum, obtained from the same area (Beauford West) as the first. When the London specimen died in 1881, analysis of its skull found no difference from a normal cheetah. Three years later, Sclater received another woolly cheetah pelt from Beaufort West, this one from a smaller specimen that proved to be female. Conservative zoologists insisted that the South African cats merely displayed aberrant color morphs, but that explanation ignored variations in size and length of legs. The woolly cheetahs of Beauford West, South Africa are now apparently extinct. Mammalogists Daphne Hills and Reay Smithers in 1980 found no local cats resembling the 19th-century specimens.

Source: Shuker, *Mystery Cats of the World*.

Woollybooger   This nickname was applied to a BIGFOOT-type HOMINID reported from North Carolina's Burke County in January 1972. An Associated Press report of 14 January claimed two sheriff's deputies had seen the 6-foot hairy creature cross a road near Drexel, but the officers changed their minds in time for a follow-up report on 26 January. In that amended version, they identified the creature as "a bear that covered its face with its paws as the lights of the moving car hit it." Nonetheless, local police departments were "flooded" with calls reporting the Woollybooger through late January. Researcher JOHN GREEN reports that the Woollybooger name "crops up in print from time to time" across the southern U.S., but he cites no further examples. It is probably derived from BOOGER, a term used in Dixie not only for SASQUATCH, but also for other cryptids.

Sources: Berry, *Bigfoot on the East Coast*; Bord and Bord, *The Bigfoot Casebook*; Green, *Sasquatch: The Apes Among Us*.

Woronora River, Australia   The Woronora River flows through Australia's Heathcote National Park, south of Sydney (New South Wales). Cryptozoologist REX GILROY reports sightings of an aquatic cryptid from the area, but no details are presently available. Curiously, the same region spawned reports of a 7-foot "apeman" resembling the YOWIE in July 1987, but local police identified the "creature" as a Yugoslav hermit with unruly hair.

Sources: "Apeman turns out to be 'Rambo' the hermit." *Brisbane Telegraph* (28 July 1987); Gilroy, "Search for the Hawkesbury River monster"; Smith, *Bunyips & Bigfoots*.

Wouwai   In the 19th century, Lake Macquarie, north of Sydney in New South Wales, Australia was a source of LAKE MONSTER or BUNYIP reports. Aborigines called the resident creature(s) Wouwai, and while the unknown animals have apparently died out at Lake Macquarie, authors Paul Cropper and Tony Healy call the nearby Macquarie river "the greatest bunyip hot-spot of modern times."

Sources: Healy and Cropper, *Out of the Shadows*; Whitley, "Mystery animals of Australia."

Wright, Bruce Stanley (1912-75)   Québec native Bruce Wright earned a degree in forestry from the University of New Brunswick in 1936 and served with the Dominion Forest Service, publishing his first articles on conservation issues in 1938. At the outbreak of World War II, he joined the Royal Canadian Navy and helped create its Sea Reconnaissance Unit. Upon release from military service, Wright completed graduate studies in wildlife management and continued writing while he served as director of the University of New Brunswick's Northeastern Wildlife Station (1947-74). Wright's private passion was a lifelong pursuit of the supposedly extinct EASTERN COUGAR. His masterwork on the subject, *The Ghost of the Americas*, was published in 1959, then revised and expanded in 1972 as *The Eastern Panther: A Question of Survival*. New Brunswick today lists cougars as endangered, rather than extinct, thanks in large part to Wright's work. Other cryptids investigated by Wright include BIGFOOT and the Bahamian LUSCA. Failing health forced his retirement in 1974, and he died in April 1975.

Sources: Coleman and Clark, *Cryptozoology A to Z*; Atlantic Society of Fish & Wildlife Biologists Virtual Wall of Fame, http://www.chebucto.ns.ca/Environment/ASFWB/wright.*html*.

Wudéwású   The Wudéwású ("wood man," in Old English) were WILDMEN reported from various parts of Europe through the Middle Ages. Although some scholars dismiss them as entirely mythical, depictions of the Wudéwású in artwork and literature provide a wealth of realistic detail. Most are portrayed as HOMINIDS covered entirely with hair, often sporting wild beards, though some — like the couple portrayed on Earl Poulett's coat of arms in *Burkes Peerage* — wear brief garments made of leaves or animal hides. (About 200 European families have Wudéwású featured in their coats of arms.) An illustration from Queen Mary's Psalter, drawn in the 14th century, depicts a Wudéwású beset by dogs wearing collars. Some Wudéwású were alleged to build crude shelters in the forest, and to hunt with weapons that included clubs and spears. Other traditions suggest that Wudéwású sometimes engaged in barter with civilized men, but such interaction could be dangerous. In 1691, a Swedish defendant was condemned and executed on charges of having sex with a female Wudéwású he met in the forest.

Wudéwású were sighted with some regularity through the late 17th century, and a 2-foot-tall female specimen was reportedly captured near Chemnitz, Germany in August 1644. Ninety-one years later, several Wudéwású were seen prowling the woods around Gröditsch, in Germany's Brandenburg State. More startling yet is the report of two apelike creatures at large near Neubrandenburg in 1938. (Newspapers reported that no primates had escaped from German zoos.) Some Scandinavians insist that Wudéwású still survive, and Swedish cryptozoologist JAN-OVE SUNDBERG has collected reports of a SASQUATCH-type creature at large in Gavelborg County, as recently as 1985. Another large, hairy hominid was seen by multiple witnesses around Ventimiglia, Italy between December 1996 and July 1997.

As with Wildmen elsewhere, skeptics insist that the Wudéwású is a mythical creature that never existed in fact. Sightings throughout history are explained as hallucinations, deliberate HOAXES, or cases of mistaken identity (involving hermits, bears, "escaped MONKEYS," etc.) Some cryptozoologists disagree, suggesting that such proto-humans as NEANDERTAL MAN or *Homo erectus* may have survived into historic times — or even to the present day. To win that argument, a specimen must be produced, but thus far the Wudéwású has failed to cooperate.

Sources: Richard Bernheimer, *Wild Men in the Middle Ages*. Cambridge, MA: Harvard University Press, 1952; Coleman and Huyghe, *The Field Guide to Bigfoot, Yeti, and Other Mystery Primates Worldwide*; Sanderson, "*Things*"; Shackley, *Still Living?*

Wulasha *see* **Ulak**

Wurrum   Ireland's Lough Bran (or Brin), in County Kerry, has a long tradition of LAKE MONSTER sightings, involving creatures collectively known as the Wurrum. Unlike some Celtic "monster" lakes, however, sightings here have continued into modern times. In 1940, a 14-year-old boy allegedly saw one of the creatures, a black beast with four stumpy legs, basking on shore. Farmer Timothy O'Sullivan was grazing cattle near Lough Bran, on 24 December 1954, when he saw what he took for two ducks on the water. Moments later, the "ducks" were revealed as two humps or fins, 12 feet apart, each two feet long and two feet high. By the time O'Sullivan retrieved his shotgun and another witness, the creature had vanished. In the summer of 1979, two brothers glimpsed a black 10-foot creature swimming in the lough, from a distance of 600 yards. Their father had seen the Wurrum several years earlier, describing it as "black as soot" and resembling a cross between "a giant seal and a DRAGON out of the pictures."

Sources: Costello, *In Search of Lake Monsters*; McEwan, *Mystery Animals of Britain and Ireland*.

——X——

Xing-Xing   An unknown anthropoid APE reported from southern China, the Xing-xing is described in some accounts as a man-eater. A site located in the Xinjiang Uygur Autonomous Region, at 41° 48' north latitude and 95° 9' east longitude, is apparently called Xing-xingxia (Ape Ravine) in honor of the creatures, though some skeptics note that a different pronunciation of *xingxing* in Mandarin translates as "stars." Witnesses typically describe the Xing-xing as arboreal, but some report bipedal locomotion when it leaves the trees. The creature is hairy overall, with a pale humanoid face and pointed ears. Its cry resembles the wailing of a child. More fanciful accounts claim the Xing-xing enjoys drinking wine and is capable of speech.

Source: Heuvelmans, "Annotated checklist of apparently unknown animals with which cryptozoology is concerned"; Tchernine, *The Yeti.*

Xipe   An unclassified cave-dwelling HOMINID reported from Nicaragua, the Xipe draws its name from the Nahuatal dialect, variously interpreted as "the flayed one" or "he with the penis." The variant name Xiximique is also used. Witnesses describe the typical Xipe as between two and four feet tall, covered in dark hair, and possessing "backwards feet" (a curious trait claimed for mystery hominids in various parts of Latin America and elsewhere). Reports claim that a group of Nicaraguan peasants tracked a Xipe to its cave in 1968 and killed it by burning the underbrush outside, thus asphyxiating the creature, but no remains were preserved. A fondness for water is suggested by another report, this one from November 1990, wherein fisherman watched a Xipe crawl out of El Palacio Lake, north of Matagalpa. This cryptid may be identical to the TRAUKO and SHIRU reported from Nicaragua, Panama and Colombia.

Source: Heuvelmans, "Annotated checklist of apparently unknown animals with which cryptozoology is concerned"; "The Xipe of Nicaragua," *Fortean Times.*

Xochitl Elena sea creature   In May 1954 crewmen aboard the Mexican shrimp boat *Xochitl Elena* spied a strange creature floundering in the Gulf of Mexico. Harpoons initially rebounded from the animal's thick hide, but it was finally transfixed and hauled aboard, where it tipped the boat's scales at 550 pounds. Witnesses described the thing as four feet long and six feet wide, with stubby fins and a mouth filled with long, sharp teeth. Uncertain what to do with the creature, the shrimpers threw it back into the water and moved on. It remains unidentified today.

Source: Keel, *The Complete Guide to Mysterious Beings.*

Xuĕ-Rén *see* **Yeren**

——Y——

Yabalik-Adam   An unknown HOMINID or WILDMAN of Central Asia, the Yabalik-adam reportedly dwells in the Pamir and Kunlun mountain ranges, overlapping the borders of northeastern Afghanistan, eastern Tajikistan, and western China's Xinjiang Uygur Autonomous Region. Variant regional names for the creature include Yaboi-adam, Yavan-adam and Yavo-khal'g. Described by witnesses as man-sized, covered in light brown or yellowish hair, with feet larger than a human's, the Yabalik-adam appears to bridge the territories normally inhabited by the ALMAS and the YEREN. Chinese hunters allegedly captured a specimen in 1912 and kept it alive on a diet of raw meat, until authorities learned of the creature and seized it. No further information is available on the captive animal's fate, if in fact it ever existed.

Source: Heuvelmans and Porshnev, *L'homme de Néanderthal est toujours vivant.*

Yagmort   An unknown HOMINID or WILDMAN reported from the eastern sector of European Russia, the Yagmort allegedly dwells in a region west of the Urals, from the Komi Republic in the north, southward to Perm' and Kirov. Witnesses describe hairy, manlike creatures between 5 foot 6 inches and 6 foot 6 inches tall, covered in light gray hair. Footprints left by the Yagmort typically measure 12.5 inches long and five inches wide. Some witnesses report Yagmorts mimicking human voices or employing a guttural "language." Others describe the Yagmort as a cave-dweller and strong swimmer, rumored to light fires by striking stones together. An apparent fondness for horses — also displayed by the ALMAS in Russia's Kabardin-Balkar Republic — leads the Yagmort to lurk around stables.

Modern reports of the Yagmort date from 1920, when two of the creatures frightened villagers at Ust'-Tsil'ma. In August 1974, a teenage witness watched two Yagmort — one of them a pregnant female — browsing and "talking" beside the Chusovaya River. Twelve years later, in August 1986, a lone Yagmort reportedly invaded a hut occupied by hay mowers near Timenskoye Ridge, in the Komi Republic. As recently as August 1999, two groups of hunters logged sightings around Sovetsk, in the Kirov district. Kirov's regional environmental agency launched an investigation of the Yagmort, but the results of that study (if any) remain unpublished.

Sources: Bayanov, *In the Footsteps of the Russian Snowman*; Shackley, *Still Living?*

Yahoo *see* **Yowie**

Yamamaya   The Yamamaya is an unclassified CAT, reported from Iriomote-jima, southernmost of the Ryukyu Islands (southwest of Japan). In 1965, zoologists discovered a new wild cat on Iriomote, known to locals as *pingimaya* and formally named *Prionailurus iriomotensis* in 1967. That species ranks as the most primitive living felid known to science, but it is a veritable dwarf beside the Yamamaya, which Iriomote natives describe as a TIGER-striped cat the size of a sheepdog. The discovery of a new dwarf wild pig on Iriomote, in 1975, suggests that the island holds more secrets in store for cryptozoologists, but the Yamamaya remains elusive. Potential candidates thus far suggested include a new subspecies of clouded leopard (*Neofelis nebulosa*) or an unknown subspecies of tiger (*Panthera tigris*).

Source: Shuker, *Mystery Cats of the World.*

Yamana *see* **Gnéna**

Yana Puma   Quechua tribesmen from the mountains of central Peru describe this unclassified CAT as jet black and twice the size of a normal JAGUAR (*Panthera onca*). A nocturnal hunter, it is said to be ferocious and an occasional man-eater, recognized from a distance by its roars. True pumas are incapable of roaring, they do not reach sizes matching those reported for the Yana Puma, and black specimens are extremely rare. Melanism is slightly more common among jaguars, though the cat's normal spots remain visible, and once again the size is wrong. Thus far, the Yana Puma remains unidentified.

Source: Hocking, "Large Peruvian mammals unknown to zoology."

Yangtze River serpent   British ship's pilot J.H. Hoar was stationed at Ningpo, China in 1880, when he sighted an unidentified SEA SERPENT at the mouth of the Yangtze River. He estimated that the creature was 120 to 140 feet long, "resembling two masts of a junk end to end, but with a slight interval" between them. The beast's head was flat on top, Hoar recalled, and its slate-colored eyes were "as big as a coffee-saucer."

Source: Heuvelmans, *In the Wake of the Sea Serpents*.

Yaquaru   South America's mysterious "WATER TIGER" is known by various names throughout its range in southern Paraguay and northern Argentina. Its regional names, all apparently describing the same ferocious animal, include Yaguaro, Yaguaron, Yaquiaruigh and *tigre de agua*. Jesuit Thomas Falkner glimpsed the creature in 1752, as it leapt into Argentina's RIO PARANÁ. He published this account of the beast in 1774 (strangely omitting his personal impressions):

> It is described by the Indians to be as big as an ass; of the figure the size of a large, over-grown river-WOLF or otter; with sharp talons, and strong tusks; thick and short legs; long, shaggy hair; with a long, tapering tail. The Spaniards describe it somewhat differently; as having a long head, a sharp nose, like that of a wolf, and stiff, erect ears....It is very destructive to the cattle which pass the Paraná; for great herds of them pass every year, and it generally happens that this beast seizes some of them. When it has once laid hold of its prey, it is seen no more; and the lungs and entrails soon appear floating upon the water. It lives in the greatest depths, especially in the whirlpools made by the concurrence of two streams, and sleeps in the deep caverns that are in the banks.

Despite a superficial similarity in names, the Yaquaru's size, color and shaggy coat distinguish it from the more familiar

Karl Shuker suggests that South America's Yaquaru may be a relict saber-tooth cat.

JAGUAR. Likewise, although native otters (*Lontra longicaudis*) are sometimes called "water tigers" in parts of Panama and French Guiana, they bear no resemblance to the ferocious, much larger Yaquaru. Cryptozoologist KARL SHUKER suggests that the creature may be a surviving SABER-TOOTHED CAT (*Smilodon*) which has assumed aquatic habits, similar in aspect and behavior to the African "WATER LION."

Sources: Basaldúa, *Monstruos Argentinos*; Thomas Falkner, *A Description of Patagonia and the Adjoining Parts of South America*. London: T. Lewis, 1774; Heuvelmans, *On the Track of Unknown Animals*; Shuker, *Mystery Cats of the World*.

Yara-Ma-Yha-Who   The Yara-ma-yha-who is an unknown Australian primate surrounded by aboriginal mythology. Typical descriptions portray a creature covered in reddish hair, perhaps four feet tall, which lives primarily in fig trees. Although ungainly on its feet and described in most reports as toothless, the Yara-ma-yha-who is still feared by aborigines for its alleged habit of leaping at people from branches, clasping them with sucker-bearing hands and feet. Those suckers allegedly drain victims of their blood, while even more fanciful stories depict the Yara-ma-yha-who swallowing victims whole and regurgitating them alive. Cryptozoologists speculate that Australia may host an unknown (or "alien") species of tarsier, a curious primate native to Southeast Asia which reaches an average length of five inches, with a 10-inch tail. The tarsier's small face and huge eyes — reminiscent of Gollum in the cinematic *Lord of the Rings* trilogy — presents an eerie sight when peering from a leafy branch, and the toes on all four feet are tipped with harmless suction cups.

Sources: Heuvelmans, *On the Track of Unknown Animals*; Whitley, "Mystery animals of Australia."

Yarri   Semantic confusion surrounds this mystery CAT reported from Australia. In the Warlpiri language of Australia's Northern Territory, *yarri* is a verb meaning "to attack" or "to threaten." It is used in parts of Queensland as an alternative name for the spotted-tailed quoll or "TIGER-cat" (*Dasyurus maculatus*), a kind of marsupial weasel averaging less than four feet in length. Confusing matters further, in Western Australia the name is applied to the Blackburt eucalyptus tree (*Eucalyptus patens*). Its most common usage, though, seems to be as an alternative name for the cryptid more commonly known as the QUEENSLAND TIGER. In 1883, German zoologist Carl Lumholtz recorded an aboriginal account of the Yarri from natives of the Herbert River valley, who described a creature dwelling in Queensland's Coast Mountains.

> From their description I conceived it to be a marsupial tiger. It was said to be about the size of a dingo, though its legs were shorter and its tail long, and it was described by the blacks as being very savage. If pursued, it climbed up the trees, where the natives did not dare to follow it, and by gestures they explained to me how at such times it would growl and bite their hands. Rocky retreats were its favourite habitat, and its principal food was said to be a little brown variety of wallaby common in northern Queensland scrubs. Its flesh was not particularly appreciated by the blacks, and if they accidentally killed a *yarri* they gave it to their old women. In western Queensland, I heard much about an animal which seemed to me to be identical to the *yarri* here described, and a specimen was once nearly shot by an officer of the black police in the regions I was now visiting.

Sources: Healy and Cropper, *Out of the Shadows*; Smith, *Bunyips & Bigfoots*.

Yawt   A mystery primate reported from Papua New Guinea, the Yawt reportedly inhabits dense forests in the Waina-Sawanda district, south of Imonda. The creatures — described as "little people" in some native accounts — are short, covered with hair, and utter a distinctive "hu-hu" call. They remain unidentified today.

Source: Alfred Gell, "The language of the forest: Landscape and phonological iconism in Umeda," in Eric Hirsch and Michael O'Hanlon, eds. *The Anthropology of Landscape*. New York: Oxford University Press, 1995.

Yeahoh This name of uncertain origin is applied to various large, hairy HOMINIDS reported from Kentucky. Cryptozoologists disagree on whether creatures sighted in the Blue Grass State represent a southern variant of BIGFOOT or an unknown primate which LOREN COLEMAN has named the NORTH AMERICAN APE. Kentuckians met their first hairy biped in 1878, when a "wild man of the woods" was captured in Tennessee and transported to Louisville for exhibition. The fate of that specimen is unknown, but Kentucky later produced its own series of sightings, including the following:

May 1894— A hairy "man-beast" clad in sheepskin was blamed for stealing chickens and livestock around Deep Creek. Hunters tracked the prowler to a nearby cave but failed to smoke it out.

1940s-1950s— Hunters tracked the elusive POPE LICK MONSTER in Jefferson County, without success.

October 1953— A group of children in Liberty reported an apelike creature "digging for food" in their yard.

June 1962— A Trimble County farmer's dogs were mauled by a 6-foot hairy creature described as "not quite a dog, a panther, or a bear."

July 1962— Four Mount Vernon teenagers were frightened when a man-sized creature shambled up to their car on a rural lover's lane.

1968— Dr. Richard Young and Charles Denton spotted the creature at Murray, in Calloway County.

1972— A nocturnal deer hunter met a huge creature outside Russellville. He described the animal as seven or eight feet tall, weighing some 500 pounds.

Autumn 1973— A 6-foot creature with an "ape/human" face and a bushy black tail raided farms around Albany, killing livestock on several occasions. It left three-toed tracks and was sometimes accompanied by a smaller animal. The raids and sightings ceased after farmer Charlie Stern reported wounding the prowler.

August 1975— A child in Calloway County reported his encounter with an apelike creature at a rural creek.

Late 1975— A sighting was reported at Spottsville.

Spring 1976— Five witnesses around Pembroke reported three sightings of a shambling 6-foot creature. Sixty miles to the northeast, in Ohio County, a "big, black and hairy" creature startled a farmer at work in his yard.

January 1977— Multiple witnesses in Simpson County included a police officer who watched the creature cross a road in front of his patrol car.

July 1977— Two sightings were recorded from Jefferson County.

August 1978— A group of youths near Owensboro fired on a large apelike creature with a .45-caliber pistol, allegedly striking it three times before the animal fled.

1978— Nearly 100 miles northeast of the August shooting site, two Lockport farmers watched "very tall, hairy creature" that fled their property with "very smooth and graceful" strides.

March 1979— An "apeman" seven or eight feet tall was sighted several times along the Pennyrile Parkway, in Christian County.

1 April 1980— A flat-faced, broad-shouldered creature prowled around the Boone County mobile home occupied by David Stultz and Jackie Jones. As they emerged to investigate, the 4-foot-tall animal fled on all fours.

4 October 1980— Maysville farmer Charles Fulton reported his encounter with a 7-foot, 400-pound creature with "long white hair and pink eyes." The creature fled under fire from a .22-caliber weapon.

10 October 1980— An apelike creature chased a woman around her car at Maysville's Central Shopping Center. Later that day, in nearby Fleming County, the creature scattered meat from J.L. Tumey's outdoor freezer. Once again, it fled from gunfire, leaving behind long white hairs and 16-inch footprints.

1993— Motorists reported Bigfoot sightings at Mayfield and Wickliffe, in the far-southwestern corner of Kentucky. Six months later, a hiker on Bear Mountain (Estill County) studied the creature through binoculars. The witness described "a giant, hair-covered man with no neck. ...The hands looked human, four fingers and a thumb, the skin a dark grayish color" under red-brown hair.

10 September 1998— A couple jogging in Jefferson County met a large apelike creature.

1999— A teenage couple hiking at Cumberland Lake, in Clinton County, reported a frightening encounter with an 8-foot hairy creature.

1 May 2000— Bigfoot reportedly lunged from roadside shrubbery at a passing car in Eddyville.

11 November 2000— A resident of Caldwell County claimed he shot Bigfoot. The creature escaped.

7 November 2001— A motorist in Hazard saw a large apelike animal cross the road in front of his car. Days later, witnesses in Lincoln County reported a large hominid throwing sticks into a tree.

20 February 2003— A Bigfoot-type creature was seen by hikers in the McCreary County woods.

Several organizations collect reports of hominid sightings in Kentucky and environs. One noteworthy group is the Southeast Kentucky Bigfoot Information Center.

Sources: Bord and Bord, *The Bigfoot Casebook*; Rife, *Bigfoot Across America*.

Yednia Tiger A variant name for the elusive QUEENSLAND TIGER, this label was applied to the mystery CAT(S) sighted repeatedly in the 1930s and 1940s, among the craggy mountains and thick subtropical forest surrounding the source of the Brisbane and Mary Rivers. As late as 1954, a Bidwell resident related the following account:

My husband was riding through the bush when suddenly he rode upon the cat on a high stony bank of a creek. [It] climbed up a wattle sucker and sat there snarling and spitting. My husband was greatly taken by the markings. Some of the stripes, he said, were nearly a dark orange and the animal was just like a very large cat in shape and size. It in no way resembled a native cat. Eventually it leaped out of the tree and faced my husband. He said that he has never seen anything so savage and...such big fangs on any animal of that size before and since. He thought for a moment that the animal was going to tear him to pieces.

Source: Healy and Cropper, *Out of the Shadows*.

Yeho A primate or HOMINID reported from Andros and Long Island in the Bahamas, the Yeho apparently derives its name from the African terms *yáhue* and/or *yoho* ("devil"). It is also sometimes called Whahoo, Yay-hoo or YAHOO — the latter an occasional point of confusion with Australia's YOWIE. Bahamian natives describe the Yeho as a night-prowling creature, covered with dark hair and armed with claws like those of a bear. As with other hominids in Africa, Asia and South America, the Yeho is said to abduct human females for breeding purposes. Opinions differ as to whether Yeho reports constitute distorted memories of African GORILLAS or represent a real-life cryptid in the West Indies.

Sources: Gardiner, "Alligators in the Bahamas"; Raynal, "Yahoos in the Bahamas."

Yellow River, Wisconsin

Wisconsin's Yellow River flows between Chippewa Lake (Taylor County) in the northeast and Lake Wissota (Chippewa County) to the southwest, a distance of some 25 miles. Reports of a "water monster" have been logged by witnesses along the river, but details are unfortunately lacking.

Sources: Coleman, *Mysterious America*; Kirk, *In the Domain of the Lake Monsters.*

Yemische

This cryptid, reported from Argentina, is also called Hym-che by the Tehuelche Indians. By any name, it is described as a ferocious, nocturnal, amphibious predator. Author Andre Tournouer collected native legends and first-hand sightings of the creature in 1900. So fearsome was the animal's reputation that some tales described it as bulletproof. A confusion of dialects in the region mingles stories of the Yemische with another "WATER TIGER," variously known as IEMISCH or Jemische, and it may be credited as well with depredations committed by the ferocious YAQUARU.

Sources: Picasso, "South American monsters & mystery animals"; Shuker, *Mystery Cats of the World*; Andre Tournouer, "Le neomylodon et le animal mysterieux de la Patagonia." *Cosmos* 1 (1900): 122.

Yeren

China's version of BIGFOOT or YETI is an unknown HOMINID most commonly called Yeren, though its regional names vary with location and dialect. It is Xuĕ-rén in Mandarin and Sūet-jùen in Cantonese—both meaning "snowman." Other variant names include Dà-mao-rén ("big hairy man"), Mao-gong, Mao-jùen, Mao-rén ("hairy man"), Mo-zhyn and Suēt-jùen ("snowman"). Many Chinese simply call it "WILDMAN" or "man-bear." Descriptions of the Yeren are nearly as diverse as its names. Witnesses report creatures ranging from four to 10 feet tall, with an average height of 6 feet 6 inches. The shaggy Yeren's coat of hair ranges from one to four inches long; its reported colors include jet black (in Yunnan Province), snow white (Tibet), reddish-brown (Hubei Province), with some individuals sporting gray hair or blond. The Yeren's hair is longest on its head, typically shoulder length or longer. Its bare face combines features of both APE and human. The footprints left in Yeren's wake are likewise variable: some are 12 to 19 inches long, six or seven inches wide at the ball and narrowing toward a tapered heel; others are ape-like, averaging eight inches long, with a widely separated big toe.

Chinese wildman reports are found in the nation's earliest recorded history (poet Qu Yuan wrote of "mountain ogres" in the third century B.C.) and sightings have continued unabated to the present day. The epicenter of modern Yeren sightings is the Shennongjia Forest Reserve, spanning parts of Hubei and Sichuan Provinces, but encounters are also reported from the provinces of Anhui, Fujian, Gansu, Guizhou, Shaanxi, Yunnan and Zhejiang. Unlike most countries, China's government has taken a positive interest in solving the hominid riddle. Official Yeren-hunting expeditions were launched from Beijing in 1961, 1977, 1980 and 1982. The 1977 effort lasted nearly a year and involved 110 searchers. One participant in the 1980 expedition—a geologist

A 16th century sketch of the Chinese wildman or Yeren.

This modern Chinese poster solicits eyewitness sightings of the Yeren.

who glimpsed two Yeren in a Shaanxi mountain forest, in 1950—donned a gorilla suit and carried a bag of dates as "an introductory gift" when he returned to the site 30 years later. No Yeren came to greet him, but teammates collected the severed hands and feet preserved of a supposed Yeren killed in 1957 at Jiulong Mountain, in Zhejiang Province. An unofficial Wildman Study Association was founded at Wuhan, in 1981, but its members failed to find their quarry. Official conferences in 1980 and 1982 left government researchers bitterly divided on the status of existing evidence.

A new spate of sightings in 1994 prompted a new expedition the following year, led by members of an official COMMITTEE FOR THE SEARCH OF STRANGE AND RARE CREATURES. Simultaneously, the China Travel Service placed a bounty on Yeren's head, offering free provisions and 500,000 yuan ($60,000) for a dead specimen, 40,000 yuan ($4,800) for photos or videotape of the creature, and 10,000 yuan ($1,200) for Yeren hair or feces. The 30-man scientific team glimpsed no Yeren, but its members collected several hairs from a site where peasants saw one of the creatures. Another search, in June 1997, turned up hundreds of Yeren footprints. More suspect hairs, along with 16-inch footprints and gnawed corn cobs, were found by government searchers in August 1999.

Results of tests performed on "Yeren" evidence so far have ranged from disappointing to ambiguous. Researcher ZHOU GUOXING examined the hands and feet collected in 1980, finally concluding that they belonged to an unknown species of stump-tailed macaque (*Macaca* sp.). In 1984, the "wildman" captured in Hunan Province also proved to be a macaque. Ten years later, a supposed Yeren was filmed in Shennongjia, but scientists determined that the "creature" depicted was a microcephalic human being. Analysis of Yeren stool samples proved inconclusive, with test results stating that "the feces could not have come from humans as we know them, nor from a carnivorous animal." A hair sample tested in 1982 matched the golden MONKEY (*Rhinopithecus roxellanae*), but an August 1988 report on other samples, performed by Dr. Wenhui Bao in Shanghai, declared that "an analysis of hair samples allegedly taken from the wildman prove[s] he exists."

Anecdotal evidence for Yeren includes several reports of specimens captured or killed—all without bodies, so far, except for the macaque caged in 1984. Biologist Wan Zelin allegedly saw a female Yeren killed by Gansu Province hunters in 1940 or 1944 (reports vary); he described the animal as six feet tall, covered in

Severed "Yeren" hands and feet collected in 1980 belonged to an unknown species of macaque.

gray hair, with pendulous breasts. In 1947, Kuomintang soldiers reportedly tracked eight Yeren for 10 days, finally slaying one, but the specimen was lost during China's long civil war. Road workers in Yunnan's Xishuangbanna Nature Preserve supposedly killed another Yeren in 1961, but they failed to preserve its remains. Witness Yin Hongfa was attacked by a Yeren on 1 May 1974, near Dahei Mountain (Yunnan Province), and defended himself with a machete. Three years later, in June 1977, commune leader Pang Gensheng lobbed stones at a Yeren that menaced him in the Qinling-Taibaishan Reserve (Shaanxi Province).

The Yeren surfaced again on 29 June 2003, crossing a road in the Shennongjia nature reserve (Hubei Province) before a Jeep with six persons aboard. One of the witnesses, journalist Shang Zhengmin, described the fast-moving creature as apelike, gray with shoulder-length black hair, and roughly 5 feet 6 inches tall. The witnesses left their vehicle and discovered 12-inch footprints on the shoulder of the road, beside a 10-foot patch of "foul-smelling urine-like liquid." On 30 June, Chinese authorities announced that "an investigation is in full swing." Ultralight aircraft were reportedly deployed to aid the search, without result. No analysis of the alleged urine had been published at press time for this work.

After decades of studying the subject, Zhou Guoxing believes that China hosts at least two different unknown hominids. The smaller species, he suggests, may be a yet-unclassified monkey; Zhou's candidate for the larger Yeren is *GIGANTOPITHECUS*, a huge ape known from fossil remains in China and Vietnam, presumed extinct for the past 500,000 years. Other proposed Yeren candidates from prehistory include *Homo erectus* (proposed by GROVER KRANTZ), *Paranthropus robustus* (an Early Pleistocene inhabitant of Africa), and *Ramapithecus* (presumed extinct since the Late Miocene, 5 million years ago). Skeptics insist that all Yeren sightings are either HOAXES or hysterical mistakes involving macaques, golden monkeys, or Asiatic black bears (*Ursus thibetanus*).

Sources: Bord and Bord, *Unexplained Mysteries of the 20th Century*; "China's 'Bigfoot' seen again, agency reports." *Toronto Star* (30 June 2003); "Chinese wildman returns," *Fortean Times*; Dong, *The Four Major Mysteries of Mainland China*; Greenwell and Poirier, "Further investigation into the reported *Yeren*"; "'Half-man' beast reported." *Sydney Morning Herald* (30 June 2003); "Hunt for 'wild man' of Hubei." *Sydney Morning Herald* (4 July 2003); Krantz, "The 1997 Yeren investigation in China"; "Latest Chinese hunt for Bigfoot." *China Daily* (6 December 1999); Lin, "On the trail of China's Bigfoot"; "Man-beast hunts in the Far East." *Fortean Times*; Poirier and Greenwell, "Is there a large, unknown primate in China?"; Poirier, et al., "The evidence for Wildman in Hubei Province, People's Republic of China"; Karl Shuker, "Menagerie of mystery." *Strange Magazine* 15 (Spring 1995): 32; Shuker, "Menagerie of mystery." *Strange Magazine* 16 (Fall 1995): 29; "Yeren urine sample." *Fortean Times* 175 (November 2003): 20-21; Yuan Zhenxin and Huang Wanpo, *Wild Man: China's Yeti*; Zhou Guoxing, "The status of wildman research in China"; Zhou Guoxing, "Morphological analysis of the Jiulong Mountain 'Manbear' (Wildman) hand and foot specimens"; Zhou Liu, "Wildman: No wild fancy."

Yeti With BIGFOOT and NESSIE, Central Asia's Yeti (or "ABOMINABLE SNOWMAN") ranks as one of cryptozoology's superstars. The most familiar name of this unknown primate or HOMINID is a Sherpa term combining the words *yeh* ("rocky place" or "snowy mountain") and *teh* ("animal"). As with the Chinese YEREN, though, a surfeit of regional names and conflicting descriptions exacerbate confusion throughout the Yeti's range. In India, the creature is often called Rakshi-bompo ("powerful demons"), while residents of neighboring Bhutan and Sikkim call it Sogpa or Jungli-admi ("wild man"). Russians have called it Chelovek medvied, Chelovek mishka ("bear man"), Osodrashin and Snezhniy chelovek ("snowman"). To the Chinese, it is Peeyi, P'ei or Pi. In Nepal and Tibet, where Sherpas know it best, names abound: Ban-jhankri ("forest wizard"), Chu-mung ("mountain spirit"), Dzu-teh ("hulking thing"), Khya, Metoh-kangmi ("snow man"), Mi-gö ("wild man"), Mi-chen-po ("big man"), Mi-teh ("man bear"), Pyar-them, Samdja ("man animal"), Teh-lma ("manlike thing") and Ui-go. BERNARD HEUVELMANS christened the Yeti *Dinanthropoides nivalis* in 1958, but application of a Latin name did not result in scientific recognition.

In fact, most cryptozoologists now agree that Heuvelmans was premature in naming a single species of Yeti. Himalayan Sherpas recognize no less than three distinct and separate kinds of Yeti, including the Mi-teh (true Yeti), Dzu-teh (a larger species) and Teh-lma (a smaller variety). Some researchers consider the Dzu-teh a large and perhaps unknown species of bear, while the Teh-lma is variously treated as a juvenile Yeti or some species of primate. Observers of the "true" Yeti typically describe it as bipedal, with bowed legs and arms dangling to its knees. Most accounts describe a creature six or seven feet tall, weighing an estimated 200-400 pounds, fully covered in hair that ranges from reddish-brown to gray. The Yeti's head is conical, with a prominent sagittal crest. Its face, largely devoid of hair, features a flat nose and wide mouth filled with large teeth. Yeti footprints measure eight to 13 inches long and four to six inches wide, with the big toe widely separated (and sometimes crooked inward).

While aboriginal peoples of the Himalayas and Tibetan Plateau have known Yeti from time immemorial, Westerners "discovered" the creature in 1832. That year saw the first published reference to a Himalayan cryptid, penned by Brian Hodgson, the British minister to Nepal. A half-century later, in 1887 or 1889 (reports vary), Major Lawrence Waddell found Yeti tracks at 17,000 feet, while mountain climbing in Sikkim. Botanist Henry Elwes was apparently the first Westerner to sight a Yeti, while scaling the Himalayas in 1906. British mountaineers found more tracks in 1921 and 1922, and sighted the Yeti itself on Mount Everest in 1923. Two years later, another sighting was logged by A.N.

Yeti footprint found by Eric Shipton in 1951.

Tombazi, leader of a photographic expedition to Sikkim. Famed climber Eric Shipton was one of five explorers to report Yeti tracks in 1936-37; Shipton found more tracks in 1951, as did climber Edmund Hillary in 1953.

Lured by curiosity, a yen for adventure and the prospect of financial reward, Yeti-hunters swarmed over the Himalayas between 1954 and 1960. London's *Daily Mail* financed two expeditions, in 1954 and 1955, and reported discovery of more Yeti tracks. Norman Dyhrenfurth, part of a Swiss expedition, photographed footprints in 1954. The following year, geologist Abbe Bordet took more photos of Yeti tracks while climbing with a French company. A group of Argentinean climbers said one of their porters was killed by a Yeti in 1955, but they offered no further details. Members of the Royal Air Force Mountaineering Club found still more tracks that year, and lone explorer JOHN KEEL claimed to have stalked a howling Yeti for two days through Nepalese marshes, in 1956. Millionaire adventurer TOM SLICK led his first search for the Yeti in 1957, with team members Bryan and PETER BYRNE reporting a personal sighting. Slick's second expedition (1958), recording a *Teh-lma* sighting and examining supposed Yeti relics at the Pangboche monastery. The third Slick expedition (1959) competed with two Japanese teams, all three reporting discovery of more Yeti tracks. (Slick's major coup that year was smuggling pieces of the PANGBOCHE HAND out of Nepal, for scientific study in the West.) No less than seven Himalayan climbing parties sighted footprints in 1960, while Edmund Hillary's Himalayan Scientific and Mountaineering Expedition ironically found nothing, devoting its time to debunking supposed Yeti artifacts.

Western interest in the Yeti faltered during the chaotic 1960s, but close encounters have continued to the present day. Mountaineer Don Whillans sighted Yeti twice while scaling Nepal's Mount Annapurna, on consecutive days in March 1970. On 11 July 1974, 19-year-old Lhakpa Dolma was attacked by a Yeti near Tengboche, Nepal; after knocking her unconscious, the creature killed five of her yaks by breaking their necks. Russian biologist

The manlike features of a Yeti, based on eyewitness descriptions (*William Rebsamen*).

Arkady Tishkov saw and photographed a Yeti on 22 September 1991, on the southeastern slope of Tibet's Mount Xixiabangma, but the long-distance photos (and a 4-inch clump of feces found nearby) proved inconclusive. Five years later, videotape of an 8-foot-tall "snow walker," allegedly taken by Flemish-Belgian hikers in the Himalayas, aired on a U.S. television network (UPN), but neither the cameramen nor their precise location were ever identified. Four months after that event, zoologist Pavel Marikovsky announced that a Yeti had been seen well outside its normal range, near the Kazakhstan capital of Almaty. Marikovsky's report to the London *Sunday Telegraph* (21 July 1996) described the creature as "a terrifying, hairy being as tall as a fir tree but with very kind eyes." No kindness was apparent in the hairy creature that attacked 20-year-old Raja Wasim outside his Kashmir home in January 2003. "There is no mistake about what I saw," Wasim said. "The monster had the face of a man with monkeylike features. It was four feet tall, but extremely sturdy. It was the Snowman." Fortunately for Wasim, his cries for help summoned friends and the animal fled. In August 1993, a Japanes expedition led by 60-year-old Yoshiteru Takahashi embarked on a 6-week campaign to photograph the Yeti and "shake hands if [we] meet him," but the team went home empty-handed. Meanwhile, fellow countryman and mountaineer Matako Nabuka caused a furor of his own with the announcement that Yeti legends represent "a case of linguistic mistaken identity" based on mispronunciation of the Tibetan word *meti*, a name applied to the Himalayan brown bear (*Ursos arctos isabellinus*).

Analysis of Yeti evidence over the past half-century has produced mixed results. Photos taken of a Yeti on 6 March 1986, in the Garwhal Himalaya of India's Uttar Pradesh State, depicted nothing more than snow-cloaked jagged rocks. The pelt of a Yeti allegedly killed by Nepalese soldiers in fact belonged to a sloth bear (*Melursus ursinus*), while two other "Yeti" skins procured in 1959-60 were traced to a subspecies of Himalayan brown bear (*U. a. pruinosis*). Three "Yeti scalps" preserved at remote monasteries proved to be facsimiles hand-stitched from goat hide (though monks and other witnesses insisted they were accurate replicas of Yeti's pointed head). Tests performed on pieces of the Pangboche hand, meanwhile, revealed that its bones belonged neither to a human being nor any primate known to science. British zoologist Rob McCall collected Yeti hairs from a hollow cedar tree in Bhutan, during 2001, and shipped them off for analysis at the Oxford Institute of Molecular Medicine. There, DNA expert Bryan Sykes told reporters, "It's not human, not a bear, nor anything else we have so far been able to identify. It's a mystery, and I never thought this would end in a mystery. We have never encountered DNA that we couldn't recognize before."

Another piece of evidence, still highly controversial at press time for this volume, emerged from Altai, Siberia in October 2003, when Russian mountaineer-scientist Serghiei Semenov announced his discovery of a mummified leg with a 9.4-inch foot. "I examined the sole of the foot, and I thought it looked unusual," Semenov said, "so I decided to bring it back with me." On previous climbs, Semenov claimed discovery of ribs and pelvic fragments, which apparently were not preserved. Scientists from Siberia's Veterinary Academy and Altai Agrarian University declared that the shaggy limb resembled a human leg, including a knee joint typical of bipeds and a humanlike big toe with three phalanges. According to a press release of 8 October, X-rays suggested that "the bones did not belong to any known animal." Russian cryptozoologist Michael Trachtengerts contradicted that

finding two days later, informing LOREN COLEMAN that the relic was "for sure the hind right leg of a bear." Three months later, on 8 January 2004, Russian scientists declared once more that the truncated leg "does not belong to any species of man."

Ten days after that announcement, Nevada resident Doug Tarrant posted a message to various Internet newsgroups which well illustrates the Yeti's tenacious grip on human imagination — and the elusive nature of proof. Tarrant briefly recounted a 1974 interview with retired big-game hunter Fred Bear, once retained by the Smithsonian Institution to provide mounted specimens of various exotic animals. Bear allegedly told Tarrant that Smithsonian curators had held "the answer" to the Yeti mystery since 1925, when showman Clyde Beatty's circus toured Europe with a captive snowman in its menagerie. According to Bear and Tarrant, Beatty planned to exhibit the Yeti upon his return to the U.S., but federal authorities banned its importation while the Scopes "MONKEY trial" was in progress, headlining the clash between evolution and Biblical creationism in a Tennessee courtroom. Washington's supposed fear: The appearance of a real-life "missing link" would "blow the roofs off churches" and destroy fundamentalist faith in the Genesis fable. Accordingly, Bear claimed, "the Smithsonian told the Beatty Circus that they would have to let the Yeti stay in Europe." Where it went from there — and how Smithsonian scientists usurped the authority of the U.S. Customs Service — remains unexplained.

Skeptics insist that all Yeti sightings result from HOAXES, superstition or misidentification of known indigenous species — including bears, snow leopards, wolves, monkeys and Hindu pilgrims (*sadhus*) tramping through the Himalayan snows on mystic quests. Cryptozoologists theorize that the riddle's solution may involve one or more unknown species of primate. Bernard Heuvelmans suggested *Gigantopithecus* as a Yeti candidate, despite its presumed extinction some 500,000 years ago. Researchers Loren Coleman and MARK HALL suggest *Dryopithecus*, found throughout Europe in the Late Miocene (and thus presumed extinct for some 8 million years). Professor W.C. Osman Hill, after studying the Pangboche hand, suggested that it might belong to a NEANDERTAL. In any case, one thing is clear: the Yeti mystery remains unsolved.

Sources: "Best proof Yeti." *Daily Record* (8 January 2004); Bord and Bord, *Alien Animals*; Bord and Bord, *Unexplained Mysteries of the 20th Century*; Coghlan, "Mystery beast"; Coleman, "Not so abominable now"; Coleman, *Tom Slick and the Search for the Yeti*; Hall, *The Yeti, Bigfoot and True Giants*; Henderson, "'Yeti's Hair' defies DNA analysis"; Heuvelmans, *On the Track of Unknown Animals*; Hill, "Abominable Snowmen: The present position"; "Japanese team to leave on quest for Yeti." Australian Broadcasting Corp. (15 July 2003); LoBaido, "In search of the Yeti"; Lorenzi, "Scientists claim Yeti DNA evidence"; Sanderson, *Abominable Snowmen*; "Mountain-climbers discover mummified leg of unknown creature in Altai." *Gateway to Russia* (8 October 2003); Karl Shuker, "Alien zoo." *Fortean Times* 147 (July 2001): 16; Slick, "The Yeti expedition"; "Snow elusive, but not mysterious Kashmir Snowman." *The Anomalist* (10 January 2003); "Tibetan Abominable Snowman remains unsolved riddle." Xinhua News Agency (30 April 2001); Tishkov, "Observation of a Yeti in the Himalayas of Tibet"; Wooldridge, "First photos of the Yeti"; "Yeti's 'non-existence' hard to bear." BBC News (26 September 2003).

Yeti Research Society   Confusion surrounds the brief career of this Florida organization, which despite its title was apparently created to investigate sightings of the Sunshine State's SKUNK APE. In February 1974, the *National Tattler* identified Gordon Prescott at the group's director, and LOREN COLEMAN reports that Prescott teamed with L. Frank Hudson, while the group's early members included EUGENIE CLARK. Matters had clearly degenerated by November 1975, when 18-year-old John Sohl and six teenage companions claimed that three large apelike creatures had approached their campfire in Citrus County, Florida. Sohl embellished the story by telling a reporter from the *St. Petersburg Times* that he was "thrown" by one of the beasts when he tried to snap their photograph. The youths described themselves as members of the Yeti Research Society, allegedly organized among students at St. Petersburg's Northeast High School. More than a quarter-century later, in August 2002, Sohl (then a university physics professor) read an account of the incident on BOBBIE SHORT'S Internet website and sent Short an e-mail, confessing that the incident was a deliberate HOAX.

Source: Coleman and Clark, *Cryptozoology A to Z*; John Sohl e-mail communication to Bobbie Short. http://www.n2.net/prey/bigfoot/hoaxes/sohl.htm.

Yevpatoriya sea serpent
In January 1934, Russian fishermen from Yevpatoriya, on the Black Sea, cut their nets in panic and fled to shore after a huge SEA SERPENT with a horselike head disturbed their labors. No further description of the beast is presently available.

Source: Bord and Bord, *Unexplained Mysteries of the 20th Century.*

Yoho
A still-unclassified primate reported from Nicaragua, the Yoho may be similar (if not identical) to the ULAK inhabiting that nation's Cordillera Isabella. Its description general conforms to that of the Ulak, though it may enjoy a broader range. A variant of the Yoho's name (written as "Yo-ho") was used in newspaper reports of a "WILDMAN" seen at Sackets Harbor, New York in September 1818. Perhaps the name "traveled" with African slaves imported to the U.S. via the West Indies, where a similar apelike creature is known to this day as YEHO.

Sources: Eduard Conzemius, "Ethnographical survey of the Miskito and Sumu Indians of Honduras and Nicaragua," *Bulletin of the Bureau of American Ethnology* 106 (1932): 168; *New York Columbian* (14 September 1818).

Yokyn
An unidentified predator reported from Australia, the Yokyn is described by aborigines and ranchers as a stocky doglike beast with long claws. Its color varies and is sometimes brindled. Although widely known in the Outback, with hundreds of sightings recorded in the 1960s and 1970s, the Yokyn is still unrecognized by science. Some researchers suggest it represents a mainland THYLACINE, while Dr. Ralph Molnar (curator of the Queensland Museum) proposed a dog-dingo hybrid.

Source: "Bears on two legs?" *Fate* 30 (May 1977): 34; Shuker, *Mystery Cats of the World.*

York, William (1932-2000)
British native William York moved to Africa as a teenager, pursuing a dream of adventure as a big game hunter and guide. After numerous safaris and a stint of military service (which included seven combat wounds), York retired from hunting and earned his Ph.D. as a wildlife biologist. In middle age, York moved to the United States, where he served as an animal consultant to Disney World and later helped develop Winston, Oregon's Wildlife Safari park. Intrigued by reports of BIGFOOT in the Pacific Northwest, York began research on the creature as a skeptic and participated in his first expedition during August 2000. Soon convinced of the creature's existence, York joined Dr. Matthew Johnson and others in founding the SOUTHERN OREGON BIGFOOT SOCIETY. More expeditions

followed, and while York never personally sighted Bigfoot, he remained optimistic to the end, counseling fellow searchers that "persistence is the most important attribute to a Bigfoot researcher." York died in November 2002.

Sources: Matthew Johnson, "Dr. William 'Bill' York, Wildlife Biologist (1932-2002)." Sasquatch Internet newsgroup posting (13 November 2002); William York, "Persistence is the Most Important Attribute to a Bigfoot Researcher." Bigfoot Internet newsgroup posting (20 September 2002).

Yorkshire sea serpents
No precise date is available for the first of two SEA SERPENT sightings reported from Yorkshire, England in the mid-20th century. Witness Joan Borgeest later recalled that the incident occurred "shortly before World War 2, when there was a severe earthquake felt in many parts of the country"—from which BERNARD HEUVELMANS concluded that the year was 1938. Initial teasing from her friends was so severe that Mrs. Borgeest kept silent on the sighting until 1961, when she described it on a BBC radio broadcast. As recalled on that occasion, she was on the beach at Skiffing, babysitting several children, when—

> Suddenly I saw a huge creature rise [from the sea]. It was of a green colour, with a flat head, protruding eyes, and a long flat mouth which opened and shut as it breathed. It was a great length and moved along with a humped glide.

Mrs. Borgeest prepared two sketches of the creature, one depicting three vertical humps between its head and tail, while the second sketch portrayed only one hump.

The war was barely finished when Spilsby resident B.M. Baylis sighted another cryptid swimming off the Yorkshire coast. As Baylis recalled the event in 1966:

> On an afternoon in early August, 1945, we were sitting on the edge of the low mud cliffs at Hilston between Hornsea and Withernsea. There we saw a creature with a head and four or five rounded humps each of which was leaving a wake. It was moving rapidly but quite silently along short northwards in face of a northerly wind.

Source: Heuvelmans, *In the Wake of the Sea Serpents.*

Yoshi
Although graced with a provisional scientific name (*Fuegopithecus pakensis*) by researcher Manuel Palacios, this primate from the extreme southern tip of South America is still unrecognized by zoologists, its very existence debated. Descriptions of the creature—also known as Cushpij and Hanush—date from the 19th century, portraying a bipedal creature less than three feet tall, covered in hair of a distinctive yellowish-green. The back of Yoshi's head is often bald, reports allege, because it habitually rubs its skull against trees. Some accounts describe the Yoshi wearing FOX skins and brandishing a club. A few reports make it a social creature, entering camps at night to crouch beside a fire. No sightings have been logged since 1928, when a hunter encountered a Yoshi at Caleta Yrigoyen, Chile.

Sources: Bruce Chatwin, "El unicorno de la Patagonia." Córdoba, Argentina's *La Voz del Interior* (13 February 2001); Nicasio Tangol, *Leyendas de Karukinka.* Mexico City: Fondo dé Cultura Economica, 1982.

Yowie
Australia's version of BIGFOOT or YETI is known by many names throughout the continent Down Under. Aborigines know the creature as Jimbra, Jingera or Tjangara in Western Australia; as Dulugal, Gooligah, Thoolagal, Moomega or Yaroma in New South Wales; as Noocoonah in South Australia; and as QUINKIN in Queensland. White pioneers in Australia initially called the beast Yahoo, a name applied to a race of fictional prim-

itive people in Jonathan Swift's *Gulliver's Travels* (1726). The first published reference to the Yahoo is found in J. Holman's *Travels* (1835), wherein he states: "The natives are greatly terrified by the sight of a person in a mask, calling him 'devil' or Yah-hoo, which signifies evil spirit." Another 36 years elapsed before the first white settler claimed to have sighted a Yahoo, near Avondale, in April 1871. Witness George Osborne gave the following account of that incident to the Sydney *Empire*:

> [A]fter sunset, my horse was startled at seeing an animal coming down a tree...and when it got to within about eight feet of the ground it lost its grip and fell.

> My feelings at the moment were anything but happy, but although my horse was restless I endeavoured to get a good glimpse of the animal by following it as it retreated until it disappeared into a gully. It somewhat resembled the shape of a man, according to the following description:

> Height, about five feet, slender proportioned, arms long, legs like a human being, only the feet being about eighteen inches long, and shaped like an IGUANA, with long toes, the muscles of the arms and chest being well developed, the back of the head straight, with the neck and body, but the front or face projected forward, with MONKEY features, every particle of the body except

A 19th-century sketch of Australia's Yowie.

the feet and face was covered with black hair, with a tan-colored streak from the neck to the abdomen. While looking at me its eyes and mouth were in motion, after the fashion of a monkey. It walked quadruped fashion, but at every few paces it would turn around and look at me following it, supporting the body with the two legs and one arm, while the other was placed across its hip. I also noticed that it had no tail.

The next report was filed from the Jingeras, near Cooma, in December 1871. Sightings continued sporadically thereafter, with a total of nine more between May 1881 and autumn 1912. Subsequent Yahoo encounters, occurring from the 1920s through the early 1950s, were not reported at the time but surfaced decades later, after the beast resurfaced in the 1970s with a new name. Henceforth, while purists argued for retaining "Yahoo," the Aussie cryptid was more commonly called Yowie, perhaps derived from the Yuwaalaraay word *yuwi* ("dream spirit").

Cryptozoologist REX GILROY claimed the first Yowie sighting of the new era — one of three or four personal sightings, he says — in the Blue Mountains of New South Wales, on 7 August 1970. By 1978, Gilroy claimed to have more than 3,000 sightings on file at his Australian Yowie Research Center, but most researchers doubt that claim, citing far more conservative numbers. Some, like authors Graham Joyner and Malcolm Smith, frankly question whether any of the modern sightings are legitimate. Others note a wide disparity in Yowie descriptions, suggesting that witnesses may be describing more than one unknown creature.

Authors Paul Cropper and Tony Healy analyzed 85 Yowie sightings in 1994, reporting that the creature's height was estimated in 43 reports. Of those witnesses, 22 (51 percent) placed the Yowie's height between five and seven feet; 17 thought it was taller (with four claiming heights of 11 or 12 feet); while four claimed it was less than five feet tall. Of 32 witnesses who recalled a particular hair color, 10 said it was brown, eight chose black, gray and "mixed" tied with five sightings each, three claimed red or reddish-brown, and one recalled the Yowie being white. While some Yowies leave relatively normal footprints, many tracks show only three or four toes — and those sometimes measure five inches long. Otherwise, size and shape of the tracks are widely variable.

Yowie sightings continue to the present day, as do attempts to solve the mystery. Larry Lesh, a U.S. Bigfoot hunter, announced his plan to zap Yowie with an electric stun gun in September 1999, but Australian authorities banned importation of the weapon. Six months later, on 11 March 2000, AUSTRALIAN HOMINID RESEARCH spokesman Dean Harrison claimed a Yowie had attacked a camper occupied by elderly monster hunters, somewhere west of Gympie. "We are over the moon, we are so excited," Harrison said. "This thing had run up to the van and given it such a bang that the man inside, George, had almost fallen out of bed." The creature fled into darkness as George lurched outside. "He didn't get a good look at it," Harrison admitted, "but he heard the foliage breaking and the footsteps." Photographs and plaster casts preserved a set of 16-inch footprints at the scene.

Doubters remain unconvinced, and one group of self-styled Australian Skeptics has offered a reward of $10,000 (or $100,000, reports vary) for proof that Yowie exists. The cash is safe, since terms of the offer dictate that any evidence must satisfy specific members of the skeptics' society. Yowie hunters, meanwhile, continue their long-running debate over the creature's possible identity. Gilroy and Harrison favor the extinct APE *GIGANTOPITHECUS* or a close relative, though fossil remains are known only from China and Vietnam. (Gilroy claims to have found a fossil footprint from *Gigantopithecus* near Kempsey, New South Wales, but the claim remains unverified.) Other candidates include an unknown apelike marsupial and a relict population of Kow Swamp people, primitive *Homo sapiens* known from 40-odd skeletons found at Victoria's Kow Swamp in the 1960s. The skulls of those specimens, carbon-dated between 9,000 and 14,000 years old, included certain features shared by earlier *Homo erectus*, reportedly including low foreheads and prominent brows, large jaws and teeth, and sagittal crests. Some anthropologists suggest that the skull deformities may have been deliberately inflicted, as with North America's "Flathead" Indians, and Dr. Gail Kennedy notes that the Kow Swamp femurs show no variation from normal *Homo sapiens*. Aussie cryptozoologists were briefly encouraged in September 2003, when DNA tests on the alleged skeletal remains of missing hiker Peter Falconio, vanished in South Australia, identified the bones as those of an unspecified "large animal." Speculation that the remains might be a Yowie's, mistaken for those of a human, remains unsubstantiated.

Sources: Bord and Bord, *Alien Animals*; Bord and Bord, *Unexplained Mysteries of the 20th Century*; Boyd, "Zowie! Where's the Yowie?"; Cropper, "Two Yowie reports"; Donnan, "On the trail of Yowie"; Gilroy, *Giants from the Dreamtime*; Groves, "The Yahoo, the Yowie, and reports of Australian hairy bipeds"; Tony Healy, "Yowie challenge." *Fortean Times* 141 (January 2001): 50; Healy and Cropper, *Out of the Shadows*; Joyner, *The Hairy Man of South Eastern Australia*; "Remains not those of missing Briton." BBC News (22 September 2003); Karl Shuker, "Alien zoo." *Fortean Times* 128 (November 1999): 19; Smith, "Analysis of the Australian 'hairy man' (Yahoo) data"; Smith, "Apes Down Under?"; Smith, *Bunyips & Bigfoots*; "Yowie attacks campervan." *Fortean Times*.

Yunwi Tsundí   It is difficult to separate fact from legend in the case of the Yunwi Tsundí, a "little people" described in Cherokee folklore. Generally described as a tribe of mountain- or forest-dwelling primitives, the Yunwi Tsundí may in fact represent a form of unclassified primate. Individual Yunwi Tsundí were said to be two feet tall on average, with black hair long enough to reach the their feet — perhaps an allusion to hair-covered bodies. Some traditional reports describe the creatures wearing skins and dancing to the music of crude drums. No sightings or reports suggest survival into modern times.

Sources: Fogelson, "Cherokee little people reconsidered"; Reed, *Stories of the Yunwi Tsundí*; Witthoft and Hadlock, "Cherokee-Iroquois little people."

Yuuri *see* **Junjadee**

— Z —

Zabairo   An unclassified primate reported from Côte d'Ivoire, West Africa, the Zabairo is described as an APE of great size, known for nocturnal habits. Some fanciful reports describe the creature carrying a torch to light its way. The nearest known GORILLA population is found in the Congo, some 1,500 miles southeast of Côte d'Ivoire. Researchers disagree on whether the Zabairo represents a misplaced gorilla colony, an unknown species of ape, or simply a legend based on exaggerated descriptions of gorillas.

Source: Gaston Joseph, "Notes sur les Avikams de la lagune de Lahou et les Didas de la région du Bas-Bandama." *Bulletins et Mémoirs de la Société Anthropologique de Paris* 6, no. 1 (1910): 234-247.

Zachrast'any, Czech Republic   A large, serpentine creature once inhabited a river near this town in the East Bohemian region, according to local accounts. No sightings have been recorded since the 19th century.

Source: Marie de Vaux Phalipau, *Les chevaux merveilleux dans l'histoire, la légende, le contes populaires*. Paris: J. Peyronnet, 1939.

Zana   A female ABNAUAYU was allegedly captured near Ajaria, Georgia in the mid-19th century by a certain Prince Achba (or Achbe). After displaying the creature at his palace for a season, the prince gave it to a friend, one Edgi Genaba, who took it to his home village of Tkhina, in Abkhazia. Genaba named the animal "Zana" and kept her under guard for several months, until the regimen of warm shelter and regular meals apparently domesticated her. Over time, Zana was trained to perform simple tasks in the village, such as carrying firewood, buckets of water and sacks of grain. Zana's great strength and marginal intelligence made her a superior beast of burden, but she also allegedly fulfilled another function in Tkhina. Over time, locals say, she was impregnated at least four times by village men and delivered mixed-breed offspring. At Zana's death, around 1884, Tkhina's residents named a nearby spring in her honor, reporting that the creature often bathed there.

BORIS PORSHNEV investigated Zana's story in 1964 and succeeded in locating two of her alleged grandchildren. Although "relatively normal," one of them — a man named Shalikula — was able to lift a chair and the man sitting in it by using his teeth alone. Two reports, published in 1969 and 1970, claim that Porshnev located Zana's grave and exhumed her remains, afterward drafting a report that read, in part: "The bones are those of a womanlike creature. A brief study of the skeleton reveals some differences from the skeletal structure of modern humans." Another Russian report, issued in 1987, claimed that Zana's grave could not be found, but said the remains of her son Khwit had been exhumed, revealing a skull that combined "modern and ancient features." Porshnev and BERNARD HEUVELMANS cited Zana's case as evidence of a relict Neandertal population surviving in parts of Asia. GROVER KRANTZ disagreed, reporting that Khwit's skull was modern *Homo sapiens*, albeit with abnormally large jaw and cheekbones.

Sources: Bayanov, *In the Footsteps of the Russian Snowman*; Heuvelmans and Porshnev, *L'homme de Néanderthal est toujours vivant*; Norman, *The Abominable Snowmen*; Smith, *Strange Abominable Snowmen*.

Zandvoort sea serpents   An unidentified SEA SERPENT was sighted offshore from Zandvoort, a Dutch coastal town on the North Sea. Zandvoort's postmaster subsequently told the *Oprechte Haarlemsche Courant* that such creatures were "very commonplace," and that he had personally seen one several years earlier, while lounging outside the Germania café with that establishment's proprietor. On that occasion, the café owner had remarked, "I see it go by at midday every day at the same time, and at about 4 o'clock it comes back."

Six months later, in June 1906, several workmen standing on the Zandvoort beach saw a creature they described as a giant EEL, at least 60 feet long, swimming near the hull of the wrecked ship *Alba*. The animal submerged briefly, then reappeared with a second swimming in tandem. In July 1906, a pupil of ANTOON OUDEMANS, one F.J. Knoops, reported sighting a similar 50-foot creature 500 yards offshore at Katwijk, 10 miles south of Zandvoort. Witness P.W. Deems, standing on the roof of Zandvoort's Zeerust boarding house, saw the "serpent" at 5:45 a.m. on 7 August 1907. Deems glimpsed only 12 feet of the creature's body, but described it moving "faster than a train." He also claimed to have seen a similar beast in 1904.

Source: Heuvelmans, *In the Wake of the Sea Serpents.*

Zarzynski, Joseph W. (1950–) New York native Joseph Zarzynski began his study of LAKE MONSTERS in 1974, while serving as a full-time social studies teacher for the Sarasota Springs City School District. Although he has spent time in Scotland, researching "NESSIE" and other unidentified freshwater creatures, his primary interest lies closer to home, with "CHAMP" in Lake Champlain. As founder and head of the LAKE CHAMPLAIN PHENOMENA INVESTIGATION, Zarzynski has logged more than 300 eyewitness sightings of Champ to date. Beginning in 1979, he collaborated with technicians from Rochester Engineering Laboratories to scan the lake with sonar, filing annual progress reports in the journal *Cryptozoology* between 1982 and 1990.

In addition to his work with LCPI, Zarzynski has at various times been a member of the INTERNATIONAL SOCIETY OF CRYPTOZOOLOGY, the LOCH NESS AND MORAR PROJECT, the SOCIETY FOR THE INVESTIGATION OF THE UNEXPLAINED, and the International Fortean Organization. He has published several books, and served as executive director of Bateaux Below Inc., a nonprofit educational corporation that studies historic shipwrecks. Zarzynski received a New York State Historic Preservation Award in 1992, and a Beneath the Sea Diver of the Year Award for Education in 1997.

Sources: "Man devotes time to finding monster." Associated Press (14 October 1981); Zarzynski, *Champ: Beyond the Legend*; Zarzynski, "LCPI work at Lake Champlain" (1982-90).

Zeegangsa In summer 1907, several English businessmen were hunting CROCODILES from a steam launch on the Kali Miring River, near Surabaya, on Java, Indonesia, when they met a SEA SERPENT at the river's mouth. At first, a swanlike neck rose from the water near the river's eastern bank, but they mistook it for a floating tree-trunk. Through binoculars, they saw the creature's head, mouth opening and closing, while an arch or coil as thick as a man's thigh broke the surface. They fired at the animal, whereupon it sank from view and did not reappear. The hunters estimated its total length at 30 feet. Local fishermen knew the beast as Zeegangsa and considered it harmless. BERNARD HEUVELMANS speculated that its name might derive from the Dutch word *zeegans* ("sea goose").

Source: Heuvelmans, *In the Wake of the Sea Serpents.*

Zemlemer An unknown HOMINID reported from Siberia, the Zemlemer ("land surveyor") is typically described as a manlike creature covered with dark hair, six feet or taller, sometimes with iridescent eyes. A report filed from Siberia's Yamal-Nenets Province in September 1917 described an 8-foot specimen fighting with dogs in the village of Puyko, on the River Ob'. Given its reported size, the Zemlemer seems to resemble the YETI more closely than the ALMAS reported throughout much of Asia.

Source: Bayanov, *In the Footsteps of the Russian Snowman.*

Zemo'hgú-Ani A LAKE MONSTER named by Kiowa tribesmen in New Mexico, the Zemo'hgú-ani has not been assigned to any particular body of water in the Land of Enchantment. No sightings by white settlers are recorded, and reports from Native American inhabitants apparently ceased in the early 19th century, thus consigning the Zemo'hgú-ani to legend.

Source: Gatschet, "Water-monsters of the American aborigines."

Zerleg Khün *see* **Khün Görüessü**

Zeuglodon Zeuglodon is the former name for a prehistoric whale, now called *Basilosaurus*, whose fossil remains were first discovered in North America, in the 1830s. Its eel-like body, known to reach 82 feet in length, made the creature a natural SEA

The extinct whale Zeuglodon has been proposed as both a lake monster and sea serpent candidate.

SERPENT suspect, and its bones were used to construct an apparent monster skeleton in a famous 19th-century HOAX. Paleontologists believe *Basilosaurus* (and a 20-foot relative, *Zygorhiza*) swam with the same vertical undulations reported by many "serpent" witnesses at sea, but neither species possessed the long neck reported in numerous sightings. *Basilosaurus* and its relatives lived in the late Eocene, and are presumed to have become extinct around 38 million years ago. Nonetheless, cryptozoologists including BERNARD HEUVELMANS, ROY MACKAL, GARY MANGICOPRA and JOSEPH ZARZYNSKI have proposed the survival of relict populations as a partial solution for sightings of large serpentine cryptids at sea.

Sources: Heuvelmans, *In the Wake of the Sea Serpents*; Mackal, *Searching for Hidden Animals*; Zarzynski, *Champ: Beyond the Legend.*

Zhabayi-Adam *see* **Adam-Dzhapais**

Zhou Guoxing (n.d.) A Chinese paleoanthropologist and archaeologist, Zhou Guoxing was educated at Shanghai's Fudan University. In 1962 he was appointed to the scientific staff of the Institute of Vertebrate Paleontology and Paleoanthropology of the Chinese Academy of Sciences, in Beijing. Seventeen years later, Zhou joined the Beijing Natural History Museum, where he currently serves as deputy director and head of the Anthropology Department. Zhou joined the INTERNATIONAL SOCIETY OF CRYPTOZOOLOGY as a board member in 1982 and remained in that capacity through 1996, when the ISC ceased publication of its yearly journal.

Chinese cryptozoologist Zhou Guoxing.

Zhou's primary contribution to cryptozoology has been intensive study, since the 1970s, of "WILDMAN" or YEREN reports from various parts of China. In December 1980 he examined the preserved hands and feet of an alleged "manbear," killed in Zhejiang Province on 23 May 1957. Zhou initially concluded that the relics belonged to "a large unknown MONKEY species," but in 1984 he revised that assessment to suggest that the hands and feet belonged to "a large stump-tailed macaque resembling the Huang

Mountain monkey." Still, Zhou insisted that identification of the relics did not solve the Yeren riddle, since unknown Chinese primates have been reported in two distinct forms: one, commonly reported from western Yunnan Province and the Shengnongjia region of Hubei Province, averaged four feet in height; the other, seen more often in the Jiulong Mountain area, is commonly described as seven feet tall, leaving 12-inch footprints.

Sources: Bord and Bord, *Unexplained Mysteries of the 20th Century*; Zhou Guoxing, "Morphological analysis of the Jiulong Mountain "manbear" (wildman) hand and foot specimens"; Zhou Guoxing, "The status of wildman research in China."

Zugersee, Switzerland   Located in Canton Zug, this Swiss lake was the scene of "monster" sightings in 1509, when startled witnesses reported a FISH "the size of a boat." Possibly explained by the presence of a giant sturgeon, the sightings have nor been repeated in modern times.

Source: Johann Cysat, *Beschreibung dess berühmbten Lucerner-oder 4. Waldstätten Sees.* Lucerne: David Hautten, 1661.

***Zuiyo Maru* sea serpent**   On 25 April 1977 the Japanese fishing boat *Zuiyo Maru* netted a startling catch while trawling for mackerel off Christchurch, New Zealand. The boat's net, ascending from a depth of 1,000 feet, contained a two-ton rotting carcass that measured 33 feet long. The creature resembled an ancient PLESIOSAUR, complete with slender neck, a head nearly five feet long and 18 inches wide, and flippers one meter (39 inches) in length. Photographs were taken of the carcass, while a biologist aboard the *Zuiyo Maru*, Michihiko Yano, collected samples of its flesh. Captain Akiro Tanaka then returned the creature to its watery grave, to prevent infecting his catch and crew.

By the time Yano delivered his samples to experts from Japan's National Science Museum and Tokyo University's Marine Research Center, a combined fleet of 20 Japanese boats, 30 Russian and eight South Korean vessels were trawling the sea off Christchurch, hoping to snare the carcass again or capture a living relative. In 1978, Dr. Shigeru Kimora announced that the tissue samples contained elastodin, a kind of protein found only in

Three views of the *Zuiyo Maru* carcass. (Michihiko Yano)

SHARKS, thus concluding that the carcass belonged to a basking shark (*Cetorhinus maximus*). In fact, cryptozoologists had long recognized that basking sharks decay in a manner which causes their normally stout bodies to resemble long-necked reptiles — what author Daniel Cohen once dubbed a "pseudoplesiosaur."

The official verdict was not well received in all quarters. Religious advocates of "creation science," determined to prove their theory of a "young Earth" wherein humans and dinosaurs existed simultaneously no more than 6,000 years in the past, cite various perceived discrepancies in an English translation of the Japanese report. Oddly, however, the tracts insist that the creature netted was a mammal, rather than a plesiosaur — which clearly does nothing to prove man's coexistence with prehistoric reptiles.

Sources: Malcolm Bowden, *The Japanese Carcass*; Coleman and Clark, *Cryptozoology A to Z*; Koster, "Creature feature."

Zwischenahner Meer, Germany   Located in Germany's Niedersachsen State, this lake produced multiple sightings of an unknown 12-foot creature during April 1979. The most likely suspect is the wels CATFISH (*Siluris glanis*), found throughout central and eastern Europe into Russia, which may grow to lengths exceeding 15 feet.

Sources: Magin, "A brief survey of lake monsters of continental Europe"; Shuker, *From Flying Toads to Snakes with Wings*.

Glossary

ABC—ALIEN BIG CAT

ABSM—ABOMINABLE SNOWMAN (coined by IVAN SANDERSON)

abundism—Abnormal multiplication of body markings

albinism—Abnormally pale coloration. Animals with this condition are called albinos (adj. = albinistic)

allopatric speciation—Evolution of a new, separate species caused by geographic isolation from the original species

amphibian—Any member of the class *Amphibia* (e.g., frogs, toads, salamanders, etc.)

amphibious—Living or able to live both on land and in water

anthropoid—Resembling man (e.g., anthropoid APE)

anthropology—The study of man's origins, physical and cultural development, racial characteristics, social customs and beliefs

aquatic—Living or growing in water (often presumed to be fresh water)

arboreal—Living primarily in trees, above the ground

archaeology—The study of historic or prehistoric peoples and their cultures by analysis of artifacts, monuments and inscriptions

arthropod—Any segmented invertebrate of the phylum *Arhtropoda*, having jointed legs (e.g., insects, arachnids, crustaceans, etc.)

ASS—Abominable Swamp Slob, a facetious alternate term for BIGFOOT-type creatures found outside the Pacific Northwest (coined by JOHN KEEL)

avian—Adjective describing bird-like qualities or characteristics

back-crossing—Mating a hybrid with one of its own pure-blood parents

BHM—Big Hairy Monster (see also ABSM above)

bifurcate—Forking or branching into two separate prongs, as with antlers

big cat—Scientifically, any felid species (regardless of overall size) possessing a hyoid apparatus not composed wholly of bone. Such CATS can roar, but cannot purr continuously

Bigfooter—A person involved in BIGFOOT research

bipedal—Walking solely or primarily on the hind limbs

bird—Any member of the class *Aves*, having a body covered with feathers and forelimbs modified into wings

black panther—A common but inaccurate term for any large black cat, typically a melanistic JAGUAR or leopard

botany—The study of plants

caecilian—A legless, burrowing amphibian. Caecilians are divided into six families with over 150 species

canid—Any member of the family *Canidae* (e.g., coyotes, dogs, FOXES, JACKALS, WOLVES)

canine—(1) Adjective, describing creatures of dog-like appearance. (2) Noun, describing the fang-like teeth possessed by many mammals, used for grasping prey (often misused in place of *canid*)

carnivore—Any flesh-eating mammal of the order *Carnivora*. More generally, any animal whose diet consists chiefly of flesh (adj. = carnivorous)

cephalopod—Any mollusk of the class *Cephalopoda*, having tentacles attached to the head (e.g., OCTOPUS, squid, etc.)

cetacean—Any member of the order *Cetacea*, including such aquatic mammals as whales, dolphins and porpoises

chordate—Any member of the phylum *Chordata*, including the true vertebrates and animals having a notochord (e.g., lancelets and tunicates)

class—A taxonomic subdivision of a phylum. The animal kingdom includes more than 60 classes

crocodilian—Any reptile of the order *Crocodilia* (e.g., ALLIGATORS, CROCODILES, CAIMANS, etc.)

cross-breeding—Mating between animals of different species, subspecies or breeds

cryptic markings—Body markings normally visible as dark patterns against a lighter background, obscured in melanistic specimens by abnormally dark background coloration

cryptid—Any "hidden" animal studied by cryptozoologists

cursorial—Adapted for running at high speeds

dimorphism—Occurrence of two distinct morphs within one species

distal—Adjective describing the part of a limb or bone located farthest from its point of attachment to the body

diurnal—Active by day (as opposed to *nocturnal*)

dorsal—Pertaining to or situated on the back, as with a shark's dorsal fin

dracontology—The study of SEA SERPENTS and LAKE MONSTERS

dwarf—A specimen affected by *dwarfism*

dwarfism—Abnormally small size or stature in comparison to the normal size for members of a particular species

ecology—The study of relationships between living organisms and their environment

ectotherm—An animal, often termed "cold-blooded," whose body temperature depends entirely on external heat sources (adj. = ectothermic)

endemic—Peculiar to a particular locality

endotherm—An animal, generally termed "warm-blooded," whose body temperature is internally regulated (adj. = endothermic)

entomology—The study of insects and arachnids

erythrism—Abnormally reddish coloration

eutherian—Belonging or pertaining to the group *Eutheria*, comprising the placental mammals

exotic—Noun or adjective, describing any animal presently existing outside its normal, native range of distribution

extant—Presently existing (as opposed to *extinct*)

extinct—No longer existing

family—A taxonomic subdivision of an order (e.g., the order *Carnivora* includes five families of flesh- eating mammals)

felid—Any member of the family *Felidae*, including all CATS

feline—Adjective describing anything with catlike characteristics (often misused in place of *felid*)

feral—Pertaining to animals which have lapsed from a domesticated condition to life in the wild

fish—Any completely aquatic, cold-blooded vertebrate having gills, typically (but not always) with an elongated body, fins, and a body covered with scales

fossil—Any remains, impression or trace of an animal or plant from a former geological age, left in stone

fossorial—Digging or burrowing, as in the case of animals that live or hunt underground

genus—A taxonomic subdivision of a family or subfamily, pluralized as genera (e.g., the family *Canidae* includes seven genera)

giant—A specimen affected by *gigantism*

gigantism—Abnormally great development in size or stature of a particular individual, beyond normal limits for the species

herbivore—An animal that feeds on plants (adj. = herbivorous)

herpetology—The study of reptiles and amphibians

hominid—Any member of the family *Hominidae*, including man and his ancestors

hominoid—A member of the superfamily *Hominoidea*, including the great APES and man

hybrid—Offspring of any mating between members of two different species, subspecies or breeds

hyoid apparatus—Bony structure of the throat, whose composition determines the nature of sounds made by an animal

hybridization *see* **cross-breeding**

icthyology—The study of FISH

indigenous—Native to a particular region

insectivore—An animal that feeds on insects (adj. = insectivorous)

invertebrate—Any animal lacking a spinal column

kingdoms—The broadest categories of living organisms, including animals, plants and fungi

leucism—A rare genetic mutation combining two recessive genes that produce white color, distinct from *albinism*; leucistic specimens have pigmented eyes, usually blue

mammal—Any vertebrate of the class *Mammalia* (including man) that feeds its young with milk from the female mammary glands, that has a body more or less covered with hair, and that (with the exception of the monotremes) is viviparous

mammalogy—The study of mammals

mandible—The lower jaw of any animal; in BIRDS, the lower part of the beak; in arthropods, one of the first pairs of mouthparts, typically a biting organ

marsupial—Any member of the order *Marsupialia*, whose birth cycle includes a short gestation period, birth in an immature state, and maturation within a pouch on the mother's body

melanism—Abnormally dark background color, as seen in black leopards and JAGUARS (adj. = melanistic or melanic)

metatherian—Alternative name for *marsupial*

mollusk—Any invertebrate of the phylum *Mollusca*, typically having a calcareous shell of one or more pieces enclosing a soft, unsegmented body

monotreme—Modern egg-laying mammals (i.e. the echidna and PLATYPUS)

montane—Pertaining to mountains (e.g., montane forest)

morph—One of two or more physically different (but taxonomically identical) forms of individual found within the same species (e.g., the *black panther* is a melanistic morph of the leopard)

morphology—An animal's physical appearance and structure

mozaicism—Abnormal coloration including aberrant patches of pigment over an animal's body

mustelid—Any member of the family *Mustelidae* (i.e., badgers, martens, otters, skunks, weasels, WOLVERINES, etc.)

mutant—A product of *mutation*

mutation—A sudden deviation from the parent type, as when an individual differs from its parents in one or more heritable traits, caused by deviation in genetic material

naturalized—Adjective describing any wild animal species that becomes established in an area outside its normal range, either by escape from captivity or deliberate introduction

nigrism—Abnormal fusion of body markings

nocturnal—Active primarily at night (as opposed to *diurnal*)

omnivore—An animal that eats both flesh and plants indiscriminately (adj. = omnivorous)

order—A taxonomic subdivision of a class (e.g., the class *Mammalia* includes eight different orders)

oviparous—Reproducing via eggs that mature and hatch after being expelled from the body, as with BIRDS, most reptiles and FISH, and monotremes

ovoviviparous—Producing eggs that hatch within the body, so that young are born alive but without a placenta

paleobiology—The study of fossil plants and animals

paleobotany—The study of fossil plants

paleontology—The study of prehistoric life forms as represented by fossils

paleozoology—The study of fossil animals

pelage—The furry coat of mammals

pelagic—Living or growing in the sea, an adjective applied to salt-water organisms

phylum—A major primary subdivision of a kingdom (plural = phyla); the animal kingdom includes 36 phyla

pinnigrade—Adapted to movement by means of finlike flippers, typically in water

pinniped—Any member of the suborder *Pinnipedia*, including seals and walruses, with limbs adapted to aquatic life

plantar pad—The pad found on the palm of an animal's paw

poikilothermal—Cold-blooded

polymorphism—The occurrence of more than two distinct morphs within a single species

pongid—Any anthropoid APE of the family *Pongidae*, including CHIMPANZEES, gibbons and GORILLAS

predator—Any organism that survives by trapping and devouring others. Those devoured are *prey*; the act of hunting and killing is *predation* (adj. = predatory)

primate—Any mammal of the order *Primates* (e.g., man, APES, MONKEYS, lemurs)

primatology—The study of primates

primitive—The first or earliest of a kind or in existence

prosimian—Any "lower" primate of the suborder *Prosimii* (i.e., lemurs, lorises, pottos, tarsiers and BUSHBABIES)

proximal—Adjective describing the part of a limb or bone located nearest its point of attachment to the body

pseudo-melanism—Abnormally dark coloration produced by fusion and multiplication of body markings, rather than by any excess of pigment

pug mark—The impression left by a mammal's plantar pads on contact with the ground

relict—A remnant or survivor; a plant or animal species living in an environment that has changed from its typical habitat

reptile—Any vertebrate of the class *Reptilia*, including TURTLES, lizards, SNAKES, crocodilians and the tuatara

retractile—Capable of being retracted, either passively or actively, as with the claws of most cats

sirenian—An aquatic, herbivorous mammal of the order *Sirenia* (i.e., dugongs, manatees, etc.)

small cat—Scientifically, any felid species (regardless of overall size) possessing a hyoid apparatus composed wholly of bone; Such CATS can purr continuously, but cannot roar

species—The major subdivision of a genus or subgenus, regarded as the basic category of biological classification, composed of related individuals that resemble one another and are able to breed among themselves but not able to breed with members of another species

specimen—An individual organism exemplifying its species

spoor—Trail or track comprising an animal's pawprints

subspecies—A subdivision of a species, typically a morphologically similar population inhabiting a geographical subdivision of the species' normal range, taxonomically distinguished from other populations of the species

sympatric speciation—Occurring when members of one species evolve into a new, separate species without first being geographically isolated

taxonomic—Pertaining to the scientific classification of organisms

taxonomy—The science of classifying and naming organisms

terrestrial—Living and moving on the ground

type specimen—The original example of a species, preserved for study and reference, from which the species identified and scientifically classified

ungulate—Any hoofed animal

venom—Poisonous fluid produced by some animals and introduced into the bodies of victims by biting or stinging (adj. = venomous)

ventral—Pertaining to the underside or lower surface of an animal's body

vertebrate—Any member of the subphylum *Vertebrata* (or *Craniata*), comprising animals with brains enclosed in a skull or cranium and a segmented spinal column

vestigial—A degenerate or imperfectly developed organ or structure having little or not utility, but which performed some useful function in an earlier state of evolution (e.g., a vestigial tail)

vibrissae—A mammal's whiskers

viverrid—Any mammal of the family *Viverridae* (i.e., civets, genets, etc.).

viviparous—Producing live young without eggs, as most mammals, some reptiles and FISHES

xenarthran—Any mammal of the order *Xenarthra*, including ARMADILLOS, anteaters and sloths

zoology—The study of animal life

Appendix A
Cryptozoology Timeline

The following timeline notes significant zoological discoveries and rediscoveries of species deemed extinct (indicated by an asterisk) since Baron Georges Cuvier declared the search for new large animals fruitless. Some animals appear twice, having been pronounced extinct and then rediscovered since 1812. Major cryptozoological events are also included. Animals are identified by the following key: A = amphibian; B = bird; C = cephalopod; F = fish; J = jellyfish; M = mammal; Ma = marsupial; P = primate; R = reptile; X = xenarthran. Latin names indicate animals with no common names.

1812 — Baron Cuvier's "rash dictum": large animal search over
1818 — Bristle-spined porcupine (M-Brazil)
    First reported north american APE sighting (New York)
1819 — American TAPIR (M-South America)
1824 — Hourglass dolphin (M-South Pacific)
1827 — Pygmy killer whale (M-England)
1828 — Heaviside's dolphin (M-South Africa)
    Whale SHARK (F-South Africa)
    Sei whale (M-Atlantic Ocean)
    Long-finned pilot whale (M-North Pacific)
    Dusky dolphin (M-South Africa)
    Spinner dolphin (M-Eastern Pacific)
1829 — Finless porpoise (M-Indian Ocean)
    Atlantic spotted dolphin (M-West Africa)
1833 — Striped dolphin (M-Pacific Ocean)
1834 — CHIMPANZEE (P-Africa)
1838 — Pygmy sperm whale (M-North Atlantic)
1839 — Western snake-necked TURTLE (R-Australia)
    Peale's dolphin (M-South Atlantic)
1840 — Gervais's whale (M-English Channel)
1846 — Clymene dolphin (M-Atlantic Ocean)
    Arnoux's BEAKED WHALE (M-New Zealand)
    Pygmy right whale (M-Indian Ocean)
    Pantropical spotted dolphin (M-Pacific Ocean)
    Short-finned pilot whale (M-South Pacific)
    Chilean dolphin (M-Chile)
1847 — Lowland GORILLA (P-Africa)
1852 — Pygmy mouse lemur (P-Madagascar)
1853 — Tucuxi dolphin (M-Amazon River)
1857 — GIANT SQUID (Denmark)
1861 — Giant otter shrew (M-West Africa)
1862 — Atitlán grebe (B-Guatemala)
1865 — Burmeister's porpoise (M-South America)
    Straptoothed whale (M-South Africa)
1866 — Dwarf sperm whale (M-South Atlantic)
1868 — Giant panda (M-China)

1869 — Hector's dolphin (M-New Zealand)
1870 — Pygmy hippopotamus (M-Liberia)
1871 — Hector's BEAKED WHALE (M-Australia)
1876 — Gray's BEAKED WHALE (M-New Zealand)
1878 — Earless MONITOR LIZARD (R-Indonesia)
    Bryde's whale (M-South Africa)
1880 — New Caledonian owlet nightjar (B-New Caledonia)
1882 — Longman's BEAKED WHALE (M-Australia)
    Grévy's zebra (M-Africa)
1883 — Baird's BEAKED WHALE (M-North Pacific)
1885 — Dall's porpoise (M-North Pacific)
    Stejneger's BEAKED WHALE (M-Alaska)
1887 — First Western YETI report (Nepal)
    Ryuku kingfisher (B-Ryuku Islands)
1892 — Atlantic hump-backed dolphin (M-Atlantic Ocean)
1893 — Siamese fighting FISH (F-Thailand)
1896 — Remains of giant OCTOPUS beached (Florida)
1898 — Goblin SHARK (F-Pacific Ocean)
1899 — Jeweled squid (C-Atlantic Ocean)
1900 — Cotton's white RHINOCEROS (M-Sudan)
    Sturdy hairy FROG (A-Equatorial Guinea)
    Golden FROG (A-Madagascar)
1901 — Giant genet (M-Uganda)
    Okapi (M-Uganda)
    Rothschild's giraffe (M-Uganda)
    Fearful OWL (B-Solomon Islands)
1902 — Mountain GORILLA (P-Congo)
    Bangs's mountain squirrel (M-Panama)
    Riverine RABBIT (M-South Africa)
    Rothschild's peacock pheasant (B-Malaysia)
1903 — Guizhou snub-nosed MONKEY (P-Madagascar)
    Kloss's gibbon (P-Indonesia)
    Mountain peacock-pheasant (B-Malaysia)
    Wake Island rail (B-Wake Island)
    Yellow-headed temple TURTLE (R-Thailand)
    Jack Dempsey (F-Mexico)
    Pancake TORTOISE (R-Tanzania)
    Chavez's macristiid (F-Azores)
    Dwarf siamang (P-Indonesia)
1904 — Goeldi's MONKEY (P-South America)
    Galápagos fur seal (M-Galápagos Islands)
    Giant forest hog (M-East Africa)
    Mindanao mountain rat (M-Philippines)
    Pacarana* (M-Colombia)
1905 — Hawaiian monk seal (M-Hawaiian Islands)
    PYGMY ELEPHANT captured (Congo)
1906 — Mindanao shrew rat (M-Philippines)

Bermuda petrel (B-Bermuda)
Goliath FROG (A-Cameroon)
Mikado pheasant (B-Taiwan)
1907 — Allen's swamp guenon (P-Congo)
Emperor tamarin P-South America)
Golden langur (P-India)
Pygmy slow loris (P-Vietnam)
Hispaniolan solendon (M-Hispaniola)
1908 — Gunning's golden mole (M-South Africa)
Dawson's caribou (M-Canada)
African broadbill (B-Congo)
New Guinea crocodile (R-Papua New Guinea)
Spined pygmy SHARK (F-Philippines)
Andrew's BEAKED WHALE (M-New Zealand)
1909 — Siamese fighting FISH (F-Thailand)
PALUXY TRACKS discovered (Texas)
Cuban solendon (M-Cuba)
1910 — Hero shrew (M-Uganda)
Quarles's mountain anoa (M-Indonesia)
Dollman's tree mouse (M-Cameroon)
Mountain nyala (M-Ethiopia)
Blind cirrate octopus (C-North Atlantic)
Hero shrew (M-Uganda)
1911 — Owston's banded civet (M-China)
Large-toothed hairy-tailed rat (M-Philippines)
Bali mynah (B-Indonesia)
Rothschild's mynah (B-Molucca Islands)
Goeldi's MONKEY (P-Brazil)
1912 — Spectacled porpoise (M-Argentina)
Goldman's water mouse (M-Costa Rica)
Komodo DRAGON (R-Indonesia)
Spiny-finned dwarf SHARK (F-Philippines)
1913 — Aquatic genet (M-Congo)
First MOKELE-MBEMBE expedition (Congo)
True's BEAKED WHALE (M-North Carolina)
Congo peacock (M-Congo)
Congo shrew (M-Congo)
Water civet (M-Congo)
1914 — Red goral (M-China)
Giant roughy (F-Australia)
Big-eared BAT (M-Papua New Guinea)
PASSENGER PIGEON officially extinct (USA)
1916 — Crested shelduck (B-Korea)
Baiji/Yangtze River dolphin (M-China)
Hamilton's FROG (A-New Zealand)
1917 — Crump's dormouse (M-India)
Dwarf hutia (M-Cuba)
Taiwan bush-warbler (B-Taiwan)
Scaly-tailed opossum (Ma-Australia)
Wyulda (Ma-Australia)
1918 — Pygmy tarsier (P-Indonesia)
Lesser Sulawesian shrew rat (M-Indonesia)
CAROLINA PARAKEET officially extinct (USA)
1920 — DE LOYS'S APE photographed (Venezuela)
Ceram bandicoot (Ma-Indonesia)
1921 — "ABOMINABLE SNOWMAN" coined as name for YETI
Montane fish-eating rat (M-Ecuador)
Golden lancehead (R-Brazil)
1923 — Edwards's pheasant (B-Vietnam)

Inaccessible Island rail (B-South Atlantic)
Hawaiian morwong (F-Hawaiian Islands)
Taipan* (R-Australia)
Morelet's CROCODILE* (R-Belize)
1924 — Purple-necked rock wallaby (Ma-Australia)
South American spiny mouse (M-Ecuador)
APE CANYON incident (Washington)
Imperial pheasant (B-Vietnam)
1925 — COLOSSAL SQUID (C-Indian Ocean)
1926 — Armored stickleback (F-Myanmar)
First pelt of KING CHEETAH collected (Zimbabwe)
1927 — First pelt of ANDEAN WOLF collected (Argentina)
1928 — Thomas's water mouse (M-Mexico)
Fire-maned bowerbird (B-Papua New Guinea)
Crocodile lizard (R-China)
Oaxacan caecilian (A-Mexico)
Baker's regent bowerbird (B-New Guinea)
1929 — Bonobo/pygmy CHIMPANZEE (P-Congo)
Venezuelan fish-eating rat (M-Venezuela)
Roraima mouse (M-Venezuela)
Giant pied-billed grebe (B-Guatemala)
"SASQUATCH" coined by press (Canada)
Sillem's mountain finch (B-Tibet)
Relict gull (B-Inner Mongolia)
Panamanian golden FROG (A-Panama)
Sinai leopard (M-Palestine)
1930 — Golden hamster* (M-Syria)
Tate's shrew rat (M-Indonesia)
Giant CATFISH (F-Vietnam)
Lafrentz caecilian (A-Mexico)
1931 — Desert rat kangaroo* (Ma-Australia)
Julia Creek dunnart (Ma-Australia)
1932 — Delacour's langur (P-Vietnam)
Drygas guenon (P-Congo)
Sichuan hill partridge (B-China)
Long-nosed bandicoot (M-Indonesia)
Lowe's servaline genet (M-Tasmania)
1933 — Miss Waldron's red colobus MONKEY (P-Ghana)
First photo of NESSIE (Scotland)
Shepherd's BEAKED WHALE (M-New Zealand)
1934 — "SURGEON'S PHOTO" of NESSIE (Scotland)
Dwarf bharal (M-China)
Santo Mountain starling (B-Espiritu Santo Island)
Black toad (A-California)
1935 — Philippine CROCODILE (R-Philippines)
Camotillo (F-Chile)
Cahow/Bermuda petrel (B-Bermuda)
1936 — THYLACINE declared officially extinct (Tasmania)
Jackson's fat mouse (M-Ghana)
Mexican blind cave FISH (F-Mexico)
Neon tetra (F-Colombia)
1937 — Philippine pygmy fruit BAT (M-Philippines)
Kouprey (M-Cambodia)
Cabanis's tanager* (B-Mexico)
Iran cave barb (F-Iran)
LIZZIE photographed at Loch Lochy (Scotland)
Bali TIGER officially extinct (M-Bali, Indonesia)
1938 — Van Zyl's golden mole (M-South Africa)
COELACANTH* (F-South Africa)

*An asterisk denotes a rediscovered species thought to have been extinct.

Desert dormouse (M-Kazakhstan)
First ONZA killed (Mexico)
Ribbon-tailed bird of paradise (B-Papua New Guinea)
First color film of NESSIE (Scotland)
Stresemann's bush crow (B-Ethiopia)
1939 — Georgia blind SALAMANDER (A-Georgia, USA)
Archbod's bowerbird (B-Papua New Guinea)
1940 — Palestinian painted FROG (A-Palestine)
1941 — White-tailed swallow (B-Ethiopia)
Rackham's xenosaur (R-Mexico)
1942 — Archey's FROG (A-New Zealand)
Prince Ruspoli's touraco (B-Ethiopia)
1944 — Sakhalin myotis (M-Sakhalin Island, Siberia)
1945 — Vietnam leaf-nosed BAT (M-Vietnam)
Northern water rat (M-Indonesia)
1946 — Small-toothed fruit BAT (M-Indonesia)
1947 — Widemouth blindcat (F-Texas)
1948 — Takahe* (B-New Zealand)
Jentink's duiker (M-Liberia)
1949 — Newman's xenosaur (R-Mexico)
1950 — Black-shouldered opossum (Ma-Peru)
Visagie's golden mole (M-South Africa)
One-toed amphiuma (A-Georgia, USA)
1951 — Don Filipés aquatic weasel (M-Colombia)
Cretan wildcat (M-Crete)
Mindanao hairy-tailed rat (M-Philippines)
African bay OWL (B-Congo)
Blomberg's giant toad (A-Ecuador)
1952 — Second living COELACANTH* (F-Comoros)
1953 — Ruwenzori otter shrew (M-Congo)
Iraq blind barb (F-Iraq)
Black dorcopsis WALLABY (Ma-Australia)
1954 — Nimba otter shrew (M-Côte d'Ivoire)
Pygmy killer whale* (M-Japan)
First sonar tracing of NESSIE (Scotland)
Lamotte's pygmy otter shrew (M-Guinea Republic)
1955 — Dwarf African water shrew (M-Congo)
Golden langur (P-India)
Sea wasp (J-Australia)
1956 — Hairyfish (F-Azores)
James's flamingo* (B-Chile)
Fraser's dolphin* (M-Indonesia)
Cardinal tetra (F-Brazil)
1957 — White-headed langur (P-China)
Gingko-toothed BEAKED WHALE (M-Pacific Ocean)
Golden-crowned manakin (B-Brazil)
Wood bison* (M-Canada)
Galápagos finch (B- Galápagos Islands)
1958 — Banana BAT (M-Mexico)
Liberian mongoose (M-Liberia)
Yellow-lipped cave BAT (M-Australia)
"BIGFOOT" nickname coined (California)
Vaquita porpoise (M-Gulf of California)
SOVIET SNOWMAN COMMISSION founded (Russia)
Javelin spookfish (F-British Columbia)
Liberian mongoose (M-Liberia)
Six-eyed spookfish (F-Pacific Ocean)
1959 — Fragment of PANGBOCHE HAND smuggled from Nepal
Mexican water mouse (M-Mexico)
Colombian grebe (B-Colombia)

Bolsón TORTOISE* (R-Mexico)
Ufiti (P-Malawi)
Seychelles scops OWL* (B-Seychelles Islands)
Denticle herring (F-West Africa)
1960 — Pipistrelles BAT (M-Israel)
TIM DINSDALE films NESSIE (Scotland)
Candango mouse (M-Brazil)
Banana BAT (M-Mexico)
Tarabundi vole (M-Mexico)
Jimi River FROG (A-Papua New Guinea)
Red goral (M-Myanmar)
Agak (A-Papua New Guinea)
1961 — Leadbeater's possum* (Ma-Australia)
Puerto Rican whippoorwill (B-Puerto Rico)
Eyrean grasswren* (B-Australia)
Irukandji JELLYFISH (J-Australia)
Noisy scrub-bird* (B-Australia)
Western bristlebird* (B-Australia)
Salamanderfish (F-Australia)
1962 — MANIPOGO photographed (Canada)
Nduk eagle owl* (B-Tanzania)
Bavarian pine vole (M-Germany)
LOCH NESS PHENOMENA INVESTIGATION BUREAU founded (Scotland)
1963 — Monjon (Ma-Australia)
Pittier's crab-eating rat (M-Venezuela)
Rufous-headed robin* (B-China)
Pygmy blue whale (M-Antarctic)
Hubbs's BEAKED WHALE (M-North Pacific)
1964 — Vu Quy's pheasant (B-Vietnam)
Catahoula SALAMANDER (A-Mississippi)
Greater yellow-headed vulture (B-Guyana)
Gabon shellear (F-Gabon)
Black-footed ferret* (M-Wyoming)
One-toed amphiuma (A-Florida)
1965 — Parma WALLABY* (Ma-Australia)
Iriomote CAT (M-Ryuku Islands)
White-throated WALLABY* (Ma-Australia)
Sokoke scops OWL (B-Kenya)
Lina's sunbird (B-Philippines)
1966 — Mountain pygmy possum (Ma-Australia)
Hairy-eared dwarf lemur* (P-Madagascar)
Auckland Island rail* (B-New Zealand)
Hispid hare (M-India)
Melon-headed whale (M-Pacific Ocean)
James Island rice rat (M- Galápagos Islands)
1967 — Long-footed potoroo* (Ma-Australia)
Southern dibbler* (Ma-Australia)
PATTERSON FILM of BIGFOOT (California)
Grey grasswren (B-Australia)
First photo of OGOPOGO (Canada)
Garrido's hutia (M-Cuba)
1968 — Somali golden mole (M-Somalia)
OGOPOGO filmed (Canada)
Black grasswren* (B-Australia)
Lamington free-eared BAT (M-Papua New Guinea)
MINNESOTA ICEMAN controversy
Woolly forest dormouse (M-Turkey)
Aldabran brush warbler (B-Seychelles Islands)
Juan Fernandez fur seal (M-Juan Fernandez Islands)
Xenosaurus platyceps (R-Mexico)

1969 — Sandhill dunnart* (Ma-Australia)
    Luzon fruit BAT (M-Philippines)
    Hartweg's soft-furred mouse (M-Nigeria)
    Lakeland Downs short-tailed mouse (M-Australia)
    Mt. Kahuzi climbing mouse (M-Congo)
    Black wallaroo* (Ma-Australia)
1970 — Hà Tinh langur (P-Vietnam)
    Large-eared hutia (M-Cuba)
    San Filipe hutia (M-Cuba)
1971 — Pygmy hog* (M-India)
    WHITEY photographed (Arkansas)
1972 — Anderson's mouse opossum (Ma-Peru)
    Mcilhenny's four-eyed opossum (Ma-Peru/Brazil)
    NESSIE "flipper" photograph (Scotland)
    Greater bamboo lemur* (P-Madagascar)
    Abingdon Island TORTOISE* (R-Galápagos Islands)
1973 — Kitti's hog-nosed BAT (M-Thailand)
    Marshall's horseshoe BAT (M-Thailand)
    Po'o-uli (B-Hawaiian Islands)
    Gastric brooding FROG (A-Australia)
    Limestone rat (M-Thailand)
    KUSSIE photographed (Japan)
    Parduco (B-Peru)
    Silver rice rat (M-Florida)
    Fijian barred-wing rail (B-Fiji)
    Fitzroy River TORTOISE (R-Australia)
    Golden poison FROG (A-Colombia)
1974 — Golden-crowned sifaka (P-Madagascar)
    Yellow-tailed woolly MONKEY* (P-Peru)
    Chacoan peccary (M-Paraguay)
    Peruvian fish-eating rat (M-Peru)
1975 — Long-tailed dunnart* (Ma-Australia)
    Ningaui — 2 species (Ma-Australia)
    El Hierro giant lizard* (R-Canary Islands)
    Pygmy short-tailed opossum (Ma-Bolivia/Brazil)
    Kabylian nuthatch (B-Algeria)
    Ridley's roundleaf BAT* (M-Malaysia)
    Dinagat bushy-tailed cloud rat (M-Philippines)
    Helmet dolphin (M-Gulf of Mexico)
    Pilliga mouse (M-Australia)
    Mountain pygmy possum (Ma-Australia)
    Sulawesti dawn BAT* (M-Malaysia)
    Fossil fruit BAT* (M-Papua New Guinea)
1976 — Proserpine rock WALLABY (Ma-Australia)
    Five photos of OGOPOGO (Canada)
    Andrews's BEAKED WHALE* (M-Catalina Island)
    Setzer's mouse-tailed dormouse (M-Iran)
    Long-whiskered owlet (B-Peru)
    Blind loach (F-Iran)
    Lesser BEAKED WHALE (M-Peru)
    Brown-plumaged yellow-billed duck* (B-New Zealand)
    Passage of Britain's Dangerous Wild Animals Act
    Megamouth SHARK (F-Hawaii
    Gray's MONITOR LIZARD (R-Philippines)
1977 — Zaire diana MONKEY (P-Congo)
    CHAMP filmed by Sandra Mansi (New York)
    White-winged guan* (B-Peru)
    Fea's muntjac* (M-Thailand)
    CHESSIE photographed (Potomac River, USA)
    Neill's long-tailed giant rat (M-Thailand)
    Sonar tracing of PONIK (Canada)

1978 — Sulawesi palm civet (M-Indonesia)
    Oyapock's fish-eating rat (M-French Guiana)
    Lear's macaw* (B-Brazil)
    SELMA filmed (Norway)
    Muisk vole (M-Siberia)
    Magenta petrel* (B-South Pacific)
    Giant palm civet* (M-Celebes)
    Golden poison FROG (A-Colombia)
    Water weasel (M-Colombia)
    Bronzeback (R-Australia)
1979 — Cinnamon antechinus (Ma-Australia)
    Slim-faced slender mouse opossum (Ma-Venezuela)
    Arnhem sheathtail BAT (M-Australia)
    OGOPOGO photographed and filmed (Canada)
    Chinese dormouse (M-China)
    Delcourt's giant gecko (R-New Zealand)
    Cabrera's hutia (M-Cuba)
    Lake Cronin SNAKE (R-Australia)
    Ruschis rat (M-Brazil)
    Fijian crested IGUANA (R-Fiji)
1980 — Chacoan naked-tailed ARMADILLO (X-Bolivia)
    Rosevear's striped grass mouse (M-Zambia)
    Mallorcan midwife toad* (A-Spain)
    Bulmer's fruit BAT* (M-Papua New Guinea)
    Six-gill stingray (F-South Africa)
    New Guinea glider (Ma-Papua New Guinea)
    Campbell's fairy wren (B-Papua New Guinea)
    Baachyaspis atriceps (R-Australia)
1981 — Handley's slender mouse opossum (Ma-Colombia)
    Sanje mangabey (P-Tanzania)
    Golden-fronted bowerbird* (B-Indonesia)
    Dusky musk deer (M-China)
    Laughing OWL* (B-New Zealand)
    Rufous-winged sunbird (B-Tanzania)
    Eskimo curlew* (B-Texas)
    White-headed steamer duck (B-Argentina)
    Ilin bushy-tailed cloud rat (M-Philippines)
    O-o* (B-Hawaiian Islands)
    Ash's lark (B-Somalia)
    Mindoro climbing rat (M-Philippines)
    Okinawa rail (B-Okinawa)
    Cloudforest screech OWL (B-Peru)
    Smallmouth char (F-Siberia)
1982 — INTERNATIONAL SOCIETY OF CRYPTOZOOLOGY founded
    First OGOPOGO videotape (Canada)
    Cochin Forest cane TURTLE (R-India)
    Amsterdam albatross (B-Indian Ocean)
    CHESSIE videotaped (Maryland)
    Bornean yellow muntjac (M-Borneo)
    Arnold's giant TORTOISE (R-Seychelles Islands)
    Orange-eyed flycatcher (B-Peru)
    Cox's sandpiper (B-Australia)
    Indian cave TURTLE* (R-India)
1983 — MEMPHRÉ photographed (Canada)
    MacGillivray's petrel* (B-Fiji)
    STORSJÖODJURET photographed (Sweden)
    Chao Phrya giant STINGRAY (F-Thailand)
1984 — Flat-headed cusimanse (M-Nigeria)
    First KELLAS CAT killed (Scotland)
    New Caledonian woodrail (B-New Caledonia)
    Red Sea cliff swallow (B-Sudan)

Sun-tailed guenon (P-Gabon)
Couresse* (R-Maria Islands)
1985 — Blackish squirrel MONKEY (P-Brazil)
Golden bamboo lemur (P-Madagascar)
Amazonian parrotlet (B-Peru)
HEUVELMANS's blenny(F-Adriatic Sea)
RI identified as a dugong (Papua New Guinea)
Deniliquin wombat* (Ma-Australia)
Eskimo curlew* (B-Texas)
Vanzolini's squirrel MONKEY (P-Brazil)
Queen of Sheba's gazelle (M-Ymen)
Cinnabar hawk-OWL (B-Indonesia)
El Oro parakeet (B-Ecuador)
Sangihe scops OWL* (B-Indonesia)
1986 — Giant-striped mongoose (M-Madagascar)
Bahamonde's BEAKED WHALE (M-Peru)
Jerdon's courser* (B-India)
Gurney's pitta* (B-Myanmar)
Thin-spined porcupine rat* (M-Brazil)
TESSIE filmed (Nevada)
Sumatran RHINOCEROS* (M-Indonesia)
Aye-aye* (P-Madagascar)
1987 — Second OGOPOGO video (Canada)
Black-hooded antwren* (B-Brazil)
Panay bushy-tailed cloud rat (M-Philippines)
Yemen MONITOR LIZARD (R-Yemen)
Freshwater whipray (F-Thailand)
Teleformin cuscus (Ma-Papua New Gunea)
Helmeted woodpecker* (B-Brazil)
Bronze quoll (M-Papua New Guinea)
St. Vincent whipsnake (R-St. Vincent Island)
1988 — Bronze quoll (Ma-Indonesia)
Crab-eating mongoose* (M-Hong Kong)
Slater's guenon* (P-Gabon)
First KELLAS CAT caught alive (Scotland)
Javan RHINOCEROS* (M-Vietnam)
Tsushima CAT (M-Tsushima Island)
Madagascar serpent-eagle* (B-Madagascar)
Black tree KANGAROO (Ma-Papua New Guinea)
1989 — Tenkile tree KANGAROO (Ma-Papua New Guinea)
Tonkin snub-nosed MONKEY (P-Vietnam)
Third OGOPOGO video (Canada)
Orangeblotch gaper (F-Caribbean Sea)
Three-banded ARMADILLO* (X-Brazil)
1990 — Black-faced lion tamarin (P-Brazil)
Nechisar nightjar (B-Ethiopia)
Ramsey Canyon leopard FROG (A-Arizona)
Red-finned blue-eye (F-Australia)
Opal allotoca (F-Mexico)
Night parrot* (B-Australia)
Hoffmann's titi (P-Brazil)
Jamaican IGUANA (R-Jamaica)
Harlequin FROG (A-Madagascar)
Emerald tree FROG (A-Madagascar)
Electric FROG (A-Australia)
Blond titi (P-Brazil)
Chinese otter* (M-Hong Kong)
1991 — Dian's tarsier (P-Indonesia)
IGOPOGO videotaped (Canada)
São Thomé grosbeak (B-Gulf of Guinea)
Canopy goanna (R-Australia)

ISSIE videotaped (Japan)
Bogert's MONITOR LIZARD (R-Papua New Guinea)
Udzungwa forest partridge (B-Tanzania)
Ucayli spiny mouse (M-Peru)
SOUTH BAY BESSIE videotaped (Ohio)
Nepal wren-babbler (B-Nepal)
Desert warthog* (M-South Africa)
Schomburgk's deer (M-Laos)
Western red colubus (P-Africa)
Venezuelan skunk FROG (A-Venezuela)
Bulo Burti boubou shrike (B-Somalia)
Western fork-crowned lemur (P-Madagascar)
Sambirano fork-crowned lemur (P-Madagascar)
Amber Mountain fork-crowned lemur (P-Madagascar)
1992 — Bulmer's fruit BAT* (M-Papua New Guinea)
Black-headed marmoset (P-Brazil)
Bay CAT* (M-Indonesia)
Tyne petrel (B-North Atlantic)
Saola/Vu Quang ox (M-Vietnam)
Lobatolampea tetragona (J-Japan)
Foothill elaenia (B-Ecuador)
Ka'apor capuchin (P-Brazil)
Cryptic warbler (B-Madagascar)
Fourth OGOPOGO video (Canada)
Fakfak paradigalla (B-Indonesia)
Río Maués marmoset (P-Brazil)
Anjouan scops OWL* (B-Comoro Islands)
Nepalese giant elephant (M-Nepal)
Vu Quang river carp (F-Vietnam)
Mozama bororo (M-Brazil)
Koopman's tree porcupine (M-Brazil)
Pygmy bluetongue skink (R-Australia)
Sumatran sureli (P-Indonesia)
1993 — Linh duong (M-Vietnam)
Nangchen horse (M-Tibet)
Koopman's porcupine (M-Brazil)
Salim Ali's fruit BAT* (M-India)
HOLADEIRA photographed (Brazil)
Forest spotted owlet* (B-India)
Lamprogrammus shcherbachevi (F-Atlantic Ocean)
Hainan leaf warbler (B-Hainan Island)
Helcogramma vulcanum (F-Indonesia)
Southern tokoeka (B-New Zealand)
Okariot brown kiwi (B-New Zealand)
Rufous mouse lemur* (P-Madagascar)
Ramsey Canyon leopard FROG (A-Arizona)
Marca's marmoset (P-Brazil)
1994 — Dingiso (Ma-Indonesia)
Gilbert's potoroo* (Ma-Australia)
Vampire FISH (F-Brazil)
Fonseca's acrobat BIRD (B-Brazil)
Giant muntjac (M-Laos)
Pink-legged graveteiro (B-Brazil)
Gray-crowned crocias* (B-Vietnam)
GUÀI WÙ photographed and videotaped (China)
Lesser brocket (M-Brazil)
HOAX alleged in SURGEON'S PHOTO of NESSIE (Scotland)
Bahian nighthawk (B-Brazil)
MIGO filmed (New Britain)
Mary River TORTOISE (R-Australia)
Madagascan red OWL* (B-Madagascar)

Ammoglanis diaphanus (F-Brazil)
Udzuniga forest partridge (B-Tanzania)
Cyclotryphlops dejarvengi (R-Indonesia)
1995 — Alexandra's cuscus (Ma-Molucca Islands)
Gray-shanked duoc langur (P-Vietnam)
First CHUPACABRA reports (Puerto Rico)
Subtropical pygmy OWL (B-Ecuador)
Siberut macaque (P-Indonesia)
Riwoche horse (M-China)
Woolly flying squirrel* (M-Pakistan)
Laos striped RABBIT (M-Laos)
Vietnamese warty pig (M-Vietnam)
Oman moray (F-Arabian Sea)
Xenoophidion acanthognathus (R-Antigua)
Xenoophidion schaeferi (R-Antigua)
Cerulean paradise flycatcher (B-Indonesia)
Roosevelt's muntjac* (M-Laos)
YEREN hair samples defy analysis (China)
Juruá spiny mouse (M-Brazil)
Marsh antwren (B-Brazil)
Vietnamese striped RABBIT (M-Laos)
Mascarene shearwater (B-Indian Ocean)
Invisible rail* (B-Indonesia)
Eastern quoll* (Ma-Australia)
Wulsin's ebony leaf MONKEY (P-Indonesia)
1996 — Black-crowned dwarf marmoset (P-Brazil)
Río Manicoré marmoset (P-Brazil)
Gulf snapping TURTLE* (R-Australia)
MARTIN'S FALSE POTTO (P-Cameroon)
Lowland tapaculo (B-Brazil)
Barbary lion* (M-Ethiopia)
GUÀI WÙ filmed (China)
Central rock rat (M-Australia)
Five photos of OGOPOGO (Canada)
Eleutherodactylus iberia (A-Cuba)
Sangha forest robin (B-Central African Republic)
STORSJÖODJURET videotaped (Sweden)
Martin's false potto (P-Cameroon)
Ghost knifefish (F-Brazil)
Matundu dwarf galago (P-Tanzania)
Río Acarí marmoset (P-Brazil)
Wetland tapaculo (B-Brazil)
Satere marmoset (P-Brazil)
Rondo dwarf galago (P-Tanzania)
Velvet climbing mouse (M-Congo)
Scarlet-banded barbet (B-Peru)
1997 — Golden-brown mouse lemur (P-Madagascar)
Indonesian COELACANTHS discovered
Taingu civet (M-Vietnam)
LAKE MONSTER videotaped at LOCH LOMOND (Scotland)
Northern talapoin (P-Democratic Republic of Congo)
Moluccan yellow MONITOR LIZARD (R-Molucca Islands)
Phantom FROG (A-Costa Rica)
Black sea nettle (J-Pacific Ocean)
Hololissa (R-Seychelles Islands)
Leaf muntjac (M-Myanmar)
Siamese algae eater (F-Vietnam)
Truong Son muntjac (M-Vietnam)
MEMPHRÉ videotaped (Canada)
Jocotoco antpita (B-Ecuador)
Borneo river SHARK (F-Malaysia)

TEGGIE videotaped (Wales)
Brush-tailed rat (M-French Guiana)
Cajas water mouse (M-Ecuador)
Forest owlet (B-India)
San Felipe Gambusia (F-Texas)
Fishing mouse (M-Ecuador)
Campbell Island snipe (B-South Pacific)
Eleutherodactylus pluvicanorus (A-Bolivia)
Gray-shanked douc langur (P-Vietnam)
1998 — Golden-headed langur (P-Vietnam)
Peruvian mounatin coati (M-Peru)
Rothschild's parakeet* (B-India)
Leopard chimaera (F-New Zealand)
Giant sawbelly* (F-Australia)
Leopard chimaera (F-New Zealand)
Mimic OCTOPUS (C-Australia)
Big-fin squid (C-Pacific Ocean)
Tricolored MONITOR LIZARD (R-Molucca Islands)
COELACANTH* (F-Indonesia)
Ancient antwren (B-Peru)
Hoan Kiem TURTLE (R-Vietnam)
Nicobar scops OWL (B-India)
Dinagat hairy-tailed rat (M-Philippines)
Rock firefinch (B-Nigeria)
Talaud Island rail (B-Indonesia)
Cherry-throated tanager* (B-Brazil)
Alice Springs mouse (M-Australia)
Attenborough's echidna (M-Australia)
Ateles kamayurensis (P-Brazil)
Thylophis ayarsaguenai (R-Venezuela)
Hubei golden snub-nosed MONKEY (P-China)
Slender-billed curlew* (B-England)
Qinling golden snub-nosed MONKEY (P-China)
1999 — MORGAWR videotaped (Cornwall, England)
Cerro de Petlalcala pit viper (R-Mexico)
Vespucci's rat (M-Brazil)
Nigerian white-throated guenon (P-Nigeria)
Inca tomb rat (M-Peru)
Pílos chameleon (R-Greece)
Niger Delta red colubus (P-Nigeria)
First Internet sighting of NESSIE
Coimbra-Filho's titi (P-Brazil)
Cloudforest pygmy owl (B-Ecuador)
Turquoise MONITOR LIZARD (R-Indonesia)
Mountain coati (M-Colombia)
Cinnabar hawk-OWL (B-Indonesia)
Shoal bass (F-Alabama)
Peacock MONITOR LIZARD (R-Indonesia)
Jocotoca antpitta (B-Ecuador)
Ngotto mustached MONKEY (P-Central African Republic)
2000 — Southern dwarf lemur (P-Madagascar)
Furry-eared dwarf lemur (P-Madagascar)
Sibree's dwarf lemur (P-Madagascar)
Large iron-gray dwarf lemur (P-Madagascar)
Lesser iron-gray dwarf lemur (P-Madagascar)
Unicolor woolly lemur (P-Madagascar)
Sclater's monal pheasant (B-Tibet)
Berthe's mouse lemur (P-Madagascar)
Sambriano mouse lemur (P-Madagascar)
Northern rufous mouse lemur (P-Madagascar)

Gunnison sage grouse (B-Colorado)
Alleged SKUNK APE photo and videotape (Florida)
Chinese crested tern (B-East China Sea)
Hussain's night FROG (A-India)

2001 — Pygmy three-toed sloth (X-Isla Escudo de Veraguas)
Bernardi's titi (P-Brazil)
Bavarian vole* (M-Austria)
COELACANTH* (F-Kenya)
Wild Bactrian CAMEL (M-China)
Pygmy sloth (M-Panama)
Bruijn's megapode* (B-Papua New Guinea)
ORANG PENDEK hair sample defies analysis (Indonesia)
Perrin's BEAKED WHALE (M-Atlantic Ocean)
Stephen Nash's titi (P-Brazil)
Mouse-eared BAT* (M-England)
Chestnut-capped piha (B-Colombia)
HESSIE videotaped (Norway)
Vizcaha rats — 2 species (M-Argentina)
Jaragua sphaero gecko (R-British Virgin Islands)
Mljet moon jelly (J-Adriatic Sea)
Arias's dwarf GECKO (R-Dominican Republic)
Sri Lankan scops OWL (B-Sri Lanka)
Carrizal seedeater (B-Venezuela)

2002 — OGOPOGO filmed (Canada)
LAKE MONSTER photographed at Dulverton Lake (Tasmania)
Lowe's servaline genet* (M-Tasmania)
Little Sumba hawk-OWL (B-Indonesia)
Batura FROG (A-Pakistan)
Golden-crowned manakin* (B-Brazil)
100 new FROG species (A-Sri Lanka)

2003 — Almiqui* (Cuba)
Dusky hopping mouse* (Australia)
Lavarack's TURTLE* (R-Australia)
Gulbaru GECKO (R-Australia)
Chinese crested tern* (B-China)
Unnamed FROG species (A-India)
Daniel's caecilian (A-India)
Bhutanese shou (M-Bhutan)
Omura's whale (M-Japan)
Bloodfin tetra (F-Venezuela)
Long-legged warbler* (B-Fiji)
Pygmy seahorse (F-Indonesia)

2004 — Wangi Wangi white eye (B-Indonesia)
Cockrum's shrew (M-Arizona)

Appendix B
Filography

The following films feature cryptids or cryptozoological themes. Excluded are any films involving manmade monsters (i.e., products of radiation, pollution, "mad science," etc.) and creatures from outer space. An exception to that rule admits films wherein human meddling with legitimate cryptids (e.g., living DINOSAURS) produce unexpected results. Whenever possible, the dates given reflect a film's original release and may conflict with dates of a foreign film's first release in the United States.

Aberration (1997) — Small-but-deadly lizards threaten a gangster's girlfriend on the run when she hides out in the forest cabin they infest. Cast: Pamela Gidley, Simon Bossell, Valery Nikolaev. Director: Tim Boxell.

Abominable Snowman of the Himalayas (1957) — This vintage British film remains the best fictional treatment of the YETI to date. Cast: Peter Cushing, Forrest Tucker, Maureen Connell. Director: Val Guest.

America's Loch Ness Monster (2003?) — No details were available at press time on this made-for-TV feature, reportedly still in production.

Anaconda (1997) — A documentary film crew runs afoul of unscrupulous SNAKE hunters and 40-foot ANACONDAS in the Amazon jungle. Cast: Jennifer Lopez, Jon Voight, Ice Cube, Eric Stoltz, Jonathan Hyde, Owen Wilson, Kari Wuhrer. Director: Luis Llosa.

Arachnophobia (1990) — A new species of South American SPIDER breeds with a common U.S. specimen to produce killer offspring and terrorize a California town. Cast: Jeff Daniels, Harley Jane Kozak, John Goodman, Julian Sands. Director: Frank Marshall.

At the Earth's Core (1976) — This low-budget adaptation of an Edgar Rice Burroughs novel takes explorers to the center of the Earth, where they encounter living DINOSAURS and primitive humans. Cast: Doug McClure, Peter Cushing, Caroline Munro, Godfrey James. Director: Kevin Connor.

Baby — Secret of the Lost Legend (1985) — The legend in question is Africa's MOKELE-MBEMBE, appearing in both adult and juvenile form as hunters with mixed motives pursue the elusive cryptids. Cast: William Katt, Sean Young, Patrick McGoohan. Director: B.W.L. Norton.

The Beast (1996) — The television mini-series adaptation of Peter Benchley's novel features GIANT SQUIDS on a rampage in a straightforward pastiche of *Jaws*. Cast: William Peterson, Karen

Sillas, Charles Martin Smith, Missy Crider, Larry Drake. Director: Jeff Bleckner.

Beast from Haunted Cave (1959) — Thieves on the run in South Dakota encounter a blood-sucking creature that resembles a forklift covered with cobwebs. Cast: Michael Forrest, Sheila Carol, Frank Wolff, Richard Sinatra. Director: Monte Hellman.

The Beast from Hollow Mountain (1956) — Cowboys clash with a predatory DINOSAUR. Cast: Guy Madison, Patricia Medina, Carlos Rivas, Mario Navarro. Directors: Edward Nassour, Ismael Rodríguez.

The Beast from 20,000 Fathoms — Nuclear tests in the Arctic thaw out a frozen DINOSAUR ("rhedosaurus"), which wreaks havoc with humans en route to its ancestral breeding grounds near New York City. Cast: Paul Christian, Paula Raymond, Cecil Kellaway, Donald Woods, Kenneth Tobey. Director: Eugene Lourie.

Beauties and the Beast (1974) — A voyeuristic BIGFOOT catches various young women in backwoods sexual encounters. Cast: Jean Gibson, Uschi Digard, Marius Mazmanian, Bob Makay. Directors: Marius Mazmanian, Ray Nadeau.

Beneath Loch Ness (2001) — A disgruntled NESSIE terrorizes locals, and a hunter is dispatched to kill her. Cast: Brian Wimmer, Patrick Bergin, Lysette Anthony, Lysa Apostle. Director: Chuck Comisky.

The Bermuda Depths (1978) — A mysterious young woman and her giant TURTLE take the blame for Bermuda Triangle disappearances in this made-for-TV feature. Cast: Leigh McCloskey, Carl Weathers, Connie Sellecca, Julie Woodson. Director: Tom Kotani.

Beware of Yeti! (1961) — Mountaineers meet the YETI in this Polish feature. Cast: Wieslaw Golas. Director: Czekalsk.

Bigfoot (1970) — BIGFOOT clashes with bikers to rescue women in distress. Cast: John Carradine, John Mitchum, Christopher Mitchum, Joi Lansing. Director: Robert Slatzer.

Bigfoot (1987) — A family vacation in the mountains leads to a meeting with BIGFOOT in this made-for-TV feature. Cast: Adam Carl, Lucy Butler, Candace Bure, Jerry Chambers. Director: Danny Huston.

Bigfoot: Man or Beast? (1971) — This documentary features interviews with GROVER KRANTZ and clips from the PATTERSON FILM. Director: Lawrence Crowley.

Bigfoot: The Unforgettable Encounter (1995) — A youth finds fame and trouble from ruthless bounty hunters after he meets BIG-FOOT in the wild. Cast: Zachery Ty Brian, Matt McCoy, Crystal Chappell, Clint Howard, Rance Howard. Director: Corey Michael Eubanks.

The Black Scorpion (1957) — Volcanic eruptions unleash giant prehistoric scorpions on the Mexican countryside. Other cryptids abound when scientists pursue the monsters into their subterranean habitat. Cast: Richard Denning, Mara Corday, Carlos Rivas, Mario Navarro, Fanny Schiller. Director: Edward Ludwig.

Blood Surf see *Krocodylus*

Boa see *New Alcatraz*

Bog (1983) — Mayhem ensues when wilderness travelers run afoul of a recently defrosted monster. Cast: Gloria De Haven, Aldo Ray, Marshall Thompson. Director: Don Keeslar.

Boggy Creek II (1983) — A mismatched team of university researchers pursue the FOUKE MONSTER in this low-budget sequel to *The Legend of Boggy Creek*. (Title notwithstanding, it's the third Boggy Creek feature, and the last to date.) Cast: Charles Pierce, Chuck Pierce, Cindy Butler. Director: Charles Pierce.

The Boogens (1981) — Subterranean monsters resume their predation when a long-abandoned mine shaft is reopened. Cast: Rebecca Balding, Fred McCarren, Anne-Marie Martin. Director: James Conway.

Bride of the Monster (1955) — A giant OCTOPUS steals the show in this unintentionally hilarious offering from schlock-meister Ed Wood Jr. Cast: Bela Lugosi, Tor Johnson, Tony McCoy, Loretta King. Director: Edward Wood Jr.

Brotherhood of the Wolf (2001) — Cryptozoology mixes with revolutionary politics mix in this above-average French film based on the real-life BEAST OF GÉVAUDAN. Cast: Samuel Le Bihan, Vincent Cassel, Émile Dequenne, Monica Bellucci. Director: Christophe Gans.

Bug (1975) — An earthquake unleashes hordes of large, super-intelligent beetles that set fire to anything (and anyone) they touch. Cast: Bradford Dillman, Joanna Miles, Richard Gilliland. Director: Jeannot Szwarc.

The Capture of Bigfoot (1979) — After BIGFOOT is sighted near a ski resort, a local businessman schemes to cage the beast as a tourist attraction. Cast: James Raudkivi, Randolph Rebane, Stafford Morgan, Katherine Hopkins. Director: Bill Rebane.

Cave Girl (1985) — Lost during a subterranean field trip, a high school student finds herself stranded among living DINOSAURS and primitive humans. Cast: Cindy Ann Thompson, Daniel Roebuck. Director: David Oliver.

Congo (1995) — Deadly mutant GORILLAS guard the ruins of an ancient African civilization in this screen adaptation of Michael Crichton's best-selling novel. Cast: Dylan Walsh, Laura Linney, Ernie Hudson, Joe Don Baker. Director: Frank Marshall.

The Crater Lake Monster (1977) — A living DINOSAUR emerges from CRATER LAKE, OREGON to ravage the surrounding countryside in this film inspired by local LAKE MONSTER reports.

Cast: Richard Cardella, Glenn Roberts. Director: William Stromberg.

Creature from Black Lake (1976) — Echoes of real-life cryptid sightings from the HONEY ISLAND SWAMP abound in this low-budget drama of a "missing link" at large in the Louisiana bayou country. Cast: Jack Elam, Dub Taylor, Dennis Fimple, John David Carson. Director: Joy Houck Jr.

Creature from the Black Lagoon (1954) — A prehistoric "gill man" menaces explorers in a remote Amazon backwater, launching a trilogy of 1950s horror films. Cast: Richard Carlson, Julie Adams, Richard Denning, Nestor Paiva, Whit Bissell, Antonio Moreno. Director: Jack Arnold.

The Creature from the Haunted Sea (1960) — A laughable sea monster interferes with shady treasure-hunters in this horror-comedy feature. Cast: Anthony Carbone, Betsy Jones-Moreland. Director: Roger Corman.

The Creature Walks Among Us (1956) — The prehistoric "gill man" of *Creature from the Black Lagoons* remains homicidal despite a surgical makeover, in the trilogy's final installment. Cast: Jeff Morrow, Rex Reason, Leigh Snowden. Director: John Sherwood.

Crocodile (1981) — A giant CROCODILE flattens Pacific island villages in this Thai-Korean import. Cast: Nat Puvanai, Kirk Warren, Angela Wells, Tiny Tim. Director: Sompote Sands.

Crocodile (2000) — A huge CROCODILE stalks irresponsible teenagers around a remote California lake. Cast: Mark McLachlan, Caitlin Martin, Chris Solari, D.W. Reiser, Julie Mintz. Director: Tobe Hooper.

Crocodile 2: Death Swamp (2001) — Armed robbers and their hostages share a common peril after their plane crashes in a swamp occupied by a giant CROCODILE. Despite the title, this is not a sequel. Cast: Heidi Lenhart, Chuck Walczak, Jon Sklaroff, Darryl Theirse. Director: Gary Jones.

Daikaijû Tôkyô ni arawaru (1998) — Yet another living DINOSAUR rises from Tokyo harbor to ravage the city. Cast: Daori Momoi, Hirotaro Honda, Yûki Hirano, Kimiko Imai. Director: Takeshi Miyasaka.

The Deadly Mantis (1957) — A giant prehistoric praying mantis thaws out in the Arctic and wings its way to a violent finale in New York City. Cast: Craig Stevens, William Hopper. Director: Nathan Juran.

Death Bite see *Spasms*

Deep Rising (1998) — A marine salvage crew battles a sea monster for control of an abandoned ocean liner. Cast: Treat Williams, Famke Jansen, Anthony Heald, Kevin O'Connor, Wes Studi. Director: Stephen Sommers.

Deepstar Six (1989) — A sea monster makes life difficult for underwater researchers. Cast: Taurean Blacque, Nancy Everhard, Greg Evigen, Miguel Ferrer, Nia Peeples, Matt McCoy, Cindy Pickett. Director: Sean Cunningham.

Devil Fish (1984) — Misguided scientists transform a giant prehistoric "protoshark" into an even more fearsome predator by adding OCTOPUS tentacles. Motives and methods remain obscure in this low-budget Italian horror film. Cast: Michael

Sopkiw, Valentine Monnier, Gianni Garko, William Berger. Directors: Lamberto Bava, Sergio Martino.

Dinosaur Island (1994) — A team of army rejects encounters nude women and living DINOSAURS on the titular island in this bargain-basement horror film. Why it needed *two* directors is anyone's guess. Cast: Ross Hagen, Richard Gabi, Antonia Dorian, Toni Naples. Directors: Jim Wynorski, Fred Olen Ray.

Dinosaur Valley Girls (1996) — Horror and nudity mingle to no good effect in another low-budget treatment of living DINOSAURS. Cast: William Marshall, Griffen Drew, Karen Black. Director: Donald Glut.

Dinosaurus! (1960) — Two DINOSAURS and a caveman emerge from suspended animation to bedevil inhabitants of a remote island. Cast: Ward Ramsey, Paul Lukather. Director: Irvin Yeaworth Jr.

DNA (1997) — Scientists extract DNA from the bones of an unknown creature found in Borneo and recreate the animal, with predictably tragic results. Cast: Mark Dacascos, Jügen Prochnow, Robin McKee, Thomas Taus Jr. Director: William Mesa.

Dragonheart (1996) — A disillusioned DRAGON slayer learns a valuable lesson from the last of the Medieval species. Cast: Dennis Quaid, David Thewlis, Peter Postlethwaite, Dina Meyer, Sean Connery (as the dragon's voice). Director: Rob Cohen.

Dragonheart: A New Beginning (2000) — An orphaned stable boy befriend's Europe's last living DRAGON in this made-for-TV sequel to *Dragonheart*. (Alternate title: *Dragonheart II*) Cast: Christopher Masterson, Harry Van Gorkum, Rona Figueroa, Matt Hickey, Robby Benson (dragon's voice). Director: Doug Lefler.

Dragonslayer (1981) — A novice DRAGON hunter strives to rescue the reptile's latest royal victim. Cast: Peter MacNicol, Caitlin Clarke, Ralph Richardson, John Hallam, Albert Salmi. Director: Matthew Robbins.

Drawing Flies (1996) — A group of hard-luck youths join a search for BIGFOOT in the Canadian wilderness. Cast: Joey Lauren Adams, Martin Brooks, Renée Humphrey, David Keeps. Directors: Matthew Gissing, Malcolm Ingram.

Earth vs. the Spider (1958) — A giant SPIDER emerges from its cavern to wreak havoc in a small American town. Cast: Ed Kemmer, June Kenney, Gene Roth. Director: Bert Gordon.

Ganjasaurus Rex (1988) — This prodrug propaganda vehicle features a DINOSAUR that wakes to save the day when police burn marijuana crops. Cast: Paul Bassis, Dave Fresh, Rosie Jones. Director: Ursi Reynolds.

Gargoyles (1972) — A predatory race of winged gargoyles wakes every 500 years to challenge mankind's dominion on earth. This time around, they're foiled by a college professor and his daughter. Cast: Cornel Wilde, Jennifer Salt, Bernie Casey. Director: Bill Norton.

The Giant Behemoth (1959) — A resurrected DINOSAUR attacks England in a virtual remake of *The Beast from 20,000 Fathoms*. Stop-motion FX artist Willis O'Brien does his best with a marginal budget. Cast: Gene Evans, Andre Morell, Jack MacGowan. Director: Eugene Lourie.

The Giant Claw (1957) — A huge prehistoric BIRD battles Air Force jets and generally raises Hell in a bona fide turkey from Hollywood's Cold War era. Cast: Jeff Morrow, Mara Corday, Morris Ankrum. Director: Fred Sears.

The Giant Gila Monster (1959) — The titular cryptid pursues hot-rodding teenagers in Arkansas, far from its normal desert range. Cast: Don Sullivan, Fred Graham, Lisa Simone, Shug Fisher. Director: Don Sullivan.

Gigantis, the Fire Monster (1955) — Godzilla wears a pseudonym in this second installment of the long-running Japanese film series (originally titled *Godzilla Raids Again*). This time around, it battles another living DINOSAUR dubbed Anguirus, wreaking double havoc on urban Japan. Cast: Hiroshi Koizumi, Minoru Chiaki, Setsuko Wakayama. Director: Motoyoshi Oda.

Godzilla, King of the Monsters (1954) — H-bomb tests in the Pacific transform a living DINOSAUR ("Godzillasaurus") into a huge fire-breathing DRAGON, which then proceeds to terrorize Japan. Cast: Raymond Burr, Frank Iwanaga, Takashi Shimura, Akihiko Hirata. Directors: Ishirô Honda, Terry Morse.

Godzilla 1985 (1984) — Living DINOSAUR Godzilla returns to menace Tokyo after 30 years of hibernation. In addition to his flaming breath, giant "sea lice" from his body also threaten hapless victims. Cast: Keiju Kobayashi, Ken Tanaka, Yasuko Sawaguchi. Director: Koji Hashimoto.

Godzilla vs. Destroyer (1995) — The 22nd episode of Japan's longest-running film series pits living DINOSAUR Godzilla and his/her offspring against deadly crustaceans. Cast: Megumi Odaka. Momoko Kochi, Yasufumi Hiyachi, Yoko Ishino. Director: Takao Okawara.

Godzilla vs. the Sea Monster (1966) — The seventh entry in this Japanese film series finds irrepressible DINOSAUR Godzilla mixing it up with a huge crustacean (Ebirah) and a giant insect (Mothra) in a three-way battle royal. Cast: Akira Takarada, Toru Watanabe, Kumi Mizuno, Jun Tazaki. Director: Jun Fukuda.

Godzilla's Revenge (1969) — This peculiar 10th episode of the Japanese film series is chiefly a child's dream sequence, wherein living DINOSAUR Godzilla and various other huge cryptids lock horns on Monster Island. Cast: Tomonori Yazaki, Eisei Amamoto, Kenji Sahara. Director: Ishirô Honda.

Gorgo (1961) — British fisherman are pleased with their capture of a living DINOSAUR, until Mama turns up to rescue her offspring. Cast: Bill Travers, William Sylvester, Vincent Winter, Martin Benson. Director: Eugene Lourie.

Graveyard Shift (1990) — This film adaptation of a Stephen King short story finds a giant rat-BAT creature stalking disgruntled employees at a factory in Maine. Cast: David Andrews, Kelly Wolf, Stephen Macht, Andrew Divoff, Brad Dourif. Director: Ralph Singleton.

Grizzly (1976) — It's *Jaws* in the big woods, as an 18-foot GRIZZLY bear terrorizes campers and forest rangers. Cast: Christopher George, Andrew Prine, Richard Jaeckel. Director: William Girdler.

Half Human (1958) — A YETI runs amok on Mount Fuji in this Japanese film with strong echoes of real-life cryptid HIBAGON.

Cast: John Carradine, Morris Ankrum, Stephen Morris. Director: Ishirô Honda.

Harry and the Hendersons (1987) — Wackiness ensues when a suburban family hits BIGFOOT with their car, then takes him home. Cast: John Lithgow, Melinda Dillon, Don Ameche, Lanie Kazan, David Suchet. Director: William Dear.

Horror Express (1972) — Scientists unearth a prehistoric HOMINID, which revives and terrorizes its captors aboard the Trans-Siberian Express. Cast: Peter Cushing, Christopher Lee, Telly Savalas. Director: Eugenio Martin.

Iceman (1984) — Arctic explorers find a prehistoric man trapped in ice and revive him for study in this reworking of a familiar theme. Cast: Timothy Hutton, Lindsay Crouse, John Lone, Josef Sommer. Director: Fred Schepisi.

It Came from Beneath the Sea (1955) — Ray Harryhausen's special effects highlight this tale of a giant OCTOPUS emerging from the Pacific to menace San Francisco. Cast: Kenneth Tobey, Faith Domergue, Donald Curtis, Ian Keith. Director: Robert Gordon.

Jaws 3 (1983) — While the other films in this series dramatized encounters with "normal" great white SHARKS, this 3-D installment features a fish the size of *CARCHARODON MEGALADON* demolishing an underwater amusement park. Cast: Lou Gossett Jr., Dennis Quaid, Bess Armstrong, Simon MacCorkindale. Director: Joe Alve.

Journey to Prehistory (1955) — This curious Czech production follows four boys from a New York museum into Central Park, where they discover the entrance to a hidden world of living DINOSAURS. Cast: Vladimir Bejval, Victor Betral, Charles Goldsmith, Petr Herrman. Directors: Karel Zeman, Fred Ladd.

Journey to the Center of the Earth (1959) — DINOSAURS survive at the Earth's core in this film adaptation of the Jules Verne novel. Cast: James Mason, Pat Boone, Arlene Dahl, Diane Baker. Director: Henry Levin.

Journey to the Center of the Earth (1976) — This Spanish version of Jules Verne's story was released two years later in the U.S., as *Where Time Began*. Cast: Kenneth More, Pep Munné, Ivonne Sentis, Frank Braña. Director: Juan Piquer Simón.

Journey to the Center of the Earth (1987) — Adding a super model to the cast won't help this tepid remake of the Jules Verne classic. Cast: Nicola Cowper, Jan Michael-Smith, Paul Carafotes, Kathy Ireland, Emo Philips.

Kappa (1994) — A KAPPA troubles humans in this Japanese horror tale. (Alternate title: *Water Creature*) Cast: Tatsuya Fuji, Ryuuki Harada, Keisuke Funakoshi, Takonori Jinnai. Director: Tatsuya Ishii.

King Kong (1933) — The original is still the greatest, as Willis O'Brien delivers classic special effects in the story of a giant GORILLA found on a remote island with living DINOSAURS. Cast: Robert Armstrong, Fay Wray, Bruce Cabot, Frank Reicher, Noble Johnson. Directors: Merian Cooper, Ernest Schoedsack.

King Kong (1976) — A modern remake of the 1933 classic loses the original DINOSAURS and most of its audience appeal. Cast: Jeff Bridges, Jessica Lange, Charles Grodin. Director: John Guillermin.

King Kong Lives (1986) — The giant GORILLA is revived and furnished with a mate (Lady Kong) in this unfortunate continuation of the series. Cast: Brian Kerwin, Linda Hamilton, John Ashton, Peter Michael Goetz. Director: John Guillermin.

King Kong vs. Godzilla (1962) — It's difficult to say if living DINOSAUR Godzilla shrank or huge GORILLA Kong quadrupled in size for this Japanese slug-fest that also features a giant OCTOPUS. Cast: Tadao Takashima, Mie Hama, Kenji Sahara, Yu Fujiki. Director: Ishirô Honda.

Komodo (1999) — Transplanted (and inflated) Komodo dragons overrun an island off the coast of North Carolina. Cast: Jill Hennessy, Billy Burke, Kevin Zegers, Paul Gleeson. Director: Michael Lantieri.

Krocodylus (2000) — Members of a documentary film crew in the South Pacific fall prey to a giant CROCODILE. (Alternate title: *Blood Surf*.) Cast: Dax Miller, Taryn Reil, Kate Fischer, Duncan Regehr. Director: James Hickox.

Lake Placid (1999) — Eccentric characters and snappy dialogue (by *Ally McBeal*'s David Kelley) enliven this story of a huge Asian CROCODILE that's somehow found its way to a lake in rural Maine. Cast: Bill Pullman, Bridget Fonda, Oliver Platt, Brendan Gleeson, Betty White, Meredith Salenger. Director: Steve Miner.

The Land That Time Forgot (1975) — A paltry budget and mediocre performances hamstring this adaptation of the Edgar Rice Burroughs novel, complete with living DINOSAURS and prehistoric humans. Cast: Doug McClure, Susan Penhaligon, John McEnery. Director: Kevin Connor.

The Land Unknown (1957) — While investigating reports of a warm-water zone in Antarctica, researchers are trapped in a volcanic crater inhabited by DINOSAURS and other prehistoric reptiles. Cast: Jock Mahoney, Shawn Smith, William Reynolds. Director: Virgil Vogel.

The Last Dinosaur (1977) — A millionaire big-game hunter tunnels underground to stalk a living DINOSAUR in this made-for-TV sci-fi feature. Cast: Richard Boone, Joan Van Ark, Steven Keats, Luther Rackley, Masumi Sekiya. Directors: Alexander Grasshoff, Tom Kotani.

The Last Late Night (1999) — In the midst of a housewarming party-cum-orgy, a guest reveals his personal relationship to the YETI. Cast: Christine Steel, Graham Galloway, Aaron Waiton, Melanie Salvatore. Director: Scott Barlow.

The Legend of Bigfoot (1976) — Suspected hoaxer IVAN MARX produced this pseudo-documentary featuring unnamed actors in baggy APE suits and a hilarious sequence wherein a car's headlights are passed off as BIGFOOT's glowing eyes.

Legend of Boggy Creek (1972) — This quasi-documentary is the first in a series of films about the FOUKE MONSTER. Cast: Willie Smith, John Nixon. Director: Charles Pierce.

The Legend of Gator Face (1999) — A LIZARD MAN in the southern bayou country proves more humane than some of the humans who stalk him. Cast: John White, Dan Warry-Smith, Charlotte Sullivan, C. David Johnson, Paul Winfield. Director: Vic Sarin.

Legend of Loch Ness (1976)—A documentary of NESSIE, narrated by Arthur Franz. Director: Richard Martin.

Legion of Fire: Killer Ants! (1998)—A colony of South American army ants swarms over rural Alaska in this made-for TV feature. (Alternate title: *Marabunta*.) Cast: Eric Lutes, Julia Campbell, Mitch Peleggi, Jeremy Foley. Directors: Jim Charleston, George Manasse.

Little Bigfoot (1997)—A family vacation turns to high adventure when the campers meet a young BIGFOOT. Cast: Ross Malinger, P.J. Soles, Kenneth Tigar, Kelly Packard. Director: Art Camacho.

Little Bigfoot 2: The Journey Home (1997)—BIGFOOT helps members of a dysfunctional family learn to appreciate one another. Cast: Stephen Furst, Taran Smith, Michael Fishman, Chuck Borden. Director: Art Camacho.

Loch Ness (1995)—A skeptical scientist investigates reports of NESSIE and finds romance in the process. Cast: Ted Danson, Joely Richardson, Ian Holm, Harris Yulin, Kristy Graham. Director: John Henderson.

The Loch Ness Horror (1981)—NESSIE gets a bad rap in this story of a bloodthirsty monster on a rampage. Cast: Sandy Kenyon, Miki McKenzie, Barry Buchanan, Eric Scott. Director: Larry Buchanan.

The Loch Ness Monster: Proof at Last! (1936)—This early documentary couples eyewitness interviews with "authentic" NESSIE footage shot by producer Malcolm Irvine.

The Lost Continent (1951)—Air Force pilots tracking a lost missile find themselves trapped on an uncharted island with living DINOSAURS. Cast: Cesar Romero, Hillary Brooke, Chick Chandler, John Hoyt, Acquanetta, Sid Melton, White Bissell, Hugh Beaumont. Director: Sam Newfield.

The Lost World (1925)—This silent version of Arthur Conan Doyle's DINOSAUR classic, inspired by conversations with explorer PERCY FAWCETT, still outshines other entries in a long-running series of remakes. Cast: Wallace Beery, Bessie Love, Lewis Stone. Director: Harry Hoyt.

The Lost World (1960)—A retelling of Doyle's DINOSAUR tale by disaster-film mogul Irwin Allen. Cast: Michael Rennie, Jill St. John, David Hedison, Claude Rains. Director: Irwin Allen.

The Lost World (1998)—Yet another version of the classic DINOSAUR saga. Cast: Patrick Bergin, Jayne Heitmeyer, Julian Casey, David Nerman. Director: Bob Keen.

The Lost World (1999)—Made-for-TV version of the DINOSAUR classic. Cast: Peter McCauley, William de Vry, William Snow, Michael Sinelnikoff, Rachel Blakely. Director: Richard Franklin.

The Lost World (2001)—Living DINOSAURS return in the second TV version (and fifth filming) of Arthur Conan Doyle's novel. Cast: Bob Hoskins, James Fox, Tom Ward, Matthew Rhys. Director: Stuart Orme.

Magic in the Water (1995)—A benevolent LAKE MONSTER bestows surprising gifts on harried humans in this family film. Cast: Mark Harmon, Harley Jane Kozak, Joshua Jackson, Sarah Wayne. Director: Rick Stevenson.

Man Beast (1956)—A low-budget expedition stalks YETI in the Himalayas. Cast: Rock Madison, Asa Maynor, George Skaff, Tom Maruzzi. Director: Jerry Warren.

Marabunta see *Legion of Fire: Killer Ants!*

Megalodon (2002)—Seagoing adventurers encounter "60 feet of prehistoric terror" in the form of a living CARCHARODON MEGALODON. Cast: Robin Sachs, Al Sapienza, Leighanne Littrell, Mark Sheppard. Directors: Pat Corbitt, Gary Tunnicliffe.

Mermaid Chronicles Part 1: She Creature (2001)—A greedy showman and his girlfriend have problems transporting a seductive and deadly MERBEING across the Atlantic in this made-for-cable feature. (Alternate title: *She Creature*) Cast: Rufus Sewell, Carla Gugino, Rya Kihlstedt, Jim Piddock, Reno Wilson. Director: Sebastien Gutierrez.

Mighty Joe Young (1949)—Special effects master Willis O'Brien teamed with protégé Ray Harryhausen to produce this film about a giant GORILLA transplanted from Africa to Hollywood. Cast: Robert Armstrong, Terry Moore, Ben Johnson, Frank McHugh. Director: Ernest Schoedsack.

Mighty Joe Young (1998)—A better than average remake of the 1949 giant GORILLA classic, incorporating an environmentalist moral without intrusive preaching. Cast: Charlize Theron, Bill Paxton, Rade Serbedzija, Naveen Andrews, David Paymer. Director: Ron Underwood.

Mighty Peking Man (1977)—This unintentional laugh riot sends hunters in search of an unknown Himalayan HOMINID and his blond wild-woman girlfriend. Cast: Danny Lee, Evelyne Kraft, Hsiao Yau, Ku Feng. Director: Ho Meng-Hua.

Moby Dick (1930)—The first film version of Herman Melville's classic, depicting an obsessed man's pursuit of a giant albino sperm whale. Cast: John Barrymore, Joan Bennett, Lloyd Hughes, Noble Johnson. Director: Lloyd Bacon.

Moby Dick (1956)—The most famous big-screen treatment of Captain Ahab's disastrous obsession. Cast: Gregory Peck, Richard Basehart, Leo Gena, Harry Andrews. Director: John Huston.

Moby Dick (1998)—The Melville classic receives fair treatment in this made-for-TV version of the giant whale's saga. Cast: Patrick Stewart, Henry Thomas, Bruce Spence, Hugh Keays-Byrne. Director: Franc Roddam.

Monster from Green Hell (1957)—Giant wasps imperil members of an African safari. The gimmicky introduction of color footage in the final reel fails to salvage a lackluster script. Cast: Jim Davis, Barbara Turner, Eduardo Ciannelli. Director: Kenneth Crane.

Monster from the Ocean Floor (1954)—A giant cyclopean OCTOPUS rises off the Mexican coast to terrorize mankind. Cast: Anne Kimball, Stuart Wade, Wyott Ordung. Director: Wyott Ordung.

The Monster of Piedras Blancas (1958)—A lonely lighthouse keeper's offerings of food fail to placate a pelagic head-hunting LIZARD MAN. Cast: Les Tremayne, Forrest Lewis. Director: Irvin Berwick.

Monster on the Campus (1959)—Contact with a preserved COELACANTH causes deadly "prehistoric" reversion in humans and animals alike. Cast: Arthur Franz, Joanna Moore, Judson Pratt, Troy Donahue. Director: Jack Arnold.

El Monstruo de los volcanes (1963) — A hairy HOMINID with hypnotic powers prowls the mountains of Mexico. Cast: Armando Acosta, Victor Alcocer, Magdaleno Barba, José Chávez. Director: Jaime Salvador.

Mothman (2000) — West Virginia's MOTHMAN received its first big-screen treatment in this feature described by its cinematographer as "a blend of comedy, drama, science-fiction and horror." Cast: Edward Schofield, Douglas Langdale, Jill McLean, Vince Campbell. Director: Douglas Tennapel.

The Mothman Prophecies (2002) — Little of JOHN KEEL'S original study remains in this fictional treatment, as a barely-glimpsed MOTHMAN plays telephone pranks and warns of impending disaster. Cast: Richard Gere, Debra Messing, Laura Linney, David Eigenberg. Director: Mark Pellington.

My Friend the Yeti (2001) — A German made-for-TV feature in which the lead player befriends a YETI. Cast: Oliver Stokowski, Ines Nieri, Sophie von Kessel, Peter Rühring. Director: Thorsten Schmidt.

Mysterious Island (1961) — Most of the oversized creatures in this cinematic sequel to *20,000 Leagues under the Sea* are manmade, but special effects wizard Ray Harryhausen provides an epic giant cephalopod for the finale. Cast: Michael Craig, Joan Greenwood, Michael Callan, Gary Merrill, Herbert Lom. Director: Cy Endfield.

The Mysterious Monsters (1975) — A documentary covering BIGFOOT, YETI and NESSIE includes psychic readings and eyewitness testimony elicited under hypnosis. Narrator: Peter Graves. Director: Robert Guenette.

The Neptune Factor (1973) — Gigantic FISH figure briefly in this lukewarm story of a deep-sea rescue mission gone awry. Cast: Ben Gazzara, Yvette Memieux, Walter Pidgeon, Ernest Borgnine. Director: Daniel Petrie.

Nessie, the Monster of Loch Ness (1985) — An obscure German "thriller" sends monster-hunters in search of NESSIE. Cast: Gerd Duwner, Christian Hanft, Ulli Kinalzik, Tobias Meister. Director: Rudolf Zehetgruber.

New Alcatraz (2002) — While building a new maximum-security prison in Antarctica, construction workers revive a giant prehistoric SNAKE and mayhem ensues. (Alternate title: *Boa*) Cast: Dean Cain, Elizabeth Lackey, Mark Sheppard, Dean Biasucci, Craig Wasson. Director: Philip Roth.

Night of the Demon (1980) — College students investigating BIGFOOT'S link to "countless deaths" stumble into a black magic ritual. Cast: Joy Allen, Bob Collins, Michael Cutt, Shane Dixon. Director: James Wasson.

Night of the Howling Beast (1975) — YETI tangles with a werewolf in this forgettable Spanish horror film. Cast: Jacinto Molina, Grace Mills, Silvia Sola, Gil Vidal. Director: Miguel Iglesias Bonns.

Nightwing (1979) — Vampire BATS invade the U.S. Southwest from Mexico, at a time when none were acknowledged north of the Rio Grande. (Today, their presence is scientifically recognized.)

Cast: David Warner, Nick Mancuso, Kathryn Harold, Strother Martin. Director: Arthur Hiller.

Octopus (1998) — A huge OCTOPUS threatens mankind in this Japanese horror film. Cast: Miyako Maeda, Kakinuma Takeshi, Kiyomi Ito, Ooki Hitomi. Director: Gou Suzuki.

Octopus 2: River of Fear (2002) — A giant OCTOPUS disrupts life along New York City's East River, in this film with no connection to *Octopus* above. Cast: Michael Burke, Meredith Norton, Frederic Lehne, John Thaddeus. Director: Yossi Wein.

Orca (1977) — A super-intelligent killer whale seeks vengeance for the wanton slaying of its mate and unborn offspring by a money-hungry fishing crew. Cast: Richard Harris, Keenan Wynn, Will Sampson, Bo Derek, Robert Carradine, Charlotte Rampling. Director: Michael Anderson.

The People That Time Forgot (1977) — Yet another low-budget treatment of an Edgar Rice Burroughs adventure featuring cave men and living DINOSAURS. Cast: Doug McClure, Patrick Wayne, Sarah Douglas, Thorley Walters. Director: Kevin Connor.

Prehysteria (1993) — A clutch of prehistoric eggs hatches in modern times, disgorging miniature DINOSAURS that lead a youth and his family into unexpected adventures. Cast: Crett Cullen, Colleen Morris, Samantha Mills, Austin O'Brien. Directors: Albert and Charles Band.

Prehysteria 2 (1994) — The midget DINOSAURS return in this sequel, helping their human friend avoid an undeserved trip to military school. Cast: Jennifer Harte, Dean Schofield, Bettye Ackerman, Greg Lewis. Director: Albert Band.

Prehysteria 3 (1995) — The sight gags start to wear thin in these further adventures of miniature DINOSAURS and their young human friends. Cast: Whitney Anderson, Fred Willard, Pam Matteson, Dave Buzzotta. Director: David DeCoteau.

The Private Life of Sherlock Holmes (1970) — England's most famous fictional sleuth tracks NESSIE in one segment of this episodic film. Cast: Robert Stephens, Colin Blakely, Genevieve Page, Christopher Lee, Irene Handl, Stanley Holloway. Director: Billy Wilder.

Q (1982) — Quetzelcoatl, the flying reptile god of the Aztecs, visits modern New York City to feed on humans and lay its eggs. Cast: Michael Moriarty, David Carradine, Candy Clark, Richard Roundtree, James Dixon. Director: Larry Cohen.

Razorback (1983) — A giant hog rampages through the Australian Outback in a film much stronger than its premise might suggest. Cast: Gregory Harrison, Arkie Whiteley, Bill Kerr, Chris Haywood. Director: Russell Mulcahy.

Reap the Wild Wind (1942) — A GIANT SQUID provides the surprising climax for this drama of 19th-century salvage divers. Cast: John Wayne, Ray Milland, Raymond Massey, Paulette Goddard, Robert Preston, Susan Hayward. Director: Cecil B. DeMille.

Reign of Fire (2002) — Construction workers in London unearth a female DRAGON, whose offspring terrorize mankind and inaugurate a new Dark Age. Cast: Christian Bale, Matthew McConaughey, Izabella Scorupco, Gerard Butler, Scott Moutter. Director: Rob Bowman.

The Relic (1996) — A reptilian monster accidentally imported from South America wreaks havoc in Chicago's Field Museum. Cast: Tom Sizemore, Penelope Ann Miller, James Whitmore. Director: Peter Hyams.

Reptilicus (1962) — A Scandinavian oil-drilling crew unearths a piece of frozen prehistoric flesh, which soon grows into a huge DINOSAUR with corrosive saliva. Cast: Carl Ottoson, Marla Behrens, Mimi Heinrich. Director: Sidney Pink.

Return of the Ape Man (1944) — Scientists resuscitate a NEANDERTAL MAN, who promptly runs amok. Cast: Bela Lugosi, John Carradine. Director: Phil Rosen.

Return to Boggy Creek (1978) — The FOUKE MONSTER returns, sans documentary format, in this low-budget feature unconnected to the Boggy Creek films of Charles Pierce. Cast: Dawn Wells, Dana Plato, David Soviesk, Marcus Claudel. Director: Tom Moore.

Return to Loch Ness (1998) — This made-for-TV documentary chronicles the 1997 expedition led by ROBERT RINES. Director: Kirk Wolfinger.

Return to the Lost World (1992) — Professor Challenger tries again in this Canadian sequel-of-sorts to Arthur Conan Doyle's classic tale of living DINOSAURS. Cast: John Rhys-Davies, Tamara Gorski, Eric McCormack, Darren Mercer. Director: Timothy Bond.

Revenge of Bigfoot (1979) — BIGFOOT offers a lesson in tolerance when he stops a racist bully from running an Indian out of town. Cast: Rory Calhoun, Mike Hackworth, T. Dan Hopkins, Patricia Kane. Director: Harry Thompson.

Revenge of the Creature (1955) — Scientists revisit the Amazon jungle and capture the prehistoric "gill man" in this sequel to *Creature from the Black Lagoon*. Transporting him to Florida isn't the best idea they ever had. Cast: John Agar, Lori Nelson, John Bromfield, Clint Eastwood. Director: Jack Arnold.

Rodan (1956) — Japanese miners accidentally wake huge PTEROSAURS from suspended animation, with predictable disastrous results. The U.S. version includes stock footage on the dangers of radioactive experiments not seen in the original. Cast: Kenji Sahara, Yumi Shirakawa, Akihiko Hirata, Akio Kobori. Director: Ishirô Honda.

Sam and Max Hit the Road (1993) — Two hard-luck private eyes are called to investigate after BIGFOOT and a giraffe-necked girl disappear from a freak show. Cast: Bill Farmer, Nick Jameson, Marsha Clark, Denny Delk. Directors: Sean Clark, Michael Stemmle.

Sasquatch (2003) see *The Untold*

Sasquatch Hunters (1997) — A comic "mockumentary" follows hapless hunters on the trail of BIGFOOT. Cast: John McDermott, Paul Reasbeck, Melinda Messenger, David Richmond. Director: Marc Messenger.

Sasquatch Odyssey: The Hunt for Bigfoot (1999) — This made-for-TV documentary features interviews with BIGFOOT hunters PETER BYRNE, JOHN GREEN, GROVER KRANTZ and RENÉ DAHINDEN. Director: Peter von Puttkamper.

Sasquatch, the Legend of Bigfoot (1978) — A group of forest campers discover that BIGFOOT is real. Cast: George Lauris, Steve Boergadine, Jim Bradford, Ken Kenzle. Director: Ed Raggozino.

Schlock (1973) — A BIGFOOT-type "missing link" falls in love with a blind girl who thinks he is a giant dog. Cast: John Landis, Saul Kahan, Joseph Piantadosi, Eliza Roberts, JOHN CHAMBERS. Director: John Landis.

Search for the Mothman (2002) — This made-for-TV documentary, written and directed by David Grabias, was plainly inspired by the theatrical release of *The Mothman Prophecies*.

Shark Attack 3: Megalodon (2002) — The latest in a "series" of unconnected horror films pits scientists against a living CARCHARODON MEGALODON. Cast: John Barrowman, Jenny McShane, Ryan Cutrona, George Stanchev. Director: David Worth.

She Creature see *Mermaid Chronicles*

Shriek of the Mutilated (1974) — College students tracking BIGFOOT fall prey to a madman in a MONKEY suit, with low-budget bloodshed resulting. Cast: Alan Brock, Jennifer Stock, Dawn Ellis, Michael Harris. Director: Michael Findlay.

Six Million Dollar Man: The Secret of Bigfoot (1975) — A made-for-TV feature spun off from the popular sci-fi series pits America's quasi-robotical man against BIGFOOT. Cast: Lee Majors, Richard Anderson, André the Giant, Hank Brandt. Director: Alan Crosland.

Skullduggery (1970) — Researchers pursue mystery HOMINIDS (the "Tropi") in New Guinea. Cast: Burt Reynolds, Susan Clark, Robert Carmel, Paul Hubschmid. Director: Gordon Douglas.

The Snow Creature (1954) — A captive YETI escapes and leads pursuers on an ambling chase through the sewers of an American city. Even the Snowman looks bored. Cast: Paul Langton, Leslie Denison. Director: W. Lee Wilder.

Snowbeast (1977) — An albino BIGFOOT terrorizes victims at a ski resort in this made-for-TV "thriller." Cast: Bo Svenson, Yvette Mimieux, Robert Logan, Clint Walker, Sylvia Sidney. Director: Herb Wallerstein.

Son of Godzilla (1967) — This eighth installment of the Japanese film series finds living DINOSAUR Godzilla defending his/her offspring from a giant SPIDER and huge praying mantises on a South Pacific island. Cast: Tadao Takashima, Akira Kubo, Beverly Maeda, Akihiko Hirata. Director: Jun Fukuda.

Son of Kong (1933) — The greedy showman from *King Kong* revisits Skull Island in search of another giant GORILLA, but learns the error of his ways. Cast: Robert Armstrong, Helen Mack, Victor Wong, John Marston, Frank Reicher. Director: Ernest Schoedsack.

Spasms (1983) — A PYTHON-sized venomous SNAKE (whose victims literally explode) is captured on a remote island and transported to a U.S. college for study, where it soon escapes. Cast: Peter Fonda, Oliver Reed, Kerrie Keane, Al Waxman. Director: William Fruet.

Special Investigations: Mothman (1996) — This short documentary links West Virginia's MOTHMAN to the "Mad Gasser" of Mattoon, Illinois and UFOlogy's Men in Black — all in 29 minutes! Cast: Sam Summerville, Cecil Lawson, Tom Byron, Linda Denton. Director: Tom Byron.

Splash (1984) — An alluring MERBEING comes ashore on Manhattan in this popular romantic comedy. Cast: Tom Hanks, Daryl

Hannah, Eugene Levy, John Candy, Dody Goodman. Director: Ron Howard.

Tentacles (1977)—A stellar cast flounders in this Italian feature about a giant OCTOPUS. Cast: John Huston, Shelley Winters, Henry Fonda, Bo Hopkins. Director: Ovidio Assontis.

They Call Him Sasquatch (200-)—This comic/adventure film, allegedly completed in November 2002, had not been released at press time. Cast: Neal McDonough, Tom Bresnahan, Warren Berlinger, Garry Marshal. Director: David Venghaus Jr.

To Catch a Yeti (1993)—The emphasis is solidly on "cute" in this made-for-cable children's film about a hunter's quest for YETI and the kids who intervene. Cast: Meat Loaf, Chantellese Kent, Jeff Moser, Rick Howland, Jim Gordon, Leigh Lewis. Director: Bob Keen.

Tremors (1990)—Subterranean predators stalk the residents of a small desert town in this above-average homage to the Big Bug genre films of yesteryear. Cast: Kevin Bacon, Fred Ward, Finn Carter, Michael Gross, Reba McEntire, Victor Wong. Director: Ron Underwood.

Tremors II: Aftershocks (1995)—Prehistoric "graboids" from the original film return and evolve into a new, more mobile form of predator. Cast: Fred Ward, Christopher Gartin, Michael Gross, Helen Shaver, Marcelo Tubert. Director: S.S. Wilson.

Tremors 3: Back to Perfection (2001)—The dreaded "graboids" mutate once again, this time into flying "ass-blasters." Cast: Michael Gross, Shawn Christian, Susan Chuang, Ariana Richards. Director: S.S. Wilson.

Tremors 4 (2003)—Prehistoric "graboids" are on the prowl again, this time in a 19th-century prequel to the original feature. Cast: Michael Gross, Sara Botsford, John Dixon, Brent Roam. Director: S.S. Wilson.

Trog (1970)—Spelunkers discover a prehistoric "troglodyte" and bring it to the surface with disastrous results for all concerned. Cast: Joan Crawford, Michael Gough, Bernard Kay, Kim Braden. Director: Freddie Francis.

20,000 Leagues under the Sea (1916)—A groundbreaking silent version of Jules Verne's undersea novel, merging elements of the sequel (*Mysterious Island*) to chart the course of Captain Nemo's life at odds with society and submarine cryptids. Cast: Louis Alexander, Curtis Benton, Wallace Clarke, Allan Holubar. Director: Stuart Paton.

20,000 Leagues under the Sea (1954)—The Disney version of Jules Verne's sci-fi novel is still most famous for its sequence of a GIANT SQUID attacking Captain Nemo's futuristic submarine. Cast: Kirk Douglas, James Mason, Paul Lukas, Peter Lorre. Director: Richard Fleischer.

Twenty Thousand Leagues under the Sea (1996)—An adequate made-for-TV retelling of the Jules Verne story, including episodes with undersea cryptids. Cast: Michael Caine, Patrick Dempsey, Mia Sara, Adewale Akinnouye-Agbaje. Director: Rod Hardy.

Twenty Thousand Leagues under the Sea (1997)—Yet another made-for-TV version of Captain Nemo's undersea adventures. Cast: Richard Crenna, Ben Cross, Julie Cox, Michael Jayston. Director: Michael Anderson.

Two Lost Worlds (1951)—After a run-in with pirates, the passengers and crew of a 19th-century clipper ship are stranded on an island where DINOSAURS survive. Cast: James Arness, Kasey Rogers, Bill Kennedy, Gloria Petroff. Director: Norman Dawn.

Unknown Island (1948)—DINOSAURS survive and threaten explorers on a South Pacific island. Cast: Virginia Grey, Philip Reed, Richard Denning, Barton MacLane. Director: Jack Bernhard.

Untamed Women (1952)—An American bomber pilot is found adrift at sea in World War II. Using truth serum, doctors extract his tale of crash-landing on an island occupied by DINOSAURS and cave women. Cast: Mikel Conrad, Doris Merrick, Richard Monahan, Morgan Jones. Director: W. Merle Connell.

The Untold (2002)—Chaotic camera work and editing further confuse this muddled direct-to-video tale of a curiously bald BIGFOOT seeking revenge for the death of its mate. (Alternate title: *Sasquatch*) Cast: Lance Henriksen, Andrea Roth, Russell Ferrier, Philip Granger. Director: Jonas Quastel.

Up from the Depths (1979)—A tired plot is rehashed in this ill-conceived remake of *Creature from the Haunted Sea*. Cast: Sam Bottoms, Susanne Reed, Virgil Frye. Director: Charles Griffith.

Valley of Gwangi (1969)—Special effects master Ray Harryhausen pulls out all the stops in this story of cowboys vs. DINOSAURS in Mexico. Cast: James Franciscus, Richard Carlson, Gila Golan. Director: Jim O'Connolly.

Varan, the Unbelievable (1958)—A living DINOSAUR (strangely called Obaki, despite the title) emerges from hibernation to menace a U.S.-Japanese scientific team in the Pacific, before laying siege to Tokyo. Cast: Jerry Baerwitz, Myron Healey, Tsuroko Kobayashi. Directors: Ishirô Honda, Jerry Baerwitz.

Viking Women and the Sea Serpent (1957)—A group of lonely Viking women build a ship and sail off in search of their missing husbands. The SEA SERPENT shows up late, and only briefly. Cast: Abby Dalton, Susan Cabot, Bradford Jackson, June Kenney. Director: Roger Corman.

Voyage to the Bottom of the Sea (1961)—A GIANT SQUID and huge OCTOPUS briefly attempt to enliven this tepid sci-fi film, which inspired a later television series. Cast: Walter Pidgeon, Joan Fontaine, Robert Sterling, Barbara Eden, Michael Ansara, Frankie Avalon, Peter Lorre. Director: Irwin Allen.

War of the Colossal Beast (1958)—This preposterous tale of an army officer grown huge after exposure to radiation takes an even stranger turn when he is attacked by a giant SNAKE of unexplained origin. Cast: Sally Fraser, Roger Pace, Russ Bender. Director: Burt Gordon.

White Buffalo (1977)—Wild Bill Hickock and Chief Crazy Horse join forces to kill a giant white bison on the 19th-century American frontier. Cast: Charles Bronson, Kim Novak, Will Sampson, Clint Walker, Jack Warden, Stuart Whitman, Slim Pickens, John Carradine. Director: J. Lee Thompson.

White Pongo (1945)—A blond GORILLA plays the "missing link" in this classic turkey. Cast: Richard Fraser, Lionel Royce, Al Ebon, Gordon Richards. Director: Sam Newfield.

Wolfen (1981)—An unknown species of super-intelligent urban WOLVES devour the homeless and anyone who suspects their existence in New York City. Cast: Albert Finney, Diane Venora, Gregory Hines, Tommy Noonan, Edward James Olmos, Dick O'Neill. Director: Michael Wadleigh.

Yeti—Cry of the Snowman (2000)—The YETI gets another send-up in this feature made for French TV. Cast: Nar Banhadur, Pasang Chilime, Charles Maquignon. Director: Jérôme-Cecil Auffret.

Yeti—il gigante del 20. secolo (1977)—A young Italian woman befriends a 30-foot YETI in this Italian "fantascientific" film, shot primarily in Canada. Cast: Antonella Interlenghi, Mimmo Crao, Jim Sullivan, Tony Kendall. Director: Gianfranco Parolini.

Yongary—Monster from the Deep (1969)—This Korean entry to the sci-fi genre features a living DINOSAUR with a suspicious resemblance to Godzilla. Cast: Yeong-il Oh, Jeong-im Nam, Sun-jae Lee, Moon Kang. Director: Kim Ki-duk.

The Young Man and Moby Dick (1978)—A Czech cast and director try their hands at retelling Herman Melville's tale of Captain Ahab and the great albino whale. Cast: Ivan Vyskocil, Eduard Cupák, Jana Brejchová, Zlata Adamovská. Director: Jacomil Jires.

Appendix C

Cryptozoology on Television

The following television series featured cryptozoological themes. Individual episodes are listed when a series itself was only occasionally related to cryptozoology. Unless otherwise noted, all series listed were produced and aired initially in the United States.

Bigfoot and Wildboy (1977)—This adventure series follows the adventures of an orphan ("Wildboy") raised by BIGFOOT in the Pacific Northwest wilderness. A total of 20 half-hour episodes were aired. Cast: Ray Young, Joseph Butcher, Monika Ramirez, Yvonne Delgado. Directors: Donald Boyle, Leslie Martinson.

Dinotopia (2002)—This miniseries follows the adventures of two brothers marooned on a "hidden continent" where humans and DINOSAURS coexist. Cast: Erik von Detten, Shiloh Strong, Michael Brandon, Georgina Rylance. Directors: Mario Azzopardi, David Winning.

Eerie, Indiana (1991-92)—BIGFOOT scavenges from garbage cans during the credit sequence of this short-lived series about an Hoosier town with roots in the Twilight Zone, but otherwise no cryptids appear in the 19 episodes broadcast. Cast: Omri Katz, Justin Shenkarow, Julie Condra, Francis Guinan. Directors: Bob Balaban, Greg Beeman.

Freaky Links (2000-01)—Low ratings doomed this series about young people who investigate weird phenomena and post their findings to an Internet website. Advance publicity included a hoaxed THUNDERBIRD photo that appeared in *Fortean Times* magazine. Cast: Ethan Embry, Lisa Sheridan, Karim Prince, Lizette Carrion. Directors: David Barrett, Stephen Cragg. Cryptic episodes include:

"COELACANTH This!" (27 October 2000)—A 150-year series of deaths is traced to a living PTEROSAUR.

"Desert Squid! Myth or Legend?" (3 November 2000)—The team visits New Mexico to expose a mythic creature.

"Sunrise at Sunset Lake" (15 June 2001)—The investigators pursue Florida's SKUNK APE.

"Subject: The Final Word" (22 June 2001)—A convicted killer blames his crime on a flying monster.

Harry and the Hendersons (1991-93)—Spinning off from the popular film of the same title (See Appendix B), this series follows the misadventures of the Henderson family and their pet BIGFOOT. Cast: Bruce Davidson, Molly Cheek, Carol-Ann Potter, Zachary Bostrum. Directors: Don Amendolia, Scott Baio.

Land of the Lost (1974-77)—Three members of the Marshall family are sucked through a time warp to a world dominated by DINOSAURS and reptilian HOMINIDS called "Sleestaks." The series included 43 half-hour episodes. Cast: Spencer Milligan, Wesley Eure, Kathy Coleman, Philip Paley. Directors: Rick Bennewitz, Bob Lally.

Land of the Lost (1991)—Advanced special effects highlight this revived series, as the Porter family drives through a time warp into a prehistoric realm of living DINOSAURS and cave men. Cast: Timothy Bottoms, Tom Allard, Shannon Day, Jennifer Drugan. Directors: Anthony Bona, John Buechler.

The Lost World (1999-2002)—Filmed in Canada, this spin-off from the 1999 made-for-TV movie leaves Professor Challenger's expedition stranded in a world of living DINOSAURS and buxom cave women. Cast: Peter McCauley, Rachel Blakely, David Orth, Jennifer O'Dell, William Snow. Directors: Colin Budds, Richard Franklin.

Mysterious Encounters (2003-04)—This series of half-hour quasi-documentaries on the Outdoor Life Channel follow cryptozoologist AUTUMN WILLIAMS in search of unknown HOMINIDS across the U.S.

Tremors (2003-04)—The Sci-Fi Channel produced this small-screen adaptation of the popular film series (See Appendix B), pursuing the further adventures of humans and "graboids" in Perfection Valley, Nevada. Cast: Michael Gross, Victor Browne, Marcia Strassman, Gladise Jiminez. Directors: P.J. Pesce, Whitney Ransick.

Uncle Jack and the Loch Ness Monster (1991)—This British series starring NESSIE and a human friend combined elements of comedy, fantasy and mystery. Cast: Paul Jones, Fenella Fielding, Vivian Pickles.

Voyage to the Bottom of the Sea (1964-68)—Irwin Allen's film of the same title (see Appendix B) did well enough to warrant this spin-off series, dispatching the submarine *Seaview* on sundry fantastic adventures. Seventeen of the 110 episodes featuring cryptozoological themes are described below, with their original air dates. Cast: Richard Basehart, David Hedison, Del Monroe, Paul Trinka. Directors: Irwin Allen, Jus Addiss. Cryptic episodes include:

"The Ghost of Moby Dick" (14 December 1964)—The *Seaview* pursues a giant whale.

"Secret of the Loch" (5 April 1965)—The crew tackles NESSIE after a submarine lab is destroyed at Loch Ness.

"Jonah and the Whale" (19 September 1965)—More giant whales get up to mysterious antics.

"Terror on DINOSAUR Island" (26 December 1965)—Footage from Allen's film *The Lost World* (1960) is recycled here.

"Deadly Creature Below" (9 January 1966) — A sea monster threatens the crew.

"The Monster's Web" (27 February 1966) — A giant undersea SPIDER snares the *Seaview*.

"Monster from the Inferno" (18 September 1966) — Another sea monster on a rampage.

"Night of Terror" (9 October 1966) — As if one island inhabited by living DINOSAURS wasn't enough ....

"Thing from Inner Space" (6 November 1966) — Another sea monster threatens the crew.

"The Creature" (1 January 1967) — It's hard to tell the sea monsters apart without a program in Season Three.

"The Fossilmen" (22 January 1967) — Prehistoric men jeopardize the *Seaview*.

"The Mermaid" (29 January 1967) — A close encounter of the fishy kind enlivens this episode.

"No Escape from Death" (19 February 1967) — Divers are swallowed by a giant JELLYFISH.

"Doomsday Island" (26 February 1967) — A giant egg hatches aboard the *Seaview* and chaos ensues.

"Fatal Cargo" (5 November 1967) — An albino GORILLA hitches a ride on the *Seaview*.

"Deadly Amphibians" (24 December 1967) — This time around, the sea monster is half-man, half-fish.

"The ABOMINABLE SNOWMAN" (4 February 1968) — While investigating a "tropical paradise" in the Antarctic, the *Seaview* picks up a hitchhiking YETI.

"Secret of the Deep" (11 December 1968) — Yet another sea monster threatens the intrepid crew.

The X-Files (1993–2002) — Most of the 202 episodes in this popular series featured FBI agents in pursuit UFOs, alien kidnappers and government conspiracies, but a handful showcased cryptozoological themes. Cast: David Duchovny, Gillian Anderson, Mitch Pileggi, Robert Patrick. Director: Chris Carter. Cryptic episodes include:

"The JERSEY DEVIL" (8 October 1993) — Primitive forest-dwelling humans prowl the outskirts of Atlantic City in this episode bearing no resemblance to the original legend.

"Darkness Falls" (15 April 1994) — Predatory prehistoric insects emerge from trees cut by loggers.

"Quagmire" (3 May 1996) — A LAKE MONSTER called Big Blue is blamed for deaths around HEUVELMANS Lake.

"Detour" (23 November 1997) — En route to an FBI conference, the agents are sidetracked by humanoid predators.

"Patience" (19 November 2000) — A creature half-man and half-BAT unaccountably waits 40 years to stalk the slayers of its mate.

Appendix D

Cryptozoological Fiction

Cryptozoological themes are fairly common in the literature of fantasy, horror and science fiction. A volume longer than the work in hand would be required to list all novels containing any mention of SEA SERPENTS, LAKE MONSTERS, living DINOSAURS or other cryptids. Accordingly, the list below is merely a representative sampling of titles, limited to stories set on Earth during real-life historical times, wherein cryptids or the search for unknown animals are major themes; (J) indicates a work intended for juvenile readers. Plot summaries were unavailable for some titles.

Abels, Hariette. *The Creature of Saxony Woods* (Chicago: Childrens Press, 1979). Children on summer vacation meet a SASQUATCH family. (J)

Adams, Samuel. *The Flying Death* (Landisville, PA: Arment Biological Press, 1908). Adams expands a short story of the same title in this romantic adventure with a living PTEROSAUR as the title character.

Alten, Steve. *Meg: A Novel of Deep Terror* (New York: Doubleday, 1997). A surviving CARCHARODON MEGALODON devours everyone in sight, while scientists try to devise a safe aquarium display for their catch.

_____. *The Trench* (New York: Kensington, 2000). The giant SHARK from *Meg* meets prehistoric reptiles in the Pacific Ocean's abysmal depths.

Althea. *Desmond Goes to Scotland* (Windermere, FL: Rourke Publications, 1981). A young adventurer meets NESSIE. (J)

Anderson, Ken. *Nessie and the Little Blind Boy of Loch Ness* (Nashua, NH: Laughter Publications, 1992). NESSIE inspires a visually handicapped child. (J)

Arment, Chad (ed.). *Strange Creatures: Classic Cryptofiction* (Landisville, PA: Arment Biological Press, 2000). The first in a series of online anthologies collects 14 short stories with cryptozoological themes, by authors including Stephen Vincent Benét, E.F. Benson, Ambrose Bierce, Arthur Conan Doyle, William Hope Hodgson, Willis Knapp Jones, Rudyard Kipling, Jack London and H.G. Wells.

_____. *Strange Creatures II: Chambers' Works* (Landisville, PA: Arment Biological Press, 2000). Arment's second anthology presents two novels by Robert W. Chambers, *In Search of the Unknown* (1904) and *Police!!!* (1915).

_____. *Strange Creatures III: Pulp Cryptids* (Landisville, PA: Arment Biological Press, 2000). This time around, Arment includes 12 short stories from various pulp magazines, including works by E.F. Benson, Wardon Allan Curtis, Richard Dehan, Arthur Conan Doyle, Lord Dunsany, William Hope Hodgson, Charles John Cutcliffe Hyne, Fitz James O'Brien, Will A. Page and H.G. Wells.

_____. *Strange Creatures IV: False Shadows* (Landisville, PA: Arment Biological Press, 2000). A different take on cryptozoology presents nine tales of mistaken identity, misidentification and outright HOAXES from authors Jane Barlow, Frank Welles Calkins, Bret Harte, William Sidney Rossiter, Robert Service, Frank Richard Stockton, Edward William Thomson and H.G. Wells.

_____. *Strange Creatures V: Critters Great and Small* (Landisville, PA: Arment Biological Press, 2000). True to its title, the nine stories in this volume cover beasts ranging in size from insects to SEA SERPENTS. The authors include Charles J. Finger, Alexander Harvey, William Fryer Harvey, Edward HeronAllen, Capt. Henry Toke Munn, Planché, Alfred Lord Tennyson and Fred M. White.

_____. *Strange Creatures VI: Double Take* (Landisville, PA: Arment Biological Press, 2001). In this volume, the 12 selections include both cryptozoological tales and "peripheral" stories of HOAXES and frauds. Authors include Samuel Hopkins Adams, Hans Christian Andersen, John Buchan, F. Norreys Connell, Charles De Kay, E. Erckmann (with A. Chatrain), W.W. Jacobs, Robert S. Lemmon, John M. Oskison, Henry Wallace Phillips, Sax Rohmer and Thomas Charles Sloane.

_____. *Strange Creatures VII: Wildmen and Wendigos* (Landisville, PA: Arment Biological Press, 2001). The eight tales in this series anthology focus on unknown HOMINIDS. Included authors are Algernon Blackwood, Mary Hartwell Catherwood, William Henry Drummond, H.P. Lovecraft and Arthur Machen.

_____. *Strange Creatures IX: Fables & Quirks* (Landisville, PA: Arment Biological Press, 2002). Editor Arment counts this volume as an "odd one" in the series, following an anthology devoted to cryptobotany (Vol. VIII) and focused this time on legendary beasts. Authors of the seven tales include Algernon Blackwood, Agnes Grozier Herbertson, William Hope Hodgson, the Rev. Dr. Jamieson, Lake Shore Kearney, A. Merritt and H.G. Wells.

_____. *Strange Creatures X: Amazing Indeed* (Landisville, PA: Arment Biological Press, 2002). Twelve cryptotales from the pulp magazine *Amazing Stories* are showcases in this volume. Authors include Anthos, Hal Grant, David H. Keller, Irvin Lester (with Fletcher Pratt), Bob Olsen, Jul. Regis, Phil Robinson, Curt Siodmak, H. de Vere Stacpoole, H. Tukeman and A. Hyatt Verrill.

Bateman, John. *Loch Ness Conspiracy* (New York: R. Speller & Sons, 1987).

Bateman, Teresa. *The Merbaby* (New York: Holiday House, 2001). Fishermen discover evidence of a MERBEING. (J)

Bear, Greg. *Dinosaur Summer* (New York: Warner Books, 1998). Decades after the discovery of living DINOSAURS in Arthur

Conan Doyle's *Lost World*, an expedition returns giant zoo specimens to their native South American habitat.

Beelart, J. Hector. *The Great Sasquatch Conspiracy, or Blood on Bigfoot Mountain* (Hillsboro, OR: Western Bigfoot Society, 1998). Published as a limited- edition fund-raiser for the WESTERN BIGFOOT SOCIETY, this novel explores the problems faced by hunters who procure a SASQUATCH specimen.

Benchley, Peter. *Beast* (New York: Random House, 1993). Author Benchley follows his successful *Jaws* formula in this tale of a GIANT SQUID plaguing Bermuda fishermen. The book spawned a TV miniseries, *The Beast* (See Appendix B).

Biro, Val. *Gumdrop and the Monster* (London: Hodder & Stoughton Children's Books, 1980). An adventure set at Loch Ness. (J)

Bogner, Norman. *Snowman* (New York: Dell, 1978). A huge, predatory YETI proves impervious to normal weapons. Boston, John. *Naked Came the Sasquatch* (New York: TSR, 1993). A newspaper editors tries to solve a series of grisly murders in this comic mystery.

Brassey, Richard. *Nessie, the Loch Ness Monster* (London: Orion, 1996). (J)

Brumpton, Keith. *Look Out, Loch Ness Monster* (New York: Simon & Schuster, 1992). (J)

Burroughs, Edgar Rice. *At the Earth's Core* (New York: A.C. McClurg, 1913). This novel presents the first tale of Pellucidar, a prehistoric kingdom inside the hollow Earth where DINOSAURS and primitive humans survive.

_____. *Back to the Stone Age* (New York: Ace Books, 1963). This fourth installment of the Pellucidar series was first serialized in 1937.

_____. *Land of Terror* (New York: Canaveral, 1963). While it was serialized in 1944, the fifth Pellucidar tale did not seek publication in book form while Burroughs was alive.

_____. *The Land That Time Forgot* (New York: Grosset & Dunlap, 1925). This volume includes three short novels about the lost continent of Caprona, somewhere in the South Pacific, where humans, DINOSAURS and a race of winged HOMINIDS vie for survival. Serialized years earlier, the stories include the title piece and two sequels, *The People That Time Forgot* and *Out of Time's Abyss*.

_____. *Pellucidar* (New York: Grosset & Dunlap, 1928). Second installment of the inner-earth series.

_____. *Savage Pellucidar* (New York: Canaveral, 1963). Burroughs initially published the last installment of his inner-Earth series in 1942-44.

_____. *Tanar of Pellucidar* (New York: Canaveral, 1962). The third tale of prehistoric inner Earth, initially serialized in 1930.

_____. *Tarzan at the Earth's Core* (New York: Metropolitan, 1930). Burroughs's most famous character travels from Africa to prehistoric Pellucidar.

_____. *Tarzan the Terrible* (New York: Whitman, 1942). First serialized in 1921, this adventure follows Tarzan of the APES to Pal-ul-don, a secret realm of Africa where DINOSAURS and prehistoric HOMINIDS survive.

Child, Lincoln, and Douglas Preston. *The Relic* (New York: Tor Books, 1996). A voracious South American cryptid stows away in a shipment of unknown plants bound for a U.S. museum, where it soon wreaks bloody havoc.

Conan Doyle, Arthur. *The Lost World* (London: Hodder and Stoughton, 1912). Inspired by conversations with PERCY FAWCETT, Conan Doyle launches a fictional expedition to find living DINOSAURS in the Amazon jungle.

Cooper, John. *Sasquatch* (New York: Scott Foresman, 1980). A wounded BIGFOOT seeks revenge on humans.

Cooper, Susan. *The Boggart and the Monster* (New York: Margaret K. McElderry Books, 1997). A mischievous Scottish spirit, the Boggart, tries to save his cousin NESSIE. (J)

Cotter, John, and Judith Frankle. *Nights with Sasquatch* (New York: Berkley, 1977). The first work of cryptopornography follows the alleged "true story" of a woman kidnapped and impregnated by BIGFOOT.

Crow, Elmay. *Ronny Meets the Sasquatch* (Victoria, B.C.: Crow Publishing, 1972). An adventure with BIGFOOT, illustrated by the author. (J)

Crowe, Ray. *The Bigfoot Bar & Grill* (Portland, OR: The Author, 1991). Veteran researcher RAYMOND CROWE'S short novel about a SASQUATCH who rapes a Washington cocktail waitress was self-published after the original publisher went bankrupt.

Darnton, John. *Neanderthal* (New York: Thorndike Press, 1997). Researchers discover a relict NEANDERTAL colony graced with surprising extrasensory powers.

Dicks, Terrance. *Doctor Who and the Loch Ness Monster* (New York Pinnacle, 1979). A Scottish installment in the venerable British sci-fi series.

Dickson, Jack. *Still Waters* (London: Prowler Gooks Publishing, 2000). An unusual piece of gay erotica set at Loch Ness.

Disney, Walt. *Donald and the Loch Ness Monster: An Adventure in Scotland* (Danbury, CT: Grolier Enterprises, 1992). Disney cartoon character Donald Duck becomes embroiled with NESSIE on a Scottish golfing holiday. (J)

Duquennoy, Jacques. *The Ghosts' Trip to Loch Ness* (San Diego: Harcourt Brace, 1996). Four ghosts travel to visit NESSIE in this English translation of a French novel. (J)

Eldridge, Jim. *Uncle Jack and the Loch Ness Monster* (New York: Red Fox, 1991. (J)

Fisher, Duncan. *That's Just What Happened* (London: Minerva, 1998). An adventure set at Loch Ness. (J)

Foster, Alan Dean. *Dinotopia Lost* (New York: Ace Books, 2002). No good can come of exposing a lost continent where DINOSAURS coexist with humans, as revealed in this sequel to the popular James Gurnsey novels.

Gentle, Gary. *The Lurking* (New York: Charter, 1989). Blood flows freely in this tale of a BIGFOOT-type predator roaming New Jersey's Pine Barrens.

Gramatky, Hardie. *Little Toot and the Loch Ness Monster* (New York: Putnam, 1989). Little Toot, a sentient tugboat, befriends NESSIE. (J)

Gurney, James. *Dinotopia: A World Apart from Time* (New York: Turner Publishing, 1992). Adventurers find a lost continent where living DINOSAURS coexist with human beings.

_____. *Dinotopia: The World Beneath* (New York: HarperCollins, 1999). The sequel presents further adventures of wayfarers in the land where DINOSAURS and humans live in harmony.

Horse, Harry. *The Ogopogo, or, My journey with the Loch Ness Monster* (Loanhead, England: Macdonald, 1983). The author mixes continents and cryptids in this adventure tale. (J)

Hoyle, Fred, and Geoffrey Hoyle. *The Molecule Men* (London: Heinemann, 1971). Two short novels for the price of one, including the title piece and a companion story, "The Monster of Loch Ness."

Hunter, Mollie. *The Kelpie's Pearls* (New York : Harper & Row, 1976). NESSIE makes a guest appearance in this tale of Scottish Highland magic. (J)

_____. *The Mermaid Summer* (New York: HarperCollins, 1988). Scottish MERBEINGS interact with humans ashore. (J)

_____. *A Stranger Came Ashore* (New York: HarperTrophy, 1977). A MERBEING poses as a shipwreck survivor for nefarious reasons. (J)

Hutchinson, Don (ed.). *Northern Frights* (Oakville, Ontario: Mosaic Press, 1995). This horror anthology includes the short story "Sasquatch," by Michael Ames, and several other quasi-cryptozoological selections.

Hyslop, Maitland. *Drummadrochit Dorit Meets Nessie* (London: Pentland, 1996). First in a series recounting a Scottish child's adventures with NESSIE. (J)

_____. *Drummadrochit Dorit, Nessie and the Plane Crash* (London: Pentland, 1996). (J)

_____. *Drummadrochit Dorit and Nessie Save Christmas* (London: Pentland, 1996). (J)

Janney, Rebecca. *Mystery at Loch Ness* (Sisters, OR: Multnomah Fiction, 1997). While visiting a virtual reality exhibit on NESSIE, Christian home-school students travels back in time to Scotland in 1934. (J)

Joyce, John. *Captain Cockle and the Loch Ness Monster* (Dublin: Poolbeg, 1995). (J)

Kenny, Kathryn. *Trixie Belden #25: The Sasquatch Mystery* (Racine, WI: Golden Press/Western, 1979). Part of a long-running mystery series. (J)

Kerr, Philip. *Esau* (New York: Henry Holt, 1997). Discovery of an unknown HOMINID'S skull in the Himalayas sends competing expeditions in search of the first live YETI.

King-Smith, Dick. *The Water Horse* (New York: Crown, 1988). An 8-year-old girl finds a huge egg at Loch Ness, which hatches to reveal NESSIE. (J)

Klement, Jan. *The Creature: Personal Experiences with Bigfoot* (Elgin, PA: Allegheny Press, 1976). The late author's use of a pseudonym is the first clue that this short (70-page) tale of meetings with BIGFOOT in Pennsylvania does not merit its nonfiction label. Improbable events and a complete lack of documentation sink the leaky ship.

Knerr, M.E. *Sasquatch: Monster of the North Woods* (New York: Belmont Tower, 1977).

Konvitz, Jeffrey. *Monster: A tale of Loch Ness* (New York: Ballantine Books, 1982). An attempt to capture NESSIE backfires on the hunters.

Leigh, Julia. *The Hunter* (Sydney, Australia: Penguin Books Australia, 1999). A hunter stalks surviving THYLACINES in Tasmania.

Logan, N.R. *Children of a Lost Spirit: A Tale of Sasquatch, a Tale of Love and Grace* (Mercer Island, WA: Kideko House Books, 1991).

Long, Jeff. *The Descent* (New York: Crown, 1999). War erupts underground as a race of gargoyle-type HOMINIDS threaten human supremacy on Earth.

Maddux, Marlaine. *The Loch: Part 1— Facing the Future* (Houston, TX: Penny-Farthing Press, 2000). First in a series of novels involving NESSIE. (J)

_____. *The Loch: Part 2—The Knowledge Journey* (Houston, TX: Penny-Farthing Press, 2001). The series continues. (J)

_____. *The Loch: Part 3—Discovery* (Houston, TX: Penny-Farthing Press, 2002). (J)

Miller, Warren. *The Black Panther of the Navaho* (Landisville, PA: Arment Biological Press, n.d.). Hunters stalk a mysterious black CAT in Arizona.

Minters, Frances. *Princess Fishtail* (New York: Viking, 2002). A MERBING rescues a drowning surfer. (J)

Montgomery, R.A. *Choose Your Own Adventure #13: The Abominable Snowman* (New York: Bantam, 1982). Readers chart their course through a Himalayan search for YETI. (J)

Murphy, Lee. *Naitaka* (Toronto: Defining Moments, 2002). This second installment of Murphy's crypto-adventure series pits protagonist George Kodiak against a Canadian LAKE MONSTER.

_____. *Where Legends Roam* (Toronto: Defining Moments, 2001). The premiere novel in this series follows cryptozoologist George Kodiak in pursuit of SASQUATCH.

Newsham, Wendy. *The Monster Hunt* (London: H. Hamilton, 1983). Searchers seek NESSIE in Scotland. (J)

Nye, Nicholas. *Return to the Lost World* (New York: Images Booksellers, 1991). Professor Challenger and company revisit Brazil in a belated sequel to Arthur Conan Doyle's *Lost World*.

Page, Jack. *Cavern* (Santa Fe, NM: University of New Mexico Press, 2003). A prehistoric carnivore emerges from the Carlsbad Caverns in this atypical offering from a scholastic publisher.

Pia, Jacklyn. *Woops and Friends* (New York: Vantage Press, 1989). Woops, the "sporting gentleman-mouse of Glasgow," relates his adventures and mishaps in a castle overlooking Loch Ness. (J)

Piper, H. Beam. *Fuzzy Sapiens* (New York: Ace Books, 1964). This novel of unknown HOMINIDS inspired the film *Skullduggery* (See Appendix B).

Popescu, Petru. *Almost Adam* (New York: William Morrow, 1996). Greed and unstable African politics complicate the search for living pithecanthropoids.

Powell, Ann. *Heather Meets the Loch Ness Monster* (Hamilton, Ontario: Wee Giant Press, 1984). (J)

Reese, Michael. *Double Danger, Double Deep* (Southfield, MI: Mars Publishing, 1999). Astronauts find more adventure than relaxation during a Loch Ness holiday.

Roberts, J.R. *Sasquatch Hunt* (New York: Charter, 1983). Sportsmen track BIGFOOT across the Old West in this 21st episode of the "Gunsmith" series.

Rovin, Jeff. *Fatalis* (New York: St. Martin's Press, 2001). SABER-TOOTHED CATS emerge from hidden caverns to prey on humans in modern-day California.

Schofield, Sandy. *Quantum Leap: Loch Ness Leap* (New York: Boulevard Books, 1997). A novelization of the popular TV science fiction series.

Schreiber, Ellen. *Teenage Mermaid* (New York: Katherine Tegen Books, 2003). Follows the adventures of a young MERBEING. (J)

Sheldon, Walter. *The Beast* (New York: Fawcett, 1980). Members of a BIGFOOT-hunting expedition face personal demons while stalking a creature "less than human, larger than life."

Smith, Martin Cruz. *Nightwing* (New York: W.W. Norton, 1977). Decades before science admitted the presence of vampire BATS in the U.S. Southwest, this horror novel tracked their invasion of New Mexico.

Smith, Roland. *Sasquatch* (New York: Hyperion Books, 1998). BIGFOOT finds itself in conflict with humans. (J)

Spruill, Steven. *Hellstone* (Chicago: Playboy Books, 1980). Modern-day Druids use dark rituals to rouse NESSIE for a predatory frenzy.

Steele, Jason. *Shadow Over Loch Ness* (Worthington, OH: Worthington Press, 1990). "Dark and forbidden secrets" are exposed on an adventure tour. (J)

Stine, R.L. *The Abominable Snowman of Pasadena* (New York: Scholastic, 1995). An urban YETI tale. (J)

Tanner, D.L. *Shadow of the Thunderbird* (Booklocker.com, 2002). Funded by the enigmatic Chimaera Foundation, cryptozoologist Ian McQuade tracks THUNDERBIRDS in Pennsylvania's Black Forest.

_____. *Track of the Bigfoot* (Booklocker.com, 2003). This second installment of Tanner's trilogy finds Ian McQuade hunting BIGFOOT from Ohio to Washington State.

_____. *Wake of the Lake Monster* (Booklocker.com, 2005). This finale to the author's trilogy had not been released at press time.

Thompson, Derek. *Timothy and the Loch Ness Monster* (Ilfracombe, England: Stockwell, 1976). (J)

Todd, E.H. *Sasquatch—The Man* (New York: Carlton Press, 1978). This short (63-page) volume follows SASQUATCH through the Canadian wild.

Tremayne, Peter. *The Curse of Loch Ness* (London: Sphere Books, 1979).

Vandersteen, Willy. *The Loch Ness Mystery* (Edinburgh: Intes International, 1999). A children's adventure with NESSIE, translated from Dutch. (J)

Verne, Jules. *Journey to the Center of the Earth* (London: Griffith and Farran, 1872). This was the first English edition of Verne's 1864 novel about an expedition to the Earth's core, where living DINOSAURS survive.

_____. *20,000 Leagues Under the Sea* (London: Sampson Low, Marston, Low and Searle, 1873). Another delayed English publication of Verne's 1869 novel about Capt. Nemo, the submarine *Nautilus*, and GIANT SQUIDS on a rampage.

Wahl, Jan. *S.O.S. Bobomobile* (New York: Delacorte Press, 1973). A young inventor and an aging scientist invent a "bobomobile" to locate NESSIE. (J)

Wallace, Karen. *Uncle Douglas and Aunt Doris Go Loopy* (London: Puffin, 1999). Mysterious adventures at Loch Ness. (J)

Wandelmaier, Roy. *Mystery at Loch Ness* (Malwah, NJ: Troll Associates, 1985). Scottish adventures with NESSIE. (J)

Waterton, Betty. *Quincy Rumpel and the Sasquatch of Phantom Cove* (Toronto: Douglas & McIntyre, 1990). An episode in the Quincy Rumpel series. (J)

Werper, Barton. *Tarzan and the Abominable Snowmen* (Derby, CT: New International Library, 1964). YETIS surface on Kenya's Mount Kilimanjaro and meet Tarzan of the APES.

Wilson, Charles. *Extinct* (New York: Arrow, 1997). Another living *CARCHARODON MEGALODON* surfaces to snack on modern humans.

Yolen, Jane. *The Sea Man* (New York: Philomel Books, 1998). Crewmen aboard a 17th-century sailing ship encounter a MERBEING. (J)

Zindel, Paul. *The Loch* (New York: Hyperion, 1995). Title notwithstanding, this tale of a man-eating PLESIOSAUR and its playful offspring is set in Vermont. (J)

_____. *Night of the Bat* (New York: Hyperion, 2003). A giant BAT terrorizes teenagers and their scientist and their scientist father. (J)

_____. *Raptor* (New York: Hyperion, 1999). Trouble hatches from a DINOSAUR egg, menacing a scientist and his son. (J)

_____. *Reef of Death* (New York: Hyperion, 1999). A man-eating sea monster terrorizes the Australian coastline. (J)

Appendix E
Internet Links

The Internet websites listed below were fully functional in mid–2004, but cyberspace is fluid by definition, and some may have changed addresses or vanished entirely by the time you read these words. The links are grouped by categories, for the reader's convenience. A website's listing here does not certify the accuracy of any information presented therein, nor does it constitute endorsement of any particular group, individual or viewpoint by the author or his publisher.

General information and news

American Monsters
http://www.americanmonsters.com/monsters.html

Anomalies
http://anomalyinfo.com/index.htm#sa00001s

The Anomalist
http://www.anomalist.com/

Beast Watch U.K.
http://www.beastwatch.co.uk/

Creature Chronicles
http://home.fuse.net/rschaffner/

The Cryptodominion
http://www.angelfire.com/bc2/cryptodominion/frames.html

Cryptozoological Realms
http://www.cryptozoologicalrealms.com/

Cryptozoology
http://www.crystalinks.com/cryptozoology.html

Cryptozoology
http://www.pibburns.com/cryptozo.htm

Cryptozoölogy
http://www.sniggle.net/cryptozoo.php

Cryptozoology.com (Spanish/English)
 http://www.fortunecity.com/roswell/daniken/62/index.html

Crypto Centre (French)
http://perso.wanadoo.fr/cryptos/

Crypto Cumbria — Animal Mysteries in Cumbria
http://web.ukonline.co.uk/bransty/index.html

Crypto Resources
http://dinojoe.8m.com/crypto/resources/cryptoressources.html

The Crypto Web: An Online Encyclopedia of Cryptozoology
http://come.to/the_cryptoweb/

The Enigma Project
http://www.enigmaproject.org/

Farshores: Worldwide Anomalous Phenomena Resource
http://www.100megsfree4.com/farshores/index.htm

Fortean Times
http://www.forteantimes.co.uk/

Joe's Cryptozoology Pages
http://dinojoe.8m.com/crypto/crypto1.html

Kentucky Cryptids
http://www.geocities.com/cryptidwrangler/index.html

Kryptozoologie (German)
http://www.alein.de/iep/

Lost Worlds Exhibition
http://unmuseum.mus.pa.us/lostw.htm

Monstrous.com
http://www.monstrous.com/

Mysterious Britain
http://www.mysteriousbritain.co.uk/index.html

Mystery Animal Research Centre of Australia
http://www.webace.com.au/~pwest/marca/

Reports in the British Isles
http://homepage.ntlworld.com/chris.mullins/reports.htm

The Shadowlands
http://theshadowlands.net

Taking a Hard Look at Cryptozoology
http://www.ncf.carleton.ca/~bz050/HomePage.cryptoz.html

Tang's Cryptozoology Page
http://cryptozoology.tk/

Under The Bridge — True Encounters with Mysterious Creatures
http://home.austarnet.com.au/buzby/creatures.html

Utah Creatures/Lake Monsters/Other
http://www.aliendave.com/UUFOH_Creatures.html

The Virtual Institute of Cryptozoology (French)
http://perso.wanadoo.fr/cryptozoo/

Weird Wisconsin — Creatures!
http://www.weird-wi.com/creatures/index.htm

X-Project Cryptozoology Archive
http://www.xproject-paranormal.com/archives/cryptozoology/index.html

Alien Big Cats

Alien Big Cats
http://www.pcfe.ac.uk/cats/index.html

Big Cat Monitors
http://www.bigcatmonitors.co.uk/index.htm

Big Cats
http://wintersteel.homestead.com/Cats.html

Big Cats: *cats.html*

Big-Cats UK
http://www.big-cats.co.uk/

British Big Cat Society
Chad 2000
http://members.aol.com/mokelembe/

Kent Big Cat Research
http://www.tudor34.freeserve.co.uk/KentBigCatResearch.htm

Scottish Big Cat Society
http://www.scottishbigcats.org

Scottish Big Cat Trust
Some Recent Sightings of the Beast(s) of Gloucester
http://www.deville.demon.co.uk/glosabc.htm

Chupacabra
Chupacabra Where Are You?!!!
http://www.oftm.com/chupa.html

El Chupacabra
http://www.cralcrusade.50g.com/chupacabra.html

El Chupacabra Online
http://www.kingkongvsgodzilla.com/chupa/

Creationist (religious) perspectives
Analysis of Kent Hovind
http://www.geocities.com/kenthovind/

Are Dragons Alive Today?!
http://www.anzwers.org/free/livedragons/index.html

Genesis Park
http://www.genesispark.com/genpark/home.htm

William Gibbons: Creation Generation
http://www.kingkongvsgodzilla.com/chupa/

Jesus, Dinosaurs and More
http://www.angelfire.com/mi/dinosaurs/

Kent Hovind
http://www.drdino.com/

The Kent Hovind Page
http://home.austarnet.com.au/stear/kent_hovind_page.htm

Scott T. Norman Website
http://www.scottnorman.com/

Sea Monsters!
http://www.wwy.org/wwy0995.html

Cryptozoologists

Jon-Erik Beckjord
http://www.beckjord.com/

Loren Coleman — The Cryptozoologist
http://www.lorencoleman.com/

Rex Gilroy's Mysterious Australia Homepage
http://www.internetezy.com.au/~mj129/Mysterious_Australia_Homepage.html

Mark A. Hall Publications
http://home.att.net/~mark.hall.wonders/

The William Rebsamen Gallery
http://www.rebsamenwildlife.com/index.html

Dr. Karl Shuker
http://members.aol.com/karlshuker/

Cryptozoology Groups

American Anthropological Research Foundation
http://www.trueseekers.org/

Australian Yowie Research
http://www.yowiehunters.com/

Bigfoot Field Researchers Organization
http://bfro.net/

Blue Mountains Cryptid Research
http://members.ozemail.com.au/~mhallett/

British Big Cats Society
http://www.britishbigcats.org/

British Center for Bigfoot Research
http://british-bigfoot.tripod.com/

British Columbia Scientific Cryptozoology Club
http://www.cryptosafari.com/bcscc/index.htm

Centre for Fortean Zoology
http://www.cfz.org.uk/

Chattahoochee Bigfoot Organization
http://www.chattahoocheebigfoot.org/

Eastern Cougar Network
http://www.easterncougarnet.org/

Global Underwater Search Team
http://www.cryptozoology.st/

Gulf Coast Bigfoot Research Organization
http://gcbro.com/

Loch Ness Monster Fan Club
http://www.lochness.co/uk/fan_club/

Society for the Investigation of the Unexplained
http://www.tje.net/para/organizations/situ.htm

Southern Oregon Bigfoot Society
http://www.sasquatchsite.com/link_frame/frameset.asp?url=www.geocities.com/bigfootlegends

Texas Bigfoot Research Center
http://www.texasbigfoot.com/

Washington Bigfoot Research Group
http://www.w-b-r-g.com/home.html

The Washington State Sasquatch Search Group
http://www.angelfire.com/wa/sasquatchsearch/

Cryptozoological Fiction

Cryptofiction Author D.L. Tanner
http://webpages.charter.net/dltanner/

Strange Creatures
http://www.herper.com/ebooks/titles/Crypto.html

StrangeArk.com
http://www.strangeark.com/czfiction.html

Dracontology
Champ: A Brief History
http://members.tripod.com/~seanclogston/history.html

Champ Quest: The Ultimate Search
http://www.champquest.com/

The Cryptozoo Archives: Lake Monsters
http://www.ncf.carleton.ca/~bz050/HomePage.lm.html

Database of Norwegian Sea Serpents
http://www.mjoesormen.no/english.htm

Dragon in the Loch: Lake Cryptid Data Base
http://www.geocities.com/nessie_hunter/LakeCryptids.html

Find Ogopogo
http://www.ogopogosearch.com/index.html

Irish Lake Monsters
http://irishlakemonsters.com/Homepage.htm

The Lake Monster of Weatherford, Texas
http://www.geocities.com/Area51/Hollow/1776/parker.htm
LakeNormanMonster.Com http://www.monsterinthelake.com/norman/

The Legend of Nessie
http://www.nessie.co.uk/

Legend of Nessie Website
http://www.myspace.co.uk/nessie/menu/nesscont.html

The Legendary Champ
http://mistwebdesign.com/Champsite.html

The Loch Ness Inquirer
http://www.loch-ness.com/Inquirer/Inquirer.asp

Loch Ness Investigation
http://www.lochnessinvestigation.org/

Loch Ness Researchers
http://www.lochnessresearch.co.uk/researchers.htm

Morgawr
http://www.nexusdomain.org/paranormal/m/mor.html

Mysteries of the Deep
http://www.ncf.carleton.ca/~bz050/HomePage.sserp.html

Nessie's Grotto
http://www.simegen.com/writers/nessie/monsters.htm

Nessie's Loch Ness Times
http://www.thefrasers.com/nessie/news/nesspapr030301.html

NOVA Online: The Beast of Loch Ness
http://www.pbs.org/wgbh/nova/lochness/

The Online Lake Cryptid Directory
http://dive.to/lakemonsters

Sea Monsters
http://www.strangescience.net/stsea2.htm

Sea Serpents & Lake Monsters
http://members.tripod.com/Celedriel2/seaserpents.html

South Bay Bessie: A Monster in Lake Erie
http://users1.ee.net/pmason/Bessie.html

Strange Science: Sea Monsters
http://www.strangescience.net/stsea2.htm

Unpublished Stories of Ogopogo
http://sunnyokanagan.com/ogopogo/index.html

Welcome to Ogopogo Country
http://collections.ic.gc.ca/ogopogo/index.html

Hominology

Adirondack Research Organization
http://squatchdetective.freeyellow.com/

The Alabama Ape-Man
http://expage.com/alabamaapeman

Almas
http://www.alamas.ru/

Arizona Bigfoot Project
http://members.cox.net/gregazbfp/

Arkansas Primate Encounter Studies
http://www.geocities.com/Arkansas_Bigfoot/

The Australian Yowie Research Centre
http://www.theaustralianyowieresearchcenter.com/

Bigfoot: America's Ape?
http://www.ratsnest.net/bigfoot/skunkape.htm

Bigfoot and the Yeti
http://freespace.virgin.net/brian.goodwin/bigfoot.htm

Bigfoot au Quebec (French)
http://membres.lycos.fr/bigfootquebec/

The Bigfoot Chronicles
http://bigfoot.itgo.com/

Bigfoot Encounters
http://www.n2.net/prey/bigfoot/

Les Bigfoot et Yéti (French)
http://www.chez.com/facteurx/bigfoot.htm

Bigfoot: Fact or Fantasy?
http://www.netcomuk.co.uk/~rfthomas/bigfoot.html

Bigfoot in Illinois
http://www.webspawner.com/users/bigfootinillinoisinv/

Bigfoot in Kentucky
http://www.bigfootinkentucky.com/

Bigfoot in New York?
http://www.angelfire.com/ny4/nyout/nybf.html

Bigfoot Internet Library
http://www.ratsnest.net/bigfoot/library/featured.htm

Bigfoot Sightings in Ohio
http://www.angelfire.com/oh/ohiosasquatch/ohsi.html

Bigfoot Museum
http://bigfootmuseum.com/

Bigfoot Northwest/American Primate Foundation
http://members.aol.com/_ht_a/bfnorthwest/myhomepage/

Bigfoot Ranger Team
http://www.rangerforce.com/brt.htm

Bigfoot-Sasquatch FAQ
http://home.nycap.rr.com/wwilliams/BigfootFAQ.html

Bigfoot-Sasquatch Revealed
http://www.bigfoot-sasquatch.com/

Bigfoot Searcher:
http://www.geocities.com/Bigfootsearcher68/BigfootSearcher.html

Bigfoot, Skunkape & Me
http://www.geocities.com/sutek316/

Bigfoot Surplus
http://www.bigfootsurplus.com/

Bluenorth.com
http://www.bluenorth.com/

British Center for Bigfoot Research
http://british-bigfoot.tripod.com/

British Hominid Research
http://www.lincolns.org.uk/

Cascade Hominology Research Project
http://www.geocities.com/cascadehominid/cascade1.html

Crypto-bipedal-Primatology…Sasquatch
http://ourworld.compuserve.com/homepages/dtrapp/bigfoot.htm

The Eyes of the Forest
http://www.geocities.com/eezebra/

Eastern Ohio Bigfoot Investigation Center
http://www.angelfire.com/oh/ohiobigfoot/home.html

Florida Bigfoot Page
http://kiwi.digitalrice.com/bf/index.htm

The Florida Skunk Ape
http://www.floridaskunkape.com/

Forest People: The Bigfoot Reality
http://www.forestpeople.biz/links.html

Friends of Bigfoot
http://www.friendsofbigfoot.org/articles/southlist.shtml

Gulf Coast Bigfoot Research Organization
http://www.gcbro.com/

High Desert Bigfoot Research Society
http://www.geocities.com/bigfootrus/

Les Hommes Sauvages en France (French)
http://perso.wanadoo.fr/cryptos/europe.htm

The Honey Island Monster
http://www.geocities.com/primateer/honeyisland.html?1041472128880

Honey Island Swamp Monster
http://jmichaelms.tripod.com/HIS/

Intermountain Research Center — The Sasquatch Zone
http://www.cactusventures.com/saswatch.htm

The International Bigfoot Society
http://www.internationalbigfootsociety.com/

John's Bigfoot Picture Page
http://www.sasquatchsite.com/link_frame/frameset.asp?url=www.bright.net/~jbmcghee

J. Vaughn's Bigfoot/Sasquatch Page
http://www.geocities.com/Heartland/Ranch/9681/bigfoot.html

Kentucky Bigfoot
http://www.network54.com/Hide/Forum/208573

Kentucky Sasquatch Sightings
http://www.geocities.com/WestHollywood/Heights/8451/sasquatch.html

Kiamichi Bigfoot Research
http://www.angelfire.com/ok5/kiamichibigfoot/

The Legend of Yeti
http://www.legendofyeti.com/

Logan Payne's Bigfoot Site
http://bigfoot_res.tripod.com/main.html

Maryland Bigfoot Digital Digest
http://www.herper.com/ebooks/titles/bfdigest.html

Michigan Bigfoot Information Center
http://www.michiganbigfoot.org/

Minnesota Bigfoot Website
http://www.angelfire.com/mn2/mnbf/

MonkeyChasers Bigfoot Information Group
http://www.network54.com/Hide/Forum/99679

New England Sasquatch Research Center
http://maxpages.com/bigfoot2001

Nguoi Rung — Vietnamese Forest People
http://coombs.anu.edu.au/~vern/wildman.html

North Louisiana Bigfoot
http://www.geocities.com/northlabigfoot/index.html

Northeastern Ohio Bigfoot Research
http://www.neobfr.org/

Northeastern Ohio's Researchable Kryptids Accounts
http://www.geocities.com/saqatchr/index3.html

Ohio Bigfoot Research and Study Group
http://users1.ee.net/pmason/obrsg.html

The Ohio Bigfoot Research Team
http://get-me.to/bigfoot

Ohio Bigfoot Search Group Club
http://www.angelfire.com/co4/OBSC/page1.html

The Ohio/Pennsylvania Bigfoot Research Group
http://members.tripod.com/sasquatchsearch/

Ohio Valley Bigfoot Research
http://www.expage.com/ohiovalleybigfootresearch

Oregon Bigfoot.com
http://www.oregonbigfoot.com/index.php

Paranormal Bigfoot Research Organization
http://www.geocities.com/bigfootrus/index.html

Pennsylvania Bigfoot Society
http://www.pabigfootsociety.com/

The Quest for Bigfoot
http://www.trailhunter.com/

Rocky Mountain Bigfoot Research Project
http://www.geocities.com/ivb4/

Russian Hominoid Website (Cyrillic)
http://almas.ru/

Sasquatch Information Society
http://www.bigfootinfo.org/

Sasquatch Northwest
http://www.ratsnest.net/sasquatch/

Sasquatch of the Pacific Northwest
http://www.geocities.com/bcsasquatch/

Sasquatchsite
http://www.sasquatchsite.com/

Shaawanoki, The Mystery of the Swamp Apes
http://www.andreaswallach.com/news.html

Skunkape: Florida's Bigfoot
http://www.geocities.com/Colosseum/Ring/3414/ape.html

Smokey and the Fouke Monster
http://www.smokeyandthefoukemonster.com/

The Southeast Kentucky Bigfoot Information Center
http://www.webspawner.com/users/sekybfinfo/

Southern Indiana Bigfoot Research
http://members.tripod.com/hyperspaztic0/index.htm

Sur les Traces du Bigfoot (French)
http://www.geocities.com/CollegePark/Union/3039/14.html

Tennessee Bigfoot Lady's Website
http://www.tnbigfootlady.com/

Texoma Bigfoot Research & Investigation
http://www.ratsnest.net/texoma/

Tracking Bigfoot
http://www.n2.net/prey/bigfoot/articles/trackingbf.htm

Unusual Research: Cryptozoology
http://users1.ee.net/pmason/cryptozoology.html

The Western New York Bigfoot Investigation Center
http://wnybic.freeyellow.com/index.html

The W-Files: Bigfoot in Wisconsin
http://www.ufowisconsin.com/wfiles/bigfoot.html

Wildmen of the World
http://home.twcny.rr.com/bigfootsasquatch/index.html

Yeti, Bigfoot, Yowie, Yeren, Barmanu, Etc.
http://perso.wanadoo.fr/daruc/indexa.htm

Miscellaneous Cryptids

The Beast of Gévaudan
http://www.answerorb.com/gevaudan/

Drop Bears: Terror of the Australian Bush
http://library.trinity.wa.edu.au/subjects/english/fant/drop.htm

The Quest for Thylacaleo
http://www.thylacoleo.com/

Appendix F

International Society of Cryptozoology

Membership inquiries, new and renewing memberships, new and renewing institutional subscriptions, orders for back issues, and changes of address should be mailed to the Society at the following address:

Membership Department
International Society of Cryptozoology
P.O. Box 43070
Tucson, AZ 85733, U.S.A.
Telephone/Fax: (520) 884-8369
Email: isc-rg@cox.net

The following submissions — (a) cryptozoological materials for the Society's archives, such as sighting reports, copies of newspaper and magazine articles, and relevant printouts from the Internet; (b) items for possible use in *The ISC Newsletter*, which will eventually also be deposited in the archives; and (c) manuscripts for possible publication in the journal *Cryptozoology* — should be mailed directly to the Secretary of the Society, J. Richard Greenwell, at this address:

J. Richard Greenwell
Secretary, International Society of Cryptozoology
Department of Zoological Collections
International Wildlife Museum
4800 West Gates Pass Rd
Tucson, AZ 85745, U.S.A.
Telephone: (520) 629-0100, ext. 479
Fax: (520) 618- 3561
Email: rgreenwell@thewildlifemuseum.org

Additional information on the Society, including updated membership fees and complete listings of back order availability of both *The ISC Newsletter* and the journal *Cryptozoology,* may be found on the Society's Internet Website at: http://www.cryptozoologysociety.org.

Bibliography

Agnagna, Marcellin. "Results of the first Congolese Mokele-mbembe expedition." *Cryptozoology* 2 (1983): 103–112.

Akins, William. *The Loch Ness Monster*. New York: Signet, 1977.

Aldrovandi, Ulisse. *Serpentum et Draconum Historiae Libri Duo*. Bononiae, 1640.

Allen, Benedict. *Hunting the Gugu: In Search of the Lost Ape-Men of Sumatra*. London: Macmillan, 1989.

Allen, Judy, and Jeanne Griffiths. *The Book of the Dragon*. London: Orbis, 1979.

Alley, Robert. *Raincoast Sasquatch: Bigfoot, Sasquatch Evidence from Indian Lore*. Seattle: Hancock House, 2002.

Ameghino, Florentino. "An existing ground sloth in Patagonia." *Natural Science* 13 (1898): 324–326.

Andrews, Roy. "The trail of the blue tiger." *North American BioFortean Review* 6 (May 2001): 80–91.

Arave, Lynn. "Mythical beasts lurk in 5 Utah lakes." *Deseret News* (24 September 2001).

Arment, Chad. "Bipedal lizards in North America." *North American BioFortean Review* 2 (December 2000): 10.

_____. *Cryptozoology: Science & Speculation*. Landisville, PA: Coachwhip Publications, 2004.

_____. "Devil monkeys or wampus cats?" *North American BioFortean Review* 2 (2000): 45–48.

_____. "Dinos in the U.S.A." *North American BioFortean Review* 2 (2000): 32–39.

_____. "Giant centipedes in the Ozarks." *North American BioFortean Review* 2 (June 1999): 5–6.

_____. "Giant snake stories in Maryland." *INFO Journal* 73 (Summer 1995): 15–16.

_____. "Giant snakes in Pennsylvania." *North American BioFortean Review* 2 (December 2000): 36–43.

_____. "Notes on Lummis' Pichu-cuate." *North American BioFortean Review* 2 (December 2000): 5–10.

_____. *The Search for Enigmatic Animals*. Tipp City, OH: The Author, 1995.

_____. "Virginia devil monkey reports." *North American BioFortean Review* 2 (2000): 34–37.

_____, and Brad La Grange. "Crypto-varmints." *North American BioFortean Review* 2 (December 2000): 18–20.

_____, and _____. "A freshwater octopus?" *North American BioFortean Review* 2 (December 2000): 47–51.

Armstrong, Edward. *The Folklore of Birds*. London: Collins, 1958.

Armstrong, Perry. *The Piasa, or The Devil Among the Indians*. Morris, IL: E.B. Fletcher, 1887.

Ashley-Montague, Francis. "The discovery of a new anthropoid ape in South America?" *Scientific Monthly* 29 (1929): 275–279.

Ashman, Malcolm, and Joyce Hargreaves. *Fabulous Beasts*. London: Paper Tiger, 1997.

Ashton, John. *Curious Creatures in Zoology*. London: John C. Nimmo, 1890.

Averbuck, Philip. "The Congo water-dragon." *Pursuit* 14 (Autumn 1981): 104–106.

Aylesworth, Thomas. *Science Looks at Mysterious Monsters*. New York: Julian Messner, 1982.

Aymar, Brandt. *Treasure of Snake Lore*. New York: Greenberg, 1956.

Bagley, Will. "Maybe there is a monster in Utah Lake." *Salt Lake Tribune* (31 March 2002).

Baird, Donald. "Sasquatch footprints: A proposed method of fabrication." *Cryptozoology* 8 (1989): 43–46.

Bakker, George. "Dakuwaqa." *Transactions of the Fijian Society* (1924): 30–36.

Bakova, Maya. "Black Sea serpents." *Fortean Times* 51 (Winter 1988–89): 59.

Barber, Dylan. *The Horrific World of Monsters*. London: Marshall Cavendish, 1974.

Barber, Richard, and Anne Riches. *A Dictionary of Fabulous Beasts*. London: Macmillan, 1971.

Barloy, Jean-Jacques. "Le Bête du Gévaudan soumise á l'ordinateur." *Science et Vie* 131 (June 1980): 54–59.

_____. *Man and Animal*. London: Gordon & Cremonesi, 1978.

_____. *Merveilles et Mystères du Monde Animal* (2 vols). Paris: François Beauval, 1979.

_____. *Serpents de Mer et Monstres Aquatiques*. Paris: Famot/François Beauval, 1978.

_____. *Les Survivants de l'Ombre*. Paris: Arthaud, 1985.

Barloy, Jean-Jacques, and Pierre Civet. *Fabuleux Oiseaux de la Préhistoire à Nos Jours*. Paris: Robert Laffont, 1980.

Barnaby, David. *Quaggas and Other Zebras*. Plymouth: Basset, 1996.

Barrett, Charles. *The Bunyip and Other Mythical Monsters and Legends*. Melbourne: Mail Newspapers, 1946.

Bartels, Ernst, and Ivan Sanderson, "The one true Batman." *Fate* 19 (July 1966): 83–92.

Bartholomew, Paul and Bob. *Monsters of the Northwoods*. Utica, NY: North Country Books, 1992.

Bass, Rick. *The Lost Grizzlies*. New York: Houghton Mifflin, 1995.

Bauer, Aaron, and Anthony Russell. "A living plesiosaur? A critical assessment of the description of *Cadborosaurus willsi*." *Cryptozoology* 12 (1993–96): 1-18.

_____. "Osteological evidence for the prior occurrence of a giant gecko in Otago, New Zealand." *Cryptozoology* 7 (1988): 22–37.

_____. "Recent advances in the search for the living giant gecko in New Zealand." *Cryptozoology* 9 (1990): 66–73.

Bauer, Henry. *The Enigma of Loch Ness: Making Sense of a Mystery*. Urbana, IL: University of Illinois Press, 1986.

_____. "The Loch Ness monster: Public perception and the evidence." *Cryptozoology* 1 (1982): 40–45.

Baumann, Elwood. *Bigfoot: America's Abominable Snowman*. New York: Franklin Watts, 1975.

_____. *The Loch News Monster*. New York: Franklin Watts, 1972.

Bayanov, Dmitri. *America's Bigfoot: Fact, Not Fiction*. Moscow: Crypto-Logos, 1997.

_____. "A field investigation into the relict hominoid situation in Tajikistan, U.S.S.R." *Cryptozoology* 3 (1984): 74–79.

_____. *In the Footsteps of the Russian Snowman.* Moscow: Crypto-Logos, 1996.

_____. "A note on folklore in hominology." *Cryptozoology* 1 (1982): 46–48.

_____. "Why cryptozoology?" *Cryptozoology* 6 (1987): 1–7.

Bayless, Mark, "The Artrellia, dragon of the trees: Meet New Guinea's crocodile monitor (*Varanus salvadorii*)." *Reptiles* 6 (June 1988): 32–47.

Beck, Jane. "The giant beaver: A prehistoric memory?" *Ethnohistory* 19 (Spring 1972): 109–122.

Becker, John. "Towards an etymology of Maori *Waitoreke.*" *Cryptozoology* 4 (1985): 28–36.

Beebe, William. *Galápagos, World's End.* New York: G.P. Putnam's Sons, 1924.

_____. *Half Mile Down.* New York: Harcourt, Brace, 1934.

Beer, Rüdiger R. *Unicorn: Myth and Reality.* London: James J. Kery, 1977.

Beer, Trevor. *The Beast of Exmoor: Fact or Legend?* Barnstaple, England: Countryside Productions, 1984.

Beisner, Monika, and Alison Lyrie. *Fabulous Beasts.* London: Jonathan Cape, 1981.

Benedict, W. Ritchie. "The dragons that stalked America." *Fate* (November 2002): 14–20.

_____. "The unknown lake monsters of Alberta." *Strange Magazine* 5 (1990): 47–49.

Benjamin, Phyllis. "Batsquatch, flap, flap." *INFO Journal* 73 (Summer 1995): 29–31.

Benton, J.R. *The Medieval Menagerie: Animals in the Art of the Middle Ages.* New York: Abbeville, 1992.

Benwell, Gwen, and Arthur Waugh. *Sea-Enchantress: The Tale of the Mermaid and Her Kin.* London: Hutchinson, 1961.

Beresford, Quentin, and Garry Bailey. *Search For the Tasmanian Tiger.* Sandy Bay, Australia: Blubber Head Press, 1981.

Bernheimer, Richard. *Wild Men in the Middle Ages.* Cambridge, MA: Harvard University Press, 1952.

Berry, Rick. *Bigfoot on the East Coast.* Stuarts Draft, VA: The Author, 1993.

Berton, Jean. *Les Monstres du Loch Ness et d'Ailleurs.* Paris: France-Empire, 1977.

Betts, John. "Wanted dead or alive!" *Fortean Times* 93 (December 1996): 34–35

Bille, Matthew. "Recent discoveries: Unknown horses." *Exotic Zoology* 3 (January-February 1996): 1–2.

_____. *Rumors of Existence.* Blaine, WA: Hancock House, 1995.

_____. "What lies beneath Lake Iliamna?" *Crypto Dracontology Special* 1 (November 2001): 66–69.

Bindernagel, John. *North America's Great Ape: The Sasquatch.* Courtenay, B.C.: Beachcomber Books, 1998.

Binns, Ronald. *The Loch Ness Mystery Solved.* Shepton Mallet, England: Open Books, 1983.

Binyon, Laurence. *The Flight of the Dragon.* London: John Murray, 1911.

Bisi, Anna. *Il Grifone.* Rome: Universita di Roma, 1965.

Blackman, W. Haden. *The Field Guide to North American Monsters: Everything You Need to Know About Encountering Over 100 Terrifying Creatures in the Wild.* New York: Three Rivers Press, 1998.

Blashford-Snell, John. *Mysteries: Encounters with the Unexplained.* London: Bodley Head, 1983).

_____, and Rula Lenska. *Mammoth Hunt: In Search of the Giant Elephants of Nepal.* London: HarperCollins, 1996.

Bölsche, Wilhelm. *Drachen: Sagen und Naturwissenschaft.* Stuttgart: Franckh'sche Verlagshandlung, 1929.

Bonney, Neville. *The Tantanoola Tiger.* Blackwood, Australia: Lynton, 1976.

Bord, Janet. "Big shot." *Fortean Times* 96 (March 1997): 32–33.

_____, and Colin Bord. *Alien Animals.* London: Panther, 1985.

_____, and _____. *The Bigfoot Casebook.* London: Granada, 1982.

_____, and _____. *The Evidence For Bigfoot and Other Man-Beasts.* Wellingborough, England: Aquarian Press, 1984.

_____, and _____. "Strange creatures in Powys." *Fortean Times* 34 (Winter 1981): 18–20.

_____, and _____. *Unexplained Mysteries of the 20th Century.* Chicago: Contemporary Books, 1945.

Bordner, Robert. "The Peninsula Python: An absolutely true story." *Atlantic Monthly* 176 (November 1945): 88–91.

Borgaard, Per. *Mysteriet om Spøgelseskattene.* Copenhagen: Gyldendal, 1993.

Borges, Jorge, and Margarita Guerrero. *The Book of Imaginary Beings.* London: Jonathan Cape, 1970.

Bose, Hampden du. *The Dragon, Image and Demon.* Richmond, VA: Presbyterian Committee of Publications, 1899.

Bottriell, Lena. *King Cheetah: The Story of the Quest.* Leiden: Brill, 1987.

Boulay, R.A. *Flying Serpents and Dragons: The Story of Mankind's Reptilian Past.* Escondido, CA: Book Tree, 1997.

Boulenger, E.G. *Animal Mysteries.* London: Duckworth, 1927.

Bouras, Laskarina. *The Griffin Through the Ages.* Athens: Midland Bank, 1983.

Bousfield, Edward, and Paul LeBlond. "An account of *Cadborosaurus willsi,* new genus, new species, a large aquatic reptile from the Pacific coast of North America." *Amphipacifica* 1 (1995): 3–25.

Bowden, Malcolm. *The Japanese Carcass: A Plesiosaur-type Mammal?* Portsmouth, England: Creation Science Movement, n.d.

Boyd, I.L., and M.P. Stanfield. "Circumstantial evidence for the presence of monk seals in the West Indies." *Oryx* 32 (1998): 310–316.

Braddock, John. "Monsters of the Maritimes." *Atlantic Advocate* 58 (January 1968): 12–17.

Bradley, Michael. *More Than a Myth: The Search for the Monster of Muskrat Lake.* Willowdale, Ontario: Hounslow Press, 1989.

Brelsford, Vernon. "Some northern Rhodesian monsters." *African Observer* 4 (1936): 58–60.

Brierly, Nigel. *They Stalk by Night: The Big Cats of Exmoor and the South-West.* Bishops Nympton, England: Yeo Valley Productions, 1989.

Bright, Michael. "Meet Mokele-mbembe." *BBC Wildlife* 2 (December 1984): 596–601.

_____. *There Are Giants in the Sea.* London: Robson, 1989.

Brodu, Jean-Louis, and Michel Meurger. *Les Félins-Mystère: Sur les Traces d'un Mythe Moderne.* Paris: Pogonip, 1984.

Brookesmith, Peter, ed. *Creatures From Elsewhere.* London: Orbis, 1984.

Brown, Charles. *Sea Serpents: Wisconsin Occurrences of These Weird Water Monsters.* Madison, WI: Wisconsin Folklore Society, 1942.

Brown, Malcolm. "In Indochina, tantalizing traces of an elusive pig." *New York Times* (30 May 1995).

Brown, Robert. *The Unicorn: A Mythological Investigation.* London: Longmans, 1881.

Brussard, Peter. "The likelihood of persistence of small populations of large animals and its implications for cryptozoology." *Cryptozoology* 5 (1986): 38–46.

Buckland, Frank. *Curiosities of Natural History.* 3 vols. London: Richard Bentley: London, 1858–1888).

Buehr, Walter. *Sea Monsters.* New York: W.W. Norton, 1966.

Buffetaut, Eric. "Vertical flexure in Jurassic and Cretaceous marine crocodilians and its relevance to modern 'sea serpent' reports." *Cryptozoology* 1 (1983): 85–89.

Buol, Peter von. "'Buffalo lions': A feline missing link?" *Swana: The Magazine of the East African Wildlife Society* 23 (July-December 2000): 20–25.

Burney, David, and Ramilisonina. "The *Kilopilopitsofy, Kidoky,* and *Bokyboky*: Accounts of strange animals from Belo-sur-Mer, Madagascar, and the megafaunal 'extinction window.'" *American Anthropologist* 100 (1998): 957–966.

Burns, J.W. "Introducing B.C.'s hairy giants." *Macleans* (1 April 1929): 9, 61-62.

____, and C.V. Tench, "The hairy giants of British Columbia." *Wide World Magazine* (January 1940): 296–307.

Burr, Malcolm. "Sea serpents and monsters." *Nineteenth Century* 115 (1934): 220–230.

Burton, Maurice. *Animal Legends*. London: Frederick Muller, 1955.

____. *Curiosities of Animal Life*. London: Ward Lock, 1952.

____. *The Elusive Monster: An Analysis of the Evidence from Loch Ness*. London: Rupert Hart-Davis, 1961.

____. "Is this the Surrey puma?" *Animals* 9 (December 1966): 458–461.

____. *Living Fossils*. London: Thames & Hudson, 1954.

____. *More Animal Legends*. London: Frederick Muller, 1959.

____. "The supposed 'tiger-cat' of Queensland." *Oryx* 1 (1952): 321–326.

Burton, R.G. "A wild beast in Russia." *The Field* 82 (9 December 1893): 882.

Bynum, Joyce. "Bigfoot — A contemporary belief legend." *A Review of General Semantics* 49 (Fall 1992): 352–357.

Byrne, Peter. *The Search For Bigfoot: Monster, Myth or Man?* Washington, D.C.: Acropolis, 1975.

____. *Tula Hatti: The Last Great Elephant*. Boston: Faber & Faber, 1990.

Cachel, Susan. "Sole pads and dermatoglyphics of the Elk Wallow footprints." *Cryptozoology* 4 (1985): 45–54.

Caldwell, Harry. *Blue Tiger*. London: Duckworth, 1925.

Campbell, Elizabeth, and David Solomon. *The Search For Morag*. London: Tom Stacey, 1972.

Campbell, John. *The Celtic Dragon Myth*. Edinburgh: John Grant, 1911.

Campbell, Steuart. *The Loch Ness Monster: The Evidence*. London: Aberdeen University Press, 1991.

Campion-Vincent, Véronique. "Appearances of beasts and mystery-cats in France." *Folklore* 103 (1992): 160– 183.

____, ed. *Des Fauves dans Nos Campagnes: Légendes, Rumeurs et Apparitions*. Paris: Imago, 1992.

Cantagalli, Renzo. *Sasquatch Enigma Anthropologica*. Milan: SugarCo, 1975.

Caputo, Philip. *Ghosts of Tsavo: Stalking the Mystery Lions of Tsavo*. Washington, DC: National Geographic 2002.

Carmony, Neil. *Onza! The Hunt for a Legendary Cat*. Silver City, NV: High-Lonesome Books, 1995.

Carrington, Richard. *Mermaids and Mastodons: A Book of Natural and Unnatural History*. London: Chatto and Windus, 1957.

Carruth, J.A. *Loch Ness and Its Monster*. Fort Augustus, Scotland: The Author, 1971.

Carter, Frederic. *The Dragon of the Alchemists*. London: E. Matthews, 1926.

Cazeils, Nelson. *Monstres Marins*. Rennes, France: Editions Ouest-France, 1998.

Chambers, Paul. "Indonesian cœlacanths." *Fortean Times* 144 (April 2001): 66.

Champagne, Bruce. "A preliminary evaluation of a study of the morphology, behavior, autoecology, and habitat of large, unidentified marine animals, based on recorded field observations." *Crypto Dracontology Special* 1 (November 2001): 93–112.

Chapman, Simon. *The Monster of the Madidi: Searching for the Giant Ape of the Bolivian Jungle*. London: Aurum Press, 2001.

Cheesman, Evelyn. *Six-Legged Snakes in New Guinea*. London: Harrap, 1949.

Cherry, John, ed. *Mythical Beasts*. London: British Museum Press, 1995.

Chevalley, Abel. *La Bête du Gévaudan*. London: Gallimard, 1936.

Choden, Kunzang. *Bhutanese Tales of the Yeti*. Bangkok: White Lotus Company, 1997.

Chorvinsky, Mark. "The Lake Worth monster." *Fate* 45 (October 1992): 31–35.

____. "The makeup man and the monster." *Strange Magazine* 17 (Summer 1996): 6–11.

____. "The search for the Thunderbird photo continues." *Strange Magazine* 15 (Spring 1995): 44.

____. "Update: Makeup master John Chambers and the Patterson Bigfoot suit." *Strange Magazine* 19 (Spring 1998): 5, 57.

Chorvinsky, Mark, and Mark Opsasnick, "Notes on the Dwayo." *Strange Magazine* 2 (1988): 28–29.

____. "The Selbyville swamp monster exposed." *Strange Magazine* 4 (1989): 6–8.

Ciochon, Russell, John Olsen, and Jamie James. *Other Origins: The Search For the Giant Ape in Human Prehistory*. New York: Bantam, 1990.

Citro, Joseph. *Green Mountain Ghosts, Ghouls and Unsolved Mysteries*. Montpelier, VT: Vermont Life, 1994.

Clair, Colin. *Unnatural History: An Illustrated Bestiary*. London: Abelard-Schuman, 1967.

Clark, Anne. *Beasts and Bawdy*. London: J.M. Dent, 1975.

Clark, Jerome. *Encyclopedia of Strange and Unexplained Physical Phenomena*. Detroit: Gale Research, 1993.

____. "On the trail of unidentified furry objects." *Fate* 26 (August 1973): 56–64.

____. "Unidentified flapping objects." *Oui* (October 1976): 94–100, 105–106.

____, and Loren Coleman. "America's lake monsters." *Beyond Reality* 14 (March-April 1975): 28, 52.

____, and ____. *Creatures of the Outer Edge*. New York: Warner, 1978.

____, and ____. "On the trail of pumas, panthers and ULAs: Part 2." *Fate* 25 (July 1972): 92–99.

____, and ____. "Swamp slobs invade Illinois." *Fate* 27 (July 1974): 84–88.

____, and ____. "Winged weirdies." *Fate* 25 (March 1972): 80–89.

Clarke, C.H.D. "The Beast of Gévaudan." *Natural History* 80 (April 1971): 44–51, 66–73.

Clarke, Sallie. *The Lake Worth Monster*. Fort Worth, TX: The Author, 1969.

Clausen, Lucy. *Insect Fact and Folklore*. New York: Macmillan, 1954.

Clebert, Jean-Paul. *Bestiaire Fabuleux*. Paris: Albin Michel, 1971.

Coffin, Tristram (consultant). *The Enchanted World: Dragons*. Amsterdam, NY: Time-Life, 1984.

____. *The Enchanted World: Magical Beasts*. Amsterdam, NY: Time-Life, 1985.

____. *The Enchanted World: Night Creatures*. Amsterdam, NY: Time-Life, 1985.

Coghlan, Andy. "Mystery beast." *New Scientist Online News* (2 April 2001).

Cohen, Daniel. *The Encyclopedia of Monsters*. New York: Dodd, Mead, 1982.

____. *A Modern Look at Monsters*. New York: Tower, 1970.

____. *Monsters, Giants, and Little Men From Mars: An Unnatural History of the Americas*. New York: Doubleday, 1975.

Colarusso, John. "Ethnographic information on a wild man of the Caucasus," in Marjorie Halpin and Michael Ames, eds. *Manlike Monsters on Trial* (Vancouver, B.C.: University of British Columbia Press, 1980), pp. 171-174.

____. "Further notes on the role of folklore in hominology." *Cryptozoology* 2 (1983): 90–97.

____. "*Waitoreke*, the New Zealand 'otter': A linguistic solution to a cryptozoological problem." *Cryptozoology* 7 (1988): 46–60.

Colbert, Edwin. "The enigma of Sivatherium." *Plateau* 51 (1978): 32–33.

____. "Was the extinct giraffe (*Sivatherium*) known to the early Sumerians?" *American Anthropologist* 38 (1936): 605–608.

Coleman, Loren. "Big cats down under." *Fortean Times* 85 (February-March 1996): 38.

____. "Bigfoot in the snow." *Fortean Times* 124 (July 1999): 46.

____. "Caught on the hop." *Fortean Times* 84 (December 1994/January 1995): 50.

_____. "The colour of mystery." *Fortean Times* 96 (March 1997): 41.

_____. "Cryptozoology in the land of shadows: Yeti, the CIA and Tibet." *Strange Magazine* 5 (1990): 11-17.

_____. *Curious Encounters*. London: Faber & Faber, 1985.

_____. "Debunking a racist hoax." *Fortean Times* 90 (September 1996): 42.

_____. "Footage furor flares." *Fortean Times* 91 (October 1996): 39.

_____. "Gorillas in the midst." *Fortean Times* 101 (August 1997): 44.

_____. "Hunting hyenas in the US." *Fortean Times* 87 (June 1996): 42.

_____. "In the name of the father." *Fortean Times* 102 (September 1997): 46.

_____. "Into the rabbit hole." *Fortean Times* 128 (November 1999): 48.

_____. "It's hairy on the outside." *Fortean Times* 104 (November 1997): p. 44.

_____. "Jersey Devil walks again." *Fortean Times* 83 (October-November 1995): 49.

_____. "Kangaroos across America." *Fortean Times* 37 (Spring 1982): 25–28.

_____. "Lake monsters' fate sealed?" *Fortean Times* 88 (July 1996): 40.

_____. "Living fossils return." *Fortean Times* 117 (December 1998): 46.

_____. "Loco for tzuchinoko." *Fortean Times* 142 (February 2001): 45.

_____. "Longing to find a giant anaconda." *Fortean Times* 99 (July 1997): 44.

_____. "Maned mystery cats." *Fortean Times* 31 (Spring 1980): 24–27.

_____. "Monkey, men and worms." *Fortean Times* 114 (September 1998): 45.

_____. *Mysterious America*. New York: Paraview Press, 2001.

_____. "Mystery animals invade Illinois again." *Strange Magazine* 14 (Fall 1994): 32.

_____. "Necrolog: Crypto-crypt." *Fortean Times* 158 (June 2002): 20.

_____. "New stirrings in Loch Ness." *Fortean Times* 110 (May 1998): 45.

_____. "Not so abominable now." *Fortean Times* 89 (August 1996): 42.

_____. "On the trail of giant snakes." *Fortean Times* 33 (Autumn 1980): 38–40.

_____. "Planet of the ape suits." *Fortean Times* 86 (May 1996): 38.

_____. "Promises of giants." *Fortean Times* 103 (October 1997): 43.

_____. "Rising from the deep." *Fortean Times* 95 (February 1997): 40.

_____. "Roaring at the mane event." *Fortean Times* 92 (November 1996): 40.

_____. "Suits you, sir!" *Fortean Times*: 106 (January 1998): 48.

_____. "Telling horny stories." *Fortean Times* 97 (May 1997): 45.

_____. "Three toes are better than five." *Fortean Times* 98 (June 1997): 44.

_____. *Tom Slick and the Search For the Yeti*. London: Faber & Faber, 1989.

_____. "TV's creature feature." *Fortean Times*: 112 (July 1998): 48.

_____. "Was the first 'Bigfoot' a hoax?" *The Anomalist* 2 (Spring 1995): 8–27.

_____. "The Wisconsin werewolf." *Fortean Times*: 108 (March 1998): 47.

Coleman, Loren, and Jerome Clark. *Cryptozoology A-Z: The Encyclopedia of Loch Monsters, Sasquatch, Chupacabras, and Other Authentic Mysteries of Nature*. New York: Fireside Books, 1999.

Coleman, Loren, and Mark Hall. "Some Bigfoot traditions of the North American tribes." *INFO Journal* 7 (Fall 1970): 2–10.

Coleman, Loren, and Patrick Huyghe. *The Field Guide to Bigfoot, Yeti, and Other Mystery Primates Worldwide*. New York: Avon, 1999.

_____, and _____. *The Field Guide to Lake Monsters, Sea Serpents, and Other Mystery Denizens of the Deep*. New York: Tarcher/ Penguin, 2003.

Coleman, Loren, and Michel Raynal. "De Loys' photograph: A short tale of apes in Green Hell, spider monkeys, and *Ameranthropoides loysi* as the tools of racism." *The Anomalist* 4 (Autumn 1996): 84–93.

Collins, Andrew. *The Brentford Griffin*. Wickford, England: Earthquest, 1985.

Constable, Trevor. *Sky Creatures*. New York: Pocket Books, 1978.

Conway, D.J. *Magickal, Mythical, Mystical Beasts*. St. Paul, MN, 1996.

Cooke, David, and Yvonne Cooke. *The Great Monster Hunt: The Story of the Loch Ness Investigation*. New York: Grosset & Dunlap, 1969.

Cooper, J.C. *Symbolic and Mythological Animals*. London: Aquarian Press, 1992.

Cordier, Umberto. *Guida ai Draghi e Mostri in Italia*. Milan: SugarCo, 1986.

Corliss, William. *Biological Anomalies: Birds*. Glen Arm, MD: Sourcebook Project, 1998.

_____. *Biological Anomalies: Humans III*. Glen Arm, MD: Sourcebook Project, 1994.

_____. *Biological Anomalies: Mammals I*. Glen Arm, MD: Sourcebook Project, 1995.

_____. *Biological Anomalies: Mammals II*. Glen Arm, MD: Sourcebook Project, 1996.

_____. *Incredible Life: A Handbook of Biological Mysteries*. Glen Arm, MD: Sourcebook Project, 1981.

_____. *Science Frontiers: Some Anomalies and Curiosities of Nature*. Glen Arm, MD: The Sourcebook Project, 1994.

_____. *Strange Life*. Glen Arm, MD: Sourcebook Project, 1975.

Cornell, James. *The Monster of Loch Ness*. New York: Scholastic Book Services, 1977.

Corrales, Scott. "Aluxoob: Little people of the Maya." *Fate* 54 (June 2001): 30–34.

_____. *Chupacabras and Other Mysteries*. Murfreesboro, TN: Greenleaf, 1997.

_____. *The Chupacabras Diaries: An Unofficial Chronicle of Puerto Rico's Paranormal Predator*. Derrick City, PA: Samizdat, 1996.

_____. *Chupacabras Rising: The Paranormal Predator Returns*. Derrick City, PA: The Author, 2000.

_____. "How many goats can a goatsucker suck?" *Fortean Times* 89 (August 1996): 34–38.

Costello, Peter. *In Search of Lake Monsters*. London: Garnstone Press, 1974.

_____. *The Magic Zoo: The Natural History of Fabulous Animals*. London: Sphere Books, 1979.

Cottrell, Annette. *Dragons*. Boston: Boston Museum of Fine Arts, 1962.

Courtenay-Latimer, Marjorie. "Reminiscences on the discovery of the coelacanth, *Latimeria chalumnae* Smith." *Cryptozoology* 8 (1989): 1-11.

Cousins, Don. "No more monkey business." *Fortean Times* 136 (August 2000): 48.

Cox, Molly, and David Attenborough. *David Attenborough's Fabulous Animals*. London: BBC, 1975.

Cremo, Michael, and Richard Thompson. *Forbidden Archeology: The Hidden History of the Human Race*. Los Angeles: Bhaktivedanta Book Publishing, 1996.

Cropper, Paul. "The panthers of southern Australia." *Fortean Times* 32 (Summer 1980): 18–21.

_____, and Malcolm Smith. "Some unpublicized Australian 'sea serpent' reports." *Cryptozoology* 11 (1992): 51-69.

Crowe, Richard. "Missouri monster." *Fate* 25 (December 1972): 58–66.

Cunningham, Gary. "The legend of the Dobhar-chú." *Fortean Times* 168 (April 2003): 40–45.

Curtler, M.S. "Carolina parakeet not extinct?" *Animals* 7 (23 November 1965): 532.

Daegling, David. "Cripplefoot hobbled." *Skeptical Inquirer* 26 (March-April 2002): 35–38.

Dammerman, K.W. "The Orang Pendek or ape-man of Sumatra." *Proceedings of the Fourth Pacific Science Congress* 3 (1930): 121-126.

Dance, S. Peter. *Animal Fakes and Frauds.* Maidenhead, England: Sampson Low, 1976.

Danquah, Joseph. "Living monster or fabulous animal?" *West African Review* 10 (September 1039): 19–20.

Dash, Mike. *Borderlands.* Woodstock, NY: Overlook Press, 2000.

_____. "Dinosaur caught on film?" *Fortean Times* 86 (May 1996): 32–35.

_____. "The dragons of Vancouver." *Fortean Times* 70 (August-September 1993): 46–48.

_____. "Mystery moggies." *Fortean Times* 64 (August- September 1992): 44–45.

_____. "The reporting of a lake monster." *Fortean Times* 44 (Summer 1985): 42–43.

_____. "Status report: Lake monsters." *Fortean Times* 102 (September 1997): 28–31.

Davies, Adam. "I thought I saw a sauropod." *Fortean Times* 145 (May 2001): 30–32.

Davis, Ann. *The Tale of the Altamaha "Monster."* (Waverly, IA: G&R, 1996.

De Loys, François. "A gap filled in the pedigree of man?" *Illustrated London News* 84 (15 June 1929): 1040.

Dethier, Michel, and Ayako Dethier-Sakamoto. "The *Tzuchinoko,* an unidentified snake from Japan." *Cryptozoology* 6 (1987): 40–48.

Deuel, Richard, and Dennis Hall. "Champ quest at Lake Champlain, 1991-1992." *Cryptozoology* 11 (1992): 102–108.

Dhakal, Shiva. *Folk Tales of Sherpa and Yeti.* New Delhi: Nirala, 1991.

Dickinson, Peter. *The Flight of Dragons.* London: Pierrot Publishing, 1979.

Dimmick, Adrian. Worme Worlde: The Dragon Trivia Source *Book.* London: The Dragon Trust, 1994.

Dinsdale, Tim. *The Leviathans.* London: Futura, 1976.

_____. *Loch Ness Monster.* London: Routledge & Kegan Paul, 1982.

_____. *Monster Hunt.* Washington, D.C., 1972.

_____. *Project Water Horse: The True Story of the Monster Quest at Loch Ness.* London: Routledge & Kegan Paul, 1975.

_____. *The Story of the Loch Ness Monster.* London: Allan Wingate, 1973.

Dixon, Roland. "Water monsters in northern California." *Journal of American Folklore* 19 (1906): 323.

Donnan, Shawn. "On the trail of Yowie: Bigfoot Down Under." *Christian Science Monitor* (22 January 2001).

Dougan, Michael. "The Tahoe monster and other legends of the lake." *Image* (12 June 1988): 2–6.

Douglas, Athol. "The Thylacine: A case for current existence on mainland Australia." *Cryptozoology* 9 (1990): 13–25.

Dower, Kenneth. *The Spotted Lion.* London: William Heinemann, 1937.

Downes, Jonathan. "The big hairy monster of Bolam Lake." *Fortean Times* 169 (May 2003): 24–25.

_____. "Born to be wild." *Fortean Times* 84 (December 1994– January 1995): 55.

_____. *Only Fools and Goatsuckers.* Exeter, England: Centre for Fortean Zoology, 1999.

_____. *The Owlman and Others.* Exwick, England: CFZ Publications, 1997.

_____. *The Smaller Mystery Carnivores of the Westcountry.* Exwick, England: CFZ Publications, 1996.

_____. "Super furry animals in Hong Kong." *Fortean Times* 94 (January 1997): 48.

_____. "Whale of a time with a dragon." *Fortean Times* 95 (February 1997): 46.

Downing, Robert. "The search for cougars in the eastern United States." *Cryptozoology* 3 (1984): 31–49.

Dragons: An Anthology of Verse and Prose. London: Lorenz, 1996.

Dratch, Peter, et al. "Molecular genetic identification of a Mexican Onza specimen as a puma (*Puma concolor*)." *Cryptozoology* 12 (1993–96): 42–49.

Duncan, Will. "What is living in the woods, and why it isn't Gigantopithecus." *Crypto Hominology* (7 April 2001): 44–49.

Eber, Dorothy. "The scientific search for a prehistoric monster." *Macleans* 74 (12 August 1961): 1.

Eberhart, George M. *Mysterious Creatures: A Guide to Cryptozoology.* Santa Barbara, CA: ABC-CLIO, 2002.

Edgerton, Harold, et al. "AAS underwater elapsed time camera silhouette photography experiments at Loch Ness, 1989." *Cryptozoology* 8 (1989): 58–63.

Eggleton, Bob, and Nigel Suckling. *The Book of Sea Monsters.* Woodstock, NY: Overlook Press, 1998.

Elliot-Smith, Grafton. *The Evolution of the Dragon.* Manchester, England: University Press, 1919.

Ellis, Richard. "How big does the giant squid get?" *Cryptozoology Review* 3 (Summer 1998): 11-19.

_____. *Monsters of the Sea.* New York: Alfred A. Knopf, 1994.

_____. *The Search for the Giant Squid.* New York: Lyons Press, 1998.

El-Mallakh, Rif. "Cloning extinct genes." *Cryptozoology* 6 (1987): 49–54.

Elwes, H.J. "On the possible existence of a large ape, unknown to science, in Sikkim." *Proceedings of the Zoological Society of London* (1915): 294.

Epstein, Perle. Monsters: *Their Histories, Homes, and Habits.* Garden City, NY: Doubleday, 1973.

An Essay on the Credibility of the Existence of the Kraken, Sea Serpent, and Other Sea Monsters. London: W. Tegg, 1849.

Evans, Hilary, Karl Shuker, et al. (Consultants). *Almanac of the Uncanny.* Surry Hills, NY: Reader's Digest, 1995.

Fanerenbach, Wolf. "Sasquatch: Size, scaling and statistics." *Cryptozoology* 13 (1997–98): 47–75.

Farson, Daniel. *The Hamlyn Book of Monsters.* London: Hamlyn, 1984.

_____, and Angus Hall. *Mysterious Monsters.* London: Aldus, 1978.

Fawcett, Percy. *Exploration Fawcett.* London: Hutchinson, 1953.

Fenton, Alexander, and David Heppell, "The Earth Hound: A living Banffshire belief." *Scottish Studies* 31 (1992–93): 145–146.

Flannery, Tim. *Throwim Way Leg: Adventures in the Jungles of New Guinea.* London: Weidenfeld & Nicolson, 1998. Flett, Josie. *A History of Bunyips, Australia's Great Mystery Water Beasts.* Tylagum, Australia: Free Spirit Press, 2001.

Fox, E.B. "The mysterious 'Jhoor.'" *Journal of the Bombay Natural History Society* 27 (1920): 175–176.

Francis, Di. *The Beast of Exmoor.* London: Jonathan Cape, 1993.

_____. *Cat Country: The Quest for the British Big Cat.* Newton Abbot, England: David & Charles, 1983.

_____. *My Highland Kellas Cats.* London: Jonathan Cape, 1993.

Freeman, Richard. "In the coils of the Naga." *Fortean Times* 166 (February 2003): 30–35.

Frenz, Lothar. *Riesenkraken and Tigerwolfe: Auf der Spur Mysterioser Tiere.* Berlin: Rowohit, 2000.

Frizzell, Michael. "The Chesapeake Bay serpent." *Crypto Dracontology Special* 1 (November 2001): 129–157.

Fugleberg, Paul. *Flathead Lake Nessie Log: A Listing of Reported Sightings, 1889–1999.* Polson, MT: The Author, 2000.

_____. *Montana Nessie of Flathead Lake.* Polson, MT: Treasure State Publishing, 1992.

Fuller, Errol. *The Lost Birds of Paradise.* Shrewsbury, England: Swan Hill, 1995.

Futch, Michael. "Beast of Bladenboro put town on map." *Fayetteville* (NC) *Observer* (23 July 2000).

Gaal, Arlene. *Beneath the Depths: The True Story of Ogopogo, Okanagan Lake Monster.* Kelowna, BC: Valley Review, 1976.

_____. *In Search of Ogopogo: Sacred Creature of the Okanagan Waters.* Surrey, BC: Hancock House, 2001.

_____. *Ogopogo: The True Story of the Okanagan Lake Million Dollar Monster.* Surrey, BC: Hancock House, 1986.

Gable, Andrew. "The Beast of Gévaudan and other 'maulers'." *Cryptozoology Review* 1 (Winter-Spring 1997): 19–22.

_____. "Two possible cryptids from pre-Columbian Mesoamerica." *Cryptozoology Review* 2 (Summer 1997): 17–25.

Gachot, Theodore. *Mermaids: Nymphs of the Sea.* London: Aurum Press, 1996.

Gallehugh, Joseph Jr. "The vampire beast of Bladenboro." *North Carolina Folklore* 24 (1976): 53–58.

Gantes, Rémy. *Le Mystère des Hommes des Neiges.* Paris: Etudes Vivantes, 1979.

_____. *Le Mystère des Pieuvres Géantes.* Paris: Etudes Vivantes, 1979.

_____. *Le Mystère du Loch Ness.* Paris: Etudes Vivantes, 1979.

Gardner, Ray. "Caddy, king of the coast." *Maclean's Magazine* 63 (15 June 1950): 24, 42–43.

Garner, Betty. *Canada's Monsters.* Hamilton, Ontario: Potlatch, 1976.

Gatschet, Albert. "Water-monsters of American aborigines." *Journal of American Folklore* 12 (1899): 255–260.

Gesner, Conrad. *Historiae Animalium* (4 vols). Zurich: Christoph Froschauer, 1551, 1554, 1555, 1558.

Gibbons, Bill. "Dinosaurs in the Congo." *Fortean Times* 125 (August 1999): 66.

_____, and Robert Rickard. "Operation Congo returns." *Fortean Times* 47 (Autumn 1986): 22–25.

Gibbons, William. *Missionaries and Monsters.* Calgary, Alberta: Creation Generation Publications, 2003.

_____, and Kent Hovind. *Claws, Jaws, and Dinosaurs.* Pensacola, FL: CSE Publications, 1999.

Gibson, John, and David Heppell, eds. *Proceedings of the Symposium on the Loch Ness Monster: "The Search for Nessie in the 1980s."* Foremount House, Scotland: Scottish Natural History Library, 1988.

Gilroy, Rex. "Australia's lizard monsters." *Fortean Times* 37 (Spring 1982): 32–33.

_____. "Australia's marine colossus." *Psychic Australian* (February 1977): 6–9, 28–30.

_____. "Giant lizards of the Australian bush." *Australian Ufologist* 4, no. 4 (1982): 17–20.

_____. *Giants from the Dreamtime: The Yowie in Myth and Reality.* Katoomba, Australia: Uru Publications, 2001.

_____. *Mysterious Australia.* Mapleton, Australia: Nexus, 1995.

_____. "Mystery lions in the Blue Mountains." *Nexus* 2 (June-July 1992): 25–27, 64.

Godfrey, Laurie. "The tale of the Tsy-aomby-aomby: In which a legendary creature is revealed to be real." *The Sciences* 26 (January-February 1986): 48–51.

Gonzalez, Silvia, Andrew Kitchener and Adrian Lister. "Survival of the Irish elk into the Holocene." *Nature* 405 (2000): 753–754.

Gordon, David. *Field Guide to the Sasquatch.* Seattle: Sasquatch Books, 1992.

Goss, Michael. "Alien big cat sightings in Britain: a possible rumour legend?" *Folklore* 103 (1992): 184–202.

_____. "Do giant prehistoric sharks survive?" *Fate* 40 (November 1987): 32–41.

_____. "Tracking Tasmania's mystery beast." *Fate* 36 (July 1983): 34–43.

Gotfredsen, Lise. *The Unicorn.* London: The Harvill Press, 1999.

Gould, Charles. *The Dragon.* [Malcolm Smith, ed.]. London: Wildwood House, 1977.

_____. *Mythical Monsters.* London: W.H. Allen, 1886.

Gould, Rupert. *The Case For the Sea-Serpent.* London: Phillip Allen, 1930.

_____. *Enigmas: Another Book of Unexplained Facts.* New Hyde Park, NY: University Books, 1965.

_____. *The Loch Ness Monster and Others.* London: Geoffrey Bles, 1934.

Graffigna, Carlo. *L'Énigme du Yéti.* Paris: Julliard, 1964.

Grant, John. *Monsters.* London: Apple Press, 1992).

Gray, Affleck. *The Big Grey Man of Ben MacDhui.* Bankhead, Scotland: Lochar Publishing, 1989.

Gray, Annie. *Bird Hybrids.* Farnham Royal, England: Commonwealth Agricultural Bureaux, 1958.

_____. *Mammalian Hybrids: A Check-List With Bibliography.* Farnham Royal, England: Commonwealth Agricultural Bureaux, 1972.

Green, John. "The case for a legal inquiry into Sasquatch evidence." *Cryptozoology* 8 (1989): 37–42.

_____. *On the Track of the Sasquatch.* Agassiz, BC: Cheam, 1968.

_____. *On the Track of the Sasquatch: Encounters with Bigfoot from California to Canada* (2 vols). Harrison Hot Springs, BC: Cheam, 1980.

_____. *The Sasquatch File.* Agassiz, BC: Cheam, 1973.

_____. *Sasquatch: The Apes Among Us.* Seattle: Hancock House, 1978.

_____. *Year of the Sasquatch.* Agassiz, BC: Chea, 1970).

_____, and Sabina Sanderson. "Alas, poor Jacko." *Pursuit* 29 (January 1975): 18–19.

Green, Roger, ed. *A Cavalcade of Dragons.* New York: H.Z. Walck, 1970.

Greenwell, J. Richard. "A classificatory system for cryptozoology." *Cryptozoology* 4 (1985): 1-14.

_____. "Colonel Fawcett and the giant anaconda." *ISC Newsletter* 11, no. 2 (1992): 8–10.

_____. "Congo expeditions inconclusive." *ISC Newsletter* 1 (Spring 1982): 3–5.

_____. "Hippoturtleox." *ISC Newsletter* 5 (Spring 1986): 10.

_____. "Mokele-mbembe: New searches, new claims." *ISC Newsletter* 5 (Autumn 1986): 1–7.

_____, and Frank Poirer. "Further investigations into the reported Yeren— the wildman of China." *Cryptozoology* 8 (1989): 47–57.

Griffiths, Bill. *Meet the Dragon: An Introduction to Beowulf's Adversary.* Wymeswold, England: Heart of Albion Press, 1996.

Griffiths, Jeanne, ed. *Unicorns.* London: W.H. Allen, 1981.

Grimshaw, Roger, and Paul Lester. *The Meaning of the Loch Ness Monster.* Birmingham, England: Birmingham University, 1976.

Groves, Colin. "The case of the pygmy gorilla: A cautionary tale for cryptozoology." *Cryptozoology* 4 (1985): 37– 44.

_____. "The Yahoo, the Yowie, and reports of Australian hairy bipeds." *Cryptozoology* 5 (1986): 47–54.

Grumley, Michael. *There Are Giants in the Earth.* Garden City, NY: Doubleday, 1974.

Gubernatis, Angelo de. *Zoological Mythology: or, The Legends of Animals* (2 vols). London: Trübner, 1872.

Guenette, Robert, and Frances Guenette. *The Mysterious Monsters.* Los Angeles: Sun Classic, 1975.

Guiler, Eric. *The Tasmanian Tiger in Pictures.* Hobart, Australia: St. David's Park Publishing, 1991.

_____. *Thylacine: The Tragedy of the Tasmanian Tiger.* Melbourne: Oxford University Press, 1985.

_____, and Philippe Godard. *Tasmanian Tiger: A Lesson to Be Learnt.* Perth: Abrolhos, 1999.

Gupta, Madan, and Tribhuvan Nath. *On the Yeti Trail: The Search For the Elusive Snowman.* New Delhi: UBSPD, 1994.

Gutierez, Gregory. "On the trail of monsters." *Fortean Times* 162 (October 2002): 50–51.

Guynn, David, Jr., Robert Downing and George Askew. "Estimating the probability of non-detection of low- density populations." *Cryptozoology* 4 (1985): 55–60.

Hall, Dennis. *Champ Quest—The Ultimate Search: Field Guide and Almanac of Best Search Dates for Lake Champlain.* Jericho, VT: Essence of Vermont, 1999.

Hall, Mark. "Bighoot: The giant owl." *Wonders* 5 (September 1998): 67–79.

_____. "Contemporary stories of 'Taku He' or 'Bigfoot' in South

Dakota as drawn from newspaper accounts." *Minnesota Archaeologist* 37 (1978): 63–78.

____. "Giant snakes alive!" *Wonders* 4 (March 1995): 80–89.

____. "Giant snakes and mystery mounds in North America." *Wonders* 3 (December 1994): 93–116.

____. "Giant snakes in the Twentieth Century." *Wonders* 4 (March 1995): 11–29.

____. *Living Fossils: The Survival of* Homo gardarensis, *Neandertal man, and* Homo erectus. Minneapolis: The Author, 1999.

____. "More giant snakes alive!" *Wonders* 4 (September 1995): 80–89.

____. *Natural Mysteries: Monster Lizards, English Dragons, and Other Puzzling Animals*. Bloomington, IL: M.A.H.P.,1991.

____. *Natural Wonders*. Minneapolis, The Author, 1991.

____. "Stories of 'Bigfoot' in Iowa during 1978 as drawn from newspaper sources." *Minnesota Archaeologist* 38 (1979): 2–17.

____. "Thunderbirds are go." *Fortean Times* 105 (December 1997): 34–38.

____. *Thunderbirds! The Living Legend of Giant Birds*. Bloomington, IL: M.A.H.P., 1994.

____. "The vampire beast of Bladenboro." *Wonders* 7 (March 2002): 3–22.

____. *The Yeti, Bigfoot and True Giants*. Minneapolis: M.A.H.P., 1997.

Hall, Sian. "Legend of the falls." *Fortean Times* 123 (June 1999): 42–44.

____. "Rumble in the jungle." *Fortean Times* 111 (June 1998): 24–27.

Halpin, Marjorie, and Michael Ames, eds. *Manlike Monsters on Trial*. Vancouver, B.C.: University of British Columbia Press, 1980.

Halstead, Richard, and Paul Sieveking. "An ABC of British ABCs." *Fortean Times* 73 (February-March 1994): 41–44.

Hamel, Frank. *Human Animals*. London: William Rider & Son, 1915.

Hamilton, Mary. *A New World Bestiary*. Vancouver, BC: Douglas & McIntyre, 1985.

Hamilton-Snowball, G. "Spotted lions." *The Field* 192 (9 October 1948): 412.

Hansen, Kim. *Mysteriet om Nessie—Søslangen i Loch Ness*. Copenhagen: Gyldendal, 1988.

Hansen, Robert. "I killed the ape-man creature of Whiteface." *Saga* (July 1970): 8–11, 55–60.

Hapgood, Charles. *Mystery in Acambaro*. Kempton, IL: Adventures Unlimited Press, 2000.

Hargreaves, Joyce. *The Dragon Hunter's Handbook*. London: Granada, 1983.

____. *Hargreaves New Illustrated Bestiary*. Glastonbury, England: Gothic Image, 1990.

Harrison, Paul. *The Encyclopedia of the Loch Ness Monster*. London: Robert Hale, 1999).

____. "Loch Ness: The tip of the iceberg." *Crypto Dracontology Special* 1 (November 2001): 49–54.

____. *Sea Serpents and Lake Monsters of the British Isles*. London: Robert Hale, 2001.

Harter, Andrew. "Bigfoot." *Skeptic* 6, no. 3 (1998): 97–99.

Hartley, William, and Ellen Hartley. "The 'Abominable Snowman' of Florida's Everglades." *Men* (July 1974): 16–18, 78–79.

Hastain, Ronald, and Nicholas Witchell. *Loch Ness and the Monster: A Handbook for Tourists*. Inverness: J. Arthur Dixon, 1971.

Hauck, Dennis. *Haunted Places: The National Directory*. New York: Penguin, 1996.

Hay, Oliver. "An extinct camel from Utah." *Science* 68 (1928): 299–300.

Hayes, L. Newton. *The Chinese Dragon*. Shanghai: Commercial Press, 1922.

Headon, Deidre. *Mythical Beasts*. London: Hutchinson, 1981.

Healy, Tony, and Paul Cropper. *Out of the Shadows: Mystery Animals of Australia*. Chippendale, Australia: Pan Macmillan Australia, 1994.

Heaney, Michael. "The Mongolian Almas: A historical reevaluation of the sighting by Baradiin." *Cryptozoology* 2 (1983): 40–52.

____. "A more appropriate procedure for naming Sasquatch." *Cryptozoology* 9 (1990): 52–56.

Heinselman, Craig. "Hairy *Maeroero*." *Crypto* 4 (January 2001): 23–26.

Helm, Thomas. *Monsters of the Deep*. New York: Dodd, Mead & Co., 1962.

Heuvelmans, Bernard. "Annotated checklist of apparently unknown animals with which cryptozoology is concerned." *Cryptozoology* 5 (1986): 1-26.

____. *Les Bêtes Humaines d'Afrique*. Paris: Plon, 1980.

____. "The birth and early history of cryptozoology." *Cryptozoology* 3 (1984): 1-30.

____. *Dans le Sillage des Monstres Marins: Le Kraken et le Poulpe Colossal*. Paris: François Beauval, 1975.

____. *Les Derniers Dragons d'Afrique*. Paris: Plon, 1978.

____. *Le Grand Serpent-de-Mer*. Paris: Plon, 1975).

____. "How many animal species remain to be discovered?" *Cryptozoology* 2 (1983): 1-24.

____. *In the Wake of the Sea-Serpents*. London: Rupert Hart-Davis, 1968.

____. "Lingering pterodactyls." *Strange Magazine* 117 (Summer 1996): 18–21, 56–57.

____. "The metamorphosis of unknown animals into fabulous beasts and fabulous beasts into known animals." *Cryptozoology* 9 (1990): 1-12.

____. *On the Track of Unknown Animals*. London: Kegan Paul, 1995).

____. "The sources and method of cryptozoological research." *Cryptozoology* 7 (1988): 1-21.

____. *Sur la Piste des Bêtes Ignorées* (2 vols). Paris: Plon, 1955.

____. "What is cryptozoology?" *Cryptozoology* 1 (1982): 1-12.

____, and Boris Porshnev. *L'Homme de Néanderthal est Toujours Vivant*. Paris: Plon, 1974.

Hewkin, James. "Continuing Sasquatch investigations in the Pacific Northwest." *Cryptozoology* 8 (1989): 73–74.

____. "Investigating Sasquatch evidence in the Pacific Northwest." *Cryptozoology* 5 (1986): 27–37.

____. "Observation of two lines of Sasquatch tracks in Oregon." *Cryptozoology* 6 (1987): 78–84.

____. "Sasquatch investigations in the Pacific Northwest, 1990." *Cryptozoology* 9 (1990): 82–84.

____. "Sasquatch investigations in the Pacific Northwest, 1991." *Cryptozoology* 10 (1991): 76–78.

____. "Sasquatch investigations in the Pacific Northwest, 1992." *Cryptozoology* 11 (1992): 109–112.

____. "Sasquatch investigations in the Pacific Northwest, 1993." *Cryptozoology* 12 (1993–96): 72–75.

Hichens, William. "African mystery beasts." *Discovery* 18 (1937): 369–373.

____. "Africa's mystery beasts." *Wide World* 62 (1928): 171-176.

____. "On the trail of brontosaurus: Encounters with Africa's mystery animals." *Chambers's Journal* 17 (1927): 692–695.

Higgons, Jim. *Irish Mermaids*. Galway, Ireland: Crow's Rock Press, 1995.

Hill, W.C. Osman. "The Ufiti: The present position." *Symposia of the Zoological Society of London* 10 (1963): 57–59.

Hill, William. "Nittaewo, an unsolved problem of Ceylon." *Loris* 4 (1945): 251-262.

Hobley, C.W. "On some unidentified beasts." *Journal of the East Africa and Uganda Natural History Society* 6 (1912): 48–52.

____. "Unidentified beasts of East Africa." *Journal of the East Africa and Uganda Natural History Society* 7 (1913): 85–86.

Hocking, Peter. "Further investigations into unknown Peruvian mammals." *Cryptozoology* 12 (1993–96): 50–57.

____. "Large Peruvian mammals unknown to zoology." *Cryptozoology* 11 (1992): 38–50.

Hogarth, Peter, and Val Clery. *Dragons*. London: Allen Lane, 1979.

Hoke, Helen, ed. *Dragons, Dragons, Dragons*. New York: Franklin Watts, 1972.

Holliday, F.W. *Creatures from the Inner Sphere*. New York: Popular Library, 1973.

_____. *The Dragon and the Disk*. New York: W.W. Norton, 1973.

_____. *The Great Orm of Loch Ness*. New York: W.W. Norton, 1969.

_____, and Colin Wilson. *The Goblin Universe*. St. Paul, MN: Llewellyn, 1986.

Holman, Felice, and Nanine Valen. *The Drac: French Tales of Dragons and Demons*. New York: Charles Scribner's Sons, 1975.

Hopley, C.C. *Snakes: Curiosities and Wonders of Serpent Life*. London: Griffiths & Farran, 1882.

Hoult, Janet. *Dragons: Their History and Symbolism*. Glastonbury, England: Gothic Image, 1987.

Howey, M. Oldfield. *The Horse in Magic and Myth*. London: William Rider, 1923.

Humphreys, Charles. *Panthers of the Coastal Plain*. Wilmington, NC: Fig Leaf Press, 1994.

Hunter, Don, and René Dahinden. *Sasquatch*. Toronto: McClelland & Stewart, 1973.

Husband, Timothy. *The Wild Man: Medieval Myth and Symbolism*. New York: Metropolitan Museum of Art, 1972.

Hutchison, Robert. *In the Tracks of the Yeti*. London: Macdonald, 1989.

Hulme, F. Edward. *Natural History Lore and Legend*. London: Bernard Quaritch, 1895.

Huxley, Francis. *The Dragon: Nature of Spirit, Spirit of Nature*. London: Thames & Hudson, 1979.

Huyghe, Patrick. "Deep secrets: Is the Navy telling Idaho residents a whopper of a fish story?" *The Anomalist* 5 (Summer 1997): 8–27.

_____. "The inner life of lake monsters." *Omni* 17 (January 1995): 80.

_____. "Not necessarily Nessie." *Omni* 16 (September 1994): 78–79.

Ineich, Ivan, and George Zug. "*Tachygya*, the giant Tongan skink: Extinct or extant?" *Cryptozoology* 12 (1993–96): 30–35.

Ingersoll, Ernest. *Birds in Legend, Fable and Folklore*. London: Longmans, Green, 1923.

_____. *Dragons and Dragon Lore*. New York: Payson & Clarke, 1928.

Izzard, Ralph. *The Abominable Snowman Adventure*. London: Hodder and Stoughton, 1955.

_____. *The Hunt for the Buru*. London: Hodder & Stoughton, 1951.

Izzi, Massimo. *Il Dizionario Illustrato dei Mostri*. Rome: Gremese Editore, 1989.

_____. *I Mostri e l'Immaginario*. Rome: Manilo Basia, 1982.

Jacobs, Louis. *Quest for the African Dinosaurs*. New York: Villard Books, 1993.

James, C.G. "Congo swamps mystery." London *Daily Mail* (26 December 1919).

James, David. *Loch Ness Investigation*. London: Loch Ness Phenomena Investigation Bureau, 1968.

Janis, Christine. "Fossil ungulate mammals depicted on archaeological artifacts." *Cryptozoology* 6 (1987): 8–23.

Jeffreys, Mervyn. "African pterodactyls." *Journal of the Royal African Society* 43 (1944): 72–74.

Johnsgard, Paul, and Karin Johnsgard. *Dragons and Unicorns: A Natural History*. New York: St. Martin's Press, 1982.

Johnson, Paul, and Joan Jeffers. *The Pennsylvania Bigfoot*. Pittsburgh: The Authors, 1986.

Johnson, Stan. *Bigfoot Memories: My Life With the Sasquatch*. Newberg, OR: Wild Flower Press, 1996.

Jolly, Ben. "Enter a dragon that's queerer than Nessie." London *Daily Telegraph* (28 May 1994).

Joly, Éric, and Pierre Affre. *Les Monstres sont Vivants*. Paris: Grasset, 1995.

Joyner, Graham. *The Hairy Man of South Eastern Australia*. Kingston, Australia: The Author, 1977.

_____. "The orang-utan in England: An explanation for the use of *Yahoo* as a name for the Australian hairy man." *Cryptozoology* 3 (1984): 55–57.

_____. "Scientific discovery and the place of the Yahoo in Australian zoological history." *Cryptozoology* 9 (1990): 41-51.

Jullien, Franz. "La deuxième mort de la Bête du Gévaudan." *Annales du Muséum du Havre* 59 (August 1998): 1–9.

Kaharl, Victoria. *Water Baby: The Story of Alvin*. Oxford: Oxford University Press, 1990.

Keating, Don. "Active Sasquatch in Cohocton County, Ohio." *North American BioFortean Review* 1 (April 1999): 5, 41.

_____. *The Eastern Ohio Sasquatch*. Newcomerstown, OH: The Author, 1989.

_____. *The Sasquatch Triangle*. Newcomerstown, OH: The Author, 1987.

Keel, John. *The Complete Guide to Mysterious Beings*. New York: Doubleday, 1994.

_____. *The Mothman Prophecies*. New York: Saturday Review, 1975.

_____. *Strange Creatures from Time and Space*. Greenwich, CT: Fawcett, 1970.

Keller, Mark. "An attempt to obtain a specimen of Sasquatch through prolonged fieldwork." *Cryptozoology* 3 (1984): 84–88.

Kenji Chōno. "Issie of Japan's Lake Ikeda." *Elsewhen* 2 (1991): 9.

Kildare, Maurice. "Winged terror of the Oklahoma hills." *True Frontier* (October 1972): 29–30, 50–53.

Kilpatrick, Cathy. *Mysteries of Nature*. London: Aldus, 1979.

King, James, and J. Richard Greenwell. "Attitudes of biological limnologists and oceanographers toward supposed unknown animals in Loch Ness." *Cryptozoology* 2 (1983): 98–102.

Kirk, John. "BCSCC report on Okanagan Lake, 1989." *Cryptozoology* 8 (1989): 75–79.

_____. "BCSCC report on Okanagan Lake, 1990." *Cryptozoology* 9 (1990): 85–87.

_____. "BCSCC report on Okanagan Lake, 1991." *Cryptozoology* 10 (1991): 72–75.

_____. *In the Domain of the Lake Monsters: The Search for the Denizens of the Deep*. Toronto: Key Porter, 1988.

Klein, Martin, et al. *Underwater Search at Loch Ness*. Belmont, MA: Academy of Applied Science, 1972.

Knerr, Michael. *Sasquatch: Monster of the Northwest Woods*. New York: Belmont Tower, 1977.

Knott, John. "Crowing snake." *African Wildlife* 16 (September 1962): 170.

Koestler, Arthur. *The Case of the Midwife Toad*. London: Hutchinson, 1971.

Koster, John. "Creature feature." *Oceans* 10 (1977): 56–59.

Krantz, Grover. "Anatomy and dermatographics of three Sasquatch footprints." *Cryptozoology* 2 (1983): 53–81.

_____. *Big Footprints*. Boulder, CO: Johnson Books, 1992.

_____. *Bigfoot Sasquatch Evidence*. Blaine, WA: Hancock House, 1999.

_____. "A reconstruction of the skull of *Gigantopithecus blacki* and its comparison with a living form." *Cryptozoology* 6 (1987): 24–39.

_____. "A species named from footprints." *Northwest Anthropological Research Notes* 19 (1986): 93–99.

Krumbiegel, Ingo. *Von Neuen und Unentdeckten Tierarten*. Stuttgart: Kosmos, 1950.

LaGrange, Brad. "Cryptoherps in Indiana." *North American BioFortean Review* 1 (April 1999): 27.

_____. "The Gowrow vs. Occam's razor: An exercise in folklore." *North American BioFortean Review* 2 (2000): 4–5.

Lall, Kesar. *Lore and Legend of the Yeti*. Thamel, Nepal: Pilgrims' Book House, 1988.

Landsburg, Alan. *In Search of Myths and Monsters*. London: Corgi, 1977.

Lange, P. Werner. *Seeungeheuer: Fabeln und Fakten*. Leipzig: Edition Leipzig, 1979.

Lapseritis, Jack. *The Psychic Sasquatch and Their UFO Connection.* Mill Spring, NC: Blue Water Publishing, 1998.

Laycock, George. *Strange Monsters and Great Searches.* London: Piccolo, 1976.

LeBlond, Paul. "Another Caddy carcass?" *Crypto Dracontology Special* 1 (November 2001): 55–59.

_____. "An estimate of the dimensions of the Lake Champlain monster from the length of adjacent wind waves in the Mansi photograph." *Cryptozoology* 1 (1982): 54–61.

_____. "A previously unreported 'sea serpent' sighting in the South Atlantic." *Cryptozoology* 2 (1983): 82–84.

LeBlond, Paul, and Edward Bousfield. *Cadborosaurus: Survivor from the Deep.* Victoria, BC: Horsdal & Schubart, 1995.

LeBlond, Paul, and John Sibert. *Observations of Large Unidentified Marine Animals in British Columbia and Adjacent Waters.* Vancouver, BC: University of British Columbia, Institute of Oceanography, 1973.

Lee, Henry. *Sea Monsters Unmasked.* London: William Clowes, 1883.

Lee, John, and Barbara Moore. *Monsters Among Us: Journey to the Unexplained.* New York: Pyramid, 1975.

Lehner, Ernst, and Johanna Lehner. *A Fantastic Bestiary.* New York: Tudor, 1969.

Lennon, David. "Loch Ness monster or myth?" *Europe* 420 (October 2002): 44–41.

Lester, Paul. *The Great Sea-Serpent Controversy: A Cultural Study.* Birmingham, England: The Author, 1984.

Ley, Willy. *Dragons in Amber: Further Adventures of a Romantic Naturalis.* New York: Viking, 1951.

_____. *Exotic Zoology.* New York: Viking, 1959.

_____. *The Lungfish and the Unicorn: An Excursion into Romantic Zoology.* New York: Modern Age, 1941.

_____. *The Lungfish, the Dodo and the Unicorn.* New York: Viking, 1948.

_____. *Salamanders and Other Wonders.* New York: Viking, 1955.

Lilius, Aleko. "I saw the monster of Umfolozi Lake." *True* (July 1944): 20–23, 92–94.

Lin, Rosanne. "On the trail of China's Bigfoot." *Shanghai Star* (21 July 2002).

Linden, Eugene. "Ancient creatures in a lost world." *Time* (20 June 1994): 56–57.

Lofmark, Carl. *A History of the Red Dragon.* Llanrwst, Wales: Gwasg Carreg Gwalch, 1995.

Long, Greg. *The Making of Bigfoot: The Inside Story.* Amherst, NY: Prometheus Books, 2004.

Lorenzi, Rossella. "Scientists claim Yeti DNA evidence." *Discovery News* (6 April 2001).

Lorenzoni, Silvano. "Extant dinosaurs a distinct possibility." *Pursuit* 10 (Spring 1977): 105–109.

_____. "More on extant dinosaurs." *Pursuit* 47 (Summer 1979): 105–109.

Louis, Michel. *Le Bête du Gévaudan: L'innocence des loups.* Paris: Perrin, 1992.

Loyd, Lewis. *Bird Facts and Fallacies.* London: Hutchinson, 1927.

Lum, Peter. *Fabulous Beasts.* London: Thames & Hudson, 1952.

MacDonald, Fiona. *Monsters.* London: Lorenz Books, 2001.

MacInnes, Hamish. *Look Behind the Ranges.* London: Hodder and Stoughton, 1979.

Mackal, Roy. "Biochemical analyses of preserved *Octopus giganteus* tissue." *Cryptozoology* 5 (1986): 55–62.

_____. *A Living Dinosaur? In Search of Mokele-Mbembe.* Leiden: Brill, 1987.

_____. *The Monsters of Loch Ness.* London: Macdonald and Janes, 1976.

_____. *Searching for Hidden Animals: An Enquiry into Zoological Mysteries.* Garden City, NY: Doubleday, 1980.

_____, J. Richard Greenwell and M. Justin Wilkinson. "The search for evidence of Mokele-mbembe in the People's Republic of the Congo." *Cryptozoology* 1 (1982): 62–71.

Mackerle, Ivan. "In search of the killer worm." *Fate* 49 (June 1996): 22–27.

_____. *Mongolské Záhady.* Prague: Ivo Zelezny, 2001.

MacKinnon, John. *In Search of the Red Ape.* New York: Ballantine, 1974.

Macrae, F.B. "More African mysteries." *National Review* 111 (1938): 791–796.

Magin, Ulrich. "A brief survey of lake monsters of continental Europe." *Fortean Times* 46 (Spring 1986): 52–59.

_____. "Continental European big cats." *Pursuit* 71 (1985): 114–115.

_____. "Danger under the waged: The giant octopus of the Mediterranean." *Pursuit* 71 (1985): 128–129.

_____. "Duck! It's a plesiosaur." *Fortean Times* 92 (November 1996): 28–30.

_____. "European dragons: The Tatzelwurm." *Pursuit* 73 (1986): 16–22.

_____. "The European Yeti." *Pursuit* 74 (1986): 64–66.

_____. "In the wake of Columbus' sea serpent: The giant turtle of the Gulf Stream." *Pursuit* 78 (1987): 55–56.

_____. "Living dinosaurs in Africa: Early German reports." *Strange Magazine* 6 (November 1990): 11.

_____. "The Oldenwald beast." *Fortean Times* 55 (Autumn 1990): 30–31.

_____. "The Saarland panther." *INFO Journal* 68 (February 1993): 22–23.

_____. *Trolle, Yetis, Tatzelwürmer.* Munich: C.H. Beck, 1993.

Magraner, Jordi. *Notes sur les hominidés reliques d'Asie centrale, district de Chitral, NWFP, Pakistan.* Paris: The Author, 1992.

Mangiacopra, Gary. "Canada's la bête du lac: The beast of Lake Pohénégamook." *Of Sea and Shore* 12 (1982): 138–140, 181.

_____. "The great unknowns into the 20th century." *Of Sea and Shore* 11 (Winter 1980–81): 259–261.

_____. "The great unknowns of the 19th century." *Of Sea and Shore* 8 (Fall 1977): 175–178.

_____. "Lake Champlain: America's Loch Ness." *Of Sea and Shore* 9 (Spring 1978): 21-26.

_____. "More on *Octopus giganteus*." *Of Sea and Shore* 8 (Fall 1977): 174, 178.

_____. "*Octopus giganteus* Verrill: A new species of cephalopod." *Of Sea and Shore* 6 (Spring 1975): 3–10, 51-52.

_____. "Sharlie: A preliminary report of possible large animals in the Payette Lakes of Idaho." *Of Sea and Shore* 12 (Spring 1980): 43–46.

_____. "The two monsters of Flathead Lake, Montana." *Of Sea and Shore* 12 (1981): 93–96.

Mangiacopra, Gary, Michel Raynal, Dwight Smith and David Avery. "'Him of the hairy hands': *Octopus giganteus* rebuttal — again!" *Of Sea and Shore* 21 (Winter 1999): 233–234.

Mangiacopra, Gary, and Dwight Smith. "Connecticut's mystery felines: The Glastonbury Glawackus, 1939–1967." *The Anomalist* 3 (Winter 1995–96) 90–123.

Marchant, R.A. *Beasts of Fact and Fable.* London: Phoenix House, 1962.

Mares, Jaroslav. *Po Záhadnych Stopách.* Prague: Orbis, 1994.

_____. *Svet Tajemnych Zvírat.* Prague: Littera Bohemica, 1997.

Markotic, Vladimir, and Grover Krantz, eds. *The Sasquatch and Other Unknown Hominoids.* Calgary, Alberta: Western Publishers, 1984.

Marks, William. *I Saw Ogopogo!* Peachland, BC: The Author, 1971.

Marshall, Robert. *The Onza.* New York: Exposition Press, 1961.

Martin, David, and Alistair Boyd. *Nessie: The Surgeon's Photograph Exposed.* East Burnet, England: The Authors, 1999.

Martín, Jorge. "Tambien animales impossibles: ¿Que ocurre en Puerto Rico?" *Evidencia OVNI* 6 (1995): 32–33.

Martyr, Deborah. "An investigation of the *orang-pendek,* the 'short man' of Sumatra." *Cryptozoology* 9 (1990): 57–65.

Mawnan-Peller, A. *Morgawr: The Monster of Falmouth Bay.* Exwick, England: Centre For Fortean Zoology, 1996.

Maxwell, Jessica. "Seeing serpents." *Pacific Northwest* 27 (April 1993): 30–34.

Mayor, Adrienne. "Griffin bones: Ancient folklore and paleontology." *Cryptozoology* 10 (1991): 16–41.

_____. "Paleocryptozoology: A call for collaboration between classicists and cryptozoologists." *Cryptozoology* 8 (1989): 12–26.

McBride, Chris. *Operation White Lion*. London: Collins/Harvill, 1981.

_____. *The White Lions of Timbavati*. London: Paddington, 1977.

McCleod, James. *Mysterious Lake Pend Oreille and Its "Monster": Fact and Folklore*. Couer d'Alene, ID: North Idaho College Cryptozoology Club, 1987.

McCloy, James, and Ray Miller. *The Jersey Devil*. Wallingford, NJ: Middle Atlantic, 1976.

McCormick, Bob. *The Story of Tahoe Tessie: The Original Lake Tahoe Monster*. Sparks, NV: Tahoe Tourist Promotions, 1991.

McEwan, Graham. *Mystery Animals of Britain and Ireland*. London: Robert Hale, 1986.

_____. *Sea Serpents, Sailors and Sceptics*. London: Routledge & Kegan Paul, 1978.

McGowen, Tom. *Hamlyn Book of Legendary Creatures*. London: Hamlyn, 1982.

McLeod, James. *Mysterious Lake Pend Oreille and Its "Monster": Fact and Folklore*. Coeur d'Alene, ID: North Idaho College, 1987.

Means, Ruth (ed.). *The Piasa*. Alton, IL: Arts Council, 1970.

Megged, Matti. *The Animal That Never Was: In Search of the Unicorn*. New York: Lumen, 1994.

Meijaard, Erik. "The Bornean tiger: speculation on its existence." *Cat News* 30 (Spring 1999): 12–15.

Ménatory, Gérard. *La Bête du Gévaudan: Histoire, légende, réalité*. Mende, France: Chaptal, 1976.

Mercatante, Anthony. *Zoo of the Gods: The World of Animals in Myth and Legend*. New York: Harper & Row, 1974.

Meredith, Dennis. *The Search at Loch Ness: The Expedition of the New York Times and the Academy of Applied Science*. New York: Quadrangle, 1977.

Merrill, George. *Uriah Jewett and the Sea Serpent of Lake Memphremagog*. Newport, VT: The Author, 1917.

Messner, Reinhold. *My Quest For the Yeti*. New York: St. Martin's Press, 2000.

Meurger, Michel. *Histoire Naturelle des Dragons*. Rennes, France: Terre de Brume, 2001.

_____. "A hyena for the Gévaudan: Testimonial reports and cultural stereotypes." *Fortean Studies* 4 (1998): 227– 229.

_____, and Claude Gagnon. *Lake Monster Traditions: A Cross-Cultural Analysis*. London: Fortean Times, 1988.

_____, and _____. *Monstres des Lacs du Québec: Mythes et Troublantes Réalités*. Montréal: Stanke, 1982.

Michell, John, and Robert Rickard. *Living Wonders: Mysteries and Curiosities of the Animal World*. London: Thames & Hudson, 1982.

Miller, Carey. *A Dictionary of Monsters and Mysterious Beasts*. London: Piccolo, 1987.

Miller, Marc. *Chasing Legends: An Adventurer's Diary*. Stelle, IL: Adventures Unlimited, 1990.

_____. *The Legends Continue: Adventures in Cryptozoology*. Kempton, IL: Adventures Unlimited, 1998.

Miller, Marc, and William Cacciolfi. "Results of the New World Explorers Society Himalayan Yeti expedition." *Cryptozoology* 5 (1986): 81-84.

Miller, Marc, and Khryztian Miller. "Further investigation into Loy's 'ape' in Venezuela." *Cryptozoology* 10 (1991): 66–71.

Moiser, Chris. *Mystery Cats of Devon and Cornwall*. Launceston, England: Bossiney Books, 2001.

_____. "Ninki Nanka: The dragon of the Gambia." *Animals and Men* 24 (2001).

Moon, Mary. *Ogopogo: The Okanagan Mystery*. Vancouver, B.C.: J.J. Douglas, 1977.

Moore, John. "What are the globsters?" *Cryptozoology Review* 1 (Summer 1996): 20–29.

Moore, Steve. "Water dragons." *Fortean Times* 36 (Winter 1982): 47.

Moreau-Bellecroix, Marie. *Le Bête du Gévaudan*. Paris: Éditions Alsatia, 1945.

Morgan, Elaine. *The Aquatic Ape*. London: Souvenir Press, 1982.

Morgan, Robert. *Bigfoot: The Ultimate Adventure*. Knoxville, TN: Talisman Media Group, 1996.

Morrell, Virginia. "Roy Mackal, dinosaur hunter." *Reader's Digest* 123 (July 1983): 108–113.

Morris, Ramona, and Desmond Morris. *Men and Snakes*. London: Hutchinson, 1965.

Morris, Tom. *California's Bigfoot/Sasquatch*. Pleasant Hill, CA: Bigfoot Investigations, 1994.

Muirhead, Richard. "The flying snake of Namibia: An investigation." *CFZ Yearbook 1996*. Exeter, England: Centre for Fortean Zoology, 1996.

_____. "Some Chinese cryptids." *Cryptozoology Review* 3 (Winter-Spring 1999): 23–25.

_____. "Some Chinese cryptids (Part Two)." *Cryptozoology Review* 4 (Summer 2000): 19–20.

Murphy, Christopher, et al. *Bigfoot in Ohio: Encounters with the Grassman*. New Westminster, B.C.: Pyramid, 1997.

Murphy, Daniel. *Bigfoot in the News*. New Westminster, B.C.: Progressive Research, 1995.

_____. "Grassman — the Ohio conspiracy." *Unsolved UFO Sightings and Other Unexplained Mysteries* 4 (Summer 1996): 30–35.

Murphy, John, and Robert Henderson. *Tales of Giant Snakes: A Historical Natural History of Anacondas and Pythons*. Malabar, FL: Kireger, 1997.

Naish, Darren. "Another Caddy carcass?" *Cryptozoology Review* 2 (Summer 1997): 26–29.

_____. "Big bad killer eagles." *Fortean Times* 122 (May 1999): 48.

_____. "Cryptozoology of the Moa: A review (Part one)." *Cryptozoology Review* 2 (Winter-Spring 1998): 15–24.

_____. "Further notes on unrecognized British mustelids." *Cryptozoology Review* 2 (Autumn 1997): 28–31.

_____. "Probable sighting of a silver pheasant (*Lophura nycthemera*) in south-western England." *Cryptozoology Review* 3 (Winter-Spring 1999): 26–27.

_____. "The walrus whales." *Exotic Zoology* 5 (July-August 1998): 1–2.

_____. "Thar she's blown away." *Fortean Times* 104 (November 1997): 47.

_____. "Where be monsters?" *Fortean Times* 132 (March 2000): 40–44.

Napier, John. *Bigfoot: The Yeti and Sasquatch in Myth and Reality*. London: Jonathan Cape, 1972.

Nelson, Michael, and James Madsen Jr. "The Hay-Romer debate: fifty years later." *University of Wyoming Contributions to Geology* 18 (1979): 47–50.

Nevill, Hugh. "The Nittaewo of Ceylon." *The Taprobanian* 1 (February 1886): 66–68.

"New Chinese wildman investigation." *ISC Newsletter* 9 (Summer 1990): 8–9.

Newall, Venetia. *Discovering the Folklore of Birds and Beasts*. Tring, England: Shire, 1971.

Newman, Paul. *The Hill of the Dragon: An Enquiry into the Nature of Dragon Legends*. Ottawa: Rowman & Littlefield, 1980.

Newton, Michael. *Monsters, Mysteries and Man*. Reading, PA: Addison-Wesley, 1979.

Nigg, Joseph, ed. *The Book of Fabulous Beasts: A Treasury of Writings From Ancient Times to the Present*. Oxford: Oxford University Press, 1999.

_____. *The Book of Gryphons*. Cambridge, MA: Apple-wood, 1982.

_____. *A Guide to the Imaginary Birds of the World*. Cambridge, MA: Apple-wood, 1984.

Nobbe, George. "Forget the fins — this Caddy's got a flipper." *Omni* 16 (August 1994): 26.

Noe, Allen. "ABSMal affairs in Pennsylvania and Elsewhere." *Pursuit* 24 (October 1973): 84–89.

Nolane, Richard. *Monstres des Lacs et des Océans*. Paris: Dossiers Vaugirard, 1993.

_____. *Sur les Traces du Yéti et Autres Animaux Clandestins*. Paris: Dossiers Vaugirard, 1994.

Norman, Eric. *The Abominable Snowmen*. New York: Award, 1969.

Norvill, Roy. *Giants: The Vanished Race of Mighty Men*. Wellingborough, England: Aquarian Press, 1979.

Nugent, Rory. *Drums Along the Congo: On the Trail of Mokele-Mbembe, the Last Living Dinosaur*. New York: Houghton Mifflin, 1993.

_____. *The Search For the Pink-Headed Duck: A Journey Into the Himalayas and Down the Brahmaputra*. New York: Houghton Mifflin, 1991.

Nutku, Mustafa, and Unal Kozak. *Van Gölü Canavari*. Van, Turkey: Y.Y.U. Matbaasi, 1996.

O'Hanlon, Redmond. *Congo Journey*. London: Hamish Hamilton, 1996.

Oliver, James. *Snakes in Fact and Fiction*. New York: Macmillan, 1958.

Olsson, Peter. *Storsjöodjuret, Framställning af Fakta och Utredning*. Östersund, Sweden: Jamtland postens Bocktrykeri, 1899.

O'Meara, Stephen. "The Loch Ness monster: Anatomy of a hoax." *Odyssey* 9 (December 2000): 20–24.

O'Neill, June. *The Great New England Sea Serpent: An Account of Unknown Creatures Sighted by Many Respectable Persons Between 1638 and the Present Day*. Camden, ME: Downeast Books, 1999.

Opasnick, Mark. "On the trail of the Goatman." *Strange Magazine* 14 (Fall 1994): 18–21.

O'Reilly, David. *Savage Shadow: The Search for the Australian Cougar*. Perth, Australia: Creative Research, 1981.

Oren, David, "Did ground sloths survive to recent times in the Amazon region?" *Goeldiana Zoologia* 19 (20 August 1993): 1-11.

Oscarsson, Ulla. *Storsjöodjuret: The Great Lake Monster*. Östersund, Sweden: Jämtland County Museum, 2000.

Oudemans, Antoon. *The Great Sea-Serpent: An Historical and Critical Treatise*. Leiden: E.J. Brill, 1892.

_____. *The Loch Ness Animal*. Leiden: E.J. Brill, 1934.

Ouellette, Trevor. "Where in the world…?" *Fortean Times* 155 (March 203): 48–49."

Owen, David. *Thylacine: The Tragic Tale of the Tasmanian Tiger*. London: Allen & Unwin, 2003.

Owen, William. *Loch Ness Revealing Its Monsters*. Norwich, England: Jarrold, 1976.

Owens, Bruce. "The strange saga of the Emmaville panther." *Australian Outdoors and Fishing* (April 1977): 17–19.

Paddle, Robert. *The Last Tasmanian Tiger: The History and Extinction of the Thylacine*. London: Cambridge University Press, 2001.

Panday, Ram. *Yeti Accounts: Snowman's Mystery and Fantasy*. Kathmandu: Ratna Pustak Bhandar, 1994.

Paré, Ambrose. *Of Monsters and Marvels*. Chicago: University of Chicago Press, 1982.

Park, Penny. "Beast from the deep puzzles zoologists." *New Scientist* 137 (23 January 1993): 16.

Parker, Eric. *Oddities of Natural History*. London: Seeley, Service, 1943.

Parker, Gerry. *The Eastern Panther*. Halifax, Nova Scotia: Nimbus, 1998.

Parrish, J.K. "Our country's mysterious monsters." *Old West* (Fall 1969): 25, 37–38.

Patterson, John. *The Maneaters of Tsavo and Other East African Adventures*. London: Macmillan, 1907.

Patterson, Roger. *Bigfoot*. Yakima, WA: Northwest Research Association, 1968.

_____. *Do Abominable Snowmen of America Really Exist?* Yakima, WA: Franklin Press, 1966.

Pearl, Jack. "Monster bird that carries off human beings." *Saga* (May 1963): 29–31, 83–85.

Peattie, Noel. *Hydra and Kraken: Or, The Lore and Lure of Lake-Monsters and Sea-Serpents*. Oakland, CA: Regent Press, 1996.

Pennick, Nigel. *Dragons of the West*. Chieveley, England: Capall Bann, 1997.

Perera, Victor. *The Loch Ness Monster Watchers*. Santa Barbara, CA: Capra Press, 1974.

Perez, Danny. *Big Footnotes: A Comprehensive Bibliography Concerning Bigfoot, the Abominable Snowman and Related Beings*. Norwalk, CA: Perez Publishing, 1988.

_____. *Bigfoot at Bluff Creek*. Norwalk, CA: Perez Publishing, 1994.

_____. *The Bigfoot Directory*. Norwalk, CA: Perez Publishing, 1986.

Peterson, David. *Ghost Grizzlies*. New York: Henry Holt, 1995.

Phillips, Henry. *Basilisks and Cockatrices*. Philadelphia: E. Stern, 1882.

Phillpotts, Beatrice. *Mermaids*. New York: Ballantine, 1980.

Pic, Xavier. *La bête qui mangeait le monde en pays de Gévaudan et d'Auvergne*. Mende, France: Chaptal, 1976.

Picasso, Fabio. "Infrequent types of southern American humanoids — Part III." *Strange Magazine* 11 (Spring- Summer 1993): 19–20.

_____. "South American monsters & mystery animals." *Strange Magazine* 20 (December 1998): 28–35.

Pilichis, Dennis, ed. *Bigfoot: Tales of Unexplained Creatures*. Rome, OH: Page Research Library, 1978.

Pilkington, Mark. "Chupacabras fever." *Fortean Times* 140 (December 2000): 22–23.

Place, Marian. *Bigfoot All Over the Country*. New York: Dodd, Mead, 1978.

_____. *On the Track of Bigfoot*. New York: Dodd, Mead, 1974.

Plaskett, James. "Plumbing the depths." *Fortean Times* 133 (April 2000): 47.

Poirier, Frank, and J. Richard Greenwell. "Is there a large, unknown primate in China? The Chinese Yeren or wildman." *Cryptozoology* 11 (1992): 70–82.

Poirier, Frank, Hu Hongxing and Chung-Min Chen. "The evidence for wildman in Hubei Province, People's Republic of China." *Cryptozoology* 2 (1983): 25–39.

Porshnev, Boris. "Borlba za Trogloditov." *Postor* no. 6 (1968): 13–16.

_____. *Sovremennoe Sostoyanie Voprosa o Relikhtovykh Hominoidakh*. Moscow: VINITI, 1963.

_____, et al. *Snomannens Gata*. Gottenburg, Sweden: Fram, 1986.

Potter, Marjorie. "Lake Champlain monster." *Vermont Life* 24 (Summer 1970): 47–50.

Potts, Marc. *Mythology of the Mermaid and Her Kin*. Chieveley, England: Capall Bann, 2000.

Powell, Thom. *The Locals: A Contemporary Investigation of the Bigfoot/Sasquatch Phenomenon*. Seattle: Hancock House, 2003.

Priest, George. *The Great Winged Monster of the Piasa Valley*. Dallas: The Author, 1998.

Pyle, Robert. *Where Bigfoot Walks*. Boston: Houghton Mifflin, 1995.

Quast, Mike. *Big Footage: A History of Claims for the Sasquatch on Film*. Moorhead, MN: The Author, 2001.

_____. *The Sasquatch in Minnesota*. Fargo, ND: The Author, 1990.

Radford, Benjamin. "Bigfoot at 50: Evaluating a half- century of Bigfoot evidence." *Skeptical Inquirer* 26 (March-April 2002): 29–34.

Radka, Larry. *Historical Evidence for Unicorns*. Newport, DE: Einhorn Press, 1995.

Rafinesque, Constantin. "Dissertation on water snakes, sea snakes and sea serpents." *American Monthly Magazine* 1 (1817): 431-435.

Ratsch, Christian, and Heinz Probst, eds. *Namaste Yeti—Sei Gegrusst, Wilder Mann*! Munich: Knaur, 1985.

Raynal, Michel. "The case for the giant octopus." *Fortean Studies* 1 (1994): 210–234.

_____. "Debunking the debunkers of the giant octopus." *INFO Journal* 74 (Winter 1996): 24–27.

_____. "Do two-finned cetaceans really exist?" *INFO Journal* 70 (January 1994): 7–13.

_____. "Does Steller's sea cow still survive?" *INFO Journal* 51 (February 1987): 15–19, 37.

_____. "Jordi Magraner's field research on the Bar-manu Evidence for the authenticity of Heuvelmans's *Homo pongoides*." *Crypto Hominology Special* (7 April 2001): 98–103.

_____. "The mysterious bird of Hiva-Oi." *INFO Journal* 73 (Summer 1995): 17–21.

Raynal, Michel, and Gary Mangiacopra. "Out-of-place coelacanths." *Fortean Studies* 2 (1995): 153–165.

Raynal, Michel, Dwight Smith and David Avery. "*Octopus giganteus*: Still alive and hiding where?" *Of Sea and Shore* 18 (Spring 1996): 5–12.

Raynal, Michel, and Jean-Pierre Sylvestre. "Cetaceans with two dorsal fins." *Aquatic Mammals* 17 (1991): 31-36.

Regusters, Herman. "Mokele-mbembe: An investigation into rumors concerning a strange animal in the Republic of the Congo, 1981." *Munger Africana Library Notes* 12 (July 1982): 1–27.

_____, and Kia Vandusen, "An interim report on the search for Mokele Mbembe." *Pursuit* 72 (1985): 174–180.

Reinstedt, Randall. *Mysterious Sea Monsters of California's Central Coast*. Carmel, CA: Ghost Town, 1979.

_____. *Shipwrecks and Sea Monsters of California's Central Coast*. Carmel, CA: Ghost Town, 1975.

Rickard, Bob. "The Exmoor beast and others." *Fortean Times* 40 (Summer 1983): 52–61.

_____. "Florida's penguin panic." *Fortean Times* 66 (December 1992-January 1993): 41-43.

_____. "Monster man." *Fortean Times* 67 (February-March 1993): 28–31.

_____. "The Mothman special." *Fortean Times* 156 (April 2002): 26–32.

_____. "The Scottish 'lioness.'" *Fortean Times* 26 (Summer 1978): 43–44.

_____. "The Scottish lions.: *Fortean Times* 32 (Summer 1980): 23–26.

_____. "The 'Surrey' puma." *Fortean Times* 26 (Summer 1978): 42–43.

_____. "The 'Surrey Puma' and friends: more mystery animals." *Fortean Times* 14 (January 1976): 3–9.

_____. "Will the real Bigfoot please stand up?" *Fortean Times* 93 (December 1996): 37–38.

Rickard, Bob, and John Blashford-Snell. "The expeditionist." *Fortean Times* 70 (August-September 1993): 30–34.

Rickard, Bob, and John Michell. *Unexplained Phenomena*. London: Rough Guides, 2000.

Rickard, J.M. "Birdmen of the apocalypse!" *Fortean Times* 17 (August 1976): 14–20.

Rife, Philip. "Almas still exist in Mongolia." *Genus* 20 (1964): 186–192.

_____. *America's Loch Ness Monsters*. Lincoln, NE: Writers Club Press, 2000.

_____. *Bigfoot Across America*. Lincoln, NE: Writers Club Press, 2000.

Rinchen. "Almas: Mongol'skii rodich snezhnogo cheloveka." *Sovremennaya Mongoliya* 5 (1958): 34–38.

Rines, Robert. "Summarizing a decade of underwater studies at Loch Ness." *Cryptozoology* 1 (1982): 24–32.

_____, Harold Edgerton and Robert Needleman. "Activities of the Academy of Applied Science related to investigations at Loch Ness, 1984." *Cryptozoology* 3 (1984): 71-73.

Ritvo, Harriet. *The Platypus and the Mermaid*. Cambridge, MA: Harvard University Press, 1997.

Rizzi, Jorge. "Existen aun animales prehistoricos?" *Nueva Acrópolis Revista* 158 (March 1988): 23–30.

Roberts, Andy. "The Big Grey Man of Ben MacDhui and other mountain panics." *Fortean Studies* 5 (1998): 152–171.

_____. *Cat Flaps! Northern Mystery Cats*. Brighouse, England: Brigantia, 1986.

Robinson, Margaret. *Fictitious Beasts: A Bibliography*. London: The Library Association, 1961.

Rodriguez Rivera, Virginia. "Los duendes en Mexico (el alux)." *Folklore Americano* 10, no. 10 (1962): 68–85.

Roesch, Ben. "A review of alleged sea serpent carcasses worldwide (Part one —1648–1880)." *Cryptozoology Review* 2 (Autumn 1997): 6–27.

_____. "A review of alleged sea serpent carcasses worldwide (Part two —1881–1891)." *Cryptozoology Review* 2 (Winter-Spring 1998): 25–35.

_____. "A review of alleged sea serpent carcasses worldwide (Part three —1897–1906)." *Cryptozoology Review* 3 (Summer 1998): 27–31.

_____. "A review of alleged sea serpent carcasses worldwide (Part four —1907–1924)." *Cryptozoology Review* 3 (Winter-Spring 1999): 15–22.

_____. "'The Thing': A cryptic polychete of St. Lucia." *Cryptozoology Review* 1 (Autumn 1996): 5–6.

Rogo, D. Scott, and Jerome Clark. *Earth's Secret Inhabitants*. New York: Tempo, 1979.

Rolland, Will. *The Tasmanian Tiger: The Elusive Thylacine*. Kenthurst, Australia: Kangaroo Press, 1997.

Romer, Alfred. "A 'fossil' camel recently living in Utah." *Science* 68 (1928): 19–20.

_____. "A fresh skull of an extinct American camel." *Journal of Geology* 37 (1929): 261–267.

Ronecker, Jean-Paul. *Animaux Mysterieux*. Puiseaux, France: Pardès, 2000.

_____. *Monstres Aquatiques*. Puiseaux, France: Pardès, 2000.

Rosén, Sven. "The dragons of Sweden." *Fate* 35 (April 1982): 36–45.

_____. "Out of Africa: Are there lions roaming Finland?" *Fortean Times* 65 (October-November 1992): 44–45.

Rosenblatt, Ronald. "Car park lizard." *Fortean Times* 92 (November 1996): 50.

Rothovius, Andrew. "Who or what was the Beast of Gévaudan?" *Fate* 14 (September 1961): 31-37.

Roumeguère-Eberhardt, Jacqueline. *Dossier X: Les Hominidés Non-Identifiés des Forêts d'Afrique*. Paris: Robert Laffont, 1990.

Rowland, Beryl. *Animals with Human Faces: A Guide to Animal Symbolism*. Knoxville, TN: University of Tennessee Press, 1973.

Rubio-Muñoz, Sergio. "Wild men in Spain." *INFO Journal* 72 (Winter 1995): 22–25.

Rudd, Elizabeth, ed. *Dragons*. London: W.H. Allen, 1980.

Rupp, Diana. "Looking for Mr. Bigfoot." *Sports Afield* 214 (Winter 1995–96): 14–15.

Rutter, Gordon. "The Lambton worm: A cryptozoological story from the past." *Cryptozoology Review* 3 (Autumn 1998): 29–31.

Salkin, Howard. "Mysterious water monsters of North America." *Sea Monsters* (Spring 1977): 22–25, 57–58.

Salverte, Eusebe de. *Des Dragons et des Serpents Monstrueux qui Figurent dans un Grand Nombre de Récits Fabuleux ou Historiques*. Paris Rignoux, 1826.

Samuelsen, Espen. "In search of the Norwegian Nessie." *Fortean Times* 154 (February 2002): 42–44.

Sanborne, Mark. "An investigation into the Duende and Sismite of Belize: Humanoids of myth?" *Cryptozoology* 11 (1992): 90–97.

_____. "On the trail of the Duende and Sisimite of Belize." *Strange Magazine* 11 (Spring-Summer 1993): 10–13, 54–57.

Sánchez-Ocejo, Virgilio. *Miami Chupacabras*. Miami: Pharaoh Production, 1997.

Sanders, John. "Titans below!" *Fortean Times* 113 (August 1998): 47.

Sanders, Tao. *Dragons, Gods and Spirits From Chinese Mythology*. New York: Schocken Books, 1983.

Sanderson, Ivan. *Abominable Snowmen: Legend Come to Life*. Philadelphia: Chilton, 1961.

_____. "Don't scoff at sea monsters." *Saturday Evening Post* (8 March 1947): 22–23, 84–87.

_____. "First photos of 'Bigfoot,' California's legendary Abominable Snowman." *Argosy* (February 1968): 23–31.

_____. "The five weirdest wonders in the world." *Argosy* (November 1968): 21-23, 83–85.

_____. "Hairy primitives or relic submen in South America." *Genus* 18 (1962): 60–74.

_____. *Investigating the Unexplained: A Compendium of Disquieting Mysteries of the Natural World.* Englewood Cliffs, NJ: Prentice-Hall, 1972.

_____. "Monster on the beach." *Fate* 15 (August 1962): 24–35.

_____. *More "Things."* New York: Pyramid, 1969.

_____. "The strange story of America's Abominable Snowman." *True* (December 1959): 40–43, 122–126.

_____. "That forgotten monster: Old Three Toes." *Fate* 20 (December 1967): 66–75.

_____. "There could be dinosaurs." *Saturday Evening Post* 220 (3 January 1948): 17, 53, 56.

_____. *"Things."* New York: Pyramid, 1967.

_____. "Wisconsin's Abominable Snowman." *Argosy* (April 1969): 27–29, 70.

Sapunov, Valentin. "A mathematical analysis of 'snowman' (wildman) eyewitness reports." *Cryptozoology* 7 (1988): 61-65.

_____. "Results of chimpanzee pheromone use in snowman (wildman) field investigations." *Cryptozoology* 8 (1989): 64–66.

Schaffner, Ron. "South Bay Bessie: A continuing investigation into an alleged Great Lakes serpent." *North American BioFortean Review* 1 (April 1999): 35–41.

Schmidt, Karl. "A new crocodile from the Philippine islands." *Zoological Series of the Field Museum of Natural History* 20 (1935): 67–70.

Schönherr, Luis. "The Tatzelwurm: Mythical animal or reality?" *Pursuit* 85 (1989): 6–10.

Schroering, Gerard. "Swamp deer resurfaces." *Wildlife Conservation* (December 1995): 22.

Scibanicus, Marcus. "Strange creatures from Slavic folklore." *North American BioFortean Review* 3 (October 2001): 56–63.

Screeton, Paul. *The Lambton Worm and Other Northumbrian Dragon Legends.* Fulham, England: Zodiac House, 1978.

_____. *Whisht Lads and Haad Yor Gobs: The Lambton Worm and Other Northumberland Dragon Legends.* Pennywell, England: Northeast Press, 1998.

Searle, Frank. *Around Loch Ness: A Handbook for Nessie Hunters.* The Author, 1977.

_____. *Nessie: Seven Years in Search of the Monster.* London: Coronet, 1976.

Sehm, Gunter. "On a possible unknown species of giant devil ray (*Manta* sp.). *Cryptozoology* 12 (1993–96): 19–29.

Sergent, Donnie, Jr., and Jeff Wamsley. *Mothman: The Facts Behind the Legend.* Point Pleasant, WV: Mothman Lives Publishing, 2002.

Shackley, Myra. "The case for Neanderthal survival: Fact, fiction, or faction?" *Antiquity* 56 (1982): 31-41.

_____. *Wildmen: Yeti, Sasquatch and the Neanderthal Enigma.* London: Thames & Hudson, 1983.

Sharp, H.S. *The Transformation of Bigfoot: Maleness, Power, and Belief Among the Chipewyan.* New York: Smithsonian Institution Press, 1988.

Shepard, Odell. *The Lore of the Unicorn.* London: George Allen & Unwin, 1930.

Shermer, Michael. "Show me the body." *Scientific American* 288 (May 2003): 37.

Shiels, Tony. *Monstrum!* London: Fortean Tomes, 1990.

_____. "The owling." *Fortean Times* 156 (April 2002): 44–46.

_____. "Surrealchemy vs. cryptozoology." *Strange Magazine* 8 (Fall 1991): 13.

_____. "That owl devil moon." *Fortean Times* 101 (August 1997): 46.

Shircore, J.O. "Two notes on the crowing crested cobra." *African Affairs* 43 (1948): 183–186.

Shoemaker, Michael. "The day they caught 'Chessie.'" *Strange Magazine* 3 (1988): 30–31.

_____. "The mystery of Mono Grande." *Strange Magazine* 7 (April 1991): 2–5, 56–60.

Short, Bobbie. "Examination of the nomenclature of Indonesian mystery hominids." *Crypto* 3 (August 2000): 10–16.

Shuker, Karl. "All new talon show." *Fortean Times* 105 (December 1997): 49.

_____. "Angel feathers and feathered snakes." *Strange Magazine* 19 (Spring 1998): 24–25.

_____. "Another missing photo?" *Fortean Times*: 107 (February 1998): 48.

_____. "Are our high-flying kin batty?" *Fortean Times* 97 (May 1997): 48–49.

_____. "Bay cat reborn in Borneo." *Fortean Times* 99 (July 1997): 50.

_____. "The Beast of Bodmin, and a lesson in skull-duggery." *Strange Magazine* 16 (Fall 1995): 29–30.

_____. *The Beasts That Hide from Man: Seeking the World's Last Undiscovered Animals.* New York: Paraview Press, 2003.

_____. "A belfry of crypto-bats." *Fortean Studies* 1 (1994): 235–245.

_____. "Bemused in Bili." *Fortean Times* 148 (August 2001): 18.

_____. "Beware: Flesh rotter." *Fortean Times* 96 (March 1997): 44.

_____. "Beware — valleygator!" *Fortean Times* 126 (September 1999): 48.

_____. "Big birds in Scandinavia." *Fortean Times* 139 (November 2000): 23.

_____. "'Big birds' update." *Fortean Times* 141 (January 2001): 23.

_____. "The Big Grey Man." *Fate* 43 (May 1990): 58–68.

_____. "Black is black…isn't it?" *Fortean Times* 109 (April 1998): 44.

_____. "Blue tigers, black tigers, and other Asian mystery cats." *Cat World* 214 (December 1995): 24–25.

_____. "Bring me the head of the sea serpent!" *Strange Magazine* 15 (Spring 1995): 12–17.

_____. "Cat flaps." *Fortean Times* 78 (December 1994– January 1995): 32–33.

_____. "Catch a kilopilopitsofy." *Fortean Times* 131 (February 2000): 48.

_____. "The cave time forgot." *Fortean Times* 88 (July 1996): 42.

_____. "Close encounters of the cryptozoological kind." *Fate* 53 (May 2000): 26–29.

_____. "Death birds and dragonets: In search of forgotten monsters." *Fate* 46 (November 1993): 66–74.

_____. "The Dobhar-chú." *Strange Magazine* 116 (Fall 1995): 32–33, 49.

_____. *Dragons — A Natural History.* New York: Simon & Schuster, 1995.

_____. *Extraordinary Animals Worldwide.* London: Robert Hale, 1991.

_____. "Fins, fangs and poison." *Fortean Times* 93 (December 1996): 44.

_____. "Flying graverobbers." *Fortean Times* 154 (February 2002): 48–49.

_____. "Flying snakes." *Strange Magazine* 17 (Summer 1996): 26–27.

_____. "Freshwater monsters: The next generation." *Fate* 51 (February 1998): 18–21.

_____. "The frog with the luminous nose." *Strange Magazine* 19 (Spring 1998): 23.

_____. "From dodos to dimetrodons." *Strange Magazine* 19 (Spring 1998): 22.

_____. *From Flying Toads to Snakes with Wings: From the Pages of FATE Magazine.* St. Paul, MN: Llewellyn Publications, 1997.

_____. "From voo moos to potoroos." *Fortean Times* 100 (August 1997): 44–45.

_____. "Gallinaceous mystery birds." *World Pheasant Association News* 32 (May 1991: 3–6.

_____. "Gambo: The beaked beast of Bungalow Beach." *Fortean Times* 67 (February–March 1993): 35–37.

_____. "A giant owl and a giant hyrax…?" *Strange Magazine* 21 (Fall 2000).

_____. "Hairy reptiles and furry fish." *Strange Magazine* 18 (Summer 1997): 26–27.

_____. "Hatching controversy." *Fortean Times* 165 (January 2003): 50–51.

_____. "Headless and petrified." *Fortean Times* 103 (October 1997): 50.

_____. "Here be dragons." *Fate* 49 (June 1996): 31-34.

_____. *The Hidden Powers of Animals: Uncovering the Secrets of Nature.* London: Marshall Editions, 2001.

_____. "Hoofed mystery animals and other crypto-ungulates, Part III." *Strange Magazine* 11 (Spring-Summer 1993): 25–27, 48–50.

_____. "Horned jackals and devil birds." *Fate* 42 (January 1989): 57–64.

_____. "A horse of a different color." *Fate* 47 (May 1994): 66–69.

_____. "Horseplay in Tibet." *Fortean Times* 86 (May 1996): 42.

_____. "How dead are the dinosaurs?" *Strange Magazine* 16 (Fall 1995): 6–11, 52–55.

_____. "How dead is the dodo?" *Fate* 42 (May 1989): 62–69.

_____. "If cats could fly…" *Fortean Times* 168 (April 2003): 48–49.

_____. "Identity charade." *Fortean Times* 89 (August 1996): 44.

_____. *In Search of Prehistoric Survivors.* London: Blandford, 1995.

_____. "The Kellas car: Reviewing an enigma." *Cryptozoology* 9 (1990): 26–40.

_____. "Land of the lizard king." *Fortean Times* 95 (February 1997): 42–43.

_____. "Lion around the beach." *Fortean Times* 101 (August 1997): 49.

_____. "Living dinosaurs?" *Me* (28 July 1993): 56–57.

_____. "Long may the coelacanth reign as king of the sea in Indonesia." *Strange Magazine* 20 (December 1998): 36–37.

_____. *The Lost Ark: New and Rediscovered Animals of the 20th Century.* London: HarperCollins, 1993.

_____. "The lovecats." *Fortean Times* 68 (April-May 1993): 50–51.

_____. "Making monsters." *Fortean Times* 134 (June 2000): 47.

_____. "Meet Mongolia's death worm: The shock of the new." *Fortean Studies* 4 (1997): 190–218.

_____. "Melanism, mystery cats, and the movies." *Strange Magazine* 19(Spring 1998): 23, 54–55.

_____. "Monkeying around with our memories?" *Strange Magazine* 20 (December 1998): 40–42.

_____. *Mysteries of Planet Earth.* London: Carlton, 1999.

_____. *Mystery Cats of the World.* London: Robert Hale, 1989.

_____. "New beasts from Brazil?" *Fortean Times* 139 (November 2000): 22.

_____. "New Britain's lake monster." *Fortean Times* 82 (August-September 195): 38–39.

_____. "The new squid in town." *Fortean Times* 160 (August 2002): 47.

_____. *The New Zoo: New and Rediscovered Animals of the Twentieth Century.* Thirsk, England: House of Stratus Ltd., 2002.

_____. "Not such a fish out of water." *Fortean Times* 113 (August 1998): 43.

_____. "Pity about the pelt." *Fortean Times* 145 (May 2001): 23.

_____. "Potty about pottos." *Fortean Times* 94 (January 1997): 42.

_____. "Puzzling monkeys." *Fortean Times* 92 (November 1996): 42.

_____. "A real pen and ink." *Fortean Times* 90 (September 1996): 44.

_____. "Return of the Sandwell Valleygator?" *Fortean Times* 155 (March 2002): 22.

_____. "A rose-horned, snow-furred, claw-footed controversy." *Fate* 45 (April 1992): 59–60.

_____. "Sarajevo's jumping snake." *Fortean Times* 123 (June 1999): 46.

_____. "A scaly tale from Rintja." *Fortean Times* 116 (November 1998): 45.

_____. "The search for monster sharks." *Fate* 44 (March 1991): 41-49.

_____. "The search for the Thunderbird photo." *Strange Magazine* 16 (Fall 1995): 40.

_____. "The search for the Thunderbird photo continues." *Strange Magazine* 20 (December 1998): 44–45.

_____. "The secret animals of Senegambia." *Fate* 51 (November 1998): 46-5.

_____. "Sideshow." *Strange Magazine* 15 (Spring 1995): 32.

_____. "Sounds fishy to me!" *Strange Magazine* 17 (Summer 1996): 23.

_____. "A supplement to Dr. Bernard Heuvelmans' checklist of cryptozoological animals." *Fortean Studies* 5 (1998): 208–229.

_____. "A surfeit of civets?" *Fortean Times* 102 (September 1997): 17.

_____. "Teggie and the Turk." *Strange Magazine* 17 (Summer 1996): 25–27.

_____. "Thylacines in New Guinea?" *Fortean Times* 108 (March 1998): 16.

_____. "Tracking a Turkish tiger." *Fortean Times* 146 (June 2001): 46.

_____. *The Unexplained: An Illustrated Guide to the World's Natural and Paranormal Mysteries.* London: Carlton. 1996.

_____. "A water vampire." *Fate* 43 (March 1990): 86–88.

_____. "A whiter shade of pale." *Fortean Times* 102 (September 1997): 50.

_____. "Who's afraid of the big bad wolverine?" *Fortean Times* 85 (February-March 1996): 36–37.

_____. "Wild kthing, I think I love you." *Fortean Times* 91 (October 1996): 42–43.

_____. "Worthy birds in the bush." *Fortean Times* 98 (June 1997): 49.

_____ (consultant). *Man and Beast.* Pleasantville, NY: Reader's Digest, 1993.

_____ (consultant). *Secrets of the Natural World.* Pleasantville, NY: Reader's Digest, 1993.

Sieveking, Paul. "Beasts in our midst." *Fortean Times* 80 (May 1995): 37–43.

_____. "Cats in the hats." *Fortean Times* 111 (June 1998): 14–15.

_____. "Cool cats." *Fortean Times* 88 (July 1996): 28–31.

_____. "The Dakuqaqua." *Fortean Times* 58 (July 1991): 28.

_____. "Millennium moggy survey." *Fortean Times* 146 (June 2001): 16–17.

_____. "Not as simple as ABC." *Fortean Times* 83 (October- November 1995): 44–45.

_____. "Nothing more than felines." *Fortean Times* 121 (April 1999): 20–21.

_____. "Watch out: Big cat about." *Fortean Times* 101 (August 1997): 23–26.

_____. "Where the wild things are." *Fortean Times* 133 (April 2000): 18–19.

Simmons, Ian. "The abominable showman." *Fortean Times* 83 (October-November 1995): 34–37.

_____. "Close, but still no cigar." *Fortean Times* 147 (July 2001): 48.

Simpson, Jacqueline. *British Dragons.* London: B.T. Batsford, 1980.

Singh, Lala. *Born Black: The Melanistic Tiger in India.* New Delhi: World Wide Fund for Nature-India, 1999.

Skinner, Doug. "John Keel: A biography." *Fortean Times* 156 (April 2002): 33–35.

Skjelsvik, Elizabeth. "Norwegian lake and sea monsters." *Norveg* 7 (1960): 29–48.

Slate, B. Ann. "Florida's rampaging man-ape." *Saga UFO Report* 4 (July 1977): 32–34, 65–67.

Slate, Barbara, and Alan Berry. *Bigfoot.* New York: Bantam, 1976.

Smith, Alfred. *Trader Horn.* London: Reader's Library, 1931.

Smith, Dwight, and Gary Magiacopra. "Carl Hagenbeck and the Rhodesian Dinosaurs." *Strange Magazine* 6 (1990): 50–52.

Smith, Malcolm. "Analysis of the Australian 'hairy man' (Yahoo) data." *Cryptozoology* 8 (1989): 27–36.

_____. *Bunyips & Bigfoots: In Search of Australia's Mystery Animals.* Alexandria, Australia: Millennium, 1996.

_____, ed. *Mythical and Fabulous Creatures.* Westport, CT: Greenwood, 1987.

Smith, Richard. "Investigations and systems tests in the Lake Champlain basin." *Cryptozoology* 5 (1986): 85–88.

_____. "Investigations in the Lake Champlain basin." *Cryptozoology* 4 (1985): 74–79.

_____. "Testing an underwater video system at Lake Champlain." *Cryptozoology* 3 (1984): 89–93.

_____, and William Konrad. "Investigations and sonar testing at Lake Champlain, 1987." *Cryptozoology* 6 (1987): 85–87.

Smith, Warren. *The Secret Origins of Bigfoot.* New York: Zebra/Kensington, 1977.

_____. *Strange Abominable Snowmen.* New York: Popular Library, 1970.

Smullen, Ivor. "Do dinosaurs still exist?" *Weekend* (7 October 1981).

Snyder, Gerald. *Is There a Loch Ness Monster? The Search for a Legend.* New York: Julian Messner, 1977.

Somer, Lonnie. "New signs of Sasquatch activity in the Blue Mountains of Washington State." *Cryptozoology* 6 (1987): 49–54.

Soule, Gardner. *The Maybe Monsters.* New York: Putnam, 1963.

_____. *The Mystery Monsters.* New York: Ace, 1965.

_____. *Mystery Monsters of the Deep.* New York: Franklin Watts, 1981.

_____. *Trail of the Abominable Snowman.* New York: G.P. Putnam's Sons, 1966.

South, Malcolm, ed. *Topsell's Histories of Beasts.* Chicago: Nelson-Hall, 1981.

Spaeth, Frank. "The Everglades Skunk Ape." *Fate* 50 (December 1997): 53.

Sparks, Everett. *In Search of the Piasa.* Alton, IL: Alton Museum of History and Art, 1990.

Spassov, Nikolai. "The musk ox in Eurasia: Extinct at the Pleistocene-Holocene boundary or surviving to historical times?" *Cryptozoology* 10 (1991): 4–15.

Speight, W.L. "Mystery monsters of Africa." *Empire Review* 71 (1940): 223–228.

Spittel, Richard. "Leanama, land of the Nittaewo." *Loris* 1 (1936): 37–46.

_____. "Legend of the Nittaewo." *Loris* 10 (June 1964): 19–22.

Sprague, Roderick, and Grover Krantz, eds. *The Scientist Looks at the Sasquatch.* Moscow, ID: University Press of Idaho, 1977.

_____. *The Scientist Looks at the Sasquatch II.* Moscow, ID: University Press of Idaho, 1979.

Stap, Don. *Parrot Without a Name: The Search for the Last Unknown Birds of the Earth.* New York: Alfred A. Knopf, 1990.

Startzman, Paul. *The Puk-Wud-Jies of Indiana.* Pittsburgh, PA: Dorrance, 1998.

Steenburg, Thomas. *In Search of Giants: Bigfoot Sasquatch Encounters.* Surrey, BC: Hancock House, 2000).

_____. *Sasquatch: Bigfoot—The Continuing Mystery.* Blaine, BC: Hancock House, 1993.

_____. *The Sasquatch in Alberta.* Calgary, Alberta: Western Publishers, 1990.

Steiger, Brad. *Bizarre Cats.* London: Pan, 1993.

_____. *Monsters Among Us.* Rockport, MA: Para Research, 1982.

Stephens, Harold. "'Abominable Snowman' in Malaysia." *Argosy* (August 1971): 37–44.

Stone, Reuben. *Monsters and Mysterious Places.* Enderby, England: Blitz, 1993.

Stonor, Charles, *The Sherpa and the Snowman.* London: Hollis & Carter, 1955.

Strasenburgh, Gordon. *Paranthropus: Once and Future Brother.* Arlington, VA: Print Shop, 1971.

Streicher, Sonnfried. *Fabelwesen des Meeres.* Rostock, Germany: Hinstorff Verlag, 1984.

Strickland, Hugh. "Supposed existence of a giant bird in Madagascar." *Annals and Magazine of Natural History* 4 (1849): 338–339.

Stringer, Chris. "Wanted: One wildman, dead or alive." *New Scientist* (11 August 1983): 422.

Stuttaford, Andrew. "Loch Roswell?" *National Review* 49 (15 September 1997): 24–25.

Sucik, Nick. "Just when you thought it was safe to go snorkeling: Hawaii's giant octopuses." *North American BioFortean Review* 2 (December 2000): 11-17.

Suckling, Nigel. *The Book of the Unicorn.* Limpsfield, England: Paper Tiger, 1996.

Sundberg, Jan-Ove. "The Kalimantan monster." *Pursuit* 9 (Summer 1976): 66.

_____. *Storsjöodjuret, Seljordsormen, Nessie och Andra Sjömonster.* Täby, Sweden: Larson Förlag, 1995.

Suttles, Wayne. "On the cultural track of the Sasquatch." *Northwest Anthropological Research Notes* 6 (Spring 1972): 65–90.

Sweeney, James. *A Pictorial History of Sea Monsters and Other Dangerous Marine Life.* New York: Nelson-Crown, 1972.

_____. *Sea Monsters: A Collection of Eyewitness Accounts.* New York: David McKay, 1977.

Swords, Michael. "On the possible identification of the Egyptian animal-god Set." *Cryptozoology* 4 (1985): 15–27.

_____. "The Wasgo or Sisiutl: A cryptozoological sea- animal of the Pacific Northwest coast of the Americas." *Journal of Scientific Exploration* 5 (1991): 85–101.

Tandory, Barbara. "The original apes of the galaxy." *Alberta Report* 20 (8 February 1993): 25.

Tassi, Franco. *Animali a Rischio.* Milan: Giorgio Mondadori, 1990.

Taylor, Dabney. "Sea monster swims again." *Scenic Idaho* 2 (1956): 8–9, 56–58.

Taylor, David. *David Taylor's Animal Monsters.* London: Boxtree, 1987.

Taylor-Ide, Daniel. *Something Hidden Behind the Ranges.* San Francisco: Mercury House, 1995.

Tchernine, Odette. *In Pursuit of the Abominable Snowman.* New York: Taplinger, 1971.

_____. *The Snowman and Company.* London: Robert Hale, 1961.

_____. *The Yeti.* London: Neville Spearman, 1970.

Teresi, Dick. "Monster of the tub." *Discover* 19 (April 1998): 86–92.

Terry, James. *Sculptured Anthropoid Ape Heads Down In or Near the Valley of the John Day River, a Tributary of the Columbia.* New York: J.J. Little, 1891.

Theil, Hjalmar, and Gerd Shriever. "The enigmatic DISCOL species: A deep sea pedipalp?" *Senckenbergiana Maritima* 20 (October 1989): 171-175.

Theiss, Henry. "World's biggest snake." Copley News Service (24 February 1969).

They Saw Nessie (Or Thought They Did!): Eye-Witness Sightings of the Monster Over the Years. Gartocharn, Scotland: Northern Books, 1984.

Thomas, Charles. "The 'monster' episode in Adomnan's *Life* of St. Columba." *Cryptozoology* 7 (1988): 38–45.

Thomas, Larry. "The search for the thunderbird photo." *Strange Magazine* 18 (Summer 1997): 34–35.

Thomas, Lars. *De Skjulte Dyr.* Copenhagen: Forlaget Klematis, 1997.

_____. *Fantasiog Virkelighed i Naturen.* Hillerød, Denmark: 1987.

_____. *Mysteriet om Enhjørningen og Andre Fabeldyr.* Copenhagen: Gyldendal, 1996.

_____. *Mysteriet om Havuhyrerne.* Copenhagen: Gyldendal, 1992.

_____. *Mystiske Dyr* (3 vols). Vanl se, Denmark: Anderse Bogservice, 1989.

Thompson, Richard. *Wolf-Hunting in France in the Reign of Louis XV: The Beast of the Gévaudan.* Lewiston, NY: Edward Mellen Press, 1991.

Tischendorf, Jay. "The eastern panther on film? Results of an investigation." *Cryptozoology* 9 (1990): 74–78.

Tischendorf, Jay, and Susan Morse. "The puma in New Brunswick, Canada: A preliminary search." *Cryptozoology* 12 (1993–96): 66–71.

Tischendorf, Jay, and Steven Ropski, eds. *Proceedings of the Eastern Cougar Conference, 1994.* Fort Collins, CO: American Ecological Research Institute, 1996.

Tishkov, Arkady. "Observation of a Yeti in the Himalayas of Tibet." *Cryptozoology* 12 (1993–96): 58–65.

Tobin, Mitch. "Wandering jaguar shakes things up." *Tucson* (AZ) *Daily Star* (24 February 2002).

Tokuharu Takabayashi. "The first Japanese-Congolese Mokele-mbembe expeditions." *Cryptozoology* 7 (1988): 66–69.

Topsell, Edward. *The Historie of Foure-Footed Beastes.* London: William Iaggard, 1607.

_____. *The Historie of Serpents.* London: William Iaggard, 1608.

Trubshaw, Bob. *Dragon Slaying Myths Ancient and Modern.* Wymeswold, England: Heart of Albion Press, 1993.

Truzzi, Marcello, and J. Richard Greenwell (Consultants). *Mysterious Creatures.* Amsterdam, NY: Time-Life, 1988.

Van Dover, Cindy. *The Octopus's Garden: Hydrothermal Vents and Other Mysteries of the Deep Sea.* New York: Helix, 1996.

Vembos, Thanassis. "A prehistoric flying reptile?" *Strange Magazine* 2 (1988): 29.

Verrill, Addison. "Additional information concerning the giant cephalopod of Florida. *American Journal of Science* 4 (February 1897): 162–163.

_____. "The Florida sea-monster." *American Naturalist* 31 304–307.

_____. "A gigantic cephalopod on the Florida coast." *American Journal of Science* 4 (January 1897): 79.

_____. "The supposed giant octopus of Florida: certainly not a cephalopod." *American Journal of Science* 4 (April 1897): 355–356.

Vibe, Palle. *Gaden I Loch Ness.* Copenhagen: Rhodos, 1970.

Vickers-Rich, Patricia, and Gerard Van Tets, eds. *Kadikamakara: Extinct Vertebrates of Australia.* Lilydale, Victoria: Pioneer Design Studio, 1985.

Vinycomb, John. *Fictitious and Symbolic Creatures in Art.* London: Chapman & Hall, 1906.

Visser, Marinus de. *The Dragon in China and Japan.* Amsterdam: Johannes Müller, 1858.

Vlček, Emanuel. "Old literary evidence for the existence of the 'Snow Man' in Tibet and Mongolia." *Man* 59 (1959): 133–134.

Wade, Jeremy. "Hell's teeth." *Fortean Times* 99 (July 1997): 24–26.

_____. "Snakes alive!" *Fortean Times* 97 (May 1997): 34–37.

Wagner, Roy. "The *Ri*— unidentified aquatic animals of New Ireland, Papua New Guinea." *Cryptozoology* 1 (1982): 33–39.

_____, J. Richard Greenwell, Gale Raymond and Kurt Von Nieda. "Further investigations into the biological and cultural affinities of the Ri." *Cryptozoology* 2 (1983): 113–125.

Walker, Paul. *Bigfoot and Other Legendary Creatures.* San Diego: Harcourt Brace, 1992.

Wall, Coleman. "Dakuwaqa." *Transactions of the Fijian Society* (1917): 6–12, 39–46.

Wallach, Van, and Gwilym Jones. "*Cryptophidion annamense*, a new genus and species of cryptozoic snake from Vietnam (Reptilia: Serpentes)." *Cryptozoology* 11 (1992): 1–37.

Wallis, James. "British big cats." *Fortean Times* 54 (Summer 1990): 30–31.

Walters, Michael. "The cryptozoological implications of old bird names in native vocabularies." *Cryptozoology* 12 (1993–96): 36–41.

Ward, Peter. *On Methuseleh's Trail: Living Fossils and the Great Extinctions.* Oxford: W.H. Freeman, 1991.

Warren, Nick. "The end of the auk." *Fortean Times* 145 (May 2001): 48.

Wasedadaigaku Tankenbu. *Maboroshi no Kaiju Mubenbe o Oe.* Tokyo: PHP Kenkyujo, 1989.

Wasson, Barbara. *Sasquatch Apparitions: A Critique on the Pacific Northwest Hominoids.* Bend, OR: The Author, 1979.

Watkins, M.G. *Gleanings From the Natural History of the Ancients.* London: Elliot Stock, 1885.

Watson, Nigel. "No pussyfooting around." *Fortean Times* 135 (July 2000): 49.

Weber, Charles, James Berry and J. Richard Greenwell. "Mokele-mbembe: Proximate analysis of its supposed food source." *Cryptozoology* 1 (1982): 49–53.

Welfare, Simon, and John Fairley. *Arthur C. Clarke's Mysterious World.* London: Collins, 1980.

Wen Jiao. "Does China have a Loch Ness monster?" *China Reconstructs* 35 (April 1986): 28–29.

Wendt, Herbert. *Out of Noah's Ark.* London: Weidenfeld & Nicolson, 1956.

Wettig, Hannah. "Return of the unicorn." London *Daily Star* (29 August 2002).

Whalen, Dwight. "Monster in Niagara River?" *INFO Journal* 43 (January 1984): 9–11.

Wharton, Violet. *Dragons and Fabulous Beasts.* London: Pavilion, 1994.

White, T.H. *The Book of Beasts.* London: Jonathan Cape, 1954.

Whitley, Gilbert. "Mystery animals of Australia." *Australian Museum Magazine* 7 (1940): 132–139.

Whitlock, Ralph. *Here Be Dragons.* London: George Allen & Unwin, 1983.

Whyte, Constance. *More Than a Legend: The Story of the Loch Ness Monster.* London: Hamish Hamilton, 1961.

Wignell, Edel, ed. *A Boggle of Bunyips.* Sydney: Hodder & Stoughton, 1981.

Wilkins, Harold. *Monsters and Mysteries.* St. Ives, England: James Pike, 1973.

Williams, Geoffrey. "An unknown animal of the Uasingishu." *Journal of the East Africa and Uganda Natural History Society* 4 (1912): 123–125.

Williams, Thomas. "Identification of the Ri through further fieldwork in New Ireland, Papua New Guinea." *Cryptozoology* 4 (1985): 61–68.

Willis, Ronald. "Ben MacDhui: The haunted mountain." *INFO Journal* 15 (May 1975): 2–5.

Winn, Edward. "Physical and morphological analysis of samples of fiber purported to be Sasquatch hair." *Cryptozoology* 10 (1991): 55–65.

Witchell, Nicholas. *Loch Ness and the Monster.* Newport, Wales: J. Arthur Dixon, 1975.

_____. *The Loch Ness Story.* London: Corgi Books, 1989.

Woodbridge, Anthony. "First photos of the Yeti: An Encounter in North India." *Cryptozoology* 5 (1986): 63–76.

Wootton, Anthony. *Animal Folklore, Myths and Legend.* Poole, England: Blandford, 1986.

Wright, Bruce. *The Eastern Panther.* Toronto: Clark, Irwin, 1972.

_____. "The Gougou: Bigfoot of the East." *Bigfoot Bulletin* 25 (1971).

_____. *The Ghost of North America.* New York: Vantage Press, 1959.

Wyckoff, Charles, et al. "An unmanned motion-sensitive automatic infrared camera tested in a Pacific Northwest quest for possible large primates." *Cryptozoology* 11 (1992): 98–101.

Wylie, Kenneth. *Bigfoot: A Personal Inquiry into a Phenomenon.* New York: Viking, 1980.

Wyman, Walker. *Mythical Creatures of the U.S.A. and Canada.* Park Falls, WI: University of Wisconsin-River Falls Press, 1978.

Yasushi Kojo. "Distributional patterns of cryptid eyewitness reports from Lake Champlain, Loch Ness, and Okanagan Lake." *Cryptozoology* 11 (1992): 83–89.

_____. "Some ecological notes on reported large, unknown animals in Lake Champlain." *Cryptozoology* 10 (1991): 42–54.

Yuan Zhenxin and Huang Wanpo. *Wild Man: China's Yeti.* London: Fortean Times, 1981.

Zarzynski, Joseph. "'Champ': A personal update." *Pursuit* 54 (1981): 51-53.

_____. *Champ: Beyond the Legend.* Port Henry, NY: Bannister, 1984.

_____. "The Lake George monster hoax of 1904." *Pursuit* 51 (Summer 1980): 99–100.

_____. "LCPI work at Lake Champlain: 1982." *Cryptozoology* 1 (1982): 73–77.

_____. "LCPI work at Lake Champlain: 1983." *Cryptozoology* 2 (1983): 126–131.

_____. "LCPI work at Lake Champlain: 1984." *Cryptozoology* 3 (1984): 80–83.

_____. "LCPI work at Lake Champlain: 1985." *Cryptozoology* 4 (1985): 69–73.

_____. "LCPI work at Lake Champlain, 1986." *Cryptozoology* 5 (1986): 77–80.

_____. "LCPI work at Lake Champlain, 1987." *Cryptozoology* 6 (1987): 71-77.

_____. "LCPI work at Lake Champlain, 1988." *Cryptozoology* 7 (1988): 70–77.

_____. "LCPI work at Lake Champlain, 1989." *Cryptozoology* 8 (1989): 67–72.

_____. "'Seilag': The unknown animal(s) of Loch Shiel, Scotland." *Cryptozoology* 3 (1984): 50–54.

_____, and M. Pat Meany. "Investigations at Loch Ness and seven other freshwater Scottish lakes." *Cryptozoology* 1 (1982): 78–82.

Zhou Guoxing. "Morphological analysis of the Jiulong Mountain "Manbear" (wildman) hand and foot specimens." *Cryptozoology* 3 (1984): 58–70.

_____. "The status of wildman research in China." *Cryptozoology* 1 (1982): 13–23.

Zingg, Robert, and J.A.L. Singh. *Wolf-Children and Feral Man.* New York: Harper, 1939.

Index

Page numbers for main entries are shown in **bold type**. Pages with illustrations are shown in *italics*. Page numbers for main entry and a picture are shown in ***bold italics***.